To: Dick Craig:-

My best wishes, Dick, and tell that outfit over at Penn State, "Hello."

My best,

Norm Childers

4/15/74

Upper, Courtesy Don Curlee, Western Fruit Grower; lower, Paul Stark Jr., Stark Nurseries and Orchard Co., Louisiana, Missouri. 63353.

(Upper) In the Wenatchee-Yakima fruit growing region of Washington, USA, most of the orchards are located along river bottom land or low plateau areas near water. This is east of the Cascade Mountains and on the Columbia River from which much of the irrigation water comes. High sunlight, adequate water, and cool nights near harvest aid in the production of the highest quality fruit.

(Lower) This scene in the Yakima area shows pears in the background, sweet cherries in the center and spur Golden and Red Delicious in the foreground and at right.

Courtesy S. A. Pieniazek, Institute of Pomology, Skierniewice, Poland.

Origin of many of our cultivated fruits was in China over 4000 years ago. Commercial fruit growing in China began in earnest in 1949, the Chinese Revolutionary Victory year. This is an apple orchard on Malus baccata seedlings in Liaoning Province in eastern China, interplanted with peanuts. The Chinese were the first to use contour orchard planting.

U. S. Library of Congress
Catalogue Card No. 68-63552

This is a group of graduate students at Rutgers University in a fruit breeding class taught by Dr. L. Fredric Hough (third from left). These students are working toward masters and doctorate degrees in horticulture and come from Brazil, Scotland, Lebanon, Poland, Puerto Rico, Germany, Guatamala and Yugoslavia, aside from those from USA. Many of these special trained students are and will be World leaders and researchers in the fruit industry.

This book is dedicated to
THE YOUNG PEOPLE OF TODAY
Who will be the leaders of
the fruit industry tomorrow

Modern Fruit Science

Modern Fruit Science

Orchard and Small Fruit Culture

❦

NORMAN FRANKLIN CHILDERS

M. A. Blake Professor and Research Specialist of Horticulture
Rutgers University — The State University of New Jersey, New Brunswick
Formerly Assistant Director and Senior Plant Physiologist
United States Department of Agriculture Experimental Station in Puerto Rico
Associate in Horticulture, Ohio Agricultural Experiment Station
Assistant Professor in Horticulture, The Ohio State University
Instructor, Cornell University

PLEASE ORDER ADDITIONAL BOOKS FROM:

HORTICULTURAL PUBLICATIONS
Rutgers University—The State University, Nichol Avenue
New Brunswick, New Jersey, 08903

Courtesy F. Hilkenbaumer, Institut Fur Obstbau der Universitat der Bonn, Germany.

This is a deciduous fruit growing region in West Germany. Vineyards are contoured on the river bank. Fruit trees on the level area are largely on EM and MM dwarfing stocks.

Courtesy Blue Star Growers, Inc., and Paul Stark, Jr., nurseryman-grower, Wapato, Washington.

This is a typical cooperative apple-pear packing and storage plant in the Wenatchee-Yakima deciduous tree fruit growing area of the Northwest, USA. This Blue Star Growers, Inc., plant at Cashmere has 70 members, 500,000 bu. cold storage, 100,000 bu. CA storage, and daily packing capacity of 7,500 bu. loose.

Printed by Somerset Press, Inc., Somerville, New Jersey
(Please order copies through Horticultural Publications,
Rutgers University, New Brunswick, New Jersey, 08903, U.S.A.)

Agricultural Photography by Grant Heilman, Lititz, Pa.

This is part of a 1000-acre orchard owned by John Peters and his four sons near Gardners, Pa. They grow mainly apples, peaches, and cherries with 50 acres of pears and plums. They have some plantings of dwarf Red and Golden Delicious and Red York trees. Pond stores pumped well water for irrigation of contoured orchard blocks at declining lower levels. Wooded areas are unsuited for fruit trees and modern machinery.

Courtesy Colin E. Cole, Div. of Hort., Dept. of Agric., Victoria, Australia.

This is a high-density apple orchard in bloom and on dwarfing stock in the Huon Valley, Tasmania. This is an important island of deciduous fruit growing off the southeast corner of Australia.

P_{reface}

❖ ❖

This book has been prepared primarily for undergraduate *fruit and nut growing courses in colleges*. The author has made a special attempt, however, to make the book not only complete and technically accurate but interesting and easy-to-read so that it can be used as a text or reference in *vocational agriculture* and *short courses*. In addition, it is hoped that the book will be of value to the *grower* of fruits and nuts who believes that he has not mastered certain details of his business and who desires to keep abreast with trends and research developments.

While considerable information and research data are given in this text, it is left largely to the teacher to challenge his students with additional research data, theories, depth of discussion and assignments, depending upon their experience and scholastic level. A special effort has been made to present the subject material in an attractive logical manner, using numerous photographs and charts to keep the attention and interest of the reader so that he will not become bored and later fail to take active part in class discussions.

The subject matter presentation in this book is different from most fruit growing texts. The first two chapters are general and refer to all deciduous fruits to be discussed. The next few chapters are devoted to the apple since it is grown widely, and, being important, it has the most and best research background. The apple chapters cover in detail the important subjects from planting to marketing. Thus, the student has an opportunity to become acquainted with the scientific principles upon which the different practices in apple growing are based and with this foundation he should be able to understand and devise solutions for problems with other fruits. Actually, for all practical purposes, there are few basic differences among fruit and nut crops with regard to their growth processes, fruiting responses and cultural requirements.

A LABORATORY MANUAL for the MODERN FRUIT SCIENCE book is available, containing over 30 two- to three-hour exercises which supplement information given in this book. The MANUAL can be used 15 exercises in the basic course and about 15 exercises in the advanced pomology course. The MANUALS are available from the same source as the above book.

The remaining chapters in the tree-fruit section cover the management of other important temperate-zone fruits which are grown widely in the United States and many foreign countries. This section is followed by two general chapters covering pest control and fruit judging. Each of the important small fruits or groups of small fruits then is covered in a single chapter complete in itself.

The appendix has been broadened considerably to give the reader detail information that cannot be found in other books, such as a list of world publications carrying pomological information, cost-of-production data, and a list of books, nut nurseries and U.S. and Canadian experiment stations, and universities experimenting with and teaching deciduous fruits. The appendix also includes a glossary and an additional set of technical references on key subjects plus other pertinent information.

There is much variation in methods of teaching pomology and results obtained. The teacher's organization and *method of presentation* of material appear to be the most important factors governing student interest. Actually, the professor is probably more than 50 percent responsible for the success of his course; I often have thought 75 percent responsible. But the teacher obviously should not try to carry most of the weight; he must call upon and stimulate his students to contribute since by such an approach they will retain more information and generate more interest.

Each teacher has a personal pattern of presentation. The system which works well for one may make a poor showing for another. In the author's experience the above system of presenting a full picture of one fruit at a time seems to be less confusing to the student than when, for example, several pruning methods for a wide variety of fruits are jumbled together in one or two lectures. When such a discussion is concluded most students cannot seem to recall what practice is used on which fruit and why. If a student studies and thinks only one fruit from the time the varieties are selected until the product is sold, the entire picture unfolds as a story with a beginning and an end and experience seems to indicate that he retains more basic information about that fruit during and after the final examination.

The plan of presentation in this book also should lend itself to certain regions where some fruits are of little or no importance. For example, much less time would be devoted to cherries in Maine than in Michigan. The cranberry merely would be mentioned in Missouri whereas it is of outstanding importance in Massachusetts, Washington and Wisconsin. The subject matter is readily available to the fruit grower specializing in but one or two fruits. If a peach grower desires information on pruning, soil management, harvesting and other practices he finds it all in one chapter and thus it is not necessary for him to thumb through long general chapters on each orchard management phase to pick out those particular practices relating to the peach.

Pomology teachers should gradually build up a file of 2 x 2 color slides for each lecture and laboratory to break the monotony of straight lectures. An opaque projector is good to reflect bulletins and books, 8-½ x 11 inches or smaller, tables, pictures, and live material on the screen (Chas. Besler Co., Photo. Proj. Equip., E. Orange, N. J. Write for information.)

The portable-overhead-transparency projector with equipment to copy charts and tables on transparencies enables the teacher to operate the equipment on his desk in front of the class, pointing to numbers, bars on a graph, etc., and to draw diagrams while the class watches. The chart and pencil are reflected on a standard projection screen against the front wall. (Minnesota Mining and Manufacturing Co., Visual Products, 2501 Hudson Rd., St. Paul Minn. 55119.)

In the future, professors of pomology must increase their efforts as much as possible to attract promising young people to this field, for colleges and universities now are falling far short of meeting the needs for well-trained capable pomology graduates. It is hoped that this book will help the teacher in capturing at least a few more of the better students.

Professional men who reviewed and assisted in the chapters of the *first* to *third editions* were: Victor R. Gardner, John T. Bregger, Andrew E. Murneek, Melvin B. Hoffman, Louis J. Edgerton, H. A. Cardinell, M. T. Hilborn, Robert M. Smock, Archie Van Doren, Fred W. Burrows, Luther D. Davis, Frank P. Cullinan, A. M. Musser, L. L. Claypool, C. J. Hansen, Max McFee, William E. Young, Jr., W. H. Childs, Nelson J. Shaulis, George M. Darrow, W. P. Judkins, George L. Slate, and Paul L. Koenig. Also assisting were the *late* (in each case) David G. White, J. Lupton McCartney, Jr. K. Shaw, Karl D. Brase, J. H. Waring, Roy E. Marshall, D. F. Fisher, Leif Verner, Henry Hartman, Walter S. Hough, Frank H. Beach, I. C. Haut, Harold B. Tukey, Sr., and Stanley Johnston. Hayao Iwagaki, Japan, and S. A. Pieniazek, Poland, gave valuable help.

My colleagues at Rutgers University who assisted at the time of writing the first to third editions were: Carter R. Smith, L. Fredric Hough, Warren C. Stiles, Catherine H. Bailey, James N. Moore, Ernest G. Christ, Abdul Kamali, Laszlo Somogyi, A. B. Wills, Udar Mahal, Miklos Faust, W. B. Collins, M. W. Borys, W. J. Kender, and Mrs. Vera DeHart.

Professional workers who assisted in the revision of the chapters or parts of chapters of the *fourth* and *fifth editions* are given in the footnotes in the respective chapters. Others were William G. Doe, grower and representative of Marwald, Inc., Ayer Rd., Harvard, Mass. and Paul Stark, Jr. of Stark Nurseries and Orchards Co., Louisiana, Missouri both of whom gave considerable advice and help on a number of chapters, based on their background of wide experience. The late H. B. Tukey, Sr. of Michigan acted in a similar manner. Other professional state or federal people who assisted in one way or another and to whom I am grateful were R. Paul Larsen, Washington; James A. Beutel, California; Ewell A. Rogers, Colorado; Cecil Stushnoff, Minnesota; Ronald B. Tukey and Robert A. Norton, Washington; Donald V. Fisher and James Marshall, British Columbia; Chesley Smith, New Brunswick, Canada; George M. Kessler, Jordan Levin, H. P. Gaston, R. F. Carlson and A. L. Kenworthy, Michigan; Robert G. Hill, Jr., Ohio; Roy K. Simons and C. C. Zych, Illinois; Frank H. Emerson, Purdue; Hollis H. Bowen, Texas; Earl F. Savage, Georgia; David W. Buchanan and L. Gene Albrigo, Florida; Walter E. Ballinger and Gene J. Galletta, North Carolina; Ray S. Marsh, West Virginia; Hubert C. Mohr, Kentucky; Aubrey D. Hibbard and Delbert D. Hemphill, Mo., Justin R. Morris and A. A. Kattan, Arkansas; the late B. A. Dominick, Jr., Cornell; Lloyd A. Mitterling, Connecticut; F. W. Southwick, Massachusetts; V. G. Shutak, Rhode Island; W. J. Kender, New York; and my colleagues at Rutgers: Ernest G. Christ, Catherine H. Bailey, L. Fredric Hough and Paul Eck. Mrs. Karen Heller, my secretary for the Fifth Edition, did most of the typing. C. Palmer Bateman, Sr. and Jr., Ollie Welsh, and Artie Clark all have been very cooperative over the years in publishing the several editions of this and other horticultural books, manuals and related materials. All of these people gave more of their help than I probably should have accepted.

My wife, Lillian Coyne Childers, gave me considerable help and encouragement which I very much appreciate.

January 1973   Norman F. Childers

NOTE: The following are the "Ten Commandments for a Good Teacher" by Victor H. Wohlford in Better Farming Methods, October 1958: (1). PREPARE YOUR LESSON WELL. A lack of proper preparation is the unpardonable sin of a teacher. Nothing will inspire the confidence of his class so quickly as the teacher who makes adequate preparation of his lesson. (2). BE PRESENT WHENEVER POSSIBLE. Unnecessary absences will not teach your students to be punctual in their attendance, and will hinder interest and progress in your class. When it is necessary to be absent, always advise your substitute in sufficient time for him to make necessary preparation. (3). BE ON TIME. Negligence and indifference on the part of the teacher will soon be absorbed by the class. Be present several minutes before the time set for the class to begin. (4). BE PERSONALLY INTERESTED IN EACH MEMBER OF YOUR CLASS. Call members by their names. Be interested in the limitations and problems of each member of your class, and willingly give such attention or assistance to those problems as you can. (5). BE ATTENTIVE OF THE PHYSICAL CONDITIONS OF YOUR CLASSROOM. Before beginning the lesson, make necessary adjustment of the lights, ventilation, window shades, seating arrangements, maps, charts, blackboard, etc. (6). BEGIN AND CLOSE PROMPTLY. Do not wait for late comers, and do not extend the lesson beyond the time set to end the class. A violation of either of these points will distract interest from your class. Your promptness will beget promptness in your pupils. (7). DO NOT DO ALL THE TALKING. Do not make your lesson a lecture, as it takes a near genius to give an interesting lecture. Encourage class discussion. Never tell anything you can get your class to tell. (8). DO NOT PERMIT ARGUMENTS IN YOUR CLASS. Nothing will kill interest more quickly. Permit discussions of differences, but when they turn into arguments, pass on to the next question or point of discussion. (9). REALIZE YOUR SERIOUS RESPONSIBILITIES. Be as serious as possible about your teaching. Realize that what and how you teach may lead your pupils to fuller understanding and appreciation, or discourage their acceptance of the facts presented. (10). BE INTERESTED IN YOUR CLASS. Consider your students, and be wise in your teaching. A good slogan for teachers is: "If the student hasn't learned—the teacher hasn't taught."

—*Victor H. Wohlford*

Contents

  I: INTRODUCTION 3

 II: APPLE REGIONS, PRODUCTION, AND VARIETIES 16

III: ESTABLISHING THE FRUIT PLANTING 31

 IV: PRUNING APPLE TREES 66

  V: SOIL MANAGEMENT FOR APPLES 99

 VI: FLOWER-BUD FORMATION, POLLINATION, AND FRUIT SET
     IN THE APPLE 128

VII: THINNING APPLE FRUITS AND ALTERNATE BEARING 146

VIII: GRAFTING AND BUDDING TREES 162

 IX: FREEZING INJURY TO APPLES 180

  X: HARVESTING, PACKING AND PROCESSING APPLES 191

 XI. STORING APPLES 238

XII: MARKETING APPLES 274

XIII: PEAR AND QUINCE CULTURE 296

XIV: PEACH, NECTARINE, APRICOT, AND ALMOND 328

 XV: CULTURE OF PLUMS 388

XVI: CHERRY CULTURE 413

XVII: EDIBLE NUTS, MINOR TREE CROPS 450

XVIII: CONTROL OF INSECTS AND DISEASES 507

XIX: FROST AND DROUTH CONTROL 638

 XX: GRAPE GROWING 666

XXI: STRAWBERRY GROWING 714

XXII: BUSH BERRY CULTURE 759

     APPENDIX 815

     INDEX 953

Courtesy Colin E. Cole, Div. of Hort, Dept. of Agric., Victoria, Australia.

Main fruit regions of New Zealand are: Auckland (extreme North); Hawkes Bay (above; east side of North Island); Nelson (north end of South Island); and Central Otago (southern South Island), each producing 18-24% of total fruit crop. New Zealand is one of the finest and most picturesque fruit growing regions of the World.

Modern Fruit Science

An orchard in full bloom is a beautiful sight. This scene is in Berks County, Pennsylvania.

CHAPTER I

Introduction

❖ ❖

The many delicious fruits we grow, eat and ferment today originated for the most part, we are told, in the old countries: *Abyssinia*: gave us coffee; *Afghanistan*: the pear, apple, and walnut; *Brazil - Paraguay*: cocoa, pineapple, Brazil nut, cashew, and passion fruit; *China*: the peach, apricot, orange, and mulberry; *Mexico*: the guava; *North America*: cultivated blueberry, cranberry, pecan; *Persia*: cherry, plum, grape, almond, fig, date, persimmon, pistachio nut, and pomegranate; *Peru*: the papaya; and *Siam-Malaya-Java*: banana, coconut, and pomelo.

Early settlers landing on the east coast of America brought with them many of these fruit plants and seeds from native lands. The different kinds and varieties of fruits, many of which are commercially important today, were rapidly propagated and distributed to the South and West by religious workers, travelers, pioneer farmers, and such well-known characters as Johnny Appleseed. Gradually, interested individuals and later the Federal and state agricultural experiment stations, through chance selection or scientific breeding, enlarged the list of high-quality varieties commercially grown today.

The technique of growing fruits has undergone a marked change during the past sixty years. In the early 1900's, fruit growing was rather simple as compared with the many steps and different types of machinery involved today. Where formerly little or no spray material was applied, now as many as ten to fifteen sprays are applied to apples in one season. The need for more spraying was brought about by an increase in number of insects and diseases and greater resistance of some species to standard spray materials. Much of the apple crop was formerly harvested and sold directly out of the orchard with comparatively little grading and packing. Now, most of the commercial crop is carefully brushed or washed, graded, sized, and packed

Dr. Arthur H. Thompson, University of Maryland, assisted in revision of this chapter, with William G. Doe, grower-commercial sales, Harvard, Massachusetts.

3

Figure 1. An orchard scene in California, the leading fruit state. Although citrus comprises a large part of its fruit industry, California also leads in grapes, peaches, plums, prunes, nectarines, pears, sweet cherries, apricots, almonds, walnuts, persimmons, olives, figs, avocados, strawberries, and dates. California also ranks high (fourth) in apple production in the United States. California is about 750 miles long, 200 miles wide.

with the aid of specialized machinery. A large part of the crop then may be placed in storage for weeks or months before being sent through established marketing channels. Obviously, the amount of labor and equipment required to grow and prepare fruit for sale has increased. Also, about thrice as many bushels of apples are required to pay the annual wages of a hired man as compared with the amount required in 1910. Although modern machinery has made it possible to increase man's efficiency in output, this gain often has been passed on to labor in awarding higher wages. Thus, the fruit grower must be increasingly more efficient in the use of his labor if he is to continue to enjoy profits above the wages paid.

Shortly after 1940, great advancements were made in new machinery designed to reduce high labor costs in fruit growing. An example is the modern power sprayer which requires only one or two men to spray a large orchard, whereas formerly, five to seven or more men were needed to do the same job in triple the period of time. Although the initial cost of such machinery is relatively high, the greater output and long-time saving in labor costs justify its use. It should be pointed out, however, that only

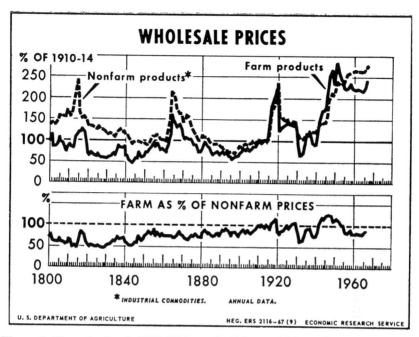

WHOLESALE PRICES

% OF 1910-14

Nonfarm products*

Farm products

FARM AS % OF NONFARM PRICES

*INDUSTRIAL COMMODITIES.   ANNUAL DATA.

U. S. DEPARTMENT OF AGRICULTURE   NEG. ERS 2116-67 (9)   ECONOMIC RESEARCH SERVICE

Figure 2. The price level (1910-1914 equals 100) at which goods are bought and sold in the U. S. is either going up or down. The four price peaks and depressions are associated with four wars. Farm product prices fluctuate wider than non-farm prices; they also lead in a trend. Note farm prices have gradually risen over non-farm prices (lower chart) from 1800 to the 1960's, with wider fluctuations since 1920.

those growers who can obtain *high production per acre of high-quality* fruit will be able to adopt the improved but more expensive production machinery and methods.

Some economic principles. A chief concern of the man who desires to plant or buy an orchard is the future likelihood of profits. Obviously, no one can predict accurately the profits of an orchard due to so many variables. There are, however, some economic principles which frequently hold and which may be considered.

The most important factor influencing cash returns to fruit growers is the general price level, which is usually going up or down, as history shows in Figure 2. Note that the major rises in price level are correlated with six wars: the War of 1812, the Civil War, World War I, World War II, and the Korean - Vietnam Wars. These price reactions to wars are similar worldwide. Foreign imports of fresh and processed fruits, as shown in Figure 3, also influence domestic prices and movement of fruit.

In present-day agriculture, the fruit grower must buy supplies on the market in order to produce and sell his products. When prices are falling, the fruit growers, as with all farm operators, are at a disadvantage because they must pay a higher price for things they buy than the price they receive

5

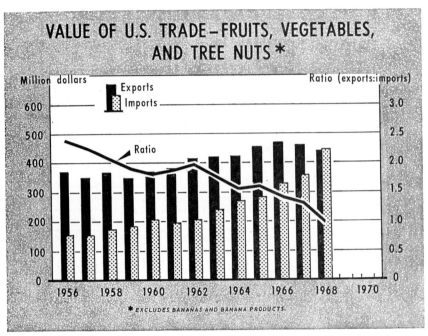

VALUE OF U.S. TRADE—FRUITS, VEGETABLES, AND TREE NUTS *

Million dollars — Exports, Imports, Ratio — Ratio (exports:imports)

* EXCLUDES BANANAS AND BANANA PRODUCTS.

Figure 3. Imports of fruits, vegetables and tree nuts into the U.S. are causing competition to U.S. farmers. Foreign production costs tend to be lower, putting U.S. farmers at a disadvantage.

for things they sell. Before a man makes a long-time investment in an orchard, it would be well for him to determine if the price level is high or low, and if it is going up or down. There undoubtedly will be less foreclosures in the next 10 to 20 years if fruit growers will remember that rising prices at one time mean falling prices at some later date. The profitableness of an orchard set in 1973 will be determined by prices obtained for fruit products and the cost of things from 1980 to 2000. With small fruits such as strawberries, however, which bring full crops in two years after planting, the grower is in a better position to take full advantage of peak-price-return periods by increasing acreage accordingly.

The fruit industry. In the 1960's, the United States accounted for about 25 percent of the combined world crops of apples, pears, peaches, plums, prunes, oranges, grapefruit, lemons, limes and other citrus. Of the individual fruits, the United States produced about the following percentages; apples, 10; pears, 11; peaches, 30; plums and prunes, 18; oranges and tangerines, 26; other citrus, 20. All U.S. noncitrus fruits and nuts were valued at 1.5 billion dollars in the late 1960s; citrus over $600 million; nuts over $182 million.

Regions in which fruits and nuts are grown in large commercial quantities in the United States are shown in Figure 4. The heaviest producing areas are located in the Far West and the eastern half of the United States. The

6

TABLE 1

World Deciduous Fruit Production in Thousands of Metric Tons (1964-68) [1]

Crop	U.S.A.	Canada	Mexico	South America [2]	Western Europe [3]	Central and Eastern Europe (Socialistic) [4]	Oceania [5]	Asia [6]	Africa [7]	World 1964-68
Apple (+cider apples)	3,190	430	125	565	10,621	2,324	476	2,025	225	19,981
Apricot	182	6	7	20	370	200	46	160	108	1,102
Berries (unspecified)	2.2	—	—	—	—	—	0.9	102	—	105
Blueberry	33	11	—	—	0.5	—	—	—	—	44
Cherries (all)	234	19	—	6	775	72	8	92	—	1,206
Cranberry	66	9	—	—	—	—	—	—	—	75
Currant	0.6	—	7	—	195	101	0.7	—	—	298
Fig	52	—	94	29	919	13	1	364	174	1,559
Grape	3,318	58	—	3,936	29,227	7,658[4]	644	4,642	2,556	52,183
Gooseberry	—	—	—	—	96	52	1.5	—	—	16
Nuts [8]	309	—	—	—	364*	—	0.2	145*	—	818
Peach, Nectarines	1,498	47	75	342	2,085	276	134	436	182	5,075
Pear (+cider var.)	626	39	34	170	3,155	613	160	669	103	5,569
Persimmon	3	—	—	—	—	—	—	465	—	468
Plums & Prunes	518	12	62	81	1,195	702	30	198	38	2,836
Raspberry	33	9	—	—	51	38	2.7	—	—	134
Strawberry	225	16	76	2	273	215	5	96	—	903

1 U. S. ton is 2000 lbs; Metric English ton is 2204.6. Accurate World data are difficult to obtain. Figures here approximate productive capacity of country or area around 1967. Data from USSR are limited. Detail production data for a country can be found for apple, pear, peach, plum, grape, cherry, fig and apricot in: (a) Production Yearbook Vol. 23:184-217. 1969. FAO of United Nations Rome, Italy; and limited data for certain other fruits in (b) Proc. XVII Internat. Hort. Congr., College Park, Md., USA. Vol. IV. 1966, Dr. S. A. Pieniazek of Poland and Dr. F. Hilkenbaumer of W. Germany helped to assemble these data.
2 Includes: Argentina, Chile, Uruguay, Brazil, and Ecuador.
3 Includes: Belgium, France, Fed. Repb, W. Berlin, Finland, Italy, Luxemburg, Netherlands, Denmark, Norway, Portugal, Sweden, Spain, Switzerland, Greece, United Kingdom, and Austria.
4 Includes: Albania, Poland, Rumania, Bulgaria, Yugoslovia, Czechoslovakia, Eastern Germany, and Hungary. (Russian data unavailable except for grapes — which is 3,528).
5 Includes: Australia, Tasmania, and New Zealand.
6 Includes: Cyprus, Israel, Jordan, Lebanon, Syria, Turkey, Iran, Japan, China, Rep. of Korea, Taiwan, Pakistan, and sometimes, Mainland China.
7 Includes: Algeria, Libya, Morocco, Tunisia, U.A.R., Madagascar, and So. Africa.
8 Consists of filbert, E. walnut, chestnut, pecan and almond for most part.
* Filberts in Turkey (Asia) 112; chestnuts 33; the 364 in W. Europe accounts for 70-100 tons of filberts in Spain and Italy.

7

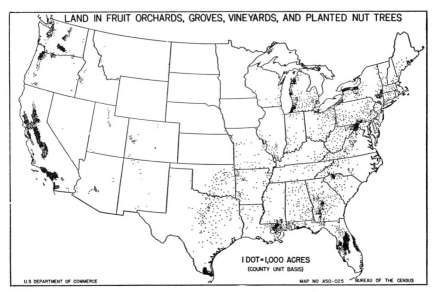

Figure 4. Fruits are grown in every state of the Union, but there are definite well suited areas where each fruit reaches peak production. The particular fruit or fruits involved in the concentrated areas shown above are pointed out in subsequent chapters. See Appendix for maps of world apple and pear regions.

densely speckled areas in the Northwest and Northeast can be largely attributed to apples, whereas those in the southeastern states, with the exception of Florida, largely represent peaches and pecans. In Florida, southern Texas, and southern California (Figure 4), the concentrated areas are principally citrus.

California is the leading fruit state, producing over one-fourth of the total United States fruit and nut crop. Almost every kind of fruit and nut produced in the United States can be grown in California due to its many climates, fertile soils, and elaborate irrigation systems. California produces both temperate fruits, such as the apple and peach, and tropical and subtropical fruits, such as citrus, avocados, figs, dates and olives.

On a tonnage basis, the leading deciduous fruit grown in the United States is grapes, as indicated in Table 3. It is closely followed by apples and then, in order, by peaches, pears, prunes, strawberries cherries and apricots.

TABLE 2

Per Capita Consumption of Fresh Fruits (fresh weight basis). Annual Averages, 1960-69

Fruit	Consumption	Fruit	Consumption
Bananas	18.09	Grapefruit	8.41
Apples	16.54	Peaches	7.25
Oranges	15.87	All other (16 fruits)	15.64
Total			81.80

Note: Fresh peaches compete well considering they are marketed 44 weeks a year; from domestic sources only 31 weeks; major volume in 20 weeks. Other fruits are available in volume year round.

In about the past fifty years, the production of citrus has increased

8

Fruit Crops	Commercial Production (based on 1964-71 average)	Approx. Trend over 15 yrs. previous
	Tons	
1. Oranges, tangerines, etc. (5)*	8,257,000	Way Up
2. Grapes (14)	3,631,000	Steady
3. Apples (34)	2,992,000	Steady
4. Grapefruit (4)*	2,070,714	Up
5. Peaches (34)	1,621,215	Steady
6. Pears (11)	627,125	Steady
7. Lemons (2)*	609,000	Steady
8. Prunes & Plums (5)	580,250	Steady
9. Strawberries (31)	244,500	Way Down
10. Cherries: all (12)	225,125	Steady
11. Apricots (3)	191,750	Steady
12. Pecans: All types (12)*	100,000	Steady
13. Walnuts, Eng. (2)	97,000	Up
14. Almonds (1)	94,125	Up
15. Cranberries (5)	81,250	Way Up
16. Olives (1)**	67,666	Up
17. Nectarines (1)	65,875	Up
18. Avocado (2) **	57,600	Way Up
19. Figs: all (1)*	57,000	Down
20. Blueberries (5)**	38,400	Up
21. Limes (1)*	25,571	Way Up
22. Dates (1) **	18,633	Steady
23. Filberts (2)*	10,142	Up
24. Macadamia Nuts (1) *** (Hawaii)	5,339	Way Up
25. Pomegranates (1) **	3,166	Steady
26. Persimmons (1) **	1,500	Down

1 Number of states commercially producing in parenthesis; U.S. ton is 2000 lbs.
* Figures for 1964-70.
** Figures for 1968-70.
*** Figures for 1969, 1970 only.

rapidly until the orange leads all other fruits in tonnage, with grapefruit and lemons also ranking high. On the other hand, the production of apples and peaches, two leading deciduous fruits, has remained approximately at the same general level since 1919.

Fruits, particularly strawberries, have a relatively high value on the basis of amount of land occupied. Some crops, such as hay, wheat, and oats, on the other hand, have a comparatively low value. Also, the value and tonnage of apples and peaches are closely related, but the value of grapes is much less than that of apples and peaches on a tonnage basis. Cultivated blueberries, on the other hand, have a high value per land unit.

During and after World War II, record crops of many of the deciduous fruits were attained, due to the great world need for food and to the high prices being paid for fruits. The increased production was largely attained

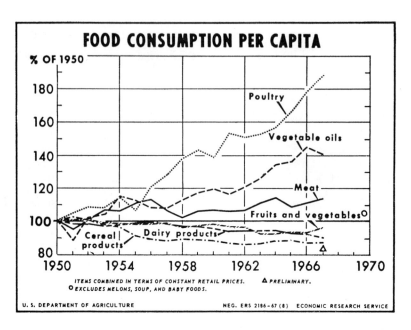

FOOD CONSUMPTION PER CAPITA

% OF 1950

Poultry

Vegetable oils

Meat

Fruits and vegetables○

Cereal products

Dairy products

ITEMS COMBINED IN TERMS OF CONSTANT RETAIL PRICES. △ *PRELIMINARY.*
○ *EXCLUDES MELONS, SOUP, AND BABY FOODS.*

U. S. DEPARTMENT OF AGRICULTURE   NEG. ERS 2186-67 (8)   ECONOMIC RESEARCH SERVICE

Figure 8. Per capita consumption of fruits and vegetables has held steady or dropped slightly, whereas meat, poultry and vegetable oil have increased. Dairy products have dropped due, apparently, to the cholesterol-heart problem. Poultry has shown a marked increase in consumption (above) while price paid has shown the greatest drop (20-30%) since 1950; fruits and vegetable prices, however, have jumped 50% in price.

by over-all better care of plantings, by renovating old orchards and vineyards, and new plantings. Inasmuch as general over-all increases in fruit acreage are attended with some risk, the individual grower might well exercise caution in increasing his own acreage during such periods.

Trends in fruit growing. Those people who believe in the philosophy of "an unfinished world" will be constantly looking into the future and making plans accordingly. The following trends in fruit growing indicate a wholesome symptom of progress.

Production costs have reached a point where a fruit grower *must increase production by increasing acreage or by using high-density compact trees to reduce costs/bushel.* Also, he must keep careful cost accounting of each orchard block to be sure it is profitable.

In the past, many fruit growers have made it a practice to devote full time to raising only one fruit such as apples. Some growers are continuing this practice with good success. But there is a trend toward diversification in fruit growing because it frequently results in better year-round use of labor, a wider and more profitable market outlet, and better distribution of cash returns for the year as a whole. Perhaps not everyone should diversify, but some growers may have an interest in raising several different

M. C. Audsley and P. A. Wells, U.S.D.A.

Figure 9. This Eastern Regional Research Laboratory at Philadelphia, Pennsylvania (there are four in the United States) is an indication of the great research effort being made by the U. S. Department of Agriculture to find new and better uses for fruit and other agricultural by-products.

kinds of fruits or a certain amount of vegetables, bees, nursery stock or livestock, such as beef, depending upon local opportunities and markets in these lines. It would be well to exercise caution, however, and not expand these activities to the point where the fruit planting suffers from lack of proper attention.

During recent years there has been an increasing tendency of the apple grower to rotate his orchard with respect to age. This gives him opportunity to plant new varieties, perhaps dwarf trees. Also, young or smaller trees with good orchard care tend to produce a better quality product at less cost. Under this system, the land available for orcharding is planned so that a new block of trees is set every five to ten years and an old block removed at about the age of 30 to 40 years.

Several valuable new chemicals are being introduced to control growth, flowering, fruit set, and size, color, maturation, and quality of the fruit. Alar, Ethrel and Ethephon are examples showing promise particularly in connection with mechanical harvesting.

In spite of the best orchard management, there will always be a certain amount of low-grade fruit. This fruit should be processed, but today considerable *good* fruit also is processed by demand. Fruit processing will no doubt undergo considerable future expansion. The importance of this field is emphasized by the fact that over half of the deciduous fruits produced are processed. A slight increase was noted in fruit processing during World War II and this increase is continuing in light of the growing interest in quick freezing, and powdered and pure fruit juices, the latter of which will undoubtedly furnish increasingly stiff competition for synthetic drinks. It is doubtful if dehydrated fruits will make much headway, but it is certain that some kind of new fruit products will be devised as a result of the vast amount of research being conducted in this field.

Much needs to be done in improving transportation and marketing systems for deciduous fruits, all of which are more or less perishable. The importance of the fruit marketing field is evidenced by the fact that about 60 cents of the consumer's dollar for apples goes into marketing channels, and the remaining 40 cents goes to the grower. Fruits that unquestionably find the quickest sales at the highest prices are those that are tree-ripened, of high quality and undamaged. In the past, the merchandiser and the fruit grower have blamed each other for bruised unattractive fruit, but this does not solve the problem for the consumer who wants a top product and is usually willing to pay a good price. The handling of fruit from tree to table needs increasingly more study and careful attention by the grower, experiment station worker, and by the merchandiser. Definite advancements are being made in fruit grading and sizing machinery and in special packaging to reduce bruising. There is also a trend toward more storages on farms in which the ripening processes of harvested fruit can be quickly reduced to a minimum. Controlled atmosphere storage has shown a marked increase in some apple sections. Precooling and better refrigeration conditions for fruit in transportation are receiving more widespread use. Air freight is growing rapidly in quick long-distance transportation of some fruits such as strawberries at the "eating-ripe" stage of maturity. There is a strong trend toward mechanization and use of materials such as herbicides to cut labor costs. All-red mutations of standard apple varieties and "spur-type" sports are being widely planted. Small acreage growers in suburban areas now are making good profits with improved roadside marketing techniques and/or Public-pick-your-own fruit.

The field of consumer education is in need of more attention. It is surprising how little the general public knows about the proper buying and use of fruits. Cooking schools offer a good opportunity for teaching housewives how to buy the different varieties of fruit in season and for specific uses. Also, a more widespread educational program for retail dealers is greatly needed on how to handle and display deciduous fruits in the stores and markets. Each deciduous fruit is an individual problem, unlike citrus.

Corporates are assuming management of large fruit and nut growing areas such as walnuts in California and grapes in western New York. Computer analysis of financial data is being used increasingly, also by individual large growers for better data evaluation and to save labor.

The fruit grower. In spite of great advancements in ways and means of growing fruit and in the amount of scientific knowledge available, the most important factor in successful fruit growing is the grower himself. In order to make a good living today, a fruit grower or any business man must have first a thorough and well-rounded practical knowledge of his business which comes only with considerable experience. If a good practical know-

Figure 10. Growers should make a special effort to attend and take part in local and national fruit meetings. If only one new idea is obtained, it is well worth your time. This is a New Jersey apple and peach meeting to which Fred W. Burrows of the International Apple Institute, Inc., is speaking.

ledge then can be reinforced with a college training or its equivalent in such subjects as botany, horticulture, plant pathology, plant physiology, chemistry, entomology, and agricultural economics and engineering, the grower is in a much better position to lead and compete with the best men in the business. A technical training in fruit growing is becoming increasingly important because of the many technical problems arising in what has become a scientific business. Among numerous other things, the fruit grower today must understand the complicated mechanisms of tractors and spray machines; he must be a semi-expert on refrigeration; he must understand the fundamental physiology and anatomy of his plants, the chemistry of his spray materials and the physics of their applications; and he must be acquainted with the life cycles of the important insects and diseases encountered in fruit plantings. Furthermore, he must have a basic knowledge of the economics and marketing of his fruit. Hence, a good fruit grower today is as keen as the best of city businessmen.

Growers, to keep abreast, must spend a lot of time in reading and developing a collection of bulletins, books, professional magazines, and weather and crop reports. In addition, growers should make it a practice to attend and take part in local and state horticultural society meetings. Such meetings not only provide an opportunity to study new developments in fruit growing, but to compare notes with other growers, and to discuss special problems with professional and commercial men. Horticultural meetings, as well as competitive exhibitions of fruit, usually have the fine quality of stimulating a real ambition among growers to go home and do a better job of producing higher quality fruit.

In every group of growers, there are invariably some who are outstandingly more successful than the group as a whole, even during the most trying years. True, they may have a large established physical unit and sufficient capital to back the business, but there are usually other more important reasons in the final analysis. Among other qualities, including those suggested above, the successful grower is usually a steady hard worker and thinker; he is systematic in performing every job from pruning and spraying to keeping an accurate account of expenses, cash income, and net returns; and above all, he is a good administrator in picking able assistants

13

and laborers, keeping harmony among them, and in accomplishing the maximum amount of work with the labor and facilities at hand. He is always open to new developments, but usually seeks first the advice of qualified professional men, then experiments cautiously in his own orchard before entirely discarding the old and tried methods for the new.

An interesting business. Most everyone has a certain leaning toward country life and some kind of farming. Boys raised on a fruit farm often continue their life work as fruit growers if the business is bringing satisfactory returns. The city boy who desires to specialize in fruit growing must recognize at the outset that he is at a disadvantage among young men who have been raised on the farm. It requires hard work for the city boy entering college to acquire the practical knowledge of fruit growing and at the same time gain a technical training in college. Young men from the city who want to specialize in fruit growing should make every effort to get practical orchard experience during summer vacations or by taking a full year off from college if necessary before attempting to enter the fruit growing business. Practical experience is equally essential before entering the fields of research, teaching, or the commercial sales and handling of materials used in fruit growing. Thus, the young city man who becomes interested in fruit growing while attending college should by no means be discouraged from continuing with this field for his life work.

It may be of interest to cite some figures regarding the fruit growing business. According to the U. S. Census, about 2 per cent of the farms in the United States are devoted principally to production of fruits and nuts. In comparison with other farms, the value of the land and buildings on these fruit farms is about twice as great as on the average farm. The expenditure for labor in an orchard is nearly three times as much. Also, on the average there are more automobiles, motor trucks, and tractors on fruit farms. There are more dwellings which are lighted with electricity and considerably more fruit farms with telephones. This analysis from the Census is an index of the cultural development of orchard folk. In fact, probably no one has a better vocation, a more delectable product, or more desirable associates than the fruit grower. A good home with all modern conveniences, which sets his family off as a cultured, comfortable group, is fully in the picture, together with good vacations and job improvement trips to foreign fruit growing areas.

Review Questions

1. How has the general price level in the United States behaved, and how has it affected the fruit grower's income? Explain foreign import effects on domestic fruit growing.
2. Considering present economic conditions, would you recommend a moderate expansion in fruit plantings?
3. How does the United States rank in world fruit production?
4. Briefly describe where the fruit regions of the United States are located, and what are the major fruits produced in these regions?

5. What is the leading fruit state in the United States, and how do you account for this?
6. List the five leading deciduous fruits grown in the United States and the world.
7. How does citrus production compare over the years with the production of leading deciduous fruits?
8. What is the relative importance of the processing field in deciduous fruit growing?
9. Discuss briefly (a) trends in fruit growing and (b) qualifications of a successful fruit grower.

Suggested Collateral Readings

Alleger, D. E. Retirement income and expectations of rural southerners — a survey in Florida and the rural south. Fla. Agr. Exp. Sta. Bull. 729 26 pp. 1969.

Anonymous. Johnny Appleseed, by one who knew him. F. J. Heer Printing Co., Columbus, Ohio. 1922.

Anonymous. Farm Economics. Dept. of Agr. Econ., Cornell University, Ithaca, N. Y. This is a bulletin issued several times a year, keeping all types of farmers up-to-date economically.

Anonymous. "Crop report for fruits," "The fruit situation," and other fruit crop data. U. S. Department of Agr., Agricultural Marketing Service. Washington, D. C. (Issued several times a year).[1] Fruit production in foreign countries is available through this source in "World Agricultural Production and Trade." Statistical Report.

Australia — Fruit production data. Commonwealth Bur. of Census, statistics. Canberra.

Burrows, Fred W. International Apple Institute Special Letters. Bi-weekly to monthly. (Must be a member to receive them). 1302 18th St., N.W., Washington, D. C. 20036

Darlington, C. D. Chromosome botany, 186 pp. George Allen and Unwin Ltd., Museum St., London, England.

Garman, C. G. How to make a fruit farm pay. Cornell Ext. Bull. 1013. 1958.

Hoofnagle, W. S. Conversion factors and weights and measures for agricultural commodities and their products. Statistical Bull. 362. USDA/ERS. 87 p. 1965.

Reed, A. Doyle. Business organization for modern farms. Univ. of Calif. Agri. Ext. Serv. AXT-49 Rev. (Feb.) 1970.

South Africa — Fruit Production Data. P.O.B. 1298, Cape Town.

Turkey, H. B. Horticultural horizons and humanity. Reprint from The Journal of the Royal Horticultural Society Vol. XCV, Part. 7. July 1970.

Vavilov, N. I. Origin, variation, immunity and breeding of cultivated plants. (Translated to English by K. S. Chester). Chronica Botanica Co., Waltham, Mass. USA. 364 pp. 1935, 1949/50.

---

[1]Fruit growers, teachers, and commercial distributors of fruit growing equipment and materials may be interested in having their names placed on the mailing list to receive these fruit crop data.

A laboratory manual with over 30 exercises is available for laboratory use by students. Request, "Modern Fruit Science Laboratory Manual" by Norman F. Childers and Dennis A. Abdalla, Horticultural Publications, Nichol Avenue, New Brunswick, N. J., U.S.A., 08903. Price $2.95 + 28c postage, domestic; foreign 48c.

United States agricultural economics depts. who are contributing regularly to fruit growing production and costs-and-returns data are New York at Cornell Univ., Michigan, Washington, U. S. Dept. of Agr., Ohio, Pennsylvania, Rutgers Univ. (N. J.), Georgia and Florida. (See appendix for addresses).

CHAPTER II

Apple Regions, Production, and Varieties

❖ ❖

There are natural forests of fruit and nut trees, including apples, still covering millions of acres of the Caucasus Mountains of southern Asia. This is a fruit breeders Paradise to search for desired new characters of growth, fruiting, season of ripening, resistance to pests and diseases, tolerance of adverse soils and drouth, and resistance to cold or heat, and others. These new characters, when found, are bred into our already high quality fruits to make them still better.

The apple has been cultivated in Europe for over two thousand years. Seed and grafted trees of the better European varieties were brought to North America and planted by the earliest settlers. Seed from these trees were disseminated westward by the Indians, traders, missionaries and the well known Johnny Appleseed (John Chapman).

Today, it is interesting to note that most of the deciduous fruit growing regions have been determined largely on the basis of apple growing. It is true, however, that some plants, particularly commercial peaches, will not thrive in all apple sections due to low winter temperatures.

The relative importance of each World area in apple production has been shown in Table 1, Chap. I, and the Appendix map. The leaders are: Western Europe, USA, Eastern Europe, Canada, Japan, Australia, and Argentina. Leading states in the USA in millions of pounds are: Washington, 1,280; New York, 911; Michigan, 676; California, 520; Pennsylvania, 491; Virginia, 464; West Virginia 247; North Carolina, 192; Ohio, 143; 192; New Jersey, 110.

Figure 2 shows the percent production of apple trees by region in the United States. This map has been divided into six regions mainly on the basis of climate and varieties grown. It is apparent that over 90 per cent of the apple crop is obtained from the Northeastern (I), Central Atlantic

---

[1]Assistance of Howard J. Brooks, U. S. Dept. of Agr., in revising this chapter is appreciated.

16

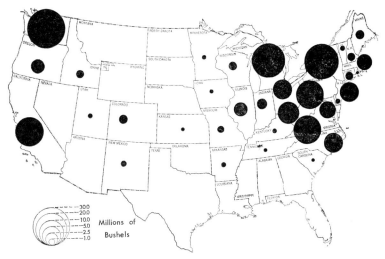

Kenneth A. Wightman, Rutgers University

Figure 1. The relative production of apples by state in the United States. See Appendix for world apple distribution map.

(II), and West Coast states (VI). During the 1940-50's there was a slight shift of the apple crop from the Midwest to the Eastern and Western sections of the United States. The sections in Figure 2 will be described separately in order to bring out the important factors governing apple regions and some of their respective problems. It is suggested that frequent reference be made to Figure 2 in order to "picture" the areas under consideration.

Northeastern section (I). About 30 per cent of the apple crop in the United States is produced in this area. Temperatures during the growing season are moderately cool, ranging between 65 and 70° F. from June to August, inclusive. Along the southern boundary of this section, the time from apple bloom in spring to the first freeze in fall allows the use of apple varieties which will mature within from 155 to 160 days from time of bloom. In the northern regions of this section where the growing season is shorter, as well as across the border in Canada, it is necessary to select varieties maturing in 140 to 150 days. In western New York 60 percent plus of the crop is processed. Varieties being suggested are: McIntosh, Cortland, Spartan and Delicious. For Processing: Twenty Ounce and Rhode Island Greening and for dual purpose Wayne, Golden Delicious, Idared and Rome. Monroe is losing favor. For eastern New York and New England where the crop is stored largely and packed out: McIntosh, Cortland and Delicious for upper New England. For lower New England and Hudson Valley: McIntosh, Red Delicious, Golden Delicious, Idared, Cortland, Jonathan, Spartan and Rome in this order.

The rainfall in New England and eastern New York averages about 45 inches. In western New York, northern Ohio, and Michigan, the average is between 30 and 35 inches annually. About half of this rainfall comes

17

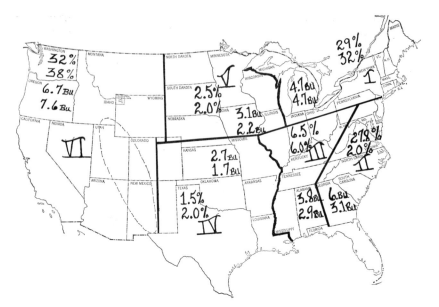

Figure 2. This map is divided into six regions on the basis of climate, varieties, and other factors. The percentage production of the total United States crop and the yield per bearing tree are indicated in each region. Upper number in each case is for 1961-67; lower for 1954, showing shifts. Yield per tree rose in Region II, remained about the same in other areas.

during the growing season between April and September, inclusive, and it is unusually dependable—more so than in any other major apple section in the United States. In orchards on moderately deep and well-drained soil, there is little danger of serious moisture shortage. This is due to a combination of dependable rainfall conditions and cool growing season. The Great Lakes have an important moderating effect on the temperature.

Central Atlantic section (II). This section produces about 28 per cent of the crop, showing a big jump (Fig. 2). The average summer temperatures are about five degrees higher than in the Northeastern section, (I), ranging between 70 and 75° F. Some orchards are planted as high as 2000 feet above sea level in the Appalachian Mountains, and the temperature at this height ranges between 65 and 75° F. Relatively few apples are grown in the area of South Carolina and southward due to warmer temperatures, averaging above 75° F. Most of the apples grown in the southern parts of this section are necessarily located at higher altitudes in the Appalachian Mountains. Winter freezing of trees is hardly a factor in this region due to the fact that minimum temperatures rarely go below —10 to —15°. In the mountainous areas, there are many orchard sites which permit good air drainage where there is less possibility of spring frosts.

Rainfall ranges between 40 and 45 inches for most of the section with the exception of the Potomac Valley where it is somewhat lower. From April to September, inclusive, about 22 inches of rain fall, but long periods of drouth seem to occur more frequently than in the Northeastern section (I).

18

Soils which permit deep rooting and cultural methods for conservation of moisture are necessary. Irrigation is being used increasingly.

Varieties should be selected for the northern part of this section which require 165 days or less for maturity. Varieties requiring longer periods of development can be grown in the southern section. Processing varieties are gaining favor. York is widely grown but has a cork spot problem. Delicious and Golden Delicious have been widely planted. Stayman and Rome also are grown in the northern area. Winesap in the southern area is losing favor. North Carolina has shown a sharp rise in production. The early Mollie Delicious is being planted in South Carolina and Georgia.

The Ohio Basin section (III). About 6.5 per cent of the apple crop in the United States is produced in this region. The June to August temperature averages about 75° F. The length of the growing season is approximately the same as that in the Central Atlantic section (II) for the northern and southern areas. Along the Ohio River where many apple orchards are concentrated, the annual precipitation is around 40 inches with about 20 inches occurring during the growing season. In the southern section, rainfall may reach 50 inches. However, due to the fact that temperatures are higher during the growing season, there is greater need for water than in northern sections of the United States. The drouth periods under these conditions tend to be more injurious to the trees. If the orchards are in soils of good water-holding capacity to a depth of three to four feet, serious damage is not likely to occur. Portable irrigation is on the increase.

Several varieties are popular throughout the region; namely, Golden Delicious, Delicious, Rome Beauty, Grimes Golden, Jonathan, Stayman Winesap, Winesap, Ben Davis, and Yellow Transparent. In Tennessee, early summer varieties, Yellow Transparent and Early Harvest, are widely planted in commerical orchards. In Illinois, Jonathan is the most important with Golden Delicious second. Delicious and Golden Delicious have gained prominence rather fast in all areas.

Southwestern section (IV). About 1.5 per cent of the apple crop is produced in this section. The temperatures between June and August are high, averaging between 75 and 80° F. The growing season is relatively long. Most of the rainfall occurs in Arkansas, with an annual precipitation of 45 to 50 inches; in southern Missouri, 40 to 45 inches; in northern Missouri and eastern Kansas, 35 to 40 inches; and in Nebraska, western Kansas, and western Oklahoma, below 35 inches. In regions where precipitation is under 30 inches per year, relatively few apples have been planted.

Jonathan is important and Golden Delicious and Delicious are being widely planted. Other varieties are Stayman, Winesap, Grimes Golden, York Imperial and Wealthy.

Northcentral section (V). About 2.5 percent of the apples are produced here. Through most of the section, summer temperatures range from 65 to 75° F. In the southern section, however, the range is between 70 and 75°, whereas in northern Wisconsin, it is relatively cool, or under 65°. Varieties with moderately long growing seasons can be grown in the southern section, whereas in the northern areas, it is necessary to plant varieties which are outstandingly resistant to low winter temperatures. Rainfall in the apple sections is relatively low, ranging from 25 to 35 inches. In the western part of this section, rainfall is less, and apples are grown primarily in home plantings. In general, less water is needed, however, due to the lower mean temperatures. Extreme winter cold is the main hazard. States in this region are conducting breeding programs for winter resistant varieties.

In southern Iowa and along Lake Michigan in Wisconsin, varieties commonly grown are McIntosh, Wealthy, Cortland and summer varieties such as Oldenburg and Yellow Transparent. Delicious, Jonathan, and to some extent Stayman Winesap and Winesap are grown. Special cold resistant varieties have been developed; namely, the Harlson, Honeygold, Red Baron in Minnsota, Joan, Secor in Iowa, Anoka in South Dakota and Regent.

Western section (VI). This section grows 32 per cent of the entire apple crop and based on new high-density plantings will rise markedly. The apple regions are concentrated in scattered areas which usually occur in valleys surrounded by mountains. Commercial apple production for the region as a whole has increased rapidly during the past 45 years; it is characterized by a relatively high production per tree and per acre. The production from one year to the next has been relatively uniform due, primarily, to the clear almost cloudless days throughout the summer, regular water supply from irrigation, and less trouble from spring frosts and freezes. The production for this area on an acre basis is generally higher than for other apple sections of the United States. In Washington State, the average yield is over seven bushels per bearing tree which, for an average of all orchards in a state is considered good. Size and color of the apples also are generally good. Circled area (Fig. 2) has a lower per tree yield. Winter freezes have killed many older trees in recent year.

It is true that western fruit usually sells for better prices than the eastern fruit, but the returns to the western grower on a bushel basis have been generally less than that obtained by the eastern growers, especially when apple prices are low. However, with high apple prices since World War II, the good productiveness of the western orchards has resulted in good returns.

Predictions are that Washington will average 38 million bushels in the 1970's with a 41 to 50 million crop every third year.

The *Wenatchee district* is in northcentral Washington along bench land of the Columbia River and tributaries. Spring frosts are rare, summer temperatures are 65 to 70° F, nights cool, precipitation 7 to 10 inches annually and mostly in winter as snow, soils deep and irrigation extensively practiced using 40 to 45 inches.

The *Yakima* district lies along the Yakima River about 100 miles south of the Wenatchee district, ranking second to it in Washington. Frosts may occur in low wide areas, and irrigation timing is important due to light rather shallow soils.

Delicious (50%), Winesap (30%), and Golden Delicious are 99% of the varieties. Other varieties are Rome, Jonathan, Stayman, and Yellow Newtown, but with CA storage these varieties and Winesap are declining.

In Oregon, the *Hood River Valley* in the northcentral area is important. Winter injury is a problem, but production is relatively good. Summer temperatures are around 65° F. Delicious, and Yellow Newtown are the leading varieties with Rome, Jonathan, Winesap and Gravenstein of minor importance; Golden Delicious plantings are on the increase.

Apple trees have been largely replaced by pear trees in the Rogue River Valley and the nonirrigated Willamette Valley because the climate is more favorable for pears.

California ranks high in apple production, rising rapidly in recent years. The Sebastapol area is north of San Francisco where it is cool, rainfall about 40 inches and irrigation rarely needed. Gravenstein is harvested in July and the best apples are distributed widely throughout the United States as an early summer apple; most Gravenstein, however, are processed to sauce and other products. Other varieties include Rome, Jonathan, and Yellow Newtown.

Another district is south of San Francisco in the Watsonville area. Rainfall is 25 to 30 inches and some irrigation is practiced. Main variety is Yellow Newtown, which is largely placed in CA storage. Yellow varieties are used because of fogginess and poor coloring of red varieties, although red strains of Delicious are being planted.

Idaho orchards are located at 700 to 3000 feet altitude along the tributaries of the Snake River near the Oregon line. Summer temperatures average about 70° F. Frost is a factor in the broad valley floors. High water table, also, has been a detrimental factor. Leading varieties are Delicious, Rome, Jonathan and Golden Delicious.

Utah orchards are located adjacent to the Great Salt Lake on the south and southeast shores. Production is limited. Altitude is about 4500 feet; average summer temperature is 70° F. Frosts and irrigation water are limiting factors. Delicious, Golden Delicious and Jonathan dominate with some Rome, McIntosh, and Lodi.

Western Colorado apple regions are in the valley of the Colorado River and its tributaries. Orchards are being planted at higher elevations to overcome poorly drained soils in the valleys. Delicious, Jonthan, Golden Delicious and Rome are popular.

21

TABLE 1. TREND AND IMPORTANCE OF APPLE VARIETIES IN THE UNITED STATES
(DATA FOR ORCHARDS OF 100 OR MORE TREES)

VARIETY LISTED BY IMPORTANCE 1969-71	PRODUCTION (MILLIONS OF LBS.)[1]				PROBABLE FUTURE TREND
	1942-48	1949-55	1961-67	1969-71	
1. Delicious	940.4	1074.1	1494.6	1846.2	Marked Increase
2. Golden Delicious	115.5	161.5	510.1	814.8	Marked Increase
3. McIntosh	414.9	580.9	721.4	693.2	Steady
4. Rome Beauty	313.5	336.5	442.3	510.6	Increase
5. Jonathan	350.5	331.9	394.5	424.4	Increase
6. York Imperial	253.6	239.7	289.3	352.1	Increase
7. Stayman Winesap	235.1	198.2	277.4	299.8	Steady
8. Winesap	534.7	502.5	343.5	207.8	Marked Decrease
9. Yellow Newtown	202.8	207.5	190.6	173.1	Slight Decrease
10. Cortland	69.2	119.9	157.1	160.6	Stabilize
11. R. I. Greening	87.6	113.7	141.6	151.4[2]	Slight Increase
12. Northern Spy	78.4	101.4	140.1	137.8[2]	Steady
13. Gravenstein	124.5	133.7	104.7	108.4[2]	Steady
14. Baldwin	147.5	147.5	84.7	51.3[2]	Decrease
15. Grimes Golden	96.8	96.8	38.5	30.6[2]	Decrease
16. Ben Davis & Gano	101.4	87.6	39.0	22.7[2]	Decrease
17. Wealthy	96.8	92.2	49.5	21.8[2]	Decrease
18. Miscelleaneous	567.0	497.9	412.2	131.3[2]	
19. Miscellaneous	——	——	——	675.2[3]	Increase

[1] In 1967 USDA Crop Reporting Service changed from bushels to pounds for apples due to so many different containers; e.g. 12 3-lb. poly bags in a carton weigh 38 lbs; 12 4-lb. bags in a carton weigh 50 lbs. A tray pack carton of apples weighs 43 lbs. USDA is using the figure 46.1 lbs. for one bushel of apples.

[2] Data are averages for 1969-70. Data for these varieties for 1971 and later are included under "miscellaneous." Other varieties include: Esopus Spitzenburg, Wagener, Stark, Winter Banana, King David, Limbertwig, Tompkins King, Yellow Bellflower, and recently named varieties that have not been fully evaluated for wide planting.

[3] Data for 1971.

In *Montana* the winter hardy McIntosh is planted along the Bitterroot River.

In *New Mexico,* planted along the San Juan River, Delicious, Rome, Jonathan, Golden Delicious and Winesap are planted.

World Apple Regions. The map in the Appendix gives a quick view of where apples are grown in the World. Western Europe dominates. This includes, for the most part, France, Federal Republic of Germany, United Kingdom, Italy, Belgium, Denmark, Norway, Sweden, Luxembourg, the Netherlands, Portugal, Switzerland, and Austria.

Eastern Europe includes the Soviet Union (to the Ural Mountains), Poland, Rumania, Bulgaria, Yugoslovia, Hungary, Czeckoslovakia, and the German Democratic Republic.

Japan, South Korea and Australia (includes Tasmania) are shown on the map, as is New Zealand.

In China apples grow mainly in two regions: (a) Liaoning province, Southern Manchuria and (b) in the loesslands of Shansi, Shensi, and Kansu provinces, Southwest of Peking.

Canada's apple regions are principally in Ontario Province near Lake

Ontario and British Columbia in the Okanogan Valley, although there are scattered plantings in other provinces near U. S. borders.

In South America, apples dominate in Argentina in (a) the Rio Negro and Neuquen area (largest), (b) the Mendoza and (c) Buenos Aires and Sante Fe area. Other countries grow apples on a minor scale at suitable altitudes and climate including Chili, Columbia, and in a very limited way in Peru and others.

Mexico, in the middle and upper areas toward the United States border and at proper altitude and climate, grows around 100 million pounds annually.

Trend in apple trees and production. Since 1910, there has been a marked decrease in apple tree number with relatively less decrease in U.S. apple production. However, with the elimination of the marginal orchards, the decline in apple production has been very little vs. tree numbers since the year 1930. Records show almost as many apples were produced in 1949 as in 1909 with about one-fourth the number of trees. This is due, no doubt, to the better selection of sites and soils in recent years and to the use of better management practices. Recent surveys indicate U.S. apple production will rise in future years. The general decrease in number of apple trees and production in recent years can be accounted for by a decrease in demand for apples as a result of a somewhat greater consumption of other fruits, such as citrus. The per capita consumption of apples in recent years has been dropping to around 16 pounds and for citrus, it is around 30 pounds, or about twice as much as for apples.

Trend in varieties. Since the 1920's there has been a definite trend toward the selection of apple varieties having high dessert quality. Table 1 gives the trend in popularity of apple varieties since 1942 in the United States and production trends in recent years. It will be noted that of 17 varieties, only Delicious and Golden Delicious have shown marked increases since 1942 while Winesap has shown a marked decrease. Many varieties, formerly important, such as Baldwin, Grimes, Northern Spy and Wealthy have fallen into the "miscellaneous" class since 1971. Delicious and Golden Delicious have shown a spectacular increase in planting in the U.S. and in most apple regions of the World. Jonathan also is widely favored and in some countries, such as Hungary, it leads. The bright red mutations are in demand over the standard red varieties.

Red Delicious, half of which is produced in Washington, accounts for about 27% of the U.S. crop and is rising; McIntosh, 12% with 45% in New York and 32% in New England; Golden Delicious, 12%; Rome 8%; Jonathan, 6%; and the York, 5%. These six varieties account for 70% of the U.S. crop. About 90% of the U.S. crop is winter varieties, 8-9% fall, and 2-4% summer varieties.

A national survey by Washington Apple Commission showed United

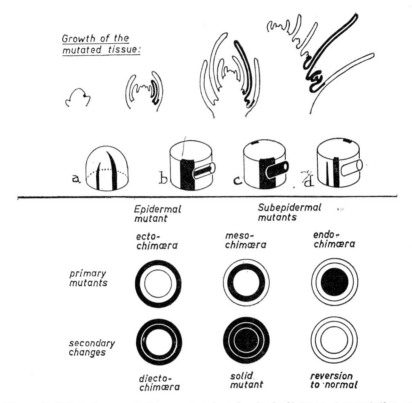

Figure 3. This is how mutations or sports arise in fruit trees. A vegetative cell mutates (black, upper row left) in a growing point of a shoot and continues dividing to right to "a" (second row left). Limb "b" carries only part of mutant and fruits developing on limb are variable for the standard and mutant character, as, e.g., scarlet red skin of fruit. At "c" mutant redder fruits on this limb will be alike. Side limb at "d" bears fruits like parent tree. (lower chart) Different types of periclinal (circular) chimaera mutants are shown on cross-cut spurs or limbs. (The late Nils Nybom, Sweden)

States housewives preferred in order: Delicious and Golden Delicious, with Jonathan and McIntosh preferred over Winesap.

While the market demand and the prices for Delicious have been generally good, there is always the danger of overplanting it.

With the holding of high quality fresh apples in controlled atmosphere storage most months of the year, the number of leader varieties may be reduced, for the most part, to only three, four or so, as e.g., Delicious, Golden Delicious, McIntosh, and Jonathan. Possibly one or two summer varieties may be included since they can be produced economically, spread the season, and are sold soon. With a growing amount of apples being processed, it is possible that such varieties as York, Northern Spy, Idared, Rome Beauty and Rhode Island Greening will continue to show increased planting, as indicated in Table 1. Winesap, a former leader and good keeper, is gradually losing to better quality CA stored varieties. About

TABLE 2. Some Fruit Characteristics of the More Important World Apple Varieties.

Variety	Where Mostly Grown[1]	Days Bloom to Picking	Fruit[2] Size	Fruit[3] Color	Fruit[4] Shape	Acidity[5]	Dessert or Cooking	Cold Storage Season Days[8]	Scald[6] Tendency	Age of Bearing (Yrs.)	Ann. or Bien. Bearing Tendency	Standard Tree Size[7]
Y. Transparent	US, USSR, WG	70-95	S-M	Y	Co	H	Cooking	0(90)	None	4-6	Bien.	M-S
Oldenburg	US	90-95	M	SR	Ro-Ob	H	Cooking	0-30(90)	SI	4-6	Intermed.	M
Gravenstein	US, N	110-115	M	SBR	Ob-Ang	M-H	Cooking	0-30(90)	SI	6-8	Ann.	M-L
James Grieve	C, WE, N, S, At, NE	110-120	M-L	YRS	Ro-Co	M	Dessert	60-90	SI	4-6	Ann.	M-S
Antonovka	USSR	110-120	M	Y	Ro-Co-Ang	H	Cooking	60-90	M	4-6	Bien.	M
Wealthy	US, P	120-125	M	MR	Ro-Ob	M-H	Both	0-30(90)	SI	4-6	Bien.	M-S
Winter Banana	US	120-125	M-L	YBl	Ro-Co	M-L	Both(fair)	90-120(150)	SI	4-6	Intermed.	M
Cortland	US	125-130	M-S	MR	Ob	M	Both	90-120(150)	M	4-6	Ann.	M
McIntosh	US, USSR, P	125-130	M	MR	Ro-Ob	M	Both	60-90(150)	SI[9]	4-6	Ann.	L
Goldpairmain	C, WE, Sw, B, USSR, C	125-135	M-S	YRS	Co	M	Both	100-120	M	4-6	Intermed.	M
Ingrid Marie	D, S, NE, WG	130-140	M	G-Y,R	Ro,Ob	M-L	Dessert	90-120	SI	5-7	Intermed.	M
Landsberger R.	EE, C	130-140	M-L	YMR	Co	H-M	Both	120-140	SI	4-6	Intermed.	M
Cox's Orange	S, EE, WE, D, H, UK, SA, C, At, NE	130-150	S-M	YSR	Ro	M-L	Dessert	90-120(150)	SI	4-6	Intermed.	M
R.I. Greening	US, USSR	135-145	M-S	GY	Ro-Ob	M-H	Cooking	90-120(180)	Sev.	6-8	Intermed.	M-L
Bramley's Se.	UK, Be	135-145	L	GYS	Ro-Ob-Co	H	Cooking	150-180	Sev.	5-7	Bien.	L-M
Landsberger Rtte.	EE, ME	130-150	M-L	Y	Ob-Ang	H	Cooking	30-60(90)	–	6-8	Intermed.	L
Wagener	US	135-145	M	BR	Obl-Ang	M	Both	90-120(150)	Sev.	4-6	Intermed.	M
Ralls	J, K, Ch	–	M-S	R	Ro-Co	M-L	Dessert	120-150(250)	M	6-8	Bien.	M
Kidd's Orange Red	NZ	140-150	M	BSR	Co	M	Dessert			5-8		M
Go. Delicious	W	140-145	M-L	Y	Co	M	Both	90-120(150)	SI	4-6	Intermed.	M
Grimes Golden	US	140-145	M-S	Y	Ro-Ob	M	Both	60-90(120)	Sev.	4-8	Intermed.	M
Baldwin	W	140-150	M-L	MR	Ro-Co	M	Cooking	120-150(200)	M-Sev.	8-10	Bien.	M-L
Jonathan	W	140-145	M-S	UBR	Ro-Co	M-H	Both	60-90(120)	SI[9]	4-6	Ann.	L
Delicious	W	140-150	M-L	MR	Ob-Co	L	Both	90-100(180)	SI	5-8	Intermed.	L
Stark	US	140-150	M-L	MDS	Ro-Co	M	Both	120-150(180)	SI	6-8	Intermed.	L

25

Variety	Country		Size[2]	Color[3]	Shape[4]	[5]	Use	Storage days[8]	Scald[6]		Type	Size[7]
Esopus Spitzen.	US	145-150	M-L	BR	Ob-Co	M	Both	90-120(180)	Sl	6-8	Intermed.	L
Boskoop	C,WE,D,Sw NE,UK	145-155	L	G-YMR	Ob-Ro	H	Both	120-140(180)	Sl	8-10	Intermed.	L
No. Spy	US	145-155	L	BSR	Ro-Co	M	Both	120-150(180)	Sl	10-14	Intermed.	M-L
Bancroft	P	145-155	M-S	RS	Ro	H	Dessert	140-170	Sl	5-8	Ann.	L
Ayvanya	B	145-155	S	Y	Ro-Co	L	Cooking	180-210	Sev.	8-10	Bien.	L
Ontario	EG	150-160	L	YS	Ob-Co	H-M	Both	120-140	Sl	4-6	Intermed.	S
Glockenapfel	S,WG	150-165	M-L	Y	Ro-Co	H	Dessert	150-180	–	6-8	Bien.	M
Ben Davis	US	150-155	M-L	SMR	Ro-Co	M	Cooking	120-150(240)	M	4-6	Ann.	M
York Imperial	US	155-165	M-L	LR	Ob-Obl	M	Cooking	120-150(180)	Sev.	6-8	Bien.	M
Roter Boskoop	WE	160-170	L	G-Y,R	Ro	H	Both	120-150	–	8-10	Intermed.	L
Rome Beauty (Imperatore)	US,I	160-165	L	MR	Ro-Ob	M-L	Cooking	120-150(210)	M	4-6	Ann.	M-S
Yellow Newtown	US	160-165	M	Y	Ro-Ob	M-H	Both	150-180(240)	Sl	8-10	Bien.	M
Winesap	US	160-170	M-S	DR	Co	M	Both	150-210(240)	M	6-8	Intermed.	M
Stayman	US	160-165	M-L	MR	Ro-Co	M	Both	120-150(180)	Sev.	4-6	Ann.	L
Sturmer Pip.	B,P,USSR,Au	160-165	M-L	YG MR	Ro-Co	M	Both	180-200				
Black Twig (Paragon)	US	165-170	M-L	MDR	Ro-Ob	M	Both	120-150(180)	Sev.	8-10	Bien.	L
Granny Smith	A,Au,NZ,Chili	180-200	M-L	Green	Ob-Ro	L-M	Both	150-180(210)	Sev.	5-7	Ann.	M-L
Democrat	Au	190-195	L	R	Ob	M-H	Dessert	150-180(240)	Sl	8-10	Intermed.	M
Splendour	NZ											

Symbols:

1 Abbreviations for countries. (Where a country is listed for a variety, neighboring countries, or those of similar environment, also may grow it.) Dr. S. A. Pieniazek of Poland, Dr. M. Zwintzscher of Germany, and Dr. J. R. Magness, USA, furnished data for this table. A-Argentina; At-Austria; Au-Australia; B-Bulgaria; Be-Belgium; C-Czechoslovakia; Ch-China; D-Denmark; EE-Eastern Europe; EG-Eastern Germany; H-Hungary; I-Italy; J-Japan; K-Korea; ME-Middle Europe; N-Norway; Ne-Netherlands; NZ-New Zealand; P-Poland; S-Sweden; SA-South Africa; Sw-Switzerland; UK-United Kingdom; US-United States; USSR-Russia; W-of fairly world wide importance; WE-Western Europe; WG-Western Germany

2 S-small; M-medium; L-large.
3 Y-yellow; S-striped; R-red; B-bright; M-medium; D-dull; Bl-blush.
4 C-conic; Ob-oblate; R-round; Obl-oblique; Ang-angular.
5 M-medium; H-high; L-low.

6 Sl-slight; M-medium; Sev-severe.
7 L-large; M-medium; S-small.
8 Maximum storage days in parenthesis.
9 Susceptible to soft scald.

C. E. Chase, Washington State Apple Adv. Commission

Figure 3. Delicious is the most widely planted apple variety in the World. It accounts for 27% of the U. S. crop. This is because it has a good combination of tree characters and popular high-quality fruit.

50 percent of the U.S. crop is processed and up to 70 percent in some areas; processing probably will continue to increase.

Desired characteristics. On the basis of experience during the past two or three decades, it would appear that the most important characteristics of an apple variety to consider when making a selection are these: it should be an annual bearer, good to very good in dessert quality, very attractive in appearance, relatively pest-resistant, productive, and hardy. In addition, if the fruit is of good storage and good handling quality, and a good processor, the value of the variety is greatly increased. Some of the important characteristics which should be considered in the selection of a variety are given in Table 2. Also indicated is the region or areas of the world where the variety is popular.

Color strains. There are a number of bud sports of popular varieties which are supposedly the same as the parent except they are redder, less russetting, etc. However, a considerable degree of caution should be taken in the use of any or all color strains. There are some cases where they have been propagated with relatively little preliminary trial. Although the best color strains of the red apple varieties appear to have considerable merit, there is no assurance that these strains are identical in every respect except color, etc., to the parent variety. The size, storage quality of the fruit, and other factors may also be different. In some cases, the shade of color in the strain appears to be deeper than the parent, and, in fact, so deep that the color is dull and unattractive. Thus, it is important that the prospective grower of such color strains make every effort to see bearing trees of the strain under his conditions and make his own decision if it is better than the parent. Red color is important in good sales appeal. Most of the apple trees now being planted are of red strains, a few have been grown rather extensively under commercial conditions and can be evaluated briefly as follows:

Delicious strains. Starking and Richared are widely planted. Starking reddens about two weeks ahead of the standard Delicious, but the date of maturity of the fruit is the same; hence, one must be careful not to pick the variety too soon, which has been a problem with red strains. At picking time the Starking develops a dark maroon red when it is fully mature. Richared does not color as early as Starking and at picking time it is more completely colored than the standard variety.

GROUP I
(Lowest Color)

Variety	Color Pattern	Type of Growth
Earlired	Stripe	Standard
Hi Red	Blush	Standard
Starking (Old)	Stripe	Standard
Wood	Stripe	Spur

GROUP II
(Intermediate Color)

Variety	Color Pattern	Type of Growth
Wellspur	Blush	Spur
Red Rich (Scacco)	Blush	Standard
Hardispur	Blush	Spur
Starking (Franks)	Stripe	Standard
Harrold	Stripe	Standard
Redspur	Blush	Spur
Huebner	Stripe	Standard
Imperial	Blush	Standard
Royal Red	Blush	Standard
Red King	Stripe	Standard

GROUP III
(Greatest Color)

Variety	Color Pattern	Type of Growth
Top Red	Stripe	Standard
Starkrimson (Bisbee)	Blush	Spur
Red Prince	Stripe	Standard
Chelan Red	Blush	Standard
Ryan Red	Stripe	Standard
Hi Early	Stripe	Standard
Houser Red	Blush	Standard
Red Queen	Stripe	Standard

The general rule of thumb was to choose from Group III if in a poor coloring area and Group II or I if in a good coloring area. Growers and researchers have been on the lookout for a high-color striped spur, considered most desirable. The spur-type trees are more open with long limbs with numerous fruiting spurs; apparently they are mutations. A new Red King spur strain shows promise.

Over 150 red strains have been named, and they continue to come, but they have not been fully tested. Washington specialists have given a tentative evaluation (see above) of some of their many more promising strains, based on color categories.

Rome Beauty strains. Gallia Beauty is a seedling, apparently, and Cox Red Rome is of bud sport origin. Both strains have a bright attractive red color more uniform than the standard Rome Beauty. The fruits are smaller, earlier maturing, and possibly not quite so good in storage quality as the standard Rome Beauty, although more experimental data are needed to verify this. The Black Rome was originated and propagated to some extent in the Pacific Northwest. It appears to be considerably darker than the standard Rome Beauty.

Stayman Winesap strains. Stamared and C & O Stayman are popular. Their color is apparently similar to that of Stayman except it averages somewhat more color at maturity. Both strains crack. The overall medium red Carlough strain in New Jersey has shown little or no cracking.

Jonathan strains. Jonared and Blackjon are the common strains. Jonared appears to have a somewhat brighter color, the Blackjon being blacker than the parent. Jonared carries considerable more color than the parent variety. Jonnee shows promise.

Other varietal strains. There are red color strains of other red apple

28

Figure 4. There is increased world planting of high-density orchards. Cion wood is of high-color strains of standard varieties or of "spur-growth-type" strains grafted on stocks of various degrees of dwarfing. The earlier-bearing spur strains on seedling roots form a three-quarter size tree and, hence, also are being close-planted. Above is a high-density orchard of Delicious and Golden Delicious near Ashville, North Carolina.

varieties, such as York Imperial, Baldwin, Northern Spy, McIntosh, Esopus Spitzenburg, Gravenstein, and Oldenburg.

The original and earlier trees of the McIntosh variety apparently were of a good solid red type of color. However, in recent years there have been mutations to a striped type which is not very attractive. It would be well to avoid the striped strain.

Golden Delicious. This is one of the highest quality apples. The main problem is russeting and obtaining a bright yellow at harvest. Many substitutes have been suggested. Mutsu (Golden Delicious x Indo) or Crispin from Japan; Sungold (apparently a seedling) from New Jersey and Spigold (Red Northern Spy x Golden Delicious) from New York are being planted and tested. VPI No. 8, Missouri A-3071 and A-2071; Sundale Sturdy Spur, PrimeGold (B. Hoekman, Wash.) and Stark's Blushing also are under test.

Promising New Varieties. It is said that it takes about 40 years to evaluate fully an apple variety. The following varieties are being planted commercially. It would be well for you to check your specialist on local performance. *Early Varieties.* Puritan (McI. x R. Astra.) from Mass.; and Viking (Jon., Del., Williams, E. McI., Starr) from Wisc. are planted in resp. areas. Tydeman Red (Worchester Pearman x McIntosh) from England shows promise in the Northwest. Mollie's Delicious (mix of Golden Delicious, Edgewood, Red Gravenstein, Close) from N. J. and Paulared (Mich. seedling) are commercially planted. *Later Varieties.* Idared (Jonathan x Wagener) from Idaho has been rather generally planted in apple regions; Wayne (Northwestern Greening x Red Northern Spy), Macoun (McIntosh x Jersey Black) and Monroe (Jonathan x Rome) all from New York are being planted generally in regions where their parents are grown. Melrose (Jonathan x Delicious) from Ohio is planted in the midwest area. Spartan (McIntosh x Yellow Newtown) from British Columbia shows promise in the northern tier of states and the northwest. Crandall (Rome x Jonathan) from Illinois is being planted in the midwest. Regent (Daniels Red Duchess x Delicious) from Minnesota is hardy, late, a good dessert and processor. The A1379 (Cox x Jonathan) from England looks good in W. Europe.

Review Questions

1. List five leading states in apple production; what is the approximate total apple production of the United States?
2. What important factors govern the selection of varieties in Minnesota as compared with selection for Virginia?
3. How do you account for the fact that apple production in the East in recent years is more uniform from year to year than in earlier years; Why is production in Wenatchee district of Washington higher per tree and per acre than in the eastern districts?
4. What is the general trend of apple trees and apple production since 1910; how do you account for this?
5. What are the three leading apple varieties in the United States?
6. What apple varieties are showing increase in popularity; how do you account for this?
7. What is the general situation and recommendations regarding the planting of color strains of standard varieties?
8. Discuss in general the World apple variety situation.
9. Point out the apple regions of the World.

Suggested Collateral Readings

Anonymous. Agricultural Outlook Charts, Agr. Marketing Service, U.S. Dept. of Agr., Washington, D. C.

Anonymous. Foreign Crops and Markets. Office of Foreign Agricultural Relations, Circular, U.S. Dept. of Agr., Washington, D. C.

Anonymous. Monthly crop report for fruits and supplemental publications on production, use and value of noncitrus fruits in the U.S. and world. U.S. Dept. of Agr., Agricultural Marketing Service, Washington, D. C.

Beach, S. A. Apples of New York. Vols. I & II, N. Y. Agr. Exp. Sta. 1903.

Berti-Petrovici, I. et al. Apple variety and tree descriptions (Pomologia II) 1007 pp. Editura Academici Repub. Populare Romine. 1964.

Bittner, C. S. et al. Golden Delicious Apple in Pennsylvania. Penna. Agr. Ext. Serv. Cir. 547, 31pp. 1970.

Blair, D. S. Apple growing in Eastern Canada. Dept. of Agr. Public. 847 (Ottawa) Request recent edition.

Blodgett, E. C. and Aichele, M. D. Apple variety notes. Wash State Hort. Bull. No. 3. 46 pp. Oct. 1960.

Brown, D. S., C. O. Hesse, E. C. Koch. Red sports of Delicious - reversion to stripes. Calif. Agric. Oct. 1959.

(See additional references under Chapter II, Appendix)

30

CHAPTER III

Establishing the Fruit Planting

◆ ◆

LOCATING THE ENTERPRISE

It is a serious mistake to locate an orchard improperly. An error in planting annual crops can be corrected the following year, but with fruit trees it is a long-time proposition. Careful orchard planning at the beginning pays dividends later. In the early 1900's during boom periods, orchards were indiscriminately planted, many on sites where climate and soil were not suited to fruit growing, and, as a result, these orchards proved unprofitable and sooner or later were abandoned. Today, commercial fruit growing is limited to definite regions which have proven over many years to be adapted to profitable fruit growing.

Before selecting a region for fruit growing, it is important to make a careful study of the transportation and marketing facilities, winter and spring temperatures, moisture, soil and site conditions, and suitability of a certain kind of fruit for a given region and site. There are many advantages in locating the fruit enterprise in a region where fruit growing is well established and where there are big centers of population. The advantages are:

1. There are definite savings in co-operative purchasing of supplies and equipment on a large scale.

2. Repairs for machinery and general orchard supplies are readily available from near-by dealers.

3. In well-established regions, there is considerable local interest and inspiration to be gained from intelligent and alert fellow workers.

Paul Stark, Jr., Vice President and world traveler, Starks' Nurseries and Orchard Co., Louisiana, Missouri, assisted in this chapter revision.

4. There is a more stable market with efficient selling organizations where buyers of quantity are available to fill their requirements.

5. Shipping charges to distant markets are held to a minimum.

6. Commercial storage space, processing plants for fruits, and outlets for the by-products are likely to be favorable.

7. Broad and heavily traveled roads near large cities afford excellent sites for roadside markets; public-pick-your-own program also is possible.

8. Transportation facilities in and out of the region, when needed, are usually adequate and rapid.

9. In general, there is better quality and more extensive public service from recognized agencies, such as the experimental stations, agricultural colleges, county agricultural agents, and large commercial firms dealing in orchard equipment and supplies.

10. In major fruit states, a greater percentage of a grower's tax money and investment in equipment come back to him in service from public agencies interested in fruit growing.

There always will be scattered orchards away from centers of population and fruit growing, and they have their definite advantages. Such growers usually manage smaller acreages and enjoy a more or less independent local market where fruit prices are often better than in heavily supplied general markets, provided the business is not overdone. Good fruit land in such areas is often less expensive to buy and carries less taxes, which makes for better profit in production. Furthermore, there is less danger from insect and disease contamination from neighboring unkept orchards, or from buildup in certain insect populations such as mites and codling moth.

Climatic factors. *Temperature* is the most important climatic factor affecting the geographic distribution of fruits and varieties of the fruits. Man has little control over temperature and, therefore, it is wise to check carefully with local growers, horticultural extension service specialists, and the government weather station regarding frequency of frosts and extreme temperatures in past years. An increase in altitude results in lower temperatures the same as a change in latitude from the equator northward or southward. Extremely cold winters where the temperature falls to 20° or 40°F. below zero, or violent fluctuations from relatively warm temperatures in winter to extremely cold temperatures are not desirable for deciduous fruits. Long hot dry summers are not favorable to successful fruit growing. Adequate hours of temperature below 45°F. must occur, however, to break the *rest period* for specific fruits and varieties (Table 1).

Spring frosts or freezes shortly before, during, or after bloom constitute one of the most important hazards in fruit growing. They are far more destructive to the fruit industry than autumn frosts. The possibility of an occasional frost is a hazard on which many fruit growers take a chance regardless of how successful a given region may be in fruit production. It is

(Left) National Frost Protection Co., Inc., Glendale, Calif. (Right) E. A. Richardson, Utah Agr. Exp. Sta.

Figure 1. (Left) A California dual "Tropic Breeze" machine for drawing warmer air from above and spreading it over up to 20 acres of the orchard floor to prevent frost damage. Helicopters are serving a similar role. (Right) Orchard heaters are most effective in a large orchard and where trees are medium-large and the air movement is slow or still.

hard to find orchards that do not suffer from them at one time or another. Dwarfs being low should be planted on the higher sites. The average peach grower in the midwestern states expects an average of three good crops of peaches in five years, with two entirely or partially lost to spring frosts or winter freezes. Injury from spring frosts are less likely within a mile or two of large bodies of water like the Great Lakes which have a tempering effect.

TABLE 1. WINTER CHILLING TEMPERATURE RANGE REQUIRED BY FRUITS TO BREAK THE REST PERIOD

Fruit Species	Hours Below 45°F Needed	Fruit Species	Hours Below 45°F Needed
Apple	1200-1500	Peach (Texas)	500- 950
E. Walnut (No. Calif.)	1200-1500	Peach (General)	50*-1200
E. Walnut (So. Calif.)	700	European Plum	800 -1200
Pear	1200-1500	Jap. Plum	700 -1000
Cherry, Sour	1200	Apricot (No. Amer.)	700 -1000
Cherry, Sweet	1100-1300	Almond	200- 500
Peach (Fla.)*	200- 400	Fig	200

*Flordawon, Univ. of Florida, Gainesville, has a very low chilling requirement.

Wind machines work best under quiet air conditions by mixing warm air above the trees (so-called temperature inversion) with colder air among the trees. *Firing* is of two types: (a) burns as open flame (petroleum bricks, logs, rubber tires, etc.) and (b) heats metal objects, such as stacks that radiate heat (Fig. 1). Firing is effective if enough fuel is burned to keep the plant and air temperatures above danger levels. Heating is more effective in big orchards with large trees, which tend to hold the heat in the orchard. Freezing of tissue reaches the danger point around 28°F, so

33

Figure 2. A hail storm while the fruit is developing results in bruised, malformed fruit, most of which must be classified as culls. The trees also may be severely damaged. Sites where hail storms are known to frequently occur should be avoided. Spring hail damage may afford fire blight entry particularly on pear.

that heating or wind machines should start at around 32°F. *Sprinkling* by an irrigation system protects trees by the water releasing heat as it freezes (heat of fusion), holding the plant temperature at around 32°F as long as water is applied. Tree breakage, of course, can be a problem with big trees but not so much with dwarfs. Icicles indicate an adequate application rate. Florida Circular 287, California Circular 400, and USDA Farmers' Bull. 1588, cover these subjects. Michigan has a bulletin on sprinkling.

Heavy winds which blow more or less continuously over a site are definitely undesirable. It is difficult to do a good job of spraying when the wind blows continuously from one direction. Dry winds during the blossoming period affect the fruit set and may result in frequent reductions in the apple crop. Also, there is a tendency for young trees to grow one-sided and lean with the prevailing wind. This more or less throws the tree off balance and may cause it to break apart with a heavy crop.

Amount of *sunshine* is important in governing the rate of food manufacture by fruit-tree leaves which, in turn, affects the size and amount of color of apples and the regularity with which the tree bears from year to year. For example, in regions of Washington State where sunshine is relatively abundant, fruit production per acre tends to be greater and alternate bearing of heavy and light crops of fruit is less pronounced than in Eastern states where there is more cloudiness during the growing season.

Hail is a hazard in fruit growing which is less likely to be destructive than spring frosts. There are some areas in fruit growing regions, however, which experience hail more frequently than others. Local growers and hail

34

Courtesy Eleanor Gilman, Middleton Springs, Vt.

Figure 3. Windbreaks may be desirable in areas where wind blows more or less continuously from one direction. Consult the local forester. This lombardy poplar windbreak grew to 50 feet in 18 years and is backed by slower-growing red pines. Located near Peru, N. Y., it reduces winterkill and windfallen fruit.

insurance companies are probably better informed on the susceptible areas. Hail can be destructive to the fruit, reducing it in grade or almost destroying it completely if the stones are large. It shatters the leaves and is also destructive to the bark, bruising and splitting it, as well as stunting growth in general (Figure 2). Hail insurance for fruit is available and some growers, especially in regions of frequent hail occurrence, have found it worthwhile. A public-pick-your-own program has helped salvage hail fruit.

Size of planting. If the grower intends to serve a large and general market, he might consider a large enterprise of 100 or 200 acres or more. This will enable him to ship in truck loads and thus receive greater consideration from large marketing agencies. If he intends to serve the local market, his business may be large or small, depending upon the size of the population to be served in the neighborhood. For example, near Cleveland, Ohio, one grower is managing 200 acres from which he sells almost his entire apple crop to the Cleveland trade. If the local market consists of scattered small towns, such a neighborhood usually will not absorb as large a quantity of fruit at a given time. However, it will purchase a continuous supply in small quantities throughout the season. Grower-

35

Figure 4. An excellent orchard site located near the heavily populated region of Columbus, Ohio. Peaches are shown in the foreground, apples in the background, with the residence, storage, and machinery sheds located in the center of the orchard next to a hard-surfaced road. Note rotation of different ages of trees in background.

owned cold storages have made it possible for fruit growers away from concentrated population centers to give a small continuous supply of fruit to a limited local market.

The fact should not be overlooked that if the grower intends to grow large tree crops, there is a period of five to ten years when the orchard will be largely an expense, and the trees will pay back little. Compact trees, however, bring quick returns, or, he might consider diversifying his business by growing other crops such as small fruits or vegetables, and perhaps some livestock. Cultivation of small fruits or vegetables between trees, especially stone fruit trees, such as peaches, cherries, and plums, is particularly beneficial to the trees, as well as to the intercrop. The same equipment and facilities in general are required for both the tree and the intercrops and, therefore, the initial cost for equipment is no greater.

It is interesting to note that there is a definite tendency away from the small orchards of 10 to 40 acres. The profit from small orchards is usually not adequate support for an average-size family, and it is necessary for the operator to have outside interests. There are cases, however, where growers can handle a small acreage, preferably diversified, together with a roadside market, purchasing additional produce to supply the trade. It is much to his advantage to be on a well-travelled highway.

Selection of site. It is important to select a good orchard site with favorable elevation. Upland rolling or sloping fields which are not too steep for efficient orchard operations are the most desirable sites (Figure 4). River bottoms or flat valley floors are usually undesirable due to the fact

36

that cold air settles in these areas and frost or freezing injury are possibilities. It is necessary that cold air move out of the orchard into land and valleys located at a lower level. On a slope, trees should not be planted lower than about 50 feet above the base of the slope, especially where cold air drains slowly from the valley floor. Under such conditions, a difference of 100 feet in elevation may make a difference of 5° to 10° in the minimum temperature encountered. In some seasons, such differences would make the difference between a full crop and a crop failure. Level land is not objectionable if frosts are not a problem or if located within a mile or so from large bodies of water so that there is a tempering effect of the deep water.

Where there is a thick woods nearby, it is unwise to plant closer than within about 75 feet of it because the timber tends to harbor cold air. In addition, the forest trees compete with the fruit plants for light, water, and nutrients. Woods on a slope below an orchard may retard movement of cold air downward, but this can be remedied to some extent by cutting 75-foot swaths through the woods at 100-yard intervals.

Although it is desirable that the orchard be located on an elevated site in order to secure good air drainage, sites on top of ridges may be unsatisfactory because of exposure to winds, and generally drier and less fertile soil conditions. The direction of slope of the land usually has little effect upon the fruit crop. However, in case of persistent prevailing winds, an orchard planted on the leeward slope would naturally be the more desirable, especially if the winds continue during extremely cold weather. Such winds will increase freezing damage at a given temperature. It is true that north slopes tend to retard bud development in the spring, whereas south slopes accelerate it, and east and west slopes fall between in this respect. But there is little specific evidence on crop yields in favor of one slope over the other.

The location of an orchard on very steep slopes presents a number of problems in later management of the orchard. On steep hillsides, spraying may be a serious problem. This can be managed by installing a central stationary spray plant and piping the orchard. The trend, however, is to pick better sites where modern air-blast spraying can be used. Cultivation of steep hillsides may be impractical because of the danger of erosion. It is fortunate, however, that the apple and pear will thrive well under permanent or semipermanent sod systems on slopes as steep as 20° to 30°, which is too steep for satisfactory growing of peaches, cherries, and plums. Many orchard operations, such as pruning, thinning, harvesting, and hauling fruit are much more difficult on steep hillsides than on gentle slopes. In fact, orchard machinery seems to get bigger and more complicated. The mechanical apple harvester is an example.

Selection of soil. The first requirement of a good orchard soil is proper water drainage which permits good aeration and extensive root development. The subsoil is probably more important than the upper layer of soil in growth and production of an orchard. When the subsoil is hard

Figure 6. The soil beneath this Schmidt sweet cherry tree is underlain with rock 18 inches below the surface. As a result of shallow rooting, the tree is shown dying during an extended drought. Fruit trees generally perform best with at least a four-foot rooting depth.

and impervious, trees may grow satisfactorily for a few years, but when the tops are large and producing fruit, they become weak, and if a dry year, very wet year, or a severe winter occurs, they may die (Figure 6). Fruit trees will not tolerate wet soils during the growing season. The roots can withstand some submergence during the winter dormant period, provided the water drains away by the time growth starts in the s p r i n g. Submergence of the root system for even a few days during the growing season, when temperatures are high, usually results in eventual death of the roots. Another period when waterlogging is disastrous is during the spring months when the buds are opening and the shoots developing.

A soil on which water stands for more than a week after a heavy rain is considered unfit for fruit growing. In most orchards, it is not unusual to find a wet spot here and there in depressed areas. These can be avoided, drained by tile, or made into ponds for water supply in spraying. There are instances where entire orchards have been drained by tile but such a practice is expensive. It is better to select land which does not need such preparation.

It is not a recommended practice to dynamite a hardpan to improve drainage and to create a greater rooting area. If the impervious hardpan is thin and underlain with well-drained sandy soil, dynamiting might prove satisfactory, but if the soil is relatively heavy throughout, the pressure of the explosion packs the soil in a bowl shape and further complicates drainage.

The rooting area for a fruit tree should be at least four to five feet in depth, but this depends somewhat on the region and soil type. Where rainfall is plentiful and well distributed over the growing season as in some sections of West Virginia, a soil three feet deep may be satisfactory for apples. In New York, fruit trees live longer and are more profitable on well-drained, even-textured, sandy or gravelly loam soils that permit root penetration to eight to nine feet than on heavy clay soils where root penetration is but three feet. In Nebraska where there is likelihood of long summer droughts and where deep loess soils are available, wider tree spacing in soils deeper than nine feet is being recommended. Generally speaking, about twice the rooting depth of soil is necessary in a medium sandy soil than would be necessary in a heavier silt loam soil to carry the trees through the same period of drought or the same interval between irrigations.

Level of the *ground water table* during the growing season, especially at blossoming time, is an important criterion of a good orchard soil. The soil is said to be unsatisfactory for orchard purposes if the water table remains within six inches or a foot of the soil surface for a week after a heavy spring rain, or within three feet of the surface for several weeks after growth starts. It is good practice to make a survey of the water table and drainage conditions previous to planting an orchard because some soils may be deceiving on the surface; also the subsoil may vary considerably within a horizontal distance of 50 to 100 feet. The survey can be made by digging about four random holes per acre, using a tractor-driven or hand digger. The holes should be about four feet deep, into which a galvanized drain pipe or four-inch tiles are placed. The water table should be studied especially in about three weeks before and after bloom. In case of the better fruit soils, the ground water may exist within a few inches of the soil surface for an hour or so after heavy spring rains, but it falls rapidly and within a day or two, it drops to three or four feet below the surface. It is important that readings be taken at least at three-day intervals during spring months. In case of a poorly drained soil, the water table will remain a foot or two below the surface for a week or so after heavy rains.

Roots must have good aeration in order to function properly. This is the reason that drainage is so important. Under optimum rooting conditions in the soil, the pore space should be occupied 50 per cent with water and 50 per cent with air. Naturally, if the soil is poorly drained, the greater percentage of the pore space will be occupied by water. The inclusion of sand or gravel in an orchard soil tends to lighten it, enables it to absorb rain or irrigation water faster, gives it better drainage, and has a tendency to make it warm. Clay gives the soil body, but when it is present in considerable amounts, it makes the soil hard to work when wet and it cracks when dry. Presence of a certain amount of clay (20 to 40 per cent) is desirable because it contains available nutrient elements and assists in retaining moisture. Decaying vegetation and humus are also valuable in a soil because they, too, help make nutrients available, greatly increase water penetration, and assist in giving the soil good tilth.

Fruit plants have a wide tolerance to soil pH. Good apple orchards have been found on soils from quite acid to very alkaline (pH 8.5; neutral is pH 7.0). Most pomologists arbitrarily have set the optimum soil pH at 6.0 to 6.5 because most intercrops and cover crops grow best in slightly acid soils. Also, laboratory research with potted fruit plants and field observations and data indicate that this pH range is most favorable.

Soil fertility from the standpoint of an orchard is not as important as the points discussed previously. Many of the fruit growing soils around the world, except the very sandy soils, are supplied with the necessary elements for tree growth, except for nitrogen. This can be applied to the soil or as a spray to the foliage in the form of nitrogen fertilizers. Other elements which may be deficient in some soils, such as boron, potassium, magnesium phosphorus, iron, and zinc, also can be supplied. Hence, the fertility of a soil is relatively less important than its physical characteristics and its location or site.

A criterion often used to pass preliminary judgment on the desirability of a soil for fruit growing is to observe the existing amount and type of plant growth. The soil shows orchard possibilities if it will grow a good crop of weeds and if the native trees are large and vigorous. Poor weed growth and trees showing weak growth with dieback in the tops are evidences of an infertile or tight soil with shallow rooting area.

The New York Agricultural Experiment Station and several other experimental stations are giving valuable soil survey service by working through the county agricultural agents to assist fruit growers in choosing good orchard soils and sites. The orchard soil specialist from the experiment station goes by appointment to the prospective farm and makes a careful study of the soil and site, making specific recommendations to the grower. This is a service that all states might well initiate to avoid cases of financial loss and disappointment and to place the fruit growing business on a higher-profit level.

PLANTING PLANS

When to plant. Early spring planting as soon as the soil can be worked is generally the best time to plant in the deciduous fruit growing areas of the world. When spring begins to break rapidly, a difference of two weeks in the date of planting often results in obviously better growth of the earlier planted trees. New roots will develop when the soil temperature is above 45°F., and if the trees are planted as soon as the frost is out of the ground, some root development will occur before the leaves appear. This early root development is highly important in getting the trees off to a vigorous start. Occasionally, there are periods of three or four weeks in spring when the weather is unduly dry. Many trees may be lost if planting has been delayed to the point where one of these dry periods follows shortly after planting. It may be necessary to haul water to the field in a spray machine, or in a large tank mounted on a truck. It may make the difference between a 100 or a 50 per cent stand. (Figure 6a).

Figure 6a. If a spring drouth occurs, or if it occurs later, watering the trees at the critical time can make the difference between heavy replanting the next year or little or no replanting.

In the milder climatic sections, if the temperature is not likely to fall below 0° F., trees may be planted any time the ground is not frozen in fall, winter, or early spring. However, it should be noted that the roots are more tender than the tops and may be killed by temperatures 20° to 24° F. It is important, therefore, to consider this fact in shipping and handling trees during the winter months.

Fall planting in the colder areas can be done more successfully with apples, pears, sour cherries, and European varieties of plums than with peaches, sweet cherries, and Japanese varieties of plums. The advantages of fall planting are (1) frequently the soil is in better condition than in spring, (2) weather conditions are more favorable in fall than spring, (3) there are usually fewer windy days, (4) nursery stock is less likely to become overheated in transit during the fall season, and (5) a fall-planted tree starts growth at the earliest time the following spring, usually earlier than spring-planted trees. In milder regions where peach trees are often planted in the fall, a common practice is to pile soil about the base of the tree in order to protect it during the winter period. It is important that the land be well drained when fall planting is practiced in order to prevent soil heaving during winter.

Varieties. The variety might be considered the keystone of American fruit growing. Probably more attention has been given to a consideration of varieties than to any other phase of fruit growing. In spite of the accumulation of much information on this subject, however, the selection of the proper varieties for a given location or condition remains a serious matter. Study the market to be served to determine varieties which bring the

41

TABLE 1. MARKET VALUE OF APPLE VARIETIES IN WASH. STATE, 1960's

	Extra Fancy/box	Fancy/box	Av. Value/box
Red Delicious	$4.11	$3.06	$3.76
Std. Delicious	3.28	2.47	2.95
Winesap	3.37	2.48	3.14
G. Delicious	4.26	4.39	4.17

higher prices (Table 1). Red improved strains of several standard varieties of apples, as well as peaches, have been well received by the trade and give definite promise of being valuable additions to the commercial list.

Quality of the fruit is becoming of utmost importance in the final selection of a variety. It is too often true, however, that high-quality fruits have shortcomings which limit the extent to which they should be planted. These shortcomings may consist of susceptibility to disease, insect and cold injury, light or tardy bearing, short life, special soil requirements, uneven ripening, high proportion of low-grade fruit, fruit easily bruised, poor storage qualities, and others. Rome Beauty, in spite of its inferior quality, is a money-maker because of its tendency to bear annually, a most important character!

Cross-pollination. Some varieties of fruits will not set fruit when planted alone or with certain other varieties of the same fruit. It is important to match varieties in order that they may cross-fertilize. As a general statement, it is unwise to plant a single variety in a large plot. Plant two to four rows of a given variety and alternate with two to four rows of another variety with the same, or an overlapping blooming period. The pollinizer variety should not be farther away than 80 to 85 feet, or two tree rows. Do not mix varieties in a row. Additional suggestions are in Chapter VI; for other fruits, see respective chapters and appendix charts.

Picking date. It is well to select about five good varieties of a fruit which ripen successively over a period of from one to three months, depending upon the kind of fruit. This facilitates many of the major orchard operations such as spraying, thinning, and especially picking and packing. The crews can spray, thin or pick continuously, shifting from one variety to the next as the trees successively bloom, the fruit increases in size, and ripens. It has been a common mistake to plant too many varieties; one should rarely plant more than ten unless for season-spread for roadside market.

Planting systems. There are several systems for planting an orchard and the selection will depend upon the topography of the land, kind and variety of fruit, the soil management practices, and if fillers are contemplated. Apple, pear, and quince will grow and produce satisfactorily in permanent or semipermanent sod. On the other hand, peaches, cherries, and plums are more satisfactory under a cultivation and cover-crop system. The sod system of management can be used in regions of the country where annual rainfall is greater than 35 inches. If rainfall is below 35 inches and irrigation is not available, herbicides or cultivation with or without cover crops or mulch will be necessary for moisture conservation for all tree fruits. Contour planting with or without terraces is one of the best systems adapted to cultivation management on rolling or sloping land. Planting systems which are better adapted to sod or semipermanent sod are square, rectangular, triangular, quincunx, and hedgerow.

The *square* system is the most common for large trees in which a tree stands in each corner of the square. The system is simple to lay out, adapted to the use of fillers or semipermanent trees, and the trees are easy to cultivate and spray. In the *rectangular* system, a tree is planted in each corner of a rectangle. In other words, the trees are farther apart in one direction than they are in the other. This system is often used where intercrops such as strawberries or vegetables are to be grown between the trees for a few years. See Tukey's book for numerous compact tree systems.

The *quincunx* system of planting is essentially the square system with a filler tree in the middle of the square.

In the *triangular* or hexagonal system, all trees are equidistant on the triangle. This plan allows for more equal distribution of tree tops and roots in a given area. About 15 per cent more trees can be planted per acre than in the square system, using the same planting distance.

Contour planting, or contour planting with *terraces,* is adapted to sloping land. With stone fruits which require an abundant supply of moisture and respond well to cultivation, it is almost imperative that they be planted on the contour where slopes are involved. If drought periods are common in a region and irrigation is not readily feasible, it might be well, also, to use contour plantings with or without terraces for apple, pear, and quince (Figure 21). Herbicidal use or cultivation under these conditions may be essential to eliminate competition of the sod or intercrop with the trees during the critical dry periods. Such cultivation also will break up compaction and allow the soil to absorb more of the rainfall.

Contour planting with terraces has some advantages, a few disadvantages. Soil and rain water are conserved, resulting in better growth and production of the tree over a longer period of time. The terrace channels are convenient for irrigation. There is more economical operation of orchard machinery on the more or less level contour runways, as compared with operating on a slope. One disadvantage is the difficulty of spraying at different angles of the wind. Also, it is unwise to cross the terraces with equipment possibly initiating washouts. When the trees become full grown, however, some growers complain of "getting lost" in the winding tree rows.

The *hedgerow* is the most efficient management system since it is well adapted to mechanical harvesting and other modern machinery and practices. In Washington, a system being followed is use of spur-type apple

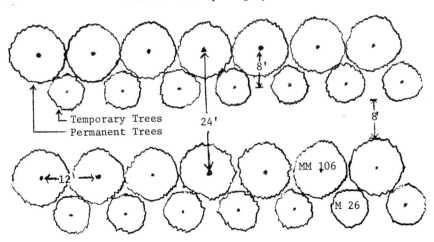

Figure 7. This "off set" planting system for compact trees should double yield per acre the first 10 years, after which temporary trees are removed. Chemical weed control is needed under trees. (R. F. Carlson, Mich. State Univ.)

varieties on seedling roots, planted 20' x 20' and held to about 14' high. Trees are held within limits by regulation of nitrogen, use of "mold and hold" pruning, and by chemical retardant sprays. The system is centered around Delicious and Golden Delicious. Hedgerow planting is used also for peaches, set about 14 feet apart in rows 22 feet apart. The system likewise is adaptable to other tree fruits, and particularly to compact trees.

Planting distances. The proper distance for planting a given fruit has never been definitely settled. Distance of planting will depend upon the region, soil type, cultural care, and the variety to be grown. Fruit trees grow larger in some sections than in others. On a deep fertile soil in the New England area, a McIntosh tree may have a spread of 50 feet at maturity, whereas on a more shallow less fertile soil, it may occupy only 30 feet. Some varieties are naturally small and do not require as much space as other varieties. Small varieties are Wealthy, Jonathan, Yellow Transparent, Golden Delicious, and Wagener. Varieties which tend to grow larger are Stayman Winesap, McIntosh, York Imperial, and Baldwin. A Montmorency cherry needs more space than a Morello, a sweet cherry more than a sour. The planting distances suggested for standard size fruit and nut trees and for compact trees are given in Table 1.

The number of plants required to plant an acre may be determined by multiplying the distance they stand apart both ways and dividing the figure into the number of square feet in an acre (43,560).

TABLE 1. PLANTING DISTANCES SUGGESTED FOR FRUIT AND NUT TREES[1]

STANDARD SIZE TREES

FRUIT	RANGE (FT.)	FRUIT	FEET
Apple	35-45	Filbert	18
Pear	25-35	English Walnut	40
Plum	20-24	Black Walnut	50
Peach	20-24	Hickory	40
Apricot	20	Pecan	70
Cherry, sour	20-25	Chestnut	40
Cherry, sweet	25-30		
Quince	18-22		

COMPACT APPLE TREES[2] [3]

SPACING IN ROWS AND BETW. ROWS (FT.)	TREES PER ACRE	CLONAL ROOTSTOCK	COMMENTS
6 x 14	518	EM IX, M26	Any Variety[4]
8 x 16	340	EM VII, MM106	Rome, York, Jonathan
10 x 18	242	EM VII, MM106, EM II	G. Del., Del., Jon., Spy
12 x 20	182	EM VII, MM106, EM II	Stay., McIn., Jon., Spy
14 x 22	141	MM 104, MM111	Rome, York, Jon. Spurs
16 x 24	114	MM 104, MM111	G. Del., Delicious
18 x 26	93	MM 104, MM111	Stayman, McIntosh
18 x 26	93	Robusta 5 (Hardy)	Canadian Varieties
20 x 28	78	MM109, EM XVI, seedling	Any Variety

COMPACT TREE SIZE BY VARIETY[3]

30' W x 20 Hi. EM 16; Std. Seedling.	25' W x 17' Hi. MM 109, 111, EM XII		22' W x 17' Hi. MM104, EM II		15' W x 10' Hi. MM 106, EM VII	
Jonathan	Jonathan		Jan.	Rome	G. Del.	N. Spy
	Spur. Del.		G. Del.	York	Mc In.	Idared
	Rome		Mc I.	Stay.	Del.	Beacon
	York		Sp. Del.	N. Spy	Stay.	S. Rambo

DWARFING CAPACITY

CLASS SIZE	ROOTSTOCK	% SIZE RELATION TREES ON SEEDLINGS	ROOT VIGOR
Full	EM IX, M-26	20-25	Weak
Compact	EM VII, MM 106	40-50	Weak to good
Semi-Std.	EM II, MM 104, 111	65-75	Fair to strong
Standard	EM XVI, MM 109	100	Strong

[1]Distances are greater with large-size varieties with favorable soil and climatic conditions, less with reverse situation. "Spur" strains are 3/4ths std. size; are suggested for MM106, MM111 and EMIX, 26, VII.

[2]See respective chapter for dwarfing stocks for other tree fruits.

[3]Adapted from tables by L. P. Batjer and C. M. Ritter.

[4]Trellis suggested, for others - hedgerow. Spur Red Delicious on EM IX develops bark "Measles", under some conditions. EM 26 preferred for G. Del.; staking or trellis support, less labor, can tie limbs down to stake.

Some commercial growers have used the square system of planting, initially spacing apples, for example, 25 feet apart. Within 15 to 20 years, when the trees begin to crowd, the diagonal rows are removed, leaving the remaining trees 35 feet apart. This is adequate spacing for moderately vigorous trees, such as Golden Delicious, Rome Beauty, and Winesap. A distance of 28 feet may be used for vigorous varieties (See Chapter II for Variety Vigor) and after filler removal, trees would be about 42 feet apart.

ORDERING AND CARE OF NURSERY STOCK

Trees should be ordered from a nursery as far in advance as possible, at least by the fall previous to planting. Nurseries become overloaded with last-minute orders in late winter and may not get your trees to you until after spring breaks and this is too late; trees in shipment at this time may be damaged by over-heating. Also, late-placed orders may find the desired varieties exhausted. Buy the better-grade larger plants in a given age. One-year whips of apple, pear, and certain other fruits are often preferred because they (a) cost less, (b) are often inherently more vigorous, (c) shipping costs less, (d) less shipping damage, (e) start growth sooner, (f) easier to plant and (g) grower can pick limbs and train framework better (See Chap. IV). One-year and two-year trees cannot be distinguished four to five years later in the orchard.

Standard varieties of fruit do not come true to seed and, therefore, it is necessary to bud or graft wood of desired varieties into selected roots. As an example, with apples it is common practice for the nurseryman to plant seed of Delicious, McIntosh, Rome, or Delcon (superior germination, uniformity at Mich.) in wooden flats and after a year transplant the seedlings to the field in spring. These seedlings may be (1) budded in the field to desired varieties the following mid to late summer, cut back the next spring above the bud, and allowed to grow in the nursery a year for one-year trees and two years for two-year trees, or, (2) the seedlings may be dug in the fall and the roots cut into sections onto which shoots of desired varieties are whip-grafted (Figure 9). This is done indoors during the winter period, generally mid to late winter, when work is slack. The grafts are then stored in the cellar in cool moist peat moss or sawdust until the following spring when they are set about 12 inches apart in nursery rows spaced three feet apart. After one season's growth in the nursery, they are cut back and allowed to grow another season, after which they are dug and sold in the spring as one-year trees. If growth is weak, they may be cut back, grown another year and sold as two-year trees.

Some growers contract with a reputable nurseryman a year or so in advance of planting, furnishing budwood from their own orchard-proven trees.

46

Piece-root grafting in apple and pear propagation, as described in Figure 9, is used instead of budding to a larger extent in the midwestern states and to a limited extent elsewhere. Advantages of this system are that in case of cold-resistant varieties, they have their grafted seedling roots which may be tender to cold, deeper in the soil and thus better protected from cold, as compared with budded stock. Often roots develop on the scion (upper piece of wood in Figure (9) which is a further advantage if it is cold-resistant.

H. B. Tukey, Michigan Agr. Exp. Sta.

Figure 8. Stages in the development of a young pear tree. (a) French pear seedlings grown in a greenhouse flat; (b) after growing one year in seedling nursery row and just before digging in fall of 1964; (c) lining-out stock in spring of 1965 soon after planting; (d) at time of budding in August 1965; (e)1-year tree with standard variety top, the fall of 1966; (f) 2-year tree, fall of 1967, ready for digging (after leaves drop) and planting to an orchard the spring of 1968, New York. Stages in the development of an apple tree are similar.

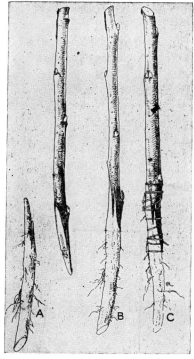

G. E. Yerkes, U. S. D. A.

Figure 9. Varieties of fruit trees do not come true to seed. During the dormant season, pieces of shoot wood are removed from the desired variety and whip-grafted on roots of seedlings of the same or a closely related fruit. Above system of propagation is commonly used for apples and pears.

Peaches, plums, cherries, and other stone fruits are budded on seedlings in the nursery in a manner similar to that for the apple. Seeds used for rootstocks for peaches are obtained from California canneries, as Halford, Lovell and Muir (Elberta may have a virus); for cherries Mazzard or Mahaleb seedlings are used; and for plums, Myrobalan seedlings. The seeds are layered in wet peat moss and given special temperature treatment during winter. In spring they are germinated

47

and grown for a year in beds, then transplanted to the nursery row 'where they are budded to the desired varieties in July or August. The following March, they are cut back a few inches above the bud, grown for a year in the nursery and sold as one-year trees. Plums and cherries may be left for another year and sold as two-year branched trees, but peaches are sold almost entirely as one-year trees. Some so-called "June-budded" peach trees are sold. They are budded in June in the nursery instead of August, and dug and sold the following spring. After three or four years growth in the orchard, particularly in the South, June-budded trees may be as large as trees one-year old at planting.

Double-worked trees. This means that the tree consists of wood from three different varieties; for example, with apple the root may be Delicious, the trunk Robusta 5, and the top McIntosh. In other words, the tree has been grafted twice, or double-worked. The reason for this is the fact that, for example, McIntosh so-grafted bears earlier, is hardier, and also will tolerate heavy soils and more moisture. Another example would be a Rome seedling root, EM IX interpiece and a Starkrimson top. Hibernal is used for the same purpose, and such trees are giving promising results with certain variety combinations. The commercial growers may buy from the nursery the Hibernal or Robusta 5 trees on Northern Spy roots, and after a year in the orchard, graft the desired varieties on them. Incompatabilities between certain standard varieties and particularly Virginia Crab are being found, however, and it thus would be well to check first desired combinations with your experiment station. (See Fig. 10).

Certified trees. Most nurseries sell certified trees which means that the trees have been checked and identified by state inspectors as true to name. This is valuable service to the customer because it protects him against planting undesirable varieties. The inspectors are able to identify given varieties of trees by the leaf, bark, and general growth characteristics of the tree. (See K. Lapins reference; also J. K. Shaw.)

Pedigreed trees or bud-selected stock means that the nurseryman has selected buds or scion wood from special highly colored or "high-yielding strains." Such "strains" may be trees that are growing on particularly fertile or well-drained soil, or that might have been growing on seedling stocks that were especially congenial. Thus, the more desirable characteristics of such trees are due to environmental influences and not to characters inherent in the scion wood from the tree. Pedigreed trees, therefore, do not have the virtues implied by the name.

Bud sport (Mutation). On a named variety of tree in the orchard, occasionally a spur, limb, or larger portion of the tree may show a distinct variation in the fruit or growth as compared with the rest of the tree. These are known as bud sports and can be perpetuated by grafting the wood of this limb upon desired stocks or roots. An example of a bud sport is spur-type Red Delicious which is a mutation of the ordinary strain of Delicious. Other well-known sports are the Starking, Richared, Jonared, Starkrimson, Gallia Beauty, and Blackjon. It is well for the orchardist to be on continual look-out for these improved bud mutations in his own orchard.

Not all varieties are obtained from bud variations. Some are developed by scientific breeding to obtain new varieties superior to the parents. Examples of varieties which have been developed by breeding programs are the Cortland a p p l e, Fredonia grape, Jerseybelle Strawberry, Coville blueberry, and the Redhaven peach.

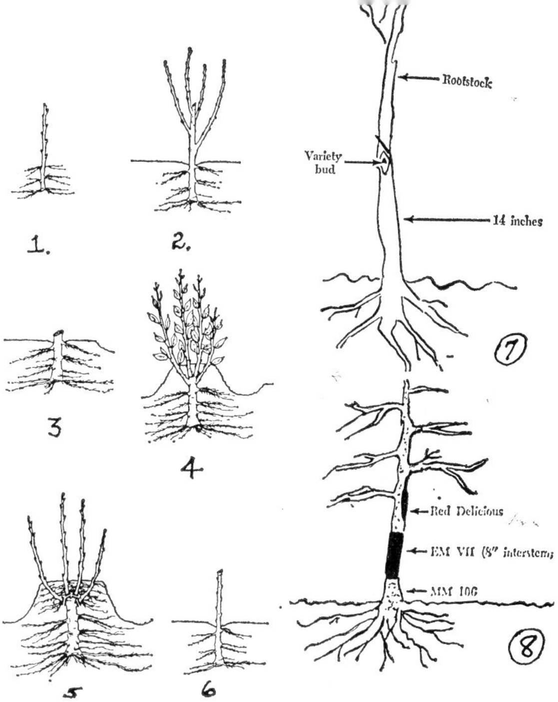

Clonal stocks are vegetative pieces from a desired parent plant and are usually propagated by mound layering. A rooted stock is planted in spring, cut back the next spring, and soil mounded around shoots as they develop.

Figure 10. How dwarf trees are propagated. (1) Rooted clonal (e.g. EM 26) branch or root is spring planted in field bed. (2) After one season's growth, the cutting is (3) cut back the next spring. (4) Rooted cutting is mounded with soil when shoots are 12 in. tall and still tender; mounded again a few weeks later to depth of 12-15 in. of soil. (5) Roots develop on new shoots the second spring, rootstock cut off at the original base, and (6) rooted cuttings are lined out in nursery row for summer budding of (7) desired variety scion or (8) interstock. At (8) double-grafting or budding is shown to get interstock effects, as well as clonal rootstock effects on the size and performance of Red Delicious top. (R. F. Carlson, Michigan State Univ., E. Lansing)

Shoots rooted at bases are removed at end of the season, bench-grafted to a desired scion variety in winter, stored, planted in a nursery row the next spring, grown for that year and sold; or the rootstock is lined out in a nursery and budded to a scion variety in summer, grown for the next year and sold. (See Figure 10).

Spur-type apples together with numerous higher colored fruit mutations (sports) largely from the Northwest, were named for the most part in the 1950-60's, although a few were named earlier as, e.g. Okanoma (spurred Delicious) in 1921. These are inherent and apparently permanent and can be propagated vegetatively. Spur-type trees are characterized by long limbs with few side branches but many spurs. Trees are more open and restricted in tree size to about ¾ of the standard trees. In the Northwest, they are being planted by hedgerow on seedling roots, clonal and dwarfing stocks; MM 111 and 106 looked good, late '60s. Examples are Goldspur (Golden Delicious) and Wellspur (or Bisbee from Starking) and a McIntosh spur being suggested by the Summerland British Columbia (Canada) Research Station. Spurs are not available as yet for some varieties. Spur types of a variety may ripen later.

Compact trees. Only in recent years has there been world-wide interest in planting of dwarf and semidwarf tree fruits. Dwarfing stocks, of course, have been used for over 40 years in Europe where they originated but other countries, particularly the United States and Canada, have turned to them because of the many advantages over the large trees of (a) reduction in labor and production costs per bushel, (b) higher production per acre (Table 2), (c) earlier bearing, and (d) improvement in color and marketability of the fruit, together with several lesser advantages. There is, however, a disadvantage in decidedly higher cost of trees and planting, plus a trellis, if used, but these are countered by advantages.

TABLE 2. TEN-YEAR PRODUCTION OF APPLES BY VARIETY AND ROOTSTOCK
(R. F. CARLSON, MICH. STATE UNIV., GRAHAM EXP. STA.)

VARIETY	ROOTSTOCK	BU./A.
McIntosh	Seedling	524
McIntosh	EM II	2046
McIntosh	EM VII	1582
Jonathan	Seedling	493
Jonathan	EM II	1902
Jonathan	EM VII	860
Red Delicious	Seedling	393
Red Delicious	EM II	1793
Red Delicious	EM VII	1370

In this book edition, an attempt has been made to up-date the discussion in all areas on compact trees, but it should be recognized that we are still "feeling our way" due to lack of experience under a broad set of conditions. Hence, suggestions should be accepted with this reservation. Growers should convert from standard trees gradually if the practice continues to look good.

A fruit tree is dwarfed to various degrees by grafting a cion variety on a clonal interstock (stem piece) or rootstock which has a dwarfing influence. In some cases there may be little or no dwarfing but there is the advantage of the trees being more uniform in character, size and fruiting. Where an interstock is used, the amount of dwarfing is proportionate to the length of the interstem which may be 3-12" or more. The following combinations are examples, and the nurseryman should so-label the trees: (a) Bartlett pear on interstem Hardy on rootstock quince, and (b) Red Delicious apple on EM VII interstock on MM 106 rootstock (Fig. 10).

Following is a brief description of several dwarfing stocks now in use. For a detailed discussion of dwarf fruit trees, see Dr. Harold B. Tukey's book. EM refers to the East Malling Research Station, Kent, England, where these stocks were collected and standardized. MM refers to the

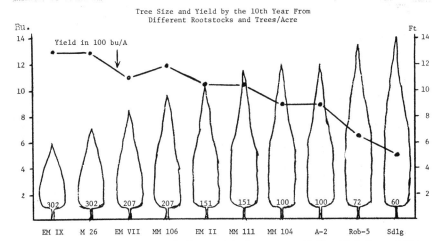

Tree Size and Yield by the 10th Year From
Different Rootstocks and Trees/Acre

Figure 10a. At least 10 dependable rootstocks are available. Relative yielding capacity of cion variety is shown by rescending curve (See Table 2), bu/tree on left, trees per acre within tree diagram, and height in ft. on right. (Courtesy R. F. Carlson, Mich. State Univ.)

Malling Merton series which resulted from a cooperative breeding program between the John Innis Horticultural Institute, Merton, England, and the Malling Station above. One of the first objectives of this program was to use Northern Spy in the breeding to get a dwarfing woolly-aphid resistant stock needed by Australian growers. The commercial stocks developed are described below. (See also Table 1.)

EM IX. Most dwarfing, wood brittle, must be staked or trellised, requires best soil in orchard, needs mulching and/or irrigation, suckering reduced by high budding and deep planting, must maintain central leader, remove fruit first two years, resistant to crown rot (*P. cactorum*).

EM 26. Showing considerable commercial promise in U.S., may use as filler tree, brittle roots, must be staked or trellised. Stock overgrows cion as EM IX and has thicker bark, susceptible to winter trunk damage in north. (See Fig. 7). Blight susceptible apples (York) may blight badly on EM 26 in blight years.

EM VII. Commercially productive, trees uniform, propagates easily, must be high-budded and planted deep to reduce suckering, some trees may need staking, susceptible to crown rot, 50% dwarfing 150 + trees/A, McIntosh, Spartan, Red Rome, Golden Delicious suited; Delicious questionable in some sites and climates.

MM 106. One of the most preferred commercial stocks, early bearing, well anchored, non-suckering, productive, susceptible to crown rot.

EM II. Does not propagate as easily as EM VII or the MMs, does best in moisture retaining loam and not a heavy clay in which it tends to lean,

Crown rot may be controlled by soil drench at trunk base with 1 lb./100 gal. maneb or ferbam.

Figure 12. A 3 or 4-wire grape trellis can be used for apple on EM IX or 26 (see Chap. XX), and for dwarf pears although not as much trellis strength is needed. Lighter wires and wider post spacing can be used. Bagging for pest protection sometimes is used in France where this photo was taken (Ernest G. Christ, Rutgers University).

fairly resistant to crown rot, well suited to Delicious, Cortland, Spy, and Jonathan. McIntosh also performs well on EM II.

MM 111 Drouth tolerant, aphis resistant, good anchorage, vigorous varieties tend toward uprightness, but suited as a general purpose rootstock.

MM 104. More vigorous than MM 111, but cion variety as Delicious produces a more spreading tree, requires well-drained soil, susceptible to crown rot, ideal for Golden Delicious and Spur Delicious.

MM 109. Trees almost as large as on EM XVI (similar to seedling stock), well anchored, may lean after summer gale in wet soil and with heavy crop, productive, best in well-drained soils, does not sucker.

EM IV. Semidwarf to semistandard, early bearing, heavy producer, common in Holland, Germany, may lean in exposed areas but well adapted to spindle bush with no staking, resistant to crown rot, liked in British Columbia.

Alnap 2(A-2). From Sweden, winter hardy, dwarfing like MM 111 or EM II, well anchored, good tree form, all-purpose stock, 90% used in Sweden, not widely tested in U. S.

Robusta No. 5. Winter hardy, should constitute about two feet of trunk, not dwarfing but as used in Canada and upper New England states where season is short, trees tend to be smaller, particularly in lighter soil types. Antanovka and McIntosh are used similarly in colder regions.

Tree specifications. In ordering nursery stock, the following specifications are suggested for the different fruits:

Standard apple and pear varieties. Vigorous four- to seven-foot one-year trees (unbranched), or five- to seven-foot two-year trees about three-fourths-inch in diameter near the base and well-branched. For pear varieties susceptible to blight, request Old Home understock (see Chapter XIII.)

Dwarf trees. One- two-year trees best, well branched, vigorous roots, and labeled: variety/root or variety/interstock/root.

Cherries (sour). Sturdy one-year trees four to five feet high, or two-year branched trees, four to six feet, with diameter of five-eighths-inch or more.

Cherries (sweet). Trees budded on Mazzard or Mahaleb stock. Sturdy one-year whips, four to five feet; or, two-year trees of five to seven feet and diameter of about three-fourths inch (see Chap. XVI).

Nuts. One- or two-year grafted stocks, large size. If the tap root has been severed about 18 inches below the ground a year before transplanting, more vigorous roots will have developed, which is desirable. Some nurserymen perform this root pruning as standard practice for nuts. Trees which are shipped with a ball of earth about the roots are more likely to succeed in transplanting.

Peaches, apricots, nectarines. Vigorous three- to four-foot yearling trees of one-half-inch diameter or more. Avoid large older trees or small one-year weak trees. Vigorous healthy "June-budded" trees can be used.

Plums. Vigorous one-year whips, four to six feet, or two-year branched trees four to five feet high.

Quince. Request two-year trees, four to five feet high, with a trunk diameter of one-half-inch or more.

Ordinarily, it is not wise to buy nursery trees older than two years. They are either so large that the shock of transplanting is too great, or, they are inherently slow-growing and ultimately will be relatively small and weak.

When the nursery stock is opened and separated, all varieties should be checked as to number, variety and grade, and those trees rejected which show crown gall, severe aphid injury on the roots, or winter killing as indicated by brittleness of wood and discoloration of the inner tissues. Since most trees are shipped in plastic-covered bundles to reduce evaporation of water, they can be placed immediately in the cold storage room and sprinkled occasionally to keep them moist before planting. Do not store with fruit, which gives off ethylene, causing buds to break. As soon as the soil can be worked, the trees should be planted.

PLANTING THE TREES

Preparation of the soil. Wherever possible, it is desirable to plant fruit trees in tilled strips, regardless of the type of soil management followed later. If the land has been in sod, fall plowing is preferable in order to permit the soil to settle and the sod to partly disintegrate during the winter

I. E. Ilgenfritz' Sons Co., Monroe, Mich.

Figure 13. This is nursery tree-digging equipment used by a large midwest nursery. As the equipment passes down the nursery row, it lifts and loosens the trees so they can be lifted out easily by hand. This equipment explains in part why millions of dollars are invested in the nursery business alone.

period. If the land is plowed in spring, it should be done as early as possible so that the ground can settle and absorb a plentiful supply of rainfall. Trees will need this moisture. Killifering in fall to a depth of 20 inches in the row and on both sides when soil is dry and cracks is good practice.

Staking the field. Building laths cut in half and sharpened on one end make satisfactory stakes. Where the land is rolling, full lengths of the lath can be nailed together to give greater height in low places. Tips of the stakes can be seen at greater distances and in hollows by dipping the ends in whitewash or by wrapping a white cloth around the tops. If timber poles are used, the bark can be peeled off the tops to expose the light colored sapwood.

Figure 15 shows a system for locating trees in a field by the square system of planting. In this case, the permanent trees are to be planted 40 by 40 feet with 30 feet between the fence and the ends of the rows in order to permit adequate space for turning with tractors and other machinery. It is important that all stakes be laid out in straight lines so that later the orchard will have a pleasing appearance from the road and will be readily accessible by machinery.

In case the triangular system of planting is employed, it is wise to use a large triangle made of heavy wire or chain with a ring in each corner. The sides of the triangle should be exactly the length of the planting distance desired. The base line is established as described previously and two of the rings are placed over two stakes in the base line while the third stake is placed in the third ring to form the second row. Each new complete row is used as a base line for setting stakes in the next row, and so on until the entire field is staked. After staking three rows, other rows may be "sighted in".

Trellis design. The design should be picked which is economical and still does a lasting job. Somewhat less strength is needed here as com-

54

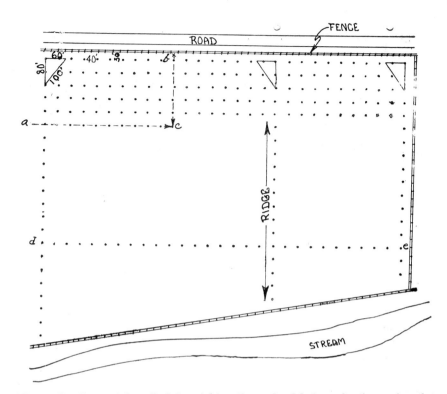

Figure 15. Suggested method for staking the orchard before planting, using the square system. Upper fence is the base line. Trees are 40 feet apart and 30 feet from fences. Right triangles are described at ends of first row to set outer left and right rows. (Metal measuring tape and stakes are used to lay out triangles.) Also, a row is established in center of field along a ridge for the man at "a" to sight upon. He cannot see row at extreme right. The line "d-e" was made for man at "b" to sight upon. Men at "a" and "b" are sighting while man at "c" sets stakes. Some growers set a minimum of stakes and plow out a furrow one direction and sight-in the trees. Tractor augers are good in medium to reavy non-docky soil. In sandy soil, hand garden shovels to set trees in a plowed-out furrow is often satisfactory.

pared with a grape trellis. As an example, a trellis for Golden Delicious on EM IX might have these specifications: 4 wires of No. 9 galvanized wire, 18 inches apart, bottom wire 18 inches from ground, treated posts 2 to 3 inches diameter at top, 9 to 10 ft. long, 3 ft. in the ground at ends, 2 to 3 ft. between, all 7 ft. above ground with dead man at end (sunken post in concrete, with screw-type powerline anchor) to hold the wire taut. Posts are 18 ft. apart, or with three trees between two posts at the 6-foot distance. See trellises, Fig. 7, and Chap. XX. For EM VII, MM 106, fan-trained on trellis, top wire is 8' high, posts larger, trees wider spaced.

Planting trees. Trees can be trucked to the field in 50-gallon drums one-third full of water. *Keep roots moist* until planted. They must not dry excessively at any time. Trim off broken or injured roots. Set standard-size trees about the same depths as they grew in the nursery (you can see the soil line). In very sandy and dry soils it may be desirable to set

55

(Left) Ohio State University Agr. Ext. Serv. (Right) H. B. Tukey, Michigan Agr. Exp. Sta.

Figure 16. (Left) The hole should be large enough to accommodate the root system. Cut back broken and long roots; set tree as deep as it grew in the nursery. (Right) In heavier soils, better tree growth is obtained if a three-gallon pail of wet peat moss is mixed with the soil as it is sifted about the roots. Lift and lower the tree slightly while filling the hole; tamp soil thoroughly as roots are covered. Where anchor posts are used, set them on the leeward tree side.

the trees deeper than they grew in the nursery. High-budded trees on dwarfing stock should be set a foot to a foot and a half deeper than grown in the nursery to get good root anchorage, but not so deep that the cion variety can root. Place the bulk of the roots toward the prevailing wind and lean the tree in the same direction. If possible, place the lowest good scaffold limb toward the prevailing wind. With peaches, place the "bud crook" toward the prevailing wind. Put the topsoil in the bottom of the hole mixed with a little peat moss if available (Figure 16). Tromp

Figure 16a. The Carl Perleberg (Quincy, Washington) fruit tree planter has planted 9,000 trees at the rate of 300 trees/hr. with a 3-man crew. The tractor-pulled plow breaker opens furrow, trees are dropped at desired distance and discs pull and pack the soil back. Disc depth is same as breaker (Courtesy C. H. Bosch, The Goodfruit Grower, Yakima, Wash., 98902).

56

Figure 17. After the tree has been sighted in place, tamp the soil solidly about the roots with topsoil replaced first and sub-soil last. Tree is leaned slightly toward the prevailing wind.

the soil solidly, leaving no air pockets (Figure 17). Apply 0.05 lb actual nitrogen (e.g. ¼ lb ammonium sulphate or 2 lbs 10-10-10) in a ring on the surface one foot from the trees. Do not put fertilizer or manure in the hole next to the roots. Burning may result.

Newly set trees should be pruned shortly after planting. This is described in subsequent chapters for each fruit.

Contour planting. In c o n t o u r planting on sloping land, all trees in any one row are in the soil at the same elevation. With this planting system, cultivation is done on the contour between the rows and not up and down the hill. Thus, cultivation tends to build up slight ridges or natural low terraces at the tree row which reduces the tendency of the water to run down the slope and increases absorption into the soil. Obviously, the tree rows will not be equally spaced in all parts of the orchard. On the slight slopes, the rows will be somewhat closer together; but on the almost level areas, they will be farther apart. In some places, a given row may be so far from another row that it is possible to insert what is known as a "spur" row as shown in Figure 19. On steeper parts of the orchard, it may be necessary to discontinue parts of rows in order to prevent the trees from becoming too close together.

The first step in laying out a contour planting is to decide upon the minimum allowable interval between rows. This minimum difference will vary with the different kinds and varieties of fruit trees. For example, it is usually 15 to 18 feet for peach trees and 25 to 30 feet for apple trees. It differs, also, according to site conditions and to the individual preference of fruit growers. The first contour line should be laid out at the highest elevation. From a given point, the line is projected on the contour in both directions by using an engineer's level and rod. The line is projected to the limits of the area to be planted. It can be marked with lath stakes at 25- or 50-foot-interval stations. The next step is to proceed to the steepest slope in the orchard below the first line and establish a point at the minimum distance between rows below the first line. Thence, with the engineer's level, another line is projected from left to right. Whenever the distance between two adjacent lines becomes twice the minimum

Figure 18. A digger attachment for tractors saves time in planting an orchard, digging post holes, or similar jobs. From 500 to 600 holes can be dug in a day, ranging in diameter from 4 to 18 inches according to bit size. A motor driven portable drill is sold by A. M. Leonard & Son, Piqua, Ohio, 45356. Tractor power-take-off back hoes are preferred by many growers.

interval, a new line is laid out on the contour between them.

On the average, the interval between contour rows of trees is somewhat greater than that between rows of trees planted by the square system. Therefore, it is desirable that the average distance between trees in a row be less (or hedgerow) than the average space between the rows in order that the number of trees per acre may not be significantly less than if the planting had been done on the square. Where two rows come close together on the steep slope, the trees can be set somewhat farther apart in the row and staggered so that the machinery can more or less zigzag between the trees. In some orchards where the slope and contour is relatively uniform, it may be possible to line up the trees across the contour line to give the orchard a better appearance and perhaps better air drainage.

In the contour system of planting, the orchard roads are placed where they will be less likely to receive and carry runoff water, resulting in erosion. Such locations will include not only the natural ridges on top of the hill, but, where terracing is used, the tree row middles just below the large terraces. The tree rows should be somewhat farther apart where roads are located to permit room for orchard trucks.

Terracing. Contour planting with terraces is used in areas where the rainfall ex-

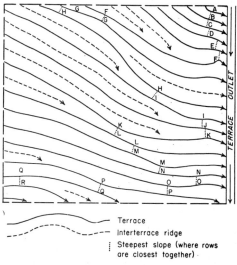

— Terrace
---- Interterrace ridge
⋮ Steepest slope (where rows are closest together)

J. T. Bregger, U.S. Soil Conservation Service

Figure 19. This is a diagram for terracing and planting an orchard on rolling topography. Points A to R were established on the steepest slopes at the minimum allowable distance between tree rows. Each point has been projected along the contour to the left and right with an enigneer's level. Terrace channels will be constructed at the lines thus established and a row of trees planted on each terrace ridge. Wherever the distance between two adjacent through rows became twice the minimum interval, a SPUR row of trees was inserted as shown by the dash line.

ceeds 35 inches a year and it is necessary at times to divert some of the water from the field. From the functional standpoint, the types of terraces may usually be classified as of either the diversion type which has one or more outlets and discharges water, or the absorption type which is level and retains water until it is absorbed by the soil. On steep land with a slope greater than 10 per cent, bench terraces may be used, but they may be more expensive to construct. They resemble large steps up the side of the hill. On slopes greater than 10 per cent it

C L. Hamilton, U.S. Soil Conservation Service

Figure 20. A terrace channel discharging water onto a well-sodded waterway. The water spreads as it leaves the terrace channel, some of which will be absorbed in the soil; the balance will move to lower areas. It is essential that such waterways be kept well sodded,

is probably better to use permanent sod with mulch. With diversion terraces, it is necessary to have a slight downward grade in the channel floor in order that the water will run toward the terrace outlet (Figure 20). The

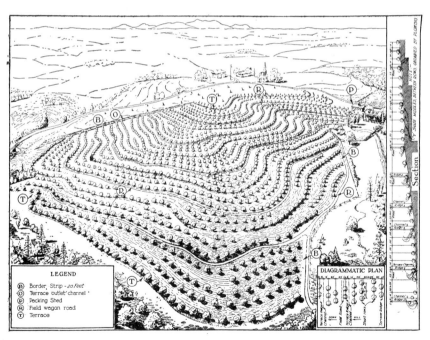

LEGEND
- B Border Strip - 20 Feet
- O Terrace outlet channel
- P Packing Shed
- R Field wagon road
- T Terrace

Clemson Agricultural College

Figure 21. Bird's-eye view of a peach orchard on sloping land showing terraces, wagon roads, placement of tree rows, terrace outlet channel, and border strips. Note the roads are located immediately below the main terraces.

59

amount of grade varies between 0.3 and about 1 per cent, depending upon the amount of slope, length of terrace, rainfall, and type of soil. From Table 3 it is possible to determine the distance between terraces based upon the land slope. If there is a water outlet at both ends of a terrace, the highest point in the channel floor usually is about midway between the ends at which point the water is directed to the left and to the right.

Before laying out the terrace or contour lines, one should go over the field carefully to determine the points of steepest slope and where the terrace outlets and drainage ways are to be located (Figure 21). Draws and swales are the natural places for discharging water from the terraces during the period of runoff and should be used wherever feasible for either a natural terrace outlet already stabilized with vegetation or as a location for a constructed waterway.

The Alabama or Nichols terrace has been used in planting orchards in the southeastern United States. This terrace has a broad shallow channel with a moderate-sized mound on the lower side (Figure 22). The lower slope of the mound is about four feet, the upper is six feet, the width of the channel is from 10 to 12 feet, and the depth of the channel is from 15 to 20 inches. As shown in Figure 22, it may not be necessary to have a terrace for each row of trees.

Terraces can be built with larger power units similar to road grading equipment (Figures 23, 25), or they can be built with ordinary plow or disk tiller. The large power units and technical assistance are available

TABLE 3

A Guide for Determining the Vertical and Horizontal Distance Between Terraces Based on the Land Slope[1]

Slope of Land in Feet Per 100 Feet	Vertical Distance or the Drop Between Terrace Ridges	Approximate Horizontal Distance Between Terrace Ridges
1 foot	2 feet 6 inches	180 feet
2 feet	2 feet 9 inches	140 feet
3 feet	3 feet 0 inches	100 feet
4 feet	3 feet 3 inches	80 feet
5 feet	3 feet 6 inches	75 feet
6 feet	3 feet 9 inches	63 feet
7 feet	4 feet 0 inches	57 feet
8 feet	4 feet 3 inches	53 feet
9 feet	4 feet 6 inches	50 feet
10 feet	4 feet 9 inches	48 feet
12½ feet	5 feet 4 inches	43 feet
15 feet	6 feet 4 inches	40 feet

[1]From Clemson Agricultural College Extension Bulletin 97, December, 1936

How to Use Table 3. After the slope of the hill has been determined, select from Table 3 either the vertical or horizontal distance that will apply to the slope determined. By use of the level and rod, locate the first terrace. Raise the target the amount of the verticle distance, then place the target down the hill until it is level with cross hairs in the level.

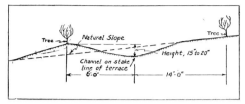

Figure 22. Cross section of a completed Alabama (Nichols) terrace after being maintained for a year or so. Recent experiments have indicated that the tree on the left should be placed at the top of the ridge. Unterraced rows, as shown by the tree on the right, should be gradually ridged by special subsequent cultivation practices.

Clemson Agricultural College

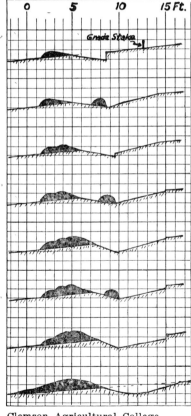

Step 1. Cut four feet below grade stake, throwing dirt downhill.

Step 2. Cut upper side of ditch, throwing dirt into ditch.

Step 3. Clean ditch and cut additional depth.

Step 4. Cut upper side of ditch, throwing dirt into ditch.

Step 5. Clean ditch and cut additional depth.

Step 6. Slope upper side of ditch and throw dirt into ditch.

Step 7. Clean out ditch—the completed terrace.

After two years. Cross section of same terrace after two years maintenance with turn plow.

Clemson Agricultural College

Figure 23. Seven steps in building the Alabama (Nichols) terrace with blade grader equipment shown in Figure 25.

61

Ohio State University Agr. Ext. Serv.

Figure 24. Steps are shown for construction of terraces with machinery and equipment found on most farms. (Top left) Advice and assistance are given by men from state agricultural extension service and an engineer from the U.S. Soil Conservation Service. Lath stakes and an engineer's target and level are used in laying out the contour lines. **(Middle left)** Using the lath stakes as markers, the contour lines are plowed out where terrace ridges will be located. **(Bottom left)** Several rounds are made with a double-bottom plow throwing dirt from either side toward the top of the ridge. **(Top right)** A disk is used to break up the large clods. **(Middle right)** One or two more rounds are made with the plow to throw the dirt farther up toward the top of the ridge to build it up. **(Bottom right)** The completed terrace. This terrace can be further built up and maintained by proper use of a one-way disk.

TABLE 4

A Guide for Giving the Terrace Grade Based on the Soil Type, Slope of Land, and Length of Terrace[1]

SANDY SUBSOIL

Number 25-Foot Stations (Stakes)	Fall per Station, Inches	Total Length Terrace of Feet	Max. Fall of Terrace Channel Per 100 Feet, Inches	Total Fall, Inches
LAND SLOPE 0—6%				
16	0	400	0	0
16	1/8	800	1/2	2
16	1/4	1200	1	6
16	3/8	1600	1 1/2	12
16	1/2	2000	2	20
LAND SLOPE 7—12%				
8	0	200	0	0
12	1/8	500	1/2	1 1/2
12	1/4	800	1	4 1/2
12	3/8	1100	1 1/2	9
12	1/2	1400	2	15
12	5/8	1700	2 1/2	22 1/2
12	3/4	2000	3	31 1/2

CLAY SUBSOIL

Number 25-Foot Stations (Stakes)	Fall Per Station, Inches	Total Length of Terrace, Feet	Max. Fall of Terrace Channel Per 100 Feet, Inches	Total Fall, Inches
LAND SLOPE 0—6%				
12	1/8	300	1/2	1 1/2
12	1/4	600	1	4 1/2
12	1/2	900	2	10 1/2
12	3/4	1200	3	19 1/2
12	1	1500	4	31 1/2
20	1 1/4	2000	5	56 1/2
LAND SLOPE 7—12%				
12	1/4	300	1	3
12	1/2	600	2	9
12	3/4	900	3	18
12	1	1200	4	30
12	1 1/4	1500	5	45
20	1 1/2	2000	6	75

[1]From Clemson Agricultural College Extension Bulletin 97. Ask for recent edition.
Note. The above table should be used as a guide and not as absolute rule, as each field may present a different problem.

63

A. F. Hallowell, U.S. Soil Conservation Service

Figure 25. Building a terrace with power blade grader equipment in New York.

through the Soil Conservation Service and if the grower desires to hire his terracing done, this type of equipment is satisfactory and reasonable in cost. Figure 24 shows the use of ordinary farm plow and disk equipment to build terraces. A small tractor bulldozer or bucket attachment is good equipment for use in opening the outlets at the end of the terraces and also for maintenance of the terraces in filling in washed-out areas.

Special attention must be given to the maintenance of terraces in order that they continue to operate properly. Maintenance can be done with terracing implements, with two-bottom terracing plows, or by using disk harrows set to throw the soil one way. During the process of cultivation of the trees, all terrace channels should be plowed or disked so that the soil will be thrown both ways from the bottom of the channel. *If breaks should occur in the terraces during periods of excessive rainfall, they should be built up immediately with soil 25 per cent higher than required in order to allow for settling.* Failure to maintain terraces in this manner is one of the greatest weaknesses of fruit growers using contour terracing.

Review Questions

1. List 5 advantages of locating the fruit enterprise in a region where fruit growing is well established near large centers of population.

2. What is the most important climatic factor to consider in selecting a region for fruit growing? Why?

3. How do large bodies of water influence temperature conditions along the shore line?

4. What program can an orchardist follow to obtain cash income while his fruit trees are coming into bearing?

5. What are the qualifications of a good orchard site?

6. What are the characteristics of a good orchard soil?

7. In colder regions, what tree fruits can be planted in spring or fall with about the same degree of success?

8. What planting systems are used for fruit trees? Which is the most common system? Which is likely to become the most popular?

9. What are the advantages and disadvantages of contour planting with terraces?

10. What factors govern the planting distance of fruit trees?

11. What are the advantages of buying 1-year apple and pear nursery trees as compared with older trees?

12. What is a double-worked tree? What are its advantages?

13. Define a certified tree, a clonal stock, an interstock, a "spurred" Red Delicious.

14. What are the advantages of semidwarf trees grafted on vegetatively uniform rootstocks? Discuss trends.

15. Briefly list the steps in properly planting a fruit tree.

16. Describe a Nichols terrace, giving approximate dimensions.

17. What tree fruits would you advise growing on land which is too steep for ter‐ racing and cultivation?

Suggested Collateral Readings

Anon. Trees against wind (windbreaks). Pacific NW Bulletin No. 5. 38 pp. Con‐ tact Wash., Ore., or Utah Agr. Exp. Sta. for copy. Jan. 1962.

Botts, R. R. Insurance for farmers. U.S.D.A. Farmers Bull. 2016. Request recent Bull.

Brase, Karl D. Rootstocks and methods used for dwarfing fruit trees. N.Y. Agr. Exp. Sta. (Geneva) Bull. 783. 1959.

Cain, John C. Optimum tree density for apple orchards. Hort Science, Vol. 5 No. 4, pp. 232, August 1970.

Campbell, A.I. Growth comparison young apple trees on virus-infected, healthy root‐ stocks. Jour. of Hort. Sci. Vol. 46 No. 1 pages 13-16, Jan. 1971.

Carlson, R. F. Dwarf and Spur-type trees. N. Y. Hort. Soc. Proc. 74-81. 1964.

Carlson, Robert F. Fruit trees — dwarfing and propagation. Horticultural Report No. 1 Dec. 1966 (revised February 1971). Mich. State University, E. Lansing.

Carlson, R. F. Root temperature effects on MM, Delicious seedlings. Proc. ASHS 86:41-45. 1965.

Cummins, N. J. and P. Fiorino. Pre-harvest defoliation of apple nursery stock using Ethrel. Hort. Sci. Vol. 4 (4): 339-341. 1969.

French, A. P. Plant characters of cherry varieties. Mass. Agr. Exp. Sta. Bull. 401. 1943. (Similar bulletins are available on apples, pears, and plums).

Hartman, H. T. and D. E. Kester. Principles Plant Propagation. Prentice Hall, Inc., Englewood Cliffs, N. J. 702pp. 1968.

History of California Apple Industry. The Blue Anchor, February/March, 1971.

Horton, R. L. Apple Hi-Density Clonal Studies (Good Rpt.) N.Y. Agr. Ext. Office. 46 pp. Mimeo. 249 Highland Dr., Rochester, N. Y. 14620. Request other reprints. 1971.

Hutchinson, A. A 13-year study with certain Malling Merton and other apple root‐ stocks. Ontario Dept. of Agric. & Food, Vineland Sta., Reports, 1968, 1970. (Re‐ quest other complete studies).

Lapins, K. Identification of nursery stock—apple, apricot, cherry, peach, pear and plum varieties and root stocks. Canada Pub. 922. Exp. Sta. Summerland, B.C. 1954.

Larsen, Fenton E. Promotion of leaf abscission of nursery stock with Bromodine. J. Amer. Soc. Hort. Sci. 95 (2): 231-232. 1970.

Ritter, C. M. and L. D. Tukey. Apple variety fruiting on clonal stocks. Bull. 649. 21 pp. July 1959.

Rogers, W. S., and M. S. Parry. Effects of deep planting on anchorage and perform‐ ance of apple trees. J. Hort. Sci. 43, 103-6, 1968.

Roosje, G. S. Experiences in handling high-density apple orchards. Res. Sta. for Fr. Growing, Wilhelminadorp, Netherlands. Publ. in Horticultural News, (New Bruns., N. J. 08903). 10 pp. May and July, 1969.

Valli, V. J. F. Freeze Prevention in Appalachian Fruit Region. The Mountaineer Grower, Martinsburg, W. Va. No. 283, pp. 3-22. 1970.

Tubbs, F. R. Tree size control. Proc. XVII Intern. Cong. Vol. II. 43-56. 1967.

Tukey, Harold B. Sr. Dwarfed fruit trees. Macmillan Co., N. Y. (Collier-Macmillan Ltd., London) 561 pp. 1964.

White, R. G. et al. Antonovka framework and apple productivity. Can. Jr. Pl. Sci. 45:455-460. 1965.

Note: Agricultural Experiment Stations with considerable experience in dwarfing rootstock studies are: E. Malling Res. Sta. (ask for publication list), Kent, Eng‐ land; Mich. State University (E. Lansing); New York (Geneva); British Columbia (Summerland); and Pennsylvania (Univ. Park), and Res. Sta. for Fruit Growing, Wilhelminadorp, The Netherlands. See earlier book editions, more citations.

CHAPTER IV

Pruning Apple Trees

❖ ❖

Most of the apple tree acreage over the world is still of the large standard trees of about 28 to 60 trees/acre, but the newer plantings are largely high-density compact trees of around 75-500-1,000 or more trees/acre. Hence the discussion of tree training and pruning in this chapter is still more or less slanted toward the large trees, although, actually, most of the principles discussed are applicable to either the large or small trees. Machine management of both large and compact trees is dictating a shift in the tree spacing designs, the training of young trees and the ultimate pruning of the mature trees. Pruning is becoming more of a bulk fast machine approach with some detail handwork rather than the former largely detail hand operation. The new approach, of course, is to reduce labor costs and problems and still get a profitable marketable product either for the fresh or the processing trade. As the "bugs" are gradually worked out of machine management of fruit trees, it is quite likely that as good or a better quality product can be placed on the market. Use of this expensive equipment, however, will be limited for the most part to the large-acreage growers.

The kind and amount of pruning to be done on a tree will depend upon (1) the age, (2) existing framework, (3) condition of bark and wood, (4) growth characteristics, (5) fruiting habits of the variety, and (6) if the tree is permanent or a filler.

Season for pruning. The majority of the pruning should be done during the dormant season (no leaves) for the following reasons: (1) The branches can be seen easily at that time; (2) Other orchard operations are less pressing; (3) There is less danger of pulling the bark away from around pruning wounds; (4) Experimental evidence has shown that dormant-season pruning has less dwarfing effect on trees than summer pruning; and (5) Pruning goes well with cool weather because the job requires much exercise.

The best time to start the pruning will depend upon the size of the job and amount of labor available. It is more hazardous to prune in early

[1]Dr. William J. Lord made suggestions for revision of this chapter, from Univ. of Mass., Amherst.

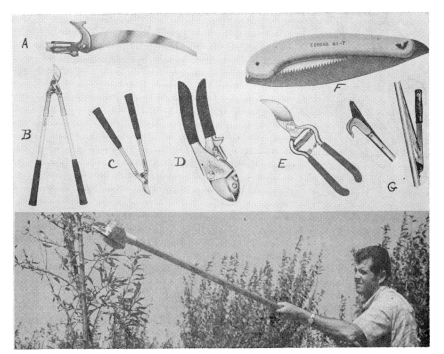

Figure 1. In the larger commercial orchards mechanical mower pruning is on the increase with some follow-up thinning-out pruning by hand tools or by hydraulically hand-operated clippers or circular saws (below) from movable "squirrels," scaffolds, or from the ground. Light weight hand tools used may be, "A", pole saws or, "G", pole pruners; "B", loppers for peach or apple; "C", miniloppers for grapes, bushes, small trees; hand shears "D" or "E" for small-wood cuts or "F", a folding pull saw. ("B-F," Corona Clipper Co., P. O. B. 730, Corona, Calif., 91720; "A," A. M. Leonard & Son, Piqua, O., 45356; "G," Seymour Smith & Son, Oaksville, Conn., 06779; below, Miller-Robinson, P.O.B. 2886, Santa Fe Springs, Calif., 90670.

winter than later in the dormant season, because evidence has shown that extremely cold temperatures following the pruning operation are likely to result in serious freezing injury to the trees. It is better, if the situation will permit, to wait until late winter when there is less danger of extremely cold temperatures. The mature apple trees should be pruned first and the young trees last, because the latter are more succulent and somewhat more subject to freezing injury. Actually, pruning wounds heal best if the cuts are made at about the time when active growth begins in the spring, but the job can be done this late only when there is a limited number of trees. Generally, it is better to play safe and start early so that the job is completed and the brush removed before spraying starts. Pruning can be performed through the blossoming period but this should be done only in an emergency.

With young or compact trees it may be advisable to do a small amount of summer training or power-mower pruning to assist the tree in assuming a better shape and to prevent it from making unnecessary growth in undesired places. During periods of severe labor shortage, a certain amount of pruning can be done at apple thinning time by using loppers

FMC Corp., Lansing, Michigan

Figure 2. Pruning machines are used in orchards over 150A. for "topping" and "siding" large and dwarf trees, using follow-up touch-up crew from platform and ground with pneumatic pruners. Relative costs/tree can be cut 35% the first year, and 55% the second, with little or no cost the third, according to Turner Ramey, West Virginia apple grower, Charles Town. Machines (a) pay for themselves in about three years, (b) do not create any great sucker problem at end of stubs, (c) enables you to keep your fillers, (d) cut trees up to 20' high, (e) work best on hedgerow planted trees and (f) greatly reduce the time to complete the job.

and removing with medium cuts the excessive twig growths along with the apples. At this season, the nonfruiting and weak wood can be spotted easily and removed. In early summer, some growers make a regular practice of "mopping-off" the succulent water sprouts which arise on the trunks and main limbs of mature trees. This can be done by hand, using leather gloves. Such water sprouts are essentially nonproductive wood which utilize water and nutrients needed by other branches, and also attract aphids. If the sprouts are left over winter, they may contain many eggs and are, therefore, a source of aphid and mite injury to the fruit and leaves in early spring.

Pruning equipment. The skill with which an operator uses pruning tools is probably more important than the tools he uses. However, the fact cannot be overlooked that good tools in first-class condition and which can be handled nimbly will offer the workmen every possible advantage in doing a rapid and high quality job with less effort. For young trees, "loppers," hand shears, and a "half-moon" saw are usually sufficient (Figure 1.). For older trees, the same equipment can be used or long-handled motor-driven 6"-8" circular saws are used by workers on maneuverable squirrels. Pruning with special machinery is shown in Fig. 2.

In commercial practice the compressed-air or pneumatic pruners with portable scaffold are becoming standard equipment for cutting labor costs to about one-third[1]. Self-propelled aerial platforms (squirrels)

[1]Contact the Dept. of Agr. Eng., Cornell University, Ithaca, N. Y. for plans for building scaffolds; for "squirrels"; Blackwelder Mfg. Co. Rio Vista, Calif. or Pitman Mfg. Co., 300 W. 79th Terrace, Kansas City, Mo.: for pneumatic tools: Miller-Robinson Co., 7007 Avalon Blvd, Los Angeles, Calif.; Bud-Air Co., Pulaski, N. Y. Corona Clipper Co., Corona, Calif. 91720; Friend Mfg. Co., Gasport, N.Y 14067.

speed the pruning, picking, etc., up to 50% faster (medium-small orchards).

It pays to buy good-quality pruning tools which will remain sharp for relatively long periods of time. The tools should be strong but as light as possible. Some lopping shears have the disadvantage of carrying too much iron which tires the pruner and reduces his daily accomplishments. Boots with rubber soles and heels, or rubber overshoes, should be worn to prevent scarring the crotches and limbs while climbing.

Making the cut. Use sharp tools at all times to make cuts clean and smooth. Ragged cuts heal slowly and often poorly. In removing branches, large or small,

Ohio State University

Figure 3. This close smooth cut is made properly. Note that it is healing satisfactorily. Avoid leaving stubs when removing branches.

make the cut close and parallel to the supporting limb, as shown in Figure 3. Stubs do not heal and result in decay which may eventually enter the trunk of the tree and weaken the entire structure if the cut has been large. Small stubs left on the periphery of the tree by pneumatic equipment, however, have caused no serious problem.

Use both hands wherever possible. Cut with one hand and hold the limb to be removed with the other, steadily pushing the limb away from the blade as the cutting proceeds. Less "fist" strength is required with hand shears when the cutting is done in this manner. In using hand or lopping shears, place the cutting blades at the side or below the crotch (but not in the crotch) to secure the best cut. Never wiggle the shears through a cut. This results in a ragged wound and may spring the shears.

If the orchard has been trained properly from the beginning, there is little or no need for removing large limbs, which is a practice to be avoided as much as possible. However, there are times when this must be done and the following procedure is recommended. Use a saw, making three-separate cuts. The first cut is made on the lower side of the limb two inches deep and about eight inches from the base of the limb. Thence, cut from above, starting about two inches closer to the base of the limb than the lower cut and continue until the limb falls. This prevents the limb from tearing bark or splitting down the trunk. The third cut is made close to the supporting limb to remove the stub.

Types of Cuts. Shoot and spur growth is stimulated around a cut,

Figure 4. (Left) A small maneuverable chain saw used by one man ahead of pruning crew to remove dead and undesirable large limbs, or to disect a bull-dozed-out tree. (Right) Heading-back cut was made at "a" the year preceding, resulting in several side shoots. Not desirable on mature trees (See Fig. 7), but used on nursery whips to force laterals for tree framework and on dwarfs to subdue undesirable growth or dwarf a shoot competing with the leader limb. (Homelite, Port Chester, N. Y.; Ohio State Univ., resp.).

but growth elsewhere in a mature tree is little affected. The cut at "a" in Figure 4 (right) is called a *"heading-back cut"* and is used (a) on nursery whips about two feet above ground to force out laterals to form tree framework and (b) on dwarfs to subdue an undesirably placed limb or one competing with the leader.

Thinning-out and bulk pruning. The term "thinning-out" in pruning is used where entire branches are removed. If these branches are large limbs, such pruning is termed "bulk" pruning. The principle behind this pruning is to admit more light and to remove unproductive branches which are producing few if any desirable fruit. See Figure 5 for a totally mech-anical system of maintaining compact tree walls and cutting swaths in the walls to admit 50% or more light and renew fruiting wood.

Thin-wood pruning. The term "thin-wood" pruning has been used by the Michigan Agricultural Experiment Station, and it refers to the removal of slow-growing, weak, underhanging branches or spurs which are either not fruiting or producing fruit of low quality. Such wood is classified arbitrarily as any four-year-old apple wood less than one-quarter-inch in diameter at the base of the fourth-year annual "ring" (a group of bud scale scars where

70

Figure 5. This Cornell hydraulically operated "slotting" saw is used to cut a 24" swath in a compact 10-foot high tree wall (10' x 20' tree spacing) to admit light and renew fruiting wood. Christmas-tree-wall shape (12 ft. base, 4 ft. top width) is maintained in dormant season by tractor-driven mower cutter bar. "Slotting" saw is operated annually in one of three levels from ground on both sides, cutting at the same level once in three years. Tests showed three times more new spurs on McIntosh on EMIX with EMVII interstems, 4-fold increase in flowering spurs, and admittance of 50% or more light in outer 2 ft. canopy compared with cutter-bar use alone. (Courtesy John C. Cain, N. Y. Agr. Exp. Sta., Geneva.)

growth started each spring). The wood is said to be intermediate in vigor if it is four-years-old, has a diameter between one-quarter- and three-eights-inch in diameter; and it is productive or thick in diameter if over three-eights-inch near the base. Data from Michigan show that the thick apple branches produce at least ten times as many desirable apples as the thin-wood branches. Varieties differ in the amount of thin-wood they should be allowed to support. It will vary, also, with the location of this wood on the tree, and other conditions.

The brush pile should consist mostly of thin-wood and branches which are "fruited out" and poorly located. Thin-wood usually appears first on the oldest wood in the center of the tree and on branches nearest the ground. Thin wood can be detected best by standing next to the tree trunk at harvest and looking upward and outward and studying which type of wood is carrying the small poor-quality fruit.

Cutting to lateral branches. Many of the cuts in pruning are of this type. A limb is shortened by cutting to a lateral branch, making the cut in line with the side branch, as shown in Figure 7. The main objective of this type of pruning is to keep the sides of the tree within bounds and to lower the tops of tall trees so that they are within easy and more economical range for pruning, spraying, thinning and harvesting. Also, branches that droop to the ground, or, those which grow closely parallel on top of other limbs are often cut back by this method to an upward- or outward-growing lat-

71

Figure 6. A Baldwin tree spilt three ways with a heavy crop because of equal-size branches arising at the same point on the trunk. This is the result of improper training methods when the tree was young. (Cornell University.)

Figure 7. A limb is shortened by cutting to a strong lateral, as shown at L. This type of cut is used to keep a tree from becoming too tall or too wide. (Ohio State Univ.)

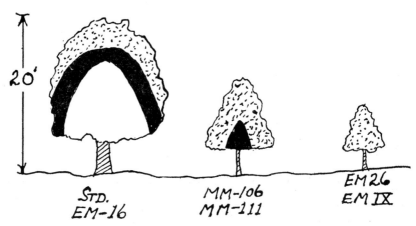

Figure 8. (left) On large standard-size fruit tree (a) speckled area is productive, (b) black is partly productive, (c) white is unpoductive "cord-wood." Center tree is semi-compact showing productive and partly productive areas, no unproductive volume. Right tree is full dwarf showing total productive area. Densely planted full-dwarf trees are generally the most productive/A. Good sunlight penetration is main factor influencing productiveness, marketable fruit quality and profitableness of compact trees. About 50% or more light penetration throughout tree is needed (After Don Heinicke, USDA, Wenatchee, Wash.)

eral. Such cuts do not dwarf the branch as much as heading-back cuts, nor do they induce many side branches to appear, and this is particularly true if the lateral shown at "L" in Figure 7 is almost the same size as the branch removed. It is poor practice to remove a relatively large limb back to a weak growing lateral, limb back to a weak-growing lateral.

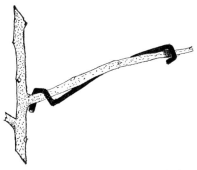

Detail pruning. This is a common practice and refers to the removal of small branches (not necessarily thinwood) with the cuts well distributed over the length of limb. Both cuts in Figure 7 are classified under detail pruning. The main purpose is to prevent the small limbs, especially on the outer portion of large limbs, from becoming thick, crowded, and forming a

Figure 9. This heavy-wire crotch former (dipped in orange paint), devised by R. L. Norton, Cornell (New York) is suggested to help widen (about 60° angle, no wider) and strengthen crotches on non-trellis compact trees the 2nd and 3rd growing season (wind won't blow them out; cost about 1.5c). Apply wires early (May) and remove in 6-7 weeks (August). Crotch angle must be changed when limbs are young. Wood-stick "spreaders" with furniture nails in each end work on about 4-year trees, causing earlier bearing with less effect on crotch angle.

canopy more or less over the center of the tree, shading it too much. A special advantage of detail pruning during the dormant season is that excessive flower buds and leaf buds are removed, thus improving the size and color of fruit developing from the remaining fruit buds. This pruning is particularly valuable when done in advance of an expected heavy crop. To some extent it takes the place of hand thinning of fruit in early summer. Popular varieties which tend to respond well to detail pruning are Yellow Transparent, Golden Delicious, Rome Beauty, Jonathan, Wealthy, Cortland.

Correction of weak crotches. Figure 6 shows an apple tree which has split apart as a result of three limbs of about equal size being allowed to develop with narrow-angled crotches. It is important that no side or scaffold branch be permitted to develop as fast as the central leader limb. If a fast-growing side branch has a wide angle in the crotch, is properly located, and worth keeping, its rate of growth can be checked by pruning it back and thinning out the remaining laterals. Such pruning will assist in dwarfing it to a lateral, and permitting the leader limb to grow upward and a few inches ahead of all side limbs.

"Mold and Hold" pruning is used mainly on spur-type strains and semi-dwarfs, forming a tree of pyramidal shape with either a delayed open center or central leader. The only early pruning is to develop tree form, correct poor crotch angles and remove criss-cross or drooping limbs. When the tree starts bearing or has reached its desired size, shoots are cut back about ¾ths their length to restrict expansion, eventually forming a sturdy tree. Concurrently, nitrogen is markedly lowered or withheld and

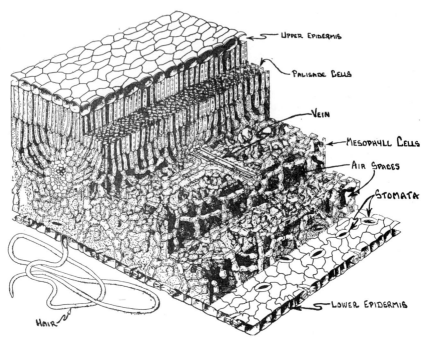

Upper Epidermis
Palisade Cells
Vein
Mesophyll Cells
Air Spaces
Stomata
Lower Epidermis
Hair

L. H. MacDaniels, Cornell University
Figure 10. A cross section of an apple leaf magnified many times, showing the principal parts. Food materials for tree growth and fruit production are manufactured in the leaves. Heavy pruning should be avoided. It reduces the -"manufacturing centers" (leaves) of the tree.

carefully manipulated thereafter to control tree size and fruiting. Pruning somewhat resembles peach pruning when tree has attained ultimate size, cutting back to strong laterals (Fig. 7).

Treating pruning wounds and cankers. W o u n d dressings are needed only for cuts larger than about two inches in diameter. The sun is probably as good a disinfectant as any for the smaller cuts. There are several good wound dressings on the market which should be applied only to the exposed wood and *not* to the bark or healing area. A satisfactory inexpensive antiseptic paint can be prepared by mixing powered bordeaux spray with raw linseed oil to the consistency of paint and applying it while fresh. Asphalt paint, grafting wax, and shellac also can be used. Water asphalt emulsions, used for roofing paint, are inexpensive and effective, but precaution must be taken to avoid those containing creosote or other toxic substances. "Flint Kote Static" and "Foster's I.B.M." are two good brands in Michigan.

In case of large diseased cankers on limbs and trunks, make a cigar-shaped or pointed cut which reaches live bark on all sides. Cuts through the bark should be vertical, not sloping; the latter retards healing. Wound dressings should be made during the dormant season, preferably in late dormancy together with necessary top-working and bridge-grafting.

C. W. Ellenwood, Ohio Agr. Exp. Sta.

Figure 11. Pruning is a dwarfing process. These 27-year Stayman Winesap trees show different growth responses following variations in pruning. The large tree at the left has never been pruned, the tree in the center has received moderate pruning, while the tree at the right has been given heavy annual pruning. Average yield in pounds per tree for the ten-year period, 1933-1942, was for the unpruned tree—553, for the lightly pruned tree—606, and for the heavily pruned tree—467. Fruit from the unpruned (left) tree was small with a large percentage in the low grades.

In case of cankers of fire blight, bitter rot, and black rot, those limbs should be removed which are dead or have been two-thirds or more girdled by the disease. Such diseases are easily spread from one tree to the next by carry-over cankers. The blighted limbs should be removed back to a lateral, if possible, at a point at least six to eight inches below the diseased areas.

In case of fire blight, it is not necessary to remove the smaller cankered areas if a special antiseptic solution is applied[1].

Effects of pruning on growth and production of young trees. There is a close relationship between the activities of the roots and the activities of the leaves of fruit plants which must be considered to understand the results from pruning. The raw materials used by the leaves in manufacturing the tree's food supply come from the soil and from the air. The water and essential mineral nutrients are absorbed from the soil by the roots. From the air the leaves absorb carbon dioxide through the open stomata (Figure 10). In the leaves, largely among the mesophyll cells, the carbon dioxide from the air and the water from the soil combine in the presence of sunlight and green coloring (chlorophyll) to form starches and sugars. This process is known as photosynthesis. The mineral nutrients from the soil then combine with the carbohydrates to form the proteins and other plant foods which are used in the growth processes of the tree. The greater the amount of healthy leaf surface on a young tree, the faster it is capable of growing.

Pruning has a dwarfing effect on young trees. The greater the amount of pruning, the greater the dwarfing effect on the tree. This has been demonstrated clearly by many experiment stations (Figure 11) and has been read-

[1] Apply the following antiseptic solution to fire blight cankers, using a small paint brush: Add one quart of hot water to four tablespoons of concentrated hydrochloric acid in an enamel kettle, and in this mixture, dissolve nine pounds of dry zinc chloride powder. Commercial grades of these chemicals can be secured at the local drug store. Add sufficient red or blue coloring, or any good dye, so that diseased areas can be checked for good coverage. After cooling, pour the above solution into seven pints of denatured alcohol and mix well. Store in tightly stoppered glass bottles or jugs to prevent evaporation.

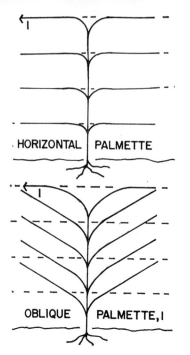

HORIZONTAL | PALMETTE

OBLIQUE | PALMETTE, I

Figure 12. Low-wire trellis training of full-dwarf trees (on EM IX or 26) by horizontal palmette gives maximum growth suppression. Oblique palmette training fits natural growth pattern of tree. Both induce early bearing, are resistant to wind and heavy-crop damage, and are suitable for commercial and particularly the home planting. Use spur-type cions on fertile ground. (L. D. Tukey, Penn State University).

ily seen in the orchards by fruit growers, themselves. It is true that one gains the impression that pruning stimulates shoot growth, but this stimulation occurs only withcut. Under these conditions, the top has been reduced in comparision with the roots and there is relatively more nutrients and water available to the remaining shoots. Experiments have shown that the total shoot growth for all terminals over a pruned tree, however, is less than if the tree had not been pruned. This effect is accumulative and after a period of four or five years with young trees, it is clearly evident that the unpruned trees are larger than the pruned trees, depending upon how much pruning was done. Light annual pruning, only for the purpose of training the tree, however, has little effect in delaying bearing.

TRAINING YOUNG APPLE TREES

The ideal tree. It is generally agreed among horticultural specialists and growers that the *modified-leader type* of tree is the strongest and easiest to manage for the large-size orchard trees. It consists of a central trunk around which scaffold or side branches, of the desired number and spacing, can be arranged with wide-angle crotches. It is difficult to point out an ideal tree-framework in the orchard since each variety and tree tends to grow differently. There are three to five scaffold branches arising from the central leader trunk. This is about the right number of scaffold limbs for a mature bearing tree. The central leader has been "modified," or cut to a side limb, at about eight to ten feet above the ground so that it no longer grows straight up but has been diverted outwardly. By so doing, the tree will be kept relatively lower and within better reach of the spraymen, the pickers, thinners, and the pruners. Also, the top center of the tree has been thinned out for light to enter throughout the inside and lower portions of the tree. For machinery usage the lowest limb is about two feet from the ground and the other scaffold limbs are spaced vertically about six to twelve inches apart. Also, the limbs are well placed around the central leader limb so that each has a definite section of the tree

76

into which it can grow. System is adapted to shake-catch machine harvesting and to chemical weed and mouse control.

Jonathan, McIntosh and Stayman have a spreading growth habit. Some varieties such as Delicious strains and Northern Spy tend to grow upright and it is somewhat more difficult to attain the desired framework. Delicious and Winesap in Washington have produced longer where about three main limbs form the tree, according to the late John C. Snyder, pomologist.

"Wedge" System. A young tree is trained into four sections, and when mature, the tree has two 1½ to 2 ft. channels maintained through the tree, running, e.g., northeast to southwest and northwest to southeast when the rows run east and west. The wedge system is used on standard large trees planted in a square, triangle, or rectangle system. Advantages are better fruit coloring and spray coverage, and facilitated hand thinning and harvesting. Details are in 1966 edition of this book.

Training Dwarf Trees. The smallest dwarfs (on EM IX or 26) are staked or trained on a trellis by any one of several systems. Semi-dwarfs, usually planted in a hedgerow, may be trained also by one of several methods. In dwarf trees, it is of utmost importance that a *leader limb* be maintained ahead of other limbs until it reaches its desired height. Also, the tree must be *defruited*[1] until it has almost reached its desired size to prevent fruiting from dwarfing it to the size of a 4-year tree when it should have 6-year size[1]. Dr. Harold B. Tukey's book describes numerous training and pruning systems. The commercial systems are discussed below.

Hedgerows or Tree Walls. Advantages are: (a) provides maximum trees per acre, (b) affords use of mechanical equipment for pruning, fruit thinning, and harvesting, and (c) easier and more efficient spray application. Adequate space must be provided between tree rows to operate machinery. Rows should run north and south for better light.

There are two types of hedgerows: (a) trees supported by individual posts or by a trellis. Where standard seedling or semidwarfing stocks are used for hedgerows, the best cion selection where available may well be the three-quarter size spur-type strains. (b) Trees are unsupported. This refers to cions on better-rooted stocks like EM II, MM 111, or 104. Stocks EM IX, VII, IV, 26 and MM 106 are not well suited. The so-called *"spindle bush"* training may be used where trees with a central leader to 12'-14' high, straight, and with numerous small fruiting side branches are tied down to ground or branches below to induce early fruiting and wide crotches. Tree spread is controlled to 6 to 7' width for machine or platform harvesting by cutting back ½ to ¾ths of shoots or to laterals as in renewal peach pruning. *"Pillar"* pruning consists of a central leader tree, unsupported on semidwarfing stock. Leader is cut back, part way each year for stiffening and forcing laterals. After 3 or 4 years growth and one fruiting year on a lateral, it is removed back to a

---

[1]Ethephon @ 250-500 ppm at petal fall should defruit trees, no harmful effects. See also Bukovac reference.

Figure 13. Palmette training, common in upper Mediterranean countries, is essentially intermeshed fan-shaped trees with a leader and side limbs tied to and interwoven with wooden or bamboo poles. Management and harvesting is facilitated. (Courtesy E. G. Christ, Rutgers University.)

stub. Hence, when mature, tree should have about an equal number of one,- two,- three,- and four-year laterals. System works best when growth is carefully controlled by fertilizer and water since heavy cutting is stimulating. System needs more testing in North America.

Palmette pruning is used mostly in upper Mediterranean countries and consists of more or less interlocking hedgerow trees trained to fan shape, with width spread a few feet thick, using poles interlaced with the limbs (Fig. 13). Branches lower than 18" above ground are removed, leader is kept dominant by removing or heading back competitors, vigorous limbs are tied down (important for slow-bearing Delicious, Winesap, Newtown, and Tydeman's Early), overly vigorous leader is cut back to force laterals, and narrow-angled crotch limbs are dwarfed by pruning or removed.

Pruning one-year nursery trees at Planting. Most of these trees come as whips with no branches except for a few varieties like York and Jonathan that have a few weak side branches. Tall whips are cut back to about 4', shoots are all allowed to attain 6-8 inches when the leader is cut back to a strong lateral, and the best wide-angle crotch shoots distributed around the trunk are retained, the rest removed (Fig. 16). Cut weaker whips to 30". If tree is hopeless after one season, cut it off at 2", drive stake nearby. Resulting growth will have many wide-angle limbs.

Deshooting one-year nursery trees. Some attention has been given to training one-year nursery trees by the deshooting method. After planting, the one-year trees are cut back as described above. When the leafy side shoots are about six inches long in early summer, select well-spaced, wide-

78

angled shoots which will develop into a desirable scaffold system (Figure 16). Remove the undesired shoots. It is preferable to have the lowest branch on the southwest side or toward the prevailing winds. Where possible, in this case, the second branch is preferred on the southeast side; the third on the northwest; and the fourth continuing the trunk into a northeast scaffold branch. This provides a main scaffold branch for each quarter of the tree. It is desirable to have from eight to twelve inches of vertical distance between the wide-angled scaffold branches. It may take longer than one year to select the main scaffold limbs for a desirable system. With careful attention the first two or three years, some excellent scaffold systems can be developed by using this training method. Experience of the Ohio Agricultural Extension Service has shown that trees tend to be remarkably uniform in an orchard from the standpoint of placement of scaffold limbs (Figure 17). With some varieties subject to weak crotches, this method of training may result in some narrow-angled crotches. Under these conditions, the limbs which have narrow-angled crotches are spread with wire formers or sticks (see Figure 9) when in their second or fourth year. The deshooting method is an

Figure 15. Pruning young compact trees. (a) Cuts shown on tree after one season in orchard. Remove branches with narrow crotches, alleviate branch crowding, space remaining branches around tree, and head back scaffold limbs and leader to balance tree. (b) Same tree with 2 seasons growth. (c) The "b" tree has been pruned, removing sharp - angled branches, branches thinned out, keeping leader dominant. (d) In 3rd and 4th year, using same approach as in "c". (R. F. Carlson, Michigan State University, E. Lansing)

improvement over the "disbudding" method originally used, where the buds were removed shortly after they "broke" in spring, and the three or four remaining shoots grew so rapidly that narrow crotches often were formed. The advantage of the deshooting system is that all buds and shoots are allowed to compete with each other for water and food materials for one to two months; and, thus, they make slower growth and tend to develop wider-angled crotches at the outset. Also, the more vigorous and desirable

79

Figure 16. A Stayman Winesap tree trained by the "deshooting" system, showing length and placement of scaffold limbs after one growing season in the orchard. The five and one-half-foot, 1-year nursery tree was cut back to the strongest growing shoot near the top when shoots were six to eight inches long about a month after growth started in the spring. Three additional shoots were selected below the top shoot, with first shoot about 20 inches from the ground, others spaced six to twelve inches apart at about equal distances around the trunk.

scaffolds can be detected by waiting for a period after growth starts.

Pruning two-year nursery trees at planting. The two-year a p p l e trees have been headed back in the nursery to about 24 inches above the ground and they come to the grower as branched trees. There are usually several branches arising close together near the point where the tree was head-ed. Two or more of the branches may already be competing for the leadership, as shown in Figure 18. Select the best and usually the most vigorous branch for the leader and cut it back as directed above for the one-year-old whip; remove the other competing leader if its crotch is narrow; otherwise, cut it back one-third and reserve it for a scaffold limb if properly placed. If additional side branches are available around the tree at distances of six to twelve inches apart, they can be retained and pruned likewise. However, one rarely finds more than two desirable side branches on a two-year nursery apple tree.

It is important to remove as early as possible all side branches which form narrow angles or which are too close to other scaffold limbs. A side limb does not move upward from the ground as the tree develops. It is true, however, that as two neighboring limbs increase in circumference, they gradually come closer to each other. This is sufficient reason for wide spacing of scaffolds on young trees. The establishment of a desirable scaffold system on a tree is a gradual process and may require three to six years in order to get the desired vertical and radial spacing between limbs.

Pruning after one year of growth in the orchard. The pruner must continually bear in mind that *narrow-angled crotches* should be elimi-

80

nated early. Therefore, with young developing trees, one must visit each tree at least once a year until the frameworks are fully established. Whorls of branches arising at about the same point on the leader should be reduced to one limb. The result of too many limbs arising at one place on the trunk is shown in Figure 8. Double and multiple leaders must be eliminated. This can be done by heavy pruning or removal of the limbs not selected for the single leader. No heading-back of lateral limbs should be done except when they are very long and unbranched, say in excess of 30 inches. Remove all water sprouts or limbs appearing at odd places on the trunk and at the base of the scaffold limbs. In general, very little pruning should be done on the secondary or side branches that arise from the scaffold limbs. In this manner, pruning can be kept light and still accomplish the purpose of the training. This management will encourage early heavy bearing.

Figure 17. Vigorous spur in early summer with terminal buds formed at A and B; scar of dropped apple at E; scars of dropped flowers at D; cluster base formed in spring at C; last years growth at F, and spring growth started at G (Cornell Univ.).

Subsequent pruning of young apple trees. The motto for pruning young apple trees might well be *"Prune lightly. If in doubt about a cut —do not cut!"* For the first eight years, one should concern himself primarily with the main scaffold and leader development of a tree. Leave the small branches and spurs on the young trees; they are the wood upon which the first fruit will develop.

Since every tree presents a different problem in pruning, nothing will substitute for common sense judgment in making cuts. For the beginner, it will be necessary to study the tree carefully before making, or not making, the cut. After considerable experience, pruning bcomes more or less second nature. Actually, it is a fascinating game.

The following suggestions are given for making the cuts on young apple trees:

1. Remove first the dead, cankered, broken or badly diseased limbs.

2. Remove as soon as possible (if they can be spared) branches which leave the leader at a narrow angle. These limbs are entirely unsatisfactory for permanent scaffolds.

Figure 18. A vigorous 2-year apple tree before and after pruning at planting. The largest and best of two central limbs was retained for the leader and cut back to about 50 inches above ground. The tree was planted with the best wide-angled lateral toward prevailing wind; lateral was cut back two-thirds. All other laterals were removed because they arose too close together.

3. Scaffold limbs may be found crowding each other. Either remove one or shorten it to a lateral that will be stunted or removed eventually.

4. Scaffold limbs may be found growing closely parallel, one above the other. If two limbs are concerned, the weaker, preferably the lower, is removed or dwarfed by heavy pruning, then eventually removed. If there are three limbs parallel one above the other, the middle one can be removed or heavily pruned. There should be a spacing of about four feet between scaffold limbs one above the other.

5. Avoid double leaders or whorls of limbs on the main leader and scaffold branches.

6. Remove water sprouts, unless they are needed to develop scaffold limbs in open areas of the tree. Sometimes, these water sprouts can be used to form a natural brace for sharp-angled crotches which, unfortunately, have been allowed to develop.[1]

7. Keep the central leading limb growing about six to ten inches above all lateral limbs. At the age of six to eight years, modify the leader and begin to open the top by cutting the leader back to a strong side lateral. This should be done only after four to six strong scaffold limbs have been developed.

---

[1]Twine the water sprouts from each limb together and leave the terminal ends loose for a period of one or two years, after which they are removed. The brace grows together quicker and increases in size more rapidly if one sprout arises several inches higher than the other. These natural limb braces will increase in size and strength as the tree grows older. In case two water sprouts are not available, a single sprout can be inlay-grafted into the other limb as described later under grafting. It is important, however, that such a limb have plenty of "spring" in order that the swaying side limbs will not dislodge the graft.

---

[1]Kwik-Way Products, No. Sacramento 15, Calif., carries bracing material for many kinds of fruit plants. Also Avistrap (rayon), FMC Corp., 1617 Penna. Blvd., Phila. 19103.

82

Figure 19. Holland growers tend toward ultra-high density plantings on EMIX to increase fruit production/man hour, using high-income varieties Beauty of Boskop, Golden Delicious, Jonathan, and Cox's Orange Pippin. "Spur-types" are used on MM stocks due to overgrowth of non-spur types. This planting is in its 5th year, 3¼ x 10 ft., staked, more or less slender-spindle-trained and pruned. Orchards should attain 90 lbs. fruit/man-hour average, with Goldens most productive and Cox's less. (R. S. Roosje, Director, Proefstation, Voor de Fruitteelt, Wilhelminadorp, Holland).

8. Remove side branches on scaffolds closer than 1 ft. to trunk on big trees, 4-6 in. on compacts. Space other side branches on scaffold limbs so that they ultimately will not interfere with each other. The less desirable branches are those growing toward the ground, straight up or into the tree center; remove these first when thinning is needed.

9. The lower limbs on the younger trees, being the oldest, come into bearing first and should be retained for fruit production as long as the fruit quality is satisfactory.

Bending or tying down branches. Northern Spy, Yellow Transparent, Delicious, and other upright growing varieties are sometimes difficult to train because almost every main limb tends to grow upright. A special practice sometimes used is to train these branches into outward-growing laterals by bending or tying them down. Crotch angles can be widened easiest while the branch is young and willowy. Heavy wire in Fig. 9 painted orange serves this purpose. Notched wood spreaders may be dislodged. Wood pieces with sharp nails in the ends can be used on limbs 4 to 5 years old, or use string from limbs to staples at trunk base. Trees flower and bear sooner so-treated.

PRUNING BEARING APPLE TREES

Before pruning a mature bearing apple tree, it is advisable to briefly study the reasons for pruning and the ultimate effects upon the tree. The

83

Figure 20. This Golden Delicious tree on medium-vigor EM VII clonal stock has well placed strong-crotch scaffold limbs on a central leader. Tree is compact yet sufficiently open for production of high-quality fruit. Arrows at right show where pruning cuts were made on the tree at left before pruning. Note also where cuts were made the years before at "o". (Robert F. Carlson, Mich. State Univ.)

purpose is to increase the quantity of high-grade marketable fruit and to keep the tree within height and width bounds for more economical management. Pruning improves color, increases size of fruit, keeps the fruiting wood vigorous on old trees, and assists in controlling insects and diseases. With some varieties such as Jonathan, McIntosh, and Rome Beauty, the detail and thin-wood pruning will largely take care of the need for fruit thinning in July, and at less cost per tree.

Shoot growth. Shoots are defined as the leafy new growths on a tree; when the leaves on these shoots are lost in autumn, they then become "twigs." It is interesting to note that terminal and lateral shoot growth on a bearing tree are often completed within a few weeks after growth starts in spring (Figure 20). As the tree becomes older and begins to bear, there is a tendency for the growth in length and diameter of the shoots to become less and less each year. Pruning, together with fruit thinning and a desirable soil management program, then become necessary to control the kind and amount of fruiting wood in order that production of marketable fruit can be maintained. In case of young trees, it is desirable to get as much terminal growth as possible, often 24 inches or more per year, but at the same time properly ripen and mature the wood for winter (wood growing vigorously into autumn is likely to winter kill). With bearing trees, it is important to obtain plump terminal shoot growth of 10 to 15 inches in length on fruiting branches, with the longer 15-inch terminals desired for such light setting varieties as Delicious and Stayman Winesap.

Fruit spurs. The term "spur" refers to the numerous short growths which are abundant over the fruit tree and upon which most of the fruit is borne (Figure 20). Large thick spurs well-supplied with leaves are correlated with large well colored fruit. Well distributed cuts over older trees are needed every one-two years to keep spurs vigorous. See Figure 5 for a mechanical means to do this. "Spur type" strains tend to grow openly with an abundance of spurs and are preferred increasingly vs. standard strains (Fig. 23).

The apple fruit bud, which contains both flowers and leaves, is usually terminal on the spur and when it sets a fruit, the new shoot growths are forced out from the sides as shown in the accompanying figure. This accounts for the fact that a fruiting spur has a zigzag growth. A nonfruiting spur, on the other hand, grows straight year after year because the terminal bud is always a leaf bud. Some varieties bear fruit terminally and/or laterally on last year's terminal shoot growth, in addition to bearing on spurs. Examples are Jonathan, Wealthy, and Rome Beauty.

An apple fruit spur usually bears fruit every other year. Pruning reduces the total number of blossoming spurs on trees which are heavily supplied with them, thus reducing the tendency to overload with fruit and inducing a

85

Figure 21. Red Delicious/EM VII before (left) and after (right) pruning in the 4th year. Some "stubbing" of last years shoots has been done to develop bearing inside tree canopy. (R. F. Carlson, Mich. State Univ., E. Lansing).

more regular bearing habit from one year to the next. When an excessive number of growing points blossom and fruit at the same time, conditions are unfavorable for fruit bud formation during the early summer of the overload period.

It is important that plenty of light reaches the leaves on the fruit spur, for these leaves will manufacture a large part of the carbohydrates that go to form the neighboring fruit. Heavily shaded spurs with two or three small leaves rarely develop well colored and good-sized fruit. Also, spurs will be thin and weak or eventually die. Thinning out pruning is needed, spread over 2 to 3 years if heavily matted. See Figure 5 for machinery and a technique to open tree wall for better light and flower bud development.

The varieties which will respond well to thin-wood pruning on mature trees include Rome Beauty, Stayman Winesap, Golden Delicious, Delicious, McIntosh, Cortland, Yellow Transparent, Jonathan, Wealthy, Rhode Island Greening, Baldwin, Northern Spy, York Imperial, and Mammoth Black Twig.

BENEFITS OF PRUNING MATURE TREES

Pruning increases fruit color. Sunlight should reach the inner leaves on a tree and the fruit itself to obtain good fruit color. With proper pruning over the mature tree, sunlight will be admitted to the fruits and leaves throughout the tree. The leaves thus are able to carry on a higher rate of food manufacture. The sugars resulting from this manufacture are used in

Figure 22. Northern Spy (variety comes into bearing late) on EM VII before (left) and after (right) pruning in 5th year with little pruning to 5th year to encourage early fruiting. Tree has been opened and headed back for better light penetration. Limb formers or spreaders are needed early to widen crotches on this variety, as Delicious, which naturally have narrow crotches. (R. F. Carlson, Michigan State University, E. Lansing).

the development of highly colored fruit. During the ripening period, the fruit must be well supplied with carbohydrates, principally sugars, beyond the requirements for growth. Apples which are red on one side and greenish on the other indicate inadequate pruning to admit light to the center and through the tree.

Pruning increases size of fruit. Judicious dormant pruning promotes the rapid development in size of fruit, starting immediately after the fruit is set in spring. Dormant pruning is more effective in obtaining size improvement in fruits than fruit thinning in early summer because by this time nutrients and carbohydrates will have gone into the fruits that are knocked to the ground by chemical or hand thinning. Thin-wood and detail pruning prevent this wastage of nutrients and food materials by diverting them to the better located apples. It is important that the pruning practice be interrelated with other practices, especially thinning, use of fertilizers, and soil management in order to secure the greatest response in size improvement. However, when pruning is carried to extremes, it reduces yields. Considerable study, experience, and skill are necessary to prune and produce the highest yield of good size, color, and all-round-quality fruit.

Pruning keeps fruiting wood young and vigorous. Every orchardist has noticed the large size, good color, and fine quality of fruit which is borne on young trees shortly after they come into bearing. Pruning must be performed on mature trees in such a way as to keep the fruiting wood similar to the ideal growth conditions usually found in the young

87

Figure 23. These are 22-year-old spurs from (left) an original "spur type" Delicious tree and (right) a standard type Delicious tree. Note difference in flowering points. "Spur type" strains of standard varieties are about ¾ths size trees whether on seedling or clonal stocks. The "spur type" strains are preferred by many growers except on full-dwarfing stocks where they, too, may be preferred on naturally vigorous varieties and on good soils. (A. H. Thompson, Univ. of Md.)

bearing trees. Essentially, this means that well-placed new growths should be encouraged, pruning them for a few years while vigorous and productive and then eliminating them when they become old, underhanging, and weak.

Pruning assists in controlling insects and diseases. If the tree is kept reasonably open, it is much easier to direct spray material into and through the tree. Effective spraying is highly important because it represents more than half the cost of growing apples. It is particularly desirable that the trees dry rapidly after rains. A dense matted condition of limbs prevents this rapid drying and encourages diseases and spray injury (particularly on sensitive-skin varieties as Golden Delicious, Jonathan) and such important apple diseases as scab, blotch, bitter rot, Brooks spot, and sooty fungus. Spray the fruits on all four sides, not just one side, to control scab, codling moth, apple maggot, and bitter rot. Likewise, proper pruning reduces aphid injury and limb rub on the fruit.

STEPS IN PRUNING BEARING APPLE TREES

One of the chief objects in pruning mature trees, in addition to increasing the amount of quality fruit, is to keep the trees within height and width bounds. In recent years, there has been a tendency to maintain the tree tops low or about 15 feet or less, because low trees are much easier and less expensive to spray, thin, pick, prune and manage in general. One of the common faults in pruning bearing apple trees is to leave a shell of unpruned branches around the outside of the tree and to remove too much inside and lower fruiting wood because it is the easiest to reach. Platform and pneumatic pruning have resulted in much better pruning in these neglected areas because they are more accessible.

The following brief suggestions are given for making cuts on mature trees:

1. A good procedure is to start at the top of the tree and work downward, cutting upward-growing limbs back to strong laterals, removing the crowding branches, and thin-wood pruning the remaining limbs. Start at the tips of the limbs and prune back to the base, leaving the vigorous fruiting wood well spaced along the length of the limbs. By working from the top of

the tree toward the ground, it is possible for the operator to remove the brush from the tree as he works downward. A stepladder or lean-to ladder will be needed to prune the high side branches and help keep the top open if a platform is not used.

2. Remove dead, broken, and diseased wood. If dead wood is allowed to remain on apple trees from one year to the next, it harbors and disseminates such diseases as bitter rot and black rot (frog-eye).

3. Remove or dwarf by relatively heavy pruning any large limbs which are crowding other limbs, growing parallel with them, or resting upon them. Use judgment, however, in making the few necessarily large cuts so that direct afternoon sunlight during hot days in summer will not sunscald remaining exposed branches.

4. Remove all water sprouts, except an occasional one which may be needed to fill a vacant space in the tree.

5. Where it is necessary to thin a thick side branch, the first cuts should be made on the under side of the limb where the weakest wood occurs. Next, thin out the "thin-wood" or badly placed interfering branches growing upward from the top of the limb. Then, thin the poorer wood which arises from either side of the limb. Divert branches to open areas and away from other branches by pruning back to desirable laterals. Be careful not to overprune. See Figure 27 for special pruning on Delicious types.

6. Bearing trees can be kept in best condition by annual pruning or, certainly, by pruning every other season. This promotes regular annual bearing. If it is difficult or impossible to give the orchard a light pruning each year, the next alternative is to arrange the pruning so that it will be done preceding the expected heavy-crop years. Such pruning largely controls blossom and fruit overloads.

7. If pruning is irregular, or at intervals of four to six years, many trees grow out-of-bounds and develop irregular bearing habits, with undesirable excessive loads of fruit that further exhaust the tree during seasons which are favorable for heavy cropping. An annual bearing tree is much easier to keep within bounds because a good crop of fruit tends to compete with and reduce vegetative growth.

8. There is less risk from winter injury when pruning is done in late winter or early spring.

9. See pages 91 to 95 for special variety requirements.

PRUNING FILLER TREES

As pointed out earlier, filler trees are planted between the permanent trees to increase the fruit production per acre before the permanent trees fully utilize the ground. Filler trees are usually retained from 15 to 18 years. Little or no labor should be expended in pruning these trees after the first two or three years in the orchard. Considerable experimental evidence is available to show that apple trees will bear more fruit of almost equally

Figure 24. Photo shows relative dwarfing effect of EM IX (left) and EM XVI (right) on Cox's Orange Pippin after 9 years. Latter stock gives a tree about standard size (courtesy F. R. Tubbs, East Malling Res. Sta., Kent, England).

good quality when no pruning is given for the first 15 or so years, after which problems of limb breakage, poorer quality fruit, and others arise. However, as these fillers begin to crowd after the first 12 to 15 years in the orchard, heavy cutting back of the side branches is needed to assist the machinery in getting through the orchard and, also, to enable the permanent trees to develop symmetrically without the slightest crowding at any time. In general, the heaviest cutting on these trees should be done before a big crop year. When an apple tree is carrying a good load of fruit, it tends to make less shoot growth.

When fillers are headed back or pruned severely, it is often desirable to ring the trunk or scaffold limbs 2-3 weeks after bloom each year.[1] This practice encourages blossom-bud formation and improves the yields and quality of fruit for 8 to 10 years of fruiting before removal.

Filler trees now are frequently being left in orchards and trained and pruned in standard hedgerow fashion.

REJUVENATING AND REPLANTING OLD OR NEGLECTED ORCHARDS

Growers sometimes can take over a neighboring neglected orchard by only paying the taxes for the owner. Neglected trees have dwarfed matted lower limbs and because of little cropping, the top-most limbs grow up-

[1] See discussion in Chapter VI on "Flower Bud Formation, Pollination, and Fruit Set" for method of ringing.

ward until out of economical reach. Cut back top limbs to strong laterals, and generally thin out dead and matted limbs to open remaining spurs to light and sprays. Do not prune a tree excessively at any one time to bring about a desired condition. Spread the pruning over 3 to 5 years. Ten lbs. of sodium nitrate or equivalent in humid regions (ammonium sulfate in arid regions) per tree before growth starts helps to set a good crop, size it and invigorate the tree.

Under most conditions, the best way to renew an old orchard is to bulldoze it out and replant a portion of the acreage each year until the entire block is replanted. Avoid planting new trees in old-tree holes unless holes are filled with trucked-in top soil. If the new planting is on dwarfing stocks, the first few acres will be in bearing when the last acre of old trees is removed and replanted.

ADAPT THE PRUNING TO THE VARIETY

Most dormant apple trees look alike to the person who has had little experience with them. However, after considerable association with trees of different varieties, it is possible to see many differences in growth habits which enable the workmen to identify one dormant apple variety from another. Because of these differences in growth and fruiting habits, it is necessary to emphasize a certain type of pruning on one variety and perform little or none of it on another. The following suggestions are given for a few of the more popular varieties including their close relatives.

Delicious, Winesap. These varieties are subject to weak crotches and grow many limbs from the same point on a branch, forming whorls. It is essential that young trees be visited once a year for the first six or eight years in the orchard to correct fast-growing, narrow-angled crotches and to reduce the number of limbs in a whorl. Trees develop numerous medium-sized branches and eventually become dense unless removal of some of these limbs is done. One must be careful, however, not to overprune. Since these varieties are more profitable when grown as fancy apples eaten out of hand, it is important to get good branch spacing to admit sunlight, and that this be followed by removal of underhanging thin-wood.

The trees have a weakness in setting light crops, which this type of pruning will assist in correcting. An interrelated program of pruning, fruit thinning, and use of adequate nitrogen should be maintained to obtain about 15-inch terminal growths. See Figure 27.

Jonathan. Due to the development of numerous branches and twigs on Jonathan trees, the lower limbs may become shaded soon after the trees begin to bear. Jonathan responds better to thinning-out than to heading-back cuts. It is best to remove undesired branches entirely and then distribute small cuts on the remaining branches. With good thinning-out and detail pruning, Jonathan will require little or no hand thinning of fruit.

John C. Snyder, Wash. State College

**Figure 27. (Left) Drooping Delicious apple tree leader bearing several "risers,"
before pruning. Note denseness because of numerous risers and presence of
secondary branches on the risers. The large riser originating at the bend of the
leader is ideal for a renewal. (Right) Most of the pruning was accomplished by
making three saw cuts shown by arrows. There was some thinning with the
loppers; more will be necessary next year. Removing the large riser was a "must."
Note that none of the remaining risers were headed. The renewal riser was left
rather heavy in the top to force it to settle into position with fruit as soon
as possible.**

This variety is susceptible to fire blight; avoid heavy pruning. Tree openness for fast drying of spray chemicals reduces russeting, a Jonathan problem.

McIntosh. The general growth habit of McIntosh is good and, therefore, it is easier to train when young. It is important, however, to have the limbs well spaced so that spray can enter the trees freely in order to control scab to which McIntosh is readily susceptible. Also, keep the tops low to facilitate effective spraying in these areas where a major portion of the crop is borne. Attention to detail pruning is needed to get Fancy fruit.

Stayman Winesap. Under good soil management, this variety develops many long leggy branches with poorly spaced scattered laterals. On young trees, some heading-back is necessary to produce laterals on terminal growths 30 inches or more in length. Stayman Winesap is an open grower and it is not necessary to make many large cuts except to avoid double leaders or weak crotches. A combination of weak crotches and wood that tends to split easily with Stayman makes it highly important to correct weak crotches early in the life of the tree. It is necessary that this variety be kept in vigorous condition by over-all annual detail pruning and a good soil management program. Stayman is an open grower. Hence, large-cut shears or long-handled motor-driven circular saws are useful.

Rome Beauty. Young Rome Beauty trees are sometimes discouraging to the pruner because most of the limbs tend to grow straight up, making a dense crowded situation. *Annual attention* to training young Rome

---

[1]For brush choppers, windrowers, etc., seek catalogues of M. Lembo & Son, Inc., Box 8, Modena, N.Y. 12548; Edwards Equipment Co., 3212 Main St., Yakima, Wash. 98902; Marwald Orch. Equipment, Ltd., Ayer Rd., Harvard, Mass. 01451.

W. Va. Exp. Sta., Morgantown.

The Gehl Mfg. Co., West Bend, Wisconsin.

Figure 26. Brush shredders are widely used to shred brush that has been placed in windrows. (Upper) Special built equipment for gathering prunings from under trees and dragging to row middles for shredding. (Lower) A rotary blade or hammer-type PTO brush shredder can be used to chew up windrowed prunings.

93

Figure 26. Cost of pruning high-density orchards is reduced in Oregon by grower-made power take-off cutter bar hydraulically manipulated up and down. Unit is raised by screw lift. Follow-up pneumatic pruning can be done from ground and/or platform. Equipment also can be used on other fruits. (Courtesy Better Fruit and Vegetables Magazine, Portland, Oregon.)

Beauty trees is highly important. As the young trees begin to bear fruit, however, the weight of the fruit pulls the limbs out and the tree gradually assumes a spreading habit. Avoid over-pruning young trees to get a desired shape. Rome wood is willowy and fairly resistant to breaking.

Rome Beauty bears much of its fruit terminally on rather long twigs at the ends of the limbs and branches. As a result of this bearing habit, the numerous small cuts must be used on mature trees to remove the excess amount of twiggy growth which develops toward the outside of the tree. Much attention must be given to thin-wood pruning. It is important to start from the outer end of the branches and work toward the base, scattering the cuts more or less evenly. It is a common mistake in pruning bearing Rome Beauty trees to start at the base of a large limb and prune outward, taking off practically all of the branches for a considerable distance, leaving a "cow tail" situation with unpruned bushy twigs at the ends of the branches.

Yellow Transparent. This variety tends to become dense by producing an excess of small and medium-size branches. A portion of these branches should be removed. The remaining branches should be detail and thin-wood pruned. Relatively little topping of the outward-growing laterals is needed under these conditions. Yellow Transparent has a tendency to set heavy crops in some years and small crops in others. One should plan his pruning particularly in advance of an expected heavy crop. In addition, trees must be fruit-thinned by hand or chemicals and completed within a few weeks after bloom. For this variety, both fruit thinning and pruning are important in order to obtain good-sized fruit.

Wealthy. Wealthy should not be permitted to overbear in any one year due to the fact that it may subsequently become a weak grower and a distinctly biennial cropper. Considerable detail and thin-wood pruning is necessary to promote good color and to prevent the tree from becoming thick. The cultural and pruning program should be regulated so that about 15 inches of annual terminal growth is obtained on Wealthy. Early fruit thinning, as with Yellow Transparent, is highly important.

Golden Delicious. This variety has the weakness of developing forks and narrow-angled crotches. In addition, its long leggy branches are brittle and break easily with the first heavy load of fruit. Therefore, special annual attention is important while the trees are young to get well-spaced scaffold limbs (12 inches apart) each of which is of good diameter and strong. Golden Delicious bears early (five to seven years) and training cuts are not likely to retard bearing. Goldens are like Delicious in having a high nitrogen need, but carefully regulated to get full harvest-yellow fruit.

It is necessary to head-back or modify the leader at a height of six or eight feet; the leader can be pulled to a side by removing the small branches on the side toward the prevailing wind. Fruit on the other side of the leader, with the help of the wind, will pull this branch to the side. In mature trees, thin-wood pruning is highly important to attain large size of fruit. Chemical fruit thinning is a standard practice with this variety to get annual cropping. Open the trees for good air movement, quick drying and high-finish fruit. Open-growing *spur* Goldens are being widely planted.

Yellow Newton and York Imperial. These varieties bear biennially if allowed to over-set fruit. In fact, in spite of all precautions, they frequently tend to alternate heavy and light crops. As trees enter the light-crop year, save as many blooming spurs as possible. But as trees enter the heavy-crop years, reduce the blooming spurs by heavier pruning. Distribute pruning over the entire tree and keep the tops fairly open.

HURRICANE DAMAGE

Trees in leaf and in soggy ground are blown over easily by high winds and are damaged much more than trees after leaf fall. Most hurricanes occur before leaf drop and during or following heavy rains. It probably is best to leave the medium-to-large trees leaning and gradually prune and train them to upright trees with a leaning trunk. The larger trees pulled upright by tractor may lose many feeding roots and it takes them years to regain vigor, if they do. Very young trees or mature trees leaning slightly may be straightened and braced immediately as in Figure 27 while the ground is still soggy.

Figure 27. Triangle tree brace made from 1-½ x 4 inch rough lumber is simple, easily placed, effective, and nonharmful to tree. Good for moderately leaning trees due to high wind, which have been pulled upright by tractor. Badly leaning tree probably should be left as is and gradually trained to upright tree with leaning trunk.

CHEMICALS TO RETARD GROWTH AND WIDEN CROTCHES

With high-density orchards there may be a need for retarding growth chemically to keep trees within bounds. A chemical which may be used is succinic acid 2, 2-dimethylhydrazide known as B-9 or Alar (Uniroyal Co., Naugatuck, Conn., USA) applied at 2000 ppm in the spray tank about two weeks after bloom time. Terminal growth will stop on Delicious soon after application whereas growth will continue to August on young trees. A spray must be applied each year for continued effect. Trees are more compact with trunk diameter little affected. Alar has many other benefits, one being to induce earlier and more flowering the year after application. TIBA (tri-idobenzoic acid; AmChem Products, Inc., Ambler, Pa., USA) at 1000 ppm is used on young trees to induce wider-angle crotches, but is not recommended for bearing trees (causes fruit cracking, early dropping, cork, other problems). A spray of cytokinin and GA also can be used to widen crotches (See Williams and Billingsley). Since use of these chemicals and similar ones are in the developmental stages, it would be well to be in contact with your governmental services for latest recommendations.

REMOVING OLD TREES

Studies at Pennsylvania State University indicate that medium to large apple trees can be removed quickest with a large bulldozer of about D-6 size. Time required to uproot a tree is about a minute. One small D-2 tractor with a twenty-five foot cable can wiggle out most trees with some maneuvering, whereas two D-2 tractors, one pushing and the other pulling is quicker. Cost for removing a tree may vary between about twenty cents and a dollar (mid 1950's), depending upon size of tree, depth of rooting, number of trees involved, type of soil, and whether the tractors are available on the farm or have to be rented and transported. Portable motor-driven saws handled by one or two men are convenient for sectioning the trees after pulling.

WILD GAME CONTROL

In some orchards deer may cause considerable damage to young and old fruit trees by browsing the new growth and by rubbing their antlers against the bark. Unfortunately, there is as yet no economical or completely satisfactory method for solving the deer problem. An eight-foot high fence around the orchard is probably the best available method for controlling deer. Some state governments (New Jersey) will supply the fencing. For young trees, three fence posts placed 1½ to 2 feet apart in an equilateral triangle around the trees are often used to prevent bucks from rubbing their antlers against the bark. The Dupont spray repellant Arasan (thiram) has been fairly effective on deer and for rabbits and mice on above-ground parts of young trees. Helicopters are used to herd elk and antelope out of Washington orchards. University of California, Davis, has a bulletin on gophers. Z. I. P. is used by some growers with trees in leaf.

Review Questions

1. What factors influence the kind and amount of pruning needed by an apple tree?
2. Why is the dormant season preferred for pruning apple trees?
3. Discuss the trend in size and training of trees and the relationship to machine management.
4. What type of pruning cuts are used to keep a mature apple tree within height and width bounds; explain how the cut is made?
5. Pruning is a dwarfing process! Why?
6. Describe the arrangement of limbs on an apple tree trained to the modified leader, central leader, palmette, spindle bush, hedge-wall, pillar systems.
7. What is meant by the "deshooting" system of training newly planted apple trees?
8. Why should the small twigs be left on the lower branches of young trees?
9. Describe a weak and vigorous apple spur; why do some apple spurs grow a zigzag fashion?
10. How can you recognize a flower bud and a leaf bud on dormant apple wood?
11. List the benefits of pruning mature bearing apple trees.
12. How does the pruning of a filler tree differ from the pruning of a permanent tree?
13. How does the pruning of a bearing Red and Golden Delicious tree differ from the pruning of a bearing Stayman and McIntosh?

Suggested Collateral Readings

Batjer, L. P. Chemical control of tree size. Proc. XVII Internat. Hort. Congr. III: 71-75. 1966.

Bukovac, M. J. *et al.* Defruiting of dwarfed fruit trees and vegetative development. Mich. Qtrly. Bull. 47:No. 3, 364-372. 1965.

Cain, J. C. Mechanical Pruning of Apple Hedgerows. ASHS: 96 (5), 664-667. 1971.

Cain, J. C. Tree spacing and orchard efficiency. Cornell Res. Cir. 15 10pp. 1969.

Carlson, R. F. Compact Fruit Trees — Roots, spur-types, cultural practices, 111pp. mimeo. Mich. State Univ., E. Lansing, May 1971.

Carlson, R. F. Intermediate stem effects on apple. ASHS 87:21-28, 1965.

Christ, E. G. Pruning apples. N. J. Agr. Ext. Serv. Bull. 377. 16 pp. 1964.

Chemical Regulation of Plant Processes. A Symposia. HortScienc 4 (2): 1969.

Developing Dwarf Apple Trees. Michigan Science in Action. Michigan State Univ. March 1971. (By R. F. Carlson)

Feucht, Walter. La Fisiologia de la Madera Frutal. Universidad de Chile, Publicaciones En Ciencias Agricolas, No. 1, 1967.

Fisher, D. V. Spur-McIntosh Strains. Offset 8pp. Summerland, B.C. 1970.

Forshey, C. G. Alar on vigorous McIntosh apple arees. J. ASHS 95 (1): 64-67, Jan. 1970.

Forshey, C. G. and M. W. McKee. Production efficiency of large vs. small McIntosh trees. HortScience 5:164-5, 1970.

Jonkers, H. Tree size control by pruning and bending (Netherlands). Proc. XVII Internat. Hort. Congr. III:57-70. College Park, Md., USA. 1966.

Llewelyn, F. W. M. Partial defoliation, fruit drop, shoot growth in Lord Lambourne apple. J. Hort. Sci. 43, 519-26. 1968.

Neely, Dan. Healing of tree wounds. J. ASHS. 95 (5):536-540. 1970.

Norton, R. L. High-density Apple Plantings (good paper). N.Y. (Albion) St. Hort. Soc. Newsletter (Suppl.) Apr. 1970.

Owens, Frank W. Training spur Delicious. Ill. Agr. Ext. Serv. Cir. 871. 1963.

Preston, A. P. Results from pruning experiments with apples at E. Malling. Bull. de l'Institut Agron. et des Sta. de Res. de Gambloux (Belgium), Hors. Serie (in English). Vol. III:1053-62. 1960.

Roosje, G. S. Extensive Tests in High-Density Apple Plantings in Holland. N. J. (New Brunswick) State Hort. Soc. News. 50:3,4, 1969.

Stembridge, G. E. and M. E. Ferree. Immediate and residual effects of Alar on young Delicious apple trees. A.S.H.S. 94:6:602-604. 1969.

Tubbs, F. R. Tree size control through dwarfing rootstocks (E. Malling Res. Sta.). XVII Internat. Hort. Congr. Proc. III:43-56. College Park, Mr. 1966.

Tukey, H. B. Dwarfed Fruit Trees. The MacMillan Co., New York City. 1964.

Wertheim, S.J. Training slender spindle apple trees. Proefstation Voor De Wilhelminadorp. No. 10, Netherlands. Nov. 1970.

Westwood, M.N. and A. N. Roberts. Relationship between trunk cross-sectional area and weight of apple trees. J. ASHS Vol. 95:1. 28-30. Jan. 1970.

Williams, Max W. and H. D. Billingsley. Increasing apple crotch angles with cytokinins and Ga. ASHS 95(5):649-651. 1970.

Williams, Max W. Induction of Spur and Flower Bud Formation in Young Apple Trees with Chemical Growth Retardants. J. Amer. Soc. Hort. Science. Vol. 97, No. 2. March 1972. p. 210.

Note: See July issues Amer. Fruit Grower Mag. Willoughby, Ohio for sources pruning equipment. Dwarf Fruit Tree Assn., Hort. Dept., Mich. State Univ., East Lansing, holds tours, meetings, issues regular reports; you must be a member.

CHAPTER V

Soil Management for Apples

❖ ❖

No one cultural program can be recommended for all orchards. A program that is satisfactory for one orchard under one set of climatic and soil conditions may be undesirable for another under a different set of conditions. Good tree performance often may be obtained under any of several different systems of management. The cultural program selected, however, must be interrelated with the pruning, fertilization, fruit thinning, and the spraying programs to obtain good shoot growth, moderate over-all tree vigor, and high production of quality fruit. It is a general observation that fruit trees respond more or less directly to the soil type in growth and yield; the more favorable the soil, the less important is the particular cultural program to be followed.

Many orchards have been planted on rolling or relatively steep land in order to secure good air drainage and freedom from frost damage. These orchards are subject to soil erosion, and special care must be exercised in the cultural program to minimize erosion as much as possible. If the slope of the land is less than 10 per cent, contour planting with or without terracing is effective in conserving both soil and moisture. However, if the slope is greater than about 10 per cent, the orchardist is almost forced to keep his land in a continuous sod in humid regions.

An orchard soil management program should meet the following objectives:

1. Provide a *favorable moisture supply* to the trees throughout the growing season.

2. Minimize or *prevent soil erosion.*

3. *Increase,* or at least *maintain,* the *organic matter* by use of cover crops or mulching to compensate for erosion loss and decomposition.

Dr. Paul Larsen, Tree Fruit Research Center, Wenatchee, Wash., helped revise this Chapter.

Figure 1. Chemical weed control and rotary hoes are being used in young and old orchards. Note comparative growth, same age trees, under herbicide treatment, left and K-31 grass sod, right. (Mich. State Univ.)

4. Supply necessary nutrients.

5. Loosen the soil for good aeration and prevent excessive compacting by heavy machinery.

It is generally agreed that the young or dwarf trees require a different type of soil management than large-size apple trees. This is because the small trees are shallow-rooted and are more likely to suffer from limited supplies of nutrients and water. The large trees, on the other hand, are less subject to competition with sod for water and nutrients because their root systems permeate the soil to a greater width and depth; also, they have greater food reserves in the bark and wood tissues to tide them over periods of stress.

Soil management: Young and dwarf trees. It is desirable to secure from 15 to 30 inches of terminal growth each year on these apple trees, the longer lengths being required for the younger trees. In order to attain this vigor, some system of management involving herbicides or *clean cultivation* is needed, beginning after growth starts in spring (Figure 1). The soil is disked only enough to keep down excessive weed growth until either three weeks after bloom when an intercrop or a summer cover crop is sown, or until mid- or late summer when a winter cover crop is planted. Both a summer and winter cover crop are often used in an orchard to increase the organic matter of the soil when disked under. In case of sloping land, it is imperative that cultivation be performed on the contour or across the slope, *not* up and down the slope. If the slope of the land is such that erosion is likely to occur when the entire area is cultivated, it may be well to use herbicides or preform shallow strip cultivation for a width of three to five feet on either side of the trees and the middles are left in sod to check erosion. Or, circular cultivation around each tree can be done with modern-type tractor equipment (Figure 1). If the uncultivated area is in orchard grass, timothy, or a hay crop, the hay can be harvested for a few years and used for mulch on sloping erosive areas or fed to livestock without deleterious effects on the apple trees. Sod strips are also convenient for operation of heavy equipment such as spray machines during soggy weather. The sod strips are gradually narrowed until the trees are about four to ten years of age, after which a new program is initiated as described

later under "Soil Management for Bearing Low - Density Apple Trees."

If the land is more or less level and can be cultivated entirely, an intensive soil management system is to grow cultivated crops between the tree rows and derive cash income from the land while the trees are coming into bearing. Strawberries and vegetables may be grown but, commercially, this is not done in the medium-and high-density orchards. Grain crops are questionable because they require considerable nitrates and moisture and may compete with the trees, especially when planted close to them. Crops such as tomatoes and beans are usually more satisfactory than early potatoes in the middle Atlantic States because they are planted later and do not compete for moisture and nitrates with the trees at a time when the trees need them most. Intercropping is being little practiced with the growing tendency

Figure 2. (Top) This management system is well adapted to steep sections of the orchard. Grass is cut one to three times a year, raked toward the trees with a side-delivery rake, and mulched about the trees by hand. If sufficient nitrogen fertilizer is applied with this system, growth is almost as good as with cultivation, and with less expense.

(Bottom) Strip usage of herbicides such as Sinbar or Paraquat in dwarf tree rows does a clean job, replacing need for cultivation. Trees make good growth. (Courtesy Mich. State Univ.)
Red fescue (Wash.) or K-31 fescue (East) make good sod strips.

toward high-density planting of dwarf and semi-dwarf trees, and use of strip chemical weed control in the rows with sod middles. Also, frost damage is a hazard when the ground under the trees has been stirred or is in a green ground cover during frosts.

On land steeper than 10 per cent slope (drop of 10 feet in 100 feet; too steep for practical terrace management), it is dubious to perform any type of cultivation, except to use herbicides or tractor-hoeing about the base of each tree. This system also cuts labor costs. One of the better soil management systems for hillside trees, according to recent experiments, is to place the land in permanent sod, cut the grass two or three times a year and place it around the base of the tree as a mulch (Figure 2). The mulch should be maintained at least six inches deep and, if necessary, additional mulch can be cut and brought from neighboring fields. Trees under this or any sod management program will require a plentiful supply of nitrogen, especially shortly after the first mulch has been applied; otherwise, the bacteria which decompose the mulch may "tie up" nitrogen and cause a deficiency of this element in the tree. In order to increase the

101

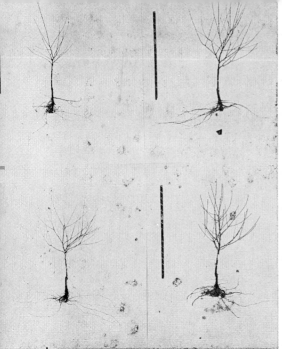

Figure 3. Photos show Cox's Orange
Pippin on M. 26 in England after three
seasons growth; trees 8' apart in rows
14' apart. Middles and 4' square areas
around trees were treated as follows:
(top left) grass, with 4' sq. grassed;
(top right) grass, with 4' sq. mulched;
(lower left) cultivated with 4' sq. hoed;
(lower right) grass, with 4' sq. treated
with herbicide sprays. Mulched trees
were most vigorous but herbicide-treated
trees grew as well as cultivated trees.
Grassed trees grew least. Tree size at
end of first year controls size of tree
next few years. (Courtesy G. C. White
and R. I. C. Holloway, E. Malling Res.
Sta., Kent)

moisture supply to young trees on slopes, some growers have plowed out or scooped out a short four- to six-foot strip about two feet above the tree which serves to catch and hold additional rain water during periods of infrequent rains.

Thus, herbicides or shallow rotary hoe usage in the tree row or in squares about the trees (boom shut off between trees) is the trend in apple regions of the world. Rodent control, cost reduction, water and nutrient conservation, and less frost hazard are key reasons.

Soil management: low-density bearing trees. In most regions of the world the horticulturists and agronomists are generally agreed that a program of continuous cultivation with cover crops throughout the life of the orchard is detrimental both to the soil and to the trees. In many of the leading apple areas, a cultural program often recommended for bearing trees and now rapidly gaining favor is *sod mulch* where the grass or legume-grass mixture is cut and placed beneath the trees, along with *additional mulch* obtained elsewhere, if needed (Figure 4).

Advantages of the mulching system where preferred are:

1. Soil moisture fluctuations beneath the trees are less, particularly during dry periods, due to reduced evaporation from the soil surface and the elimination of competition by weeds and grass growing beneath the trees.

2. The soil becomes more loose, friable, and better aerated beneath the mulch.

3. Available potassium and certain other necessary elements including phosphorus, magnesium, calcium, and boron are found to be higher in the soil beneath mulched trees.

4. There is less fluctuation in soil temperature beneath the mulch, the soil being as much as 15° cooler in summer and 5° warmer in winter as compared with tilled soil.

5. The soil organic matter in the upper two to four inches under mulch

is about 1 per cent higher than under sod and 2 to 3 per cent higher than under cultivation.

6. The mulch acts as a cushion for drop apples which are less damaged and can be sold at better prices.

7. The growth and yields of apple trees under this system have been shown to be almost as good and in some cases better than those under clean cutivation with cover crops, especially when the life period of the orchard is considered. At the Michigan Experiment Station, the clean cultivation with cover-crop system of managing apple trees was satisfactory for about the first ten years, but by the time the trees were 20-22 years of age, growth in circumference of the trees, on the average, was less per tree (Figure 5). Also, the yield and quality of the fruit were significantly less on cultivated as compared with mulched trees. Continuous cultivation in an orchard depletes the organic matter and destroys the loose structure, causing the soil to puddle, pack, crack, and be less absorptive and retentive of moisture.

Figure 4. This commerical apple grower cuts, loads, and hauls additional mulch from his neighbor's field. (Top) Hay is purchased by the acre, uncut. Mulch production often can be doubled and tripled by an application of commerical fertilizer, particularly nitrogen. Modern mechanical handling of mulch is essential to reduce labor costs.

(Bottom) Mulch collected as shown in the top picture is unloaded in June adjacent to trees bearing good crops and spread evenly beneath the branches to within two feet of the trunk.

8. The color and quality of fruit is better under a sod or sod mulch system of management, as compared with cultivation. This is because continued cultivation tends to release nitrogen in the soil which, in turn, is available to the tree throughout the growing and ripening season. This nitrogen is largely in addition to that applied as a chemical fertilizer in the spring. Relatively high nitrogen during the ripening period depresses coloring of the apple and keeps the tree growing too late in the season, resulting in greater susceptibility to winter injury. In case of the sod management system with nitrogen fertilization and additional mulch, the tree and grass normally have utilized most of the nitrogen by the middle of the summer. As the fruit begins to ripen, the carbohydrates manufactured by the leaves tend to accumulate in the fruit rather than being diverted to additional shoot growth. With the high carbohydrate condition in the apple, coloring

Walter Toenjes, Michigan Exp. Sta.

Figure 5. Grimes Golden trees in neighboring plots receiving different soil management programs. (Left) Typical tree under cultivation with cover crops for 22 years; trunk circumference was 31 11/16 inches. (Right) Tree under sod-mulch plus additional mulch for 21 years (cultivated with cover crop the first year); trunk diameter was 34 13/16 inches. Compare heights of the two trees with 20-foot pole in center of trees. Experiment demonstrated that clean cultivation with cover crops over a 22-year period was detrimental to soil structure and to size and yield of trees.

is better, provided the temperatures are cool and good light reaches the fruit during a few hours of the day.

9. A liberal supply of hay mulch furnishes adequate nitrogen and other elements after the first two or three years of use, and little or no commerical fertilization may be required thereafter, provided the layer of mulch is replenished every two or three years (based on experimental data in Massachusetts).

The sod system with mulching has some limitations:

1. The mulch and dry grass become a fire hazard during dry periods.
2. The mulch may harbor insects, diseases, and rodents.
3. The cost of additional mulch material may make the practice difficult or prohibitive.

The *fire hazard* can be minimized by strip plowing across the slope, making the strips about six feet wide in every second to fourth middle. This is particularly important near roads and railroads where cigarettes and sparks may start fires. Also, during periods of drought, the spray machine should be kept in readiness with a quickly available water supply for the purpose of fighting a fire. To avoid damage by *mice*, it is important to keep the mulch a few feet from the tree base especially during winter.

The *field* or *meadow mouse (Microtus pennsylvanicus, Figure 7)*, works on the soil surface or a few inches below the surface. Most of his damage

104

consists of bark injury to the tree near the soil surface. In some regions, such as southern New York, the Virginias, and regions of similar climates, the *pine mouse* (*Pitymys pinetorum scalopsoides*) is a serious pest, causing bark damage on the roots, as shown in Figure 8. Damage by this species of mouse is serious because it is difficult to detect the damage before it is too late to save the tree. It is also inconvenient and hard to correct the situation by bridge-grafting, as can be done for damage by the meadow mouse. (For methods on bridge-grafting, see Chapter VIII.)[1]

The environmentalists and Federal Food and Drug Administration are frowning on and disbanding the use of strong chemicals such as endrin to control mice. There is a shift back to (a) baiting and (b) the encouragement of forage for mice in the row middles such as orchard, blue and quack grasses, perennial forbs and bulb and rhizome plants (research of Frank Horsfall, VPI, Blacksburg). Ground under trees should be kept clean by frequent rotary mowing, shallow rototilling, or by herbicides. Also plastic or wire-mesh trunk guards 18" high and cinders around the tree base can be used, particularly on young trees.[1] In grassy areas apply poison bait by hand or by "trail-builder"[2] (cuts labor, time; cannot use on rocky ground) in the fall during good weather and before hard freezes. Sprinkle 1 level teaspoon of zinc phosphide rodenticide (1 oz. can treats 20 qts.; covers 8-10 acres) over each quart of cubed apples; tumble the cubes. Broadcast and/or place bait in fresh mouse runs or under fertilizer bags, etc. Use both apple cubes and zinc-phosphide or strychnine oats or wheat for pine mice. Use 10 lbs./A broadcast or 3 lbs./A trial bait. Ready-mix grain bait is available from farmer co-ops or the Wildlife Services Fund, 451 Russell St., Hadley, Mass., 01035. Wash hands thoroughly before eating.

Natural enemies of mice such as skunks, dogs, weasels, hawks, owls and foxes can be encouraged. Mow the orchard and remove dropped apples before baiting.

Waterproof tubes (mouse can enter) with poisoned grain glued to inside walls are available in quantity (Prolin Mouse Tubes, Niagara Chem. Co.).

The short-lived chlorophyacione from France is a promising mouse poison without endrin's faults (Dr. Horsfall's VPI research) but it must be cleared for grower use.

Porcupines, active in cold weather, may girdle trees. Traps, poison bait or a low (8") electric fence are controls.

---

[1] Cottontails may be a problem with young trees. Many repellents have been tried on the trunks and lower limbs. Species of cottontails vary in the West (Hildreth and Brown) and East (Hayne and Cardinell). Check your county agricultural agent for latest controls. Kitchen aluminum foil wrapped about the trunks is effective for a few trees. Thiram, as described by Hildreth and Brown, Hayne and Cardinell is effective against jack rabbits and cottontails. For deer control suggestions, contact Department of Horticulture, Pennsylvania State University, University Park, Penna.

[2] Obtain recommendations from manufacturer, your government specialist, or bulletins from Hort. Dept., VPI, Blacksburg, Va. Contact U. S. Fish and Wild Life Serv., Dept. of Interior, Rodent Control, Wash., D. C., USA for "trail-builder" recommendations; for equipment specifications, write R. R. Elston, E. 79 St., Minneapolis, Minn.

Figure 8. Injury to apple tree roots by the pine mouse (Pitymys pinetorum scalopsoides) is difficult to detect before it is too late to save the tree. A regular poisoning program is effective in preventing this damage in areas where these mice are known to exist.

Figure 7. Two species of mice injurious to fruit trees. (Top) The pine mouse has a small body, short tail, Roman nose, sunken eyes, brownish fur and tail as short or shorter than hind leg; burrows deep, damages roots. (Bottom) Meadow mouse has a large body, long tail, prominent eyes dark-grayish fur, tail longer than hind leg; makes surface marks.

Source of mulch. It is impossible to grow sufficient mulch between mature apple trees to maintain adequately the mulch at a depth of six to eight inches under the trees. Thus, it becomes necessary to collect or buy additional mulch outside the orchard. This may consist of wheat or oat straw from old stacks, spoiled legume hay, corn cobs, sawdust, leached cinders, or similar materials. Sawdust obtained from some trees may be acid, and lime should be added to the mulch to correct the acidity. (See Figure 4).

Whether the mulch is obtained between the trees or from the fields outside the orchard, it has been shown by the Ohio Agricultural Experiment Station that nitrogen fertilization often will result in greatly increased yields of mulch per acre. For example, the use of 400 pounds of ammonium nitrate/A on a rather infertile medium loam soil more than tripled the production of dry grass from 1573 to 5143 pounds per acre. Nitrogen is the fertilizer that ordinarily gives best response with grasses but on sandy soils an N-P-K mix may be needed such as a 16-16-16.

Mulch of grasses and grains decomposes more slowly than legumes, although the latter are generally higher in some nutrients. A one-to-two mixture of grass-legume hay has been shown effective by Harley of U.S. D.A. for invigorating nutritionally weak trees.

Cost of mulch. The cost of mulch varies considerably and the use of additional much in an orchard may be governed entirely by its expense. A mature tree requires about 200 to 400 pounds of straw, or two to four bales

for the first mulching, after which 100 pounds per year or 200 pounds every other year should be sufficient. Some growers have found it possible to buy molded hay at a low price or to get it for nothing for hauling it away. An average value for good straw or hay might be placed at $25.00 per ton. Where there are 30 trees per acre, this would be $35.00 to $50.00 per acre per year, with labor for applying the mulch not included. Sometimes straw can be purchased

Figure 9. A snowball bloom creates a heavy drain on both stored food and nutrients, dwarfing the foliage (right) at a period of the year when rapidly enlarging leaves are very important. Proper pruning, fruit thinning, and fertilization, are effective in attaining the ideal bloom shown at left.

cheaper, or obtained only for the hauling, but the approximate cost of mulching an orchard will need to be calculated by the grower under local conditions and prices. Take into consideration the fact that fertilizers can be reduced or eliminated after the first two to three years of mulching. Also, irrigation may be reduced or omitted.

With a mature orchard in sod alone or sod plus additional mulch, it is good practice to loosen the sod a few weeks before bloom with a stout spring tooth harrow, or use other practices (Figure 10). Some growers do this once every spring, others, once every three to five years. If done at several-year intervals, it helps to correct a more or less "sod bound" condition, stimulates growth of the sod, and loosens the soil for better absorption and penetration of rainfall. This "set-back" to the sod also reduces the water and nitrogen requirements by the grass at a time when they are most needed by the trees. The grass recovers about the middle of the summer and by winter, it is well established to prevent erosion during the dormant period. This system of management is sometimes called "short-sod rotation" when practiced at intervals of three to five years. Some growers go so far as to prepare a special seedbed for another permanent sod to be planted about the first of August. A seed mixture which has been used successfully for permanent sod in mature orchards is: four pounds each of alfalfa, red clover, bluegrass and timothy, and two pounds of alsike clover per acre. Another combination often used where more mulch is required is six to eight pounds each of timothy and red clover, two pounds of alsike, and four pounds of bluegrass. Alfalfa in orchards has lost favor as a permanent sod in the West; ladino clover in the East may be slippery for tractor wheels on sloping land. Alta fescue (Ky. 31) is being used in high-density plantings; the tight sod resists weeds, dandelions.

Figure 10. Heavy machinery used in orcharding packs soil in the rooting area. Periodic breaking of sod is needed. (Top) Tool bar to loosen soil before planting. (Bottom left) Killifer subsoiler blade loosening dry soil in fall. (Bottom right) Good soil break-up for better aeration and moisture penetration.

A word of caution should be given against mechanical injury to young and mature trees by orchard implements. Broken branches, and patches of bark knocked off the trunk, are serious injuries to a tree. The most valuable preventative of injuries to trees is a *skillful* and *careful* driver. A moment's carelessness might cause an injury that will take years to heal or, in fact, threaten the life of the tree.

Subsoiling. Heavy orchard machinery packs the soil between the trees. Some growers use the subsoiler blade (Killifer) to a depth of twenty inches on either side of the tree row at the branch spread to get better drainage and storage of water. The blade is run one direction one autumn, and at right angles the next for low-density trees. Soil shatters best in fall when dry.

Orchard cover crops. The use of cover crops between the tree rows is suggested where the soil is sandy and/or low in organic matter. Cover crops, however, are being replaced in high-density plantings by a sod strip such as Alta fescue (Ky. 31) with chemical weed control in the rows. Red fescue is used in the arid Northwest U.S. Where low-density trees are grown cover crops have these advantages:

1. Add organic matter and help maintain the soil humus content.

2. Heavy soils become easier to work and light soils are improved in physical condition and in their ability to retain moisture.

3. Nutrients are added and returned to the soil.

4. When a cover crop is competing with the trees for nutrients and water in late summer and autumn, the wood of the young vigorously growing trees is better matured and less susceptible to winter injury.

5. Cover crops protect the soil against wind and water erosion.

TABLE 1

The Amount, Relative Cost, and Time of Seeding for Orchard Cover Crops

Cover Crop	Time of Seeding[2]	Seed per Acre	Relative Cost of Seeds[3]	Nitrogen Added Before Disking In
Legumes[1]				
Alfalfa[4]	Early Spring or Aug. 1	20 Lbs.	$11.00-16.00	No
Alsike Clover	July	6 Lbs.	1.90- 2.40	No
Canada Peas	June	1½ Bu.	10.80-12.60	......
Cowpeas	June 1-15	1½ to 2 Bu.	31.50-36.75	No
Crimson Clover	July	16 Lbs.	12.80-13.60	No
Ladino Clover	Late August	2 Lbs. (+ grass)	2.00- 2.20	No
Lespedeza	June 1	20 to 25 Lbs.	7.70- 8.80	No
Red Clover	July	12 Lbs.	4.80- 5.40	No
Soybeans (drills)	June 1-15	½ Bu.	1.80- 2.10	No
Sweet Clover[4]	Early Spring or Aug. 1	15 Lbs.	3.00- 3.75	No
Winter Vetch[4]	After August 15	1 Bu.	15.00-18.00	No
Nonlegumes				
Red Fescue	E. Spring/late Summer	50 Lbs.	35.00-40.00	Yes
Alta Fescue (Ky.31)	Late August	40 Lbs.	4.00- 4.50	Yes
Barley	August 15	1½ Bu.	3.60- 3.90	Yes
Bluegrass	June 1	30 Lbs.	15.00-18.00	......
Buckwheat	June or July	1 Bu.	2.00- 2.40	No
Dwarf Essex Rape	June	2 Lbs.	0.48- 0.52	......
Millet	June 1	25 to 40 Lbs.	4.95- 6.00	Yes
Oats	August 15	1½ Bu.	3.00- 3.52	Yes
Rye	September 1-15	1½ Bu.	4.05- 4.20	Yes
Rye Grass	September 1-15	12 to 15 Lbs.	2.10- 3.50	Yes
Sudan Grass	June or July	25 to 30 Lbs.	4.20- 5.60	Yes
Timothy	June 1	20 Lbs.	6.60- 8.00	Yes
Weeds	......	......	......	Yes

[1] The seed should be inoculated before planting if the desired legume has not been grown recently and successfully on the site. The most convenient, economical, and effective means is to purchase inoculant at the seed houses and follow directions on the bottle. Legumes generally grow better in soils near the neutral point, or slightly acid. It requires between one and two tons of agricultural limestone per acre to raise the pH one point, as, for example, from 5.0 to 6.0. Grains should be treated for smut.

[2] Dates suggested for North Central and Northeastern states. Contact local county agent for dates for other areas.

[3] Varies with season and locality. Prices obtained in late 1960's, USA. Prices can change with variety, volume, general price level.

[4] Because initial growth is slow, it is best to sow also with a nurse crop such as oats or buckwheat. However, alfalfa and most legumes are being less used in orchards.

6. They moderate the soil temperature, retain snow better, and reduce the likelihood of winter injury to the roots.

7. Cover crops absorb mineral nutrients, preventing them from being leached away over winter.

8. After spring disking, the organic matter of the cover crop decays and assists in making available the mineral nutrients tied up in the soil.

9. Cover crops such as rye, which have a high water requirement are valuable in absorbing excess water in orchards which tend to be too moist in spring

There are two main types of cover crops—*legumes and nonlegumes.* The legumes, through the action of bacteria in root nodules, have the ability to store nitrogen. Legumes which have been disked in, therefore, decompose rapidly, releasing the nitrogen and other nutrients which in turn may be utilized by the trees. The nonlegumes such as the grasses are relatively low in nitrogen and, thus, decompose slowly. Nitrogen fertilizer may be needed to speed up their decomposition, and avoid a depressing effect on tree growth. Environmentalists' "fear" of chemical nitrogen may force more legume usage.

The best cover crop to use will vary with the soil, the site, and the geographical location. The most satisfactory cover crop for a given region is the one which grows well and produces considerable organic matter relatively high in nitrogen. Consult your governmental agent for the best locally adapted orchard cover crops.

Summer cover crops. Summer cover crops are usually sown two to three weeks after tree bloom and after a good seedbed has been prepared by thorough disking and dragging. A complete fertilizer of 250 to 300 pounds of a low-nitrogen mix is often helpful in getting both summer and winter crops off to a good start. Better germination is obtained if the seed is sown or drilled shortly after a shower.

Soybeans (Soja max.). Soybeans make an excellent summer cover crop for orchards under 10 years of age. They are more popular in the Midwest and South than in the extreme northern regions and Canada. Soybeans can be grown on a somewhat more acid soil than the clovers, but lime should be added if the pH is below 5.5. They respond well to fertilization in soils with medium to high organic matter. Directions for seeding this and other cover crops are given in Table 1.

Cowpeas (Vigna siness). Cowpeas are handled similarly to soybeans and will grow on somewhat poorer soils. Cowpeas are grown mainly in the southeastern quarter of the United States.

Sudan Grass (Sorghum vulgare sudanensie). Sudan grass is a valuable cover crop where water is not likely to be limiting and where considerable bulk is desired to improve soil organic matter and aeration. It is a rapid grower, germinating well in hot weather and reaching four to six feet in height; hence, it may be valuable to use in cases where soybeans have failed to grow. It is necessary to apply 200-300 pounds of nitrogen or its equivalent in an N-P-K fertilizer per acre to get good growth and to reduce competition for this element with the trees. In northern states and Canada, Sudan grass may not yield as much organic matter as Crown, Empire, and Japanese millets.

Millet (Setara italica, Panicum miliaceum, Echinochloa frumentacea, and others). Millet is a nonlegume which can be used for a summer or winter cover crop in young orchards where shading is not a factor (Figure 11). Its natural habitat includes regions north of Alabama and Texas, with heaviest use from Missouri eastward to Maine. In areas where droughts are likely to occur, however, it competes with the trees for water and under such conditions may be of questionable value. In young orchards, it should be kept at a distance of about five feet from the trees. It grows under a wide range of soil conditions and is not exacting in moisture requirements.

Figure 11. Rotary mowers with swing-out head are being used in low-and high-density sod orchards to keep the floor clean, particularly before mouse control treatment. (Courtesy R. Van Delft, Mar-wald, Ltd., Waterdown Rd., Burlington, Ont., Canada.)

Siberian millet is valuable in orchards which are generally too wet, because it will utilize much of the excess moisture. Crown, Hog, and Red Turghai are better varieties where conditions may be dry, due to the fact that they are shallow-rooted and compete less for water.

Buckwheat. This crop is sensitive to frosts but thrives best in a cool moist climate in the northern states or near the Great Lakes. It succeeds well in sandy loam soils, but also will thrive on rather poor heavy soils, improving them for subsequent legume crops. The seed is inexpensive. When sown early, seed will mature in about two months, after which a light disking will thresh out enough seed for another crop over winter. The following spring, the orchard is cultivated for a few weeks, after which a good stand of volunteer buckwheat can be obtained during late summer and autumn. This practice can be continued for about three years from the original seeding. Buckwheat straw decomposes easily and creates little nitrogen drain.

Lespedeza (L. striata). Korean lespedeza is an annual, but it is used mainly as a permanent cover to conserve the soil. It is mostly used in the South where it will grow on the poorer types of soil. It is not a bulky grower. Seed should be sown early in the spring so that it will reseed itself for the following year. On some occasions weeds may grow taller than the lespedeza, and it is necessary to mow them in midsummer to reduce competition.

Winter cover crops. Winter cover crops are sown in late summer and disked down the following spring, before they compete with the tree for nutrients and moisture.

Rye. Rye is widely used as a cover crop because it makes good growth on relatively poor and acid soils, withstands winter freezes, and is effective in preventing soil erosion during winter. With rye, however, it is highly

Figure 12. Posion ivy is a problem in some orchards, particularly to the harvest crew. Dacamine 4D, 2 qts./A. applied when weeds are growing rapidly is effective. Keep drift off tree and fruit. (Diamond Alkali Co., Cleveland, O. 44114) or use Weedone 638 (2, 4-D acid) at 2 qts./150 gals. at 20#/sq. in pressure (Amchem Co., Ambler, Pa. 19002).

important that it be disked down when it is about knee high. Otherwise, it competes heavily with trees for moisture and nitrogen at the critical growth period of the tree. The fact that rye grows so fast in spring is its biggest disadvantage because on too many occasions the land is too wet to disk, and the rye may noticeably stunt tree growth before a disk can be used. With young trees, 1- to 5-years old, rye must be disked next to the trees at the proper time. However, the middles can be allowed to reseed and form more organic matter before disking.

Wheat. Wheat is handled similarly to rye, except that it has the advantage of growing more slowly in the spring, giving the grower a better chance to disk it under before it damages tree growth. The choice of rye or wheat, however, may depend upon the price of the seed.

Domestic rye grass (Lolium multislorum). This crop has been used widely in the northern states for a winter cover crop. When seeded the middle of August, it makes enough fall growth to give ample soil cover for protection during the winter. Although it makes abundant root growth, it does not form as much top growth in the fall as common rye and, therefore, does not necessitate a cutting preceding fall harvest of winter apples, as is sometimes true with earlier planted rye. In the spring, its growth is not as rapid as rye and gives the grower an opportunity to disk it in before it competes with trees. It has a dense root system which makes up for less top growth. There has been relatively little winter killing of this crop under Michigan and Pennsylvania conditions.

Winter vetch (Vicia villosa) and rye. This makes an excellent winter cover crop because if there is a good stand of vetch, the combination produces a heavy tonnage which is relatively high in nitrogen as compared with rye alone. The winter vetch will grow in seasons which are too dry for clover and on soils too acid for a good stand of clover and alfalfa. It makes more growth in cool weather than most legumes. The price of the vetch seed, however, in some years makes it prohibitive. When vetch is used alone, it should not be plowed under until the latter part of May due to the fact that it makes slow growth in spring. It reseeds itself.

Oats. Oats should be sown about mid-August in order to attain sufficient growth before the first freeze. In the North, oats are killed by the first heavy frost. This cover, although dead, will furnish good protection for the grouna over winter. The crop is best adapted to a cool moist climate and a slightly acid soil. Oats will usually over-winter in the southern regions. Disc under a month before bloom so rain can pack the soil, reducing frost hazard at bloom.

Crimson and red clover. If good stands of crimson clover can be obtained, it makes a desirable cover crop, but it tends to kill badly in regions where freezes are severe. It withstands the winter somewhat better if seeded in midsummer. Red clover and mammoth clover are good cover crops where the soil is sweet and good stands can be secured. Seed cost is high.

Sweet clover (Melilotus alba and M. officinalis). Sweet clover is a valuable cover crop in the young orchard, provided it is kept a good distance from the trees due to the fact that it is deep-rooted and may compete with the trees for water in times of stress. It also can be used in a mature orchard where large quantities of humus are needed. Some growers make it a practice of sowing about 15 pounds of unscarified seed on wheat in January. Then shortly after the middle of March, five to six pounds of scarified seed are sown per acre. The crop should be disked down early the following year in about May to avoid competition for moisture with the trees. Biennial sweet clover has been used in Washington for a permanent cover, partially reseeding itself and resulting in a definite improvement in the physical condition and fertility of the soil. It is a tall grower, however, and sometimes interferes with spraying and other orchard operations. Its best adaptation appears to be in regions where irrigation is practiced.

Crotolaria (Giant Striata) is seeded in the southeast after the last cultivation and is knocked down if growth is too vigorous, particularly during drought. It should reseed itself and offers a good source of organic matter.

Alfalfa (Medicago sativa) Alfalfa can be used for a cover crop the same as sweet clover, but the price of seed has discouraged its use as an annual cover crop. Alfalfa is more valuable as a permanent cover, serving alone (Figure 3) or with clover and grasses as recommended previously for a permanent sod. It will take considerable rough treatment with machinery. Alfalfa alone as a permanent sod is the leading perennial legume in western orchards where irrigation is available. Irrigation is needed because this plant is deep-rooted and may compete heavily with the trees for water during dry periods. Once established, it has lasted as long as 18 years in one Washington orchard. Alfalfa may harbor the buffalo tree hopper which injures bark on young trees. Chemical weed control next to the tree reduces injury. Here again, alfalfa is losing favor in orchards.

Field Brome. From Sweden and tested in New York, this vigorous grass which resembles oats has shown promise in young orchards. Ten pounds per acre are seeded in late summer, disked when six to ten inches high in spring, leaving about four plants per square foot for reseeding.

Weeds. Where a good even crop of weeds can be obtained, they are a good source of organic matter. They should be mowed once or twice a season when about two feet in height.

FERTILIZING THE APPLE ORCHARD

The nutrients in the soil are first dissolved in the soil water and then absorbed by the fruit trees through the fine root hairs at the tips of the rootlets. Nutrients also can be absorbed by the leaves and bark when dissolved and applied as sprays. Among the more important elements absorbed are nitrogen, phosphorous, potassium, magnesium, calcium, sulphur, and iron. Boron, zinc, manganese, copper, chlorine and molybdenum are considered of lesser importance though highly important when deficient.

Nutrients needed in fruit plantings and deficiency correction. The key nutrient for deciduous fruits over the world is unquestionably nitrogen. There are a few sections of the world, such as the arid San Joaquin Valley in California, where thirty-year orchards have never had a pound of nitrogen, only zinc sprays, but these areas are limited.

In regions where rainfall is at least fifteen to twenty inches, and particularly if the soil is sandy, there is sufficient leaching of the soil to reduce the available nitrogen supply to the deficient level for most fruits. Commercially, nitrogen is the key nutrient used to control growth and fruiting. The other nutrients, such as potash, magnesium, zinc, and boron, are supplied, if needed, in adequate quantities to prevent deficiencies from occurring. Excess boron is a problem where irrigation water carries too much boron.

Magnesium is becoming more widely recognized as a deficient nutrient in deciduous orchards in humid areas. Nitrogen, potassium, magnesium, and boron are all readily soluble and thus tend to be leached in areas where annual rainfall is at least moderate—thirty to fifty inches. Boron may be found to be deficient in some areas, however, where rainfall is no more than ten inches a year. The deficiency is created by a relatively high pH of the soil which tends to tie up the boron, making it unavailable to the trees. This also can happen with other trace elements, such as zinc, iron, and manganese. As yet there has been no report of molybdenum deficiency in deciduous orchards but this is not to say that the deficiency does not exist. Trees have responded to copper in former corral areas and in light low-organic matter soils.

If zinc and manganese deficiencies occur in fruit trees growing in sandy soils in humid areas, they can be corrected either by applying sulfate forms to the soil (except in high pH soils), or quicker response can be obtained by sprays. A spray of two to five pounds of manganese sulfate such as Techmangan (Tennessee Corp., Atlanta, Ga.) is applied preferably when foilage is young to medium age.

Zinc is generally caustic to foliage and it is usually applied as a dormant spray at from 10 to fifty pounds per hundred gallons just before the buds break, depending upon severity of deficiency and the crop. Zinc deficiency is more difficult to correct on sweet cherry than apple. In desert areas where soil pH is moderately high and these nutrients are tied up, either dormant or foliar spraying or daubing the pruning cuts (grapes) is the best approach for deficiency correction, following the local government station's and extension's suggestions.

Iron chelate spray is partly effective for correcting iron deficiency in arid regions. Use ammonium sulfate if soil pH is high. In humid areas where organic matter content is low, or in sandy or overlimed soils, boron, zinc, iron, and manganese deficiencies have been noted. In these soils the major elements, such as nitrogen, potassium, and magnesium also are likely to be limited.

Does the orchard need fertilizer? Fruit trees are in good vigor if the leaves are large, plentiful, and dark green, and the shoot growth is thick and relatively long for the age of the tree (Figure 13), and the fruiting is regular and satisfactory in size and quality. With a mature bearing apple

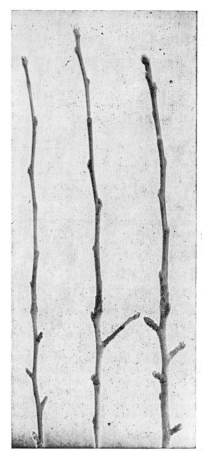

M. A. Blake, New Jersey Agr. Exp. Sta.

Figure 13. Shoot thickness is as important as shoot length in judging vigor of trees. Note the thick shoot and the plump fruit buds on the spurs of the Delicious wood at the right. Thin weak wood and spurs which contain mostly leaf buds are shown at the left. Wood of intermediate vigor is shown in the middle. Nitrogen fertilization would probably benefit growth of the trees from which the two left twigs were taken.

tree, shoot growth at the tips of the branches should be at least six to ten inches annually, preferably 12 to 14 inches. Terminal growth for young nonbearing apple trees should be from 15 to 30 inches with the longer growths on the younger trees. The trunk and scaffold limbs should be thick and stocky with a dark greenish-brown color and only a moderate amount of scaliness of the bark. The amount of growth and the number of leaves on the spurs are important indications of the vigor of the tree. The non-

115

Upper Photos, C. G. Woodbridge, Summerland, B. C.; Lower left, S. Fish, Dept. of Agr., Victoria, Australia; Lower right, T. Wallace, Kent, England.

Figure 14. Three mineral deficiences that are common in some apple sections. Upper photos show cracked and misshapen McIntosh from British Columbia on the left, as compared with fruit receiving adequate boron; right photos show a flatter Delicious with no points, internal cork and badly misshapen fruit. (Lower left) Rosetted small narrow zinc deficient leaves with some chlorosis and wavy margins. (Lower right) Magnesium deficiency on apple showing interveinal chlorosis on upper leaves grading into interveinal necrosis in mid and lower leaves. Both symptoms occur on apple, depending upon variety and growing conditions. See appendix for additional deficiency photos.

bearing spurs in good condition should make from one-half- to three-fourths-inch length growth and should have from six to ten healthy leaves.

If the trees under question do not meet the above qualifications for good vigor, the difficulty may be due to a limited supply of one of the following elements, deficiencies of which have been reported for apples. See also Figure 14 and appendix photographs and descriptions.

Nitrogen deficiency symptoms. Shoot growth short and thin; leaves small, erect and light green or yellowish in color, dropping early, and showing somewhat more red color in the veins in autumn; bark light brown to yellowish orange in color; fruit small and highly colored, good storage quality, with crop relatively light, and tree alternate bearing.

Potassium deficiency. Marginal and tip burning of the leaves; failure of lateral buds to unfold; short thin shoot growth; reduced size, color, and quality of the fruits. Potassium deficiency is more likely to occur on light soils, or shallow poorly drained soils, or in old orchards where the soil has been exploited by roots. Grain straw mulch is high in K.

Phosphorus deficiency. Dark grayish-green foliage and stems, restricted shoot growth and size of leaves; death of buds; and dull unattractive fruit which is lacking in firmness, reduced yields. Rare in orchards.

Magnesium deficiency. The leaves show some chlorosis and an interveinal scorch which may extend to the margins. This may appear suddenly in mid-summer and progress rapidly from the base toward the tip of the shoots. The basal leaves usually absciss in late summer while the tip leaves persist. On old bearing trees the scorch is generally more uniform on all the foliage. Fruit drops early, but size, yield, and quality are less affected.

Calcium deficiency. Restricted root growth, brown root tips; death of the growing shoot tips; chlorotic browning and breakdown of large spots in leaf centers; tip shoot leaves curled upward, yellowish; fruit with large lenticels, cracking, storage breakdown, more "sunscald," cork spot and bitter pit. Ca sprays beneficial. Low foliar zinc may accompany low Ca.

Boron deficiency. Water-soaked exuding spots occur in the bark near the growing tips where they enlarge, turn brown and girdle the tips, causing death of leaves beyond the girdle; bark eventually becomes rough, cracks, and has corklike patches; some shoots develop leaf "rosettes"; poorly developed root system; fruit shows sunken corky areas near the skin and core, falls prematurely. B excess resembles B shortage.

Zinc deficiency. Small mottled abnormally shaped leaves near the shoot tips with wavy margins which bunch together and form rosettes; reduced number of fruit buds, some "dieback" of shoots. Fruits small, misshapen, running high in percentage culls, and with reduced yields.

Iron deficiency. Leaves near shoot tips show complete straw yellow or a fine network of green veins on yellowish green. Some leaves may show marginal burn. Yields reduced, fruit poorly colored, flat flavor.

Manganese deficiency. Tip and mid-shoot leaves have herringbone appearance, with yellowish-green areas between main veins which are surrounded with a deeper green. The leaf size is not much affected; yields reduced; Mn excess in acid soils is associated with bark "measles," corrected by liming.

Sulphur Deficiency. Even yellowing of tip leaves first, whole tree if severe; reduced growth, fruiting and quality. Found in areas away from industry, or where pesticides and fertilizers do not contain S and irrigation water contains less than 0.75 ppm S.

Copper Deficiency. Die back of shoots, black leaves resembling fire blight, yellowing of tip leaves; reduced fruiting of poor quality; susceptible to winter injury; early leaf drop.

Molybdenum Deficiency. Soil pH generally low; interveinal yellowing of tip leaves; marginal scorching lower leaves; rare.

Note: Deficiency correction techniques vary so much with soil, crop

117

and climatic conditions, it is probably best for you to contact your government official for local recommendations. The book, *"Fruit Nutrition —*

TABLE 2. RELATIVE FERTILIZER COSTS TO SUPPLY 100 LBS. N PER ACRE MICHIGAN, 1968. (AFTER PAUL LARSEN, WASH. TREE FRUIT RESEARCH CENTER, WENATCHEE.)

Material	Amt. needed per acre lbs.	Approx. cost per 100 lbs.	Cost per acre	Cost per 10 acres
Am. nitrate - 33%	300	$4.31	$12.93	$129.30
12-6-12	800	3.68	29.44	294.40
12-12-12	800	4.02	32.44	321.60
5-20-20	2000	3.13	82.60	826.00
Am. nitrate + Muriate of Potash	300+166	4.31+2.92	17.78	177.80

Temperate to Tropical," Hort. Publ., Nichol Ave., New Brunswick, N. J., USA, is a complete treatise on this subject with 100 8" x 10" pages of photographs, 888 pp total.

Amount of fertilizer needed. It should be stressed that fertilizer will not overcome fundamental difficulties of poor drainage, rodent injury, or other root and trunk damage which frequently cause low vigor and fruit production. The amount of fertilizer to apply to an orchard will depend upon the amount of shoot growth obtained, the yield and quality of fruit, the soil type, permanent sod, cultivation or chemical weed control, and the type spray chemicals being used. Each orchard presents a different problem. Trees on the lighter sandy type of soil require more fertilizer and usually more nutrients in the fertilizer than trees on the heavier soils. Orchards with sod growing beneath the trees will require more fertilizer, especially nitrogen, than trees under mulch or cultivation. For an unmulched bearing apple tree with a 40-foot spread, about one extra pound of actual nitrogen will be needed for the grass in addition to that required by the tree. If it is desired to produce more mulch between the trees, the application must be increased accordingly. The nitrogen stored in the green grass is readily available to the tree if the sod is cut frequently.

Under sod conditions, the average amount of fertilizer for apples per year, using ammonium nitrate, is based on the thickness of the trunk. Diameter of the trunk is divided by three which gives the approximate number of pounds of ammonium nitrate to apply. For example, an apple tree measuring ten inches in trunk diameter would receive 3.3 pounds of ammonium nitrate, or equivalent in another form of nitrogen. Mixed fertilizers are applied on the basis of actual nitrogen desired per tree or acre and the percent N in the mix, e.g. a 16-16-16 has 16% N; amonium nitrate has 33.5% actual N.

Other sources of nitrogen used in orchards and percent N in each are: Urea (Nugreen is trade name for spray form), 45%; ammonium sulfate, 20%; nitrate of soda, 16%; nitrate of potash, 13% N, 44% K_2O; nitrate of soda-potash, 13% N, 15% K_2O; calcium nitrate, 15% N, 20% ws. Ca; and ammo-phos, 11% N, 48% phosphoric acid. Cost per lb. of N, of course, is important and it varies as shown in Table 2. See, also, the Appendix for fertilizer mixing techniques and problems. Sodium nitrate is quickly available but more expensive. Ammonium sulfate is slower acting, lowers pH in upper soil layer — desirable in high pH soils, but can be counteracted in humid areas by 110 lbs. lime per 100 lbs. of ammonium sulfate.

Since the last World War when nitrate of soda and sulfate of ammonia were scarce or unavailable, ammonium nitrate and urea sprays have been commonly used in orchards. Both proved satisfactory. Urea is conveniently placed in the tank with or without pesticides and applied at three pounds per hundred gallons before bloom and five pounds after. This may supplement soil applications of N, or provide the sole source. Urea applied as a spray has the advantage of the nitrogen entering the tree within a few hours. Urea is frequently used in an emergency, when in early spring it is apparent that inadequate nitrogen has been applied to the soil for a heavy fruit set, as judged by foliar color and shoot growth. Urea sprays probably should not be applied after about the second cover spray.

Continued applications of ammonium nitrate to the soil tend to increase soil acidity. For each hundred pounds of fertilizer applied, about fifty-eight pounds of lime are required. It is advisable to have samples of the soil checked every few years by state or dealer agencies, and then apply the recommended lime to raise the pH to between 6.0 and 6.5, to benefit trees and the sod, particularly if a legume is involved. Accumulation of sulfur in the soil from sprays is also a factor in increasing soil acidity. High-magnesium lime (dolomite) is best when soil test shows a Mg need.

Some apple varieties require more nitrogen than others. Delicious, Jonathan, Stayman and Winesap usually respond well to more nitrogen than Golden Delicious, McIntosh, and Rome. The latter three varieties in sod require about a pound of actual nitrogen per tree. Varieties that respond better to about half this amount are English Codling, Twenty Ounce, and Starr.

Manure of any kind is usually classified as a nitrogenous fertilizer, although it carries about as much potash as nitrogen, and is low in phosphorus. Manure used in field experiments at Pennsylvania State College was computed to carry the equivalent of 9.8 pounds of nitrogen, 2.82 pounds of phosphorus, and 7.14 pounds of potassium per ton. These figures vary for different manures and other factors. It requires about 20 times as much manure by volume to furnish the same amount of nitrogen as in sulfate of ammonia. Also, nitrogen in manure becomes available to the trees more slowly than the commercial forms and, for this reason, it seems advisable to make a light application of manure in early spring in combination with sufficient soluble nitrogen to meet the requirements.

As for phosphorus, there are only limited data indicating a response by

119

fruit plants other than strawberries to phosphorus applications. Nevertheless, in humid areas it is a common practice to use an N-P-K base mix. For fruit plantings in general, a 1-1-1 ratio seems to be the most widely used, however, where the soil is quite sandy, a 1-2-2 ratio of N-P-K is used and may be needed, although there are insufficient experimental data to back this suggestion.

On sandy soils in *humid* regions an N-P-K base mix is generally advisable. If organic matter is low, other nutrients may give response if included on an insurance basis. If this is desired, a magnesium oxide content in a complete mix should be about the same as the nitrogen percentage; for example, if a 5-10-10 is used, about four to five per cent magnesium oxide should be included. Borax can be included so that no more than about five pounds per acre per year is applied. In a 5-10-10 mix this would be about ten pounds of borax per ton. Peaches are very sensitive to excessive use of borax, whereas apples will tolerate up to a pound (or more) per mature tree, provided it is not applied more often than every third year.

Bitter pit in apples, as well as cork spot, has been reduced by calcium nitrate sprays. The addition of NAA and boron to calcium spray by Dr. F. N. Hewetson of Pennsylvania State University has further reduced cork spot, not entirely, but appreciably. Avoid heavy pruning, fruit thinning.

In the above base mix and on a ton basis, the following nutrients may also be included; twenty pounds each of manganese and zinc sulfate, ten pounds of copper sulfate, thirty pounds of iron sulfate, and one pound of sodium or ammonium molybdate. There are proprietory minor element mixes on the market, such as FTE (Ferro Corporation, Cleveland, Ohio) and Esminel (Tennessee Corporation, Atlanta, Ga.), which can be mixed with N-P-K-Mg base mixes at 50 to 100 lbs/T. A liquid complete fertilizer mix with chelated trace elements and herbicide is in use in New Jersey. (See Childers' reference.)

Annual Bearing, Quality Fruit. No one is a better judge than the grower himself as to how much nitrogen to apply to his trees each year based on their performance in the past. Growers should go through their orchards several times a season and particularly at harvest. Too little nitrogen will result in the trees becoming hard, foliage light green in color at harvest, yields down, but color, eating and storage quality of a high order. If too much nitrogen is being used, trees will become too green and healthy appearing, fruit production will be upped but fruit color will be less and the eating and storage quality likely lowered. It is true, however, that growers contracting their crop to processors will use more nitrogen for better yields and cut the spray program since finish of the fruit and full color are not as important.

Apple trees will vary in an orchard as to the amount of nitrogen required. Some trees in the row will be smaller and need less fertilizer, others may be getting too vigorous. When growing fruit for the fresh market, it may be well to check the crop at harvest and tag those trees with a plastic colored label which are too vigorous and need less fertilizer, using another colored tag for trees needing more than average fertilizer. The entire orchard may be showing less need for nitrogen, in which case it should be cut slowly, not eliminated entirely as to too often done. Cut it to three-fourths or half. Complete omission of fertilizer for two or three years may result in alternate bearing and be difficult to get the trees back into annual bearing. A major-trace elements fertilizer on medium-low fertility soils in New Jersey has brought trees to uniform vigor.

If a heavy crop is expected, both the pruning (reduce bloom points) and fertilizer may be modestly increased so that adequate nitrogen will be available to the heavy bloom to set the apples, and at the same time develop big leaves to supply food to size the apples (See Figure 9). An excessive bloom and fruit set draws heavily on the same ingredients it takes to size the leaves. Once leaves have attained a small size early, they never become larger later. If a heavy crop is set, which is likely, then use of chemical thinners can help remove the excess crop which, in turn, enables the subsequently formed leaves to size better.

Old orchards in moderately fertile soil which have lost vigor frequently can be brought back to good production by good pruning practice and by doubling or quadrupling the fertilizer applications, particularly nitrogen, and the use of trace elements if known to be deficient in the area, until vigor is restored. Borax at one half to one pound per mature apple tree may help. It may be better to pull old trees and replant with high-density trees.

Medium- and Low-Density Trees. The amount and kind of fertilizer to use varies with the variety and basic fertility of the soil. Recommendations for the kind of fertilizer to use in this chapter for low-density trees more or less hold for medium and high-density trees. Amount per tree is based on trunk diameter. For example, if a bearing low-density Golden Delicious tree in sod with a 10-inch trunk requires 1 lb. actual N (or 10 lbs. 10-10-10 or 3 lbs. am. nitr. or 5 lbs. am. sulfate), a dwarf Golden Delicious with a 2 in. trunk would require about 1/5 this amount. Somewhat less fertilizer would be needed where in-row shallow rototilling or herbicides are used. Here again, rate of fertilizer should be adjusted according to color, quality and yield of fruit the previous year or years.

Soil or Leaf Analysis? In regard to soil tests it should be stated that insofar as fruit tree crops are concerned, about the only value of soil analysis is to indicate the pH and whether the potash, magnesium, and phosporus, (calcium, boron, others when analyzed) are excessively high or low for the trees and particularly the cover crops.

The main difficulty is getting a representative sample of soil in an orchard. With perennial trees which are deeply rooted, even as deep as thirty feet in loess soil, the roots will be feeding at much lower depths than that from which the soil sample is taken. It is true that eighty to

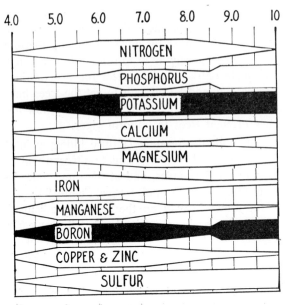

| 4.0 | 5.0 | 6.0 | 7.0 | 8.0 | 9.0 | 10 |

NITROGEN
PHOSPHORUS
POTASSIUM
CALCIUM
MAGNESIUM
IRON
MANGANESE
BORON
COPPER & ZINC
SULFUR

Figure 15. Numbers at top of chart represent pH (4.0 is very acid; 10 is very alkaline). Maximum availability of a nutrient is where the lines are widest apart. The pH under fruit trees in a humid region should be maintained between 6.0 and 6.5 by liming. (After E. Troug, Univ. of Wis.)

ninety per cent of the roots are in the upper foot of soil, but where a deficiency occurs, the lower feeding roots apparently pick up needed nutrients from lower depths.

It appears that our best indication of nutritional needs by trees and other deep-rooted plants is, in addition to soil tests, a chemical analysis of the leaves. This latter service is being offered by most states and provinces for interested growers, usually at an added cost. Contact Michigan State University, Horticulture, E. Lansing, who has pioneered in leaf analysis of deciduous fruits, and request their instructions and pamphlet on leaf analysis of fruit plants. Contact also your local governmental extension or experimental institution if you have a difficult nutritional problem.

Approximate range for essential nutrients in apple leaves obtained from the mid-shoot section (tip leaves for sulfur diagnosis) in mid-summer should be about as follows for satisfactory tree performance, according to W. C. Stiles[1], Univ. of Maine, and C. B. Shear, U.S. Dept. Agri.:

N	P	K	Mg	Ca	S	Iron	B	Zn	Copper	Molyb.
%	%	%	%	%	ppm	ppm	ppm	ppm	ppm	ppm
1.90	0.2	1.2	0.24	1.5	150	100	30	25	5	0.5
to	to	to	to	to	to	to	to	to	to	
2.25	0.3	1.95	0.40	2.0	2300	300	40	50	20	1.0 +

[1]Desirable mineral content will vary with variety, other factors. For example, McIntosh and the lighter feeders for nitrogen have better quality fruit if the per-cent is about 1.90 to 2.00; Delicious, a heavier N feeder, does better with the higher N content suggested. Healthy trees may show higher or lower contents than listed here; experience, however, has shown the ranges to be about right. Phosphorus need is similar to N while K is more standardized. Bear in mind that some pesticides, herbicides, manures and fertilizers contain nutrient impurities and may be supplementing or supplying tree needs. Golden Delicious in Massachussetts may russet if leaf N is above 2.0.

New England Lime Co., Canaan, Conn.

Figure 16. Lime or fertilizer may be distributed by dealer trucks with end-gate twirlers. It is important to get the lime and fertilizer largely under the trees where it is needed. Use 25 percent more fertilizer by this method vs hand application. Power-take-off-end-gate twirler-tractor-attach units are good for dwarf trees, bush fruits.

Time for application. Nitrogen fertilizer will do the most good if applied at least three to four weeks before the buds begin to swell in spring. This gives the nitrogen ample time to be dissolved by rain, absorbed and transferred to the spurs and shoots, resulting in early development of large leaves, good shoot growth, good set of fruit, and rapid development in fruit size.

If a heavy bloom occurs, supplemental nitrogen in urea sprays may be needed to size the leaves and carry the heavy fruit set. A heavy bloom and fruit set tend to dwarf leaves in early spring (Figure 9).

Experimental evidence has shown little or no difference in tree response with fall or spring applications of fertilizer. In fall it should be applied about a month after leaf drop to avoid trunk cold injury in Northern areas. Some fertilizer may be leached below the rootzone if soils are very light, but the saving in price of fall delivered fertilizer and better labor availability may justify fall application. Do not apply when the ground is frozen or icy. Rains and thawing may carry much of it away.

Method of application. Former commercial method was to apply fertilizer in a band or ring around the tree under the spread of the branches. No fertilizer should be applied within two to three feet of the trunk. Few feeding roots are in this area. Method is effective but laborious.

Where feasible, application of fertilizer by machinery is more rapid and labor saving than by hand. Fruit growers report satisfactory results with endgate distributors, lime drills, grain drills, and power dusting machines. With endgate distributors, the truck or PTO tractor-attached unit is driven up the row middles broadcasting over the entire area, or thrown to the right or left, one side only, directly under the trees (Figure 16).

123

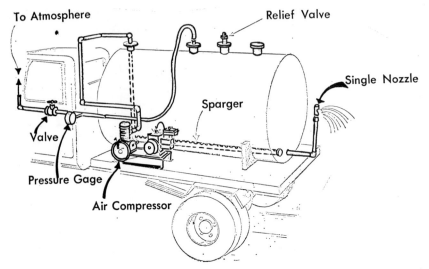

To Atmosphere

Relief Valve

Single Nozzle

Sparger

Valve

Pressure Gage

Air Compressor

Figure 17. This orchard liquid fertilizer applicator is used during the dormant season. It has one flooding jet nozzel to broadcast suspensions, a small compressor at 20-30 psi, throwing a swath up to 40 ft., with an air agitator at tank bottom (Amer. Fruit Grower, March, 1972).

Where the land is suitable, some growers apply in one direction one year and in the cross direction the next. Power pesticide dusters can be calibrated and used to apply fertilizer in half-moons under trees as it moves up the row middle. A tin lip on the discharge pipe will help direct the flow downward.

Since liquid fertilizer has become available, spray application equipment has been designed (Figure 17). Considerable time and labor can be saved, and with this job greatly reduced, only the best days need be picked. Liquid fertilizer with or without chelated trace elements also is being strip-applied by tank-truck booms or through overhead permanent irrigation pipes.

Orchard irrigation. Orchard irrigation is now common for apples east of the Rockies. For example, most of the commerical orchards in Missouri are now being irrigated. Heavy mulching and other practices for conserving moisture on the better soils, however, often have been more economical in tiding the trees over the dry periods. Irrigation should be considered in heavy shallow-rooted soils or in sandy soils if, in spite of mulching, fruit thinning, and other standard practices, the trees are making less than eight to ten inches annual terminal growth and producing small-size, poor-quality fruit. It would be well, however, for the grower to study local U. S. Weather Bureau rainfall records and determine the frequency of droughts for his region. An irrigation system is of questionable value if it can be used only once in several years. If the droughts are so severe,

[1]For liquid fertilizer foliar application, contact Leffingwell Chem. Co., P.O.B. 188, Brea, Ca. 92621; Tenn. Corp., Marietta St., Atlantic, Ga. 30303; or Miller Chem. and Fert. Co., Box 311, Hanover, Pa. 17331.

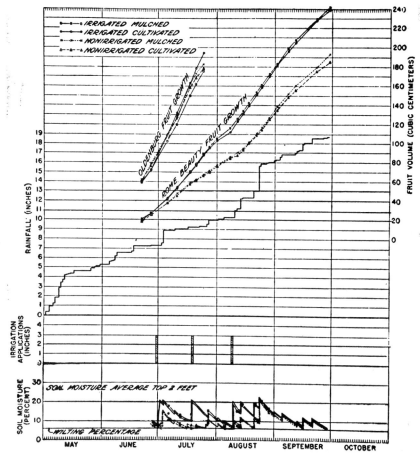

Courtesy J. R. Magness, USDA

Figure 18. This chart shows the effect of soil moisture level on rate of fruit growth of an early ripening apple, Oldenburg, and a late ripening variety, Rome Beauty. Effect of mulching, cultivation, and irrigation on size of apples was greater for the late-ripening Rome than for the early Oldenburg.

however, that the trees are badly damaged or killed, obviously the equipment should pay for itself.

The first requisite in orchard irrigation is a plentiful supply of water from a deep well, river or stream which does not go dry during the most extensive drought periods. It is not worthwhile to irrigate with less than two inches of water per acre each time, which requires 54,000 gallons. Water from wells is usually not adequate for extensive orchard irrigation. The portable or permanent pipe sprinkler systems are being used in the East and Northwest. In the West, furrow or basin (pond under tree fed by furrow) also are used.

A fairly satisfactory method used in the East for determining when and how much water to apply is to study the average monthly rainfall records

125

for the area. When rainfall becomes deficient over a two- to three-week period, two- to three-acre inches of water are applied.

Orchard irrigation is a common practice in desert regions where rainfall is deficient. Sufficient water must be supplied to secure thrifty but not extensive or rank wood growth. Excessive irrigation may be disastrous. Light sandy soils or soils underlain with a substratum of gravel require more frequent and heavier applications of water, while the heavy clay loams may need only one or two applications. More irrigation water is needed in an area where the evaporating power of the air is high than where it is low.

It is important to get even distribution of water and good penetration. Furrow system is common in western U.S. for irrigating where six to eight large furrows, six inches or more in depth are made between every two rows of trees. The contour-check system of furrow irrigation is best adapted to the foothill and mountain sections.

Most authorities agree that the soil should be wetted to a depth of about three feet for the heavier soils and to about six feet for the lighter soils, or the area in which most of the tree roots occur. For a loam to clay-loam type of soil, as an example, this would require around 100,000 gallons per acre per application. As much as 30 to 35 inches of annual irrigation water is applied in some regions in addition to the rainfall which may amount to only 8 to 10 inches annually, most of it occuring in winter. Frequent examination of the soil with an auger is the most satisfactory method in the West for determining the necessity for and the frequency of irrigation. It requires technical assistance to estimate properly when and how much water to apply. References are given at the end of this chapter for more detailed recommendations on orchard irrigation. Also, contact your local government and commercial leaders. There may be a trend toward using the permanent overhead irrigation system to apply irrigation water, fertilizer, and pesticides and to apply water for frost control and to cool trees on hot days. Trickle irrigation conserves water where limited; water drips from spaced holes in in-row plastic pipes at tree bases (see Miller and Schultz). See also photos in Appendix.

Review Questions

1. Why does a young or dwarf apple orchard require different soil management than a low-density bearing orchard?
2. Outline a soil management program for dwarf (indicate stock(s), variety) apple trees planted in hedgerows on gently rolling, relatively heavy soil.
3. Outline a soil management program for dwarf (indicate stock(s), variety) apple trees in hedgerows on gently rolling sandy-gravelly soil.
4. What are the advantages of sod mulch with additional mulch for mature bearing apple trees?
5. Discuss a control program for mice in sod-mulch orchards.
6. What is the value of a killifer or "ground ripper" in a low-density orchard?
7. List methods of irrigating orchards and advantages of each.
8. List 5 summer and 5 winter orchard cover crops which you think would be adapted to your local soil and climatic conditions; discuss one of each.
9. What is the chief disadvantage of rye as a cover crop?
10. In apple orchards, what nutrient receives most attention in the fertilization program, and why?

11. How much fertilizer would you apply to a 20-year apple tree growing in medium-heavy soil in sod with no mulch, and making annual terminal growth of from 2 to 3 inches?
12. What percentage nitrogen do the following fertilizers contain: sulfate of ammonia, nitrate of soda, urea, and ammonium nitrate?
13. What effect do continued applications of the above fertilizers have on soil acidity in the upper few inches of soil?
14. Would you advise orchard irrigation in your region? Why?

Suggested Collateral Readings

Alderman, D C., et al. New ideas on orchard fertilization. Am. Fr. Grow. Mag. Pages 8, 20, 42, 52, 53, 55. April 1967.

Allen, M. Apple leaf uptake of inorganic sprays (CU, MG). Pesticide and Science 1:152-5, 1970.

Armstrong, J. H. and W. E. Pettigrew. Price variation in fertilizer mixtures and materials. Purdue Res. Bull. No. 812 (Indiana) 10 pp. 1966.

Barlow, H.W.B., Root/shoot relationships in fruit trees. Sci. Hort. 14, 35-41, 1960.

Benson, Nels R., E. S. Degman and L. P. Batjer. 20 questions and answers on orchard fertilization. Wash. State Ext. Bull. 426. 8 pp. 1961.

Benson, Nels R., et al. Sulfur deficiency in deciduous tree fruits. ASHS 83:55-62. 1963.

Bernstein, Leon. Salt tolerance of fruit crops. USDA Agr. Inf. Bull. No. 292. 8 pp. Aug. 1965.

Bould, C., and A. I. Campbell. Virus, fertilizer and rootstock effects on young apple trees. Jour. Hort. Sci. Vol. 45, No. 3. 287-294. July 1970.

Bould, L. N. Irrigation on steep land. Calif Ext. Serv. Circ. 509, 26pp. 1962.

Boynton, Damon, A. B. Burrell, R. M. Smock, O. C. Compton, J. C. Cain, and J. H. Beattie. Response of McIntosh apple orchards to varying nitrogen fertilization and weather. Cornell Memoir 290. 1950.

Childers, N. F. A. Liquid major-trace-elements soil fertilizer mix. Hort. News (N.J.) November 1970.

Childers, N. F. Fruit nutrition-temperate to tropical. Horticultural Publications, Rutgers University, New Brunswick, N. J. Over 900 pp. 1966.

Cook, R. L., J. R. Davis and E. H. Kidder. Fertilizing through irrigation water. Mich. Agr. Ext. Bull. 324. 23 pp. 1956.

Eadie, W. R. Wildlife control in orchards. NY Ag. Ex. Srv. Bull. 1055. 1961.

Ferree, D. C. and A. H. Thompson. Bark necrosis of apple as influenced by Ca placement and soil Mn. Md. Ag. Exp. Sta. Bull. A-166, June 1970.

Fisher, V. J., E. H. Ralph and D. B. Williams. Effect of apple soil management practices upon growth, fruitfulness and fruit quality. Del. Agr. Exp. Sta. Bull. 336 (Tech.) 31 pp. Feb. 1961.

Ford, Elsie M. Studies in the nutrition of apple rootstocks. Ann of Bot. *30*: No. 120. Pages 639-655. Oct. 1966.

Ford, Elsie M. Epsom salt sprays on apple trees on two rootstocks. J. Hort. Sci. 43, 505-17, 1968.

Forshey, G. G. and B. A. Dominick, Jr. Irrigation of apples in the Hudson Valley. New York Agr. Exp. Sta. (Geneva). Bull. 809. 30 pp. October 1965.

Frink, C. R. Apple orchard soil and leaf analysis. Conn. Agr. Exp. St. Bull. 670. 11 pp. 1965.

Fry, A. D. and A. S. Gray. Sprinkler irrigation handbook. Rainbird Sprinkler Manufacturing Corp., Glendora, Calif. 41 pp.

Futral, J. G., J. L. Butler, J. H. Ford and E. F. Savage. Constant flow equipment for field application of non-pressure liquid fertilizers and soil fumigants. Geo. Agr. Exp. Sta. Mimeo. Series N. S. 35, April 1957.

Note: For information, assistance on irrigation problems, contact: Ag-Rain, Inc., S. Schrader Ave., Havana, Ill. 62644; John Bean Div., FMC Corp., Jonesboro, Ark. 72401 or San Jose, Ca. 95103; Ocoee Fla. 32671; Rainbird Sprinkler Mfg. Corp., 7045 No. Grand Ave., Glendora, Calif. 91740; Williamstown Irrigation, Inc,, Williamstown, N. Y. 13493; Drip Eze Inc., Box 953, El Cajon, Ca. 92022; Bruckner Industries, Inc. ,Box 232, Fresno, Ca. 93708; Submatic, Inc., 1361 20th Ave., Kingsburg, Ca. 93631. See also Amer. Fruit grower, July issue, Willoughby, Ohio 44094.

(See additional references under Chapter V, Appendix)

Flower-Bud Formation, Pollination and Fruit Set in the Apple

◆ ◆

FLOWER-BUD FORMATION

Time and manner of flower-bud formation. In temperate zones, the flower buds of fruit trees are more or less well developed the season *previous* to their unfolding into blossoms. The exact time when initiation of flower buds occurs in the apple varies somewhat with the geographic region and the variety. The gradual development of an apple flower bud is shown in Figure 1, starting in June of one year and reaching completion in the spring of the following year. In general, the outside parts of the flower bud develop first, and the inside last.

The observations of A. W. Drinkard on flower-bud development in Virginia are similar to those diagrammed here. The variety of apple which he used was Duchess of Oldenburg. First indication of flower-bud primordia was noticed between June 15 and 30; calyx lobes were seen, June 30 and July 7; anthers, July 7 and 14; pistils, August 7 and 14; cavities of the ovaries where the ovule is located, September 15 and 30; flower petals near base of calyx, November 15, ovules did not appear until March; mature pollen was evident in March; and differentiation of the flower was complete by April 1 shortly before it opened into a blossom.

From the above information, it is evident that June or July is the period during which it is determined whether an apple bud will be a flower bud or a "vegetative" growing point without flowers. One should bear in mind, therefore, that any cultural treatment to induce flower bud formation during these months must be performed during the previous spring or fall.

Factors affecting flower-bud formation. From a physiological standpoint, it has not been well established as to the exact factors associated with flower-bud formation in the apple and other pomological fruits. Many horticulturists and plant physiologists have explained flower-bud

Dr. I. C. Haut, University of Maryland, and Dr. L. J. Edgerton, Cornell University, assisted in revision of this chapter.

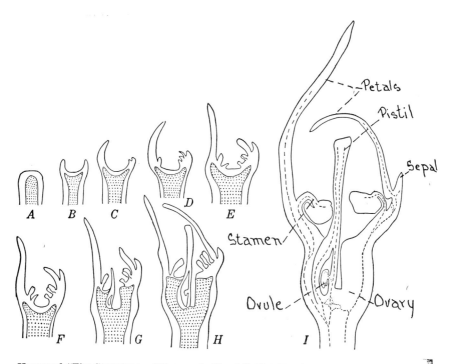

Hayward "The Structure of Economic Plants", The MacMillan Co., New York City.

Figure 1. Diagrams show the development of a flower bud of the apple, beginning at (A) in about mid-June and extending to the following April at (I). The outer parts of the flower appear first, the inner parts last. (In Virginia, U.S.A.)

formation on the basis of relative amounts of carbohydrates and nitrogen in the plant tissues. While this theory appears to be a logical explanation in that a certain balance between carbohydrates and nitrogen has been found to be correlated with flower-bud differentiation, there is insufficient clear-cut evidence at this time to fully substantiate it as a casual relationship. The concept has developed largely on the basis of work done with the tomato by E. J. Kraus and H. R. Kraybill who show by extensive chemical data the effects of different carbohydrate-nitrogen relationships in tissues on fruit setting but not on flower-bud formation. In the original work four classes were designated into which a tomato plant may be placed according to its vegetative and fruiting responses. These classes may be repeated arbitrarily for the apple, as shown in Table 1. An apple tree which has been heavily fertilized with nitrogen would be placed in Class II, whereas a neglected tree growing in sod would probably fall in Class IV. Note that high carbohydrates and high nitrogen are symbolized respectively by large "C" and large "N", whereas low carbohydrates and low nitrogen are designated respectively with a small "c" and "n". Intermediate amounts are symbolized by letters intermediate in size.

There is increasing evidence that auxins are important in flower-bud

TABLE 1

THE INFLUENCE OF DIFFERENT AMOUNTS OF CARBOHYDRATES AND NITROGEN IN
TREE TISSUES ON THE GROWTH AND FRUITING

CLASS	RELATIVE AMOUNTS OF "C" AND "N"	AMOUNT OF VEGETATIVE GROWTH	AMOUNT OF FRUIT	SITUATION DUE TO
I	$\dfrac{C}{N}$	poor	small or none	Defoliation by insects, diseases, sprays, or continued excessive summer pruning.
II	$\dfrac{C}{N}$	rank	small	Too much nitrogen fertilization or too heavy pruning, or both.
III	$\dfrac{C}{N}$	moderate	good	Judicious fertilization, pruning, fruit thinning, soil management, and spraying.
IV	$\dfrac{C}{N}$	poor	small	Insufficient nitrogen often found under sod management with little or no attention to nitrogen applications.

formation. In fact, scientists in this field of research are inclined to place more emphasis on auxins or growth substances as a factor inducing flower-bud initiation than on the carbohydrate-nitrogen concept, although the importance of the latter still may not be revealed fully. These growth substances, the chemical nature of which is not well understood, are apparently formed in the leaves and transported to and concentrated in the regions of the plant where flower buds are formed. Future research may indicate more clearly the exact nature of these substances which together with the carbohydrate food supply are influential in the initiation of flower buds. The fact still remains, however, that flowers and their end products, such as fruit and seed, are composed largely of the products of photosynthesis and of the organic nitrogen complexes. Thus, the green leaves are no doubt of utmost importance in governing flower-bud formation and should be guarded closely against injury from insects and diseases, caustic spray solutions and other agents which may tend to lower their efficiency.

There are several environmental factors under field conditions which are known to stimulate or depress flower-bud formation. These will be discussed briefly in the following paragraphs.

Under natural conditions, *light intensity* is the most important environmental factor governing the rate of carbohydrate manufacture in leaves. It is important especially from the standpoint of amount of light reaching the foliage in the center of trees. With dense trees, low light intensity is one of

130

the chief reasons for few flowers being borne in the centers of the trees. The practice of opening the top of trees by *pruning,* therefore, admits light to the centers and tends to increase flower-bud formation in this region. On the other hand, *excessive pruning* reduces the foliage to such an extent that the roots are able to supply relatively large quantities of nutrients and water to the remaining portion of the top, resulting in considerable shoot growth and water-sprouts with little or no flower-bud formation. *Root pruning,* or any injury to the roots as a result of cold, excessive moisture, deep plowing, or rodent injury, tends to increase flower formation temporarily. Root pruning reduces the root system and thus, limits the amount of water and nutrients available to the top, resulting in reduced shoot and spur growth. Such a retardation in top growth is usually associated with increased flower-bud formation. Root pruning is an amateur practice in Europe with the purpose of inducing young vigorous trees to bear earlier. It has not been commercially adopted in America.

Removal of leaves or defoliation due to injury by insects, diseases, or caustic sprays results in reduced flower-bud formation, especially if defoliation occurs prior to the period of flower-bud differentiation. In principle, this is due to a reduction in the carbohydrates available to the buds in the axils of the injured or destroyed leaves. A *deficiency of water* during the period when flower buds are forming may stimulate flower-bud formation intensely. However, if water deficiency is severe and the tree is already in weak condition due to poor cultural management or other reasons, flower-bud formation may be affected adversely. Excessive application of *nitrogen fertilizers* to young apple trees results in rank vegetative growth and tardy bearing. On the other hand, moderate nitrogen applications to low-vigor trees usually increase flower-bud formation. Zinc, copper, and boron are key deficiencies that tend to reduce normal flowering.

Bending of limbs often results in increased flower formation beyond the bend. Back of the bend, however, new and vigorous shoot growth may be induced. The theory involved is that the bend restricts the movement of carbohydrates from the outer portion of the limb toward the roots. An accumulation of carbohydrates and slowing down of growth beyond the bend is, therefore, assumed to be favorable to flower-bud formation. Back of the bend, less carbohydrates are available, but more water and nutrients from the roots are present, resulting in vigorous shoot growth in this area. Bending is sometimes practiced on vigorous young apple and pear trees to induce wide-angled crotches and earlier flowering. *Dwarfing rootstocks* for standard varieties usually cause the trees to bear much earlier in life. The dwarfing stocks reduce the rate of shoot and spur growth, probably by restricting uptake of soil moisture and nutrients, and apparently result in flower-bud formation.

Ringing is a special commercial practice that usually causes increased flower formation. Ringing is defined as the removal of a thin strip of bark from around the trunk or at the base of main limbs. "Scoring" has a similar

Figure 1a. Left young Golden Delicious tree was sprayed the previous season with Alar. (Right) No spray. (Courtesy late L. P. Batjer, USDA, Wenatchee, Wash.)

effect and consists of making two or more cuts to the sapwood around the trunk or limbs, but no bark is removed. Driving nails into the trunk or cutting out notches below buds influence flowering more or less the same as ringing. Likewise, injuries to the limbs, crotches, trunk, or roots due to low temperature, cankers, disease, fire, or rodents result in increased flower formation. If a wire label is left attached to a young tree, it becomes taut and eventually rings or constricts the tree, causing carbohydrates to accumulate above the wire; the top becomes weakened, and flower-bud formation takes place, providing the tree is older than about three years.

Ringing is a practice used occasionally to increase flower formation on vigorously growing young trees which are tardy in bearing. It is also practiced commercially along with rather heavy pruning on filler trees which are beginning to crowd the permanent trees. Ringing is done about three to five weeks before flower-bud formation usually occurs. The entire trunk may be ringed but it seems preferable to ring a few main branches one year and the rest the next year. The wounds should be covered with roofing or horticultural asphalt free of creosote or like materials harmful to the tissues. Shoots developing near the ring must be removed immediately to prevent entrance of the fire blight organism (*Erwinia amylovora*).

The ringing should not be performed on very young trees, small limbs, more or less defoliated trees, trees in very low vigor, or on peaches, apricots, cherries, or plums. The ringing of alternate bearing trees cannot be expected to induce fruit production in the so-called "off" year.

Use of *Alar* (succinic acid 2-2, dimethyl hydrazide) about three weeks after bloom on apples at 4 lbs/A or 1000 ppm in the spray tank has increased return bloom. It does not seem to affect fruit set. Alar and *TIBA* (2, 3, 5-Triiodo-benzoic acid; inhibits auxin transport) at 1000 ppm each gives good return bloom but TIBA may induce fruit corking, cracking and early dropping. Ethrel (ethephon) (2-chloro-ethyl phos-

132

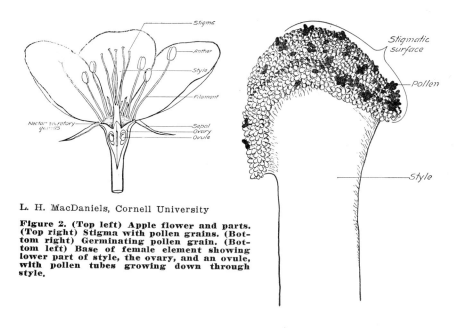

L. H. MacDaniels, Cornell University

Figure 2. (Top left) Apple flower and parts. (Top right) Stigma with pollen grains. (Bottom right) Germinating pollen grain. (Bottom left) Base of female element showing lower part of style, the ovary, and an ovule, with pollen tubes growing down through style.

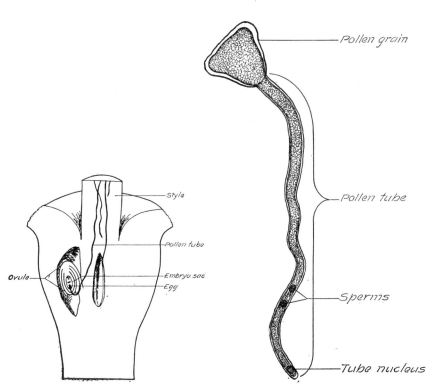

A. J. Heinicke, Cornell University

Figure 3. Some apple varieties are self-unfruitful. The McIntosh on the left was cross-pollinated with insects and bore 23 bushels of apples. Insects were excluded from the tree on the right by cheesecloth netting, with the result that it bore less than one-half bushel of apples.

phonic acid) applied shortly after bloom also increases return bloom on young trees. (See Figure 1a for Alar effect on bloom.)

By the modern radioactive tracer technique in which molecules of naphthalene acetic acid, used as a hormone fruit thinner, are "tagged", the late C. P. Harley, USDA, Beltsville, Md., found this hormone may be directly responsible for greater flower bud formation on apples when used as an apple thinner about three weeks after bloom. This may in part account for better annual bearing of apple trees thinned with this or similar hormones.

POLLINATION AND FRUIT SET

In discussing pollination, it is important to know first the essential parts of the flower. The stamen, or male organ, consists of two parts (Figure 2): (a) the anther, which is made up of two sacs containing the pollen grains and (b) the filament, or stalk which supports the anther. The three parts of the pistil, or female organ, are (a) the basal part or ovary which contains the young ovules and which, along with other parts, develops into the fruit, (b) the styles which are attached to the ovary and bear at their apexes the receptive sticky surfaces known as (c) the stigmas upon which the pollen grains are caught and germinate.

Once the flower has opened in the spring, it is necessary for pollination

134

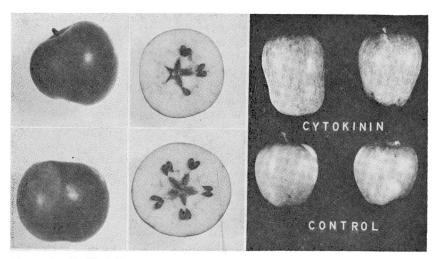

Figure 3a. (Left). Effect of seed formation on shape and size of McIntosh. The lop-sided apple (top) has been cut to show the seeds located in the cavities on the enlarged side of the fruit; no seeds were present in the cavities on the small side of the fruit. The larger, well shaped apple below has a full compliment of seeds. (L. J. Edgerton, Cornell Univ.). (Right) Use of cytokinin and/or gibberellin shortly after bloom will lengthen Delicious fruits and enhance the calyx-end points. This shows commercial promise in the warmer climates. (Geo. C. Martin, Univ. of Calif.).

to take place in order for it to "stick" to the tree and begin to develop into a fruit. If limited or no pollination occurs, the flowers will drop, or develop into a small fruit that drops early. *Pollination* is defined as the transfer of the pollen grains from the anther to the stigma. If the transfer is from anther to stigma on the same flower or to the stigma of another flower of the same variety, it is known as *self-pollination*. If the transfer is from an anther of one variety to a stigma of another variety, it is known as *cross-pollination*. The honeybee is probably responsible for over 90 per cent of the apple pollination, bumblebees and other wild bees may serve more effectively in pollination during windy or cold weather but there are too few of these insects.

Pollen grains of the apple and most fruit plants resemble minute yellow dust particles. They are round or roughly triangular in shape with a diameter of 1/1000 of an inch. Each anther contains about 3500 pollen grains, and since there are 20 stamens, this would be 70,000 grains per flower. Apple pollen is sticky and adheres to the hairy body of the honeybee as it visits the showy flowers in search of nectar. The nectar glands are located near the base of the stamens, as shown in Figure 2[1]. The number of pollen grains carried by a single bee might easily approximate 100,000. In visit-

---

[1]It has been pointed out by R. H. Roberts at the Wis. Agr. Exp. Sta. that better pollination conditions are required for Delicious. The structure of the Delicious flower is such that the bee does not need to crawl over the anthers and stigmas in obtaining nectar. In regions where weather conditions during bloom are likely to be unfavorable it may be desirable to have a pollinizer next to every Delicious row. Hand pollination also may be considered. See Preston, A. P. Bee Visits and Apple Blossom Morphology. Ann. Rpt. E. Malling Res. Sta. 1948 (1949).

TABLE 2

(Adapted from Gourley and Howlett)

Arkansas (Mammouth Black Twig)	Stark
Baldwin	Stayman Winesap, Stamared, Blaxtayman,
Canada Reinette	and Scarlet Stamared
Gravenstein, Red Gravenstein and Bank's	Summer Rambo; Spigold
Hibernal	Tompkins King
Minkler	Turley
Paragon	Virginia Crab
Rhode Island Greening	Winesap

[1]All of these varieties have a triploid number of chromosomes which is closely correlated with infertile or ineffective pollen.

ing flower after flower, however, the bee rubs off pollen onto the stigmas and picks up additional pollen, bringing about self- and cross-pollination. Wind carries very little apple pollen. There is little or no flight of honeybees during rains and heavy winds, or if the temperature is below 65° F. Therefore, the number of sunlight hours during the blossoming period when the temperature is above 70° F. and the air is fairly quiet, are highly important. A bee may visit 5000 blossoms a day.

The pollen grain germinates shortly after it comes in contact with the stigma (Figure 2), sending out what is known as a pollen tube. Germination and growth of this tube are faster when the temperature is above 70°F., but it probably is retarded at temperatures above 80° F. The pollen tube grows down the style until it reaches and penetrates the young ovule and finally finds its way to the place where the egg, or female organ, is located (embryo sac). During the growth of the pollen tube, the two male germs (sperms) are formed in the pollen tube. These are discharged into the embryo sac, where one of them unites with the egg, and by this process, *fertilization* is accomplished. Fertilization, or the union of egg and sperm, is quite similar, therefore, to that taking place in animals. When fertilization in the flower has taken place, there is an initial stimulation to the basal part of the flower tissues which prevents it from dropping.

While eating an apple, it may be noted that there are five compartments or carpels near the core which contain two, one, or no seeds. If pollination and fertilization have been good, the apple, therefore, may contain from a few to ten seeds, and such an apple will likely stick to the spur and mature. However, if pollination and fertilization have been inadequate due to poor weather conditions or other causes, only one to three seeds may develop. Seed development stimulates the apple tissue in the immediate vicinity of the seed. For example, if an apple contains three seeds on one side and none on the other, the tissues in the neighborhood of the seeds will grow normally, whereas the other side of the apple will develop slowly and the fruit subsequently will be lop-sided. (Figure 3a). Also, an apple with only a few seeds is more likely to drop to the ground before maturing, especially if there is considerable competition between the fruits for water, soil nutrients, and carbohydrates.

Most apple varieties will not set fruit by self-pollination. Much of the difficulty experienced in obtaining a set of fruit in orchards is due to the fact that many important varieties, as, for example, McIntosh and Delicious, will not form seeds nor set fruit when their blossoms are self-pollinated (Figure 3). Such varieties are known as *self-unfruitful,* and must have cross-pollination from another variety in order to set and hold their fruit. If a set of fruit results from self-pollination, the variety is said to be *self-fruitful.* Some apple varieties are considered *partly* self-fruitful but none, except perhaps Yellow Transparent, has produced full commercial crops of fruit year after year by its own pollen.

There are cases, such as the Delicious variety, where the pollen is viable or capable of germination, and the egg cells are normal, yet the variety will not set fruit after self-pollination. The variety, therefore, is said to be *self-incompatible,* as well as self-unfruitful. Some varieties may be *cross-incompatible* where fruit does not set, as for example, after Arkansas has been cross-pollinated with Grimes. They are also said to be *cross-unfruitful.*

It is apparent from the above discussion that when cross-unfruitful or self-unfruitful varieties are planted in large blocks with no other varieties in the neighborhood, the trees will not bear commercial crops of fruit, even though they may bloom profusely. In the old days when orchards contained as many as fifty varieties of apples interplanted together, there was little difficulty encountered from poor crops of fruit due to lack of cross-pollination. However, in more recent years when orchardists occasionally planted large blocks of single varieties such as McIntosh for convenience in management, difficulties immediately arose in obtaining commercial crops of fruit. This stimulated considerable experimental work over the country in the field of pollination and fruit setting. Trees were placed in cloth cages at blossom time, or individual branches or spurs were placed in cloth bags. In cross-pollination experiments, stamens of the enclosed flowers were removed before they shed pollen. Then by special technique, pollen from a different variety or the same variety was daubed with a camel-hair brush (hand-pollinated) on the pistils of the enclosed flowers to determine the percentage of fruit set. After several years of experimental work, the more common apple varieties listed above were found to have *infertile* pollen and consequently are *ineffective* in self- or cross-pollination.

Thus, if any one of the above varieties is used, the planting must consist of at least three varieties. The two other varieties must cross-fertilize each other in addition to the above variety. Pollen of commercial varieties not listed above is usually effective in cross-pollination. There are cases, however, where Grimes Golden is cross-incompatible with Arkansas

(Mammoth Black Twig); Early McIntosh is a poor pollinizer for Cortland and standard varieties are incompatible with their "bud sports." Seedlings are usually cross-fruitful with their parent varieties, except Rome Beauty and Gallia Beauty which are only partly cross-fruitful. Some varieties, like Jonathan, Delicious, and Golden Delicious produce unusually large quantities of viable pollen.

There are some varieties which are partly self-fruitful when planted in large blocks, including Jonathan, Maiden Blush, Rome Beauty, Oldenburg, Wealthy, Yellow Transparent, Golden Delicious, Yellow Newtown, Grimes Golden, York Imperial, and others. However, it is now generally agreed by horticulturists that even with these varieties, cross-pollination should always be provided in commercial plantings.

Blooming period for different varieties must overlap. In o r d e r for cross-pollination to take place, it is obviously important that the varieties bloom at approximately the same time. Length of blooming season varies from one week to slightly more than two weeks, depending upon the variety and weather conditions. Some varieties open their blossoms relatively early in spring, such as Red Astrachan, Early Harvest, Gravenstein, Fameuse (Snow), McIntosh, Melba, Milton, Oldenburg, Ohio Nonpareil, and Wagener. The late blooming varieties are Gallia Beauty, Northern Spy, Macoun, Northwestern Greening, Rome Beauty, and York Imperial with Ralls and Ingram very late blooming. Most other commercial varieties are midseason bloomers.

If the temperature is high during the blooming period, all varieties, excepting the late ones, may bloom very close together or almost simultaneously. In some years, when a sudden hot spell at the start of blooming is followed by a protracted cold and rainy period, the time of blooming of varieties may be unduly long. In such seasons, varieties that come into full bloom rather early may be past the pollination stage before the others are ready to shed their pollen freely. Thus, cross-pollination troubles may be encountered, as for example, between the relatively early blooming Duchess of Oldenburg and the late blooming Rome Beauty. This is not likely, however, between most of the midseason and late blooming varieties.

Importance of bearing age. McIntosh on seedling stock comes into bearing at the age of 4 to 6 years, whereas others come into bearing late at the age of about 12 years, as Northern Spy. Thus, the McIntosh may flower for six years without fruiting until the Northern Spy develops flowers. Under these conditions, it will be necessary to use a third variety such as Cortland to provide cross-pollination for the McIntosh. Ages at which commercial apple varieties bloom are given in Chapter II.

Consider alternate bearing habits. Under somewhat neglected cultural conditions, some varieties have a tendency to bear a large crop one

Jonathan		J	J	J	J	J	J	J	J	J
Jonathan		J	J	J	J	J	J	J	J	J
Delicious		D	D	D	D	D	D	D	D	D
Jonathan		J	J	J	J	J	J	J	J	J
Jonathan		J	J	J	J	J	J	J	J	J
Jonathan		J	J	J	J	J	J	J	J	J
Jonathan		J	J	J	J	J	J	J	J	J
Delicious		D	D	D	D	D	D	D	D	D
Jonathan		J	J	J	J	J	J	J	J	J
Jonathan		J	J	J	J	J	J	J	J	J

Figure 4. In this planting plan no tree is more than two rows from its pollinizing variety. Both varieties are cross-fruitful. Delicious must be kept in annual bearing. Plant solid variety rows for mechanical harvesting. Appendix has more charts.

year and a small or no crop the next. York Imperial and Yellow Transparent are examples. Obviously, there will be little or no source of good pollen in the "off" year from the alternate bearing variety. Under these conditions, a third variety should be employed in order to play safe. Information on the tendency of apple varieties to alternate bear light and heavy crops, is given in Chapter II.

Suggested planting plans. No tree should be planted farther than one permanent row (40 to 50 feet) from its pollinizing variety. Hence, a single variety can be planted in blocks of two rows, provided the pollinizing variety is planted on either flank, as shown in Figure 4. Exceptions to this rule may be made in case of varieties which are partly self-fruitful such as York Imperial, Rome Beauty, and possibly Jonathan, although the latter may be erratic under some conditions. These varieties may be planted in blocks of four and six rows with the pollinizing variety on either flank. In northern U. S. orchards where good pollination weather is erratic, no more than two rows of a variety flanked by its pollinator is suggested.

Delicious		D	D	D	D	D	D	D	D
Delicious		D	D	D	D	D	D	D	D
Delicious		D	J[2]	D	D	J	D	D	J
Delicious		D	D	D	D	D	D	D	D
Delicious		D	D	D	D	D	D	D	D
Delicious		D	J	D	D	J	D	D	J
Delicious		D	D	D	D	D	D	D	D
Delicious		D	D	D	D	D	D	D	D
Delicious		D	J	D	D	J	D	D	J

Figure 5. One variety is emphasized in the above planting plan, and the other is used sparingly as a pollinizer. The varieties are cross-fruitful. If this orchard were planted solidly to Delicious by mistake, every third tree in every third row could be top-worked to Jonathan. If the solid planting were McIntosh, each tree to be grafted should be top-worked to two varieties, half of the trees to one variety and half to the other, such as Cortland, Puritan, or Early McIntosh. If cold and/or wet weather during bloom may be a problem, entire rows of Jonathan should be used instead of every third tree.

2 Jonathan.

139

Pollinizers	P[1]	C[2]	C	P	C	C	P	C	Permanent trees
McIntosh		m	m	m	m	m	m	m	Semipermanent
McIntosh	M	M	M	M	M	M	M	M	trees
Pollinizers		p	c	c	p	c	c	p	
McIntosh	M	M	M	M	M	M	M	M	
McIntosh		m	m	m	m	m	m	m	
Rhode Island Green- ing	RIG	RIG	RIG	RIG	RIG	RIG	RIG	RIG	
McIntosh		m	m	m	m	m	m	m	
Rhode Island Green- ing	RIG	RIG	RIG	RIG	RIG	RIG	RIG	RIG	
McIntosh		m	m	m	m	m	m	m	
Pollinizers	P	C	C	P	C	C	P	C	

[1] Puritan

[2] Cortland

Figure 6. An apple variety with infertile or poor pollen is used in this planting (Rhode Island Greening). Two other varieties are needed to cross-fertilize this variety and each other.

If the grower desires to have the majority of his trees of one variety with as few of the pollinizing variety as possible, the planting plan shown in Figure 5 can be used. In this case, the pollinizing trees are located at every third permanent tree in every third permanent row. This has proven entirely satisfactory, providing the blooming seasons overlap, the varieties come into bearing about the same age, they are cross-fruitful, and neither variety has a tendency to bear a heavy crop one year and a light crop the next.

Where the pollen of one variety is of little or no value in cross-pollination, as with Stayman Winesap or Rhode Island Greening, and it is necessary to use three varieties, a suggested planting plan is shown in Figure 6.

Use of bees in the orchard. Due to the importance of honeybees in cross-pollination, some growers have made a habit of bringing in bees a day or so in advance of the blooming period. The hives are scattered throughout the orchard so there is one strong colony for each one or two acres (Figure 7). One hive to ten acres may be sufficient for young bearing trees. The grower sometimes owns his own bees, but attempts by growers to raise bees have usually been disappointing. It seems better for him to rent the bees from a beekeeper, due to the specialized nature of beekeeping. A medium strength colony contains 15,000 to 20,000 bees. Extra strong colonies containing eight to nine pounds of bees have been effective in pollinating over four acres of trees during good weather. During unfavorable weather, bees may travel only half a tree to two trees from the hives. The most striking results from bringing bees into the orchard will be evident in a season with only a few hours of favorable weather during bloom. It is during these seasons that apples are usually scarce and bring the higher prices.

The orchardist should take care not to spray the trees with pesticides (organic phosphate-type sprays are particularly poisonous) while the bees

140

Figure 7. (Left) The honeybee is most important in pollen transfer. One strong hive per acre scattered through the orchards and mounted above the grass at blossoming helps get a good crop. (Right) Orchardists should contract with bee-keepers early to get strong hives on time. (Left, Cornell University; right, Norman Sharp, Honeybees, Fishers, N. Y.)

are still working. Bees should not be left in the orchard throughout the year; aside from being in the way, they may bother the workmen. Broad-leaf weeds such as dandelion that compete with the apple bloom for the bee's attention can be controlled with a herbicide as 2, 4-D. A tight Ky-31 sod "squeezes out" dandelions.

Top-working to provide pollinizers. Commercial growers today rarely make the mistake of planting solid blocks of a single variety. When this situation arises, however, it is possible to top-work or graft every third tree in every third row to a pollinizing variety, as shown in Figure 5. If the solid block consists of a variety with nonviable pollen, a tree next to each of the above-grafted trees can be top-worked to a third variety which is cross-fruitful with the other two.[1] Or, every third tree in every third row can be top-worked half to one variety and half to the other. These grafts will not bloom for three years. In the meantime, it is necessary to bring in bouquets of flowers in buckets or two-quart jars of water and hang the bouquets in the grafted trees. Bees should be provided in this case to in-sure maximum pollination. Grafts are pruned as little as possible in order that they flower earlier. It is important to provide bees in the orchard at least until the grafted trees are blooming rather heavily all over.

Hand cross-pollination. Solid blocks of Delicious and Winesap in recent years have been cross-pollinated by hand in the Pacific Northwest. In New York, this system was successfully used on large blocks of Mc-Intosh. It requires one hour or less per tree to daub one to two flowers in every four flowering spurs, thus eliminating need for fruit thinning. Ap-plication of pollen by bombs, shotguns, dusters, or sprays mixed with water, sugar or *Lycópodium* (fern) spores have not given improved or

---

[1] If possible use a yellow variety for top-working on a red variety, or vice versa. This enables pickers to keep the varieties separate while harvesting.

very good results. Generally, any such method is used only as a makeshift until permanent cross-pollination can be provided.

Too much cross-pollinization. If all provisions have been made for good cross-pollination and the weather during the blooming period is quite favorable, it is probable that there will be excessive fruit set. At present, however, there is no method for obtaining a definite amount of cross-pollination and no more. It seems best to provide for a full commercial crop, then remove the overload by chemical and/or hand-thinning.

There may be sufficient wild insects in the neighborhood to provide adequate cross-pollination. Or, growers may remove the bees after one or two days of good weather.

Researchers and growers comparing the effects of chemical thinners on fruit set should be aware of control trees setting excessively, then dropping much of their crop, giving erroneous interpretation of the chemical effects on treated trees.

The effect of pollen on shape, size, and color of fruit. The shape and color of an apple are typical for the variety regardless of the source of pollen. It is true, however, that cross-pollinated fruits are often of better shape, size and color than those obtained from self - pollination. This is probably due to the fact that the cross-pollinated fruits have more seed, start growth sooner, and because of additional seed, they have more uniform shape, and better size and color at picking time. Pollen from a yellow variety, such as Golden Delicious, does not cause yellow streaks to appear on red apples, neither does the pollen of an oblong or flat apple change the shape to a round apple.

Factors affecting the set of fruit. *Nitrogen* is most frequently the limiting factor in orchards, and applications to the soil and/or as a urea spray before bloom are usually effective in increasing the fruit set on mature bearing trees. *Pruning* the winter before an expected heavy crop is a common method of increasing the fruit set. Such a practice reduces the competition between the remaining flowers for carbohydrates, water, and nutrients. The practice of *ringing* is resorted to only in particularly stubborn cases where the tree produces flowers with little or no set of fruit. In this case, ringing must be done not later than full bloom to affect the set of current blossoms.

Temperatures below 40° F. during bloom not only inhibit bee activity, but they hinder pollen germination. There is some germination at 40° to 50° F., but not until the temperature reaches 60° to 70° F. is pollen germination satisfactory. Optimum conditions for pollen germination and pollen tube growth are between 70° and 80° F., above which there is a decrease. Frosts just preceding or during blossoming may decrease the crop considerably. The farther open a blossom is when the frost occurs, the more susceptible it is to freezing. Fully opened apple blossoms may be killed at temperatures between 25° and 28° F. Delicious is quite susceptible, followed by Stayman Winesap, Arkansas, and Winesap. Although the first blossoms to open on these varieties may be killed the later blossoms set sufficient fruit to give full commercial crops. The blossoms of Rome Beauty and York Imperial usually withstand frosts quite satisfactorily and this may be due partly to their late-blooming habit. Other varieties more resistant to frost at blooming are Jonathan, Oldenburg, Grimes Golden, Summer Rambo, and Wealthy.

The pistil, or female organ, is usually killed first by low temperatures. If the buds are unopened, freezing injury to the pistil can be detected by cutting the bud in half crosswise; dead pistils will be brown, live pistils green. Pollen is more resistant to frosts and can remain viable at several degrees below 32° F. If the temperature hovers at 29° F. or below only for a few hours, injury may not result. The longer the period of cold, the more likely the injury.

Wind may affect the set of fruit by inhibiting bee activity, desiccating the stigmas, or excessively whipping the flowers and destroying their capacity to function. High *humidity* may prevent proper release of pollen. Low humidity may dry the stigmas and reduce pollen germination. *Rainfall* also inhibits bee flight and prevents release of pollen. Intermittent rainfall with periods of sunshine during the bloom period, however, ordinarily does not affect a commercial set adversely.

APPLE DROPS

Fruit growers are familiar with the fact that though an apple tree may bloom profusely, only a relatively small percentage of the flowers will mature into fruit. Actually, only about one bloom in 20 is needed for a good commercial crop on a full-blossoming apple tree. Most of the blossoms fall soon after full bloom with smaller amounts dropping later. It is true that the various drops may be so great that the final yield is reduced seriously.

Two general drop periods are usually recognized (Figure 8), one defined as the "first drop" which begins shortly after petal fall and continues for two or three weeks. The other drop is the better known "June drop" which is more obvious to the fruit grower because the fruits have developed to a larger size. The June drop begins a few weeks after the first drop and continues for two to four weeks. In some parts of the country, it may begin in late May and be completed in June, or begin in June and be completed in July.

These drops are remarkably uniform from year to year under varied weather conditions. The behavior has been regarded by some workers as an hereditary characteristic. The quantity of fruit that drops early or late varies with the variety. Some varieties have a heavy first drop shortly after bloom with a relatively light second drop. Examples of these are Stayman Winesap, Arkansas, Rhode Island Greening, Delicious, Tompkins King, and Winesap. With other varieties, the first drop is relatively light with the later drop heavier; these varieties include Baldwin, Grimes Golden, Wealthy, Yellow Transparent, Oldenburg, and Rome Beauty.

143

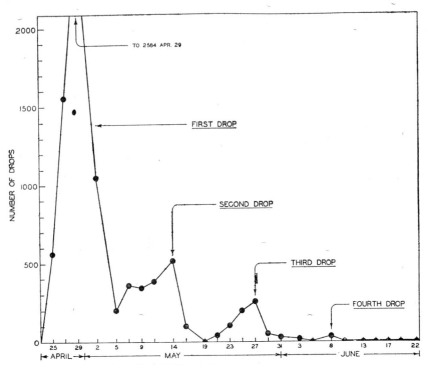

A. E. Murneek, University of Missouri

Figure 8. Murneek describes four waves of apple drops in Missouri. Horticulturists usually lump the first and second drops into the "First Drop" and the third and fourth drops into the "June Drop." Note relative size of the first drop.

Information is still quite incomplete as to the cause of the various apple drops. It seems to be clear, however, that most of the flowers that drop soon after full bloom do so because of the lack of pollination, or as a result of self-fertilization. It is possible to reduce the early drop, if that be desirable, by providing the right varieties for cross-pollination and by putting more bees into the orchard.

The June drop consists of apples one-half to one-inch diameter. Because these apples stay under the tree longer and are more conspicuous, the apple grower frequently worries more about the June drop than the more significant early drop. The cause of the comparatively late shedding of immature apples is probably due to competition among the fruits for food, water, and nutrients. It is not certain if the supply of nutrients, principally nitrogen, carbohydrates, or some other indispensable substance becomes limiting first when the fruit load is excessive for the capacity of the particular tree. One relatively weak branch on a tree may release a large number of drops, whereas an adjoining more vigorous branch may shed only a few. Fruits which contain the fewest or weakest seeds are usually the first to drop. Although there does not seem to be any practical way of controlling the June drop in apples, it is probable that the maintenance of sufficient

144

vigor and the development of healthy foliage will reduce its severity. Judicious fertilization with nitrogen and pruning may also have a helpful influence.

Review Questions

1. Distinguish between pollination and fertilization.
2. What part of the flower produces the sperms; what part bears the egg?
3. What are the agents responsible for transfer of pollen from one plant to another; which is the more important?
4. List 5 commercial apple varieties which are good pollinizers and 5 which are poor pollinizers.
5. Diagram a plan for planting a poor pollinizing variety with good pollinizing varieties so as to secure effective cross-pollination. Use varieties commonly grown in your locality.
6. What would you do to an 8-year solid block of Delicious to secure good cross-pollination? Name the variety or varieties used and practices followed subsequently.
7. How can the shape of Delicious be lengthened in warmer climates?
8. List environmental and other factors which may affect adversely pollination and set of fruit.
9. Are the "bud sports" of standard varieties generally good pollinizers for their parent varieties? Explain.
10. What is an important factor causing lopsided fruits?
11. List two chemicals used as a spray that cause return bloom.

Suggested Collateral Readings

Batjer, L. P., M. W. Williams, G. C. Martin. Effects of Alar on growth and fruiting of apple, pear, sweet cherry. Proc. A.S.H.S. 85:11-6. 1964

Bartram, R. D. et al. Alar on apples - guide to use. Wash. E.M. 3072. Revised.

Blasberg, C. H. Artificial pollination of fruits. N. J. Hort. News, New Brunswick, N. J. May 1949.

Galston, A. W. and P. J. Davies. Control mechanisms in plant development, Prentice-Hall, Englewood Cliffs, N. J. 184 p. illus. 1970. HortScience Vol. 6, No. 2, April 1971.

Gourley, J. H. and F. S. Howlett. Ringing applied to the commercial orchard. Ohio Ag. Sta. Bull. 410. 1927. Also their book, Mod. Fruit Prod., Macmillan Co., N. Y. 1941.

Griggs, W. H. Pollination requirements of fruits and nuts. Calif. Ext. Serv. Cir. 424. 35 pp. 1953.

Grower experiences with Alar. British Columbia Orchardist. 15-19. Apr. 1971.

Hartman, F. O. and F. S. Howlett. NAA, fruit setting, and apple development. Ohio Agr. Exp. Sta. Res. Bull. 920. 66 pp. 1962.

Hillman, W. S. The physiology of flowering. 164 pp. Holt, Rinehart, Winston. New York City, London. 1964.

Hoffman, M. B. Pollination, fruit development of tree fruits. Cornell Ext. Bull. 1146. 8 pp. 1965.

Indispensable pollinators, The Rpt. (Mimeo) 9th Pollin. Conf., Univ. of Ark., Agr. Ext. Serv., Fayetteville. 1970.

Kotob, M. A. and W. W. Schwabe. Induction of parthenocarpic fruit in Cox's Orange apples. Jour. Hort. Sci. 46: (1) 89-93. Jan. 1971.

Kremer, J. C. Traps for the collection and distribution of pollen in orchards. Mich. Agr. Exp. Sta. Bull. Vol. 31. Aug. 1948.

Looney, N. E., D. V. Fisher, J. E. W. Parsons. Effects of annual applications of Alar on apples. Proc. A.S.H.S. 91: 18-30. 1967.

Martin, G. C. et al. Changing apple shape with cytokinin and GA sprays, Calif. Agr. p. 14. April 1970.

(See additional references under Chapter VI, Appendix)

CHAPTER VII

Thinning Apple Fruits and Alternate Bearing

◆ ◆

Thinning is the removal of a part of the crop before it matures on the tree with the object of (a) increasing the marketability of the remaining fruit, and (b) reducing the alternate bearing tendency. Indeed, thinning may be grouped with pruning and fertilization as among the important cultural practices which tend to induce and maintain tree vigor. Horticulturists, in general, consider it sound practice to provide for a full bloom by good orchard management, and then if conditions during bloom are particularly favorable for a heavy fruit set, it becomes necessary and advisable to chemical and/or hand thin the excessive crop prospect at bloom or a few weeks after bloom. Chemical thinning of apples has been one of the most important developments gaining widespread use in commercial orchards in recent years.

Fruiting is an exhaustive process to the tree, especially if the crop is heavy. Hence, the chief goal is to permit the tree to mature as large a crop as possible and yet conserve sufficient nutrients and carbohydrates for good shoot and spur growth, leaf development, and flower-bud formation for next year's crop. If the tree is permitted to mature an excessive crop, obviously it becomes devitalized to the point where it not only produces an inferior product, but it becomes increasingly susceptible to disease and low-temperature injury.

Thinning is practiced only on trees carrying a moderate to heavy crop of fruit. It accomplishes relatively more on mature trees making small annual growth, or on trees reduced in vigor with weak leaf surface than on young vigorous trees of the same variety. Response is better on light soils deficient in moisture than on heavy loams with adequate moisture. Trees growing in

Assisting in revision of this chapter were Dr. Clive W. Donoho, Jr., N.C. State Univ., Raleigh; Dr. Max W. Williams, U.S.D.A., Wenatchee, Wash.; Dr. M. J. Bukovac, Mich. State Univ.; and Dr. L. J. Edgerton, Cornell Univ., Ithaca, N.Y.

sod alone usually respond better to thinning than trees growing under mulch or some system of cultivation or chemical weed control.

After years of commercial experience in thinning apples, it has become increasingly apparent that thinning is necessary on all small-fruited varieties which tend to retain an overload of fruit after the June drop. These varieties include Grimes Golden, Golden Delicious, Wagener, Early McIntosh, Baldwin, and Wealthy. Although varieties such as Jonathan, McIntosh, and Stayman Winesap require relatively less thinning than the above varieties, in some seasons after a particularly heavy set, thinning is a necessity in order to increase size and quality of fruits. Delicious and its bud sports require more leaf surface per fruit than most varieties in order to attain high flavor and dessert quality; otherwise, the fruit may have a "starchy" flavor.

OBJECTS OF FRUIT THINNING

The reasons for thinning may be outlined as follows:

1. Increase annual yields of marketable fruit.
2. Improve size.
3. Improve color.
4. Improve eating quality.
5. Reduce limb breakage.
6. Promote tree vigor and, where early chemical spray-thinning is practical, to induce annual cropping.
7. Minimize the handling and storage of low grade and cull fruit.
8. Permit more thorough spraying and dusting of fruits during lat-season applications.
9. Expedite all handling operations at harvest and reduce their respective costs.

Thinning increases fruit size. Probably the most pronounced effect of thinning is an increase in size of fruit, largely as a result of alloting more leaf surface for each fruit. Experimental evidence has shown that good size and quality can be obtained when fruits of most varieties are spaced to allow about 30 to 40 average size leaves in the vicinity of each fruit. If 50 or more leaves are left per fruit, there appears to be little additional increase in size and quality of the fruit. The usual commercial practice of spacing the fruits from six to eight inches apart on the branch allows about 30 average-size leaves per fruit for most varieties.

Table 1 shows the effect on size, grade, and cash returns of spacing Winesaps from three to four inches, six to seven inches, and nine to ten inches apart on 12-year trees in Oregon. Exact spacing, however, is not necessary since some cross-transfer of food within limbs allows bunched fruits to size well.

Under conditions of the above experiment, the peak returns were obtained by thinning the fruit a distance of six to seven inches on the

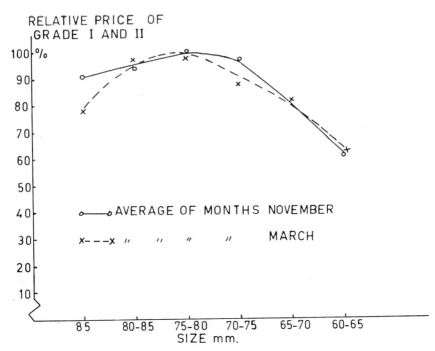

Figure 1a. Fruit thinning of apples pays. The better auction prices brought by larger size fruits is shown above for Golden Delicious in the market at Goes, The Netherlands. Fruits 75–80 mm are about 3–3¼ inches in diameter; 60–65 mm are about 2½ inches. U.S. chain stores are requesting medium size apples for bagging, over-raps, and children. (Courtesy S. J. Wertheim, Fruit Exp. Sta., Wilhelmina-dorp, The Netherlands).

branches. At this distance there were about six boxes of fruit per tree which had 163 or less apples per box as compared with one-half box in this class from the unthinned trees; gross returns were over twice as much for the thinned trees. Thinning a distance of nine to ten inches with Winesaps gave no advantage over six to seven inches.

Thinning is not the only factor which influences size of fruit at harvest.

1. Some apple varieties inherently produce small fruits and require more thinning than varieties which produce characteristically large fruits.

2. As the tree becomes older, the fruits tend to become smaller in size, as for example with Wealthy. This is because old trees set heavier crops than young trees, possibly because of the accumulation of a reproductive hormone in the older trees.

3. Fruit size may be markedly reduced under drought conditions, depending upon severity of the drought.

4. Fruits are usually larger when the trees have been pruned the winter preceding a heavy crop.

5. Vigorously vegetative growth produces larger fruit than weak growth.

6. Foliage injury by caustic sprays during the growing season may result in smaller fruit size. The relatively good size fruit being obtained on heavily cropping trees today is likely due to the mild organic pesticides as captan and also to chemical fruit thinning.

Thinning increases f r u i t color. Fruit thinning tends to increase the amount and intensity of red overcolor and yellow undercolor of apples. C. G. Brown in Oregon Circular 76 showed on Winesap trees that the more highly colored apples (Fancy and Extra Fancy) were obtained when the fruit was spaced six inches or more. Results have shown that there is a gradual increase in over- and undercolor of apples with an increase in number of leaves to 30 to 40 per fruit. This is important to consider for apple varieties such as Delicious which need considerable red color in order to fall in the higher grades. The general effect of thinning on

Ohio State University, Columbus

Figure 1. High school boys and girls, specially selected, are often used in hand thinning fruit. A foreman in charge of a group of 10 to 20 children checks the work, keeps time, and moves ladders for the girls.
With full-dwarf trees on EM-26 or EM-IX this job is greatly simplified.

color, however, is usually not as striking as its effect on size. Limb propping helps to expose fruit to the sun for better coloring. Also, fruit on dwarfed trees receives better light and colors better than on larger trees.

Thinning increases dessert quality. When a fruit is accompanied by adequate and efficient leaf surface, it is better supplied with carbohydrates and other materials which are necessary for good flavor and quality. The result is largely due to an increase in the sugar sucrose. Most apple varieties require 30 leaves per fruit for good dessert quality, except the Delicious and its bud sports which, as pointed out earlier, require about 40 leaves in order to avoid a characteristically undesirable flavor obtained at lower fruit-leaf ratios.

Thinning reduces limb breakage. A heavily loaded mature McIntosh tree may carry almost a ton of fruit. Obviously, the leverage and strain of such a crop is tremendous and much aggravated by high winds. The grower cannot afford to take chances on losing large sections of his trees by overloading. Thinning not only reduces this danger, but helps to

149

reduce the amount of necessary propping. The preparation of numerous props from saplings or branches of large trees entails considerable time and labor, but Washington growers consider it a worthwhile practice. Props can be prepared from rough-sawed boards with the following dimensions: 1 x 4 inch x 6 to 8 feet, or 1½ x 6 inch x 10 feet. A semicircular notch at one end holds the branch. Dwarfs, of course, need no propping.

Thinning reduces disease and insect injured fruits. Thinning offers an early opportunity to remove malshaped specimens and fruit injured by insects and diseases, all of which are bound to fall in the cull class in the grading operation. These fruits not only rob the better fruits of nutrients, carbohydrates, and water, but are expensive to handle during the picking and grading season. Also, spread of insects and diseases can be checked greatly by removing injured fruits which may rub against healthy fruits. Thorough spraying is difficult among unthinned groups of two and three apples.

Thinning reduces cost of handling the crop. Although there are no specific figures to demonstrate the reduction in handling costs as a result of thinning, it is obviously less expensive to handle a crop 90 per cent in the upper grades with 5 per cent culls than one 75 per cent in the upper grades with 15 per cent culls. The cost of thinning is largely counteracted by the reduction in handling costs at harvest. Also, it is cheaper to pick or knock apples off at thinning time than at harvest time, because the fruits are dropped to the ground as soon as separated from the tree.

Thinning affects yield. Experimental results of thinning on fruit yields are variable, but the majority of the experiments indicate that thinning by standard methods do not, or slightly reduce the yield. This is more or less to be expected since the practice is designed to decrease competition between fruits so that the remaining fruits will derive the benefit of increased water and food materials. The effect on yield seems to depend entirely upon the extent of reduction of the crop by thinning. With early-season chemical thinning it is probable that yields over a period of years are increased, but no supporting data are available. One must be careful not to overthin and produce oversized fruits which are often inferior in eating and storage qualities, and may be difficult to market.

Interrelation of pruning and nitrogen fertilizers. Pruning and thinning are interdependent. If a tree has been invigorated by pruning during the previous winter season, there will be less need for fruit thinning the following season. On the other hand, if there has been light or no pruning during the previous season there may be a greater need for fruit thinning. It seems desirable not to try to eliminate thinning by heavy pruning. On the contrary, pruning should be kept to a minimum consistent with its favorable effects, and the excess fruits removed by chemical and hand thinning.

It has been pointed out in the chapter on soil management that excessive application and poor timing of nitrogen fertilizers results in poor fruit color and condition. Fruit color can be controlled more easily by regulating the nitrogen fertilizer than by thinning or pruning. Therefore, from a practical standpoint, it is important to regulate carefully the nitrogen so that the color of the fruit is not affected adversely.

Alternate bearing. This is the tendency of a tree to bear heavily one year and lightly the next. The varieties York Imperial and Golden Delicious tend to do this more than Rome Beauty and Jonathan. Chemical fruit thinning to reduce the drain of a heavy fruit set on a tree early in the season has done more than any other factor in correcting "on-off" years of bearing. Other corrective practices are (a) use of somewhat more pruning before the expected heavy-bloom season to reduce flowering points, (b) use of supplemental irrigation when needed, and (c) application of more fertilizer, particularly nitrogen, before the heavy-crop year to get large green leaves as early as possible to support the heavy crop. Supplemental urea sprays are effective in getting the nitrogen into the leaves quickly and early in spite of adverse weather. One of the main problems now is for the researchers to devise a means of obtaining a good fruit set in spite of almost continuously bad weather during bloom. Growers in the eastern U. S. who are using chemical thinning and other practices listed above generally are getting good return bloom each year, but with bad bloom weather the crop may be reduced greatly because of inadequate pollination by bees, with the grower helplessly standing by. Interestingly, Bukovac's research with Gibberellins (A_3 A_4) applied to pistils of emasculated flowers induced fairly normal seedless apples.

CHEMICAL THINNING OF APPLES

Blossom or young-fruit thinning of apple and other deciduous tree fruits with chemical sprays has been a growing practice in commercial orchards of the United States for several years. Among the leading researchers have been M. B. Hoffman, Cornell; L. P. Batjer and C. P. Harley, USDA; A. H. Thompson, Maryland; F. W. Southwick, Massachusetts; and many others. The following summary and recommendations are largely those of USDA based on all results available.

The principal value of chemical-thinning sprays is to improve size and finish of the fruit and to break up biennial bearing, or "on" and "off" years of heavy and light fruiting, thus making annual crops larger and more uniform. Also, spray-thinning costs less, reduces amount of hand thinning needed, and tends to reduce fire blight (bacterial) infection.

Although much has been learned about chemical sprays for thinning, much remains to be ascertained about the actual mechanics of their operation on living trees. Their use is beset with complexities and hazards. Identical applications on the same trees in succeeding years may have very different results. Yet the use of these sprays is of such economic value that fruit growers have been willing to employ them despite the variability in results. Variation in results may be caused by timing of application, weather conditions, vigor of trees, concentration of spray material, varieties treated, thoroughness of pollination, winter injury, frost damage, and other factors.

Chemical thinners add another to the arsenal of sprays already used by commercial orchardists to produce marketable fruits. Insecticide and fungicide sprays are used to control insects and fungus diseases, nutritional sprays sometimes are applied to the dormant tree or to the leaves to make better-nurtured trees, and sprays are used to keep fruit from dropping until the orchardist is ready to pick it. Some of the stop-drop sprays are identical with some sprays used for chemical thinning. Thinning sprays are generally not recommended for use in combination with other spray materials that require uniform coverage; blossom-thinning sprays are best used selectively from tree to tree.

Spray-thinning research started in the depression years of the early 1930's, with the work of E. C. Auchter and J. W. Roberts. Growers wanted a spray that would entirely defruit apple trees of varieties that would not pay their way. This forestalled the expense of spraying and harvesting a crop for which there was no market. After this initial venture in total crop removal, emphasis passed to finding spray materials that would break up biennial bearing in varieties having that tendency. Early thinning was done with sodium dinitro cresylate and related dinitro compounds. These still are largely used in the West. Later, the hormone-type materials, particularly naphthaleneacetic acid (NAA), used originally in orchards to delay harvest drop, were found to be effective for thinning after the blossom stage and after the danger of frost had passed. NAA and related materials have been most popular in the East.

Fruit trees do a partial job of thinning themselves. Usually not more than five to twenty per cent of the apple blossoms set fruit. Thinning may be required to reduce fruit set by a relatively small percentage on some varieties. It is especially needed on varieties that tend toward "snow-ball" blossoming and to biennial bearing habits. Growers have found chemical thinning profitable, lowering hand-thinning costs from one-fourth to nine-tenths. Hand thinning of heavily loaded trees may cost up to $275 per acre, as compared with $5 or $10 an acre for the chemical spray technique. Thus, even if the chemical spray does not do a complete thinning job, and some hand thinning is necessary, the saving in cost may be substantial.

FACTORS AFFECTING RESULTS WITH THINNING SPRAYS

Hand thinning developed early in the apple-growing industry of the Northwest. Its purpose was to help produce a higher quality crop. However, it is one of the costliest operations in the production of fruit. Depression-born research using dinitro compounds to defruit unprofitable varieties and later work to reduce biennial bearing, indicated the feasibility of using chemical sprays for fruit thinning that could be applied with orchard equipment already in use.

(Upper photos) Louis P. Edgerton, Cornell University.

Figure 3. Chemical thinning in commercial apple orchards is in wide use. Golden Delicious has responded particularly well in annual cropping of larger better quality fruit. Upper left photo shows a tree with light bloom that had been hand thinned the previous year; on the right is a neighboring tree that had been chemically thinned. Both carried about 17 bushels the previous year. Note the difference in follow-up bloom. Lower photos show unthinned Golden Delicious in New Jersey in mid-August on the left; chemically thinned on the right.

Timing: Early experiments were directed toward obtaining information about timing and concentration of DNOC (dinitro or Elgetol) sprays. Experiments with DNOC on apples, which does the job by physical injury to blossoms and physiological shock to the tree, have resulted in about the same amount of thinning with applications at full bloom as at early petal fall (2 to 3 days later). Timing, therefore, is not critical with DNOC on apples, and one has 3 to 4 days to make applications under most conditions. This is long enough for growers to spray a sizable acreage of a given variety. DNOC is not adapted for use as a postbloom thinner. It can be used only in regions where postbloom frosts are not likely to occur.

Timing is rather critical when the hormonelike chemicals NAA and NAAmide are used on summer varieties. These sprays should be applied on early varieties preferably at the petal fall stage. If used much later than 10 days after bloom, stimulating effects manifested by premature

153

ripening and fruit splitting are likely to occur. Sevin has not been effective as a thinner for summer varieties. FDA may, in fact, drop Sevin.

The fact that the postbloom thinners NAA, NAAmide (best for Stayman and McIntosh types and early ripening varieties) and Sevin may thin fall and winter varieties effectively during the bloom or petal fall period is of limited commercial value. Important advantages of a postbloom thinning spray are delaying the application to avoid the frost danger and the opportunity to evaluate the degree of fruit set before applying treatments. Many timing studies on late varieties have been conducted with NAA and NAAmide. Unlike summer varieties, the results generally indicate a wide latitude in time of application. At present most sprays including these chemicals are applied from 10 to 21 days after full bloom.

Sevin, used commercially since about 1960, has as wide a range in timing as NAA and NAAmide. L. P. Batjer and B. J. Thomson, working in Australia and Washington, effectively thinned several varieties of apples when Sevin sprays were applied 5 to 30 days after full bloom. In general, results were consistent and uniform between 15 and 27 days after full bloom. Sprays applied earlier and later were somewhat more variable and in some instances failed to thin enough. How late in the season Sevin will cause thinning is likely to depend on the weather. During a cool postbloom period, "natural" fruit drop is delayed. When this occurs, the sprays are effective later in the season than if the weather is warmer.

DNOC is not generally used in the more humid fruit areas of the country. In the arid regions of the Northwest, DNOC has been used extensively. However, with the advent of Sevin the chief use of DNOC has been in a "two-spray" program.

In some apple regions Sevin has been removed from the spray schedule because it is too effective against predators of mites and, hence, mites may become more troublesome with its use.

Loren Tukey (Penna.) and Clive Donoho (formerly Ohio) report that a good index for thinning apples is by fruit dimension. Tukey suggests that fruits should be about 6/16 to 7/16 inch in diameter, the former diameter being the time when fruits can be removed more easily. Measurements are taken at the same time each day on sample trees of each variety, using either the "king" (the terminal) or lateral fruit depending on which set the earliest. A circular plastic rule can be used with proper size holes in it to check fruit diameters. If NAA is applied to Delicious after the 7/16 inch size is attained it may cause many small apples to persist to harvest. Sevin, then, may be best but it does kill mite predators.

Concentration: Since the effective concentration of thinning sprays is related to weather conditions, tree vigor, variety, and possibly other factors, no inflexible recommendation is in order. With NAA, reduction in set is greater with the stronger spray. However, with DNOC and Sevin (carbaryl)

154

one may not find any difference between ⅔ and 1-⅓ pints per 100 gallons of DNOC, or one-half and 1 pound of 50% WP or equivalent of Sevin.

Table 2 is an example of chemical fruit thinning recommendations for northeastern USA and Table 3 is typical of northwestern USA recommendations.

TABLE 1. Chemical Concentrations for Thinning Apples in New York, USA.*** (Note: Check with your local experiment station for up-to-date recommendations.) Data courtesy of L. J. Edgerton and M. B. Hoffman, Cornell University, Ithaca, N. Y.

VARIETY	(NAPHTHYLACETA-MIDE) NAD PPM*	(NAPHTHALENE-ACETIC ACID) NAA** PPM*	SEVIN** LBS/100 GALS.*
Lodi****	35 - 50	....	....
Yellow Transparent	35 - 50	....	....
Melba	35 - 50	....	....
Oldenburg (Duchess)	35 - 50	....	....
Early McIntosh	35 - 50	5 - 10	2
Milton	35 - 50	5 - 10	....
Wealthy	50	10 - 15	....
Jonathan	35 - 50	5 - 10	1
McIntosh	35 - 50	5 - 10	1 - 2
Cortland	35 - 50	5 - 10	1 - 2
R.I. Greening	35 - 50	5 - 10	1 - 2
Macoun	....	5 - 10	....
N.W. Greening	35 - 50	5 - 10	....
Delicious	....	5 - 10	1 - 2
Baldwin	35 - 50	5 - 10	....
Northern Spy	35 - 50	5 - 10	1
Golden Delicious	....	10 - 20	....
Yellow Newtown	35 - 50	5 - 10	....
Rome Beauty	35 - 50	5 - 15	1 - 2
Ben Davis	35 - 50	5 - 10	....

*Use lower concentration for conditions very favorable for thinning. Select favorable weather for treatment; i.e. warm and calm. Apply thinning spray as a separate operation. Do not concentrate, especially when using NAA. Do not spray thin young trees; i.e. those under 10-12 years of age unless they are subject to biennial bearing. Leave several representative trees unsprayed. This is the only way to evaluate the thinning results and the effects of the treatment on repeat bloom.

**Use of NAA and Sevin limited to 3 weeks following bloom. Sevin is ineffective on Baldwin and may be inadequate on the heavy setting varieties E. McIntosh, Wealthy and G. Delicious. Sevin will kill mite predators.

***When detergent is used, concentration of NAA should be reduced to one-half the amounts listed.

****Early varieties as Lodi and Y. Transparent should be sprayed within 6 days after full bloom and fall and winter varieties within the 21-day period after full bloom.

Variety: In general, chemical thinning can be used with greater safety and dependability with varieties that tend to set heavy crops. With a moderately heavy bloom, production of a commercial crop usually re-

155

Table 3. Chemical Thinning Program For Apples, Washington State, USA.

Stage	Variety	Material and Amt. Per 100 Gal.	Wetting Agent and Amt. Per 100 Gal.
Full Bloom Period	Delicious and Winesap	⅔ pint Elgetol	None
	Golden Delicious, Jonathan, and Yellow Newtown	⅔ to 1⅓ pints Elgetol	None
7 to 25 Days Past Full Bloom[2]	Golden Delicious	1½ pounds Sevin 50% powder or 17 ppm Amide or 3 ppm NAA	None ⅔ pint spray modifier ⅔ pint spray modifier
	Winesap	½-1 pound Sevin 50% powder or 17 ppm Amide or 2 ppm NAA	None ⅔ pint spray modifier ⅔ pint spray modifier
	Delicious	¼-½ pound Sevin 50% powder[3] or 2 ppm NAA	None ⅔ pint spray modifier
	Jonathan, Rome Beauty and Yellow Newtown	½-1 pound 50% Sevin powder[3] or 3 ppm NAA	None ⅔ pint spray modifier

[1]Concentrations given are regarded as conservative, but may be altered up or down as much as 50 per cent depending upon weather conditions, tree age, vigor, proximity to pollenizers, and method of spray application.

[2]Preferred timings (days following full bloom) for the various chemicals are Amide, 7 to 14 days; NAA and Sevin, 15 to 25 days.

[3]Sevin is extremely hazardous to bees. Be sure to mow, beat down, or use herbicides on blooming cover crops.

quires 20 to 35 apples per 100 blossoming spurs, depending on the variety and conditions under which it is grown. It is generally necessary to remove fruit in excess of the amount desired if satisfactory fruit size and annual bearing habits are to be obtained.

Although there are some exceptions, varieties that are generally classified as hard-to-thin set heavier than those considered easier-to-thin. The former varieties are partially self-fruitful (set fruit with their own pollen) and tend to set heavily even under rather adverse weather conditions. Conversely, varieties considered easy to thin are all self-unfruitful and may or may not set heavily.

In the fruit areas of Washington the partially self-fruitful varieties, such as Golden Delicious, Yellow Newtown, and Rome Beauty, usually set 80 to 100 fruits per 100 blossoming spurs when carrying a heavy bloom. Thus, one can expect a fruit set on these varieties of nearly three times the number considered desirable for a satisfactory crop.

On the other hand, Delicious and Winesap may or may not set heavily, depending on the season and provisions for pollination. If these self-unfruitful varieties are adequately pollinized, they usually set about 50 to 60 fruits per 100 blossoming spurs; this is only about twice the number of fruits required for a commercial crop. Therefore, because of the lighter setting tendencies of these varieties, the margin of safety is less than with the partially self-fruitful varieties mentioned. Consequently, there is more chance of overthinning.

Fruit set on most varieties growing under eastern and midwestern conditions is lighter and generally more erratic. Success with thinning sprays is based on the assumption that fruit set will be in considerable excess of that necessary for a commercial crop of good size and quality. One of the major factors in overthinning is set failure. Certain varieties are more erratic in their setting tendencies than others. Aside from other considerations, postbloom thinners rather than DNOC bloom sprays are best suited for such situations. Careful appraisal of fruit set is therefore vitally important in determining the need for, and the type of, thinning spray best adapted for a given situation.

In some instances, there may be little choice between the different chemicals, but in others a clear-cut preference is indicated. For example, Sevin has generally been the most satisfactory thinning spray on Delicious, Rome Beauty, and Jonathan in all sections of the country. It is also effective on other varieties.

Under certain conditions NAA results in severe flagging and dwarfing of foliage. This condition most frequently occurs on summer varieties. In order to partially avoid leaf injury, it is necessary to apply NAA as late as possible during the postbloom period. When this is done on early apples, premature ripening and splitting of the fruit are likely to occur. Thus, NAA is best suited for fall and winter varieties, but it should be used on these only when Sevin or NAAmide is not effective.

Under certain conditions young fruit suppressed in growth by NAAmide does not absciss. It continues to develop, but final size is greatly reduced. Because of this condition, NAAmide should not be used on the Delicious variety. This condition may also occur on other varieties.

Weather: Weather before and after spraying affects the great variability that often results from thinning sprays. Environment can affect the rate of absorption and action of the spray material and the degree and nature of the fruit set.

One hazard with DNOC is rain following the sprays. Material deposited on the leaves may be rewetted. The resultant additional absorption sometimes seriously injures the foliage and excessively reduces the fruit set.

Factors affecting the absorption of NAA and NAAmide sprays have received considerable attention. Unfavorable weather prior to and after spray applications, such as cool temperatures, excessive humidity or rain-

157

fall, or minimum sunshine, has resulted in heavier thinning with these chemicals.

Environmental factors affecting the action of chemical thinners, especially NAA are similar in many respects. The leaf is the primary organ in absorption of these chemicals. Absorption efficiency is affected in part by the physiological status of the plant and particularly by the cuticle, which is considered a major barrier to absorption. Factors such as humidity affect thickness, composition, and absorption rate through the leaf cuticle.

Sevin has been considerably more consistent than other thinning chemicals. Although the effects of environment have not been so thoroughly studied with Sevin, experiments and extensive observations indicate that weather has no consistent effects on the results obtained. This characteristic of Sevin is probably associated with the difference in mode of entry and site of action of the chemical.

Additives: Several investigators found that adding certain surfactants (wetting agents) to spray mixtures greatly enhanced foliar absorption of growth regulators. When Tween 20 (1 pint per 100 gallons) is added, NAA is suggested at half the usual rate.

This finding suggested that a surfactant might be used with relatively low concentrations of NAA and NAAmide and thereby less variability would result because of environment. However, the addition of a surfactant does not greatly reduce variability as might be expected from controlled experiments. Nevertheless, the inclusion of an additive with hormone-type thinners has become general practice in most apple-growing areas of the United States. The reduced amount of chemical used is a very substantial saving in cost of NAAmide sprays. The additive used is either Tween 20 or Collodial Spray Modifier. The latter material is preferred in the Northwest because it does not foam excessively when agitated in the spray tank.

Tree Vigor: Growth status of the tree affects results with thinning sprays. Over-thinning is less likely with these sprays when trees have normal vigor. Trees are more susceptible to the action of thinning sprays when suffering from the effects of inadequate light when closely planted and lightly pruned, winter injury, "wet feet," low nitrogen level, or any condition that may affect normal growth and fruit-setting processes.

Trees suffering from the effects of any of these conditions may set less fruit. Furthermore, the set may be "weaker" and more easily thinned with spray chemicals. All chemical thinners reduce fruit set more on weak wood lacking in food reserve. Even with normal trees, thinning is heavier on the weak, shaded wood of the lower and inside branches of the tree.

Many observations indicate that when trees have previously cropped heavily, they are usually more easily thinned, even though they have a heavy bloom that sets normally. In such instances, a lower carbohydrate reserve may result in greater thinning by the chemical.

Young trees are more easily thinned than older ones with established bearing habits. Some varieties, including Delicious (5 to 8 years old) that are just beginning to bear, may not set fruit in proportion to the amount of bloom. Even the fruit of varieties that tend to set heavily on young trees is more easily thinned than on older trees. This response of young trees to thinning sprays is perhaps related to their faster vegetative growth and a consequent reduction in carbohydrates available to the young developing fruit in the early postbloom period. Young trees, particularly Golden Delicious, are frequently thinned safely with chemicals, but the spray concentration should be adjusted to approximately one-third to one-half that for older trees of the same variety.

Pollination and Bee Activity: Since successful spray thinning depends on heavy fruit set, weather during bloom is important in determining the adequacy of pollinizers and the number of bees needed to insure a heavy set of fruit.

With favorable weather during bloom, self-unfruitful varieties such as Winesap and Delicious may set heavily at least three tree spaces away from a pollinating variety. Under cool, rainy, or windy conditions, pollination may be poor when these varieties are more than one tree space from a pollinizer. It is more important to evaluate pollinating conditions carefully when using DNOC sprays. With postbloom thinners, however, one can evaluate the degree of fruit set before spraying.

Do not use Sevin at bloom to avoid killing bees, which are needed in pollination, nor in a spray program encouraging mite predators.

Amount of Bloom: Fruit growers often ask how much bloom is required before thinning sprays should be considered. To obtain this information, several tests were conducted in Washington with trees possessing only one-half as much bloom as other trees growing under the same condition. It was found that on trees with lighter bloom, fruit set per 100 blossoming spurs was substantially greater. Also, thinning sprays had less effect in reducing the amount of fruit set. Thus, sprayed trees varying from 50- to 95-percent bloom set about the same amount of fruit per linear unit.

Generally when bloom is light, fruit set is heavy and thinning from chemical sprays is reduced. Obviously, sprays should not be applied to a bloom or fruit set that is not heavy enough to require thinning. However, if an occasional tree with a lightbloom is sprayed, there is little likelihood that appreciable thinning will result.

Number of Spray Applications: One application of a thinning spray on hard-to-thin varieties usually does not thin enough. Also, it may be desirable to apply two sprays to other varieties under conditions conducive to a heavy set. With a two-spray program there should be enough

159

time between the two sprays for the effects of the first one to be evaluated before it becomes necessary to apply the second. In the Northwest it is common practice to apply a DNOC spray during the bloom period and follow 14 to 21 days later with a postbloom thinner if needed. Such procedure provides time to evaluate the effects of the first spray. The chemical used in the second spray is either Sevin or NAAmide.

In the more humid areas of the Midwest and East, DNOC is not generally used because it is erratic. If a two-spray program is desired in those areas, the first, preferably NAAmide, can be applied at petal fall and followed 2 weeks later with Sevin or NAA. This procedure allows for a sufficient interval in which to evaluate the effects of the first spray. When a two-spray program is contemplated, it is highly desirable to have sufficient check trees in order to properly determine the amount of thinning resulting from the first spray.

Defruiting Trees. Defruiting young or dwarf trees (while developing a desired framework), ornamental crabapples, and backyard apple trees often is desired. Application of ethephon (Ethrel) at 250-500 ppm at petal fall will defruit apple trees with no adverse effect on the foliage.

EASY AND DIFFICULT-TO-THIN CONDITIONS

When undecided on a fruit thinning program for a particular orchard block, two questions frequently arise: (a) "Will thinning be necessary?" and (b) "Will the fruit be easy or difficult to thin?" Below is a list of factors to consider.

Easy-to-thin conditions. (1) Fruit spurs on lower and inside branches that are shaded and less vigorous; (2) Trees with inadequate moisture or nitrogen supply; (3) Trees with weak root systems due to freeze damage, trunk girdling, too little or too much water in soil, insect damage, or herbicide injury; (4) Trees, limbs, or spurs in low vigor caused by first three factors; (5) Trees with heavy bloom, especially following previous heavy crops; (6) Young trees with many vigorous upright branches; (7) Self-pollinated and poorly-pollinated varieties; (8) Heavy fruit set on easily thinned varieties such as Red Delicious; (9) Varieties that tend to have a heavy "June drop;" (10) Fruit set in clusters rather than singles; (11) Short bloom periods with many flowers open and susceptible to blossom-thinning sprays; (12) High temperatures accompanied by high humidity before or after spraying that cause stress on foliage and fruits and increases chemical absorption; (13) Frost before or soon after spray application that injures blossoms and young leaves, thus increasing chemical absorption; (14) Prolonged cool periods before spraying that pre-condition the foliage for increased chemical absorption;

(15) Prolonged cloudy periods before application of chemicals that reduce photosynthesis.

Difficult-to-thin conditions. (1) Trees in good vigor with 12 to 18 inches of terminal growth per year; (2) Light bloom or light fruit set after a heavy bloom; (3) Cross-pollinated varieties with adequate insect activity in orchard; (4) Older trees with a mature bearing habit; (5) Fruit on spurs in well-lighted areas of tree (tops and outer periphery); (6) Horizontal fruiting branches; (7) Slight girdling of limbs and spurs following moderate winter injury; (8) Trees in biennial bearing habit with no crop in previous year; (9) Fruit set in singles rather than clusters; (10) Heavy setting varieties such as Golden Delicious; (11) Warm, sunny weather ideal for good growth prior to and after time of thinning; (12) Decreased chemical absorption resulting from low humidity before and after spraying that causes rapid drying of the spray.

Review Questions

1. Define fruit thinning.
2. List 7 advantages of thinning fruit.
3. What appears to be the best time for thinning annual bearing trees of fall or winter varieties?
4. What are the advantages of thinning blossoms with certain chemical sprays as compared with hand thinning fruit after the June drop? What are the disadvantages of these chemical sprays at blossoming?
5. How should thinning, nitrogen fertilization, and pruning be interrelated to attain the best size and quality of fruit?
6. Discuss briefly the reasons for so much variability in results with chemical hormone-type thinning sprays on apples.

Suggested Collateral Readings

Batjer, L. P. Fruit thinning with chemicals. Agr. Inf. Bull. 289. ARS, USDA, 27 pp. 1965.
Batjer, L. P. and H. D. Billingsley. Apple thinning with chemical sprays. Wash. Agr. Exp. Sta. Bull. 651. 24 pp. 1964. (Good bibliography included.)
Bukovac, M. J. Seedless apples with gibberellins. Bot. Gaz. 124:3. 1963.
Bukovac, M. J. Gibberellin - induced asymmetric apple fruits. HortScience 3:3. 1968.
Chemical thinning of apples. Exten. Folder F-177. Mich. State Coll. Ask for latest. Also, Univ. of Mass. Spec. Cir. No. 189 4 pp. March 1958. Write your state university for latest local recommendations.
Donoho, C. W. Jr. NAA spray date and fruit size relation to thinning effectiveness. ASHS 92:55-62. 1968.
Donoho, Clive W. Jr. Translocation and breakdown of $C^{14}NAA$ in apple. 16th Intern. Hort. Cong. Belgium. 1962.
Forshey, C. G. and M. B. Hoffman. Factors affecting chemical thinning of apples. N. Y. Res. Cir. Ser. No. 4. 12 pp. (Cornell) 1967.
Forshey, C. G. Interaction of Alar and fruit thinning sprays. N. Y. Food and Life Sci. (Geneva) Apr.-Sept. 1971. Also, Alar on vigorous McIntosh trees. Jr. ASHS 95:64-67. 1970.
Growth regulators in fruit production. A Symposium. September 1972 at Long Ashton Research Station, Bristol, England. Request proceedings directly.
Haeseler, C. W. *et al.* Agr. Recom. for Penna. fruit crops. Request recent ed.

(See additional references under Chapter VII, Appendix)

CHAPTER VIII

Grafting and Budding Trees

◆ ◆

Every fruit grower should develop a technique in grafting. Sooner or later he may desire or be forced to change some trees in the orchard to another variety. There are several reasons a change may be needed:

1. The market demand for certain varieties may shift, leaving the grower with an orchard of fruit that cannot be sold at a reasonable profit.

2. With dwarfing stocks being used increasingly over the World, a knowledge and training in double-working, budding and grafting these trees is essential.

3. The varieties planted may not cross-pollinate properly. Other varieties with effective pollen must be grafted on scattered trees.

4. Although trees may have been inspected in the nursery for trueness to name, it is not uncommon for jobbers and dealers to lose and jumble the labels on bundled trees; hence, undesired varieties may be planted which will need to be grafted to another variety later.

5. The grower, himself, may make a mistake and order varieties which later prove undesirable.

A knowledge of grafting technique may be needed, also, for repairing bark damage which is not uncommon in most orchards. Bark damage may be caused by freezing temperature, cultivating tools, canker diseases, or by mice and rabbits chewing away the bark.

The meaning of frequently used grafting terms should be understood clearly at the outset in order to make later reading clear.

Stock is the root, tree, or portion of a tree into which the graft is set.

Cion (also scion) is the bud or piece of a twig which is grafted into the stock. From it grows a branch or an entire tree-top which bears the desired variety of fruit.

---

[1]Dr. Frank N. Heweston, Penn. State Univ., and Paul Stark Jr., Stark Nurseries and Orchard Co., Louisiana, Mo., assisted in revision of this chapter.

Interstock or intermediate stock is a piece of trunk or lower framework of a tree introduced between the stock below and the cion variety above. It is used in this position because it is considered more desirable than the cion variety from the standpoint of vigor, hardiness, framework form, disease resistance, and for dwarfing.

Cambium layer is a single layer of living cells which lies between the bark and the sapwood. It is constantly dividing during the growing season, forming new cells; cells produced on the inside from sapwood and those on the outside from the inner bark. The cambium is responsible for increase in diameter of all tree growth and for most callus formation. It is the most essential tissue, and its preservation is highly important for continued growth. If bark is peeled back in spring, the slippery pastelike substance on the sapwood and bark consists largely of cambium-like cells which make up the cambium region.

Bud stick is growth made during the current season at the ends of branches from which buds are removed for bud grafting. From each bud may grow a branch or an entire treetop of the desired variety.

Top-working is a form of grafting by which the top of a tree is changed from one cion variety to another.

Double-working is a form of grafting in which an interstock is introduced between the root and the top by successive budding or grafting operations. Hence, double-worked trees consist of stock, interstock, and cion variety, each of which has special characteristics which make for a better and longer-lived tree.

Triple-Worked trees consist of a rootstock, a hardy interstock, and dwarfing interstock, and then the cion variety. Robusta 5, McIntosh, Haralson, Alnap 2, Hibernal, EM VIII, IX, and 26 can be used as hardy or dwarfing interstocks, 4 to 12 inches long, the longer interstems having the greater desired effect on the cion. Dr. R. F. Carlson of Michigan State University has found greater gibberellin activity in dwarf than standard tree tissues, helping to explain the precocity of dwarfed trees.

Interstem grafting may be accomplished by bench or whip grafting. A 6- to 8-inch scion of the dwarfing stock is grafted to a one-year seedling. The grafted stock is then lined out in the nursery row in early spring. In mid-summer, the desired apple cultivar (variety) is budded onto the scion at least 5 to 6 inches above the previous graft union. This method requires two years to produce a tree suitable for planting.

In another technique, buds from the dwarfing stock are inserted in the seedling or rooted clonal rootstock while it is growing in the nursery row, at the most suitable time in mid-summer. In mid-summer of the following year, the desired cultivar (cion variety) is then budded onto the resulting whip growing from the inserted dwarf stock bud. The cultivar bud is inserted 5 to 6 inches above the previous bud union. This technique requires three growing seasons to produce a plantable tree. This disadvantage, however, may be out-weighed when large numbers of trees are propagated, since less scion wood is needed.

Bridge-grafting is a form of grafting where damaged bark is bridged with wood which is grafted into the tree above and below the injury.

SHOULD YOU GRAFT?

In the long run, is it cheaper to replace the tree or to perform the grafting operations? After surveying many top-worked bearing trees in Michigan, investigators found that there were as many failures or near failures as successes. The same is often true of trees completely or excessively girdled where numerous long cions will be needed. Usually, the younger and more vigorous the tree, the better will be the chance for successful recovery without seriously delaying the bearing life of the tree. Young trees of diameters less than two inches make excellent recovery if cut off below the girdled area and (*a*)cleft-grafted, or (*b*) allowed to send up a new trunk, provided it arises from wood of the named variety.

It usually takes from three to five years for a mature tree to recover to normal and expected production after a major grafting operation. If a tree has been girdled for a full growing season or more, its chances for satisfactory recovery after bridge-grafting are slim. Certainly, trees which have been completely top-worked never catch up with the total lapsed production that a bearing tree would have given if its limbs had not been cut back for grafting. The question might be asked, "Will the new variety after five or so years give more net profit and satisfaction to the owner than could the old variety; and with girdled trees, is the injured tree worth the repair cost?" Although bridge-grafting is relatively time consuming, when balanced against the actual future value of a good tree, the cost is generally small. With girdled trees, it is always well to examine carefully the depth of injury to the bark. If the sapwood is not exposed, the cambium is probably still alive, and painting with water asphalt emulsion (roof paint with no creosote or similar ingredients), or mounding with soil will often suffice until the bark heals and thickens.

WHEN TO GRAFT

The best time for most grafting is when the buds are beginning to swell in the spring. Where it is necessary to split the wood before inserting the cion, as in cleft-grafting, this work should be done just before the bark begins to slip. If the bark is slipping readily, the wood may split along one line and the bark along another, making proper placement of the cion difficult. Cleft- and whip-grafting can be performed with dormant cion wood while the stock is dormant and as late as blossoming or later, but the latter is considered late for best results. Under Ohio conditions, the highest percentage of successful grafts were made experimentally in May, although grafts made in April, June, and July were almost as successful. Cions for the late grafting were kept dormant in cold storage until ready for use. Bridge-grafting can be done best after growth starts when the bark is slipping readily. It is difficult to bridge-graft early before the bark slips.

SELECTION AND STORAGE OF CION WOOD

Sometime during the dormant season, the grower should make a row by row inspection of his trees to record the location, variety, and amount of grafting needed. Thence, the necessary cion wood can be collected during the pruning operation. Some growers consider it a wise practice to store cion wood regularly each year for emergency jobs discovered after growth starts in spring.

Cion wood should consist of shoot growth made during the previous season. This can be distinguished easily by starting at the tip of the branch and proceeding backward to the first ring of bud scale scars which encircles the twig. This ring denotes the point where growth started the previous season; also, older wood back of it is of a different shade in color. The percentage of success with cion wood older than one year is usually low. Good cion wood has the following qualifications: (a) growth of one to two feet during the previous season; (b) about as thick as a lead pencil (water sprouts are satisfactory, but tips should be rejected because of immaturity; water sprouts usually remain dormant longer in spring); (c) having large plump mature buds devoid of insect eggs and disease injury; (d) no discoloration of pith due to cold injury; and (e) absolutely dormant.

If a cion stick is divided into four parts, the center two parts are the best for grafting because the buds in this area are large and healthy and the wood is well supplied with stored food. The tip buds are often immature, winter injured, or may have flower buds while buds near the base of the cion are small and weak.

Proper storage of cion wood is extremely important. It must be kept continually cool and moist, but not wet. This can be done by wrapping the cions in cloth or heavy paper and burying them horizontally two feet deep in a well-drained spot, preferably on the north side of a building. Cion wood can be kept in common or cold storages in damp sawdust or peat moss, but it should be examined frequently and redampened if necessary. If cion wood dries or becomes too wet, its chances for growth are poor.

If the cion wood has been exhausted during grafting and more is needed, sometimes it is possible to obtain additional wood from dormant nursery trees in storage or from nearby nursery houses. Also, water sprouts in mature trees or shoots from young trees in the orchard may be a source since they start growth several days after the outer wood on mature trees. The farther the buds have pushed on prospective cion wood in the spring, the less likely such wood will succeed in a graft. Cion wood with swollen

165

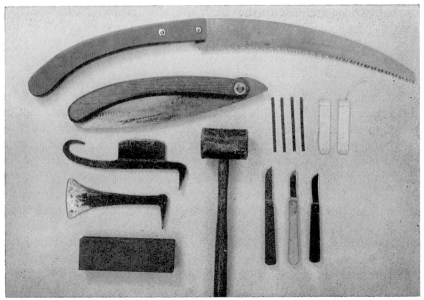

W. P. Duruz, Oregon Agr. Exp. Sta.

Figure 1. Tools for orchard grafting are shown above. Two types of saws (workers may prefer saws with finer teeth); two types of steel grafting wedges; a coarse-fine whetstone; wood mallet: rubber strips (or nurseryman's tape or shields may be used); variety labels; one grafting knife; and two budding knives are shown.

buds should be used only in a limited way in exceptional cases and then covered with asphalt emulsion and shaded with paper bags.

GRAFTING SUPPLIES AND EQUIPMENT

Equipment needed for orchard grafting is shown in Figure 1. Most of the tools can be purchased from the local hardware stores or nursery supply companies.[1] A rubber hammer can be used in place of a mallet. Rubber strips or plastic shields are superior to raffia because they maintain an even pressure, expanding with the growth of the stock. A modified carpenter's apron is convenient for holding the equipment and cions while grafting.

Asphalt emulsion paint (roofing paint) is largely used today. It is applied cold by brush and stored at a temperature above 40°F. The ideal grafting paint should have the following qualifications: (a) exclude air and fungi and retain moisture in the wood; (b) is not toxic to tender tissue; (c) does not crack in cold weather; (d) does not melt in hot weather; (e) semipermanent; (f) is somewhat elastic to accommodate differences in growth rate of stock and cion; (g) has sufficient body during application

---

[1]Companies include: A. M. Leonard and Son, Piqua, Ohio; Bartlett Manufacturing Co., 3044 E. Grand Blvd., Detroit, Mich. 48202; Diston Div., H. K. Porter Co., 701 Grant St., Pittsburgh, Pa., 15219; Seymour Smith and Son, Inc., Oakville, Conn. 06799. See July issues, Amer. Fruit Grower Mag., Tyson Orchard Service, Flora Dale, Pa. 17307.

Figure 2. Using a motor-driven chain saw, the main limbs of this 25-year apple tree were cut back and topworked to a more marketable variety two seasons previous to this photo by bark grafting large limbs, whip grafting a few well-placed suckers, and cleft grafting the small limbs. The cion variety should have about the same inherent vigor as stock (see p. 168). A fair crop was borne the third year and almost a full crop by the fifth year. Bark grafting is best on 45° angle to upright limbs; horizontal limbs give upright easily breakable cion growth (C. left, right). Note left graft in "b"; it is best to cut horizontal limb back to an upright limb for topworking: Note pruning technique in "d" to encourage desirable framework limbs and dwarf or remove others as top of stock is healed over completely. (Ernest G. Christ, Rutgers University)

to fill cracks; (h) relatively cheap; and (i) easy to handle. It is important that asphalt emulsion *not* contain creosote or similar materials toxic to plant tissues.

TOP-WORKING

As indicated earlier, the primary reason for top-working a tree is to change the variety. For the change to be successful, (a) the graft union between stock and cion must be sound, (b) big limbs must not be exposed to sunscald during the process, (c) the new variety must be compatible with the stock, and (d) the limbs to be grafted must be selected carefully.

Limbs selected properly for top-working on a mature apple tree can be (a) up to six to eight inches in diameter, (b) not shaded or exposed at right angles to sunlight, pointing upward at 45° angle or better rather than level or downward, and (c) located in a prominent position and well spaced around the tree (grafting insignificant limbs is a waste of labor and materials). The limbs should be grafted relatively low or back into the tree. (Figure 2).

Top-working of trees older than 20 years has been done successfully, as shown in Figure 2. These trees were in good bearing within 4 to 5 years. A part of a block can be done each year over a three to five-year period to maintain sales income from the block.

Special care should be taken to avoid unduly exposing large limbs to sunscald which may lead to injury by flat-headed borers and subsequent entrance of wood-destroying fungi. Danger from sunscald can be reduced by lime-spraying the limbs and leaving water sprouts for shade until about the end of the second year. Fire blight sprays may be needed if the cion variety is susceptible. A lime mixture for painting limbs can be prepared as follows: 10 lbs whiting lime (from paint stores; a carbonate form) or hydrated lime; 5 oz. soya bean flour (or caseine glue); 1 oz. salt; in 5 gallons of water. Exposed stubs and scaffolds usually escape sunscald when they run more or less parallel to the hottest rays of the sun between two and three o'clock in the afternoon.

It is best for the novice to spread top-working over a two-year period. It is true. however, that experienced grafters can spot-graft in key positions the first year so that no additional grafting is necessary. Subsequent pruning in such a case should encourage the grafted limbs to assume the main framework of the tree, while the ungrafted limbs are pruned heavily, dwarfed, and eventually removed.

Apple varieties in general can be intergrafted successfully with each other, but it is wise to use varieties of about equal inherent vigor. For example, a vigorous growing variety may be top-worked best on an equally vigorous variety, as McIntosh on Baldwin. The following varieties and their strains are listed according to inherent vigor:

VIGOROUS

Arkansas	Gravenstein	Red Astrachan	York Imperial
(Black Twig)	Hibernal	Red June	Roter Boskoop
Baldwin	Hubbardston	R. I. Greening	Ayvanya
Benoni	Lowland Rasb.	Stark	Baucroft
B. Gilliflower	Maiden Blush	Tolman Sweet	Boskoop
Boiken	Granny Smith	Tompkins King	E. Spitzenburg
Cortland	McIntosh	Twenty Ounce	Landsberger Rette
Delicious	Northern Spy	Winter Banana	Bramley's Seed.
Fallawater	N. W. Greening	Wolf River	
Fameuse	Pewaukee	Y. Bellflower	

MEDIUM VIGOR

Ben Davis	King David	Roxbury Russet	Ralls
Chenango	Sturmer	Stayman	Cox's Orange
Duchess	Glockenapfel	Winesap	James Grieve
E. Strawberry	Mann	Y. Newtown	Ingrid Marie
G. Delicious	Opalescent	Y. Transparent	Antanovka
Grimes	Ortley	Goldparmäne	
Jonathan	Red Canada	Kidds Orange Red	

RELATIVELY SMALL

Mother	Spur Strains	Wealthy	Ontario
Rome Beauty	Wagener	Williams	

168

Cleft-grafting. The cleft-graft is made by inserting a cion into the split stock, as shown in Figure 3. Limbs selected for cleft-grafting should have the following qualifications: (a) from one to two i n c h e s in diameter; limbs smaller than one inch in diameter should be wrapped firmly with string or tape for a few weeks to assure a strong union, (b) wood six inches below the cross cut must be straight-grained and free from large knots or scars, (c) accessible from the ground if possible, and (d) more or less upright; cions in horizontal stubs "take" poorly or to grow upward at right angles, forming an undesirable scaffold limb.

The cut across the stock should be square, not sloping. Fine-toothed s a w s make a smoother cut and expose the cambium zone better. Short cions with two or three buds

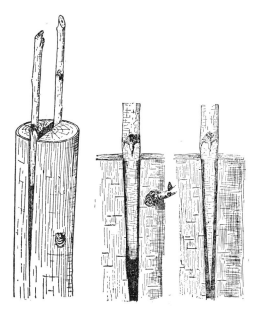

H. A. Cardinell, Michigan Agr. Exp. Sta.

Figure 3. (Left) Here is a cleft-graft complete except for asphalt. Note position of the cion buds, number of buds, and the type of cuts. Split in stock was made with grafting chisel and then held open by a wedge on back of chisel. (Middle) The cion is correctly made and placed. Note the blunt end and close contact of cambiums of stock and cion. (Right) This shows the cion improperly cut; it should not be beveled to a point; cambium contact is poor and cions may rock with the wind.

are less likely to be knocked out by birds or wind as compared with the longer cions. Cions the size of a lead pencil with plump vigorous buds contain adequate food materials and water. Discard terminal portions of cion shoots because they may contain flower buds. Prepare the base of the cion with two sloping cuts, starting at or slightly below the level of the lowest buds (Figure 3). This appears to be of value because the food stored around the bud is greater than between buds and, therefore, is thought to enhance union quickly enough to preserve the cion until internodal cion bark slowly unites. Do not bring the wedge to a point. The inside of the wedge should be thinner than the outside. This insures closer contact of the cambiums of the stock and cion. The top of the cion should be cut about one-quarter inch above a bud to reduce likelihood of the bud dying. Cion cuts should be straight and smooth with no wave. After a little experience, one stroke with a sharp knife makes the best bevel.

The stock stub is split across the center, using a chisel and a mallet. A four- to six-inch split is adequate. The split is held open by the wedge on the back of the chisel, or with a screw driver. Two cions are inserted care-

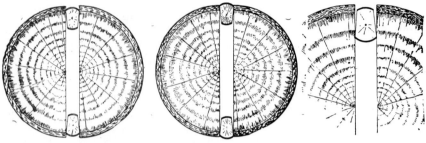

H. A. Cardinell, Michigan Exp. Sta.

Figure 4. Reasons why some grafts fail. (Left) Cleft-graft properly made and properly set with cambiums of stock and cions in perfect contact. (Middle) This shows the failure of cambium contact between stock and cion; the cions are set out too far toward the outside of the stock. (Right) This shows the failure of cambium contact because of undue thickness of inner side of cion.

fully, making sure that the cambium of the cion and the cambium of the stock come in close contact. One must bear in mind that the thickness of the bark is much greater on the stock than on the cion (Figure 4). Buds must be upright. Contact of the cambiums at the top of the stock is most important, and further contacts below should be as continuous as possible. Tilting the cion outward is dangerous because the two cambiums may cross at a point where the cion bevel waves inward, preventing contact. The top of the cion bevels should be flush with the top of the stock. If the split in the stock is accidentally made deep and the cions are held loosely, tie a strip of plastic tape string-enforced around the stock and leave it for about three months, after which it must be cut loose but not removed.

All cut surfaces should be carefully sealed with asphalt paint. Check each graft before leaving to be sure there are no pinholes left unsealed. Holes in the paint permit moisture to escape, resulting in drying of tissues and poor or no "take." Seal the split in the stock also with asphalt paint.

Over 90 per cent of the cions should take if the job has been done carefully. Common causes for failure in cleft-grafts are (a) failure to obtain proper cambial contact because of uneven bevel edges on the cion, (b) imperfect painting, (c) lack of dormancy in cion, (d) cion too thin and weak, and (e) fire blight bacteria which may infect the union.

The cleft-graft shown in Figure 5 shows an excellent "take" three months after grafting.

Bark-grafting. Bark-grafting can be understood by studying Figure 6. Although cions may be more easily blown out by wind, it is preferred by some operators to the cleft-graft because it is not necessary to split the stub and it can be used on stubs too large for cleft-grafting. Success is better with pears than apples and cherries. The job can be speeded up by making one lengthwise split in the bark, lifting it, slipping the beveled cion under, wrapping in place with a band, and asphalting.

Modified Kerf graft. This graft is useful where cion wood is small or

170

where stocks are too large for whip-grafting but too small for cleft-grafting. It is suited for top-working cherry and plum. Use a curved knife. See Figure 7.

SUBSEQUENT CARE OF GRAFTS

Careful attention to the grafts for a few years afterward is highly important for two reasons: (a) the prevention of invasion by wood-rotting fungi, and (b) to encourage correct framework development of the new top. Where two or more cions have been set in a cleft- or a bark-graft, the one making the best shoot growth should be encouraged and pruned as little as possible. The others should be nipped back over a two-year period, beginning the second year. When the stock wound has healed over, the subordinated cions are removed entirely. Presence of these subordinate cions is highly important in healing over the stump. If one cion should die, a nearby water sprout may be encouraged for a-while as the "subordinate" cion.

G. C. Pace, U.S.D.A.

Figure 5. A vigorous three-month growth of cions in a cleft-graft. Note temporary retention of nurse shoots close to the cions, and the excellent sealing of the union with wax.

Grafts should be checked periodically to repaint areas which have cracked and exposed the tissue. Asphalt, however, is pliable and is a big improvement over the old waxing materials. Sunscald on a heavily cut-back tree, as the one in Figure 2, is generally not a problem because sucker growth quickly appears over these limbs. Periodic thinning and eventual removal of most suckers is a necessary followup job.

All cions on a cleft- or bark-graft should be allowed to grow the first year. If the desired cion is growing very vigorously the second year, four to six inches of the tip should be removed about July 1 in order to induce branching if this is desirable in forming the framework of the tree. If there is likelihood of sunscald on the larger limbs, some water sprouts should be encouraged for temporary shade, then nipped and later removed.

Inlay-grafting. Inlay-grafting is a method for top-working large trees where it is difficult or impractical to cleft-graft stubs larger than two inches

171

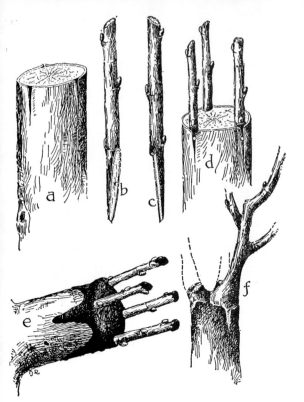

in diameter, and where growth is desired on large bare limbs.

C i o n s somewhat thicker than a lead pencil are the best for inlay-grafting purposes. The cions may be two to six inches long, including one or more buds. A one- to two-inch bevel to the pith is made at the base of the cion, with or without a shoulder (Figure 6). The stock is cut back with a motor-driven chain saw (p. 70). Actually, the cuts in Figure 2 could be made somewhat closer to the crotches. The stock is prepared for the cion by cutting one slit (if bark is thin) or two parallel slits the width of the cion (if the stock is large and the bark thick). The beveled cion is positioned under the bark and nailed with a brad. The cions are spaced an inch-and-a-half to two inches apart around the stock and painted thoroughly with asphalt. Spurs will form the second year, bloom the third. Some crop should be harvested the third year and a full crop by the fifth or sixth year. An entire block of trees can be topworked by spreading the job over a four- to six-year period.

These cions should be placed within two or three feet of the main crotch and on scaffold limbs approaching a 45° angle; almost vertical limbs are unsatisfactory. The cions should be placed somewhat on the sides of the scaffold limbs, and not on top, for best results.

After shoots from these grafts have grown two or three years, the best can be selected for permanent scaffold limbs. The top of the tree over a period of from four to six years or more can be gradually opened to admit more light and room to these new limbs, while the old unneeded limbs are gradually pruned away and eventually removed.

The tongue- or whip-graft. The tongue- or whip-graft is suited to top-working young trees in the orchard where the stock and cion are small and about the same size. It is also used for bench-grafting indoors in winter where the cion and/or interstock (double-worked) and clonal or seedling roots are grafted together, wrapped with string, stored in moist peat moss, and set in the field, as described in Chapter III. The method of match-

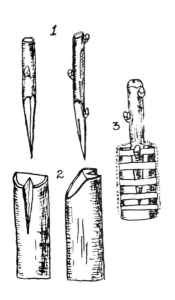

(Left) Karl D. Brase, New York Exp. Sta., Geneva
(Right) Better Fruit Magazine, Portland, Oregon

Figure 7. (Left) Steps in making a modified kerf graft. (1) Cion wedged triangularly by two equal cuts. (2) Triangular groove made in stock by two cuts the same size and angle as those on the cion. (3) Cion placed in groove and held in place by grafting tape or rubber bands; cut surfaces waxed. (Right) Topworking by cleft-graft on a young tree. Note training of leaders and side branches.

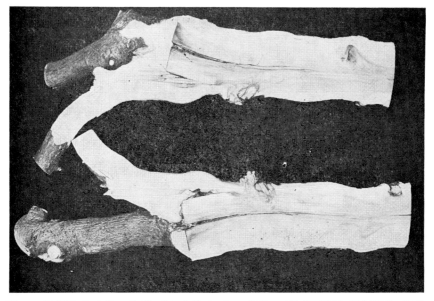

Figure 8. This is a longitudinal cut through a cleft graft (center) and bark graft (on side) after three seasons of growth. Bark grafts are satisfactory and are quicker and easier, particularly on large stocks. (Ernest G. Christ, Rutgers University).

173

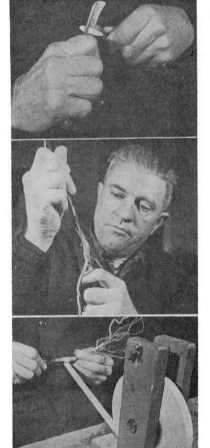

ing the stock and cion (with two to four plump buds) is shown in Figure 9. The uniformly sloping bevels are from one to one and one-half inches long. On both stock and cion, a slit is made halfway between the pith and the end or toe of the cut. The two are then slipped together as indicated. If the cion is smaller than the stock, union of the cambium should be provided on only one side. If the ends, or toes, of the stock and cions should hang over, these must be trimmed flush. In the orchard, the graft is then wrapped with rubber bands or nurserymen's tape. Exposed areas are then covered thoroughly with asphalt emulsion paint. A young apple tree top-worked in this manner is shown in Ohio in Figure 10. Whip-grafting can be done from the time before the bark slips to afterbloom, provided the cion wood is dormant.

Beginners may not be successful with this graft because of: (a) failure to make the sloping cut long enough, (b) uneven bevels arising from a dull knife or other causes, (c) improper placing of the slit, and (d) failure to press the tongues together deeply enough.

Figure 9. In whip-grafting (upper) diagonal bevel cuts are made in both the cion and stock, then (middle) joined or "meshed" together with cambium layers in contact on at least one side and (bottom) taped or wrapped with rubber strips. (Paul Stark, Jr., Stark Nurseries and Orchard Co., Louisiana, Mo.)

It requires about a month after growth starts for the union to take place, after which the rubber strips or string should be cut to prevent ringing. At this time select the best shoot from the cion, remove the others, and begin to train the tree properly as described in the pruning Chapter IV.

Budding. Budding is a form of grafting in which a bud is used as the cion rather than a section of the stem. Budding is used mostly on trees in the nursery. It also can be used in the orchard on young apple trees like the one shown in Figure 10, but whip-grafting may put you a season ahead. It is used for top-working peaches, plums, and cherries in the field because

174

gumming is not excessive and splitting of the wood is not necessary.[1]

Budding is done in late summer or early fall. Buds are selected from the middle portion of vigorous current-season growth. These growths are called "bud sticks." The leaves are trimmed off, leaving three-fourths inch of the petiole or stem attached for a handle in manipulating the bud later (Figure 11). The bud sticks are wrapped in moist burlap to prevent drying during the budding operations. Buds are more successful when inserted on the upper side and at the base of one-year wood where the bark is relatively thin. If the stock is one to three inches thick, as with peaches, a one-year side shoot is selected for budding, after which the stock is cut back the following spring just above the side shoot, and flush with it.

Using a special budding knife (Figure 1) a "T-cut" is made as described in Figure 11. The bud is removed from the bud stick by making a concave cut starting one inch below the bud. A transverse cut is made about one-fourth inch above the bud to remove it. After the bud has been inserted *upright* into the opened cut, it is snugly wrapped with a rubber band, taking care to leave the bud exposed. Ends of the rubber strips can be held in place by putting the free end back under the last turn. No asphalt emulsion paint is necessary.

C. W. Ellenwood, Ohio Agr. Exp. Sta.

Figure 10. Whip-grafting can be used to convert young trees to a more marketable variety, or, to topwork a hardy frame-work interstock such as McIntosh on seedling roots to a spur ' and/or standard Red Delicious top.

If the graft is successful, the bud should grow to the stock within about two to three weeks, after which the rubber band will begin to loosen, deteriorate, and drop. The graft was successful if the bud is plump; if shriveled, it will be necessary to rebud. The next spring before growth starts, the stock should be removed about one-half inch above the bud in order to

---

[1] See reference by Blake, Edgerton and Schneider for stub-grafting as an alternative for other methods of top-working. N. J. Agr. Exp. Sta. Cir. 507. 1947.

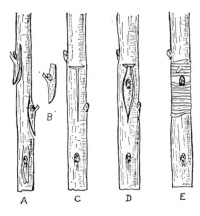

Figure 11. Budding. (A) prepared bud stick; (B) bud removed; (C) T-shaped incision in stock; (D) bud inserted; (E) bud tied with rubber strip. (R. F. Carlson, Mich. State Univ.)

force the bud into early growth. Shoots arising below the bud during the next season must be removed periodically.

REPAIR-GRAFTING

Bark repair may be necessary on the trunk or base of the main limbs as a result of injury from mice, rabbits, winter freezing, cultivating tools, or disease cankers. Repairs must be done the spring after the injury occurred for best results. Large injuries which more than halfway girdle the tree and which have gone for more than one growing season may weaken the tree seriously and take it several years to recover, if such recovery is possible.

If the bark has been removed by rodents during the winter, especially on very young trees, an application of asphalt emulsion covering exposed areas should be made immediately to prevent excessive drying until a bridge-graft can be made.

Cions for repair work should be selected from hardy disease-resistant varieties, such as Duchess, Fameuse, Northwestern Greening, Robusta 5, McIntosh, Hibernal, and the Cortland. Undesirable varieties are Baldwin, Delicious, Golden Delicious, Gravenstein, Grimes Golden, Northern Spy, Rhode Island Greening, Rome Beauty, Stayman Winesap, Winesap, and York Imperial.

Bridge-grafting. Bridge-grafting is used to bridge over a bark area where the cambium is exposed or dead (Figure 12). On relatively young trees which have been completely girdled, the best procedure may be to cut them off at the girdle, causing shoots to appear, preferably above the nursery graft on the seedling root. If shoots arise from the seedling root, it will be necessary to whip-graft or bud them to the desired variety, or, the stump may be cleft-grafted provided it is strong enough to hold the cion. Cleft-grafting these small stumps may be preferable to bridge-grafting.

Bridge-grafting should be preformed when the bark is slipping readily, which is about the time buds are unfolding. Emergency bridge-grafting can be done in the summer, but careful selection of cion wood held over in storage is necessary.

The area to be bridged should be cleaned with a knife or a special bark scraper and painted with asphalt emulsion, preferably a day in advance of grafting to prevent the sapwood from drying and to facilitate the grafting job.

Cion wood for bridge-grafting can vary in size from that of a lead pencil to one-half inch in diameter, the large and longer cions being used on larger

176

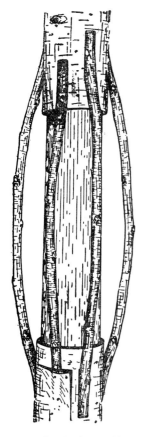

G. E. Yerkes, U.S.D.A.

Figure 12. A bridge-graft over mouse injury which extends out on the roots. Asphalt emulsion is valuable for covering remaining exposed areas, after which soil will be replaced.

H. A. Cardinell, Michigan Exp. Sta.

Figure 13. Bridge-graft showing three methods of setting cions. Cion set under flap at bottom is beveled on two sides. This method is timesaving on stocks with relatively thin bark. A bow in cions is important on young trees which sway with the wind. Cions are placed one to two inches apart around the trunk.

wounds. The cion should be cut at least four inches longer than the area to be bridged. Long cions are easier to manipulate than short cions. Therefore, if the area to be bridged is narrow, it may be better to inlay-graft the ends of the cion several inches above and below the injured area, using a long cion. The method of preparing the cion and nailing them in place is shown in Figure 13. The lower two- to three-inch bevel is prepared first, set in a slot or under a flap, and nailed. The upper bevel is than cut and placed against the stock and outlined with the knife, thence removing the bark slot. With young trees a small stick is placed between the center of the cion and the stock in order to give the cion a bow and prevent it from being pulled out as the tree sways with the wind. One must be careful to have all buds facing upward. Inverted cions have been noted growing in many cases, but the vigor and percentage "take" are lower. All exposed areas should be covered thoroughly with asphalt emulsion paint. After the bridge-graft has been made, it should be protected from future rodent injury by precautions of spray-repellent Thiram or wrap-around wire cloth (Chap. IV). No protection is necessary if the bridged area is above the reach of mice and rabbits. Remove water sprouts arising on and near the cions at frequent intervals the following seasons.

177

H. A. Cardinell, Michigan Exp. Sta.

Figure 14. (Left) A 6-year bridge-graft used for repairing fire blight damage on a mature apple tree. (Right) Inarching or approach-grafting may be used to repair pine-mouse injury to roots, or to increase the root system under shallow soil conditions, or for similar reasons. Four seedling apple trees have been planted at the base of the tree and inlay-grafted into the trunk. Grafts are 4 years old.

The approach-graft. Approach-grafts are shown in Figure 14. One or more nursery trees, from one to two years old, are planted at the base of the tree. Tops of the trees are inlay-grafted into the trunk similar to the contact made in case of the upper end of the cion in bridge-grafting. This type of grafting is useful where the mature tree has received a bark or canker injury a few years previously, and grafting has been neglected. Many of the roots may have died and the limbs in line above the injury may have become weakened. Some growers have practiced approach-grafting on trees growing on shallow soil in order to increase the amount of root system, but experimental data to confirm this practice are lacking. It is important to remove all suckers and side branches appearing on the seedling trees or the trunk of the mature tree until the young trees are well established.

Contract Budding. Fruit growers frequently contract with a reputable nursery a year or so before planting to guarantee getting desired varieties, stock, or interstocks for a specific planting date. This is good practice.

Review Questions

1. Give at least 5 reasons why a knowledge of grafting is essential in orcharding.
2. Give the qualifications of good cion wood.

178

3. When is cion wood selected and how should it be stored until used?
4. What is the cambium and where is it located?
5. List the essential equipment needed in a grafting outfit.
6. Draw a diagram to show proper insertion of a cion in cleft-grafting.
7. Why is the inserted bevel in the cleft-graft wider on one side than the other?
8. If the cion is smaller than the stock in whip-grafting, what procedure is generally followed?
9. List and discuss tools and materials used in all types of grafting.
10. What is a "bud stick?"
11. Why are grafts painted with asphalt emulsion?
12. On mature topworked apple trees what happens if there is a different inherent vigor in stock and cion?
13. For what age apple trees are the following methods of grafting best adapted?
    (1) cleft-graft   (4) whip-graft
    (2) bark-graft   (5) budding
    (3) bridge-graft   (6) kerf-graft
14. What periods of the year are best to perform grafting methods given in question 13?
15. Briefly discuss subsequent care of a (a) cleft-graft, and (b) bridge-graft.
16. Are roots ever bridge-grafted?

Suggested Collateral Readings

Banta, E. D. Fruit tree propagation. Ohio Ext. Serv. Bull. 481. 31 pp. 1967.

Brase, Karl D. Propagating fruit trees. N. Y. Agr. Exp. Sta. Bull. 773. 1956.

Brown, Gordon. A method for top-working pear trees for early maximum production and for reducing stony pit losses. Oreg. Agr. Exp. Sta. Bull. 1946.

Cation, Donald and R. F. Carlson. Determination of virus entities in an apple scion/rootstock test orchard. Rpt. I and II. Mich. Qtrly. Bull. 43-2. 435-443, Nov. 1960; 45:17. 159-166. Aug. 1962.

Doran, W. L. Propagation of woody plants by cuttings. Mass. Agr. Exp. Sta. Bull. 491. 99 pp. 1957.

Duruz, W. P. Grafting and budding contests. Ore. State College Ext. Bull. 530. 1939.

Gardner, V. R., F. C. Bradford, and H. D. Hooker. The reciprocal influences of stock and cion. Chapter XXXI, Fundamentals of Fruit Production, McGraw-Hill Book Co., Inc., New York, 1952.

Garner, R. J. The grafter's handbook, Faber and Faber, Ltd., 24 Russell Square, London. 260 pp. 1958.

Graham, B. F. Jr. and F. H. Borman, Natural roof grafts. Bot. Rev. 32: 3, 255-292. 1966.

Graham, C. D. and W. A. Goodfellow. Orchard grafting. Ont. Dept. of Agr., Toronto. Publ. 439, 21 pp. 1961

Hansen, C. J. and H. T. Hartmann. Propagation of temperate-zone fruit plants. Calif. Ext. Serv. Circ. 471. 50 pp. 1966.

Harrison, T. B. Note on the vegetative reproduction of peach cuttings. Canadian Journ. Pl. Sci. 38:515-516. 1958.

Hartmann, H. T., and D. E. Kester. Plant propagation — principles and practices. 559 pp. Prentice-Hall, Inc. Englewood Cliffs, N. J. 1968.

Hatcher, E. S. J. The use of growth-promoting substances in the vegetative propagation of plants. Ann. Appl. Bio., 36, 562-6. 1949.

Lapins, K. Cold hardiness of rootstocks and framebuilders for fruit trees. Canada Dept. of Agr., Res., Summerland, B.C. SP-32, 36 pp. Oct. 1963.

Larsen, F. E. Promotion of leaf abscission of deciduous tree fruit nursery stock with abscisic acid. HortSci. Vol. 4 (3) 216-218, 1969.

McKenzie, D. W. Apple rootstock trials. Jonathan on E. Malling, Merton and Malling-Merton rootstocks. Journ. Hort. Sci. 39:2. 69-77. Apr. 1964.

Mosse, B. Graft-incompatability in fruit trees. Com. Bur. Hort. Planta. Crops Tech. Comm. 28. 36 pp. Bucks, England, 1962.

(See Appendix for additional references and material on seed and tree propagation)

CHAPTER IX

Freezing Injury to Fruit Trees

❖ ❖

Probably the most important factor influencing the distribution of the fruit industry is minimum winter temperatures. They more or less mark the boundaries where certain fruits can be grown. In any fruit region, however, unusually low temperatures occur at times, causing widespread damage to fruit plants normally grown in that region. Also, some freezing injury occurs to nut and fruit trees in almost every region every winter. This is probably due to the fact that man tends to introduce economic fruits as widely as possible, often beyond the limits of their natural temperature tolerance.

At times, some people seem to think that the climate has changed and that more severe winters are being experienced. The available literature reveals that this is hardly true. Severe winters have been occurring periodically in the United States for at least the past 175 years at the ratio of about one severe winter in nine, but there appears to be no rhythm to their occurrence. Very cold winters may occur in succession for a few years, then none for several. Since 1900 "test winters" have occured in 1903-04, 1906-07, 1911-12, 1917-18, 1933-34, 1935-36, 1954-55, 1964-65, 1968-69.

Winter injury is not confined to the colder or semi-mild areas alone. Greatest injury to deciduous fruits[1] in mild climates may occur when rather warm spells in the winter are followed by moderately cold periods.

How freezing kills. As yet, there appears to be no complete agreement among investigators as to how freezing kills. Different workers have

---

[1] Deciduous fruits lose their leaves during dormancy.

Researchers assisting in this chapter revision were: J. Levitt, U. of Mo.; P. L. Steponkus, Cornell; Del Ketchie, E. L. Proebsting, Jr. Wash. St. U.; G. C. Martin, U. of Cal.; A. Sakai, Japan; H. Quamme, R. E. C. Layne, Res. Sta., Ontario; D. K. Wildung, C. J. Weiser, U. of Minn.; D. R. Walker, Utah St. U.; N. W. Miles, Kan. St. U.

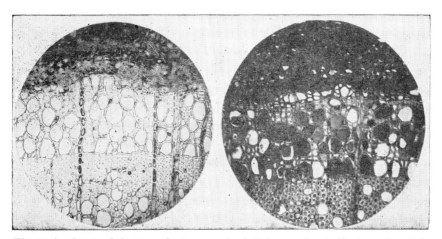

Figure 1. Sapwood from apple tree on the left is uninjured. That on the right was injured by the severe winter of 1933-34, and it shows characteristic clogging of the vessels. This injury is often termed "blackheart." (M. T. Hilborn, Maine Agr. Exp. Sta.)

presented different theories, each supported by rather extensive experiments and observations. W. H. Chandler of California has concluded that the dehydration effect of intercellular ice in plant tissues causes death by freezing. It is known that, with no jarring, plant parts can be cooled slowly without ice formation to several degrees below their normal killing temperature; if plant tissues so-treated are then warmed to above freezing without ice formation, no injury occurs. Futhermore, it is known that pollen grains which contain relatively little or no water can be subjected to temperatures as low as —328°F. without injury to them. But if these cells are permitted to absorb a little water, ice forms and they are killed.

Generally, the rapid rehydration upon fast thawing is the basis for cell damage during thawing. It is true that ice masses have been observed both inside and outside the protoplasm while the tissue is frozen. Another possible explanation for cell death is an excessive strain upon the protoplasmic layer as a result of its rapid and perhaps uneven contraction when water moves out and freezes between the cell walls, or, between the walls of each cell and its protoplasm. Some plants or plant tissues are killed by a small amount of ice formation; others can withstand considerable ice formation before they are killed.

Wood which has been injured by freezing shows not only death of many of the cells in the sapwood, but also a clogging of some vessels with a black gum formation (Figure 1). After the severe freeze in 1933-34 in Maine, it was discovered that trees showing about a 50 per cent death or clogging of cells in the sapwood usually did not recover, whereas those showing only 20 per cent damage often recovered.

The amount of injury from freezing in dormant tissue is influenced by three factors: (a) the rate at which the temperature falls, (b) the duration of the low temperature, and (c) the rate of thawing. It appears rather certain that the more rapidly the temperature falls, the greater is the injury for the minimum temperature attained. Thus, injury under such conditions may be produced at a higher temperature than if the rate of fall had been gradual. Almost everyone can remember nights when the temperature dropped exceedingly fast to low levels. It is these nights which are likely to be the most damaging to plants, and which probably account for most of the severe injury to fruit trees. If rapid drops in temperature are accompanied by strong wind, the tissues are cooled faster, and the damage is accentuated.

The longer the cold period, the more the winter injury at a given temperature. According to G. E. Potter, the increased injury under these conditions may be due to death partly from desiccation as a result of cold drying winds; water movement in the tree is very slow at low temperatures.

Freezing injury is greater the faster the frozen tissue thaws. Often, but not always, after spring frosts when the leaves have been frozen, the shaded leaves and fruits are damaged less than those exposed to bright sunlight. In addition, apple fruits show less browning and breakdown if they thaw slowly at a temperature of about eight degrees above freezing than if thawed rapidly at a higher temperature.

Hardiness of tissues. The relative hardiness of tissues is different in winter and summer. When the tree is in active growing condition, the more active the cells, the more susceptible they are to cold temperatures, which means that the cambium layer and newly developed cells on either side are the first to be killed. This was clearly shown in an unusual cold wave occurring between November 11-15, 1940, in an area following roughly the Missouri River Basin, including Iowa, Missouri, Nebraska, and Kansas. The autumn had been unusually warm with sufficient moisture to keep the plants in active metabolism. The crop of pome fruits, in general, had been heavy and the trees were still in leaf when the storm struck. At Ames, Iowa on November 11, T. J. Maney reports the morning temperature was 51° F.; by noon, a 50-mile gale of wind developed, and by night, a temperature of 9° F. was recorded. Minimum temperatures on the four succeeding dates were 4°, —2°, 2°, and —2° F. Injury assumed all forms common to low-temperature midwinter damage, except root killing. Because of the active metabolism of the cambinum in the tops at that date, many of the trees were killed out-right. Few or no sprouts grew in spring from the apparently uninjured roots, probably because limited food had been stored in them by the time of the freeze and, also, as a result of the heavy fruit crop the tree had matured shortly before.

When the tissues have become well matured by the middle of winter, the cambium becomes the most resistant to freezing, followed in order by bark, sapwood, and pith. In fact, laboratory experiments have shown that well-matured cambinum during winter cannot be injured by freezing at temperatures considerably lower than those occuring in orchards. In the roots,

CHAPTER X

Harvesting, Packing and Processing Apples

❖ ❖

One of the most important periods in the life of an apple is from the time it is picked until sold to the consumer. The grower cannot afford to become careless during this period in any one of the fruit handling operations. Actually, it costs no more to handle fruit carefully than to permit an accumulation of bruises, stem punctures, and press marks. It is not an overstatement to say that, "Fruit must be handled like eggs," for almost every bump and bruise will be readily apparent sooner or later, certainly by the time the fruit reaches the display counter. The trade quickly recognizes quality unblemished fruit and will pay a high premium for it.

PREPARING FOR HARVEST

Estimating yields. It is important to develop a "knack" for estimating crop yields several weeks before picking starts. This gives time to determine the amount of labor needed, picking equipment to provide, the amount and type of packages to purchase, grading and sizing equipment needed, and the amount of storage space to provide or engage from commercial storage houses.

The ability to estimate the yield of fruit before it is mature comes with experience in studying carefully the bearing habits of different varieties. Some varieties, such as Delicious (except in Northwest), have a tendency to fool the estimator, and fall short of expectations. McIntosh and Rome Beauty, on the other hand, are good examples of varieties which habitually do better than expected, because they bear heavily throughout the tops of the trees.

The yield from an acre of mature trees varies with the age, variety, number of trees per acre, methods of management, and the region. According to the U.S. Census, the average yield for all orchards, large and small,

---

William G. Doe, fruit grower and Marwald, Ltd., Ayer Rd., Harvard, Mass., 01451, assisted in this chapter revision.

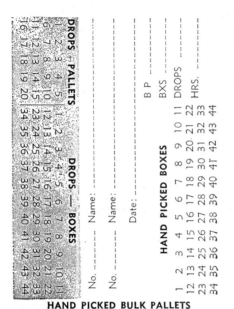

HAND PICKED BULK PALLETS

```
 1  2  3  4  5  6  7  8  9 10 11 12
13 14 15 16 17 18 19 20 21 22 23 24
25 26 27 28 29 30 31 32 33 34 35 36
37 38 39 40 41 42 43 44 45 46 47 48
```

Figure 1. Each picker may be given this type ticket (no ticket, no pay). Each foreman has his punch design in large crews. Space is provided for totals, particularly total hours worked per day. (Courtesy W. Doe, Harvard, Mass.).

well and not-so-well managed, has risen from about 1.0 bushel per tree in 1900 to 1.5 in 1925, 2.6 in 1940, about 6.0, 1970. Yields in Eastern orchards up to the 1950's were generally somewhat better than the Midwest, but not as good as the Far West. However, in recent years, with better spray materials, chemical fruit thinning, and better fertilization and pruning, yields and quality have been as good in the East and Midwest orchards as in the West.

Low-density orchards in the U.S. may produce about 15-20 bu/tree or 500 to 1000 boxes or more per acre (42 lbs./box) of packed fruit. Under high-density management on very dwarfing stocks, yields may reach 1500 to 3000 packed boxes/A or more after 4 years. To these figures must be added the cull fruit which goes into by-products, and does not justify packing costs. However, the alert grower constantly seeks to reduce the amount of low-grade fruit and increase the quantity of quality stock. One of the better growers in Ohio reports less than 5 per cent culls with McIntosh almost every year; on the other hand, some growers report 15 per cent or more culls.

A crop estimator who is new at the game must be careful to base his estimate on average yields for many years, rather than on occasional bumper crop years. It is well for the grower to determine what the average yield is for his region and then through practices better than the average try to exceed this figure as much as possible.

An estimate of the yield should be made at three periods during the year: (a) after the crop has set, (b) after the "June drop," and (c) about one month before harvest. Five random trees per acre should be inspected, being aware of the fact that heavier crops are likely to occur on outside rows, that a few trees may be carrying abnormally heavy loads, and that varieties with a limited number of trees should not be given too much weight. These estimates should be recorded in a bound notebook so that the grower later can compare them with the actual yield. If this is done year after year, he eventually can make estimates which will be of considerable value.

Providing needed equipment. On a lax or rainy day in midsummer, the grower should inventory all harvesting equipment on hand which is in usable condition. Each picker should have an assigned picking receptacle (Figure 2) which is designed to handle the fruit with as little bruising as possible. It should be light in weight, easily manipulated while the picker is standing on the ladder, and provide the picker with free operation of both hands. It is generally agreed that the half-bushel metal-or canvas-sided picking bucket with canvas drop bottom causes about the least injury to fruit under most conditions. It is suspended from the shoulder, hanging in front or slightly to the side of the picker, as shown in Figure 2. The bucket is padded on the inside and around the top with felt; the rigid sides also protect the fruit. It is easily carried and emptied.

Containers should be a v o i d e d which have sharp edges that may bruise or cut the fruit. True, any container may be satisfactory in the hands of a careful workman; any receptacle may be objectionable if used carelessly.

H. P. Gaston, Michigan State University.

Figure 2. Picking buckets of the Wells and Wade type are preferable to picking bags because they afford more protection against bruising and stem punctures. In emptying the picking bucket into the field boxes, the canvas flap should be lowered to the bottom of the box so that the apples will slip out gently. Boxes should be filled to slightly below the top so they can be stacked without bruising apples. Bulk boxes containing multiples of 5 bu as 10, 15, 20, 25 are easy to keep track of for all concerned.

A ladder which is light, strong, and well balanced should be assigned to each picker who is held responsible for its care during the picking season. Choice of an easily handled and sturdy ladder is highly important because the picker spends considerable time climbing up and down the ladder and moving it from place to place. The picker should have confidence in its strength so that it will not detract from his working rapidly and efficiently. It pays to buy good ladders.

Rung ladders flared at bottom and tapered at top are used for large trees. Ladders are set against the tree as perpendicular as safe to put most of picker's weight on the ladder and ground, and not on the tree. Ladders

Figure 3. This is one of many ideas for harvesting aids for dwarf apples in hedgerow. Tractor-mounted attachment holds man standing in front, woman sitting, both harvesting into separate chutes leading to bulk bins carried behind tractor.

should be laid against a stable limb so it settles gently against it without dislodging apples.

Twenty-eight to thirty-foot ladders are available, but these are difficult to handle for one man; a 22-foot ladder is used more commonly. Also, there is a definite tendency for growers to keep their trees around twenty feet or lower for economical management. It is surprising that the cost of harvesting tall trees is almost double the cost of harvesting low trees. Too much time and energy are spent climbing up and down a tall ladder during picking.

Research is underway to determine the value of growing semi-dwarf apple trees in hedgerows, and pruning the sides and top with a special-built cutter bar, thus making it possible to eliminate ladder use by building hydraulically operated worker seats on motor driven mobile masts. Such equipment obviously would be confined to more or less level land.

Fruit receptacles in the orchard. Although bulk-box handling of apples with tractor fork lifts has gained in popularity, there are still many orchard boxes and crates used as field containers with or without pallets and fork lifts. Use of latter equipment has brought a big saving in labor and maintained better fruit quality.

An orchard box, preferably with finger holes in the ends for lifting is a desirable container for field use. These boxes are superior to slatted crates because the walls are smooth with no sharp corners that bruise the fruit. Extra wood strips can be nailed either in the tops or bottoms of the ends so that the boxes can be stacked with less likelihood of mashing the fruit in the box below. Some growers use the final packing container as the field crate, in which case the new boxes are distributed through the orchard and the fruits drawn to the packing shed in them.

The bulk box holds sixteen to twenty or more bushels. Attempts are being made to standardize the size, but processors like to use their own size box

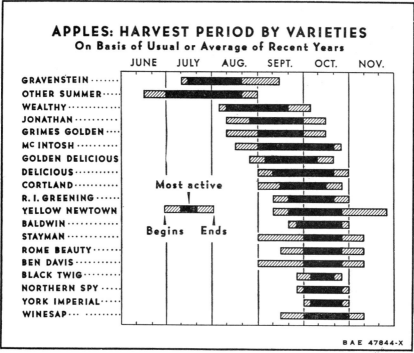

APPLES: HARVEST PERIOD BY VARIETIES
On Basis of Usual or Average of Recent Years

U.S.D.A.

Figure 4. The above listed varieties are harvested over the United States approximately within the span indicated. These dates may vary in unusual seasons.

so growers are more or less obligated to deal with them, once their boxes are distributed to them. Actually,the bulk box is a pallet too, since its floor is built to fit fork lifts. Gaston and Levin suggest the following size bulk box as being, in their experience, satisfactory: length (OD), 48″; width (OD), 48″; depth (OD), 32″; fork opening, 3.75″ capacity, 24 bu.; weight (dry) 220 lbs. A hinged door at the base is convenient when apples for processing are poured into a truck, but where much of this type handling is done, it is best to buy equipment that tips the boxes, eliminating need for hinged doors.

In advance of the harvest season, an inventory should be taken on fruit picking containers. Types of containers to be used will be discussed later. However, it is essential that the grower order his supply as early as possible so that he will receive high quality stock and have it on hand without delay.

Harvest labor. It is well to have a nucleus of capable and efficient workers, some of whom are hired throughout the year, to take the lead more or less in harvesting the crop. In established orchard sections, practically all workers have had a certain amount of experience in harvesting. In addition, there is the influx of "floating" labor which comes from distant areas to work throughout the harvest season. Contractors now provide labor from Puerto Rico, Jamaica, and Mexico, which, over the years, has proven satisfactory. A built-up-over-the years nucleus of local labor is best, using foreign help only in an emergency.

Workmen hired by the day tend to work somewhat slower and cause less injury to the trees and the fruit. It can be estimated roughly that workmen paid by the day will harvest from one-third to one-fourth less fruit as compared with those paid by the box or bushel (100-150 bushels per day). In case of a large crop, some growers may contract their entire crop to a buyer who takes responsibility for the harvesting, packing, storage, and marketing operations.

Proper time for picking. Today, a large percentage of the crop is stored in refrigerated or controlled atmosphere storages before marketing. Apples may be kept in storage for a few weeks to several months. In order that they maintain dessert quality, storage capacity, and commerical value, it is highly important that they be picked at the *proper stage of maturity*. If picked prematurely, apples are likely to be small, poorly colored, sour, tough, off-flavor, and subject to functional diseases such as bitter pit and scald. On the other hand, overripe apples may develop water core while still on the tree, or, after picking, they are likely to develop soft scald and internal breakdown (Figure 5). With overripe red varieties, in some cases the color may become dark and dull and the skin greasy or oily. Overripe apples, especially with some varieties, tend to be mealy and flat in flavor. With the advent of stop-drop hormone sprays, some growers have tended to be lax in getting the fruit off the trees or they leave it on the trees too long to try to increase color, resulting in over-ripe fruit that develops internal breakdown or similar storage disorders.

In general, there is a period of about 5 to 20 days, depending upon the variety and climatic and cultural conditions, during which the fruit can be picked with reasonable assurance that it will be free from storage disorders and develop good dessert quality. It is important to note that the fruit continues to increase in size as long as it remains upon the tree. From this standpoint, it is desirable to leave the fruit on the tree as long as dropping does not equal or exceed the total volume increase. It cannot be predicted, however, when excessive dropping is likely to occur and, therefore, picking must start while the fruit is still adhering well.

The following methods are used for determining the proper time to pick. It should be borne in mind, however, that none of these is entirely dependable under all conditions.

Time elapsed from full bloom to picking maturity. It has been found by an extensive survey among the leading commerical apple states that the number of days from full bloom to picking maturity is rather constant over a wide range of climatic and cultural conditions. According to Haller and Magness, this seems to constitute one of the most reliable indexes of the earliest maturity date of many apple varieties. According to this survey, for example, the Delicious variety requires from 145 to 150 days from full

D. F. Fisher, U.S.D.A.

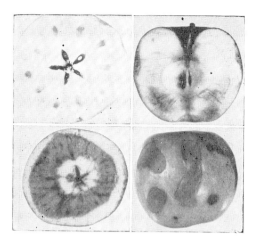

Figure 5. Common physiological diseases of apples which are apparently associated with over-maturity at picking time. (Top left) Water core, characterized by glassy or water-soaked appearance of flesh around the core or main vascular bundles. Such apples eventually may show internal breakdown. (Top right) Internal breakdown has general mealiness and brownish discoloration of the flesh. (Bottom left) Soggy breakdown. (Bottom left) Soft scald makes the apples look as if they were rolled on a hot stove.

bloom to reach picking maturity. Mean temperature seems to have relatively little effect on this time interval with apple varieties. However, relatively high temperatures just preceding harvest tend to result in more rapid abscission. Heavy nitrogen fertilization may delay fruit color development and result in scald unless picking is postponed. On the other hand, dropping may be more pronounced from heavily fertilized trees than from those receiving medium or light fertilization. A light crop of fruit tends to mature somewhat earlier than a heavy crop. The extent to which these and other factors may retard or advance maturity has not been established entirely.

Full bloom is defined as that period when the first petals begin to fall. This period is established readily if the weather is warm during bloom. However, if the weather should turn cool after the king or center blossoms open, the period may be prolonged for a week or more and confuse the specific time of full bloom.

The days from full bloom to picking maturity for several popular commercial varieties on which considerable information is available are shown in Figure 6. The apples may ripen during the early-maturity period (diagonal hatch) under conditions that would tend to hasten maturity, such as a light crop. Apples ripening during the late-maturity period (cross hatch), due perhaps to too much nitrogen, may become overmature and excessive dropping is a definite possibility. The period of optimum maturity, shown by the black area, is the number of days during which the apples can be picked for best handling and storage quality. The approximate time elasped from full bloom to maturity of varieties other than those given in Figure 6 has been given in Table 2 in Chapter II.

The results of R. M. Smock at Cornell University should be cited as an example of the fact that this method of determining fruit maturity apparently does not always hold. For over ten years previous to 1945 at Ithaca, New York, a range of at least ten days was found from year to year for the

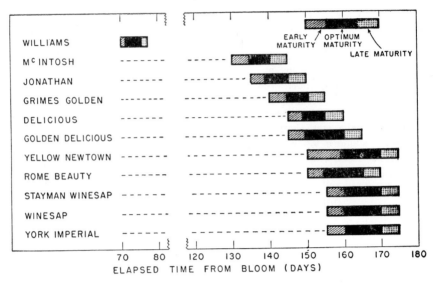

M. H. Haller and J. R. Magness, U.S.D.A.

Figure 6. Days elapsing from bloom to maturity of fruit for 11 varieties of apples. The period of early maturity, as shown above, is when barely satisfactory maturity of the fruit normally occurs, but optimum maturity may advance to this period under conditions that would tend to hasten maturity. Similarly, the period of late maturity is when overmaturity or dropping may become imminent, but optimum maturity may extend into this period under conditions that retard maturity.

period in which McIntosh should be picked. During the 1945 season, bloom occurred one month early and yet apples were picked within a few days of their usual picking date. In this case the number of days from full bloom to harvest was 154, whereas the average for McIntosh at Ithaca, New York is 127-130 days. Smock's studies have shown that ground color of McIntosh seems to be the best index for proper time to pick.

Ease of separation of fruit from the spur. When an apple is ready to pick, it can be separated from the spur without breaking the stem by lifting it with or without a slight rotating movement. There are popular varieties, however, such as McIntosh and Delicious, which may loosen and drop before maturity as a result of early frosts or other factors. On the other hand, there are certain varieties, as Jonathan and Stayman Winesap, which may retain their fruit until it is overmature. Thus, ease of separation of fruit from the spur is not necessarily an indication of proper maturity, but it may indicate when picking is necessary in order to save the crop. If no sound fruit is dropping and the fruit can be picked only with considerable effort, it is considered that the apples are still attached firmly to the tree. However, if a few sound apples are dropping and similar fruits can be separated rather easily from the tree it is definitely time to pick the crop. One should not be misled by the dropping of wormy or otherwise injured fruits.

198

In recent years harvest sprays, as described later, have been used by nearly all growers to make the apples "stick" to the tree longer. Naturally, with the use of these sprays, this index is of little value and, in fact, the fruit may tend to hang too long and become overmature, which is too often the case.

Change in ground color. The ground or undercolor of an apple is a more reliable index of maturity than the red or overcolor. When most varieties of apples become mature, the ground color changes from a leaf green to a lighter shade and eventually to a yellowish color. With most varieties, the time to pick is when the first signs of yellowing begin to appear. However, with Jonathan, and Cortland, the fruit sometimes drops excessively before the color change takes place. This criterion of maturity cannot be used on red bud sports which become red all over before they are mature, leaving no uncovered ground color for observation. The usual result is that these red sports are picked before mature, resulting in the usual storage and flavor difficulties associated with immaturity. It has been found, however, that the red bud sports do not differ greatly in picking maturity from the parent varieties. Therefore, one could use the ground color of the parent variety as an indication if such parent varieties are in the orchard. A color comparison chart has been devised by the U. S. Department of Agriculture for use in determining picking maturity by change in ground color from green to yellow. These are available through the U.S. Plant Industry Station at Beltsville, Maryland. Cornell University has a color chart for McIntosh available through the extension service.

Firmness of flesh. Firmness of the flesh can be determined by removing a thin slice of the skin and flesh with a knife and using a special hand-operated pressure tester which records the pounds pressure necessary for the plunger to penetrate the flesh. Used independently of other criteria, it is of value chiefly in determining when apples are too soft and ripe for storage, rather than when picking should begin. Publications listed at the end of this chapter should be consulted for further details as to the applications and limitations of the "mechanical thumb" or pressure tester.

Committee Decision. In Washington, e. g., a committee of growers, Federal and state workers and marketing representatives visit key orchards about harvest time to decide when fruit, mainly red sports of Delicious should be harvested. State regulatory men attempt by law to keep fruit from moving out of state before the initial harvesting date is set. This helps to keep starchy apples from depressing market sales. Flesh firmness, sugar content and general agreement among the committee based on experience are criteria used.

A simple reliable chemical technique is needed whereby a grower can determine when an apple variety is ready to harvest. Accumulated seasonal heat units and temperature near harvest are among several approaches under investigation.

Picking maturity of different varieties. Considerable information

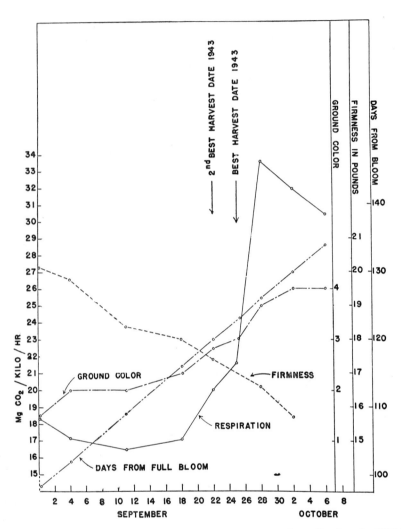

Figure 6a. Maturity changes of McIntosh apples ripened on the tree in 1943 in New York, as noted by R. M. Smock, Cornell University. The best picking date, based on ground color, firmness, and respiration rate, was found to be September 24 in this particular year.

has accumulated regarding the proper picking maturity for specific apple varieties. As examples, and to point out the special problems involved, three leading varieties will be discussed briefly. Detailed information on other varieties commercially important can be obtained from a bulletin by Haller and Magness cited at the end of this chapter.

Delicious. Delicious develops very poor dessert quality if picked in an immature state. On the other hand, it is a common mistake to leave Delicious on the tree too long in an attempt to get high red color development which is extremely important in its marketability. Overmaturity results in poor storage quality.

200

Elapsed time from full bloom to maturity, as pointed out earlier, is probably the most reliable index for picking Delicious. Studies under widely varying climatic conditions in Washington, Oregon, Illinois, Ohio, Michigan, New York, and Maryland indicate that at least 145 days and preferably 150 days should elapse between full bloom and picking. In other words, harvest should begin at about 145 days and end between 155 and 160 days for satisfactory storage holding.

Delicious may become overmature under long season growing conditions. Under these conditions, the use of the pressure tester may be advisable; apples should be picked before the pressure test drops below 15 or 16 pounds. Water core may develop if Delicious becomes overmature under long-growing season conditions. Another index in determining picking time for Delicious is the fact that the flesh turns yellowish when in proper picking condition. Delicious stores well at 31° to 32° F. At higher temperatures, it may become mealy extremely fast; thus, it is not well suited to common storage and should be placed under refrigeration.

Delicious picked prematurely may develop scald, and in Washington, from 150 to 155 days is recommended from full bloom before picking in order to prevent scald development. When picking must start early, because the crop is large and packing and storage facilities are limited, the early picked apples should not be kept for storage but sold for immediate consumption. Special attention must be given to red sports of Delicious in order not to pick them prematurely. Several states are using the Maturity Committee's decision for Delicious harvest.

Stayman Winesap. Relatively late picking is desired with Stayman Winesap in order to get full color development and to avoid scald which develops from harvesting prematurely. Fruit left on the tree too long, however, may develop water core and storage breakdown, and in some seasons, dropping may be serious. The variety requires at least 155 days from full bloom to earliest maturity, and 160 to 170 days for optimum maturity. For best storage, it should not be left on the tree until the pressure test is below 16 pounds. Fruits between 15 and 18 pounds have been found satisfactory for storage. The number of days from full bloom is probably the most reliable index of the time to start picking Stayman Winesap. This variety ripens quickly after it is picked and, therefore, should be placed immediately under refrigeration, particularly if picking has been delayed until the fruit has become slightly soft.

McIntosh. McIntosh can be picked somewhat earlier than other fruits because it is almost immune to storage scald. However, the variety should be left on the tree long enough to develop high color and command a premium price; it is not susceptible to water core. The biggest difficulty with McIntosh is that it tends to drop suddenly even before prime picking maturity has been reached. Hoffman of New York has shown that this tendency can be overcome by the application of chemical sprays shortly before harvesting, as described later. This is an important practice with

Courtesy Michigan State University, East Lansing

Figure 7. No end of ideas have been proposed for harvesting machinery and planting and training systems for trees. Paul Larsen, formerly Mich. State University has presented this idea among several for mechanically harvesting hedgerows of compact-size deciduous fruit trees. Orchards of the future likely will be planted a few feet apart in hedgerows only far enough apart for machinery passage. If the "shake and catch" system is used, trees may be trained to a "T" or "Y" shape to prevent fruit from falling through the limbs. Frame structure of above harvester may serve also as the basic unit for spraying, thinning, power pruning and weed spraying under the trees.

McIntosh because the period elapsing from full bloom to proper picking maturity is often inconsistent. According to Haller and Magness, the minimum days from full bloom to picking maturity is 130; optimum maturity is generally reached between 135 and 140 days. Within these limits, picking may be determined by development of red overcolor and yellow undercolor and the firmness of the fruit which should not drop below 15 to 14 pounds pressure before picking.

Color Development in Apples. Factors that influence anthrocyanin (red pigment) development in apples are (a) temperature, (b) nutrition, (c) moisture, (d) sunlight, (e) mite damage, and (f) its inherent tendency to become red in spite of adverse environmental factors. Weather conditions a few days or weeks before harvest, is the predominating factor. Clear days with relatively cool nights are ideal for good fruit color. These conditions can largely overcome unfavorable nutrition, such as too much nitrogen being available to the tree before harvest. A period of warm muggy and rainy weather one to three weeks before harvest can result in poor fruit color and condition. Drought for a few weeks before harvest will cause the fruit to be dull red, but the color will brighten almost overnight with a good rain. Pruning should be adequate to admit light through the tree so apples will be red on all sides.

It seems unwise for a grower to cut drastically or omit nitrogen application the year following poor fruit color. If crop size and quality have been reasonably satisfactory over the past few years, a cut of not more than 25 percent in nitrogen from one year to the next should be the limit. Adjustment in nitrogen, when such adjustment is needed, from one year to the next should be about 0.1 lb. of N per mature tree, such as Rome Beauty or Stayman that normally require about a pound of actual N per tree. Potassium applications may improve fruit color only when the nutrient is deficient in the soil. Iron deficiency may cause poor fruit color also.

There is a tendency among most growers to plant the red sports of standard varieties to try to insure acceptable fruit color every harvest season.

Courtesy of Paul Adrain, University of California and USDA, Davis, California

Figure 8. Horticulturists and engineers are combining efforts to develop harvesting aids that will reduce labor markedly and make the job less backbreaking on large trees. This is an experimental motor-propelled picking platform with decelerator chute and a track for bulk bins below. It is designed for pear trees trained to the hedgerow system.

CONTROLLING FRUIT DROP WITH HARVEST SPRAYS

Since 1939 an increasing number of commercial fruit growers have sprayed fruit trees with various chemicals before harvest to control fruit drop on varieties susceptible to dropping. Chemical sprays that retard the apple fruit drop have reduced fruit losses at harvest from twenty percent or more to only five percent and frequently less. The chemicals in these sprays, known generally as "stop-drop" sprays, so tighten a tree's hold on its crop that the fruit is not likely to drop even when jolted by ladders or shaken by the wind. Research is adding progressively to the number of chemicals that can be used to stop the fruit from dropping, and is also determining more specifically their effectiveness on particular varieties, solution strengths, times of application, and such side effects as over-ripening and softening of fruit and damage to foliage and buds. Loosening of fruit on a tree is natural in the maturing process. As fruit nears maturity, a callous abcission (separation) layer forms where the fruit stem joins the spur, and from then on the weakly-held fruit may fall.

Drop may be increased if trees are deficient in boron or magnesium, or if they have too little moisture. Trees fertilized heavily with nitrogen often drop more fruit then trees fertilized moderately.

All varieties are subject to drop, particularly the short-stem ones. Loss has been serious enough to lead growers of all commercial varieties to adopt preharvest spraying, except in the case of early summer apples which are picked before they are eating ripe. Protection against dropping by a preharvest spray may be gained at a cost of around $10 an acre (a rough approximation)for cost of material and application. Before fruit-sticking sprays were available, apple growers knew, and occasionally practiced, one drastic means of forestalling drop loss. This was to pick early, even though fruit might not have attained its best value in size, color, or storage quality.

NAA. Use of a plant-growth regulator to control fruit drop became practical in 1939 when horticulturists at the U.S. Department of Agriculture's Plant Industry Station reported that NAA—naphthaleneacetic acid or its salts or esters—would retard the drop of apples. The chief limitations of the NAA compounds is their brief effectiveness, which usually lasts not more than four weeks at the most. When the effect wears off, fruit on the tree is likely to drop quickly, often in quantities over-night. Repeating the spray to prolong effectiveness has not proven very helpful. Despite its limitations NAA has, from the first, been used widely and valued by growers. It is still chosen in some situations. It is the only fruit-sticking chemical found practical for airplane spraying.

2,4-D, 2,4,5-T, and 2,4,5-TP. Initial success of NAA has led to many experiments with growth-regulating chemicals in a search for longer-lasting control of fruit drop. These can be applied conveniently early—three to four weeks ahead of the rush work of harvest—with expectations of controlling drop during harvest, even if picking takes longer than the usual three weeks. Each of the longer-lasting compounds has some limitations in use. One protects only certain varieties. None is satisfactory for spraying from the air or in concentrate form. Experiments with 2,4-D (2,4-dichlorophenoxyacetic acid) at USDA's Plant Industry Station, Beltsville, Maryland, showed that this chemical controls drop of but two apple varieties—Winesap and Stayman. Research initially begun at Cornell University has established wide usefulness of the phenoxy compounds 2,4,5-T (2,4,5-trichlorophenoxyacetic acid) and 2,4,5-TP (2,4,5-trichlorophenoxypropionic acid). Both can be used in salt and amide forms as well as the acid. Both are satisfactory for sticking on all commercial varieties of apples.

Alar (Succinic acid 2,2-Dimethylhydrazide or SADH) applied 70-80 days after bloom (no later) on most varieties (except Golden Delicious), and particularly Delicious, at 1000 ppm provides drop control, increases firmness and delays water-core development.

Ethrel may be used for increased efficiency in mechanical harvesting of apples, coloring apples more uniformly and hastening maturity for one picking. Research is limited. Check your local fruit specialist. Use about 300 gals./A, 250 ppm to loosen early and mid-season varieties; 500 ppm for late varieties when temperatures are cooler. Apply 7-14 days before anticipated harvest. If temperature exceeds 75° F, watch fruit carefully for fast ripening. (Cornell, N. Y., suggestions by L. J. Edgerton).

Spraying versus dusting. Spraying is commonly preferred to dusting as a means of applying stop-drop chemicals. Spraying from the ground is somewhat more effective than spraying from airplane. Dusting as an alternative to spraying has been included in stop-drop experiments and often is as effective as spraying when there is enough moisture on foliage to make a deposit stick.

Spray solutions and their use. Much has been learned about advantageous use of successful stop-drop chemicals. Following are recent practices and principles, based on advances in research:

Suitable chemical and dilution to use. Success with stop-drop spraying calls for selection of a suitable chemical and in the weakest solution that will be effective. The weakest solution that gives stop-drop control is the most advantageous on several important counts: it is economical; it is less likely to cause side effects, such as over-ripening and softening of the fruit, or damage to buds and foliage; and over-strong solution can make fruit hard to pick.

NAA can be used on any of the commercial varieties of apples. An NAA stop-drop ground spray is generally kept to a standard strength of 10 ppm. (parts per million). 2,4-D is useful only for Winesap and Stayman Winesap apples. To avoid tree injury, concentrations of 2,4-D should be kept at five to seven ppm. for these varieties, never more than seven. 2,4,5-T and 2,4,5-TP can be used on any of the commercial varieties of apples.

A rate of 20 ppm. is considered the maximum strength of 2,4,5-T and 2,4,5-TP that can be used without causing apples to ripen and soften undesirably. For some varieties, weaker solutions have proved adequate—for example: ten ppm. for Delicious and Winesap; fifteen ppm. for Golden Delicious, Stayman, and York. For Rome, 20 ppm. are needed.

Quantity. In early research it was thought that spray must contact fruit stems in order to be carried to the stem-spur junction. Later work has shown that foliage is the main transmission route. To spray an acre of large trees from the ground with any of the dilute fruit-sticking solutions requires from 600 to 1,000 gallons.

With air-blast spray equipment, it is possible to apply the stop-drop chemicals as "concentrate" sprays of 4x to 6x. Washington, however, discourages concentrate plane spraying of 2, 4, 5-TP. Lateral buds in the tree tops may be damaged. Excessive fruit ripening may occur.

Timing. How far ahead of harvest to apply a fruit-sticking spray depends on the chemical chosen. Proper timing allows for a lag of some days after spraying, in which period the chemical is taking effect. NAA requires about three days to become effective; 2,4-D about ten days; 2,4,5-T and 2,4,5-TP about a week. Since NAA is dependable for no more than ten days or two weeks a preharvest NAA spray needs to be timed closely, to take effect just when drop is expected to start. 2,4,-D, 2,4,5-T, and 2,4,5-TP may be applied three to four weeks before harvest, which is often convenient timing for work management. Successful spray application is timed to keep within certain stages of plant growth. Spray applied too early may increase the chemical's effect on ripening, and fruit may be overripe when picked. A stop-drop spray is considered to be too late and is wasted if applied after the abcission process is already under way. Spray is also too late to give good effect if applied after foliage is old and faded from frost or other cause.

Combining treatments. Several varieties planted together frequently can be given drop protection by one preharvest spraying—provided the same chemical and the rate of application are suitable for all. A dual-purpose spray in which a stop-drop chemical sprayed separately, has been added to material for disease or pest control is often less satisfactory and especially so if the other spray material contains lime.

Climate considerations. Temperature will make some difference in results achieved with preharvest sprays. A relatively warm temperature, 70° F. or higher, at spraying time is an advantage, because the chemical will be absorbed more readily than when weather is cool. At warm temperatures the chemical will also take effect faster. Once a stop-drop chemical has become effective, temperature changes do not further alter its potency to any extent.

Considerable moisture from dew, fog, or rain is ordinarily an aid to the potency of the chemicals. Lack of moisture on the other hand, lowers their efficiency. Occasionally, the unexpected happens, as when McIntosh apple trees in Northeast orchards dropped fruit badly in 1955, when the growing season was rainy. Such situations are a reminder that, useful as the stop-drop chemicals are, their action is not understood completely.

Airplane spraying. Airplane spraying is ordinarily a custom arrangement with firms doing this work. The method offers advantages of speed and convenience to growers who have large fruit plantings. For airplane spraying the only practical stop-drop chemical is NAA. Drift of 2,4,5-T or 2,4,5-TP that might reach pear or other trees could damage foliage and fruit. Damage to the tops of apple trees also has been a problem with concentrate plane application of 2,4,5-TP.

Future Research objectives are: (a) to find better chemicals to serve many varieties with greater economy and convenience, (b) to gain more

H. P. Gaston, Michigan Experiment Station

Figure 9. To pick an apple, hold it as shown to left: lift to one side and up, giving a slight turn (center). Work with hands close together, making sure that the left hand does its share (right).

knowledge of how chemicals work so their effects can be predicted better, and (c) to find a chemical that will release the fruit and facilitate mechanical harvesting. L. J. Edgerton of Cornell states that Amchem 66-329 is showing promise in promoting fruit abscission. Growers should keep in touch with Federal Food and Drug Administration laws on use of these chemicals and be aware of up-to-date improvements as reported by government service men.

HARVESTING THE FRUIT

Every hour is precious during the harvest season. Make complete plans well ahead. Stop-drop sprays and the development of mechanical aids and harvesters have helped to reduce "harvest tension," particularly in the medium-size and large orchards. The early developed mechanical apple harvesters have been clumsy to handle and expensive to buy and operate (justified, however) but the the size and spacing of the large trees has necessitated this. As compact trees and hedgerow planting becomes widespread, it is likely that simplified and more efficient and lower-priced mechanical harvesters will be developed. Engineers and horticulturists are working together to perfect this equipment and cut labor to a minimum. The "shake-and catch" harvester shown in Figure 9a is doing an acceptable job for harvesting processing fruit with only about 15% of the fruit bruised or damaged which actually is but little more than found in hand harvesting. This harvester has two self-propelled frames, each with decelerator strips to break the fall of the fruit, and a floating boom limb

Figure 9a. These are two of the many ideas being tested and perfected for mechanically harvesting fruit. (Upper) Cornell "shake and catch" machine designed for apple, cherry, peach and other fruits. (Lower) Cornell's apple harvester designed to pick bruise-free apples for fresh market. There are three frames for catching fruit, two padded with inflatable plastic bags filled with air that can be inserted into the fruit laden tree. The limbs are shaken by machine to dislodge the fruit. (Courtesy Cornell Agr. Engineering Dept.)

shaker. Another type is the wrap-around, single-unit, inverted-umbrella, self-propelled machine with a Shock-Wave trunk shaker (see Peach Chap.). The Cornell oscillating tines rotated on circular drums is another idea being tested for hedgerow plantings (Figure 9a). References are given at the end of this chapter for details on this fast-growing field. Watch for improvements and developments in grower magazines.

Until mechanical harvesters are perfected and we have shifted more or less to compact trees, much of the world apple crop still must be harvested by hand as in Figure 9. Key pointers to bear in mind are: (a) Take

Figure 10. (Left) Tractor rear lift is used to line up bulk boxes for lumber type carrier. Sled carriers will reduce jolting. (Right) Fork lift (electric to avoid fumes) is used to stack boxes five to six high in modern storages.

every precaution to reduce careless handling of fruit by pickers to a minimum; (b) start with lower branches and move to the tree tops; (c) do not pull stems from the apples, or cut them with finger nails, or twist off spurs; (d) place fruit *carefully* in picking container, *don't drop it;* (e) set ladders so they fall in the tree if something slips; (f) drop adequate boxes by the trees beforehand; (g) keep the picked fruit in the shade and take it to the packing shed and get it in storage as quickly as feasible to minimize ripening; and (h) make every effort to start the picking and finish before the fruit drops excessively, is over-mature, or is damaged by cold or unexpected heavy winds.

Pick-Your-Own can be used near population centers with considerable savings in harvesting, container, and handling, storage, marketing costs. See appendix for details.

Apples Orchard-to-Store Directly. Cornell found savings up to 50 percent in costs. Pickers are instructed not to pick undersized, misshapen, or damaged apples. This "orchard-run" fruit, tested at 16 supermarkets, increased sales 45% and brought good return sales. Fruit is picked in ¼-bu. corrugated boxes, pallettized orchard to store, reducing handling from 16 to 6 times, and, hence, less damage to tender McIntosh.

THE PACKING HOUSE

Private or co-operative packing. Fruit may be (1) packed in the grower's own packing house, or (2) it may be hauled to a community or co-operative packing house.

(1) Many of the growers, especially in the Middlewest and East, own their packing house and storage. Under these conditions, the grower can hire his workmen on a year-round basis and work may go on in all kinds of weather. These grower-owned packing houses are more or less a necessity

R. W. Staples, Yakima County Hort. Union, Yakima, Wash.

Figure 11. (Top) Apple storage and packing plant in the Yakima Valley, Washington. Packing house is at the right with rounded roof. The storage plant for over 580,000 boxes is at the left of packing house. Cabins for seasonal help are shown in the foreground. (Bottom) Several ideas are under test for mechanically picking up drop apples. Apples must be washed and processed immediately. This machine operates with rubber fingers, picking up fruit without damaging it; manufactured by Koehring Inco., Grand Haven, Mich. (Courtesy Jordan Levin, USDA at Mich. State Univ., E. Lansing.)

in orchards which are scattered, and the quantity of fruit harvested within a region hardly justifies a co-operative packing house.

(2) Community packing houses operated co-operatively or as a private enterprise, are used extensively in the West for all types of fruit (Figure 11). In the East, they are used only in sections where the apple industry is more or less concentrated. The many advantages of co-operative packing houses have been pointed out in Chapter III.

In community packing houses: (a) the grower delivers tree-run fruit; (b) he is given a receipt; (c) his fruit is graded, sized, packed out, culls go to processing; (d) charges for handling, storage and packing are deducted and returns to the grower are pro-rated through all or part of a season. Advances in cash to the grower can be made if needed.

On-the-farm packing facilities. Gaston and Levin of Michigan list several advantages of providing grading and packing service at the point of production. On-the-farm packing: (1) reduces per-bushel costs—wages, taxes, and overhead are usually lower in rural areas than in towns and cities, (2) makes it possible to put up the size, grade and pack currently in demand, (3) makes it possible to use year-round farm help to advantage in the winter months, (4) keeps cull fruit off the fresh fruit market, (5) lowers transportation costs by disposing of cull fruit at nearby cider mills rather than in more distant markets, (6) makes retail sales easier and increases average net returns, (7) controls the all-important grading operation, (8) uses the packing house for several fruit crops and for other purposes during the off-season, (9) uses farm fruit storages to the best possible advantage, and (10) increases total net returns to the grower—the profit that otherwise goes to those who perform the packing service is added to that which he receives from growing the fruit.

Grower-controlled community packing houses (growers sharing risks and profits), managed by professionals, and co-operative fruit exchanges also have most of the above advantages.

Cost of building and equipment. Cost of packing facilities vary on a bushel basis with the size of the plant. Building and equipment for handling 5,000 bushels for the season generally cost four times as much as facilities for handling 40,000 bushels, which in turn costs twice as much as a unit for handling 200,000 bushels, according to Gaston and Levin.

In planning new structures, provide all of the space and capacity that can be used effectively. When amortized over a period of years (20 years is often used), the per-crate cost is relatively low. This means that it is usually more economical to provide facilities for anticipated needs than to build for the present and expand at a later time.

Location. Both the original and operating costs depend to some extent upon the packing house location. If operated with a fruit storage, it should adjoin or be close to this structure. The packing house should be in or close to the orchard so that fruit can be moved to it with a minimum of effort and expense. Ready access by truck is essential.

Grading and packing equipment are operated by electric motors; water is necessary for drinking, washing and cleaning purposes. This means that both water and 220-volt alternate current electricity should be readily available at the packing house site.

Packing house design. The efficiency with which grading and packing operations are performed depends, to a considerable extent, upon packing house design. Although no two houses are the same, there are several principles which you must consider before the packing house is built and equipped if efficiency is to be achieved.

How is your fruit to be sold. Growers who plan to sell at retail should provide a readily accessible, conveniently arranged and attractive salesroom. Provide parking space for the peak number of cars (including those which belong to the help). If you expect to sell to truckers, provide a loading dock. Growers who plan to sell to jobbers or chainstore buyers should be prepared to pack and load the volume of fruit that these outlets will demand. The method of merchandising has a direct bearing on packing house design.

An attractive sign which will identify your packing house is a distinct asset. This is especially true if you plan to make retail or "trucker" sales.

Decide how the fruit is to be packed. Apples may be packed in open returnable crates, baskets, boxes, cartons, cell, and tray packs and film bags.

Plan packing facilities around the packages that are or may be used. For example, the grower who plans to pack in plioflim bags or other consumer-size containers must provide enough space for the special equipment that will be required. Those who pack in cartons or cell-pack must also make room for the machines that will be required as well as for the storage of the empty containers.

The layout in each case will be somewhat different and should receive careful attention. The wise grower will provide enough space to shift from one method of packing to another if circumstances and demands change.

Volume packed per day per season. After choosing markets and packages, consider the number of bushels of fruit to be packed. The space required and the capacity of the equipment needed depends on the volume of fruit to be handled daily. The accompanying table will help you estimate the amount of floor space that will be required.

Grading and handling equipment to be used. If you are constructing a new packing house, it will pay to provide a structure that will accomodate standard equipment. Most concerns that make and sell grading equipment will supply the services of a qualified engineer upon request. The engineer can help design a building that will accomodate standard grading, packing and handling units without increased installation or operation costs.

Will there be a connected refrigerated storage. Growers who do not have a refrigerated storage must provide facilities to complete their packing during or shortly after the harvest season. Most growers who pack more

TABLE 1

Approximate Packing House Floor Space and Equipment Needed
(After Gaston and Levin)

Bushels Packed Per Season[1]	Capacity In Bushels Per Hour	Square Ft. Floor Space Needed[2]	Packing Equipment Generally Needed
5,000	25	1,000	12½-inch unit consisting of receiving belt, eliminator, brusher, sorting rolls, sizer, and two bins.
10,000 or 20,000 or 30,000	50	1,750	12½-inch unit consisting of receiving belt, eliminator, brusher, sorting rolls, two sizers, and three bins.
40,000	75	2,300	15½-inch unit consisting of receiving belt, eliminator, brusher, sorting rolls, two sizers, spacer belts, crossover belts, and a 20-foot return-flow belt.
50,000 or 75,000	100	3,000	19-inch unit consisting of receiving belt, eliminator, brusher, sorting rolls, two sizers, spacer belts, crossover belts, and a 20-foot return-flow belt.
100,000	150	4,000	22-inch unit consisting of receiving belt, eliminator, brusher, sorting rolls, three sizers, spacer belts, crossover belts, and a 30-foot return-flow belt.
150,000	200	5,000	24-inch unit consisting of receiving belt, eliminator, brusher, sorting rolls, three sizers, spacer belts, crossover belts, and a 40-foot return-flow belt.
200,000	250	6,500	31-inch unit consisting of receiving belt, eliminator, brusher, sorting rolls, three sizers, spacer belts, crossover belts, and a 40-foot return-flow belt.

[1]Growers will pack about two-thirds of their production on the average.

[2] If automatic baggers and combination units accomodating more than one type fruit pack are used, it will jump costs.

213

than 20,000 bushels should provide a refrigerated storage to extend their packing season over several months.

When the packing room is to be used with a refrigerated storage, it should be located in or near the storage building. When the seasonal volume is 10,000 bushels or more and the packing is done in a separate building, a lift truck to move the fruit quickly and easily is essential. The structures must be connected by suitable paved drives.

The requirements of growers who pack "out of storage" differ from those who pack at harvest time. The flow of both fruit and packages must be considered when the layout is planned.

Design for flexibility. All fruit packing operations should be flexible. The tonnage of any crop or combination of crops is likely to vary considerably from year to year. Average production in any orchard may vary as young orchards come into full bearing or old ones pass their prime. Day-to-day variations in volume during a single season are sure to occur. Thus, packing lines should operate effectively at a fraction of their capacity as well as at full load.

The facilities of any one plant can, for example, often be used to advantage to pack several different crops in succession if the shift from one to another can be accomplished quickly and economically. A shift from the use of boxes to fiberboard cartons or film bags, is often necessary. The line should be laid out in such a way that several grades of fruit and two or more types of packages can be assembled.

Layout and arrangement. From 2½ to 4 square feet of floorspace should be available for every box of fruit that will be packed in any one 10-hour day (see table on page 213).

If empty packages, supplies, and several grades of fruit are to move through a packing house in an orderly manner, two sides of the packing house floor should be readily accessible by truck. Suitable all-weather drives with ample room in which to make turns, and at least one dock of truck-bed height will be required.

When bulky packages, as fiberboard cartons or wooden boxes are used, provide ground floor storage space next to or near the packing room. This makes it possible to move the "empties" to the point where they are needed with a minimum of effort and confusion.

The layout should be arranged so that the fruit can be moved to the receiving belt of the grader line either directly from the orchard or from the storage space through the various steps in grading, packing and shipping with the least effort and expense.

The grading and packing equipment should be laid out so that all the points at which fruit accumulates can be serviced by a fork-lift truck. The area in which ungraded fruit is received and stockpiled should be separate from that in which the packed fruit is loaded for shipment. Both these areas should be readily accessible to lift equipment.

All floor space to be used for storage, grading and packing operations

may be either of the stationary or rotary type. Stationary bins (Figure 13) have been used for many years for packing boxes and consumer packs and are still in wide use. The rotary bin (Figure 15) is being used in packing houses for hand packing of boxes and cartons. The bins have a floating bottom which maintains the fruit at a specific level at all times and within easy reach of the packer. The bin rotates slowly and gives the packer opportunity to choose each apple; the rotating also facilitates equal distribution of fruit in the bin.

Figure 15. This packer is tray-packing Washington Golden Delicious. The corrugated separations give protection to each apple. Only the top layer of apples is wrapped, mainly for sales appeal (courtesy Washington State Apple Commission).

Packing apples. Under ideal conditions, apples should be packed and stored or shipped immediately after picked. If the fruit is handled when more or less hard immediately after picking, there is less danger of bruising and of subsequent bluemold infection. The sooner oiled paper is mixed among apple varieties susceptible to scald, or the apples are treated with a scald deterrent, the better. Another advantage of immediate packing is that it gives an opportunity to sort out and immediately eliminate the culls which are not only a source of infection to the quality fruit, but may take up valuable space in the packing shed or storage. Tendency, however, is to pack fruit as sold.

Under practical conditions, it is usually necessary to keep some of the crop out of storage for a few days to a few weeks before it can be packed either for storage or for market. In northern areas this can be done fairly well with the cool autumn weather. With some varieties susceptible to bitter pit, it seems advisable to delay packing for a month to six weeks to permit the disease to develop, and then eliminate affected fruit over the grading tables. If private storage space is available, most growers place the apples directly in storage, and pack them out in various containers as ordered. This practice is common today since most orchardists are growing high-grade fruit, but it is expensive for the orchardist with low-grade fruit, who pays for refrigerating a large quantity of culls which later will be discarded.

The effect of delay in storage. Temperature has a profound effect on the ripening of apples. Softening of fruit proceeds about twice as fast at 70° F. as at 50° F., and at 50° it is almost twice as fast as at 40°, while at the latter temperature, it is fully twice as fast as at 32°. About 25 per cent longer time is required for fruit to ripen at 30° than at 32°. Thus, it is clearly evident that the sooner fruit can be placed in storage and lowered to a temperature of 32° F., the longer it will keep in top-quality condition. Every effort within reasonable practical limits should be exercised to prevent the fruit from remaining in the orchard or in the packing shed longer than absolutely necessary.

Types of packages. Types of packages used for marketing apples have been everchanging. In the 1920's the barrel was almost a universal package in the Eastern areas. The barrel has been displaced by smaller packages which display better and are easier to handle and cause less bruising. The wooden box has been used in all apple sections, but has been replaced by fiberboard boxes for domestic distribution and even for export.

Baskets of the one-half or one-bushel size are used only to a limited extent. The *box* type of package is popular in the East, but it is largely fiberboard rather than wood. The Western wooden apple box has all but given way to corrugated tray packs shown in Figure 15.

Several types of fiberboard containers are in use and may be packed similarly to a standard box. Most fiberboard boxes are designed to eliminate bruising and flimsiness when packed. Other styles have egg-crate type cells for individual apples. This type of fiberboard container provides maximum protection against bruising, but the tray-type separators, as shown in Figure 16, are used widely because of relative ease of packing and safety to fruit.

Corrugated fiberboard is good insulating material, and consequently, it takes longer to cool the fruit, especially when sealed tightly. On the other hand, it takes longer for cooled fruit to warm in these containers. The original fiberboard boxes tended to moisten in storage and hold the fruit less rigidly after several months of storage, but later designs and materials have overcome this weakness for the most part.

The formerly used colored mesh bags containing a few to several pounds of fruit have been replaced by "Poly" bags, mostly of three- to five-pound sizes (Figure 16).

In the choice of containers, there are several factors to consider. Some varieties, such as McIntosh, are more tender than others and, therefore, demand a type of package which causes as little bruising as possible. In some seasons, the general crop is of higher quality than other seasons. Thus, it may justify a larger proportion of high quality containers. The grower should not be misled by the presence of a minor quantity of highly colored specimens in his crop. To pack these into the higher grades may so reduce the appearance of the remainder of the crop as to make the project uneconomical.

When the general crop situation is short, the proportion of fruit packed in closed high-grade packages might be increased to an advantage. But when the crop is average or heavy, only the better fruit is likely to pay the attendant cost of better packages. It is well for the grower to study the

Fruit Industries Research Foundation, Yakima, Washington.

Figure 16. (Left) The center attachment is used to pack apples in polyethylene bags. The bag is placed over the chute after apples have been pulled by hand into chute from bin. The chute tips apples into bag. Scale at right is used to bring bag to designated weight by adding or withdrawing apples. Bagger is now equipped with blower to hold bags open for easy quick filling. (Right) This machine is designed for quick packing in fiberboard boxes, using tray-type separators.

market preferences and make every effort to give the dealers and consumers the container and pack they like. It is too expensive and difficult to try to change the nature of the demand in order to suit the grower's own desires. Much of the fruit that is contended to be unsuitable for the better containers because of lack of uniformity, inferior color, and other reasons, is no longer profitable to grow for any purpose. The public has far passed the stage where such fruit is acceptable to it, except in the form of by-products. Growers of this type of fruit must either change their practices or be forced out of the business.

Packing in boxes. Only the best grades of apples are packed in boxes. The general box-packing procedure is as follows: The empty boxes come to the packers in reaching distance on a gravity conveyor. A box is placed upon a small stand, as shown in Figure 15, at a convenient height for the specific packer. Each stand is equipped with a hod containing wrapping paper for the apples. The paper is 12- or 14-pound weight and glazed on the surface away from the fruit. Wrapped apples pack easily, are protected from decay and injury, and give an attractive package on the market. The wrapping paper size varies with size of fruit. Largest apples are wrapped with 14 by 14 inch paper; apples which run 64 to 80 to the box require 11 by 11 inch paper; 88 to 113 require 10 by 10 inch paper; 125 to 180, 9 by 9 inches; and for smaller sizes 8 by 8 inches. Small apples are sometimes packed without wrappers. The paper may be stamped with an attractive brand or trademark. Paper impregnated with special oil is employed for varieties which tend to develop storage scald. Gloves for the packers are preferred to prevent fingernail marks on the fruit. Second finger on the left glove is removed in order that a rubber cap can be used on that finger to faciliate grabbing paper.

227

Although no two persons wrap in exactly the same manner, the general procedure is shown in Figures 17 and 18. It will be noted that there are several movements for the wrapping of each apple and, therefore, the procedure should be studied carefully and practiced in order to eliminate all unnecessary twists or turns. Detailed procedure can be found in the U. S Department of Agriculture Farmer's Bulletin No. 1457.

Packing in consumer containers. For local trade, polyethylene bags, shrink-poly trays of 4-6 apples, and small corrugated boxes of different sizes are popular consumer packages with housewives. A small package of apples fits easily in the refrigerator and usually lasts until the next trip to the store. Corrugated containers and poly-wrapped cardboard trays are manufactured to accomodate a definite number and size of apples, which are packed uniformly. Some packers may mix colored oiled paper with the fruit, mostly for effect. Polyethylene bags of three- to five-pound sizes are pouular. In the East, these small packages are packed out of storage and sold as needed throughout the winter or delivered to chain stores for their help to bag to please the trade.

Larger corrugated boxes containing about a bushel of fruit are usually jumble packed for near-by market outlets although some growers have used the uniform pack system. If an orchardist is supplying apples to a nearby dealer regularly, these containers may be used over and over if the store is making sales by paper sack out of each box.

Waxing. Waxing of apples commercially grew fast in the 1960's. Smock's Cornell studies show waxed apples to have high gloss for a week or more at room temperature, have 1-3 days longer shelf-life than unwaxed apples but little or not improved rot control. "Waxes" include Carbanauba, paraffin, liquid polyethylene and some "waxes" contain shellac and resins. Cost is about 1½-2 cents/box for 400 boxes/hr.; small operations, 5 cents/box or more. About 2½ gals. wax covers 400 boxes of fruit. Real cost comes in washing and drying (Fig. 14). Customers will be the ones who will decide if they want to pay for glossiness in waxing, since actually not much benefit is derived.

APPLE PROCESSING

Details of this phase of the apple business usually fall in food technology. It should be noted, however, that the percentage of apple crops being processed has been increasing. In fact, over forty percent of the United States apple crop goes into such products as sauce, juice and cider, regular and dehydro-frozen slices, powdered and concentrate apple juice, pies, baked, and other frozen and canned products.

With the changing habits of the housewife toward less preparation of foods before meals, it is probable that an increasing amount of the crop will be processed in future years. About one-third of the processed apples

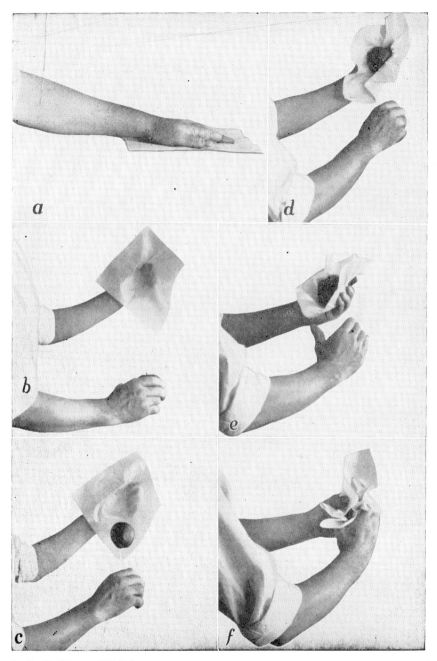

R. R. Pailthorp U.S.D.A.

Figure 17. Method for wrapping apples for box packing is shown here and in Figure 18. (a) Pick up the wrap; (b) cup the wrap and pick up apple; (c) throw the apple into the wrap; (d) position of apple upon striking wrap; (e) close left hand about apple, note position of right hand; and (f) wrapping process. See Figure 18.

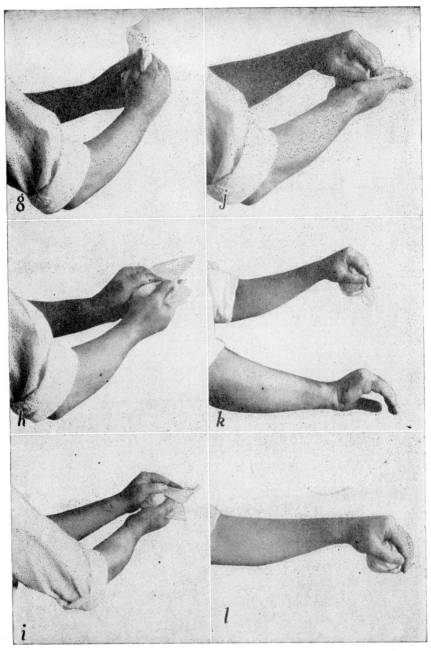

R. R. Pailthorp U.S.D.A.

Figure 18. Wrapping process continued. (g) Apple held tightly in right hand, pressing apple against cup formed by left hand; (h) apple turned within cup formed by left hand, both wrists turning toward right; (i) hands turn over completely; (j) back of left hand upward, back of right hand downward; (k) apple ready for placing in box, right hand reaching for next apple; (l) place wrapped apple in box.

are made into sauce, one-third into juice, cider and vinegar, about 9 percent frozen slices for bakery, and 5 percent dried (decreasing). Total crop processed is over 50 million bushels, and has been increasing about 1.7 million bushels a year in the U. S., which indicates this growing phase of the apple business.

Varieties for processing. Studies at the University of Maryland have shown that for apples for slicing, York and Golden Delicious rank high in wholeness and firmness, the latter having particularly good color. Jonathan ranks next. Stayman, North Western Greening, and Rome Beauty are less desirable for this use. The latter varieties, however, are good for baking. McIntosh and its relatives are generally down on the list with respect to quality for processing. Delicious is a good processer, but it generally has a good fresh market outlet.

A study was made by U.S.D.A. of the qualities of Delicious, Golden Delicious, Jonathan, Rome Beauty, Stayman, and Winesap with respect to applesauce and baking, as related to their raw qualities. Conclusions are: It is known that consumer preferences do exist for varying degrees of sweetness or tartness, firmness or softness of apples for eating raw. Nevertheless, from judges' ratings all apples in this study that were of good harvest quality were acceptable for eating raw before storage and after storage for as long as 5 months at 40° F. and for 6 months or more at 32°. In general, the same was true for apples used in making applesauce and baking. Delicious apples, though not commonly considered a cooking apple, made acceptable sauce from apples freshly harvested or stored no more than 3 months. Jonathan and Stayman apples of higher acid content made smoother, thinner sauces than the other varieties. Jonathan and Rome Beauty made better baked apples. When of good harvest quality, Golden Delicious made acceptable baked apples. Delicious and Winesap baked apples had tough skins and hard flesh textures; hence, were less acceptable, as were Stayman baked apples because of soft and mushy texture.

Experience of William Rooker of H. F. Byrd, Inc., Winchester, Va., one of the largest apple growers and processors in the U. S., is that there is not a variety now grown that cannot be used to good advantage by the processors. Although certain varieties are best for certain products, *quality* and *proper stage of maturity* are more important. Some examples cited are: Golden Delicious is the best sauce variety, but if green or overly soft, it is not as good as other varieties. Stayman is the best juice apple, but sound, fully mature Delicious, Winesap, Jonathan, Grimes Golden, Rome and York are better for juice than a poor-quality Stayman. Most processors use a mixture of varieties in an effort to keep their apple products uniform in taste and texture throughout the year.

Apple butter. Processors can use any variety, but a high proportion of Ben Davis gives a pleasing red color to the apple butter mix.

231

Apple juice. Again it is best to use a blend of varieties. Rooker prefers 25% Golden and Red Delicious, 50% Jonathan, Winesap and Stayman,, and 25% York and Black Twig. When one variety is used alone, Stayman or Winesap is preferred.

Apple sauce. A blend of at least four or five varieties is suggested in order to maintain a uniform pack through the season. By using a number of varieties, processors can drop one that becomes scarce and add another without abrupt changes in flavor, color, texture or consistency of the sauce.

Apple slices. This may surprise some growers, but a number of varieties now make just as good slices as York. Years ago, when canners started canning slices, York was the only variety that would stand up under the process. Buyers got into the habit of demanding Yorks for slicing. Processors have developed better methods, however, that permit them to make excellent slices from many varities. Stayman is the favorite variety for slicing with his company and added that "eastern Red Delicious makes some of the best apple slices I have ever inspected." But a fully mature old York apple still is the best all-around variety for processing.

Apple varieties are listed in order of preference for processing:

First, old York; second, Golden Delicious; third, new York; fourth, Stayman and fifth, Northwestern Greening. After these, all varieties are rated about the same. Three varieties that may deserve slightly higher ranking are: Ben Davis, Gano and Lowry.

What processors want most is: *Clean, sound fruit that is fully mature.* This means getting apples at the stage when their flavor and sugar content are highest. Sugar content and flavor reach their peak at the same time in apples.

Large apples. Large apples are desired. For example, suppose a processor has 40 peeling units, daily labor costs of $3,600 (early 1960s) and pays growers 85c a bushel for sauce apples. If the apples are all 2¾ inches, he can handle about 7,500 bushels in a nine-hour shift. Production will be about 10,200 cases of sauce. His fruit cost will be 62.5c a case. Total labor, 35.3c per case.

Now, if the processor has all 3-inch apples, he can handle 9,400 bushels in a nine-hour shift and production will be 13,000 cases. His fruit cost will be 60c a case and labor cost 27.1c a case. This would be a total saving (fruit and labor) of 10.7c a case or $1,400 each nine-hour shift.

Processing Grades. The Virginia Agricultural Experiment Station studied the U.S. standards for apple grades for processing which have not been changed for several decades. Labor costs during this period had increased tenfold. To do the job economically, fruit of better quality is needed to cut the trimming time, defect trim, and increase the yield of usable product. These workers found that the U. S. No. 2 grade of apples for processing was of no value to the processor, or actually cut the profit on the U. S. No. 1 grade because of excessive hand labor required to prepare the No. 2 grade of processing. The U. S. grades established in 1930 allow a maxium defect trim for No. 1 and No. 2 grades of 5 and 25 per cent, respectively. The latter figure was found to be too lenient.

Lopez *et al.* on the basis of their studies, recommended A, B, and C grades for processing apples, allowing maxium defect trim of about 3, 6, and 12 per cent, respectively. Defect trim does not include the peel trim which results from peel not removed by semi-automatic peelers. By using the more narrow grade limits suggested above, a better quality of apples is obtained for processing, cutting processing costs. Poorer quality apples not meeting the C grade should be used for cider or juice. Actually, with better growing techniques in recent years, the overall quality of the apple crops has improved, making it easier to meet these higher grade standards.

General Comments. At an apple processing conference held at the University of Maryland, College Park, a number of conclusions were drawn by processors, growers and government service workers which may be of interest. They are briefed as follows.

About 70% of the apple crop is processed in the Virginia area vs 40% for the USA. Yield per tree in the U. S. has increased dramatically since 1950 due to improved cultural practices and removal of marginal orchards. A big explosion will occur in the amount of Red Delicious on the market; previous estimates have been too conservative. Golden Delicious is showing the biggest percentage increase because it is of value as a fresh and processing variety. Apple plantings seem to be governed more by current prices than probable future trends. Since it takes apple growers longer to shift out of the business than potato growers, they go through considerable misery while over-producing before the balance of production and marketing is adjusted. Processors are planting their own orchards to supply their business. There is a trend toward storing apples for processing in CA storages because it enables the processors to spread their peaks, minimize the labor problem, and cease building bigger plants to take care of peak operation. Growers in the northwest have a growing interest in processing whereas only limited interest was shown in the past. Freight rates show that there is an advantage of over $1.00 a hundred pounds for shipping of processed West Coast apples to the rest of the country as compared with shipping East Coast processed apples.

If there is an overproduction of apples, growers can go to the U. S. government to get production-control laws similar to those in California. Future apple producing areas will be concentrated where climate, cost of production, processing and sales and distribution are the most favorable.

Processors object to buying apples on a "junk" or "salvage" basis. Processing is becoming a paying proposition for both processor and grower and a quality product is needed. Michigan studies show that when there is a 10% price reduction in fresh apples or an apple product, there is a 5%

increase in demand for fresh apples, a 44% increase in demand for apple-sauce, and a 23% increase in demand for apple juice.

Some apple growers want to produce for processors because they can "push" their trees to higher yields with more fertilizer, do less trimming, do only limited hand thinning, undergo quick sales and movement of crop with little or no storage problem and lower labor costs generally. Growers estimate that they can save from 5 to 10% on growing costs when apples are produced for processors.

Cornell finds that apples can be harvested mechanically for processing in about as good condition as they can be hand picked. Some New York growers are permitting pickers to shake the trees and pick the fruit from the ground for processing. With mechanical harvesting, one can do the work of 8 to 10 pickers. Damage to the apples is about 15% which is about the same as by hand picking. To use mechanical harvesting, a grower must be producing over 40,000 bushels. An automatic machine is needed to separate bruised apples by degree of bruising before process-ing. Bruised apples should be processed first, and good apples placed in CA storage if possible. A bruise tends to grow in size with time — faster at a warm temperature; hence, bruised apples should be kept cool. A pro-cessor stated that with CA apples, a price of $1.77 per hundred pounds of processing fruit was obtained above the price for regular storage apples. CA storage has been found to reduce or stop bitter pit development in Spy.

New York has a law that processors cannot accept fruit before a mu-tually acceptable price is reached. In western New York, 80% of the ap-ples are produced for processing. The N content of apple leaves is main-tained at 1.7% for fresh fruit sales and 2.0% for processing fruit. Growers can double their yield by applying more N and maintaining the higher N content in the leaves. Varieties processed are: Delicious, Golden Delicious, and Idared with Rhode Island Greening, McIntosh, Monroe, and Twenty Ounce of lesser importance. Cortland, Rome, Baldwin and Ben Davis also are processed. It is believed that McIntosh and Rhode Island Green-ing will continue for some time as processing varieties.

Summer varieties are generally not desired by processors. If breeders could produce an early variety adaptable to processing, growers could produce it more economically and it would help spread the processing season. An example of costs given by a Pennsylvania processor are: 35% direct cost of apples; 26% for containers; 16%, labor; 13%, sugar; 7%, overhead, 3%, cartons; and 0.6%, labels. Apple processors complain of having no organized body of growers with whom to deal. It would be an advantage to both processors and growers to have a small talking body for each group to finalize deals.

The citrus industry is using about 20 million dollars a year to promote fresh and processed citrus; processors and growers are on the same pro-motion team. California experience shows that it takes about four years to develop a product that will go well on the market. Cranberry promotion technique for juice should be used on apple juice to increase sales every month of the year, rather than having one tall peak of apple juice and cider sales at Hallowe'en. Ocean Spray Cranberry Company gives a bonus and helps finance advertising of poultry when cranberry sauce is included in the advertisement. Instruction from state agricultural extension services is needed to bring restaurant and bakery chefs up-to-date on how to bake good pies. This "gift" has been lost in recent years. Apple promotion booths should be set up at the annual national restaurant and dental meetings. Apple pie has decreased on menus due to an increase in tarts, which do not use as many apples as pies. A big volume of processed fruit goes to institutions and restaurants in No. 10 cans, and this outlet should be "nursed" and promoted more than in the past. U. S. Army personnel use more apples in fresh and processed form than the average civilian; a greater effort should be made to promote apple use by the U. S. Armed Services which is a big buyer. Consumption of canned peaches ranks first in the U. S. Army with applesauce second.

In California, there is Federal and State inspection of the fresh product before it is processed. This third party is needed for bargaining and protection.

The following variety characteristics are considered in apple processing: (a) Golden Delicious loses weight fast after harvest if not handled properly; (b) Spy has a tender skill as does Golden Delicious; (c) Stayman and McIntosh have a tough skin; (d) Rome and Idared are outstanding in storage life; (e) Rome and Monroe give high yield as peelers; (f) oblate or conical shaped varieties give less yield in processing; (g) Delicious has large seed pockets whereas Rhode Island Greening has small seed pockets; (h) York has a high ratio of processed product to initial volume of apples; (i) darkening of flesh near the core and coarseness of the fibrovascular bundles are undesirable characters; (j) McIntosh softens fast in a thermal-processing step, whereas York and Monroe are least affected; (k) Rhode Island Greening and Newtown Pippin score high in retention of juice while processing whereas McIntosh scores low; and (l) juice from McIntosh and Northern Spy changes color but little in storage, whereas juice from Red Delicious may brown. Apple juice is the biggest processed apple product in Canada with growing interest in carbonated cider; this type cider is popular in Europe. An apple cider slush (ice crystals) is boosting sales in some areas. (see Chap. XII).

Cider. For details on cider making see the U.S.D.A. bulletin by Robinson *et al.* cited at the end of this chapter.

Review Questions

1. What is the general procedure and the necessary precautions in estimating the yield of an orchard?

2. What difficulties may be encountered by harvesting apples prematurely or when overripe?
3. List and discuss briefly 3 of the apparently better methods for determining when apples should be picked.
4. List 2 hormone harvest sprays for reducing fruit drop. When and at what concentration are they applied?
5. Describe how a mature apple should be removed from the spur.
6. Why is it important to keep fruit cool after harvesting?
7. What is the present day trend in apple packages as compared with thirty years ago? How do you account for this shift?
8. List the advantages and disadvantages of the Northwestern apple box, tray-pack carton, polyethylene bags, and other consumer packs.
9. What is meant by grade of apples?
10. Upon what two principles are the methods for sizing apples based?
11. How does a co-operative packing house operate? Its advantages?
12. Briefly discuss the important factors to consider in planning a packing house for convenience and economical operation.
13. What is meant by 2-2, 3-2, and 2-1 pack in preparing boxed apples?
14. Discuss recent developments in labor saving machinery and techniques for harvesting and handling apples in the orchard and packing house. Under what conditions are they profitable to use?

Suggested Collateral Readings

Batjer, L. P. Harvest Sprays for the Control of Fruit Drop. U.S.D.A. Cir. 685. Request recent edition.

Blakeley, R. A. and J. F. Spencer. Planning your packing shed layout for production. Cornell Univ. (Ithaca) Ext. Publ. 100. Sept. 1960.

Blanpied, G. D. and Shaul Ben-David. A New York Study of 'McIntosh' apple optimum harvest dates. J. Amer. Soc. Hort. Sci. 95(2) :151-154. 1970.

Bosch, C., Ed. Electronic apple color sorter in commercial use. Eastern Fruit Grower, pp. 5-6, Dec. 1961.

Brearley, N. and J. E. Breeze. Spectrophotometric measurements of skin colours of apples. J. Sci. Food and Agric.: 17. pp. 62-64. Feb. 1966.

Brunk, Max E., B. A. Dominick, D. A. Call and O. D. Forker. Profile and prospects in apple products 1967-1975. American Can Company, 100 Park Ave., New York City, June 1967.

Carey, L. C. Containers in Common Use for Fresh Fruits and Vegetables. U.S.D.A. Farmers' Bulletin 2013. Request recent edition.

Cargo, C. A. and D. H. Dewey. Thiabendazole and Benomyl for the control of post-harvest decay of apples. HortSci. Vol. 5, No. 4. pp. 259. August 1970.

Dalrymple, D. G. and I. C. Feustel. Recent developments in production and marketing of applesauce and slices. USDA Fed. Ext. Ser. July 1965.

Dalrymple, D. G. and I. C. Feustel. Recent developments in production and marketing of apple juice and cider. USDA Fed. Ext. Ser. July 1964.

Edgerton, L. J. New compound aids regulation of fruit abscission. New York's Food and Life Sci. (Cornell) Vol. 1, No. 1. pp. 19-20. Jan.-March 1968.

Electronic color sorter for apples. Western Fruit Grower. pp. 14-15. Dec. 1961.

Ethylene and Fruit Abscission - A Symposia at Florida ASHS Meeting, Nov. 2-3, 1970. In HortSci. 6(4): August 1971.

Evans, H. C. and R. S. Marsh. Costs and Mechanical Injury in Handling and Packing Apples. W. Va. Agr. Exp. Sta. Bull. 416. June, 1958.

FMC Catalogues for Fruit Handling Equipment. Contact the Lakeland, Flordia or San Francisco, Calif. branches of Food Machinery and Chemical Corp.

French, B. C. and D. G. Gillette. Cost of assembling and packing apples as related to scale of operation. Mich. Agr. Exp. Sta. Tech. Bull. 272. 1959.

Fridley, R. B. and P. A. Adrian. Mechanical harvesting equipment for deciduous tree fruits. Calif. Agr. Exp. Sta. Bull. 825, 56 pp. July 1966.

Haller, Mark H. and J. R. Magness. Picking Maturity of Apples. U.S.D.A. Cir. 711. 1944.

Hardenburg, R. E. and R. E. Anderson. Polyethlene box liners for storage of Golden Delicious apples. USDA Mkting Res. Rpt. No. 461. March 1961.

Herrernan, R. E. Apple storage and packing facilities for southern Illinois. USDA Agr. Mkting Ser. Rpt. No. 610. July 1963.

Herrick, J. F. Jr., S. W. McBirney, and E. W. Carlsen. Handling and Storage of Apples in Pallet Boxes. U.S.D.A., Agr. Mark. Ser. Report 236. Processed 41 pp. 1958.

Herrick, J. F., Jr. et al. Apple packing and storage houses. USDA Mkting Res. Rpt. No. 602. Jan. 1964.

Hewitt, A. A. Modifications for mechanization in fruit trees. The Mountaineer Grower, W. Va. Hort. Soc., Charles Town. 1967.

Hoyt, S. C., N. R. Benson and E. C. Burts. The relationship of sulphur fumes to defoliation and fruit drop of apples. HortSci. Vol. 5 (1):27-28. Feb. 1970.

Huelin, F. E. and I. M. Coggiola. Superficial scald, a functional disorder of stored apples. V. Oxidation of a-farnesene and its inhibition by diphenylamine. J. Sci. Fd. Agric., Vol. 21, January 1970. Part IV: J. Sci. Fd. Agric., 1968, 19, 297.VI. Evaporation of a-farnesene from the fruit. J. Sci. Fd. Agric. 1970., Vol. 21, February.

Hulme, A. C. Biochemistry of fruits and their products. Food Sci. & Tech. Series of monographs. Vol. 1. 652 pp. Academic Press. New York, London, 1970. Vol. II in preparation.

Hunter, D. L. Apple Sorting Methods and Equipment. AMS-MRR No. 230 U.S.D.A. August, 1958.

Jackson, et al. Shade and apple position effects on fruit size, color, quality. J. HortSci. 46:11 pp. 1971.

Levin, J. H. and H. P. Gaston. Equipment Used by Deciduous Fruit Growers in Handling Bulk Boxes. U.S.D.A. Agr. Mark. Ser. Report 42-20. Aug., 1958.

Levin, J. H. and H. P. Gaston. The Three-team Method of Picking Apples. Mich. Agr. Exp. Sta. Qtly. Rpt. 38-65. June, 1956.

Lott, R. V. and R. R. Rice. Effect of Preharvest Sprays of 2, 4, 5-T Upon Maturation of Jonathan, Starking and Golden Delicious Apples. Ill. Agr. Exp. Sta. Bull. 589. 1955. (See also their bull. 588 on summer apple varieties.)

Markwardt, E. C. et al. Mechanical harvesting of apples used for processing. Cornell Univ., Ithaca, N. Y. Paper No. NA66-203. 155 pp. Aug. 1966.

McGrath, E. J. Marketing potential for superconcentrated apple juice, USDA Mkting Res. Rpt. No. 582. 1963.

McGrath, E. J. and Howard W. Kerr, Jr. Dehydro-frozen apple slices: their potential in selected markets. USDA Mkting Rec. Rpt. No. 578. 1963.

Mechanical harvesting of apples in New York, 1966. Reprint from N. Y. State Hort. Soc. Proc., Thomas E. LaMont, Ed., Albion. 1967.

Mohsenin, N. J. Physical properties of plant and animal materials. Vol. 1 Structure, physical characteristics and mechanical properties. Gordon and Breach Science Publishers, New York, 1970.

Murphy, Elizabeth F., C. Stiles and R. H. True. Effect of Succinic Acid-2,2-dimethylhydrazide (SADH) on the sensory quality of 'McIntosh' apples. J. Amer. Soc. Hort. Sci. Vol. 96, No. 4, p. 472. 1971.

National Canners Association. Monthly reports on canned stock of fruit. (must be a member) 1133 20th St. NW, Wash., D. C. 20036.

Nature, Mechanisms and Control of Ripening. A Symposia. HortSci. 5(1): 29-40. 1970.

(See additional references under Chapter X Appendix)

Catalogues can be obtained from these harvesting and handling equipment companies: (1) Wilde Bros. Mfg., Inc., Bailey, Mich. 49308; FMC Corp., Lakeland, Fla. 33802 and Jonesboro, Ark. 72401; Shipley Products, Box 8276, Oakland, Calif. 94608; Ramacher Mfg. Co., Linden, Calif.; H. C. Shaw Co., Fresno, Calif.; Shock-Wave-Shaker, Yuba City, Calif. 95991; Fruit and Produce Packaging Co., Box 31155, Indianapolis, Ind. 46321; see Amer. Fruit Grower Buyer's Guide issue. July each year.

CHAPTER XI

Storing Apples

◆ ◆

The price of apples during a normal storage season will gradually rise as the marketing season progresses. This normal seasonal price increase makes it desirable for the apple grower to devise a means of delaying his marketing to obtain the higher prices. In order to make the venture profitable, however, the cost of storage and any loss from decay of fruit during storage must be less than the increase in price return at the time of marketing. The venture is profitable as indicated by the increasing number of farm-refrigerated and CA storages.

Reasons given by growers for owning their own storages are: (1) cost of storage on the farm is less than that of commercial storage, (2) the grower is better able to choose and satisfy his market, (3) the necessity of grading and packing at picking time is eliminated, (4) the apple storage can be used for holding strawberries, peaches, eggs, citrus and other products for rental or better prices, (5) storage space is always available even in the heaviest crop years, (6) growers can receive the benefit of seasonal price advances, and (7) quick cooling of apples from orchard.

In the over-all picture, storages have three chief advantages whether owned by a commercial concern or by the grower himself: (1) to provide a means of holding apples in good condition for several months, thus permitting orderly distribution of the crop and preventing gluts on the market, (2) the orderly distribution of fruit tends to stabilize prices, and (3) a

Dr. George E. Mattus, VPISU, Blacksburg, Va., and Dr. Chaim Frenkel, Rutgers University, New Brunswick, N. J. assisted in this chapter revision.

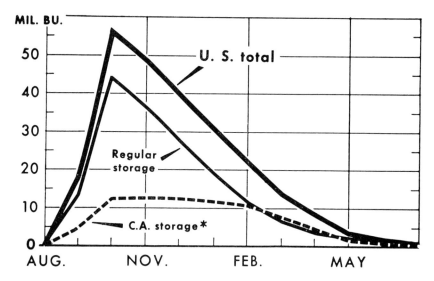

Figure 1. Curves in this chart are typical of movement of apples from regular and CA storages. Amount of controlled atmosphere (CA) apples may reach double or more the peak shown here in future years before leveling off (USDA).

continuous supply of high-quality apples is available to the consuming public every month of the year. This includes such popular varieties as McIntosh, Delicious, Golden Delicious and Jonathan which without storage would be available to the public only a few months after harvest.

In concentrated apple growing regions such as in Washington State, the fruit is largely handled and stored in huge cooperative plants where the grower more or less loses contact with the fruit once it leaves his orchard.

THE FUNCTION OF STORAGES

Harvested fruits are alive. They continue to carry on life processes which are essentially distructive. The basic object in storage is to keep these processes (ripening) at a minimum by lowering the temperature or by both lowering the temperature and modifying the atmospheric oxygen and carbon dioxide.

The respiration rate of fruit (O_2 intake and CO_2 output) is doubled or trebled for each 18° F. rise. Hence, an apple ripens two or three times as fast at 50° F. as at 32° F. and about two or three times as fast at 68° F. as at 50° F. For example, assume that apples are brought into the storage at 68° F. and are cooled to the "holding" temperature of 32° F. in one week. Assume also that the apples stay at 68° F. for four days, then the temperature is dropped to 50° F., held there for three days, and then dropped to 32° F. The first four days at 68° F. are comparable to twenty-eight days at holding temperature (32° F.), and the three days at 50° F. are comparable to six days at holding temperature. In other words, the storage

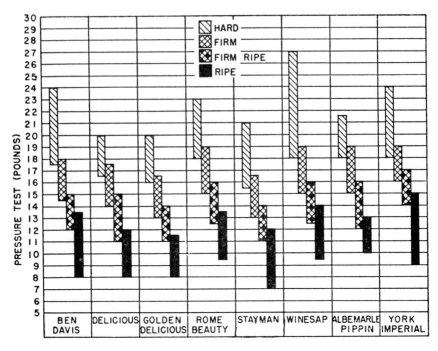

U.S.D.A.

Figure 1a. Chart shows a general range of fruit pressure tests, representing different stages of softening. Pressures of apple flesh can be obtained by using a Magness-Taylor pressure tester (see July Directory, American Fruit Grower). For maximum storage life, apples should be placed in storage at the "hard" stage. (See reference by Lott of Illinois for another interpretation of maturity terminology.)

life of apples cooled under these conditions is shortened by thirty-four days. In actual practice, the conditions would not be so extreme because the "cool down" is gradual and starts immediately, and it is not expected that the apples would remain at 68° F. for four days. On the other hand, apples are often brought into storage at temperatures exceeding 68° F. The importance of cooling the apples to holding temperature as rapidly as possible cannot be over emphasized (Figure 2). For this reason, refrigerating equipment is designed to cool the fruit in 24 hours. In actual practice the apples are not brought to storage temperature in this time, but actual practice has shown that this figure must be used to insure enough cooling capacity.

It is necessary for respiration and other ripening processes to take place in order for the fruit to reach proper eating condition. In ripening, the starch in mature firm fruit gradually changes to sugar; acids usually decrease; tannins and pectins change form; heat from respiration is given off, and the esters which are responsible for flavor and aroma of a variety, become more pronounced. As these chemical changes proceed, the fruit

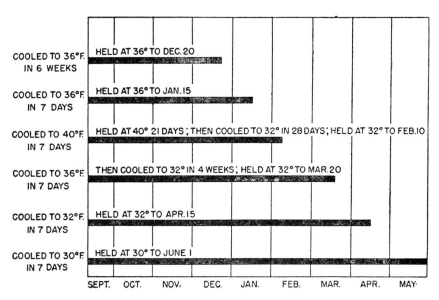

W. V. Hukill and Edwin Smith, U.S.D.A.

Figure 2. Normal storage life expectancy of Delicious apples when cooled at different rates and stored at different temperatures. For each week of exposure at 70 degrees F. before storage, deduct nine weeks of storage life at 22 degrees; for each week of delay at 53 degrees, deduct one month of storage life at 32 degrees.

tends to soften and the ground color changes from leafy green to yellowish shades. Eventually, the aroma and flavor develop fully, an optimum relationship is obtained between the amounts of sugar and acid, and the fruit softens to an ideal "eating stage." At this point, the fruit is said to be fully ripened with maximum quality.

The generation of heat during the respiration and ripening processes is greater than is commonly realized and is a factor deserving important consideration in the design and operation of fruit cold-storage houses. The faster a fruit ripens the greater the quantity of heat generated. It is of interest that a Bartlett pear ripens faster than an apple at a given temperature, and, therefore, its greater heat of respiration results in larger refrigeration demands, even when it is taken into storage at the same temperature as the apple.

IMPORTANT STORAGE FACTORS

There are three key factors contributing to the longevity of apples in storage. These are *temperature, humidity,* and *composition* of the storage atmosphere. In operation of air-cooled storages the factor of *ventilation* is important.

Temperature. Ripening processes of fruit proceed slowly if the temperature is maintained at 30° to 32° F., which is considered most satis-

241

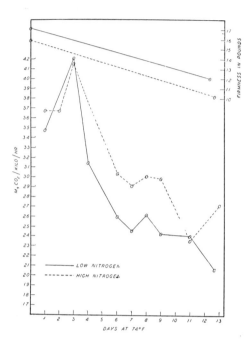

R. M. Smock, Cornell University, N. Y.

Figure 3. Respiration rate of apples is a good index of rate of ripening. Above chart shows that McIntosh from low-nitrogen trees respire more slowly and they are firmer than apples from high-nitrogen trees.

factory for apple storage, except for some varieties, such as Jonathan and Yellow Newtown which may develop soft scald or internal browning unless held at about 36° F. Grimes Golden apples that are intended for early marketing should be held at 35° to 38° instead of at 32°, in order to obtain better quality and avoid soggy breakdown.[1] These varieties preferably should be kept in a separate room if available. The average freezing temperature for most fall and winter apples is about 28.5° F. with a maximum freezing temperature of 25.3° F.

Controlled - atmosphere. CA storages may be run at a higher temperature during the holding period for certain varieties, such as McIntosh; but when the storage is opened at marketing time, the temperature is usually brought down to 32° F. Consequently, CA storage design and capacity are based on this temperature of 32°F.

Humidity. Unless humidity is regulated in a storage, fruit will lose moisture and shrivel. The minimum relative humidity should be not lower than 85 per cent. Relative humidities of 90 to 95 per cent can be maintained without excessive fungus growth if the temperature is held at 32° F. The grower can determine relative humidity by using a sling psychrometer or a wet and dry bulb thermometer with accompanying conversion tables; these are available and inexpensive.

If the inside building surfaces or refrigeration equipment are substantially colder than the humid air of the storage room, condensation of moisture on the walls is likely to take place. This situation is common during the loading-in season when there is a 10° F. or more "split" between temperature of the return and discharge air from coils. Excessive condensation in a storage is undesirable because most of the moisture in the air during the storage holding months comes from the fruit; eventually, this situation will cause shriveling. Condensation of water on the walls and ceiling can

---

[1]For relative lengths of storage season and susceptibility to storage scald for popular apple varieties, see Table 2, in Chapter II.

242

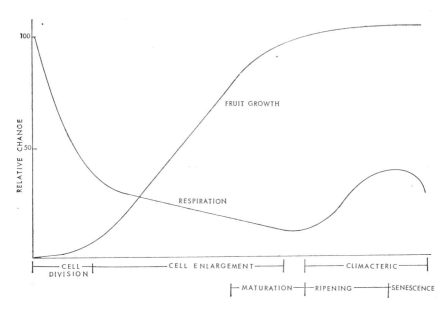

Figure 3a. Growth of an apple fruit on the tree is shown by the typical sigmoid "S" curve above. Growth, of course, stops on harvesting. Designated are the stages of (a) cell division, (b) cell enlargement and (c) maturation. The onset of the climacteric rise in respiration marks the initiation of ripening and senescence. (Adapted from J. B. Biale by Chaim Frenkel, Rutgers University).

be prevented during winter by adequate insulation in the walls to prevent the inner wall surface from becoming substantially colder than the air in the storage room.

Ventilation. Ventilation refers to the introduction of outdoor air into the storage room. Ventilation is necessary for air-cooled storages as a means of lowering temperature, as discussed later. However, ventilation for the benefit of the stored product itself is not essential. This is because in mechanically refrigerated storages of usual construction, carbon dioxide from respiration of the fruit does not build up to the point where it is toxic to the stored product, nor is oxygen reduced to the point where it is limiting in the respiratory process. However, oxygen may become so low in cold storages that some ventilation will be necessary for the comfort of men working in them. Air circulation within a storage, as differentiated from ventilation, is important in moving air away from fruit and preventing the adjacent accumulation of ethylene gas and esters which, respectively, speed ripening and cause storage scald on susceptible varieties. Do not store apples with potatoes, onions, or cabbage.

TYPES OF STORAGE BUILDINGS

There are essentially three types of storage buildings now in use: (1) storages refrigerated with mechanical equipment, (2) refrigerated and

243

TABLE 1. REQUIREMENTS FOR CONTROLLED ATMOSPHERE STORAGE OF APPLES

Variety	$\%CO_2$	$\%O_2$	Temperature°F
McIntosh	2—5	2—3	37—38
Delicious and Golden Delicious	1.5—3	2.5—3	30—32
Jonathan	3—5	3	32
Rome Beauty, Stayman Winesap	2—3	3	30—32
Yellow Newtown	5—8	2—3	38—40

controlled-atmosphere (CA) storages, and (3) air-cooled strages. A fourth approach, under experimentation, is a pressure-tight storage room where apples are held at only a fraction of atmospheric pressure. The air-cooled storages refrigerated with ice have for the most part disappeared.

The air-cooled storage. This was the predominating type of storage in the more northern areas, but nearly all of them have been converted to refrigerated storages. In Michigan in the 1960's less than 10 percent of the total apple storage space was of this type. Temperature in the storage room is reduced by opening air intakes and vents and admitting cool air when the air temperature outside is colder than the storage room temperature (Figure 10). The vents and intakes are then closed before the outside temperature rises above the storage-room temperature. Operating costs of these storages are very low. If air-cooled storages are constructed, it is wise to insulate them sufficiently so that later when additional finances are available, they can be converted to mechanical refrigeration.

Mechanically refrigerated storages. The mechanically refrigerated storage is the most popular in the major world apple producing areas. When properly designed and operated, it has the advantages of (1) prompt cooling of products, (2) maintenance of optimum relative humidity, and (3) an even holding temperature with only a one-to-two degree fluctuation. Since this type of storage is the most popular, it will be discussed in greater detail later.

Controlled atmosphere (CA) storages. Interest in this type storage was stimulated by the initial work of Kidd and West in England in the 1930's and developed commercially by Dr. Robert M. Smock, Cornell University, starting in the early 1940's. CA storages hold an important and increasing part of the apple crop stored in North America and other countries. Some 18 million bushels were CA stored in the U. S. in 1971 or about 28 percent of the stored apples. The advantages are: (1) storage life of apples can be prolonged beyond the normal life in regular cold storage, (2) some varieties subject to low temperature disorders, such as McIntosh, can be held for a long period at a temperature above 32°F., (3) fruit removed from storage keeps longer than fruit held an equal time

244

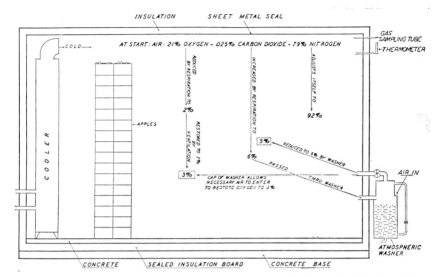

Figure 6. Vertical diagrammatic sketch of a conventional controlled-atmosphere (CA) storage room indicating how the atmosphere is controlled. With gas generators, the atmosphere machinery is outside the room flushing desired gas mixture into room. Latter system affords O₂ pull down from 20% to 3% in about 3 days vs 30 days by conventional system. (R. M. Smock, Cornell University)

in regular storage, (4) it is rodent proof, (5) a relative humidity can be maintained above 90 percent with little danger of mold growth, and (6) apples removed from CA storage have more of a firm "fresh apple" taste. CA apples may bring 80c more per bushel than regular stored apples; CA costs are 35-40c more per bushel.

The essential features of CA storage are: (1) use of mechanical refrigeration to maintain temperatures of 30-32°F. or 36-38°F., depending on the varieties stored; (2) the storage room is specially constructed *gastight* for regular CA storage or *suitably tight* for an externally generated atmosphere introduced into the room (The Arcogen System)[1], or a combination of both methods; (3) in regular CA storage oxygen is reduced and carbon dioxide is increased by the respiring apples. Nitrogen gas may be introduced into the storage by portable equipment to hasten the reduction of oxygen after the storage room is filled and sealed; (4) in regular CA storage excess carbon dioxide is removed by water scrubbing, or supplemented by caustic soda when necessary, or carbon dioxide is absorbed by dry hydrated lime; and (5) oxygen level is usually held at about 3 percent and carbon dioxide about 2 to 5 percent, depending on the apple variety. If oxygen is below 18% in a CA room, repairs by man must be made with a suitable air supplying or oxygen mask. To load or unload fruit, the atmosphere must be flushed out to raise oxygen up to at least 18% and reduce carbon dioxide to a low level.

---

[1]Manufactured by Atlantic Research Corp., Alexandria, Va. 22314.

Fruit is inspected through a window and fruit samples may be taken by temporarily opening and reaching through a small port hole. Atmosphere samples are taken daily for carbon dioxide and oxygen analysis and the scrubbing of carbon dioxide, the increase in oxygen, or changes in generated atmospheres are made in accordance with the daily atmosphere tests. The cost of CA storage is higher than regular storage. Costs vary depending on type of CA, building and storing costs, length of storage, and other factors. Good condition CA stored fruit brings a premium price but may not continue to do so. When the controlled atmosphere is terminated in a room, the fruit remains under refrigeration until sold. The later the CA storage is opened, the sooner the CA fruit should be sold. Fruit from a late season CA opening should be sold within a few weeks. Some apples are held under CA conditions for processing but most CA fruit is intended for the fresh dessert market. CA storage has extended the normal storage season of many apple varieties and has thus eased the marketing pressure through the harvest and storage season. With the advent of large CA storage holdings, (may reach 25 million bushels or more in U. S.), it is becoming increasingly difficult to market regular storage apples after the middle of the storage season.

CA storage operation since 1960 has been simplified insofar as the grower is concerned by introduction of automatic equipment that maintains the desired gas mixture inside the storage room, flushes it through the room, and recirculates the desired O_2 and CO_2 levels. Advantages over regular CA are: (1) O_2 pull-down takes 3 to 5 days compared with 25 to 30 days for regular CA; (2) rooms do not need to be as gas tight, (3) rooms can be opened and resealed after or before fully loaded; (4) much less worry and bother to the grower with daily operation details, and (5) rooms can be used for strawberries, peaches, tomatoes, etc., in off-apple-season.

A Holland gas generator (Oxydrain[1], will serve up to ½ million box storage) speeds O_2 pull-down 4 to 5 times faster by cracking ammonia at 2000° F. into hydrogen and nitrogen, then joining hydrogen with oxygen forming water. The nitrogen gas quickly displaces O_2 and CO_2 in the room which also gives better emergency hold-down with gas leaks.

Inflated CA apple warehouses have been in use since 1967 in France: 88x39x33' high, 840 denier nylon, storing 25,000 bu., erected in a month at ½ cost, white neoprene interior-coated, yellow DuPont Hypalon "rubber" exterior-coated, double door air-lock, no built-in floor but fitted with bolts sunk in concrete base and held by metal perimeter strip, sealed with

---

[1]Designed by Pieter Noordzij of Wageningen, The Netherlands, consulting engineer for Food Industries Research and Engineering, Yakima, Wash.

neoprene adhesive before inflation, and predicted to last 15 years against adverse elements.

See Appendix for CA storage construction details.

SIZE OF STORAGE BUILDINGS

In calculating storage building capacities, about 2.5 to 2.8 cu. ft. of storage space is allowed for each bushel. The 2.8 cu. ft. ratio allows ample space for aisles and for proper stacking to facilitate good air circulation. Where palleted or bulk boxes are used, from 10 to 20 per cent more fruit can be stored in a given area. Modern 25,000 box or larger storages usually have about 20 ft. of vertical stacking space for fork lift handling of crates on pallets or bulk bins.

INSULATION AND INSULATING MATERIALS

Gray and Smock of Cornell University offer the following information on this key subject. "Insulation is a material used in wall, ceiling, floor, or roof construction primarily to reduce the rate of heat transfer through the structure. The ability of a material to conduct heat through a unit thickness is called its *thermal conductivity;* the resistance of the material of unit thickness to the flow of heat is its *thermal resistivity*. The conductivity of a material is the reciprocal of its resistivity; that is, conductivity $= \dfrac{1}{\text{resistivity}}$.

The flow of heat through any structure can be likened to the flow of water through a pipe. The quantity of water that flows out of a pipe depends upon the pressure behind it, the resistance of the pipe, and the size of the pipe. The pressure is the force that moves the water; the resistance of the pipe tends to retard the flow and must be overcome by the pressure; and the size or area of the pipe determines how large a quanitity can move through the pipe at one time. In heat flow through a wall, the difference in temperature from one side to the other is the force that causes the heat to flow. The thermal resistivity of the insulation tends to retard the flow of heat, and the area of wall involved determines the total quantity of heat flowing through the wall.

The temperature inside the refrigerated storage is much lower than the outdoor temperature during loading time. Consequently, the temperature difference, or the force tending to move the heat, is relatively high. To keep the heat flow into the storage at a minimum, an insulation that has a high resistance to the flow of heat is used.

Many types of insulation materials are available. Some of them are commercial and some are native, such as sawdust, shavings, and the like. To be of greatest value, the materials should have good insulating qualities, must be dry, and should be economical, relatively easy to put in place, odor free, and vermin proof.

247

Based on physical characteristics, insulating materials may be divided into four classes: (1) reflective, (2) rigid, (3) flexible, and (4) loose fill.

Reflective insulation derives its name from the fact that it has a bright shiny surface that reflects radiant heat much as a bright shiny object reflects the sunlight. Such insulation is typified by aluminum sheets or aluminum foil. This type of insulation loses its effectiveness when placed in contact with the building or other materials. For best results, a ¾-inch air space between this insulation and any other material, and between the layers of this type of insulation, is recommended. When reflective insulation is placed between studs, precautions must be taken to prevent air movement by convection between the layers. Air next to the layer on the warm side rises and that on the cold side falls thus setting up convection currents that take up heat on the warm side and give it up at the cold. This increases the rate of heat transfer and reduces the effectiveness of the insulation. To prevent this air movement, horizontal wood strips should be placed about 30 inches apart between the layers.

Rigid insulation is made up of rigid boards of insulating material that can be laid up against the sheathing. Rigid insulation has considerable structural strength, and some types are used as sheathing.

Styrofoam has largely been replaced by Polyurethane which is within cost range and is twice as effective. (Table 3).

Flexible insulation is made up of blankets or bats of insulating material that can be laid up against sheathing between studs and joists. These blankets have no structural strength and depend upon the structure to support them.

Loose-fill insulation consists of loose or granular insulating material. This type of insulation has no structural strength and must be poured into a rigid container as the space between the inside and outside sheathing. Included in this class are native materials, such as sawdust, shavings, and buckwheat hulls.

To determine the particular insulation to use, the grower should choose the one that gives him the desired insulating value for the least expenditure for material and construction.

Materials of construction other than insulation also offer resistance to the flow of heat. Although this resistance is small compared with that for insulation, it still should be included in determining the overall rate of heat flow.

There is additional resistance to heat flow from a solid surface to air in contact with it and from air to a solid surface. In storage-wall construction two of these surfaces need to be considered, one inside and one outside. The outside surface offers less resistance because the sweeping action of wind tends to increase the rate of heat transfer.

In some types of wall construction, air spaces are left. These air spaces resist the flow of heat mainly because of the resistance of the bounding surfaces. Under most normal conditions, the resistance of an air space

TABLE 3.

Thermal insulation and conductivity practical values for various materials[1]

Material	Conductivity (k)[2]	Conductance (C)[3]	Thermal insulation	
			Resistivity (1/k)[4] (per inch of thickness)	Resistance (1/C)[5] (thickness listed)
Building materials				
Common woods (average) 1 inch thick	0.92	....	1.09	....
Common woods (average) ⅞ inch thick	....	1.05	....	0.95
Plywood, ⅜ inch thick	....	2.12	....	0.47
Stone masonry	12.50	....	0.08	....
Concrete (gravel aggregate)	12.50	....	0.08	....
Concrete (cinder aggregate)	4.90	....	0.22	....
Concrete (lightweight aggregate)	2.50	....	0.40	....
Concrete block, 8 inches thick	....	1.00	....	1.00
Concrete block, 12 inches thick	....	0.80	....	1.25
Cinder block, 8 inches thick	....	0.60	....	1.66
Cinder block, 12 inches thick	....	0.53	....	1.88
Plaster Board, Sheet Rock, Gypsum Board, ⅜ inch thick	....	3.73	....	0.27
Insulating materials Reflective				
Reflective sheets 5 thicknesses, spaced ¾ and ¾ inch between insulation and sheathing	....	0.077	....	13.02
Rigid				
Corkboard	0.30	....	3.33	....
Wood fibre board	0.312	....	3.21	....
Mineral wool board	0.321	....	3.12	....
Vegetable fibre board	0.346	....	2.85	....
Foamglass	0.40	....	2.50	....
Styrofoam	0.25	....	4.00	....
Polyurethane	0.12	....	8.33	....
Blankets				
Mineral wool	0.27	....	3.70	....
Wood fibre (Insulite)	0.33	....	3.00	....
Cellulose fibre	0.27	....	3.70	....
Glass wool (Fiberglas)	0.27	....	3.70	....
Loose-fill				
Regranulated cork (3/16-inch particles	0.31	....	3.22	....
Buckwheat hulls	0.36	....	2.78	....
Vermiculite	0.48	....	2.08	....
Shavings (ordinary dry)	0.41	....	2.44	....

Table 3 continued on next page

[1] These values are from various sources, such as United States Bureau of Standards and manufacturers specifications.

[2] *Conductivity* (k) is rate of heat transfer in B.t.u. per hour per degree difference in temperature (F.) per square foot of surface through 1 inch thickness of material.

[3] *Conductance* (C) is the rate of heat transfer in B.t.u. per hour per degree difference in temperature (F.) per square foot of surface through the thickness as manufactured and used.

[4] *Resistivity* (1/k), the reciprocal of k, is the insulating value of 1 inch of the material.

[5] Resistance (1/C), the reciprocal of C, is the insulating value of the thickness of the material as manufactured and used.

Table 3 (continued)

Thermal insulation and conductivity practical values for various materials (continued)

Material	Con-duc-tivity (k)[2]	Con-duc-tance (C)[3]	Thermal insulation	
			Resistivity (1/k)[4] (per inch of thickness)	Resistance (1/C)[5] (thickness listed)
Sawdust (ordinary dry)	0.41	....	2.44	....
Cinders (screened and fine material discarded)	1.25	....	0.80	....
Redwood bark	0.26	....	3.90	....
Miscellaneous				
Air space (vertical, ¾ inch or more, ordinary surfaces)	....	1.10	....	0.91
Surfaces (ordinary non-reflective wall)				
still air	....	1.65	....	0.61
15 mph wind velocity	....	6.00	....	0.17
Roofing materials				
Asphalt shingles	....	6.50	....	0.15
Built up roofing (⅜ inch)	....	3.53	....	0.28
Heavy roll roofing	....	6.50	....	0.15
Wood shingles	....	1.28	....	0.78

increases with the thickness of the space up to ¾ inch. Beyond that, the increase is slight and for practical considerations is neglected. For this reason, the conductance of an air space is usually given for "¾ inch or more," and includes surface conductances.

Thermal insulating values, and conductivities and conductances of some of the materials more commonly used for refrigerated storage construction are given in Table 3.

Minimum insulation requirements. Through experience, minimum insulating values for floors, walls, and ceilings have been set for refrigerated apple storages in climates such as New York State. For walls, a minimum of 4 inches of corkboard or *its equivalent in insulating value* has been recommended. Where loose-fill types of insulation are used, a minimum of 6 inches is recommended. Although some of the loose-fill types have the same insulating value as corkboard, a greater thickness is recommended because plaster protruding from the joints in masonry walls reduces the effective thickness, and it is also difficult to pack these types of insulation to optimum density.

The thickness of insulation in the ceiling should be 25 per cent greater than in the walls because roof and attic temperatures may run 30° F. higher than outdoor air temperatures in the summer and early fall. A well ventilated loft may reduce this temperature difference to 10° F. A minimum of 5 inches of corkboard or from 7 to 8 inches of loose-fill type of insulation is recommended for the ceiling.

Up to 30 per cent of the total heat leakage is through an uninsulated

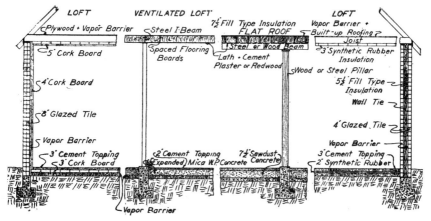

Roy E. Marshall, Michigan State College

Figure 7. Several methods of construction are shown for refrigerated farm storages. Left section shows typical construction of walls, ceiling, and floor insulated with cork board. Other sections show various materials in sufficient amounts to provide same insulating values as corkboard. Ceiling construction should provide unobstructed air flow in storage room. The insulation of junctions of walls and floors, and walls and ceilings should be continuous.

floor. For floor insulation, a minimum of 4 inches of corkboard or its equivalent is recommended."

VAPOR BARRIERS

Insulation materials must be kept dry because water is one of the best conductors of heat. Water vapor barriers in the walls, floors, and ceiling are essential. Movement of water vapor in most cases is from the outside to the inside; this is when the outside temperature is higher than the inside temperature. For storages to be operated at 32° F. throughout the year, it is recommended that a vapor barrier be applied between the outside supporting wall and the insulation. For storages operated at 32° F. from peach harvest until spring, no vapor barrier is needed if the outside supporting wall is well laid face tile. Face tile itself is a good vapor barrier.

Since there is no perfect vapor barrier, it is necessary to use a material which reduces the vapor movement as much as possible. Building papers used as a barrier should be asphalt impregnated, coated and glossy surfaced,and should weight at least 35 pounds a roll of 500 sq.ft. Rough-coated masonry walls should first be painted with two applications of cement plaster to give an even surface for the vapor barrier. Then the interior surfaces of the walls, ceilings, and floors are given a coat of asphalt paint to seal the surface, after which two layers of asphalt impregnated paper are cemented over the asphalt coated surfaces. No vapor proofing should be placed on the inside of the insulation material. If there is either natural or forced air ventilation in the loft, there is no need for a vapor barrier in

251

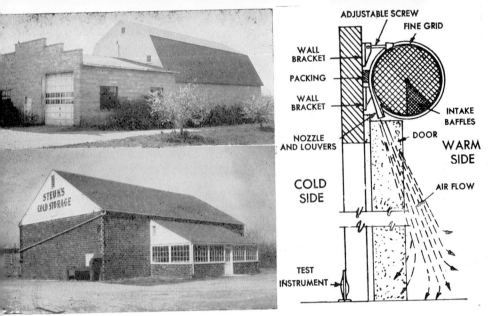

Figure 8. Farm apple storages. (Top left) Fourteen thousand bushel refrigerated storage insulated with five inches of regranulated cork in the walls and floor and seven inches in the ceiling. Storage was first air-cooled with forced ventilation, then changed to forced-air circulation through melting ice, and finally equipped with mechanical refrigeration. (Bottom left) A ten thousand bushel refrigerated storage with sales room in front. Note small entrance door for fruit at left and water-cooling system for refrigeration condenser at rear.

(Right) In large cold storage rooms this type door can be left open while loading and unloading fruit. Above-door equipment creates an air curtain that holds cold air in storage room. (Top left, courtesy Mich. State Univ.; bottom left, W. Steuk, Venice, Ohio; right, Dyfoam Corp., Cherry St., New Castle, Pa.)

the ceiling. Air-cooled storages with face-tile construction do not need a vapor barrier.

STORAGE CONSTRUCTION

Walls. In the smaller refrigerated storages, a common type of construction is a four-inch glazed tile wood frame or masonry block wall and an inner wall of the same set three to six inches inside the first wall, with the space between the two walls containing fill-type insulation material (Figure 7). Regranulated cork, expanded mica, and shredded redwood bark fiber are filling materials that are commonly used. A vapor seal, if it seems advisable, is applied to the inner suface of the outer wall. A common construction of large commercial storages consists of a masonry wall of concrete, tile, steel frame, or brick at least 8 inches thick, a vapor barrier, and 4 inches of styrofoam. Insulation is set in asphalt adhesives or mortar. Or, a 2-3 inch spray-foam layer of polyurethane insulation-vapor-barrier may be used.

Doors. A *minimum number* of doors should be used. A 5 feet wide by 8 feet high door size is most desirable to accommodate lift trucks, palletized crates and bulk boxes. Where only bushel containers are used, a considerable saving in refrigeration can be obtained if one or more doors about two feet square are provided, through which fruit can be moved on

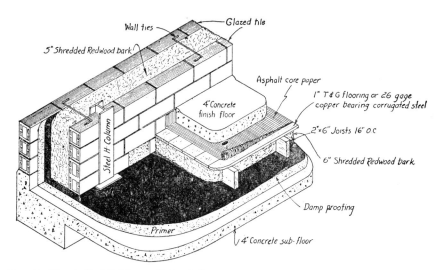

Labels in figure: Glazed tile; Wall ties; 5" Shredded Redwood bark; Asphalt core paper; 1" T & G flooring or 26 gage copper bearing corrugated steel; 4" Concrete finish floor; Steel H Column; 2"x6" Joists 16" o c; 6" Shredded Redwood bark; Damp proofing; Primer; 4" Concrete sub-floor

Roy E. Marshall, Michigan State College

Figure 9. This diagram shows the junction of wall and floor of a refrigerated storage. Instead of lumber and shredded redwood bark between concrete slabs of floor, two to three inches of cork board, rock cork, or similar materials may be used. In place of the steel H-column, masonry pilasters may be built into and outward from the outer wall unit.

roller conveyors in and out of the storage (Figure 8). Hand operated or floor tripping mechanisms may be employed to open and close doors mechanically. An air door or air curtain may be used at one door to permit easy passage through an open door with a minimum rise in cold storage temperature.

Ceiling. About 20 to 25 per cent more insulation should be provided in the ceilings than in side walls. Corkboard or other rigid type insulating materials can be applied below the joists as shown in Figure 7. Popular types of ceiling construction in Michigan are either lath (metal preferred) and cement plaster below the joists, copper-bearing sheet metal, or redwood boards. The area between the joists is filled with dry-fill insulation, allowing it to rest on the rigid ceiling construction. If a loft floor is placed above the ceiling, a two- to three-inch air space should be left between the fill-type insulation and the floor in order to provide ventilation and drying to the insulation material. Insulation should be continuous at the joints of the ceiling walls. There should be no obstructions on the ceiling surface which will interfere with a clean sweep of cold air across the top of the stacked fruit. If beams are necessary, they should run parallel with the air flow.

Floor construction. Floors in air-cooled storages are seldom insulated. The usual procedure is to level the dirt floor, fill in with several inches of clay soil, pack well, and add two inches of pea-gravel (Figure 10). If a concrete floor is used in the air-cooled storage, it should be level in order to permit water to stand to help raise the humidity.

253

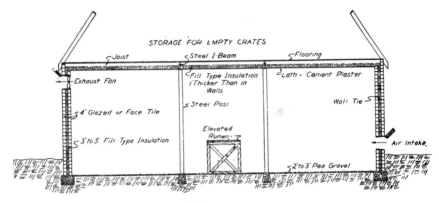

STORAGE FOR EMPTY CRATES

Joist — Steel I-Beam — Flooring

Exhaust Fan

Fill Type Insulation 1' Thicker Than in Walls

Lath - Cement Plaster

4" Glazed or Face Tile

Steel Post

Wall Tie

3' to 5' Fill Type Insulation

Elevated Runway

Air Intake

2' to 3' Pea Gravel

Roy E. Marshall, Michigan State College

Figure 10. Cross-section of an air-cooled storage showing insulated walls and ceiling and a pea-gravel floor. Cold outside air enters ducts at right, passes through stacks of stored fruit, and is exhausted by fans in upper-left ducts. These storages are still used in many European countries.

Refrigerated storages must have insulated floors because uninsulated floors may increase the refrigeration load by 30 per cent. Methods of floor construction for commercial storage floors is to pour a concrete base three to four inches thick, apply an asphalt vapor barrier on top of the concrete, apply three inches of corkboard in asphalt, mop the top of the corkboard with asphalt, and then finish with three-inch cement topping for wearing surface. If other types of construction are preferred, an equivalent insulation should be provided. Floors should be designed to support 210 pounds per square foot for a ten-foot ceiling and 260 pounds per square foot for a twelve-foot ceiling, or greater support for higher stacking.

THE AIR-COOLED STORAGE

This type of storage, as stated previously, is cooled by judiciously admitting air colder than storage-room air and excluding air warmer than that in the storage. The arrangement of air intakes and vents, as shown in Figure 10, is fast (with fans) and efficient in evenly cooling fruit throughout the storage. The cold air enters at several intakes in the lower right wall, and is drawn through the fruit and exhausted by fans in the upper left wall. Well-insulated above-ground storages are usually better than storages built into a bank or surrounded by soil. The temperature of the earth runs between 50° and 60° F. which is considerably higher than the air temperature on many days during the storage season.

Ventilation may be by gravity or by forced air using power. The fans are located in the upper wall vents or the ceiling flues. With forced air ventilation, inlet openings at the base of the walls should be two and one-half to three feet square with doors hinged at the top; with gravity ventilation, the intake areas should be at least four square feet. These entrances must be covered with hardware cloth to keep out rodents.

254

Capacity of common storages varies from 2500 bushels to 12,500 bushels or more. Cost of construction is cheaper on a per bushel basis for the larger storages.

REFRIGERATED STORAGES

Estimating refrigeration load. *A word of caution is advisable. Salesmen for refrigeration equipment are helpful in planning a storage and estimating needed equipment. The grower must be careful in quoting the rate of movement of fruit into the storage during the harvesting season. It is a common mistake for growers to underestimate this rate of movement; the grower must base his estimate upon the peak loading day. Salesmen are in competition and in order to underbid their competitors, inadequate refrigeration equipment is often sold and installed. It is, therefore, most essential that prospective owners of refrigerated storages know, or seek the advice of people who know, if the equipment in question has enough capacity to provide the desired conditions of both temperature and humidity under normal operation conditions for the storage.*

Any equipment that will handle the peak cooling load during harvest will be more than adequate for the rest of the storage season. The following quotation by Marshall gives the problems and methods involved for estimating the refrigeration load.

"The amount of refrigeration in British thermal units (B.t.u.) or tons of refrigeration (one ton of refrigeration is equivalent to a rate of heat removal of 288,000 B.t.u. per 24 hrs., or 200 B.t.u. per minute, in changing one ton of ice at 32° F. to water at 32° F. or 288,000 B.t.u.) required may be calculated rather accurately if the following information is available: (1) the area in square feet of the walls, ceiling, and floor; (2) the thermal transmission factors for the walls, ceiling, and floor or the detailed construction of each; (3) the average maximum difference between the outdoor and the storage room temperatures; (4) the maximum daily rate of loading of the product to be stored; (5) the maximum loading-in temperature of each kind of product and the length of time allowed to cool it to the desired holding temperature; and (6) the amount of heat that will be generated by workmen, motors, and lights in the storage room. In a more general way, one must calculate the amount of heat leakage through the walls, ceiling, and floor during the warmest period that the storage will be in operation, must calculate the cooling load for introduced goods, must calculate the heat generated by respiration of the stored goods, and must calculate or make an allowance for heat generated by workmen, motors and lights. Obviously, the calculation of the amount of refrigeration needed to accomplish a given job is rather complicated. Enough experience has been gained with farm storages so that it is possible to provide some more or less "rule of thumb" information that may serve as a guide in determining if the refrigeration requirements are being approximated.

TABLE 4.

EVOLUTION OF HEAT BY APPLES AT VARIOUS TEMPERATURES[1]

Temperature (F.)	Heat per ton in 24 hours
Degrees	*B. t. u.*
30 to 32	220 to 660
38 to 40	880 to 1,540
45 to 47	1,760 to 2,860
50 to 52	2,640 to 4,620
55 to 57	3,520 to 5,720
60 to 62	4,400 to 7,260
65 to 67	4,840 to 9,020
70 to 72	5,280 to 10,780
75 to 77	5,700 to 12,540
80 to 82	6,160 to 14,300
85 to 87	6,600 to 16,060

[1]These figures were taken from USDA Agr. Hdbk. 66, *The Commercial Storage of Fruits, Vegetables, and Florist and Nursery Stocks* by J. M. Lutz and R. E. Hardenburg.

"The amount of refrigeration required to take care of the daily heat leakage through walls, ceilings, and floors with *standard insulation* during the warmer portions of August and early September in Michigan for storages of 5,000, 10,000, 15,000, and 20,000 bushels capacity would approximate 0.9, 1.3, 1.9 and 2.2 tons, respectively, or from 0.11 to 0.15 ton per 1,000 bushels capacity. If the floor or ceiling insulation amounts to less than what is termed standard (standard recommendations given in this chapter), correspondingly greater refrigeration capacity would be needed to counteract heat leakage, and *if the floor is uninsulated, two to three times as much refrigeration would be needed to take care of heat leakage into the rooms.*

"The amount of refrigeration required to remove the field heat from products varies directly with the temperature range through which the fruit must be cooled and with the kind of product. Time or rate of cooling is immaterial if uniform quantities of product are loaded in daily. The same amount of refrigeration is required to do this cooling in one or two days as would be required to do the work in a week. To reduce the temperature of 1,000 bushels of peaches from 82° to 32° F. requires more than eight tons of refrigeration. The same quantity of apples maturing later when outdoor temperatures are lower, could be cooled from 72° to 32° F. with about six tons of refrigeration. The difference between the peaches and apples may be explained mostly by the ten-degree difference in initial temperatures and partly by the heavier weight of peaches.

"The heat generated by respiration of fruits must be taken into consideration (Table 4). Apples at 65° respire about eight times as rapidly as apples held at 32° F. This means that the former generate eight times as much heat as apples at 32° F. Therefore, if fruits are cooled slowly, they generate

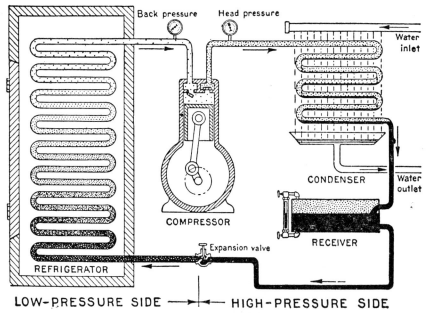

Back pressure   Head pressure

Water inlet

CONDENSER   Water outlet

COMPRESSOR

Expansion valve

RECEIVER

REFRIGERATOR

LOW-PRESSURE SIDE ⟶|⟵ HIGH-PRESSURE SIDE

G. O. Patchen, U.S.D.A.

Figure 11. Essential parts of a compression refrigeration system. Refrigerant leaves compressor as a gas (dense stippled area) under pressure; gas is cooled and condensed to a liquid (solid-black area) in the condenser and thence stored in storage room, admitting liquid refrigerant to expansion coils in storage room; liquid refrigerant gradually changes to a gas and in the process absorbs heat from the storage room; gas then returns to compressor and operation is repeated.

several times as much heat as do those that are cooled rapidly. The amount of refrigeration necessary to counteract heat generated while apples are cooling through a range of 40° F. in six days is at least one-third as much as the cooling load amounts to. If the cooling time is reduced to three days, only one-half as much refrigeration will be needed to counteract heat of respiration. This means that the 1,000 bushels of apples referred to in the last paragraph would require an additional two tons and one ton of refrigeration, respectively, for cooling during a six-day or a three-day period.

"Nearly one-fourth ton of refrigeration per day is required to neutralize the heat generated per horsepower by electric motors running continuously in the storage room. A workman generates about one-fourth as much heat in an hour as does a one horsepower motor, and nine electric lamps of 100 watts each would be the equivalent of another such motor.

"If the maximum daily rate of loading fall apples into a storage is 10 per cent of its holding capacity (it should not be more than this, preferably), there should be about one ton of refrigeration capacity for each 1,000-bushel capacity of the storage. If the loading rate is 7 per cent of the total capacity of the storage, one should be able to get good refrigeration with a machine that will deliver three-fourths ton for each 1,000-bushel capacity of the storage. These suggestions are approximations that take into con-

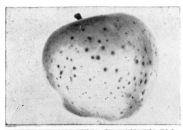

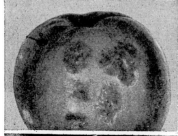

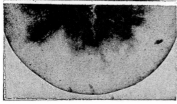

Figure 12. (Top) Injury from ammonia leakage from pipes in storage. (Middle) CO_2 external and (lower) internal injury in CA storage, occurring some seasons in spite of following recommendations. (Courtesy Ohio State and N. Y. Agr. Exp. Stas.)

sideration all the factors discussed in preceding paragraphs, but they must be regarded as rather rough measuring sticks for storages that are adequately insulated.

"Once the stored goods are cooled to a holding temperature of 32°F., little refrigeration is required to take care of heat leakage and the heat of respiration. One ton of refrigeration per day would probably be ample to maintain the temperature in a 10,000-bushel farm storage in late fall or early winter when outdoor temperatures are relatively low."

Refrigerants. A refrigerant is a liquid that evaporates or boils at low temperatures and relatively low pressures. When the liquid refrigerant boils and changes to a gas in the storage-room coils, it absorbs heat from the room and the stored product. The gas with the heat is then piped outside the storage room where it is compressed and passed through a condenser which absorbs and dissipates the heat, changing the gas back to a liquid for repeated use.

Equipment needed for circulating and changing a refrigerant from a gas to a liquid is shown in Figure 11. The *compressor sucks* the refrigerant vapor from the evaporating coils, and compresses it. The vapor under pressure is then forced by the compressor into a set of coils known collectively as the *condenser* where cool air or water extracts the heat from the vapor and reconverts it to a liquid. The liquid is stored in a tank and released to the storage-room coils by an *expansion valve which* is opened and closed by a thermostatic switch. This process is done over and over in cooling and maintaining a cold storage-room temperature.

Refrigerants commonly used are Freon, ammonia, and methyl chloride. Freon is probably the most popular refrigerant in farm storages. It is odorless and nontoxic, but leaks are difficult to locate. Ammonia gas is toxic to fruit if it escapes in large quantities (Figure 12). Methyl chloride has the disadvantage of being poisonous to man in high concentrations. Cost of equipment and the refrigerant in the long run is about the same for the three refrigerants listed.

Compressors. A compressor is essentially a pump. It somewhat resem-

258

bles a gasoline engine in that there is a crank shaft, connecting rods, pistons, and valves which require care similar to that needed by the parts in a gasoline engine. Compressors are either water-cooled or air-cooled. Those using Freon or methyl chloride are smaller, lighter, and are operated at faster speeds with less vibration as compared with the ammonia compressors. In buying compressors, company reputation is more important than mechanical characteristics, since reliable companies will guarantee and repair their equipment.

The capacity of a compressor depends upon the number of cylinders, their diameter, the length of stroke, and the speed at which the compressor operates. Capacity is usually measured in tons of refrigeration per 24 hours, but this varies with temperature of refrigerant, cooling medium surrounding the condensing coils, and the speed of rotation. For example, a compressor using Freon will deliver 9.75 tons of refrigeration at a refrigerant gas temperature of 10° F., and 20.8 tons at a gas temperature of 30° F. At twice the operating speed, the machine will produce about twice as much refrigeration. The h.p. of a motor required to operate a compressor runs about 1.5 h.p. per ton of refrigeration for farm-size installations of from 2 to 20 tons capacity.

It is more economical to install two compressors than one of the same total capacity. The chief refrigeration load comes at harvest time. Considerably less refrigeration is needed once the products are cooled to the holding temperature. Thus, with two machines, one machine should be capable of producing about two-thirds of the total required refrigeration and the other producing the remaining one-third. Both machines will operate during the loading-in period, then perhaps the larger one can carry the load for a time, and eventually, the smaller one may provide the necessary refrigeration during the colder winter months. This arrangement is better and more economical than having one machine with a change of speed of operation according to load. The compressors are operated thermostatically on not more than a two-degree range in storage temperature.

Condensers. Purpose of a condenser is to absorb and dissipate the heat which the refrigerant picks up in the storage room. In one type, a pipe is placed within a pipe with cool water running in the inner pipe and the refrigerant running in the outer pipe. This type of arrangement is usually mounted on the wall in the compressor room. In another type of condenser, there is a series of coiling pipes within a large metal cylindrical shell. Water flows through the pipe and the refrigerant on the outside through the shell.

The evaporator condenser is becoming popular where water is scarce. The coils carrying hot refrigerant gases are in a metal outside cabinet. Water is sprayed down over the coils while a fan blows air up through the coils, increasing evaporation and cooling. In winter only the fan is needed.

Expansion Coils. The coils in which the refrigerant evaporates or expands from liquid to gas may be either inside or outside the storage

(Top) H. Laney, Wenatchee, Washington
(Bottom) G. O. Patchen, U.S.D.A.

Figure 13. (Top) Height of this storage ceiling accommodates 8 stacked apple bins. Note type of refrigeration system upper left. (Bottom) Looking up at unit coolers, pipes, and catwalk located overhead in the center of a large cold-storage room. Coils are defrosted by warm water from condenser, electrical heating element, or fresh water.

room. In what is known as the "brine system" the evaporating coils are usually outside of the storage room and immersed in a bath of saturated brine solution (calcium or sodium chloride). The brine is thus cooled and then circulated by pump into the storage room through coils. This method is used for cooling some commercial storages, but rarely used in farm storages. It has several disadvantages: (1) the numerous pipes in the storage room take up considerable space, (2) they require periodic defrosting, (3) are more expensive to install and operate, (4) the brine corrodes metals, and (5) most important, there tends to be too much temperature variation throughout the room. When an attempt is made to cool the fruit to 32° F. in the center of the room, fruit next to the coils may freeze. The chief advantage is the fact that there is no danger of injuring the fruit by excessive gas leaks.

With the "direct expansion" cooling units, the refrigerant flows into coils in contact with the storage room air where it expands into a gas and absorbs heat; no brine solution is involved. In recent designs the coils are concentrated into a small space and the air is moved rapidly through them by means of a high speed fan, as shown in Figure 13. This type of forced air circulation and refrigeration is widely used in farm storages. The warmer air enters the unit at the base, is sucked over the cooling coils, and blown out through the upper vents. The advantages of this system over numerous pipes along the walls or against the ceiling are (1) the air is moved rapidly throughout the room, avoiding "dead air" spaces, (2) the smaller amount of coil system can be defrosted easily at regular intervals, (3) considerably less space is occupied in the storage room by refrigeration equipment, (4) there is less trouble from storage diseases, such as brown

260

core and internal breakdown, and (5) a uniform temperature is automatically maintained within a narrow range of 1° or 2° F.

In CA storages, the following suggestions are made: (a) cold diffuser is located near door with fan pulley in sight from door window, (b) use cloth streamers in air stream; (c) use air mask to enter room for repairs; (d) motor and fan bearings should operate without frequent greasing; (e) renew belts yearly; and (f) refrigeration controls must be on outside of room. Cool the storage to about 28° F. before loading in fruit and prop door slightly open to prevent vacuum and cave in of insulation or walls.

The following precautions should be observed in arranging the floor unit, the air ducts, and the fruit containers in the storage: (1) A minimum of 12 inches should be allowed between the tops of the containers and the ceiling joists, or beams; (2) A four- to six-inch space should be provided between the containers and the wall opposite the unit; (3) Containers should be spaced about one to two inches apart and two to five inches from the floor for air circulation; (4) Aisles or alleyways should not run parallel to the air flow because they provide flues and reduce air circulation among the stacks; if such alleyways are necessary, hang periodic heavy curtains across them to prevent flue action; (5) Alleyways which run at right angles to direction of air flow should be bridged across the top with wall boards or similar material; this prevents the air from short circuiting and developing dead-air spaces; and (6) If girders or beams are present on the ceiling, it is important that they run parallel to the air flow.

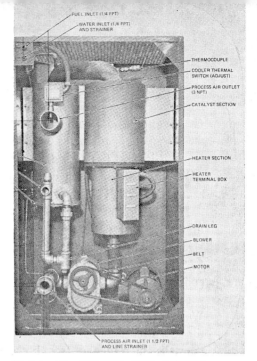

Figure 14. (Above) This catalytic oxygen converter for O_2 pull-down is located outside multiple CA rooms. Alongside (not shown) is a CO_2 dry scrubber for CO_2 removal. These units maintain the storage room atmosphere at desired levels of O_2 and CO_2 for specific varieties by intermittent recirculation of air through the equipment. Cooler tank is located at upper left. (Atlantic Research Corp., Alexandria, Va. 22314.)

Air Circulation. The fan in the blower should be large enough to move at least 100 cu. ft. per minute of air per ton of refrigeration. In other words, if the equipment is of five and one-half tons capacity, the fan should pass about 5,500 or more cu. ft. per minute.

Defrosting of blower units is necessary, up to several times daily, and less often during the storage season than during the loading period. Collection of frost on the coils not only reduces air circulation through the closely spaced coils, but also interferes with heat transmission into the pipes.[1] Defrosting can be accomplished by several methods: (1) passing hot refrigerant gas directly to and through the expansion or cooling coils; (2) shutting off the compressor and continuing to operate the fan when the storage temperature is 34° F. or higher; (3) drawing outside air over the coils by fan; (4) periodic spraying of water over the cooling coils, and (5) continuous spraying of brine water over the coils, or (6) electrical heaters.

Humidity Control. Moisture in the air must condense when the saturation or dew point (100 per cent relative humidity) is reached for a given air temperature. Thus, when air at 34° F. with a relative humidity of 88 per cent is cooled to 31° F. by coming into contact with refrigeration coils or wall surfaces, the saturation point of the atmosphere is reached; with further cooling, there is condensation of moisture on the walls or coils. Water so-collecting on the coils or walls and running out of the storage through drains must come indirectly from the stored apples or through the walls and ceiling, or from both sources. This moisture must be replaced, especially if it is coming from the fruit. With proper equipment operation, humidity can be maintained above 90% and prevent fruit shriveling.

So-called "high-humidity maintenance systems" are being used which utilize secondary refrigeration wherein water or anti-freeze solution is cooled and circulated through the room cooling unit. In CA storages this can be used as a CO_2 scrubber. The humidity loss is cut to 1% vs former 4%, or for 10,000 bu over 6 mos CA storage this would be a loss of 100 vs 400 bu weight (42 lbs/box) in fruit water-loss.

Summary Note. Materials and methods for building refrigerated and CA storages are changing constantly. Seek the help of a competent architect, builder, and refrigeration engineer.

COMMON TROUBLES IN REFRIGERATION OPERATION

Most of the common troubles encountered in refrigeration operation can be eliminated by a periodic inspection during shut-down by a good maintenance man. When contemplating buying refrigeration equipment, the prospective purchaser should always consider the service facilities in his area for that make of equipment.

Some of the more common operation troubles, with possible causes and remedies are listed below by Gray and Smock. Where the remedy is obvious, this has been omitted.

---

[1] A blower unit is recommended capable of furnishing refrigeration at peak load with a 10° F. temperature difference (T.D.) between the refrigerant and the return air. The T.D. should drop to 2° F. after field heat is removed.

Short cycling (compressor on and off for short periods)

Possible cause	Remedy
1. Too large a compressor	1. Smaller pulley on motor
2. Thermostat differential too close	2. Widen differential
3. Discharge valve leaking	3.
4. Shortage of gas	4. Look for a leak, repair, recharge
5. Leaky expansion valve	5. Replace valve—use solenoid ahead of expansion valve
6. Too much refrigerant	6. Bleed
7. Cycling on high pressure cut-out	7. Check water supply to condenser

Unit operates too long

1. Shortage of refrigerant	1.
2. Air in system	2. Purge
3. Control contacts frozen	3. Clean points or replace control
4. Dirty condenser	4. Clean
5. Inefficient compressor	5. Service valves and pistons
6. Plugged expansion valve	6. Clean or replace
7. Heavily frosted coils	7. Defrost
8. Insufficient insulation in storage	
9. Unit of insufficient capacity	

Head pressure too high

1. Too much refrigerant	1. Bleed
2. Air in line	2. Purge
3. Dirty condenser	3. Clean
4. Not enough water supply to condenser	
5. Water shut off to condenser	

Noisy or pounding compressor

1. Low oil level	1. Add oil
2. Defective belts	2. Replace
3. Loose pulley or fly wheel	3. Tighten
4. Worn bearings	4. Service

| 5. Mountings worked loose | 5. |
| 6. Liquid slugging[1] | 6. Adjust oil level or refrigerant charge |

Suction-line frosts

| 1. Expansion valve open too much | 1. Adjust expansion valve |

Hot liquid line

1. Shortage of refrigerant
2. Expansion valve open too much

Frosted liquid line

| 1. Receiver shut-off practically closed or plugged | 1. Open valve or clean |

Where ammonia has been used as a refrigerant, there have been a few explosions. Although these instances are rare, two such explosions have occurred in the Hudson Valley. From the evidence collected on the causes of one of the explosions, several conditions seem to have contributed to the explosion:

Apparently, there was liquid refrigerant in the suction line which caused the compressor head to blow and to release the ammonia to the machinery room. Because there was not enough ventilation to clear the ammonia from the room, a combustible concentration built up and the mixture ignited and caused an explosion and considerable damage. The center of the explosion seemed to be at the switchboard, indicating that an automatic switch had arced and ignited the mixture.

From this experience, it is obvious that a pounding compressor should be shut off and checked. Adequate ventilation of the machinery room prevents the build-up of dangerous concentrations of ammonia if there are leaks. A master switch on the outside of the building permits all compressors to be shut off without personnel going into the danger area and where an arc will do no harm.

If trouble arises in the operation of any equipment, it is investment in safety to cease operation until the trouble is located and remedied. If the trouble cannot be found, an experienced service man should be called.

COSTS

Surveys in Michigan indicated in the mid-1950's that costs for constructing farm storage with packing room and equipment with mechanical

---

[1]Other causes of slugging may be a leaky expansion or solenoid. It is difficult to get a solenoid tight after it has been used. If the condition persists, it may be necessary to install an accumulator or trap that collects the liquid and by-passes the compressor to the receiver. A large accumulation of liquid in the suction *line* may damage the compressor.

refrigeration and hand trucks, roller conveyors, and power elevator has varied from $1.24 to $2.40 per bushel capacity, or, 45 to 90 cents per cubic foot. The average price is $1.75 per bushel or 65 cents per cubic foot. According to Gaston and Levin, a conservative estimate of construction costs of farm storages with good walls and adequate insulation, adequate refrigeration machinery, and a sorting and handling room of adequate dimensions would be $1.25 to $1.75 per bushel capacity. Almost all of this cost would be for construction of the building.

Electric consumption by survey has ranged between 1.0 and 3.1 kilowatt hours per bushel per normal six-month season, with an average of about 1.6. Assuming an average of 2.5 cents per kilowatt hour, cost of power should be about four cents per bushel per season for winter variety apples. Total annual costs of operating farm storages including power, handling, maintenance, and overhead range between 20c and 35c per bushel.

Pflug and Brandt give typical cost-of-construction figures in the late 1950's for an apple storage 40x60 ft. in Michigan. The block walls are 20 ft. high with board form insulation. There is a 12-inch filled concrete foundation wall on concrete footings. The roof is of steel struss with wood joints and fill insulation. There is one 5x9 ft. refrigeration door. Relative cost data below must be adjusted to 1970s.

TABLE 4. COST OF 40 x 60 FT. APPLE STORAGE, MICHIGAN[1] (LATE 1950's)

Unit of building	Unit cost	No. of units	Cost
Excavating and backfilling	$ 44.50/100 lin. ft.	2	$ 89.00
Footing	$292.50/100 lin. ft.	2	$ 585.00
Foundation (12-inch block wall filled with concrete)	$392.50/100 lin. ft.	2	$ 785.00
Floor (4-inch)	$ 27.50/100 sq. ft.	24	$ 660.00
Walls	$126.00/100 sq. ft.	40	$ 5,040.00
Roof	$ 1.59/sq. ft.	2,400	$ 3,816.00
Door	$350.00 each	1	$ 350.00

Total net cost $11,325.00
Overhead plus profit (26½% of net cost) 3,000.00

Contractor cost estimate $14,319.00

[1]Electrical system and refrigeration figured separate. U. S. retail price index rose from 100 in 1959 to about 120 in 1968. Adjust prices accordingly.

The electrical cost of the above storage is estimated at approximately 5 percent of the net building cost. Cost of refrigeration is almost a straight-line drop from 41c per bushel for a 5000-bushel storage to 33c for a 60,000 bu. storage.

Construction costs for CA storages in Washington averaged about $2.50 /bu in the late 1960s.

265

Cost of storing apples is about 40 cents/bu. regular refrigerated storage and 70 cents/bu. CA (early 1970s).

STORAGE TROUBLES

Aside from fungous rots, apples held for a number of months in storage are likely to develop one or more physiological disorders. Storage conditions may or may not be responsible for these troubles, but since they manifest themselves in storage they most commonly are referred to as storage troubles. Often the basic cause of these diseases is either inherent in the apples or is due to faulty harvesting and handling before the fruit is placed in the storage room.

TABLE 5

SUSCEPTIBILITY OF APPLE VARIETIES TO PHYSIOLOGICAL DISORDERS.

(After Smock and Neubert; see also Table 2, Chapter II)

Variety	Water core	Scald	Soft Scald	Bitter pit	Miscellaneous
Delicious	Severe	Slight	None	Slight	Mealy breakdown
Winesap	Medium	Medium	None	None	
Jonathan	Medium	Slight	Severe	Slight	Jonathan Spot
Baldwin	Slight	Medium	None	Severe	
Stayman	Medium	Severe	None	Medium	Internal breakdown cracking
Ben Davis	Slight	Medium		Slight	
Rome Beauty	Slight	Medium	Medium	Slight	
York Imperial	Slight	Severe	None	Severe	
McIntosh	None	Slight	None	Slight	Brown core
Grimes Golden	Medium	Severe	Severe	Medium	Shriveling
Yellow Newtown	Slight	Medium	None	Slight	Internal browning
Wealthy	Slight	Medium	Medium	Slight	
Transparent	Medium	None	None	None	
R. I. Greening	Slight	Severe	None	Severe	Mealy breakdown
Northern Spy	Slight	Slight	None	Severe	Spy spot, breakdown
Gravenstein	Slight	Slight	None	Severe	
Oldenburg	Slight	Slight	None	None	
Arkansas	Medium	Severe	None	Slight	
Golden Delicious	Slight	Slight	Severe	None	Shriveling
Spitzenburg	Slight	Slight	None	Slight	
Wagener	Slight	Severe	None	Slight	
Stark	Slight	Medium	None	Slight	
Winter Banana	Slight	Slight	Severe	Slight	
Cortland	Slight	Medium	Slight	Slight	

The diffuse browning of the skin of apples known as **apple scald** is perhaps the most widespread physiological disease of apples. Arkansas, Stayman Winesap, Grimes, Rome Beauty, and Rhode Island Greening are particularly susceptible. It also occurs on other varieties, especially when harvested early in the season or with poor color development. Delayed storage and storage temperatures above 32° F. also favor its development. High nitrogen level in the orchard has been found to accentuate scald on some varieties, not on others; the picture is not clear. The disease seems to be worse following warm weather at harvest.

266

TABLE 6

FACTORS AFFECTING APPLE SCALD (AFTER SMOCK)

Factor	Effect on scald	Undesirable side effect of treatment
Orchard conditions		
Climate	Usually worse after warm growing season	
Nutrition		
High nitrogen	Increases it on some varieties, decreases it on others	
Pruning	Usually less with well pruned trees	
Crop size	Usually worse on large fruit	
Spray program	Uncertain	
Maturity at harvest	Immature fruit much worse	
Post-harvest conditions		
Delayed storage	Slight lessening before regular storage; may make it worse in CA storage	Ripens fruit
Waxes	Erratic effects	
Oil sprays and dips	Decrease	
Hot water dip. (30-60 sec. @ 136°F.)	Decrease	Apples injured at hotter dips
Chemical inhibitors (DPA, Ethoxyquin)	Decrease	
Oiled paper	Decreases	
Unsealed box liners	Increase	
Sealed box liners	Decreases	Possible off flavors
Storage		
Temperature	Most varieties less scald with low temperature. Cortland may have more	
Oxygen level	Rapid drop in CA storage decreases scald	
Carbon dioxide		
Carbon dioxide treatment	Decreases	Danger of injury
Controlled atmosphere Storage	Decreases	Requires CA rooms
Ventilation	Theoretical decrease but often no effect	
Circulation	Not a lasting decrease	
Air purification	Inadequate decrease	
Ozone	Possible increase	May injure fruit
Presence of other varieties	Possible increase Sometimes no effect	

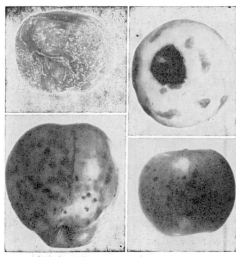

D. F. Fisher, U.S.D.A.

Figure 15. Blemishes and diseases appearing on apples during storage. (Top left) Blue-mold rot, soft and watery, has a musty odor and frequently is covered with bluish masses of spores. Benomyl dip and cleanliness in storage room controls the rots. (Top right) A partly peeled apple showing how prominent so-called "slight bruises" appear, which emphasizes importance of careful handling at all time. (Bottom left) Bitter pit, a physiological disease, occurs as brownish spongy or corky spots or pits in the flesh just under the skin and usually is the most prevalent on blossom end of apple. (Bottom right) Jonathan spot is a superficial skin disease giving the apple a freckled appearance.

Scald usually affects only the skin and therefore only the appearance of the apple, but may, in advanced stages, extend into the flesh. Fruit showing scald in storage is likely to have the trouble markedly increased within a few days after it is removed to room temperature.

Diphenylamine (DPA) and ethoxyquin (Stop-Scald) as a dip or spray or impregnated in paper wraps will markedly reduce apple scald in most years. Such treatments currently are the most effective and most widely used against scald. DPA under some conditions has been more effective than Stop-Scald, but in a critical scald year, as 1959-60, both are less effective but far better than mineral oiled wraps. The DPA dip method shortly after harvest affords good fruit coverage and is generally somewhat more effective than wraps, although wraps sometime are as effective. DPA is used as a dip or spray at 1000 ppm on Grimes, York, and Cortland; 2000 ppm is better on Delicious, Rome, Stayman and Arkansas. On latter varieties 1000 ppm may be satisfactory if fruit is late-picked or otherwise less likely to scald. Stop-Scald at 2700 ppm (3 pts/100 gals. 70% emulsion) is suggested. Coverage is better on warm fruit. Cost per bushel is small compared with possible scald losses. Good scald control can be obtained with 1.5-mg DPA oiled wraps. Preharvest tree sprays with 2000 ppm DPA are questionable. CA Apples must be pretreated for scald.

Bitter pit, in its usual form, is characterized by sunken spots on the surface of the apple resembling small bruises. These spots are usually concentrated over the blossom end of the fruit and in the early stages have a water soaked appearance. Later they become deep red or light green and finally gray or black. When the apple is peeled or cut, areas of brown, spongy tissue appear in the flesh. The affected tissues are rarely bitter in taste as the name "bitter pit" might suggest. The spots are usually most numerous in the outer portions of the flesh just beneath the skin area, but frequently, may be found deep in the flesh. Bitter pit is a physiological disease associated with calcium availability to the tree and fruit. It is most severe on apples picked immaturely; and on larger apples than on smaller ones. The severity of the disease increases in storage—new spots increasing in number and old ones enlarging. It does not spread from apple to apple. Baldwin, Rhode Island Greening, Stayman, Yellow New-town, Delicious, and Gravenstein are among the most susceptible. Check for latest controls with calicum foliar sprays and post-harvest dips.

Soft scald, which is distinctly different from ordinary scald, is charac-terized by blister-like or burned-appearing areas extending in irregular pat-terns over the fruit. The affected areas are usually brown in color, slightly sunken, and with definitely outlined edges. The flesh beneath such areas is often soft and discolored to a slight depth. Jonathan and Rome Beauty are the most susceptible varieties, but soft scald may also occur on Cort-land, Winter Banana, Golden Delicious, Northwestern Greening, and other varieties. The exact nature and cause of the trouble are unknown; but it is associated with delay in moving fruit from orchard to cold storage, low-storage temperatures, and advanced maturity. Holding at 36° F, if the fruit is well matured or over-mature when harvested, is usually recom-mended, although the trouble appears to be reduced or prevented also by early harvest and immediate storage at 30 to 32° F. Gerhardt and Sainsbury report successful control of soft scald on Delicious apples by storing eight weeks at 34° F., then 30-32°. CA storage helps.

Again as with ordinary scald, Brooks and Harley were able to control soft scald commercially on Jonathan and soggy breakdown on Grimes Golden by subjecting the fruit for several days before storage to atmos-pheres containing 25 to 35% carbon dioxide.

Soggy breakdown is a disease very similar to soft scald in cause but manifests itself in a soft watery or soggy breakdown of the flesh, often without any external symptoms. The disease is most severe on Grimes Golden and Golden Delicious, and storage at 36° F is generally recom-mended to prevent its occurrence where prevalent.

Internal breakdown is a brown more or less discoloration of the flesh characterizing the end of normal storage life of apples. In advanced stages, the skin is also discolored, and the flesh becomes soft. Large apples are usually the first to show this condition. Over-maturity at time of harvesting, delayed cooling, high storage temperatures and it often follows water core, freezing. CA storage reduces it on Spys.

Jonathan spot is manifested as dark colored, superficial spots in the skin of the fruit and is most prevalent on the Jonathan variety. It is associated with over-maturity, delayed storage, high storage temperatures, and long holding. The colored side of the fruit is more susceptible than the uncolored. Controlled atmosphere storage controls the disorder.

Shriveling is the visible evidence of excessive moisture loss from the fruit and is due primarily to too low humidity of the storage atmosphere.

Fruit harvested in an immature condition loses moisture more readily than that which is allowed to become fully mature. Polybags reduce it.

Internal browning differs from internal breakdown in that the discoloration, which at first is confined to elongated areas radiating from the core in the upper half of the apple, appears while the flesh is still firm— usually by mid-storage. Later the entire flesh may become brown. The trouble is of most economic importance on Yellow Newtowns grown in the Pajaro Valley of California. The brown core condition, important in McIntosh apples in New York and New England, is similar if not identical. Unlike internal breakdown, these two disorders are induced by minimum storage temperatures. Little development occurs at 36° F and none at 40° F. Both McIntosh and Yellow Newtown respond well to modified atmosphere storage at these temperatures. Delaying the storage of susceptible varieties for 5 to 10 days reduces the severity of the trouble but this delay at atmospheric temperature shortens the period during which the fruit can be held.

Apple Rots. Decay of apples in cold storage is caused by fungus diseases. Most storage rot is caused by blue mold (Penicillium expansum). Low storage temperatures retard decay. Riper fruit decays more readily. Most rots develop where skin breaks have occurred. To minimize apple rot in storage a prestorage treatment of apples with Benlate (benomyl) effectively reduces decay. Good storage room sanitation and disinfection between storage seasons is desired.

Mice, Rats. Methyl Bromide fumigation is preferred. Contact Pomology, Cornell, Ithaca, N. Y. 14850 for latest control.

More Information. See Cornell Bull. 440. Ithaca, N. Y. 14850.

Review Questions

1. What are the benefits to the grower of storing his fruit in a refrigerated storage?
2. What effect does lowering the temperature from 50° to 40° and 40° to 32° F. have upon the rate of ripening of apples?
3. How does humidity affect stored apples; what relative humidities are recommended?
4. What is the value of ventilation in refrigerated storages; atmospheric composition?
5. How much space should be allowed for each bushel in calculating capacities for storage buildings?
6. List two popular insulation materials used in air-cooled and refrigerated storages and what respective thicknesses are recommended for side walls, floor, and ceiling.
7. What is a vapor barrier and where is it located in a refrigerated storage?
8. Why is floor insulation recommended in cold storages and left optional for air-cooled storages?
9. Describe how a controlled atmosphere storage is built and operated. List its advantages and disadvantages.
10. What factors must be known in estimating the refrigeration load for an apple storage?

11. Under average conditions, about how many tons of refrigeration should be provided for a 10,000 bushel farm storage?
12. List three refrigerants and give a disadvantage of each.
13. Trace the path of the refrigerant through the refrigeration system naming the important equipment involved.
14. What are the advantages of using the diffuser or blower system of cooling as compared with wall-type coils in the storage room?
15. Describe the development of CA storage and discuss recent developments in construction and operation as described by your instructor.
16. Describe three of the most important apple storage diseases in your area and suggest the better control measures.

Suggested Collateral Readings

Anonymous. Apples, pears, and grapes. Chapter 27. AHRAE Guide and Data Book. 1971 Applications. Amer. Soc. Heating, Refrigerating and Air-Conditioning Engineers. 1971.

Bartram, R. et al. High-quality Delicious for late marketing. Wash. State. Univ. Em-3033. 10 pp. 1969.

Blanpied, G. D. What percentage of the stored crop should be in CA? Proc. New England, New York CA Storage Seminar. Mass. Ext. Publ. 422: 51-56. 1964.

Blanpied, G. D. and Apinthai Purnasiri. Thiabendazole control of post-harvest apple decay. Hort-Sci. 5: No. 6. p. 476. Dec. 1970.

Brooks, Charles and C. P. Harley. Soft scald and soggy breakdown of apples. Journ. Agr. Res. 49; 55-69. 1934.

Bulk Storage Processing of Fruits and Vegetables — A Symposia. HortSci. 6(3): 219-230. 1971.

Cargo, C. A. and D. H. Dewey. Benomyl control of postharvest apple decay. Hort-Sci. 5(4): 259-260. 1970.

Controlled atmosphere for plant growth. ASAE Publication Proc. 270. Amer. Soc. Agr. Engrs. HortSci. Vol 6(2). April 1971.

Dewey, D. H. Grade defects of CA apples and their effect on storage returns. Mich. Qtrly. Bull. 41: No. 1. pp. 122-129. 1958.

Dewey, D. H., and D. R. Dilley. Control of storage scald of apples. Mich. Ext. Bul. 470. 1964.

Dewey, D. H. and D. R. Dilley. Jonathan apple quality and storage life. Mich. St. Univ. Ext. Bull. 627, 4 pp. August 1968.

Faust, M. et al. Biochem. changes with cork in apples. Qual. Pl. Mat. Vet. XIX, 1-3: 255-265. 1969.

Faust, M. et al. Physiological disorders of apples. Bot. Rev. 35: (2). 169-194. 1969.

Ferris, R. T. and R. K. Bogardus. Storing fruits and vegetables on pallets in wholesale warehouses. USDA Mkt. Res. Rpt. No. 622. Agric. Res. Serv. Transp. & Facil. Res. Div. 1966.

Fisher, D. V. and S. W. Porriett. Apple harvesting and storage in British Columbia. Dept. of Agr. (Ottawa) Pub. 724. 1951.

Gray, H. E., and R. M. Smock. Farm refrigerated apple storages. Cornell Ext. Bull. 786. Request recent edition.

Hardenburg, R. E. Chemical control of scald on apples grown in eastern United States. U.S.D.A. Mkt. Res. Rep. 538. 1962.

Hardenburg, R. E. Wax, related coatings for hort. prod. ARS 51-15, U.S.D.A. Dec. 1967.

Hardenburg, R. E., and R. E. Anderson. Polyethylene box liners for storage of Golden Delicious apples. U.S.D.A. Mkt. Res. Rep. 461. 1961.

Hardenburg, R. E., and R. E. Anderson. A comparison of polyethylene liners and covers for storage of Golden Delicious apples. Amer. Soc. Hort. Sci. Proc. 82: 77-82. 1963.

Herrick, J. F. Jr. et al. Apple packing and storage houses. Layout and design. Mkt. Res. Rep. 602. 1964.

Herrick, J. F. Jr., S. W. McBerney, and E. W. Carlsen. Handling and storage of apples in pallet boxes, U.S.D.A. AMS-236. April 1958.

Hill, H., F. B. Johnston, H. B. Heeney, and R. W. Buckmaster. Relation of foliage analysis to keeping quality of McIntosh and Spy varieties of apples. Sci. Agr. 30: pp. 518-534. 1950.

Huelin, F. E. and I. M. Coggiola. Superficial scald, a functional disorder of stored apples. V. Oxidation of a-farnesene and its inhibition by diphenylamine. J. Sci. Fd. Agric., Vol. 21(1): 44-48. 1970.

Hukill, W. V., and Edwin Smith. Coordinated management for building, storing, and marketing Northwest apples. U.S.D.A. Cir. 759. 1947.

Kefford, J. F. and B. V. Chandler. The chemical constituents of citrus fruits. Advances in Food Res., Supplement II. Academic Press, N. Y. 1970. HortScience Vol. 6, No. 2. April 1971.

Lord, W. J. Proceedings of the New England-New York Controlled Atmosphere Storage Seminar. Mass. Ext. Pub. 422. 1964.

Lott, R. V. The terminology of fruit maturation and ripening. Proc. Amer. Soc. Hort. Sci. 46: 166-172. 1945.

Lutz, J. M. and R. E. Hardenburg. Commercial storage of fruits, etc. Agric. Handbook, U.S.D.A. 66, 77 pp. 1968. See also Phillips, W. R. and J. G. Armstrong. Same type inform. Canada Dept. of Agric. Publ. 1260(Ottawa). 50 pp. 1967.

Mattus, G. E., and H. A. Rollins ,Jr. Storing Virginia apples. Va. Ext. Cir. 841. 1963.

Mattus, G. E., and H. A. Rollins, Jr. Testing apple firmness. Va. Ext. Leaf. 87. 1963.

Merritt, R. H. et al. Preharvest air temperatures on apple scald. ASHS 78:24-34. 1961.

Olsen, K. L., and H. A. Schomer. Oxygen and carbon dioxide levels for controlled-atmosphere storage of Starking and Golden Delicious apples. U.S.D.A. Mkt. Res. Rep. 653. 1964.

Patchen, G. O. Air door for cold storage houses. U.S.D.A. AMS-458. 1961.

Patchen, G. O. Cooling apples in pallet boxes. U.S.D.A. Mkt. Res. Rep. 532. 1962.

Patchen, G. O. Storage for apples and pears. USDA Mkt. Res. Rpt. 924, 51pp. 1971. (Excellent bulletin).

Pflug, I. J., and D. H. Dewey. Construction for controlled-atmosphere apple storage. Agr. Eng. 40(2): 80-83, 86. 1959.

Pflug, I. J. and M. W. Brandt. Cost of Michigan fruit storage buildings as affected by size and type of construction. Mich. Qtrly. Bull. 41: No. 4, 778-790. May 1959.

Phillips, W. R. Construction and operation of a home storage for fruits and vegetables. Canada Dept. of Agr. (Ottawa) Publ. 743. 1957.

Rose, D. H., L. P. McColloch, and D. F. Fisher. Market diseases of fruits and vegetables: apples, pears, and quinces. U.S.D.A. Misc. Pub. 743. 1957.

Sainsbury, G. F. Heat leakage through floors, walls and ceilings of apple storages. U. S. Dept. of Agr. MRR-315. 65 pp. 1959.

Sainsbury, G. F. Cooling apples and pears in storage rooms. U.S.D.A. Mkt. Res. Rep. 474. 1961.

Smock, R. M. Lab studies on chemicals causing apple coloration. Jour. ASHS 94:1 49-51. January 1969.

Smock, R. M. and G. D. Blanpied. The storage of apples, (one of best). Cornell Ext. Bull. 440. Rev. 1969.

Smock, R. M. CA storage of apples. Cornell Ext. Bull. 759. Rev. 1958.

Smock, R. M., and C. R. Gross. Studies on respiration of apples. Cornell Mem. 297. 1950.

Smock, R. M., and A. M. Neubert. Apples and apple products. Interscience Publishers, Inc., New York. 486 pp. 1950.

Smock, R. M., and G. D. Blanpied. Some effects of temperature and rate of oxygen reduction on the quality of controlled atmosphere stored McIntosh apples. Amer. Soc. Hort. Sci. Proc. 83: 135-138. 1963.

Smock, R. M., and G. D. Blanpied. The use of nitrogen for cooling, flushing, and maintaining atmospheres in CA rooms. Proc. N. Y. Hort. Soc. 1965. 141-145. 1965.

Smock, R. M. and G. D. Blanpied. Handbook for CA storage rooms. Cornell Dept. Pomology Mimeo. bul. S-504. Rev. 1968.

Southwick F. W., and J. W. Zahradnik. CA apple storage. Mass. Ext. Bull. 322. June 1958.

Stevenson, C. D. Physical effect of Ca sprays on bitter pit. Queensland Jr. Agr. and Animal Sciences. 24:59-67. 1967.

Stiles, W. C., and N. F. Childers. Factors affecting fruit condition. N. J. Agr. Exp. Sta. Conference Mimeo. 190 pp. Feb. 1961.

Tindale, G. B. and C. R. Little. Picking maturity in relation to storage life of apples and pears and their susceptibility to disorders. Dept. Agr. Vic. Stor. Exp. Austr. 1961.

Williams, M. W. and E. A. Stahly, N-Malonyl-D-Tryptophan in apple fruits treated with succinic acid 2,2-dimethylhydrazide. Amer. Soc. of Plant Physio. Vol. 46, No. 1. July 1970.

Wills, R. B. H., K. J. Scott and W. B. McGlasson. A role for acetate in the development of low-temperature breakdown in apples. J. Sci. Fd. Agric. Vol. 21(1): 42-44. 1970.

Wills, R. B. H. and W. B. McGlasson. Effect of storage temperature on apple volatiles associated with low temperature breakdown. Jour. HortSci. Vol. 46: No. 1 89-93. 115-120. January 1971.

Wright, R. C., and T. M. Whiteman. Some changes in Eastern apples during storage. U.S.D.A. Tec. Bull. 1120. 1955.

Wright, T. R., and Edwin Smith. Relation of bruising and other factors to blue mold decay of Delicious apples. U.S.D.A. Cir. 935. 1954.

Additional References

Anderson, R. E. CA storage tests with eastern U.S. Delicious apples. ASHS *91*: 810-820. 1967.

Blanpied, G. D. Growing season, temperature, bloom dates, length of season and Delicious apples. ASHS *64*:72-81. 1964.

Blanpied, G. D. Measuring respiratory climacteric in apples. ASHS *87*:85-92. 1965.

Blanpied, G. D. et al. Alar, harvest dates and apple keeping quality. ASHS *90*:467-474. 1967.

Bramlage, W. J. et al. Comparison of CA and air-stored McIntosh. ASHS *89*:40-45. 1966.

Bramlage, W. J. and M. R. Shipway. Watercore and internal breakdown of stored Delicious detected by light transmission. ASHS *90*:475-483. 1967.

Deciduous Fruit Growing in World Countries. Proc. XVII Intern. Hort. Cong. Vol. IV, pp. 215-456, Univ. of Md., College Park. 1966.

Dilley, D. R. et al. CO_2 production by apples after air and CA storage. ASHS *84*: 59-64. 1964.

Dewey, D. H. and D. R. Dilley. Managing and operating a controlled atmosphere storage for apples. Hort. Rep. 10. Mich. State Univ. 1969.

Doub, J. W. CA storage for farm products. ASAE. Atlantic Res. Corp., Alexandria, Va. 22314. 1969.

Drake, M., et al. Bitter pit as related to calcium level in Baldwin apple fruit and leaves. ASHS 89:29. 1966.

Eaves, C. A. et al. O_2 with and without CO_2 on quality of McIntosh at two levels of N. Canadian J. Plant Sci. *44*:458-465. 1964.

Hardenburg, R. E. and R. E. Anderson. Post-harvest hot water and packaging treatment for apple scald. ASHS *87*:93-99. 1965.

Hardenburg, R. E. Hot-water and chemical treatments to control scald on Stayman apples. ASHS 90:484-490. 1967.

(References Con't. in Appendix, Chap. XI)

Note: The most research and bulletins on apple storage have come from Cornell University, Michigan State University, U.S.D.A., England, British Columbia (Summerland), Australia (Queensland and Tasmania), Univ. of California, Virginia Polytechnic Institute, and University of Massachusetts. Keep in contact with these institutions for the latest and future storage research. The International Apple Inst., 2430 Penna., N. W., Wash., D.C. 20037, has a special letter on storage holdings and world apple situation (you must be a member to receive it).

CHAPTER XII

Marketing Fruit

◆◆◆◆◆◆◆◆◆◆◆◆◆◆◆◆◆◆◆◆◆◆◆◆◆◆◆

The first and most important step in marketing is to *grow superior fruit*. With a high-quality and attractively packaged product, a grower's marketing problem is 90 percent solved. Michigan research clearly has shown that better growing, harvesting and handling methods are needed than now used by many growers to get the fruit quality that brings reasonable income, particularly to growers who store under refrigerated controlled atmosphere (Dewey and Schueneman, 1972).

While the apple often is used in this chapter as an example, the principles apply for the most part to all fruits. You will find additional marketing discussion for specific fruits in the respective chapters.

METHODS OF SELLING

In any system of selling, it is highly desirable for a grower to follow his fruit through the marketing channels to the consumer sometime during the year so that he can observe what happens to the product and how it is received by the consumer.

Grower to retail buyer or consumer. The most simple and direct procedure in selling fruit is where the grower deals directly with retail grocers, pie companies, and similar outlets in nearby towns and cities. As an example, an Ohio grower sells practically his entire crop of 100,000 bushels to trade in Cleveland, Youngstown, and neighboring cities. Fruit is packed out of storage through the winter and delivered in large trucks traveling a set route once or twice a week. The men in charge of these trucks and fruit sales are especially selected and serve, in addition, as managers of the cultural program for 50-acre blocks of the orchard. The trucks rarely travel to cities farther than 100 miles.

Selling to processors. About 40% of the U.S. apple crop goes to

Herschel H. Jones, Herschel Jones Marketing Service, Inc., 99 Hudson St., New York City, and Fred W. Burrows, International Apple Institute, 2430 Penna. Ave., Wash., D.C., 20037 assisted in the revision of this chapter.

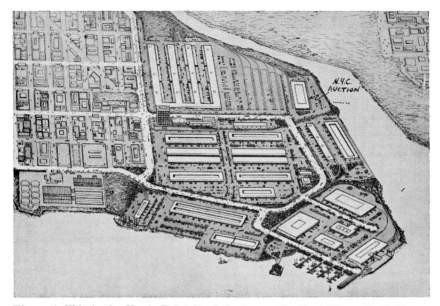

Figure 1. This is the Hunts Point Food Center on the East River, South Bronx, New York, where fresh fruits, vegetables and other foods are brought by truck, rail and ship for distribution in surrounding metropolitan areas and for some exporting. Air-conditioned space is set aside for auctions. Business is handled mainly by commission, by outright purchase and by joint account. Philadelphia, Baltimore and other large cities also have modernized their food distribution centers to facilitate handling. (Courtesy Dept. of Ports and Terminals, New York City 10474).

A large volume of fruit is purchased by chain stores directly from grower corporations and shippers and assembled at their distribution centers where orders are filled and trucked to local stores.

processors for juice, sauce, baked apples, pies, etc., each year. This is on the increase as a regular outlet, and it is particularly important in salvaging hurricane damaged fruit or when other sales outlets are flooded, although the processor outlet no longer can be regarded as a salvage deal. See processing discussion, end of Chapter X.

Co-operative selling. Co-operative selling is feasible where the apple industry is sufficiently concentrated as in the Northwest and the Shenandoah-Cumberland regions. The grower undoubtedly strengthens his position from a marketing standpoint by pooling his efforts with those of others engaged in the same business. There are many advantages in co-operative selling: (1) A standardized product can be offered; (2) the volume of produce handled is sufficiently large to attract the larger regular buyers; it is difficult for an individual grower to supply sufficient repeat orders for the big buyers unless he is a large grower; (3) an association can keep in close contact with market conditions through their specialists in the large buying and merchandising centers; (4) supplies and equipment can be purchased in wholesale lots at a considerable saving; and (5) an association can conduct advertising and publicity campaigns which are denied an individual grower. It is for the latter reason that the large apple organ-

Figure 2. This pie and bakery shop, fully equipped with modern ovens, mixers, and refrigeration, is a part of a roadside market operation in New Jersey. Wife of the orchardist operates the shop. Front part of building is brick colonial, spacious, neat, and devoted to sale of fresh fruits, some vegetables, canned goods, cold meats, and a wide variety of cheeses. Market draws over 2000 people a day and sometimes more on weekends. (C. W. Barclay, Jr., Colts Neck, N. J.)

izations in the Northwest have been so successful in moving enormous quantities of their product. There are the disadvantages of the grower losing contact with the buyers and his right in some cases to gamble on a later market.

Growers in New Jersey and other apple areas of the Northeast, even though they are on the doorstep of the largest markets, also have found it to their advantage to join together in cooperatives to move their f r u i t systematically and at a price. Where there formerly were over a thousand buyers in this general area, the number has been reduced to less than a dozen. This is due to the dominating influence of large chain stores. Under these conditions the growers must place themselves in a position to bargain by cooperative effort. Examples of these successful organizations are The Jersey Fruit Cooperative at Riverton, N. J. and several cooperatives in the Eastern U. S. Eventually it may be necessary to draw growers together in an entire large region under one co-op, in order to deal with the relatively few buyers at a better price. Also, a large volume of fruit is now sold by large grower corporations or by grower-shippers.

Henry Miller, a progressive grower in West Virginia has suggested it is better to move a more or less even volume of fruit throughout the marketing season, and take lower prices than desired on some sales, rather than to hold large volumes for better prices later, and end up taking disastrous cuts. Mr. Miller pulled old apple varieties and after a planned

TABLE 1

Revamp of an Old Orchard to Adjust Percentage of Certain Varieties to Market Demand and to Space Harvest Dates to Facilitate Handling. (After Henry Miller, W. Va.)

Variety	Production Percentage Desired in Plan	Percentage of Each Variety Produced 3 yrs. later	Approximate Harvesting Dates	Usual Packing & Marketing Dates
Summer				
Lodi	5	4.788	Jul. 1-15	Jul. 1-20
*N.W. Greening	5	6.767	Jul. 25-Aug. 15	July 25-Sept. 1
McIntosh, Roger Strain	5	2.763	Aug. 15-Sept. 1	Aug. 15-Sept. 15
Early Fall				
Red Jonathan	5	5.342	Sept. 1-Oct. 1	Sept. 1-Oct. 1
Red Delicious including super strain	25	21.462	Sept. 15-Oct. 5	Sept. 15-Oct. 15
Golden Delicious	5	5.262	Oct. 1-Oct. 5	Oct. 1-Jan. 1
Late Fall				
Stayman Winesap	10	16.571	Oct. 10-Nov. 1	Oct. 25-Feb. 15
Red York	15	17.661	Oct. 5-Nov. 1	Oct. 5-Mar. 1
Winesap	5	2.841	Oct. 10-Nov. 1	Nov. 15-Apr. 1
Red Rome	20	11.394	Oct. 10-Nov. 1	Nov. 15-Apr. 1
Totals	100	94.851		

*Greening now being gradually replaced with Miller Red, harvested and marketed at same time. Percentage of Golden and Red Delicious production by compact trees is being increased, Winesap and Rome decreased.

program planted the varieties shown in Table 1 to match more nearly the current demand at that time and space harvest dates to facilitate handling.

Roadside marketing. The happiest growers are often on well-traveled highways, moving a part or all their crop by roadside marketing. Peak sales occur during the summer months of July, August, and September, but some roadside markets are maintained all months of the year except the coldest. Most patrons are from the middle-upper incomes who buy primarily to obtain fresh and better quality produce. Second-grade goods can be sold for canning and cooking if properly priced; low-grade or cull produce should not be offered. In an attractive friendly roadside market today, most customers will pay a higher price than in supermarkets for a high quality product, in spite of your lower overhead and no delivery charges.

Saturdays, Sundays, and holidays are the best days between the hours of 2 and 5 P.M. Largest purchases are from motorists returning home. Motorists leaving the city usually buy only for consumption that day. A market located next to the in-coming lane of traffic to a city will often do twice the business of a market located near the out-going lane. The sales building should be neat, clean, orderly, but not necessarily expensively built. Adequate parking spaces on one or both sides of the road are of paramount importance.

Figure 3. This roadside stand is located on a four-lane heavily traveled highway in New Jersey. There is ample parking space, a large covered sales area, the fruit is sized and graded before the customers, and there is an attached cold storage to keep the fruit and vegetables fresh. The owner's fruit and vegetable plantings surround the stand. The sign in front of the white horse symbol indicates the owner to be a member of New Jersey Certified (Quality) Markets.

Many stands have cold storage space as a part of the stand and some grade their fruit before the customers to emphasize the fact that the seller grows his own fruit. Attractive, concise, easily understood signs should be used for advertising the market; they should be placed at an angle to the road, legible at 150 feet or more, and far enough from the stand to give the driver ample opportunity to stop. Salesmen must be courteous, accommodating, and always attendant, making every effort to develop return sales.

In several states a number of grower-operated roadside markets have teamed together. In New Jersey, e.g., they call themselves the "Jersey Certified Farm Markets, Inc," using an attractive symbol to indicate to consumers that they are of high standards, reputable, and seeking only high quality produce. This is a means of distinguishing themselves from the numerous grower or non-grower operated roadside markets of variable quality. The happiest growers financially often are marketing through roadside outlets. See (or write for) references with details.

Using marketing agencies. Although the small grower may move most of his crop at roadside market or direct to local retailers, the large grower must be prepared to move his crop in a standardized pack that can be sold on description and delivered on definite schedules to meet buyers needs.

Continuity of supply is essential to efficient marketing, as well as uniformity of pack and quality. Neither chain store buyers; purveyors who supply restaurants; steamship lines or individual retailers; nor exporters are interested any more in "one shot" deals. They all want to buy their supplies where they can come back and get more of exactly the same quality as needed. A cooperative association of growers with substantial

278

volume and uniform control over quality and condition can service customers that would have no interest in dealing with a smaller supplier. The speculative buyers who go from one orchard to another looking for bargains in tree-run fruit, which they can peddle to retailers or repack themselves are no longer an important factor.

The following are marketing means and agencies available to the grower.

Commission Houses. At one time the *commission merchant* in the terminal markets in larger cities was a big factor in the marketing of apples consigned by growers. He put them on display in his store or on his sidewalk and showed them to buyers who came to the market. He might sell one or two packages or several hundred to a customer. Price depended on quality and supply in the market and might fluctuate widely in a few hours. Now that chain stores are buying mostly for direct shipment from the country to their warehouses, there is much less volume of buying in the terminal markets.

Jobber A *jobber* is a person or firm who specializes in supplying retailers, or others who require regular deliveries of relatively small quantities. One jobber may have a clientele of independent retail stores or delicatessens that depend on him. Those who supply restaurants, hotels and steamships are usually called "purveyors". They must have dependable quality and efficient deliveries.

Service Wholesaler. A new type of jobber that has become an important factor in distribution of apples and other fruits in some areas, especially the Midwest and Southeast is the *service wholesaler*. He usually has a group of independent retailers or small chain supermarkets that depend upon him to purchase their supplies in volume lots and deliver to the stores, on a fixed margin. They are a purchasing agency for the retailers. Their service may also include assisting in making displays of fruit in the stores and helping in special promotions.

Broker. A *broker* is a selling agent who is a contact medium between seller and buyer. It is his job to offer what the shipper has to sell to a buyer who may need it, and to know where to get supplies that buyers need. Brokers usually deal only in trucklots or carlots, but they will make up mixed loads with deliveries to several customers. When a sale is completed the broker issues a confirmation of sale, with a copy to the shipper and to the buyer. If both buyer and seller accept this, it beomes a legal contract. The brokerage fee is paid by the seller. In some markets there are buying brokers employed by buyers to inspect and purchase fruits and vegetables, whose fee is paid by the buyers.

Disposal by auction. The principal items sold at large fruit auctions are citrus, Northwest apples, California grapes, and Pacific Coast pears. The boxes of fruit are available for inspection on platforms or piers prior to and during the auction (Figure 5). The contents of each lot are listed

W. C. Crow, U.S.D.A.

Figure 5. (Top) Auctions offer a rapid, convenient means of disposal of large quantities of fruit. (Bottom) A fruit auction display house in Chicago where prospective buyers first examine the various lots of fruit, take notes on a published catalog giving essential information regarding the fruit, and then proceed to an auction room for the bidding where selling proceeds item by item.

on sheets available to all persons attending. Prospective buyers make hurried inspections and mark their lists to indicate on which items they will consider making bids. These lists are watched closely as the auction proceeds.

The seller may withdraw his offering, but he may not bid himself. The fruit is available for immediate delivery and the auctions are usually finished by midafternoon.

The larger fruit auctions are located in New York City, Baltimore, Cleveland, Chicago, San Francisco, and Portland, Oregon. The buyers represent wholesale grocers, restaurants, chain stores, hotels, or brokers. The smaller lots may be taken by hucksters, and push cart men. The usual auction commission is 2½ to 3½ per cent on standard products in quantity.

In dealing through auction, the shipment is usually consigned to a commission agent or to some representative of the shipper who makes contacts with the auction company. In this transaction, the commission agent's charge is less since the auction company does the selling. Auction companies deal almost entirely with well-known and firmly standardized brands of products. Competition is usually keen enough to eliminate unfair practices. The auction method of selling is continuing as a popular system of selling fruit. Auctions also are used extensively in Europe.

Pick-it-yourself. This method of disposal is adapted to medium to small plantings. Orchardists near cities, particularly when harvest labor is a problem, advertise through radio and newspapers when fruit can be picked by local people. Supervision of pickers is needed to keep them on the right tree or row. Growers have been surprised at the care and interest taken by city people. Price can be half or greatly reduced because of no need for containers, storage, or the usual expenses from picking through marketing. Names and addresses are taken; people are notified by postcard in subsequent years. See references, specific fruit, appendix.

Vending machines. These automatic refrigerated machines are operated in schools, railroad stations, U. S. Armed Services Camps, and areas of heavy traffic and have proven successful for operators who may devote full time to the venture. Only the best apples are used, giving a choice of three or four varieties.

SHIPPING POINT INSPECTION

In addition to a government inspection certificate on grade, pack, quality, and shipping condition at point of origin, there also is provided by state or government officials an inspection certificate of the fruit upon arrival at the destination. The certificates of these inspectors are accepted in the courts in the United States as *prima facie* evidence of the truth of the statements therein contained and are the standard recognized basis for the buyer's final acceptance of quality, grade, pack, and condition. This service encourages greater care on the part of shipping concerns; it also reduces the rejection of cars at a destination because of

Figure 6. This machine was built to dispense an ice slush of "colored sugar water" but has been found to make an excellent cider slush simply by filling it with fresh cider. An operator is needed. Two small machines or one large one may be used in the market. Return sales are good the year round, and particularly on warm days. (Courtesy Wilch Factory Sales Co., Jenkins Ave., Tonkawa, Okla. 74650).

trivial reasons when the market is oversupplied. The inspection system induces stability and general confidence in the market; it is the best kind of insurance that the shipper can buy. The cost is relatively inexpensive. Further information regarding this inspection service can be obtained from The Farm Products Inspection Service, Agricultural Marketing Service, U. S. Department of Agriculture, or from the local state department of agriculture.

The Federal Inspection Service also issues a "Condition Report" upon request. This covers such factors as decay and other deterioration in a product. It is usually requested after storage. Before storage, for example, apples could be graded Extra Fancy and be within the established tolerance for decay at time of storage. Later, if decay developed in an excessive amount, they would still be Extra Fancy, but out of condition because of decay, and the "Condition Report" would so certify.

MARKET PREFERENCES

It is general knowledge among fruit growers that some varieties, particularly Delicious and Golden Delicious, are in greater demand than others such as Rome Beauty. It is becoming an increasing problem to move present summer varieties of apple since housewives in general are doing less home cooking and canning; also summer varieties generally are of too poor quality to eat out of hand. People turn to other kinds of fresh fruits in season.

Some cities are better markets for second-class fruit than others. Some orchardists consider Pittsburgh a good market for second-grade fruit, due probably to the large population of foreign workers in the mills, mines, and factories. Midwestern cities such as Kansas City, Fort Worth, and Omaha have often paid higher prices for a given pack and variety than large eastern cities, including Chicago. An eastern grower must first consider freight rates, handling, and cartage charges before shipping his fruit to the midwestern markets. Unless the price received would compensate for these additional charges and also add a profit, there would be little reason, other than gluts on the eastern markets, to warrant sending fruit to the Midwest. None but their best fruit can be shipped these distances at a profit.

The U. S. Armed Services and the USDA School Lunch Program are among the biggest buyers of U.S. fruit and fruit products.

LOADING AND SHIPPING FRUIT

The first requirement in shipping fruit successfully is to use rigid containers and pack them firmly. Containers must be stacked solidly against the car or trailer walls and against each other; ventilation should be provided in all parts of the car and throughout the stacked fruit. Packages which are defective in any way should not be loaded because the collapse of one such package may cause the entire load to shift, resulting in considerable damage to a large portion of the shipment. Railroads or trucking concerns by which fruit is shipped will furnish directions for loading of boxes, or other containers.

If the fruit has set outside over night, it should be loaded early in the morning while it is cool. If it has been in cold storage, so much the better. It may take several days to cool fruit that is warm when placed in refrigerated cars or trucks. Fruit near the top and in the center of the car requires much longer to cool in ice-refrigerated cars. If the temperature of the fruit is 75° to 80° F. when loaded, it may take 12 hours for it to reach 45° F. in the bottom layer and six or seven days for fruit in the top layer to reach 50° F. Obviously, considerable ripening can occur in this time and shorten the future storage life of the apples. Rapid precooling of fruit in special storage rooms or with portable machinery attached temporarily to the loaded car is frequently practiced. The mechanics of precooling is discussed in the chapter concerning peaches with which crop it is of paramount importance.

Rail vs. Truck. Where formerly the majority of the fresh tonnage was

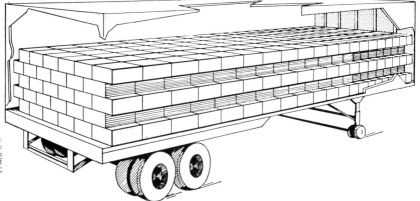

Courtesy Great Northern Railway and USDA

Figure 7. (Top) Wenatchee, Washington apples are being loaded into "piggy-back" van to be moved east by rail. (Bottom) Fiberboard boxes of apples in a motortruck semi-trailer or rail car should be loaded to provide air channels (shaded areas) for efficient refrigeration.

shipped by rail, the increased freight rates have shifted emphasis to truck. Only about one third is shipped by freight cars and most of this from the Northwest. In fact, Idaho ships fifty per cent fresh tonnage by truck and this may be 1,000 miles or more. Apples are now being trucked from Washington to Los Angeles and San Francisco and from New England to Florida. Truck and rail rates have become comparable.

Apples may be carried on unregulated trucks and it is more or less a personal bargaining arrangement between the trucker and the shipper. Trucks are invaluable for transporting fruit to and from wholesale markets in congested areas. The principal advantages of the motor truck are speedy service, less expense and less handling. The trucks are equipped with refrigerator service for the longer hauls, as shown in Figure 7. Some disadvantages have arisen with the use of motor trucks, but measures are being taken to correct them. Among the disadvantages are the following: (1) Inadequate terminal facilities for handling produce arriving by motor truck; (2) variation from one state to the next in motor-vehicle laws, (3) poor salesmanship and knowledge of market procedures on the part

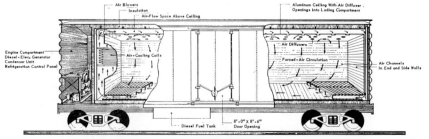

Figure 6. Most of the fruit today is being shipped by sealed refrigerated rail cars and truck-pulled refrigerated containers. The 100-ton rail car above is 57 ft. long, has a load capacity of 4,270 cu. ft. and is equipped with a self-contained refrigeration unit capable of maintaining a preset temperature level from 0° to 70°F. (Courtesy Fruit Growers and Western Express Companies, Washington, D.C. 20005). (Lower) Refrigerator car without its own cooling unit being iced.

of the grower or truck driver, (4) lack of systematic control of movement of the trucks to the market, and (5) inadequate advance knowledge of market supplies by both the grower and terminal operators.

In spite of these disadvantages the majority of the fruit in the East and Midwest is being transported by trucks, which indicates a correction of these problems.

Manner of shipment. Many apples are shipped long distances to market and frequently are in transit from one to three weeks before being unloaded. There are several services by which fruit can be shipped as outlined below. The service selected should depend upon the variety of apple, the condition of the fruit, the time it will be held in storage before selling to ultimate consumers, weather conditions, the time of year shipped, the character and facilities of the railroad, truck, or steamship and the probable length of the trip. Most shipments today are being made under refrigeration. The use of weather reports is invaluable in determining the type of shipping services which should be used.

1. Standard refrigeration. This means protective service against heat

284

by the use of ice placed in the refrigerator car bunkers (Figure 6). The insulated cars carry from 6,000 to 12,000 pounds of ice. Under standard refrigeration, the cars are re-iced to capacity by railways at all regular icing stations, or at approximately 24-hour intervals while in transit from point of shipment to destination.

2. Standard refrigeration with salt. This service is the same as outlined above, except that about 3 per cent of salt is included at each icing station at an added cost. The salt affords more intensive refrigeration and lower temperatures inside the car, and is suggested for fruit loaded warm which will be commercially stored at destination for several months.

3. Initial icing only. Under this service, the railways furnish refrigerator cars with ice tanks filled to capacity at the time of shipment, but no further ice is furnished. This service is often used with fruit coming from cold storage or which has been precooled for shipment.

There is a modification of this service known as initial icing with one or two re-icings in transit, which means that the cars are iced to capacity at point of origin and re-iced to capacity at a designated point in transit. Both, or either of these services also can be used safely with fall and winter varieties of apples being shipped during early fall or early spring when the requirement for ice in shipment is not so great. There is also what is known as "half-stage" icing used in fall, winter and spring when demand for cooling is less. Only the upper half of the bunkers are filled with ice, resulting in adequate cooling and a definite saving in cost. This is due to modern cars with thicker insulation and air circulating devices.

4. Ventilation service. This is the cheapest service available to the grower and should be used only when the fruit will be sold for immediate consumption. Under ventilation service the fruit is carried in refrigerator cars without ice. The hatch covers and plugs are manipulated so as to exclude or admit outside air according to prevailing temperatures. Fruit coming out of cold storage preferably should be shipped under refrigeration.

5. Box car service. Box cars are used only in case of extreme emergency when there is a refrigerator car shortage. Box cars are risky because they have no insulation and no provision for ventilation.

6. Carriers protective service against cold. During the period October 15 to April 15 inclusive, shipments also may be made under this service. The railways will protect the shipments against frost, freezing, or artificial overheating by thermostatically-controlled heaters with forced-air circulation. The service extends to the Atlantic seaboard.

IMPROVING THE SELLING AND ADVERTISING PROGRAMS

People normally eat about the same amount of fruit from one year to the next. If consumption of one fruit is increased by intelligent and persistent promotion, consumption of another fruit must suffer. The popularity of citrus is unquestionably due to extensive advertising programs to make the housewives conscious of the health values of citrus. The doctors' recommended pectin consumption in fruits and juices to reduce blood cholesterol and heart problems has boosted fruit sales immeasurably.

Apple research in recent years has emphasized its health values to keep pace with citrus. A Michigan study has shown that students eating two apples a day had fewer tensions, headaches, emotional upsets, skin diseases, arthritic ailments, respiratory troubles, and missed less classes than those not eating apples by a 12 to 1 ratio. Dentists claim that an apple after a meal keeps the teeth and mouth cleaner.

Promotional organizations. In order for apple sales to keep pace with competitive fruits, it has been necessary for special organizations to devote more and more time and money to extensive advertising programs. Among the groups which have played a major and highly effective part in these programs are the *Washington State Apple Advertising Commission, International Apple Institute, Pacific Northwest Fruit, Inc., Michigan State Apple Commission, California Fruit Exchange, National Apple Week Association, and United Fresh Fruit and Vegetable Association, New York-New England Apple Institute,* and several individual state organizations. Channels of promotion consist of advertising in leading national newspapers and magazines, outdoor posters, radio and TV spots, moving pictures, advertisements directed to the produce and retail grocery trade, direct messages to the trade by telegram and special bulletins, store display material sent to the trade upon request, apple books containing pertinent information of varietal and cooking uses, and "tie-in" advertising with other lines of items such as breakfast foods, cigarettes, and cooking recipes.

The *International Apple Institute* was formed in 1970 by merger of the International Apple Association and the National Apple Institute with headquarters at 2430 Pennsylvania Ave., N.W., Washington, D.C. 20037. IAI serves growers, exporters, importers, banks, ocean shipping companies and distributors. An annual meeting is held in early summer and frequent newsletters and an annual reference book are sent to paid members, covering crop estimates, storage holdings, market movements, export-import situation, advertising and promotion, and practically all key developments and problems in apple production. IAI plays a key role in bargaining where needed. There are three departments: (a) marketing, (b) education and promotion and (c) legislative and government relations.

Many of the above organizations have special year-round representatives boosting the sales of apples in cooking schools, assisting in retailer education in setting up displays, and properly handling apples for the best sales possible (see Figures 8 and 9). It is to the advantage of every grower to support one or more of these organizations. Some states, including Washington, Michigan, and New Jersey, have a tax of two to four cents a bushel on apples produced and sold. Revenue is used for promotion and production and marketing research. Eventually, there may de-

George Luke, Rutgers University

Figure 8. Apples in polyethylene bags, whether summer, fall, or winter varieties, far outsell bulk display apples, although the two types of display are usually complementary.

velop a national or international apple and pear organization like Ocean Spray for cranberries or Welch for grapes which has its own brand advertising, research and development, processing facilities and its own sales contacts and/or retail outlets. This could be owned privately or by participating growers who make their own rules and regulations, bargain for prices, and share in the total profits.

Boosting retail sales. That a vigorous revitalized sales-boost program is needed with apples is demonstrated by a survey made by the *Progressive Grocer,* covering $1,700,000 fresh produce sales over a 12-week period in six supermarkets. Only 73 cents of every $100 spent in these stores was for apples, $1.07 for oranges, $1.01 for orange juice, $1.03 for bananas, and 81 cents for potatoes. For processed items the consumer spent 8 cents for sauce, 3 cents for slices, and 5 cents for apple juice, totaling 16 cents out of every $100.

Several pointers and suggestions have been made for increasing sales once the apples reach the retailer.

1. There must be a co-ordinated program of advertising and selling efforts; high quality, well-packed fruits must be available in sufficient

Figure 9. Local and National queens help bring public attention to the merits of an important fruit crop. Rosemary Mood, daughter of a famous fruit growing family near Mullica Hill, New Jersey (Starking Delicious apple discovered in their orchard), served as a National Peach Queen. The National Peach Council sponsored her speaking and performing talents through National news media and at important meetings throughout the year.

quantities to back up the advertising program. If any one step in a promotional program breaks down, the entire program is likely to collapse.

2. Most fruit sales in retail stores are made on Wednesday, Friday, and Saturday with Sunday being a big shopping day in states so permitting. Afternoon sales are greater than morning sales.

3. The housewife buys about eighty per cent of the food for the table. She buys largely through her eyes by "impulse sales." If the apples have been carefully handled and packed, properly priced, and attractively displayed by a retail store, they are more than half sold to her. Young people under thirty years buy more apples than older people.

4. Supermarkets are predicted to move 75% of the total food sales by 1980. Concentrate promotional efforts on these stores which are in a position to influence a greater proportion of the nation's housewives. Research has shown that three key factors effect fruit movement: (a) quality, (b) service, and (c) price.

5. There is no more potent advertising of apples than a beautiful display of apples itself, particularly when a display is backed by aggressive, intelligent selling, and an adequate supply of high-quality fruit.

6. The better displays are artistic, clean, well-lighted, have an appealing color arrangement, have clearly readable variety, grade and price tags, and are well-stocked and full-looking at all times. Items closely associated with apples on menus should be included in the display when available. Apples sell better if displayed alone, not with citrus or bananas.

7. The medium to large apples of a variety may bring the quicker sales and better profit, although with polyethylene bags it has been found possible to move large quantities of medium to small size apples. Faced apples

VARIETY	FLAVOR AND TEXTURE	EATING FRESH (SALADS TOO)	SAUCE	PIE	BAKED	WHEN AND WHERE SOLD
SUMMER-TIME	SOUR, TENDER	X	X	X		JULY-AUG
JONATHAN	TART, TENDER	X	X	X	X	SEPT.-JAN.
GRIMES GOLDEN	SWEET, MELLOW	X	X	X		SEPT.-DEC.
DELICIOUS	SWEET, RICH	X				SEPT.-APR.
McINTOSH	SPICY, TENDER	X	X	X	X	SEPT.-APR.
CORTLAND	MILD, TENDER	X	X	X	X	OCT.-JAN.
GOLDEN DELICIOUS	RICH, SEMI-FIRM	X	X	X	X	OCT.-APR.
STAYMAN	SPICY, SEMI-FIRM	X	X	X	X	NOV.-MAR.
NORTHERN SPY	TANGY, TENDER	X	X	X	X	NOV.-MAR.
YORK	TART, FIRM	X	X	X	X	NOV.-MAR.
BALDWIN	MILD, FIRM	X	X	X	X	NOV.-APR.
ROME BEAUTY	BLAND, FIRM	X	X	X	X	NOV.-APR.
NEWTOWN-PIPPIN	TART, FIRM	X	X	X	X	NOV.-MAY
WINESAP	SPICY, FIRM	X		X		DEC.-JUNE

National Apple Institute, Washington, D. C.

Figure 10. This chart is published and distributed as an aid to retailers and consumers in moving apple varieties in their proper season. Similar information on basis of local varieties could be stamped on corrugated boxes or printed on folders containing other pertinent information and dropped in each container or sack of purchased apples.

(red side out) may sell three times faster and bring gross profits four times as great as jumble arrangement. Good appearance of apples with no bruising is a tremendous factor in boosting sales. Quality and condition of apples are more important than price in sales of best grades of apples.

8. The grocer may figure an average shrinkage loss of about five per cent. Although this figure is bound to vary under different conditions, the grocer in pricing his fruit at the outset should figure on this handling loss in order to compensate roughly for it.

9. The grocer should check his display frequently and sort out apples beginning to fade or show signs of deterioration. These should be sold immediately at marked-down prices before the fruits are a complete loss.

10. If possible, the clerks should receive special training in the proper handling and many uses of the different varieties of apples. Often this instruction can be obtained for sizable groups of clerks and store operators through the local state agricultural extension service or through special apple promotional organizations. Some of this type information can be placed on "talking" price cards in self-service stores.

11. Small consumer packages or poly bags containing three to six pounds of apples are suggested, although the best size bag varies with different regions. These bags are especially convenient for rapid sales. The top layer of fruit should be clearly evident and open for inspection

if in cartons. If in polybags, all apples should be seen clearly. Consumer packs prevent buyers from fingering the apples so much and bruising them with their thumbs. With these consumer packs, it has been found that there is little or no leftover fruit of poor quality. Max Brunk of Cornell University has found that polybags far outsell bulk display apples.

12. The chart shown in Figure 10, or a similar one bearing information on local varieties is invaluable to both retailers and consumers in selling and buying wisely. They should be placed prominently near the display counters.

13. The health value of apples should be stressed in posters and in discussing apples with the housewife. Apples supply carbohydrates and minerals in the diet and have important therapeutic value. In institutions for the care of children in both Europe and America, remarkable relief of digestive troubles including diarrhea, dysentery, enteritis, and dyspepsia has been reported. The number of patients was large and the control adequate. Scraped or pulped apples and apple powder are used for children to cleanse and detoxify the intestines. The dental health promotion for apples by N.A.I. has been very effective.

14. A small inexpensive folder provided either by the grocer, distributor, or retailer, is effective when placed in each package, giving details regarding uses for varieties, a few cooking recipes, health value, and better methods for keeping apples in the home (Figure 10).

15. Provisions for cold storage of apples in the retail store are highly desirable for preserving quality and condition of the fruit. Otherwise, if possible, the retailer should buy from a jobber or seller every two or three days to keep a fresh supply coming from a local commercial cold storage.

16. Handled like eggs or butter, they go through the merchandising channels with very little loss.

17. A survey in New Jersey showed that all-red apples are preferred by housewives 3 to 1 to red apples with some green showing. Women picking the fruit with some green had the definite reason that these fruits were frequently of better quality, not over-ripe or mealy as the all-red apples sometimes are. This would indicate that about one-third of a display might have fruit showing some green.

18. One N.Y. grower pays the local supermarket $25/ad to use his name with apples being advertised in a local newspaper.

Marketing CA apples. In CA (controlled atmospheres) storage, apples are held in a refrigerated and especially sealed room where the carbon dioxide and oxygen are regulated to specified levels throughout the storage period. In this way, the apples are of much higher quality when removed from storage and have a "shelf-life" approximately twice as long as apples held in regular storage. Delicious, Golden Delicious, Jonathan and McIntosh, are the most common varieties in CA storage. In the early

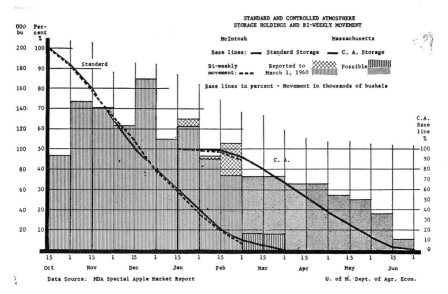

Data Source: MDA Special Apple Market Report   U. of M. Dept. of Agr. Econ.

Figure 10a. Chart shows the biweekly movement of regular and CA stored apples in Massachusetts. CA apples (McIntosh) started moving in January.

1970's around 30 to 50 percent of these varieties were held in CA storage in the U.S., according to International Apple Inst. Other varieties being held in CA storage include Rome, Newtown, Spy, Stayman, Cortland, and others.

The amount of CA apples in the U.S. is on the increase, approaching 20 million bushels in 1972-3. CA storages are owned by the larger growers. About one third of the CA capacity consists of remodeled regular storage space; the balance is newly constructed.

CA apples are marketed widely in the U.S. Chain stores have begun to demand them. The consumers apparently are not particularly concerned about the price as long as they can buy at a "reasonable" price. Demand has been strongest for all packs of 96 and 112 sizes. CA apples ("they have risen from a long sleep") are becoming well known to the public through radio, TV, newspapers, and sales-tag advertising. There has been an expanded market open for CA apples in the late spring and early summer although there may not be premium prices in late CA season.

CA apples definitely bring a premium price so long as the market is not flooded. No doubt the higher quality level maintained by CA fruit will increase over-all consumption of apples during periods when regular stored apples has waned. Figure 10a shows movement of CA apples in a typical season in Massachusetts.

By-products. Since 1934 fresh apple consumption in the United States has dropped about 40 percent, or about one-fourth pound per capita per year; processed apple products, particularly apple sauce, have increased 250 to 300 percent. Selling to the processor is no longer a salvage proposi-

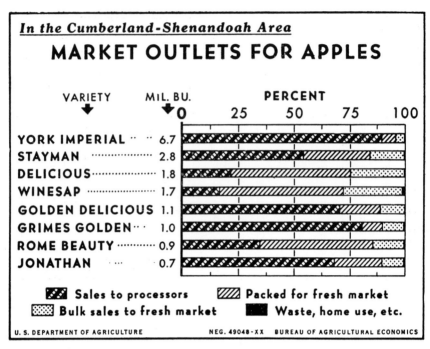

Figure 11. This chart shows the relatively large percentage of apples by lead-ing varieties in the Cumberland-Shenandoah area which move to the processors. The percentage is likely to increase. For the country as a whole about one third of the apple crop goes to processors.

tion. The processor must have quality fruit, good sizes and varieties.

Actually, about 40 percent of the total apple crop of the United States is being processed. In the Cumberland-Shenandoah region this percentage is higher (Figure 11). Most of the apples are canned, but apple juice with added vitamin C is now being sold along milk routes and in super-markets in increasing quantities. Sauce mixed with raspberries and straw-berries is a tasteful mix. Dried apples are important where they afford a convenient means of handling under adverse conditions as during wars. Other by-products consist of frozen apples, canned baked apples, fresh cider, vinegar, dried cubed apple breakfast food, juice, apple concentrate, apple powder, crisps and pumice. One processor is freezing fresh cider of a given apple variety into blocks, holding the blocks in a freezer, and later blending the cider by melting and mixing the blocks for immediate sale. Cider freezes and holds well. Various artificially fruit-flavored wines made from apple juice and the concentrate are popular.

Apple syrup has been found valuable in retaining quality and moisture in white breads, cigarettes, and smoking tobacco. The U.S. Department of Agriculture research laboratory near Philadelphia, Pa., and another in California are concentrating on new uses for by-products of fruits. Steps are now being made for better utilization of low-grade fruit which is definitely receiving less and less sympathy in the fresh fruit marketing channels. Apple, cranberry, prune and other juices are now being blended for sale.

EXPORT-IMPORT

Fruit production and processing in, e.g., Europe, Australia, New Zealand, Mexico, Canada, South Africa, Argentina and Chile have increased in recent years to the point where market disposal within the respective countries and the disruption of foreign markets by export has caused international problems. Holland has devised a plan to cut back on plantings.

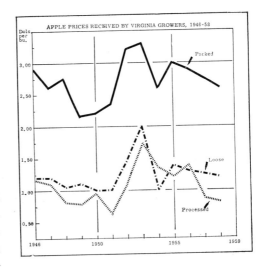

Figure 12. Prices received for processed and loose apples in Virginia have been a little more than a third of the packed price.

Australia *must* export due to its own limited population. A full crop in Italy actually could supply all of Europe; Japan is a big producer. Apple juice concentrate being imported into the U.S. is creating a local problem. Thus, some means of reducing world acreage must be taken or greater emphasis must be placed on local and international promotion.

Apples exported from the United States (2.3 million bushels in 1969-70) vary with the size of the European, U.S., and Canadian crops; much of the Canadian exports are sent into the U.S. and to England. Although Canada and Mexico are fair export customers, most of the United States trade goes to the British Isles and its possessions with fair quantities going to Germany, the Netherlands, Belgium, France, Sweden, South America, W. Indies, Philippine Is. and others. Germany and the Netherlands also serve as distributing centers for United States shipments to neighboring territories. Ports of export from the United States are Boston, New York, Philadelphia, Norfolk, Baltimore, Seattle, San Francisco, and Portland, Maine and Oregon. In Canada, Halifax is the chief port with Montreal, Quebec, and St. Johns in the East, and Vancouver on the Pacific Coast, making shipments.

Fancy or better McIntosh in uniform cell cartons of 140, 160, and 200s are demanded in England and Scotland by *brand name*. Newtown and Albermarle Pippins are also in demand. Tray-pack Red Delicious, Red Romes, and Golden Delicious, are popular, small sizes in Europe and large sizes, 88/100/113 in South America. Goldens must be clean, no russet or lenticel spots, greenish tinge for better keeping, and wrapped.

Season for export starts in August for South America and West Indies and continues until Argentine or other southern hemisphere apples fill their markets. Exports to Europe may start late August or early September depending upon competitive supplies, and continue till March or later. England has a license system with allotments to exporters based on their volume of imports in a post-war period. The allocations for the first period from August to end of December are limited for the protection of British growers, and are larger for period from January 1st to July. Southern hemisphere new-crop apples start coming in about March 1st.

Practically all apples exported now are sold at definite prices on definite specifications, f.o.b., port of shipment or C.I.F. port of destination. On an f.o.b. sale the foreign buyer pays for the fruit delivered on board the ship. On C.I.F. sales the exporter pays the ocean freight and collects by draft or "Letter of Credit" on delivered destination port basis. When a grower or shipper sells F.A.S. New York (free-along-side), or other port, he is obligated to deliver the apples onto the dock where the ship is loading but has no further responsibility. All apples sold for export must have USDA inspection at time of shipment and must not only pass the grade for which they are sold but must meet U.S. Standard Condition for Export. Exceptions as to inspection may be made on lots of less than 100, where it may be difficult to get inspection.

Future expansion of export business only can be based upon dependable supplies of quality apples in good carrying condition and attractive packages that protect the fruit.

Review Questions

1. List and discuss briefly the various methods of selling fruit.
2. Briefly describe a well-operated roadside market for fruit, vegetables and other products.
3. How do the following marketing agents or agencies operate in disposal of fruit: cooperative, commission house, jobber, broker, and auctions?
4. What is the value of shipping point inspection?
5. What part does the motor truck play in the transporting and marketing of fruit?
6. List 3 apple promotional organizations and state how they are aiding in disposal of apples and other deciduous fruits.
7. List 6 suggestions for increasing fruit sales in retail stores.
8. How important are by-products in the utilization of apples? List the principal apple by-products.
9. Discuss the general apple export-import situation, varieties, packing and countries involved.

Suggested Collateral Readings

Are We misleading ourselves about the value of bulk crop estimates? American Fruit Grower. December 1969. p. 18 & 33.
Australian apple and pear growers seek U.S. markets. USDA, Foreign Agriculture. October 25, 1971. p. 10.

Ben-David, Shaul and W. G. Tomek, Storing and marketing N. Y. apples based on intraseasonal demands. Cornell Bull. 1007. 35 pp. 1965.

Blakeley, R. A. An encyclopedia and bibliography on roadside marketing. New York Agr. Exp. Sta. (Cornell) A. E. Res. 114. 83 pp. May, 1963.

Brunk, Max E. Marketing strategy for apples in the future. Cornell Univ., Dept. of Agric. Econ., Ithaca, N. Y. 1969.

Buck, W. F. Using your fruit and vegetable co-op. U.S.D.A. FCS Educ. Cir. 7. June, 1955.

Burns, A. J., G. R. Rockwell, Jr., and E. Thigpen. Apple marketing - - a review of economic research, 1945-1960. USDA Econ. Res. Ser. 140. 36 pp. Oct., 1963.

Canadian imports of horticultural products. USDA, Foreign Agricultural Serv. Bull. FAS M-226. February 1971. 28pp.

Ceponis, M. J. and J. Kaufman. Some effects of packaging and merchandising on the quality of McIntosh apples in New York City. USDA Agr. Mkt. Ser. 494. 9 pp. Feb., 1963.

Clayton, L. Yvonne. Homemakers' use of and opinions about selected fruits and fruit products. USDA Mkt. Res. Report No. 765. 78 pp. Aug., 1966.

Cook, A. Clinton. Horticultural imports hurt U.S. producers. Better Fruit, Better Vegetables. March 1971. p. 14 & 17.

Cunningham, A. C. Marketing apples harvested in consumer containers. New York Agr. Exp. Sta. (Cornell) A. E. Res. 141. 50 pp. Feb., 1964.

Dalyrmple, Dana G. Fruit-grower experience with "pick-it-yourself." Conn. Agr. Ext. Serv. Mimeo. Rpt. 11 pp. November, 1957.

——————————. Some observations on the marketing of fruits and vegetables in the Sovet Union. USDA, Federal Ext. Serv. Bull. MUS 167. October, 1964. 12pp.

Dewey, D. H. and T. J. Schueneman. Quality and packout of storage apples— effects on cost and return. Mich. Res. Rpt. 147. 1972.

Evans, H. C. Competition and apple prices (with emphasis on processors in the Appalachian area). W. Va. Agr. Exp. Sta. Bull. 406. 1957.

Fountain, J. B. Evaluation of shipping trays and pads for pears and apples. USDA. Mkt. Res. Rept. No. 530, 20 pp. Apr., 1962.

Fresh Fruit and Vegetable Prices—1970 USDA, Fruit and Vegetable Div., Washington, D.C. Bull. 468. May 1971. 39pp.

Friedman, B. A. Market diseases of fresh fruits and vegetables. Economic Botany 14: No. 2. pp. 145-156. April-June, 1960.

Frye, R. E., and V. D. Grubbs. Promotion of farm products by agricultural groups. U.S.D.A.—A.M.S. Res. Rpt. No. 380. 27 pp. Jan. 1960.

Gifford, J. C. and A. H. Harrington. Northwest fruits and western markets—effects of grades, standards, quarantines and inspection on movement. Wash. Agr. Exp. Sta. Cir. 256. pp. 27. 1954.

Greig, W. S., C. L. Bedford and H. Larzelere. Consumer preference among apple varieties in fresh and processed forms. Mich. Quar. Bull. 44: No. 3. pp. 505-526. 1962.

Greig, W. S., Mary E. Grant, and H. E. Lozelere. The effect of methods of freezing apple slices on consumer preference for pies. Mich. Agr. Exp. Sta. Quart. Bull. 42: No. 4, 929-935. May, 1960.

Henderson, P. L., S .E. Brown, and J. F. Hind. Special promotional programs for apples, their effects on sales of apples and other fruits. USDA Mkt. Res. Rept. No. 446. 31 pp. Jan. 1961.

Higgins, W. J. and D. A. Lockhart. Market prospects for U. S. horticultural products in Japan. USDA FAS M-211. Sept. 1969.

Jones, H. H. Transport packaging technology. Inter. Fruit World, Basle, Switzerland. pp. 298-315. March, 1967.

Knapp, J. C. Fruit and vegetable bargaining co-operatives. U.S.D.A. FCS Cir. 25. 59 pp. 1958.

McColloch, L. P. Home storage of vegetables and fruits. USDA Farmers' Bull. No. 1939, 21 pp. June, 1960.

(See additional references under Chapter XII Appendix)

CHAPTER XIII

Pear and Quince Culture

❖ ◆ ❖ ◆ ❖ ❖ ◆ ◆ ◆ ◆ ❖ ◆ ◆ ❖ ◆ ◆ ◆ ◆ ❖ ◆ ◆ ◆ ◆ ◆ ◆ ❖ ◆

PEAR CULTURE

The earliest authentic record of pears in the United States is probably that of the Endicott pear tree planted near Salem, Massachusetts, about 1630. It was brought to America by the French and English colonists. Despite the early introduction and general popularity of pears, they have never become as widely grown as the apple in America. Fireblight, a bacterial disease favored by rains, has limited commercial pear production to Western U.S. areas where summer rains are rarer.

Expansion in pear growing since 1920 has been in the three Pacific Coast states where the conditions are favorable to economical and heavy production of high-quality fruit. This region and the Po Valley in Italy are the most intensive pear-growing sections in the world. Pear production in the eastern United States is of little commercial importance, except for a few regions around the Great Lakes. Production is largely limited to cannery outlets, local trade, and home orchards. In many ways, the pear is more desirable for home orchards than the apple because it grows and produces acceptable fruit with less attention. Also, pear trees such as Kieffer and Tyson are relatively long-lived. Once a Kieffer tree has become mature and well established, it may live and produce satisfactorily for 100 years or more.

Pear psylla, still a serious pest in the West, and fire blight were largely responsible for a marked decrease in pear trees in the East from 1910 to 1930. Since 1930, this reduction in pear trees has been less marked.

Pear psylla has been shown to be a vector of an extremely potent and dangerous virus to pears known as "pear decline". Pear decline reached serious proportions in the Pacific Northwest during the 1950's and first appeared in California in 1959. Since then it has killed over a quarter of a million California pear trees, and the disease is still active, although its

---

James A. Beutel, Extension Pomologist, University of California, Davis, assisted in this chapter revision.

Figure 1. Home gardners can make good use of limited space by training dwarf fruit trees on a wire trellis. This 10-year old espalier-trained Williams (Bartlett) pear is on Quince A rootstock in Victoria, Australia. Note leaf lettuce beneath. (Paul Stark, Jr., Stark Nurseries and Orchards Co., Louisiana, Mo. 63353).

intensity has dwindled in recent years. Much still remains unknown about this disease, and once established in a tree, there is no known cure. It could indeed have far reaching effects on the Pacific Coast pear industry and on the economy in many portions of this region.

Pear trees in the U.S. were close to 11 million in the 1970's of which about three million were nonbearing. The number of pear trees of all ages in the United States has decreased about one half since 1930. The decrease was about the same for both bearing and nonbearing trees.

In contrast with the above reduction in tree numbers, pear production has nearly trebled in the United States during the past seventy years, the increase having occurred largely in the Pacific Coast States. The 1969-71 three-year average production in the United States was 646,000 tons. Leading states showed the following production and rank in tons: California, 306,000; Oregon, 148,000; Washington, 137,000; Michigan, 19,000; and New York, 17,000. All other commercially important states produced together less than about 12,000 short tons. Fresh sales have comprised less than 40 percent of the production, pears canned over 60 per cent, dried and farm use about two per cent.

Commercial pear production on the Pacific Coast is confined largely to nine districts. Progressing from Washington State south, these districts are the Wenatchee and Yakima Valley areas in central Washington;

the Hood River Valley in northcentral Oregon, and the Rogue River Valley around Medford in southern Oregon; in California, the north coast area of Lake and Mendocino Counties, the Sacramento River district located southwest of Sacramento, the Sacramento Valley area around Marysville and Yuba City, the foothill district near Placerville, and the Santa Clara district south of San Francisco Bay.

Pear production is confined largely to areas within the temperate zone. World production is approaching 5.5 million *metric tons* (no data from China). Annual production in 1,000s of *metric tons* by countries for which data are available is about as follows: (a) United States, 640; (b) Canada, 35, mostly in Ontario and British Columbia; (c) Mexico, 35; (d) South America, around 165, mostly in Argentina followed by Brazil, Chili, Uraguay and Equador; (e) Europe, 3.5 to 4.5 million tons, one-third of apple production, by leading countries in order: Italy, 1400; Soviet Union, 450; Germany (FR), 400; France, 360 (excludes Perry cider pears); Switzerland, 200; Spain, 175; Austria, 150; Poland, 135; Greece, 125; Bulgaria, 115; and The Netherlands, 110, followed approximately by Belgium, Yugoslavia, Portugal, U.K., Romania, Hungary, Czechoslovakia, Denmark, and Sweden; (g) Australia, 150; and N. Zealand, 20; (h) Japan, 450; Korea, 40; and South Africa, about 75, half exported. Pear is very popular in China, more so than apple, and mainly of the Oriental types; *P. ussuriensus, P. bretschneideri, P. serotina* and some *P. pashia*. See Appendix for relative world pear production.

Most pears in Europe are eaten fresh, some are canned, and others pressed for cider known as "Perry." In the United States, more pears are eaten canned as halves or diced in fruit cocktail, than are eaten fresh. A few are dried.

Argentina and the British dominions of Australia, South Africa, and New Zealand also produce pears largely for dessert and cooking. Pear production in these southern hemisphere countries has been increasing rapidly since 1930; from February to June, their exports are beginning to dominate the world's best export market—the United Kingdom. Most of their season is opposite that of the West Coast, but they do compete with late-stored winter pear varieties like Anjou in the United States and United Kingdom.

CHOICE OF PEAR VARIETIES

Pear varieties have a great diversity in size, shape, texture, and flavor. Pear species vary from the small hard inedible fruits of the Oriental pear, *Pyrus calleryana Dec.,* to the fine-quality fruits of some varieties of the common European pear, *Pyrus communis L.* Also, there may be a considerable variation in fruit quality and shape within a variety from one region to the next. The Bartlett in Washington, for example, is longer

298

Figure 3. (Above) Bartlett (or Williams) is the most widely planted variety of pear. These trees are 3-years old, palmette trained, 4 ft. spacing, after pruning, on Quince A rootstock, producing 11 T/A the year of photo. (Courtesy, James A. Beutel, Univ. of Calif., Davis).

and more narrow than in California, but it seems to attain higher quality where the summers are relatively hot than where they are cool.

All important pear varieties grown in the United States belong to the European species, except for a few hybrids such as Kieffer, LeConte, and Garber which are crosses between the European and the Japanese pear, *Pyrus serotina Rehd.* Although there are more than 2500 minor varieties and 100 major varieties, commercial pear production is limited to a relatively few varieties. Seven varieties are commercially important on the West Coast. The Bartlett variety known as the "Williams" in Europe, New Zealand, Australia, and South Africa, usually accounts for about eighty percent of the U.S. commercial pear production. This is because the Bartlett fruit is well suited for canning, drying, and for fresh sales either locally or distant. The tree also is adapted widely to soil and climatic conditions. California has over 40,000 acres of which 95 percent is planted to Bartletts. Other varieties in order are: Hardy, Comice, Winter Nelis, and Bosc. Additional varieties comprise less than 500 acres.

In Washington the commercial varieties are Bartlett and Anjou, with Bartlett representing 2/3 of all pears. Bartletts are canned and shipped fresh August through October, while Anjous are stored and shipped December through May.

In Oregon, Bartlett, Anjou, Bosc, Winter Nelis, El Dorado, Packhams and Triumph are grown. At Hood River, Bartletts and Anjou are most important. In Medford all the above varieties are grown commercially. The Comice attains high quality there and for many years has been primarily sold in gift packages. Bosc[1] develops a fine cinnamon russet desired by the trade and has become an important variety in Medford.

The Kieffer variety is generally grown in the East. Although the variety is of inferior quality, it produces heavily, and the fruit is an attractive deep yellow. The tree is adapted widely to soil and climatic conditions and is hardier and more blight resistant than other varieties grown in the East. Michigan and New York, the two most important commercial pear producing states in the East, and possibly Pennsylvania, are the only eastern states in which the Bartlett acreage generally exceeds that of Kieffer. Other commercial varieties are Clapp, Maxine, Comice, Flemish Beauty, Bosc, Clairgeau, Seckel, Duchess d' Angouleme, and Anjou. New varieties which are being tried in the East and Northwest are Ovid, Early Seckel, Gorham and the blight resistant Magnesss (Dawn), Moonglow, and New Jersey No. 4 and 6. Magness is showing the most promise although with time for testing other blight resistant pears may gain commercial favor. Early Seckel ripens about two to three weeks earlier than the Seckel of which it is a seedling and which it otherwise resembles. The Gorham ripens about two weeks later than Bartlett, and appears to be about equal in blight susceptibility.

In the southern states, such as Texas, the Kieffer, Bartlett, and Garber are popular. The Tenneesse Station has bred several promising blight resistant selections, two of which are Morgan and Carrick.

PEAR POLLINATION

Most varieties of pears are self-unfruitful. Some varieties (Bartlett, Comice, Hardy) under ideal conditions set huge crops of parthenocarpic (seedless) fruit. These ideal conditions for parthenocarpy are several days of warm weather (maximum temperatures of 70-85°F) during bloom. When bloom occurs during cool, dry or wet weather with daytime maximums of 55-65°F, cross-pollination by bees and other insects is essential for adequate crops. In California a good correlation between parthenocarpic set of solid blocks of Bartletts and hours over 60°F during a 10-day bloom period has been determined. If more than 80 hours over 60°F occur during the 10-day bloom period, good to excellent crops are parthenocarpically set, but poor crops are set if there is less than 80 hours over 60°F. Most reports of better sets of Bartletts with cross-pollination are explainable based on this temperature relationship. In years of cool wet

---

[1]The "Beurré" and "Doyenné du" are rarely used by growers. Pear varieties carrying these names are referred to as "Hardy," "Comice," or "Bosc."

Courtesy H. Jonkers, Lab. voor Tuinbouwplantedteelt, Wageningen, The Netherlands.

Figure 4. The spindlebush training system is common for both pear and apple in Europe. This is Comice on Quince A rootstock in heavy cropping the seventh year.

bloom periods like 1965, cross-pollination by insects was most beneficial in many areas of California. However, when the temperature was too cold for bee activity in 1967 in the Sacramento River district, cross-pollination could not take place and a crop failure occurred in both orchards with and without pollinators. Hand pollination, although not economically practical, did provide fruit set under these conditions. Applications of pollen by airplane dusters or air blast sprayers have been of little or no value under these conditions. Small hand operated pollen dusters can be useful when temperatures are too low for bee flight.

For these reasons most California orchards are planted solid to Bartletts. As insurance against poor bloom conditions (cool weather which occurs about 10% of the time in the Sacramento Valley) some growers plant one pollinizer for every 16 Bartletts. Pollinizers used are Winter Nelis, which blooms ahead of Bartlett in California; Hardy, which blooms with Bartlett; Comice which blooms slightly ahead of Bartlett; and Bosc, which blooms with and after Bartlett. In California all pollinizers have less market demand than Bartlett fruit, so they are used on a limited basis in less than 25% of the orchards. In Washington, Bartletts are commonly used to pollinate Anjous and both have good market value in Washington.

Magness and Waite are pollen sterile and Bartlett and Seckel are incompatible for pollination. With these exceptions, other pear varieties will cross-pollinate each other. In the East and other areas where cool weather

301

at bloom time necessitates cross-pollination, two or more varieties should be planted. If both varietiies are equally valuable, solid rows of each variety should be used. If one variety is preferred, pollinizers may be scattered in every third or fourth row.

Bartlett in California has shown earlier and more uniform stage of bloom on Old Home stock than on *P. betulaefolia* and *P. calleryana.*

Susceptibility to fire blight must be considered in selecting a pollinizing variety in pear orchards. Varieties such as Bosc, Clapp Favorite, Flemish Beauty, and Gorham, which are relatively blight susceptible, may be of little value as pollinizers after a blight attack, necessitating the use of bouquets for several years until blooming returns. Experience has shown that where a minimum number of trees are required as pollinizers for a Bartlett planting, it might be well to use some trees of a blight resistant variety as Old Home, Magness, or of the lighter bearing Anjou variety. One tree in nine is the minimum number of a pollinizing variety that can be used. Solid pollenizer rows are better. The honeybee prefers flowers of other fruits to the pear's. Hence, supply an abundance of bees to insure a thorough cross-pollination.

Anjou fruit set is increased commercially the following year by applying 2, 4, 5-TP at 7.5 ppm dilute volume immediately after harvest. Bartlett set can be increased by using 2.5 ppm, same procedure. NAA to reduce fruit drop also may increase set the following spring, as will a boron spray at bloom if B is a marginally deficient nutrient.

LOCATING THE PEAR ORCHARD

Pears require about 900 to 1000 hours of chilling below 45° F. during winter in order to break their rest period. This is about the same amount of chilling as required for the average apple variety, except Bartlett which needs 1000-1100 hours under 45°F. In the southern United States and southern California, this is a factor to be considered. The uneven opening of flowers in spring due to insufficient winter chilling makes it difficult to time the sprays for codling moth, increases difficulty in controlling fire blight during bloom, and may interfere with cross-pollination in districts where it is needed.

Most pear varieties, properly matured, will endure winter temperatures as low as —20° F. without serious injury. Flemish Beauty, Anjou, and Clapp Favorite are the most resistant to cold; Bartlett is the least. Pear buds and wood are less resistant to cold than those of the apple but more resistant than the peach. Pear planting is generally questionable in regions where temperatures may fall lower than —20° to —25° F.

Although pear blossoms open earlier than apples and later than almonds, apricots, or peaches, spring frosts are a definite factor, and the selection of a frost-free site is important. Heaters and wind machines will pay if not

TABLE 1. CRITICAL TEMPERATURES FOR BLOSSOM BUD KILL OF PEAR* AT DIFFERENT STAGES OF DEVELOPMENT (E. L. Proebsting, Jr.)

	BUD DEVELOPMENT STAGE							
	Scales Separating	Blossom Buds Exposed	Tight Cluster	First White	Full White	First Bloom	Full Bloom	Post Bloom
Old Std. Temp.	18	23	24	28	29	29	29	30
Av. Temp. 10% Kill	15	20	24	25	26	27	28	28
Av. Temp. 90% Kill	0	6	15	19	22	23	24	24
Av. Date (Prosser)	—	3/23	3/31	4/5	4/9	4/14	4/18	4/25

*For Bartlett. Anjou is similar in hardiness but may bloom earlier and, hence, may be more tender than Bartlett at the same date. Wash. State Univ., Prosser Station.

used more than about 20 nights a year. Frosts during blossoming may hinder cross-pollination. Post-bloom frosts may kill pears and/or cause frost rings and spotting.

The pear will withstand higher summer temperatures than the apple. As stated previously, Bartlett attains highest quality where summers are hot. In cool areas, Bartlett ripens unevenly and the core tissues tend to break down before the outside of the fruit is ready for use. For this reason, Bartletts are not grown in the cooler areas.

Water supply. Although pear trees are remarkably tolerant of drought or excessive moisture for relatively long periods, better and bigger crops can be obtained by special attention to irrigation and drainage. Better fruit size can be obtained in most commercial pear regions in the West by irrigation during periods of low rainfall even though winter rainfall may be heavy. Portable sprinklers and flood irrigation are in use, but permanent under and over-tree sprinklers are being used in hedgerow plantings. Trickle irrigation from in-row plastic tubes is under study and looks promising, particularly where water is limited or expensive.

Soil. Pears will grow in a wider variety of soils and will probably do better on the heavier wet soils than almost any other fruit. However, the pear performs best on a soil that approaches the ideal fruit soil—deep, fertile, well drained, easily worked, and not too heavy. In the West, freedom from all alkali in the soil is key, also freedom from salinity in irrigation water. Kieffer will tolerate the light droughty soils in western Michigan.

ORCHARD LAYOUT

Planting distances of 18-22 feet on the square in the U.S. were common before 1960. Most plantings since have been in hedgerows with distances ranging all the way from 8 x 12 to 14 x 24 feet. These plantings have all been on vigorous seedling rootstocks but training systems have varied from modified palmette to standard vase-trained trees. Few plantings have been made on dwarfing rootstocks like quince. Dense plantings of 200-300 trees per acre make more efficient use of land and result in higher early yield per acre. To avoid overcrowding and shading, special management procedures are necessary and considerable side hedging and topping are done. The 15- to 30-year old orchard, if properly maintained, regardless of tree spacing, will produce 15-25 tons per acre consistently.

In Europe, Quince A dwarfing stock under Comice, e.g., trained in hedgerows by spindlebush, may produce over 80 T/hectare. Planting distances are close: 4 to 8 feet apart in rows 10 feet apart (see Jonkers). Interplanting old "decline" orchards, later pulling the old trees, is common practice on the West Coast, USA.

PROPAGATION AND ROOTSTOCKS

The most widely used understock for pears is the European or French pear (*Pyrus communis L.*). Relatively few trees have shown susceptibility to pear decline. Winter Nelis seedlings (Bartlett pollen) are now the preferred French-type rootstock in California. Old Home and Old Home X Farmingdale selections (*P. communis*) are highly resistant to decline and are used as rooted cuttings for pear trees in some orchards. Seedlings of *P. calleryana* and *P. betulaefolia,* both resistant to decline, are used as rootstocks, especially in difficult soil conditions.

Pear decline. Pear decline, a disease which has over the past 20 years decimated millions of trees in the West Coast U. S., from British Columbia to central California is similar to, if not identical with, the Italian pear disease called *Moria.*

Pear decline is a mycoplasma which is spread by a common pear insect, the pear psylla. Symptoms may take two forms. A sudden and utter collapse of a perfectly healthy tree may occur within 60 days, or a year or more when the tree finally dies. The former is called *quick decline,* the latter is *slow decline,* but regardless of symptoms, tree death is inevitable. Weakening and eventual death are due to blockage of the phloem vessels immediately above the graft union, which prevents the roots from obtaining nourishment. It is during this period of infection that a deterrent *brown line* forms encircling the tree in the cambial area immediately above the graft union.

Pear varieties grafted to Oriental rootstocks, such as *Pyrus serotina* and *P. ussuriensis,* are extremely susceptible to pear decline.

At least 80% of the nearly two million pear trees which have succumbed to pear decline in California were growing on these two Oriental rootstocks. However, not all Oriental rootstocks are susceptible. As a matter of fact, *P. calleryana* is highly resistant and *P. betulaefolia* so far has appeared to be immune. The European rootstock *P. communis L.* is

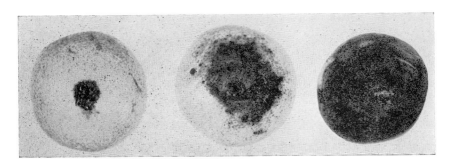

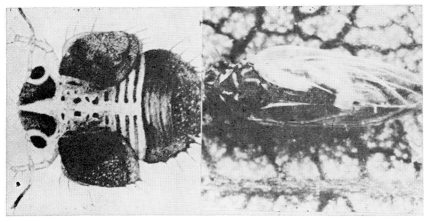

L. D. Davis, University of California; USDA

Figure 5. Bartlett pears showing varying degrees of black-end, a physiological disease aggravated by certain rootstocks, including Pyrus serotina. Varieties grafted on Pyrus communis have been relatively free from the disease. A water unbalance in the tree has been a suggested cause. (Lower) One of later nymph stages of pear psylla on left; on right is adult psylla, carrier of "pear decline" disease, a virus. (Lower, USDA).

also highly resistant. A botanical variety of this species *P. communis* var. *nivalis* has shown some slight susceptibilit yto pear decline. The Old Home variety of pear long used as an intermediate stock because of its high degree of resistance to fire blight also appears to be virtually immune to pear decline, and along with domestic rootstock is being recommended for planting in new orchards as well as replanting in old orchards. Pear decline does not apparently affect unbudded or ungrafted trees, for seedling trees of highly susceptible rootstocks (*P. serotina* and *P. ussuriensis*) have been innoculated with pear psylla which had previously fed on infected trees, and no evidence of pear decline has appeared. There are confirmed reports of pear decline in orchards where quince root is used as a rootstock.

There is as yet no known cure for pear decline. Growers with orchards grafted to Oriental rootstock cannot be certain how long their trees will escape infection. Countless observations and many experiments have shown that visible symptoms of pear decline appear to be triggered,

James A. Beutel, Univ. of Calif.

Figure 6. To avoid fireblight and decline, Old Home pear trees budded on French pear seedling roots are being recommended both in the West and in the East. After two or three years in the orchard, the Old Home trees are top-worked by budding or grafting to a commercial variety such as Bartlett, as shown above. Grafts have been made at points indicated by the arrows.

or expressed under the following set of conditions: a) susceptible rootstock, such as *P. serotina* or *P. ussuriensis;* b) a population of "decline" infected pear psylla,, and it need not be a high population; and c) conditions which will cause tree stress, in other words, excessive heat, drought, poor drainage, severe cold in the winter causing winter injury, or any combination of climatic and cultural factors which would tend to put the trees under a stress. Growers with orchards in Oriental rootstock can perhaps retard the advance of pear decline by spraying to reduce pear psylla, doubling the N, irrigating frequently, and pruning heavily, particularly in the cool foothill areas.

Dwarf and semi-dwarf pear trees on quince stock (*Cydonia oblonga*) are being used for home planting and for high-density commercial plantings. The Angers and Provence quince clones are the most widely used. The EM A Angers is preferred in Europe; EM B is slightly more dwarfing and EM C (may contain stunt virus) is the most dwarfing. Old Home is used as an intermediate stock on quince for most varieties, as Bartlett and Clapp Favorite unite poorly on quince. Some United States nurseries are using Provence in preference to EM A as an understock, which is rated second best.

Top-working. If the practice of using the Old Home variety for an intermediate stock on pear trees continues to increase in popularity, then top-working in the orchard may become a standard operation in starting a pear orchard. Clonally propagated Old Home trees are planted and grown in the orchard for two or three years until a good framework is established, as shown in Figure 6. At this time, four to six leaders should have been established, each with possibly an equal number of secondary branches. All of these branches then are either budded or grafted to the desired commercial varieties. Top-working is performed preferably about five feet above the ground. When blight susceptible varieties are used for the top, they should be inserted about ten to twelve inches from the nearest branch of the resistant stock. Old pear trees can be top-worked, using either the bark- or cleft-graft. In the East, the same system for top-working apple trees can be applied to pear trees. In California, the entire top of the old tree usually is removed back to stubs three to six inches in diameter. From two to six cions are inserted in each stub, using the bark-graft method. (See Chapter VIII for grafting and budding technique).

James A. Beutel, University of California, Davis.

Figure 7. Hedgerow Bartletts in Sacramento Valley, California, with underhead irrigation, in-row herbicides, seedling rootstocks, 8 x 15 ft. spacing, 5 yrs. old, pruned and harvested from special-built scaffolds, and sprayed with 2-way vertical mast. (See Chapter XVIII).

TRAINING AND PRUNING PEAR TREES

Young trees. The young pear tree is trained and pruned to the modified-leader system as recommended for the apple in Chapter IV. In the areas where fire blight is not so likely to be a serious problem, three or four main scaffold limbs may be left (Figure 7). However, where fire blight is a problem, as in the East, it is recommended that about six scaffold limbs be left in the event that subsequent fire blight infection may necessitate the removal of some of the branches. Light pruning is recommended, especially in humid areas, because blight is more difficult to control on trees making soft growth as a result of heavy pruning.

It is characteristic for most pear varieties to grow strictly upright, and not branch freely. Heading-back cuts to outward-growing branches should be kept to a minimum because they encourage a profusion of soft terminal shoots. It is best to confine most of the cuts to the thinning-out type. The upright branches of young pear trees can be spread manually by placing wood or wire wedges in the crotches or by using the Verner system of delayed heading (see reference). This shifting of polarity tends to induce shoots and spurs along the branch that subsequently become fruitful. Once the tree has begun moderate production, the weight of the fruit will help to give the tree a spreading habit of growth. With young trees, it is important to prevent any one branch from bearing

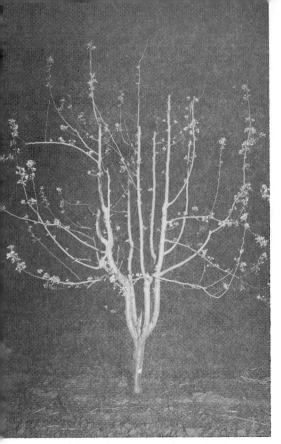

James A. Beutel, University of California, Davis.

Figure 8. A standard-trained Bartlett pear, 8 ft. spacing in a hedgerow, 4-yrs. old, on seedling rootstock, after pruning. Note vase-form a few heading-back cuts, with mostly thinning our cuts. (See Fig. 7, 5-year trees.)

so heavily that it is weighted and trained toward the ground, impairing its future usefulness. With the Anjou variety, the habit of growth is somewhat more spreading and, therefore, mechanical spreading is usually not required.

The new growing and training system being favored is the hedgerow or wall system in which a topper and side-hedger (see p. 94) is used for dormant pruning. Follow-up detail pruning from a multiple (p. 203) or 2-level moving platform, accommodating four or five workers, can be used to thin out the trees (and also used in harvesting). These close-planted trees may or may not be on dwarfing stock since in arid regions growth can be controlled by judicious fertilization and irrigation. Also, the greater competition of tree roots for water and nutrients tends to keep the trees within bounds, pariculary if they are fruited regularly and heavily.

Use of Alar in controlling growth and other characteristics in pear has shown little benefit.

Pruning mature trees. A fruit bud of the pear is similar to that of the apple, containing from five to seven flowers at the terminal of a leafy cluster base. Pear fruits are largely borne on spurs whose economic life is about seven to eight years. A given spur generally fruits from a terminal bud every other year. Some varieties such as Bartlett, also may bear fruit both laterally and terminally on one-year shoots. This is true up to the age of ten years, after which a progressively greater part is borne on spurs. Fruit buds borne on shoots usually blossom about ten days after the spur buds; thus, if spur buds have been destroyed by spring frosts, fruit buds on the shoots may give rise to the major portion of the crop. Therefore, on these varieties, shoots left for fruit production should not be headed back because the fruit buds usually exist on the outer one-third of the shoot.

With mature trees, annual thinning out of new shoots and of an occasional older branch is to be recommended over heavy heading-back that may result in succulent growth susceptible to fire blight. Thinning-out tends to stimulate spur formation. In a bearing pear tree, new growth of about 18 to 30 inches each year is desirable. The type of pruning on bearing trees may vary considerably from one region to another. For example, the mature Bartlett pear in California is pruned more heavily by heading-back cuts in the Santa Clara Valley in order to maintain sufficient renewal wood and to prevent the production of large crops of small fruits. On the other hand, in the Sacramento Valley where vegetative growth is more vigorous (Figure 8), it is advisable to prune lightly by using mostly thinning-out cuts. Wood of the Bartlett pear in the Santa Clara Valley is distinctly softer and more brittle than in the Sacramento Valley.

When the Bartlett tree is mature and fully occupies its alloted space, there is apparently little effect of any reasonable system of pruning on the size of the crop and time of maturity. Based upon experience in California, this evidently is true regardless of the region. In other words, if adequate replacement wood is obtained without severe pruning, it makes no difference whether these results are obtained by thinning-out, heading-back, or by a combination of the two.

Kieffer trees in the East are often cut back to two-year-old wood every other year, or stubbed back each year, so as to remove about two thirds of last season's growth. This can be done with this variety because it is less subject to blight than Bartlett and most other European types. Also cutting back is a fruit-thinning process, and the Kieffer needs this since it is likely to set heavily, producing small fruits.

Fire blight treatment. If it is necessary during the growing season to cut out blighted branches to save important limbs, cut a foot or more below the lowest point where blight is showing and promptly disinfect the shears, saw, and wound with a solution of 1 to 500 bichloride of mercury (poisonous) and 1 to 500 cyanide of mercury (poisonous) mixed together. Place the solution in a bottle, tie a sponge over the opening, and daub the wounds and tools with the wet sponge.

Blight can be pruned away with least danger of spreading it when the tree is dormant. It is recommended that this work begin in autumn when the blighted twigs contrast readily against normal leaves and growth. See Calif. Ext. Circ. 127 for blight control in the West.

In the East and regions where fire blight is a problem, all water sprouts and spurs should be removed regularly from the trunk and lower portions of the main limbs to eliminate this source of infection.

Other precautions include: (1) avoid the type of pruning that encourages water sprouts, (2) spray with antibiotics, copperlime dust, or weak

C. P. Har'ey,
U.S.D.A.

Figure 9. Magnesium deficiency is seen frequently on pear in the humid regions, appearing a few weeks before harvest. Intervenal yellowing and browning are the symptons along with early fruit drop.

Bordeaux, as recommended by the local experiment station, and (3) keep growth under control by judicious use of nitrogen, sod, and/or sod mulch.

SOIL MANAGEMENT

Cultivation. In regions where fire blight is not a problem, the cultivation and cover crop system of soil management is commonly employed for pears. This is true in the heavy commercial areas of arid regions. Cultivation starts in the spring by turning under weeds or cover crop. Another cultivation may be necessary before the first irrigation. If the soil does not crack badly, the same furrows are used for the second or third irrigation; if the soil cracks, cultivation may be practiced between each irrigation, reconstructing the furrows each time. Frequency of cultivation is limited to 3 to 6 a year, depending largely upon the rate of weed growth.

Strip-row chemical weed control under the trees, permanent sod in the middles and irrigation when needed is growing in popularity.

Cover crops. Voluntary weeds may be used for a winter cover if an even cover can be obtained. Otherwise, a winter cover crop such as yellow sweet clover, common vetch, and purple vetch may be used. Commonly used non-legume cover crops are the mustards and cereals such as rye, barley, and oats. Rosen rye is popular in Washington. These are generally planted in fall, early enough to give good cover before cold weather. For young trees, a nonleguminous cover crop seems to be preferable.

In humid areas, it seems advisable to cutivate the young pear trees early in the season or use strip-herbicide treatment in the rows. After the third year, the trees are placed in sod-strip-herbicide or sod-plus-mulch, both being the trend. Any subsequent cultivation, if practiced, should be on a very limited scale early in the spring. The grower should be cautious with practices which induce excessive and soft shoot growth.

Omund Lilleland, Univ. of California, Davis.

Figure 10. Potassium (K) shortage reduces fruit size, advances maturity, causes marginal burning and rolling of older leaves. Lower figures on chart refer to circumferences of fruit in cm. K deficiency may occur in sandy soils in humid regions. Deficiency also may occur in arid regions, "spotty" through the orchard, necessitating treatment of individual trees.

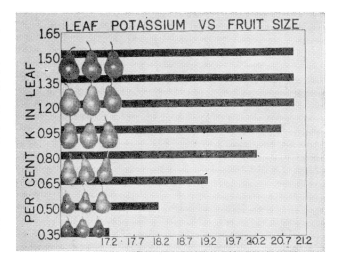

Commercial fertilizers. Nitrogen is the main fertilizer showing response in pear orchards. Phosphorus has given increased yield response in New York, and magnesium deficiency is common along the Atlantic Seaboard. Potassium shortage has appeared in many areas of arid California where 15-25 lbs. of potassium sulfate per tree or one ton/A are used to correct it. Muriate of potash tends to burn roots and kill limbs in arid areas. A 1-1-1 NPK mix such as 10-10-10 is used commonly in humid regions.

In the use of manure or commercial nitrogen, fire blight is the chief consideration. Pear trees must be fertilized with extreme caution. Too much growth may result in loss of an entire orchard in a year or less due to blight.

Leaf analysis (by local government experiment station) helps to diagnose a nutritional problem. Pear orchards in good bearing have shown approximately the following leaf nutrient contents in mid-summer: N, 2.0-2.8%; P, 0.1-0.2%; K, 1.0-2.0; Mg, 0.3-0.5%; Ca, 1.5-3.5%; S, 125-300 ppm; Fe, 100-250 ppm; Mn, 20-75; Zn, 15-40 ppm; B, 20-50 ppm; Cu, 4-10 ppm; and Mo, 0.7-1.5 ppm Deficiencies may occur at lower levels.

Some difficulty may occur with boron deficiency, (Fig. 11a); applications of thirty pounds per acre every third year of boric acid in early fall has corrected corky spot and the characteristic bronzing and rosetting of the leaves. Where aflalfa is the cover crop, use ten pounds of boric acid per acre due to its sensitivity. Boron shortage causes skin and flesh cracking and corky areas in the fruit (the stink bug in California also causes corky areas under the skin). Iron, zinc, manganese, and copper deficiencies are a problem in some arid areas, magnesium in the humid areas. Foliar ap-

311

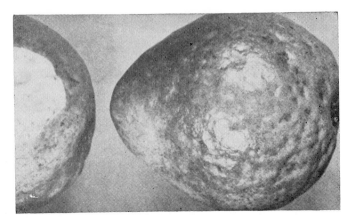

Figure 11. Cork spot of Anjou, is avoided by using French rootstocks instead of oriental and using cultural practices conducive to heavy fruit set. Similar to bitter pit in apple.

plications of trace elements are effective and easier than soil applications. Only early fall B sprays may correct "blossom blast" next spring.

FRUIT THINNING

Relatively little fruit thinning is practiced with pears. In case of such varieties as Bartlett, Hardy, and Bosc which tend to set heavy crops of fruit in clusters of three to five fruits on a single spur, it may be necessary to reduce the number of fruit per cluster to one or two each. If the set on the entire tree is not excessive, however, fruit in these clusters may reach satisfactory size and quality without thinning. With an extremely heavy set of fruit, obviously, thinning is essential to obtain good size and quality. Under these conditions, thinning should be done 50-70 days after full bloom reducing the number of fruits per cluster and excess clusters. Chemical thinning sprays have not been perfected as yet. Prices for the Hardy crop have not justified hand thinning.

In Washington, larger size fruits are required for canning and drying than for fresh fruit market. The growers usually secure this size by spot picking the larger fruit first. The remaining pears are permitted to hang on the tree for seven to ten additional days to attain adequate size. This increase in size may be 2.5 per cent per day during this period. It is important, however, that Bartlett not be permitted to remain too long on the trees to attain the desired size, or losses from core breakdown will occur in cold storage or at the time of preparation for canning.

From 20 to 30 average-sized leaves per fruit are required for proper sizing of Bartlett and most pear varieties.

An a trial basis, the Oregon Medford Station suggests 3 weeks after petal fall on Bartlett, using 16-oz. Spray Modifier wetting agent /100 gals: NAD at 25 ppm on set of 50+ fruit/100 custers or NAA at 7.5 ppm

312

on 25-35 fruits/100 clusters or 15 ppm on 35-50/100 clusters. Chemical thin half the job; complete with hand thinning.

HARVESTING AND HANDLING PEARS

Pears are unlike most deciduous fruits in that they attain highest quality when harvested in a slightly "green" stage. At this stage, they must have developed sufficiently to reach highest quality when ripened off the tree, but not so mature as to impair quality of the ripened fruit. This is principally true for the Bartlett variety. Some varieties such as Anjou and Bosc, however, develop better eating quality by being permitted to become somewhat more mature before harvesting.

Picking maturity. It is rather difficult to select the proper time to pick pears. As the fruit develops and ripens to maturity, the most obvious stages include an increase in size, increases in sugar content, soluble solids, softness and odorous constituents, and a gradual change in ground color from green to yellowish-green followed by a greenish-yellow, and finally a full yellow. Size cannot be relied upon as an index for picking because fruits of different size may be of the same maturity. Fruit harvested when immature is subject to excessive water loss and subsequent shriveling.

The better criteria for determining maturity of pears are: color change, change in firmness of flesh, and change in soluble solids, all of which indicate a change in sugar content. Color charts may be used in California to note progressive ground color changes: No. 1 is green; No. 2 is light green; No. 3 yellowish-green; and No. 4 yellow. Softness of flesh is determined with a pressure tester (see July, Amer. Fruit Grower). Pressure test limits for harvesting certain varieties of pears in Washington are given in Table 1a. These figures may vary somewhat in other states. The soluble solids are determined by using a refractometer on part of the juice obtained while making the pressure test.

The ease with which the stem can be separated from the spur by an upward twist also is used as an index of maturity. Number of days between full bloom and maturity for pears is fairly consistent within a region, but may vary between regions. In Washington, the following intervals are suggested: Bartlett, 110 to 115 days, Bosc, 130 to 135; and Anjou, 145 to 150 days. Pears on heavily loaded trees usually mature somewhat slower than those on lightly loaded trees. Pears left on the tree too long show core breakdown later.

In California an improved picking maturity standard has been developed by Claypool et al.[1] Pears with higher soluble solids are mature at

---

[1] By correspondence

VARIETY	PRESSURE IN POUNDS			LOCALITY
	Passable	Optimum	Low	
Anjou	15	13	10	Wenatchee
Anjou	15	13	11	Approx. applicable generally
Bartlett	23	20	16	Wenatchee
Bartlett	23	17	15	Yakima (canning only)
Bartlett	23	20	17	Approx. applicable generally
Bosc	16	13	11	Wenatchee
Bosc	15	14	11	Approx. applicable generally
Comice	13	11	9	Wenatchee
Comice	13	11.5	9	Approx. applicable generally
Easter Beurré	....	15		Wenatchee
Flemish Beauty	....	13	10	Wenatchee
Winter Nelis	15	14	10	Wenatchee
Winter Nelis	15	14	11	Approx. applicable generally

a higher firmness. This principle excludes weather and nutritional effects since these two indices operate in opposite ways. On Bartlett, there is no soluble solids requirements for pears having 19 pounds pressure or lower. If a pear has eleven per cent soluble solids, it is mature at twenty-one and a half pounds. For each per cent rise in soluble solids, one half pound increase in pressure is permitted up to twenty-three pounds for picking maturity. This system has been working satisfactorily for several years.

In picking pears, size of fruit is taken into consideration, in addition to the criteria mentioned above for picking maturity. Size is based on the largest cross diameter of the fruit and is determined by passing the fruit through a given diameter ring which each picker carries. After a little experience, the picker becomes proficient in estimating the size of fruit by the eye, checking occasionally against the ring. On the West Coast, rather definite sizes are requested for given purposes based on the choice of the grower, the buyer or shipper, or upon an agreement between growers and shipper. In general, Bartlett fruits which are less than two and three-eights inches in diameter are too small for harvest and are left for sizing. Handle pears with care from the time they leave the tree until packed in the box. Abrasion of the skin and discoloration of the flesh can be reduced by lining the field boxes with cardboard.

Bulk Handling. Inasmuch as the operations of pruning, fertilization and spraying of pears are now highly mechanized, there has been an almost complete shift in key areas to bulk handling with mechanical lifts, as described earlier for apples. Multiple lined picking aids for hedgerow plantings seem to be favored in the future pear harvesting picture (see p. 94).

Hormone sprays to reduce pear drop. Pears, like apples, have a tendency to drop fruits before they can be picked. Bartletts are most likely to drop, with Bosc next. Other standard varieties may not drop seriously enough to require a preharvest spray. Spray cost is around $10 an acre, materials and application.

Drop may be increased if the trees are deficient in boron, magnesium, or moisture, or if over-fertilized with nitrogen. The use of hormone sprays applied from ground or air, by pear growers has become a standard practice, using 10 ppm (25 grams/A) alpha-naphthaleneacetic acid. The manufacturer's recommendations should be followed as to quantity of material and the use of a spreader. The spray is applied about five to ten days before harvest or when there is first evidence of drop of normal fruit. These hormone sprays do not slow down the ripening process; in fact, there is evidence to indicate that ripening is accelerated whether the fruit is

Courtesy Howard J. Brooks, U. S. Dept. of Agriculture, Beltsville, Md.

Figure 11a. Boron deficiency in pear. "Blossom blast," is corrected by early fall boron spray. (Lower) Bartlett pitting at left; normal fruit, right; and split fruit at center,

on or off the tree. Pear fruits must be harvested *at the proper maturity* with little or no delay, stored as soon as possible, and the temperature of the fruit reduced quickly to 35° F. or lower within forty-eight hours if at all possible. On trees sprayed with preharvest sprays, there may be a number of overripe fruits which did not drop, making it necessary for the overripe fruit to be sorted out either by the picker or by the packing crew. It cannot be overemphasized that every effort should be made to harvest pears at the proper stage of maturity regardless of whether they have or have not been sprayed with hormone sprays. If you permit hormone-sprayed Bartletts, e.g., to hang 10 days after proper maturity, early subsequent core-breakdown may occur. *Ethrel* is under test to bunch ripening for mechanical harvesting.

Grading and sizing. In the packing house, the pears may be first run through a bath, and rinsed and dried in an air-blast before delivery to the sorting table. At the sorting table, the culls are eliminated, and the

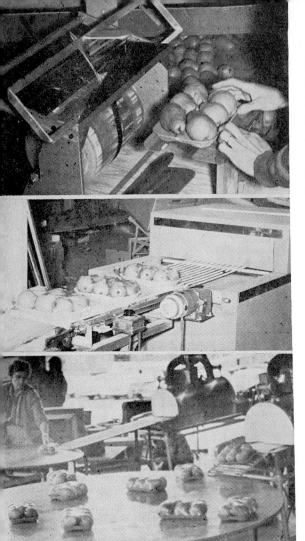

low-grade fruits are separated from the high-grade fruits. Each grade is sized into several sizes. The rotary bin and other modern types of machines, as described for apples in Chapter X, also are well adapted to pears. The machine must handle the pears with extreme care. Pears packed in boxes must be of uniform size. See "U.S. Standards for summer and Fall Pears", and "Winter Pears" obtainable from U.S.D.A.-A.M.S., Wash. 25, D. C., Roy W. Lennartson, for grades, tolerances, sizes and packs.

Containers. The standard box for pears has the same inside width and length as the peach and apple boxes (11½ by 18 inches), but it is only 8½ inches deep. These dimensions are generally accepted in all producing sections, except the state of New Mexico a n d Washington, which designate an 8-inch-depth as standard. The half-box is standard in Oregon; it is 4½ inches deep with the above length and width dimensions (this is the same size as the 4½-inch-depth peach box). There is a special 5½-inch-depth box for pears used for export shipments from

Figure 12. This grower consumer-packaging station shows (top) 6-pear molded pulp tray, filled from bin at right, resting on film that had been pulled from roll and cut; film then wrapped around pears which go by belt to hot plate that seals bottom folds, thence to cold plate to set seal, then to heat tunnel (middle) to shrink film around pears. (Bottom) Finished package on rotating table is packed in cartons in Figure 14. (Courtesy of J. F. Fountain and H. J. Brooks, USDA).

California. This same box and one that is 9½ inches deep are standard in Oregon for a three-cushion pack of pears. In California, pear containers are the standard wood pear box, telescope corrugated paper cartons and the L.A. lug. Tight-filled cartons are now gaining popularity because more of the packing can be mechanized, (Fig. 13a). The tub bushel basket in the East is losing favor to boxes, using polybags as described on the next page.

Pear packing. Each p a c k e r handles only one size of pear from the rotating bins. The pear is picked up with the right hand, while the left is grabbing a sheet of wrapping paper. The pear is thrown into the left hand, stem up, with some force so that it rests between the thumb and fore-fingers. Corners of the paper are then folded over the calyx end of the pear, and the pear is turned up with the right hand while the left hand and fingers twist the paper around the stem

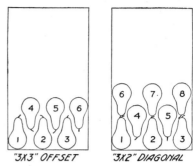

"3X3" OFFSET   "3X2" DIAGONAL

W. P. Duruz, California Agr. Exp. Sta.

Figure 13. **Two styles of pear packs commonly used. Stems in first row next to packer should point away from packer; stems of fruit in other rows point toward packer.**

of the fruit to form a point. The pear is then placed in the box with the left hand with folds down. The first row of fruit next to the packer is laid with the stems away from the packer, but for other rows the stems are all placed toward the packer. The right hand reaches for another fruit while the left hand is placing a wrapped pear in the box. The process of wrapping fruit by hand is claimed to be faster if the fruits are not wrapped. Also, wrapped pears stay in place better than unwrapped pears because, in addition they are provided with a cushion of paper which helps to restrict the spreading of rots among the pears. The two commonly used styles of packing pears are the "offset" and the "diagonal." The "offset" or "3 x 3" pack is employed for sizes of pear that will give five or more fruits across the box, as shown in Figure 13. The "diagonal" pack, or "3 x 2" is used for larger pears. The pears should be arranged in the box so there is a 1½-to-3-inch graduated bulge at the topcenter of the box.

Packed boxes are marked with the total numbers of pears contained, the grade and the shipper's name and address. The standard pear boxes may contain the following number of fruits, depending upon their size; 70, 80, 90, 100, 110, 120, 135, 150, 165, 180, 195, 210, 228, and 245.

Pears in recent years are being packed in fiberboard cartons, volume-fill, followed by vibration to settle them. On arrival in Eastern markets, they are vibrated again. These have been in better condition on the retail counters than hand-packed pears, and there is a saving in cost. This method is dominating in popularity.

Polyethylene Bags. The most significant development in packing pears for shipment is in polybox liners to which pears have proven well adapted. They extend storage life from a six- to eight-week period or longer.

Figure 13a. Wooden or fiberboard boxes with poly liners perforated (or inserted hydrated lime envelope pads to lower CO_2) are being used for pear shipment, vibrated (above) for tight fill. Hartman wraps impregnated with mineral oil or ethoxyquin (scald control) used when pears are individually wrapped. (Courtesy Wooden Box Institute, San Fransico, Cal.)

After placing pears in the bag which lines the box and surrounds the fruit, it is necessary to withdraw the air. An ordinary vacuum cleaner is rigged to do this. About 1½ gauge film is used and the bag must be air tight to provide a more or less "CO_2 gas-storage compartment." Since humidity builds to 100 per cent in the bag, the fruit should be only the best and pretreated with a fungicide such as "Stop Mold" by Dow Chemical Company. When removed from cold storage for consumption the bags must be punched within 72 hours for proper ripening and flavor, taking seven to nine days. These poly-wrapped pears have a greater shelf life than other pear packs. Sometimes no air withdrawal from bags is done. See Figure 14 for another method of shipping pears.

Precooling. The practice of precooling is becoming popular for the shipment of pears from the West to the East Coast. Methods for precooling are described in Chapter XIV. Precooling reduces ripening quickly and eliminates need for re-icing in shipment, although mechanically refrigerated cars are being used increasingly.

STORAGE OF PEARS

Due to the fact that respiration and the breaking-down processes in the pear are more rapid than the apple, it is highly important that the temperature of pears after picking be reduced as quickly as possible using the most effective means of refrigeration. If there is a delay between harvest and storage, allowing the ripening processes to become accelerated, it becomes difficult to retain pears satisfactorily in storage. A storage temperature of 30° to 31° F. is recommended for the longest storage life of pears. A temperature of 36° F. reduces the storage life to about one-third to one-half in the shorter-lived varieties, such as Bartlett, Comice, and Hardy. Pears at either temperature, however, tend to show more loss than apples under comparable conditions.

Although pears may be under-cooled in storage, their critical freezing temperature is about 27.7° F. This is only about two degrees below the minimum storage temperature recommended for retaining pears in best fresh condition. Anjou pears frozen for a week to 23° to 27° F. usually recover with little or no injury to the flesh, but if frozen for four to six weeks at these temperatures, the fruit becomes waterlogged under the skin and sometimes in the core region.

Ripening of pears in storage.

With the fall and winter varieties, such as Hardy, Anjou, Comice, Bosc, Winter Nelis, Glou Morceau, and Easter Beurré, the highest quality is attained by storing and ripening under carefully controlled conditions of temperature and humidity. Because of the need of these rather definite conditions, an increasingly common practice is to store the fall and winter varieties in rooms at 30° to 31° F., removing them as the trade requires and ripening them in special rooms at temperatures between 60° and 70° F. with the humidity well controlled between 80 and 85 per cent, before delivering to the retailer. This process insures maximum quality to the consumer. If pears are ripened about 70° F., they may not

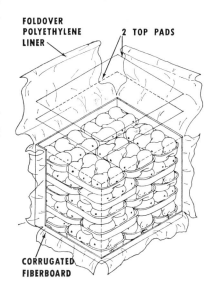

FOLDOVER POLYETHYLENE LINER

2 TOP PADS

CORRUGATED FIBERBOARD

Figure 14. This shipping carton holding 5 or 6 layers (two sizes tested), of 25-30 6-pear trays was shipped successfully in carlot from west to east coast U. S., provided pears were NOT soft at start. Costs are 1½c more/lb pears than packaging in wood boxes.

soften properly and remain slightly firm until decay or breakdown sets in. Also, they may be tough-textured and poorly flavored. These special ripening rooms have been established in the eastern terminal markets by the West Coast shippers.

It is important to have a knowledge of the limitations of each variety with respect to its storage life. For example, the Bosc is at its best from September 1 to December 15 in California and should never be held beyond the Christmas holidays. It must be held constantly at 30° to 31° F. and ripened at 60° to 70° F. The Bosc will not ripen in cold storage and will lose its ability to ripen if held for any length of time at temperatures between 34° and 35° F.

In Washington, Bosc and Clairgeau when stored at 30° to 31° F. can be utilized best from September 1 to January 15; Anjou, Conference, and Forelle, from October 1 to April 15; Comice from October 1 to February 1; and Winter Nelis and Easter Beurré are not ready until December 1 and may be kept until May.

Bartlett tends to have better more uniform color and texture for canning if stored immediately after picking for 15 to 30 days before being processed. Bartlett pears harvested at pressure tests of 18 to 15 pounds give a

TABLE 2

STORAGE LIFE OF COMMERCIAL PEAR VARIETIES

	In polybox liners, 30-31°F.*	Stored immediately at 30-31° F.	Stored at 30°-31° F. after precooling and 10-12 days in transit
	Days	Months	Months
Bartlett	107-126	1½-3	1½-2
Comice, Hardy, and Kieffer	120-135**	2 -3	2 -3
Bosc	120-130	3 -3½	2 -3
Anjou	214-216	5 -6	4 -5
Winter Nelis		6 -7	6 -7

*Data from Batier *et al.*
** Comice data only.

fairly good product when stored at 30° to 32° F. for as much as 60 days before canning. If they are retained in storage unduly long, however, core breakdown, rot, scald, softening, and browning of the tissues may result. This is particularly true if the pears are overmature when harvested, or if they are held at room temperature for three to six days after picking before they are stored. CA storage, widely used, lengthens storage life greatly.

The Kieffer pear has been shown to develop surprisingly good quality when harvested at 14 to 13 pounds pressure and stored for 90 days at 32° F., and then ripened at 60° F. Kieffer pears allowed to remain on the trees until overripe develop excessive grit cells, are apt to become dry and mealy, and soften too rapidly around the core. Pears removed from the tree can be ripened immediately at 60° to 65° F. in order to obtain full flavor and juiciness with splendid texture.

Although the pressure tester can be used effectively for determining harvest maturity of pears, it is not satisfactory for measuring the ripeness of pears during cold storage. Pears and apples should not be stored together.

Ripen pears with ethylene. Ethylene gas hastens pear ripening, except for the Kieffer variety which does not seem to be affected either by artificial treatment or by the natural emanation of ethylene gas from nearby ripening pears. The use of ethylene gas may be desirable and profitable in hastening the ripening of Bartlett pears for canning, which appear to be ripening unevenly. This has been demonstrated by placing containers of pears in a closed chamber and exposing them intermittently to concentrations of ethylene of from 1:1000 to 1:5000. At the end of each 24 hours, the ripening rooms are aerated for one hour, using a fan to exhaust the products of respiration. Treatments on four successive days are usually adequate. Where ripening of the fruit is uniform without ethylene treatment, use of this gas has no advantage. The effects of ethylene upon the

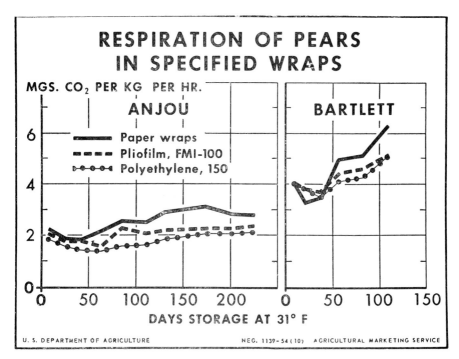

RESPIRATION OF PEARS
IN SPECIFIED WRAPS

MGS. CO_2 PER KG PER HR.

ANJOU   BARTLETT

Paper wraps
Pliofilm, FMI-100
Polyethylene, 150

DAYS STORAGE AT 31° F

U. S. DEPARTMENT OF AGRICULTURE   NEG. 1139-54(10)   AGRICULTURAL MARKETING SERVICE

Figure 15. The process of respiration is an index of the rate of ripening of pears. Note from the chart that polyethylene bags reduce respiration more than paper wraps and pliofilm. Note also that Bartlett seems to have a higher respiration rate than Anjou under comparable conditions.

ripening of pears are apparent only if the gas is used a short time after harvest. If the pears have been in cold storage for several weeks, they show little or no response to ethylene gas. Effects of ethylene are most pronounced at temperatures of 65° to 70° with little or no effect at cold storage temperatures. See L. J. Edgerton and Griggs et al. for tests with Ethrel.

Modified atmospheres storage. As in the case of apples, pears can be kept in storage for several weeks longer by manipulating the temperature and the oxygen and carbon dioxide concentrations in the storage air.

Benefits from CA storage of pears have been recognized for years, based on early work by Allen and Claypool, California, but this type storage has not been adopted extensively for pears. This may be due to the fact that similar benefits can be obtained with polyethylene box liners. A CA atmosphere with about 2% O_2 and 1% CO_2 is suggested at 30-31°F.

STORAGE TROUBLES

Although *core breakdown* is likely to be more serious in pears from some districts than others, it occurs widely. It is characterized by a breakdown of the tissues in the core area and may spread to the entire fruit. At first, the flesh is soft and watery. Later, it turns brown and

Courtesy The Wooden Box Institute, San Francisco, Calif.

Figure 16. Boxed pears palleted and stacked on their sides in a commercial storage on the West Coast. Use of fork lift with pallets has facilitated greatly the handling of pears in boxes.

the skin of the fruit may also become discolored. Affected fruit has a foul sickening odor and flavor. Core breakdown is definitely associated with harvesting in an overmature condition and with delayed cooling. Bartlett, Hardy, Bosc, and Comice are the important varieties that are especially susceptible.

Anjou scald is similar in appearance to apple scald and apparently is induced in part by the same factors; like apple scald it can be controlled by oiled wraps.

The ordinary form of *pear scald,* however, is usually associated with core breakdown and apparently is due to prolonged holding in storage. It is not controlled by use of oiled wraps. The time when pear scald appears depends upon storage temperatures. Bartletts which may be free of scald even after 90 days at 30 or 31° F. are likely to show it in 70 to 80 days at 36° or in 30 to 35 days at 43°. Bartlett and Bosc are the most susceptible varieties.

Although pears may color at low storage temperatures, they do not always ripen. This is true of Bartlett, Bosc, Anjou and Comice; if held in storage too long, they lose their ripening capacity and will fail to ripen even after removal to suitable ripening temperatures.

Pears may occasionally suffer *freezing injury,* but in the Bartlett variety at least, unless this is severe or prolonged, no subsequent damage seems to occur. A trouble of much more common occurrence is a wilting or shriveling of the fruit as a result of excessive moisture loss. A relative humidity of about 90 per cent will hold the fruit in good marketable condition although an atmosphere approaching saturation is necessary to prevent moisture loss entirely.

Where fruit is carefully handled and graded before storage, fungous rots in pears are usually not serious. However, Anjou and Winter Nelis when stored for long periods may suffer serious loss from *gray mold* rot (*Botrytis sp.*). This trouble is also known as a cluster rot because a large

Hibino, H. et al. Mycoplasma-like bodies in the psylla vector of pear decline. Virology 43:34-40. 1971. In sieve tubes of pear decline trees. Phytopath. 60:3-499-501. March. 1970.

Jensen, D. D., W. H. Griggs, C. Q. Gonzales, and H. Schneider. Pear decline virus transmission by pear psylla. Phytopathology 54 (11): 1346-1351. 1964.

Jonkers, H. Tree size control by pruning and bending. Proc. XVII Intern. Hort. Cong. XVIII, 57-70. College Park, Md. 1966.

Kenworthy, A. L. Fertilizers, fireblight and fruit disorders. Mich. State Hort. Soc. 97th Ann. Proc. 108-113. 1967.

Kidd, F., and C. West. Refrigerated gas storage of fruit. Conference, Doyenne du Comice, and Williams Bon Chretien pears. Journ. Pom. and Hort. Sc. 19: (3-4) 243-276. 1952.

Lange, A. H., and C. L. Elmore. Preemergence weed control in pear orchards. Calif. Mimeo Leaflet AXT-225. 10 pp. (Request recent edition.)

Larsen, R. Paul. Pear culture in Michigan. Mich. Ext. Bull. E-519. 1966.

Larsen, Richard. A blight resistant Bartlett. Western Fruit Grower, p. 12. July, 1961.

Lombard, P. B. et al. Relation of post-bloom temperatures to "Bartlett" pear maturation. J. ASHS 96: 6. November 1971. p. 709.

Looney, N. E. Influence of succinic acid-2, 2 dimethylhydrazide and ethylene on respiration and ethylene production by developing "Bartlett" pear fruits. J. ASHS: 97:1. Jan. 1972, p. 79.

Looney, N. E. Interaction of harvest maturity, cold storage and two growth regulators on ripening of "Bartlett" pears. J. ASHS. 87:1. Jan. 1972. p. 81.

Madsen, H. F. and M. M. Barnes. Pests of pear in California. Calif. Agr. Exp. Sta. Bull. 478. 40 pp. (Request latest edition.)

Madsen, H. F., R. L. Sisson and R. S. Bethell. The pear psylla in California. Calif. Agr. Exp. Sta. Cir. 510. 11 pp. 1962.

Martin, G. C. and W. H. Griggs. Effectiveness of succinic acid, 2, 2-dimethylhydrazide in preventing preharvest drop of "Bartlett" pears. HortSci. Vol. 5, No. 4., August, 1970. pp. 258.

McNelly, L. B., Jr. and J. A. Beutel. Pear decline on quince stocks, Santa Clara Co., Calif. Agr. Jan. 1968.

Milbrath, J. A. Pear stony pit. Ore. Tech. Bull. 93. 23 pp. 1966.

Millecan, A. A., S. M. Gotan and C. W. Nichols. Red-leaf disorders of pear in Calif. Calif. Dept. Agr. Bull. 52 (3) 166-170. 1963.

Mosse, B. and J. Herrero. Studies on incompatibility between some pear and quince grafts. Journ. of Hort. Sci. 26: No. 3. 238-245. 1951.

Motts, G. N. Pear grader's manual. Mich. Ext. Folder F-202 (Rev.)

Oitto, W. A., T. Van der Zwet, and H. J. Brooks. Rating of pear cultivars for resistance to fire blight. Hort-Sci. 5:6 p. 474. Dec. 1970.

O'Reilly, H. J. Stony pit of pear. Calif. Agr. Ext. Serv. Mimeo. AXT-1. 9 pp. 1960.

Parker, K. G., E. C. Fisher and W. D. Mills. Fire blight control on pomes. Cornell Ext. Bull. 966. 23 pp. 1956.

Patchen, G. O. Apple and pear storage. USDA-ARS-Mkt. Res. Rpt. 924. 50 pp. 1971.

Pear Rootstocks in California. Formerly Leaflet 135, 1961. Ask for recent edition.

Posnette, A. F., and R. Cropley. Quince indicators for pear viruses. Journ. Hort Sci. 33: No. 4 289-291. Oct. 1958.

Posnette, A. F., and R. Cropley. Virus diseases of pear in England. Journ. Hort. Sci. 32: No. 1. 53-61. January 1957.

Proebsting, E. L. Nitrogen use on Bartlett. Calif. Agr. June 1961.

Randhawa, G. S., and W. H. Upshall. Congeniality of some pear varieties on quince A. Sci. Agr. 29: 490-493. Oct. 1949.

Ryugo, K. The apparent reversibility of pear decline by top-grafting to clones of *Pyrus serotina*. Proc. Amer. Soc. Hort. Sci. 83: 199-204. 1963.

Sainsbury, G. F. and H. A. Schomer. Influence of carton stacking patterns on pear cooling rates. U. S. Dept. of Agr. A.M.S. Report 171. 10 pp. April 1957.

Sommer, N. F. Discoloration of Bartlett pears. Calif. Agr. II: No. 1 pp. 3-4 1957.

Southwick, L., A. P. French, and O. C. Roberts. The identification of pear varieties from non-bearing trees. Mass. Agr. Exp. Sta. Bull. 421. 51 pp. 1944.

Thorniley, M. and P. R. Lombard. Pears on quince. W. Fruit Grower. Aug., 1964.

Tukey, H. B. Dwarfed Fruit trees. Macmillan Publ. Co., New York City. See pear sections. 562 pp. 1964.

(See additional references under Chapter XIII Appendix)

CHAPTER XIV

Peach, Nectarine, Apricot, and Almond

◆ ◆

PEACH CULTURE

The peach (*Prunus persica*) originated in China where it was known to grow as far back as 2000 B.C. Three wild species still are found there, namely, *P. davidiana* in the North which is used for a rootstock, *P. mira* on the Tebetan Plateau and *P. ferganensis in* the Sinkiang province both in West China. Some species near Harbin in North China grow in the open where winter temperatures may drop to -40°; their eating quality is poor but their genes are valuable in breeding for cold resistance.

The peach gradually spread from China and is found commercially around the World between 25° and 45° latitude above and below the Equator. These limits may be extended somewhat by warm ocean currents, large lakes, or altitude. While the peach can be grown in most apple sections, it extends for the most part closer to the Equator because it is more tolerant of heat and requires less cold to break the rest period.

Data in Table 1 give the approximate peach production by country. Leaders are the United States, Italy, France, Japan, Argentina, and Korea. While no data are availble for China, production is significant, particularly in the wide area around Peking. One variety, Tung-tao (The Winter Peach), is harvested very late and stores longer than any known peach — up to four months.

Columbus and the Spaniards brought the peach to St. Augustine, Florida in their second or third visit where it spread rapidly from coast to coast in North America.

James A. Beutel, Extension Pomologist, University of California, Davis, assisted in this chapter revision with Dr. Harold W. Fogle, USDA, Beltsville, Md.

East of the Rockies, peach production has had many setbacks, largely as a result of planting on sites frequently susceptible to spring frosts and winter freezes. Drought, insufficient winter cold, and pests, have taken

TABLE I. APPROXIMATE PEACH PRODUCTION (000's Metric Tons) FOR WORLD COUNTRIES 1964-70[1]

United States	1550	South Arica	145	Canada	45
Italy	1300	Bulgaria	125	Hungary	60
France	480	Greece	125	Chili	45
Japan	260	Australia	115	Yugoslovia	45
Rpl. Korea	250	Brazil	85	USSR	30
Argentina	190	Turkey	80	Germany (W)	30
Spain	155	Mexico	75	Portugal	30
				N. Zealand	20

[1]Austria, Belgium, Czechoslovakia, Ecuador, Uraguay, Israel, Lebanon, Syria and No. African production are below 20,000 T each. Chinese production is significant but no data are available.

their tolls and caused shifts in the industry from one section to another. In spite of these setbacks, however, peaches rank second to the apple among deciduous tree fruits from the standpoint of production and value.

The upward trends in production in recent years are probably due to (a) better selection of sites and soils, (b) the introduction of somewhat hardier and better quality peaches, (c) increased marketing of the crop at the orchard or roadside stand, and (d) the use of refrigerator trucks and rail cars to haul perishable fruit quickly to adjacent or distant markets.

The first good crop of peaches can be obtained within 4 to 5 years after planting, which is sooner than for most deciduous tree fruits. Thus, the grower in many cases can benefit from the relatively higher market prices and demand in good periods.

Figure 1 shows approximate centers of tree locations and the relative production of peaches by state. California is by far the leading state and accounts for about 60 per cent of the total production, depending upon fluctuation of the crop in the East. California peach production shows little variation from year to year, but production of the states east of the Rockies may vary considerably with weather conditions. Production figures in millions of lbs, 1969-71 average, are: California, 1,530 clings, 420 freestones; South Carolina, 287; Georgia, 158; New Jersey, 100; Pennsylvania, 103; Michigan, 94; Washington, 40; Arkansas, 42; Virginia 43; Alabama, 40; and North Carolina, 43. There are about 48.6 lbs. in a bushel (USDA). Peaches grown in California are largely processed; about 87% are canned, (mostly clings); for freestones, 10% are dried, about 15% frozen, and 38% sold fresh. In the eastern states the majority of the crop is sold fresh, although fair quantities are canned in some states as in Michigan and Arkansas.

The peach, like the apple, is getting more competition from other fruits and vegetables on the store shelves. The per capita fresh consumption has

329

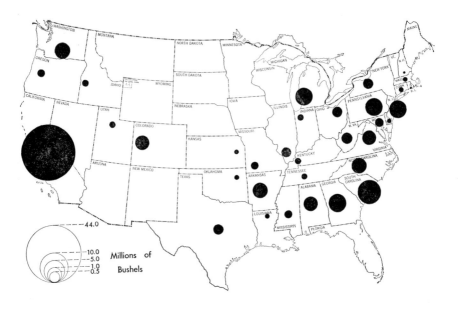

Kenneth A. Wightman, Rutgers University

Figure 1. This is the relative production of peaches by states. California, where peaches are largely processed, is by far the leading state producing 50 to 60 per cent of the total crop. Dots are located about where the state's industry is centered. Many trees are located around the Great Lakes where the deep water reduces temperature extremes. Cold dry winters limit peach growing in an area northwest of a line from Chicago to North Texas. There are about 40 million trees in the U.S.

dropped from 13.2 pounds in 1947 to around 7.0 pounds, 1970-72 average, while plums (1.7), cherries (0.5), grapes (4.2), nectarines (0.2), apricots (0.2), strawberries (1.3), and bananas (17.5) have remained about the same. About 9.0 lbs. per capita consumption are canned. (p. 8).

SELECTION OF PEACH VARIETIES

The variety list for peaches is probably changing more rapidly than for any other tree fruit. This rapid change is due to several factors: (a) the tree is relatively short-lived; (b) there is an urgent demand for varietal improvement in hardiness and quality; (c) more good seedlings are cbtained from peach crosses than with apples, pears, and most tree fruits; and (d) it takes relatively less time to develop, introduce and popularize a new peach variety.

Choice of peach varieties for any one region is governed by three factors: (a) the type of market to be served, (b) distance to the market, and (c) adaptability to local soil and climatic conditions. If the orchard is located in regions of the country where the temperatures frequently fall to -12°F., or lower, hardy varieties such as Veteran, Redhaven and Triogem are possibilities. For a particualar site in the East, it is considered good policy by growers to set the more tender varieties on the high

330

elevations and to locate the hardier varieties on the slopes and lower elevations. Due to the tenderness of Elberta buds, this variety should be planted nearer the top of the slope.

If the fruit will be sold at a roadside market, or by "pick-it-yourself," it is desirable to select a number of varieties which will ripen over a period of several weeks to give a continuous supply of fruit to the counter and pickers. The New Jersey Station is attempting to develop a series of varieties ripening through the season that look alike to facilitate marketing.

If the fruit will be sold in large quantities to a co-operative fruit packing association, few varieties are needed and only those which are suitable for processing, or which have a wide reputation in the fresh fruit markets should be grown in quantity. In the East, if the peach orchard is located a considerable distance from large fresh fruit markets, no doubt much of the crop will be sold locally, but in case it should be necessary to ship surplus quantities in the fresh state, a portion of the varieties should consist of Elberta or some well-known variety adapted to distant shipment.

Variety susceptibility to diseases, insects and other pests is an always present problem. Breeders continually watch for seedling crosses resistant to the most troublesome problems which will vary with locality. Virus diseases, bacterial spot, brown rot, several canker (fungal and bacterial) diseases, and rot (oak) are key diseases. Insects and other pests are mites, nematodes, Oriental fruit moth and plum curculio. Leaf chlorosis due to iron, zinc or manganese deficiency and spotty death of trees due to rootstock incompatability or virus may be problems in some regions (see references for details).

If the variety is to be used for canning, as is particularly true in California and certain other states, the fruit should be (a) of yellow flesh, (b) preferably a clingstone (although many freestones are canned and there is a trend in this direction), (c) a small non-splitting pit, (d) firm, (e) of good symmetrical size, (f) no red color at the pit, and (g) slow flesh-browning. The variety should mature evenly, color well and stay firm on the tree for a single (mechanical) pick.

If the fruit is to be dried, it should be a freestone and particularly sweet in addition to the characters given above for canning. A variety that gives one pound of dried peaches from five pounds of fresh fruit (Muir) is preferred over Elberta, e.g., which gives 1:7.

Home freezing of peaches has displaced home canning. Some good freezing varieties are Redhaven, Triogem, Sunhigh, Washington, Jefferson, Madison, Halehaven, J. H. Hale, Elberta, Vedette, Veteran, Golden Jubilee, Fay Elberta, and Rio-Oso-Gem (check your local experiment station).

The fresh fruit market prefers a yellow-flesh freestone peach, good annual producer, and relatively free from fuzz. It should be fairly early for the region in question, firm, of good size and roundish, bright color, and if possible, a good shipper. In addition, it has distinct advantages if it can be canned, or frozen dried. Nectarines likely will be grown more widely in the future since the public is favoring this fuzzless peach at good prices.

Table 2 gives an evaluation of most of the commercial peach varieties in the United States and Canada. Table 3 gives an evaluation of varieties in the Virginia area, together with those suggested for trial. For an in-depth evaluation of peach varieties by U. S. and Canadian peach breeders, see the proceedings of the National Peach Conference held at Rutgers University (see reference by Childers *et el.*). We are growing and market-ing over 40 peach varieties in North America; non-bearing trees comprise about 30 percent of the total.

During mild winters in the warmer peach zones difficulty may be en-countered with uneven and weak opening of flower and leaf buds of peach. For example, Elberta fruit buds need from 750 to 800 hours of temperature below 45° F. for proper breaking of the rest period. The leaf buds need around 1,000 hours below this temperature. If less cold than this is available, some trees may show considerable flowers with no leaves and uneven opening of both types of buds.

Aside from Elberta and a few others such as Redhaven and Rio-Oso-Gem, most peach varieties are regional in their adaptation, performing well in one region or locality and poorly in another. Also, peach variety lists are changing continuously. It is wise for the grower to keep in touch with his local experiment station regarding the latest and best varieties for the purpose desired.

Varieties being grown and suggested for increased plantings across the U. S. and Canada are, in brief: *Northwest*: Elberta, J. H. Hale, Redhaven, Dixired, Cardinal, Redglobe, Redtop, Vedoka and Veteran (plus other "V" peaches for B. C.), Early Red Haven, Early Elberta, and Rio-Oso-Gem. *California*: *Fresh shipping*: Springold, Springcrest, Early Coronet, Royal May, June Lady, Regina, Redtop, Angelus, Suncrest, Fortyniner, Rio Oso Gem, Fairtime, Parade and Carnival. *Freezing*: Pacifica, O'Hen-ry, Rio Oso Gem, Madera Gem. *Canning*: Loadel, Carson, Tufts, Bowen, Fay Elberta (freestone), Andross, Peak, Carolyn, Halford and Starn. *Nectarines*: Armking, May Grand, Early Sun Grand, Independence, Sun Grand, Red Grand, Fantasia, Flavortop, Late LeGrand, Autumn Grand and Flamekist.

Texas: (950 hrs. chilling) Dixired, Ranger, Loring; (750 hrs.) Key-stone, Redglobe, Loring, Redskin; (500 hrs.) Sam Houston and five seed-lings of "A" series Texas Station introductions. *Colorado*: Elberta, Red-skin, Blake. *Utah*: Redhaven, Johnson Early Elberta, Gleason Early El-berta, J. H. Hale, Halberta Giant, Rio-Oso-Gem. *Central Alabama*: Springold, Earlired, Cardinal, Dixired, Redcap, Redhaven, Sentinel, Re-

CHARACTERISTICS OF PEACH VARIETIES GROWN IN NORTH AMERICA LISTED IN APPROXIMATE ORDER OF RIPENING
(Adapted from USDA Agricultural Handbook 280 by H.W. Fogle et al.)
See also Ritter and Peterson. Peaches for the 70s. Pennsylvania State University Fruit Notes.1972

(Numerical ratings of quality characteristics range from 1 to 10; the higher values indicate more desirable characteristics)

Ripen'g Season and Cultivar	Approx. ripen'g date in days before (−) or after (+) Elberta	Color of flesh	Fruit size	Stone free-ness	Attrac-tive-ness	Flesh firm-ness	Des-sert qual-ity	Can-ning qual-ity	Bac-ter'l spot resist.	Chill'g require't (Hours below 45°F.)	Zone of Adapta-tion
Very early:											
Springtime	−61	White	3	3	7	3	6	3	6	650	Cal
Springold	−58	Yellow	4	4	8	5	6	3	6	850	SE, Cal
Springcrest	−54	Yellow	5	4	8	6	7	3	6	650	Cal
Royal May	−51	Yellow	7	5	8	6	7	4	−	−	Cal
Earlired	−50	Yellow	6	5	8	6	7	4	7	850	E, SE
Candor	−50	Yellow	6	5	7	6	7	4	8	950	SE, SE
Early Coronet	−47	Yellow	7	4	8	6	7	4	−	650	Cal, SE
Cardinal	−46	Yellow	6	5	7	6	5	3	7	950	SE, E, NW
June Gold	−45	Yellow	6	5	8	6	6	5	5	650	SE, Cal
Early Redhaven	−45	Yellow	6	5	8	7	7	5	4	−	NW, NE
Garnet Beauty	−44	Yellow	6	4	8	7	6	4	5	850	NW, E
Dixired	−42	Yellow	6	4	7	6	6	4	8	1000	SE, E, NW
Maygold	−42	White	7	6	7	6	8	4	6	650	SE
Erly-Red-Fre	−40	Yellow	7	6	6	7	7	5	6	900	E
Merrill Gemfree	−40	Yellow	7	6	7	7	7	5	9	850	Cal
Sentinel	−39	Yellow	7	6	7	6	7	5	7	950	NE, SE
Royalvee	−37	Yellow									
Early											
Harbelle	−35	Yellow	7	7	8	7	8	7	7	750	E
Coronet	−33	Yellow	7	7	9	8	9	7	6	−	SE, Cal
Babcock	−31	White	6	7	7	6	7	6	−	(low)	Cal
Redhaven	−30	Yellow	7	7	8	8	8	7	8	950	E,SE, NW
Regina	−30	Yellow	8	8	7	8	8	7	6	850	Cal, NW
Norman	−28	Yellow	7	7	7	7	8	7	8		SE
Raritan Rose	−27	White	8	8	8	6	9	7	9	950	E

333

Variety	Days	Flesh								Size	Region
Ranger--------	-25	Yellow	9	8	8	8	7	8	8	950	SE, E, NW
Suwanee	-24	Yellow	5	—	8	8	8	8	8	650	SE
Washington	-23	Yellow	—	8	8	7	7	8	8	950	E
Redtop	-23	Yellow	6	8	8	8	8	7	8	850	Cal
Velvet--------	-22	Yellow	5	7	7	7	7	7	8	750	NE
Triogem-------	-22	Yellow	6	7	8	7	8	8	8	850	E
Envoy---------	-22	Yellow	6	7	7	8	8	7	8	—	NW
Mideeason:											
Sunhigh-------	-17	Yellow	4	9	9	8	8	8	9	750	E
Glohaven------	-16	Yellow	7	—	8	9	8	8	8	850	Central
Redglobe------	-14	Yellow	7	9	9	10	10	9	9	850	E, SE
Southland-----	-14	Yellow	6	9	9	9	9	8	9	750	SE
Roza----------	-14	Yellow	4	9	8	8	9	9	9	—	NW
Earlihale-----	-13	Yellow	4	8	9	9	8	8	8	750	NW
Canadian Harmony	-12	Yellow	—	8	9	9	9	9	9	800	Central
Loring--------	-11	Yellow	8	9	9	10	10	9	10	750	Central, E, SE
Summergold----	-11	Yellow	—	9	9	8	8	8	9	850	SE
Suncrest------	-10	Yellow	4	9	9	9	9	9	8	850	Cal, NW
Cresthaven----	-8	Yellow	—	6	8	9	9	9	9	850	Central
Madison-------	-7	Yellow	—	8	8	8	8	8	7	850	E
Merrill Fortyniner	-7	Yellow	—	8	9	8	9	9	8	—	Cal
Sullivan Early Elb.	-5	Yellow	5	9	9	9	9	9	9	900	E, NW
Blake---------	-3	Yellow	6	8	9	9	8	9	9	750	SE, E
Early Elberta (Gleason)	-3	Yellow	6	8	8	8	9	8	9	850	NW, E
Redskin-------	-1	Yellow	8	7	9	7	7	8	9	650	E, SE
Elberta-------	-0	Yellow	9	10	9	10	10	9	9	900	NW, Colo
Dixiland------	+0	Yellow	7	8	8	8	7	9	9	750	SE, E
J.H.Hale------	+1	Yellow	8	9	9	7	9	9	10	900	NW, Colo
Fay Elberta---	+2	Yellow	6	7	8	9	9	9	9	750	Cal, NW
Jefferson-----	+2	Yellow	—	7	9	8	8	8	9	850	E
Jerseyqueen---	+3	Yellow	5	10	9	9	10	9	9	850	E
Late:											
Shippers Late Red	+3	Yellow	5	7	9	9	9	10	10	850	Cal
Fayette-------	+6	Yellow	6	8	9	10	8	9	9	850	Cal, NW
Tyler---------	+7	Yellow	—	7	8	8	7	8	8	900 (high)	E, NW, SE
Rio Oso Gem---	+8	Yellow	5	8	9	10	8	9	10	(high)	E
Monroe--------	+12	Yellow	7	7	9	9	9	9	9	(low)	Cal
Kirkman Gem---	+25	Yellow	7	6	8	9	8	9	9	(high)	Cal
Marsun--------	+26	Yellow	8	6	9	9	9	9	9	750	Cal
Summerset-----	+30	Yellow	7	—	8	8	8	8	9	850	Cal
Fairtime------	+37	Yellow	6	7	7	8	8	8	8	(low)	Cal

Table 3. Evaluation of peach varieties suggested for planting in Virginia. (After George D. Oberle, Va Polytechnic Inst., Blacksburg)

	Days ripe before Elberta	Frost hardiness of blossoms	Flesh color	Firmness	Pit adherence	Remarks
Marcus	-64	Probably tender	Yellow	Soft	Clingstone	Fruits are too small and too soft for other than local markets. The earliest yellow peach.
Earlired	-46	Medium tender	Yellow	Med.	Semicling to cling	An attractive early yellow peach of good quality. Must be thinned early.
Erly-Red-Fre	-42	Hardy	White	Med. -	Semicling to cling	Usually sells well on roadside stands and local markets.
Sunhaven*	-36	Medium	Yellow	Med.+	Semicling	A promising new variety to precede Redhaven.
Redhaven***	-28	Hardy	Yellow	Firm	Near free to semi-cling	Still the best of its season if thinned early.
Triogem***	-25	Tender	Yellow	Med.	Free to near free	Should be a useful variety in many Virginia peach orchards.
Washington*	-21	Hardy	Yellow	V.Firm	Free	A promising new variety from V.P.I.
Redglobe	-16	Med. to tender	Yellow	V.Firm	Free	Susceptible to bacteriosis and brown rot.
Sunhigh**	-16	V.tender	Yellow	Firm	Sticks badly some years	Very susceptible to bacteriosis and buds are tender to winter cold and blossoming season frosts.
Loring*	-10	V.tender	Yellow	Med.+	Free	Subject to blossoming season frost damage.
Madison*	-7	Hardy	Yellow	V.Firm	Free	New variety from V.P.I.
Blake*	-6	Med. to tender	Yellow	Med.+	Free	Tender to winter cold and blossoming season frosts.
Redskin***	0	Tender	Yellow	Med.+	Free	Subject to blossoming season frost damage.
Elberta***	0	Tender	Yellow	Med.+	Free	
Jefferson	+3	Hardy	Yellow	V.Firm	Free	Bud and blossom hardy; new variety from V.P.I.
Rio OsoGem*	+7	Medium	Yellow	Firm	Free	Best late variety for Virginia.
V.P.I. 58	+12	Hardy	Yellow	V.Firm	Free	To be named and released in 1966. Tolerant to blossoming season frosts.

*** Recommended for commercial planting.   **Special purpose variety.   *Promising new variety.

Figure 2. Peach varieties differ in winter chilling requirements. For Elberta a duration of 750-800 hours below 45 degrees F. is required to induce opening of buds in the spring. (Left) Elberta tree shows symptoms of insufficient winter chilling. (Right) Ramona variety bore a good crop, indicating a lower winter-chilling requirement.

J. W. Lesley, California Agr. Exp. Sta.

gina, Ranger, Redtop, Loring, Washington, Blake, Redskin, Rio-Oso-Gem, Dixiland. *Midwest*: Elberta, Redhaven, Halehaven, Redskin, J. H. Hale, Rio-Oso-Gem and under promising trial, Collins, Comanche, Sunhigh, Glohaven, Merrill Hale and Madison. *Michigan*: Sunhaven, Redhaven, Glohaven, Cresthaven, Kalhaven, and Redskin, Babygold 5, Ambergem, and Suncling for processing. *Virginia*: See Table 3. *South Carolina*: Cardinal, Coronet, Redhaven, Ranger, Keystone, Sunhigh, Loring, Blake, Elberta, Redskin. *Florida*: (300-400 hrs.) Early Amber, Flordasun, nectarine Sunred, Flordawon and Tejon; (650 hrs.) Maygold, Swannee, Sunhigh, Springtime, and June Gold. *Mid-Atlantic States*: Sunhaven, Collins or Sunrise, Triogem, Jerseyland (Newday), Sunhigh, Redqueen, Halehaven, Loring, Blake, Elberta, Jerseyqueen, Rio-Oso-Gem; Babygold (N. J.) series planted widely in East for processed baby food; and Nectared (N. J.) series of nectarines (Nectared 7 is best) covering a 2-month ripening period, are on wide trial. *New York, New England area, Eastern Canada*: Earlired, Collins, Cardinal, Dixired, Garnet Beauty, Sunhaven, Jerseyland, Redhaven, Golden Jubilee, Envoy, Richhaven, Vineland No. 46108, Washington, Glohaven, Loring, Early Elberta, Elberta, Redskin; Babygolds for cling processing.

POLLINATION REQUIREMENTS

Practically all commercial peach varieties are self-fertile. Only a few varieties are self-sterile, including J. H. Hale, June Elberta, Halberta, Candoka, Chinese Cling, Alamar, and Giant. Only J. H. Hale has received wide planting, and it is giving way to better varieties. If a self-sterile variety is used, it should be planted in double rows, alternating with two rows of a self-fertile variety. Bees in the orchard at blossoming provide greater assurance of cross-pollination during adverse weather.

ROOTSTOCKS FOR PEACH TREES

There is a definite rootstock problem with peaches in some commercial areas due to apparent transmitted viruses, incompatability between rootstock and cion with the ever-changing variety picture, lack of uniformity of seedling vigor and/or nematode suscept-

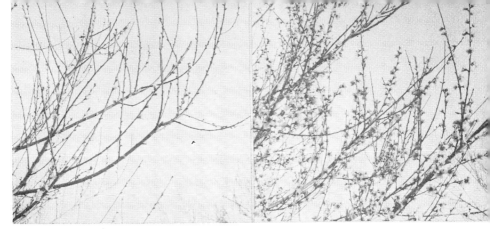

Figure 3. In mild climates as Israel and Mexico, inadequate chilling of a variety occur. Dormancy was broken (above right) in Israel by spraying the Robin variety not later than 4 weeks before expected bud opening with 2% thiourea and 0.2% Triton x-100 emulsifier, followed after drying by a "winter wash" of medium heavy mineral oil UR-75 emulsified with 20% water containing 1.5% DNOC. A spray mixture of 10% KNO_3 with the thiourea-Triton above also has given good results. The mixtures are timed according to fruit species. (Left, untreated tree). Courtesy I. Eres, S. Lavee, R. Samish, Volcani Inst. of Agr. Res., Bet Dagan, Israel).

ability. After a few years in the orchard, scattered trees may gradually weaken and die. Most rootstocks come from open-pollinated pits collected from canneries (Lovells, Halfords), wild trees, and from commercial varieties such as Elberta, but these supplies have diminished; Elberta is in question. Almost all peach varieties over the years have been budded on seedlings in the nursery row. However, rooting of peach and almond cuttings is now successful and this should make it possible to select interspecific hybrids for hybrid vigor that provide uniform rootstocks free from and/or resistant to viruses, the several harmful nematode species, and to crown gall. These are the main rootstock problems today together with hardiness in Canada. Ontario workers believe a Siberian peach and their Harrow Blood may be the answer to hardiness and canker resistance and also give some dwarfing for dense planting of trees. Researchers in W. Virginia, New Jersey, Pennsylvania and USDA are concentrating on the virus-transmission problem and/or incompatibility approach. Michigan has been using Suncling seed from local canneries with uniform results. The Harrow Exp. Sta., Canada, has found Siberian C stock to be fairly tolerant of low fluctuating winter temperatures.

The West Virginia Experiment Station recommends that the grower visit the nursery and select his own trees and tag them, choosing the larger more vigorous trees of a variety. It is a 15-year investment and is considered to be worth this trouble. Smaller trees may be small because of virus, incompatability, or other reasons. Some nurserymen grow their own stock from seed to be sure the trees are uniform, true to type and free from virus.

There is no proven dwarfing stock for commercial peach, almond or apricot. For peach, St. Julien A stock gives intermediate vigor; common Mussel is a traditional stock for semidwarfness; and *P. besseyi* and *P. tomentosa*, (the better) dwarfing. Use only clonally propagated dwarfing stock.

The Nemagard (USDA) rootstock is quite resistant to the two more common root-knot nematodes and has replaced other stocks used previously where nematodes are a problem, but it is sensitive to bacterial canker and, hence, where nematodes are not a problem, Lovell stock is preferred.

Figure 4. Deep soil fumigation with Nemagon (Shell) before planting is effective in arresting nematodes and getting peach trees off to a good start. Liquid is pumped from tank on back of tractor through tubes behind the two soil breakers which are hydraulically operated. Nematodes may account for part of the replant problem in old peach growing regions. (Courtesy Stuart Race and Ray Kienzle, Rutgers University).

PLANTING RECOMMENDATIONS

Planting recommendations in Chapter III also apply to the peach. Sites with good air drainage, good top soil, and not previously planted to peach are best. Do not plant in holes left by pulling old trees; plant in centers and run rows across a slope. Planting on the square about 18 to 24 feet with strip herbicides or cultivation in the young tree rows and sod middles with irrigation available when needed is being favored in both arid and humid regions. Peaches can be interplanted with apples provided the site is suitable for peaches and arsenic sprays will not be used which burn peach foliage. *Early* spring planting in northern areas and fall planting in milder climates are suggested.

At the Summerland Research Station, B.C., spacing for 2-arm palmette trees on seedling roots and "trellis" is about 11 x 17 ft. (see Fig. 10). On *P. tomentosa* stock, trees are set 6 x 11 ft. on trellis.

Trees planted on old apple tree sites may encounter arsenic accumulation in the soil which retards growth and production. Peaches after peaches has been a longtime World problem. Nematodes has been a likely factor but there may be other undetermined problems. Tractor drills, or better,

Figure 5. Small peach trees are developed by (a) a dwarfing rootstock as P. to-mentosa, (b) training and fertilizer control, and (c) new or compact strains of a variety. Above are Fred Anderson's several genetic dwarf peaches at Merced, Calif., of possible interest to home gardeners. They attain 4-6 ft. height in 10-15 years with fruit of acceptable quality. (Courtesy Paul Stark, Jr., Stark Nur. and Orch. Co., Louisiana, Mo. 63353).

a backhoe may be used to dig holes rapidly. Plow furrowing also is popular, using garden spades to set the trees. Latter approach is used best in the sandier soils.

PRUNING

Pruning at planting. Most peach trees are trained to the open-vase form. See Figure 6 for description. About 18 inches of trunk is needed for borer control. The side-leader method of starting trees which was initiated and now is widespread in Michigan is shown in Figure 7. Tree is planted with a wide-angled good limb 18-24" high pointing into the prevailing wind. Tree is cut back to this limb which, in turn, is cut back to 10-12 inches; all other limbs are removed. The first season select 3 wide-angled limbs from the side limb; remove others. Develop the tree from this framework. Michigan growers have found these trees to be strong and long-lived[1].

In some orchards of the milder peach growing sections, June-budded trees are set. Trees budded in the nursery in June and dug the same year for fall or winter-planting are usually only three to four feet in height and may be more or less weakly branched. The side branches are frequently too low for framework use, and these are pruned flush to leave only a whip. Vigorous branches formed the first year in the orchard then are selected for the scaffold.

---

[1]See Chapter IV for principles and methods of pruning.

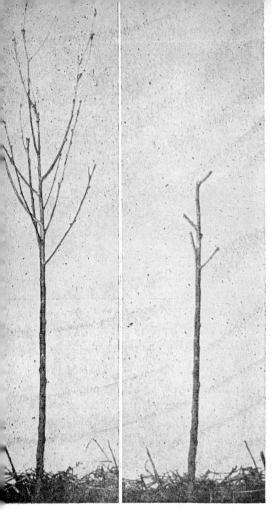

Figure 6. (Left) One-year peach tree after planting. (Right) Same tree after pruning. The tree was cut back to 30 inches. Four well-distributed side branches were left and cut back to short stubs to assist in developing an open-center head.

The California "Long" System. In the San Joaquin Valley where most of the California peaches are grown, the season is long, the soil deep and fertile, and adequate water is provided by irrigation. Thus, trees grow relatively large and reach maximum size early. An essentially open-vase system of pruning is used in which three main scaffold limbs with strong crotches are selected (Figure 8). From five to seven secondary limbs are selected on the primary limbs. When bearing starts the third to fourth year, double bindertwine or small rope is used to encircle the main limbs to prevent the crop from spreading the tree. The next year No. 11 galvanized wire is used to encircle the outside secondary limbs about ¾ the distance up to hold the tree together to avoid breakage.

The advantages of this system are: (a) longer-lasting trees that have reduced breakage of important limbs; (b) greater bearing surface that helps account for the higher yields per acre; and (c) reduced over-all pruning on mature trees vs. the relatively heavier pruning in the standard open-center tree to keep the trees low, particularly on the better soils.

The first concern of growers using the open-center pruning is the height of these trees, necessitating the extra expense of reaching the top fruit. However, growers using the "Long system" claim it is worthwhile to go higher for the fruit if the yields per acre can be increased appreciably. This system of pruning probably would not work satisfactorily elsewhere, except in those areas where peach trees could reach maximum height with good soil and fertilization and with plenty of sunshine and adequate water. As compared with most California varieties some varities grown elsewhere naturally have small thick and spreading type trees, which may be difficult to train by this system. Early tree training and

340

R. Paul Larsen, Michigan State
University

Figure 7. A newly planted peach tree, pruned to start its training by the side-leader method (bottom). One strong lateral branch is selected that is as nearly horizontal as possible. In planting, this branch should be placed opposite the direction of the prevailing wind. Three shoots to be used as scaffold branches are allowed to develop the first season (top). Others should be removed.

manipulation of the bracing wires may be too tedious and expensive for some growers, although the longer life of the tree should justify the effort.

California growers have ceased "flat topping" their trees by cutter bar. Cost data showed little saving in labor or pruning costs.

Pruning the second year. In training the peach tree from the second year to maturity, *prune as lightly as possible to attain the desired shape.* It is a common mistake of growers to prune young trees heavily either in an attempt to develop stocky trunks or because of a misunderstanding of the effect of such pruning on subsequent growth. Actually, heavy pruning results in smaller trunks, delays commercial bearing, and drastically decreases profits.

After the first season's growth, select the best three or four strong *wide-angled* scaffolds which are well spaced around the tree; most of these limbs will be the same ones which were selected immediately after planting. The branches should be spaced from about six inches apart vertically along the trunk for the open-head tree and a little farther apart for the modified-leader tree. Remove all other branches arising on the trunk. Remove any strong upright-growing central shoots, or, limbs that grow from one side of the tree across to the other side. The principal object is to train the tree to a symmetrical open-bowl tree, as shown in Figure 9.

The lateral scaffolds which have been selected should be headed back lightly only where growth has exceeded about 30 inches with little or no branching. If length growth of the scaffolds is less than 30 inches and heavily branched, several thinning-out cuts will need to be made along the scaffolds. Two or three strong secondary laterals are usually sufficient at this age, with none left closer than about 15 inches to the trunk. In this thinning-out operation, side branches on the scaffolds which grow toward the ground, toward the center of the tree, or straight to the sky are usually the first to be removed. Laterals on a scaffold limb which grow out and slightly up from the left and right are the most desirable.

341

W. P. Tufts, Univ. of Califorina, Davis

Figure 8. (Upper left and right). Two-year peach tree before and after pruning by California or "Long" system, named after the man who devised it. (Lower) Four-year mature trees, trained by same system, showing strong crotches on primary limbs, well-placed secondary limbs (5 to 7 per primary limb), bracing wire at 10 to 12 feet, and outer side "arms" from which willowy drooping "hanger" branches are developing. Overall shape of tree in leaf is an upright rectangle vs. an horizontal rectangle for low-headed trees. Willowy hanger limbs are removed if mechanical tree shakers are used for fruit thinning and harvesting.

342

Figure 9. (Top) A 6-year old Elberta peach tree with strong framework.

(Bottom) The same tree after pruning. The tips of all strong growing branches were cut back 12 to 24 inches to a side branch to keep the tree within a height and width spread of about 13 feet. The center was opened for light (medium-sized limb in center of tree will be removed in a few years). Lower limbs which tend to droop to the ground with fruit have been removed entirely or pruned to an upward-growing lateral. Dead twigs in center of tree which may harbor disease also were removed. Wood removed is shown near ladder. Some growers in Pennsylvania prune their trees low so all operations can be performed without ladders.

In regions where Oriental fruit moth is a problem and modern insecticides are not being used, the worms characteristically enter the tips of the growing shoots in early summer and stunt the length growth, causing many lateral branches to appear back of the injury. If this injury is excessive, the trees tend to become dense, necessitating several thinning-out cuts. With very dense vigorous young trees, some thinning-out during the summer may be helpful in speeding the development of a desirable framework.

The Street System. In Kentucky, Frank Street, a grower, has described a method of training peach trees where only sharp-angle crotches are removed on the young tree until the tree reaches full size. The advantage is heavy bearing earlier. It should be noted, however, that the soil in this area is unusually good, and that the main variety, Elberta, tends to thin its limbs more than most varieties and attains good fruit size even when cropped heavily. This training system may not work well on many leading varieties and on light sandy soils; additional experimentation is needed.

Special problems in starting the head. In some cases, a large part of the top may die in recently planted trees due to winter injury during the first year, or to an excessively dry period the first summer after planting. Under these conditions, a vigorous shoot may appear during the course of the season near the base of the tree and grow ahead of the originally selected trunk and laterals. This vigorous shoot can be used to develop the new head provided it arises *above* the point where the seedling root was budded in the nursery. A new framework is developed from this vigorous shoot, and the old head is removed flush with the base of the vigorous growth.

Pruning the third year. If proper precautions have been taken prev-

343

Figure 10. Dr. Donald V. Fisher, Canada Research Station, Summerland, B.C., finds the 2-arm palmette training system on seedling roots and "trellis," 6 x 11 ft., to show promise. This is Redhaven, end of third year before and after pruning, which bore 80 lbs. fruit the fourth season. Note training wire (poles can be used) from posts to anchor wire (attached to 40 lb. rock in planting hole) at base of tree and straps (or plastic chains) to hold the two arms in position. The growing season is shorter and cooler in Canada and, thus, it may be easier to hold threes within bounds.

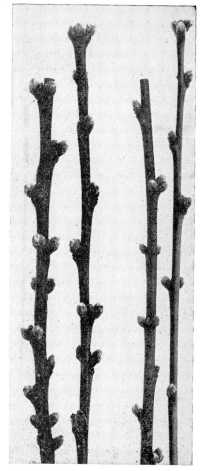

Figure 11. (Left) A thick vigorous annual twig of Elberta peach cut in two sections. (Right) A relatively thin twig of the same variety cut in two sections. Note that the fruit buds on the left shoot are larger and more numerous. Thick wood also is capable of producing more and larger leaves and fruit. (Where three buds are located at a node, the center bud is usually a leaf bud.)

iously, the tree should have its main framework well formed by the third year. Pruning then will consist largely of keeping the center of the tree open and spacing the lateral limbs and shoots on the main scaffold limbs. All short spurlike growth should be left which is not likely to become a competitive problem. These limbs contribute to fast development of the tree and are often the first to bear fruit. They should be maintained until the tree becomes large, at which time they may be removed because of reduced vigor as a result of overshading and competition.

During the third summer, some thinning-out pruning may help to keep the center of the tree open, admitting more light for better fruit-bud formation in this area. Fruit buds of the peach are formed in late summer, later than those on the apple. If the pruning and soil management programs have received proper attention, some fruit buds should form the third summer for a light crop the following year. This is particularly true in milder climates where the growing season is longer and the trees develop somewhat faster than farther North. There is considerabde experimental evidence from Ohio and other states to show that heavy pruning of peaches in the third, fourth, and fifth years greatly reduces the yield. The peach tree usually does not attain its full size until the fifth or sixth year. Therefore, *light to moderate annual pruning attention* to attain strong desirable framework should be practiced so that the tree will attain its full size and production as soon as possible.

PRUNING THE BEARING PEACH TREE

Bearing habit. Peach trees bear fruit laterally on wood that grew the previous year. Thus, the terminal and lateral shoots which have developed over the outer surface of the tree are the most important in fruit production. The best and most fruit is produced in the upper third of the tree. If the practice has been followed of leaving the center of the tree relatively open, as shown in Figure 9, a considerable number of new shoots and short growths or spurs will develop also near the center of the tree. The open-bowl type of head should be maintained, and the height and width of the tree also should be kept within easily managed bounds. About a 13-foot height and a 13-foot spread is acceptable but the soil, planting system, climate and convenience for mechanical harvesting govern this.

Fruit buds of the peach are plump and roundish; on the other hand the leaf or shoot buds are small, narrow, and pointed (Figure 11). On the vigorous shoots, fruit buds at a given node may occur in numbers of one, two, or three, depending upon the variety and tree vigor. Where three buds are at a node, the usual arrangement is for the center bud to be a leaf bud while the two outer buds are fruit buds. On the shorter growths and spurs fruit buds are often borne singly beside a leaf bud. On very vigorous shoot growth of 30 inches or more, the lateral buds may consist almost entirely of leaf buds, particularly on the lower portion of such a shoot.

Well-grown bearing trees seldom fail to make enough fruit buds for a heavy crop of fruit the following year. Ordinarily, far too many fruit buds are produced and, therefore, dormant pruning is helpful in thinning the crop as well as inducing proper renewal of fruiting wood throughout the tree. If a bearing peach tree 8 to 12 years of age is making from 12 to 16 inches of shoot growth on the majority of the outer branches, this is sufficient for maintaining good fruit production.

Bearing peach trees *must be pruned every year*. If regular annual pruning is not performed, the tendency is for the fruiting wood to develop farther and farther out and higher up each year. Eventually, a thick-topped leggy tree develops almost devoid of low-fruiting wood. In order to bring such a tree down to economical range and fruiting, it will be necessary to make some heavy heading-back cuts on the main limbs which may destroy a large part of the crop in the first and second years following.

When and how severely to prune. In regions where winter killing of wood and buds is a factor, the presence or absence of freezing damage more or less governs the pruning procedure with bearing peach trees. If the temperature reached 10° F. below zero during the winter, at least some and perhaps all fruit buds may be killed, depending upon the variety. In a mild climate, a temperature of -10° F. could be expected to cause more damage than in the North unless the trees had been hardened by cold weather sometime prior to this low temperature. The critical temperature for killing dormant peach wood in the colder peach growing areas is around 20° F. below zero, although there may be considerable variation in amount of injury, depending upon the variety and previous growth conditions. Winter injured wood can be identified by a browning of the inner sapwood to the pith. Fruit buds killed by low temperatures have dark brown centers when cross-sectioned. Some estimate of the percentage

346

damage can be obtained by sectioning 100 buds on each variety in different exposures in the orchard.

In northern areas in small orchards, it is best to delay pruning until after danger of winter killing of buds and wood is passed. If there has been no winter injury to the fruit buds, a general over-all pruning then is recommended. If a portion of the buds has been killed, a relatively light pruning should be given because heavy pruning may reduce yield without improving quality. Under most conditions, however, the majority of the living buds will be found on wood in the top of the tree; pruning in this area, therefore, should be relatively light and so-governed to make the best of the prospects.

If practically all of the fruit buds appear to be killed in small orchards, delay pruning until blossoming time. If no blossoms appear, use this opportunity to thin out and moderately cut back in order to keep the tree within desirable height and spread. Special attention should be given also to proper branch distribution in order to space evenly the fruiting wood throughout the tree.

If the orchard is large, the grower must proceed with his pruning regardless of possible cold injury in order to cover his orchard completely. In mild regions tempered by the ocean or by a large body of water, it is usually safe to prune any time during the winter when most of the work is commonly done.

In regions where spring frosts are a greater risk than winter injury, the necessary thinning-out cuts can be made during the dormant season, but the amount of heading-back cuts can be deferred until after danger of frost injury is over. At this time, the degree of heading-back which is needed can be done with more certainty.

If the crop is lost entirely and the wood is injured severely, there may be temptation on the part of some growers to "dehorn" the trees. "Dehorning" is a term used to describe large heading-back cuts four to six feet or more from the tips of the branches, leaving little more than stubs of the main branches. This practice was recommended back in the early 1900's, but experience has shown that these large cuts drastically reduce the crop for several years and may be fatal or severely weakening to the tree. The best treatment for severely winter-injured trees is not to prune, or, to prune lightly after growth starts, in combination with an early and rather heavy spring application of a quickly available nitrogen fertilizer, such as nitrate of soda. This should be accompanied by cultivation, if possible, to restore growth conditions. After growth starts, the dead wood can be spotted and removed. If the trees recover, a moderate amount of pruning can be made the following spring to lower, thin out, and spread the top.

If uninjured peach trees are dehorned heavily, the resulting growth is so rank that it is difficult to train the tree properly. This heavy pruning also practically eliminates bearing for two or three years. A moderate amount of dehorning may have a place in cases where trees have become "leggy" from neglect and the crop has been killed, but the wood uninjured. The large cuts should not be made in wood older than three or four years. All heading-back cuts should be made to prominent side branches on which rather light heading-back also is given. When some dehorning is practiced, the vigorous upright branches should be removed entirely which, in some cases, may be growing into and through the center of the tree. All cuts should be directed toward forming a low open and spreading type of framework where the low open-center type of tree is the standard.

Placing renewal cuts. As a tree reaches the height of about ten feet, it is important to cut the main upward-growing branches back to outward laterals, as shown in Figure 9. The point at which this cut is made is known as the "renewal point" near which similar cuts will be made in future years. A renewal cut should be placed at the end of every main branch as soon as it reaches sufficient height or width spread. The summer after this type of cut is made, one or more side shoots will appear below the cut. During the next winter pruning period, the more vigorous and outward-growing lateral of these can be retained; the other laterals are removed, including the large side branch left the year before. Some growers make these first heading-back cuts on a tree when it has attained a height of eight feet. This usually is done on soils relatively low in fertility or on varieties that are naturally small. While this may somewhat reduce the bearing surface of a tree, in subsequent years it is possible for the workmen to make most of the renewal cuts without a stepladder. Also, with the bearing surface closer to the ground, the harvesting and thinning operations are facilitated.

See Figure 12 for the mower-cut pruning that peach growers are using to reduce labor and speed-prune a large acreage.

General recommendation. Peach pruning should be somewhat lighter during the first three or four years after the trees come into bearing. Later, a somewhat heavier heading-back type of pruning is desirable every third or fourth year in order to keep the bearing wood low. When the bloom has evidence of being heavy, the thinning-out pruning will assist considerably in reducing the need for thinning of the fruit later. However, this thinning-out pruning should not be excessive to the point of reducing yield.

Dormant pruning throughout the tree should be sufficient to admit several sun spots on the ground beneath the tree during the growing season. Thick annual terminal growth of 10 to 15 inches is desirable for maintaining good production and sizing of the fruit. The pruning, fertilization, and soil management programs must be interrelated carefully to promote this type of terminal growth. Short slender shoot growth is generally unproductive and is characteristic of declining trees (Figure 11). On the other hand, trees which are overly vigorous and producing annual growth of over 30 inches are not only less productive but are difficult to manage in pruning. The accumulation of many dead twigs in the center and lower

Figure 12. (Upper) "Flat-top" tractor-mower-pruned peach trees, thinned-out by hand loppers or pneumatic equipment. Method is quick, labor-saving, cutting costs about 10 percent. (Mid) The apparently initial "flat-top" mower on front-end-lift tractor, built by J. F. Hendrickson, grower, New Jersey. (Lower) Sophisticated equipment that both hedges and tops. (Courtesy Ernest G. Christ, Rutgers University, N. J.)

349

part of a tree is good evidence of too little pruning throughout the top center of the tree.

Pneumatic Platform Pruning. Costs can be reduced within the 10 to 15% range by use of power pruning tools, as described for the apple. Four men usually work together, two on the ground pruning as high as they can reach and two on the platform with kickboards to walk into the trees to reach the tops. In hilly orchards the platform is built to be tilted level. Workers favor this power equipment because it speeds, improves, and eases the job. In California, however, growers have almost quit using platforms as it is not adaptable to large crews and affords a saving of within the 10% range only.

"Flat-top" Mower Pruning. Many peach orchards are being topped at about 8 to 11 ft. and some are side-hedged with cutter-bar equipment as shown in Figure 12. About 4 minutes per tree is required to mow the top and thin out by hand loppers (pneumatic platform pruning is better) as compared with 12 minutes for hand-lopping only. A canvas flap tied to and trailing the cutter bar helps collect and drop the prunings between the trees.

Mice damage. Occasionally field mice will damage peach trunks, particularly during extended snow cover. Peach prunings left in the row middles may reduce damage to trunks if the snow comes in late winter. Mouse precautions taken for apple generally hold for peach. (Chap. V).

SOIL MANAGEMENT

Young trees. Cultivation or chemical herbicides should be used for young peach trees for at least the first two or three years after planting in order to obtain good survival, vigorous growth, and earlier commercial production. Common systems of management for young trees are shown in Figure 13. If the orchard is planted on the contour, either the entire middles or only narrow strips on either side of the trees can be kept bare during the spring and most of the summer, discontinuing any cultivation in late summer or earlier. Middles of the rows may be sown at the outset to a semi-permanent cover as fescue or alfalfa, or they may be sown each year to a summer and winter cover. If the land is fertile and suitable to the growing of intercrops as vegetables or small fruits, such a practice is feasible and it affords cash income until the peaches start bearing the fourth or fifth year.

During the first two or three years in an orchard, summer cover crops are often planted if some cash intercrop is not grown. These are sown in late spring. Soybeans or cowpeas are common, both in the colder and warmer climes; in the latter, crotolaria also is popular. These crops are disked into the soil in late summer in preparation for a winter cover.

Winter cover crops are rye, rye grass, bromegrass, or wheat. Hairy vetch, Austrian peas (Figure 14), rye, oats, barley, or crimson clover are popular in the South. Where the winter cover crop is a grain, it is im-

(Top) D. F. Brown, U.S. Soil Conservation Service. (Middle) Roy E. Marshall and U.S. Soil Conservation Service. (Bottom) A. B. Beaumont, U.S. Soil Conservation Service.

Figure 13. (Top) A 2-year peach orchard planted on the contour in a medium-sandy loam soil, Gloucester County, New Jersey. Narrow strips are cultivated or treated with herbicides with fescue or alfalfa strips in the centers. (Middle) Michigan peach orchard in the first year of growth. Trees planted on the rectangle, 18 by 24 feet, using a grain cover crop drilled about the middle of August. (Bottom) A 2-year peach orchard planted on Merrimac coarse sand in Massachusetts, using a drilled rye cover to assist in maintaining or building up needed organic matter.

In regard to contour planting, the earlier designs sometimes were too rigid to be wholly practical. Curves in the contours were too sharp. SCS in recent years has made the curves wider or used sodded areas to accomodate the traffic and large machinery.

Clemson Agr. College, and U.S. Soil Conservation Service, Clemson, S.C.

Figure 14. (Top) Oldest peach orchard in South Carolina planted in 1901. Rows were on contour; bench terraces have been built up gradually. Slope averages from 6 to 15 per cent. Trees are still vigorous and produce from 350 to 400 bushels per acre. (Bottom) A good stand of Austrian winter peas in South Carolina. Hairy vetch, rye, and Crotalaria are also popular in this region. Winter covers are more important in the South to help control soil erosion; in the North they reduce root damage to trees during severe freezes when no snow protection covers the ground. In Georgia more frost damage to bloom has been noted by Dr. E. F. Savage in orchards with heavy winter covers of rye or crimson clover. Georgia growers thus are using winter covers only in young orchards or discing them down early in spring in mature orchards so the soil will be bare and hard-packed at bloom. Soil heat apparently moves upward better thru a rain-packed soil with no cover crop than one filled with air pockets due to recent cultivation, or one with a substantial plant cover.

Strip-row chemical weed control with fescue sod middles and overhead portable irrigation is growing in popularity as a soil management system for peaches.

Figure 14a. (Upper left). Zinc deficiency is the easiest to identify: wavy leaf margins, main veins remaining green the longest, area between main veins a "dirty" white, leaves bunched, small (little leaf), early drop; fruits misshapen, small, flesh browns faster, off quality. (Upper right) Iron deficient leaves have fine network of green veins in yellowish field, shoot tip leaves first affected, fruit flat in flavor, off color, some branches and trees showing deficiency more than others. (Lower left). Boron deficient young lateral shoots show death, oozing 1-3 inches from tip, then dieback like oriental fruit moth injury; fruits flat in flavor, poor quality with center corking; bark splitting, large lenticils; (lower right) boron deficient trees flushing late in spring, then many soft shoots dying back. (Lower right, H. R. McLarty and C. G. Woodbridge, formerly Summerland, B.C., Canada; others, Hector R. Cibes, fomerly Rutgers University).

353

E. F. Savage, Georgia Exp. Sta.

Figure 15. Four-year June Elberta peach trees at Experiment, Georgia. Typical tree on (left) clean cultivated plot and (right) on adjoining alfalfa sod plot. Alfalfa is deep-rooted and competitive for moisture; it should be kept a few feet form the tree trunk and used only in regions of adequate moisture or where irrigation is available. Both trees were well fertilized with nitrogen, Tree-row chemical weed control with fescue strip centers is replacing row cultivation.

portant that disking or mowing be done early in the following spring, preferably when the growth is about knee high and before it has had opportunity to compete with the trees for water and nitrogen. This is especially true for rye which may grow so fast in spring that it is difficult to complete disking before the crop has interfered with growth of the trees. The danger of such a situation in humid regions is not great, however, if adequate nitrogen has been applied for both the cover crop and the trees. Where spring frosts are a problem, land should be disced and packed by rain well before bloom to afford heat movement from soil upward on cold nights.

Polythylene plastic mulch sheets have shown promise for weed control around young fruit trees. Peach and nectarine having shown in one test 45 to 571 per cent increase over cultivated trees. There is a moisture control benefit, but mice tend to nest under the mulch, making a place to bait and trap them, which may or may not be a favorable situation.

Bearing trees. If strip-in-row herbicides or cultivation is used in orchards, some type of cover cropping is recommended in order to maintain or increase organic matter in the soil, reduce erosion, and to reduce the possibility of winter injury. Shortly before or after bearing has started, however, it may be desirable to shift the soil management program from a cultivation cover-crop system to some form of sod management, depending upon the soil type and rainfall conditions in the region. It is generally agreed among horticulturists that cultivation should be reduced to a minimum; there is considerable evidence accumulating to show that excessive cultivation is eventually detrimental to the soil and to tree growth. What the minimum amount of cultivation should be cannot be stated definitely;

it may vary from orchard to orchard, depending upon the tendency of the soil to become compacted, the slope, and the moisture holding capacity. For example, an orchard on a fertile soil with high moisture retaining capacity might be managed to a good advantage under a system of semipermanent sod with annual row-herbicide treatment and the sod allowed to grow with one or two mowings in summer, using irrigation when needed. On the other hand, an orchard on a lighter and somewhat less fertile soil probably could not be handled successfully by this method. Undoubtedly, under sandy soil conditions in a mild climate, it would require longer periods of cultivation to remove competition between the trees and the cover crop for moisture. Heavy clays may be entirely unsatisfactory because they present a drainage problem and are likely to be too wet at times and too dry at others. Irrigation is used more and more to adjust deficient water.

If a semipermanent cover is desired, such as shown in Figure 15, it is well to consider annual rainfall as well as the moisture retaining capacity of the soil. Such a system undoubtedly would have more chance to succeed under annual rainfall conditions of about 50 inches or more, as compared with 30 inches or less.

There is clear evidence from experiment stations in humid regions that peaches can be grown satisfactorily under sod mulch in the moderately heavy types of soil, provided a heavy mulch is maintained and two and three times the nitrogen is applied as recommended under cultivation. Mulch, however, is becoming difficult to find at a reasonable price. Hill of Ohio has shown under long-term test that good quality yields can be obtained in sod if ample nutrients and water are supplied.

Herbicide use in modern peach orchards is becoming standard practice. See Chapter XVIII for details of chemicals used and application methods. See in Table 3 below how N is higher in foliage where chemical weed control is used as compared with hoeing and black plastic cover. This is to be expected since trees with chemical-strip-weed control often look better and darker green than those cultivated.

TABLE 3.

EFFECT OF NITROGEN AND WEED CONTROL METHOD ON LEAF NITROGEN OF 5-YEAR RICHHAVEN AND REDHAVEN PEACH TREES.
(Michigan State University)

Nitrogen applied/tree lb.	Weed Control Method and % N (DW)		
	Hoed %	Black Plastic %	4# Simazine + 2# Amitrole-T per A %
1/8	2.35	2.59	3.19
1/4	2.97	2.85	3.65
1/2	3.71	3.64	3.92

On sloping land which has not been contoured, it may be desirable to leave narrow strips of sod between the rows across the slope, using strip-tree-row herbicides early in the spring and summer, and leaving the soil

355

A. C. McClung, University of North Carolina

Figure 15a. Two types of magnesium deficiency in peach as developed under field conditions in the Sand Hill section of North Carolina. (Upper) Marginal and interveinal yellowing and burning; (Lower) Marginal and interveinal dying which appears suddenly and the leaves drop.

356

Figure 16. Manganese deficiency is characterized by a herringbone appearance of leaves (left) due to light green areas between the main veins; areas adjacent to main veins remain a darker green. A spray of three to five pounds of manganese sulfate in 100 gallons should correct the deficiency in two to three weeks.

bare or sowing a winter cover. It has been demonstrated that these narrow sod strips have little influence on yields and do not materially increase the disease and insect problem. The width of the sod strips would depend largely on the erosiveness of the soil. Cultivation between the rows in any event should be only enough to discourage weed growth until a cover crop or permanent sod strip is sown.

The size of the peach crop more or less governs the time of seeding the cover crop in late summer. If the trees are carrying a light or no crop, the cover can be sown earlier for the purpose of competing with the tree, reducing its growth, and thus reducing the likelihood of winter injury. On the other hand, if the trees are carrying a heavy crop of fruit and the weather is somewhat dry, the cover crop can be sown later in order to reduce competition for water with the maturing crop of peaches.

Rye grass and wheat have been popular winter cover crops in bearing orchards in the Northeast because they grow more slowly in spring and give the grower opportunity to mow or disk them down before they compete heavily with the trees. Rye is a popular cover crop because the seed is cheap, available, and will germinate and take hold better under adverse conditions. Sudan grass is frequently used but it has the objection of growing too rapidly shortly after sown, thus competing with the trees. It also may become so high as to interfere with the harvesting operations unless mowed. See Table 1 in Chapter V for cover crop seeding.

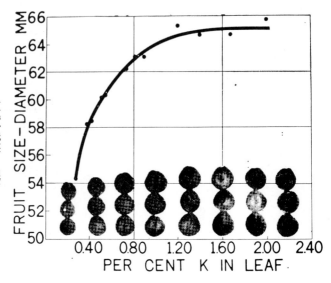

Figure 16a. Maximum size of Cortez peach fruits and yield is reached at midseason potassium leaf levels of about 1.2%.

Courtesy Omund Lilliland, Univ. of Calif., Davis.

Fertilization, with or without lime, of the cover crop at seeding time is now being generally practiced to obtain good covers. Most cover crops and especially legumes grow best in soils with a pH of about 6.0 to 6.5. Rye will grow on soils too acid for other cover crops. An application of 100 to 150 pounds per acre of a high-grade complete fertilizer is recommended on areas where the cover is sown, using a 5-10-5 for loamy soils of a moderate fertility and a 10-10-10 for sandy soils, or those of low fertility. Caution is needed against over-liming a peach orchard; much damage to the trees can result.

Fertilization. Most peach growers rely on commercial fertilizers as a source of nutrients. Nitrogen is the element which gives the best response in peach trees; in some soils it may be the only element needed. In fact, for a given amount of nitrogen, more response is obtained in peach trees than almost any other fruit crop.

Application of nitrogen should be governed by variety and character of the shoot growth. If young peach trees are making approximately 18 inches of terminal growth and the foliage is of good color without fertilizer application, they do not need fertilizer. The same can be said for bearing orchards if the annual shoot growth is 10 to 15 inches, the girth of the shoots is thick, and the yields good. If the growth exceeds this length for mature trees by several inches, it would be well to reduce the nitrogen for awhile. There are instances of where careless use of nitrogen on peach trees has resulted in damage by overstimulating the trees. *Each tree should be considered separately as to its fertilizer needs.* Trees growing on the lower more fertile areas will require less fertilizer than those growing on somewhat eroded knolls.

It is difficult to recommend a definite amount of nitrogen-carrying fertilizer for a given orchard, or, for a given peach tree. When growth of the trees has been uniform, the problem is easier. However, tree growth in most orchards tends to be quite variable. Sulfate of ammonia, or ammonium nitrate is generally used at the rate of one-fourth to one-third pound of sulfate of ammonia per year of age of trees or its equivalent in actual nitrogen. Nitrate of potash or soda is used widely in some humid regions. When the trees have reached maturity after about six years, the application thereafter is three to five pounds per tree of sulfate of ammonia or its nitrogen equivalent, depending upon annual shoot growth, amount of pruning, condition of the tree, and type and native fertility of the soil. On the basis of pure nitrogen, this is about one-half to one-pound per mature tree. Varieties with highly colored fruits such as Jerseyland and Redhaven can use higher rates of nitrogen to get higher yields and still not hinder color commercially.

O. W. Davidson, Rutgers University

Figure 17. Potassium deficiency on peach is characterized by crinkling, marginal burning, and speckled dead spots between the main veins of the leaf.

Leaf analysis is used widely to govern fertilizer applications to peach, particularly where a nutrient problem is apparent. Following are average contents found in good yielding trees by standard laboratory procedure.

Contents below minimum figures may result in deficiencies.

N	P	K	Mg	Ca	S	Fe	Mn	B	Zn	Cu	Mo
%	%	%	%	%	ppm	ppm	ppm	ppm	ppm	ppm	ppm
2.5	0.15	1.25	0.25	1.9	100	124	20	20	15	4.0	0.5
to	to	to	to	to	to	to	to	to	to	to	to
3.36	0.30	3.00	0.54	2.5	150	152	142	80	30	11.9	1.0

There is evidence in humid and dry regions that potassium may be a problem on young as well as old trees, particularly in the lighter soils. This is characterized by limited growth with curling leaves which show considerable tip and marginal burning (Figure 17). Phosphorus is most important to the cover crop. Other nutrients which may be deficient in peach orchards are zinc, manganese, and iron, particularly in arid regions;

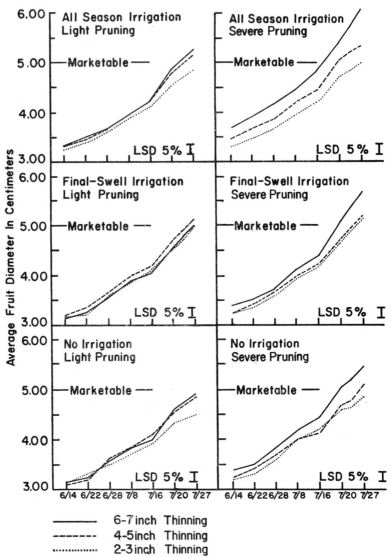

Figure 18. Morris et al. in Arkansas show in a three-year test that heavy pruning and/or fruit thinning may replace irrigation within limits, from the standpoint of fruit size. Actually, an attempt should be made to get maximum crop and fruit size with the proper irrigation (if needed), pruning and fruit thinning. This is a delicate situation to manipulate and comes only with experience.

and magnesium in humid areas. In humid sandy soil areas where organic matter is low, the following nutrients in a ton of fertilizer are used by some growers in a 5-10-10 mix at 1000 lbs./A.: manganese, zinc, and iron as sulfates, 20 lbs. each; borax and copper sulfate, 10 lbs. each; ammonium or sodium molybdate, one lb.; Mg oxide, 2%. See Ritter for his reference on Pennsylvania long-term NPK test.

Irrigation. Peach trees respond well to readily available water throughout the growing season. Fruit which has fallen behind in size because of insufficient moisture during the growing season, even as early as two to four weeks after bloom, will never regain the size obtained on other trees receiving adequate moisture. Irrigation is a regular practice in peach orchards where low annual rainfall makes it a necessity. Where water is plentiful, low in cost and the land level, furrow or flood irrigation are used because initial installation is 25% the cost of portable sprinklers, although water application can

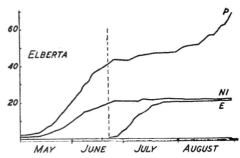

New York Agr. Exp. Sta., Geneva

Figure 19. Growth curves of Elberta peach from full bloom to maturity for (P), pericarp or edible part; (NI), nucellus and integuments of pit; and (E), embryo in the pit. Note period of about five weeks after dotted line and during embryo development when the edible part, (P), shows little increase in volume size. Length of period from full bloom to dotted line is about the same for early, medium, and late varieties, but period from dotted line to final increase in fruit size may vary from a week for an early variety (Greensboro) to six weeks for a late variety (Chili).

be controlled better with sprinklers. Where water is scarce or expensive plastic pipe in-row "trickle" irrigation shows promise. See Chapter XIX.

Results of Feldstein and Childers on a deep medium loam soil near Doylestown, Pa., reported through Rutgers University, indicated that irrigation paid well five out of six years in the 1950's. In two of the years the fruit from nonirrigated trees was so small that over 75 per cent was unsaleable, whereas fruit from irrigated trees was all saleable. B. L. Rogers in Maryland obtained an average of 29% larger fruit size for Sunhigh and 26% for Elberta over a seven-year irrigation test. Morris *et al.* in Arkansas in Figure 18 show interrelationship between irrigation, fruit thinning, pruning. Texas tests doubled crop value by irrigation.

The soil moisture content should not become less than 1 atmosphere by a tensiometer in all rooting areas (top 5-8 ft.). Excessive water usage causes root and crown rots.

THINNING PEACH FRUITS

Fruit thinning is a standard practice on peach trees carrying a moderate to heavy crop. However, in spite of the many benefits from thinning which have been demonstrated through long years of experience, fruit thinning is too often one of the most inefficiently conducted operations in peach growing. Johnston of Michigan gives the following reasons for growers slighting this job: (a) Failure to realize at thinning time how much the young fruits will expand in size before the harvesting season if they are given the proper opportunity; it is important to consider that it takes twice as many peaches of two-inch size as of two and one-half inch size to fill a

361

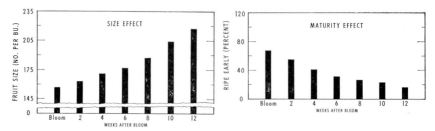

Figure 20. Graphs show effects of time of thinning Redhaven peaches (2-week intervals after bloom) on ultimate fruit size (left) and maturity time (right). Note that each successive thinning time caused smaller and later maturing peaches. Early thinning also increases leaf size and shoot growth. Among other early ripening varieties that set heavily and so-benefit are Mayflower, Earlired, Cardinal, Coronet, Golden Jubilee and Triogem. (After Fogle et al., USDA.)

bushel basket; (b) failure to realize that it is better economy to pick the excess fruits after the June drop and throw them on the ground than to be compelled to pick them at the regular harvesting season with the resultant extra handling costs and lower value of small peaches; (c) it is a monotonous job when done only by hand and it is only natural to hurry through or to find excuses to do something else. Thinning crews must have constant and careful supervision for best results.

Hand and Mechanical Thinning. Start thinning after the June drop (5-8 wks. after full bloom). Extent of the thinning task can be determined better at this time than earlier because peach trees generally retain practically all fruit to maturity which are attached to the tree after the June drop. Where certain insects are a problem, most of the injury is over by this time, and damaged peaches can be removed in the thinning operation.

Early maturing varieties are thinned first. (Figure 20). Next, thin the varieties and the trees within a variety which are carrying the heaviest crop. In order to obtain the greatest benefit from thinning, the job should be completed as soon after the June drop as possible, although it has been shown that for many of the medium- to late-maturing varieties, some benefit from thinning can be obtained as late as eight to ten weeks before picking. Fogle et al. of USDA state, "How many peaches should be removed from a tree by thinning depends chiefly on the size of the tree and its bearing capacity. If a tree cannot bear more than 1 or 2 bushels, only enough of the peaches that can develop to desirable size (those with a diameter of 2¼ to 2½ inches) should be left to make up this quantity. When a tree has a uniformly heavy set of fruit, it can be thinned to a fixed spacing, such as 6 to 8 inches along the twig. Usually, it is best to thin not according to a fixed spacing but according to leaf area, tree vigor, and bearing capacity. After a spring freeze, sometimes the only blossoms left alive are those at the bases of terminal shoots. When this happens, the fruits are not thinned even where they touch each other, because the leaf area is sufficient for all.

Where labor costs are high, peach growers may choose to reduce the

362

number of peaches that will be produced on their trees by pruning off a large number of shoots either before or at blossomtime. In localities where spring frosts occur, some detailed pruning may be postponed until blossomtime, when crop prospects are more certain."

In California, an attempt is made to grow fruits as nearly uniform in size as possible for canning purposes. In thinning, a more or less definite number of peaches is left on a tree of given vigor and size. If 2-½ inch peaches are desired from a 20 x 20 foot planting, it will be necessary to leave the following number of peaches per tree for a given yield; about 700 peaches per tree yields 10 tons/acre; 1,050 peaches yield 15 tons and 1,250 peaches give 18 tons. Based on a measurement at *Reference Date* (10 days after pit hardening) cling peach sizes can be predicted accurately so heavy thinning is necessary if peach diameter is 33 mm, moderate thinning if diameter is 36 mm, and only touch-up if sizes exceed 38 mm, at reference date.

The largest and best-colored peaches are produced on the more vigorous new wood. Thus, more peaches should be left on the outside and especially in the tops of the trees than on the inside and lower branches. Fruit on "hanger"[1] branches around the lower part of the tree should be thinned more heavily, perhaps picking all fruits from thin weak wood.

About 30-35 average size peach leaves are required to size a peach to marketable size. Generally, the smaller the natural size of the fruit for a variety at harvest, the more leaves and wider spacing of the fruit is needed.

Because of the high labor costs, considerable thinning has been done in recent years by rapid mechanical methods rather than by the older hand method. Some growers use poles 4 to 8 feet long or longer, with about 12 inches of hard rubber hose over one end. With such poles, the excess fruits are removed by tapping the branch or twig first at right angles and then lengthwise. A teenage boy can do about 65 trees a day. Wire or brush brooms (dogwood or apple limbs one-inch at base) sometimes are used to thin peach blossoms, especially those of early ripening varieties. A stream from a spray gun at 600 lbs. pressure can be run up and down the branch knocking off most of the bloom. Blossom thinning, of course, is risky where frost damage is a factor. (See 1966 edition of this book for details.)

Trunk shakers are an effective means of removing fruits on a large scale and where chemical thinning has been inadequate. The trunk is grasped by a cushioned arm, tightened, and the entire tree vibrated, shaking off the fruit in seconds.[2] Avoid over-thinning in the tree tops and do not

---

[1]In the East this term refers to wood which has fruited for several years and becomes low-hanging and unproductive, whereas in California it means branches arising from the main limbs on heavily cut back stubs. These produce good size fruit. Where mechanical harvesting is used, however, these are removed because they do not release their fruit well in tree shaking.

[2]Orchard Machinery Corp., Yuba City, California. 95991

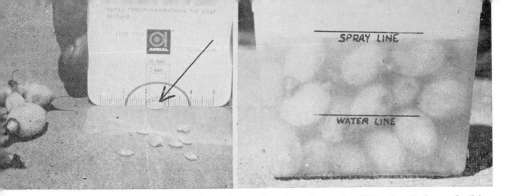

Figure 20a. Two methods to determine time to apply CPA chemical peach thinner. (Left) About a dozen average size peaches are harvested at 3-day intervals from the variety in question, starting about 3 wks after bloom. When the ovules (kernels) reach 8.5-10 mm in length, (arrow) the CPA spray is applied, weather permitting. (Right) In the volume method, 100 peaches are harvested at random, the plastic cup is filled with water to the water line, peaches are dropped in, and if the water rises to the spray line (displacing 300-400 ml) it is time to apply CPA. These suggestions are subject to change; keep in touch with your local specialist. Triogem variety is shown. Some other varieties may have a different timing of application.

rely on trunk shakers to do the complete job. Motor-driven hand operated limb shakers are favored by some growers.

Chemical thinning. Many chemicals have been tested and discarded because of too much foliage and shoot damage, premature fruit softening along the suture, or due to necessity of applying at or too shortly after bloom in regions where post-bloom frosts may occur, further reducing set. In the arid mild climates or sections of the world where post-bloom frosts are a low-risk, Elgetol from 1 pt. (J. H. Hale) to 1½ pts. (Elberta) to 1 qt. (most varieties) in 100 gals. of water is used with fair success, depending upon weather, tree vigor, intensity of bloom, and other factors. Spray is applied when 60-75 per cent of the blossoms are open. Exact timing is important. Complete thinning is not recommended; excess fruits are knocked off manually with clubs.

Auxin (hormone) spray-thinning of peaches is showing the most promise as a quick, easy, and economical method of peach thinning. Many auxins have been tested and discarded. No chemical as yet is fully satisfactory.

CPA (2-3 chlorophenoxy propionamide)* is used by some growers 3 to 4 weeks after bloom and, hence, after most danger of frost damage. Methods tested and proposed for proper timing of CPA are: (a) by fruit volume—2.8 mi; (b) by fruit weight—2.0 gm; (c) by ovule (kernel) length—8.5-10 mm; and (d) by degree days—about 1000. All methods are based on the stage of fruit development when cells of the kernel are just beginning to form and when the fruit is highly susceptible to CPA. At this time the auxin will kill the embryo, causing abortion and fruit drop. By allowing fruit of early bloom, which is the largest size at harvest, to pass this critical stage, then spray with CPA, the smaller and weaker

---

*Initially, Fruitone, sold by Amdal Co., Abbott Lab., No. Chicago, Ill.

fruits are "shocked" and soon will drop. The remaining best fruit are larger at harvest than fruit from hand-thinned trees.

Ethephon** applied at full bloom to petal fall or when ovule is 9-15 mm long results in ethylene development which causes flower or fruit thinning. Excess amounts cause overthinning of fruit, excessive leaf drop and gumming of shoots. Nearly all peach varieties can be thinned with Ethephone if properly timed, but subsequent frosts may be a problem in frost-prone areas.

FROST DAMAGE AND WINTER INJURY

In California the only injury from cold, which is not frequent, is due to spring frosts during bloom or after the fruit has set. Open blossoms are very tender, but small fruits are more tender, becoming increasingly so until one-half-inch in size. The seed is usually killed, causing the fruit eventually to drop. Blossoms and fruit can be protected by orchard heating, but the grower must decide whether the increased returns brought by saving the crop over a period of years more than offset the cost of heating.

East of the Rocky Mountains, the most important factors influencing peach growing are spring frosts and winter injury in one form or another. Winter injury in its broadest aspects is experienced in peach regions above the Mason and Dixon Line. In South Carolina and neighboring states, the so-called "winter injury" is not so much due to low temperature as to cold March weather following a warm period in February which has induced growth activity. The results of winter injury in a region like Michigan and New York, however, are very clear-cut when a peach crop is lost or when the trees themselves virtually are killed by one extreme drop in temperature. Of almost equal importance to the trees in those regions are secondary effects of winter injury, including the resultant entrance of peach borers and the canker disease, which together may shorten considerably the life of a tree.

The most common form of winter injury to peaches is the destruction of fruit buds. Leaf buds are usually not injured unless the twigs are killed. It is impossible to give a definite critical temperature for fruit buds of each variety. The danger point for Elberta during midwinter is usually between —10° and —12° F. and other varieties are compared with it. Fruit buds of Elberta and J. H. Hale are among the most tender in bud; Halehaven, Redhaven, and Golden Jubilee are medium hardy; whereas those of Rochester, Veteran, Cumberland and Erly-Red-Fre are among the more hardy to low temperature. A variety like Redhaven that produces many buds per foot of limb may come through cold weather when others that produce relatively few will not come through. Alar foliar spray

---

**Ethrel sold by Amchem. Co., Ambler, Pa. 19002.

has been reported in Indiana to increase fruit bud hardiness the following winter.

The farther the blossoms have opened, the more susceptible they are to cold; peaches in full bloom may be injured at about 25° F., whereas just before the petals open, they may survive 20° to 23° F.

Table 3a. CRITICAL TEMPERATURES FOR PEACH BUDS (ELBERTA).
E. L. PROEBSTING, JR., WASH. STATE UNIV., PROSSER.

Bud Development Stage*	1	2	3	4	5	6	7
Old Standard Temp.[1]	23	—	—	25		27	30
Ave. Temp. for 90% Kill[2]	1	5	9	15	21	24	25
Ave. Temp. for 10% Kill[2]	18	21	23	25	26	27	28
Average Date (Prosser)[3]	3/7	3/16	3/19	3/29	4/3	4/11	4/18

*Stage 1 is first swelling; 4 is first pink and 7 is postbloom.

[1]Critical temperatures as previously published in WSU EM 1616.
[2]Average temperatures found by research at the WSU Research and Extension Center, Prosser, to result in 10% and 90% bud kill.
[3]Average date for this stage at the WSU Research and Extension Center, Prosser.

Winter injury is more a factor in weakening peach trees than most growers realize. Injury to roots due to extended periods of low temperature in the North may not appear for one or two years after the damage. Such injury tends to be greater in light sandy soils with no cover crop. Trees in weak condition seem to be the most susceptible to severe winters, whereas those receiving light to moderate applications of fertilizer are more hardy. Trees excessively vigorous late in the growing season, however, are tender.

Following are given comments for reducing loss from winter injury in Michigan, and, in whole or in part, are applicable to many other areas of similar climate.

1. Do not plant commercial peach orchards in areas where the temperature frequently drops below —12° F.

2. The peach site should have a moderately fertile well-drained soil with good elevation above surrounding country (except when near large bodies of water). Exceptionally fertile soils may be hazardous and should receive minimum fertilizer and cultivation.

3. Select varieties which are most hardy in fruit bud and wood.

4. Perform moderate to light pruning; avoid severe heavy pruning. Where peach canker disease is likely to be a problem, delay pruning until the first of March. *Do not prune in fall with trees in leaf.*

5. Apply fertilizers cautiously if the foliage has good color and the terminal growth on young trees is about 18 inches, and on old trees about 12 inches. If there is doubt as to how much fertilizer to apply, it is best to apply too little than too much. Peach trees making moderate growth live longer. Whitewash reduces winter trunk temperature fluctuations.

6. Start cultivation early in spring and stop early (late June or July) if the trees are young, or if the mature trees are not carrying a crop. Cultivation may continue for one to one and one-half months longer if the mature trees are carrying a good crop.

7. At the last cultivation sow a cover crop covering the soil area to the trunks to give root protection. Herbicide usage may preclude this.

8. Level the soil about the trunks to prevent water accumulation and ice formation next to the trunk.

9. Thin the fruit of healthy bearing trees to conserve tree vitality.

10. Keep the foliage in a healthy condition by proper spraying. Any insect or disease injury which damages the foliage weakens the trees.

TOP-WORKING AND BRIDGE-GRAFTING

It may be desirable to top-work peaches for the purpose of changing trees which did not come true to name, or, in an unusual case, when a pollinizer variety is needed. Peach varieties are compatible with one another. Top-working is usually done on the younger trees which have an abundance of small pencil-sized branches close to the center of the tree and fairly close to the ground. These branches may be top-worked by budding in late summer and cut back the following spring.

Rodents usually do not injure peaches except during extended periods when the ground is covered with snow. Methods and materials for bridge-grafting are given in Chapter VIII.

HARVESTING PEACHES

Because the first fresh peaches on the market bring good prices, there is a tendency among growers to flood the early market with immature peaches. Green, hard, starchy, shriveled peaches receive little or no demand, or, if bought, do not bring return sales and consequently the price often drops quickly. If the consumer were given his choice, he would prefer that the peach be removed from the tree at the peak of its color and quality. The grower, on the other hand, cannot afford to wait until the peach reaches this stage of ripeness because such peaches bruise easily, lose condition rapidly, and may result in considerable loss during the handling operations. The grower knows that firmness is a primary factor in safety of handling; the degree of firmness at which the peach should be harvested depends upon the variety, size of the crop to be handled, availability of hydrocooling, and refrigeration for holding and in shipment, and distance to the market.

Probably the best time to harvest peaches is just as the ground color is beginning to change to yellow for yellow-flesh peaches or to white for white-flesh peaches. Also, just prior to maturity, there is a swelling of the flattened sides of a peach. It is usually necesssary to pick the trees more than once during the harvesting season in order to attain the desired degree of ripeness. Some growers go over the trees "spot" picking two or three times, each time removing the fruits which are of first-grade size and color. Other growers may go over their trees five or ten times, removing only the largest, best-colored fruits and leaving the smaller ones to gain size and color before being picked. South Carolina tests show alar (N-dimethylamins succinamic acid) applied as post-bloom sprays and near pit hardening to cause accelerated maturity by 5 days and reduced pickings from 5 to 2, causing no adverse effects on under- or overcolor, soluble solids, pH, titratable acidity and soluble solids - acid ratio of fruit. Reduced pickings favors mechanical harvesting of peaches.

Where the fruit are to be shipped a long distance, the growers usually pick the fruit up to about a week before it would be ready to eat. This is under average weather conditions. If the weather has been cool and suddenly turns hot and muggy, ripening will be speeded up considerably. On the other hand, if weather has been hot and turns cool shortly before harvest, the ripening may be retarded.

The variety must be considered. Golden Jubilee for example, is of high quality but too soft and it is not well suited to shipment and should be sold locally. Elberta is adapted to long shipment but must be picked promptly at a certain stage of maturity to avoid loss from dropping. With a little experience with different varieties and different weather conditions, it is not so difficult to judge the proper stage of maturity with a fair degree of accuracy.

In commercial areas where peach orchards are located relatively close to the consumption centers, there is a trend toward picking the fruit at the firm-ripe stage, and using much greater care in packing and handling of the crop. Work at the Illinois Experiment Station has shown that if peaches are harvested when firm-ripe, which is around seven days later than many growers harvest peaches in Illinois and neighboring states, the size of the fruit, sugar content, and total yield can be increased considerably with little or no effect on keeping quality. Fruit picked firm-ripe and held in storage two weeks had good quality and better color and flavor than fruit picked somewhat immature. Such fruit sells easily with little waste. The results indicated that too early picking may result in sufficient loss of cash income to make the difference between operating the orchard at profit or a loss in good seasons.

Peaches are highly perishable and require the most careful handling to prevent cuts and bruises. Picking containers such as the metal one-half-bushel drop-bottom type should be padded and lined with canvas. The pickers must be cautioned beforehand on carefully filling and emptying the picking containers. Temperature is the most important factor affecting the ripening processes. Once peaches are removed from the tree they must be handled quickly and kept cool or as near to 32° F. as possible until they reach the consumer's table. Trucks and trailers for transporting peaches in the orchard or to the market should be equipped with rubber tires and springs to reduce jolting to a minimum.

Mechanical Harvesting, Bulk Handling. Increasing labor problems and costs have stimulated the development of mechanical harvesting equipment on the West Coast for processing clings and in the east for free-stones. Mechanical harvesters cost $25,000 to $40,000 each, and one harvester unit with a 3-man crew can harvest in California the tonnage of peaches that could be picked in a 9-hour day by a 20 to 25-man crew with ladders. Lower limbs must be removel so fruit can fall directly and uninjured to the padded catching frame. Under these conditions mechanically harvested firm peaches show no more defects when canned within 24 hours of harvest than do hand-picked fruit. A harvester consists of 2 parallel catching and separately operated frames which close under the tree. The fruit is shaken off the tree with a trunk shaker and all fruit is conveyed from the bottom of the catching frame conveyor belt to bulk bins of 1000-pound capacity. Usually sorting and sizing facilities are available on the frame, so only first-grade peaches reach the bin. All peaches are picked in a single pick. Those not wanted are dropped on the ground (Fig. 21).

In the East, an over-tree, single unit harvester (Fig. 21) developed by USDA and South Carolina agricultural engineers is used for freestones. A trunk shaker is mounted under the catching frame which closes under the tree. Trees must be pruned so fruit can fall directly to the catching frame. Firm peaches with 14-16 pounds pressure as measured by Taylor-Magness tester with 5/16 each tip are harvested.

Development in these fields is fast and similar to that for the apple; any detailed discussion here soon would be obsolete. The reader is referred to the references and also to the concurrent research of the agricultural engineering departments of California, Davis, and South Carolina, Clemson, with the USDA cooperating.

Pick-your-own-peaches. For peach orchards near population centers and where the manager enjoys dealing with many types of people, this system has worked with success. See Chapter X and its references for details; see also the Appendix and Index.

Yields. In California where trees are 15 feet high and 16-18 feet in diameter, production from 100 trees per acre averages 12-15 tons per acre for midseason freestones or canning clings. In the best orchards, some varieties in certain years will produce 30 tons/acre, but 20-25 tons/acre of processing peaches is common for the better orchards. With the lower trees in the humid east, yields are generally 400-800 bu/A depending upon many factors.

Split Pits. Any treatment or environment that favors fruit growth during the starting of pit hardening tends to increase split pits, namely (a) early excessive thinning of the fruit such as frost and immediate irrigation or rains, (b) girdling of tree limbs by wire, etc., (c) early maturing

Figure 21. This is the over-tree harvester for fresh peaches (canners too) developed by Clemson University and USDA. Canvas halves lift hydraulically between trees, then settle in place for the trunk shake, taking about a minute/tree. Fruit are collected from conveyor belt in bins and dropped behind harvester to be picked up by tractor lift, carried to truck at end of row. Lower photo shows Durand model built from above design and being perfected with grower help, government engineers. (Courtesy Bud Webb, Clemson University and Durand Machinery, Inc., LaGrange, Ga. 30420). See Plum Chapter for harvester being used in California for cling peaches, other fruit crops.

370

Figure 21a. (Upper left) This corrugated master carton holds 8 four-lb. consumer packs of molded pulp, plastic trays or other consumer packs for shipment to terminal market or local retail outlet. (Right) This 38-lb. corrugated fiberboard container can be passed through the hydrocooler, retaining stacking strength and insulating qualities in transport. Other types of 38-lb. corrugated containers are available, with or without stitching, gluing, or taping needs, two compartments for stacking strength for packing after bulk hydrocooling. (Lower) Corrugated container holding 3 trays of 20 fancy peaches each for retail trade. Trays can be stacked 3 deep on sales counter for display and sale by the pound. (Courtesy George A. Shuttleworth, New Jersey representative Fruit and produce Packaging Co., Indianapolis, Ind.)

of some varieties, (d) varieties in which pit hardening is relatively late as Elberta, Dixon, and Phillips Cling, and (e) excessive N.

PACKAGING

Selecting packages. In some areas, peaches are still sold in wood boxes of various sizes. One used is about 11-½ x 18 inches and 3-½ to

Figure 21b. This is a modern Georgia peach packing house. The bulk-bin line starts outside the extreme right door, goes into far room by conveyors, eventually entering room shown here. From the field, bulk bins are placed in cold storage first, then the steps are: (a) hydrocooling; (b) submerged in hydrofeeder; (c) over trash eliminator; (d) hydrobrusher to remove fuzz; (e) over a one-size belt roll for presizing; (f) preliminary hand sorting as elevated to waxing machine (using special Johnson wax, Recine, Wis.) to help preserve freshness; (g) hand sorted on roller table, rejecting culls; (h) thence down the 6-lane weight sizer shown in this photo, equipped with 3 sizing and one eliminator sections; (i) right line is packing in consumer trays which are placed on belt at hand height and carried to overwrap machines at extreme right; (j) thence to rotating accumulation table where they are hand packed in corrugated master cartons for refrigerated shipment to northern markets. This equipment also handles apples, plums, and nectarines. (Contact FMC, Lakeland, Fla. for modern equipment and packing house plans.)

six inches deep, in diagonal or offset rows, carefully sized 2 to 3 layers deep. One-half and one-bushel-baskets still can be found in limited use. Various size hampers or "peach baskets" are used for local trade, placing the fruit in brown paper bags after a sale.

The trend for shipping peaches is toward corrugated and fiberboard cartons and boxes, as described in Figures 21a and 21b. These are changing somewhat from year to year with perfection for specific needs.

Packing. Where peaches are raised in quantity, packing houses are essential. In the Southeast, these houses are located in the orchards or near railroad switches in order to reduce hauling. A two-story frame house with the top floor for containers and other storage space is typical. The lower floor is used for packing and is usually open on at least three sides with a covered driveway. The fruit is delivered at one side and moved across the house during the packing operation, eventually going into refrigerated railroad cars or trucks at the opposite side. The steps discussed and shown in Figure 21b cover fully the modern peach packing line. Some steps may be eliminated depending upon local needs.

Peaches in most of the states are packed under the United States grades, specifications for which can be secured from the Agricultural Marketing Service, U. S. Department of Agriculture in Washington. Peach growers should follow carefully the Federal specifications where possible in order to stabilize the market and provide a uniform and dependable basis for doing business.[1]

STORING PEACHES

Firm-ripe peaches which are not overgrown may be held in cold storage for two to four weeks at a storage temperature of from 30° to 32° F. and 85 per cent humidity. If peaches are held too long in cold storage, the fruit tends to lose flavor.

Time to remove peaches from storage is determined by the variety. J. H. Hale, if cooled promptly to 31°F can be held 3 to 4 weeks. Elberta, Redhaven and Golden Jubilee will hold 2 to 3 weeks. Tissues freeze at just below 30°F. Hence, it is risky to drop the temperature much below 31°F.

If peaches are harvested at the shipping stage (Elberta testing 10-14 lbs pressure with a 5/16-inch plunger with the Magness-Taylor tester on paired cheeks), they will become ripe in 2 to 4 days at 70-80°F. Ripening will proceed about as fast at 60° as at 70° or 80° and about half as fast at 50°. At 60° and above most peaches will ripen with good flavor, while if held at 50° for more than a week, the flavor may be poor. At 40° ripening is half as fast as at 50° and if held at 40° very long internal breakdown may occur. If held at 32 to 36° ripening is almost stopped, but if held at 36 to 50° for 10 days or more, internal breakdown, off-flavor and mealiness will occur. If held at 31 to 32°F peaches will hold up longer than at 32° to 36°, and they can be ripened at room temperature without loosing flavor.

CA Storage. Early USDA tests showed that Redhaven, Sunhigh and Loring peaches and the LeGrand nectarine can be stored successfully at 1 percent oxygen and 5 percent carbon dioxide. Fruits were juicer, had better flesh color and flavor and softened like freshly harvested peaches. It is likely that CA storage rooms will be used for peaches before the apple season starts but more study and experience is needed to perfect the practice.

SHIPPING PEACHES

In the U. S., e. g., Georgia begins the shipment of peaches to northern markets in May, followed by California, North Carolina, and Texas. The harvest season extends gradually northward until the peaches of Ohio, New York, and Michigan are marketed in September with a few late varieties available in October. Breeders are trying to spread the ripening season both ways with high color and flavored varieties.

---

[1]Contact your local governmental marketing agency for specifications on packaging and labeling for shipping peaches.

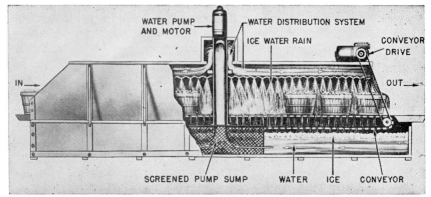

Figure 23. Diagram shows how a Stericooler or hydrocooler quick-cools peaches and sterilizes them with a fungicide in the bath to control brown rot. The same equipment can be used to quick-cool vegetables such as sweet corn. Chain stores and other large buyers of fresh peaches are beginning to request hydrocooled fruit, having experienced its better hold-up on the market counters.

The storage life of peaches may be increased several days by precooling to 30° to 32° F. before shipment; also, quick precooling requires less refrigeration in the long run because there is less heat of respiration developing from the fruit. Precooling of a perishable fruit such as peaches can be done with special hydrocooling machinery (Figure 23), or by portable or stationary mechanical refrigeration equipment. The portable equipment on trucks is driven alongside refrigeration cars, attached, and by a special system of ducts in the door, air throughout the car is circulated rapidly over the refrigeration coils. In the stationary precooling rooms more time is available for cooling than with the portable refrigeration on trucks. Thus, fruit loaded into the precooling rooms late in the afternoon at 75° F. require 24 to 30 hours to reach 32° F. Opposite walls of the rooms are provided with several windows through which cold air is moved rapidly into and through the fruit stacks. After precooling, peaches are loaded into refrigerated cars kept cool to destination by ice.

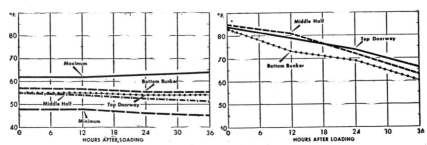

Figure 24. The charts show the effect of hydrocooling before loading (left) and no hydrocooling (right) on temperature of peaches in transit from South Carolina to the North. Shelf life of peaches can be increased by hydrocooling; also, the peaches can be harvested firm-ripe and of better eating quality. Where formerly dubious of "wet" peaches, buyers now are demanding hydrocooled fruit.

By precooling the temperature is reduced at the outset to a level which hardly could be attained by ice and salt after one or two weeks or more in transit. Also, less expense for icing in shipment is needed with precooling.

Mechanically refrigerated cars and trucks are more desirable because they provide better control of transit temperatures than do ice refrigerated vehicles which have almost disappeared.

Hydrocooling has been used for many years by the larger peach growers who ship in quantity. Temperature of field fruit can be reduced by about 24° F. in the range 68-84° F. by passing it through an ice or mechanical refrigerator and flood type machine. (Figure 23).

The charts in Figure 24 show the advantages of hydrocooling peaches. Respiration and tissue breakdown are slowed markedly. A fungicide is used in the dip to help reduce disease development. Request U. S. Dept. of Agr. Inform. Bull. 293, U. S. Gov. Print. Off., Wash., D. C. to help check the efficiency of your hydrocooler.

USDA tests indicate that peach rots can be reduced effectively by treating fruit in hot water at 130° F for 2 to 3 minutes. The technique is still under study. Benlate, botran and captan are effective against rots.

CANNING AND DRYING

Over 90 per cent of the canned peaches originate in California, principally the San Joaquin and Sacramento Valleys. The California fruit growers being far removed from large fresh fruit markets in the East, discovered early the merits of the clingstone peach for canning and increased this industry to a large scale. California produces practically all the dried peaches, except for a small amount from Washington. It also packs about half of the frozen peaches.

In California, the canning trade requests a fruit two and three-eighths inches or more in diameter for Grade 1; it must be firm, ripe, clean, and free from blemishes. Canners accept nothing but No. 1 fruit, except during periods of great demand. When canned, the fruit must be of a pleasing golden color, firm texture, and good quality.

Peaches for drying are picked when fully mature, though still reasonably firm. They are machine-cut about the suture with a knife, the pit removed, and the two halves laid on a clean tray with cut surfaces up. The full trays are treated with sulfur fumes for three to five hours, then exposed to the sun in the drying yard. Drying requires from two to six days until the fruit has a leathery texture. Total drying time varies, but 4 to 7 days is about an average. The fruit is then cleaned and sorted, and sweated in a storage building to equalize the moisture before delivery to the packer. The drying ratio varies from four to one for some varieties and from eight to one with others. Average yield of dried peaches is about one and one-half tons per acre. The market for dried peaches has been on a decline for 30 years.

peaches also have been dried. Common varieties are Fay Elberta and Lovell; clings are not dried.

In the East, there are several advantages in growing peaches for the canning trade which tempts the grower to enter the business. The Babygold series of cling peaches from New Jersey is being grown increasingly and processed for baby food. Freestones also are being canned and sold increasingly. Processors want fruit of good size and quality.

MARKETING PEACHES

The greater majority of the peach crop, whether processed or sold fresh, is marketed through co-operative organizations and regular marketing channels as described in Chapter XI. Still, however, there is a place for the independent grower/shipper who delivers a quality peach packed as the buyer desires it.

With the larger buyers (chain stores) becoming fewer (half dozen, e.g., on the East coast), the growers must group together to hold their price at a uniform and reasonable level rather than to remain independent and cut prices to each other's disadvantage. The ultimate answer to this situation may be for all growers in a general area, perhaps as much as a third of the country, to join together in a cooperative selling agency. It has been the experience in the area of New Jersey that cooperative selling agencies, although handling over a million bushels each of apples and peaches, and serving a great purpose in the industry, may cut each other on price in critical seasons.

Peaches must be handled fast with little delay. Some co-operatives in the East send their own representatives or agents to the large wholesale markets during the harvesting and marketing season to check the peaches on arrival and assist in routing them through the wholesale or auction channels. Chain store buyers in the field have been buying directly from growers in the New York City-Philadelphia area; these buyers may practically "sit" on the doorstep of growers of fine peaches to get first option on their crops. Near population centers a vast amount of fresh peaches are sold through roadside stands owned by growers or former growers who have decided to devote full time to roadside marketing and buy from other growers or sources.

Retail sales. Because of the perishable nature of peaches, there is often much dissatisfaction among retail chain stores and merchants because of waste due to excessive bruising in handling and shipment, to rotting, and to immature green peaches.

There is considerable difference of opinion in the trade about the proper type of containers for shipping firm-ripe fruit. The Illinois and Michigan Experiment Stations have shown that firm-ripe, well-colored peaches can be handled satisfactorily in shipment and retail stores with little or no bruising, and that they can be sold with much less difficulty at definitely

higher prices than the general run of immature green peaches. Merrill's results are typical. He used cell-type corrugated boxes to protect the firm-ripe peaches for distant shipment. Several thousand bushels were shipped to distant Michigan markets. The sales of these packages were followed and compared with the typical run of peaches sold in standard bushel baskets on the Michigan markets. There was a decided consumer preference for the fruit picked firm-ripe and shipped in the cell-type boxes. Reasons given by the consumers for buying peaches from these containers were either because of the greater degree of ripeness or the absence of bruises, or both. Bulk and pound sales were made from both the cell-type box and bushel basket. From the cell-type box in Store No. 1, 1368 pounds of fruit were sold in six consecutive days, whereas in the bushel basket, 858 pounds were sold. In Store No. 2, 3781 pounds of fruit were sold from the cell-type box and 1985 pounds from the bushel basket in 13 consecutive days.

Fruit shipped by bushel basket showed 31.3 per cent bruising, whereas fruit in cell-type boxes showed less than 0.1 per cent bruising. Amount of unsaleable fruit from the bushel baskets due to bruising was 5.4 per cent; in the cell-box, all fruits were saleable.

Cost of packing the box and basket was about the same; four minutes and ten seconds were required for facing, filling, and covering a bushel basket, and about four minutes were necessary for filling and completing two one-half-bushel cell-type corrugated boxes. It is indicated that the cell-type corrugated box when manufactured in large quantities can be purchased for about the same price as baskets of equal size.

Tray-packs are very popular peach containers because they are easy to pack, display the fruit well and are not too expensive to construct. Prepackaging peaches in small consumer packs has made good progress. Six peaches in a pulp tray covered with shrink film is popular[1].

At Clemson University an Information Filter Center, coordinated by a Filter Center Staff, gathers, condenses and distributes information sheets to buyers, brokers and growers, enabling them to predict crops and evaluate current situations affecting peach marketing in the eastern markets.

COST OF GROWING PEACHES

There are many factors influencing the cost of peach production, but yield per acre is undoubtedly the most important single factor; the higher the yield, the lower the cost of production per bushel. This was clearly shown in California in a cling peach district comprising 653 acres. The orchards were divided into two groups — high and low producing. Net profit of the high-producing orchards was over sixteen times greater than for low-producing orchards. The approximate man-hours required and

---

[1]Note: Commercial peach growers should support the National Peach Council by being members and attending annual meetings. Objective is to boost peach sales, primarily. Address: P.O. Box 1085 Martinsburg, W. Va. 25401.

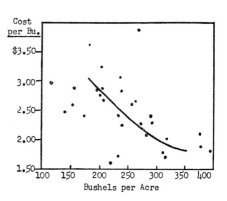

Rutgers University, New Jersey

Figure 26. It is evident from this chart that as the production of peaches per acre goes up, the production costs per bushel go down. Data are from 30 New Jersey commercial peach orchards averaging 25 acres each.

cost to do each job in an average Virginia peach orchard are given in Table 4. From the machine and man-hour data, up-to-date costs for doing the various jobs can be calculated on the basis of prevailing wages. Jobs requiring the most labor are pruning, thinning, and picking. Irrigation, where practiced, probably would rank fourth in labor required. The following practices were associated with high yields and good profits: frost-free sites, well-drained soils, suitable varieties, fertilizaton to get 10-12 inches terminal growth yearly, adequate annual pruning, economical brush disposal with chopper or pusher, adequate cultivation with cover crop to reduce erosion, adequate spray program, economical fruit thinning by pole method. Chemical thinning and use of mechanical tree shakers are reduce these costs as will careful picking, grading and packing to deliver a high-quality product.

Wilbur Yates, Indiana grower, reported at the National Peach Council Meeting that to establish a 101-acre peach orchard from 1953-55 inclusive, the first three years before bearing, cost $649.62 an acre, including land and tenant house. This cost can be adjusted to the current price level.

Figure 26 shows, as has been demonstrated in most cost-of-production figures, that with higher yields production costs go down. Table 5 gives cost-of-production figures for clings, California (1971); see appendix.

NECTARINES

Peaches and nectarines are quite similar in appearance of the trees, growth responses, bearing habits, and other general characteristics. The chief difference is that peaches have a fuzzy skin, while nectarines are fuzzless and smooth. Also, nectarines are usually smaller in size, have greater aroma, are, in general, less melting in flesh, less suited for shipment to distant markets, more skin and flesh cracking, and because of lack of fuzz are more susceptible to curculio and thrip damage. Breeders in recent years, however, have improved nectarine fruit quality and size markedly. Nectarines can be grown in almost all regions where peaches are grown, but in humid areas, they are more susceptible to brown rot. With great

378

	Man labor		Tractor		Material	Total Cost per acre
	Hrs.	Cost	Hrs.	Cost		
Fertilization	2	$ 1.20	1	$ 1.50	$ 5.00**	$ 7.70
Pruning and Brush Removal	30	18.00	2	3.00		21.00
Cultivation and Mowing	4	2.40	4	6.00		8.40
Spraying	8	4.80	4	16.00	18.00	38.80
Thinning	30	18.00				18.00
Picking and Hauling	56	33.60	6	9.00		42.60
Grading and Packing	16	9.60			75.00	84.60
Marketing and Hauling	6	3.60	2	3.00		6.60
Overhead, Interest, Misc.						33.00

Total Cost	$260.70
Value of Packed Fruit — 150 Bu./Acre at $2.20/Bu.***	$330.00

* Man labor at 60c/hour: tractor and attached equipment (except sprayer) at $1.50/hour; tractor and sprayer at $4.00/hour; packages and accessories at 50c/bu.
   Obviously, these figures give you only a relative estimate of costs. They can be adjusted according to the current price level.
** This covers nitrogen only; where 1000 lbs./A. of a 5-10-10 is used on sandy or infertile soils of low organic matter, this cost may be four to six times this figure.
*** This yield includes average to above-average producing orchards. The best orchards may yield considerably more bushels per acre, showing better profit.
   Note: Use of mechanical harvesting equipment should cut harvest costs markedly when perfected. Also, fruit thinning by chemicals or by tree shakers should cut this greatly over hand thinning.

improvement in fungicides and insecticides, brown rot, curculio, and thrip damage have been reduced to the point where nectarine growing is encouraging, for many customers will choose fresh nectarines over fresh peaches, if quality is about the same.

Origin of the nectarine is unknown, but its history goes back for 2000 years and merges into that of the peach. Genetically, the nectarine is an interesting phenomenon in horticulture. Peach trees may develop from nectarine seeds, and nectarine trees from peach seeds, or, peach trees may develop nectarines by bud sports and nectarine trees may develop peaches in a similar manner.

California is the largest commercial producer of nectarines, particularly in the southern San Joaquin Valley where large quantities of nectarines are shipped consisting mainly of the LeGrand series (May, Early Sun, Red, Late and Autumn Grand). Since Fred Anderson's (private breeder, Merced, Calif.) firm, yellow-flesh, commercial quality varieties were introduced the number of trees increased from 400,000 in 1950 to over 1,400,000 in 1971 in California, where over 90% of the U.S. crop is grown in hot dry summers favorable to nectarine quality. Most nectarines are sold fresh and a few are canned and dried. Nectarine production is on the increase in many peach states.

L. F. Hough of Rutgers University, New Jersey, has a number of large-fruited, good quality nectarine seedling crosses that look promising for the East, under the name Nectared Nos. 1 to 9.

YIELD — 16 TONS #1 FRUIT   109 TREES PER ACRE

Operation	Hours per Acre	Cash and Labor Cost per Acre				Total	% of Cash Cost
		Labor	Fuel and Repairs	Materials Kind and Quantity	Cost		
Cultural Costs							
Prune, $ .90 per tree		$ 98.10	$ 1.40			$ 99.50	12
Brush removal	2.0	3.80	3.40			7.20	
Wire and prop.	4.0	7.60	.25	Wire	$ 2.00	9.85	
Spray, 5X (2M)	5.0	10.38	9.63	Chemicals	65.00	85.01	10
Fertilizer		application $1.50 + 150 N @12c			19.50	19.50	
Thin, $1.60 per tree		174.40				174.40	21
Cultivate, 4X (2 ways)	4.0	9.00	6.00			15.00	
Ridge, 4X	.8	1.80	1.16			2.96	
Knock ridges	.4	.90	.58			1.48	
Irrigate, 6X	12.0	22.80	power to pump		9.75	32.55	4
Misc.	3.0	5.70	1.50			7.20	
TOTAL CULTURAL COSTS		$334.48	$23.92		$96.25	$454.65	55
Harvest Cost: Pick & Haul, 17 2/3 tons @ $14.00		$247.33				$247.33	
TOTAL HARVEST COSTS		$247.33				$247.33	30

Cash Overhead		
Misc., office, etc.		$ 42.11
Taxes		
Land, $1200 x 25% x 7% rate	=$21.00	
Trees, $1200 x 25% x 7% rate	= 21.00	
Equipment, $288 ÷ 2 x 25% x 7% rate	= 2.52	
Total	$44.52	44.52
Marketing order $2.25 per ton		36.00
TOTAL CASH OVERHEAD		$ 122.63
TOTAL CASH COST		$ 824.61
Management, 5% of 16 tons @ $75.00		$ 60.00 7

Investment	Per Acre	Annual Cost		
		Depreciation	Interest (7%)	
Land	$1200.00		$ 84.00	
Trees	1200.00	$ 85.71	42.00	
Irrigation system	110.00	5.50	3.85	
Buildings	75.00	3.00	2.63	
Equipment	288.00	28.81	10.12	
TOTAL	$2873.00	$123.02	$142.60	$ 265.62 32

TOTAL COST PER ACRE		$1150.23
Cost per ton	@ 16-ton yield	$ 71.89

For recommendations on the culture of nectarines, the reader is referred to the previous discussion on peaches, since, in general, cultural practices for nectarines are the same as for the peach.

Harvesting and handling nectarines. Nectarines are shipped primarily for dessert purposes. Gower and the New Zealand seedlings are outstanding for home canning, but being tender, they tend to fall apart more than peach varieties adapted to canning.

One and two-layer tray packs in wood or corrugated boxes are used for nectarines shipped fresh. Fruit sold locally is generally unpacked in various size lug boxes.

APRICOTS

The apricot probably came from western China while certain hardy strains known as Russian apricots came from Siberia. The apricot was brought to Rome about the time of Christ. Apricots were grown in Virginia as early as

Figure 27. This type tree trunk shaker is being used to thin peaches, nectarines and other fruits and nuts, taking only seconds per tree. It also is used with a catching frame to harvest stone fruits. The trunk clasp, as constructed, causes little or no injury to the trunk. (Courtesy Orchard Machinery Corp., Yuba City, California, 95991).

1720. The commercial culture of this fruit is limited largely to the semi-arid irrigated districts on the Pacific slope (Figure 28).

Based on the approximate available production data in the 1970s, the Soviet Union leads in apricot production, namely (000's metric tons) 450; USA, 170; Spain, 150; France, 110; Hungary, 100; Turkey, 80; and Italy, 70. Countries producing between 15-50,000 metric tons are Bulgaria, Romania, Yugoslavia, Czechoslovakia, No. and So. Africa, Argentina, Australia, Greece, Syria, Iran and Israel. China is a significant producer in the Liaoning, Shantung, and Hopei provinces but no production data are available. Natural forests of apricots can still be found near Lanchow in Kansu province.

New varieties (No. 6) from Michigan may encourage eastern plantings. Outlook in California which produces over 95% of the crop or 200,000 tons (Washington, 3%; Utah, 1%) is: plantings steady, concentrating in major districts; yields rising; production fluctuating; 75% going to cans; 20% dried; fresh sales down; exports and prices steady.

The most important varieties in California are Blenheim, Royal (the two varieties are so similar they have lost separate identities) and Tilton; in Washington, the large Early Montgamet and Wentachee Moorpark are grown; the Large Early Montgamet is the leading variety in Utah. Kernels of some varieties of apricots such as the Early Montgamet are almost as pleasant in flavor as almond kernels. All apricot varieties grown commercially in America are self-fruitful.

The open flowers of the apricot are about as resistant to spring frosts as the peach, but they are more likely to be killed because they tend to open earlier. For eastern conditions, Michigan's South Haven Nos. 6, 7, and 50 and the Curtis variety are the most promising. It appears that

F. P. Cullinan, U.S.D.A.

Figure 28. Apricots and peaches constitute important industries in California. Rows in this orchard are three miles long, with apricot trees in the foreground and peach trees in the background.

limited production may be possible for local fresh markets, where the best frost protection sites are used.

The total commercial crop of apricots tends to vary more in California from year to year than the peach crop, largely because the flowers and young fruits are very susceptible to brown and green rot in those regions where the blossoms are not killed by frost.

Rootstocks for commercial apricot plantings consist of peach, plum, and apricot seedling roots. Apricot roots seem to be better in sandy soils because of greater resistance to nematodes, although there are now available some nematode-resistant peach stocks which are used. Myrobalan plum rootstocks are used frequently for apricot trees grown on the heavier more impervious soils. In Michigan, the Manchurian and South Haven No. 6 apricots were best. Peach roots (Lovell and Nemagard) cause apricots to mature 3 days earlier than apricot roots.

Fruit thinning and pruning. Apricot fruits develop rapidly and ripen early in summer. Like the peach, the fruits have a period of retarded growth about the time the pit is hardening. The trees blossom and set fruit heavily, resulting in small size of the fruit at harvest. Since the practice of fruit thinning does not increase the size of apricot fruits to the extent that it does for peach, pruning is used to reduce the number of flower buds and fruit competition. Chemical blossom thinning with dinitro sprays can be used provided no Federal regulations are against DNOC. Spray when blossoms are 90% open. Recommended concentration for apricots is 1-½ to 2 pints of sodium dinitro ortho cresylate to 100 gallons of water for Blenheim and Tilton varieties; 1 pint per 100 gallons for Wenatchee Moorpark. The risk of overthinning may be lessened by reducing the concentration or by delaying the spray application until full bloom or 1 to 2 days thereafter. Hand thinned, the fruits are spaced 1½-2 inches apart. Chemicals on apricot have generally caused gumming and leaf drop. Thinning with trunk shakers or hand thinning with poles are the most common in California.

The apricot tree tends to develop large heavy branches, more so than the peach. Therefore, the modified-leader system of training, as described

for apples in Chapter IV, appears advisable, although the vase-form tree has proven satisfactory in most areas. Mature apricot trees are pruned somewhat less than peach trees, although more than the apple. The fruit is borne on short one-year spurs and largely toward the tip of last year's shoot growth. After the branch containing these spurs has borne fruit for about three years, they tend to die and the object of the pruning is to induce new growth in these areas for subsequent fruit production.

A. J. Schoendorf, California Fruit Exchange, Sacramento

Figure 29. Packing fresh apricots in California, showing empty box supply at top left; moving fruit supply belt below; the packers and the conveying equipment at right.

For young trees, pruning should be light and only sufficient for properly training the tree. For mature trees, it should be directed mainly at maintaining the proper height and width spread. Heavy pruning delays bearing and reduces yield. Mechanical topping of trees as for peach is used in California, with hand thinning of old wood inside the tree every third year to stimulate new wood.

Cultural systems for the apricot are similar to those for the peach, except that apricot trees appear to require somewhat less nitrogen. There is also some evidence to indicate that they will grow and produce with a lower supply of potassium. Excess sodium and chloride in some California soils cause leaf scorch and low yields. Coastal California N suggestions are: 50 lbs/A for Blenheims; Central Valley, 80 lbs; and for Tiltons, 120 lbs. Too much N results in green shoulders and uneven ripening on Blenheims and Royals, delaying ripening on all varieties. Heavy irrigation with contour basin checks has improved these orchards. Mechanized harvesting is used, but uneven maturity and problems in bin handling have limited its use.

ALMONDS

The almond probably came from western Asia. Leading countries are Italy, Spain, Iran, Morocco, Portugal, in order. Its culture in North America is limited to California; acreage has jumped to over 16 million trees. Production is under 200,000 tons. Yields may fall to half this figure in some years. The California varieties are from local seedlings of strains brought from southern Europe and northern Africa. The most extensively grown variety is the Nonpareil. Other varieties are Mission, and Ne Plus Ultra, Peerless, and Eureka. Kapareil is a promising new variety

Ramacher Mfg. Co., Nut Harvesting Equipment, Linden, Calif.

Figure 30. This type mechanical harvester with trailer for bulk handling of almonds is being used to cut labor costs in California. Note the smooth land preparation necessary before the trees are shaken.

developed by the USDA and the University of California. Thompson, Ballico and Merced are being widely planted.

Climatic adaptions. Commercial almond growing in California is limited to those areas where there is little or no frost hazard, due, in part, to an early blossoming characteristic of the almond. The almond is also susceptible to injury by rainy weather in spring and summer which increases blossom and fruit infection by brown and green rot organisms; rains in midwinter are apt to cause infection by a shot-hole disease, while foggy and rainy weather during the summer results in brown stains on the shells of the ripening nuts, lowering their market value.

Pollination. Important almond varieties in America are self-sterile; some are cross-incompatible. Pollination is almost entirely by insect activity, and in view of the fact that almonds blossom early while the weather is likely to be too cool for insect activity, it is necessary to interplant pollinizing varieties closely. In some orchards, every tree is adjacent to a pollinizing variety, whereas in other orchards, blocks of one variety may be four rows wide if the rows are no farther apart than 25 feet. Differences in time of blossoming tend to be wide among almond varieties. Therefore, the orchard should consist of more than two varieties, preferably three or four. Nonpareil, Ne Plus Ultra, and Mission are often interplanted for cross-pollination. Other combinations are: (a) Peerless, Nonpareil, Mission; (b) Ne Plus Ultra, Peerless, Nonpareil; (c) Davey, Nonpareil, Mission; (d) Ne Plus Ultra, Nonpareil, Davey; (e) Merced, Nonpareil, Mission (see California Leaflet 150 by Kester).

Rootstocks. Almond trees grow best on almond roots. According to

experienced growers, bitter almond stocks are slightly better than the sweet almond stocks. Almond trees on peach roots have been shorter-lived in California, especially on soils high in lime and sodium. Marianna $\overline{2}624$ stock is compatible with some varieties and tolerant of oak root fungus. Nemaguard roots are used where nematodes are a problem,

Cultural requirements. Almond orchards produce best on the lighter sandy types of soils. Although the almond is more resistant to dry soils than most other orchard trees, it shows definite response to standard summer irrigation on all soils. The almond has a high nitrogen requirement simliar to the peach. However, it will tolerate a lower available potassium content of the soil than prunes and apples and its zinc requirement seems to be a little lower than for most other fruits in California. The soil management program for the almond is similar to that of the peach in California. Chemical strip weed control is used.

Pruning. In general, almond trees are pruned lighter than peach trees, because more fruiting wood is necessary for a crop, and because almond growing is usually on a more narrow margin of profit. Most growers prune every second or third year only, because the benefits of pruning every year are usually not great enough to pay for the extra labor. Due to lighter pruning, almond trees tend to become large with long branches which may be very heavily loaded. For this reason, a modified-leader system of training seems best. Larger and fewer cuts are made on almond trees as compared with peaches. Cuts are made where the wood is three-quarters to one and one-half inches in diameter near a strong outward-growing lateral branch.

Yields and harvesting. Almond trees will bear some nuts the third or fourth year in the orchard, and by the eighth year will yield as much as 2000 pounds of nuts per acre. Yields of 3000 pounds or better per acre are occasionally reported but this is unusual. Fruit thinning is not practiced with almonds.

Harvesting starts when almonds in the shady portions of the tree show shriveling and cracking of the hulls. The usual sequence of events in the harvesting operation is to knock the almonds to the ground, usually with mechanical shakers or knockers; however, some growers are still using the rubber headed mallets. After several days of drying on the ground the almonds then are picked up with the hulls still attached to the shell. They are then run through the huller to remove the hulls; however, practically all of the shells remain intact. The nuts are then dried in almond dryers or dehydrators to the point where they can be broken without bending the kernel and then are delivered to the processing plants. At that point the almonds are either shelled if they are to be sold as kernels or bleached if they are to remain intact and sold as inshell almonds.

The land leveling preparation (Figure 30) which is found to be necessary in order to facilitate the use of pickup machines has resulted in some breakdown of the soil structure which impairs the infiltration of irrigation water and also causes a delay in harvesting, if there happens to be a few days of rain in the early fall when the crops are ready to be harvested. California workers have made considerable progress in solving this problem by adopting a non-tillage and strip weed control program for almond orchards. This seems to be an ideal soil management program where the irrigation water is applied by sprinklers. (See Meith and Rizzi.)

A small portion of the crop in California is harvested in early June at the time when the embryos first fill the seed coat. These more or less green kernels are a delicacy with some people. Hulls of soft-shell almonds are mixed with alfalfa and barley for livestock feed.

Review Questions

1. Compare peach production in California and in the eastern states.
2. Discuss the peach variety situation, in general, and under your local conditions.
3. Descrbe a good soil management program for young peach trees growing in a moderately fertile sandy loam soil.
4. Give a good soil management program for mature bearing peach trees growing in a moderately fertile medium-loam soil in your locality.
5. What system of training is employed for peach trees in your area? Compare with the training systems elsewhere.
6. What is meant by the "renewal system" of pruning bearing peach trees, and what is the purpose? Discuss mechanical "topping" of stone fruit trees.
7. Describe a fertilization program for a bearing peach orchard which is making 6 to 8 inches of thin terminal growth under a system of clear cultivation with a non-legume cover crop. The soil is moderate to low in fertility.
8. Prepare an orchard planting plan for a 10-acre peach orchard located on a 10 per cent slope within a few miles of a large city. Disposal of the crop will be through a roadside market and trucking to neighboring markets.
9. When is the proper time for picking peaches for (1) local sale, (2) truck shipment to large cities within a distance of 200 miles, and (3) shipment by railway several hundred miles? Discuss hydrocooling.
10. Discuss the various aspects and techniques of (a) hand, (b) club, (c) shaker, and (d) chemical fruit thinning of the peach.
11. Discuss mechanical harvesting of cling and freestone peaches.
12. How long can peaches be stored; factors involved? Discuss CA storage.
13. What type of peach does the customer prefer to buy based on survey experiments? Explain. Discuss modern peach sizing, grading and packaging.
14. Discuss costs of peach production and point out how the best profits can be made.
15. Discuss important precautions against winter injury to peach fruit buds.
16. How does a nectarine differ from a peach? What is the future of the nectarine?
17. In what ways does the apricot and its management differ from the peach?
18. How does the almond and its management and requirements differ from the peach?

Suggested Collateral Readings
Peach

Anderson, R. E., C. S. Parsons, and W. L. Smith, Jr. Controlled atmosphere storage of eastern-grown peaches and nectarines. USDA, ARS Marketing Res. Report No. 836, 19p. illus. 1969.

Banta, E. S. and F. S. Howlett. Pruning fruit trees. Ohio Agr. Ext. Serv. Bull. 313, 32 pp. 1962.

Bedford, C. L. and W. F. Robertson. Harvest maturity and ripening of peaches in relation to quality of the canned and frozen products. Mich. Agr. Exp. Sta. Tech. Bull. 245. 31 pp. 1955.

Bennett, A. H. et al. Hydrocooling peaches — management guide. USDA Ag. Inf. Bul. No. 293. 11 pp. 1965.

Blake, M. A. Classification of fruit bud development on peaches and nectarines and its significance in cultural practice. N. J. Agricultural Exp. Sta. Bull. 706. 1943.

Browne, P. and M. H. Gerdts. Rootknot nematodes in stone fruits. Calif Agr. Ext. Serv. Mimeo Rpt. (Fresno County) 1965.

Buchanan, D. W., C. B. Hall, R. H. Biggs, and F. W. Knapp. Influence of Alar, Ethrel, and Gibberellic acid on browning of peaches. HortSci. Vol. 4(4):302-303. 1969.

Bukovac, M. J. et al. Fruit thinning peaches with machines. Mich. Quart. Bul. 45:3 pp. 518-532. 1963.

Carlton, C. C. et al. Peach variety evaluation in central Alabama. Agr. Exp. Sta. Auburn Univer. Leaflet 72, 7 p. 1966.

Chandler, W. H. and D. S. Brown. Deciduous orchards in California winters. Calif. Ag. Ext. Cir. 179, 38 pp. 1951.

Childers, N. F. (Editor) Fruit Nutrition. Chap. on Peach Fertilization. Horticultural Publications, Rutgers University, New Brunswick, N. J. Sec. Ed. 1966.

Childers, N. F., L. Gene Albrigo and E. G. Christ. The Peach — varieties, culture, marketing and pest control. Summary Nat'l. Peach Conf., Rutgers Univ., New Brunswick, N. J. Mimeo, 281 pp. Revised 1973.

Claypool, L. L. et al. Split-Pit of 'Dixon' Cling peaches in relation to cultural factors. J. ASHS. Vol. 97, No. 2. March 1972. 181p.

Cline, R. A. and O. A. Bradt. Effects of several fertilizer and cultural treatments on growth, yield and leaf nutrient composition of peaches. Hort. Res. Inst. of Ontario. Report for 1969. p. 37-45.

Cowart, F. F. and E. F. Savage. The effect of nitrogen fertilization on yield and growth of Elberta peach trees. 16 pp. 1947.

Cooper, J. R. Factors that influence production, size, and quality of peaches. Ark. Agr. Exp. Sta. Bull. 547. 63 pp. 1955.

Craft, C. C. Evaluation of maturity indices based on pressure-test readings for eastern-grown peaches, 1954. U. S. Dept. of Agr. A. M. S. Mimeo. Rpt. 34, 8 pp. April 1955.

Cullinan, F. P. Improvement of stone fruits. U. S. Dept. of Agr. Yearbook Separate. 1588. 1937.

Culpepper, C. W., M. H. Haller, K. D. Demaree, and E. J. Koch. Effect of picking maturity and ripening temperature on the quality of canned and frozen peaches. U. S. Dept. of Agr. Tech. Bull. 1114: 32 pp. April 1955.

Edgerton, L. J. Studies on cold hardiness of peach trees. Cornell Bull. 958. 30 pp. 1960.

Emerson, F. H. Increasing peach bud hardiness with Alar. Ind. Hort. Soc. Transactions. pp. 29-33. 1966-67.

Erez, A., S. Lavee and R. M. Samish. Improved methods for breaking rest in the peach and other deciduous fruit species. J. ASHS Vol. 96, No. 4. July 1971. p. 519.

Erez, A. and S. Lavee. The effect of climatic conditions on dormancy development of peach buds. J. ASHS. Vol. 96, No. 6. November 1971. p. 711.

Faris, Edwin and A. Doyle Reed. When to replace cling peach trees. Calif. Ag. Ext. Serv. Circ. 512, 29 pp. 1962.

Feldstein, Joshua and N. F. Childers. Effect of irrigation on fruit size and yield of peaches in Pennsylvania. Amer. Soc. Hort. Sci. 87:145-153. 1965.

Fogle, H. W. et al. Peach production east of the Rocky Mountains. USDA Ag. Handbook 280, 70 pp. Revised 1973.

Fogle, H. W. and F. L. Overley. Winter hardiness of stone fruit varieties. Wash. Agr. Exp. Sta. Bull. 553: 20 pp. 1954. See also Bull. 576.

Forbus, W. R., Jr. Guide lines for peach packing houses. USDA-ARS 52-19, 31 pp, 1967.

Forbus, W. R. Handling peaches in pallet boxes. USDA-MRR. No. 875. pp. 1-18. April 1970.

Fridley, R. B. et al. Mechanization research of cling peach harvesting. Res. Prog. Rpt. Univ. of Calif., Davis, 31 pp. 1966.

(See additional references under Chapter XIV Appendix)

CHAPTER XV

Culture of Plums

◆ ◆

Plums are adapted more widely in the U. S. and world than almost any other deciduous fruit. This is because there are many species and varieties which are adapted to one or another of the different climatic and soil conditions. Plums will thrive where winters are cold and the summers hot, or where it is dry or the rainfall is heavy. For home use, they are suitable for most orchards throughout the temperate zone. But, commercially, their production is restricted to rather definite areas. In the United States this is largely on the Pacific coast.

In Europe, it is a question if plums rank first or second in importance among the deciduous tree fruits, whereas in the United States they are exceeded by apple, peach, and pear. In the eastern U. S., plums are grown largely for the local market, and with improved pesticides, there is a moderate increase in commercial plantings.

The approximate capacity of countries in plum and prune production in thousands of *metric* tons is given below for the early 1970s:

Country	Production	Country	Production
Yugoslavia	860,000	France	180,000
Rumania	760,000	Poland	150,000
Germany (FR)	520,000	Italy	140,000
USA	480,000	Austria	100,000
USSR	325,000	Turkey	100,000
Bulgaria	280,000	Czechoslovakia	100,000
Hungary	225,000	Japan	75,000

Other countries producing plums and prunes are: Mexico, Argentina, German Democratic Republic, Australia and New Zealand, Canada, most other countries in western Europe, South Africa, and limited acreage in North Africa, Chili, Israel, Lebanon and Taiwan. Plums in the Far East generally are of minor importance.

U. S. production of plums and prunes by leading states in thousands of tons is approximately: California—435; Oregon—25; Washington—15; Idaho—15; and Michigan—12. Fruit largely for local markets is produced

---

Dr. Claron O. Hesse and James A. Beutel, University of California, Davis, assisted in the revision of this Chapter.

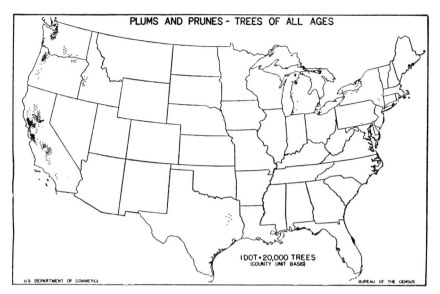

Figure 1. Distribution of bearing plum and prune trees in the United States. Commercial prune and plum growing is confined largely to the West Coast where over 85 per cent of the trees are located and about 93 per cent of the crop is produced. There has been a modest increase in home and some commercial plantings in the East, largely localized in Texas, Michigan, and New York. Total U. S. trees have been around 15.5 million.

in Texas and states bordering the Great Lakes on the south and east. Per capita consumption of plums and prunes has decreased appreciably since 1935. Fresh consumption dropped from 2.5 lbs. to 1.5, processed from 5.5 to about 2.5 lbs.

Prunes are produced in greater quantities than plums.[1] The four leading states in prune production are California, Washington, Oregon, and Idaho. Over three-fourths of the total crop is raised in California, mainly in the Sacramento Valley, central coastal valleys, and the San Joaquin Valley. In Idaho and Washington about ¾ of the crop is sold fresh with the balance canned; in Oregon 1/5 is dried and 1/3 canned with some frozen, but this varies widely from year to year. Michigan may can ½ the crop with some frozen.

Almost the entire commercial crop of plums is produced in California and Michigan. Michigan cans over half the crop with 300-900 tons frozen.

Plum trees in the U.S. have decreased from 35 million in 1925 to about 15 million in the 1970s, but production has been maintained at around 20 to 25 million bushels (56 lbs. bu.) due to improved practices and elimination of marginal trees.

---

[1] A prune is a plum which because of higher sugar content can be dried whole without fermentation at the pit. Growers in California who ship their fruit to canneries are known as plum growers, while those producing drying varieties are known as prune growers. Commercially, the prune is largely dried, but it is also canned and sold fresh. Plums are sold fresh, canned, or split and dried with the pit removed.

Figure 3. One of the largest centers of plum production in California is in the Sierra foothills. This district has developed because fruit ripens early, and there are good irrigation and transportation facilities. Trees are planted closer because soil is relatively shallow.

GROUPS OF PLUMS

Over 2000 varieties of plums, referable to some 15 species, have been grown in the United States. Few of these species and only a few of the varieties are important commercially; namely, *Prunus domestica* (European plums), *Prunus salicina* (Japanese plums), and hybrids of the latter.

European type. This is the most important group of plums in the United States. The plum is characterized by a moderately vigorous tree with thick leaves which are glossy dark green above and pale green with considerable pubescence beneath; the leaf edges are coarsely notched or sawtoothed. The fruit is borne largely on spurs, is variable in size, color, and shape, and the stone either clings to or separates from the flesh. Due to the rather wide variation of color, shape, and flesh characteristics of the fruit, the European plums have been divided into the following subgroups:

(A) Prune group is usually distinguished from the other European plums because they can be successfully dried without removal of the pit. It includes such popular varieties as French, Sugar, Italian, German, Imperial Epineuse, and all varieties of plums grown for drying.

(B) Reine Claude (Green Gage) group is characterized by more or less round fruit which has a very slight suture and of green, yellow, or slight red color. The flesh is sweet, tender, and juicy. Varieties include Reine Claude, Jefferson, and Washington which are important among canning varieties.

(C) Yellow Egg group is a comparatively small and relatively unimportant group which is desirable for canning only. Best known variety is Yellow Egg.

(D) Imperatrice group is a large group, including practically all of the blue plums. Chief fruit characteristics are blue, heavy bloom,[1] medium-size,

390

oval shape, firm flesh, and thick skin with only fair quality. Important varieties include Grand Duke, Diamond, Tragedy, and President.

(E) Lombard group is similar to the above group, except that the fruits are red in color instead of blue, probably of smaller size, and of somewhat lower quality. Varieties include Lombard, Bradshaw, and Pond.

Japanese type. Trees of the Japanese plums are early blooming and susceptible to frost. Many of the varieties are about as hardy to winter cold as the peach and can be grown under a wide range of conditions. Fruits of the Japanese varieties are quite variable but easily distinguished from other types of plums by their large size, oblate to heart - but rarely oblong - shape, and their bright yellow, red, or purplish-red color. Fruits are never blue. Flesh color is yellow, amber, or red in the so-called blood plums, juicy, and firm. The dessert quality ranges from fair to excellent, depending upon the variety. There is considerable variation in character of tree growth; some varieties are spreading in habit while others grow upright. The bark is rough, even when young; peach-like as compared to the smooth gray bark of European plums. Leaves are medium-sized, sharp-pointed, and nearly free of pubescence. The Japanese sorts are distinguished also by their abundant flowers which are produced three in a bud on many-budded spurs and on one-year shoots.

The American plums. Native to America, include several species used for fresh or culinary purposes, in breeding, or as a stock. A few of the more important are:

P. americana, Marsh. is native from Conn. to Montana, south to Fla., Tex., and Colo.; resistant to cold; varieties are Hawkeye, Wyant, DeSoto, Weaver, Terry.

P. hortulana, Bailey is thorny, bushy, more vigorous than the plum native farther south to Miss. Valley, less flavored, more resistant to brown rot, and makes good jellies and jams; varieties Golden Beauty, Wayland.

P. Munsoniana, Wight and Hedr., is resistant to spring frosts and fruit to brown rot; widely planted in lower Miss. Valley; variety Wild Goose.

P. Besseyi, Bailey, or "sand cherry," native Kansas to Manitoba, is used for hybridizing and as a dwarfing stock for stone fruits.

P. Maritima, Marsh. or "beach plum" grows well on beaches and sand dunes from Va. to N. Bruns., Canada, and is used in jams and jellies commercially.

P. subcordata, Benth., or Pacific plum is native and wild mostly in southwest Oregon and northwest California; is used in preserves and sauces, some eaten fresh.

Other plum types. In addition to the above species and types of plums, the following are worthy of mention because they: (a) are used as root-

---

[1] This refers to powdery film over skin, not to blossoming.

stocks for commercial varieties, (b) have desirable characteristics for hybridizing, or (c) are often found in home orchards.

The *Myrobalan* or cherry plum (*Prunus cerasifera*) is used widely as a rootstock for European and Japanese plums. Seedlings are hardy, vigorous, and tolerant of wet soil. Fruit of the Myrobalan tree is small, round or oval, yellow or red in color, and with rather insipid flesh. A form with red foliage is called *Pissardi*. The chief value of the fruit is the seed from which the seedling rootstocks are grown. Some selected types, as Myro 29C, are propagated from cuttings.

The *Simon* plum (*Prunus simoni*) has been used as a parent in the development of many so-called Japanese plums, e.g., Climax and Wickson.

Damson plums (*Prunus insititia*) are found occasionally in home orchards where the fruit is limited to culinary purposes because of its small size and sour or acid flavor. Trees resemble European plums but are smaller; they are hardy, productive, relatively free from diseases, require little care, and come nearly true from seed although varieties, as Frogmore and Shropshire, are known and are propagated by budding or grafting. St. Julien is a type whose seed is used for rootstocks.

CHOICE OF VARIETIES

The geographical region and varieties of plums selected will depend upon the proposed market outlet. If a distant grower intends to ship a large portion of his crop on a fresh basis, it is important that he plant not more than six or eight varieties of well-known shipping quality. Practically all miscellaneous sorts should be eliminated. The buying market is interested in obtaining large quantities of relatively few varieties, and not limited amounts of a large number of varieties. Many small shipments of from 10 to 20 boxes are undesirable and discriminated against by most big-scale buyers. In California, the early varieties give greater promise of satisfactory returns than most midseason or late sorts.

The following varieties are grown commercially for shipping in California and are listed for the most part according to peak sales, June to September (100,000 packages or more): *Early* — Beauty, Burmosa, Red Beaut, Santa Rosa (1/3 of acreage); *Midseason*—Wickson, Laroda, Eldorado, Nubiana; *Late* — Queen Ann, Late Santa Rosa, Kelsey, President, and Casselman. Many minor varieties are sold throughout the season.

The following varieties are used primarily for canning: Jefferson and Reine Claude (not commercial). The canning trade desires the large, firm, green or yellow plums. Large plums which are not smaller than 12 to a pound bring a premium as first-grade canning stock; plums not smaller than 20 to a pound are rated second class for canning. Varieties for drying are grown mainly in the Interior Valleys and near the Pacific Coast.

The Pacific Northwest does not compete with California in the plum crop. A premium exists, however, for earliness of prunes in the Milton-Freewater area, Oregon; Yakima, Washington and Payette, Idaho, where growers plant early strains of the Italian prune such as Richard's Early Italian and Milton Early Italian. In general, California meets only limited competition from plums grown in other states. However, the early varieties meet considerable competition in the eastern markets with Georgia peaches, and the midseason and later varieties come into competition with California Bartlett pears and with shipping prunes from the Pacific Northwest.

For drying, the French Prune (Prune D'Agen) accounts for over 90 per cent of the California acreage. Other important drying varieties are Imperial, Sugar, and Robe de Sergeant. Varieties for drying are grown mainly near the Pacific Coast and in the Sacramento Valley.

If the plums are to be sold at the roadside market or at local stores, plant a number of varieties ripening over several weeks. In the East, the only varieties grown commercially and usually on a relatively small scale are Italian and Stanley prune.

Other varieties suggested by the New York Experiment Station for trial for roadside market and local trade are, in the order of ripening: Early Laxton, Beauty, Formosa, Santa Rosa, California Blue, Clyman, Oullins, Utility, Washington, Prinlew, Yakima, Reine Claude, Albion, and French or Shropshire Damsons. Varieties recommended for home and market in Texas are America, Compass Cherry[1], Gold, Munson, Omaha, and Opata. Popular varieties in Missouri are Munson, Red June, Gold, Wild Goose, Green Gage, Shropshire Damson, Lombard, Omaha, French Damson, President, German Prune, and Italian Prune.

Contact your local governmental agency for local variety suggestions. Also, contact the Federal Plum Commodity Committee, 701 Fulton Ave., Sacramento, Ca. 95825, for color folder of key varieties and ann. rpts.

POLLINATION

European plums. European varieties of plums fall into either one of two groups, self-fruitful or self-unfruitful. It has been shown that about 30 per cent of the flowers will set fruit on self-fruitful varieties whether the flowers are cross- or self-pollinated; this is considered more than a sufficient set for a commercial crop. Flowers of the self-unfruitful varieties, however, set only about 1.5 per cent; this is insufficient for a commercial crop, necessitating interplanting with pollinizing varieties.

Among the self-fruitful varieties are the following: Agen, Bavay, California Blue, Coates 1418, Czar, Drap D'Or, Early Mirabelle, French Damson, German Prune, Giant, Goliath, King of the Damsons, Monarch, Ontario, Ouillins, Pershore, Purple Pershore, Sannoir, Shropshire Damson, Stanley, Sugar, Victoria, and Yellow Egg.

---

[1]Compass is a synonym.

Among the self-unfruitful varieties are: Altham, Allgrove's Superb, Anita, Arch Duke, Belgian Purple, Blue Rock, Bradshaw, Burton, Cambridge Gage, Clyman, Coe's Violet, Conquest, Crimson Drop, De Monfort, Diamond, Esperen, Frogmore Damson, Golden Drop, Grand Duke, Hall, Hand, Italian Prune,[1] Imperial Epineuse, Imperial Gage, Jefferson, Late Orange, Late Orleans, Miller Superb, McLaughin, Pond, President, Quackenboss, Reine Claude, Rivers' Early, Rivers' Early Prolific, Sergeant, Silver, Standard, Sultan, Tragedy, Transparent, and Washington.

Due to the fact that some of the above self-fruitful varieties apparently have different strains in different regions, or the same strains respond differently under varied environments, it is probably safer to interplant with at least one pollinizing variety. Varieties which tend to be variable include Italian Prune, Agen, Reine Claude, and German Prune, which may be self-fruitful in some regions. All varieties listed above in both groups, except for the variety Esperen, have good pollen for cross-pollination, if blooming seasons overlap sufficiently. Some combinations are cross-unfruitful because of close relationship. These include Golden Drop, Coe's Violet, and Allgrove's Superb. Another cross-incompatible group is Cambridge Gage, Late Orange, and President.

The European plums in the East usually overlap sufficiently in blooming periods to provide adequate cross-pollination. In some localities, however, Italian Prune and Imperial Epineuse may bloom too late for adequate cross-pollination by such early-blooming varieties as Reine Claude, Lombard, or Grand Duke. In this case, another late-blooming or midseason-blooming variety should provide cross-pollination for the late-blooming varieties.

European varieties grown in California, with the exception of Tragedy, fall into rather distinct groups with relation to season of blooming. Midseason-blooming varieties are Agen, Clyman, Grand Duke, Diamond, Quackenboss, Jefferson, Standard, Sugar, Imperial, and President. Late-blooming varieties are California Blue, Hungarian, Pond, Giant, Italian Prune, Yellow Egg, and Washington. In normal seasons, those varieties blooming after President are not cross-pollinated effectively by varieties of the early group. Tragedy, however, having a long blooming period, usually blooms along with several of the late-blooming Japanese varieties and extends into the blooming period of Grand Duke and Diamond.

Japanese plums. Most of the varieties in the Japanese group are self-unfruitful. These include Mariposa, Inca, Wickson, Eldorado, Queen Ann, Laroda, Formosa, Kelsey, Red Beaut, Redheart, Duarte, Gaviota, Elephant Heart, Becky Smith, and Burbank.

Although Redroy, Red Rosa (Late Santa Rosa), Santa Rosa, Climax, Beauty, Nubiana, and Methley produce more fruits from self-pollination than other Japanese plums, they also should be interplanted with pollinizers unless their local self-fruitfulness is established.

---

[1] Italian prune is self-fruitful in the Pacific Northwest.

Following varieties are not recommended for pollinizers because their pollen tends to be low in viability: Burmosa, Mariposa, Red Ace (Florida), Eldorado, Formosa, Gaviota, Red Beaut, and Kelsey. Shiro probably should be placed also in this classification. Varieties which are considered somewhat more dependable as pollinizers are Wickson, Laroda, Santa Rosa, Redheart, and Eleaphant Heart. Several cross-and inter-incompatible combinations are known. See Griggs and Hesse's Calif. Leaflet 163. Japanese plums bloom 3 to 4 weeks earlier than most European plums and are subject to frosts in northern latitudes where bee activity also may be restricted by cold weather at bloom.

European and native plum varieties as cross-pollinizers. European plum varieties are not consistently effective in pollinizing Japanese plum varieties. Fair to good sets on Japanese varieties have been obtained by cross-pollination from Clyman, Ouillins, Reine Claude, Victoria, and Yellow Egg. Tragedy is fairly effective for cross-pollination of Japanese varieties, but the reciprocal relationship is unfruitful. American species of plums (see below) which possess viable pollen have been found to be most effective as pollinizers for Japanese varieties.

American species and hybrid plums. The following varieties of the American species are self-unfruitful: *Prunus Americana:* De Sota, Hawkeye, Rollingstone, Wyant Var. Mollis, and Wolfe; *Prunus hortulana:* Wayland Var. mineri, Miner, and Surprise; *Prunus munsoniana:* Wild Goose and Newman; and *Prunus nigra:* Cheney. Some hybrids between American and Japanese species are self-unfruitful largely because of nonviable pollen; they include Red Wing, Monitor, Underwood, Elliott, La Crescent, Tonka, Radisson, and Fiebing; these varieties are obviously of no value as pollinizing varieties. The following varieties can be used for pollinizers, although they, too, contain considerable nonviable pollen: Assiniboin, Cheney, De Sota, Newman, Miner, Surprise, Rollingstone, Wyant, and Wolfe. The Surprise variety is the best single pollinizing variety for all the hybrids grown in the Mississippi Valley. Hybrids of the Sand Cherry *(Prunus besseyi)* produced by Hansen of North Dakota are also self-unfruitful, namely: Oka, Saca, Zumbra, and Compass. Compass can be used for a pollinizing variety, *P. subcordata* trees are self-unfruitful but the various selections or varieties are inter-fruitful.

Planting plans for plums. For pollination purposes, as a whole, it is recommended in plum plantings that at least every third tree in every third row be planted to a pollinizing variety. Two to six rows of a variety alternated with one or two pollenizer rows is desirable when both are important commercially and to facilitate use of mechanical equipment. About one strong beehive/A through the orchard is needed for pollination.

In California, trees planted 8x12 ft or 454 trees/A, cordon-trained, have yielded the 3rd, 4th, and 5th years approximately 2-½-3, 5-½-6, and 7½-16 tons/A, respectively. Yields of trees in standard orchards are 6-10 T/A. Labor/Ton was reduced markedly. Future plum orchards, like the pear, peach and apple, may be set in hedgerows. Most orchards, however, are planted on the square 18 x 22 ft., depending upon soil fertility and vigor of variety. Various types of hedgerow plantings with trees spaced 8 to 10 ft. in rows, 16 to 22 ft. apart, are under observation.

In milder climates as Mississippi, some varieties require less winter chilling for good bloom and set, including Methley, Santa Rosa, Bruce, America, and Starking Delicious (See Overcash).

ROOTSTOCKS FOR PLUMS

Plum varieties do not come true from seed. They are propagated by budding on seedlings in the nursery similar to peach propagation. The plum is grown mostly on plum stocks (Myrobalan). It can be grown on seedlings of peach, Japanese apricots and to some extent on almond. Seedlings are compatible with a variety of both Japanese and European plum varieties.

Myrobalan stock also is tolerant to poor soil aeration and is adapted to a wide range of soils. In California, it is not so inclined to produce suckers from the roots, but in some of the areas it may sucker badly. It is hardy, long-lived, and deep-rooted, although not particularly vigorous. It also gives very satisfactory results on deep comparatively dry soils. The brown color of the roots usually distinguishes the Myrobalan seedlings from other stocks used for plums. In Western Europe the St. Julien stock frequently is used in addition to *P. domestica* and *P. cerasifera* clones (not stolon propagated because of a virus transmission). *P. cerasifera divaricata* is used in Poland. Myrobalan, Marianna and Buck plums are used in Australia.

In California, selected nematode resistant stocks of Myrobalan (Myro 29C) and Marianna (also resistant to oak-root fungus) plums propagated vegetatively are among the preferred rootstocks for the standard variety plums.

In New York, the Myrobalan seedlings may show "chlorotic fleck," a leaf virus. These should be rogued. Stanley is particularly short-lived on "flect" seedlings. Japanese-American hybrids should be grafted on American plum seedlings. The Western Sand Cherry (*P. besseyi*) is a dwarfing stock for European plums such as Stanley and Italian. Japanese varieties are very small on this stock, making suitable home grounds trees.

Peach. In California, the nematode resistant stocks of peach (see Peach chapter) also have been gaining popularity as desirable stocks for plums.

About half the plum acreage is on peach except where soils are heavy, wet and oak-root fungus (*Armellaria melea*) exists. Possibly 50 per cent or more of the Italian prune trees in Idaho are on peach rootstocks.

Courtesy Ernest G. Christ,
Rutgers University

Figure 3a. A plum tree being early trained in Italy to the palmette system (eventual tree wall) with bamboo poles, tape or string and an upper wire (arrows). These are high-density plantings on standard stocks, managed from the ground and from wheeled scaffolds.

Apricot. Before the advent of rootknot nematode resistant plum and peach stocks, plums were budded on apricots because of high immunity to nematodes. However, apricot stock is not generally recommended because of frequent unsatisfactory unions between stock and cion. Some growers, however, have reported success.

Almond. Few commercial varieties of plums are propagated on almond stock, although some varieties can be grafted successfully, others cannot. The almond as a rootstock is suited chiefly to deep, light soils.

TOP-WORKING

There is often considerable interest in top-working plum trees to change the variety or to provide cross-pollination. There is a wide variation in compatibility among varieties of plums in top-working. Most Japanese varieties can be top-worked successfully on European varieties, but the reciprocal is not satisfactory. Do not top-work Italian prune on Damsons (latter carries dwarfing virus). See Calif. Cir. 34 by Allen for additional information, or contact the Pomology Dept. at Davis, Cailfornia. Plums can be top-worked on peach, other stocks suggested above.

PRUNING PLUMS

Young trees. One-year European trees are sold as unbranched whips; the two-year and one-year Japanese trees are branched. Whips can be trained best by the "deshooting system" as described for the apple in Chapter IV.

Subsequent training and pruning of these trees is similar to the plan outlined for the apple in the case of the modified leader system, or for the peach (Chapter XIV) in case of the open-center system. The open-center system of training has been common for most species of plums. Choice of a training system, however, should be governed by growth habit of the variety; those varieties that have a spreading habit, such as Burbank and many Japanese varieties, are perhaps better adapted to the open-center training system,

Figure 4. A Stanley prune tree trained to modified-leader system with the central trunk larger than any lateral branch. The five or six strong lateral branches have wide-angled crotches and are well spaced. European plums tend to form good framework naturally.

whereas those which grow upright, such as Stanley, Santa Rosa, and Wickson might be trained easier and better to the modified leader system. Generally, for Japanese varieties, 4 to 5 main scaffolds are developed plus a few more secondaries than on the peach in the open center system. Also, these trees produce many lateral shoots and water sprouts, necessitating much wood removal.

See Figure 3a for the palmette system. The hedgerow system developed less systematically and mechanically pruned and harvested as for the apple may be the future system in commercial plum and prune orchards.

With upright growing varieties special attention is necessary to cut the branches back to outward-growing branches to develop a more spreading tree. With the naturally spreading varieties, such as Burbank, it is necessary to cut back the branches which are growing straight out or downward to upward- and outward-growing branches. Most European varieties develop into well-shaped trees even if very little pruning is done (Figure 4). In general, plum trees require relatively little pruning while young.

Mature trees. The plum bears fruit laterally on one-year wood and on the vigorous spurs on older wood. It is important to encourage shoot growth of 10 to 24 inches on young trees and at least 10 inches on bearing trees. With trees making this much shoot growth, spur development also is encouraged and the productive capacity of the tree is increased considerably. Bearing Domestica plum trees are pruned lighter than the peach or apricot.

If the fruit will be dried, trees are pruned less than if it will be sold on the fresh market. After the trees have borne many crops, terminal growth may tend to become short and spur growth weak unless moderate pruning, fertilization, and good soil management have been practiced. With these trees, a thorough thinning out of the small thickly spurred branches is necessary; lower limbs and tops of main limbs also should be thinned out and headed back to vigorous laterals. Larger and fewer cuts are made on sugar prune trees, such as Agen and Imperial Epineuse, because it is less expensive and the margin of profit is usually too narrow to justify expensive practices on these varieties. Also, the branches tend to be brittle and break easily if allowed to become too long. About one-inch cuts are made back to laterals.

Prune the prune trees annually or, at least, bi-annually. Tree rejuvenation also can be done by thinning out thickly spurred branches.

Because of the tendency of many Japanese varieties to overbear, a heavier pruning is recommended on this group of plums than for most European varieties; amount of pruning is about the same as recommended for the peach. The Japanese varieties bear fruit laterally on one-year wood similar to the peach; they also bear laterally and heavily on spurs. Judicious pruning of these varieties will reduce materially the subsequent expense and need for hand thinning of the fruit. Japanese trees growing on the more shallow soils may require somewhat heavier cutting in order to reduce the size of the crop, but increase the individual size of the fruits. The varieties in California which tend to set a particularly heavy crop, and should be pruned somewhat heavier are Beauty, Nubiana and Wickson. Moderate pruning is required for Formosa, Queen Ann, Duarte, Gaviota, Eldorado, and Kelsey. On upright-growing varieties, it is important to thin the branches and the center top of the tree sufficiently to admit sunlight to the center and induce

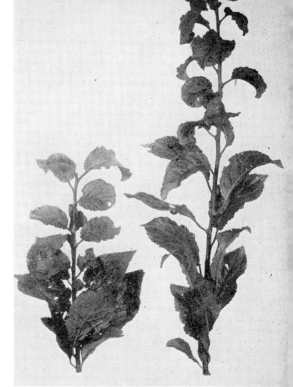

Michigan Agricultural Experiment Station

Figure 5. The effect of thinning a heavy crop of Lombard plums on size of fruit in Michigan (Bottom left) Twelve fruits from an unthinned tree. (Bottom right) Twelve fruits from a thinned tree. The effect of this thinning carried over to the following year in spite of crop failure the second year due to adverse weather. Note (top left) corresponding shoot from the tree which was unthinned the previous year, and (top right) shoot from the tree thinned the previous year.

more vigorous spur growth and better coloring of the fruit in this area.

In pruning both the young and mature trees, it is important to prune as little as possible to attain the desired results. Heavy pruning in any case should be avoided.

THINNING THE FRUIT

Thinning for fresh market is a must. Good fruit size is paramount for good prices. Hand thinning is delayed until after the so-called June drop. With plums, thinning not only increases the size and uniformity in color of the fruit, but also reduces or prevents breakage of the tree, maintains good vigor (Figure 5), reduces insect injury, reduces spread of brown rot just prior to harvest, and decreases the labor required for handling the crop during and after harvest.

Prune plums in California have been thinned chemically and successfully with 1½ pints of DN-289 or Elgetol 30 or 318, to 200 gallons of water. Size of fruit may be increased markedly, but sometimes at the expense of a lower yield. Better results may be accomplished when 70 to 80 per cent of the blossoms are open. Caution should be exercised against over-thinning. Varieties on which promising results have been obtained are: Beauty, Kelsey, Santa Rosa, Wickson, and certain of the Japanese varieties that have a biennial bearing tendency. Lower concentrations are needed for these plums than for apricots. Ethephon at 50 to 100 ppm 3 wks after bloom is showing promise as a thinner. Trunk shaking or poleing, followed by hand thinning to the desired tree load is the common practice. A saving of $1-4/tree has been reported by using hand-held pneumatic driven shaker rods from a moving platform. See your farm adviser and the Appendix (trunk shaking and fruit thinning cost).

Although rather heavy pruning is practiced with varieties which tend to set fruit heavily, it is usually desirable to supplement this pruning by fruit thinning. European varieties will usually attain better size in clusters than the Japanese and, thus, are thinned less heavily. In favorable years for heavy production by Japanese varieties, they tend to set so many fruits that they are unable to size properly. Japanese varieties are probably thinned heavier than any other deciduous fruit.

In order to secure large uniform well-colored fruit, plums usually require a thinning of from one to three inches apart when mature, with the heavier thinning being recommended for the Japanese varieties. Burbank tends to set very heavy crops and requires relatively heavy thinning. Beauty probably demands the heaviest thinning of any. The varieties Santa Rosa and Climax tend to thin themselves as the fruit develops, and fruit thinning where necessary is usually light. In sections of the country where strong winds are likely to occur while the crop is maturing, the thinning may be much lighter than otherwise.

SOIL MANAGEMENT

The same soil management systems as outlined for the young and bearing peach trees in the previous chapter will apply for the young and bearing plum trees. However, plum trees tend to perform somewhat better under sod

A. J. Heinicke, Cornell University

Figure 6. Cultivated plum trees in New York on medium-heavy soil showed little or no response to applications of sodium nitrate. Trees in sod, however, which received 900, 900, and 1800 pounds per acre of sodium nitrate in successive years showed response to nitrogen but averaged only two-thirds as large as those on the cultivated plots. (Far left) cultivated; (middle left) cultivated with nitrate of soda; (middle right) timothy-rye sod with nitrate of soda; and (far right) timothy-rye sod without nitrogen fertilization.

or sod mulch than the peach. They withstand neglect and, thus, do well in home grounds. The future commercial management system likely will be herbicides in the row, sod middles of fescue, and irrigation when needed.

Fertilization. Plum trees planted on the heavier types of soil, in general, do not show the response to fertilizer applications that most deciduous trees exhibit. Where cultivation or herbicides in the row are used, the need for nitrogen is reduced, as indicated in Figure 6. Plum trees growing in sod without nitrogen fertilization definitely are dwarfed as compared with those in sod receiving nitrogen. Plum trees will respond well to a system of sod-mulch plus additional mulch, although there may be increased difficulty from curculio with this system in eastern orchards.

Leaf analysis is being used to determine fertilizer needs, particularly where a nutritional problem exists. Approximate nutrient contents of leaves by standard analysis are: N, 1.80-2.10; P, 0.14-0.25; K, 1.50-2.50; Mg, 0.18; Ca, 2.00-4.00; S, 125-175 ppm; Mn, 53-93 ppm; B, 33-50 ppm; Zn, 25-50 ppm; Cu, 7-10 ppm; Fe, 50-100 ppm; Mo, 0.7-1.0 ppm. Ammonium sulfate, nitrate of soda (not in arid regions), ammonium nitrate, or potassium nitrate should give good response. In California the usual

M. E. McCollam, American Potash Institute, San Jose

Figure 7. Potassium deficiency is shown on Agen prune in the Sacramento Valley of California in the Northern Interior section. Note poor foliar development, scortching and dieback in the top.

rate of application is from one to two pounds of ammonium sulfate for trees two to five years of age and from four to six pounds for bearing trees. The fertilizer is spread evenly over the ground surface under the branches and during the dormant season. Trees in a sod system may require double or triple the N for cultivated or herbicide-treated plantings. A 10-10-10 mix frequently is used in humid areas, liming to pH 6.0-6.5.

Boron deficiency in California causes dry hard pockets in the fruit flesh and may be corrected by a half-pound application of borax about every third year to a mature tree. Avoid areas where B is high in the soil or irrigation water.

Copper deficiency in South Africa has been described to cause interveinal chlorosis or complete yellowing of young leaves and necrotic spotting between veins of old leaves. Soil applications of 1-2 pounds copper sulphate per tree may correct the trouble in one to two years. "Little leaf" or zinc deficiency is prevalent in some sections of the world and is corrected by dormant sprays of zinc sulphate (36 per cent) before the buds break in spring, using 10 to 18 pounds per 100 gallons, depending upon severity of deficiency. Annual applications may be necessary. Potassium (Fig. 7) and magnesium deficiencies have been reported both in humid and arid regions. Potassium shortage in arid areas may necessitate heavy applications of 25-50 lbs/tree sulphate of potash every three years, plus heavy pruning and thinning to secure good growth.

Irrigation. Irrigation is practiced only rarely in the East or in some counties along the west coast of California. In the largest plum producing sections of the West, however, irrigation is a necessary practice. It may be done by furrows, portable pipe, or basin flooding. Application of water by the furrow system in California varies from a 24-hour application every 12 to 14 days in some sections to a 72-hour application only two or three times a season in other regions, depending chiefly upon soil type and topography. Sprinkler irrigation is now the commonest method of water application in arid and humid regions. Total water applied in the entire season varies from 15 to 36 acre inches. A 5/32-9/64-inch nozzle is best on clay loams and a 1/8-7/64-inch nozzle on heavy clay loams to avoid compaction and get better penetration. Actually, strip-row herbicides + sod middles is good management where heavy orchard machinery is used on level land. On the sloping Sierra foothills sprinklers with sod culture are used to cut erosion. Trickle irrigation at tree bases by in-row plastic pipe shows promise where water is limited and/or expensive.

The soil about the tree roots should be kept moist and this can be determined by using a soil auger at weekly intervals during periods of drought. Trees should never be allowed to show signs of foliage wilting before irrigating. Where a deep-rooted alfalfa cover crop is used, special attention is necessary to see that the trees do not suffer from water deficiency through severe competition with the alfalfa.

RESISTANCE TO FROST AND WINTER INJURY

The average variety of European plum is about as resistant to cold as the Winesap or Baldwin apple. Lombard trees may be a little more resistant. Resistance to cold of flower buds varies considerably, with some less and others more resistant than apple flower buds.

Trees of the Japanese varieties may vary in cold resistance from the Kelsey, which is less resistant than peach trees, to Burbank, Abundance, and First which may be almost as resistant as European plums. Under good care, the flower buds of Japanese varieties are about as resistant as European plums. However, if the trees are in poor condition, the buds may be more

BUD KILL OF ITALIAN AND EARLY ITALIAN PRUNES AS RELATED TO TEMPERATURES
AND BUD DEVELOPMENT
(E. L. PROEBSTING, JR., WASHINGTON STATE EXP. STA. PROSSER).

Bud Development Stage	First Swelling	Side White	Tip Green	Tight Cluster	First White	First Bloom	Full Bloom	Post Bloom
Old Standard Temp.	-	-	-	-	23	27	27	30
Ave. Temp. 10% Kill	14	17	20	24	26	27	28	28
Ave. Temp. 90% Kill	0	3	7	16	22	23	23	23
Averge Date (Prosser)	3/13	3/20	3/27	4/3	4/8	4/12	4/16	4/23

Obtain color bud development chart from Wash. State Exp. Sta., Prosser.

tender than peach buds. Most flowers of Japanese plums are somewhat more resistant to cold than apple flowers and the young fruits appear to be at least

403

as resistant as apple fruits of the same age. However, with Japanese varieties, the flower buds tend to open much earlier than apple flowers and are, therefore, more likely to be killed by the late spring frosts.

After relatively warm winters in California, some varieties of European plums, such as President, may be very slow to begin growth and many flower buds may be abscissed. On the other hand, trees of some varieties, such as Tragedy, may not be delayed to any extent. Chilling requirements of the Japanese plums, except for Climax, are considerably less than that for most varieties of European plums. After warm winters when President shows considerable injury, trees of Japanese varieties also may be delayed in starting, but, except for Climax, not enough to prevent their making good growth and setting a fair crop of fruit.

Prunus nigra, the Canada plum, is one of the most hardy to winter cold of the deciduous fruits grown in North America.

HARVESTING

The stage of maturity at which plums should be picked depends upon how they are to be utilized. For local trade, roadside markets, and for canning, it is best to pick plums when they are well colored and firm-ripe. For jams and jellies the fruit should be fully ripe when picked. For long-distance shipping, plums must be hard and the early varieties should be only partially colored. They should arrive at wholesale buyers or jobbers before fully ripe, and thence, at retailers' stands in good, firm-ripe attractive condition. Temperature at which the fruit is handled is the most important factor governing rate of ripening.

Most varieties of plums undergo rather marked changes in color within a period of about ten days to several weeks before becoming fully mature. Although these changes are gradual, they may be divided into several more or less distinct stages. With the Japanese varieties, the earliest stage occurs when the green of the stilar-tip changes to a lightish or yellowish green; this stage is often spoken of as "breaking." With most varieties, this yellowish green changes to a more decided yellow or straw yellow, after which the plums gradually assume their characteristic yellow or red. Commercially, the fruits are described as "straw tip," "slight color," "red tip," "three-fourths red," etc. With the blue or purple varieties, the color changes proceed from green, to greenish-blue, or reddish-purple, followed by dark blue or purple.

Color changes are especially noticeable and, therefore, have been considered one of the main indices for maturity. As the color increases, there is normally a softening of the flesh. The firmness of the fruit when picked is the best correlation with the way the fruit will hold up in transit. In California, a combination color-and-firmness-of-flesh standard has been suggested for a few of the leading plum varieties, as shown in Table 1.

The above table shows that plums can be picked somewhat more mature if they are to be shipped under precooled conditions. If the fruit will be

TABLE 1
Picking Conditions for Plums (Does Not Apply to Prunes), Based Upon Temperatures in Transit in the Upper Half of Refrigerator Cars
(Adapted from Allen)

Variety	When Shipped Standard Refrigeration		When Precooled and Shipped	
	Color Range	Pressure Test[1] Range (Pounds)	Color Range	Pressure Test[1] Range (Pounds)
Beauty ..	Straw tip to trace pink tip	13— 9	Pink tip to ½ red	8— 6
Formosa	Straw tip to trace pink tip	13— 9	Pink tip to ½ red	8— 6
Climax ..	Straw to pink tip	18—13	¼ to ½ red	12— 8
Santa Rosa	Trace red to ½ light red	18—12	½ to full light red	12— 9
Burbank .	Straw tip to full straw slight red	20—14	Yellow to ¼ red	13— 8
Wickson .	Straw tip to yellow tip	15—12	½ to ⅔ yellow	11— 8
Duarte ..	⅓ to ¾ light red	15—11	Full light to medium red	10— 8
Diamond	Trace to ¾ light blue	10—15	Full light to medium blue	14—10
Giant ...	¼ to ¾ light red	16—11	Full light red	10— 8
President	½ to full light blue	16—11	Full blue	10— 7

[1]The figures given in this column refer to the number of pounds pressure required to force the plunger point of a fruit pressure tester 7/16-inch in diameter into the flesh of the fruit 5/16-inch in depth. The pressure tester is described in U. S. Dept. of Agr. Cir. 627, "Fruit pressure testers and their practical applications" by M. H. Haller. 1941.

shipped under standard refrigeration, it is best to place the more mature fruit at the base of the car where the temperature is 8° to 10° cooler. The later maturing firm-fleshed European varieties may be allowed to become more mature than the earlier more juicy thin-skinned varieties. Canning factories usually specify that the fruit for canning must be firm-ripe, and with maximum sugar content.

It is usually necessary to pick the trees from two to three times due to the fact that most varieties do not ripen uniformly. Commercially, the tendency is to rush the first picking of the earlier varieties, allowing some of the midseason varieties to become slightly overripe. The fruit should be picked slightly firmer and with less color as the season advances.

Mechanical devices have been developed for harvesting prunes and plums (Fig. 8).

Yields. In Eastern orchards, a mature plum orchard may yield between three and five tons per acre or one to one and a half bushels to a tree. Prune trees yield somewhat more than plum trees, or two to three bushels per tree. Japanese varieties bear at from three to five years of age, while the Domestica varieties bear about two years later. Native American plums require a somewhat longer period to come into bearing.

The trees tend to come into bearing earlier on the Pacific coast and yield

Figure 8. (Upper Left). Two parallel individually operated catching frames, one with a trunk shaker, are run along the tree row, "hitched," and the tree shaken as above in California's Sacramento Valley area. Prunes, largely French for drying, are conveyed to carrier behind (upper right). Bins carry the fruit to washer, grader, sugar testing, hot water dip, prickle-board, thence dried on trays in ovens at a temperature up to 165°F (lower right), or sun-dried for 3 to 5 days.

much larger crops. The average yield per acre in California runs six to 10 tons per acre. High density orchards may reach 16 or more tons.

Picking and handling methods. Special precautions should be taken to remove shipping plums with stems intact and to avoid breaking the skin. Due to the perishable nature of plums, they must be handled with extreme care. In filling the picking receptacle and sizing, grading, and packing, it is important to preserve as much of the bloom on the skin surface as possible. Keep the fruit in the shade of the trees immediately after picking. Handle the fruit from tree to storage with little or no delay. Plums may be transported from the orchard to the packing shed in either picking baskets or in pails, boxes or bins; the fruit receives one less handling when picking baskets or pails are used.

Picking for distant shipment should be done early in the day and the fruit taken immediately to the packing shed, or, picking can be done in late afternoon and the fruit left in the orchard to cool overnight. If the plums are to be used in canning, they are handled mostly in lug boxes or bins with somewhat less care.

For prunes several weeks are required for harvest in the coastal areas of California, where fruit matures slowly with ripe fruit dropping while immature fruit is still on the tree.

In interior valleys, harvest is a once-over operation, and begins about a week after sampling shows that chlorophyll has disappeared from the flesh and skin and under most conditions should permit completion of

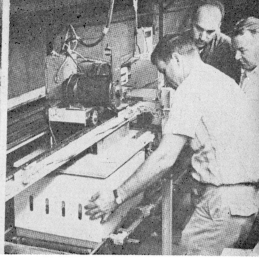

Figure 10. (Left) Partial view of Santa Rosa plums in a vibrated "tight-fill" fiberboard contained as they arrived in New York City from California. Injury was equal to or less than hand or conventionally packed fruit. Note bloom intact. (Right) Fruit was settled into permanent position by vibrating machine, as used for pears, before shipment.

harvest before the flesh color has darkened seriously, exclusive of periods of heat above 100° F. (Claypool and Kilbuck).

Flesh firmness at 3 to 5 pounds may be an aid to color index as to when to start harvest, but the soluble solids is a better index. When the crop is of normal size or less, harvest may start when soluble solids attain 24 per cent. If the crop is heavy, s.s. may not reach 20 per cent while the fruit

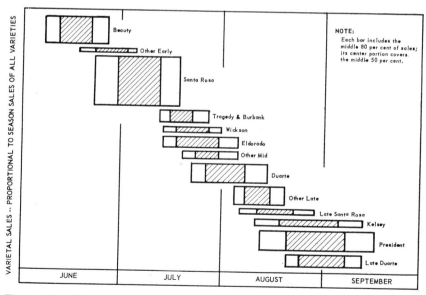

Figure 10a. Varietal plum marketing periods on the New York market. A bar includes 80% of sales with cross-hatched area covering mid 50% of sales (University of Calif., Davis).

407

is turgid, and thus the s.s. index is of little value, according to Claypool and Kilbuck.

Where dehydrating, rather than sun-drying is used, the natural toughness of the skin, particularly in French prunes, is a problem. Investigations are under way to determine the cause of toughness and how to correct it.

About 2-½ to 3 pounds of fresh prunes are required to give one pound of dried fruit; sugar content is probably the most important factor affecting the drying ratio. Machine-pitted dried prunes store better with improved quality.

PACKING[1]

Although some of the large growers in California individually pack their own fruit, there is a strong tendency toward community packing. Plum sizing is done mechanically by weight or by size (minimum dimension). The fruit is sorted into one or two grades by maturity, color, and blemishes according to the requirements of the U.S. Standard or the particular state standards. These qualifications usually are established by the growers themselves in order to protect and maintain a standard and quality of fruits from a given state or region. Some growers and packing concerns have been exceeding the minimum requirements of the standard law

Goodloe Barry, U.S.D.A.

Figure 11. Research is underway to improve fiberboard boxes for shipment of plums because they are easier to pack and less expensive than the four-basket crates. An indented pad in the bottom into which plums fit help position the plums. Upper: The face tray has been removed to show orderly fill. Note cut-down sides which give the box a full appearance after shipment shake-down of plums.

by issuing an extra fancy grade. Returns from this higher grade usually have been justified, especially during heavy crop years.

Containers. In the East, plums are often sold locally in Climax baskets

---

[1] A bushel of plums weighs about 56 lbs. net.

of the four- and twelve-quart size. One-half and one bushel tub baskets also are used. Small plums may be shipped in berry crates.

Plums shipped from California are packed in four-basket crates, fiberboard cartons, or peach boxes for larger sizes. The standard four-basket crates are from four to five inches deep with two or three layers, depending upon the size of the fruit; the count may range from 112 to 340 fruits per crate. This crate holds four three-quart till baskets and is 16 inches wide and 16⅛ inches long. Each basket may be sold as a separate unit in the retail trade. Peach boxes as described in Chapter XIV also are used with the standard packs.

Fiberboard containers are the standard shipping container because they are less expensive, require less packing labor, and afford savings in loading, and costs of rail shipments. One popular type is a two-piece full telescope box with roll ends which fold into place (see Figure 11).

Changes in packing equipment are needed for the random-fill fiberboard containers, machine vibrated and settled before shipment (Figure 10.) Costs are reduced appreciably. The "tight-fill" packs require careful grading, sizing, weighing, top padding, and lid fastening under some pressure. This packaging is increasing in popularity.

A cooling experiment by the California Experiment Station with 25-lb. fiberboard boxes of plums showed that the rate of cooling was speeded up by use of a 3 cu. ft. per minute cold air blast. The fiberboard boxes with open hand holes required about one-third longer to cool than the standard 4-basket crate or field lug; if poly liners were used in the fiberboard boxes, two and one-half times longer to cool was required. Fruit in the center of the box took the longest to cool.

Corrugated and fiberboard containers vary too much in size and content. Attempts are being made to meet the needs of handling for shipment, export and store movement with as few standardized containers as feasible for all fresh fruits.

Marking. Each container is marked on the outside with the name and address of the orchard, the packer, the variety, net weight, and approximate number of fruits (within four of the true count in California) in the container or the subcontainer.

Transporting. In transporting plums from the packing house to the shipping point, place each box squarely on top of the box below. The boxes should be stacked firmly so that there will be no possibility of shifting. A light canvas over the top of the load will protect the fruit from sun and dust. Hauling by truck to local markets is done largely during the cool night hours.

STORAGE

Fruit of most varieties of Domestica plums can be held from two to four weeks at 30° to 32° F. during floods on the market. At higher temperatures of 37° to 50° F., which is usually the temperature range in a refrigerator car, plums will not keep so long. Fruit of certain varieties, such as Tragedy, Grand Duke, and President, will keep for nine weeks if they are harvested when full-grown and somewhat sweet, and held at a temperature of 30° to 32° F. If harvested greener, they may show various injuries at these temperatures; better flavor is obtained if plums are held at the higher temperatures of 37° to 50°F. Plums in storage and/or shipment may show jellying and/or internal browning which are slowed at 33°-34°F. Idaho research shows *internal browning* on the standard Italian prune to be reduced by fewer irrigations, avoiding any compression of the fruit, using sprays of GA (gibberellic acid), and with high N and high light intensity (latter controls skin color, as does storage temperatures — 33-38°F no increases; 43-49°F, increases).

Natural modification of storage atmosphere by use of sealed 1.5 ml poly box liners by USDA in California has provided a favorable environment for Nubiana plums at 32-34°F. The enclosed atmosphere of an average of 7.8% CO_2 and 11% O_2 reduced fruit decay, softening and loss of soluble solids up to 10 weeks. The longer the storage period, the greater the beneficial effects. Eldorado plums respond similarly but Santa Rosa was injured, indicating need for tests with each variety.

SHIPPING PLUMS

Most West Coast plums have been shipped to the East. With increased population in the West Coast, it appears that relatively more will be sold fresh on local markets early in the season before other fruits become plentiful.

Precooling of fruit to 40°F. before loading the rail car is highly desirable. By this system, it requires from 20 to 24 hrs. Fruit is precooled in a special room or cold storage before loaded in refrigerator cars. If precooling is to be most efficient, fruit temperatures in the center of the packages should be reduced to 40° F. or below.

Many refrigerator cars are equipped with blower fans under the floorboards of the bunkers. These fans can be driven for precooling by motors attached outside the car, or they can be operated while the car is in motion by a friction wheel against the car wheel. Precooling is now generally used on California.

In California shipping plums must meet the requirements for U.S. No. 1 Grade to be eligible for inter- or intra-state shipment. In addition, a minimum size standard is applied to each variety, varying in accordance with the normal sizing ability of the variety. For example, an eight-pound sample of Santa Rosa plums must number no more than 69 fruits, which is roughly equivalent to a 4 x 5 standard four-basket crate pack.

MARKETING

Plums grown in the East are sold mostly to local markets or on roadside stands, for fresh consumption or for canning. Appearance of small baskets of fresh plums can be improved on the counter by mixing plum varieties of different color and/or by mixing plums with peaches, grapes, and perhaps other currently ripening fruits.

In the West, plums are sold through shipping agencies which deal with brokers, or which have their special representatives in the East. The fruit may be sold to an individual at a private sale, or it may go to public auction; this is usually determined by the sales manager of the shipping agency. Although plums are a perishable fruit, they are being shipped to all parts of the United States and some are being exported.

Frozen prunes are a product with steady demand. Washington, Michigan and Oregon freeze several hundred tons a year. Both dried and fresh prune juices, nectars, and purees for babies, are available, alone or combined with other fruit juices in punches, affording a broadening outlet for this fruit.

One of the major problems in normal times with marketing of plums is to move the large quantities of fruit from the West at prices satisfactory to the growers and shippers. This situation is being met by advertising campaigns put on by the marketing agencies, by improved packaging to get Mrs. Housewife's eye, and by sending special representatives to the Eastern markets to encourage and maintain good will. Efforts also are being made to distribute California plums, for example, to the smaller cities and towns throughout the United States. In this selling program, the grower himself must realize that small fruits of miscellaneous varieties and of inferior quality will bring a price but not a profit. Informational signs on the sales counter help to move this less-known fruit, such as "Plump juicy Duarte plums — fine for school lunch, —c lb."

Cost of Production. See literature citations.

Specifications for maturity standards, packaging and other shipping details can be obtained from the shipping agency of Federal or state marketing offices.

Review Questions

1. State briefly where plums are grown in the United States on a commercial basis, and for home consumption and local trade. List key world countries.
2. Name and differentiate briefly the different groups and subgroups of plums.
3. What is the difference between a plum and a prune?
4. List leading plum varieties in your general area, stating to which group each variety belongs.
5. What governs the choice of varieties of plums in California; in New York?
6. What is the most common rootstock for plum trees? What other stocks are used for plums in California? Why? Name a dwarfing stock?
7. Can European varieties of plums be top-worked successfully on Japanese varieties? Why would such grafts be desired?
8. Differentiate between the pruning received by Japanese and European type plums.

411

9. Describe the precautions necessary in training the Wickson variety of plum.
10. At what time and at what distances are Japanese and European plum fruits thinned? Discuss chemical fruit thinning.
11. What is a good system of soil management for young plum trees growing on a 10 per cent slope in medium heavy soil in your state?
12. Where and when is irrigation practical with plum trees?
13. At what stage of maturity should plums be harvested for long distance shipping, for roadside markets, for drying, and for canning?
14. Discuss mechanical harvesting — machinery, maturity desired, techniques.
15. What types of containers are popular for shipping plums? Discuss the merits of fiberboard containers; vibrating and cooling before shipment.
16. Discuss storage conditions required by plums, dependent upon variety and ultimate use. How about CA storage of plums?
17. Discuss briefly how plums are shipped from California to the eastern market?

Suggested Collateral Readings

Alderman, D. C. *et. al.* Managing and harvesting the mature prune orchard. Calif. Pub. AXT-159, Nov. 1964: J. J. Smith, Water and soil management for prune orchards, Calif. Pub. AXT-67: Alderman, D. C. and W. M. Anderson and C. J. Hansen, Developing the prune orchard. Calif. Pub. AXT-104. 1963.

Alderman, W. H. and T. S. Weir. Pollination studies with stone fruits. Univ. of Minn. Tech. Bull. 198. 16 pp. 1951.

Bailey, John S. The beach plum in Massachussetts. Mass. Agr. Exp. Sta. Bull. 422. 16 pp. 1944.

Bark-split—A virus disease of plums. Ann. Applied Bot. *45*:No. 4. 573-579. December, 1957.

Benson, Nels, R. C. Lindner, and R. M. Bullock. Plum, prune and apricot nutrition. In Childers, N. F. Fruit Nutrition, Chap. XIV. Horticultural Publications, Rutgers University, New Brunswick, N. J. 1966.

California Agriculture. This monthly resumé of experimental research at the California Agricultural Experiment Stations frequently contains items on plums and prunes. The following subjects can be found in the respective months: Nematode resistance in plums, October, 1957; Mechanical fruit tree shaking, October, 1958; Time study of plum packing, May 1955; Quality of dried French prunes, August 1955; Improving prune dehydration, May 1952; Cooling fruit (plums and pears) in fiberboard, Febuary 1955; Prune harvest methods, costs, July 1955; Prune harvesting cost methods, July 1958; Boron requirements of prunes; August 1958; Fertilizer trials with plums, February 1958; Factors in prune skin texture, November 1958; Quality of dried French prunes, August 1955; Parallel-flow prune dehydration, Aug. 1965; Fresh-pitted dried prunes, Apr. 1963.

Claypool, L. L. *et al.* Physical and chemical changes in French prunes during maturiation in coastal valleys and the influence of harvesting procedures in storage on the quality of dried French prunes from coastal regions. Hilgardia 33:8, 311-348. 1962.

Claypool, L. L. and John Kilbuck. The influence of maturity of Interior Valley French prunes on the yield and quality of the dried product. Proc. Amer. Soc. Hort. Sci. 68: 77-85. 1956.

Couey, H. Melvin. Modified atmosphere storage of Nubiana plums. Proceedings ASHS. Vol. 86, 1965. On Eldorado plums. ASHS 75:207-15, 1960.

Crane, M. B. and A. G. Brown. incompatibility and sterilty in the Gage and dessert plums. Jour. Pom. and Hort. Sci. 17: 51-66. 1939.

Cullinan, F. P. Improvement of stone fruits. U. S. Dept. of Agr. Yearbook, separate 1588. 665-748. 1937.

deGoede, C. Australian dried prune industry. USDA-FAS-M-97. 12 pp. 1960.

Elmore, C. L., *et al.* Annual weed control in young prunes. HortSci. Vol. 5, No. 4. pp. 263. Aug. 1970.

Foytik, Jerry. California plums—economic status. Calif. Agr. Exp. Sta. Circ. 493. 34 pp. Request recent work.

Gaston, H. P., S. L. Hedden and J. H. Levin. Mechanizing plum harvests. Mich. Quart. Bul. 42:4. 779-783. 1960.

(See additional references under Chapter XV Appendix)

CHAPTER XVI

Cherry Culture

◆ ◆

Sweet and tart[1] cherries always have played a more or less important part in home fruit gardens, but it was not until the 1920's-30's and 1950's-60's that extensive commercial cherry plantings were made. The increased plantings were due to development of the canning and frozen-pack industries and to mechanized growing and handling. Cherries now are available to domestic and foreign consumers every day of the year instead of for only a four- to six-week period within a short distance of where they were grown. With the tendency of the housewife to do less canning and cooking of fresh fruits, commercial processing of cherries is continuing to grow; almost half the sweets and nearly all the sours are processed.

Approximate cherry production figures for the World in thousands of *metric tons* are:

Soviet Union	475*	Austria	85*	Switzerland	53
Germany (FR)	270	Turkey	80	Portugal	45**
United States	235*	Czechoslovakia	65**	Germany (DR)	42*
Italy	222	Rumania	65	Hungary	41**
France	122	Hungary	60*	Canada	15
Poland	85*	Bulgaria	60**	Belgium	10
Yugoslavia	85*	Spain	54	Australia	8
				New Zealand	8

*Tart cherries predominate.
**Sweets predominate.

It is apparent that cherries are widely grown around the World and that the Soviet Union, United States, Germany (FR), Italy and France are leaders in cherry production. Except for the Far East where there is limited interest, cherries are grown commercially in Sweden, Netherlands,

---

[1]"Tart" is preferred to "sour" in marketing channels, although the words still are used interchangeably among growers and professional workers.

Dr. Charles D. Kesner, Dist. Hort. Agt., Traverse City; George A. McManus, Jr., Traverse Co. Ext. Dir., Michigan State Univ.; and Dr. Harold W. Fogle, USDA, Beltsville, Md. gave considerable assistance in revision of this chapter.

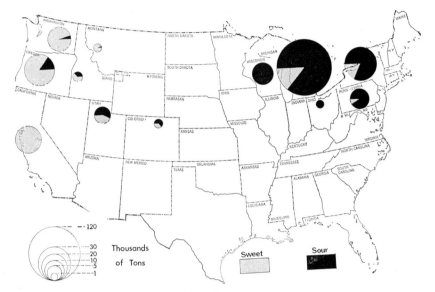

Kenneth A. Wightman, Rutgers University

Figure 1. The leading states in commercial cherry production are Michigan, Oregon, California, New York, Washington, Wisconsin, and Pennsylvania. The solid portion of the circles indicates tart varieties and the cross-hatch areas sweet cherries. Tart cherries are largely grown in the East whereas sweet cherries are concentrated in the West. (Numbers at lower left represent thousands of tons.)

Australia, Japan, Norway, Denmark, Argentina, New Zealand and Luxembourg.

U. S. cherry production has increased since 1890 from 90 to around 700 million pounds in the 1970s, while tree population generally has dropped from a peak of 15 million in 1935 to about 10 in recent years.

Commercial cherries are grown principally above the Mason and Dixon line in the United States. This is mainly because cherry diseases and insects are difficult to control in the southern United States, and because the summer climate is too hot, except at higher altitudes. In the northern states, commercial cherry orchards are very much localized. Thus, most of the bearing trees in Wisconsin are in Door County; Oregon (after Albino virus problem) is up in production in the Williamette, Umpqua, and Walla Walla Valleys, and The Dalles. In Michigan, most of the cherry trees are grouped along the shores of Lake Michigan; in Utah, in the Great Salt Lake area, and in Colorado, along the Arkansas River Valley. In New York, cherry trees are largely confined to Wayne County and along the shores of Lake Ontario, while in Washington trees are in the Yakima and Wenatchee Valleys and below Seattle.

Although sweet and sour cherries are grown both in the East and West, sour cherries are largely grown east of the Rocky Mountains, whereas sweet cherries are concentrated in the West (Figure 1). The ranks of states in

414

production of all varieties of cherries (1967-71 average, short tons) and sweet and sour varieties separately are as follows:

Area	All Varieties	Rank	Sweets	Rank	Tarts	Rank
U. S.	231,792		112,144		119,648	
Mich.	98,100	(1)	19,600	(4)	78,500	(1)
Oregon	36,200	(2)	32,100	(1)	4,100	(6)
Calif.	25,360	(3)	25,360	(2)	0	
Wash.	22,804	(4)	22,140	(3)	664	(7)
New York	20,420	(5)	4,820	(5)	15,600	(2)
Utah	8,536	(6)	3,400	(6)	5,136	(5)
Penn.	7,967	(7)	707	(7)	7,260	(3)
Wisconsin	5,446	(8)	0		5,446	(4)

U. S. CHERRY PRODUCTION BY DECADES (TONS)

	Total	Sweets	Tarts
1940 - 49	184,812	91,064	93,748
1950 - 59	219,290	88,979	130,311
1960 - 70	246,146	101,992	144,154

CHERRY VARIETIES[1]

Most of the cultivated cherries grown today have been derived from two species; namely, the sour cherry (*Prunus cerasus*) from which both the light- and dark-colored sour cherries have developed, and the sweet cherry *(Prunus avium)* from which the sweet varieties and the Mazzard types have arisen. The Duke cherries, intermediate in type, are considered to be hybrids between the sweet and sour groups. Other species of cherries have not produced varieties which are grown extensively on a commercial scale for their fruit. The Mahaleb cherry *(Prunus mahaleb),* native to Europe, is used as a rootstock upon which standard cultivated varieties are budded. The Mazzard wild sweet cherry is also used for this purpose. A Chinese species *(Prunus tomentosa)* has been grown to some extent in the Upper Mississippi Valley and in the Canadian prairie provinces where winters are too adverse for common sweet and sour varieties. Several of the Japanese species of cherries are grown widely for ornamental purposes in the United States (notably near the Washington Monument). The Bird cherry (wild sweet) is valued only for its wood. The Western wild cherry (*Prunus besseyi*) is used as a dwarfing stock for plum, prune and peach, but not for cherry.

Most of the important cherry varieties grown in the United States are of European origin, coming from France, England, Holland, and Germany. Because of the fact that the cherry is inclined to reproduce comparatively true to type from seed, many similar seedlings have developed which hardly can be placed under the same variety heading. As a result, one speaks of a cherry as Morello-like, Napoleon-like, or Montmorency-like.

The cherry variety list has probably undergone less change than almost any other deciduous fruit. Northwest growers, due to uneasiness with

---

[1] Request H. W. Fogle, et al. up-dated detail USDA handbooks on (a) sour and b) sweet cherries, Plant Industry Station, Beltsville, Md., 20705.

TABLE 1

Days From Full Bloom to Harvest for Cherry Varieties in
New York (After Tukey, H. B.)[1]

Variety	No. Seasons	Length of Seasons			Maximum day differences
		Shortest	Longest	Average	
Sweets					
Bing	5	60	74	71	14
Black Tartarian	7	49	63	57	14
Gov. Wood	9	43	50	47	7
Knight	12	44	55	51	11
Lambert	7	61	72	69	11
Napoleon	6	67	74	68	7
Rockport	8	42	56	52	14
Schmidt	0	62	74	72	12
Windsor	6	65	76	75	11
Y. Spanish	6	60	70	67	10
Red (Sours)					
E. Richmond	17	47	57	50	10
E. Morello	29	60	74	70	14
Montmorency	14	54	64	62	10
Dukes					
Late Duke	5	60	72	66	12
May Duke	9	41	55	51	14

[1] Tukey, H.B. Proc. Amer. Soc. Hort. Sci. *40*: 133. 1942.

winter injury and several virus problems, however, are testing the new sweet cherries Van, Sam, Ebony, Spaulding, Lamida, Chinook, Ranier, Corum, Macmar, and Compact Lambert (smaller than Lambert). California is testing the Mona, Larian, Jubilee, Berryessa, Bada; and New York, the Ulster and Hudson (very little cracking). Vista and Vega are promising sweets from Ontario, Canada.

There are at least 1,145 cherry varieties (as described by Hedrick), which have been grown at one time or another in America. There are only a few, however, which can be grown commercially and which meet a ready market demand. Commercially important varieties belong to either the sweet or sour (tart) group. Sweet cherries are used, about 40%, for fresh-fruit dessert, although increasing quantities are being brined and made into maraschino cherries. Sour cherries constitute much of the frozen pies and pie filling and canned cherries for use in restaurants, soda fountains, bakeries and in homes for pies, ice cream, sauce, preserves, and other desserts. A few sours also are being processed into maraschino cherries.

The sweet varieties. Most of the sweet cherries belong either to the "Heart" or "Bigarreau" group. Those varieties belonging to the Heart group have a comparatively soft flesh and many of them are heart-shaped, although some varieties are globose or oblate. Heart cherries may be divided further into dark-colored varieties with reddish juice and light-colored varieties with colorless juice. Among the light-colored Heart varieties are Coe, Ida, Elton, and Governor Wood. Dark-colored varieties are represented by Black Tartarian and Early Purple.

J. A. Milbrath, Oregon State College

Figure 4. (Left) Montmorency leaves are shown with various types of necrotic ring pots and necrotic (dead) areas which have resulted from a first-year invasion of the ring spot virus. The Yellows Virus, according to K. G. Parker, usually follows ring spot in New York. (Right) Comparison of height of virus-free Royal Ann (A10) on the left and ring-spot virus-infected Royal Ann (A11) on the right.

Varieties of the Bigarreau group are usually roundish in shape and of firm crisp flesh. There are some, however, that are as typically heart-shaped as those of the Heart group. Examples of the black Bigarreau type are Windsor, Schmidt, Hedelfingen, Bing, Lambert, while light type varieties include Y. Spanish, Napoleon, Emperor Francis, Ranier, Gold. The Bigarreau group is the most commercially important. Those of the Heart group, as a whole, tend to have poor-keeping and shipping qualities, although some are excellent for home use and local market sales.

In the Northwest U. S. Lambert, Bing and Royal Ann are widely planted. The Compact Lambert, under test, is smaller, blooms later, fruit ripens 3-5 days later and is smaller with a shorter stem than regular Lambert. Van is used as a pollenizer.

In California, the Bing,[1] Lambert, Republican, and Napoleon are the leading commercial varieties of sweet cherries. In New York, the Black Tartarian, Schmidt, Napoleon and Windsor are grown commercially, while the Early Rivers, Victor (yellow flesh ripening before Napoleon), Emperor Francis, and Geant D'Hedellingen are recommended for trial. In Michigan, Schmidt, Napoleon, Emperor Frances and Hedelfingen are recommended, with Napoleon having the most acreage. In Ohio, Windsor has been the most dependable sweet variety. Lambert and Napoleon also are suggested. It is interesting to note that Bing tends to crack at maturity more than other sweet cherry varieties under Ohio and eastern conditions, whereas Bing is one of the more resistant varieties to cracking in Idaho, followed by Black Tartarian, Napoleon, Lambert, and Republican. Cracking of cherries is

---

[1] Long-stem Bing is apparently resistant to buckskin virus and may prove of value in such virus-infected areas. Other viruses in the West are "twisted leaf," "albino," "little-cherry Western X complex," and "Lambert mottle," all of which are causing many sweet cherry trees to be removed.

Figure 5. Both sweet and sour cherries grow poorly or die on heavy soils with poor drainage, particularly sweet cherries. (Top) Note missing Montmorency trees in low poorly drained area in center of orchard. (Bottom) Ten-year Montmorency trees dying in July in heavy poorly drained soil following an unusually wet spring in northern Ohio.

associated with high humidity caused by heavy dew or rainfall shortly before harvesting. The Napoleon variety is probably the most widely planted sweet cherry in America.

Sweet cherry varieties which have originated in America as seedlings include Governor Wood and Waterhouse of the yellowish varieties; and Burbank, Chapman, Oregon, Bing, Lambert, and Republican of the dark-red good-shipping varieties.

The tart cherries. The tart cherries contain many varieties, but only three receive attention from a commercial standpoint and of these, the Montmorency is outstanding. It is used chiefly for canning and freezing. The Early Richmond ripens a week to ten days earlier than Montmorency, but it yields less and the fruits are slightly more acid and somewhat smaller in size than Montmorency[1]. Early Richmond is planted mainly to extend the ripening season for local fresh market trade. English Morello is a relatively small spreading tree which bears medium to small, dark red to almost black cherries that are tart and of good quality. English Morello matures relatively late and will hang on the tree for a long time after maturity without deteriorating. It requires thorough spraying because the foliage is highly susceptible to the leaf spot disease. English Morello has a limited demand on local markets and a very limited demand for commercial canning.

The Duke cherries contain less important varieties than the sweet or sour groups. Only three Duke varieties are planted to any commercial extent in the United States; namely, May Duke, Royal Duke, and Late Duke. Other varieties grown occasionally in the East are Brassington and Reine Hortense.

---

[1]Long-term Bing is apparently resistant to buckskin virus and may prove of value in such virus-infected areas. Other viruses in the West are "twisted leaf," "albino," "little-cherry Western X complex," and "Lambert mottle," all of which are causing many sweet cherry trees to be removed.

Dr. Robert Carlson, Mich. State Univ., is evaluating several Montmorency strains for bud hardiness, spur-type, lateness or earliness of bloom and ripening, fruit quality and virus tolerance.

General variety considerations. As pointed out previously, the cherry varieties, like other fruit varieties, are limited in commercial adaptability to rather definite areas. Disadvantages of the sweet cherry are the fact that although it is as hardy in wood as the peach, it does not recover as well from winter injury; it blossoms early in the spring, and hence, is more likely to be damaged by cold and frost injury. The trees do not thrive on heavy or poorly drained soils. Likewise, the sour cherry is affected adversely by poor soil drainage (Figure 5).

The sour cherry tree is about as hardy as some apple varieties, but its flowers are tender to cold in the "water-bud" stage. In Michigan, although there has been a shift to better sites, one crop out of about three in the average commercial orchard is lost to spring frosts; in the one-third of the orchards on the best sites, crop loss from frosts occurs less frequently than once in five years. Gardner states that "most growers, if asked to name their most serious problems or limiting factors (in cherry growing), would mention frost injury to blossoms in the spring, yellow-leaf virus, and the difficulty in obtaining what they regard as a satisfactory price for their product." The yellow-leaf virus disease has become one of the most important limiting factors in sour cherry production in the East and Northwest (Figure 4). Cherries have a number of viruses. See suggested Collateral Readings for descriptions and controls.

There has been relatively little work in cherry breeding in the past decade. The failure to develop new varieties of cherries, particularly the sweet cherry, may be due to the fact that cherries cannot be grown over such a wide area of the country as the peach and the plum, and to the failure of the seed to germinate and grow, especially with the sweet varieties. Modest breeding programs are underway in N.Y., Mich., Canada, California, Washington — USDA cooperating. The objectives are high-quality sweet varieties that will prove more hardy in trees and blossom characters than many of those now available for planting. Even in the limited areas where sweet cherries will grow, there is definite need for firm-fleshed varieties that do not crack and that will ripen over a long season. At present, there is no firm-fleshed early-ripening variety of the Bigarreau type. The Duke varieties are excellent cherries, but there is a definite need for higher-producing varieties.

POLLINATION

Sweet varieties. All sweet cherry varieties appear to be self-unfruitful in that little or no fruit develop following self-pollination. All commercial varieties of sweet cherries have viable pollen, but not all varietal combinations are fruitful. There are many cross-incompatible groups of sweet cherries. Varieties within a group should not be planted together without a pollinizer. The cross-incompatible groups include: (1) Bing, Lambert, Napoleon, Emperor Francis, and Ohio Beauty; (2) Wind-

Figure 6. Sweet cherry trees (right) in Ohio may be in full bloom ten days before the sour cherries (left) begin to bloom. Hence, sour cherry trees will not provide cross-pollination needed by sweet cherry trees. In Idaho sweet cherries bloom before sours.

sor and Abundance; (3) Black Tartarian, Black Eagle, Knigth's Early Black, Bedford Prolific, and Early Rivers; (4) Centennial and Napoleon; (5) Advance and Rockport; (6) Elton, Governor Wood, and Stark's Gold; and (7) Early Purple and Rockport; (8) Black Tartarian, Early Rivers, V29023; (9) Sodus, Van, Venus, Windsor; (10) Bing, Emperor Francis, Lambert, Napoleon, Vernon; (11) Velvet, Victor, Gold, Merton Heart; (12) Hedelfingen, Vic; (13) Hudson, Giant, Schmidt, Ursula; (14) Valera and (15) Seneca, Vega, Vista, V35033, V35038 (compatible with groups 8-14). Note: No. 8-14 from Publication 430, Fruit Varieties, Ontario Department of Agriculture and Food.

Sweet cherries must be interplanted for cross-pollination. Tarts cannot be used as pollinizers for sweet cherries since their blooming periods do not overlap in most regions. (Figure 6). The Duke varieties are not reliable in cross-pollination with sweet cherries.

In the East, blooming seasons of the commercially grown sweet cherry varieties usually overlap sufficiently to provide good crops. However, in the West, somewhat more care is needed in the selection of varieties on the basis of blooming dates. Early-blooming sweet cherries include Black Tartarian, Black Republican, Advance, Burbank, Chapman, Black Heart, and Early Purple. Napoleon, Rockport, Bing, Pontiac, Longstem Bing, and Lambert are considered late-blooming, and Deacon has been interplanted among these varieties in Washington and British Colombia as a pollinizer. The Black Republican and Black Tartarian usually overlap sufficiently in blooming period to pollinize most of the late-blooming sweet varieties.

Tart varieties. The common varieties of tart cherries; namely, Early Richmond, Montmorency, and the Morellos are sufficiently self-fruitful to give commercial crops when planted in solid blocks, provided sufficient pollinizing insects are available.

Duke varieties. The Dukes are similar to the sweet varieties in that cross-pollination is needed for commercial crops. With good cross-pollination, however, Duke varieties in general are relatively low-producing, apparently due to the unbalanced constitution of the reproductive cells. The May Duke and Royal Duke are usually the most productive. The late-blooming sweet cherry varieties are used for cross-pollinating the early-blooming Duke varieties, such as May Duke. Among the late-blooming sweet varieties are

Napoleon, Windsor, and Governor Wood. The Early Richmond and Montmorency sour cherries are effective as pollinizers for most late-blooming Duke cherries, Olivet being one exception.

Planting plan. In both the East and the West, it is recommended that where cross-pollination is required, every third row be a pollinizing variety, or that two rows of the pollinizing variety be planted between every four rows of the variety needing pollination. This system facilitates mechanical harvesting.

ROOTSTOCKS FOR CHERRY TREES

Three rootstocks are used for cherry: Mazzard and Mahaleb seedling cherries and Stockton Morello softwood cuttings or suckers. Mazzard is a sweet cherry type with small black bitter fruits; it is native to Central and Southern Europe. Mazzard seed for rootstocks are obtained from Europe and from trees which have escaped cultivation in sections of the United States where the sweet cherry is grown. The Mahaleb variety is native in southwestern Europe and is probably more closely related to the sour cherry types than to the sweet types. The tree tends to be thick, bushy-topped, spreading, and small in size. Seeds for rootstocks are obtained from trees in southern Europe. Seedlings from standard commercial varieties of sweet cherries are used sometimes by nurserymen for rootstocks, but the trees are often less vigorous, less uniform, and less satisfactory than the true Mazzard. The sour and native "pin" or "bird" cherry seedlings are not considered satisfactory for rootstocks.

Mazzard is the main stock on the Pacific Coast for sweet cherries and to a considerable extent for other types. Trees are larger, root-knot nematode resistant, semi-resistant to oak-root fungus, gophers, mice, trunk borers, and out-produces trees on Mahaleb roots. Mazzard stock is preferred for both sweet and sour varieties in Eastern sec-

Figure 7. A vigorous Montmorency sour cherry tree growing on a Mazzard rootstock in western Pennsylvania. Note difference in vigor of root and top. Where extremely cold temperatures are not likely to be a factor in the East, sour cherries on Mazzard stock are usually more vigorous, higher yielders, and longer lived than those on Mahaleb stock. In areas as Northwest Michigan, Mazzard roots are satisfactory where snow cover prevents soil freezing.

421

tions where winter temperatures are not extreme. Results obtained at the New York Agricultural Experiment Station have shown that the sweet, sour, and Duke cherries grown on Mazzard stock are larger, more vigorous, more productive, longer-lived, and show less mortality among young trees. In the East, however, it is clearly evident that the Mahaleb stock is hardier and more drought-resistant than the Mazzard, and in regions where droughts are common and extreme temperatures are likely to occur, the Mahaleb stock is recommended. In California the Morello stock is used for sweet cherries in soils likely to become wet, or as a semi-dwarfing stock. Specify *virus-free* stock.

In Utah, Coe has shown that the Mahaleb stocks are better than Mazzard for commercial use with sweet cherries in the typically porous gravelly orchard soils. Trees on Mahaleb stock proved to be much superior in vigor, size, hardiness, survival, yield, and are earlier bearing as compared with those on Mazzard.

The F-12-1 Oregon Mazzard is fairly resistant to bacterial canker where it is a problem. Van and Bing perform best on Mazzard in Washington. In Pennsylvania Napoleon survived best on Mahaleb. In Michigan, Mazzard is recommended for Hedelfingen.

In New York, nematodes may be a serious pest on cherry, reducing growth and production and increasing susceptibility to cold damage. Soil fumigants often are used before planting.

Where available, as in Missouri and New York, state-inspected nursery stock *certified-free* of the common *viruses should be sought.*

RESISTANCE TO COLD

Sweet cherry trees in general are somewhat more resistant to cold than the average variety of Domestica plum. There is no great difference in cold resistance among varieties grown extensively in the United States. Windsor, Governor Wood, and Yellow Spanish are more resistant than the average sweet cherry. Lyon has shown the most resistance, but it is a minor variety. Blossoms of the sweet cherry open somewhat earlier than the peach and, therefore, are more likely to be killed by spring frosts. The amount of cold required by the sweet cherry for breaking the rest period is slightly more than for most peaches. (1100-1300 hrs. below 45°F.; sours - 1200)

Many orchards are being heated to protect them against frost damage. Smudge pots, wind machines, and petroleum bricks are being used with varied degrees of success. Portable propane fueled systems are being used in the Northwest with the propane gas and irrigation water sharing the same main laterals.

The sour cherry varieties, except for the Russian varieties, are about as resistant to cold as the medium-hardy varieties of apple, such as the Northern Spy. Russian varieties of sour cherries may be as resistant as the Mc-

CRITICAL TEMPERATURES FOR SWEET CHERRY BLOSSOM BUDS*
(E. L. PROEBSTING, JR., WASH. STATE AGR. STA., PROSSER).

Bud Development Stage	1	2	3	4	5	6	7	8	9
Old Standard Temp.[1]	23	23	25	28	28	29	29	29	30
Ave. Temp. for 10% Kill[2]	17	22	25	26	27	27	28	28	28
Ave. Temp. for 90% Kill[2]	5	9	14	17	21	24	25	25	25
Average Date (Prosser)[3]	3/5	3/13	3/23	3/27	4/1	4/4	4/8	4/13	4/21

*For Bing. Lambert and Rainier approximately 1 to 2 degrees hardier through Stage 6.

[1] Critical temperatures as previously published in WSU EM 1616.

[2] Average temperatures found by research at the WSU Research and Extension Center, Prosser, to result in 10% and 90% bud kill.

[3] Average date for this stage of the WSU Research and Extension Center.

Intosh apple and, therefore, should be a good parent for hybridizing to extend the commercial sour cherry region northward.

If growth of the sour cherry tree has ceased relatively early in the growing season due to leaf spot disease, low nitrogen, or drought, the buds may be more tender to cold during the winter than peach flower buds. In orchards under good management, however, much less trouble from winter killing of fruit buds is experienced. English Morello has shown less bud killing due to cold than Montmorency or Early Richmond. In view of the fact that sour cherries ripen early in the season and that a short season is required for maturing the buds and wood, they can be grown at relatively high latitudes, provided large bodies of water are available for moderating temperature during extremely cold nights.

PLANTING RECOMMENDATIONS

A good peach orchard site is an equally good cherry orchard site. Vigorous one-year nursery trees are desired for sweet cherries as well as for tarts and Dukes. In the milder climates, fall planting is suggested. In the colder climates *early* spring planting is recommended to avoid winter damage, except where snow may protect the tree into late winter. Root killing by winter cold and winter injury due to chemical or hand defoliation of nursery trees for early-fall digging can be problems in fall-planted trees in the colder climates.

Spring-planted cherry trees should be set as early as possible on fall-plowed ground. Delay in spring planting of cherry trees is probably responsible for the loss of more cherry trees the first season than all other factors put together. This may be due to the fact that cherry buds open relatively early and that evidently the cherry roots are a little slow in becoming established. This results in a greater demand for water by the tops than the roots can supply. Thence, the opening buds dry, the wood and bark shrivel, and the tree soon dies. This is one of the main reasons

Figure 8. Efforts are underway to develop compact cherry trees. (Above) A compact Bing and Lambert high-producing sweet cherry orchard near Wapato, Washington with Montmorency trunks and Mazzard rootstocks. "Stub Pruning", as indicated, induces large-size fruit bringing premium prices (courtesy Paul Stark, Jr., Stark Nurseries, Louisiana, Mo.). (Low-left) Hedge-row planting of Bing sweet cherry high-budded on Mahaleb rootstocks in mid California gives insurance against "buck-skin" virus and also affords an easy-to-train early-bearing tree held to a desirable height (courtesy Kay Ryugo, Univ. of Calif., Davis). (Right) Radiation treatment with X-rays, gamma rays, and thermal neutrons induces dwarf mutant trees. Center two trees are compact Lamberts in seventh year, so-treated, as compared with standard Lamberts at side and rear (courtesy K. O. Lapins, Agr. Research Sta., Summerland, B.C., Canada).

why fall planting is desirable in those sections where winter killing of the roots is not a factor.

Special care should be exercised in handling cherry trees during transit, storage and planting. Cherry buds are easily rubbed off being large and prominent.

Standard planting distances have been 15 x 15 for Morellos, 20 x 20 ft. for tarts and Dukes and 20 x 20 to 36 x 36 for sweets, depending on variety, vigor and soil. A shift to hedgerow planting is occurring to increase acre yields where mechanization of orchard operations will be used.

Tarts are set 12 to 13 feet in the row and sweets about 17 to 20 feet in a row with 22 to 24 ft. between rows.

Where cherries are replanted on old fruit plantings, fumigation of the soil in fall when its temperature is 50-80°F is suggested to get healthy vigorous trees. See page 338.

PRUNING YOUNG CHERRY TREES

Tart cherry. If the trees are one-year whips, they should be cut off 30+ inches above the ground. A selection of the scaffolds can be made the following year. If the nursery trees are branched two-year-olds, about two or three well-spaced laterals should be selected around the leader, with the lowest limb 30-36 in. above ground (mechanized harvesting) on the southwest side of the tree or toward the

Figure 9. An excellent start in the framework of a sour cherry tree beginning its second season in the orchard. Lowest limb should be about 24 inches from the ground where mechanical harvesting will be used.

prevailing winds (Figure 9). Heading-back cuts should be avoided on the branches left to form the head, because such practice has a definite stunting effect on sour cherries.

The sour cherry tree naturally has an open spreading growth habit and for this reason many commercial trees are trained to the open-center system. However, the general experience with open-center sour cherry trees has been too many weak rotting crotches. In recent years, there has been a definite trend toward the modified-leader system of training sour cherries, similar to that described for apple in Chapter IV. Although the modified-leader system of training trees requires somewhat more care and attention during the first four or five years in the orchard, it should add years to the life of the average sour cherry orchard.

Three or four scaffolds distributed over about three or four feet of the trunk above the lowest branch are desirable (Fig. 10a). The leader is then modified by cutting it to an outward-growing lateral. In sour cherries, it is particularly important to give attention to the elimination of branches originating parallel with one another on the trunk. It is important, also, to avoid if possible two scaffold limbs originating at the same height. If two scaffolds are permitted to develop close together on the same side or opposite

425

to each other on the trunk, later development of the leader and branches above may be considerably subdued and choked. The moderately vigorous sour cherry tends to develop numerous lateral shoots on the scaffold limbs and leader, and one must take special care not to prune these too heavily. It is particularly important with young cherries to prune as little as possible to attain the desired scaffold arrangement. Heavy pruning may delay full bearing several years.

Sweet cherries. Sweet cherry trees often come from the nursery as one-year whips which should be cut at a height of 30 to 48 inches from the ground, depending upon the vigor of the tree. The deshooting system of training one-year whips is often practiced with the sweet cherry as described for the apple in Chapter IV. If allowed to grow without training, the sweet cherry will usually develop into a central-leader type of tree which becomes too high for economical production. It is important to prevent the leader and upper branches from being choked by opposite or closely placed scaffold limbs. Three or four later scaffolds with about 12 inches vertical distance between limbs, in addition to the leader which is modified to an outward-growing limb, will make a desirable framework for sweet cherry trees. The sweet cherry is susceptible to crotch splitting and, thus, it is especially important to eliminate at an early stage any scaffolds with narrow-angled crotches. Wide-angled scaffolds not only develop a strong head but also reduce the hazards of winter injury and decay on the body of the tree.

Wayward limbs. On young cherry trees, frequently one finds a limb which has started to outgrow the others, and, if left alone, may result in a one-sided unsymmetrical top. This limb can be subordinated by heading it back more or less severely. However, if this vigorous side limb has gained considerable dominance over the other limbs, it may be advisable to gradually prune away the weak limbs and permit the new growth to replace them.

PRUNING THE BEARING CHERRY TREE

Tart cherry. Fruit buds of the tart cherry are produced laterally on one-year terminal growths and spurs (Figure 10). The terminal buds of shoots and spurs are leaf buds. If the terminal growth on sour cherries is less than about seven inches, nearly all lateral buds on such shoots will be fruit buds. After fruiting, this wood becomes largely bare. On the other hand, when terminal shoots are about 7 in. in length, $\frac{1}{4}$ in. thick, some of the lateral buds will be leaf buds from which spurs and lateral shoots develop. Trees with numerous spurs are very productive and the flowers open over several days, hence, some of them dodging a current frost.

Moderate pruning and good soil management are needed to encourage spur development. Dr. J. C. Cain of the New York Station, Geneva, finds that 20 to 50 ppm of gibberelic acid 4 to 5 wks. after bloom (Mich. - 2 wks.) reduces fruit on one-year growth but encourages spur development

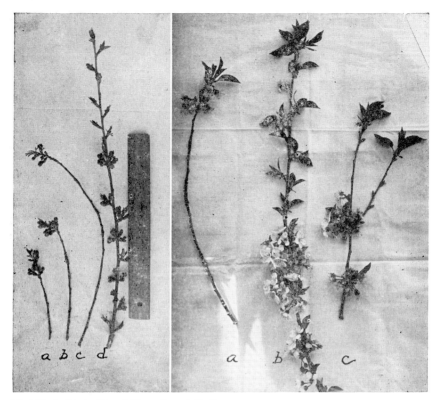

New York Agricultural Experiment Station.

Figure 10. (Left) Short annual growth (two to four inches) is associated with unproductive cherry trees; long shoot growth (seven to twelve inches) is associated with productive trees. Long 2-year growth at D has numerous fruiting spurs on lower 2-year wood; upper 1-year wood has mostly leaf buds which will form shoots and fruiting spurs in the following year. The three weak terminal growths of A, B and C are from 4 to 6 years old and have produced only 2- to 4-inch shoot growth each year. Note lack of spurs, due to practically all buds being fruit buds each year; such wood has low productive capacity. (Right) Terminal growths at A and B show flowering and leaf development on wood similar to C and D, respectively, in left photo. Note at C that fruit buds on 1-year wood have been killed by low temperature, whereas those on spurs were not injured.

and bloom throughout the tree the following year on wood best adapted to mechanical harvesting. GA also will negate some of the effect of yellows virus, but the economics is doubtful.

For Mechanical Harvesting. When trees that are designed for hand harvesting are to be harvested mechanically, they must be pruned rather drastically the first year to change them from a system that encourages fruit wood close to the ground to a system as shown in Figure 10a for quick machine shaking and adjustment of the catching frame under the tree. Willowy limbs do not free the cherries well during shaking and must be removed. Bark damage results if the shaker arm rubs against one main limb while shaking another, hence, the main limbs *must* be freely accessible to shaker arms over a 30° arc while operating from one posi-

427

Courtesy J. C. Cain in Farm Research, N. Y. Agr. Exp. Sta., Geneva

Figure 10a. (Left) Conventionally pruned Montmorency tart cherry tree suitable for hand harvesting. White bands (4) indicate main limbs easily accessible for machine shaking which will be left; others will be removed. (Right) From 30-40% of the productive area of the tree has been removed to adapt tree to mechanical shaking and quick adjustment of catching frame under the tree from one side of tree. Tree will regain productive capacity in two to three years. Strip row herbicide treatment under tree is facilitated by this pruning, as are other orchard practices. This severe pruning is not so essential with modern trunk shakers that cause little or no bark injury.

tion. The shaker arm (some equipment has two arms, Fig. 15) is attached to the catching frame, both of which are operated and moved by the same motor. Increasing popularity of trunk shakers that do not harm the bark are making the positioning of main lateral limbs less important.

Subsequent pruning of the above trees is based for the most part on principles outlined below. Cutter bar mowing of dormant trees, as for the peach, is under test to keep trees within bounds and cut pruning costs.

For Hand Harvesting. It is important to correct or eliminate any limbs with sharp crotch angles or those that crowd others, or grow across the center of the tree. Only sufficient pruning should be done to keep the tree from becoming dense and to thin out lightly through the top and sides for efficient light and spray penetration. Neglected dense trees result in considerable dying of spurs and limbs in the center and lower sections of the tree. Good air circulation through a tree is important in reducing the amount of brown rot developing shortly before and during harvest. Sour cherries, generally speaking, require relatively little pruning. In fact, in Michigan even light pruning over a period of years has been found to reduce yields slightly. This is because with the main variety, Montmorency, the fruit spurs are relatively short-lived. Also, regardless of the pruning treatment, the major portion of the crop is borne within a comparatively thin rim around the

428

outside of the tree. The greater majority of the fruiting spurs are found on two- and three-year wood, with some on four- and five-year wood. After the first good crop of cherries on a spur, it seems to become less and less productive. Moderately-heavy pruning does not seem to invigorate these spurs; in fact, it has the opposite effect with sour cherries.

Sweet, Duke cherry. Fruiting habit of sweet cherry is mainly on the tree's spur system. The trees grow more or less upright and the main limbs form much less lateral growth as compared with tart cherries. It is important to head-back the main upright limbs when they attain a height of about 15 to 18 feet in order to keep the tree within a 20-foot maximum height, or preferably lower for economical management. The main upright and spreading limbs should be cut back to strong laterals to keep the tree within bounds. Some Yakima growers tip back shoots to induce branching, better fruiting and hold the tree in bounds.

Sweet cherry trees tend to form long limbs with a whorl of side limbs located at long intervals. Whorls of from three to five limbs should be reduced to two or three at the most the first dormant season after they have formed. It is difficult to correct such whorls if allowed to remain for two or three years. Big cuts at the whorl have a "ringing" or stunting effect.

Duke varieties resemble the sweet cherry in growth habit. The pruning system recommended for the sweet cherry thus is applicable to the Duke cherries.

Smooth flush cuts that heal quickly are important because cherry wounds are more susceptible to wood-rotting fungi.

Pruning to adapt sweet cherry trees to harvesting machinery is needed as described above for the tart cherry.

SOIL MANAGEMENT

Cherry trees are almost as responsive to nitrogen and clean cultivation as the peach. A system of shallow cultivation with cover crops, as described for peach trees, generally has been suggested for young and mature sweet and sour cherries. The cultivation consists of a shallow plowing or early disking followed by only a sufficient number of cultivations with a spike- or spring-tooth harrow to keep down the weeds. The early cultivation either should be done several weeks before blossoming or after the fruit has set. The soil surface should be rain-packed (not loose and preferably with no ground cover) at bloom time to permit radiation of ground heat to reduce frost damage, as described for peach. Actually, there has been a general shift to strip chemical weed control under the trees with permanent sod cover in the middles and irrigation available if needed. In some areas, alta or creeping red fescue make good sod middles.

Cover crops frequently used in cherry orchards are millet, rye, oats,

A. J. Heinicke, Cornell University

Figure 11. Montmorency sour cherry trees respond well to cultivation and nitrogen. The two left rows are under cultivation and the two right rows are in sod. The first row and the third row were fertilized the previous three years with 900, 900 and 1800 pounds per acre of nitrate of soda, respectively. The second and fourth rows received no fertilizer. On cultivated plots, nitrated trees were one-third larger than unnitrated trees. On sod plots, fertilized trees were almost twice as large as unfertilized trees. Cherry trees on heavily nitrated sod plots were almost as large as unfertilized trees on cultivated plots. This is on a fairly fertile loam. In sandy soils response to N should be greater and to cultivation less.

buckwheat, and Sudan grass. Rye grass has been used as a winter cover in western Pennsylvania and New York.

A study of the effects of cultivation and nitrogen applications on young Montmorency trees is shown in Figure 11. These results are typical.

Leaf analysis by standard procedure may be used with the help of the local government experiment station to diagnose what appears to be a nutritional problem. While data for mineral content of good bearing cherry trees is scanty for some nutrients, the following contents are considered approximately normal for New York.

N*	P*	K*	Mg*	Ca	S	Fe	Mn	B	Zn	Cu	Mo
		%						ppm			
2.33	0.23	1.25	0.49	1.62	124	119	44	38	20	8	0.5
to	to	to	to	to	to	to	to	to	to	to	to
3.27	0.32	1.92	0.74	2.60	150	203	60	54	50	28	1.0
2.95**	0.25	1.67	0.68	2.09	—	203	150	50	—	57	—

*Values established in personal communication with Dr. J. C. Cain, N. Y. Agr. Exp. Sta., Geneva, for Montmorency.

**Values in this line are for Michigan from A. L. Kenworthy. Nutrient element balance in fruit tree leaves. Amer. Inst. Biol. Sci. Publ. No. 8. 1961.

In order to establish and maintain productivity in sour cherry trees, Gardner recommends:

"(1) For their first few years in the orchard, the trees should be grown so that their shoot growth averages 12 to 24 inches in length. While making

430

Figure 12. Zinc deficiency on sweet cherry (above) is characterized by whitish or dirty-white chlorosis between the main veins, rosetting of small narrow leaves, and dieback of limbs. Manganese deficient (lower) leaves have light-green areas between the main veins with areas near main veins remaining a darker green. Zn and Mn deficiencies may be found in the same leaves as, e.g., in Utah.

Franklin A. Gilbert, University of Wisconsin

Figure 13. Potassium deficiency on cherry is characterized by marginal scorching of leaves, moving from the lower to upper leaves on shoots. Scorch usually starts mid to late summer on older trees but may appear early on newly planted trees. Leaves are undersized when deficiency is severe, with limb dieback.

such a vigorous growth, they bear little fruit but increase rapidly in size and develop a large bearing surface for later production.

"(2) Then, until they attain full size, they should be grown so that their shoot growth averages six to twelve inches in length. While making growth of this type, they bear heavily and gradually increase in productivity.

"(3) After attaining full size and productivity, they should be grown so that their shoot growth averages four to eight inches in length. This will provide for a practically indefinite maintenance of yields."

No attempt should be made to produce the above growth and fruiting conditions by pruning alone. In fact, pruning should play only a minor role, with most emphasis placed on soil management, particularly fertilization. In the East, there has been a trend toward use of an NPK fertilizer mix of a 1-2-2 or 1-1-1 ratio, especially on gravelly or sandy soils. Spotty reports of manganese, iron, and zinc shortages have been noted. Potassium now is generally used in humid regions on the lighter soils. This deficiency has been reported to be common in the north central U.S. cherry regions. (Figure 13). In the western arid sections, zinc, manganese (Figure 12), and iron shortages may be a problem; nitrogen is the only major nutrient used as a general rule, although occasional cases of P and K deficiencies are reported. Nu-Iron, an organic iron product (Tennessee Corp., Atlanta), applied with standard pesticides in New York has increased the sugar content and quality of sour cherries; it is not certain if this is a nutritional effect of the iron or a safening of certain pesticides. See Chapter IV in Childers' *Fruit Nutrition* book for corrective measures for trace element deficiencies. In Michigan, Mg is often deficient and is corrected by dolomitic lime to adjust soil pH if needed, plus syrup of epsom salts.

In general, young non-bearing trees of most sour varieties should make an annual shoot growth of 12 to 24 inches, whereas young non-bearing sweet varieties should make from 22 to 36 inches. Mature bearing sour and sweet varieties should make a new shoot growth approaching eight inches each year to maintain high production. Failure to obtain this growth most often is due to lack of sufficient fertilizer (nitrogen mainly), although drought and certain types of winter injury may cause the same result. The uneven ripening of fruit more likely is due to inadequate leaf area to accommodate a heavy set than to too much nitrogen, as some growers surmise. Experimental evidence indicates that the more nitrogen added, up to the point where vegetative growth is excessive, the higher the yields and the more profitable the orchard. The rate of nitrogen applications for cherries is similar to that recommended for peaches in Chapter XIV.

It should not be implied from this discussion that clean cultivation is being recommended unconditionally for mature cherry trees. There is a definite trend in Michigan, eastern states, and the west toward the use of sod, strip-row herbicides, and trickle or overhead irrigation if needed. This system is giving excellent results, provided sufficient nitrogen is applied; it has the main advantages of checking soil erosion, cutting costs, conserving soil structure and facilitating movement of mechanical harvest equipment.

The nitrogen requirement of sweet cherry trees is probably somewhat less than for the peach and sour cherry trees. On the West Coast, sour cherry trees apparently can obtain sufficient potassium from soils in which apple trees and some varieties of Domestica plums will show potassium deficiency. However, according to Chandler the sweet cherry trees, especially the old ones, are more apt to show zinc deficiency symptoms in semiarid districts of California than are other fruit trees, and it is more difficult to correct. Moderate liming of cherry orchards to maintain a pH of about 6.0 is suggested in humid areas, using high magnesium lime, principally for the cover crop. Avoid excessive liming; trace element deficiencies may be induced.

Irrigation is practiced only rarely for sour cherry trees in the East because the fruits mature early in the season before the soil is apt to become deficient in moisture. However, if early dry periods occur, sour and sweet cherry fruits appear to be more sensitive to high transpiration and high daily water deficit than other deciduous fruits. This may be because the fruits are small and numerous and a higher percentage of the water within them can be removed by the leaves during hot dry periods of the day.

On the West Coast where sweet cherries are grown widely, irrigation is a regular practice in some orchards. Sweet and Duke cherries are quite

Courtesy Paul Stark, Jr., Wapato, Washington and R. T. Meister, American Fruit Grower.

Figure 14. Young sweet cherry trees in sod treated with a herbicide (Paraquat + spreader) on the square. Strip-row chemical weed control will be used as the trees enlarge. An orchard soil management system used in the Northwest is creeping red fescue permanent sod middles with strip-row herbicide treatment and portable overhead irrigation. Cool water spray during hot weather (105°F) has been found to induce better fruit sizing, finish and quality.

sensitive to drought (P. 38). Tarts are less sensitive but respond well to irrigation when needed. In the cool coastal areas of California, sweet cherries can be grown without irrigation in regions of about 15 inches of annual rainfall where other deciduous fruits ripening later in the season cannot be grown. Sweets are highly sensitive to deficient and excessive soil moisture. In Washington, large fruit growers are welding irrigation pipe with risers together in about 630 ft lengths and dragging the pipe by tractor from block to block to cut labor.

In Michigan, "trickle" or "daily flow" irrigation at tree bases from perforated in-row plastic pipe is popular. Limited water is applied under low pressure (15 lbs/sq. in. or less) at 1-2 gals/hr. to hold the soil for a part of the root system at near field capacity.

Fruit thinning of sour cherry trees is not practiced because they ripen early in the season when soil moisture is usually adequate, and also because size of cherries is not as important in market sales and prices as it is for larger fruits, such as the peach and apple. Furthermore, Gardner has shown an apparent lack of correlation between size of fruit and size of crop on sour cherry trees. Chemical thinning of sweet cherries with dinitros for better fruit size is in the experimental stages. New York experiments have shown that tripling the nitrogen rate will increase yields by 13 to 20 per cent on sour cherry trees showing "yellows" virus.

See Chapter XVIII for chemical weed control in cherry orchards.

HARVESTING CHERRIES

There is no standard degree of maturity for picking the cherry. Flavor and over-all color as determined by sampling a few fruits of each variety, furnish the best guides for time to harvest. Cherries, like peaches, increase in size until ripe and should be left on the tree as long as feasible to attain the maximum poundage per tree. With firm-fleshed sweet cherries, there is some tendency among growers to harvest early to obtain better prices. This practice, however, results in less flavor and color and smaller size. Furthermore, cherries picked before fully mature will not ripen off the tree; if picked half ripe, they remain half ripe. Red tart cherries are harvested when they have obtained sufficient size and color for the canning market. However, it is usually determined by the ease of mechanical harvesting. Many sour cherry processors require less than 10 percent of the fruits to have stems attached. Maturity of cherries in Michigan can be hastened one week with applications of Alar at 15 days post-bloom. Rates of 2000-4000 ppm are suggested for tart cherry and 1000-2000 ppm on sweets. In addition to hastening maturity, application of Alar results in more even ripening of the fruits, more uniform color, and slightly smaller firmer fruits. Alar is not recommended on brining sweet cherries because of the earlier enhancement of color. However, in the case of sweet cherries for canning and tart cherries for canning and freezing, quality is greatly improved with Alar.

Investigations show that the final increase in fruit size may be 35 per cent from the time they might first be picked (although premature) until full maturity. Fully mature cherries are less subject to shrinkage in volume when canned than those picked early. In fact, there is actually little reason for early picking of cherries for the cannery.

The period for picking cherries may be shortened by hot dry weather during ripening. The soft-fleshed juicy varieties tend to mature and deteriorate more rapidly than the firm-fleshed varieties which generally provide a longer period for picking and handling. Of the sour cherries, English Morello will hang on the trees longer without deterioration than Montmorency or Early Richmond. Deterioration of the crop from brown rot at harvest can be prevented to a large extent by dusting with sulfur prior to picking. Precooling as soon after harvest as possible is also important in reducing brown rot and general deterioration.

More and more tart and sweet cherries are being harvested by machines. As machine harvesting is perfected and a chemical (see below) is found to release the tighter-sticking stems of sweet cherries together with already perfected destemming equipment, it is probable that most of the commercial sweets will be harvested mechanically, as are the tarts.

Ethephon. Research indicates application of Ethephon at 250-500 ppm 7-14 days prior to harvest will significantly reduce fruit removal force

Courtesy R. P. Larsen, Michigan State Univehsity, East Lansing

Figure 15. Mechanical harvesting and handling of tart cherries has reduced costs markedly and improved quality. Increased tree plantings in leading cherry states has resulted from this key advancement. (a) Self-propelled mobile catching frame has been moved into place and the attached two shaker-arms are positioned and ready to shake two of four main limbs. Equipment can harvest 25 to 40 trees an hour. (Mfg. by Friday Tractor Co., Hartford, Mich.). (b) Care is needed to keep an even but not excessive flow of cherries on conveyor; latter condition causes rolling, crushing and bruising of fruit, marring processed product. (c) Some growers use the trailer tank shown here for transporting cherries to the processor; others use the tanks (holding 1000 lbs. cherries shown in a & d) which are handled by fork lift. Water is held below 60°F in tanks with ice to firm the cherries and reduce scald. (d) Cold water is circulated through the tanks for several hours at cooling station before transporting them to processor. Similar equipment is being used on sweet cherries except they are not handled in water.

of sweet cherries. Thus, it greatly assists in mechanically harvesting the fruit (without stems), especially at immature stages of ripening as are common in the brined cherry industry, according to Dr. John Bukovac, Michigan researcher.

Hand Harvesting. Where cherries are to be harvested by hand, either by grower-hired help or by pick-it-yourself customers, the grower must prepare well ahead to be supplied adequately with ladders, a weighing station, picking buckets, lugs, containers, and other equipment to get the crop off within 10-14 days. A high school teacher with his students may be contracted to do the job, releasing the grower for sales and other details. A picker in a commercial orchard may harvest 300-400 lbs. of tart cherries per day (highest on record, 1,357 lbs of Napoleons). With mechanical harvesting taking over, commercial hand harvesting will become almost non-existant.

Mechanical Harvesting — Bulk Handling. Michigan State University, USDA and cooperating commercial companies and growers have led in the development of mechanical harvesting techniques during the 1950's-60's to cut harvest costs, simplify and speed the operation, and improve the product for processing where nearly all tarts now are utilized.

Tart Cherries. One type of equipment used to shake and catch tart cherries and get them to the processor quickly and in cooled condition is shown in Figure 15. Improvements in equipment are being made yearly. Average equipment can harvest 25 to 30 or more trees an hour. It is more efficient on: (a) well loaded trees (it takes as long to harvest a tree with 50 lbs. as 100 lbs, (b) on mowed or short ground cover, (c) on trees well pruned, and (d) on ground that is fairly level. In the early 1970's cost of harvest by machines was generally about 3.0 cents a pound and by hand picking about 5 cents. The money saved by machine harvesting 100,000 tons of tarts in Michigan, figuring amortization charges on equipment, was well over six million dollars.

H. P. Gaston of Michigan State University makes the following suggestions for machine harvesting cherries:

"**Prune** to reduce main limbs to 4, open lower part of the tree, eliminate willowy hanging branches, induce uniform ripening, reduce excessive tree spread. **Spray, fertilize,** (and heat during frosts if necessary) to induce heavy yields of firm, well colored, high grade fruit. **Level the ground** by cultivation tools and keep ground cover low during harvest. **Obtain machines early** with adequate spare parts. Check **water supply** and **containers. Discuss plans** thoroughly with processor field man to schedule arrival of cherries at plant. **Before harvest:** employ good responsible harvest crew, train them well, pad surfaces where cherries fall, arrange for plenty of ice, check fruit maturity and decide in what tree block to start harvesting, make a "shake-down run" to train crew and check equipment. **When harvest starts:** supervise closely, avoid undue haste, attach shaker arm claw to limb at right angle, shake in short bursts (1/2 - 3 sec.) at frequences of 1000-2000/min. Allow fruit to clear collecting frame between bursts, obtain steady light flow of fruit, leave fruit on tree that does not free easily, stop shaker if leaves begin to fall, keep fabric tight on collecting surfaces, watch for oil leaks and keep any trace of oil away from fruit. **After picking:** avoid unnecessary handling, skim trash off tanks, keep water below 60°F with ice if needed, move fruit promptly to cannery on schedule. **Encourage processor at plant to:** hold fruit in cooled tanks until processing, handle fruit carefully avoiding drops, use well-designed water-filled flumes or well-adjusted conveyor belts, limit soak time (including orchard soak) to 10 hours, remove small and crushed cherries with eliminator, keep fruit one layer deep on eliminator, use mechanical destemmer for early-harvested fruit and provide a bypass for late-harvested fruit when stems are not a problem, keep electric fruit sorters (see reference by Whittenberger **et al.**) in proper adjustment, help growers avoid and solve any mutual problems, provide adequate fieldmen, discourage late night-harvesting and on hot afternoons, and find a method to weigh-in fruit without draining the water away; latter procedure damages the fruit."

Scald can be kept to a minimum by maintaining O_2 content at 2 ppm in water in which cherries are held.

Sweet Cherries. Harvesting machines developed for tart cherries are being used to harvest sweets, but more power is needed to shake effectively

Table 2. Comparison of results in machine (sloping-surface type) harvesting tart and sweet cherries in Michigan (adapted from H. P. Gatson, R. T. Whittenberger and J. H. Levin, 1967)

No in crew	Kind of Cherry	Variety	Tree age	Trees per hour	lbs. per tree	lbs. per hour	% Fruit Removed	% Fruit Bruised
4	Sweet	Schmidt	11	30	79	2370	94	18
4	Tart	Mont-morency	16	36	83	2988	97	21

the larger trees, particularly on older trees. Future training, pruning, and other techniques on young sweet cherry trees no doubt will help adapt the trees better to machine harvesting.

Since sweets are not usually collected and transported in water, improved techniques are needed to fill the bins (46 x 46 x 24 inches deep filled to 16-20 inches) gently to avoid bruising. Improved trash elimination is needed either by blower as the fruit goes into the orchard bin or over graders in the processing plant. Dilute brine handling of cherries from orchard to processor improves quality.

Time to harvest is judged by pull or "feel." When fruit is ready to harvest, a sample of 15-20 fruit on a typical tree should detach "rather easily." Size and skin and flesh color and a "test shake" on one or two trees are also indices. A chemical spray, Ethephon, referred to earlier, at 500 ppm cuts the stem "hold" on the tree. When sweets are harvested without Ethephon, there is more bruising, more cherries left on the tree, and less total size and weight of fruit, which generally is less desired by processors. Left on the tree too long, there is risk of fruit cracking, more brown rot, and the cherries becoming undesirably dark in color for the maraschino packers. Cherries brined for maraschinos immediately after harvest have significantly better processed quality than when there is a delay of 4 to 8 hours in brining.

Tension to pull cherries from the tree decreases from 450 to 300 grams pull for Schmidt over the two-week period before harvest. A simple device to take these measurements is available and known as a pull-force gauge. Vareties being mechanically harvested in Michigan include Schmidt, Napoleon, Emperor Francis, Hardy Giant, Black Tartarian, Hedelfingens, Gold and Windsor.

Volume Measurement. It became necessary with the advent of mechanical harvesting and bulk handling of cherries to find a new method for measuring the raw fruit before sale to processors and handlers.

Historically, cherries were sold by weight which was readily ascertained by determining the gross weight of a load of cherries, removing the fruit and determining a tare weight of containers and usually hauling equipment. However, in the case of mechanically harvested cherries in water (or brine) this became difficult and expensive. Thus, a method was devised whereby the fruit could be sold by volume.

Courtesy Great Lakes Fruit Grower News, Sparta, Michigan.

Figure 16. This is a tart cherry processing plant in Michigan. Cherries are washed, graded, and prepared for canning or frozen pack.

A standardized container (pallet tank holding approximately 1000 lb.) in terms of cubic feet per inch of depth plus a standardized calibrated gauge rod (dipstick) were devised. Subsequently a conversion factor "weight per cubic foot" of cherries was determined.

In Michigan 47.45 lb. per cubic foot is the conversion factor for red tart cherries. The conversion factor for sweet cherries in brine varies from 39-45 lb. per cubic foot depending upon stems, maturity, etc. In the early 1970's the average-agreed-upon conversion factor for sweet cherries in brine in Michigan was 42 lb. per cubic foot.

Michigan weights and measures regulations permit the purchase of cherries by volume but do not permit the conversion of volume to weight. Thus, it is necessary for the industry to determine price by volume as well as by weight. The determination of price per cubic foot utilizes the pertinent conversion factor.

Pick-Your-Own. Where small orchards are located near cities, this method as described for peach and apple earlier, has worked satisfactorily for cherries. (See index.)

Birds and Bear. Robins, starlings, and other birds may become a serious problem in cherry orchards during the harvest season. The birds often damage as many or more cherries than they eat. Recommended practices for a

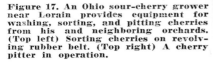
Figure 17. An Ohio sour-cherry grower near Lorain provides equipment for washing, sorting, and pitting cherries from his and neighboring orchards. (Top left) Sorting cherries on revolving rubber belt. (Top right) A cherry pitter in operation.

few backyard cherry trees have consisted of (a) planting a mulberry tree nearby whose fruits are more attractive to the birds than the cherries; (b) placing pieces of glistening tin or heavy tin foil in the trees to dangle and shift with the wind; (c) using a scarecrow, and (d) placing a cat in a cage in the center of the tree. If birds become a problem in large orchards, an automatic acetylene exploder or 2- to 3-inch firecrackers tied at intervals into a small rope "fuse" (obtainable on the market) should accommodate two to four acres of cherry orchard. The exploder or crackers are timed to explode once every four or five minutes. Trapping of starlings in large special-built wire cages (U. S. Fish and Wild Life design) and cyaniding is permitted in most states. One company sells tapes of starling distress calls that frightens them away when played back on a loud speaker. Orchards should not be located near a woods or hedgerow whiich encourage depredation by birds. Ultra high frequency alarm systems are on the market that reportedly "jam" the birds audio system.

In Idaho and the Flathead River area of Montana, bear may cause heavy breakage of limbs while seeking sweet cherries in season. No fool-proof control has been devised.

DISEASES AND INSECTS

Most important fungus diseases of cherry East of the Rockies are *leaf spot* of foliage and *brown rot* of fruit. *Powdery mildew* may be a problem in both the East and West. *Leaf spot* overwinters on fallen leaves which eject spores to the wind in spring, eventually germinating on new leaves and causing yellowish then brown spots in great numbers. *Leaf spot* is aggravated by damp weather. *Brown rot* is the number one problem in Eastern orchards, particularly where fruit has been injured by curculio or cracked by excessive rain or hail. Where infection is present, cracking can become a real problem in mechanically harvested tart orchards. Other fungus diseases include

440

black rot, powdery mildew, and *leaf rust,* which are controlled by standard sprays for *leaf spot* and *brown rot. Virus yellows,* frequently following *ring spot virus,* is a growing problem. Leaves show green and yellow mottling with waves of defoliation starting three to four weeks after petal fall. Trees infected for several years develop abnormally large leaves and few spurs and bear small crops of large fruit. The tree gradually deteriorates. Specify *virus free* trees from the nursery.

Insect pests include *black cherry aphis, plum curculio, leaf roller, fruit flies,* (cherry maggot), *Mineola moth, mites, scales, sawfly, lesser peach tree borer, American plum borer,* and *slugs.* The sweet cherry "pitting" problem (wrinkled sunken areas on fruit) is thought to be due to the sucking damage of the *green soldier beetle.* See chapter XVIII for controls.

CONTAINERS, GRADING, STORAGE

Containers. Cherries, particularly sour cherries, are packed in many types of containers, ranging from 16- and 24-quart crates of individual quart baskets to 4-quart climax baskets and various types of lugs. Most sour cherries for the fresh market are loose-packed with the stems on.

The most widely used containers for sweet cherries from the Pacific Coast continue to be the Calex Lug and the Campbell Lug, both standardized by California. The Campbell Lug, measuring $3\frac{3}{4}$ x $11\frac{1}{2}$ x $14\frac{1}{8}$ and containing 15-16 pounds net, is the most popular shipping package for fancy cherries. The fruit is packed in rows with the top layer, or two top layers, faced. The row count across the width of the container is marked on the package, also the variety and net weight. The Calex Lug, measuring $3\frac{3}{4}$ x $13\frac{1}{2}$ x $16\frac{1}{8}$ and containing approximately 18 pounds net, is extensively used for loose, bulk and bunch-faced packs. Bunch-faced cherries are arranged carefully to look much like the faced row-pack, and must be marked with the row size or minimum diameter in terms of inches.

There has been an increase in the marketing of fresh sweet cherries in transparent film bags and folding boxes or trays, either overwrapped or with film windows. The packages are shipped in master-containers. Fiberboard containers are the rule although some shippers use a slatted-type wooden box. There is no standard master-container. California cherries, if packed in other than master-containers, must be marked "Irregular Container." The film bags and over-wrapped trays usually hold one pound or one-half pound. In Washington State, studies by U.S.D.A. showed that poly liners for the standard 15-pound lug reduced decay markedly and improved stem freshness and fruit brightness after simulated conditions of shipment and a two-day store treatment. (See Gerhardt *et al.*)

Grading. Cherries for fancy packs, canning, or freezing are graded from canvas trays or a moving belt (Figure 16). Fruits are removed which show evidence of insect damage such as curculio, fruit fly (maggot), brown rot, or cracking. Cherries showing wind bruising (brown discoloration of the

TABLE 3
Utilization of Sweet and Sour Cherries in the United States
(5 Year Period). In Tons.

	Fresh Market	Canned	Frozen	Brined	Juice
Tarts* 1966-70	4,458	36,376	67,283	Negligible	8,044
Sweets* 1965-69	38,888	14,097	431	50,243	Negligible

*Utilization of tart cherries is primarily frozen and canned whereas sweet cherries are primarily fresh market and brined.

skin) also are eliminated. All cherries that pass this inspection are put in Grade 1. Larger cherries may bring a premium. Sweet cherries for fresh trade frequently are sorted into several grades according to size after the blemished fruits have been removed. Highest prices usually are obtained for the largest fruits.

Storage. Cherries are not adapted to long storage, but may be held 10 to 14 days while the market is being cleared of an excess supply. They should be stored at a temperature of 31°-32° F. and 85-90% humidity to reduce wilting and brown rot. Sweet cherries can be held 31° F for 25 days in 10% CO_2, then ripened for 2 days at 70°F to fair quality with good appearance and comparable to fruit held in sealed polyethylene liners. It is preferable to grade and pack cherries before storing.

Prior to storage, research in Michigan indicates that a three-minute dip in hot water at 125° F. plus an appropriate fungicide such as Benlate eliminates brown rot and lessens other rots so that cherries may be stored satisfactorily in coolers for over three weeks.

Cherries which are to be shipped to distant markets should be precooled, by hydrocooling or by pressure cooling to reduce field temperature from 80° to 40°F in an hour, before shipping in refrigerated cars. Firm-fleshed sweet cherries may be shipped for a distance of a thousand miles under conditions of non-refrigerated express. Soft-fleshed cherries hardly could be shipped successfully a quarter of that distance. Some growers truck soft-fleshed cherries 100 to 300 miles over good roads, and firm-fleshed sweet cherries as much as 350 miles during the night and early morning hours to save cost of a refrigerator car and cartage at destination.

MARKETING

The largest percentage of both the sweet and sour cherries reach the consumer either directly or indirectly through the tin can, the frozen pack, or the glass jar. The relative amount of sweet and sour cherries sold fresh, canned, frozen, or brined may vary somewhat from year to year. Table 3

Note: For up-to-date fruit container specifications, contact Agent-in-charge, 516 W. Jackson Blvd., Chicago, Ill. 60606.

gives the relative importance of these four outlets for cherries. Only a small amount of the cherry crop is candied or used for juice, wine, and preserves.

Table 3 shows the relative amounts of tart and sweet cherries sold fresh and processed in the United States.

A large part of both the sweet and sour cherry crop is processed. Although the grower may not obtain a cannery or frozen-pack price which he considers entirely satisfactory, his crop is usually contracted before harvesting begins. The final problem of finding a consumer for the fruit rests mostly with the processor or re-manufacturer and not the producer.

Bargaining Tart cherries in eastern U.S. are bargained to processors by American Agricultural Cooperative Marketing Association and its state affiliates. Similar organizations, such as the Flathead Lake Sweet Cherry Growers (cooperative) Association, and the Flathead Lake Cherry Growers, Inc., in Idaho, assist grower members in their marketing problems.

Promotion. The National Red Cherry Institute headquartered at East Lansing, Michigan and its state affiliates, the New York Cherry Growers Association, the Michigan Association of Cherry Producers, and Wisconsin Red Cherry Institute carries on National promotional activities to asssit in selling processed tart cherries. February has been declared National assist Cherry month and many cherry promotion activities center around George Washington's birthday in remembrance of his chopping down a cherry tree. The National Cherry Festival is held in July each year at Traverse City, Michigan, the center of the nation's cherry industry. The industry wide promotion of sweet cherries is under the direction of the National Sweet Cherry Growers and Industries Foundation headquartered in Corvallis, Oregon. Many processors, pie bakers, maraschino manufacturers and other manufacturers of cherry products also carry on promotion programs aimed primarily at selling their own brand of product.

If fresh shipments are made to distant points, the cherry growers must follow trade channels similar to those described for apples in Chapter XII. Due to the perishable nature of cherries, the major portion is precooled and shipped by express. Sweet cherries washed and in poly bags move well in supermarkets.

Processing cherry outlets in the U.S. have been shifting somewhat over the years. The amount of sweet cherries brined has been increasing. In the late 1960's, the percentage consumption of total sweet cherries produced was approximately: canned, 12%; fresh, 40%; brined, 48%; and frozen, insignificant.

Per capita consumption of tart cherries has shown increases in the amount canned and frozen but a decrease in the amount sold fresh. In the late 1960's, per capita consumption was: canned, 0.9 lb; frozen, 0.6 lb; and fresh, 0.1 lb. During World War II, tart cherry consumption was depressed markedly whereas sweet cherries showed little change.

In big centers of consumption such as Cleveland and Detroit, a large amount of cherries are sold fresh-frozen as slush-pack. Restaurants use a sizeable percentage of these shipments in cherry pies and cobblers during the fresh cherry season. Some fresh cherries may be sold to hucksters who peddle the fruit for small sales. Roadside markets offer a good outlet for fresh cherries on well traveled highways. In fact, cherries come at a time in the season when the roadside markets, restaurants, and retail stores are not well supplied with other fresh fruit. In order to cater to this type of trade, however, the medium to small cherry grower should plant a considerable number of varieties, beginning the season with an extra early variety, such as Vista or Valera and closing it with Hedelfingen, Vic or Van, or another equally late and equally good variety. Good roadside market trade will depend upon high-quality cherries packaged attractively.

Housewife's needs. Cornell University conducted a study in which 3,000 housewives in five scattered New York cities were interviewed regarding their use of cherries. About 75 per cent of all cherries bought were used in pies. Most of the balance was used in various desserts. Type of packs bought in order of preference were: canned, cherry pie filler, frozen cherry pies, and frozen cherries. Most popular size pie tin for cooking was 8 to 9 inches diameter and 1¼ inches deep. There appeared to be a need for a can that held the amount of cherries for this size tin; available sizes were generally considered too small; 53 per cent of the wives would like a larger size. While size of package was their chief concern, some objected to poor color of water packed cherries, the small amount of cherries in pie filler, and the small size of individual cherries. Convenience products such as frozen pies, frozen pastries, cherry cheesecakes, cherry shortcakes and "high" pies show increasing promise in cherry marketing.

Dried tart cherries or "chaisins" (instead of raisins) has a potential sales outlet in fruit bars, coffee cake, etc. They have advantages of a dried product in storing and handling.

Federal Order in Tart Cherries. The tart cherry industry of Eastern U.S. voted in 1971 to utilize provisions of the Federal Marketing Order legislation of 1937 permitting supply control. A board of six growers and six processors elected by their geographic constituency administer provisions of this program in cooperation with the USDA to improve the marketing of tart cherries. The order in this industry was set up to correct the historical problem of widely fluctuating crops of tart cherries from one year to the next due to weather conditions. The order utilizes the provisions of storing a portion of the crop in years of heavy supply (thus removing it from the market) and subsequently re-entering the frozen stored cherries into the market in years of short supply. The order is intended to assist the industry in providing the market with a more stable supply of fruit than has historically been true, thus, over the long run increasing product and market development and ultimately consumption of the product.

COST OF GROWING CHERRIES

The amount of profit that a grower can make from a cherry orchard will depend upon three factors: (a) yields, (b) production costs, and (c) current prices. Yields vary considerably from one area to another and from one orchard to another. Over a period of 30 years, the average yield per acre for Washington, Oregon, and California, was estimated to be 2200 pounds. In the eastern states, where most of the trees are of the sour varieties, the average production is about 1200 pounds per acre. These figures for both the East and West include comparatively young-bearing trees as well as those in full-bearing, and likewise, those with poor care as well as the better orchards. Experienced cherry growers will recognize these figures as being very low and not representative of good commercial orchards. In order to arrive at these averages, however, there are some orchards obviously bearing less than the average.

Good commercial orchards in Michigan begin to bear at five to six years and reach 6000 to 10,000 pounds/A/year over a 10-year period, beginning with the 8th or 9th year at which time the orchard usually reaches full production. Trees continue at this production until about 20 to 22 years, after which they decline more or less rapidly as the case may be. There are authentic Montmorency yields in Michigan of 22,000 lbs./A. These figures give some idea of what a Montmorency orchard can do when conditions are reasonably favorable with good cultural practices.

Sweet cherries produce 1000 lbs/A at 8 to 9 years with an increase of from 7000 to 8000 when 14 yrs. old.

When the harvesting was accomplished by hand, the expected commercially productive life of sour cherry trees in New York was estimated at 30 to 40 yrs. and for sweet cherries, 50 to 60 yrs. However, mechanical harvesting has reduced this significantly. In Michigan these estimates are now as follows: Montmorency, 25 yrs; sweet cherries, 30 yrs. The commercially productive life of a cherry tree may vary widely according to cultural practices, insects and diseases, regions, and other factors affecting tree vigor.

In Michigan, Montmorency is the only commercially tart variety. The English Morello has given satisfactory results in some regions, whereas in other regions it did not prove profitable. Early Richmond and Louis Phillipe were doubtful for extensive planting. Sweet cherries such as Windsor, Schmidt, Napoleon and like varieties are the commercial sweet cherry varieties. However, sweet cherries only do well in the north part of the state. Because of fruit cracking, the Lambert and Bing varieties are a liability.

The itemized man-hours per acre for growing and harvesting sour cherries in Michigan are given in Table 4. Picking (non-mechanized) required the most labor, followed in order by pruning and brush removal, and spraying. With machine harvesting, costs can be reduced 75 to 80%. In the late

TABLE 4

AVERAGE HOURS OF MAN LABOR REQUIRED BY OPERATIONS IN 69 SOUR CHERRY
ORCHARDS IN MICHIGAN
(ADAPTED FROM WRIGHT AND JOHNSTON)

OPERATION	HOURS PER ACRE
Growing	
Pruning and brush removal	17.3
Spreading fertilizer	2.1
Spraying	11.7
Cultivating	4.8
Other	3.7
Total	39.6
*Harvesting**	
Picking (hand)	64.4
Total to grow and pick 1102-pound yield	104.0
Total to grow and pick 1937-pound yield	162.7

*Machine harvesting covers about 30 trees an hour, crew of four (1967 data from H. P. Gaston, Mich. State Univ.).

1960's machine costs were 1.1 cents/lb. as compared with 5 cents/lb. hand harvest. Or a crew of 4 can harvest, conservatively, about 30 trees/ hour or an acre of trees in about 4 hours, totaling 16 man hours per acre as compared with 64.4 hours hand harvest in Table 4. Hours devoted to cultivation in Table 4 also may be reduced where herbicides are used in the row and the middles are mowed.

Itemized costs of growing tart cherries in New York orchards are given in Table 5 for small, medium and large enterprises. While costs vary considerably from year to year, one can gain from these data an idea of the relative importance of the different operations.

The average cost of growing an acre of red tart cherries up to harvest showed a steady decline as the size of enterprise increased (Table 5). The small enterprises had the highest cost with an average of $156 per acre. Medium sized enterprises had a cost of $145 per acre to grow while the large enterprises were lowest with an average of $136 per acre to grow an acre of cherries.

Considering the various charges for growing one acre of red tart cherries, the land charge was one-quarter to one-third the total cost. Farm labor was another important item of the growing cost, accounting for about one-fifth of the total. It was not as important in the large enterprises as charges for sprays and dusts. Charge for power declined from 14 to seven per cent of the total cost of growing. This was in part due to the more efficient use of larger tractors. Sprays and dusts comprised a little less than one-fifth of the total growing costs and ranged from 14 per cent of the budget in small enterprises to 20 per cent for medium enterprises. The larger growers used the more recent chemicals which cost less per acre in some cases. Commercial fertilizer use constantly rose as size of enterprise increased reaching eventually 12 per cent of the budget in large enterprises.

TABLE 5

Item	Size of enterprise		
	Small	Medium	Large
Number of farms	12	24	21
Yield — tons of saleable cherries per acre	3.6	3.4	3.3
Growing costs per acre:		dollars	
Labor	34	31	21
Land	40	35	42
Power	22	13	10
Truck and auto	7	2	3
Special equipment	12	15	10
All sprays and dust	22	28	24
Fertilizer and manure	12	13	18
Other	4	4	5
General overhead	2	2	2
Interest	1	2	1
Total	156	145	136
Growing cost per pound of saleable cherries	.0220	.0219	.0220

These costs need to be adjusted upward with increases in price level in the 1970s.

Prices received for cherries obviously fluctuate with supply and demand. Average price paid per ton for tart cherries (farm disposition in 1970 in leading states) according to USDA figures were: Michigan, $143; Pennsylvania, $152; Wisconsin, $143; and New York, $155. For sweet cherries, prices were: Oregon, $329; California, $293; Washington, $325; Michigan, $180; New York, $180; Montana, $310 and Idaho, $467.

Higher prices may be obtained for early and particularly fancy products sold in small packages. However, the extra handling charges for the small packages usually absorb much of the difference so that in the end, the net profit obtained for a fancy packed product is not much more than that obtained for the product at the packing house or delivered to a cannery.

In order to make a profit, it is usually necessary for the yield of cherries to exceed 2500 to 3000 pounds per acre. Cherry orchards producing as little as 1200 pounds per acre are unquestionably a losing proposition, except perhaps during war periods when there is great need for food. Substantial profits can be realized from Montmorency orchards only where production costs per pound can be kept low by obtaining yields well over a general average of 50 pounds per tree.

In Michigan, Gardner states: "Indeed, it may be questioned if the producer of any other kind of fruit has within his ability to obtain greater net profit than the cherry grower. This is far from stating the profits as certain. Probably as large a percentage of cherry growers fail to make expenses as is true with most fruits. Nevertheless, the possibility of a profitable industry exists where soil and climatic conditions are favorable for heavy and regular

447

TABLE 6

GROWING AND HARVESTING COSTS FOR 10 ACRES OF TART CHERRIES
WESTERN MICHIGAN, 1971

Item	Southwest	West Central	Northwest
Growing Costs			
Variable:			
Labor	$ 275.05	$ 302.46	$ 272.24
Machinery	178.69	87.64	70.72
Spray Material	250.72	357.75	280.48
Other Material	307.11	226.00	198.00
Other	144.46	142.96	136.86
Total Variable	$1156.03	$1116.81	$ 958.30
Fixed:			
Machinery	$ 299.98	$ 184.35	$ 134.80
Orchard Overhead	1040.00	1163.33	1173.33
Total Fixed	$13339.98	$1347.68	$1308.13
Total Growing	$2496.01	$2464.49	$2266.43
Harvest Costs			
Labor	$ 482.40	$ 482.40	$ 611.20
Machinery	189.70	189.70	189.70
Fixed	1043.10	1043.10	1043.10
Total Harvest	$1715.20	$1715.20	$1844.00
Total Cost	$4211.21	$4179.69	$4110.43
Total Cost Per Lb.	$.070	$.070	$.069

Agricultural Economics Report No. 188, July 1971. ECONOMICS OF TART CHERRY PRODUCTION IN WESTERN MICHIGAN. By Myron Kelsey, Donald Ricks, Dept. of Ag. Econ., Michigan State University, East Lansing.

yields and where good marketing facilities are available; and this may become a certainty where cultural methods are employed that promote a vigorous growth and provide protection from injurious insects and diseases."

Review Questions

1. Discuss the leading World and U. S. commercial cherry producing areas.
2. Why has U. S. cherry production increased in some areas and decreased in others?
3. Discuss any changes in the tart and sweet cherry variety situation in recent years, giving reasons.
4. What is a Duke cherry?
5. List 2 important varieties of sour, sweet, and Duke cherries.
6. What are the climatic and soil requirement of sour and sweet cherries?
7. What are the pollination requirements of the tart, sweet and Duke cherries?
8. Are sour cherry varieties generally used for cross-pollination of sweet and Duke cherries? Why?
9. What three rootstocks are frequently used for cherries? What are the respective merits? What dwarfing stocks are available?
10. What is the relative resistance to cold of commercial varieties of sweet and sour cherries as compared with the peach?
11. What system of training the trees is suggested for sweet and sour cherries in your general area? Discuss training and pruning for mechanical harvesting.
12. With regard to other deciduous fruits, what is the relative amount of pruning recommended for cherries?

13. What is the approximate length of shoot growth desired in young and mature sour cherry trees? Should the desired shoot growth be obtained by pruning, cultivation or nitrogen fertilization?
14. Describe a good soil management system for young and mature cherry trees on a medium sandy-loam soil in your area.
15. Discuss hand and chemical fruit thinning of sweet and sour cherries.
16. When is the proper time to harvest: (a) tart cherries for canning, (b) sweet cherries for fancy pack? Discuss techniques, problems, advantages of mechanical harvesting and bulk handling for fresh and processing cherries.
17. List the growth regulator chemicals being used before harvest; describe effects.
18. Under what conditions and how long should cherries be stored?
19. What is the approximate amount of sour and sweet cherries processed and sold fresh?
20. Discuss factors influencing net returns in cherry growing?
21. What is an approximate yield one may expect from a well-managed orchard of sour, sweet, and Duke cherry trees in full bearing?
22. At about what year do sour cherries reach full production?
23. At what age under Michigan conditions do sour cherries begin to show a decline in production?

Suggested Collateral Readings

Anstey, T. H. Full bloom prediction for apple, pear, cherry, peach and apricot based on air temperature. ASHS 88:57-66. 1966.

Banta, E. S. Success with pick-your-own harvesting (cherries). American Fruit Grower. pp. 12, 13. September, 1953.

Bass, L. N. Cherry Seed Storage. (USDA, Ft. Collins, Colo.) J. ASHS. To be published 1973.

Bedford, C. L. and W. F. Robertson. Effect of handling and processing methods on the firmness and quality of canned and frozen red cherries. Mich. Qtrly. Bull. 40:(1) pp. 51, 58. 1957.

Bolen, J. S. and B. F. Cargill. Mechanized harvest systems for red tart cherries. Ext. Bull. E-660, Farm Sci. Ser. Cherry Harvest Mechanization. (2). June, 1970.

Bontrager, H. L. and H. M. Hutchings. Cherry brining costs as affected by container type. Ore. Agr. Exp. Sta. Spec. Rpt. 191. Apr. 1965.

Bukovac, M. J., et al. Effects of (2-Chloroethyl) phosphonic Acid on development and abscission of maturing sweet cherry. J. ASHS. Vol. 96, No. 6. Nov. 1971. p. 777.

Cain, J. C. and K. G. Parker. Virus disease of sour cherries cuts yields—nitrogen may help. Phytopathology 41: (8) pp. 661-664. 1951.

Chaplin, M. H. and A. L. Kenworthy. The influence of Alar ripening of 'Windsor' sweet cherry. J. ASHS 95 (5):536.

Childers, Norman F. Fruit nutrition — Temperate to tropical. Cherry nutrition, Chap. VI, by M. N. Westwood and F. B. Wann. pp. 158-173 Hort. Publ., New Bruns., N. J. 1966.

Cline, R. A. and J. A. Archibald. Nutritional factors and low temperature injury in peach and tart cherry. Ontario Hort. Exp. Sta. Ann. Rpt. 1967.

Cline, R. A. and O. A. Bradt. Soil drainage and compaction effects on growth, yield and leaf composition of cherries and peaches. Hort. Res. Inst. of Ontario. Rep. 1969 #45-52.

Cochran, L. C. et al. How nurseries get virus-free fruitstock. USDA Yearbook for 1953. pp. 152-158.

Costs of cherry production. Contact departments of agricultural economics at Cornell Univ., Ithaca, N. Y.; Mich. State Univ., E. Lansing; Wash. State Univ., Pullman; Pa. State Univ., Univ. Park.

Curwen, D., F. J. McArdle and C. M. Ritter. NPK effects on fruit firmness, pectic content of Montmorency cherry. ASHS 89:72-79. 1966.

Davidson, T. R. and J. A. George. Necrotic ringspot yellows effects on growth, yield of young sour cherry trees. Canada Jour. of Pl. Sci. 45:525-535. 1965.

Dawson, D. G. and P. C. Bull. Survey of bird damage to fruit. New Zealand JL Agric. Res. 1970. pp. 362-371.

(See additional references under Chapter XVI Appendix)

CHAPTER XVII

Edible Nuts, Minor Tree Crops

❖ ◆ ❖ ◆ ❖ ◆ ❖ ◆ ❖ ◆ ❖ ◆ ❖ ◆ ❖ ◆ ❖ ◆ ❖ ◆ ❖ ◆ ❖ ◆ ❖

EDIBLE NUTS

The important edible nuts produced in the United States are pecan, English walnut, filbert and almond (Figure 1). The almond, because of its close relationship to the peach, was discussed in Chapter XIV. Combined, the total commercial production of nuts, including the almond, is about 300,000 tons a year which places the nut crop among the ten important evergreen and deciduous fruits in the U.S.

Almonds, filberts and walnuts are grown in other countries, principally those in and bordering the Mediterranean; pecans are produced mainly in the U. S. and Mexico.

In addition to the commercially grown nuts listed above, there are several kinds of nuts in North America found growing for the most part in the wild and in home yards which are harvested largely for home use. These include the black walnut, the hickories, butternut, and the chestnut. The American chestnut was commercially important until the famous blight eleminated nearly all the trees as they grew in their natural habitat, particularly through the Appalachian Mountain range to Alabama.

In Figure 2 it is apparent that commercial nut growing is confined to the Southern States and the West Coast. The pecan predominates in the Southern States; on the West Coast, the English Walnut is important in California and Oregon; and the filbert is grown largely in Oregon and Washington. Filbert, English walnut and pecan can be grown to a limited extent in other areas of the United States and Canada but hardly in a commercial sense due to no or undependable cropping.

It is interesting to note that the commercially important nut trees in the United States are of the catkin-bearing type. This is examplified best in Figure 3, showing the long staminate catkins of the pecan with the in-

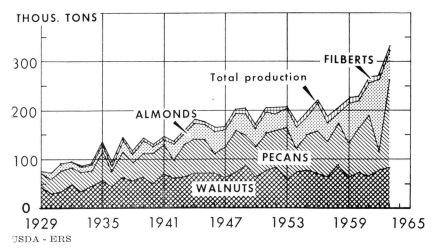

THOUS. TONS

300 ── FILBERTS

Total production

200 ── ALMONDS

100 ── PECANS

WALNUTS

0

1929   1935   1941   1947   1953   1959   1965

USDA - ERS

Figure 1. Total production of walnuts, pecans, almonds and filberts in the United States has about doubled since the mid-1930's. Most of the increase occurred before 1949. Production of each kind of tree nut has trended upward, with the largest increase in almonds. Walnuts and pecans usually lead in annual production. In recent years, these four tree nuts have comprised about half of the U. S. supply, and imports such as cashews, pistachios, and Brazil nuts the rest.

conspicuous pistillate flowers being born separately at the tip of the shoot. Several catkins originate from one compound bud at each node; there also is a vegetative growing point in this bud, but it will soon abscise unless the branch has been pruned back above the bud before it starts growth. Flower buds undoubtedly are formed by the end of a growing season for the crop the next year, since a heavy crop of nuts one year is likely to reduce both the staminate and pistillate flowers appearing the next spring. When the staminate and pistillate flowers are borne separately on the same plant, it is said to be monoecious.

The pecan, walnut and hickories belong to the family Juglandaceae; the filbert, hazelnut or cobnut belong to the family Corylaceae, the chestnut to Fagaceae. The botanical name of the commercially important English or Persian walnut is *Juglans regia,* L.; of the pecan, *Carya illinoensis,* Koch. (*Carya pecan,* Engl. and Graebn.), and of the filbert, *Corylus avellana* (*maxima*), L.

CARYA SPECIES

The pecan is the most important of about twenty species of *Carya* found in an area from eastern North America to Mexico (Figure 2). Belonging to this group also are pignuts (*Carya blabra,* Sweet; C. *ovalis,* Sarg., the small pignut) and the shellbark (C. *laciniosa,* Loud.) and shagbark (C. *Ovata,* Koch.) hickories. Except for the pecan, all of these nuts are class-

Dr. F. R. Brison, Emeritus Professor, Dr. J. Benton Storey, and Dr. J. P. Overcash of the Texas, and Mississippi Stations, respectively, gave valuable help on the pecan section.

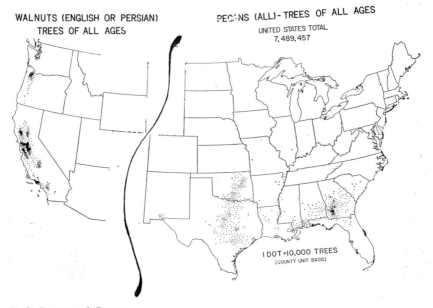

WALNUTS (ENGLISH OR PERSIAN)
TREES OF ALL AGES

PECANS (ALL) - TREES OF ALL AGES
UNITED STATES TOTAL
7,489,457

I DOT = 10,000 TREES
(COUNTY UNIT BASIS)

U. S. Bureau of Census

Figure 2. Commercial nut growing is confined to the southern states where the pecan predominates, and to California and Oregon where the English walnut is grown. Filberts are largely confined to Oregon and Washington on a commercial basis.

ified as hickory nuts which have shells that are harder and more roughened than pecan, and are shorter and rather flattened instead of being round like the pecan. All species have a four-lobed husk that develops from an involucre and when mature, dries, splits apart and pulls away from the nut.

Nearly all hickory trees are seedlings from the wild which generally have a long tap root, making them difficult to transplant. Young trees grow and come into bearing slowly. While there are several named varieties of hickory, it is essential to select those for a given region which have come from the wild in that region. This is because southern selected seedlings are not likely to mature their nuts in the shorter growing season and reduced summer heat found in the northern areas.

There are hybrids between the pecan and the hickory known as hicans. The nuts are longer than hickory nuts but the shell tends to be thick and rough like the hickory nut; they have gained but little interest in view of the fact that the pecan is being accepted so well.

Commercial production of pecans from native seedlings, and from improved grafted varieties each total around 50,000 tons, but both fluctuate widely from year to year. The commercially important pecan producing states and their respective 3-year average total production (in 1,000's of lbs.) from 1969-71 were: Georgia, 76,300; Texas, 28,000; Alabama, 28,000; Louisiana, 23,400; Oklahoma, 16,200; Mississippi, 11,300; Arkansas,

Figure 3. Nature of growth and blossoming habits of hickories and walnuts as illustrated by the pecan. A, Twig showing staminate flowers (a) borne axillary on growth of the past season and (b) pistillate flowers borne terminally on growth of the current season. B, Section of a catkin showing three staminate flowers of the many that form on each catkin (usually two 3-stalked catkins in each bud — three buds per node). C. Enlarged staminate flower containing several anthers (a); b, sepals. D. Single pistillate flowers with rough stigma at a. Drawing should show catkins at point where current season growth starts since catkins are in terminal bud.

7,700; New Mexico, 6,600; South Carolina, 3,600; Florida, 3,400; and North Carolina, 2,800.

In the western arid regions, the native[1] pecan trees are found along streams, whereas in humid areas they are found in well-drained deep soils, also along streams, and occurring in clumps and over considerable areas from Mexico to as far north as southern Iowa, Illinois, Indiana, and western Tennessee and Kentucky.

Varieties. The pecan is one of the few tree fruits that has such extensive native distribution in North America. Varieties now grown were selected from natives for their superior qualities. Controlled USDA-Texas breeding also has introduced Barton, Comanche, Choctaw, Wichita, Sioux, Apache, Mohawk and Cherokee varieties. The Oklahoma station intro-

---

"Wild" and "Native" seedlings are used interchangeably; "Native" is preferred.

453

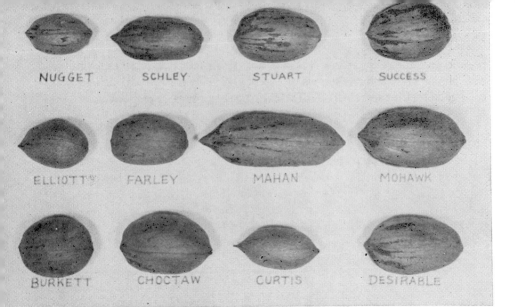

Jean P. Overcash, Mississippi State University, State College

Figure 4. The commercial and promising varieties of pecan above show variation in size, shape and markings. Among the more popular commercially are Stuart, Schley, Success, Mahan and Desirable.

duced several small-nut varieties with excellent shell-out and unusually fine kernel qualities. Many of the earlier commercial selections were made from the wild in Florida in the mid 1800's by John Hunt of Bagdad, Florida, others by E. E. Risien, Texas.

Varieties which have originated from natives in the drier western area of the pecan growing section are not adapted to the eastern growing pecan sections because they tend to be more susceptible to scab. With the advent of good scab control chemicals such as dodine, maneb, du-ter or polyram, scab control is not the problem it was.

Native so-called "paper-shell" strains selected in the southern part of United States are not well suited to northern sections because they have a longer required growing season of from 205 to 215 days in New Mexico, for example, although some varieties are said to require an even longer growing season to fill their shells with kernels. Pecans selected from the wild in Northern areas generally have a smaller nut with a thicker shell, but they will mature and fill the shell in 180 to 200 days. Pecans are quite tolerant of heat, producing satisfactorily in the 110° to 120° F. temperatures, but best around 80° with warm days and nights. There are no pecan varieties that will mature their nuts in the relatively short growing season from about New Jersey, North to New York and Canada, although the trees will flower and develop attractive foliage that can be used in a limited way for shade.

Since the introduction of named pecan varieties, more than 200 seedlings have been advertized and sold. Only a few meet the standards of a good commercial variety, namely: (a) come into bearing early, (b) be a prolific and annual producer, (c) has nuts of large size that crack easily with plump straw-colored kernels of good flavor and quality, (d) high percentage kernel for total weight (Table 1), and (e) be resistant to diseases or at least sufficiently so that it can be sprayed economically.

Most varieties under good management require four to seven years to begin bearing and seven to 12 years to produce commercial crops. The trade that likes unshelled pecans will favor the larger thin-shelled varieties with high quality kernels. However, much of the pecan crop is now going to the shelling plants. Thus, prolific varieties that produce small to medium-sized nuts of good quality are in demand by shellers. Low-quality nuts, whether large or small, generally bring low prices and are hard to move in heavy production years. Planters should choose probably not more than three or four of the best varieties for their respective area.

In Florida, Curtis and Stuart (more resistant to scab than Schley) are first choice with Elliott and Desirable among the newer most promising varieties. Other varieties commonly planted are Success (quite subject to scab), Mahan (subject to scab), Moneymaker (somewhat scab susceptible), Schley (the most generally grown variety east of the Mississippi River, not highly susceptible to scab), Moore (requires scab control), and Kennedy.

The nine leading varieties in New Mexico are Delight, Onliwon, Success, Barton, San Saba Improved, Ideal, Texhan, Western, and Burkett. Key characteristics of some of these varieties plus others grown in Texas are given in Table 1. The shape of the nut for a given variety and the superficial markings on the shell are characteristics for that variety and can be used in identifying it.

Important varieties coming from Mississippi are Schley, Stuart, Success, Pabst, Mahan and Russell. From Louisiana, the Moneymaker, Fortscher, and Van Deman have come, while from Texas were introduced the Burkett, San Saba, Halbert and Sovereign. From Florida came the Curtis, Moore, Kennedy, Santos, Acme, Rising, and Ramble. The Stuart variety (Figure 4) is probably the most widely planted because it is relatively more scab resistant. The Mahan bears very large nuts the first 15 years but may not fill well later; hence it is used as a filler-tree variety. Desirable has become a leading variety.

In the northern regions, probably the best known varieties which grow from Missouri to Kentucky are Busseron, Indiana, Butterick, Green River, Kentucky, Posey, Major and Niblack. The southern varieties can be grown as far north as southern Missouri. Since the pecan is relatively late to leaf out and flower in the spring it is seldom injured in commercial growing areas by late spring frosts. The wood also becomes dormant well before freezing weather in the fall. Where winter freezing damage does occur it is usually on young trees which will sprout at the base and form a new tree. Check the local government station for up-to-date varieties.

Soils and sites. The natural habitat for the pecan seems to be along

TABLE 1
TABLE OF VARIETAL CHARACTERISTICS (Texas Bull. 162).

| VARIETY | Kernel content of well filled nuts | Number of nuts per pound | Relative dates of | | Relative time of season when nuts ripen |
			Pollen Shedding	Stigma Receptivity	
WESTERN VARIETIES	Percent				
Burkett	54-58	40-60	Late	Early	Mid-season
Clark	53-56	60-80	Early	Late	Past mid-season
Halbert	57-60	60-80	Early	Late	Early
Ideal (Bradley)	54-58	55-75	Late	Early	Mid-season
Nugget	56-59	80-100	Late	Early	Mid-season
Onliwon	58-61	55-75	Early	Late	Mid-season
San Saba Improved	58-61		Early	Late	Early
Squirrel Delight	53-56	50-70	Early	Late	Early
Sovereign	52-55	50-70	Early	Late	Mid-season
Western Schley	56-59	55-75	Early	Late	Before mid-season
EASTERN VARIETIES					
Desirable	54-58	40-60	Early	Late	Mid-season
Mahan	53-57	40-60	Late	Early	Late
Moore	47-50	60-80	Early	Late	Early
Odom	54-57	40-60	Late	Early	Mid-season
Schley	57-60	50-70	Late	Early	Mid-season
Success	51-54	40-60	Early	Late	Mid-season
Stuart	48-50	45-60	Early	Late	Mid-season

the deep fertile soils next to streams, particularly in arid regions where possibly the lowest cost production is possible. Profitable pecan orchards also are being grown on high-priced irrigated land. Pecans will thrive on either high or low ground provided it is deep, well drained, and moisture is adequate; trees may survive and fruit for over a hundred years if the soil meets these requirements. Pecan trees will grow and fruit satisfactorily on the sandy to sandy loam soils of Florida to the heavier types in other areas. The sandy type soils may require more fertilizer attention as pointed out later.

Size of the tree, tree tops, and spread of the roots at different ages is shown in Table 2 from Georgia. It is apparent that mature pecan trees should have a four- to six-foot or better rooting depth.

Propagation. The stronger growing pecan seedlings are used for stocks. Seedlings from varieties which are known to be resistant to scab are used in the humid areas. Seedlings are lined out in the nursery and grown for two or three years. The roots grow about twice as fast as the

TABLE 2

HEIGHT AND SPREAD OF BRANCHES IN RELATION TO DEPTH AND SPREAD
OF ROOTS OF TREES OF DIFFERENT AGES (Ga. Exp. Sta. Bull. 176).

Age of Trees (years)	Height of Tree (feet)	Spread of Branches (feet)	Depth of Roots (feet)	Spread of Roots (feet)
1	1	0	1-3	1-2
2	2-3	1-2	2-4	3-4
3	4-5	2-3	3-5	6-8
4	5-6	3-4	4-5	15-20
6	6-8	3-6	4-6	20-30
10	15-20	25-35	4-6	40-60
20	35-45	55-60	4-6	80-120
25	45-55	70-80	4-6	100-150

tops. Trees are budded in mid-summer, 2nd or 3rd year, using the patch bud as shown later for the Persian walnut. The tongue-graft can be used on small seedlings in humid areas, (Chapter VIII). When the bud is fitted into place on the stock, it is held tightly in place by rubber or plastic strips, and coated with an air-tight material (water asphalt emulsion) to keep the patch from drying until it grows to the stock.

The bud-wood is collected in winter and stored at 32° F. in cold storage in moist peat moss. Cions are removed from storage about a week before they are to be used and held at a temperature of 80° to 85° F. in moist peat moss. The higher temperature facilitates peeling of the bark. If all bud sticks are not used they can be stored again at 32° F. for use during the next two- to three-week period.

The inlay graft is used in dry regions (Chapter VIII) on one- to two-inch stubs, differing from apple by covering 4-6 inches of the stock stub after grafting with aluminum foil, then pulling a poly bag over the cion and securing it at the base of the cion and 4-6 inches below with poly tape to reflect heat and keep good humidity. Tip of cion is coated with orange shellac. See Texas planting and grafting pamphlets.

Planting. Permanent tree spacing is generally 60 feet or more on the square, depending upon moisture supply and soil fertility. Trees sometimes are planted 30 x 60 feet to provide space for intercropping and after about 20 years every other tree in the row is removed, leaving about 12 trees to the acre. High-density plantings are under test of 72 (17½x35 ft.) to 193 (15x15) trees per acre, with the trees pruned to small size. A search is underway for dwarfing stocks. Tree training is not as exacting, offering several intriguing advantages. This system should be watched as more experience is gained. Machine mowing of sides and tops is under test, costing under a dollar a tree. It is suggested that the *Pecan Quarter-ly** be checked often for this and other key research developments.

Since the pecan has a long tap root it is necessary to dig a hole about 3

---

*Edited by Dr. J. Benton Storey, Horticulturist, Texas A & M University, College Station. 77843.

R. E. Harper and J. V. Enzie, N. Mex. Exp. Sta., Las Cruces

Figure 5. (Left) The far better root system is shown on the right pecan tree where success from early vigorous growth is more likely to occur. At right is shown the graft union between a seedling pecan and the improved cion variety; the seedling was top-worked when young.

feet deep using, if available, a tractor back hoe. Growth the first year may start late and be slow.

Pecan trees budded to known varieties are sold by nurseries with the rootstock three to five years old and the tops one to two years old. The tops may be three to eight or ten feet in length and ¾ to 2" in diameter about six inches above the bud union. There is no advantage in planting trees larger than this. Pecan trees are rather difficult to transplant and thus should be transplanted as soon after dug as possible with no drying of the roots during the process. Good and poor pecan trees for transplanting are shown in Figure 5.

It is important to remove about half of the top in transplanting to reduce the water requirement of the tree. Mulching is advantageous to conserve water particularly in arid regions. Because the trees are slow to start growth they may be sun scalded. This can be prevented by wrapping or tying burlap or a cylinder of kraft paper around the trunk, or by whitewashing the trunks with a lime-water solution.

Many branches are likely to develop in the area where the top was cut back. The best of these which grows in an upright position is left and the remainder are removed at this point. However, this should not be done until there is adequate foliage to prevent the trunk from sun scalding. The permanent branches should arise from five to six feet above the ground to provide for mechanical shaker attachment below the lowest branch.

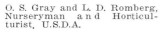

O. S. Gray and L. D. Romberg, Nurseryman and Horticulturist, U.S.D.A.

Figure. 6. These trees are high-density planted (35 by 35 ft) and machine pruned on the sides, top (right). The system shows promise with strip-chemical-weed-control, irrigation as needed, and sod middles replacing former intercropping and pasturing practices.

Trees should be pruned as little as possible to attain the desired shape, since the more foliage left, the faster they will grow.

CULTURAL MANAGEMENT

Young trees. Strip chemical weed control or strip cultivation should be practiced next to the trees. If an organic mulch such as sawdust, wood shavings, or hay is available, this applied to a depth of six or more inches keeps the soil about the roots cooler and moist. Additional nitrogen may be needed at first to assist in the decomposition of the mulch and prevent nitrogen deficiency in the tree.

Fertilizer generally is applied the second season after transplanting since the tree grows so slowly the first year it is unable to make good use of fertilizer. In the arid sections of the West only nitrogen and zinc are used. One-half to one pound of urea, amonium nitrate, or an equivalent nitrogen fertlizer is applied for each year of age of the tree, broadcasting it in a zone from two to six feet from the trunk and working it in with a disc. A zinc foliar spray is used at 2 pounds of 36% zinc sulfate in 100 gals. (use 2 lbs. hydrated lime in humid areas) as needed to eliminate "rosette." In humid areas, an 8-8-8 can be ringed under the tree at ½ to 2 lbs. for each year of tree age in early spring. ZN-EDTA (12%) sprays also are effective. Consult your government specialist.

Since pecan trees are widely spaced in the beginning, it is common to grow for several years intercrops such as cotton, corn, small fruits, truck crops, and even peaches, pears and Satsuma oranges where they can be grown. Intercrops in the mature orchard are limited to early spring vegetables that can be grown before the trees leaf out. Some growers lease their land for this purpose, the main value being that the fertilizer and

459

Figure 7. Pecan tree on the left shows dieback and rosetting of small leaves, On the right is the same tree after receiving three early-season zinc sulfate spray applications.

cultivation benefit the trees, in fact necessitating no separate fertilization of the trees, especially when winter and summer legumes are grown. Winter legumes in the Southeast are crotoloria, beggar weed, and hairy indigo; summer legumes are crimson clover, lupine, and white and Hubam clovers.

Bearing trees. Strip-row chemical weed control under the branch spread year round is a trend, which also facilitates nut pick-up at harvest.

In case of pecans alone, a common practice is to grow a winter legume of lupine, or crimson, giant bur, white or Hubam clover fertilized with 300-500 lbs. of an 0-10-12 or 0-14-14. The legume may or may not be disced down in spring with the native cover taking over during summer. Basic fertilizer applied to pecan usually includes NP and K. The 1 - 1 - 1 ratio or 10 - 10 - 10 is common, with additional N where needed.

By standard leaf analysis technique, the following mineral contents are suggested for "normal" producing pecan trees.

N	P	K	Mg	Ca	S*	Mn	B	Zn	Cu*	Fe*	Mo*
2.3	0.11	1.0	0.3	0.7	100	150	20	50	5	75	0.7
to	to	to	to	to	to	to	to	to	to	to	to
2.9	0.16	1.5	0.6	1.5	150	500	45	100	15	150	1.0

Data supplied by Dr. Ray E. Worley, Ga. Coastal Plain Exp. Sta., Tifton. Contact this station for up-to-date pecan leaf analysis recommendations.
*No data available for these nutrients; suggested amounts based on "normal" content of other fruit and nut trees. Data for NPK, Mg, Ca in %; others in ppm.

Nitrogen deficiency is the most common for pecan in all commercial growing sections. Symptoms first appear as a light green color in the leaves followed by a yellowish even green, then a greenish yellow and finally a uniform yellow as the deficiency becomes acute. Here again small reddish brown dead spots will develop between the veins giving the leaves a russet appearance. The leaves drop earlier as the deficiency increases. From year to year the leaves become smaller in size, shoot growth progressively shorter, with some shoots dying. For mature trees, the rate of actual N per acre is about 100 lbs. for trees alone. Where sod is envolved, additional nitrogen will be needed to feed both the trees and sod.

Phosphorus deficiency is noted in South Carolina as a delay in opening of the spring foliage. Old leaves later in the season will change to a dull green and then to a yellowish green with some parts of the leaves losing green color. Small areas die and turn brown and the leaves take on a bronzed appearance. Under acute conditions shoot growth is short and slender. Tip and marginal burning of the leaves is apparent with subsequent drop of the leaves while many of the younger leaves will be unaffected. Where complete NPK mixes ar being used, phosphorous should not be a problem.

U. S. D. A.

Figre 8. A pecan leaf showing typical severe zinc deficiency symptoms. The leaflets show wavy margins and have become narrowed, and crinkled, and the necrotic areas between the veins have dropped out, leaving a perforated condition.

Potassium deficiency rarely occurs in pecan to the point where marginal and tip burning and upward rolling of the leaflets occur on older leaves; but yields may be reduced. From 25 to 50 lbs. of K_2O or 40-80 lbs. of 60% muriate of potash should provide the needs on an acre.

Pecan trees were among the first on which *zinc* deficiency, or leaf "rosette", was discovered and corrected. The pecan ranks with sweet cherry, salicina plum, and the apple as being among the most apt to show zinc deficiency. Soils in the arid regions of the West have a high fixing power for zinc, making it necessary to use larger quantities for correction of deficiency. In arid regions, rosette is most economically controlled with 2-3 lbs 78% ZnEDTA wettable powder/100 gals. when the leaves are 1/8 grown and before pollen shedding.

Spray applications of zinc are used more or less in all pecan areas and while quick response is obtained, the effect is not as lasting nor as uniform as soil applications where effective. In New Mexico, 2 lbs. of a 36% $ZnSO_4$ in 100 gals. is used, but no leaf burn resulted in experiments where 6-8 lbs. were used. Applications are made starting after pollination at 4 to 6-week intervals as needed, and continuing each year until full correction. In humid areas, as Florida, 2 lbs. to 100 gals. of water with 2 lbs. hydrated lime are used, or where copper Bordeaux is being used as a fungicide, 4 lbs. of $ZnSO_4$ is added to the mix. Correction is better on young growing foliage.

In South Carolina, rule of thumb for soil zinc application is ½ to 1 lb. for each year of tree age, or 1 to 2 lbs. per inch of trunk diameter. Application in late February or early March is recommended for the soils in Georgia.

In Florida where soils are on the acid side 2½ lbs. of zinc sulphate per tree, spread evenly under the branches is usually sufficient on sandy soils. Sandy loams and heavier textured soils may require 5 to 10 lbs. of zinc sulphate per tree to accomplish the same result. For young trees 2 to 4 ounces should be sufficient. Once the deficiency is corrected additional zinc applications should not be more often than once in five to ten years since high zinc levels are quite toxic to plants.

Manganese, boron, calcium, and magnesium levels should be watched particularly in sandy type soils of humid areas. In the Southeast, yields have been increased by USDA worker, J. H. Hunter at Albany, Georgia, by maintaining the pH of the soil around 6.0 with the application of lime, preferably dolomite (contains a higher percentage of magnesium as well as calcium). Pecan growers generally have avoided the use of lime because of fear of aggravating zinc deficiency. However, this worker and others in Florida have found that yields can be increased by double or more by holding the soil pH at a slightly acid level by lime applications.

When leaf *manganese* in pecan is less than 100 parts per million "mouse-ear" or little leaf may be observed particularly in door yard plantings in Florida. Manganese levels in pecan leaves should be rather high, or from 150-500 parts per million. Manganese deficiency may be particularly noticeable in marl soils. A broadcast of 2 to 10 lbs. of manganese sulphate with 15 lbs. of ammonium sulphate or 5 lbs. sulphur per tree to lower the pH should be adequate to correct the deficiency in such soils, depending upon tree size.

Normal content of *boron* seems to range from 10 to 90 parts per million in pecan leaves and while no deficiency symptoms have been reported in the Florida area, they do recommend that boron be included in the pecan fertilizer for the cover crop using 10 to 15 lbs. per acre of borax or its equivalent.

Boron deficiency in South Carolina is characterized by small water-soaked spots appearing on normal leaves which later turn a purplish reddish brown. Younger leaves may become misshapen, and smaller in size as the deficiency becomes acute. Later, ends of the shoots together with buds will die.

Sulphur deficiency also has been reported in South Carolina resulting in loss of color of the young leaves. Loss of green occurs first on the sides of the mid-rib of the leaves extending toward the margins with green spots surrounded by yellow developing as the deficiency advances. This is followed by small reddish necrotic spots, marginal burning and loss of leaves. Later, the new and very small yellow leaves will appear. This deficiency is found only in unattended trees, since fertilizers and spray materials used in good orchard management contain sulphur.

Pollination, fruit set, alternate bearing. Mature bearing pecan trees will normally produce large quantities of pollen which is shed when the humidity is below 85%. Pollen may be carried 3,000 ft. by wind. The flowers are wind pollinated. However, since the male and female flowers do not mature at the same time, known as dichogamy, the trees often are not adequately self-pollinated. Some varieties will shed most of their pollen before their pistillate flowers are receptive, and in others the situation is the reverse. A given variety may be dichogamous one year and not the next. Where the orchard consists of many trees of one variety, there probably is sufficient overlapping in pollen shedding and receptiveness of the pistils between the individual trees to get normal crop setting. However, where only a few trees are planted it may be advisable to select a combination of varieties which will provide pollen from early until late in the flowering season as shown in Table 1.

Romberg and Smith at the USDA Field Station near Austin, Texas found that where cross-pollination between varieties was accomplished, this resulted in more nuts per cluster at harvest than where self-pollination occurred; also, the nuts from cross-pollination were generally larger in size and contained heavier kernels. It, therefore, seems advisable to interplant two or more varieties in commercial orchards, alternating groups of rows of each variety to facilitate machine harvesting and pick-up.

In New Mexico alternate bearing of light and heavy crops seems to be more of a problem than in the eastern areas where the pecan nut casebearer is a factor in thinning the fruit. Harper and Enzie were unable to correct alternate bearing by thinning the nuts experimentally on three common varieties. Random branches in accessible areas of the trees were thinned to one, two and three nuts per cluster. There was a local increase in size of kernel due to thinning. In pruning trials preceding the heavy crop year where the main branches were cut back into second year wood, some improvement in the "off" year was obtained. Early-season chemical thinning of pecan, as with apple may be more effective in securing annual production, but the technique has not been perfected. A study is being made at Texas A & M of seasonal fluctuations of endogenous growth substances to try to manipulate fruit set and thinning.

As with the apple there are about three waves of dropping of flowers and young fruits. The first drop consists of pistillate flowers at about pollination time due sometimes to imperfect development of the apical flower and the one next to it. This may be associated with a heavy crop the preceding year or to unfavorable soil or weather conditions. The second drop consisting of fruit takes place due to the eggs not being fertilized; this may be due to insufficient pollen at pollination time and can be corrected by interplanting different varieties. The third drop will occur later and into the month of September in Georgia. This occurs particularly on trees that are heavily loaded with nuts and may be caused by embryo abortion in some nuts. Water or nutrient deficiencies also may be factors as well as insect and disease injury.

It is rather surprising in the pecan that fertilization of the egg does not take place until five to seven weeks after pollination; in fact, the embryo is not readily apparent until 9 weeks or more after pollination.

The hard shell of the pecan is essentially the ovary wall and the hull or husk develops from the involucre. The kernel or embryo starts rapid enlargement about 12 weeks after pollination and continues for six to eight weeks. This period of rapid growth does not occur until the shell is almost full size and the seed coat or integument has reached the size and form of the mature kernel. The endosperm which is largely the edible portion and is inside the seed coat is essentially a storage area for the embryo to draw upon when it starts to grow into a seedling tree.

The shells may not be filled with kernels if, during the period of their rapid growth, nutrient or water deficiencies occur or the leaves become unhealthy for one reason or another, or there is an excessive crop. These same factors may result in small nuts if they occur early in the development period of the nut. Also, if the growing season is too short and there is inadequate heat, the nuts will not fill properly. Too close planting of trees without proper pruning may cause poor filling of nuts.

When the nut matures, the husk begins to dry and split four ways starting at the apex. This accelerates the drying of the shell and the kernel, which is desirable. If the growing season retards the proper drying and opening of the husk, the embryo may germinate within the nut and start growth before it falls which indicates of course that the nut, like many other seeds, is capable of germinating without a rest period.

Pruning. The pecan tree naturally forms a relatively strong framework. Limbs are well-spaced with wide-angled strong crotches, generally speaking. An effort is being made by some growers to control tree size by pruning and use of dwarfing spray chemicals to keep them in workable range as is done with apple. Lowest limb at tree maturity should be at 6-7 feet. When weak, broken, or dead branches are removed, the technique described in Chapter IV should be followed. Due to their size, actually it is difficult to prune pecans regularly as with apple or peach. Texas research shows that Alar and heading-back pruning on 18-year trees

R. E. Harper and J. V. Enzie, N. Mex. Agr. Exp Sta., Las Cruces
(Lower) Ramacher Manufacturing Co., Linden, California, 95236

Figure 9. (Above) Special-built screens which are tractor-propelled are used
to center wide-falling nuts as pecan trees are shaken by tractor and cable.
(Below) Special-built pickup machines, as used for English walnuts, are labor
savers. High-lift clearance facilitates movement in rough areas. Bulk bins
handled with tractor lifts speed the operation from orchard to grading and packing house.

will maintain a smaller regular bearing pecan tree, permitting initial hedge-row or closer planting of trees.

Pest control. In the arid sections of New Mexico leaf diseases are not a problem, but two aphids, the black pecan and the black-margined aphids, must be controlled to keep the foliage normal and active.

In most other pecan areas there are a number of pests. Scab is the problem disease of the nut and foliage. Other pests attacking the nuts include pecan weevil, hickory shuck worm, stink bugs and pecan nut casebearer. Other foliage pests are webworm, walnut caterpillar, aphids, and several minor diseases. The twig girdler, trunk borer, crown gall, sun scald, and winter injury may be minor wood problems. The squirrel is controlled by mounting an outward and downward slanted galvanized 6- to 8-inch wide iron band on the trunk to prevent the squirrels from climbing the trunks. Rats and mice during storage are controlled by poison, trapping, and rodent-proof room construction. Shading by heavy growth of Spanish moss is controlled by a regular spray program where a caustic fungicide such as 6-2-100 Bordeaux is used.

Helicopters, fixed-wing airplanes and air-blast sprayers are widely used in pesticide applications. Southern experiment stations and USDA have up-to-date spray recommendations and pest descriptions. (See references).

Harvesting. Most of the pecan crop is jarred, shaken, or bamboo-poled from the trees. Increased labor costs has resulted in greater use of tractor shakers, as described for cherry and walnut, or the simpler use of a padded cable attached to limbs by hand and jerked by an eccentric and piston on a tractor. Two sheets are used under the trees to catch the nuts, or, as shown in Figure 9, special built screens, each tractor-propelled from tree to tree, are used to catch and center nuts that fall beyond the sheets. Pick-up machines (Figure 9) on previously smoothed ground and use of bulk boxes has replaced burlap bags for handling.

Ethylene (Ethrel) spray shows promise in getting uniform and quick husk dehiscence.

After harvest the nuts are dried and shrunk in weight by 10 to 20 percent by placing in racks or trays or in a 6-inch layer on the floor, or by placing in used gunny sacks. Pecans will keep for several months if held in a cool dry place, but they become rancid quicker than the English walnut. For costs of growing pecans, see Farris and Allen; Seals; Fowler, others in suggested collateral readings.

Marketing. Pecans are marketed through auctions, private sales, and co-op associations. Some are sold directly to consumers in 5, 10, 25, 50 and 100 lb. packages and bags. Growers generally deliver the nuts orch-ard-run to distributors who do the sizing, grading, and blending, but in heavy crop years it may pay growers to do the latter jobs themselves prior to marketing. About six percent of the production goes to distribu-tors as whole nuts to be moved before Thanksgiving and Christmas. These nuts are cleaned, bleached, then processed to restore color before sold.

Fla. Agr. Exp. Sta., Gainesville

Figure 10. At left are motor-driven pecan crackers and at right a kernel grader in a Florida shelling plant. These machines separate nearly all of the kernels from the shells after cracking.

U. S. and state (where established) standards are followed in sizing and quality grading. Size varies by 1/16 inch within a range of 12/16 to 16/16 inch. Nuts within these sizes may be small, medium, large, extra large and oversize. Grades are U. S. No. 1, U. S. Commercial, and Unclassified. U. S. No. 1, as an example, calls for the following: Ninety percent of nuts uniform in color, fairly well shaped, and free of external defects such as stains, adhering hulls, split and broken shells, loose hulls and other foreign material. Up to 10 per cent may be off-quality in external appearance, but only 3 percent may show serious damage caused by stains, adhering hulls, and other factors. Eighty-five percent of kernels by count must be free from internal defects that affect quality such as moisture, rancidity, worm injury, shriveling, discoloration, and other factors. Of the 15 percent permitted below U. S. 1 requirements, only 6 percent may have serious damage.

Around 94 percent of the pecan crop goes to the shellers, who sell them as half and piece kernels for baking, confections, ice cream, and other products. Pecan shelling equipment is highly mechanized (Figure 10), consisting of sizers, crackers, cleaners, hand-picking belts, and driers. Driers bring the kernels to constant weight by reducing moisture 10 to 20 percent.

An increasing proportion of the crop is being stored at about 32° F.; short storage periods of two to three months at 37° to 40° F. and 85% humidity is satisfactory for early deliveries. At 32° F. nuts should store for about a year; at 5° F. they will hold and not become dark and rancid in two years. If kernels are allowed to dry below 3.5 to 4.0% moisture, the normal percentage for cured kernels, rancidity and brittleness will develop. Above this moisture, undesirable texture and blue mold will develop. Kernel flavor is retained better if stored in sealed cans, glass jars, or moisture-proof bags. The nitrogen and vacuum packs in glass containers in Florida were satisfactory at 32° F. but none would keep kernels fresh for more than two to four weeks at room temperature in summer months; under cool room temperature or in air-conditoined stores rancidity should not develop for several weeks after removal from cold storage.

Pecan kernels are high in energy (fat) and fairly high in vitamins B_1 and B_2. From waste pieces of kernels about 75 percent of the oil can be recovered by heating to 200° F. and pressing with 12 tons psi. Pecan oil as a liquid or emulsified is a good cooking fat and salad oil and it has good keeping qualities. Crushed pecan shells can be mixed equally with builders' sand to form a good rooting medium for greenwood cuttings.

WALNUTS[1]

The genus *Juglans* includes all walnuts. The only commercially important walnut is the English or Persian, *J. regia,* L., which is grown for the most part in California and eastern Oregon (Figure 2), although it is found growing in the East as far north as Niagara Falls, N. Y. Total commercial production is approximately the same as for pecans (Figure 1). The 3-year average for 1969-71 was: California, 114,000 tons; and Oregon, 2,800 tons. Crop size fluctuates considerably from year to year. In one year for California, for example, production was 132,000 tons (all-time high) while in the previous it was 108,000. Around 35% of the crop is sold in-shells and the balance shelled. Price has been $400-450/T with a total U. S. value of 45-55 million dollars. Only about one percent of the crop is exported.

Europe no longer dominates the walnut industry of the western hemisphere, as was the case a few decades ago when the United States produced only about 20,000 tons. In those days France produced alone twice this much and Italy another 10,000 tons. Since then, there has been a decline in the French crop with an increase in walnuts in Italy.

Walnut production in California has moved from southern counties to north of the Techachipi mountains to the central coast and San Joaquin and Sacramento Valleys where production and quality are better. Trend of total bearing acreage and production of walnuts to 1963 are shown in Figure 11, but note total production has jumped to over 130,000 tons in the 10 years since.

There are many kinds of walnuts, other than the Persian walnut, growing both in the wild and in dooryards in the United States. The eastern American black walnut, *J. nigra.* L. is by far the most important in this group. The kernels are among the richest in flavor but the large hulls are

Dr. George C. Martin, Pomology Department, University of California, Davis, assisted in revision of the walnut section.

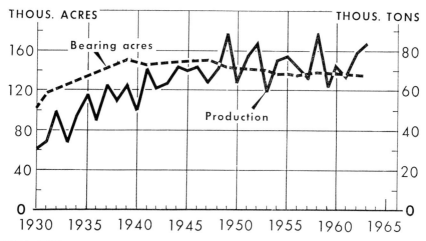

Figure 11. English walnut production in California and Oregon has gradually risen to over 130,000 tons. The big increase in production, not shown here, came in the late 1960's and early 1970's with large plantings of Hartley, the leading variety in California, upping total bearing acreage to around 145,000.

difficult to separate from the nuts and the shells are thick and hard to crack without getting a black pungent powder mixed with the kernels. The trees are difficult to propagate and transplant and come into bearing slowly. Varieties have been selected from the wild. Among the better grafted varieties available from nurserymen in the East are Thomas, Ohio, Stabler, and Rohwer.

Roots of the eastern black walnut are thought to create a toxic substance, possibly juglone, which stunts growth of apple, tomato, potato, blackberry, alfalfa, the heaths and some wild species of plants when their roots come in contact with or grow near the walnut roots.

The butternut, *J. cinerea,* L., which is the most cold resistant species, is native from Arkansas and Georgia to New Brunswick, Canada. The tree is slow growing and has richly flavored nuts but the shells are thick and the kernels slim and small. Varieties selected from the wild and propagated in a limited way by nurserymen include Van der Poppen, Kenworthy, Sherwood, Thill, Love, and Irvine.

J. ailantifolia, Carr., the Japanese walnut, produces smooth-shelled nuts for the most part although there are some strains that bear rough-shelled nuts, suggesting hybridity. The heartnut (*J. ailantifolia,* var. *cordiformis,* Rehd.) is closely related and bears heart-shaped nuts. These species are fairly hardy in the Northeast but may show tree damage in severe winters and occasional crop loss.

Walnut species hydridize readily. Some hybrids make acceptable rootstocks for the Persian walnut.

469

The Persian Walnut

Climatic Limitations. The main climatic limitations for Persian walnuts in the West are: (a) spring and fall frosts, (b) extreme summer heat, and (c) insufficient winter chilling.

Sites should be avoided where spring frosts below 30° F. are likely to occur. Catkins, new growth, and young fruits may be injured. Early fall frosts are likely to injury young shoots causing them to fail to leaf out the next spring. Winter temperatures in the West rarely injure dormant walnut trees. The varieties Mayette and Franquette have endured winters without severe injury when the minimum temperature fell to 0° F. which explains why these varieties are occasionally seen growing in dooryards in the Eastern United States.

In the Northeast, varieties of Carpathian origin, introduced from Poland, are hardy, particularly the variety, Broadview. Other grafted varieties available from nurserymen in this area are Schafer, Little page, McKinster, Metcalfe, Colby, and Jacobs.[1]

If temperatures above 100°F. are accompanied by low humidity, sunburning of the exposed walnuts is likely to occur. If sunburn occurs early in the season the nuts may become "blanks" (no kernels), but if it occurs later the kernels may be partly shriveled, dark in color, or they stick to the shell and stain it, classifying it as a cull.

In the warm coastal areas of southern California some walnut varieties do not receive adequate chilling, causing them to leaf out and bloom late. Nuts will be small and the crop greatly reduced. The soft-shell types of the Santa Barbara group are better suited to the southern areas of California whereas the French varieties such as Franquette and Mayette which require more chilling are better adapted to central and northern California and Oregon.

Soil. The ideal walnut soil is a well-drained silt loam at least five to six feet deep containing abundant organic matter, free from a high or fluctuating water table, and free from alkali. Soils not well suited to walnut orchards are those which are coarse and sandy, heavy adobe, and clay underlain with adobe.

It is true that most of the high-water tables in arid regions of California carry some alkali. If the water table is within nine to ten feet of the surface, deep-rooted trees are likely to be injured by the salts even though there seems to be a substantial layer of good soil above the water table. Some orchards are being grown with success on land with a high-water table but the injury is reduced by more rainfall, careful application of irrigation water, a well-drained soil, and irrigation water relatively free from salts. Orchards that have been damaged by alkali water table have been improved to some degree by installation of drains. Walnut trees are among the most sensitive to alkali.

---

[1] A list of nurserymen handling nut trees is given in the appendix.

470

Only a small amount of boron in irrigation water will cause leaf scorch and occasional severe defoliation with a reduction in yield and quality. It is well to seek competent advice and run tests for the site and irrigation water before planting.

Winter irrigation will be needed in those areas where the rainfall (a) is insufficient to produce a winter cover crop and (b) to penetrate the soil to a depth of six feet.

Varieties. Walnut varieties grown in southern California largely originated from nuts (probably from Chile) planted by Joseph Sexton near Santa Barbara in 1867. While nuts of some of the seedlings had hard shells, it is the so-called Santa Barbara soft-shell types that now comprise the industry. Nearly all commercial varieties except Payne and Eureka are descendants of this original planting; they include Placentia, Pride of Ventura, Neff, Prolific, Wasson, Ehrhardt and Chase.

Key characters desired in a walnut variety are good annual yields of high-quality nuts which have a strong well-sealed shell that withstands handling, packing and shipping without cracking. Proportion of kernel to total weight of nut should be 50% or greater in crack-out.

Ten promising new varieties have been released by the University of California, namely, in order of ripening starting 5 days after Payne: *Lompac* (best in Santa Ynez Valley); *Serr* (San Joaquin-Sacramento Valleys, hotter areas); *Gustine* (west San Joaquin Valley); *Chico* (Sacramento Valley); *Vina* (Vina-Red Bluff area); *Midland* (Stockton-Sacramento); *Amigo* (same as Chico; a good pollinizer); *Pioneer* (upper Sacramento Valley); *Tehama* (Tehama county); and *Pedro* (a good pollinizer). USDA and Oregon State University introduced the promising varieties Hartley, Spurgeon, Adams UC 49-46, Adams No. 10, Chambers No. 9 and Webster No. 2 for limited commercial testing.

Hartley is the leading variety in California. Nuts are large, shells bleach well, kernels reasonably light colored, good flavor, blooms before Franquette, small pin hole in end of nuts (entering moisture discolors kernels in Oregon), and a lateral bearing habit that increases production. Seasons, plus other problems, are not wholly adopted to this variety in Oregon.

Placentia. This variety is grown in Southern California. The trees grow rapidly, are precocious yielders, bear annually but the nuts blight badly in some areas, and may spring open at the apex if dried too rapidly. The nuts do have a desirable size, a smooth shell that is usually oval, thin and strong, with a smooth, plump, light-colored kernel. It is considered the standard of quality and appearance. The kernel attains best quality in coastal areas in southern California; it is not suited to central or northern California. *Eureka* trees grow vigorously, come into bearing relatively late, bloom late and escape spring frosts, ripen three weeks later than Placentia, nuts long and parallel with sides rounding to square ends, and kernels may show "shrivel tip", particularly in inland districts. *Franquette,* second in California and the leader in Oregon, blooms four weeks later than Payne

471

and after Eureka escaping spring frosts, is slow to reach bearing; nut elongated, pointed, moderately rough; shell well-sealed, very well filled with light-colored kernels; recommended for central and northern California and Oregon. Trees by this name vary considerably. While tree population is high in California, very few are being planted. *Mayette* trees are large, spreading, starting growth about two weeks before Franquette. Kernels are relatively small in proportion to shell size, good color; tree holds catkins late and may be used for pollinizer for Franquette; grown in central and northern California and Oregon. There are several strains of Mayette: Triple X strain has a heavy shell and is well sealed, not bearing consistently large crops; San Jose is poorly sealed, requires packing in cartons, and has a round hard-shelled nut; Tribble has a long-type well-sealed nut which gives high yields in some districts. *Payne* was discovered by G. P. Payne near Campbell, California; it is grown in most walnut areas. Trees bear early and heavy, and make slow growth when young due to heavy cropping; nuts exposed prominently on outside of trees and subject to sunburning; shell of medium thickness, pitted, well sealed; kernel of full good quality. Payne or Payne types (10 new ones recently released from Calif. breeding program) are the most prominent varieties in the recent California plantings. Payne is highly blight susceptible.

Other commercial varieties include Blackmer, Ehrhardt, Wasson, Pride of Ventura, and Concord. Oregon is testing Manregian (Manchuria) seedlings in search of a better variety. New varieties for testing in the Northeast are Clinton, Gratiot, Greenhaven and Somers.

Rootstocks. The best rootstock for the Persian walnut has been *J. hindsii,* the northern California black walnut. It makes a good graft union, shows some resistance to oak root fungus (*Armillaria*), is apparently resistent to the common rootknot nematode (*Heterodera marioni,* Cornu) and the nematode, *Cacopaurus pestis,* but may be injured by the Meadow nematode (*Pratylenchus pratensis,* De Man). It is susceptible to crown rot. Care must be exercised by the nurseryman to be sure he gets the northern California black walnut since it can be confused with the southern California black walnut (*J. californica,* S. Wats.); they are found growing together. Manregian seedings are used as stocks in Oregon.

Hybrid rootstocks known as Paradox, a cross between the Persian and any of the black walnuts, and Royal hybrid, a cross between Eastern black walnut and either of the California black walnuts, are being used only in a limited way. Paradox is used only where added vigor of the hybrid is of special importance. Royal hybrid is limited by the difficulty encountered in producing the hybrid seed stock.

Persian walnut seedlings are being used for stocks in southern California; they are vigorous, but are susceptible to oak root fungus and alkali soil; they make a smooth graft union free from constriction; are more resistant to crown rot and root rot; more subject to injury by the common root lesion nematode than northern California black walnut; and they are objectionable to nurserymen because of slow initial growth.

Unfortunately, all stocks are susceptible to root-lesion nematode, and all but Persian are susceptible to Black-line, a real problem in the Santa Clara region and creeping into other areas.

Propagation. Walnut trees are propagated in the nursery by grafting in southern California and by budding in northern California. High budding on the black walnut trunk gives a short section of black walnut trunk and decreases sunburn and entrance of oak root fungus where these are problems.

A year after planting when the trunk is one inch or more at ground

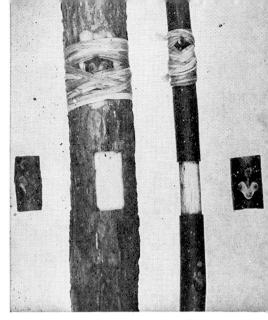

L. H. MacDaniels, Cornell University

Figure 12. Technique for patch-budding nut trees is shown on the left; a bud tied in place is shown above. On the right, a shield bud is shown before and after (above) placement.

level, soil is hoed away from the tree crown to two or three inches and the scion is grafted into the stock just below ground level. The scion is tied, asphalt coated, and the soil hoed back to cover the scion to a depth of one to two inches. Grafted trees are grown another year in the nursery, trained to a leader with no laterals and tied to stakes 1 x 2 inches by 8 feet.

Patch budding in late summer (Fig. 12) can be used on fast-grown one-year trees. Preripen the bud by removing the leaf blade (not petiole) 10 days before removing the bud (Figure 13). Plastic or rubber bands may be used to tie the bud firmly in place on the stock. Grafting by anyone of several methods is more successful in Oregon than budding.

A premium price is placed on the larger trees. Small nursery trees may have a poor root system and never make a first class orchard tree. Medium trees 8 to 10 feet in height may be preferrable to larger trees because of less shock in transplanting.

Starting Young Orchards. Old orchards that have been the most productive are planted 50 to 70 feet apart for permanent trees. Trend, however, is toward high-density plantings 30 x 30 ft. which with high-bearing lateral buds (Hartley), proper pruning, irrigation, and nitrogen control will prove satisfactory and high-yielding per acre. Trees are planted in late winter allowing adequate depth of 18" to 30" for the tap root; width of the hole should be sufficient to accommodate lateral roots of 6" to 8" length.

In the northern walnut areas of the west coast, some growers plant

L. H. MacDaniels, Cornell University

Figure 13. Homemade knives on the left are used for shield- or patch-budding nut trees. Tool on right is used for patch-budding and is obtainable from nursery supply houses.

black walnut trees, then top-work them in the orchard. Considerable skill and consistent follow-up care are needed. One-year black walnut trees may be planted in the orchard, the preferred way, or the seed may be planted. When seed are planted, two to four nuts are set at each location, leaving the most vigorous one for grafting. Trees should be top-worked when they are young to avoid the need for propping and tying on the older trees. A single graft on the young trunk is easiest although individual budding may be done on several main limbs. Patch budding is most common and is done when the bark slips well in midsummer although early spring may be satisfactory.

Grafting is done in spring just after growth starts using either the side or whip grafts (See Chapter VIII) on small branches or the bark cleft or kerf grafts for stubs 3" to 5" in diameter. Usual care of the grafts as described in Chapter VIII is suggested.

Because of the *blackline* disease (line forms at xylem of scion and stock), Oregon growers do not use the black walnut as a stock (see reference).

Training Young Trees. Nursery trees are headed five to six feet above the ground at planting and protected from sunburn by whitewashing or special tree wraps or protectors. Buds and growth are rubbed off the lower section of the tree as growth starts. Where sunburn is a problem in hot

474

interior districts, trees may be cut back to 5 to 7 buds above the root-stock union (about 18"). The most vigorous upright branch is selected after one year of growth, removing the others, but leaving one or two small lower branches on the southwest side to protect the tree from sunburn. The tree is trained to either a vase-shape with a high head or the central or modified leader (Chapter IV). The main advantage of the central-leader type tree is that there is greater strength of the framework. Laterals are spaced about two feet apart vertically and spirally around the tree. Vase-shaped trees, which have most of their branches developing within a limited area, tend to be weaker and are subject to more breakage. In a vase-shaped tree there should not be more than three or four main branches. Eureka and Franquette can be trained to the central leader easier than Placentia, Payne and Mayette, which tend to be spreading and are somewhat better adapted to the vase form. The first main framework branch should be four to six feet from the ground. Secondary laterals on the main limbs tend to become horizontal eventually and should not arise closer than eight feet from the ground, except where the tree is naturally small such as Payne, or where there are strong prevailing winds.

Whether the grower selects the central leader, the modified leader, or the vase shape for his trees, the framework of the tree should be selected so that the branches are spaced as far apart as practicable, both vertically and horizontally. Excess branches should be removed at winter pruning during the first few years, but in interior districts a few small low branches on the southwest side of the trunk should be stubbed back and left for shade until the top is fully developed.

Soil Management. Cultivation insofar as a deep-rooted walnut tree is concerned is of relatively little importance. It is practiced mainly to disc in cover crops and organic matter, to keep down summer weed growth, to permit better penetration of irrigation and rain water, to smooth the soil for harvesting, and to prepare a good seed bed for cover crops. Subsoiling is not recommended in walnut orchards nor should the soil be worked when wet or excessively dry.

Strip-row herbicide applications under the limb spread in the fall before rains is being used in walnut orchards to control mainly annual weeds. Simazine and diuron in initial tests were best. Consult local government service for up-to-date recommendations. (See reference).

Common cover crops and pounds per acre to plant are: (a) melilotus clover—20 lbs.; (b) purple vetch—40 lbs.; and (c) mustard—5 to 10 lbs. Slow-growing legume crops such as vetch and melilotus clover should be planted immediately after harvesting. Fast-growing crops such as mustard and rape may be planted later. They grow very rapidly and will produce a heavy tonnage of organic matter in 90 to 100 days (Figure 14). An application of nitrogen may be needed with the latter crops. Cover cropping in the drier sections may necessitate one winter irrigation to replace that used by the cover crop.

Irrigation. Walnuts need adequate moisture most during the five to six weeks immediately following bloom (Figure 14). No amount of mid-summer or late irrigation will compensate for a deficiency during this period. With inadequate moisture after bloom, nuts at harvest will be small and of poor quality due to lack of plumpness of the kernels, reducing yields.

Since walnuts are deep-rooted the grower must use a soil tube or auger to sample the soil at depths up to six feet. Most observations indicate that soil moisture control to a depth of nine feet in walnut orchards is sufficient to maintain proper vigor and production. About 80% of the moisture used by the tree to a depth of nine feet comes from the upper six feet. In heavier soils most of this water comes from the upper three feet, whereas in lighter soils, withdrawal is about equal in the 0-3 and 3-6 feet depths.

In the interior valley areas soil may dry during the harvest period necessitating an irrigation after harvest to mature the wood properly and avoid killing-back from winter frosts. If rainfall during the winter does not wet the soil to a depth of six feet, a late winter irrigation will be necessary to make up for the deficiency and provide adequate moisture for the trees when they leaf out and bloom. The nuts make nearly all of their volume increase in size within the first six weeks of their growth, after which the shells begin to harden.

Intercrops. With the trend toward high-density plantings and a greater effort to initiate high early production, intercropping with vegetables, etc., has become rare.

Fertilization. Soils in the arid walnut regions of the West have a larger natural supply of nitrogen than soils in humid areas. Frequently the amount of nitrogen available in these soils will maintain good growth of walnut trees for many years. Legume cover crops also will supply a small amount of nitrogen. When nitrogen begins to become deficient, however, the foliage will be smaller and lighter overall green, sparse, with some twig dieback and a reduction in yield.

A nitrogen test in Oregon showed that 6 lbs. actual N/mature tree increased yields 14-25 lbs./tree, and increased size of nut and the percentage kernel and filling, covering by several times the cost of the ammonium nitrate. Kernel weight from N-treated trees was increased 5 times as much as the shell weight.

California volcanic soils are deficient in P but control is difficult.

Zinc deficiency or "little-leaf" occurs in the interior districts and for some obscure reason is particularly troublesome on spots where corrals were formerly located, regardless of soil type. When severe, there is no normal foliage; leaves are small, yellow, twisted and showing chlorosis between the main veins with dieback of the shoot tips. Where less severe there will be good shoot growth only in spring but yellowing and curling of leaves will appear in midsummer. Treatment consists of foliar sprays of zinc sulfate (1 lb/100-36%) or chelate (2 lbs. Zn EDTA/100) 2-3 times at 2-3 wk. intervals after the foliage is about ¾ full size in spring. One treatment lasts for several years.

Soil treatments can be used where the fixing power of the soil is not high such as in very sandy soils. Zinc sulphate is placed in a trench about four to six inches deep and about two feet from the trunk, using 5 to 10 lbs. for trees two to eight inches in diameter and up to as high as 30-50 lbs. for larger trees. Apply in early winter. Spray treatments of zinc have not been satisfactory on walnuts.

Mn deficiency may be found in the central and south-coastal areas of California. Herringbone leaflet chlorosis and scorch are typical. Apply 5 lb. $MnSO_4/100$ gal when leaves are almost fully expanded.

Cu deficiency may be found in the areas of Mn deficiency in California. Shriveled kernels, die-back, yellowing and dropping of tip leaves are typical. Bordeaux foliar sprays (10-10-100) at end of pollination to only deficient trees is a corrective.

Boron deficiency or die-back is occasionally a problem in Oregon, resulting in brown-spotting of the tip leaflet between the veins; elongated leafless shoots or shoots with misshapen leaves; and nuts not setting well, dropping off when the size of peas.

Boron toxicity also may occur where the irrigation water is high in boron, or excess borax has been used. Symptoms are more or less similar to deficiency symptoms.

Boron deficiency is corrected by applying to the soil in late winter about three lbs. of borax or equivalent for a 12- to 14-year tree or four to six lbs. for an 18- to 24-year tree. The borax is broadcast under the tree. Correction may last for about three years.

Suggested mineral contents of leaves of "normal" producing walnut trees follow:

N	P	K	Mg	Ca	S	Mn	B	Zn	Cu	Fe*	Mo*
2.5	0.12	1.2	0.3	1.25	170	30	35	20	4	75	0.7
to	to	to	to	to	to	to	to	to	to	to	to
3.25	0.3	3.0	1.0	2.5	400	350	300	200	20	155	1.0

N, P, K, Mg, Ca expressed in % D. W.
*No data available in literature; values are approximate amounts found in other woody fruit and nut plants; values for S, Mn, B, Zn, Cu, Fe and Mo are in ppm.

Pruning Bearing Trees. Good yields are associated with good vigor in mature walnut groves. In interior districts from 8 to 12 inches of shoot growth is desired in the top-most shoots, whereas in coastal districts, 4 to 6 inches is a desirable minimum. Trees with less vigor may be due to a deficiency of nitrogen or another of the nutrient elements listed above, or inadequate irrigation, or an accumulation of injurious salts, or scale insects. Detail pruning throughout the periphery of the tree sometimes has given beneficial results on weak trees.

In general, there are two types of pruning on walnut trees. One is the removal of the lower limbs to facilitate cultural practices. In the other,

(Upper left). Caterpillar Tractor Co., Peoria, Ill.; upper right, lower right, Diamond Walnut Growers, Inc., Stockton, Calif.; lower left, Ramacher Mfg. Co., Linden, Calif.

Figure 14. (Upper left) This crawler tractor is knocking down a vigorous mustard cover crop in a California walnut orchard, using a tandem heavy disc with a heavy spike-tooth harrow following. **(Upper right).** Contour-check irrigation; oil burners are on islands in the row for frost control. **(Lower left).** Brush for sweeping nuts in window for early pickup by nut harvester at lower right; a screen trailer is catching nuts at rear. A standard tractor is used to motivate the harvester. Due to fall rains and inability to use pick-up machinery, most of the Oregon crop is still tree-shaken and hand-picked off the ground. With little bark injury to tunk, "Shock-Wave" type shaker i snow widely used.

the trees are thinned throughout the tops to admit more light to the center of the tree and to develop more fruiting wood in this section. As trees become older the periphery tends to be the only bearing area with the center of the tree more or less shaded out.

Walnut Insects and Diseases. Major insects are the codling moth, walnut aphid, walnut husk fly and the red spider; there are a number of minor pests. Among the key diseases are walnut blight, melaxuma (canker), crown gall, crown rot and winter injury or dieback. Consult references for details and seek the latest spray schedules from local government services.

Harvesting and Marketing Walnuts. *Factors effecting Crop Quality.* Walnuts drop naturally over about a two-month period. Trees are shaken by mechanical shakers, as shown in Figure 14, before they drop naturally in order to obtain the highest quality. Number and vigor of shakings depend upon the climatic conditions and variety; it varies from two to four times. In cooler areas the nuts mature more slowly and over a longer period of time. Cracking of the hull and maturity of the kernel occurs about the same time in cool areas and because of this three to four light shakings are usually desirable. In hot interior areas, however, kernel maturity usually precedes hull cracking; earlier and more vigorous shakings bring better quality in these areas.

The nuts should be gathered, hulled and dried immediately after shaking to avoid damage from rain and/or fog, increasing the percentage of culls.

Husks on some nuts adhere tightly and are called "sticktights"; kernels in these nuts are likely to be inferior to nuts where the husks fall away clean. "Sticktights" are likely to be greater during seasons of high temperature and sunburning. Droughts during the latter part of the growing season, aphids, red spiders or any factor causing leaves to drop prematurely will result in a higher percentage of "sticktights" and inferior nuts.

Commercial grades are set according to the percentage of edible kernels, light-colored kernels, and shell appearance. Use of mechanical shakers and harvesters to pick up the nuts from the ground have aided considerably in reducing the number of moldy nuts and culls resulting from slower harvesting techniques. This mechanical equipment also reduces labor costs considerably. Mechanical harvesting has been more effective in the interior sections where the nuts ripen over a shorter period and where more vigorous shaking is required. Mechanical shakers also do a more thorough job of removing the nuts from the trees. They are particularly effective with Payne, Eureka, Mayette, and Franquette varieties. The ground must be smoothed before harvest (Figure 14).

Hulling. Careful judgment is needed to shake the trees at the proper time so that most of the hulls will be ready to fall away from the nuts naturally. If shaking is done too early there will be a high percentage of hulls sticking to the nuts. Hulling is done by hand or by machine. Machine hulling is quicker and more economical and removes the hull before the shell cracks open. Oregon tree shaking starts when 75% of hulls split.

Use of Ethylene Gas. Once the kernel is mature the biggest obstacle to rapid harvesting is the large amount of green "sticktights" that fall at the first shaking. In some interior sections the kernel will mature two to three weeks ahead of hull loosening. While water-sweating can be used to assist in removing the hull it is not always satisfactory. Use of ethylene gas is more rapid and effective. But it has been used successfully only in the warm interior districts of southern California, mostly on Placentia and Eureka varieties. In coastal districts it may cause darkening of the outer veins on kernels. To be effective the kernels must be mature. The green nuts are separated out and placed in an airtight bin equipped with forced draft ventilation. The gas is injected at the rate of one cubic foot of ethylene to a thousand cubic feet of air with the temperature ranging

479

between 70° and 80° F. The bin is ventilated with fresh air, every twelve hours for twenty minutes to one and a half hours, regassing after each ventilation. Treatment is continued until 96 to 98 percent of the hulls are removed, requiring 24 to 72 hours.

Ethephon. Encouraging research is underway in California by Dr. George C. Martin with the chemical, 2-chloroethylphosponic acid (ethephone), which may eliminate many of the steps outlined above in the harvesting and hulling of walnuts. When the packing tissue* had turned brown on key varieties, ethephon foliar sprays at 500-1,000 ppm were applied 27-10 days before normal harvest. The sprays caused dehiscence of hulls and enabled complete nut removal from trees with a single mechanical shake as much as 3 wks. earlier than normal. Walnuts were hullable and the quality generally superior to controls. Costs reduction are obvious. In some instances considerable leaf drop resulted. It is suggested that the reader keep current with this work.

Washing. The nuts are washed after the hulling to remove juice of the crushed hulls which otherwise will stain the shell and make bleaching difficult or impossible. Sunburned or blighted hulls will retain their stain. Large, cylindrical drums are used with coarse wire netting to wash the nuts. The nuts are revolved in this cylinder under a stream of water for two to three minutes.

Dehydration. After hulling and washing the nuts must be dried immediately to remove excess moisture from the kernels and shells, (a) bringing the nut to a stable weight, (b) preventing molding and darkening of the kernels and (c) to permit efficient bleaching. Nuts adequately dried should average about 6 percent moisture and not exceed 8 percent. Use of dehydrators has replaced sun drying because they can be operated in all kinds of weather, giving (a) uniform drying within twenty-four hours, (b) minimizing molding, darkening of kernels and splitting of shells, (c) reducing labor and (d) speeding walnuts to the consumer. Walnuts have a critical temperature of 110° F. Higher temperatures will cause rancid kernels to develop within a few weeks.

Packing and Selling. After curing, the nuts are delivered to a local packing house such as the one shown in Figure 15. This plant[1] processes about 75 percent of the California crop.

On reaching the packing house the nuts are passed under a vacuum hood which removes the "blanks" or improperly filled nuts. Nuts with

---

*Packing tissue is the white, pithy material that fills all the space between the lobes of the cotyledons and between the cotyledons and the shell of an immature nut. In the mature, dry walnut the remains of the packing tissue form the major septums and the thin layer that lines the shell.

---

[1]A brochure is available, giving details of history, organization and operation. It is the largest walnut packing house in the world. Write Diamond Walnut Growers, Inc., Stockton, California. 95201

Figure 15. (Upper left) Headquarters of Diamond Walnut Growers, Inc. at Stockton, California, covers 14 acres of a 50 acre site showing cold storage tower and receiving bins at right; offices and cafeteria are at left with mechanized handling of walnuts in main plant in center of picture. This is one of the most efficient and best organized plants handling fruits or nuts in the country. This highly automated plant will process 50,000 to 75,000 tons of nuts each year or approximately 55% of walnuts produced in the U. S. 98% of U. S. production is in California. (Upper right) New products are developed and tested. (Lower left) Close-up of electronic kernel sorting machine which accepts walnut kernels of specified color and rejects others. (Mid-bottom) Forty electronic color sorting machines handle 90,000 pounds of nut meats per eight hour shift. (Lower right) Constant check on kernel quality is maintained in the standards laboratory. (Courtesy Diamond Walnut Growers, Inc., Box 1727, Stockton, California, 95201.)

full kernels pass on to an endless belt where they are hand-culled to remove those which are obviously imperfect. The nuts then pass through a revolving drum containing a bleach solution of sodium hypochlorite for two to three minutes. The bleach is harmless to humans and the kernels; it removes dirt and stains leaving them uniformly bright and clean. The nuts then pass to a belt where women pick out those with imperfections revealed by the bleaching, such as wormy, sunburned or moldy nuts. The nuts are then sized mechanically into three standard grades: large, med-

481

ium and baby. Since the larger size nuts bring the higher prices it is obvious that the best cultural practices should be used to get the bigger nuts. Each size grade of nut is run through a large thoroughly ventilated bin where the moisture is removed which was absorbed in the bleaching process. From the drying bins the nuts pass on to another culling belt before they are individually labeled as shown in Figure 15 for this particular brand, then packed mechanically into one- to two-pound cello-phane bags or larger cartons. Over 80 percent of the in-shell walnuts are marketed in cellophane bags, the rest in bulk cartons.

Many of the walnuts picked out as culls have good kernels and are cracked along with others by machine. The kernels in the factory shown in Figure 15 are separated electronically on a color basis and sold as shelled walnuts which comprise about 40 percent of the crop. Surveys indicate a declining willingness of customers to crack nuts; they are preferring high-quality meats ready to use.

Kernels are sold in 4- and 8-ounce vacuum cans. In vacuum canning, machines do the filling, weighing, pulling of the vacuum and sealing. In recent years, research has developed a tasteless chemical substitute, an antioxidant, for the "pellicle" or skin of the nut that prolongs keeping quality of the broken kernels. Kernel life also can be prolonged by re-ducing the moisture to 3.2 to 3.7 percent.

Kernels not used in consumer packages are packed in cartons for com-mercial use in ice creams, cookies, cakes, and the like. Inedible kernels and shells are processed into various by-products, such as oil for paints, walnut meal (shells and meat particles) for poultry and cattle, and a good percentage of shells, of course, are burned in the plant's furnaces for fuel.

Walnut kernels contain a high proportion of unsaturated fatty acids to the saturated types. In one cup of kernels, aside from oil, water, and other minerals in the ash, there are the following: 15% protein, 15.6% carbohydrates, 30 International units of Vitamin A, 480 micrograms of thiamin (B group), 130 micrograms of riboflavin (B group), 1.2 mg of niacin (B group), 380 mg. of phosphorus, 2.1 mg. of iron, and 83 mg. of calcium.

From 75 to 85 percent of the walnut crop is packed and sold by the Walnut Growers' Association which is a noncapital, nonprofit, coopera-tive and composed of local associations in all walnut districts. In Cal-ifornia the Board of Directors of the Central Association is composed of one representative from each local association. Association members re-ceive the market price of the particular grades of their delivery, less the cost of packing and marketing. Those growers who are not association members sell their crops to commercial packers.

FILBERTS[1]

The commercial filbert industry is centered primarily in Oregon and Washington. The U. S. crop has increased markedly since the 1920's when it totalled around 50 tons. The 1969-71 average for Oregon was, 8,750 tons, and 442 tons for Washington. In 1961 the crop rose to 13,000 tons in Oregon. As shown in Figure 1, however, total production is only a fraction of that for almond, pecan and Persian walnut.

In the world picture, Turkey produces about 133,000 short tons of filberts although the crop fluctuates considerably; Italy about 60,000, and Spain around 19,000 short tons. The United States imports about 2,500 tons and exports around 300. World production trend is upward.

Filberts also are found in the Northeast where people may grow a few trees on odd bits of fertile ground around farm and home buildings. Filberts also can be grown as a tall hedge, but hedges are not likely to bear as heavily as single-trunk trees. In the area of Geneva, New York, winter injury of shoots and catkins is likely to be severe and occur frequently enough to reduce yields below a profitable level. Filbert breeding projects at the New York Agricultural Experiment Station and by U.S.D.A. at Beltsville, Maryland, have as a major object the development of hardier and more productive varieties for the Northern climates.

The hazel tree goes far back into history. Garden culture of this tree seemed to have begun in Italy where six varieties were grown as far back as 1671. Many varieties were known in England in 1912. Kentishcob (known also as DuChilly) was from a seedling grown about 1830. Hazelnuts or filberts (*C. colurna* L.) are grown extensively in northern Turkey, as summarized in a comprehensive report by Schreiber.

Botany. The filbert (sometimes called cobnut[1]) and native hazelnuts belong to the genus *Corylus* (family, Corylaceae) which includes a number of species, but only one, the European filbert (*C. avellana*), is cultivated extensively for its nuts. The varieties of this species are numerous and are the basis for the rapidly expanding filbert industry in Oregon and Washington. Varieties of this species also are cultivated extensively in southern and central Europe. Two species of *Corylus* are indigenous in eastern North America, namely: *C. cornuta* (*C. rostrata* in Gray's *Manual of Botany*), the horn or beaked hazel, and *C. americana,* the American hazel. Both of these species grow as low shrubs, sucker freely and are common along fence rows and in wasteland. While *C. cornuta* is of little value for its nuts, it is the more hardy of the two. *C. americana* is the more promising; a few varieties such as Winkler and Rush have been se-

Robert L. Stebbins, Extension Horticulturist, Oregon State University, Corvallis, assisted in the filbert section revision.

[1]Cobnuts often are described as short round nuts that are not entirely covered by the husk or involucre; the filbert is entirely covered (Figure 16).

lected from the wild by those who are interested in the improvement of native nuts. But the best varieties are inferior to the European filbert. Because of their hardiness and fruitfulness, however, they are useful in breeding.

The Turkish tree hazel (*C. colurna*) is of interest only as an ornamental large tree reaching a height of sixty feet or more and having a rough, corky, rather picturesque bark with handsome foliage. Since the tree does not sucker, grows rapidly, and is very late coming into bearing, the species is being tested in the Northwest as a rootstock for commercial varieties.

Varieties. There are some 220 varieties of filberts tested in the United States and of these there are perhaps only a dozen of commercial interest. In Oregon the main variety is Barcelona with Daviana as a pollinizer. In New York, varieties suggested by Slate of the New York Exp. Station are Cosford, Medium Long, Italian Red and Royal.

Pollination. The filbert is monoecious which means that the staminate and pistillate flowers are born separately on the same plant, such as in corn (See Figure 16). The pistillate flowers are born in small scaly buds with the stigmas being visible during the flowering season only. They are reddish, threadlike, and appear in very small short bundles. The pistillate flowers usually appear a few days before the catkins begin shedding pollen. Nearly all varieties of the filbert are self-unfruitful, which means that in commercial plantings there should be two or more varieties interplanted. Filberts are wind-pollinated, not needing bees in the orchard. The same pistil may be receptive for over a period of several weeks. After pollination, the pollen tube is found to grow to the stigma base, enters a resting stage of four to five months, when the pollen tube resumes growth and the eggs are fertilized. The filbert shell is the ovary wall and the kernel is largely embryo. It takes several months after pollination for the nut to show development after which the shell sizes rapidly and then the embryo develops.

In California, filberts seem to fruit at high elevations up to 2000 feet better in past experience but Paul Marianni, one of the largest fruit and nut growers, says that filberts at Davis, California, a much lower elevation, may fruit satisfactorily in his experience. Flowers when fully open often endure considerable frost with no injury being noted to either flower when the temperature dropped to 16° F. during the pollinating season at Geneva, New York. If high winds accompany this temperature, however, the staminate flowers almost certainly will be destroyed.

Climatic Requirements. Chilling requirements for such varieties as DuChilly and Cosford is about the same as for that of most apple varieties such as Delicious. With inadequate chilling, however, filbert flowers will open together better than for apple or peach. When filberts are not located near large bodies of water or near similar site protection, the pistils

George L. State, N. Y. Exp. Sta., Geneva

Figure 16. (Upper left) Filbert flowers: (1) Catkin or staminate flower, (2) pistillate flowers at shoot tip, with tiny flower parts protruding from bud tips, and (3) a winter-killed catkin, above. (Right) types of husks on filberts: (top) cluster, Italian red; top row, left to right, Barcelona, Kentish Cob, and Nottingham; lower row, White Aveline, C. americana, and C. Cornuta. (Lower left) Filbert varieties showing shapes and sizes: (1) Cosford, (2) Medium Long, (3) Italian Red, (4) Barcelona, (5) Kentish Cob, (6) Red Lambert, (7) Noce Lunghe, (8) Neue Riesennuss, (9) Red Aveline, (10) Purple Aveline, (11 White Aveline, (12) Bixby, (13) Rush, (14) Winkler, (15) C. Cornuta and (16) C. Colurna.

frequently are killed in many parts of the United States and Canada because of opening too early.

Site, Soils, and Planting. It is possible to plant filberts on frosty locations not suitable for other fruits, although, of course, it is safer to plant at higher locations. In Oregon they are grown in the foothill and river bottoms, whereas in the East, they should be grown near large bodies of water that will delay opening of the flowers. Northern slopes are preferred. In the East a search should be made for native filberts to destroy them since they will harbor the Eastern filbert blight which will quickly spread to the European species.

It is best to plant filberts on soils considered good for apple or peach growing, avoiding the light sands and very heavy clays, although the filbert is more tolerant of heavy clays than the pecan or walnut. The filbert is not tolerant of excessive soil moisture, however, and may prove uneconomical on such soils.

Since filberts do not have a tap root they are much easier to transplant than other nuts; they more nearly resemble the apple in this respect. Most propagation is by tip-layering from stool beds. It is one orchard tree in which the top and root of a tree are of the same variety. Growers can obtain these trees by heaping soil around the trunks of orchard trees where suckers have formed. After the suckers have developed roots the soil is removed, the tree is cut away and transplanted.

Except when grown in hedge rows or as bushes the tree should be set in the orchard about twenty feet apart.

Fertilization, Pruning. The fertilizer and pruning program for filberts is about the same as that used for peach in a particular area. Diligent removal of suckers at the base of the trunk as promptly as they appear is necessary. The filbert bears its fruit laterally and terminally on wood of the previous season's growth and pruning after the tree has come into bearing should be such as to stimulate a moderate amount of new growth each year, as in the case of the peach. Some thinning out of the tree is necessary to admit light to the center and prevent the tree from bearing only on its periphery. Pruning, however, is not as severe as in case of the peach. Where frost is likely to be a factor as in New York, pruning is delayed until near the close of the blossoming period. Oregon tests show 6 pounds KC1 per mature tree every third year increases yields and quality of nuts, provided the soil or leaf test shows a deficiency. NPK on cover crops should supply PK needs on valley floorland. A mature tree requires about 1.5-2.0 pounds N applied February-March.

Mineral content of "normal" filbert leaves follows:

N*	P*	K*	Ca*	Mg*	S[1]	Fe	Mn	B	Zn	Cu	Mo[1]	Cl*
2.3	0.10	0.9	0.6	0.2	100	236	100	20	23	8	0.7	0.06
+	to	+	to	+	to	to	to	to	to	to	to	to
	0.22		1.4		150	500	600	50	50	11	1.0	0.36

Data suggested by Dr. O. C. Compton and Dr. H. Lagerstedt, Oregon State University, Corvallis.

*In percent; others in ppm.

[1]No data available; figures are based on reasonable amounts found in other fruit and nut trees.

Pests. Bud mite, leafroller, aphids and bacterial (Oregon) and fungal (New York) blights are problems. The main pest in Oregon is filbert worm.

Note: The Filbert Control Board of growers and handlers regulate through USDA the disposal of filberts from Oregon and Washington. The Oregon Filbert Commission is a research (new uses) and promotion body.

Yields. Filberts reach maximum production between fifteen and twenty-five years of age. Yields in some years may reach 3000 or more pounds per acre. In New York 5 to 10 lbs per tree may be expected.

Harvesting and Marketing. Filberts are permitted to drop to the ground before harvesting. Most of the time the shells are well sealed and may lie on the ground half of the winter without serious damage. Usually there is a once-over harvest after all nuts are down. After drying they are stored but should not be held in a dry room for long periods because they tend to lose flavor: however, they will regain the flavor if held in a humid atmosphere. If Barcelona nuts are held at 80 percent humidity, they will contain between 12 and 15 percent water, which is about the desired amount. Filberts will absorb and release water readily to the atmosphere causing the weight and volume of the nuts to vary with humidity in the storeroom.

Standard grades have been established by the U. S. Department of Agriculture. The first and second grade in general must consist of unshelled filberts which are clean, dry, bright, uniform in color and shape, sound and free from foreign material, well-cured with plump kernels that are free from damage caused by insects, mildew or other means, and not rancid or badly discolored. Cracking tests of the nut should show at least 90 percent plump kernels. Separate size specifications are set up for the round-type nuts such as of the Barcelona variety, and for the long-type such as of the Daviana. Mechanized harvesting, cracking, and processing of nuts, and bagging is, as with walnuts, becoming a part of this industry to cut and save labor costs. It is probable that with more advertising and sales boosting that the demand for in-shell and shelled filberts can be increased considerably. Where mixed nuts are offered to the general public many people frequently will pick out the filbert first.

Miller and Devlin of Oregon conducted experiments in the processing of filberts. Their conclusions were as follows: "Hot lye-acid baths followed by a cold water blast was found to be the most satisfactory process for peeling raw filberts. Even this process left a slight off-flavor and the color of the nuts was somewhat altered by the peel dye.

"Roasting facilitates the peeling of filberts. Of the several roasting methods tried, oil roasting proved superior as far as peeling ease was concerned. A mechanical device was developed for peeling roasted filberts.

"The optimum oil roast was obtained by roasting the nuts for 3 minutes at 300° to 320° F. in cocoanut oil.

"The best oven roast was obtained at 400° F. for 7 minutes.

"A filbert-nut-butter spread was developed. Basic considerations in the development of this product were: Obtaining a satisfactory grind; finding a stabilizer of the desired stiffening power; finding a material compatible with filbert nuts for use as a filler; and producing a finished filbert spread of suitable color, flavor, and texture."

CHESTNUTS

The chestnut belongs to Fagaceae, the same family as the beech and oak. *Castanea dentata,* Borkh., the American Sweet Chestnut, is native to the area of the United States east of the Mississippi River and particularly from the northeast to south through the Appalachian Mountain range. Nuts of this species were prized because they were richer and sweeter in flavor than most other chestnut species. The tree was stately and produced good timber, but was destroyed in the early 1900's by chestnut blight, a fungus which is still active on the young seedlings not permitting them to reach full bearing.

The Oriental species, *C. mollissima.* Bl. is not only highly resistant to chestnut blight but some trees are known to produce nuts of good flavor. Trees of this species should be valuable in breeding to obtain blight resistant varieties of possible commercial importance. *C. crenata,* Sieb, and Zucc., the Japanese chestnut also is highly resistant to blight, bears earlier, is a smaller tree, and has larger-sized nuts which also may be valuable in breeding for blight resistance.

C. sativa, Mill., known as the Spanish or European chestnut, is cultivated to some extent in southern Europe and has been widely planted in homeyards in America. Its nuts are not of the best quality but they do comprise an important food supply in southern Europe.

The Golden Chinquapin, *C. chrysophyllum,* (Douglas) A. DC, grows native in Nevada, California and Oregon and is not attacked by the blight fungus under its natural conditions but it has been killed when subjected to the fungus under greenhouse tests. The American Chinquapin, *C. pumila,* Mill., is relatively resistant to chestnut blight and the fruit is sweet but hybrids with other chestnut species have shown little promise.

The Oriental species of chestnuts can be grown in the northeastern part of the United States but they must be located in protected areas for they are more susceptible to cold than *C. dentata;* the American chestnut. *C. mollissima* trees have more resistance to cold than most peach trees.

Three chestnuts are borne in a hull known as a burr which has numerous spines. At maturity the burr splits open releasing the nuts. The pistillate flowers are born at the shoot tips and the staminate flowers at the mid or basal portion of the previous season's growth (Figure 16).

The Connecticut Station (New Haven) introduced nine (C1-C9) blight resistant hybrids for home-yard plantings in 1963, scions of which are available for the asking (See Jaynes and Graves). USDA in 1963 introduced the two Chinese orchard blight resistant varieties Crane and Orrin (Beltsville, Md.).

Most chestnut trees will set fruit without cross-pollination but there is an indication that cross-pollination is desirable to get better yields. There is evidence that the pollen from large-fruited chestnut varieties may cause nuts to be larger on a tree than when from flowers fertilized with pollen from a small-fruited variety.

THE FIG

The common fig, *Ficus carica,* L., belongs to the same family as the mulberry, Moraceae, which includes many tropical fruits and ornamental species. Fruits of this family are composed of small achenes or drupes attached to a fleshy axis which form an aggregate fruit known as a syncarp. Although the fig and mulberry are of the same family they cannot be hybridized, nor can the rootstocks of one be used for the other.

The fig has been grown since prehistoric times in the Mediterranean Basin. It is mentioned in the Bible and eulogized by the well-known Greek writers, Homer and Plato. At one time the fruit was so highly prized in Greece that by law its export was forbidden. In several southern European countries today the fig is thrown at newlyweds much the same as rice in America.

Mission fathers of Spain brought the fig to California in the mid eighteenth century. Fig trees now are grown mainly in California, although many trees are found in the region south of a line extending roughly from Norfolk, Virginia; through Raleigh, North Carolina; Columbia, South Carolina; Augusta, Georgia; Tuscaloosa, Alabama; Shreveport, Louisiana; and Austin, Texas. North of the cotton belt figs may give satisfactory results where the growing season between killing frosts is 190 days or more and a temperature as low as 5° F. is not experienced every winter. The bearing wood can be killed by a considerably higher temperature than 5° F. if the winter weather is not sufficiently cold to maintain the trees completely dormant.

Occasional fig trees in backyards are seen as far north as New Jersey but they must be planted in protected areas, on a southern slope with good air drainage, or at the side of a building, wall or hedge. Young trees can be protected by banking the trunks with soil to a height of 18", or by bending them to the ground and pegging and covering them with one foot of soil. Tops of larger trees can be drawn together and tied, then wrapped in heavy paper or sacking, or covered with pine boughs or corn stalks. A removable frame sometimes is placed around the trees and filled with straw or leaves and then a waterproof cover placed over the tree to shed the rain and snow. Where winters are severe the figs can be grown in tubs and stored over winter in a cool cellar.

Commercial fig orchards generally have been unsuccessful in the more humid parts of the southeastern states, but a small home planting will supply family needs and any surplus can be used for cash return. The figs must ripen on the tree and for this reason they are too soft and short-lived to ship well except with special precautions. The fruit can be eaten fresh, canned, preserved and dried. It is easily digested, palatable and a helpful sweetener. Figs are popular in cakes, candies and salads.

According to the 1959 census there were 1,130,625 bearing trees in the United States and 197,156 non-bearing trees. Of the bearing trees, California had 994,280, followed by Texas, 58,266; Mississippi, 18,975; Georgia, 17,243; Alabama, 14,522; Louisiana, 12,015; Florida, 4,316; North Carolina, 3,891; and South Carolina, 3,593. Total average production of figs in California from 1969-71 was 49,500 tons of which 14,500 were dried and 6,000 canned and sold fresh.

Botany. Both the fig and the mulberry fruit develop from an entire inflorescence of many flowers, the tissue of which is merged with tissue of the flowering axis or peduncle. Flowers of the mulberry, however, are attached on the outside of the peduncle while flowers of the fig are located on the inside of the peduncle. The inflorescence axis of the fig and the mulberry often is termed the receptacle. Actually, each flower in the entire inflorescence has its own receptacle attached to the axis. The fruit of the fig is called a syconium.

Another way to view the fig botanically is as a fleshy hollow receptacle bearing flowers on the interior surface. At the apex of all fig fruits is an ostiolum (eye or mouth) which is usually more or less closed by scales. Within certain receptacles of most if not all species of *Ficus* there are various species of insects whose larvae develop from eggs to adults inside the individual flowers. When the fig wasp (*Blastophaga psenes*) abandons the fruit through the ostiolum, it is dusted with pollen if the staminate flowers near the mouth are mature. This pollen is carried to other figs into which the insects enter to lay eggs, and pollination then is accomplished unwittingly.

Type of figs. There are four general horticultural types of figs: (a) The largely inedible caprifig has flowers and short-styled pistils while the (b) Smyrna, (c) White San Pedro, and (d) the common types have flowers with long-styled pistils, making it practically impossible for the fig wasp to lay eggs among them.

The *caprifig* is the primitive type of fig indigenous to southwest Asia. It is quite probable that the three types of edible figs grown in the United States have evolved from the caprifig type. The short-styled flowers of this fig produce pollen and are adapted to egg laying by the fig wasp. The receptacles of the three successive crops during a season harbor the larvae, pupae, and temporarily the adults of the insect. Caprifigs, with few exceptions (Croisic and Cordelia) are not eaten by man because of very poor quality.

The edible figs listed below do not produce pollen.

The *Smyrna* type figs will mature only after their long-styled flowers have been pollinated and the seeds develop. Without such stimulus, most of the immature figs of both the first or *breba* crop and the main crops

490

will shrivel and drop when about an inch in diameter; a few brebas may develop without this stimulus. Presence of the fertile seeds, however, is necessary to develop quality.

Pollination of the Smyrna fig is accomplished by the fig wasp which carries the pollen from the June crop of caprifigs to the Smyrna figs. This process is called *caprification*. Man actually modifies the normal life history of the fig wasp by placing mature June-crop caprifigs in perforated bags in trees of the Smyrna type and thus causing the pollen-dusted wasps to enter Smyrna figs instead of other caprifigs. The female which generally loses her wings as she pushes her way between the scales of the eye in the end of the fig, crawls over the long-styled flowers in a *vain* attempt to deposit her eggs, and pollination thus is inadvertently accomplished.

The *common type* figs are parthenocarpic. They do not require caprification to mature their fruits. Varieties of this type include the important Mission, Adriatic, Kadota, Celeste, and Brown Turkey. Probably all common figs could produce fertile seeds if the flowers were caprified.

The *White San Pedro* type fig is actually a combination of characters of the common type and the Smyrna-type figs. Figs of the first (breba) crop on the San Pedro type trees are parthenocarpic (without seeds) whereas figs of the second crop are non-parthenocarpic and like those of the Smyrna type, fail to set and mature unless their flowers are pollinated and fecundated (fertilized). King is a variety recently introduced into California. San Pedro type figs are of relatively poor quality.

Varieties. There are six commercial varieties grown in California all of which originated in the Old World. In the order of importance they are: Adriatic, Calimyrna (California Smyrna or Lob Injir), Kadota, Mission, Turkey (San Pedro, Brown Turkey, or known as Brunswick in the Southern States) and Brunswick. In the Gulf and Southeastern States varieties grown for the most part are Brown Turkey, Brunswick (Magnolia in Texas) and Celeste.

The *Adriatic* variety is the principal drying fig in California although its product is not of the highest quality. The *Calimyrna* is identical with the principal drying fig of Smyrna. It is of the highest quality for fresh consumption locally, for distant shipping, and for drying. The *Kadota* (Dottato of Italy) has been planted mainly for fresh-fruit canning in California and Texas although large tonnages are being dried. The *Mission* is an excellent fig both fresh and dried but the black color is objectionable to the baking trade and to eastern dried fruit markets. The *Turkey* variety is best grown in the Coachella Valley of California and in the vicinity of Los Angeles. It is a heavy producer of large figs for the fresh fruit market. It is worthless as a dried fig and is quite susceptible to souring in the San Joaquin Valley where it cannot be grown successfully. The *Brunswick* (Magnolia) fig has been grown for many years in England

491

and is characterized by narrowly lobed leaves, particularly in the foliage of sucker wood. It is grown in Texas as a canning and preserving fig under the name Magnolia. Texas figs are largely canned in glass whereas California figs are canned in tins. The *Celeste* variety, eaten fresh, is best suited to the Gulf States because the ostiolum (eye) is tight, making it difficult for insects to enter and cause souring or other troubles. Celeste has good flavor.

A promising new seedling fig called *Conadria,* developed from a 30-year fig breeding program in California, is showing promise both for fresh and dried fruit markets. See references by Condit for detailed descriptions of these and other varieties.

Climatic Requirements. The fig is a deciduous subtropical tree which loses its leaves for only a very short period in the climate of California. It is a native of the arid semi-desert regions of the Old World where successful culture is limited more by low temperatures of winter than by high heat of summer. In California there are three seasons when serious frost damage may occur to young trees: the fall season during October and November while the foliage is still green, the dormant winter period, and the season of early spring when the new growth is appearing. In California dormant fig trees can be expected to withstand winter temperatures of 15° F. without injury but usually suffer at temperatures lower than this.

Figs for drying are produced best in regions which have long sunny days and relatively low humidity. Figs for preserving and canning are being produced in regions where summer showers occur and there is a fairly high humidity. Vigor of the fig tree can be controlled by cultural methods, particularly irrigation, so that they can withstand extremes of heat without serious injury to fruit quality. Windy weather and rains during the caprification season may interfere with normal flight of the fig wasps. Gentle breezes during the drying season, however, are desired since they favor the proper maturing of the fruit.

Soils. Deep clay loam soils are best for fig culture but during the first few years vigorous tree growth may occur on these soils at the expense of fruitfulness. Trees can be grown successfully on sandy soils but they are likely to become unprofitable because of nematodes. Some of the best Adriatic orchards are found on a very heavy, sticky clay soil at Merced, California, where there is a hard pan about 28" beneath the surface.

Propagation. The only method of propagation used, because it is so successful, is rooted woody cuttings. In California, cuttings are made during the pruning season in January and February. Bundles of the cuttings are placed butt end up in a well-drained trench and covered with several inches of sandy soil, well packed. They are set in the nursery about March 15 and the soil kept moist to maintain steady even growth.

Culture. Establishment of fig orchards in California and the southern states is much the same as for peach or other deciduous fruits.

Unlike the peach tree which bears its fruit on wood of the previous season's growth, the fig normally bears two crops each year—the first crop appearing on wood of the previous season, and the second crop on new wood of the current season's growth. Since the fruiting habits of different fig varieties vary, they are pruned differently. For example, the Mission tree is notably unproductive under a system of very heavy pruning or stubbing back of the branches, while trees of the Turkey and Kadota usually produce best under such pruning treatment. (See appendix photos.)

The young Adriatic tree is pruned very little except to remove the lower spreading branches and a certain amount of thinning out of the interior branches when they become too thick. Mature trees are pruned annually or biennially throughout the top to induce new vigorous wood and to prevent the accumulation of dense growth of short weak twigs. The Mission fig forms a tall many-branched tree requiring little pruning except for an occasional thinning out and removal of interfering branches. Calimyrna trees produce long upright branches without laterals on current season's wood. These branches are inclined to become top heavy with the weight of fruit and leaves and the pruning problem therefore is to produce stocky branches which are capable of standing upright under future heavy crops. Either heavy winter pruning or light summer pruning may be used to shorten the intervals between laterals in such trees. In the bearing Calimyrna trees an occasional thinning out and heading back of the top is needed to stimulate a succession of new vigorous wood on the main framework branches. Annual or biennial pruning of the top will help to prevent early decline of the tree and encourage production of fruit-bearing wood.

Since the Kadota fig is grown primarily for fresh fruit, the trees are trained low to facilitate economical harvesting. A low, nearly flat top tree is produced by pruning the inside branches shorter than the outside branches. The amount of wood left and the extent of the cutting depends upon the vigor of the tree. Harvesting in the tree center is facilitated by a pruned opening in one side (see appendix photos).

Irrigation of fig orchards is necessary in California except where there is a relatively high water table.

Winter cover crops and spring and summer clean culture has been the practice. As with other fruits, strip-row herbicides under the trees, sod or no-sod middles with sprinkler irrigation are under test.

N fertilizer is applied in the San Joaquin Valley only to trees with poor color. Too much N causes frost susceptibility and fruit splitting and souring.

Maxie and Crane, California, found fruit growth stimulation from 2, 4, 5-T sprays to be due to ethylene production. They suggest ethylene as a regulator to speed growth period III, and quicker maturation of fruits.

In the process of caprification, perforated paper bags containing the caprifigs are attached to the trees requiring pollination by the fig wasps. Calimyrna figs are receptive to pollen when about ¾-inch in diameter and remain receptive over a period of several days. The fig wasp carries with the pollen the spores of injurious fruit diseases as well; therefore, the number of caprifigs and wasps distributed to Calimyrna trees should be reduced to a minimum to insure a reasonable crop of edible fruit. It is generally considered better to obtain a light crop of clean figs by caprification, rather than a heavy crop inclined to rot on account of greater fungus infection. About one caprifig is needed for each 18 square feet of bearing tree surface as experiments have demonstrated in the Fresno area. Four distributions of caprifigs are needed over a period of about 15 days.

Because caprification is expensive and the wasps may induce souring of the fruit, ways have been sought to develop fruits without caprification, such as use of growth regulator sprays to enduce parthenocarpic fruit setting. Many substances have been tried by California workers (see references) but none has been commercially acceptable.

Harvesting. While fig trees may bear as early as the fourth season in the orchard, commercial bearing starts at about seven years of age. Calimyrna trees will produce from 1.25 to 1.5 tons of dried figs per acre while the Mission and Adriatic orchards will produce 2 to 2.5 tons per acre. Kadota trees are heavier producers than other varieties except the Turkey. Trees three to four years of age will produce a few hundred pounds of fresh fruits per acre while those from five to seven years of age will produce from 1.0 to 2.5 tons per acre; older orchards will produce from 5 to 7 tons of fresh figs.

Harvesting of figs is one of the most tedious of all fruits. Fruit of some varieties will not drop until overripe and rather dried and because of this it holds to the tree tightly when harvested for fresh fruit or canning. Pickers wear cotton gloves to protect them from the exuding latex which may irritate the skin. Since the figs are rather soft at harvest they must be handled very carefully for they crack easily and are not protected by a waxy skin like apples.

Fresh figs are usually available from June to October as follows: June, 9%; July, 9%; August, 35%; September, 28%; October, 19%. The average per capita consumption of fresh figs is less than 0.05 pound. More than 87% of the fig crop is sold dried. Texas production goes almost entirely into canned figs and preserves.

Fresh figs from California are shipped in one-layer boxes in which cardboard fillers are used to provide a separate cell for each fruit. The number of cells varies with the size of the fruit but the boxes are uniformly 1⅞" deep, 11" wide, and 16⅛" long, inside. Weight is five pounds net per flat. Shallow baskets with a top dimension of approximately 8 square inches and bottom dimension of 6¾" and a depth of 1¼" sometimes are used. The baskets are packed with a single layer of fruit and shipped four to a crate.

Figs are highly perishable because they must be fully ripe to be of good quality. A ripe fig is rather soft and varies in color from greenish yellow to purplish or almost black according to the variety. Over-ripeness is detectable by a sour odor which is due to fermentation of the juice. Bruised or mechanically injured fruit should be avoided because such fruit breaks down rapidly in shipment and marketing. There are no U. S. Standard grades.

For commercial storage, figs should be held at 31°-32° F. and a relative humidity of 85 to 90 percent. Under these conditions, however, they cannot be expected to keep satisfactorily for more than about ten days. The reserve stocks in retail stores should be kept cold and if possible the stock on display should be refrigerated. Figs on display counters should be watched carefully because any decay will spread rapidly from one fruit to another.

In a pound of figs there are 357 calories; 6.4 gms. protein; 1.8 gms. fat; 89 gms. carbohydrates; 245 mgs. calcium; 145 mgs. phosphorus; 2.7 mgs. iron: Vitamin A, 360 International Units; thiamin .25 mg.; riboflavin .23 mg.; niacin 2.5 mgs.; and ascorbic acid, 7 mgs. Figs have a definite laxative effect due probably to fiber and bulk of seeds together with some specific solvent in the juice. They also have an high excess alkalinity of ash.

Fruits of varieties other than Calimyrna can be frozen in syrup at 0° F. and are about as good eating as fresh fruits but they are highly perishable upon thawing.

The canning trade prefers fruit without crunchy seeds such as the Kadota of California and the Brunswick (Magnolia) in Texas. A variety is desired that does not become too soft at maturity and that holds its yellow color on canning. Canned figs are necessarily higher in price than canned peaches and apricots because they are more expensive to grow, harvest and process.

Drying. Fruit for drying is permitted to hang on the tree until it drops. It loses some water while still on the tree just before dropping and also on the ground before it is picked up. Methods of drying vary with the variety and district in California. The light colored figs such as the Kadota and Calimyrna are picked up frequently and dried on trays in the sun. Adriatic and Kadota figs are sulphured lightly to hold the bright color while Calimyrna figs when carefully handled will dry naturally to a straw color. Mission figs in some districts are placed in half-full sacks and left open in a sunny place to dry. About 3 pounds of fresh figs are required to make one pound of dried.

Pests and Diseases. Pests and diseases affecting the tree are the root knot nematode, the Mediterranean fig scale, fig mites, Pacific red spider and a leaf mosaic disease to which the Mission variety is especially susceptible. Pests and diseases affecting the fruit include birds such as

J. F. Cooper, Fla. Agr. Exp. Sta., Gainesville

Figure 17. (Upper left) Young Japanese persimmon tree of the Tanenashi variety, the leading variety in the Southeastern United States; trees may reach a height of 40 feet, but not ordinarily. At right is a cluster of fruit. (Lower left) Fruit of the Hachiya variety which leads in California and is grown to a limited extent in Florida.

the house finch, characteristic splitting of immature fig fruits of certain varieties such as Calimyrna, souring due to yeasts and bacteria, smut or mold on dried Adriatic and Calimyrna figs, and endosepsis or internal rot due to a fungus carried by the fig wasp. See leaflet No. 70 for figs of the California Extension Service, or contact your local experiment station for a pest control calendar.

California Fig Institute. In 1935 the California fig growers organized the California Fig Institute at Fresno with a general objective of improving the industry. About three-fourths of the California industry is in this general area. A marketing control program has operated to set a standard each season for figs going into the fresh and dried trade. All lots testing less than the minimum standard are diverted into by-products such as animal feed, alcohol, brandy and syrup. The Fig Institute has a Director of Research and a staff located in a well-equipped laboratory at Fresno. Research is being conducted on such subjects as caprification, control of pests and diseases and irrigation and fertilization. Active advertising and publication of recipe booklets is a part of the promotional program of the Institute.

PERSIMMONS

The Oriental or Japanese persimmon. (*Diospyros Kaki, L.*) is the only commercially important persimmon in the United States. It is probably native to China for it was introduced into Japan from China. In Japan it ranks next to citrus in importance and is considered their national fruit. The Oriental persimmon was first introduced into the United States by Commodore Perry's expedition which opened world commerce to Japan in 1852. It later was introduced as grafted trees of better varieties by the U. S. Department of Agriculture in 1870.

Almost all of the crop comes from California where the average production is between 1500 and 2000 tons. The size of the crop may fluctuate considerably from year to year. Other states reporting Oriental persimmons and their approximate tonnage are: Texas, 40; Florida, 15; Hawaii, 11; Louisiana, 3; Mississippi, 3; Alabama, 2; and Missouri, 1. The following states produce less than a ton: Arizona, Georgia, Indiana, Kansas, Oklahoma, Pennsylvania, South Carolina and Utah. The 1959 census showed about 70,000 trees in the United States which is considerably less than reported in 1930 and 1940, which were 257,913 and 138,000 trees, respectively. Yield per tree according to the Census varies between 30 and 50 pounds but on well-managed trees production should be appreciably better. Retail value of the U. S. crop is around a half-million dollars.

There are several problems in the southern states which have limited the persimmon commercially. Some of the problems, of course, apply to California. These include a lack of concentration of plantings with no organization for handling and vigorously advertising the fruit, as, for example, has been the case with avocados. This, in turn, has been largely responsible for unsatisfactory returns to shippers. Shipments to the markets have been sporadic with no effort to maintain a steady supply or demand in any one market; hence the prices have fluctuated widely and have been generally uncertain. Fancy prices obviously cannot be expected from a fruit that has no U. S. standard grades and is generally unknown to the public. While there is a limited but loyal public buying persimmons there are those who have tried the fruit for the first time and found it hard, astringent and puckery. This is due to lack of instructions on when and how to eat it, and has discouraged them from further purchases. This, of course, could be overcome by proper advertising. Also, the growers have planted small acreages of numerous varieties, some of which were not suited for marketing because of lack of good size or dark-color flesh. Poor fruiting or heavy dropping of the young fruits due to inadequate cultural knowledge has resulted in poor returns to the grower. If the above difficulties could be overcome, and it seems possible, a satisfactory and growing demand for this fruit undoubtedly could be developed.

Not all the Oriental persimmons are astringent when hard. Generally

J. F. Cooper, Fla. Agr. Exp. Sta., Gainesville

Figure 18. The small Japanese persimmon flower on the left is staminate; the larger ones on the right are pistillate. Perfect flowers having both stamens and pistils sometimes are borne. A tree may have only one or more of these types of flowers.

speaking the varieties which have dark-colored flesh are sweet and non-astringent, and may be eaten before they become soft. Varieties that have a light-colored flesh, which are preferred by the public, tend to be astringent until they soften, with one exception, the Fuyu variety. Astringency is due to tannin, the same substance found in tea. Frost is not necessary as an aid in reducing the tannin and in softening and ripening the persimmon. With time, the tannin will disappear and the fruit ripen and sweeten naturally. The fruit will ripen as well off the tree as on the tree. The Japanese have a special method of removing the pucker by placing the fruit in casks that have been used for sake, Japanese beer. Depending upon weather they remove the fruit from the casks when it loses its astringency in five to fifteen days. In this country the persimmons are allowed to sweeten naturally at room temperature, although they can be held in firm condition for periods of two to three months at 30°-32° F. and 85% to 90% relative humidity. Average freezing point of the flesh is 28.2° F.

Varieties. The leading commercial variety in California is Hachiya, mainly because of its large handsome fruit. It is usually seedless in California but may contain one or more seeds when grown in Florida. Hachiya, as shown in Figure 17 is oblong-conic, apex rounded, terminating in a black point; skin glossy, deep orange-red; flesh deep yellow, astringent until soft, rich and sweet when ripe.

The Tanenashi is the leading variety in the southern states. The fruit is medium to large (Figure 17), broadly conical with a somewhat pointed apex; skin a light bright orange changing to light red when ripe; flesh yellow, nearly always seedless, astringent until ripe and with a pasty texture.

Descriptions of other varieties can be found in Fla. Ext. Bull. 124. They include Zengi, Taber No. 23, Okame, Fuyu, Jumbu, Triumph, Hyakume, Yemon, Tamopan, Costata, Eureka, Tsuru and Ormond.

The Oriental persimmon tree may reach a height of 40 feet, is a beautiful tree in the home landscape, will survive winters where grown, and has but few insect and disease enemies. The chilling requirement is only slight, with the buds opening with but little delay even after the warmest winters in southern California. Trees are grown in all parts of California and Florida and as far north as Missouri, southern Indiana and Virginia.

Flowering and Pollination. Buds on last year's wood contain indeterminate shoots, some of which will have flowers in the axils of the leaves. The basal flowers on the shoots, according to Japanese studies, may have been formed as early as July of the previous summer, whereas flowers near the tips of the shoots may have been formed in late winter or early spring of the year growth starts. These later flowers are not as vigorous as the early flowers, but they may set fruit. The staminate flowers are about a third of the size of the pistillate flowers (Figure 18).

Three kinds of flowers may be borne on Oriental persimmon trees: (a) perfect flowers having both stamens and pistil, (b) pistillate flowers having a pistil and no stamens, and (c) staminate flowers having stamens but no pistil. In the early classification of Oriental persimmons difficulty was encountered because one or more of these types of flowers was being borne on any one tree. H. H. Hume in Florida showed that in one group of varieties only pistillate flowers are borne which he characterized as "pistillate constants." In the second group of varieties both pistillate and staminate flowers are borne regularly, and he designated these, "staminate constants."

The "pistillate constants," include such commercial varieties as Tanenashi, Hachiya, and Tamopan. Some varieties in this group are parthenocarpic, setting fruit without seeds and pollination. In other varieties the fruits are usually seedy and pollination is necessary for setting the fruit. With the latter varieties it is necessary to interplant a variety from the group of "staminate constants," the variety Gailey being most frequently used because of its profusion of staminate flowers. It should be noted that the native American persimmon, *D. viriginiana* will not cross with the Oriental varieties and thus cannot be used as a source of pollen.

Pollination problems are not as important in California as in Florida.

499

This, no doubt, is due partly to the fact that three of the main varieties, Hachiya, Tanenashi and Tamopan, will bear fruit without pollination.

After Hume had conducted his pollination experiments he found it possible to classify the fruits according to whether they were light-fleshed or dark-fleshed. In the one group which he called "pollination constants" the fruit was destined to be light-fleshed whether it bore seeds or not. In the second group, termed "pollination variants" the varieties had fruit that was light-fleshed when seedless (unpollinated), but dark-fleshed when seedy (pollinated). It is interesting to note in the latter group that a fruit with only one seed showed a dark area around the seed but the remaining flesh was light in color. If the fruit had two seeds, side by side, the flesh was dark in the area of the seeds and light in the remainder of the fruit. On the other hand, if the two seeds were opposite each other, the entire fruit was dark fleshed.

Hume classified the varieties under the following headings:

Pollination Constants (Light-fleshed whether seedless or seedy)		Pollination Variants (Light-fleshed when seedless, Dark-fleshed when seedy)	
Costata	Tanenashi	Gailey	Taber's 23
Fuyu (Gaki)	Tamopan	Godbey	Yemon
Hachiya	Triumph	Hyakume	Yeddo
Ormond	Tsuru	Okame	Ichi
		Taber's 129	Zengi

The main commercial varieties in both Florida and California are among the left list above, due to the fact that the public has not as yet accepted the dark-fleshed fruits. In the right column, however, are varieties which usually bear an abundance of staminate flowers; the variety Gailey is interplanted among light-fleshed varieties as a source of pollen.

Propagation and Rootstocks. In China the *D. kaki and D. lotus* seedling rootstocks produce large trees of grafted *D. kaki* of almost indefinite life. But by experience, seedlings of the native American persimmon, *D. virginiana,* have been found best and are used almost exclusively in the southern United States as a rootstock for *D. kaki*. This rootstock, however, still falls short of being completely desirable since it is difficult to transplant due to a long large tap root and the trees tend to be short-lived (10 years, occasional trees older) and dwarfed. The trees, however, come into bearing early, two to three years after grafting. Seedlings with crown gall, to which persimmon is highly susceptible, must be discarded.

In California, while *D. lotus* seedlings are generally used as a rootstock, *D. kaki* appears to be the best rootstock for a number of varieties including the Fuyu. Since opinion is changing, check your local agricultural advisor.

Nearly all propagation is done by grafting the scion on the seedling root, using the whip-graft for small-diameter stocks and the cleft-graft on large stocks. It is considered better to replant with young stock rather than to try to topwork old trees to new varieties.

General Culture. The Oriental persimmon seems to perform best on the well-drained lighter soils which have a good subsoil containing some clay. They are not tolerant of poorly aerated soils. Trees are transplanted during the winter months at distances of 15' x 15' to 20' x 20'. The same cultivation and cover cropping system can be used as for the peach. In California the amount of nitrogen used is about the same as for the peach to obtain shoots about a foot long. Excessive nitrogen, however, will cause a high percentage of the young fruits to drop. In Florida, an N-P-K fertilizer is suggested of a 1-2-1 ratio, using about one pound of fertilizer per year of age of the tree; some difficulty with zinc deficiency is encountered and this is corrected by applying two ounces of zinc sulphate for each year of age of the tree under the leaf spread.

Since the wood of the Oriental persimmon tends to be brittle and breaks easily with a load of fruit, the trees should be trained as nearly as possible to the modified leader system (Chapter IV). When the trees begin to occupy their full allotted space it will be necessary to head them back annually as with the peach to keep them within width and height bounds.

For those varieties which require a good annual source of pollen, one tree of the Gailey variety is used for eight trees of the pistillate flowering type.

On some varieties the young fruits tend to drop rather heavily early in the season. To some extent this is an advantage in sizing up the remaining fruits at harvest, for the large fruits draw a premium. If dropping becomes excessive, however, scoring or girdling of the trunks in late May or early June (Chapter VI) in southern California will help reduce the drop; also a reduction in nitrogen supply should help. Hand thinning of the fruit would be difficult since it adheres tightly to the calyx and stem making the job tedious and expensive.

Fruit Handling. Fruits are harvested when they have attained a yellow to reddish color but are still firm. They are clipped from the tree with shears leaving the calyx attached to the fruit together with a short stem. Great care is needed to avoid bruising since bruising eventually will show up clearly and encourage decay. The fruits are wrapped individually in paper and packed in a six-basket peach crate or in the two-layer California crate, size 5"x13½"x16⅛", weighing 20-24 lbs. net. Large fruits are packed in a single-layer crate, size 3½" x 13½" x 16⅛". A polystyrene box, 6⅜" x 13½" x 16½", with 2 polyvinyl trays is gaining popularity.

Since the general public is uninformed on how to ripen the fruit before it is eaten, the proper wraps on each fruit should carry instructions on how to avoid astringency. Instructions such as follows might be used: "Persimmons—delicacy of the Orient. Let the flesh become very soft, then eat it with cream. It is delicious and different." Or, perhaps the following label could be used: "Ripe persimmons are delicious. Flesh is sweet and jelly-like. Chill, and eat out of hand or in a bowl with cream."

Marketing. Some marketing problems already have been noted in the introduction. The marketing season from California as percentage of the total annual supply is: October 24%; November 55%; and December 21%. Most of the persimmons are eaten from Halloween to Christmas to New Year's. Fruits shipped should be well-shaped, plump, smooth, highly colored, with unbroken skin and with stem cap attached. An ideal way to display persimmons on a sales counter is in a single layer nested in wrapping paper to prevent bruising. By displaying in this manner it prevents the customer from digging among the fruits; she usually takes the first fruit picked, or gently puts it back in the nest. Persimmons are so delicate that it is essential to minimize handling as much as possible. Reserve stock can be stored at 30°F up to 2 months at 85-90% humidity.

In a pound of seedless Oriental persimmons there are: 344 calories; 3.5 gms. of protein; 1.8 gms. of fat; 88 gms. of carbohydrates; 26 mgs. of calcium; 114 mgs. of phosphorus; 1.3 mgs. of iron; 11,900 International units of Vitamin A; 0.22 mg. of thiamine; 0.2 mg. of riboflavin; 28 mgs. of ascorbic acid.

American Persimmons. *D. virginiana,* L. is a native from Texas to Florida and north to latitude 38° which runs through southern Missouri; some varieties may grow as far North as 40°. The trees grow wild over the countryside, spreading like a weed in pastures, but there is a fungus, *Cephalosporium diospyri,* which may kill many wild persimmons in large areas.

The fruits when ripe are one to one and a half inches in diameter, full of seeds, sweet and rather pasty. They are very astringent before ripe and do not lose this until they are too soft for marketing. The tree has no commercial importance but it is liked by many people in the areas where it grows.

The bell-shaped staminate and pistillate flowers are almost always on separate trees. The staminate trees not having to bear a crop are usually somewhat more upright and vigorous in appearance than the pistillate trees. Some varieties have been picked from the wild and named, including Early Golden, Ruby and Miller. Pollination is by insects and it has been noted that pistallate trees may be pollinated from staminate trees several hundred feet away. Parthenocarpic (seedless) fruits are occasionally set on some varieties as Early Golden and Ruby. John Rick variety shows promise in the midwest.

Suggested Collateral Readings

PECANS

Barnes, G. L. Effectiveness of Benomyl for control of Pecan Scab. Plant Disease Reporter. 55:(8). 711 pp. Aug. 1971.
Brison, F. R. Patch-budding pecans. Texas Ag. Progress 5:1, 5-7. 1959; Top working pecan trees by inlay grafting. Texas Ag. Progress 4:2, 12-15. 1958.

Brison, F. R., R. E. Brason, W. W. Clark, A. H. Krezdorn, and J. B. Storey. Improved Grades and Consumer Demand for In-Shell Pecans. Texas Agr. Expt. Sta. Bull. 932. 14 pp. May, 1959.

Brison, F. R. The Storage of Shelled Pecans, Texas Agr. Expt. Sta. Bull. 667. 16 pp. March, 1945.

Bryant, M. D. Pecan propagation. Plant Science Guide - Extension Service New Mexico State University, Las Cruces 400H-604. p. 4. 1969.

Burke, G. M. and Sydney C. James. Economics of pecan marketing in New Mexico. N. M. Ag. Exp. Sta. Res. Rpt. 82, 13 pp. July 1963.

Crane, H. L., and C. A. Reed. Nut Breeding. U.S. Dept. of Agric. Yearbook Section 1590. 827-890. 1937.

Farris, D. E. and E. J. Allen. Pecan production in Arkansas; marketing, costs. Ark. Ag. Exp. Sta. Bull. 680, 25 pp. 1964.

Fowler, M. L. Early-season pecan production forecast. Okla. Ag. Exp. Sta. Mimeo Series P-440, 18 pp. Feb. 1963; Factors affecting U. S. pecan prices. Okla. Ag. Exp. Sta. Tech. T-100, 26 pp. 1963.

Going, W. D. The pecan in Rhodesia. Hortus Rhodesia 11:7-10. 1969.

Hansen, C. J. and H. T. Hartmann. Propagation of Temperate-Zone Fruit Plants. Univ. of Calif. Agr. Ext. Ser. Cir. 471, 51 pp. 1958.

Lipe, John A., and Page W. Morgan. Ethylene: Involvement in shuck dehiscence in pecan fruits. HortSci. 5(4):266. August 1970.

MacDaniels, L. H. Nut Growing. Cornell Agr. Ext. Ser. Bull. 701. 31 pp. 1958.

Marloth, R. H. The Pecan in South Africa. Dept. of Agr. Hort. Series 10. Bull. 274. 12 pp. 1946-7.

McElroy, R. C. and J. V. Powell. Economic aspects of pecan production, marketing. USDA Ag. Econ. Rpt. 41. Sept. 1963.

Nakayama, Roy M. Pecan variety characteristics. N. M. Ag. Exp. Sta. Bull. 520, 13 pp. Apr. 1967.

Norton, J. A., and J. B. Storey. Dalapon for Johnsongrass in pecan orchards. Pecan Quarterly. 6(1). Feb. 1972.

_____. Herbicidal effects on growth of pecan trees. Weed Science Vol. 18. p. 522-524. 1970.

Norton, J. A., et al. Effects of herbicides on roots and pecan nut quality. Weed Science Vol. 18. p. 520-522. 1970.

Osburn, M. R. et al. Insects, diseases and control on pecan. USDA Ag. Handbook 240, 55 pp. Sept. 1966 (very good bulletin).

Payne, J. A., et al. Aerial infra-red photography to locate pecan orchards. Pecan Quarterly. Vol. 6 (1). February 1972.

The Pecan Quarterly published by Texas Pecan Growers Assoc. $2./year. Contains research, industry developments. Drawer CC, College Station, Texas 77840.

Powell, J. V. Domestic tree nut industries-economic appraisal. USDA Ag. Econ. Rpt. 62, 41 pp. Nov. 1964.

Powell, J. V. Pecan nursery industry, structure, economic aspects. USDA Ag. Econ. Rpt. 44. Oct. 1963.

Powell, J. V. and D. A. Reimund. Pecan shelling and processing industry, practices, problems, prospects. USDA Ag. Econ. Ppt. 15. Sept. 1962.

Proebsting, E. L. and E. F. Serr. Edible Nuts. Chapter in Fruit Nutrition. Horticultural Publications, New Brunswick, N. J. N. F. Childers, editor .1966.

Purcell, J. C. and J. C. Ellrod. Supply, price, utilization of pecans. Ga. Ag. Exp. Sta. Mimeo. N. S. 182, 24 pp. Aug. 1963.

Reed, C. A. and John Davidson. The Improved Nut Trees of North America and How to Grow Them. The Devin-Adair Co. New York City. 404 pp. 1954.

Rosberg, D. W. and J. C. Schaffner, Pecan diseases, insects, control. Texas Ag. Exp. Sta. Bull. MP-313, 19 pp. 1964.

Rosborough, J. F., F. R. Brison, S. L. Smith and L. D. Romberg. Propagation of Pecans by Budding and Grafting. Texas Agr. Expt. Sta. Bull. B-166. 27 pages. 1949.

Seale, A. D., Jr. Costs-returns of pecan enterprises. Miss. Ag. Exp. Sta. Bull. 686, 20 pp. 1964.

Search for hardier fruits and nuts. USDA-ARS 22-87, 15 pp. Jan. 1964.

Smith, C. L., J. Hamilton, C. J. B. Thor and L. D. Romberg. Root Composition and Top Development in Large Pecan Trees, Headed to Various Degrees of Severity and Top-Working. Journal of Agr. Research 58: No. 11, pp. 821-842. June 1939.

Smith, M. W. *et al*. I. Nitrate enhancement of Zn absorption in pecan leaves. II. washing Zn from pecan foliage. JASHS. (Tex. A. & M.) In press. 1973.

Southeastern Pecan Growers Ass'n Proceedings. Contains current research, industry developments. Contact Hort. Dept., Univ. of Ga., Athens.

Storey *et al*. Alar and heading-back pruning effects on pecan trees. ASHS (in Press), 94. About 1969.

Storey, J. B. Flowering habits of pecan tree. Pecan Quarterly. 3(2):4-6. 1969.

Strong, W. J. Nut Culture in Ontario. Ontario Dept. of Agr. Bull. 494. 25 pp. Sept. 1952.

Taylor, Glenn G., and R. E. Odom. Some biochemical compounds associated with rooting of pecan stem cuttings. J. ASHS. 95(2): 146-150. 1970.

Thomson, H. J. Flowering Habits of Pecans in Oklahoma. Okla. Agr. Exp. Mimeo. Circular M-289. 3 pp. June, 1957.

Upson, J. R., Jr., and D. Sparks. Pecan seedling response in sand culture to levels of potassium. J. ASHS. 94(2):125-127. March 1969.

Woodroof, J. G. Tree nuts—production, processing, products. Vol. I, Almonds, Brazil nuts, cashnew, chestnuts, filberts, Macadamia (available). 356 pp. 1967. Vol. II, Pecans, walnuts. 1967.

Woodroof, J. G. and E. K. Heaton. Pecans for processing. Ga. Ag. Exp. Sta. Bull. N. S. 80, 91 pp. (very good bulletin) Mar. 1961.

Worley, Ray E. Effects of defoliation date on yield, quality, nutlet set, and foliage regrowth for pecan. HortSci. 6(5). 1971.

Worley, Ray E., and Glenn G. Taylor. An abnormal nut splitting problem of pecan. HortSci. 7(1). February 1972.

Note. State agricultural stations in Southern U. S. have bulletins on local pecan growing recommendations. Contact them for free publications.

WALNUT

Batchelor, L. D., O. L. Braucher and E. F. Serr. Walnut Production in California. California Agricultural Experiment Station Circular 364. 34 pp. 1945.

Black walnuts for home use. USDA Leaflet 525, 8 pp. 1963.

Brooks, Maurice G. Effect of Black Walnut Trees and their Products on Vegetation. W. Virginia Agricultural Experiment Station Bulletin 347. 31 pp. 1951.

Brooks, R. M., and H. P. Olmo. Register of New Fruit and Nut Varieties. List 6. Proceedings American Society Hort. Sci. 58:386-407. 1951.

Burlingame, Burt B., Walnut Harvesting—Methods, Equipment and Costs. California Agricultural Experiment Station Circular 416. 24 pp. 1952.

California Agriculture. This popularized monthly report from the University of California contains from time to time up-to-date research and developments on English walnuts. A sample of these are are follows: B Vitamin in Walnuts, Nov., 1954; Blackline in Walnut, March, 1959; Walnut Aphid Investigations, March, 1959; Vitamins in Walnut Meats, August, 1959, Filbertworm Injury to Walnuts, September, 1957; Migrating Aphids on Walnuts, June, 1953; Walnut Aphid Investigations, July, 1954; Walnut Branch Wilt, October, 1955; The Walnut Husk Fly, May, 1956; Navel Orangeworm on Walnuts, June, 1956; Frost Damage to Walnut Kernels, June, 1956; Root—Lesion Nematode on Walnuts, May 1958; Frosted Scale on Walnuts, April, 1956; Fumigation of Walnuts, July, 1952; Mites on Walnuts, February, 1951; Timing of Spray Treatments for Codling Moth, March, 1950; Walnut Aphid Studies in 1955, March, 1956; Control of Walnut Blight, March, 1956; Spider Mite on Walnuts, Nov., 1957 and July, 1956; and Filbertworm Injury to Walnuts, January, 1956. Pre-emergence herbicides for weed control in walnuts, 1967. (Spraying with zinc, April 1970).

Clark, F. B. Black walnuts for timber. USDA Forest Serv. Leaflet 487, 8 pp. 1966.

Day, B. E. *et al*. Weed control in walnuts. Calif. Agr. Exp. Sta. Leaf. 194. 1966.

Forde, H. I., et al. Walnut crack tests. Diamond Walnut News (Stockton, Calif.) February 1969.

Gagnaire, J., and C. Vallier. Variations in leaf K of grafted walnut trees, *Juglans Regia/Juglans Nigra*, grown under natural conditions (in French). C. R. Ocd. Agr. France. 54(2):81-86. 1968.

Hansche, P. E., V. Beres, and H. I. Forde. Estimates of quantitative genetic properties of walnut and their implications for cultivar improvement. J. ASHS. 97(2): 279. March 1972.

Kuhlman, F. W. Cost of Producing Filberts and Walnuts in Oregon. Oregon Agricultural Experiment Station Circular of Information 499, 1951.

504

Lee, K. C., and R. W. Campbell. Nature and occurrence of juglone in *Juglans nigra* L. HortSci. 4(4):297-298. 1969.

Martin, G. 2-Chloroethylphosphonic acid as an aid to mechanical harvesting of English walnuts. J. ASHS. 96(4):434. July 1971.

Martin, George, et al. The movement and fate of 2-chloroethyl phosphonic acid in walnut. J. ASHS. 97(1):51. Jan. 1972.

Michelbacher, A. E., and J. C. Ortega. A Technical Study of Insects and Related Pests attacking Walnuts. California Agricultural Experiment Station Bulletin 764, 86 pp. 1958.

Miller, P. W., C. E. Schuster and R. E. Stephenson. Diseases of the Walnuts in the Pacific Northwest and Their Control. Oregon Agricultural Exp. Station Bulletin 435 42 pp. 1947.

Miller, P. W. *et al*. Blackline of walnuts. Ore. Ag. Ext. Serv. Circ. 644. Mar. 1963.

Nast, C. G. Morphological Development of the Fruit of *Juglans Regia*. Hilgardia 9-7. 345-381, 1935.

Norton, J. A., et al. Herbicide effects on nut quality and lateral root development. Weed Science 18(4):520-524. July 1970.

Painter, J. H. Walnut nutritional experiment. Ore. St. Hort. Soc. 44th Ann. Rpt. 179-182. 1952.

Perry, E. J. and A. D. Rizzi. Whitewash sprays against walnut sunburn. Calif. Agr. April 1970.

Proebsting E. L. Fertilizers and Cover Crops for California Orchards. California Agricultural Experiment Station Circular 466, 19 pp. 1958.

Reed, A. D. Walnut production Costs. Calif. AXT. 333. 1970.

Reed, C. A. and John Davidson. The Improved Nut Trees of North America and How to Grow Them. The Devin-Adair Company, New York City. 404 pp. 1954.

Reimund, D. A. Bibliography, Tree nuts, 1945-60. USDA-ERS. Misc. Pub. 862. 1961.

Seidel, K. W. and K. A. Brinkman. Walnuts on strip-mine land, Kansas. USDA (Forest) Tech. Paper 187. 1962.

Serr, E. F. *et al*. Nutrient deficiencies (G4564L)VL; Training young trees, AXT-86; Combined old and new plantings, Leaf. 143; Suitable varieties, Leaf. 144; Rootstocks, AXT-120. All walnut. Calif. Ag. Exp. Sta., Davis. 1966; '67; '62; '62; '65, resp.

Serr, E. F. and H. I. Forde. Ten new walnut varieties. Calif. Ag. 8-9. Apr. 1968.

Sherman, L. W. and C. W. Ellenwood. Top-Working and Bench-Grafting Walnut Trees. Ohio Agr. Exp. Sta. Special Circular 69 16 pp. March, 1944.

Spray calendar. California Agr. Ext. Serv. Leaflet 80. Request latest edition.

The California Walnut. Published and distributed by Diamond Walnut Growers Inc., Stockton, California. 72 pp. 1959.

Tesche, W. C. The Walnut and Filbert Industries of the Mediterranean Basin. U. S. Department of Agriculture. Foreign Agriculture Report 93, 48 pp. 1956.

Tufts, W. P., and R. W. Harris. Pruning Deciduous Fruit Trees. California Agricultural Extension Service Circular 444, 47 pp. Request latest edition.

Wilson, E. E. The Branch Wilt of Persian Walnut Trees and Its Cause. Hilgardia 17:12. 413-436. 1947. Calif. AXT-18. 1962.

FILBERTS

Johansson, Emil. Variety trial with hazelnuts at Alnap. 1938-50. (English summary). Middlelande NR-63 Fran Statens Tradgardsforsok. Lundgrens Soners Boktr. Malmo 1951.

Jones, S. C. *et al*. Filbert insect pest control. Ore. Ag. Ext. Circ. 728. (Seek latest).

Kuhlman, G. W. Cost of producing filberts and walnuts in Oregon. Ore. Agr. Exp. Sta. Cir. of Info. 499. 8 pp. 1951.

MacDaniels, L. H. Nut growing. Cornell Ext. Bull. 701. p. 12. 1958.

Miller, P. W. *et al*. Control of filbert blight in Oregon. Ore. Ag. Ext. Circ. 645. Mar. 1963.

Miller, R. C. and K. A. Devlin. Processing filbert nuts. Ore. Agr. Exp. Sta. Tech. Bull. 15. 16 pp. 1948.

Painter, J. H. and H. E. Hammar. K and B fertilizer effects on filbert. ASHS 82:225-230. 1963

Painter, J. H. and H. S. Hammar. N, P, K, Mg, B fertilizers on filbert and leaf concentration. ASHS 80:315-326. 1962.

Reich, J. E. and H. B. Lagerstedt. The effect of paraquat, dinoseb and 2,4-D on filbert (*Corylus avellana* L.) Suckers. JASHS 96:5 554-60, 1971.

Schreiber, W. R. Filberts in Turkey. U.S. Dept. of Agr., For. Agr. Rpt. 73. 35 pp. 1953.
Schuster, C. E. and J. H. Painter. Filberts in Oregon. Ore. Ag. Ext. Sta. Bull. 628, 24 pp. Revised 1961.
Slate, G. L. Filberts. The Cornell (Ithaca, N. Y.) Plantations 4: No. 4, pp. 52-55. Summer 1948.

CHESTNUT

Chestnuts resistant to blight. USDA Farmers Bull. 2068. 21 pp. 1954.
Crane, H. L., C. A. Reed and M. N. Wood. Nut Breeding, Yearbook of U. S. Department of Agriculture, Pages 827-889. 1937.
Jaynes, R. A. and A. H. Graves. Connecticut hybrid chestnut culture. Conn. Ag. Exp. Sta. Bull. 657. 29 pp. Apr. 1963.
Jaynes, R. A. Buried-inarch technique for rooting chestnut cuttings. Northern Nut Growers Assoc. 52nd Annual Rept., 37-39. 1961.
Jaynes, R. A. Chestnut chromosomes. Forest Science 8:4. 372-377. Dec. 1962.
McKay, J. W. and H. L. Crane. The immediate effect of pollen on the fruit of the chestnut. Proceedings Amer. Soc. of Hort. Sci. 36. pages 293-298. 1939.

FIG

Beutel, James A. Home fig growing. Calif. Agr. Ext. Serv. Publ. AXT-123. 1965.
Blondeau, Rene and J. C. Crane. Early maturation of Calimyrna fig fruits by means of synthetic hormone sprays. Sci. 108: 719-20. December 24, 1948. See, also, Crane, J. C. Bot. Gaz. 114: p. 102. 1952.
California Agriculture. This monthly publication from the University of California, Berkeley, contains progress reports on fig research from time to time. Subjects covered include: Promising new seedling fig. June, 1956; Biological control of fig scale. August, 1954; Phomopsis canker of fig. November, 1949; Parathion tested on fig pests. September, 1949.
Condit, Ira J. Fig culture in California. Calif. Agr. Ext. Ser. Cir. 77. 67 pages. Request recent edition.
Condit, Ira J. Fig characteristics useful in the identification of varieties. Hilgardia. 14: 1-69. May, 1941.
Condit, I. J. The fig. A book. Chronica Botanica Company, Waltham, Mass. 222 pages. 1947.
Condit, I. J. Fig varieties: a monograph. Hilgardia 23: 11. 323-538. February, 1955.
Condit, I. J. and J. Enderud. A bibliography of the fig. Hilgardia 25: 1-663. July, 1956.
Crane, Julian C., Nasr Marei and M. M. Nelson. Growth and maturation of fig fruits stimulated by 2-chloroethylphosphonic acid. J. ASHS 95(3):367-370. 1970.
Davey, A. E. and R. E. Smith. The epidemiology of fig spoilage. Hilgardia 7:13 523-551. July, 1933.
Davis, C. S. et al. Pest and disease control program for figs (published frequently) Calif. Ag. Exp. Sta. Leaflet 70. Ask for recent edition.
duPreez, Daneel. The dropping of immature fruits. Farming in South Africa. Reprint No. 77. December 1948.
Krezdorn, A. H. and G. W. Adriance. Fig growing in the south. USDA Ag. Handbook 196, 26 pp. 1961 (popularized version, "Growing figs in the south for home use," Home and Garden Bull. 87, USDA, 11 pp., 1962.)
Kolbe, M. H. Fig culture in North Carolina. No. Car. Ag. Ext. Folder 115, Oct. 1963.
Marei, Nasr and J. C. Crane. Ethylene effects on fig. Plant Physiol. Vol. 48. September 1971.
Mehr, Stanley and H. K. Ferguson. Dried fig industry of Portugal. U. S. Dept. of Agr. FAS-M-40. 18 pages. August, 1958.
Phillips, E. L. Figs for Virginia. Va. Ag. Ext. Serv. Circ. 1035. Jan. 1967.
Prest, R. L. The fig. Queensland Agr. Jour. Pages 137-142. September, 1955.
Simmons, Peres, C. K. Fisher, I. J. Condit, H. N. Hansen and J. G. Tyler, Caprification of Calimyrna figs—Summary of three years research. Calif. Dept. of Agr. Bulletin. pp. 115-121. August, 1947.
Sission, R. F. The wasp that plays cupid to a fig. National Geographic. 138(5):690-697. Nov. 1970.
Smith R. E. and H. N. Hansen. Fruit spoilage diseases of figs. Univ. of Caiif. Agr. Expt. Sta. Bull. 506. 84 pages. 1931.

(See additional references under Chapter XVII Appendix)

CHAPTER XVIII

Control of Insects and Diseases

❖ ❖

Because of favorable soil and climatic conditions, fruits are grown year after year in the same regions. Thus, there is a tendency for insects and diseases to build up in these regions and for certain species to develop increasing resistance to spray chemicals used against them. Examples of this buildup of resistance to spray chemicals are the mites, codling moth, and, in the West, pear psylla. While the introduction of DDT in the early 1940's brought remarkable control of the worst apple pest, codling moth, it killed predators, particularly those of mites, and left the mites little affected. Mites now are one of the main problems, necessitating a shift among miticides and techniques to avoid resistance buildup.

As a result of initial entomological research in Nova Scotia, several stations now are studying the development of apple spray programs that control serious pests but also encourage predators of these pests, in an attempt to reduce the cost and amount of spraying needed. There are chemicals on the market that more or less meet this requirement. Another approach is the release of millions of male codling moths sexually sterilized by radio-active cobalt. A 99% control has been attained in test orchards.

Synthetic female sex attractants (insect pheromones—or sex lures) are now being used to attract males to traps to disclose their presence and population.

In order to fight orchard pests intelligently and economically, and to adjust the program to changing conditions, the fruit grower must have a thorough knowledge of spraying and dusting equipment, spray and dust materials, and modern methods of applying them. Changes have been rapid over the years in spray and dust machinery, materials and control methods

William G. Doe, fruit grower and Marwald Ltd., Harvard, Mass.; William E. Young, FMC representative, Summit, N. J.; and Dr. W. H. A. Wilde, Univ. of Guelph, Ontario, Canada, made many suggestions for revision of this chapter.

but this has slowed somewhat in recent years due to a Federal requirement for thorough evaluation of a chemical before it is released for general use.

Although there are many key practices in successful fruit growing, spraying probably is the most important cultural practice. Between 25 and 50 per cent or more of the total cost of commercial production of tree fruits is devoted to insect and disease control. Without this expenditure of money and effort in spraying, the trees would be relatively short-lived and the fruit almost worthless. In previous chapters, it has been emphasized that the general public is becoming critical of the fruit it buys. Buyers are no longer dependent on a few sources of supply and if the product is inferior, they turn to citrus, vegetables, or to other sources for their needs.

Spraying may be defined as the application of chemicals in liquid form to fruit plants as a preventative and combative measure against attacks by insects and diseases. Dusting is the application of chemicals in the form of dust for the same purposes. Although the grower may use other measures in combating insects and diseases, he relies mainly upon the spraying program for a large measure of the control.

Some pests make a more or less regular appearance year after year and occur in sufficient quantities to require standard control measures. Others are considered minor and may be destructive only under certain conditions or when a new spray chemical is used that is relatively ineffective against them or kills their predators.

Insects and diseases can be divided into groups, depending upon distinct characters of the organism and the type of injury it causes to the plant.

Types of insects. Insects may be grouped on the basis of their mouth parts, namely, (1) chewing, (2) sucking (and rasping in case of mites), and (3) lapping.

The chewing insects possess hard mouth parts with which they bite off parts of the plant (Figure 1). Examples of chewing insects are the worm stage of the codling moth which feeds largely on the fruit, and the tent caterpillar which feeds on the leaves. Other examples are the red banded leaf roller that causes damage mainly to apple fruits, the grape flea beetle which is destructive to grape leaves, and the plum curculio which attacks stone fruits and apples.

Sucking insects have tubelike mouth parts which they insert through the epidermis and tissues of the leaves, fruits and stems (Figure 1). The juices of the plant are thus withdrawn and digested. Examples of sucking insects are the aphids (plant lice), scales, red bugs, and leafhoppers. The red mite and two-spotted mite have sucking and rasping mouth parts that cause leaves to lose color and become bronzed.

B. A. Porter, U. S. D. A.

Figure 1. Types of fruit insects: (a) Plum curculio on peach, (b) tent caterpillar on apple, (c) rosy apple aphids on opening apple bud, (d) spring cankerworm on apple, (e) cherry leaf beetle on cherry, (f) black cherry aphis causing leaf curling on sweet cherry, and (g) pear slug on pear. Biting insects are represented at a, b, d, e, and g. Sucking insects are shown in c and f.

a

b

c

d

e

f

g

THE EGG

THE LARVA

HIBERNATING LARVAE

THE PUPAE

THE ADULT

Dow Chemical Co., Midland, Mich.

Figure 2. Four stages in the life cycle of the codling moth, a major apple insect, are shown. Eggs are laid on the leaf by adult moth; small larvae crawl to fruits, enter, gain full size; leave fruit, crawl down trunk or drop to ground, spin a cocoon; pupate; emerge as a moth; and start the life cycle again.

The third group of insects possess lapping mouth parts with which they lap up liquids from the outer surfaces of the plant. Common fruit insects of this type are the cherry fruit fly and the adult fly of the apple maggot.

An insect may pass through several stages during its development (known as metamorphosis); as for example, egg, larva, pupa, and adult (Figure 2). An insect of this kind may have different types of mouth parts while passing through different stages. For example, in the larva stage, the cherry fruit fly has biting and chewing mouth parts, whereas the adult fly has relatively harmless lapping mouth parts. The same is true for the apple maggot. The aphid has sucking mouth parts from the time it is a small nymph to a full-grown adult.

Types of diseases. A fruit disease may be caused by a fungus, bacteria, or virus (Figure 3), or it may be due to a physiological disorder. Most fruit diseases controlled by sprays or dusts are caused by fungi which are the lower plant forms lacking chlorophyll or green coloring matter found in higher plants. Fungi exist as parasites in or on the tissues of living plants. They are usually microscopic in size, although when vigorously present, they may be apparent to the naked eye. Examples are scab lesions on apple leaves and fruit, blue mold on apples in storage, and brown rot on peaches, plums, and cherries. Propagation of fungus diseases is by microscopic spores wihch may be transported by wind, light air currents, rain, insects, or other agents. Moist surroundings are favorable for spore germination and fungus development under most conditions. In the spraying program, it is desirable to cover the fruit and foliage with spray or dust materials before rainy periods occur in order to prevent or inhibit spore germination and fungus growth.

The bacterial diseases of fruits are difficult to control by spraying and usually are combatted by other means. Best example of a bacterial disease of fruit trees is fire blight of apple, pear, and quince. Bacterial spot on peach, particularly hybrids from the J. H. Hale parent, is a difficult bac-

510

(a and d) Michigan State College, (c) Botany Dept., Purdue University, (b) New York Agr. Exp. Sta.

Figure 3. Typical fungus, bacterial, and virus diseases of fruits: (a) Peach leaf curl (fungus) (b) crown gall on raspberry (bacterial), (c) brown rot on plum (fungus), and (d) red suture virus on peach.

terial disease. The usual means of control of bacterial diseases is to rogue out and burn the plants or remove infected areas and disinfect the pruning wounds thoroughly.

Virus diseases are caused by ultra microscopic organisms which cannot be controlled directly by spraying. Plants affected by virus often are removed from the planting and destroyed by burning. Probably the best approach to combatting these diseases is by cross-breeding for development of resistant varieties. Examples of virus diseases are Peach Yellows, Leaf Pucker and Russet Ring on apple, Streak disease of brambles, and Yellows disease of the strawberry.

Virus diseases have been of commercial importance mainly on raspberry, strawberry, cherry and peach. But in recent years they are being identified on most fruits, where their importance may be greater than heretofore thought. A number of virus diseases of apple have been noted in the United States; a total of 15, in fact, have been described in the world, mostly in Europe. A blueberry stunt virus has caused some concern. Pears

511

and grapes have their share. More research attention now is being directed toward these problems.

There are many physiological diseases which may be due to unbalanced nutrition, adverse weather conditions, poor stock-cion relationship, or other factors. Common examples are scald, internal breakdown and bitter pit of apple fruits, black-end of pear fruits, cork in apple fruits, Jonathan spot in apple and "little leaf" of many fruit trees caused by zinc deficiency.

ROLE OF EXPERIMENT STATIONS AND OTHER AGENCIES

The governmental experiment stations play a vital role in the testing and search for new spray chemicals and better methods of applying them. The large spray machinery and spray chemical companies likewise play an indispensable role. In fact, their field representatives are effective in advising and helping growers, while experiment station and extension workers are devoting more time to research and unbiased published material, and to coordination of grower meetings. It is only through the co-operation between these agencies, the fruit journals, and the growers themselves that outstanding progress has been made during the past half century.

From 1940 to the early 1950's the fruit industry probably underwent its greatest transformation on methods of insect and disease control that has occurred in human history. In order to keep well informed on rapidly changing methods, it is essential that the grower make frequent contacts with his local experiment station, and that he attend fruit meetings, subscribe to progressive fruit journals, and contact representatives of commercial companies as a safeguard and insurance in his orcharding program. The state and provincial experiment stations are particularly valuable because of their nonbiased recommendations based upon sound research.

The agricultural extension service or similar service groups provide punctual and rapid communication to the growers on *when* and *what* to apply in the insect and disease control program. Under typical conditions, the extension service distributes spray information to the growers through two channels: (a) by letters, and (b) by radio broadcast. Spray schedules are distributed to the growers before the spray season starts. The schedule contains information on concentration of sprays, approximately when they should be applied, and the insects and diseases they are designed to control. The grower orders the necessary spray materials well in advance and overhauls his spray equipment to place it in good working condition. When the spray season begins, the growers are informed by radio broadcast during critical periods exactly when (within hours) they should start spraying. Time of spraying is governed mainly by occurrence of rains, prevailing temperature conditions, and other factors which influence germination of disease spores and the emergence of codling moths and other pests.

The above information on "when to spray" is obtained through the co-operation of several key growers in important fruit regions throughout the area. During critical spray periods, these growers regularly send samples of leaves to the plant pathologists of the extension service, who examine them microscopically to ascertain the rate of development of scab spores. The key growers also maintain codling moth bait traps and report by phone to the extension service the number of emerging codling moths plus any other important data. From this information and weather forecasts, the extension service prepares special radio broadcasts for specific fruit regions. In the USA these are telegraphed or phoned to the county agricultural agents who broadcast them over local radio stations at a specified and regular time. This information is available to all growers free of charge.

SPRAY MATERIALS

Pesticide chemicals are classified according to use into three groups: (a) *Fungicides*—materials to control fungus diseases; (b) *insecticides*— materials to control insects; *Miticides*—materials that are effective against mites; and (d) *accessory materials (adjuvants)*— materials used as correctives, stickers, spreaders, activators, flocculators, and emulsifiers.

A chemical may be effective against one insect but ineffective against another, and it may be useless against diseases. On the other hand, there are some chemicals which control both insects and diseases. The grower must know the merits and weaknesses of the various materials, and in addition, their relative costs. New chemicals are being placed on the market continually and, again, the grower must decide if he should discard the old materials and adopt the new. He must base his decision as much as possible upon known facts and not upon opinions, then proceed with judgment with as little risk as possible.

MATERIALS FOR INSECT AND MITE CONTROL
(Read all container labels carefully before using)

There are two general types of *insecticides*: (a) stomach poisons, and (b) contact insecticides. Most insecticides for fruits are of the contact type, although some may act as both a contact and stomach poison. Acid lead arsenate which has been a standard insecticide for decades is an example of a stomach poison; the phosphates may act as either.

Insects that obtain food by biting and chewing or by lapping commonly are controlled by stomach poisons. Insects that obtain food by sucking sap from the plant tissues are largely controlled by contact insecticides which kill by suffocating, burning, or paralyzing them. Contact insecticides also will control many chewing and lapping insects. A stomach poison is of little or no value for controlling sucking insects because they insert their mouth parts through the layer of poison and suck sap from beneath the epidermis. Insects with lapping mouth parts, however, can be controlled with a stomach poison since they obtain food from the outer surfaces of plant parts.

Miticides are chemicals which are effective against mites, as e.g., Kelthane and Morestan (both chemicals effective against powdery mildew).

Fumigants often are used in fruit growing, mainly as soil fumigants that are directed against nematodes and soil borne insects.

Some poisons used against insects and mites are *systemic* which means that they are absorbed directly into the plant and translocated to all aerial parts. These chemicals are highly effective against pests such as aphids and mites. Obviously, the material may be absorbed into the fruit, creating a hazard to human consumption and this is studied carefully by the Pure Food and Drug Administration before permission for its specific use is given.

The following is a discussion of the kinds of insecticides, miticides, and fungicides available on the market, based largely on a discussion provided by Michigan State specialists, W. W. Thompson, Chm. To this list new materials are being added yearly. The best place to keep up-to-date on pesticides is at the local spray meetings conducted by government service men.

Unrelated Materials

Carzol (m-dimethylamino) methylene) amino) phenyl) methylcarbamate mono-hydrochloride). Non-phosphate, miticide pre- or post-bloom apples, pear; residual to 30 days; prevents egg hatch; repeat sprays needed; up to 7 days to harvest; moderately toxic to bees; relatively non-toxic to life; compatible with most products (a formamidine).

Lead Arsenate was the standard stomach poison years ago and now is coming back in fruit spray schedules. Acid lead arsenate should not be used on peaches, cherries, plums, or after Second Cover on apples without a corrective. Acid lead arsenate may be used safely with most pesticides. It should not be combined with weak concentrations of lime-sulfur (less than 1 gallon of lime-sulfur in 100 gallons of water, or less than 4 pounds of dry lime-sulfur) without the addition of hydrated lime, using equal amounts of lime and lead arsenate. It adheres well to the fruit and should not be used within 30 days of harvest. It is used in early season sprays against curculio, leaf roller, and other pests.

Other types of arsenates used in the past but little used on fruit now are calcium, magnesium and zinc arsenates. The cryolites, barium and sodium fluosilicate and sodium aluminate, were stomach poisons formerly used in the Northwest, but, since, replaced. It should be noted, however, that there is a tendency to go back to some of the formerly used pesticides when pest resistance or other problems arise with newer materials.

DN Compounds, Dinitro chemical compounds (e.g. Elgetol) are effective against aphids and mite eggs, scale, bud moth, and mineola moth as dormant applications. Follow the manufacturers' directions carefully. Foliar applications of DN compounds are now largely supplanted by other materials and are no longer generally suggested. El-318 and DN-289 are not used with oil. Elgetol and Dry Mix No. 1 may be combined with oil for dormant spraying and will increase toxicity of oil to aphid eggs.

Dormant Oils can be used to control European red mite, scale insects, and pear psylla. In general, the amount of oil in a spray varies from 3 to 4 percent. Oils should be used at manufacturers' directions. Dormant oils should have a viscosity (Saybolt at 100° F.) of 90 to 120 seconds; a minimum viscosity index (Kinematic) of 65; a minimum-gravity (A.P.I. degrees) of 28; a pour point not greater than 30° F., and an unsulfonated residue of above 78 percent. DN compounds should not be used in the same spray mixtures with 3 or 4 percent oil emulsions.

The 70-second superior oil is being recommended for mite eggs at green tip and PrePink stages for early effective kill. Apply spray from four sides of trees for best control.

Morestan (6-methyl-2-oxo-1, 3-dithio (4, 5b) quinoxaline), 25% WP, is effective against mites (not cyclamen mite), mite eggs, pear psylla and powdery mildew.

Rotenone is an insecticide derived from the roots of certain plants (*derris* from the East Indies and Malaya and *cubé* from South America). Being relatively safe, rotenone is exempt from the requirement of a tolerance. On fruits, its major usage is against pests immediately before or during harvest.

CHLORINATED HYDROCARBONS

Chloropropylate (Acaralate) (isopropyl 4, 4-dichlorobenzilate), 25% EC, is compatible with most insecticides and fungicides on apple and pear, but is not compatible with tri-basic copper sulfate, phosphamidon (WP) or Dyrene (WP). No toxicity observed on apple and Bartlett or Seckel pear. Use caution but no protective devices needed on body.

Dieldrin (hexachloroepoxyoctahydrodimethanonaphthalene) has proved very effective against the plum curculio on tree fruits and spittle bug on strawberries. It has a persistent residue and should not be applied after *First Cover* spray on peaches, plums, or cherries nor after *Third Cover* on apples, nor should it be used after *Bloom* on strawberries. It also controls apple sawfly, tarnish plant bug and tent caterpillars.

Endosulfan (Thiodan) (6-10, 10-Hexachloro-1, 5, 5a, 6, 9, 9a-hexahydro 6, 9-Methano-2, 4, 3-benzodioxathiepin 3-oxide . . .) is very toxic to skin and wildlife, emulsifiable formulation, stays in suspension well; used for peach tree borer during early and late season. Used to dip nursery peach trees before planting against borers; 5 lbs./100 gals.

Galecron-Fundal (N-N4-chloro-o-totyl)-N, N-dimethylformamidine monohydrochloride). Twin pre-post-bloom mites, c. moth, psylla, on apple, pear (new class of miticides-formamidines) outstanding on all mite strains eggs to adults; don't apply 14 days before apple harvest, 28 days

515

before pear harvest; slow killing; compatible most products, harmless to man, animals, bees, plants, other useful insects.

Kelthane (1, 1-bis (chlorophenyl) trichloroethanol) is a specific miticide. The residual action of this material is sufficiently long to control mite infestations with one application in many instances. For best results, apply Kelthane when the average temperature is predicted to be above 70° F. for 5 to 7 days. Not effective against insects.

Methoxychlor (1, 1, 1-trichloro-2, 2-bis (paramethoxyphenyl) ethane), a close relative of DDT, is also sold under the trade-name Marlate. It exercises control against such pests as the plum curculio, codling moth, apple maggot, splittlebug, and cherry fruit fly. It is available as a wettable powder and as a liquid emulsion. The wettable form is best for tree fruits, while the emulsion works better against spittlebug on strawberries. Do not use the emulsion form in the same spray mixture with fungicides.

Omite (2-(p-tert-butylphenoxy) cyclohexyl - 2 - propynyl - sulfite) Good control mites on apple, peach, pear, plum, prune; needs complete coverage upper-lower leaf surfaces, fruit; after bloom at temp. 70°F above; long residual action; not ovicide; little toxicity to predators, man, animals.

Perthane (1, 1-dichloro-2, 2-bis (p-ethylphenyl) ethane). Lowest toxicity, unstable, early pear psylla control where other chemicals no longer effective; *must* be timed for adults before egg laying.

Tedion (2, 4, 5, 4'—tetrachlorodiphenyl sulphone) is a specific miticide. It offers long residual effectiveness and a high degree of safety to man and plants. A Pink-stage application controls phosphate-resistant red mites. Sprays at pink, first-, third- and fifth-cover control red and two-spotted mites.

Thiodan (hexachloro-hexahydro-methano-2, 4, 3-benzo-dioxathiepien-oxide). Peach tree borers (both), on plums, cherries, too; post-harvest sprays for late season infestation; for pear psylla, aphids, t. plant bug, rust mites, moderate toxicity to mammals, usual precautions.

CHOLINESTERASE-INHIBITING COMPOUNDS
INCLUDING ORGANIC PHOSPHATES

Demeton (O-(2-ethylmercapto) ethyl)-O, O-diethy thiophosphate) commonly called Systox, is a systemic aphicide and miticide formulated as an emulsion concentrate. Do not use it more than three times during the growing season nor within 21 days of harvest. Demeton has been cleared for apple, pears, and strawberries but this may change in the future; check your local spray literature. Like parathion, this chemical is highly toxic to man and precautions on the label should be followed. Not effective against insects.

Diazinon (O, O-diethyl-O-(2-isoproyl-4-methyl-pyrimidyl (6) thio-phosphate) is intermediate between parathion and malathion in tox-icity to humans. It is effective against a wide range of insect pests, and has a residual action of 11 to 14 days. Diazinon is cleared for use on apples, pears, cherries, peaches, plums, strawberries and grapes.

Ethion (0, 0, 0, 0-tetraethyl S, S-methylene bisphosphorodithioate) with oils on apples for red mites, mite eggs, aphids, scale; not used on varieties ripening before McIntosh.

Gardona (2-chloro-1 (2, 4, 5-trichlorophenyl) vinyl dimethyl phos-phate). Low toxicity to man, animals, wildlife; hazard to fish; moderate damage to benefitual insects; for apples on codling moth, red banded leaf roller, curculio, plant bug, leaf roller, maggot. For late season prob-lems on apple, giving good finish quality.

Guthion (O, O-Dimethyl S-(4-oxo-1,2,3,-benzotriazinyl-3-methyl) phosphorodithioate) continues to give outstanding results in research plots and grower orchards. Almost all common fruit insects and mites are controlled with sprays applied at 14-day intervals.

Guthion has not performed well as a late clean-up material for two-spotted mites.

Guthion has been cleared for use on apples, pears, peaches, cherries plums, and strawberries. To avoid prohibitive residues, do not use more than 8 applications of Guthion per season and do not use it later than indicated by official schedule.

Experiences in Michigan to date have indicated a greater degree of fruit safety with the wettable powder than the emulsifiable formulation.

Guthion is similar to Parathion in toxicity to humans.

Imidan (0, 0-dimethyl S-phelhalimindomethyl phosphorodithioate). Relatively low toxicity to mammals, early on apples, pears, peaches, gives broad control codling moth, r.b. and f.t. leafrollers, *maggot,* curculio, plant bug, g. and r. aphid, peach t. borer, O. F. moth, *pear psylla,* non-existant strains, suppresses mites without damage to predators, in integrated pro-gram. Soon dissipates and harmless to man.

Malathion (S-(1, 2-dicarbethoxyethyl), O, O-dimethyl dithiophos-phate) is useful against many insect pests and is especially effective against many forms of aphids. Its period of effectiveness is only 2 to 3 days. Because of its short residual action, it often can be used to good advantage in late season sprays.

Parathion (O, diethyl O-p-nitrophenylthiophosphate) is highly toxic to man and animals. It has been widely used since 1949 and has given good control of aphids, bud moth, pear psylla, curculio, codling moth, oriental fruit moth, and grasshoppers. Some effectiveness is exhibited against mites and red-banded leaf roller. Parathion permits effective foliage treatment against insects that, in the past, have required dormant sprays. No injury from this material has been observed on peaches, plums, or cherries. Apples have been injured when parathion was used in amounts greater than generally suggested. Parathion can often be used to good advantage in combination with other insecticides.

Phosalone (O,O-diethyl S — (6 chloro—2-orobenzoxazolin-3-yl-methyl) phosphorodiethioate) or Zalone, contact or stomach poison; apples, pears, grapes for aphid, c. moth, maggot, r.b. leafroller, curculio, psylla, 1. hopper, mites; near harvest or cover sprays for apples; dissipates rapidly.

Phosdrin (alpha isomer of 2-carbomethoxy-1-methylvinyl dimethyl phosphate) has shown outstanding effectiveness against the red-banded leafroller. Although phosdrin controls a wide range of pests, its effectiveness lasts only about 24 hours. From this standpoint, it is more useful as a clean-up material than as a protective insecticide. Phosdrin is labeled for most fruits. Since it is highly toxic to humans, all safety precautions and a special mask are necessary when phosdrin is used.

Phosphamidon (2-chloro-2-diethyl-carbamoyl-1-methyl vinyl dimethyl phosphate). Controls aphids, mites, leafhopper as contact and systemic, early apple sprays.

Trithion (O, o-diethyl S-p-chlorophenylthiomethyl phosphorodithicate) is a phosphate material showing long residual effectiveness against certain pests. In experimental plots, aphids, scales, and mites have been controlled for periods longer than three weeks with one application. Michigan research studies indicate that trithion is effective against other fruit pests, but the protection is for a shorter period of time— approximately 10 days. Trithion is cleared for use on most fruits. It is suggested for trial in apple and cherry orchards where serious aphid, scale, and European red mite problems exist. However, Trithion has injured the leaves of Delicious and has russeted the fruit of Jonathan and Golden Delicious in Michigan when used after *Bloom*. Check your spray specialist for use under your conditions.

Sevin (1-naphthyl N-methylcarbamate), a relatively safe insecticide, controls a wide range of insects at dosage rates from 1 to 2 pounds of 50 percent wettable Sevin per 100 gallons. While not a phosphate, Sevin is considered a cholinesterase-inhibiting compound to a mild degree. Its effectiveness ranges from 10 to 14 days depending on the insects to control. Sevin is not effective against mites. It is compatible with most other pesticides. Sevin offers a high degree of safety to animals and plants and gives good control of certain pests resistant to other frequently used insecticides. Sevin should not be used before the second cover spray because of its fruit thinning tendency on McIntosh, Jonathan, Delicious, and N. Spy.

Chemicals which control fungus diseases by their chemical action are known as *fungicides*. Sulfur and copper are still active ingredients for fungicides but much of their former use has been replaced with organic-type fungicides. The fungicides primarily prevent germination of the spores and the establishment of the fungus upon the host, although some of the fungicides such the organic mercuries, phygon, and liquid-lime sulfur may "burn out" the fungus after it is established.

COPPER FUNGICIDES

Copper fungicides are usually divided into two groups: (1) Bordeaux; and (2) proprietary or low-soluble copper compounds.

Bordeaux is a tank-mix of copper sulfate (bluestone or blue vitriol), hydrated lime, and water. It is identified by a characteristic formula, an example of which is 4-6-100. The "4" means 4 pounds of copper sulfate; the "6" means 6 pounds of hydrated lime; and the "100" means that the total volume of spray mixture is 100 gallons.

There are various formulae for bordeaux mixtures, such as 1-16-100, 4-2-100, 4-4-100, etc. When bordeaux is suggested in the spraying schedules in this publication, the first figure always refers to the amount of copper sulfate in pounds, the second figure to the amount of hydrated lime in pounds, and the third figure to the quantity of spray mixture in gallons, with the liquid always water.

Copper sulfate can be obtained in several forms, based on size of particles. The rather fine, granular, and pulverized forms are easier to use in making tank-mix bordeaux. These forms are referred to by the trade as "powdered", "snow", "small crystals", and "large crystals". The powdered or snow forms are recommended for convenience.

Preparation of Bordeaux. There are several methods for preparing bordeaux. The one most common is the "instant bordeaux" method. It is convenient to use and the mixture is entirely satisfactory. *One precaution should always be remembered in making bordeaux: Never mix concentrated solutions of copper sulfate and hydrated lime.* Such a mixture is coarse and does not adhere well to the fruit or foliage.

The "instant method" requires the use of copper sulfate in the "powdered" or "snow" forms. The hydrated lime should be fresh. Make "instant bordeaux" as follows:

1. Fill the spray tank almost full of water (12 to 14 inches from the top of the tank).

2. Dissolve the amount of copper sulfate to be used in the tank of spray in a pail of water, using a porcelain pail.

3. With the agitator running, pour the dissolved copper sulfate into the tank.

4. Remove the screen of the spray tank and, with the agitator running, slowly pour the required amount of hydrated lime into the tank.

5. Add any other chemicals to be included with the bordeaux.

6. Replace the screen in the spray tank and finish filling the tank with water.

Proprietary Copper Compounds are fungicides or bactericides containing copper in a low-soluble, slowly available form. They are sold under various trade names, such as Basicop, COCS, Spray-Cop, Tennessee 26, Tribasic Copper, Copisol and Tennessee 34. In general, they are not as effective as bordeaux for control of diseases, but they are less injurious to fruit and foliage.

Because they vary in copper content, these compounds should be used at manufacturers' directions. To guard against possible injury from soluble copper, include 1 pound of fresh hydrated lime with each 0.24 to 0.26 of a pound of actual metallic copper used in the spray mixture.

SULFUR FUNGICIDES

Elemental Sulfur means sulfur in pure form. For disease control, the sulfur is reduced to extremely small particles by mechanical grinding or by other processes. Dry, powdered sulfur which is used for dusting contains an inert material to improve the flowing properties of the sulfur. Wettable powdered sulfur is elemental sulfur with a wetting agent added, so that the particles of sulfur can be wetted and dispersed in water. Sulfur pastes are finely divided sulfur particles, less than 5 microns, combined with enough water and wetting agent to make a paste. "Bentonite sulfur" is elemental sulfur fused chemically with bentonite clay; it is considered a form of wettable sulfur in this book.

Proprietary sulfur products vary in particle size and in sulfur content. Thus, it is favorable to follow the recommendations of the manufacturer. In general, 4 to 8 pounds of wettable sulfur are used per 100 gallons of spray. "Flotation paste" contains 32 to 42 percent elemental sulfur, compared to 95 to 98 percent elemental sulfur for the common, dry wettable form. Flotation paste is generally used at the rate of 8 to 10 pounds of paste per 100 gallons of spray. A sulfur paste common in some states is Magnetic 70 paste. This product contains 70 percent elemental sulfur and is used at the rates of 5 to 8 pounds per 100 gallons of spray.

The amount of sulfur paste or wettable sulfur used per 100 gallons of spray depends on the disease to be controlled and the season. The higher amounts are used early in the season for the control of apple scab, and for the control of brown rot on peach and plum. The lower amounts are used when diseases are more easily controlled, and during those periods favorable for sulfur burn.

The adhesiveness and fungicidal value of wettable and paste sulfurs depend, within limits, upon the size of the sulfur particles and the content of sulfur in the product. Sulfur, referred to as 325-mesh sulfur is coarse, with a maximum allowable particle size of 40 microns (a micron is equal to 1/25,000 of an inch). Paste sulfur and some of the wettable sulfurs have particles which range in size from 1 to 4 microns.

Wettable sulfurs and paste sulfurs are principally protective in their action against disease organisms. All parts of the fruit and foliage must be kept covered during infection periods.

Wettable and paste sulfurs are virtually noninjurious to apple fruit and foliage at cool temperatures. At temperatures above 85° F., sun scald may occur on the fruit and scorch on the foliage of apple trees. This is especially likely to happen in warm, humid weather. However, wettable sulfurs and paste sulfurs are safe to use in all applications on peaches, plums, and cherries even under conditions injurious to apple.

Lime-sulfur is available in both the liquid and dry forms. In this book, the term lime-sulfur refers to commercial concentrated solutions testing 32° to 33° Baume. Liquid lime-sulfur is a true solution consisting of caustic calcium polysulfides and thiosulfates as the toxic ingredients. The caustic action of the polysulfides kills certain fungous spores which are germinating or partly established, giving the material some eradicative as well as protective properties. Soon after being exposed on the leaf surface, the polysulphides and thiosulfate break down into finely divided sulfur, which has a protective action similar to elemental sulfurs.

Lime-sulfur, because of its caustic property, is more injurious to fruit and foliage than elemental sulfurs and must be used with caution.

ORGANIC FUNGICIDES

Dithiocarbamates

Benomyl (methyl 1-(butycarbamoyl)-2-benzemedazole carbamate). *Benlate,* peach, nectarine, apricot, cherry, prune, plum for brown rot, p. mildew, p. scab, b. l. spot; not effective p. l. curl; preharvest spray, postharvest dip or spray; not control *Rhizopus* or *Alternaria* rots.

Dikar (zinc ion and manganese ethylene bisdithiocarbamate, dinitro (1-methyl heptyl) phenylcrotonate and other phenols, derivatives). Active ingredients of Dithane M-45 + Karathane. P. mildew, scab on apple with spreader-sticker; mite suppression; good fruit finish except moderate russet on McIntosh, Cortland at high concentrations; incompatible with oil; compare costs other products before using.

Ferbam (ferric dimethyldithio-carbamate) is a black bulky powder

521

sold under the names of Fermate, Karbam, and Coromate. This material is suggested to control leaf spot on sour cherries, black rot on grapes, currant leaf spot, and is as effective as elemental sulfur in controlling scab on apples. It may be used also with glyodin and with actidione as a safening agent when these chemicals are used with lead arsenate. Less fermate is being used than formerly, due to russeting on some apple varieties.

Zineb (zinc ethylenebisdithiocarbamate) is a formulated wettable powder sold under the tradenames Dithane Z-78 and Parzate. It may be used on apples as a protective fungicide to control scab, and for early season rust and with captan for sooty blotch and fly speck.

Other Organic Fungicides

Botran (2, 6-dichloro-4-Nitroanaline) specific for water molds such as *Rhizopus* rot, brown rot, and leak on strawberry. FDA cleared.

Captan (N-trichloromethylmercapto-4-4 cyclohexene-1, 2-dicarboximide) is a 50 percent wettable powder sold as Orthocide 50 Wettable and Stauffer's Captan Fungicide. This material has given good control of apple scab, cherry leaf spot, brown rot on stone fruits, and fruit rots on strawberries. It is generally "kind" to foliage (Figure 3a).

Captan is suggested specifically for use on Golden Delicious during the period *Pre-Pink* through *Second Cover* to aid in the development of good fruit finish. Captan has caused leaf injury on Delicious in some orchards when applications have been too heavy or when used with incompatible materials. It requires one-half pound of captan to safen one pound of lead arsenate.

Cracking of Stayman was a serious problem in the early 1950's, but captan largely solved this problem from a spray standpoint in the East.

Cyprex or dodine (n-dodecylquanidine actetate) has given very good control of scab on red apples and leaf spot on sour cherries. May cause fruit injury on yellow apple varieties. Good protection before rains with moderate "back-action" if applied soon after a rain. Treated apples not useable for pomace for livestock.

Cyprex is not compatible with lime. Read the manufacturer's label carefully before using Cyprex.

Dichlone or Phygon (2,3-dichloro-1, 4-naphthoquinone). Phygon is a fungicide with both protective and eradicative properties. It is used against apple scab in cases where control has been difficult either alone or in combination with a protective fungicide. It is suggested in blossom sprays to control brown-rot blossom blight on peaches, plums, and cherries. Phygon is a caustic, irritating chemical and should be handled carefully. Operators who are sensitive to this material can obtain special non-oily ointments to overcome skin irritation.

Dinocap (Karathane) (2-capryl-4-6-dinitro-phenyl crotonate) specific for powdery mildew with some mite control. Frequent sprays at low concentrations are preferred to fewer at higher concentrations. In hot weather a scorch like sulfur burn may develop, but can be used at 10° F. higher temperature than sulfur. Do not use with oils. A spreader may be desirable to wet young foliage.

Folpet (Phaltan) (N-Trichloromethyl thiophthalimide . . .). Excellent for nearly all summer diseases on apple and peach. Closely related to captan but less safe on tree tissue early in season. May cause some injury on peach and young foliage.

Glyodin (2-heptadecylglyoxalidine acetate) is a liquid fungicide sold as Crag Fruit Fungicide 341 for use as a protective fungicide on apples to control scab and on cherries to control leaf spot. It has resulted in good finish of apples of all varieties, except Golden Delicious. It should not be used on Golden Delicious during the period *Pre-Pink* through *Second Cover*. When lead arsenate is used with glyodin, include one-fourth pound of ferbam for each pound of lead arsenate in the spray mixture to guard against arsenical injury. Glyodin and the combination of glyodin plus ferbam have performed creditably on sour cherries for control of leaf spot. *Glyoxide* (heptadecylimadazoline) and glyodin may be used interchangeably.

Guthion (Azinphosmethyl) (O, O-dimethyl S [4-oxo-1, 2, 3-benzo-triazin-3(4H) ylmethyl] phosphorodithioate) Controls most major insects from bloom to harvest. Widely used. Highly poisonous.

Niacide M (formerly Vancide M) is a mixture containing the following: 53.9 percent manganous dimethyldithiocarbamate, 10.9 percent thiram, 2.9 percent benzothiazyl disulfate, and 2.3 percent manganous benzothiazylmercaptide. It is suggested for use on apples any time throughout the growing season. In contrast to Niacide A, the "M" form is white or light gray in color, and leaves no undesirable visible residue on the harvested fruit. Niacide M has performed well throughout the season on Golden Delicious with no unfavorable russeting.

APPLE SCAB CONTROL

Since apple scab is the main fungus disease confronting apple growers in many apple regions and since good control is highly important, the following information is gleaned largely from the Michigan recommendations.

Scabby apples are culls. Also, the fungus, if not controlled, can cause early fruit and leaf drop which may reduce yields seriously.

The apple scab fungus develops during the winter and early spring in the old leaves on the ground that were infected the previous season. Ascospores, similar to small seeds, are produced and are usually ripe about the time the first green apple tissue is exposed in the spring. Rain is necessary for spore discharge, and enough rain to wet the surface of the leaves will cause some of the ascospores to be shot into the air. The air currents then carry these spores upward into adjoining trees; or the wind may carry the spores long distances. If they land on green apple foliage or fruit, they cause infection when they stay wet for a few hours. Ascospores may continue to be discharged as late as 2 to 4 weeks after Petal Fall in some seasons, but are usually all gone by First Cover.

The spores (ascospores or conidia) will germinate and penetrate into the green tissue — if the green tissue is wet, and if the spores on the green tissue remain wet long enough. The time required for the discharged ascospore to germinate and cause infection depends upon the temperature during the wet period. This relationship is shown in Table 1.

TABLE 1

THE APPROXIMATE NUMBER OF HOURS OF CONTINUED WET FOLIAGE REQUIRED FOR PRIMARY APPLE SCAB INFECTION AT DIFFERENT AIR TEMPERATURE RANGES

Air temperature range during wet period	Number of hours of continuous wet period required for primary apple scab infection
32°—40° F.	48 hours
40°—42° F.	30 hours
42°—45° F.	20 hours
45°—50° F.	14 hours
50°—53° F.	12 hours
53°—58° F.	10 hours
58°—76° F.	9 hours
76°—	11 hours

Primary apple scab infection is soon followed by the formation of secondary spores that are produced abundantly in established scabbed spots. Table 2 gives the time of expected appearance of the secondary spores (called conidia) after primary scab infection. Once primary infection is established, it is possible to have both ascospores and conidia present at the same time. The conidia or summer spores are not scattered by the wind, but are spread only by dropping or splashing water. Therefore, conidia reinfect only nearby fruit and foliage. Infection by conidia requires a wet period about 3 hours shorter than that given for ascospore infection in Table 1. The 3-hour lag in ascospore infections is based on the time the ascospores spend floating around in the air.

TABLE 2

THE EFFECT OF TEMPERATURE FOLLOWING PRIMARY APPLE SCAB INFECTION ON
THE LENGTH OF TIME REQUIRED FOR THE DEVELOPMENT OF CONIDIA
(SUMMER SPORES OR EGGS CAUSING ADDITIONAL INFECTION).

Average temperature following primary apple scab infection	Approximate period of time required for conidia (summer spores) development following primary apple scab infection
30°—40° F.	18 days
41°—45° F.	16 days
46°—50° F.	13 days
51°—55° F.	14 days
56°—60° F.	12 days
61°—65° F.	10 days
66°—70° F.	8 days
71°—75° F.	7 days

Control. By knowing the temperature from the time the green tissue first becomes wet until it dries again, you can determine (from Table 1) if infection is likely and judge whether spray materials already applied are adequate for the control of scab. If weather predictions indicate that the wet period will extend beyond the time given for apple scab infection in Table 1, it is advisable to apply a protective cover before or during the wet period, or an eradication spray immediately after the wet period. Renewed protection or eradication is particularly necessary if the protective cover already present is questionable.

To protect against apple scab infection, protective fungicides such as sulfurs or ferbam must be on the foliage before infection occurs. However, eradicative fungicides — such as lime-sulfur or phenyl-mercury compounds — kill the fungus after it has entered and penetrated for some distance into the apple leaf or fruit tissue; at full strength, these materials are usually effective for about 72 hours after the infection has taken place. Phygon is an effective eradicative fungicide when used at one-fourth pound per 100 gallons within 30 to 36 hours from the beginning of an infection period and in combination with a protective fungicide.

The performance expected of the several types of fungicides for scab control is illustrated, for all practical purposes, in Fig. 4. In this diagram, the organic mercuries—such as Tag, Coromerc, Phix, and Puratized Apple Spray—are shown eradicating infections that were established during the 3 days previous, or about 72 hours before the time of application. These organic mercuries are not, however, considered reliable for much further continued protection.

Lime-sulfur has an eradicative action equal to that of the mercuries, but the eradicative action of Phygon is considered to be somewhat less— or about 36 hours when used at one-half pound per 100 gallons. In addi-

Mich. Agr. Exp. Sta. E. Lansing

Figure 4. Approximate periods of control of apple scab by different kinds of fungicides. (T-time of application.) The time to the left of the vertical line indicates the approximate period of eradicative action; that to the right indicates the approximate period of protective action.

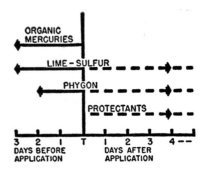

tion, lime-sulfur and Phygon leave protective fungicidal deposits. The fungicides, such as the wettable sulfurs, ferbam, and glyodin, are considered to be protective only, having rather limited or no eradicative properties. Captan is classed as a protectant, but does have eradicative action from 18 to 24 hours, depending on the prevailing air temperature.

For a protective spray program to be effective, the developing fruit and leaves must be covered before an infection period of wet weather The effective period of protection for the different fungicides is variable, depending on the amount of spray coating washed off by rains and the amount of new unprotected growth developed since the last spray. In general, a protectant spray coating in the prebloom period should be considered insufficient after a period of over 7 days, or after 1 inch of rainfall.

The following are spray chemicals specifically for the control of apple scab and are grouped according to their best use.

PROTECTIVE FUNGICIDES	ERADICATIVE OR PROTECTANT-ERADICANTS	FUNGICIDE MIXTURES WITH BOTH ERADICATIVE AND PROTECTIVE PROPERTIES
Lime-sulfur	Lime-sulfur	Sulfur, Ferbam, or Captan at half-strength combined with half-strength Phygon
Wettable sulfur		
Sulfur paste	Phygon (dichlone)	
Ferbam	Cyprex (dodine)	
Captan	Captan	
Phygon (dichlone)		
Cyprex (dodine)		

Purdue and Rutgers Universities are cooperating in the development of scab-resistant apple varieties by cross-breeding standard high-quality varieties with small-fruited scab-resistant crab apples, as the Siberian crab. Five promising hybrids were released for grower trial in the mid 1960's.

Precautions in Selecting Chemicals. Newly-established apple scab infection can be eradicated effectively within 30 to 36 hours from the beginning of a wet period—using either ¼ pound of dichlone (Phygon XL) with a protective fungicide at half-strength — or within 72 hours

526

from the beginning of an infection period, using full-strength mercury. When mercury is used at half-strength in combination with a protective fungicide, the effective period for eradication is usually reduced to 40 to 45 hours. However, the period of effective eradication may be somewhat longer for all concentrations of eradicative fungicides if the temperature during the time of infection is under 50° F. Remember also that liquid lime-sulfur has effective eradicative properties if used

TABLE 3. EFFECTIVENESS AND SAFETY OF APPLE SCAB FUNGICIDES
(BASED ON TESTS AT THE OHIO AGRICULTURAL EXPERIMENT STATION)

Fungicide	Dosage in 100 gal. (Delayed Dormant through 1st cover)	Scab Control	Foliage Safety	Fruit Finish
Captan (50%)	¼ lb.	Good	Excellent[1]	Excellent
Dichlone (50%)	2 lbs.	Good	Good	Fair[2]
Dodine (65%)	½ lb.	Excellent	Good	Good[3]
Liquid lime-sulfur	1-½ gal.	Good	Fair[4]	Fair[4]
Microfine sulfur (95%)	6 lbs.	Fair	Good[5]	Good[5]
Thiram (65%)	2 lbs.	Fair	Excellent	Excellent

[1] May cause some leaf spotting if used following heavy sulfur applications.

[2] Has caused excessive fruit injury on some varieties when applied after freezing temperatures. Has caused excessive russet on Golden Delicious.

[3] Has caused excessive russet on Golden Delicious.

[4] Has caused excessive foliage and fruit injury when used beyond the early prebloom periods.

[5] May cause foliage and fruit injury when applied during or just preceeding periods of very high temperatures.

[6] Used primarily as eradicatives after rain periods.

at 2 gallons per 100 gallons of spray within 72 hours from the beginning of the infection period.

Mercurial compounds may be most valuable as an emergency measure after rains, when protection against possible apple scab infection is questionable. Use a protective fungicide with the mercury.

It is generally conceded among plant pathologists that apple trees over-fertilized with nitrogen are more susceptible to scab infection.

ORDERING SPRAY MATERIALS

Spray materials must be ordered several months in advance of the spray season. The first consideration in ordering is to determine as nearly as possible the spray schedule to be followed, especially during the early part of the season. This schedule can be obtained from the local agricultural extension service or at the principle winter fruit meeting. It will suggest the number of sprays to be applied, the materials to be used, and the dilutions. Every grower should request that his name be placed on the reg-

THE THIRD GENERATION WORMS OF A SINGLE OVERWINTERING LARVA ARE CAPABLE OF DESTROYING 27,676 APPLES OR 138 BU. CONTROL THE FIRST BROOD AND PREVENT THESE LOSSES

C. E. Lehker, Purdue University, LaFayette, Indiana

Figure 4a. In the controlling of any pest, it is wise to take extreme precautions to time the early sprays properly. Once a disease or insect becomes established it is difficult to control for that season. Early scab, curculio, and mite control are as important as early codling moth control.

ular mailing list for spray schedules and other spray information from the local county agricultural agent.

Considerably more spray material will be required for the afterbloom than for the prebloom applications. Table 4 gives the average gallons of dilute spray solution required for the season for different fruit trees of different ages.

Table 4a shows a sample concentrate spray schedule for apples, as compared with a dilute spray program for mature apple trees in Ohio.

TIME AND AMOUNTS OF SPRAY APPLICATIONS

Most insects and diseases tend to build up as the growing season advances. It is, therefore, particularly important that the correct materials be applied thoroughly at the proper time early in the season in order to reduce as much as possible the early generations of insects and diseases. Burkholder and Lehker state that the progenies of a single overwintering codling moth, if uncontrolled, can destroy about 140 bushels of apples in one season. To control codling moth effectively, it is often good judgment early in the season to apply "top off" sprays between the regular cover sprays[1] in order to cover adequately the treetops and to keep the rapidly expanding surface of the young apples covered with spray material. As shown in Figure 5, the surface area of young apples may double every seven days early in the season.

Most fungus diseases thrive best in the presence of moisture from continued rains. During such periods, the spores readily germinate and the

[1] A cover spray is one applied after the blossom petals fall, the chief purpose of which is to keep the fruit surfaces covered as they grow and enlarge with a protective layer of spray.

TABLE 4.

Age of Trees	Average Amount per Application for Season in Gallons			
	Apples	Peaches	Sour Cherries	Sweet Cherries
2 to 3 years	.5	.7	.5	.5
5 years	1.5	3.0	2.5	1.5
10 years	6.0	5.5	6.0	6.0
12 years	8.0	6.0	8.0	8.0
15 to 20 years	12 to 20	6.0	10.0	10.0
21 to 25 years	20 to 35		12.0	15 to 18

TABLE 4a.

Dilutions for Wettable Powder and Emulsifiable Concentrates

TYPE OF MATERIAL	Quantities of Material for Indicated Quantities of Water			
	100 Gallons	5 Gallons	3 Gallons	1 Gallon
Wettable Powder	5 pounds	15 tablespoons	10 tablespoons	3 tablespoons
	4 pounds	13 tablespoons	8 tablespoons	8 teaspoons
	3 pounds	10 tablespoons	6 tablespoons	2 tablespoons
	2 pounds	8 tablespoons	4 tablespoons	4 teaspoons
	1 pound	3 tablespoons	6 teaspoons	2 teaspoons
	½ pound	5 teaspoons	1 tablespoon	1 teaspoon
Emulsifiable Concentrate	5 gallons	1 quart	1¼ pints	13 tablespoons
	4 gallons	1½ pints	1 pint	10 tablespoons
	3 gallons	1¼ pints	¾ pint	¼ pint
	2 gallons	¾ pint	½ pint	5 tablespoons
	1 gallon	½ pint	8 tablespoons	3 tablespoons
	1 quart	3 tablespoons	2 tablespoons	2 teaspoons
	1 pint	5 teaspoons	1 tablespoon	1 teaspoon

organism becomes established on the host, provided temperature is satisfactory. With most fungicides used today, it is important to have the spray materials on the foliage and fruit prior to the rainy period in order to prevent the spores from germinating. If in case of apple scab, the disease has made considerable headway, it may be advisable to use a "back-action" spray such as lime-sulfur to "burn-out" the established fungus.

RESIDUE TOLERANCES ON FRUITS

According to regulations established under "The Miller Bill (Federal)", certain small amounts (tolerances) of pesticides may remain legally on harvested fruits. The grower alone is responsible for producing legally marketable fruit.

By following three rules, the grower can be reasonably sure his harvested fruit will be "within the limits of the law":

Rule 1. Do not increase dosage rates above those currently recommended.

TABLE 4b.

QUANTITIES OF MATERIALS TO USE PER 100 GALLONS FOR VARIOUS RATES OF APPLICATION

Units of Material desired/A (lbs, gals, etc.)	Gallons of Spray to be Applied per Acre									
	60	75	100	200	300	400	500	600	800	1000
2	3-1/3	2-2/3	2	1	2/3	½	2/3	1/3	¼	1/5
3	5	4	3	1½	1	3/4	3/5	½	3/8	3/10
4	6-2/3	5-1/3	4	2	1-1/3	1	4/5	2/3	½	2/5
5	8-1/3	6-2/3	5	2½	1-2/3	1¼	1	5/8	5/8	½
6	10	8	6	3	2	1½	1-1/3	1	3/8	3/5
8	13	11	8	4	2-2/3	2	1-3/5	1-1/3	1	4/5
10	17	13	10	5	3½	2½	2	1-2/3	1¼	1
12	20	16	12	6	4	3	2-2/5	2	1½	1-1/5
15	25	20	15	7½	5	3¼	3	2½	2	1½
16	27	21	16	8	5-1/3	4	3-1/5	2-2/3	2	1-3/5
18	27	24	18	9	6	4½	3-3/5	3	2¼	1-4/5
20	33	27	20	10	6-2/3	5	4	3-1/3	2½	2
24	40	32	24	12	8	6	4-4/5	4	3	2-2/5
25	48	33	25	12	8-1/3	6¼	5	4¼	3-1/8	2½
28	46	37	28	14	9-1/3	7	5-2/3	4-2/3	3½	2-4/5
32	53	40	32	16	10	8	6-2/5	5½	4	3-1/5
40	67	53	40	20	13	10	8	6-2/3	5	4
48	80	64	48	24	16	12	10	8	6	4-4/5
55	92	73	55	28	18	14	11	9	7	5-½

TABLE 4c.

TREE SPACING—MILES PER HOUR

Miles per hour	Tree spacing						
	10 feet	15 feet	20 feet	25 feet	30 feet	35 feet	40 feet
	tree spaces per minute						
1.0	8.8	5.8	4.4	3.5	3.0	2.5	2.2
1.5	13.2	9.0	6.6	5.3	4.4	3.8	3.3
2.0	17.6	11.7	8.8	7.0	6.0	5.0	4.4
2.5	22.0	14.7	11.0	8.8	7.3	6.3	5.5
3.0	26.4	18.0	13.2	10.6	8.8	7.5	6.6

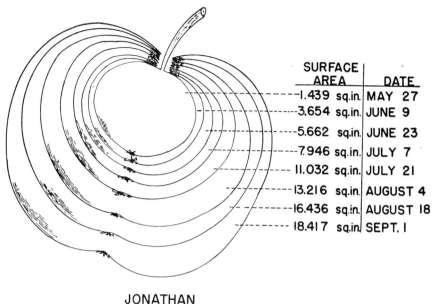

SURFACE AREA	DATE
1.439 sq.in.	MAY 27
3.654 sq.in.	JUNE 9
5.662 sq.in.	JUNE 23
7.946 sq.in.	JULY 7
11.032 sq.in.	JULY 21
13.216 sq.in.	AUGUST 4
16.436 sq.in.	AUGUST 18
18.417 sq.in.	SEPT. 1

JONATHAN

New Mexico Agr. Exp. Sta.

Figure 5. It is shown here that Jonathan apples about double their surface area every two weeks to a month during early development. Thus, there is a great need for frequent sprays to keep the fruit surface covered.

Rule 2. Do not use materials on crops not listed in current schedules for fruit.

Rule 3. Do not use materials closer to harvest than is indicated by the latest recommendations.

Materials used in the dormant, pre-bloom, and post-harvest periods ordinarily do not present a residue problem on harvested fruits.

Pesticides are grouped into several chemical classes such as unrelated materials, chlorinated hydrocarbons, cholinesterase-inhibiting compounds, and carbamate compounds. As an example, where residues of two or more chemicals in the same chemical class are present on a fruit, a "chemical class" tolerance becomes effective. Neither can combined amounts of materials in the same class exceed 100 percent of tolerances for component materials. For instance, if apples have a residue of 6 ppm of malathion (75 percent of its tolerance), only 0.25 ppm of parathion (25 percent of its tolerance) is allowed.

Materials of different chemical classes are considered separately; therefore, an apple can have a legal residue of 14 ppm methoxychlor, 8 ppm malathion, 7 ppm arsenate, and 7 ppm ferbam, as an example.

Since these tolerances and allied regulations are changing by month and year, contact your experiment station for the latest published data, or the Pesticide Chemical Regulations Section 120.3 of Sub-Part A of

Days Between Final Spray and Harvest for FDA Tolerances.
(As of the early 1970s)

	Apples	Pears	Cherries	Peaches	Plums	Black-berries	Grapes	Rasp-berries	Straw-berries	Blue-berries
ACARALATE	14	14	..	..	..	..	..	..	..	..
AZINPHOSMETHYL	7	7	15a	21	15a	14	10a	14	5	14
BHC	60b	60b	ab	60	60	..	b	..	b	b
BINAPACRYL	60a	60a	..	..	60a	..	45a	..	..	..
BORDEAUX MIXTURE	NTL	NTL	NTL	NTL	NTL	NTL	NTL	NTL	NTL	..
CAPTAN	NTL	NTL	NTL	NTL	NTL	NTL	NTL	NTL	NTL	NTL
CARBARYL	1	1	1	1	1	7	NTL	7	1	NTL
CARBOPHENOTHION	30	30	30	30	30	d	30	..	3	..
CHLOROBENZILATE	14	7	d	..	..	..	..	..	..	..
COPPER, FIXED	h	h	h	h	..	..	h	..	..	..
DEMETON	21a	21a	c	30a	30a	d	21	d	21	..
DIAZINON	14	14	10	20	10	..	10	..	5	7
DICHLONE	1	a	3	7	3	..	..	c	3	..
DICOFOL	7	7	7a	14	7a	2	7	2	2	..
DIELDRIN	90	a	a	45	30	c	14	c	b	c
DIMETHOATE	28	28	..	..	..	..	..	..	..	..
DNOC	e	e	ef	e	ef	..	..	e	..	..
DODINE	7	7	NTL	15	..	..	..	..	14	..
ENDOSULFAN	30a	7a	21a	30a	7	..	7	..	4a	a
ETHION	30a	30a	de	30a	21a	..	30a	..	2	..
FERBAM	7	7	NTL	21	7	40	7	40	14	40
FOLPET	NTL	..	NTL (sour)	..	..	NTL	NTL	NTL	NTL	NTL
GARDONA	7	..	..	..	..	..	..	..	..	..
GENITE	b	b	a	b	b	..	..	..	..	..
GLYODIN	NTL	NTL	7	NTL	..	..	..	..	..	..
IMIDAN	7	7	..	14	..	..	..	..	..	..
KARATHANE	21	21	..	45	..	..	21	7	21	..
LEAD ARSENATE	30	30	g	30	30	..	b	b	b	b
LIME	NTL	NTL	NTL	NTL	NTL	NTL	NTL	NTL	NTL	NTL
LIME SULFUR	NTL	NTL	NTL	NTL	NTL	NTL	NTL	NTL	NTL	NTL
MALATHION	3	1	3	7	3	1	3	1	3	NTL
MERCURY, ORGANIC	a	..	..	..	..	..	..	..	ab	..
METHOXYCHLOR	7	7	7	21	7	3i	14	3i	3i	14
MEVINPHOS	1	1	2	1	1	..	2	3	1	..
MORESTAN	35a	35a	cd	cd	cd	..	..	..	..	..
OIL, SUPERIOR	NTL	NTL	NTL	NTL	NTL	NTL	NTL	NTL	NTL	NTL
OMITE	7a	14a	..	14a	28a	..	..	..	..	..
OVEX	30	30	cd	30	30	..	b	..	cd	..
PARATHION	14	14	14	14a	14	15	14	15	14	14
PHOSALONE	14	14	..	..	..	..	..	..	..	..
PHOSPHAMIDON	30	..	df (sour)	..	..	..	..	..	..	..
STREPTOMYCIN	50	30	..	..	..	..	..	..	..	..
SULFUR, WETTABLE	NTL	NTL	NTL	NTL	NTL	NTL	NTL	NTL	cd	NTL
TDE	30	30	30	30	30	14	40a	14	5	14
TEPP	a	a	a	a	a	a	a	a	a	a
TETRADIFON	a	a	a	a	a	a	a	a	3a	a
THIRAM	NTL	..	..	7	..	..	..	..	3a	..
ZINEB	NTL	7	7	30	30	14	7	14	7	..

KEY TO TABLE
(Use each material as recommended in spray charts.)

NTL = no time limitations.
a = see label restrictions on use.
b = do not use after fruit begins to form.
c = use only at pre-bloom.
d = use only at post harvest.
.. = not labeled for use on this crop.

e = use only at dormant.
f = use only at one-half inch green.
g = 14 days processing, 30 days fresh.
h = exempt when used as recommended herein.
i = if more than 1.75 lbs. actual is used per acre, wait 14 days.

Federal Food, Drug and Cosmetic Act, U. S. Dept. Agr., Washington, D. C.

HEALTH HAZARDS
(Suggestions from Washington State Ext. Bull. 419 U. S.)

Each year there are a number of poisonings, and in some years deaths, attributable to the use of organic phosphorus insecticides. This should make every grower pay particular attention to the health hazards involved.

Research indicates that all pesticides, even the most hazardous, can be used with safety provided that recommended safety precautions are followed. The accompanying table shows the relative hazard to spraymen of the various pesticides.

TABLE 6. THE RELATIVE HAZARD OF PESTICIDES TO SPRAYMEN (WASHINGTON EXT. BULL. 419).

Most Dangerous¹	Dangerous	Less Dangerous	Least Dangerous	
Di-Syston (OP)²	Aldrin (CO)	BHC (CO)	Alar (M)	Morestan (M)
Furadan (Carbo-furan) (C)	Delnav (OP)	Dibrom (Naled) (OP)	Aminotriazole (Amitrole) (M)	NAA (M)
Lannate (C)	Dieldrin (CO)	Chlordane (CO)	Aramite (M)	Oil (M)
Parathion (OP)	DNOC (dinitrocresol) (N)	Cygon (OP)	Calcium Nitrate (M)	Omite (M)
Phosdrin (Mevinphos) (OP)	DNOSBP (dinitro-butylphenol) (N)	Diazinon (OP)	Captan (M)	Ovex (CO)
Schradan (OMPA) (OP)	Endrin (CO)	DN-111 (N)	Casoron (Di-chlobenil) (M)	Perthane (CO)
Strychnine (M)	EPN (OP)	Ethion (OP)	Chlorobenzilate (CO)	Phostex (M)
Systox (Demeton) (OP)	Methyl Parathion (OP)	Fundal (M)	Copper sprays (M)	Phygon XL (Dichlone) (M)
TEPP (OP)	Nicotine (M)	Galecron (M)	Cyprex (dodine) (M)	Rotenone (M)
Thimet (Phorate) (OP)	Paraquat (M)	Guthion (OP)	Dalapon (M)	Sevin (carbaryl) (C)
Zinophos (Cynem) (OP)	Phosphamidon (OP)	Imidan (OP)	Diuron (Karmex) (M)	Simazine (M)
	Trithion (Carbo-phenothion) (OP)	Lead Arsenate (M)	Ferbam (D)	Sinbar (Terbacil) (M)
	Zectran (C)	Lindane (CO)	Gardona (OP)	Sodium polysulfide (M)
	Zinc phosphide (M)	Meta-Systox-R (OP)	Glyodin (M)	Solubor (M)
	Zolone (OP)	Morocide (Bina-pacryl) (N)	Iron Chelate (M)	Sulfur (M)
		Thiodan (Endo-sulfan) (CO)	Karathane (N)	Tedion (Tetradifon) (CO)
		Toxaphene (CO)	Kelthane (CO)	2,4,D (CO)
			Lime-sulfur (M)	2,4,5-T (CO)
			Malathion (OP)	2,4,5-TP (CO)
			Maneb (D)	Urea (M)
			Methoxychlor (CO)	Zinc Sulfate (M)
				Zineb (D)
				Ziram (D)

¹These estimates are based primarily on the observed acute dermal and, to a less extent, oral toxicity of these compounds to experimental animals. Where available, experience has also been considered. The classification into toxicity groups is both approximate and relative.

²The chemical class to which the pesticide belongs is designated as follows: C, carbamate; CO, chlorinated organic; D, dithiocarbamate; M, miscellaneous; N, nitro; and OP, organic phosphorus.

Safe use of compounds in the "Most Dangerous" category requires full attention to all recommended precautions. Materials in the less hazardous categories may be used safely with correspondingly less protective clothing and equipment.

The more toxic materials easily enter the body through contact with the skin as well as through breathing. Ingestion of any of these compounds may be fatal. Repeated exposures may, even without symptoms, increase susceptibility to poisoning.

Take These Precautions: 1. If you plan to apply any of the more dangerous pesticides, make sure your physician knows the types of compounds you are using. If you anticipate using the more toxic organic phosphorus materials, he may suggest that you have a pre-seasonal blood test to determine your normal cholinesterase activity level. He then will be in a better position to deal with a sudden illness. If he should provide you with a supply of atropine tablets for organic phosphorus poisoning, do *not* take them before definite symptoms occur. If you ever take atropine tablets, call your physician as soon afterward as possible. Any person who is ill enough to receive a single dose of atropine should be kept under medical observation for 24 hours, because atropine may produce only temporary relief of symptoms in what may prove to be a serious case of poisoning. Keep atropine tablets away from children. An antidote for treating organic phosphorus poisoning, 2-PAM, has been developed. This antidote should be available at the U.S. Public Health Service Toxicolgy Laboratories and at hospitals and clinics serving your major agricultural area.

2. Wear protective clothing, preferably water repellent, while spraying hazardous materials as toxic pesticides can be absorbed into the body through the skin. Change and launder clothing and bathe daily.

3. Wear a respirator mask when loading or mixing wettable powders or when applying dusts. *The respirator should be approved for the material in question by your federal government services.* An approved respirator should be worn whenever the more volatile of the toxic compounds are being used, especially one such as Phosdrin. The filters and pads should be changed at regular intervals.

4. *Burn empty insecticide bags or other combustible containers, but do not stand in the smoke. Metal or glass containers should be rinsed with water immediately after emptying. The glass jars should be broken and metal containers crushed or punched with holes for permanent disposal. Bury them in an isolated place where water supplies will not become contaminated. A sanitary landfill type dump could be used for this purpose if the caretaker is cautioned to cover the pesticide containers as soon as possible. Never measure or leave mixtures of insecticides in beverage bottles or in labeled cans or boxes which have formerly contained food products. Each year tragic, preventable poisonings occur when children get ahold of "empty" insecticide containers or obtain food containers filled with insecticide.*

5. Keep your pesticide storage room locked (empty cans too).

6. Do not smoke, chew tobacco, or eat while spraying or while your hands are contaminated, especially with concentrate materials.

7. Mix insecticides according to directions and apply at the recommended rate.

8. Experience shows that poisoning occurs most often in hot weather. Spray with the more toxic materials during cooler periods insofar as possible. Take extra care when it is necessary to spray during periods of high temperature.

9. Fruit thinners and others have been poisoned by working in orchards treated with parathion less than 72 hours earlier. Therefore, it is advisable to wait longer than 72 hours before beginning work in treated orchards.

10. Bury spilled insecticide and wash the contaminated area with soap and lots of water. The breakdown of these insecticides can be speeded up by using a weak lye solution.

11. Cover crops should not be fed to livestock.

12. Do not feed insecticide-contaminated apple or pear pomace to livestock.

13. There have been a number of cases of irritation of skin, eyes, and respiratory tract from the use of ziram. These cases have occurred to sprayers from direct contact with the material and to thinners and pickers whose only exposure was to residues on fruit. There have also been a number of cases of skin irritation as a result of contact with Morestan.

Watch for These Symptoms: The initial symptoms of organic phosphorus poisoning are giddiness, headache, nausea, vomiting, excessive sweating, and tightness of the chest. These are followed by or accompanied by blurring of vision, diarrhea, excessive salivation, watering of the eyes, twiching of muscles, especially in the eyelids, and mental confusion. One of the most characteristic signs is constriction of the pupils, but this may be preceded by dilation. Late signs are fluid in the chest, convulsions, coma, loss of urinary or bowel control, and respiratory failure.

The symptoms of poisoning by the chlorinated organic compounds, such as dieldrin and endrin, are primarily due to their effect on the nervous system and include hyperexcitability, tremors, and convulsions. General symptoms are malaise, headache, fatigue, and possible lack of appetite and weight loss.

What to Do for Poisoning: 1. In severe cases of organic phosphorus poisoning, breathing may stop. In such a situation *artificial respiration is the most important first aid until breathing has resumed.*

2. Get the patient to a hospital or physician as soon as possible. Give artificial respiration on the way if the patient turns blue or stops breathing. If you know which pesticide may be involved, *take along a label for the doctor's information.* If the label cannot be removed easily, take along the entire pesticide container.

3. Never try to give anything by mouth to an unconscious patient.

4. If the insecticide has been swallowed but the patient has not vomited, induce vomiting by giving a tablespoonful of salt dissolved in one-half glass of warm water.

5. Where excessive amounts of the insecticide, especially in concentrate form, have come into contact with the skin, immediately remove all clothing and bathe the patient with generous amounts of soap and water, rinsing thoroughly.

6. If the eyes have been contaminated with spray, especially with insecticide concentrate, wash them immediately with flowing water.

7. Make the patient lie down and keep him warm.

BEE POISONING

Bees are necessary for the pollination of fruit trees. Orchardists should make a sincere effort to protect them. The following precautions will not only protect both domestic and wild bees, but also will help insure better pollination.

1. Do not place bees in an orchard until 10 to 20 per cent of the blossoms are open.

2. *Never apply* insecticidal sprays or dusts when blossoms are open or when drift of the material may get on open blossoms in adjoining orchards or interplants.

3. Mow, beat down, or use herbicides on cover crops before applying sprays toxic to bees. This will reduce bee poisoning from insecticide runoff on the cover crop. Grass sod cover crops should be encouraged to prevent bee losses, using 2-, 4-D to control dandelions.

4. Ask beekeepers to remove bees from your district before starting your spray program.

5. Parathion and most other organic phosphorus insecticides as well as dieldrin, lead arsenate, and Sevin are the most hazardous to bees. See Wash. State Agr. Ext. Bull. 419 for listing of chemicals hazardous to bees under various conditions.

COMPATABILITY OF SPRAYS

Every year several organizations including the experiment stations and the American Fruit Grower Magazine publish up-to-date compatability charts to show which combinations of chemicals, new and old, are (a) compatible (no injury resulting on fruit or foliage), (b) incompatible, or (c) should be tried with caution on a limited scale. On page 537 is a compatibility chart published by the Michigan Experiment Station, annual fruit spray and orchard care recommendations.

SPRAY SCHEDULES

Spray chemicals and ways of using them are changing every year. The commercial manufacturers are performing an excellent service in developing new and better pesticides. Experiment stations also are an important link in testing the chemicals and reporting results in an unbiased manner. But with the Pure Food and Drug Administration's increasing scrutiny with these chemicals from the standpoint of human consumption and the rulings of the Miller Bill, it is probable that new and improved chemicals now will enter the market more slowly and spray schedules will change less rapidly. This is due to the added expense and time required of industry to check any ill effects on rats of the proposed new pesticides.

	Lead Arsenate	Methoxychlor	Kelthane	Chloropropylate	Parathion, Ethion	Systox	Malathion, Trithion	Diazinon	Guthion	Captan	Dichlone (Phygon)	Bordeaux	Fixed Copper	Lime Sulfur	Elemental Sulfur	Ferbam, Thiram	Ziram, Zineb	Niacide M	Lime	Dinocap (Karathane)	Rotenone	Sevin	Tedion	Dodine (Cyprex)	Superior Oil	Morestan	Thiodan	Phosphamidon	Dimethoate	Imidan	Omite	Phosdrin	Perthane	Gardona	Zolone	Galecron-Fundal	Dikar	Carzol
Lead Arsenate		+	+	+	+	+	+	+	+	+	+	+	+	+	+	+	+	+	±	+	+	+	+	+	N	Q	+	+	+	+	+	+	+	+	+	+	+	Q
Methoxychlor	+		+	+	+	+	+	+	+	+	+	±̲	+	+	+	+	+	Q	+	+	+	+	Q	+	+	+	Q	Q	+	+	+	Q	Q	+	Q
Kelthane	+	+		+	+	+	+	+	+	N	N	N	+	+	+	+	N	+	+	+	+	+	Q	+	+	+	+	Q	+	+	+	+	Q	+	Q
Chloropropylate	+	+	+		+	+	+	+	+	N	Q	N	Q	N	+	Q	+	Q	+	+	+	N	N	Q	+	+	Q	Q	Q	Q	Q	Q	+	Q
Parathion, Ethion	+	+	+	+		+	+	+	+	+	+	+	±	+	+	+	+	+	+	+	+	+	+	Q	+	+	+	+	+	+	+	+	+	+	+	Q
Systox	+	+	+	+	+		+	+	+	+	Q̲	Q	Q	+	+	+	+	±	+	+	+	+	Q	+	+	+	+	;+	+	Q	+	+	+	+	Q
Malathion, Trithion	+	+	+	+	+	+		+	+	+	+	+	+	+	+	+	Q	+	+	+	+	+	Q	+	+	+	+	Q	N	+	Q	Q	Q	+	Q
Diazinon	+	+	+	+	+	+	+		+	+	Q̲	Q	Q	+	+	+	+	±̲	+	+	+	+	Q	+	+	+	Q	N	+	Q	+	+	N	Q	+	+
Guthion	+	+	+	+	+	+	+		. +	Q	Q	Q	+	+	+	+	±	+	+	+	+	Q	+	+	+	Q	+	+	Q	+	+	N	Q	+	+
Captan	+	+	+	+	+	+	+	+		Q	Q	+	N	N	N	+	+	+	N	+	+	N	+	+	+	+	+	+	+	+	+	+	+	+	+
Dichlone (Phygon)	+	+	N	+	+	+	+	+		Q	Q	+	+	+	Q	+	+	+	Q	N	Q	+	+	+	Q	+	+	Q	Q	+	+	+
Bordeaux	+	+	N	Q	±̲	Q	±̲	Q	Q	N	Q		+	N	Q	Q	Q	+	Q	N	N	Q	N	+	Q	N	Q	N	Q	+	N	N	N	+	Q	Q	N	Q	N
Fixed Copper	+	+	N	Q	±̲	Q	±̲	Q	Q	N	Q	+		N	+	Q	Q	Q	+	Q	N	+	Q	N	+	Q	N	+	+	+	+	Q	Q	Q	+	Q
Lime Sulfur	±̲	Q	N	Q	±̲	Q	±̲	Q	Q	N	Q	N	N		+	Q	Q	Q	N	N	N	+	N	N	N	Q	N	+	N	N	N	Q	Q	+	N	±̲	N
Elemental Sulfur	±̲	+	N	±̲	±̲	+	+	+	+	+	+	+	+	+		+	+	±	N	Q	+	+	+	+	+	±	+	+	+	+	+	N	+	Q
Ferbam, Thiram	+	+	+	+	+	+	+	+	+	+	Q	Q	Q	+		+	+	N	+	+	+	+	+	Q	+	+	+	+	+	+	+	+	+	+	+	Q
Ziram, Zineb	+	+	Q	+	+	+	+	+	+	Q	Q	Q	+		+	N	+	+	+	Q	+	+	Q	+	+	+	+	+	+	+	+	+	Q
Niacide M	+	+	+	+	+	+	+	+	+	+	Q	Q	Q	+	+	+		N	+	+	+	+	+	+	Q	+	+	+	Q	+	+	+	+	+	Q
Lime	+	Q	N	Q	±̲	±̲	+	±̲	+	N	Q	+	+	+	N	N	N		Q	N	N	Q	N	+	Q	N	+	N	+	N	N	N	Q	Q	Q	N	Q	N
Dinocap (Karathane)	+	+	+	+	±̲	Q̲	±̲	+	+	+	Q	Q	Q	+	+	+	+	Q		+	+	+	N	Q¹	+	+	+	Q	+	+	+	+	+	Q
Rotenone	+	+	+	+	+	+	+	+	+	+	+	N	N	N	+	+	+	+	N		Q	Q	N	Q	+	+	Q	+	+	+	Q	Q	Q	+	Q
Sevin	+	+	+	+	+	+	+	+	+	N	+	N	+	+	+	+	+	N	+	Q		+	+	+	Q	+	+	+	+	+	+	+	Q	+	+
Tedion	+	+	+	+	+	+	+	+	+	Q	Q	Q	+	+	+	+	Q	+	Q	+	Q	+		N	+	Q	+	+	+	+	+	+	+	Q	+	Q
Dodine (Cyprex)	+	+	N	+	N	+	+	+	+	N	N	N	+	+	+	N	+	+	+	+		Q	+	+	+	+	+	N	+	+	Q
Superior Oil	N	+	N	+	+	+	+	+	N	N	+	+	N	N	+	+	+	N	N	+	N	+		N	+	+	+	Q	N	+	Q	+	+	+	N	+
Morestan	Q	Q	Q	Q	Q	Q	Q	Q	Q	Q	Q	Q	Q	Q	Q	Q	Q	Q	Q	Q	Q	Q	Q	Q	N		Q	Q	Q	+	Q	Q	Q	+	Q	+	Q	Q
Thiodan	+	+	+	+	+	+	+	+	+	+	N	+	N	+	+	+	+	N	+	+	+	+	+	+	+	Q		+	+	+	+	+	+	+	+	Q
Phosphamidon	+	+	+	+	+	+	+	+	+	Q	+	+	+	+	+	+	+	+	+	+	Q	+		+	Q	Q	+	+	+	+	+	Q
Dimethoate	+	++	+	+	+	+	+	+	+	Q	+	+	+	+	+	+	+	+	+	+	Q	+		+	Q	+	Q	+	+	+	+	Q
Imidan	+	Q	+	Q	+	+	Q	Q	+	Q	N	Q	N	+	+	Q	N	+	Q	+	+	Q	+	+		+	Q	Q	Q	Q	+	+	+
Omite	+	Q	Q	Q	+	+	N	+	+	+	N	+	N	+	+	+	N	Q	N	Q	+	+	Q	+	N	Q	+	+	+		+	Q	Q	+	Q
Phosdrin	+	+	+	+	+	+	+	+	+	N	+	N	+	+	+	N	+	+	+	Q	+	+	Q	+	+	Q	+		+	+	Q	Q	+	Q
Perthane	+	+	Q	+	+	+	+	+	+	+	Q	+	+	+	Q	+	+	+	+	Q	Q	+	+	Q	Q	+		Q	Q	+	Q
Gardona	+	+	+	Q	Q	N	Q	Q	Q	+	+	+	Q	+	+	+	+	Q	Q	+	+	Q	Q	+	Q		+	+	Q
Zolone	+	Q	+	Q	+	Q	Q	Q	+	+	+	N	Q	Q	+	N	Q	Q	+	Q	Q	Q	Q		+	+	Q
Galecron-Fundal	+	Q	Q	Q	+	+	+	Q	+	+	N	Q	N	N	+	+	+	N	+	Q	+	Q	+	+	+	+	+	+	Q	+	Q	+	+		+	Q
Dikar	+	+	+	+	+	+	+	+	+	Q	+	+	+	+	+	+	+	+	N	Q	+	+	+	+	+	+	+	+		Q
Carzol	Q	Q	Q	Q	Q	Q	Q	+	+	+	N	Q	N	Q	Q	Q	Q	N	Q	Q	+	Q	Q	+	Q	Q	Q	+	Q	Q	Q	Q	Q	Q	Q	Q	Q	

Q = Questionable; compatibility not clear.
N = Not compatible.
± = Decomposes on standing; residual action reduced.
+ = Materials compatible.

*Compatible materials are those which can be mixed together in a spray tank without: (1) loss of effectiveness of the materials, or (2) unfavorable chemical reactions between the materials which might harm the plants.

Except when using ferbam, streptomycin is most favorably applied as a separate application, although it is compatible with ferbam or captan when necessary for scab control. Urea formulated for foliar applications is compatible with the commonly used pesticides. However, it doesn't seem to be compatible with fixed copper or Bordeaux.

Spray schedules that are listed here, namely, for apple, pear, and peach, are given only as examples of the problems and pests involved and how schedules are designed and executed. For other fruit and nut schedules contact the experiment stations (addresses in Appendix) of states which have substantial production of the crop in question.

In some states, for example Virginia, there is a trend toward devising spray programs for special needs, rather than present one general program for average needs. The Virginia Agricultural Experiment Station

APPLE SPRAYING SCHEDULE

NOTE: See end of schedule for intervals between final spray and harvest. Chemicals are not necessarily listed in order of preference in the spraying schedule.

The rates of materials for use on apple are based on a standard of 400 gallons per acre dilute spray for trees pruned 20 to 22 feet high in rows 40 feet apart.

Silver Tip to Pre-Pink
Non-Oil Schedule

DISEASES

Sepal and Leaf Scab only*

	Rate/100 gallons	Rate/acre
LIME SULFUR	2 gallons	8 gallons
	or	
DODINE (CYPREX)** (65% WP)	¾ to ½ pound	1½ to 2 pounds
	or	
DICHLONE (PHYGON) (50% WP)	¼ pound, plus	1 pound, plus
PROTECTANT	½ strength	¼ strength
	or	
CAPTAN (50% WP)	2 pounds	8 pounds
	or	
DIKAR (80% WP)***	2 pounds	8 pounds
	or	
WETTABLE SULFUR	6 pounds	24 pounds

INSECTS

Climbing Cutworms

	Rate/100 gallons	Rate/acre
PARATHION (15% WP)	2 pounds	8 pounds
	or	
PARATHION LIQUID	0.30 pounds active ingred.	1.20 pounds active ingred.

NOTE: Special Dylox (5%) and Sevin (5%) baits are available for cutworm control, applied at 2-4 ounces per tree in an area 6 feet by 6 feet around the base of the tree.

Green Tip to Pre-Pink
Oil Schedule

Sepal and Leaf Scab*

DODINE (CYPREX)**
(65% WP) ....¾ to ½ pound ....1½ to 2 pounds

NOTE: Do not use SULFUR compounds, DICHLONE (Phygon), CAPTAN, DIKAR or DINOCAP (KARATHANE) with oil.

European Red Mite (preventive program)
San Jose Scale, Aphids, Tarnished Plant Bug, Leafroller

Superior Oil, 70 sec. vis. ....2 gallons ....8 gallons
NOTE: Oil must be used as a dilute spray at the rate per acre shown for effective mite and scale control. Superior oil, 70 sec. vis. plus ETHION ¼ pound actual or FLOWABLE PARATHION 0.15 pounds actual, has given better control of San Jose scale than oil applied alone. Better mite control has been achieved by spraying 4 sides of the tree. In this case an additional application using 4 gallons of oil in 400 gallons of water is applied immediately after the first application or later before bloom. Do not add parathion to oil when spraying McIntosh and related varieties. When sulfur compounds are used in pre-bloom disease control, follow a non-oil schedule for mites to avoid plant injury.

Rosy apple aphid, other aphids*

	Rate/100 gallons	Rate/acre
PHOSPHAMIDON (8 pounds/gallon)	¼ pint	1 pint
	or	
DEMETON (SYSTOX) (6 pounds/gallon)	¼ pint	1 pint
	or	
DIMETHOATE (2.67 EC)	1 pint	4 pints
	or	
DIMETHOATE (25% WP)	1 pound	4 pounds

Tarnished Plant Bug, Green Fruit Worms, Leafrollers, Climbing Cutworms

	Rate/100 gallons	Rate/acre
PARATHION (15% WP)	1 pound	4 pounds
	or	
PARATHION LIQUID	0.15 pounds active ingred.	0.50 pounds active ingred.
	or	
GUTHION (50% WP)	½ pound	2 pounds
	or	
IMIDAN** (50% WP)	1 pound	4 pounds

*Scab spray may be necessary if infection period occurs from Silver Tip to Green Tip.
**Use Cyprex, ½ pound for longer back action.
***NOTE: DIKAR is suggested primarily when scab, powdery mildew and mites are problems together.

*NOTE: Aphid control at pre-pink to early pink offers the best protection against fruit injury.
**NOTE: IMIDAN also controls Rosy and Green Apple Aphids.

Pre-Pink and Pink
Non-Oil Schedule

Scab

	Rate/100 gallons	Rate/acre
DODINE (CYPREX) (65% WP)	¾ to ½ pound	1½ to 2 pounds
or		
DICHLONE (PHYGON) (50% WP)	¼ pound, plus	1 pound, plus
PROTECTANT	½ strength	½ strength
or		
CAPTAN (50% WP)	2 pounds	8 pounds
or		
DIKAR (80% WP)	2 pounds	8 pounds
or		
WETTABLE SULFUR	6 pounds	24 pounds

NOTE: DIKAR is suggested primarily when scab, powdery mildew and mites are problems together.

European Red Mite, Rosy Aphid, Tarnished Plant Bug, Green Fruitworms, Fruit Tree Leafroller.

	Rate/100 gallons	Rate/acre
European Red Mite		
MORESTAN (25% WP)	½ pound	2 pounds
or		
TEDION (1EC)	1 quart	4 quarts
or		
CHLOROPROPYLATE (ACARALATE) (2EC)*	1½ pints	6 pints
or		
GALECRON SP and FUNDAL SP (Soluble powder)	½ pound	2 pounds
or		
GALECRON (4EC) and FUNDAL (4EC)**	1 pint	4 pints
Rosy Aphids, Other Aphids***		
PHOSPHAMIDON (8 pounds/gallon)	¼ pint	1 pint
or		
DEMETON (SYSTOX) (6 pounds/gallon)	¼ pint	1 pint
or		
DIMETHOATE (2.67 EC)	1 pint	4 pints
or		
DIMETHOATE (25% WP)	1 pound	4 pounds
Tarnished Plant Bug, Green Fruitworm, Fruit Tree Leafroller		
PARATHION (15% WP)	1 pound	4 pounds
or		
PARATHION LIQUID	0.15 pound active ingred.	0.50 pound active ingred.
GUTHION (50% WP)	½ pound	2 pounds
or		
IMIDAN (50% WP)	1 pound	4 pounds

*NOTE: If mite eggs have not started to hatch, delay ACARALATE application until First Cover.

**NOTE: Liquid formulation of GALECRON and FUNDAL are not compatible with DODINE (CYPREX). Do not mix SP or EC with the combination of DIMETHOATE and DODINE (CYPREX).

***NOTE: PHOSPHAMIDON or DEMETON or DIMETHOATE application at pink to late pink offers systemic control of white apple leafhopper through bloom. Later problems with this insect may thus be reduced. Refer to rates given under petal fall.

NOTE: See Russetting of Golden Delicious when selecting pesticides — page 12.

Period of Bloom

Fire Blight

On susceptible varieties*

BORDEAUX 2-6-100

or

STREPTOMYCIN .... 50 to 100 ppm

Timing of bloom sprays: Use STREPTOMYCIN when maximum temperatures above 65°F exist or are anticipated to occur and are accompanied by precipitation or follow rainy days. Use 100 ppm in orchards prone to blight. Dormant pruning of overwintering cankers ½ inch or larger is a must. Remove all cankers on young trees and lightly infected mature trees. (See bloom schedule under PEARS, page 27.)

Post-bloom sprays: STREPTOMYCIN can now be used to within 50 days of harvest. The following suggestions are provided on a trial basis for those wishing to attempt early and mid-summer control of shoot, leaf, and fruit blight. Apply 100 ppm sprays on a 7-day protective schedule starting at petal fall or 5 to 7 days after the last in-bloom spray. During periods of wet, humid weather shorten interval to 5 to 7 days. Continue program until terminal growth stops. Spray during the evening or early morning hours to increase effectiveness.

Compatibility: Use protective compatible fungicides with STREPTOMYCIN if scab infection periods occur (see page 17). If BORDEAUX is used, fog-spray and apply only under fast drying conditions. Do not use STREPTOMYCIN after a BORDEAUX spray.

*Susceptible varieties include: Wagener, Tompkins King, Twenty Ounce, Rhode Island Greening, Yellow Transparent, Jonathan, Idared, Fenton (Beacon), and many Crab apple varieties. In some years, Golden Delicious and Stayman will develop twig infections.

Do not use insecticides in bloom as they are toxic to bees. Remove bees from the orchard before applying Petal Fall Spray.

Petal Fall
(Three-fourths of the petals fallen)

Fruit Scab and Leaf Scab	Rate/100 gallons	Rate/acre
CAPTAN (50% WP)	2 pounds	8 pounds
or		
DODINE (CYPREX) (65% WP)	¾ to ½ pound	1½ to 2 pounds
or		
DICHLONE (PHYGON) (50% WP)	¼ pound, plus	1 pound, plus
PROTECTANT	½ strength	½ strength
or		
DIKAR (80% WP)	2 pounds	8 pounds
or		
WETTABLE SULFUR	6 pounds	24 pounds

Red-Banded Leaf Roller, Plum Curculio,* White Apple Leafhopper, Aphids	Rate/100 gallons	Rate/acre
Red-Banded Leaf Roller,** Plum Curculio		
GUTHION (50% WP)	½ pound	2 pounds
or		
IMIDAN (50% WP)	1 pound	4 pounds
or		
GARDONA (75% WP)	2/3 pound	2¾ pounds
White Apple Leafhopper, Aphids***		
DEMETON (SYSTOX) (6 pounds/gallon)	1/3 pint	1 1/3 pints
or		
DIMETHOATE (2.67 EC)	1½ pints	6 pints
or		
DIMETHOATE (25% WP)	2 pounds	8 pounds
or		
THIODAN (50% WP)	1 pound	4 pounds
or		
THIODAN (2 EC)	1 quart	4 quarts

*NOTE: IF CURCULIO IS A PROBLEM, INCREASE GUTHION OR IMIDAN OR GARDONA RATE BY 25%. APPLY A SECOND SPRAY 7 DAYS LATER.

**NOTE: PHEROMONE TRAPS may be used to detect red-banded leafroller and determine spray timing.

***NOTE: MAXIMUM KILL OF NYMPHS BY THOROUGH COVERAGE OF UPPER AND LOWER LEAF SURFACES IS MOST ESSENTIAL FOR EFFECTIVE LEAFHOPPER CONTROL. An additional application of DEMETON or DIMETHOATE or THIODAN may be needed in late August or September to control a second generation of leafhoppers.

NOTE: See sections on Russetting of Jonathan and Golden Delicious on page 14 and Fruit Thinning, pages 15 and 16.

First Cover
(7 to 10 days after Petal Fall)

Scab	Red-Banded Leaf Roller, Plum Curculio, White Apple Leafhopper, Aphids
Same fungicides as in Petal Fall	Same insecticides as in Petal Fall
	NOTE: A repeat application of DEMETON or DIMETHOATE or THIODAN advised if leafhoppers are a major and continued problem.

Second Cover
(10 to 14 days after First Cover)

Scab	Rate/100 gallons	Rate/acre
CAPTAN (50% WP)	1½ to 2 pounds	6 to 8 pounds
or		
DODINE (CYPREX) (65% WP)	¾ pound	1 pound
or		
DIKAR (80% WP)	1½ to 2 pounds	6 to 8 pounds

Codling Moth,* Aphids, Plum Curculio	Rate/100 gallons	Rate/acre
GUTHION (50% WP)	½ pound	2 pounds
or		
SEVIN (50% WP)	1 pound	4 pounds
or		
SEVIN LIQUID	0.5 pound active ingred.	2 pounds active ingred.
or		
IMIDAN (50% WP)	1 pound	4 pounds
or		
GARDONA (75% WP)	2/3 pound	2¾ pounds
or		
DIAZINON (50% WP)	1 pound	4 pounds
or		
PHOSALONE (ZOLONE)** (3 EC)	1 pint	4 pints

*NOTE: PHEROMONE TRAPS may be used to detect codling moth and determine spray timing.

**NOTE: PHOSALONE (ZOLONE) will control non-phosphate resistant mites.

SUMMER MITE PROGRAMS

Summer mite control is best accomplished by spraying before the mites have a chance to build up. Where mites have increased to large numbers, eradication of these populations is extremely difficult. The following "eradicative" programs are suggested to reduce populations of European red mite, two-spotted mite and four-spotted mite.

Two sprays spaced 7 to 10 days apart required.

	Rate/100 gallons	*Rate/acre*
OMITE (30% WP)	1¼ pounds	5 pounds
or		
KELTHANE (18.5% EC)	1 quart	4 quarts
or		
KELTHANE (35% WP)	1¼ pounds	5 pounds
or		
PHOSDRIN (4 EC)	¼ pint, plus	1 pint, plus
TEDION (1 EC)	1 quart	4 quarts
or		
MORESTAN* (25% WP)	½ pound	2 pounds
or		
CARZOL SP (Soluble powder)	¼ to ½ pound	1 to 2 pounds
or		
CHLOROPROPYLATE (ACARALATE)	2 pints	8 pints
or		
GALECRON SP and FUNDAL SP (Soluble powder)	½ pound	2 pounds
or		
GALECRON (4 EC) and FUNDAL (4 EC)**	1 pint	4 pints

*NOTE: *To prevent fruit injury, do not tank-mix with other materials.*

**NOTE: *Liquid formulation of GALECRON and FUNDAL is not compatible with DODINE (CYPREX).*

NOTE: *GALECRON and FUNDAL applied in post-bloom cover sprays for mites will control codling moth as well.*

NOTE: *Complete coverage of upper and lower leaf surfaces is important for maximum control with OMITE.*

NOTE: *If DIKAR is used as a fungicide program, its mite suppression may make other miticides unnecessary at this time.*

Third Cover

(10 to 14 days after Second Cover)

Scab

CAPTAN (50% WP)	1 to 1½ pound	4 to 6 pounds
or		
DODINE (CYPREX) (65% WP)	¼ pound	1 pound
or		
DIKAR (80% WP)	1½ pounds	6 pounds

Codling Moth, Aphids

GUTHION (50% WP)	½ pound	2 pounds
or		
SEVIN (50% WP)	1 pound	4 pounds
or		
SEVIN LIQUID	0.5 pounds active ingred.	2 pounds active ingred.
or		
IMIDAN (50% WP)	1 pound	4 pounds
or		
GARDONA (75% WP)	2/3 pound	2⅔ pounds
or		
DIAZINON (50% WP)	1 pound	4 pounds
or		
PHOSALONE (ZOLONE) (3 EC)	1 pint	4 pints

Fourth Cover

(Time to be announced by District Horticultural Agents between June 20 and July 15—based upon special bait trap detection)

Scab

DODINE (CYPREX) (65% WP)	¼ pound	1 pound
or		
CAPTAN (50% WP)	1 pound	4 pounds
or		
DIKAR (80% WP)	1½ pounds	6 pounds

Apple Maggot, Codling Moth, Aphids

GUTHION (50% WP)	½ pound	2 pounds
or		
SEVIN* (50% WP)	2 pounds	8 pounds
or		
SEVIN LIQUID*	1 pound active ingred.	4 pounds active ingred.
or		
GUTHION (50% WP)	¼ pound, plus	1 pound, plus
SEVIN (50% WP)	½ pound, or	2 pounds, or
SEVIN LIQUID	0.25 pound active ingred.	1 pound active ingred.
or		
LEAD ARSENATE	2 pounds, plus	8 pounds, plus
PARATHION (15% WP)	1 pound, or	4 pounds, or
PARATHION LIQUID	0.15 pounds active ingred.	0.50 pounds active ingred.
or		
LEAD ARSENATE	2 pounds, plus	8 pounds, plus
SEVIN (50% WP)	1 pound, or	4 pounds, or
SEVIN LIQUID	0.5 pounds active ingred.	2 pounds active ingred.
or		
LEAD ARSENATE	2 pounds, plus	8 pounds, plus
PHOSPHAMIDON (8 pounds/gallon)	¼ pint	1 pint

Apple Maggot, Codling Moth, Aphids (Continued)

	Rate/100 gallons	Rate/acre
IMIDAN (50% WP)	1 pound	4 pounds
or		
GARDONA (75% WP)	2/3 pound	2¾ pounds

CAUTION: Use ½ pound FERBAM as an arsenical corrective if DODINE is used with LEAD ARSENATE. (See Arsenical Injury, page 14.)

	Rate/100 gallons	Rate/acre
DIAZINON (50% WP)	1 pound	4 pounds
or		
PHOSALONE (ZOLONE)	1 pint	4 pints
(3 EC)		

Do not use LEAD ARSENATE on varieties ripening before Wealthy.
NOTE: SEVIN may be used alone on a 10-day schedule only where Apple Maggot is not a severe problem.

APPLES

Fifth Cover
(10 to 14 days after Fourth Cover)

Scab

Codling Moth, Apple Maggot, Red-Banded Leaf Roller,* Aphids

Same fungicides as for Fourth Cover

Same insecticides as for Fourth Cover
NOTE: PHEROMONE TRAPS may be used to detect red-banded leafroller and determine spray timing.

Sixth Cover
(10 to 14 days after Fifth Cover)

Scab

Codling Moth, Apple Maggot, Red-Banded Leaf Roller,* Aphids

Same fungicides as for Fourth Cover

Same insecticides as for Fourth Cover
NOTE: To avoid possible excess residues do not apply lead arsenate after July 25 on varieties to be harvested before September 15, and do not use lead arsenate after August 10 on varieties to be harvested after September 15.

Two-spotted mite may attack in extreme numbers at this time. Adults may over-winter in the calyx end of the fruit. Adults of the European red mite may deposit eggs in the calyx end of fruit. Excessive insects in or on fruit constitutes an adulteration of food products. To prevent excess insects in or on the fruit at harvest, follow the directions given for the control of mites listed under the Summer Mite Programs on page 24.

Seventh and Eighth Cover
(10-14 day intervals after Sixth Cover)

Scab

Codling Moth, Apple Maggot, Red-Banded Leaf Roller, Aphids

Same fungicides as for Fourth Cover

	Rate/100 gallons	Rate/acre
GUTHION (50% WP)	½ pound	2 pounds
or		
GUTHION (50% WP)	¼ pound, plus	1 pound, plus
SEVIN (50% WP)	½ pound, or	2 pounds, or
SEVIN LIQUID	0.25 pounds	1 pound
	active ingred.	active ingred.
or		
IMIDAN (50% WP)	1 pound	4 pounds
or		
GARDONA (75% WP)	2/3 pound	2¾ pounds
or		
DIAZINON (50% WP)	1 pound	4 pounds
or		
PHOSALONE (ZOLONE)		
(3 EC)	1 pint	4 pints

Codling Moth, Apple Maggot, Red-Banded Leaf Roller, Aphids, White Apple Leafhopper*

	Rate/100 gallons	Rate/acre
SEVIN** (50% WP)	2 pounds	8 pounds
or		
SEVIN LIQUID**	1 pound	4 pounds
	active ingred.	active ingred.

NOTE: SYSTOX or DIMETHOATE or THIODAN will also control second generation leafhoppers. Refer to rates given under Petal Fall.
**NOTE: Refer to use of SEVIN for apple maggot under Fourth Cover.*

542

SPECIAL APPLE DISEASE CONTROLS

(Controls are suggested where these diseases are economic problems)

Silver Tip to Petal Fall

Powdery Mildew (on susceptible varieties)*

	Rate/100 gallons	Rate/acre
Scab fungicide plus		
WETTABLE SULFUR	2 pounds	8 pounds
or		
Scab fungicide plus		
DINOCAP (KARATHANE)		
(25% WP)	½ pound	2 pounds
or		
DIKAR (80% WP)	2 pounds	8 pounds

NOTE: When LIME SULFUR is used, do not use SULFUR or DINOCAP (KARATHANE). Add wetting agent if necessary to wet fungal growth.

Cover Sprays Starting at Third Cover

Sooty Blotch, Fly Speck and Scab

	Rate/100 gallons	Rate/acre
CAPTAN (50% WP)	1 pound, plus	4 pound, plus
ZINEB (75% WP)	1 pound	4 pounds

First Cover to Third Cover (or cessation of terminal growth)

Powdery Mildew

	Rate/100 gallons	Rate/acre
Scab fungicide plus		
WETTABLE SULFUR		
(325 mesh)	2 pounds	8 pounds
or		
Scab fungicide plus		
DINOCAP (KARATHANE)		
(25% WP)	½ pound	2 pounds
or		
DIKAR (80% WP)	1½ pounds	6 pounds

Pink to Third Cover

Cedar-Apple Rust

	Rate/100 gallons	Rate/acre
FERBAM (76% WP)	2 pounds	8 pounds
or		
FERBAM (76% WP)	¾ pound, plus	3 pound, plus
SCAB FUNGICIDE	½ strength	¾ strength
or		
THIRAM (THYLATE)		
(65% WP)	2 pounds	8 pounds

*Susceptible varieties to mildew include: Jonathan, Rome Beauty, Cortland, Baldwin, Mornoe, and Idared.

Northwestern Anthracnose (Bull's Eye Rot). Where this disease is a problem, use ZIRAM 1½ pounds or CAPTAN

(50% WP) 2 pounds in the late cover sprays, starting in early August until 1 or 2 weeks before harvest at 2-week intervals.

DAYS BETWEEN FINAL SPRAY AND HARVEST

Insecticides: IMIDAN—7, GARDONA — 7, PHOSDRIN—1, OMITE—7 and no more than 3 applications per year. DIAZINON—14, PHOSALONE (ZOLONE)—14, GALECRON and FUNDAL—14 and no more than 3 applications while fruit is on the tree, DYLOX—do not apply after fruit has formed, THIODAN—21 when not more than 3 applications are used. CHLOROPROPYLATE (ACARALATE)—14; DIMETHOATE—28; DEMETON (SYSTOX)—21; GUTHION—7; KELTHANE—7; LEAD ARSENATE—30; MORESTON—35; PARATHION—14; PHOSPHAMIDON—30; SEVIN—1; TEDION—apply no more than 4 treatments after petal fall if the rate is either 1 pound of TEDION (25% WP) or 1 quart of TEDION (1 EC) per 100 gallons.

Fungicides: CAPTAN—0; DICHLONE (PHYGON)—1; DODINE (CYPREX)—7; DINOCAP (KARATHANE)—21; SULFUR—0; THIRAM (THYLATE)—0; ZINEB—7; STREPTOMYCIN—50. DIKAR—21.

TABLE 8. PEST CONTROL PROGRAM FOR PEARS
(FROM WASHINGTON AGRICULTURAL EXTENSION SERVICE BULLETIN 419)

Pest or disease to be controlled	Use any one of the listed materials or the listed combinations	Amount per acre	Amount per 100 gallons	Minimum days between last use and harvest, restrictions, remarks
DORMANT SPRAY (Stage 1)—Based on 400 gallons per acre (for average size trees). Use at least 5 gallons per acre for aerial applications				
Pear psylla	1. Perthane 4 lbs./gal. EC	1 gallon	1 quart	Apply when first psylla eggs are found. For aerial application use 3 gallons of oil and 5 quarts of Perthane 4 lbs./gal. EC per acre. This oil application can be followed by a delayed-dormant or cluster-bud oil as shown later in this schedule.
	2. Perthane 4 lbs./gal. flowable	1 gallon	1 quart	
	3. Perthane 4 lbs./gal. EC +	1 gallon	1 quart	
	Superior type oil 98%	4 gallons	1 gallon	
	4. Perthane 4 lbs./gal. flowable +	1 gallon	1 quart	
	Superior type oil 98%	4 gallons	1 gallon	
	5. Fundal SP or Galecron SP	2 pounds	½ pound	
	6. Fundal SP or Galecron SP +	2 pounds	½ pound	
	Superior type oil 98%	4 gallons	1 gallon	
DELAYED-DORMANT SPRAY (Stages 2, 3, 4, apply before new growth is exposed to minimize spray injury)—Based on 500 gallons per acre (for average size trees)				
European red mite, brown mite, San Jose scale, blister mite, rust mite, lygus bugs, stink bugs	1. Superior type oil 98% +	7½ gallons	1½ gallons	Use no more than 5 gallons of oil per acre in concentrate sprays. If San Jose scale is moderate to severe, use dilute spray.
	Ethion 25% WP or	5 pounds	1 pound	
	Trithion 4 lbs./gal. flow. or	2½ pints	½ pint	
	Parathion 25% WP or	5 pounds	1 pound	
	Diazinon 50% WP or	5 pounds	1 pound	
	Lime-sulfur	15 gallons	3 gallons	
Pear psylla	1. Perthane 4 lbs./gal. EC +	5 quarts	1 quart	
	Superior type oil 98%	7½ gallons	1½ gallons	
Pear scab	1. Lime-sulfur (not on Anjou)	30 gallons	6 gallons	
	2. Cyprex (dodine) 65% WP	3¾ pounds	¾ pound	

544

Pest or disease to be controlled	Use any one of the listed materials or the listed combinations	Amount per acre	Amount per 100 gallons	Minimum days between last use and harvest, restrictions, remarks
Grape mealybug	1. Superior type oil 98% + Parathion 4 lbs./gal. EC or Diazinon 50% WP	7½ gallons 2½ pints 5 pounds	1½ gallons ½ pint 1 pound	
Cutworms	1. Dieldrin 1.5 lbs./gal. EC	5 pints	1 pint	Dieldrin may be combined with oil, Perthane, and an organophosphate compound, or applied to the trunk and ground as a separate spray. If the latter method is used, the gallonage per acre should be reduced.

PRE-PINK SPRAY (Stages 5, 6)—Based on 500 gallons per acre (for average size trees).

Pest or disease to be controlled	Use any one of the listed materials or the listed combinations	Amount per acre	Amount per 100 gallons	Minimum days between last use and harvest, restrictions, remarks
Tent caterpillar, European red mite, brown mite, San Jose scale	1. Superior type oil 98% + Ethion 25% WP or Trithion 4 lbs./gal. flow. or Parathion 25% WP or Diazinon 50% WP	5 gallons 5 pounds 2½ pints 5 pounds 5 pounds	1 gallon 1 pound ½ pint 1 pound 1 pound	
Pear psylla	1. Perthane 4 lbs./gal. EC 2. Perthane 4 lbs./gal. flow.	5 quarts 5 quarts	1 quart 1 quart	
Pear psylla, McDaniel mite, European red mite, brown mite, rust mite	1. Morestan 25% WP + Parathion 25% WP	5 pounds 5 pounds	1 pound 1 pound	
Cutworms, leaf roller, lygus bugs, stink bugs, thrips, green fruitworm	See pest control program on apples			

Pest or disease to be controlled	Use any one of the listed materials or the listed combinations	Amount per acre	Amount per 100 gallons	Minimum days between last use and harvest, restrictions, remarks
PINK SPRAY (Stages 7, 8)—Based on 600 gallons per acre (for average size trees).				
Pear scab	1. Lime-sulfur (not on Anjou)	18 gallons	3 gallons	
	2. Ferbam 76% WP	4½- 6 pounds	¾-1 pound	
	3. Cyprex (dodine) 65% WP	4½ pounds	¾ pound	
Pear mildew, rust mite	1. Karathane 25% WP (+ spreader)	3 pounds	½ pound	
	2. Karathane 50% EC (+ spreader)	1½ pints	4 ounces	
	3. Lime-sulfur (not on Anjou)	12 gallons	2 gallons	
Pear mildew (Anjou)	1. Ferbam 76% WP	4½- 6 pounds	¾-1 pound	
BLOSSOM SPRAY (Stages 10, 11)—Based on 600 gallons per acre (for average size trees).				
Fire blight (Anjou)	1. Streptomycin 17%	28.8 ounces	4.8 ounces	See page 14. Do not use streptomycin closer than 30 days before harvest.
Fire blight (other pears)	1. Fixed copper 53%	3 pounds	½ pound	If copper content differs from 53%, convert so that there is ¼ pound metallic copper per 100 gallons. See page 14 for use of streptomycin. Do not use closer than 30 days before harvest.
	2. Copper sulfate + Lime.	3 pounds	½ pound	
	3. Streptomycin 17%	28.8 ounces	4.8 ounces	
PETAL-FALL SPRAY—Based on 600 gallons per acre (for average size trees)				
Fire blight	Same as blossom spray			
Pear scab	Same as pink spray			

Pest or disease to be controlled	Use any one of the listed materials or the listed combinations	Amount per acre	Amount per 100 gallons	Minimum days between last use and harvest, restrictions, remarks
Pear mildew	1. Karathane 25% WP (+ spreader)	3 pounds	½ pound	Avoid killing bees on blooming cover crops.
	2. Karathane 50% EC (+ spreader)	1½ pints	4 ounces	

LATE SPRING AND SUMMER (May to August)—Based on 600 gallons per acre (for average size trees).

Pest or disease to be controlled	Use any one of the listed materials or the listed combinations	Amount per acre	Amount per 100 gallons	Minimum days between last use and harvest, restrictions, remarks
Pear psylla	1. Perthane 4 lbs./gal. flowable	1½ gallons	1 quart	7	Two Perthane applications, 7 to 14 days apart, are usually necessary for control. Apply Perthane no more than 4 times after petal fall. Allow 30 days between second and third application. EC formulations may cause russeting. See sections on spray injury and compatibility for precautions with summer oil sprays. Interval before harvest for ethion is 30 days if 3 applications made after first cover spray, 20 days if 2 applications made after first cover spray. Do not make more than 3. Do not apply Galecron or Fundal more than 3 times during fruiting period. See discussion of Thiodan on page 13. Make only 2 applications of Thiodan during fruiting period. Use no more than 5 pounds per acre (500 gallons of spray).
	2. Perthane 4 lbs./gal. EC	1½ gallons	1 quart	7	
	3. Superior type oil +	4½ gallons	3 quarts	0	
	Guthion 50% WP or	2¼ pounds	⅜ pound	7	
	Ethion 25% WP or	6 pounds	1 pound	30/20	
	Imidan 50% WP	6 pounds	1 pound	7	
	4. Galecron SP or Fundal SP	3 pounds	½ pound	28	
	5. Thiodan 50% WP	5 pounds	1 pound	7	
	6. Dithane M45 or Manzate 200	9 pounds	1½ pounds	15	

Pest or disease to be controlled	Use any one of the listed materials or the listed combinations			Minimum days between last use and harvest, restrictions, remarks
Apple aphid	See pest control program on apples			Do not use phosphamidon on pears.

547

Pest or disease to be controlled	Use any one of the listed materials or the listed combinations	Amount per acre	Amount per 100 gallons	Minimum days between last use and harvest, restrictions, remarks
Codling moth, pear sawfly	1. Guthion 50% WP 2. Imidan 50% WP 3. Galecron SP or Fundal SP	1½-3 pounds 6 pounds 3 pounds	¼-½ pound 7 1 pound 7 ½ pound 28	Timing is critical. See discussion in text. Do not apply Galecron or Fundal more than 3 times during fruiting period.
European red mite, brown mite, pear rust mite	1. Ethion 25% WP 2. Morestan 25% WP 3. Galecron SP or Fundal SP	6 pounds 1½ pounds 3 pounds	1 pound 30/20 ¼ pound 35 ½ pound 28	Interval before harvest for ethion is 30 days if 3 applications made after first cover spray, 20 days if 2 applications made after first cover spray. Do not make more than 3. See Morestan under spray injury. Do not apply Galecron or Fundal more than 3 times during fruiting period.
Two-spotted mite, McDaniel mite	1. Fundal SP or Galecron SP 2. Kelthane 35% WP	3 pounds 6 pounds	½ pound 28 1 pound 7	Do not apply Galecron or Fundal more than 3 times during fruiting period.
Pear leaf blister mite, pear rust mite	1. Sevin 50% WP 2. Systox 26% EC 3. Thiodan 50% WP 4. Ethion 25% WP 5. Galecron SP or Fundal SP	6 pounds 6 pints 4½ pounds 6 pounds 3 pounds	1 pound 1 1 pint 21 ¾ pound 7 1 pound 30/20 ½ pound 28	Do not apply Systox more than 3 times per season. Interval before harvest for ethion is 30 days if 3 applications made after first cover spray, 20 days if 2 applications made after first cover spray. Do not make more than 3. Do not apply Thiodan more than twice during fruiting season. Do not apply Galecron or Fundal more than 3 times during fruiting period.
Grape mealybug (when crawlers are present)	1. Parathion 25% WP 2. Diazinon 50% WP	6 pounds 6 pounds	1 pound 14 1 pound 14	

Pest or disease to be controlled	Use any one of the listed materials or the listed combinations	Amount per acre	Amount per 100 gallons	Minimum days between last use and harvest, restrictions, remarks
Bull's eye rot	1. Ziram 4 lbs./gal. flow.	6 quarts	1 quart	0
Fire blight	Same as blossom spray			
San Jose scale (mid-June or early July)	1. Parathion 25% WP	6 pounds	1 pound	14 — Do not apply Galecron or Fundal
	2. Diazinon 50% WP	6 pounds	1 pound	14 — more than 3 times during fruiting
	3. Galecron SP or Fundal SP	3 pounds	1/2 pound	28 — period.
Scab (every 12 days until dry weather)	1. Ferbam 76% WP	6 pounds	1 pound	7
	2. Cyprex 65% WP	4 1/2 pounds	3/4 pound	7
Phytophthora rot	1. Zineb 75% WP	6 pounds	1 pound	7
Stink bugs, lygus bugs	1. Parathion 25% WP	6 pounds	1 pound	14 — Do not apply Thiodan more than
	2. Thiodan 50% WP	4 1/2 pounds	3/4 pound	7 — twice during fruiting season. Spraying orchard borders will improve control.

POST-HARVEST SPRAY—Based on 600 gallons per acre (for average size trees)

Pest or disease to be controlled	Use any one of the listed materials or the listed combinations	Amount per acre	Amount per 100 gallons	Minimum days between last use and harvest, restrictions, remarks
Pear leaf blister mite, pear rust mite	1. Diazinon 50% WP	6 pounds	1 pound	
	2. Sevin 50% WP	6 pounds	1 pound	
	3. Thiodan 50% WP	4 1/2 pounds	3/4 pound	
Pear psylla	Same as summer sprays			
Fire blight	1. Fixed copper 53%	3 pounds	1/2 pound	If copper content differs from 53%,
	2. Copper sulfate +	3 pounds	1/2 pound	convert so that there is 1/4 pound
	Lime	3 pounds	1/2 pound	metallic copper per 100 gallons.

TABLE 9. DORMANT PEACH SPRAY PROGRAM (SOUTH CAROLINA, CLEMSON COLLEGE, CLEMSON, S. C.)
Roy J. Ferree, Assoc. Professor (Horticulture); W. C. Nettles, Assoc. Professor (Entomology and Economic Zoology); C. A. Thomas, Assoc. Professor (Entomology and Economic Zoology); R. W. Miller, Asst. Professor (Plant Pathology)

PEACH SPRAY SCHEDULE

(To be used only by those who will observe all precautions especially with parathion or Guthion)

Spray Name	When Applied	Materials For 100 Gallons of Spray	To Control	Remarks
Blossom	Begin when 10 percent blossoms open	Dichlone (½ lb. Phygon XL) or 1 gal. liquid lime sulfur (32 degrees Baume) or 6 lb. wettable sulfur or 2 lb. captan or ½ lb. Benlate 50 W (Benomyl)	Blossom blight caused by the brown rot fungus	Sprays during bloom may aid in reducing blossom blight. If bloom sprays are applied, sprays at 2-3 day intervals are required, except that two sprays of Benlate (early and full bloom) are sufficient.
Petal-fall	After all petals are off and before peach is showing	6 lb. wettable sulfur, or 2 lb. captan (50%) plus 2 lb. parathion* (15%), or Guthion 50% ½ to ⅝ lb.	Curculio Brown Rot Catfacing Insects	Thorough spraying absolutely necessary if good control is expected. If catfacing is a problem, use Guthion.
Shuck-fall or First Cover	Three-fourths of shucks off	6 lb. wettable sulfur or 2 lb. (50%) captan or 2 lb. (15%) parathion* or ½ to ⅝ lb. 50% Guthion*	Curculio Brown Rot** Catfacing Insects	Spray thoroughly trunks and larger limbs to aid in control of lesser peach tree borers.
Second Cover	7-10 days after first cover	6 lb. wettable sulfur or 2 lb. captan (50%) or 2 lb. (15%) parathion* or ½ to ⅝ lb. 50% Guthion*	Curculio Brown Rot Scab**	"Cover" sprays are very important in control of scab, curculio, and brown rot. If captan is not used throughout the season, wait until 6 weeks before harvest before substituting it for wettable sulfur (especially important where scab was severe the year before).
Third Cover	12-14 days after second cover	6 lb. wettable sulfur, or 2 lb. captan (50%) plus 2 lb. parathion* (15%), or Guthion 50% ½ to ⅝ lb.	Curculio Brown Rot Scab	
Fourth Cover	14 days after third cover	6 lb. wettable sulfur, or 2 lb. captan (50%)	Brown Rot Scab	
Fifth Cover	6 weeks before harvest of each variety	6 lb. wettable sulfur, or 2 lb. captan (50%) plus 2 lb. parathion* (15%), or Guthion 50% ½ to ⅝ lb.	Oriental Fruit Moth Curculio Brown Rot Scab	Apply spray 6 weeks before the first heavy picking. Do not apply more than 5 lb. actual parathion per acre per year.

550

	Timing	Materials and rates	Pests controlled	Remarks
Sixth Cover	4 weeks before harvest of each variety	6 lb. wettable sulfur, or 2 lb. captan (50%) plus 2 lb. parathion* (15%), or Guthion 50% ½ to ⅝ lb.	Oriental Fruit Moth Curculio Brown Rot	Apply spray 4 weeks before first heavy picking. Do not apply Guthion within 3 weeks of harvest.
Seventh Cover	2 weeks before harvest of each variety	6 lb. wettable sulfur or 2 lb. (50%) captan or 1 lb. (50%) captan plus 1 lb. Botran (75%) ½ lb. Benlate 50 W (Benomyl) plus 2 lb. parathion* (15%)	Oriental Fruit Moth Curculio Brown Rot Rhizopus Rot‡	Apply spray 2 weeks before first heavy picking. Do not apply parathion within 14 days of harvest; malathion 7 days; Sevin 1 day. If brown rot is a problem and dichloran is used, add 2 lb. captan instead of 1 lb.
Pre-harvest	7 days before harvest of each variety	6 lb. wettable sulfur or 2 lb. (50%) captan or 2 to 3 qts. liquid lime sulfur or sulfur or captan dust. 1 lb. (50%) captan plus 1 lb. (75%) (Botran)‡ plus ½ lb. Benlate 50 W (Benomyl)	Brown Rot Rhizopus Rot‡	Apply additional sulfur or captan, preferably as dusts, before and during harvest if brown rot is present or if rainy, humid weather occurs. Under certain conditions liquid lime-sulfur may injure leaves. Use malathion or Sevin if needed to control green June or Japanese beetles.
	1 day before harvest of each variety	Same, but omit benomyl if it was used in the preceeding 2 sprays.	Brown Rot Rhizopus Rot	Apply no more than 2 pre-harvest sprays of Benomyl. Benomyl will not control Rhizopus rot.
Harvested fruit	Postharvest dip	Botran (75%) 1 lb. per 100 gal. water in hydrocooler or Botran (75%) 1 lb plus ½ lb. Benlate 50 W (Benomyl)	Brown Rot Rhizopus Rot‡	Add 1 lb. Botran (75%) plus ½ lb. Benlate to each additional 100 gal. of water added to hydrocooler during operation. Flush and clean hydrocooler every 1 to 2 days.
		Botran (75%) 2 lb. per 100 gal. water in hydrocooler.	Brown Rot Rhizopus Rot	Only to fruit which is going to be processed.

*If liquid formulations of parathion or Guthion (liquid concentrate) are used, apply them at equivalent concentrations of actual toxicant. Observe waiting periods for each material. This is for protection of picker as well as consumer.

**½ lb. Benlate 50 W (Benomyl) is the most effective material for the control of scab. It will also control powdery mildew. In problem orchards, growers may want to consider using Benlate. Growers are advised that cost for this material is considerably higher.

Note: Wettable sulfur recommended in this schedule should contain a minimum of 80 percent sulfur.

‡Harvest — Benomyl is effective in control of brown rot — Dichloran (Botran) is effective in control of Rhizopus rot — See Circular 360, Peach Pest Control. Maximum benefit will result when peaches are not subject to brushing and to dirty hydrocooling water. Least reduction in benefit will occur when only dry brushing is used.

D. H. Peterson, USDA and Pennsylvania State University

Figure 6. Many plant diseases such as fire blight on apple and pear and bacterial canker on peach can be transferred from tree to tree on pruning tools. Several peach trees in row above were infected with canker and died after pruning tools were used on a diseased tree. Where a serious disease as peach canker is prevalent, dip tools in strong disinfectant after each tree.

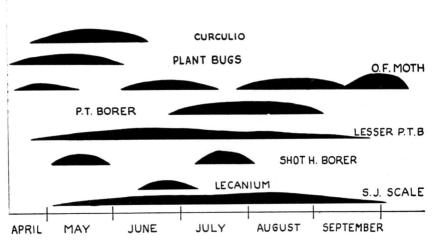

Lee Merrill, Rutgers University

Figure 7. This chart shows when certain peach pests are most active under New Jersey conditions, and at what periods control is most important. Relative emergence periods should be about the same under conditions of other regions where these pests are present.

Figure 8. Adult cicada shortly after shedding nymphal skin. When wings and body are dry, the insect will turn darker. This is a troublesome pest which damages orchard and nursery trees by laying eggs in the bark. Nymphs suck sap from roots, weaken trees particularly year before emergence. Do not prune young trees winter before scheduled emergence.

is suggesting separate type pest control programs, in an effort to reduce cost wherever possible, for (a) orchards where the chlorinated hydrocarbons are still effective and pest resistance is not an important problem, (b) maximum protection, (c) for varieties grown for processing (principally York Imperial); and (d) for non-bearing blocks (York alternate-bears in spite of all precautions in some orchards).

In nearly all apple states, it has been found necessary to use different materials on different varieties to get maximum finish on fruit of particularly sensitive varieties such as Golden Delicious, Jonathan and Grimes Golden.

PROGRAM FOR YOUNG NONBEARING FRUIT TREES

Dormant trees showing scale on the bark and eggs of aphids or red mite near young buds should receive a dormant oil spray. A dormant spray for peaches for leaf curl and a summer borer trunk spray are needed. Young apple trees need late bloom and first cover scab sprays in scab areas, plus a green aphis spray if they are heavy. A spray for canker or measuring worms may be needed at pink and calyx-cup periods. Tree hoppers (particularly from an alfalfa cover) may slit young bark to lay eggs, damaging growth. Sprays, mowing the cover or cultivation are controls. Young cherry trees need a leaf spot and slug spray, rarely a dormant spray.

Check young peach trees early fall and early spring for white grub borers in bark near soil surface. Remove with wire or knife or use PDB, EDC or Thiodan sprays for large scale treatment.

Special precautions are necessary among all young fruit trees in years when the periodical cicada (17-year locust in the North, 13 years in the South) is due to appear. Specific dates and years they will appear can be secured from the entomologist at the local agricultural experiment station. Control is especially needed for young trees located near

SMALL FRUITS

PRODUCT	RATE PER ACRE	TIME OF APPLICATION	WEEDS CONTROLLED	REMARKS
Dow General Weed Killer (dinoseb)	2-3 pts.	In fall after harvest, or spring before bloom. Apply when weeds are growing well but before 6" tall.	Early spring and fall weeds.	Use as directed spray. **Blackberries, raspberries, brambles.**
2,4-D amine salt	¼-1 lb. acid equivalent.	First application, preemergence. Second application, when weeds are small and new growth is tall enough for spraying around base.	Early spring weeds.	Do not apply to flowers or fruiting canes. Be careful not to get spray on new plant growth. **Raspberries, brambles.**
Chlorpropham (CIPC)	4-6 lbs./20 gals. water.	Prior to weed emergence in fall or early winter.	Winter annual grasses and broadleaved weeds.	Especially effective in controlling chickweed after emergence. **Blackberries, raspberries.**
Princep 80W (simazine)	2-4 lbs. a.c. (2½-5 lbs. 80W).	Spring, before weed emergence.	Most annual and broad-leaved weeds.	Do not apply to foliage or while fruit is present. **Blackberries, boysenberries, raspberries, blueberries, loganberries.**
	2 lbs. a.c. (2½ lbs. 80W).	Spring and fall.		
	4 lbs. a.c. fall, or 2 lbs. a.c. fall and 2 lbs. a.c. spring.		Quackgrass.	
Princep 4G (simazine)	2-4 lbs. a.c. (50-100 lbs. 4G).	Spring, before weed emergence.	Most annual and broad-leaved weeds and grasses.	
Chlorpropham EC (CIPC)	6 qts./40 gals. water.	Late winter or early spring.		Direct spray on weed-free soil. Avoid wetting canes. **Raspberries, dormant. Blackberries, dormant.**
Chlorpropham 10% (CIPC)	6 lbs. a.c. (60 lbs. 10%).			
Chlorproham 20% (CIPC)	6 lbs. a.c. (30 lbs. 20%).			

a.c. = active chemical   EC = emulsifiable concentrate   WP = wettable powder   G = granule

*Read all labels on containers carefully before using. Keep in touch with local government recommendations, as they change frequently. These recommendations are general; local recommendations may work better due to different climates, soils and weed species.

Product	Rate	Timing	Weeds Controlled	Remarks
Chlorproham EC (CIPC)	8-12 qts./40 gals. water.	Late fall and again in early spring if needed.		Direct spray to base of plants in weed-free soil. **Blueberries, dormant.**
Sinox General or Basanite (dinoseb, DNBP)	1.25-1.875 lbs. a.c. (2-3 pts.)/10-20 gals. oil plus enough water to make 100 gals. spray. Apply 150 gals./A.	Spring (prebloom) and fall (post harvest).	Annual broadleaved weeds and annual grasses.	Apply as directed spray to weeds and soil. Avoid contacting foliage, blossoms or fruiting clusters. **Grapes, blueberries, blackberries, currants, gooseberries, raspberries.**
Casoron G-4; W-50 (dichlobenil)	4 lbs. a.c. (100 lbs. G-4 or 8 lbs. W-50).	Preemergence or on clean cultivated soil.	Annual grasses and broadleaved weeds.	Apply early spring as a surface application, band over row or broadcast; in southern areas, shallow incorporation immediately after application. Apply only on established plantings; do not apply during new shoot emergence. Do not apply within 4 weeks after transplanting. Do not graze treated areas. **Blackberry, raspberry.**
Ansar 529 (MSMA)	2 lbs. a.c.	Non-bearing; directed spray in interspaces and around vine bases.	Johnsongrass, dallisgrass, nutsedge, cocklebur, ragweed, sandbur, puncturevine.	If regrowth occurs, respray as required, however, do not exceed 3 applications per year. Keep spray solution from contacting leaves, stems and bark of vines. Do not apply around vines from which fruit will be harvested within one year of treatment. **Grape vineyards.**
Ansar 529 H.C. (MSMA + surfactant)	2 lbs. a.c.			
Casoron G-4; W-50 (dichlobenil)	4-6 lbs. a.c. (100-150 lbs. G-4 or 8-12 lbs. W-50).	Preemergence or on clean cultivated soil. Do not spray foliage or fruit of bearing plants.	Annual grasses and broadleaved weeds.	Apply early spring as a surface application, band over row or broadcast; in southern areas, shallow incorporation immediately after application. May be used in new plantings 4 weeks after transplanting. Do not graze treated areas. **Grapes, blueberries.**
Casoron G-4 (dichlobenil)	6 lbs. a.c. (150 lbs. G-4).	Late fall, early winter, Nov. 15-Feb. 15.	**Quackgrass, artemisia,** (mugwort or wild chrysanthemum), Canada thistle, curly dock, fescue, leafy spurge, timothy, wild artichoke, orchardgrass, **wild aster, wild carrot.**	Apply to soil surface, non-incorporated on plantings established at least one year. Do not graze livestock in treated areas. **Grapes, blueberries.**
Karmex 80W (diuron)	1.6-3.2 lbs. a.c. (2-4 lbs. 80W).	Late fall or winter prior to weed seed germination.	Annual weeds.	Use as band treatment in vine row. Apply only to established vineyards, with trunk diameter 1½" or more, bearing vines 3 years or older. Use restricted to east of the Rocky Mountains. Do not replant treated areas to any crop within 2 years after application. **Grapes.**

PRODUCT	RATE PER ACRE	TIME OF APPLICATION	WEEDS CONTROLLED	REMARKS
Princep 80W (simazine)	2-4.8 lbs. a.c. (2½-6 lbs. 80W).	Late fall, following harvest to early spring, prior to weed emergence.	Most annual broadleaved weeds and grasses.	Plants must be established for 3 years or more before treating. **Grapes.**
Dowpon or Basfapon (dalapon)	10 lbs./100 gals. water.	Spot application, when Bermudagrass is 4-6" tall; when Johnsongrass is 12-18" tall.	Johnsongrass and Bermudagrass (in Western Irrigated grapes).	Avoid application to grape foliage and young vines that haven't developed a coating of loose bark. Grapes are extremely sensitive to the phenoxy compounds such as 2,4,5-T, silvex, and MCPA. Do not use spray equipment that has been used for these herbicides unless it is known to be completely free from them. Do not apply within 30 days before harvest. Do not graze livestock on treated areas. **Grapes.**
Treflan 4EC (trifluralin)	½-1 lb. a.c. (1-2 pts. EC), depending on soil type. Check label; rates vary for preplant incorporated vs. established.	Preemergence (applied prior to planting) or as directed spray in established plantings.	Annual grasses; many broadleaved weeds.	Must be incorporated. Do not injure plants when incorporating. Does not need rain or irrigation to activate; resists leaching. Uses restricted to Western States for bearing and non-bearing vines; central and eastern states for non-bearing vines only. Do not apply within 60 days before harvest. Check label. **Grapes.**
Treflan 5% G (trifluralin)	½-1 lb. a.c. (10-20 lbs. 5G) depending on soil type and location. Check label.	Preemergence. Applied prior to planting.	Annual grasses; many broadleaved weeds.	Apply and incorporate Treflan before planting. **Grapes.**
Eptam (EPTC)	3 lbs. a.c.	After cultivation. Applied in irrigation water.	Annual grasses, Johnsongrass seedlings, dead nettle, lambsquarters, purslane, redroot pigweed, hairy nightshade, common chickweed and nutgrass (nutsedge).	Do not apply within 40 days before harvest. Check label for local region recommendations. **Grapes.**
2,4-D wax bar	1.5 lbs. a.c.	When bindweeds start to bloom and before grapevines reach the ground.	Bindweed.	Drag wax bar over bindweeds in 30-36" wide band under trellis of bearing crop. Keep wax bar off grapevines. **Bearing grapes.**
Treflan 4EC (trifluralin)	Non-bearing ½-1 lb. a.c. (1-2 pts. EC). Established plantings 1-2 lbs. a.c. (2-4 pts. EC).	Apply and incorporate before planting. Apply directly to soil around plants after cultivation.	Annual grasses; many broadleaved weeds.	In established vineyards use incorporation methods not injurious to plants. Do not apply within 60 days of harvest. **Grape vineyards.** Western United States only.

Dymid 80W (diphenamid)	4-6 lbs. a.c. (5-7½ lbs. 80W) depending on soil type. Check label.	New plantings: Apply after transplantings. Caution: Transplants on light soil should be established and showing active growth before application. Established plantings: Apply after plants become dormant or apply after harvest following renovation of beds.	**Wide variety of annual grasses, broadleaved weeds.**	Can be applied directly over top of transplants. Do not apply within 60 days before harvest. **Strawberries.**
sesone	3-5.5 lbs.	On established plantings apply before blooming and after harvest following each cultivation.	**Annual grasses and broadleaved weeds.**	Varietal responses to herbicides vary and should be determined locally in each case. Do not apply within 7 days of, or during, harvest season. **Strawberries.**
Premerge or Basanite (dinoseb, DNBP)	4-6 lbs. a.c.	In early spring and immediately following harvest.	**Chickweed and germinating winter annual grasses.**	On **established strawberries** in Northwest only.
2,4-D	½-1½ lbs./10-40 gals. water.	After transplanting or post-harvest (limit to one application per season).	**Established broadleaved weeds.**	On established beds apply after harvest but before runners form. Do not apply during bud, flower or fruit stage. **Strawberries.**
Tenoran 50WP (chloroxuron)	4 lbs. a.c. (8 lbs. 50WP). Broadcast.	Postemergence (spring and/or fall) in established beds and in new transplants as soon as plants are established.	**Annual grasses and broadleaved weeds.**	For best results, apply immediately after renovation of beds in fall and repeat application in spring. Do not apply more than 2 applications in one year. Do not apply within 60 days of harvest. **Strawberries.**
Dacthal W-75 (DCPA)	9 lbs. a.c. (12 lbs. W-75).	On newly-planted or established beds. Additional applications of 8-12 lbs. may be made to control susceptible weeds germinating in late summer and early fall.	**Annual grasses and broadleaved weeds.**	Do not apply after first bloom. Lower rates should be used on sandy soils. **Strawberries.**
Enide 50W (diphenamid)	4 lbs. a.c. (8 lbs. 50W), light soil; 6 lbs. a.c. (12 lbs. 50W), heavy soil.	Newly planted: Apply 2-6 weeks after planting, but not before new foliage has appeared. Established: Apply while strawberries are dormant or semi-dormant, or after renovation. Additional applications may be made at intervals of 6 months or more.	**Wide variety of annual grass and broadleaved weeds.**	A temporary delay in rooting of daughter plants may occur but will not affect yield. Do not use on the herbicide sensitive variety Shasta. No application should be made within 60 days prior to harvest. **Strawberries.**

a.c. = active chemical   EC = emulsifiable concentrate   WP = wettable powder   G = granule

557

PRODUCT	RATE PER ACRE	TIME OF APPLICATION	WEEDS CONTROLLED	REMARKS
Sinox PE (DNBP)	3-4½ lbs. a.c. (1-1½ gals. 3E).	Dormant application.	Most annual weeds and grasses.	Dormant application in early spring and immediately after harvest to established beds. Use restricted to Northwest. **Strawberries.**
Princep 80W (simazine)	Massachusetts: 4 lbs. a.c. (5 lbs. 80W). Other areas: 2 lbs. a.c. (2½ lbs. 80W).	After fall harvest or before spring growth begins. In the spring before growth begins.	Most annual broadleaved weeds and grasses.	**Cranberries**
Chlorpropham (CIPC)	Not over 20 lbs. a.c.	Apply to dry plants.		**Cranberries, dormant, established plantings.**
Casoron G-4 (dichlobenil)	4-6 lbs. a.c. (100-150 lbs. G-4). 4 lbs. a.c. (100 lbs. G-4).	Late fall only, after harvest. Early spring only, on dormant crop.	Wide range of perennial and annual broadleaved weeds and grassy weeds including ferns, rushes and sedges.	Spring application is made early while perennial weeds are still dormant, preemergence to annual weeds. Do not apply after blooming starts. Do not graze treated areas. **Cranberries.**
Dowpon or Basfapon (dalapon)	20 lbs. 10 lbs.	Early June and mid-July. After harvest.	Grasses, sedges, rushes.	For ditches and shores. Do not contaminate crops. **Cranberries.** **Cranberries.**

TREE FRUITS
(Deciduous)

PRODUCT	RATE PER ACRE	TIME OF APPLICATION	WEEDS CONTROLLED	REMARKS
Dowpon or Basfapon (dalapon)	2-6 lbs./50-100 gals. water.	Directed spray on grass foliage in a radius of 3-4 ft. from trunk of trees. Repeat in 2-3 weeks.	Annual and perennial grasses.	Do not graze meat or dairy animals. Do not spray within 30 days of harvest. **Apples, apricots, peaches, pears, plums.**
Ortho Paraquat (2 lbs. cation per gal.)	½-1 lb. a.c. (1-2 qts.)/50-200 gals. water. Add 8 ozs. (such as Ortho X-77).	Best results when weeds are young and succulent (1-6" tall). Mature woody weeds are less susceptible. Repeat application as necessary.	Most annual and broadleaved weeds. Perennial weed desiccation.	Apply as a directed spray for thorough weed coverage. Spray drift will cause injury. Do not allow spray to contact foliage, fruit, or stems. Do not graze livestock on treated areas. Consult label. **Fruit trees and vines, such as apples, apricots, citrus, peaches, grapes.**

558

Material	Rate	When to apply	Weeds controlled	Remarks
Sinbar 80W (terbacil)	1.6-3.2 lbs. a.c. (2-4 lbs. 80W). Not to exceed 3.2 lbs. a.c./A.	Single application In spring before weeds emerge or during early seedling stage. Apply as a direct spray on a band or broadcast (40 gals. water/A. actually sprayed).	Annual weeds and grasses; quackgrass, yellow nutsedge, horse nettle, sheep sorrel.	Lower rates for light soils; higher rates for clay loam. Do not use on loamy sand or gravelly soils; do not apply to eroded areas where tree roots are exposed. Do not allow drift to come in contact with fruit; do not spray foliage. Use only where apples and peaches have been established for the last 3 years. Do not replant to any treated area within 24 months after treatment. **Peaches and apples, bearing and non-bearing.**
Princep 80W (simazine)	2-4 lbs. a.c. (2½-5 lbs. 80W).	Prior to weed emergence, one application per year.	Most annual broadleaved weeds and grasses.	Trees must be established one year or more. Do not contact foliage or fruit. **Apples, pears, sour cherries.**
Karmex 80W (diuron)	3.2 lbs. a.c. (4 lbs. 80W). Do not use on apples where organic matter is less than 1%.	In spring. Do not treat dwarf varieties.	Most annual weeds and grasses.	**Far West:** Treatment may be made in winter or apply 2 lbs. as post-harvest treatment followed by 2 lbs. in the spring. Avoid contact with foliage or fruit. Do not replant treated areas to any crop within 2 years after application. **Apples, pears.**
Ammate X (AMS)	60 lbs./100 gals. water. Rate must not exceed 57 lbs. actual product/100 gals. water for apples and pears.	When poison ivy plants are in full leaf.	Poison Ivy.	Add 4 ozs. Dupont spreader-sticker per 100 gals. spray. Wet poison ivy thoroughly. Keep spray off foliage and fruit. **Apples, pears.**
Premerge or Basanite (dinoseb amine)	9-10.5 lbs. a.c. (3-3½ gals.).	Early spring, during dormant period, and prior to bloom.	Annual weeds and seedling grasses.	Repeat application when weeds reappear. Avoid spraying foliage and trunks. Dormant application only. Do not graze treated areas. **Cherries, peaches, plums, pears.**
2,4-D amine	2 qts. (1 lb. acid equiv.)	Apply to floor of orchard when weeds are rapidly growing.	Canada thistle, poison ivy, marestail, pigweed, sunflower, velvetleaf, dandelion, plantain, dock.	Avoid spray drift or direct spraying to foliage, limbs or trunks of fruit trees. **Apples, pears.**
Enide 50W (diphenamid)	4 lbs. a.c. (8 lbs. 50W), light soil; 6 lbs. a.c. (12 lbs. 50W), heavy soil.	Any time of year except when fruit is on tree or within 90 days of harvest.	Wide variety of annual grass and broadleaved weeds.	Following clean cultivation, apply to soil around established trees. Caution: On peaches do not use on sandy soils. Do not graze livestock in treated areas. **Apples, peaches.**
Dymid 80W (diphenamid)	4-6 lbs. a.c. (5-7½ lbs. 80W), depending on soil type. Check label.	Apply any time for pre-emergence weed control.	Wide variety of annual grasses and broadleaved weeds.	Work all weed growth into soil prior to application. Do not apply within 90 days of harvest. Do not graze livestock on treated areas. **Apples.**

PRODUCT	RATE PER ACRE	TIME OF APPLICATION	WEEDS CONTROLLED	REMARKS
Treflan 4EC (trifluralin)	1-2 lbs. a.c. (2-4 pts. EC) depending on soil type. Check label.	Preemergence. Apply and incorporate before planting.	Annual grasses; many broadleaved weeds.	New plantings. Must be incorporated. Use restricted to western states. **Apricots, nectarines and peaches.**
Princep 80W (simazine)	2-4 lbs. a.c. (4-8 pts. EC) depending on soil type. Check label.	Use as a directed spray around trees.	Annual grasses; many broadleaved weeds.	Bearing or non-bearing (established). Must be incorporated. Use incorporation methods not injurious to trees. Restricted to western states. **Apricots, nectarines and peaches.**
Princep 80W (simazine)	2-4 lbs. a.c. (2½-5 lbs. 80W).	After final preparation of grove.	Most annual broadleaved weeds and grasses.	In California only. Do not apply to sandy soils. **Avocados.**
	1.6-4 lbs. a.c. (2-5 lbs. 80W).	Late fall or early spring.	Most annual broadleaved weeds and grasses.	Consult label for recommendations for specific areas. **Peaches, plums, sweet cherries.**
Ansar 529 (MSMA)	2 lbs. a.c.	Non-bearing; directed spray in interspaces and around tree bases.	Johnsongrass, dallisgrass, nutsedge, cocklebur, ragweed, sandbur, puncturevine.	If regrowth occurs, respray as required, however, do not exceed 3 applications per year. Keep spray solution from contacting leaves, stems and bark of trees. Do not apply around trees from which fruit will be harvested within one year of treatment. **Apple, peach, pear, plum, prune, apricot, cherry.**
Ansar 529 H.C. (MSMA + surfactant)	2 lbs. a.c.			
Casoron G-4; W-50 (dichlobenil)	4-6 lbs. a.c. (100-150 lbs. G-4 or 8-12 lbs. W-50).	Preemergence or on clean cultivated soil. Do not spray foliage or fruit of bearing trees.	Annual grassy and broadleaved weeds and certain perennial weeds such as crabgrass, redroot pigweed, henbit, smartweed, wild mustard, pineapple weed, knotweed, chickweed, shepherdspurse, lambsquarters, groundsel, carpetweed, purslane, annual bluegrass (poa annua), bluegrass, cudweed, dandelion, evening primrose, peppergrass, plantain, ragweed, Russian thistle, Texas panicum (hurrahgrass), yellow woodsorrel, spurge, horsetail and foxtall.	Apply early spring as a surface application, single tree, band over tree row or broadcast; in southern areas, shallow incorporation immediately after application. May be used in new orchards 4 weeks after transplanting. Do not graze livestock on treated areas. For cherries, peaches, and prune plums. Do not make application within 1 month before harvest. For figs (California only). Do not make application within 5 months before harvest. **Bearing, nonbearing: apples, avocados, cherries, figs (California only), mangoes, peaches, pears, prune plums.**

a.c.=active chemical   EC=emulsifiable concentrate   WP=wettable powder   G=granule

560

PRODUCT	RATE PER ACRE	TIME OF APPLICATION	WEEDS CONTROLLED	REMARKS
Casoron G-4 (dichlobenil)	6 lbs. a.c. (150 lbs. G-4).	Late fall, early winter, Nov. 15-Feb. 15.	Perennial weeds such as quackgrass, artemisia, Canada thistle, curly dock, fescue, leafy spurge, orchardgrass, timothy, wild artichoke, wild aster, yellow rocket and wild carrot.	Apply to soil surface, non-incorporated on trees established at least one year. Do not graze livestock on treated areas. For cherries, peaches, and prune plums. Do not make application within 1 month before harvest. For figs (California only). Do not make application within 5 months before harvest. Bearing, non-bearing: apples, avocados, cherries, figs (California only), mangoes, peaches, pears, prune plums.
Sinox General (dinoseb, DNBP)	1.25-1.875 lbs. a.c. (2-3 pts.)/10-25 gals. diesel or any suitable weed oil plus enough water to make 100 gals. of spray.	Directed spray to ground cover. Completely cover all weed foliage.	Annual broadleaved weeds and annual grasses.	Avoid spraying fruit, destroy any fruit accidentally sprayed. Avoid spraying base of young trees. Do not graze livestock on treated areas.

NUTS

PRODUCT	RATE PER ACRE	TIME OF APPLICATION	WEEDS CONTROLLED	REMARKS
Princep 80W (simazine)	2-4 lbs. a.c. (2½-5 lbs. 80W).	Before weeds emerge. Do not apply when nuts are on ground.	Most annual broadleaved weeds and grasses.	Do not use on orchards less than one year old, or on sandy soils. One treatment per crop cycle. Do not apply to foliage. **Walnuts.**
	2-4 lbs. a.c. (2½-5 lbs. 80W)/50 gals. water.	Preemergence. Repeat as necessary, but not when nuts are on ground.		Cover soil thoroughly. Do not use on orchards less than one year old. Do not apply to foliage. **Macadamias.**
	2-4 lbs. a.c. (2½-5 lbs. 80W, fall or 2½ lbs 80W, fall, and 2½ lbs. 80W, spring.).	Fall or split application fall and spring.		Oregon and Washington only. **Filberts.**
Premerge or Basanite (dinoseb, DNBP)	9-10½ lbs. a.c. (3-3½ gals.).	Apply during dormant period and prior to bloom.	Annual weeds and seedling grasses.	Repeat application when weeds reappear. Avoid spraying foliage and trunks. Do not graze livestock on treated areas. **Almonds.**
Sinox General or Basanite (dinoseb, DNBP)	1.25-1.875 lbs. a.c. (2-3 pts.)/10-25 gals. diesel or any suitable weed oil plus enough water to make 100 gals. of spray.	Directed spray to ground cover; completely cover all weed foliage.	Annual broadleaved weeds and annual grasses.	Avoid spraying base of young trees. Do not allow livestock to graze on treated ground cover.

PRODUCT	RATE PER ACRE	TIME OF APPLICATION	WEEDS CONTROLLED	REMARKS
Ortho Paraquat (2 lbs. cation per gal.)	½ lb.-1 lb. a.c. (1-2 qts.)/ 50-100 gals. Add non-ionic surfactant at 8 ozs./100 gals. spray liquid.	Best results when weeds are young and succulent 1-6″ tall. Mature woody weeds are less susceptible. Repeat application as necessary.	Most annual and broadleaved weeds. Perennial weed desiccation.	Apply as a direct spray for thorough weed coverage. Spray drift will cause injury. Do not allow spray to contact foliage, fruit or stems. Do not graze livestock on treated areas. Consult label under "Trees and Vines."
Treflan 4EC (trifluralin)	New plantings: ½-1 lb. a.c. (1-2 pts. EC). Established plantings: 1-2 lbs. a.c. (2-4 pts. EC), depending on soil type.	New plantings: Apply and incorporate before planting. Established plantings: Apply as a directed spray to soil around plants.	All annual grasses; many broadleaved weeds.	Use incorporation equipment not injurious to the trees. Central and Eastern U.S., **pecan trees;** Western U.S., **almond, pecan, walnut.**
Eptam (EPTC)	3 lbs. a.c.	After cultivation. Applied in irrigation water.	Annual grasses, Johnsongrass seedlings, nettle, lambsquarters, purslane, redroot pigweed, hairy nightshade, common chickweed and nutgrass (nutsedge).	Do not apply within 14 days before harvest. **Almonds.**
Casoron G-4, W-50 (dichlobenil)	4-6 lbs. a.c. (100-150 lbs. G-4 or 8-12 lbs. W-50).	Preemergence or on clean cultivated soil. Do not spray foliage or fruit of bearing trees.	Annual grassy and broadleaved weeds and certain perennial weeds such as evening primrose.	Apply early spring as a surface application, single tree, band over tree row or broadcast; In southern areas, shallow incorporation immediately after application. May be used in new orchards 4 weeks after transplanting. Do not graze livestock on treated areas. Do not apply within 6 months after transplanting to pecans only. Do not make application to within one month before harvest. **Bearing and nonbearing: almonds, filberts, pecans, English walnuts.**
Casoron G-4 (dichlobenil)	6 lbs. a.c. (150 lbs. G-4).	Late fall, early winter, Nov. 15-Feb. 15.	Perennial weeds such as quackgrass, artemisia, Canada thistle, curly dock, fescue, leafy spurge, orchardgrass, timothy, wild artichoke, wild aster, yellow rocket, and wild carrot.	Apply to soil surface, non-incorporated on trees established at least one year. Do not graze livestock on treated areas. Do not make application within one month before harvest. **Bearing and nonbearing: almonds, filberts, pecans, English walnuts.**

a.c. = active chemical   EC = emulsifiable concentrate   WP = wettable powder   G = granule

562

old apple trees or woodlands which have maintained a heavy brood of cicadas in previous years. The insecticide Sevin has controlled the cicada satisfactorily under Maryland conditions; it has a relatively long residual effect. See adult cicada in Figure 8.

In midsummer, colonies of caterpillars, such as the red-humped apple caterpillar, yellow-necked datana, and fall webworm, may defoliate certain limbs or the entire tops of small trees. A prompt spray with lead arsenate should suffice.

Grasshoppers may defoliate young trees. An application of a spray, such as chlordane to the cover crops should control them.

Bark beetles and shot-hole borers may be attracted to the general area if prunings of removed-trees are left piled near young trees; these should be burned or destroyed.

SPRAY AND WEATHER INJURY

Spray and weather injury to leaves and fruit are confused frequently. It may be necessary to examine neighboring unsprayed trees before the relative amount of spray injury can be determined on sprayed trees. Spray injury develops when improper materials have been employed or when the correct materials have been applied in the wrong way, or when certain weather conditions tend to increase spray injury. Weather injury results from exposure of the fruit to extremes of temperature or moisture. Apple varieties vary greatly in susceptibility to spray injury and diseases as shown in Table 14.

TABLE 14.
Degrees of Susceptibility of Apple Varieties to Diseases and Spray Injury
(From Ohio Agr. Exp. Sta. Bull. 655)

Variety	Scab	Bitter Rot	Blotch	Brooks Spot	Fire Blight	Cedar Rust	Bordeaux Russet	Lime-Sulfur Russet
Baldwin	Moderate	Moderate	Slight	Slight	Slight	Slight	Very	Very
Ben Davis	Very	Very	Moderate	Slight	Slight	Slight	Very	Very
Cortland	Very	Very	Very	Slight	Very	Moderate	Slight	Slight
Delicious[1]	Very	Moderate	Slight	Moderate	Slight	Moderate	Slight	Moderate
Duchess	Moderate	Slight	Very	Slight	Slight	Slight	Slight	Slight
Golden Delicious	Slight	Very	Moderate	Very	Slight	Slight	Very	Very
Grimes	Slight	Very	Slight	Very	Very	Slight	Very	Very
Jonathan	Slight	Very	Slight	Very	Very	Moderate	Very	Moderate
McIntosh	Very	Very	Very	Slight	Slight	Slight	Slight	Moderate
N. Spy	Very	Moderate	Slight	Slight	Slight	Slight	Slight	Slight
R. I. Greening	Moderate	Very	Slight	Slight	Very	Slight	Moderate	Moderate
Rome	Very	Moderate	Moderate	Moderate	Moderate	Very	Slight	Slight
Stayman	Moderate	Moderate	Slight	Moderate	Slight	Slight	Moderate	Moderate
Wealthy	Moderate	Slight	Slight	Slight	Very	Moderate	Slight	Slight
Winter Banana	Very	Very	Slight	Slight	Slight	Moderate	Moderate	Moderate
Yellow Transparent	Moderate	Slight	Slight	Slight	Very	Slight	Slight	Slight

[1] Varieties like Delicious, Rome, Stayman, etc., include the red sports of those varieties.

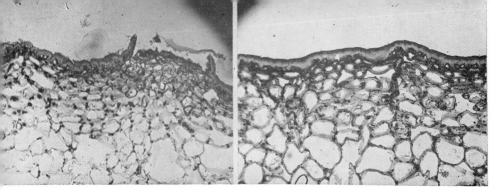

R. R. Little, U.S.D.A.

Figure 9. The cuticle or skin on the left apple has been dissolved or broken by adverse external factors; the one on the right is unharmed. Caustic spray materials can cause such damage, russeting the apple and causing it to shrivel quickly in storage.

Trees low in vigor are frequently injured more by spray and weather conditions than moderately vigorous trees. Also, foliage which has been injured by insects, diseases, wind whipping, or hail, is more susceptible to spray injury than healthy foliage.

Lime-sulfur injury. It is well known that liquid-lime sulfur will burn most foliage and small apples if the spray is applied during hot weather or in strong concentrations, or under weather conditions resulting in slow drying of sprays. Lime-sulfur injury is characterized by deforming, edge-burning, crimping, and scalding of the leaves. Foliage may be dwarfed in size both during the early and later stages of development. This results in reduced leaf area, reduced fruit size, and poor quality and finish of the fruit. Foliage crimping and dwarfing are also caused by low temperatures in early stages of leaf development.

It has been shown that even very dilute lime-sulfur sprays, such as 1 to 100, may markedly reduce the photosynthetic activity of apple leaves. Older trees are usually affected more than trees 10 to 15 years of age. Liquid- or dry-lime sulfur are not considered safe for summer spraying of peaches. The wettable sulfurs or organics are preferred under these conditions.

Copper injury. Russeting is a characteristic injury of a copper such as Bordeaux mixture on apples. Very susceptible apple varieties are Grimes Golden, Golden Delicious, Jonathan, Baldwin, Ben Davis, Gano, and Ensee. Varieties comparatively resistant to russet injury are Rome Beauty, Gallia Beauty, Delicious, Northwestern Greening, Duchess, and Wealthy. Most russeting is caused by applications of copper as a fungicide or bactericide (for fire blight) in the preblossom, petal-fall, and ten-day sprays. The chances for russeting continue until about six weeks after petal fall in northern climates. By adding hydrated lime to spray mixtures of copper sulfate, the resulting product is Bordeaux mixture. When using "fixed" copper, one pound of lime is added to the mixture for every 0.24 to 0.26 pound of *actual* copper. For example, when using 3 pounds of Tennessee 26 per 100 gallons(Tennessee 26 contains

0.26 pound of *actual* copper per pound), you would add also 3 pounds of hydrated lime per 100 gallons of spray.

Cool wet weather is most inducive to copper injury, which results in slow drying of the spray. The best time to spray with copper is when the trees are dry and the weather favors quick drying of the spray material on the trees. Moderately high temperatures tend to reduce Bordeaux injury.

Arsenical injury. Peaches are the most susceptible to arsenical injury, especially when acid lead arsenate is used alone or combined with sulfur fungicides. Leaf damage may appear in two ways: (*a*) The leaves may exhibit many small injured areas, giving a general "shot hole" appearance; or (*b*) They may turn yellow and drop prematurely, or both. Tender peach twigs are injured most, especially in areas where the spray material tends to accumulate, such as at the base of leaf petioles and in crotches. As the wood ages, scaly bark may develop from this injury. Fruit may be injured both directly and indirectly. Arsenical injury to the foliage and wood reduces food manufacture by the leaves which in turn reduces fruit size, results in poor quality and color, and some fruits may drop prematurely. Arsenical injury on the fruit appears as cracks and gummy exudations.

Apple foliage may be injured in two ways by arsenical sprays: (*a*) tip and marginal burning which may result from an accumulation of arsenic at the margins and tips of the leaves, and (*b*) a yellowing of the foliage due to absorption of the arsenic by the leaves or by injury to the petiole. In extreme cases of burning, the damage may result in almost total defoliation.

Arsenical injury on apple fruit appears as blackened areas around the calyx end, which later becomes sunken. Secondary rots tend to develop in these injured areas. Arsenical burning on apples can be prevented by the addition of excess lime, or zinc sulfate and lime, to the lead arsenate-sulfur combination. The finish of the fruit is usually improved where excess lime is added. It should be noted, however, that organic fungicides also safen against arsenical injury and are replacing hydrated lime in many formulae. The following organic fungicides will safen against arsenical injury (in Michigan) when used in the same spray mixture with acid lead arsenate.

- One-fourth pound of ferbam will safen one pound of lead arsenate.

- One-half pound of captan will safen one pound of lead arsenate.

- One-half pound of Ziram will safen one pound of lead arsenate.

- One-half pound of Niacide M will safen one pound of lead arsenate.

Thiram or dodine will *not* safen lead arsenate. When you are using these fungicides with lead arsenate, reduce the amount by 1/3 or ½ per 100 gallons and add either ferbam, captan, Ziram or Niacide M in amounts recommended above.

Russeting and weather injury. Low temperature and frost during the blossoming period and early part of the growing season may cause varying amounts and kinds of russet injury to fruits. This injury usually takes the form of a belt of russet around the apple. Weather injury to the leaves is characterized by dwarfing, crimping, and when severely injured, blisters may develop on the under surfaces. Such leaves may turn yellow and drop prematurely. During extremely hot days in midsummer, exposed fruit may show sunburning on one cheek. A discoloration of the skin is evident and in extreme cases blistering, cracking of the skin and sunken corky areas the size of a nickel, may occur on the exposed areas. Very hot weather may also cause a bronzing of the red color and a whitening of the green color of the fruit.

Stayman cracking is worse where russeting is present.

G. Delicious, Delicious and Jonathan are easily russeted by spray chemicals and freezing air temperatures (32° F. or lower) which occur frequently in northern areas after Pre-Pink. Under Michigan conditions which are typical of much of the apple regions east of the Rockies, the following suggestions have been made.

Golden Delicious: If smooth finish on Golden Delicious is important, do not use ferbam, wettable or 1. sulfur, or Cyprex during the time of Pre-Pink through Second Cover. These pesticides, plus wettable and lime-sulfur, may russet G. Delicious when no freezing occurs particularly during Pre-Pink through Second Cover. Ferbam, glyodin, or Cyprex may be used on Golden Delicious before Pre-Pink and after Second Cover. Captan, Niacide M, and Thylate may be used on this variety any time during the growing season. Plant Golden Delicious where aeration is good, drying fast and use mist concentrates if possible.

Jonathan: Although not as easily injured as Golden Delicious, this variety is russeted by certain pesticides when temperatures 32° F. and lower occur just before, during or shortly after *Bloom*. When the air temperature drops to 32° F. or lower at *Bloom* or shortly thereafter, use captan through *Second Cover,* or dodine (Cyprex) no higher than ¼ pound per 100 gallons.

If back action beyond 25 hours is required to control scab, use Phygon at ¼ pound plus Captan at 1 pound per 100 gallons. If no freezing temperatures occur at Pink or after, any fungicide suggested for apple may be used.

Beginning with Third Cover, any fungicide or any fungicide combination may be used on Jonathan at the rates suggested in the Michigan Apple Spraying Schedule without danger of increasing fruit russeting.

Use of bordeaux or fixed copper and hydrated lime on Jonathan for the control of fireblight following freezing temperatures (32° F. or lower) after Pre-Pink may cause unfavorable fruit russeting.

Delicious: Wettable sulfur, sulfur paste, lime-sulfur or dichlone

(Phygon) as a spray after *Bloom* may cause fruit russeting. If freezing conditions (32° F. or lower) occur close to *Bloom* and/or if humid, rainy, cool conditions prevail after *Bloom*, the use of sulfur pesticides or over-spraying with dichlone (Phygon) *will russet Delicious,* including the red sports.

The following comments on spray injury in an arid climate come from Washington State:

Faulty spray equipment, highly concentrated materials, or extremes of weather during or following spraying may lead to fruit or foliage injury. The risk of spray injury is greater when drought stress exists.

Cool, rainy, or humid weather in the early growing season may cause russeting of Golden Delicious or Jonathan apples. Russeting may be increased by pesticides or nutritional sprays if they are applied when such conditions occur or if sprays are applied at night. Emulsifiable materials are more likely to cause injury than wettable powders.

The following is a list of some of the common pesticides and the injury observed following their use: *Benzene Hexachloride (BHC)* — May russet Golden Delicious and has caused off-flavor to apples. *Captan* — May cause injury to leaves and fruit following summer oil combinations, especially if the Captan spray or sprays have been applied after an early frost or during slow drying conditions. *Chlorobenzilate* — Has russeted pears when used at more than 1½ pounds actual per 300 gallons of water. Do not use on Delicious apples or peaches. *Demeton (Systox)* — Has caused injury to pears, and Golden Delicious apples if used in excess of ½ pt/100 gallons.

Oil — The following conditions may aggravate injury: cool, damp and extremely dry weather; broken emulsions; applications of oil or oil-lime sulfur at the pre-pink stage; summer applications preceding or following many organic insecticides or fungicides within two weeks or during hot weather; and faulty application. Winter-injured trees may be particularly susceptible to damage by oil. *Ovex* — May cause injury to apples and pears if applied in excess of ½ pound actual per 100 gallons of water or during slow drying conditions. *Parathion* — causes fruit and foliage injury to McIntosh apples and under certain conditions has caused russeting of Golden Delicious. *Perthane* — Emulisifiable concentrate formulations may cause russeting or spotting of pear fruits. Store chemical away from major buildings — has properties of spontaneous combustion. *Phosphamidon* — May cause injury to apple foliage. Do not use or allow to drift on cherries. *Phygon* — May cause severe fruit and foliage injury when applied to apricots after petal fall. *Schradan (OMPA)* — Has caused foliage burn, defoliation, on drouthy young apples. *Sevin* — If used as a first cover spray may cause marginal foliage burning of Bartletts and usually causes fruit thinning of apples. *Sulfur and Sulfur Compounds* — Do not use at temperatures above 90° F., or on apricots. On Delicious and Anjous, use only during prebloom. *TEPP* — Has caused injury to fruit and foliage as a spray on apple, cherries, and pears. *Trithion* — Has caused injury to apples as cover spray. *Urea* — May harm stonefruits, pears.

Cygon may damage apples; prevent drift on stone fruits. *Galecron* may damage fruit-leaves with EC formulations of other ag. chemicals or surfactants. *Imidan* will injure cherry, peach foliage. *Morestan* may russet Bartlett, Anjou pears; summer sprays may defoliate G. Delicious and injure fruit of several varieties when combined with other pesticides or at temperatures above 90°F. Oil before or after Morestan causes damage. *Karathane* may burn or defoliate apples under extreme conditions or slow drying or if oil was applied; use oil only after 21 days. *Omite* may damage fruit and foliage in hot weather; may severely hurt pears, or if oil was applied before or after. *Plictran*: do not *use oil, except after* 28 days. *X-77* with other materials or in cool slow-drying weather causes damage. *Zinc sulfate* defoliates apricots as post-harvest spray.

Mechanical injury. Mechanical injury to the foliage and fruit results from improper use of spray equipment or guns. Injury consists of russeted fruit, dwarfed or torn leaves, and in some cases a lack of finish and quality of the fruit. Mechanical injury is caused by (*a*) poor breakup of the liquid at the nozzle, (*b*) coarse particles in the spray materials, (*c*) drenching of the foliage, and operating air-blast equipment too close to the trees.

Importance of lime in preventing spray injury. The main purpose of lime in summer sprays, when and where recommended, is to prevent spray injury. It also may serve as a guide to the spray operator to see where the foliage is covered thoroughly with spray materials. Freshly manufactured hydrated lime is preferred which is free from grits and is so finely divided that 99 per cent of the particles will pass through a 325-mesh sieve; all particles should pass through a 300-mesh sieve. Lime kept over 90 days in the spray shed should be added to the soil and not used for spraying purposes. A supply of specially hydrated spray lime obtained in the spring should be satisfactory throughout the season.

Effect of sprays on color, quality, and yield. More emphasis is being placed by state and federal research workers on the effect of spray materials and combinations of materials on yield and quality of fruit, since many workers are finding a pronounced effect by some materials.

Garman and coworkers in Connecticut report typical results. They drew the following conclusions: (*a*) No significant effect of the insecticides on sugars could be detected but there was a slight trend toward increased sugars from the non-arsenicals. Some fungicides increased sugars strongly. *Crag* 341 was the most notable in this regard. (b) Total acidity appeared to be depressed slightly by arsenicals. This was more apparent from analyses of the pressed juice than of the whole apple, and was more apparent in one year than another. Some fungicides also effect acids strongly; for example, a complete schedule of *Phygon*-lead arsenate reduced acid content. Others such as lead arsenate-*Captan* or lead arsenate-*Crag* 341 gave no indication of depression; in fact, a slight increase was noted for *Captan*. (*c*) No differences could be detected in ascorbic acid content due to treatments. (*d*) Minerals were depressed by arsenical sprays. Other elements in the spray mix have not been demonstrated to have any effect. Depression of boron in particular appeared to be important from a number of standpoints. (*e*) Both insecticides and fungicides may affect the physical appearance of the apple as by russeting (arsenates, sulfur), sun scald (sulfurs), color reduction (any black spray too late in the season), and bleaching (sulfurs). Some combinations reduced yield (parathion-sulfur, lead arsenate -sulfur); others had little effect (lead arsenate-thiram, parathion-thiram) while others containing nitrogen (fermate) may increase it. (*f*) Lead arsenate has consistently affected flavor unfavorably in Baldwin and Gravenstein, but not so much in McIntosh. Very significant preferences for thiram-sprayed fruit when compared with sulfur (in combination with both lead arsenate and parathion) developed over the three-year period and were relatively consistent from year to year. (*g*) Flavor tests require careful operation and are sometimes difficult to evaluate. Complete examination of fruit, processed and unprocessed, refrigerated and fresh, is indicated. Examination for off-flavors as well as general preferences should be considered.

Some chemicals such as the mercuries and Sevin will reduce set if applied improperly (follow recommendations). Since new spray chemicals are appearing continually on the market, and many combinations of them are possible, the grower should keep in close touch with his local experiment station's annual recommendations.

Air pollution damage. Damage to foliage from air pollution has been known for over 200 years. The problem became more apparent after World War II with increased and widespread industrial development and a great increase in automotive equipment on highways. Early pollution damage was believed to be limited to that caused by sulfur dioxide, ethylene and illuminating gas. With new war industries, heretofore unknown other pollutants were discovered, including chlorine, hydrogen flouride ozone mixtures, titanium, and others. Some states are passing laws to enforce filtering of pollutants on smoke stacks and exhaust pipes.

Damage usually becomes apparent during seasons when the air becomes heavy, foggy and quiet, as in autumn. Heavily industrialized areas such as Los Angeles, New Jersey, and sections of the Northwest have registered complaints. Injury involves leaf speckling, marginal and interveinal scorch, premature yellowing and leaf drop, silvering, and chlorosis.

Figure 10. This is John Bean, the man who started the present well-known spray (and fire engine) company. He is holding the sprayer he invented in 1883 and started manufacturing in 1884.

Tender leaves of vegetables are affected first. There is resemblence to magnesium deficiency in some cases.

Fruit Growers must be fully cognizant of any pollutants they may be contributing to the environment in view of the public's awareness of this topic. Every effort should be made to develop a good image for the farmer.

HISTORY OF ORCHARD SPRAYING

Since the 1880's when early efforts were being made to control insects and diseases, spraying equipment has shown tremendous improvements, particularly since the early 1940's. Howard G. Ingerson, former official of the John Bean Division of Food Machinery and Chemical Corporation has covered this interesting progress in a brief history cited below.

"Back in the period of commercial orchard hand spraying from 1884 to the late 1890's, the regular spray crew included two men who alternated at pumping and holding the 10- to 14-foot long spray "rod." The spray material was usually discharged through one or two nozzles at the end of this long rod. At the end of a long hard day's work, only 1 acre of mature apple orchard had been sprayed.

Today, two men *riding* comfortably, one on tractor and one on supply truck, and operating "push buttons" or valves, protect 60 to 70 acres of mature apple orchard in 10 hours.

From hand pumps, the evolution of spraying methods and equipment took a step forward when, at the turn of the century, gasoline engines were adapted to farm use. Power sprayers were shown and demonstrated in the early 1900's.

The period from 1910 to 1920 was one of rapid expansion of orchard acreage. Large individual and company-owned orchards were coming into bearing. The labor shortage of World War I called for the development of larger, faster sprayers. Pumps of 12 to 15 gallons per minute became regular equipment, with tank sizes to 300 gallons. Gasoline engines had been improved, made lighter in weight, and 6- to 10-hp sizes were available for these larger pump sizes. Using the larger of these sprayers, a two- or three-man crew protected 10 to 15 acres of mature orchard per day.

One of the most important contributions to labor saving came in 1916 with the invention of the *adjustable type spray gun* which made it possible to change the spray pattern quickly and to secure effective spray coverage at greater distances.

Even with improved spray guns, it was difficult under some wind conditions to spray the tops of large fruit trees with the sprayman on the ground. It logically developed that spray "towers" or platforms were mounted on the sprayers. These devices were usually homemade.

In the period from 1920 to 1935, pump capacities were increased to 45 gpm and tank sizes, to 600 gallons. In the early 1920's crawler tractors were beginning to be used for hauling orchard sprayers, and by the late 20's wheel tractors were coming into this service.

The next step was the replacement of the sprayer engine with tractor power take-off drive under favorable operating conditions. As larger-capacity, heavy-duty pumps were available and larger tractors put into orchard use, this combination of tractor with power take-off driven sprayer became almost universal in many orchard sections.

In the period from 1920 to 1935, with larger-capacity pumps available and suited to pressures of 500 to 600 pounds, stationary sprayers found a place in orchards too steep or too closely planted to permit the use of portable equipment. In some of these piped orchard installations the most distant hose connection was more than a mile from the sprayer, and high pressure was required at the pump to overcome loss of pressure in the long pipe lines.

While steel sprayer frames, axles, and wheels had been regular construction for some years, wooden spray tanks were still regular equipment until 1935. The first line of all-steel portable sprayers was offered in 1935, and within a few years steel had largely replaced all wood in sprayer construction.

With 35 gpm pump capacity and 500-gallon tank size, and a two-man spray crew, it became regular procedure to protect 20 to 30 acres of mature apple orchard in a day's work.

The period from 1935 to 1945, including the labor shortage of World War II, showed the need for still greater labor saving devices in orchard spraying. By 1947 rapid conversion began from hand directed spray guns to semi-automatic and then to entirely automatic spray devices, known as spray masts or booms.

The use of air as the carrier for spray chemicals was practiced in a limited way for many years. This was done as dusting, mist-dusting, mist-spraying, and various other combinations of application methods.

All the methods and equipment used until 1937 were dependent on relatively low volumes of air, in the range of 3000 to 8000 cubic feet per minute, usually at relatively high velocities of 100 to 150 mph at the air outlet. This combination of low volume air with high velocity had limited carrying power or penetration, and, accordingly, its use was limited to the few hours in the day or night when there was little or no wind.

Fortunately for the orchard industry, a grove caretaker in Florida, with several thousand acres of groves to be sprayed several times a season, started on a new approach to air spraying equipment. This was the use of a large volume (30,000 cfm or more) at medium velocity (90 to 100 mph). From this start in 1937 has come the almost complete changeover from hydraulic to air spraying, with a reduction of labor costs.

In reviewing the evolution of high pressure or hydraulic spraying, experienced spraymen know that as pump and nozzle capacity is increased the rate of travel of the sprayer and the "rate of work" is increased. For this reason, the grower with large acreage selects the hydraulic sprayer with large pump capacity, while the medium-acreage grower can protect his smaller acreage in the same limited time with less pump and nozzle capacity.

This same principle applies to air spraying. Accordingly, air sprayers of different air capacities are available for different acreage requirements, including air attachments for hydraulic sprayers.

After the principle of modern air spraying was proven, several so-called "air attachments" were developed for use on high pressure sprayers. These attachments served to convert a medium to large capacity high pressure sprayer into a one-man air-type sprayer. The first of these air attachments was lacking in air volume and was suited only to spraying of small trees. As larger units with more air capacity were developed and put into service. they helped to bridge the changeover from hydraulic to the present type complete air sprayer.

The completely automatic Speed Sprayer was introduced in the period from 1937 to 1945 during the acute labor shortage of World War II—first into the citrus groves of Florida, then into the apple and peach orchards of the East and Central states, and by mid-1940's into the orchards and groves of California and the Pacific Northwest. This development was the most revolutionary in spraying methods and equipment since the introduction of power sprayers.

The Speed Sprayer was unique in that it used a *large volume of medium velocity* air to carry the finely atomized spray liquid into and through the trees. The spray pattern was quickly adjustable to size and shape of trees and adequate to completely spray one side of each of two rows of trees as the sprayer was hauled between the rows at speeds to 3 mph.

While the Speed Sprayer was being developed and refined, research workers at federal and state experiment stations and in laboratories of spray chemical manufacturers were mixing and testing spray solutions in more concentrated forms than the regular "dilute" solutions used up to that time.

Sprayer manufacturers worked closely with all researchers to design and adapt sprayers to the most practical and economical application of these concentrated solutions.

Attention was then focused on the design of the air and liquid discharge sections of large volume air sprayers for greatest efficiency and economy.

After several seasons of field use with concentrations of from 2x to 10x regular dilute-strength material, the concentrations generally recommended by research and extension departments were 3x to 4x the original dilute strength. Both theory and commercial practice showed that at these concentrations, complete coverage and practical rate of travel could be combined. At higher concentrations, it was usually necessary to reduce the rate of travel to a point where maximum acreage could not be sprayed in a day.

Use of these air sprayers with air volume in excess of 50,000 cfm has made it possible for one tractor-sprayer operator to protect from 60 to 70 acres of mature apple orchard in a 10-hour day with spray material hauled to the sprayer by a supply unit, usually motor-truck mounted.

The change from hydraulic to modern air spraying with concentrate materials represents the greatest saving in orchard costs of any change in orchard practices during the history of the fruit industry.

The transition of large air volume sprayers has also brought several other important advantages to the commercial grower. He now is able to cover his entire acreage within the short period when insects and diseases are most effectively controlled. One large air volume sprayer usually replaces two to three hydraulic sprayers, which in turn reduces the number of tractors required and the number of year-around employees."

"During the 1950's and early 1960's there was a trend toward air sprayers of still greater air volume which in turn allowed more rapid spraying with further reductions in labor costs. However, in the late 1960's and continuing into the 1970's the trend has shifted to smaller units and use of higher concentrations of spray materials.

The newer plantings are generally on dwarf or semi-dwarf rootstocks with smaller trees and many more trees per acre. Large pruning machines, hedgers, and toppers have been utilized to materially reduce the size of older trees and to maintain the smaller size trees. Picking labor has refused to pick tops of tall trees, or insist on higher wages making large tall trees uneconomical. Irrigation has made possible higher density plantings in many areas, too. All of these changes in cultural practices have lessened the need for larger air sprayers.

Another trend has been to use Tractor Power Take-off (PTO) machines because of the availability of larger tractors with "live" PTO in the 50 to 70 h.p. class. The grower will tend to purchase PTO units if he has enough other needs for a large tractor.

In many areas the larger air sprayers now spray 2 complete rows of trees with one pass. They drive in *every other row* of trees, alternating each spray, with satisfactory results because of smaller trees and a saving in time and labor. Also, where local water supplies permit, sprayer operators are hauling their own water, dispensing with the portable supply units. With large wheel tractors with appropriate road gears they can make trips to water lines much faster." (Latter 4 paragraphs by William E. Young, FMC Repr., Summit, N. J.).

SPRAY MACHINERY AND EQUIPMENT

There are three fundamental requirements for good spray equipment: (1) obtain a complete spray coverage of the tree or plant; (2) apply the spray materials during the most effective period, and (3) obtain good coverage at the lowest cost possible. There is no set method of application and no one piece of equipment which will assure these results for all growers. A satisfactory method and piece of equipment for one set of conditions may be entirely unsatisfactory for another. In order to make a wise choice of equipment to suit conditions, the grower must have a fundamental knowledge of different types of spray equipment, their advantages and limitations and know how to operate them for best insect and disease control.

BASIC MECHANICS OF SPRAYERS

Spray atomization. It is the purpose of all sprayers to atomize a liquid with or without solids into small droplets and to force this finely divided spray onto the plants, fruit, or leaf surfaces. Adequate coverage should be obtained with a mimimum of material. The most common method of atomizing liquid sprays is by direct hydraulic pressure which forces the liquid rapidly through a nozzle, causing it to disintegrate into minute droplets. Another more or less opposite means of producing sprays is to use a high or moderately-high velocity air stream which picks up a jet of liquid or a coarsely or finely atomized liquid and deposits it in a fine mist on the plant.

Types of pumps. All spray pumps are essentially similar in basic principles with the exception of pumps used with knapsack sprayers of the compressed air and diaphragm type. Knapsack sprayers of the compressed-air type contain a simple air-displacement pump inside a small cylindrical tank (Figure 11). The tank is filled about three-quarters full of spray, the lid replaced, and the air within the tank compressed with the hand pump to a pressure of 50 to 75 pounds per square inch. When the spray nozzle is opened, the air pressure forces the liquid through the nozzle. The chief disadvantage of the compressed-air knapsack sprayer is the fact that the spray pressure will decrease as the liquid level decreases and the air expands. While these sprayers are handy for home garden use and for a limited scale in weed control in orchards, they are not suitable where a uniform spraying pressure is desired.

The knapsack sprayers which have constant pressure pumps are of two types, plunger and diaphragm, both of which are of the positive-displace-

F. E. Myers and Bros. Co., Ashland, Ohio

Figure 11. (a) The knapsack sprayer (diaphragm-type) is carried on the back of the operator with straps over the shoulders. The operator pumps continuously and an air chamber provides an even flow of solution from the nozzle. (b) The compressed-air knapsack sprayer holds from two and one-half to four gallons. The tank is filled three-quarters full of solution and the air compressed to 50 to 75 pounds. It is necessary to stop spraying and pump at intervals in order to keep up pressure. Cross-cut of pump unit is shown at lower right.

ment type (Figure 11). These pumps are fitted with a small air-cushion chamber within the tank to maintain uniform pressure. With this type sprayer, it is not necessary for the tank to withstand any pressure because the pump may be mounted either on the inside or the outside of the tank. The tank serves only as a reservoir of spray solution for the pump. The equipment is mounted on the sprayman's back and he must pump slowly but continuously while spraying. The pump maintains a more or less uniform pressure of from 50 to 75 pounds per square inch. Knapsack sprayers are suitable for low-growing crops and weed control.

The type of pump used in hydraulic power sprayers is of the displacement single-acting reciprocating type, examples of which are shown in Figure 12. They are available in a wide range of sizes and capacities with working pressures up to 1000 pounds per square inch or higher (Table 15). The capacity of these pumps depends upon: (a) the number of cylinders; (b) diameter of each cylinder; (c) length of stroke; (d) number of strokes of plunger per unit of time; and (e) the volumetric efficiency of pump.[1] All spray rig manufacturers rate pumps ac-

---

[1]This is defined as the actual volume of spray discharged divided by the plunger displacement.

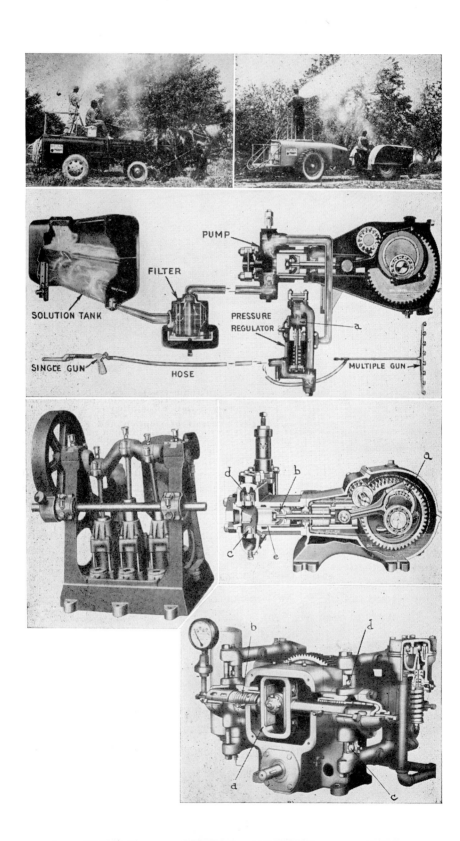

PUMP

FILTER

SOLUTION TANK

PRESSURE
REGULATOR

a

SINGLE GUN

HOSE

MULTIPLE GUN

d

b

a

c

e

b

d

d

c

cording to their maximum capacity in gallons per minute at a given pressure. With very little leakage past the valves or plunger packings, the volumetric efficiency of reciprocating-type pumps on sprayers should be 90 per cent or more. During spraying, the pumps are under considerable strain and much research has been done to prolong the life of plunger packing, valves, and cylinder walls.

Valves. In small hand sprayers and dusters, the "poppet" air valve is common. It usually consists of a leather flap held in place over the hole

TABLE 15.

Size of Pump to Purchase for Given Quantities of Spray per Application
(After Ohio Agr. Exp. Sta. Bull. 655.)

Spray Material Required for One Application	Pump Size Required in Gallons per Minute on Portable Rigs
Less than 500 gallons	Hand pumps
500 to 3000 gallons	Power pumps rated up to 10 gallons
3000 to 6000 gallons	Power pumps rated at 12-15 gallons
6000 to 10,000 gallons	Power pumps rated at 15-22 gallons
Above 10,000 gallons	Power pumps rated at 35 gallons or more according to need or air-blast sprayers

by a small spring. Under pressure the spring gives and the valve opens, allowing air to pass one way, but not the other. In the simplest type of poppet valve on dusters, no spring is used. The flap is attached at the side of the hole, allowing the air current to pass one way.

The modern power sprayers have shifted for the most part from hardened stainless steel ball-type valves in the pressure regulator to the seating plunger-tip type valve shown in Figure 13. This modern regulator is more simplified in construction and operation. The balls in ball-type valves where used (Figure 12), the plunger tips, and the value seats are all corrosion resistant. No gaskets are used with the modern valve seat assembly which eliminates a source of leakage formerly troublesome.

Legend for photos at left.

(Top three) FMC, Jonesboro, Arkansas. (Middle left) The Hardie Div., Lockwood Corporation, Gering, Neb. (Middle) F. E. Myers and Brothers Co., Ashland, Ohio. (Bottom) Friend Mfg. Co., Gasport, N. Y.

Figure 12. (Top left) This equipment was used in the early 1940's; gun and multiple nozzel broom spraying by hand is still used in small plantings and some foreign countries. (Top right) Power take-off sprayer attached to tractor. (Middle) Channels through which spray solution flows from solution tank through the filter, the pump, the pressure regulator, and out through a single nozzle gun (left) or multiple nozzle boom gun (right). When nozzles are shut off, spray solution by-passes from pressure regulator back to tank (return pipe at a to tank not shown). (Middle left) A 3-cylinder vertical-type spray pump, showing crank shaft and connecting rods. Inlet and outlet ball valves are housed on either side of base of each cylinder. (Middle right) Horizontal-type pump with eccentric drive shown at a, connecting-rod drive and removable rubber-fabric plunger-cap packing at b, porcelain cylinder walls at e, inlet valve at c, and outlet valve at d. (Bottom) Spray pump using Scotch-yoke drive at a, to which horizontal opposing plungers are attached. In operation, yoke moves back and forth. At b the stationary outside-type packing for cylinders is shown. Spray inlet-ball valve is shown at c and outlet valve at d.

577

Plungers. There are two types of plunger-displacement mechanisms in use in high-pressure rigs: (*a*) A plunger with an expanding cup fitted to the end of the plunger; thus, the cup moves with the plunger, as shown in Figure 12; and (*b*) a plunger which operates through a stationary packing which acts as the cylinder wall for the displacement chamber (Figure 12). Neither of these two systems is free from wear by abrasive chemicals manipulated under high pressure. On the pressure stroke, the plunger cups which are constructed of molded rubber and fabric, expand against the cylinder walls. This seals and prevents leakage past the cup. Although most cylinder walls are coated with acid-resistant porcelain, there eventually is some abrasion and wear of the cylinder walls. When this occurs even the plunger packing will not prevent leakage entirely.

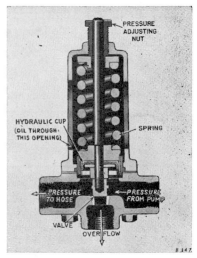

FMC, Jones, Arkansas

Figure 13. Modern pressure regulator for power sprayers with a rubber fabric diaphragm-type regulator; when solution pressure on diaphragm exceeds pressure desired, spring raises the valve stem which allows solution to by-pass back to spray tank.

Plungers which operate through packing in the walls of the cylinders are made of stainless steel, inasmuch as abrasion and erosion of the plunger must be avoided as much as possible to prevent leakage. The packing should be adjusted so that there is a very slight leakage which indicates that the packing is not so tight as to cause scoring of the plunger.

The reciprocating motion of plungers in high-pressure spray pumps can be obtained by several different mechanisms, the most common of which are (*a*) crank shaft and connecting rods, (*b*) eccentric and connecting rods, and (*c*) the Scotch-yoke assembly (Figure 12). The Scotch-yoke assembly has two opposing plungers, operating from one reciprocating mechanism; sprayers using this system must be either two or four cylinders. The other two systems usually involve three cylinders. It is immaterial whether the cylinders are vertical or horizontal.

The working parts of a high-pressure pump are enclosed to provide for self-oiling systems and to afford protection from dust. In purchasing this type rig, it is important to consider the ease with which the pump can be taken apart and repaired.

The pressure regulator. Perfection of the pressure regulator by the Bean Spray Pump Company in 1914 was one of the biggest advances in spray machinery. In power systems, some type of automatic by-pass is needed to divert spray solution back to the tank when the spray nozzles are shut off suddenly but the pump continues to operate. In other words,

578

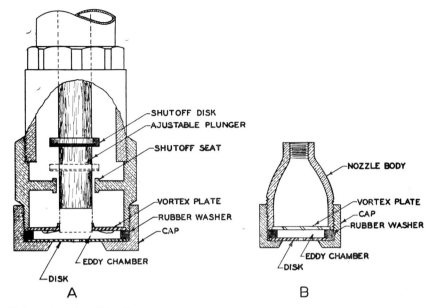

Figure 13a. Two types of eddy-chamber on disk spray nozzles: A, variable-depth type used in spray guns, adjustable plunger regulates width of cone and fineness of spray; B, fixed-depth type of eddy-chamber nozzle found on multiple nozzle booms, or as a single nozzle on small-capacity sprayers.

the pressure regulator serves as a safety device. It also has two other functions: (*a*) to maintain a uniform pressure at the spray nozzles; and (*b*) to permit the pump to operate at a greatly reduced load when no material is being discharged through the nozzles.

The construction of a modern widely used type pressure regulator is shown in Figure 13. When pressure builds up against the hydraulic cup, over and above the tension on the spring as determined by the pressure adjusting nut, the spring gives, lifting the seated plunger tip and allowing solution to flow back to the supply tank.

In the older type pressure regulators two stainless steel ball valves were used as diagramed in Figure 12, middle and bottom photos. When in these types, the pressure of the liquid exceeds the resistance offered by the compression spring, the spring gives and lifts a rod which in turn lifts a ball valve and permits excess liquid to by-pass under the ball and through a pipe back to the supply tank. A check valve (Figure 12) is employed between the diaphragm or plunger and the pump discharge line to assist the pressure regulator in acting as an unloading device as well as a pressure release valve. The release-valve ball and check-valve ball must fit perfectly in their seats in order that they function sensitively. If the check valve were removed from the system, the pressure regulator would then function merely as a release valve.

579

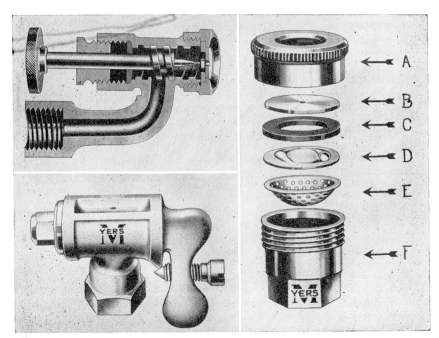

F. E. Myers and Bros. Co., Ashland, Ohio

Figure 14. (Top left) Vermorel nozzle emits a variable fine spray mist by regulating the screw plunger. If the nozzle becomes plugged, it can be disgorged with screw plunger. (Bottom left) Bordeaux nozzle throws a fan-shaped mist or a solid stream, or it may be shut off entirely by manipulating the cock handle and lock screw. Nozzle is unclogged by twisting the cock handle. (Right) Disk-type nozzles are the most popular; parts consist of: A cap, B stainless steel disk, C rubber gasket or washer, D stainless steel vortex or whirl plate, E brass cone strainer, and F body.

A spray machine is functioning properly when a little liquid is by-passing through the pressure regulator and going back to the supply tank while the spraying is in progress. If no liquid is by-passing back to the spray tank, the discharge of the spray guns is probably too great for the capacity of the spray pump, provided the pressure regulator is properly adjusted and the valves are not leaking.

Nozzles, guns, and brooms. Nozzles of the eddy-chamber type are used today on spray guns, rods, multiple-nozzle brooms or in a battery of nozzles on air-carrier sprayers (Figure 13). Vermorel and Bordeaux nozzles also are used on hand sprayers and a few power sprayers (Figure 14.) The integral parts of the eddy-chamber or disk nozzles are shown in Figure 14. The spray solution under high pressure comes up against and passes through a vortex plate which contains spiral or tangental channels. These channels set up a whirl of the spray solutions in the eddy chamber. Purpose of this whirl is to rotate the spray stream to facilitate breakup after it is discharged through the disk orifice, or port. The angle of the spray cone can be changed to narrow or wide by varying the depth of the eddy chamber or the speed of rotation of solution within it. A shallow chamber will produce a wide-angled cone. In case of a very deep eddy chamber, a jetlike spray stream will be emitted through the nozzle disk with considerable driving power and distance. With a single nozzle spray gun, the depth of the eddy chamber in the nozzle can be varied by means of an adjustable plunger, as shown in Figure 13. Thus, while spraying close to the plant, the cone is made wide and with less driving power by reducing the depth of the eddy chamber. On the other hand, if it is desired to spray the top of a tree several feet distant, the eddy chamber can be adjusted deeper to obtain a jetlike stream.

A spray cone may become unsymmetrical if the hole in the disk plate becomes worn irregularly, or if the vortex openings assume an unsymmetrical shape. It is, therefore, important to renew the spray disk or vortex plate when such a condition arises.

There are two types of spray patterns: (a) a ring type, or (b) a solid-pattern type. The solid cone is obtained by a hole arranged in the vortex plate so that it is in direct line with the disk hole.

Gunkel of Cornell has stated that a simple nozzle urgently is needed that will produce a fairly homogeneous mist cloud of *controllable* droplet size. This would permit orchard spraying with the larger 150 micron droplets in cold spring weather and changing to the 100 micron size later to improve the resulting deposits, using air-blast mist-concentrate spraying.

Pressure effects. With *high-pressure* orchard power sprayers, pressures of 450 to 600 pounds are used. This has proved advantageous as compared with the lower pressure of 250 to 400 pounds. Use of the higher pressures speeds up spraying operations without requiring additional man hours of labor and without requiring any increase in the quantity of spray material, provided the spraying is handled properly. Under the higher pressures, the liquid is broken into finer droplets which give a more uniform coverage at a rapid rate. Under high pressures, it is important that the operator be alert at all times in order to prevent wastage of spray materials.

Factors which influence spray nozzle operation are summarized as follows:[1]

Disk-orifice diameters affect:
1. Diameter of spray cone (the smaller the orifice the smaller the cone).
2. Carry (Carrying distance increases with diameter)
3. Quantity of discharge.

Pump-pressure increases cause:
1. Smaller spray droplets (pressure is the most important factor governing size of droplets).

[1]Davis, Cornelius, and G. R. B. Smyth-Homewood. Investigations on machinery used in spraying. Journ. Southeast Agr. Coll. (Wye, Kent, England), No. 34: 39-52. 1934.

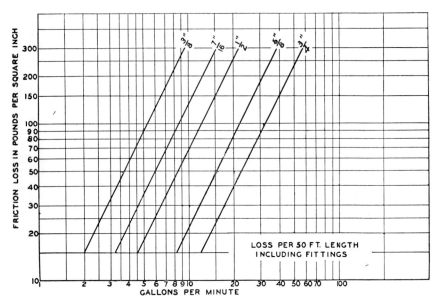

Figure 15. Friction losses which occur in different sizes of spray hose at various rates of flow. Plastic hose may have one-half friction loss of rubber hose.

    2. Increased carry of droplets (if pressures do not decrease size of droplets).

    3. Increased included angle of spray cone.

Eddy-chamber depth increases cause:

    1. Increased carry.

    2. Increased output.

    3. Decreased atomization.

    4. Decreased included angle of spray cone.

Vortex-opening size increases cause:

    1. Increased carry.

    2. Increased output.

    3. Decreased atomization.

    4. Decreased included angle of spray cone.

    If the thickness of the disk is increased, the included angle of the spray cone is decreased.

    Pressure losses in hose and rod. Pressure loss from pump to nozzle outlet is due to friction of the liquid against the inside walls of the hose or rod. The amount of this pressure loss varies with (*a*) the length of hose or rod, (*b*) roughness of the inside walls of the hose, couplings, and rod, and (*c*) the square of the velocity of flowing liquid. Figure 15 gives the average pressure losses for various sizes of hose carrying different volumes of solution. Tables 16 and 17 give approximate rate of

TABLE 16.

AVERAGE RATES OF DISCHARGE OF A SHORT GUN ADJUSTED FOR

LONG-RANGE SPRAYING[1]
(Adapted from French)

Pressure at gun in Pounds per Square Inch	Gallons per Minute Discharge Using Disks with the Given Sizes of Orifice					
	3/64 inch	4/64 inch	5/64 inch	6/64 inch	7/64 inch	8/64 inch
200	0.64	1.10	1.70	2.40	3.33	4.10
300	0.79	1.32	2.06	2.90	4.15	5.05
400	0.91	1.55	2.40	3.40	4.75	5.75
500	1.02	1.72	2.69	3.75	5.30	6.40
600	1.13	1.90	2.94	4.12	5.80	7.00

[1]Short guns adjusted for close-range spraying will deliver approximately 5 to 10 per cent less volume than that shown in the table.

TABLE 17.

AVERAGE RATES OF DISCHARGE OF A MULTIPLE-NOZZLE GUN
HAVING THREE OR MORE NOZZLES (Adapted from French)

Pressure at gun in Pounds per Square Inch	Gallons per Minute per Nozzle with Vortex Plates Having No Central Orifice—for Disk Sizes Given				Gallons per Minute per Nozzle Vortex Plates Having Also Central Orifice of Same Diameter as Disk Sizes Given			
200	0.64	1.25	1.61	2.13	0.67	1.37	1.81	2.41
300	0.79	1.53	1.97	2.60	0.83	1.67	2.23	3.00
400	0.92	1.77	2.27	3.00	0.97	1.93	2.57	3.47
500	1.03	2.00	2.57	3.40	1.08	2.17	2.87	3.87
600	1.13	2.17	2.80	3.70	1.17	2.37	3.17	4.23

spray discharge of short guns and multiple nozzle rods. By means of these tables and Figure 15, it is possible to estimate the pressure loss in hose lines equipped with different type nozzles.

Due to construction, some guns may create more friction and "kick" while operating than others. The gun that is most desirable is one which is easy to manipulate and less tiring, does a good job, and has relatively little kick.

583

Agitators. Some kind of agitation is needed in all spray tanks in order to provide a more or less uniform concentration of spray solution from the time the tank is full until empty. Agitation for hand sprayers and small power sprayers may be obtained by: (*a*) swishing of the solution as the operator moves, (*b*) small by-pass spirt of solution from pump chamber back into supply tank (Figure 11), or (*c*) simple paddles connected to the pump handle which swish the solution as the pump handle operates.

Agitation is usually provided in power-sprayer tanks by two or more paddles mounted on a lengthwise shaft in the tank, as shown in Figure 12. The paddles may be of the propeller or flat type. To obtain the same degree of mixing, propeller-type paddles require a greater speed of rotation than square-end flat paddles. However, for certain spray mixtures, the square-end agitators tend to whip an excess of air into the liquid when the tank is almost empty; this causes the pump to operate less efficiently toward the end of the tank supply.

The agitator shaft may be driven either by chain and sproket, V-belt, or by gears on the spray pump. The agitator shafts are usually mounted so that the paddles sweep within one-half inch of the bottom of the tank. Some spray solutions require greater agitation than others. For example, oil sprays and especially tank-mix oil sprays require considerable agitation. On the other hand, some spray mixtures in which the suspended materials tend to separate, such as lead arsenate, oil and detergent, will require a reduced amount of agitation. It is important that obstructions, such as pipes, braces, and filler screens be reduced to a minimum because they tend to produce quiet spots and lower the efficiency of agitation. Some larger power sprayers provide agitation by jets of spray solution which are pumped under pressure out of a pipe located near the bottom of the supply tank.

For the same amount of agitation, the circular-bottom type of solution tanks require more agitator-shaft speed and horsepower (80 and 50 per cent, respectively) than the semiflat bottom tanks.

SMALL HAND AND POWER SPRAYERS

These sprayers for fruits may be grouped under the following headings: (*a*) knapsack and (*b*) wheelbarrow. The knapsack sprayer has been discussed previously under "Type of Pumps."

Estate or greenhouse sprayer consists of a spray tank of 5- about 50-gallon capacity, mounted on 1 or 4 wheels. (Figure 16). The pump may be operated by hand or by a gasoline or electric motor. The advantages are: (*a*) the operator carries only a part of the load while moving the sprayer, (*b*) the tank is readily cleaned, (*c*) has efficient agitation, (*d*) *pressure* is fair and even, and (*e*) it is useful for spraying one or two fruit trees and a few grapevines and bush fruits. The sprayer

Figure 16. There are several types
of small estate or greenhouse
sprayers on the market. This
one (Peerless) is a 3-wheel type
pulled by hand (some motor-
driven), gasoline motor driven
pump (some equipped with electric motor), with 5 gpm capacity
and 50-gallon corrosion-resistant
tank. A heavy-duty model is a-
vailable and also 2-wheel or skid
models.

has the disadvantage of accommodating only one or two acres of low plants. It is useful around the home grounds or greenhouse.

The pump is the cylinder-plunger type. When equipped with an air chamber, a continuous even supply of spray solution is provided. Steel or rubber-tired wheels are available.

LARGE PORTABLE POWER SPRAYERS

Rigs with auxiliary engines. This type of power sprayer is a complete unit with tank, pump and auxiliary engine, all mounted on a chassis and pulled by a tractor. With this type of equipment, the capacity and pressure of the pump are independent of ground conditions or of the type of power used for transportation. The tank, pump, and auxiliary engine may be mounted on a motor truck. This arrangement is preferred by operators of custom sprayers who may travel a considerable distance from one small orchard or homegrounds to another making spraying their business part of the year.

Auxiliary engines of power outfits should be capable of operating the spray pump at maximum output without being loaded to more than 75 per cent of their rated horsepower. The engine should be provided with a governor to regulate its speed according to the pump load. Water-cooled engines are employed on all sprayers except some of the smaller port-able outfits. Some engines are cooled not by radiators and fans, but by pipe coils installed in the spray tank. This method is satisfactory provided the sprayer is not operated for long periods with one tank of spray material, in which case the spray solution may be injured by the heat absorbed from the coils. There is also the additional disadvantage of the pipe coils reducing the effectiveness of agitation in the spray tank. The chief advantage of this cooling system is the fact that the pump and engine can be completely enclosed under a hood which protects them from dust and spray materials.

585

Power take-off sprayers. Inasmuch as the majority of sprayers are pulled by tractors, the power from the tractor also can be used for operating the spray pump, as shown in Figures 12, 17, and 34. The chief advantage of this arrangement is the lower initial cost of the spraying equipment. The main disadvantage is that power take-off outfits may lack the flexibility of an auxiliary engine-driven sprayer. Manufacturers have improved the power take-off arrangement, however, by providing the sprayer with a transmission having two gear ratios so that with any given tractor speed, a choice of two speeds is available for the pump operation. This gives added flexibility in the choice of ground speeds for spraying on the move. *In fact, PTO sprayers are increasing in popularity with dwarf trees, with smaller sprayers, and where a larger tractor can be used for other purposes.*

The tractor must have ample reserve power for spraying while moving. With most tractors, the master clutch controls the power take-off shaft and, therefore, it is necessary to disengage the clutch, shift to neutral, and re-engage the master clutch in order to operate the sprayer at each stop. Success with power take-off sprayers depends upon correct selection and operation of the tractor power units, and upon the uniformity and size of trees. Field representatives of spray machine companies are able to furnish information on correct matching of tractor with power take-off equipment.

Speed, air-carrier, or air-blast sprayers. This type of spraying (Figure 17) has largely displaced other types in commercial fruit growing in North America and is gaining favor in foreign countries. It is well adapted to concentrate as well as dilute spraying. The advantages over high-pressure spraying are: (*a*) saves 70% labor, (*b*) saves 30-50% time, and (*c*) saves 20% material.

The principle is based on a low-pressure centrifugal pump which delivers the spray material to a battery of nozzles in fixed positions. A powerful motor-driven fan discharges a strong air blast in excess of 50,000 cu. ft. per minute past the nozzles which carries the spray as an enveloping fog drive over and through the trees. It is designed for rapid coverage and saving of labor on large acreages, as one operator can drive the tractor and operate the sprayer. The rigs are usually equipped with a 500-gallon tank and serviced by a tank truck (Figure 17) for rapid refilling which takes about three minutes. These rigs can spray out from 1500 to 2000 gallons per hour, covering from three to five acres, or more if a concentrate mix is used, of bearing apple orchard. Up to about 70 acres of mature apple trees can be covered in a 10-hour day.

Air-carrier spraying has shown outstanding performance with peaches. The double head which throws spray from left to right, as shown in

FMC, Jonesboro, Arkansas

Figure 17.   Types of air-carrier sprayers used by U. S. orchardists (Upper photos) These machines are available in four sizes: (1) 95,000 CFM total air volume @ 100-120 MPH, 232 HP engine, 100 GPM pump @ 100 PSI; (2) 67,000 CFM total air @ 95 MPH, 188 engine, 100 GPM pump @ 100 PSI; (3) 52,000 CFM @ 100 MPH, 100 HP Engine, 100 GPM pump @ 75 PSI; and (4) 35,000 CFM @ 100 MPH, 70 HP engine, 25 GPM pump @ 400 PSI. The larger machines have 500 gal. tanks; smaller ones, 300-400 gal. tanks. (Mid-photos) On the left is a 500-gal. tank tender loading water through a strainer while attendant dumps in spray material. At right is shown the type of clothes and "breather" mask spray-men should use when applying highly toxic materials as parathion. (Lower photos) At left is a multiple-row nozzles air-blast sprayer applying both sides, mist concentrate and (at right) a PTO, 300-500 gal. tank inside fiberglass coated, 20 gpm pump, 400 psi, 29-inch fan.

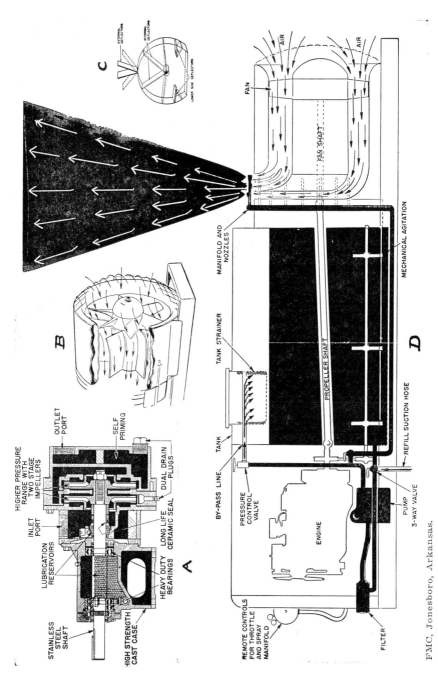

OUTLET PORT

SELF PRIMING

HIGHER PRESSURE RANGE WITH TWO STAGE IMPELLERS

INLET PORT

DUAL DRAIN PLUGS

LUBRICATION RESERVOIRS

LONG LIFE CERAMIC SEAL

STAINLESS STEEL SHAFT

HIGH STRENGTH CAST CASE

HEAVY DUTY BEARINGS

A

B

C

EXTERNAL DEFLECTORS

INTERNAL DEFLECTORS

LOWER SIDE DEFLECTORS

D

AIR

AIR

FAN

FAN SHAFT

MANIFOLD AND NOZZLES

TANK STRAINER

TANK

BY-PASS LINE

PRESSURE CONTROL VALVE

ENGINE

PROPELLER SHAFT

MECHANICAL AGITATION

REFILL SUCTION HOSE

3-WAY VALVE

PUMP

FILTER

REMOTE CONTROLS FOR THROTTLE AND SPRAY MANIFOLD

FMC, Jonesboro, Arkansas.

Figure 18. These charts show how an air-carrier mist sprayer is built. The spray pump is shown at "A", the fan and vanes at "B", and the deflectors to guide the mist at "C". At "D" is a full-length cross section.

588

William E. Young, FMC Repr., Summit, N. J.

Figure 19. This air-blast sprayer can be adjusted for orchard floor coverage for mouse control. Field representatives of such spray equipment can advise on size of nozzle disks, ground speed, angle of nozzles and other adjustments.

Figure 17, is preferred for low-growing trees. The equipment also can be adjusted for ground spraying for mouse control (Figure 19).

Accurate control of the air stream is provided through a system of fins or guide vanes (Figure 18). These fins can be adjusted easily and quickly from a panel to direct the air stream higher or lower, according to the shape and height of the tree and the wind condition. The amount of spray material being discharged can be regulated inasmuch there are several nozzle pipes on each side of the delivery head. Each nozzle pipe supplies a varied number of nozzles depending upon its location in the air stream. Certain nozzle pipes are equipped with pet-cocks which may be turned on or off as needed. A master control gate valve is provided for instantly feeding or cutting off the material to all nozzles. Provision also is made for adjusting the number of nozzles to avoid waste of material and drenching of foliage and fruit when travel-ing at slow speeds. The speed usually ranges between one to four miles per hour. A computor or "slip stick" is available for adjusting the factors that govern efficiency of spraying (Figure 20). A remote control box (Figure 25) is mounted on the tractor, providing the ignition-starter switch, engine throttle and controls for the two spray-control valves, plus engine and engine air-cleaner gauges.

Effective spraying can be done by this equipment against more wind than is possible with a spray gun. This is because the air-blast sprayer can discharge sufficient air to displace the air in the tree and to replace it with air carrying the spray material. For example, the space occupied

589

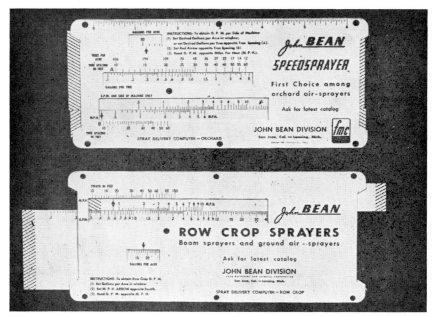

FMC, Jonesboro, Arkansas.

Figure 20. A computer or "slip stick" has been designed to assist growers in coordinating the proper speed of machine, gallons per tree or per acre, tree spacing, and trees per acre receiving concentrate or dilute spraying.

by an apple tree with a 35-foot limb spread and 20 feet high is 24,500 cubic feet. If the sprayer is moving past the tree at a rate of two miles per hour, it passes a 35-foot tree in about 12 seconds, in which time over 25,000 cu. ft. of air is discharged.

Experiences have shown that air-blast sprayers are no more, or, less wasteful of spray material than the conventional portable high-pressure sprayers in orchards uniformly planted and having trees of uniform size. However, the sprayman must be alert in regulating spray output and direction according to tree size and shape. Sufficient time should be given in passing a tree for the fog to penetrate throughout the tree. Trees must be opened properly by pruning to derive the greatest benefits from this type of spraying.

Based on spraying capacity, a single unit should be able to service from 60 to 70 acres of average bearing apple trees and about double this acreage of peaches and cherries. Some growers who have only 50 to 75 acres of orchard are using air-blast sprayers because they reduce the spray job to a minor operation and, thus, give more free time for attention to other tasks on a diversified farm. These growers apparently

Request "Orchard and Field Crop Spray Computer" (plastic disc cards) for determining tree spacing, MPH, No. trees, time, gpt, gpm, swath width, etc. F. E. Myers, Co., Ashland, Ohio 44805.

Figure 21. Spray equipment used in Europe. (a) 24-meter wide spray boom for dwarf fruit trees, nursery row trees, or trees in beds; (b) mist blower elevated for spraying experimental trees in beds. (Courtesy E. W. M. Vorhey, Instituut Voor Tuinbouwtechniek, Wageningen, The Netherlands). Note: Fruit Machinery Co, Mercersburg, Penna., 17236, handles Holland-built sprayers in the U.S.A.; (c) Nozzle direction and cone width can be varied for row-crop strawberry spraying; and (d) mist blower for standard size trees.

F. E. Myers & Bros. Co., Ashland, Ohio

Figure 22. (Left) This air sprayer has twin 36-in fans, delivering 70,000 cfm air volume with gasoline or diesel engine. (Right) Air sprayer with one 36-inch fan, delivering 30,000 cfm air volume, PTO, corrosion-proof GlasStran parts. Designed for orchard crops. Left machine can be used on the larger pecan trees.

charge the extra initial expense of the sprayer to over-all operations, rather than to the orchard alone.

Every effort and adjustment should be made to avoid two possible disadvantages of the air-blast sprayers: (a) in the foliage sprays the top-centers of tall trees may not be sprayed thoroughly even though the spray mist may be blown high above the top, and (b) in the dormant or delayed dormant sprays the twigs and branches may not wet on all sides because each side (two sides) of the tree is sprayed from a fixed position.

Power-Take-Off (PTO) Rigs. These rigs are popular where the tractor not only pulls the rig but also provides the power for the spray pump. The PTO connection between the tractor and sprayer has been perfected and with the current use of tractors with adequate power, the combination works well. A comparison of PTO and engine-driven rigs is below:

PTO	Engine - Drive
1) lower initial cost	higher initial cost
2) lower operating & maintenance	higher operating & maintaining
3) requires higher tractor H.P.	less H.P. requirement
4) less flexibility	more flexibility
5) greatly affected by terrain	not as affected by terrain
6) less soil compaction	more soil compaction
7) can operate on moist ground	limited to relatively dry ground
8) smaller, more maneuverable	larger, less maneuverable
9) more affected by wind	less affected by wind
10) generally concentrate only	dilute capabilities

Spray tanks. A tank should be selected with as large a capacity as can be pulled to advantage in order to save time in refilling. Spray tanks are now largely steel and are available in standard sizes up to 500 gallons, although larger tanks are available. Steel tanks have gained popularity over wood because they last longer, require less maintenance and permit rigid attachment to the frame, which in turn provides greater strength and compactness of the outfit. Fiberglass is being used for tanks up

592

(Upper left) Friend Mfg. Co., Inc., Gasport, N. Y.; (Upper right) Hardie Div., American Pulley Co., Philadelphia, Pennsylvania; (Lower left) FMC, Jonesboro, Arkansas; (Lower right) N. F. Childers, Rutgers University.

Figure 23. Several types of sprayers on the market. (Upper left) 80 GPM pump, 500 gal tank epoxy-resin coated inside, hand-gun attachment air-blast type. **(Upper right)** This is a dual-fan sprayer having two 40-inch 11-blade fans, 97,500 CFM, 100 GPM pump @ 125 PSI, self-priming, 500-gal. tank, 5500 lbs. **(Lower left)** High pressure air-carrier sprayer for hedgerows and compact trees, small orchards, bush fruits, and up to 10x concentrate spraying; 20 gpm pump, 400 psi, 300 gal tank, 21" axial fan, narrow overall width of 53½"; 1420 lbs total. **(Lower right)** Spray mast, home-made by pear grower in Sacramento Bay area for both sides spraying of hedgerow-trained trees 16 ft. high, planted 12 x 14 ft.

to about 150 gallons; the tanks consist of top and bottom halves seamed and bolted at the center. Single or double plastic coating on the inside of the bigger tanks is available for protection against rust and corrosion. Flat-bottom tanks may have a slanted bottom for complete drainage at the lower side. Some steel tanks have been known to last through more than twenty years of service.

Transport trucks and wheel equipment. The power take-off rigs are usually mounted on a two-wheel trailer-type chassis (Figures 12, 17a, 21). With this arrangement, the tractor wheels assume a part of the load of the sprayer, and this additional weight increases traction of the tractor wheels. Double wheels, large airplane rubber tires (Figure 19), tandem wheels, or crawler-type tracks may be used for the larger units. The chief advantages are that they distribute the load better on the soil surface and facilitate moving of the equipment over ridges, and moist, rough ground. The crawler tracks are best used for the larger sprayer units when ground conditions are soft or muddy.

As stated previously, motor trucks often are used to carry sprayers

(FMC, Jonesboro, Ark.).

Figure 24. Centrally located in orchard blocks, large water storage tanks can be used to fill rapidly the sprayer tank. Used oil storage tanks or railroad tank cars can be mounted on concrete piers. A layer of oil on top of the water reduces rusting of tank. With high-geared tractors, and concentrate PTO sprayers for compact trees, the tender to carry spray solution to sprayers in the orchard has been eliminated; no need for it.

where the soil terrain permits. Commercial sprayer operators sometimes use this system because sprayers can be transported between orchard units separated from each other by miles. Also, if water-supply trucks are not used in the orchard, motor-truck sprayers can save considerable time in returning to the water supply tank for refilling.

Pneumatic rubber tires are used almost exclusively for spraying equipment because: (a) They increase the life of the sprayer if much traveling is required on hard-surfaced or gravel roads; (b) draft is less on loose or sandy soils; (c) on wet soils, the large-diameter tractor-type tires clean themselves and do not ball up with mud as do steel wheels; and (d) the equipment can be pulled at higher speeds either for refilling or highway transporation. The small-diameter truck or bus tires are not satisfactory under muddy orchard conditions because they tend to slide along rather than roll. In case of motor-truck outfits, the oversize ballon tires are a distinct advantage because: (a) They do not break down irrigation furrows; (b) they have better traction; and (c) they cause less packing of the soil.

The chief disadvantage of pneumatic rubber tires is the initial cost and depreciation. Some farmers have avoided the higher initial cost by purchasing used truck, airplane or bus tires which are satisfactory if muddy conditions are not a problem. Pneumatic tires installed new should last as long as tractor tires, or about seven years or longer. The

(Upper) FMC, Jonesboro, Ark., (Lower left) Bell Aircraft Corp., Buffalo, N. Y. (Lower right) The Hardie Division, American Pulley Co., Philadelphia, Penna.

Figure 25. (Upper left) Narrow sprayer (Bean 2106) built for close-planted dwarf or semi-dwarf fruit trees, for grapes, raspberries and for 10x concentrate application; 300 gal. tank, 20 gpm pump at 400 psi, 21-inch axial-flow fan at 3000 rpm. See in operation in Figure 23. **(Upper right)** Control panel for hydraulic and electrical manipulation of sprayer from tractor seat. **(Lower left)** Helicopter equipped for concentrate spraying for cranberries, weed control, etc. **(Lower right)** This air-blast sprayer is equipped for single-gun spraying for such jobs as borer control in peach trunks.

extra initial cost of rubber tires may not be justified if the sprayer will be used only a few days each year.

Spraying towers. High spray towers which still may be needed for tall trees such as in walnuts are used on level or moderately rolling ground, altho large-capacity air-carrier sprayers are being used increasingly. The so-called "pest nest" is in the top center of the tree where it is difficult to spray throughly. Furthermore, most of the highest-quality fruit is usually carried through the top one-third of the tree.

For such tall trees as walnuts, heights of from 15 to 30 feet may be necessary. Telescoping hydraulic towers are in use in California. With these units, the operator in the "crow's nest" can control his height by opening or closing a hydraulic valve. Some "crow's nests" have a "catwalk" which permits the spray operator to stand almost over the top center of the tree. The extremely tall "catwalk" towers which can accommodate two men and which are used for spraying walnut trees from a height of 30 feet, are mounted on special trailers with wheel treads considerably wider than used for most sprayers to give stability. Pecan and walnut trees, however, are being trained lower and older trees are mowed mechanically to lower them, so that standard sprayers can handle them adequately.

SPRAY MIXING PLANTS AND REFILLING EQUIPMENT

In some orchards, considerable time is wasted in returning to the water tower for refilling. In fact, half of the day may be utilized in the refilling operations. Timeliness of application is a prime factor in effective spraying and, therefore, the time required for refilling should be reduced to an absolute minimum. The usual refilling time is about 20 minutes, but this may be reduced to three to five minutes by operating a special portable water-supply tender truck in conjunction with the spray rig (Figure 17a). Refilling time also can be reduced by locating water tanks throughout the orchard. A common recommendation is one tank of sufficient size to accommodate each 20-acre block of the orchard. These tanks which are about 3000-gallon capacity may be supplied by gravity or pressure pumping from a larger master tank, which in turn is filled by pumping from a spring or similar water supply. Discarded railroad oil tanks often are used for these water supply tanks. They are mounted on about eight-foot concrete or brick pillars. Some growers use a one-half inch layer of oil on the water surface in these tanks to prevent corrosion of the walls as the water rises and falls. It is important, however, never to drain completely a supply tank into the sprayer tank in order to avoid oil contamination in the spray solution.

The size of the storage tank needed for an orchard or a block of trees will depend upon the supply of water and upon the amount of water needed for one spray period. If the supply of water is small, a pump of small capacity should be used, and the tank should be large. If the pump must operate 24 hours a day, the tank should hold nearly one day's supply of water. If the supply is so small that the pump cannot deliver enough water in 24 hours, then the storage tank should have a capacity sufficient for two or more days of spraying. The following problems are typical for calculating the size of tank, based upon water supply and water needed.

Example 1. What size tank should be installed to supply 9000 gallons of water for one spray if the water supply furnishes only 1½ gallons of water per minute?

A water supply of 1½ gallons per minute, if pumped for 24 hours, delivers 1½ gallons × 60 minutes × 24 hours, or 2160 gallons per day. For three days the pump will deliver 2160 × 3, or 6480 gallons. Since 9000 gallons are needed for one spray and the pump delivers only 6480 gallons in three days, the storage tank at a minimum should hold the difference, 9000 — 6480, or 2520 gallons. In this case the pump is supplying less than is needed or used and a surplus must be stored. The storage tank should hold twice the amount needed, or approximately 5000 gallons.

Example 2. What size storage tank should be used to supply 9000 gallons of water for one spray if the water supply is three gallons per minute?

Three gallons × 60 minutes × 24 hours = 4320 gallons per day. In this case the pump is supplying in 24 hours a sufficient amount of water for one day's spraying, but one must have a reservoir to hold the water pumped during the night, or as a minimum one half of 4320, or approximately 2000 gallons. A 3000-gallon storage space should be provided.

Example 3. When the water supply is large so that a large-capacity pump can be used, the elevated storage tank may be comparatively small. If a pump is used, the capacity of which is equal to the rate used for spraying, the elevated storage tank need be only twice the size of the sprayer tank and the pump may be run only during the daytime. For example, suppose that 9000 gallons are needed for one spray and that the water supply furnishes five gallons per minute. Five gallons × 60 minutes × 10 hours = 3000 gallons per day. Since this is equal to the amount needed, storage space is actually needed only for one spray tank, or 500 gallons. An 800- or 1000-gallon storage tank should be used. Of course, a larger tank may be used but it is not needed except in case of a breakdown of the water pump.

Additional information on water supply for the orchard can be obtained from a Cornell bulletin by Jennings (see references).

As stated previously, the most rapid means of refilling a portable spray tank is to use a portable tender tank which is pulled alongside the sprayer and quickly emptied into the spray tank. Transfer of the water may be done by a low-pressure rapid operating pump which is driven by a special one-cylinder motor or by a power take-off from the truck motor (Figure 17a). These portable supply tanks carry spray material previously mixed which is well agitated and ready for transfer.

Mist concentrate spraying has reduced the need for water considerably.

STATIONARY SPRAY PLANTS

The stationary spray system consists of a permanently and approximately centralized pumping and mixing plant and a connected piping system in the orchard through which the spray solution is forced. The pipelines are equipped with hydrants to which the rubber spray-hose lines are attached; a sprayman thus can spray a block of several trees from a single hydrant. Stationary spray systems are used in steep orchards where portable equipment cannot travel. However, there are so few of the stationary systems now in use that the reader is referred to the 1949 edition of this text and to references at the end of this Chapter for such details as layout, plans of buildings, and operation. Growers now are planting orchards on level or rolling land with good air and soil drainage that is better adapted to labor-saving modern machinery,.

such as air-blast sprayers and mechanical pruning and harvesting equipment.

AIRPLANE AND HELICOPTER SPRAYING

Airplane and helicopter spraying of fruit plantings in Canada and the United States generally is drawing increased interest and use. Machines equipped with devices for atomizing liquids have been used for several years on the West Coast for applying concentrated oil base sprays and for application of preharvest stop-drop sprays. They are frequently employed in emergencies at seasons when ground conditions are too wet for operation of ground machines. The atomizing devices are located under each wing. A rolling cloud of atomized liquid is dispersed while the plane flies as close to the crop as possible at a speed of 90 to 115 miles per hour. The chief disadvantage of air spraying is that weather conditions must be more nearly perfect than for ground rigs. Consequently, the spray application may be delayed seriously. Furthermore, airplane spraying is limited to commercial operators, since most farmers do not own and operate their own plane. The helicopter is proving well adapted for the job (Figure 25). Spray droplets produced by airplanes should be relatively large, ranging from 150 to 300 microns in diameter. Very small droplets may evaporate before they reach the desired surface. (Figure 30).

WEED SPRAYERS[1]

Chemical weed control is a well established practice in orchards. Two types of herbicides are generally used, preemergence and postemergence. A preemergence herbicide is applied and controls weeds before they emerge from the ground. A postemergence herbicide is applied to the foliage of plants that are already established. A postemergence herbicide may be selective or non-selective. An example of a selective herbicide is 2,4-D, which kills broadleaf weeds, such as dandelion and dock, while leaving the grasses unharmed. An example of a non-selective herbicide is paraquat. Care must be taken to keep all herbicides off the foliage of tree and fruit. Shift herbicides for difficult-to-control weeds.

The equipment needed for applying herbicides as sprays consists of a pump, a supply tank, and a boom having a series of nozzles which emit either a flat fan-type spray or a cone spray, all mounted on some type of chassis for transportation (Figures 25a and 25b). Synthetic rubber parts must be installed in sprayers using oil.

Tractor tracks or large diameter pneumatic tractor tires may be necessary for the weed sprayer to prevent bogging down during muddy weather in the spring. A track-layer chassis is more satisfactory for tanks containing more than 400 gallons.

---

[1]Dr. W. V. Welker, Rutgers University, advised on weed sprayers and control.

Courtesy (a, c, e, and f) E. W. M. Vorhey, Institute voor Tuinbouwtechniek, Wageningen, The Netherlands; (b) R. Paul Larsen, Michigan State University; and (d, d-l) Rutgers University.

Figure 25a. Equipment for orchard and small fruits weed and ground cover control in the U. S. and Europe. (a) Hoods for herbicide strip-application between strawberry rows; cloth flaps at rear of hoods drop down to confine mist. (b, e, d-l) Boom weed sprayers with pump, motor and tank mounted on tractor rear. Operator can shut off spray between young trees, giving square control area around tree. (d) Young Delicious on EM VII in western Pennsylvania under a comparison of mulching and chemical weed control around trees. (e) Orchard rotary mower with adjustable working width for narrow-row plantings of dwarf trees. (f) Another version of a home-built two-blade rotary mower for dwarf plantings in Holland.

The triplex reciprocating orchard spray pump can be used for weed sprayers. However, a high pressure orchard spray pump is not necessary, inasmuch as only 75 pounds per square inch pressure is needed. Rotary pumps may be satisfactory for nonabrasive materials, but they may wear rapidly if abrasive materials are used. They can be run from the fan belt of automobile trucks or pickup trucks. The tank with boom also may be mounted on the truck.

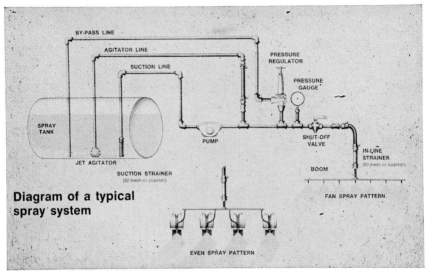

Diagram of a typical spray system

BY-PASS LINE
AGITATOR LINE
SUCTION LINE
PRESSURE REGULATOR
PRESSURE GAUGE
SPRAY TANK
PUMP
SHUT-OFF VALVE
IN-LINE STRAINER
(50 mesh or coarser)
JET AGITATOR
SUCTION STRAINER
(50 mesh or coarser)
BOOM
FAN SPRAY PATTERN
EVEN SPRAY PATTERN

Courtesy Geigy Agricultural Chemicals, Ardsley, N. Y.

Figure 25b. This diagram shows the essential parts of a weed sprayer for row crops and strip-row applications, in case a grower wishes to build his own sprayer. A solenoid shut-off valve, triggered by hand at the tractor seat, can be installed for "spot" application on either side of young trees.

Special acid-resistant centrifugal pumps are available on the market for applying dilute sulfuric acid sprays.[1] Cost of these sprayers may be high due to special construction materials. The ordinary cast iron pumps are satisfactory for noncorrosive liquids. A single-stage centrifugal pump is satisfactory, provided its speed is between 2400 and 3600 r.p.m. in order to develop sufficient pressure. About three-fourths to one gallon of spray material will be required per minute per foot of boom used. The length and design of the boom will need to be governed by the crop sprayed.

The better booms have been constructed of one and one-quarter-inch extra heavy pipe. The pipe should be brass for acid sprays and of black iron for noncorrosive sprays. Booms often consist of three sections: one section extending out from each side of the sprayer and one middle section mounted either in the rear or the front of the machine. The sections which extend to the side of the rig must be supported both vertically and horizontally in order to prevent whipping, and they must be arranged so that they can be folded forward while passing through a gate or a narrow pass. The mounting of the boom should be made adjustable for height.

---

[1]Manufacturers and distributors of sprayers for weed killing include: FMC, Jonesboro, Arkansas; Friend Mfg. Co., Gasport, N. Y.; 14067; Hardie Mfg. Co., 4200 Wessahicken Ave., Philadelphia, Pa., 19144; F. E. Myers & Bros. Co., Asland, Ohio, 44805; Skibbie Mfg. Co., Sodus, Michigan 49126; California Heater Co., 1511 W. Second St., Pomona, Calif., 91766. To construct your own weed sprayer, contact your county extension agent or your local agricultural experiment station (see Fig. 25b).

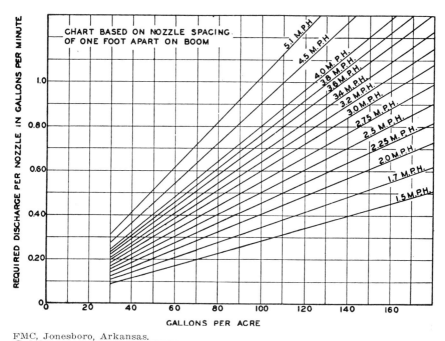

FMC, Jonesboro, Arkansas.

Figure 26. A chart showing required discharge per nozzle in a boom to give quantity per acre at various field speeds. If nozzles are spaced 18 inches apart on the boom, multiply the indicated discharge per nozzle by 1.5; if spacing is 2 feet, multiply by 2.0.

Under trees, it may be necessary to spray within a few inches of the ground.

Nozzles which give a flat fan-shape spray are available on the market. They may be attached to the boom by means of quarter-inch short nipples tapped into the one and one-quarter-inch main pipe. Nozzles that deliver spray at an included angle of 60° should be spaced one foot apart; 80°, 18 inches apart; 90°, two feet apart. The wide spacing of nozzles is more desirable because the cost is then smaller and larger orifices in the disks tend to reduce the danger of clogging. Figure 26 should be of assistance in selection of nozzles for a given boom and of different field speeds for various quantities of spray materials per acre. Figures in this chart are based on a nozzle spacing of one foot. For 18-inch spacing, multiply the discharge per nozzle by 1.5; for two-foot spacing, multiply by 2.0.

It is important to calibrate the boom before taking it into the field. This can be done by placing a trough or small containers under the nozzles and calculating the total discharge per minute. Discharge can be varied somewhat by adjusting the pressure. Nozzle disks of several sizes are available on the market.

For more detailed information on weed control see references at end of Chapter. See also fruit chemical weed control charts on previous pages, this chapter.

Courtesy Solo Industries, Inc., 5100 Chestnut Ave., Newport News, Va., 23605.

Figure 27. This mist blower is used in the U. S. and Europe in the smaller plantings, greenhouses, etc. Several models are available. Specifications for one model are: 5 H.P. engine; fuel, 1 qt/hr; weight, 25 lbs; horizontal spray to 35 ft, vertical to 25 ft; spray tank, 3 gals; fuel tank, 3½ pts. The Junior 410 model is on the left.

DUSTING MACHINERY AND EQUIPMENT

Hand dusters. Hand dusters contain only a small quantity of dust, have a limited and uneven dusting range, and some models are difficult to clean. There are several kinds: (a) shaker, (b) telescope, (c) plunger, and (d) bellows.

In the shaker duster, dusting material is placed in a cheesecloth bag, or gallon tin can with holes punched in the bottom and a wooden handle nailed to one side and shaken above the plants.

The telescope hand duster consists of two cardboard cylinders, one telescoped within the other. One-way poppet air valves control the flow of air and dust as cylinders are pulled apart and pushed together in a pumping action.

The plunger hand duster is operated like a hand bicycle pump. The dust may be located in the plunger cylinder or in a glass or metal container attached to the lower end of the cylinder, or it may be located in a bulge at the end of the plunger cylinder. The plunger is pulled back until it passes an air intake port in the cylinder. As the plunger then is forced down, air is pushed out through a side delivery tube, carrying the dust blend with it.

The bellows duster is useful for the same jobs as the bucket-type and small compressed-air sprayers. The dust is carried by gravity through a hole in the base of a small dust container and as the bellows operates by hand, a current of air is driven through the same passage, picking up the dust and carrying it to the plants.

In Figure 27 is shown a type of mist knapsack applicator used widely.

Ohio State University

Figure 28. The fan-type of knapsack duster, driven by a crank, gives an even and plentiful flow of dust. It is particularly effective in dusting for currant worm, and it can be used for peach, cherry, and other backyard trees.

The larger unit may be tiring for some operators due to weight when filled. The unit can be used for other jobs such as melting snow and frozen water pipes, using special attachments.

Knapsack dusters. More work can be done with a knapsack duster than with a knapsack sprayer in a given time. As compared with the above types of hand dusters, the knapsack duster has more capacity and wider use, but the initial cost is greater.

A knapsack duster is operated from the operator's back by a bellows or by a blower fan (Figure 28). Different types of mouth pieces may be attached to the dusting pipe to obtain different angles and patterns of dust distribution. The bellows and fan dusters are about equal in efficiency, but the bellows type may be somewhat easier to operate. In the fan-type duster, the hand crank drives a blower fan and an agitator.

Power dusters. The power duster is simple as compared with the power sprayer. It consists essentially of a gasoline engine, a hopper for the dusting materials and a fan or blower which forces the material through the discharge pipe and onto the trees. The duster may be mounted on a truck on skids, or PTO on the rear of a tractor.

Auxiliary engines of four to eight or more horsepower are used to

Courtesy FMC, Jonesboro, Arkansas.

Figure 29. (Top) Power take-off Bean-Niagara duster attached to standard wheel tractor. (Bottom) Cut-away illustration of power duster. Agitator stirs the dust in hopper and feeds it through lower right pipe. A 16-inch steel-bladed fan, operating at 3600 rpm, picks up dust and discharges it through pipe at upper right of fan. Operator regulates rate of dust flow by lever at right.

develop strong air blasts, depending upon the size of the machines. The fans are about 12 inches in diameter and consists of six blades, making 3500 or more revolutions per minute. The hopper should hold at least 100 pounds of dust and be air tight. The opening for filling the hopper with dust should be large.

Airplane and helicopter dusting. Airplane dusting has been practiced for many years on citrus and recently there is increasing usage of airplane and helicopter dusting on deciduous trees and other fruit plants (Figures 30 and 31). It is a common sight to see airplane dusting of pesticides on blueberry and cranberry fields. Fertilizers also are spread on cranberries by plane.

Airplane dusting is best adapted to large rather level acreage of a given crop. The field and borders should be free of interfering power lines, buildings, and similar dangerous obstacles. Airplane dusting is largely performed between daybreak and about eight or nine o'clock in the morning when wind velocity is low. Due to poor visibility at daybreak, it is well for the pilot to practice flying over the field during daylight hours the previous day in order to "spot" any obstacles. The airplane must travel about 100 m.p.h. within a few feet of the treetops. Special precautions are necessary to spread dust on the plants at the edge of the field.

The dust hopper may contain from 500 to 2000 pounds of the dust blend, and is located low on the fuselage between the engine and the pilot. The agitator in the hopper is rotated by a separate wind-driven propeller. The agitator pushes the

Michael Szkolnik, New York Agr. Exp. Sta., Geneva.

Figure 30. Airplane spraying and dusting for pests and diseases is on the increase, particularly in fruit regions where land is relatively level and weather is more or less reliably good as in desert areas, although plane and helicopter pest control is now seen frequently in the humid East. Helicopter and biplane spray and dust application can be made when ground travel is too soggy in the spring as frequently happens in the Northeast U. S. and Quebec, Canada. Biplanes are better than monoplanes. Scale should be controlled by ground spraying, or, half the oil can be applied by air, half from the ground.

dust mixture into a small chamber immediately above the delivery slot. The amount of dust coming through the small sliding valve at the delivery slot can be regulated by the pilot. The so-called "venturi" acts as a metal air guide to catch and concentrate a flow of air past the delivery slot. There are several shapes and sizes of venturis which may be classified in either of two groups: (a) The modified-cone type which catches the air current at the large end of the metal cone and increases the air speed past the dust delivery slot, discharging it through the small end of the cone, and (b) the miniature airplane wing type. This wing is mounted on the base of the airplane so that air passes between the plane body and the miniature wing, increasing the speed of the air current, picking up the dust, and discharging it in a cloud behind.

The advantages of airplane dusting, where feasible, are (a) large acreage of fruit crops can be covered with dust in a few hours, (b) no labor and equipment are needed by the orchard owner, eliminating depreciation and cost of upkeep, and (c) the expense is not much greater than ground spraying. Disadvantages are (a) weather conditions may be too hazardous for flying at a time when the dust is needed most on the crop, and (b) a damaged or broken down plane may be in repairs for

Bell Aircraft Corp., Buffalo, N. Y.

Figure 31. Dusting by helicopter has several advantages; it is on the increase. Due to better control it is more widely adopted than the airplane, but initial cost of equipment is greater. (Right) Dusting a low-bush blueberry field.

several days during a critical period. The helicopter is showing some advantages over the airplane, particularly from the standpoint of safety.

Airplane dusting is being used in the New England states to supplement ground applications for scab and when ground is soggy. Control generally has not been as good as ground spraying, but is useful where the grower adopts another block of trees down the road, and cannot afford to buy new and larger equipment at the time.

A point of interest in airplane dusting is the fact that the dust is given an electrical charge on leaving the plane. If the charge is the same as that held by the leaf, the dust is repelled; if the charge is different, they attract each other and the dust will stick. As yet, this charge cannot be controlled in a practical way.

CARE OF MACHINERY AND EQUIPMENT

Frequent and thorough lubrication of all working parts of spray machinery is highly important during the operating season. At the end of each day of use, thoroughly rinse the tank, and pump clean water through the system. Open the nozzles until the water is discharged. Do not drag the hose on the ground except when actually spraying. When going for a refill, either disconnect the hose from the rig or coil it upon hangers at the rear or sides of the machine. Do not permit kinks to form in the hose.

At the end of the spray season, it is highly important to do a thorough job of rinsing the machine with clean water, then drain the pump, the engine, and the tank. In order to prevent rusting of the pump during the winter, pump used lubrication oil through it. Store hose in a cool dark place. Drain it completely and coil it over an elevated barrel or stretch it out on a bench or shelf. Do not suspend it on nails or similar objects which cause it to kink and crack.

The spray machine should be gotten out ahead of time in the spring and gone over completely, thoroughly cleaned, and "tuned up" ready for use. The following suggestions are given by the John Bean Division of Food Machinery and Chemical Corporation for trouble-shooting, adjustment, overhauling, and care of Bean air-blast sprayers. While these suggestions do not apply strictly to all makes of spray equipment, they may act as a guide for care of air-blast sprayers in general.

PROBLEMS, DO'S AND DONT'S[1]

Pressure Losses

1. If no spray solution comes from the nozzles, make certain that:
    a) There is liquid in the tank.
    b) All valves are in their proper positions.
       (The by-pass valve is not open.)
    c) The water level is above the level of the pump.
    d) Air is not trapped in the suction line of the pump.
    e) The packing gland on pump shaft is tight, and that the pump is not drawing air through this gland.
    f) The packing is well lubricated and not dried out.
    g) Drive belts are not slipping.
    h) Cover on suction strainer is sealed.

2. If insufficient spray solution comes from the nozzles, make certain that:
    a) All valves are in proper position.
       (The by-pass valve is closed.)
    b) Nozzles are not clogged.
    c) Main strainer is not clogged.
    d) Pipe and hose lines are not clogged.

3. If the pressure drops rapidly upon opening the valves, its generally an indication that the impeller vanes on the centrifugal pump are plugged. The pump must be disassembled and the impeller cleaned to correct this trouble. Indications similar to this can also be caused from a collapsing suction line between the strainer and pump.

Care of the Sprayer tank. The 500-gallon spray tank if steel, is treated on the interior with a rust inhibitor type finish.

(a) *Flush Daily.* To avoid plugging of the spray nozzles it is important to prevent scale build-up on the inside of tank and piping system.

Immediately after each day of operation, if spray other than oil has been used, run sufficient clean water through to flush the tank, pump, and piping system. After cleaning the tank, flush with straight spray oil.

---

[1] Each spray machine manufacturing company can provide a complete instruction manual for the proper care of the respective equipment owned.

(*b*) *Interior*. At the end of the spraying season the tank interior should be cleaned thoroughly.

When working inside the tank, it is suggested that a sack or mat be used on which to stand to prevent damage to the protective coating.

Use a fiber brush when washing the interior surfaces.

Coat with oil or grease if the sprayer is to be idle more than one week.

(*c*) *Exterior*. Many spray materials are very corrosive and damage paint and metal surfaces. When spraying with other than oil spray, it is suggested that the entire outside of the sprayer be cleaned and coated with oil after each day's spraying. Regular lubricating oil, reduced with kerosene or tractor fuel can easily be sprayed with an air pressure chassis sprayer, or even an insect hand sprayer.

A coating of oil on the sprayer will prevent the corrosive material from adhering to the sprayer, protect it from the corrosive action and also make the entire sprayer easier to clean.

(*d*) *Agitator*. The mechanical agitator provides sufficient mixing for either dilute or concentrate spray materials. Four paddles are employed which are mounted on a 1-3/16" diameter shaft carried in packed and lubricated bearings at each end of the tank.

When mixing extremely heavy solids it may become necessary to advance engine throttle a little to speed agitation; also open the by-pass valve for additional pump agitation.

Tighten the packing nut on the front agitator bearing as necessary to prevent leakage. When the packing nut has been turned all the way in, unscrew and insert an additional packing ring.

If leaking persists, disassemble packing nut agitator shaft, and remove packing. Clean and inspect the shaft and replace if worn sufficiently; replace old packing with new, being sure to stagger ends, and to coat rings with grease when installing.

Drain to prevent freezing. Open all valves in the piping system. In addition, remove plugs (or open petcocks) and drain at the following points:

1. Radiator (at bottom on radiator)
2. Engine Block (both sides)
3. Strainer Assembly (remove cover)
4. Pump and Piping
5. Spray Tank
6. Spray Manifold and Hose Lines
7. Remove the fitting on the line "to Pressure Gauge" to drain the water from the pressure gauge line.

Preparing gas engine for storage. A manual of instructions is available for diesel engines.

The operator will avoid serious repairs and will be money ahead by rust proofing engines that are to stand idle.

Most engines are stored in places where they are subject to temperature changes. As the temperature falls and rises, condensation coats the engine's inner surfaces with moisture. The resulting water plus metal results in rust.

The following materials will be needed:

1) Engine rust preventive oil. Suggested brands are Texas Oil Company (their #651 and 652), Sinclair Refining Company (their #10-Rust-O-Lene), or equivalent.
2) Rust Inhibitor for the cooling system.
3) Masking tape.

The following procedure is recommended:

1) Drain lubricating oil from the engine. Then add 2½ quarts of the rust preventive lubricant.
2) Drain the cooling system. Add good grade "Rust Resistor" and fill with clean water.
3) Run the engine at idle speeds for 3 or 4 minutes. This will do several things:

   (a) The rust resistor in the cooling system will coat the radiator and the inside of the engine.
   (b) The rust proofing oil will be distributed throughout the system and on the cylinder walls. Avoid overheating. (If it is not possible to run the engine on its own power, turn it over with the starter several times.)

4) Remove the top of the carburetor air cleaner elbow. Run the engine at approximately 1000 RPM. Pour about ½ pint of engine rust preventive oil through the carburetor air intake. This should choke the engine. If not, shut off the ignition as soon as the ½ pint has been drawn into the system. Smoke coming from the exhaust will indicate when this has been done. (If it is not possible to run the engine under its own power, pour the ½ pint rust preventive into the carburetor air intake while the engine is being turned over with the starter.)

5) Drain the rust proofing oil from the crankcase. This oil may be re-used until five cycles are completed. Replace the drain plug.

6) Remove the spark plugs. Pour into each cylinder through the spark plug hole, one (1) ounce of engine rust preventive oil (the same as

listed on previous page). Turn the engine over 4 or 5 revolutions with the starter. Replace the spark plugs.

7) Drain the cooling system by opening the radiator drain. *Caution*: Remember to open the drain in the side of the water jacket on the cylinder block (starter side.)

8) Drain the excess gasoline from (1) the carburetor, (2) the fuel pump, and (3) the gasoline tank. Gasoline standing over periods of time tends to "gum".

9) After the above steps have been completed, seal all vents which permit air to enter the idle engine.

   1. Carburetor air intake.
   2. Oil filter pipe.
   3. Oil vent pipe at manifold side of the engine.
   4. Manifold exhaust opening.

   A good seal can be made with masking tape or adhesive.

10) Place a warning tag on the engine to serve as a reminder that the oil and coolant have been drained; and that the engine should be properly serviced before using.

In case of a power duster, drain the engine at the end of the season, clean the hopper thoroughly, and coat all corrosive parts with heavy oil or grease.

Accurate scales and measuring cans should be available. It is a wise investment to have a good stock of repair parts for the engines, pumps and rig frames before the season begins. Although some manufacturers attempt to give air-express service on repair parts from the factory, as much as a day or two may be lost in securing these parts during a critical period. In most fruit growing areas, there are sales outlets of the major spray machine companies; these distributors carry a full stock of parts which can be gotten in hours. However, it is wise for growers to carry a stock of key parts such as agitator paddles, gaskets, connecting rods, spare belts, disks and vortex plates for nozzles, gaskets for nozzles, hose clamps, connections and washers, extra nozzles, spark plugs, stove bolts, suction strainer for hose, valve balls, seats, springs, repair tools and possibly other items suggested by the field representative. If several outfits are working in an orchard, it may be well to have in reserve an extra engine and pump, both in good working condition with all connections. The spray machine parts should be pigeon-holed by classification and those subject to corrosion should be protected by a heavy coating of oil or grease.

APPLICATION OF SPRAYS AND DUSTS

Applying spray. The most important factor in efficient spraying is the sprayman himself. He must start each application on time, finish on

610

time, and use the equipment and methods skillfully so that every tree is sprayed thoroughly inside and out, top to bottom, with finely-broken spray fog or mist applied in such a way as to give safe uniform coverage. There is no substitute for a skillful, alert thorough-working sprayman.

It is relatively easy to do a good spray job on small trees, but as the trees reach 15 feet or higher, the tops and especially the top centers become increasingly difficult to cover thoroughly. Scabby and wormy fruit at the end of the season often tell a bad story of poor spraying in this section of the trees.

Most spraying failures can be attributed to too much speed and "skimpy gallonage". After what appears to be a thorough spray application, the top of the tree often carries one-third less spray material than the bottom. The top third, or "pest nest," must receive special attention during the spraying operation. As shown in Figure 5, apples may double their surface area a week or two soon after fruit set and applications made as close as a week apart may be necessary to build up effective spray barriers where codling moth is a problem. Some varieties increase rapidly in size early in the season, such as Delicious, Rome, and Rhode Island Greening, and they need somewhat more frequent coverage than varieties which tend to grow more slowly at this period, such as Grimes Golden and Winesap.

Timely, speedy applications are needed in early season scab sprays to cover the upper surfaces of the expanding leaves and blossoms. It is especially important to cover all sides of the apples for controlling such pests as codling moth, bitter rot, Brook's fruit spot and blotch.

Large trees with bushy interiors and branches hanging to the ground cannot be covered by any practical method of spraying. It is highly important that the pruning program be co-ordinated with the spray program to lower tops of tall trees, eliminate underhanging branches, and thin out dense areas to permit thorough penetration and application of sprays. This is especially important where large capacity rigs are used, such as the air-blast sprayers, which apply spray while moving continuously.

A good method for the grower to check efficiency in spray coverage is to hang two- to three-inch diameter sponge rubber balls by wire hooks in different parts of typical trees. This method can also be used to check on the efficiency of different types of spray equipment.

Although a better job can be done by spraying with the wind with high-pressure equipment, many difficulties may be encountered when growers insist on spraying only with the wind, because often the orchard is not completely sprayed within the necessary time interval for best control of pests. With large-capacity equipment, it is possible to develop a technique of spraying at an angle into the wind and securing adequate coverage without wasting material. It is highly important that applications be completed on time and that methods be employed to secure prompt complete coverage. The equipment must be adequate to cover the orchard in three days or less, especially for apple scab sprays,

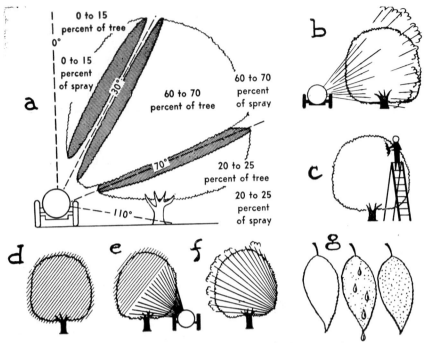

John Bean Div., Food Mchy. & Chem. Corp., Lansing, Mich.

Figure 32. In order to spray a tree effectively the nozzles and nozzle sizes on an air-blast sprayer should be located about as shown at "a" on the upper left; slight variations in this pattern will be needed to conform with individual orchard conditions. At "d" is a tree with the contained air all quiet. At "e" the air sprayer is moving too fast; this is about as far as the mist may carry. At "f", nozzle sizes, distribution of nozzles and sprayer speed are about right for thorough penetration of the entire tree; good penetration is shown at "b" also. At "c" it is well to check a few trees in tops and on all sides to be sure coverage is adequate. At "g" the right leaf is sprayed correctly; the middle leaf is over-sprayed and dripping, wasting material, time and money.

and on some occasions during critical scab development periods, it may be necessary to cover the orchard within 24 hours for best control.

In previous photos in this chapter modern machinery is described which is adapted to hedgerow or "wall" plantings and compact trees, mostly concentrate sprayers.

Suggestions for Speed, air-blast or air-carrier spraying. Since air-carrier spraying essentially uses air to give spray-mist coverage, it is important for air in a tree to be replaced completely with spray-carrying air from the machine. If the sprayer is moved past the tree too fast, the tree will NOT be filled with spray mist; conversely, if the sprayer moves too slowly, the trees are over-soaked, they drip, and expensive material is wasted (Figure 32).

There is an inaccurate belief that injection of more spray material into the air stream will increase the rate of spraying; actually, the standing air in the tree will not be replaced any sooner. The result will be to place more spray material into those areas of the tree already being reached by

612

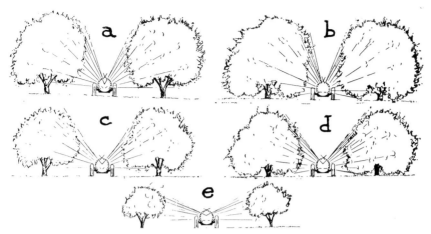

John Bean Div., Lansing, Mich.

Figure 32a. Diagrams show how an air-carrier sprayer is adjusted for different sizes and pruned trees. At "a" with 25-ft. tall high pruned lower limbs, top nozzle petcocks are open, external vanes raised, internal upper deflectors raised, internal lower diverters raised slightly, bottom nozzle petcocks closed (see also Figure 18-c). At "b", for 25-ft. tall trees with unpruned lower branches, top nozzles are open, external vanes raised, internal upper deflectors raised, internal diverters lowered, bottom nozzle petcocks open. At "c" and "d" for 15- to 20-ft. trees, the 4 top petcocks are closed; at "c" the external vanes are partially lowered, internal upper deflectors partially lowered, internal lower diverters raised slightly, and bottom nozzle petcocks closed; while at "d" the external vanes are raised slightly, internal upper deflectors raised about 45°, internal diverters about horizontal, and bottom nozzle petcocks open. At "e" for dwarf, young, or low-growing trees, the top nozzle petcocks are closed, external vanes aimed at tree tops, internal upper deflectors lowered, internal lower diverters about horizontal, with bottom nozzle petcocks closed.

the spray. Failures in pest control with air-blast spraying usually can be traced to traveling too fast while spraying.

The air pattern achieved by a machine forms the spray pattern and determines the sprayer performance. In order to control 30,000 to 60,000 cu. ft. of air per minute at 100 miles per hour, it is essential to gain control of the air while it is still in the machine. Every engineering feat must be employed to guide the air through the sprayer smoothly. Turbulent, uncontrolled air wastes fuel and increases engine wear because the air "fights" to leave the sprayer. Whirling and rolling air currents after leaving the sprayer are without control and may miss parts of the tree; also, such air does not travel as far as straight-flowing air.

For good movement of air through a large air-blast sprayer, the air should enter a more or less bell-shaped opening. The fan then pushes the air in almost a straight line, thus keeping control while it packs and accelerates the air. The U.S. Air Force uses the axial fans and flow principle in its jet engines because it moves the most air for its size.

Any sharp entrance corner in the sprayer is likely to start loss of control of the air, and also reduces the amount of air entering the blower. A centrifugal type fan is not the best type because it whorls the air off the blade tips, starting a boiling action like that in a clothes washing machine.

An air-straightening tunnel is used in some sprayer types (Figure 18)

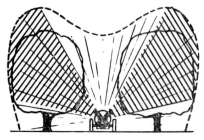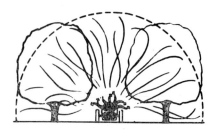

Figure 33. Spray pattern on the left is giving good efficient coverage; note the shoulder areas where volume and velocity are needed. Spray pattern on the right is not fitting the need. Bottom 1/3 of air is poorly directed. Because the shoulder area is not reinforced with air from the lower portion of the sprayer, part of the tree is not sprayed thoroughly, and some parts are over-sprayed.

after the fan to gain control of the air and prevent it from leaping, twirling and fighting itself. As the air is discharged, it is turned by curved metal. Air hurled against a flat surface, sharp corner, or against another air stream before leaving a sprayer is splintered and may go out of control.

The amount of air moved per minute is a useless figure unless its speed is known. If there is no means of measuring the air speed, the width of the air discharge area should indicate it. A large volume of slow-moving air must have a large discharge area. Such a large "river" of air tends to carry far because it holds momentum. It should cause a "leaf-turning" action on the far side of the tree, getting good coverage.

In buying a sprayer, check the size of the discharge opening in relation to the cubic feet of air moved. A narrow discharge area indicates that high air velocities are used to achieve the same cu. ft./min. figure of air moved. A thin stream of air traveling at high speed from a narrow opening will lose momentum rapidly. It loses its speed through turbulence. High air-spray velocity near the discharge also may damage fruit on the outside of trees.

The largest portion of the spray material should reach the "10 o'clock to 2 o'clock" shoulders of the spray pattern (Figures 32 and 33). Up to 70% of the tree's bulk is in these shoulders. With this shape spray pattern, the sprayer does not work as hard in reaching all parts of the tree, thus saving gas, oil, and wear and tear.

Size air-carrier machine needed. First, determine the shortest time likely to be required to cover the orchard thoroughly under the most difficult conditions. Find the size sprayer that will do this job. A small volume sprayer will cover almost any orchard but will take a long time if the trees are big and the orchard large. It is better to make the mistake of buying a machine on the large size for the job at hand, than to buy one too small. The sprayer must be powerful enough to blow through the heaviest foliage on the tallest trees against a strong wind. On such a day, a small sprayer could spray only with the wind and thus take twice as long or longer to cover the trees.

A large sprayer moving fast will save labor and fuel and does not tie up the tractor and refill trucks for long periods. A sprayer with a large tank needs less refilling time.

Adjusting the air-carrier sprayer. The following steps outline methods useful in planning the best use of the air-carrier sprayer. It is suggested that new owners of air-blast sprayers fill the tank with water, if practical, and go into the orchard for practice spraying. This will enable the operator to note: (a) type of coverage obtained with the nozzles used, (b) the time required to empty the tank, and (c) the number of trees covered in a definite period of time.

Coverage should not be checked until both sides of the tree have been sprayed. When using only water, coverage should be checked just after a turn where the trees have been sprayed completely, and before evaporation has taken effect.

One-side delivery and two-side delivery of spray material from the sprayer are discussed separately in most of the steps below.

First Step: Determine Ground Speed

1. Test run the sprayer to find ground speed at which spray is blown completely through tree under the most adverse wind condition that is expected.

2. If tractor speed is not known or cannot be guessed accurately the following formula will help.

$$\frac{S \times N}{88} = MPH$$

Where: MPH = Miles per hour
S = Tree spacing in feet
N = No. of trees passed in one minute

Example: If trees are on 22 ft. centers and tractor passes 8 trees in one minute, then:

$$\frac{22 \times 8}{88} = 2 \text{ miles per hour}$$

Second Step: Determine Acres Sprayed Per Hour

One Side Delivery:

$$\frac{6 \times MPH \times S}{100} = APH$$

Two Side Delivery:

$$\frac{12 \times MPH \times S}{100} = APH$$

Where: APH   Acres sprayed per hour
MPH   Tractor speed in miles per hour
S   Tree spacing in feet

Example: If tractor speed is 2 MPH, and tree spacing is 22 ft., then:
(One
Side) $\dfrac{6 \times 2 \times 22}{100} = 2.64$ acres per hour

Example: If tractor speed is 2 MPH, and tree spacing is 22 ft., then:

(Two Sides) $$\frac{12 \times 2 \times 22}{100} = 5.28 \text{ acres per hour}$$

NOTE: Step 2 is not needed in steps 3 and 4, but is very important in planning the time needed for completeing a spray application. It is therefore valuable in finding the size of sprayer which will be needed for a certain acreage. Remember, this is time required for actual driving and makes no allowance for filling time.

Third Step: Determine Gallons Per Minute of Spray Material When Gallons Per Acre Is Known:

One Side Delivery: $$\frac{\text{GPA} \times \text{MPH} \times \text{S}}{1000} = \text{GPM}$$

Two Side Delivery: $$\frac{2 \times \text{GPA} \times \text{MPH} \times \text{S}}{1000} = \text{GPM}$$

Where:
GPA = Gallons per acre of spray material to be applied
MPH = Tractor speed in miles per hour
S = Tree spacing in feet
GPM = Gallons per minute of spray material

Example: If you want to apply 500 gallons per acre, and the tractor speed is 2 MPH and the tree spacing is 22 ft., then:

(One Side) $$\frac{500 \times 2 \times 22}{1000} = 22 \text{ GPM}$$

Example: If you want to apply 500 gallons per acre, and the tractor speed is 2 MPH and the tree spacing is 22 ft., then:

(Two Sides) $$\frac{2 \times 500 \times 2 \times 22}{1000} = 44 \text{ GPM}$$

When Gallons Per Tree Is Known:

One Side Delivery: $$\frac{44 \times \text{GPT} \times \text{MPH}}{\text{S}} = \text{GPM}$$

Two Side Delivery: $$\frac{88 \times \text{GPT} \times \text{MPH}}{\text{S}} = \text{GPM}$$

Where:
GPT = Gallons per tree of spray material to be applied
MPH = Tractor speed in miles per hour
S = Tree spacing in feet
GPM = Gallons per minute of spray material

Example: If you want to apply 5.5 gallons per tree, and the tractor speed is 2 MPH and the tree spacing is 22 ft., then:

(One Side) $$\frac{44 \times 5.5 \times 2}{22} = 22 \text{ GPM}$$

Example: If you want to apply 5.5 gallons per tree, and the tractor speed is 2 MPH and the tree spacing is 22 ft., then:

(Two Sides) $\dfrac{88 \times 5.5 \times 2}{22} = 44$ GPM

Fourth Step: Determine Arrangement of Nozzles on Machine. See diagram in Figure 32.

1. The GPM is now known for nozzling each side of machine.
2. Place the proper number of gallons per minute in each sector of the spray head. These sectors will usually include more than one nozzle.
3. Divide the GPM of each sector by the number of nozzles in the sector to find out how big a nozzle disc or cap is needed. Now the total discharge of these discs or caps will add up to the total gallons per minute from this sector.
4. Refer to your service manual for disc or nozzle cap size corresponding to desired GPM from each. Remember that some nozzles may be plugged entirely or shut off by convenient valves.

LOW-VOLUME CONCENTRATE SPRAYING

Interest in the low-volume method of applying insecticides, fungicides, and other spray materials has increased markedly with dwarf fruit trees. Experimental work has shown that with this method many orchard pests can be controlled with savings in time, labor, and materials which will vary with the individual orchard. To insure success, as with any new technique, it must be approached with a full understanding of its possibilities and limitations. It has *not* been proved beyond a doubt that pest control equal to that of dilute spraying will be obtained under all circumstances, according to A. A. LaPlante of Cornell University. Present information indicates that a conservative approach is the best key to the successful use of the method. The experience of a number of growers during the past few years has shown clearly that careful and intelligent use of many of the available low-volume machines has resulted in excellent pest control. The converse also has been true, as there have been miserable failures.

James Marshall of the Canadian Experimental Station at Summerland, B. C. has stated that, "In the 67-year history of the British Columbia tree fruit industry it is doubtful whether any production method has contributed so much to the welfare of the fruit grower as concentrate spraying." He states further that the cost of pest control was reduced to about half and the job greatly simplified with this technique (Figure 34).

Much of the experimental as well as the commercial work has been on apples. Enough work has been conducted, however, with peaches, pears, cherries and similar tree fruits to indicate that they, too, can be treated successfully by this method. Aside from the initial cost saving on the ma-

James Marshall, Summerland, B. C.; (middle left) E. W. M. Vorhey, Wageningen, The Netherlands.

Figure 34. In the Okanagan Valley of British Columbia the orchardists are demanding relatively lightweight inexpensive but efficient mist sprayers that are easily maneuvered through their low acreage mostly hilly orchards, where formerly stationary spray equipment was used. (Upper left) McIntosh sprayed with 50% DDT wettable powder at 6 lbs. in 65 gals. of water. Left apple, DDT-surfactant (spreader) mixture; right apple, DDT alone. (Upper right) Very small power take-off rig, 100 Imp. gal. steel tank, spraying 2 acres at a filling, and costing $1000 less than a turbo-mist sprayer with an auxiliary engine. (Mid photos) Left machine is a low-volume PTO mist blower; sprays two sides; of European design (The Fruit Machinery Co., Mercersburg, Pa., dealer). Right machine is a 50-gpm Victair low-volume sprayer, PTO, 2-sides (or all nozzles adjustable to one-side spray), 150 mph air velocity, steel tank, diaphram pump 100-400 psi, 4A filling, squirrel cage blower, made in British Columbia. (Lower photo) Left machine is a one-side concentrate sprayer applying 50 gals. per acre. Right photo shows a spray-frame used in assessing orchard sprayers to eliminate inefficient types. Targets are distributed on the rack; dyed water is sprayed at them under different wind and weather conditions.

TABLE 17.
Number of Trees Passed at Different Driving Speeds

MPH	Feet per minute	Different spacings (feet)						
		20	25	30	33	35	40	45
		Number of trees passed per minute						
1	88	4.4	3.5	2.9	2.7	2.5	2.2	2.0
1½	132	6.6	5.3	4.4	4.0	3.8	3.3	2.9
2	176	8.8	7.0	5.9	5.3	5.0	4.4	3.9
2½	220	11.0	8.8	7.3	6.7	6.3	5.5	4.9
3	264	13.2	10.6	8.8	8.0	7.5	6.6	5.9

zles, special metering devices or shearing nozzles to break up sprays. operating costs low but high HP tractors needed, appear to be satisfactory for mite and insect control. 3. Be sure pump has adequate pressure, adequate air volume, coverage, fits your needs, compatible with tractor HP, gearing, proper type and arrangement nozzles to give good deposit, distribution, has proper tank, fittings to handle concentrates.

Ultra-high concentrates. ULV has potential for covering tremendous acreages with few gallons of pesticide with smaller less elaborate equipment. Lack of available chemicals, however, leaves this equipment impractical for the present.

Converting high-volume machines to concentrates. (a) Machine must be in good mechanical shape; (b) adequate screening devices; good screening is essential in concentrate spraying; (c) sludge, rust or corrosion needs to be sandblasted and refinished; (d) pump must produce pressure of at least 80 to 100 psi; (e) the machine needs an air volume of at least 15,000 to 20,000 cubic feet per minute. A greater volume of air may be needed to obtain adequate coverage on large trees or for locations having continual windy conditions; (g) the machine must produce air velocity of between 110 and 130 miles per hour; (h) the machine needs to be fitted easily with 6 to 10 equally spaced hollow-cone disc type nozzles. The equipment supply dealer and the sprayer manual can aid in making the above decisions and adjustments.

General information. Most of the materials now available to use as mist concentrates are in the form of wettable powders or pastes. These materials are more or less abrasive when used at 6 to 8 times the usual concentration and may cause serious wearing to the pumps, pressure regulators, and nozzles. Thus the pumps should be of a type that will handle such materials without undue wear and the worn parts should be replaced with the least expenditure of time and money. The abrasive action of these materials is less at lower pressure.

The efficient application of concentrates demands a careful regulation of the rate of delivery. When the orifice in a liquid nozzle becomes worn, the rate of discharge at a given pressure increases and in some cases the spray pattern changes. When the orifice is worn too much, the distribution of the spray or the droplet size may no longer be entirely satisfactory where the spray pattern has changed.

Conditions that affect the rate of application are the gallons of liquid discharge per minute and the speed of travel through the orchard. The means of controlling the rate of delivery vary with the type of nozzle used. A grower should fully understand how to control the rate of delivery on the machine with which he is working and should know what his machine is delivering before attempting to spray with it.

Low-volume spraying is effective against such pests as apple scab, coddling moth, plum curculio and red-banded leaf roller, but where complete coverage is needed control is more difficult with mites, aphids, scales, mildew, peach diseases and the like.

High concentrate spraying (above 10x has some drawbacks and limitations as well as assets: 1) High concentrate application (over 5X) must be applied with extreme accuracy and under ideal conditions. This means that a well-trained, conscientious operator is a MUST. A hesitation in forward travel can mean burned or damaged fruit. The higher the concentration the less tolerance of human, mechanical, and natural errors. 2) As stated earlier, the rate of travel must be held to an absolute minimum to permit thorough coverage. The slower rate of travel decreases the detrimental effect of any wind condition, but increases the time spent per application. 3) High concentrate applications are more readily affected by humidity conditions. If distribution is to remain the same for concentrate as for dilute, the number of droplets must be increased as the volume applied is reduced. Thus, smaller droplets are mandatory for high concentrate spraying. The smaller droplets are more susceptible to evaporation than larger droplets. 4) Coverage in tree tops is marginal under the best conditions. Coverage of this area becomes even more difficult with smaller droplets. The smaller the droplets, the higher the velocity required to obtain impingement (adhering the droplets to the foliage or fruit). Since air velocities in the tree top are usually in the order of 12 to 17 miles per hour, there is a practical minimum to droplet diameter where impingement can be obtained. Thus, the small droplets tend to drift around the foliage in the slowly moving air, possibly repelled by the static charge of the tree, and may be picked up by rising air currents and carried out of the orchard and 5) High concentrations result in an almost invisible spray pattern with some chemicals. Growers trying it for the first time may feel as though they are shooting in the dark because they cannot see the coverage.

Rate of Travel. Judgement in speed of driving often determines whether a grower succeeds or fails in concentrate spraying. A proper speed can

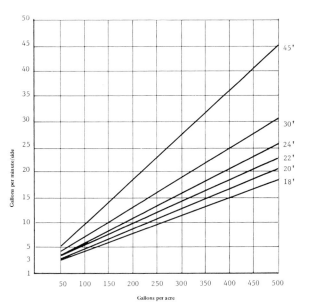

Figure 36. Orchard sprayer calibration chart showing gallons per minute discharge necessary from each side of sprayer at 2 mph for 50 to 500 gpa at each of 6 different row spacings.

be chosen only by observing coverage in all parts of the tree (Figure 32).

In the application before bloom and at petal fall, with the larger machines it may be possible to get coverage at 3 miles per hour on trees of small or moderate size. With somewhat smaller machines or with very large trees, a speed of 2 miles per hour may be suitable. Under most conditions where foliage is fully developed, the rate of travel should not exceed 2 miles per hour. Any machine when operated at too great a speed eventually loses penetration through shearing of the air stream. Under good conditions the spray pattern should pass about ¾ way through the tree, and the tractor speed adjusted accordingly. Depending upon the sprayer size and the type crop, this speed with present-day concentrate sprayers may vary between 2-7 mph.

For machines with manually operated outlets where the distribution of the material within the tree depends on the operator, care should be taken that several times more material be directed at the tops of the trees than at the lower portion (Figure 32). It is necessary to proceed slowly to accomplish this objective.

Few if any of the machines that have been or are now being sold are equipped with speedometers. Some manufacturers realize the necessity of this device and are planning to make available special speedometers suited to their particular piece of equipment.

Speedometers are available that are adaptable to most machines. They employ a small wheel that can be placed on any smooth tire. Growers who lack a speedometer will have to check their speed by counting the number of trees sprayed, and comparing it with the number of gallons of material used.

625

TABLE 18.

	Dilute materials		Concentrate material		
Concentration of materials (times)	IX	2X	4X	6X	8X
Rates of application	1	½	1/5	⅛	1/10
Gallons per tree	5	2½	1	⅝	½
	10	5	2	1¼	1
	15	7½	3	1-⅞	1½
	20	10	4	2½	2
	25	12½	5	3-⅛	2½

Rate of Application. In several experiments where the same amount of toxicant was applied per tree, the mist-concentrate method using from 4 to 8 times concentrations laid down from 20 to 25 per cent more deposit than did the hydraulic sprayer using the dilute material. This increase in deposit can be attributed to the fact that the mist-concentrate application has no run-off while with the hydraulic sprayer there was some run-off. Thus for an equivalent deposit, the mist-concentrate method, when 4 or more times concentration is used, requires only from 75 to 80 per cent as much material as the dilute spray. On the other hand, because there is no run-off from trees treated with concentrates, the materials applied in this manner tend to deposit in direct proportion to the rate at which they are applied. Thus 2 gallons of a given concentration lays down approximately twice the deposit laid down by 1 gallon of the same material applied to the same tree. This means that the rate at which a concentrate is applied is extremely important. If too much is applied, some material will have been wasted, and with certain materials, foliage or fruit injury may result. On the other hand, if too little is applied, insect or disease control may not be adequate. This differs entirely from the dilute spray method where trees are sprayed to the point of dripping to assure adequate coverage and where run-off tends to prevent the laying down of excessive deposits.

The number of gallons of dilute spray that would normally be applied to a tree is the best basis on which to calculate the rate to apply a mist of any desired concentration. If 2 times concentration is used, one-half the number of gallons, or slightly less, should be applied per tree. If 4, 6, or 8 times concentrations are used, their respective rates of application should be 1/5, 1/8, or 1/10 the gallons usually applied as a dilute spray.

The above Table 18 gives the approximate gallons of concentrate to use for several concentrations on trees of various sizes.

Any sprayer outlet that cannot be pointed toward the tree as one approaches and leaves, wastes material if there is space between trees in the row yet not enough to permit shutting off the spray. Therefore, in some circumstances, it may be necessary to discharge as much toxicant per tree in concentrate spraying as in spraying with hand-operated guns or brooms.

Spray Concentrations. Mist-concentrate formulations have used from 2 to 16 times the concentrations in the high-pressure sprayers. Up to 8 or more times concentration has been used efficiently on fruit trees with those machines designed primarily for mist applications. Machines of the Speed Sprayer type that have been designed primarily for dilute spraying have been most widely tested at 2 to 4 times concentrations under northeast U. S. conditions. Virginia specialists suggest 4x to 5x concentration to start for a grower, then use gradually higher concentrations with experience.

When concentrations higher than 8 times have been used, it has not always been possible to get adequate distribution and deposit within the trees with the small volume of liquid applied and with the equipment now available. Evaporation during hot, low humidity days, sometimes prevents adequate deposit of sprays even at 6 or 8 times concentration. Night spraying alleviates this difficulty. See Figure 35 for very high concentrate rig now being used successfully in some deciduous orchards.

Materials. The materials available for mist-concentrate application to fruit trees are the same as those used in the hydraulic high-pressure sprayers. Although there have been some indications that special formulations may be desirable in the future, experimental work has shown that the standard preparations can be used satisfactorily except as indicated in the following paragraphs. Since materials are changing constantly, it is well to keep in close contact with the local spray specialist as to what can and cannot be used.

DNC materials such as Elgetol are satisfactory for aphid control but mite eggs may not be completely reached in rough bark. *Superior oil* (70 seconds) must be thoroughly emulsified so as not leave free oil droplets and the spray machine must be able to handle the concentrate, (ask the dealer). Careful application is needed to kill mite eggs. *Wettable powders* are safe and effective. Sticker-spreader may be added to get good coverage; amount depends on water hardness. *Copper* materials can be concentrated but some mechanical difficulties may be encountered. *Glyoxaldine* fungicides may foam but otherwise are satisfactory. *Nicotine sulfate* and TEPP must be handled very carefully to avoid toxicity through the skin of the operator who must stay out of the drift; otherwise are satisfactory.

Parathion and like materials will mist and float and are very hazardous to man; their use as concentrates is questionable for this reason. Lime-sulfur, Phygon, and DNBP are dangerous to the tree as concentrates. Too little experience is available with urea, magnesium, boron and other nutritional sprays as concentrates to give their use an unqualified recommendation; proceed with caution and trial. *Fruit thinning and "stop-drop" sprays should be applied dilute.*

Some chemicals are not registered for low volume or concentrate applications. Check the product label or your local governmental agricultural agency.

Timing sprays. The timing of concentrate applications is the same as the timing of dilute sprays except that there is still greater advantage in spraying during calm weather. Concentrate spraying is especially efficient for in-the-rain applications of such protectants as the sulfurs during the early part of any scab infection rain.

General suggestions. Mist concentrates should be applied to both sides of the row to be effective. Spraying with the wind from one side only has the same limitations as in dilute spraying. Wind-borne drift does not give adequate coverage. Good results, however, sometimes have been obtained by spraying from one side for control of apple scab in the spring.

Under good weather conditions it may be possible to spray alternate rows one time, then the next application start the next row over and spray alternate rows, cutting the travel in half each application.

Just as with the hydraulic sprayer, concentrates can be most effectively applied when there is no wind, but winds from 4 to 8 miles an hour can be combated if the machine has enough air blast. The design and location of the air outlet also affects the ability to combat a wind. Concentrates tend to deposit slightly better when the humidity is high and when there are no thermal currents to distort the spray pattern. Against scab, spraying in the rain with concentrates is effective and *may give a longer period of protection than dusts or dilute sprays applied at the same time.* For best results, the concentration of mists applied in the rain should be increased from 25 to 50 per cent without reduction in gallonage.

For some fruit growers, the use of mist concentrates in their orchards is an entirely new experience. It offers possible savings in time, labor, and materials, but must be handled properly if a good job is to be done. Therefore, it is advisable to take some of the time that is saved to make sure that the equipment is working properly and that the cover is satisfactory.

The air-blown mist concentrates are practically invisible in the air so that it is essential that frequent checks be made on the number of gallons applied per tree. Mist concentrates can do an excellent job of insect and disease control. They are, however, similar to dilute sprays in one respect. They give satisfactory results only when the right amount of material is applied to the right place at the right time.

TABLE 19. SPRAYING COSTS IN DOLLARS PER ACRE OF POME FRUIT IN SOME ONTARIO ORCHARDS, 1969. (W. H. A. WILDE, UNIV. OF GUELPH, ONTARIO, CANADA).

Factors	Low Volume Spraying	Medium Volume Spraying	High Volume Spraying	Average
Number of Growers	8	8	14	
Fixed Costs Sprayer	8.85	11.89	7.46	9.01
(Depreciation, Tractor	4.54	3.48	2.84	3.46
Interest, Total Insurance)	13.38	15.37	10.30	12.47
Maintenance Costs (Sprayer & Tractor)	1.82	4.96	4.01	3.67
Labour Costs	5.10	6.80	6.87	6.38
Cost of Materials (Fungicides & Insecticides)	51.84	69.11	58.13	59.38
Total Cost	72.15	96.24	79.32	81.92

Costs of Conventional and Concentrate Spraying. The cost of any type of orchard spraying is influenced by a number of factors such as length of rows, capacity of sprayer tanks, and rate of travel in spraying, according to Purdue specialists. Costs are also influenced by the use of one or two gunmen on the conventional sprayer and the possible use of a supplementary tank wagon to carry water and chemicals to the sprayers in the orchard. The actual field data given in Table 19 are based on records taken in the Horticultural Farm plots, Purdue University, Lafayette, Indiana, where conventional spraying was done with a tractor driver and one gunman.

Whether the amount of spray chemicals per tree or per acre can be reduced safely below what previously has been considered to be necessary, depends upon several factors such as disease and insect carry over, size of trees, pruning, and how evenly the particular applicator distributes the spray throughout the entire tree. In the work, the control of apple scab was the major problem and for this reason it was decided that the amount of fungicide should not be reduced until the danger of primary scab infection was practically over. However, the 12-gallon per tree base used throughout several seasons actually resulted in a saving of approximately 20 per cent in spray chemicals, after the first cover spray. On the other hand it might not be possible to obtain satisfactory codling moth control where insecticides are reduced below recommended rates in orchards or areas where this insect is a serious problem.

The fact that concentrate spraying makes it possible to cover a much larger acreage per day is one of the most important points in favor of this

	3x (2 men)		33x (one man)	
	per hr.	per yr.	Per hour	per year
Depreciation	$3.00	$1200	$2.75	$1100
Maintenance	2.00	800	1.00	400
Fuel (gas, diesel)	1.00		0.30	
Labor	3.30		2.00	
Total cost	9.30	$2000	$6.05	$1500
Acreage covered:				
Apple	5.8		4.75	
Peach	5.0		6.00	

method of disease and insect control. The rate of travel and concentrations naturally have a direct relationship to the acres that can be covered in a day. Beginning with the first cover spray, a reduction in rate of travel may be necessary, and this must be determined in each individual orchard and according to the type of concentrate applicator used. The top rate of travel in the Lafayette work was 3 mph. for the large air volume concentrate sprayers. The records in Table 19 do not include cost of spray chemicals. However, when the 12-gallon base is used throughout the season, there is a saving of approximately 20 per cent in materials beginning with the second cover spray.

John Linde, Jr., grower, Orefield, Pennsylvania, over several years compared spray application with a Speedsprayer at 3x and a high concentrate sprayer (EconOMist) at 33x (Fig. 35; Hart-Carter). With 90 acres of apples and 68 of peaches, his data were as follows in the mid 1960's:

Costs/A/application for apples were $1.60 for 3x and $1.28 for 33x; for peaches costs were $1.86 and $1.01, respectively. Total savings in a year for the 33x over the 3x on both apples and peaches was $2,759.00 for 158 acres.

Control of current pests was satisfactory on apple trees no higher than 18 ft. or farther apart than 35 ft. Wind was not a problem on peaches but could be on larger apple trees. Operators on 33x machines must be well protected from drift.

Low-volume spraying is popular on dwarf trees, bush fruits and grapes. Also, less fruit russetting occurs with mist spraying due to quick drying.

Night spraying. As a result of high winds and occasional high temperatures, it is often difficult or impossible to apply all the spray during the day. In order to finish the spray job on time, it may be necessary during such periods to spray at night after the wind has died down and conditions are generally more favorable. However, if high humidities should occur during the night and the spray is not drying before morning, severe burning or russeting of the foliage or fruit may occur. It is necessary, therefore, for the operator to check carefully to be sure that the spray is drying at night in a moderate length of time.

Custom spraying. In some fruit regions, it is not uncommon to find many small orchards or vineyards, each of which hardly justifies good power spraying equipment. As a result, pest control with too-small or poorly maintained pumps is unsatisfactory. A truck-mounted or tractor-pulled sprayer owned by a custom sprayman can service many such orchards or vineyards, and in most cases the results are a definite improvement in market quality of the fruit. Custom spraymen know how to spray properly and are familiar with materials which should be used and when they should be applied. The best results are usually obtained where the operator supplies the materials and charges the owner on a gallon basis for the material applied with a flat rate as the minimum charge. Custom spraymen will find that spray rigs equipped to cover potatoes and vegetables as well as tree fruits are operated more profitably than those equipped to spray only trees. By such an arrangement, the sprayman is able to operate his outfit over a longer season. Charge for this service varies considerably in different communities and from year to year. Cost per tree is less, however, where there are over 25 or more trees than where there are only one or two to be sprayed.

Applying dusts. The best time for dusting is when the air is still at the beginning and end of the day. Under these conditions, there is little waste of material and the dust hangs in a cloud or dry fog about the trees for a considerable period (Figure 29). The presence of dew on the leaf surfaces early in the morning and late in the evening, helps the dust to stick better than at periods during midday. Sulfur dusts will adhere to the foliage even though it is dry. Many of the dusts contain adhesive materials.

The dusting machine may move constantly over the ground, going fast for small trees and slower for large trees. A puff of dust is usually sufficient for small trees; the feed lever is opened and closed quickly as the discharge pipe passes the tree. For large trees, the discharge pipe must be moved sufficiently to cover the entire top, including the projecting exterior tips. The trees are dusted[1] by giving an upward and downward sweep of the discharge pipe, using a horizontal stroke across the top and another across the bottom as the machine is leaving the tree. This gives an even coverage with a minimum of material. For very high trees, it may be necessary to use an extension pipe and give the pipe a sudden upward fling at the top of the stroke. The entire operation is a matter of seconds and, therefore, the operator must be agile to do a good job and conserve materials.

Peach trees or other trees of similar size and openness can be dusted from one side only when air conditions are good. However, it is a good

---

[1]This refers to the 4-inch hand manipulated pipe in use before the type shown in Figure 29, and still in use in some areas.

TABLE 20

QUANTITY OF DUST TO USE PER PLANT AT EACH APPLICATION
(Adapted from Beach and Childers)

Crop[1]	Age of Trees in Years				
	1 to 5	5 to 10	10 to 15	15 to 20	20 and over
	Ounces	*Ounces*	*Ounces*	*Pounds*	*Pounds*
Apples	2	4.8	16	1½-3	3-4
Cherries	2	4	8-12	1	1-1½
Peaches	2	4.8	8	½	½
Pears	2	4.8	8-12	1	1
Plums and Prunes	2	4	8-12	1	1

[1]Amount of dust required for currants, gooseberries, and grapes is about 2 ounces per plant.

idea to make successive applications from alternate sides; for example, dusting the east side during one application and dusting the west during the next. Large trees should be dusted from both sides during each application. Thus, about half of the quota is applied to one side and half to the other side.

Careful adjustment of the speed control lever is important in order to get a good coverage but still not waste material. The amount of material applied per tree can be checked by dividing the number of trees covered by the poundage of material placed in the hopper for a given application. The quantity of dust ordinarily required for different fruit plants by age is given in Table 20.

Growers may do considerable dusting at night using lights maintained by a special generator. Air conditions are good at night and the job can be hastened by almost continuous operation of the machine.

Dusting versus spraying. Spraying is considered the standard practice in most fruit regions. Dusting frequently will suffice as a control program for apples and pears when the orchard is coming into bearing, but in mature orchards, dusting is limited chiefly to supplementary applications for scab control when it is not feasible to use sprayers. Growers who own dusting machines in addition to sprayers use the sprayer during the dormant and early foliage sprays, then employ the duster during summer applications, or hold it as an insurance and safety factor against an emergency need. In large orchards, dusting as supplementary to spraying or between sprays is considered a sound practice where the length of time to complete a spray is too long to give adequate control. However, if the apple or pear planting is not big enough to justify ownership of both a sprayer and a duster, a grower should place dependence on spraying.

The dusting of peaches, plums and sweet cherries for control of brown rot has produced good results and is recommended in most states when timed properly. Here again, however, the enterprise must be large enough to justify the ownership of both a duster and a sprayer. A duster cannot be used effectively for dormant control of insects and diseases of stone fruits.

CONTROL MEASURES OTHER THAN SPRAYING AND DUSTING

Natural control measures. A common and important means by which insects and diseases are controlled are natural factors which operate without the assistance of man. These include inherent resistance of the species, or immunity; environmental conditions, as unfavorable temperatures, moisture and light; and the natural plant and animal enemies of horticultural pests, included under the subject, "Biological Control." As indicated earlier, the releasing of male sterilized codling moths, e.g., and the use of synthetic sex attractants to reduce populations may be practical in the future.

Different varieties of the same fruit exhibit different degrees or resistance toward insect and disease pests. The exact cause or causes of resistance and immunities are not known but certainly some of them are hereditary. Different degrees of resistance will be exhibited by the same kind of plant at different seasons of the year, and by different parts of the same plants in different stages of growth and development of the plant or plant parts. Natural factors which may contribute to the immunity of a plant to attacks by plant and animal pests are thickness of the cuticle and cell wall, the size and abundance of stomata and lenticels, the presence or abundance of hairs and other physical structures on the plant, and numerous other factors may contribute to resistance. Growth and germination of fungi may be inhibited on some plants because of their chemical composition. Likewise, such a plant may be repellent or even toxic to insect pests and be a barrier to the development of bacterial and virus diseases. It is generally true that a moderately vigorous plant is more resistant to insect and disease attacks than a weak one. The most progress in developing resistance in plants to animal and plant pests is through crossbreeding and selection of mutations.

Sooner or later, almost all insects and diseases have natural enemies which prey upon them so that a natural system of checks and balances exist. Shortly after cottony-cushion scale was introduced into the United States, it became a serious pest in orchards until its natural enemy, the lady bird beetle, was introduced, after which the scale pest was reduced to one of minor importance in fruit orchards. Entomologists are on continual look-out for predatory insects which can be propagated and disseminated for the purpose of reducing major insect pests of fruit crops. The pomologist, as well as the entomologist, encourage the perpetuation and multiplication of birds, fungi, bacteria, and insects that aid in keeping the plant and animal pests of fruit plants under control. Researchers also are attempting to find pesticides that control the major pests but cause little or no harm to their predators, thus reducing need for expensive materials and cutting spray costs. Ryania is one such pesticide.

Artificial control measures. There are several physical means of controlling insect pests and diseases, namely, (a) destroying or burning the diseased plant or portion of a plant, (b) mechanical guards, (c) soil cultivation, (d) sanitation, (e) crop rotation, (f) official nursery inspection of propagation material, (g) sterilization of pruning tools and the pruning wounds where disease portions have been removed, and (h) the releasing of males sterilized by radio-active cobalt to cut certain insect populations.

Many pests of orchard crops overwinter in plant refuse, such as dropped leaves and fruits, weeds and other plants about the trees and along fence rows. These harboring areas should be cleaned up and burned each dormant season, which also lessens the danger of mice and rabbits. Disposal of cull fruits by burying or similar means is highly important in controlling insects and diseases. Also, sanitation around the packing shed is important to prevent spring emergence of codling moths harbored over winter in old boxes, crates, and packing rooms. Old boxes should be placed in a tightly closed room and fumigated to kill adhering cocoons. Some insects and diseases, such as the Oriental fruit moth of peaches, the grape berry moth and brown rot of stone fruits, are partly controlled by spring disking. Wire guards around the base of trunks of trees are helpful in reducing mouse and rabbit injury.

About the only effective control available for some pests and diseases is roguing and destroying affected plants. Examples are cedar rust of apples, crown gall of nursery stock and mosaic diseases of brambles and peaches. The cedar tree, the so-called alternate host, is rogued.

Official nursery inspection service is highly effective in reducing the dissemination of diseases and insects from nurseries.

Applying pesticides by Over-Tree Irrigation Equipment

The obvious advantages of applying pesticides through over-tree sprinklers include—less expense in spray equipment and operation of equipment, enables more precise timing of pesticide applications, less soil compaction from heavy equipment travel, and less bruising of fruit by equipment traveling through the orchard. In addition, the spray operator is not exposed to toxic pesticides during the application. But more information is needed on the deposit and residual life of pesticides in over-tree applications. Approach is under test in Washington State.

Defruiting Trees in Dooryards. Two lbs Sevin/100 gals, or fraction thereof as needed, applied at blossom petal fall should remove most of the undesired fruit. Sevin aggrevates red mite damage in dry hot season.

Review Questions

1. List the 3 types of insects (based on mouth parts), with examples, as found in fruit plantings.
2. What groups of diseases, with examples, are found in orchards and small fruit plantings?
3. Give the types of insecticides used for controlling the insects listed under question 1, with specific examples.
4. Explain "Insect Pheromones".
5. What is the purpose of dinitro compounds when mixed with petroleum oil for dormant spraying?
6. What apple varieties are particularly susceptible to scab, to spray injury, and to adverse weather injury?
7. Why do wettable sulfurs cause little or no burning of apple foliage as compared with liquid-lime sulfur?
8. What is meant by a 1-6-100 Bordeaux mixture?
9. What are the purposes of the pressure regulator and describe briefly how it works?
10. Give the parts of a disk nozzle and state briefly the purpose of each.
11. What effect does varying the depth of the eddy-chamber have on the type of spray cone?
12. What effect does an increase in pump pressure have on size of spray droplets and angle of spray cone?
13. What type of spray tank and agitator require the least power for an equal amount of agitation? Give advantages and any disadvantages of the types of agitators available.
14. How do you account for the popularity of the air-blast orchard sprayer?
15. Describe the air-blast sprayers and their principles of operation.
16. What type concentrate sprayers are on your market today? Advantages, disadvantages of each.
17. What is the quickest method for refilling a portable orchard sprayer? Why have stationary spray systems more or less disappeared?
18. What is the trend in PTO concentrate sprayers? Advantages, disadvantages.
19. Under what conditions is the purchase of a power duster advisable in deciduous fruit growing?
20. Give pertinent recommendations for effective spraying of mature apple trees with a modern air-blast sprayer.
21. How much dust is necessary to cover an acre of mature peach trees? How much spray? What factors govern the amount of each needed?
22. Describe how the spray service of the state agricultural extension service may operate to assist the fruit grower in using the correct materials at the critical time.
23. Describe techniques for night spraying and when is such spraying advisable?
24. From cost figures from your local supply house, calculate the cost of materials for a season of spraying a 100-acre peach or apple orchard, following the spray schedule of your local extension service, or the schedule cited in this chapter. Calculate also the man-labor costs, gasoline, grease, oil, depreciation on equipment and other costs if such data are available to you. (Your local air-blast orchard sprayer representative can give you basic data, or consult with a local commercial grower.)
25. Under what conditions do copper and sulfur cause foliage injury?
26. What is meant by a cover spray?
27. Discuss methods other than spraying and dusting that are effective in reducing insect populations.
28. Discuss low and high concentrate spraying, advantages and disadvantages.
29. Discuss advantages and disadvantages of aerial spraying and dusting.

Suggested Collateral Readings [1]

GENERAL

Anderson, H. W. Diseases of fruit crops. McGraw-Hill Book Co., Inc., New York City. 501 pp. 1956.

Asquith, Dean and F. H. Lewis. Mite control by helicopter in Pennsylvania. Pa. Fruit News, 4 p. March 1965.

Avery, D. J., and J. B. Briggs. Damage to leaves caused by fruit tree red spider mite. J. Hort. Sci. 43:463-473. 1968.

Backyard Fruits—Disease and Insect Control. Write your state experiment station. Following stations are known to have recent editions: Ohio, New York, Michigan, Missouri, and Indiana.

[1]Catalogs and operation manuals from spray equipment companies are valuable for study and comparison of the various types of equipment on the market. Companies include: FMC, Jonesboro, Arkansas; Marwald, Ltd., Ayer Rd., Harvard, Mass.; Dobbins Manufacturing Co., North St. Paul, Minn.; Friend Manufacturing Co., Gasport, N. Y.; Hardie Manufacturing Co., 4200 Wissachickon Ave., Phila., Pa.; H. D. Hudson Manufacturing Co., Chicago, Ill.; Messinger Manufacturing Co., Tatamy, Pa.; The F. E. Myers and Bros. Co., Ashland, Ohio; Root Manufacturing Co., Cleveland, Ohio; Tecnoma, P.O.B. 195, 51-Epernay-France; KWH Whirlwind Holland NV. Wadenoyen-Netherlands P.O.B. 47. See also the July issues of the American Fruit Grower Magazine, Willoughby, Ohio, for up-to-date indexes of spray and dust materials and machinery manufacturers.

Barnes, M. M., and H. F. Madsen. Insect and mite pests of apple in California. Calif. Ext. Cir. 502, 31 pp. Request latest edition.

Bell Aircraft Corp. The utility helicopter. Request descriptive literature. Bell Air craft Corp., Buffalo 5, N. Y.

Boulanger, L. W. The effect of E. red mite feeding injury on certain metabolic activities of Red Delicious apple leaves. Me. Agr. Exp. Sta. Bull. 570. 34 pp. 1958.

Chapman, P. J. Petroleum oils for the control of orchard pests. N. Y. Agr. Exp. Sta. Bull. 814. 22 pp. 1967.

Child, R. D. Bullfinch damage to pear buds. Long Ash. Hort. Res. Sta., England. Report 110. 1967.

Curtis, O. F. Jr., J. M. Hamilton, E. H. Glass, and M. Szkolnik. What effect are newer spray materials having on apple yield and quality? N. Y. State Hort. Soc. 102: 253-258. 1957.

Cutright, C. R. Rotational use of spray chemicals in insect and mite control. Journ. of Econ. Entom. 52: 3, 432-434. 1959.

Davidson, J. B. and C. H. Van Vlack. Ponds for farm water supply. Iowa Agr. Exp. Sta. Bull. P. 17 58 pp. 1940.

Donoho, C. W. et al. Cicada and soil pH effects on apple-tree decline. HortScience II: 4. 149-150. 1967.

Fisher, W. B., A. H. Lange and J. McCoskill. Growers need identification. Handbook Univ. of Calif., Berkeley (up-dated regularly). 1971.

Fridlund, P. R. Temperature effects on virus symptoms in *Prunus Malus,* and *Pyrus* cultivars. Wash. Agr. Exp. Sta. Bull. 726. p. 1-6. Sept. 1970.

Fruit Diseases. Following agricultural experiment stations have good general bulletins or specific circulars by disease or by fruit crop. New York (Cornell), Michigan, Ohio, California and Illinois.

Gardner, V. R., R. H. Pettit, C. W. Bennett, and W. C. Dutton. Diagnosing orchard ills. Mich. Agr. Exp. Sta. Spec. Bull. 164. 70 pp. 1924.

Garman, P., L. G. Kierstead, W. T. Mathis. Quality of apples as affected by sprays. Conn. Agr. Exp. Sta. Bull. 576. 46 pp. 1953.

Groves, A. B. Weather injuries to fruits and fruit trees. Va. Poly. Inst. Bull. 390. 39 pp. 1946.

Gunkel, W. W. Durabilty tests of some agricultural sprayer pumps. Cornell Univ. Agr. Exp. Sta. Bull. 915. 23 pp. 1955.

Gunkel, W. W. The effect of droplet size on spray deposit. Presented at No. Alt. Sec., Amer. Soc. Agr. Eng., Newark, Dela. August 27-29. 1957.

Heald, F. D. Introduction to Plant Pathology, McGraw-Hill Book Co., Inc. New York City and London. 603 pp. 1943.

Health Hazards. Wash. Agr. Ext. Ser. EM-3300. 11 pp. Mar. 1971.

Hickey, K. D., et al. Apple diseases and their control in Virginia. Virginia Ext. Pub. 374. 20 pp. May 1970.

Hildebrand, E. M. Perennial peach canker and the canker complex in New York, with methods of control. Cornell Univ. Agr. Exp. Sta. Mem. 276. 61 pp. 1947.

Hough. W. S., A. B. Groves, and C. H. Hill. Effects of some spray mixtures on toxicity of DDT, parathion, and malathion. Va. Agr. Exp. Sta. Tech. Bull. 143. 26 pp. 1959.

Kasting, R. and J. C. Woodward. Persistence and toxicity of parathion when applied to the soil. Sci. Agr. 31: 133-138. 1951.

Knipling, E. F. Guide for insectide use to control insects affecting crops, livestock and household. USDA Agr. Handbook 290, 200 pp. 1965.

Lagerstedt, H. B. Tree trunk spray boom. HortSci. 6(5). 1971.

Manis, H. C. Sterile male coddling moth release program (Idaho). East Fruit Grower Mag. June 1968.

Marshall, J. and A. D. McMechan and K. Williams. Low-volume air-blast spraying in British Columbia. Can. Dept. Agr. Publ. 111191, 18 pp. 1963.

Marshall, J. Nozzle abrasion in orchard spray applicators. Sci. Agr. 31: 470-474. 1951.

Massee, A. M. Problems arising from the use of insecticides: effect on balance of animal populations. Rept. E. Malling Res. Sta. for 1964 (1965)). p. 137-140.

Metcalf, C. L. and W. P. Flint, Distructive and useful insects—their habits and control. McGraw-Hill Book Co., Inc., New York City. Fourth edition. 1962. Request latest edition.

Michelbacher, A. E., et al. Ridding the garden of common pests. Calif. Ext. Cir. 479, 47 pp. 1957.

Newcomer, E. J. Insect pests of deciduous fruits in the west (U. S.) USDA Agr. Handbook 306, 57 pp. 1966.

Oberly, G. H. et al N. Y. tree fruit recommendations. N. Y. Agr. Ext. Serv., Ithaca, N. Y. Request latest (annual) edition.

Parker, K. G., E. G. Fisher, and W. D. Mills. Fire blight on pome fruits and control. Cornell Univ. Agr. Ext. Serv.Bull. 966. 23 pp. 1956.

Payne, J. A., et al. Aerial photography with infra red film to locate pecan pests and diseases. Pecan Quarterly. Nov. 1971.

Pollutant impact on horticulture and man. HortSci. 5(4):235-254. 1970.

Powell, D., B. Janson and E. G. Sharvelle. Diseases of apples and pears in the midwest. North Central Reg. Publ. 16. Ill. Ext. Serv. Cir. 909, 26 pp. April 1965.

Principles of Plant and animal pest control. Div. of Bio & Agr. Nat. Res. Council. 6 vols. 2101 Constitution Ave., Washington, D. C. 20418. 1971.

Rasmussen, E. J., W. Toenjes, and F. C. Strong. Effect of spray treatment on foliage injury, pest control, and yield and quality of apples. Mich. Agr. Exp. Sta. Spec. Bull. 347. 26 pp. 1948.

Robinson, D. E. and W. J. Lord. Response of "McIntosh" apple trees to soil incorporated Simazine. J. ASHS 95 (2):195-198. 1970.

Sirois, et al. Fungicide effects on photosynthesis of entire apple tree. Me. Agr. Exp. Sta. Bull. 629, 18 pp. Dec. 1964.

Spray schedules for fruit. All state experiment stations will provide local published recommendations on request. Among the more complete and detail recommendations are those of *Michigan, Ohio, California, Washington, New York, Virginia* and *Illinois.*

Stier, E. F. et al. Flavor of fresh, canned and frozen foods as influenced by herbicides, fertilizers, fungicides and insecticides. N. J. Agr. Evp. Sta. Bull 808, 34 pp. 1964.

Verloop, N. A. The mist blower-origin, uses of low-volume mist blower. Contact Marwald, Ltd., Ayer Rd., Harvard, Mass.

Walter, T. E. Russeting and cracking in apples: a review of world literature. Rep. E. Malling Res. Sta. for 1966 (83-95 pp). 1967.

WEED CONTROL

Herbicide Handbook, J. Weed Sci. Soc. of Amer. "Monthly," Dept. of Agronomy, Univ. of Illinois, Urbana. 61801.

Putnam, A. R. Chemical Weed Control for horticultural crops. Mich. Agr. Ext. Bull. 433. 1971.

Skroch, Walter A. Effects of five herbicides on young apple and peach trees. HortSci. 5(1):41. Feb. 1970.

Weed Control. Vol. II. Principles of plant and animal pest control. Publ. 1957, 472 p. Nat. Acad. of Sci., Wash., D. C. 1968.

Weed Control Manual and Herbicide Guide, Meister Publ. Co., Willoughby, Ohio. 44094. Annual.

(See additional references under Chapter XVIII Appendix)

CHAPTER XIX

Frost and Drouth Control

❖ ❖ ❖ ❖ ❖ ❖ ❖ ❖ ❖ ❖ ❖ ❖ ❖ ❖ ❖ ❖ ❖ ❖ ❖ ❖ ❖ ❖ ❖ ❖ ❖

To make a comfortable living, a grower must try every way possible to insure a full fruit crop every year. Periodic frost (freeze) and/or drouth damage in fruit growing regions have been something with which many growers in the past have been willing to take a gamble. The money loss, however, can be heavy when a frost or drouth does occur and when the grower is not prepared for them. Today, most growers are taking steps to minimize as much as possible the money loss from these acts of nature.

This chapter reviews frost and irrigation problems in the business of fruit growing and their suggested solution. Elsewhere in the book (see the index) you will find brief discussions pertinent to the crops in question. Sources of information also are listed at the end of the chapter for a more thorough study of a specific problem.

FROST CONTROL[1]

Frost control is becoming more involved due to air pollution ordinances, increased labor costs, high-density orchard management practices and new techniques in frost prevention.

Factors Influencing Frost (Freeze) Damage. A *radiation frost* occurs on cloudless relatively quiet nights. Ground heat radiates to the sky; air near the soil level is cooled and the heavy cold air will drift to low spots in the orchard. At a peak, heat loss from the ground on cold clear nights may reach 900,000 BTU/A/hr. About sundown, input of heat is

---

[1]Much of this information is from Extension Bulletin 634 by J. K. Ballard (Yakima) and E. L. Proebsting, Jr. (Prosser), Washington State University, to whom appreciation is expressed for use of the material and the photographs and diagrams. California Bull. 723, "Effectiveness of orchard heaters" by R. A. Kepner, Univ. of Calif., Davis, contains helpful information.

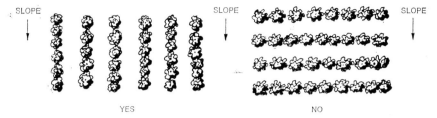

Figure 1. Hedgerow planted trees should run downward on a slope for best air drainage. This can be done without a soil erosion problem by using strip-chemical-weed control in the rows and permanent sod between rows. Natural draws should be kept open for air drainage by removing trees and brush.

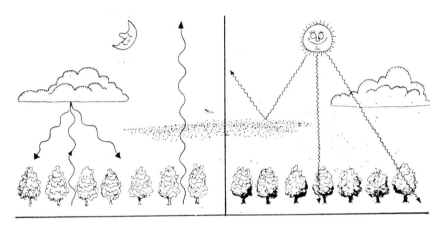

Figure 2. Energy radiated from the ground at night is in the form of long-length waves. Long waves are absorbed and radiated back by natural clouds, but pass right through smoke. Energy radiated from the sun during the day is in the form of short-length waves. Short waves pass through natural clouds, but do not pass through smoke.

equal to output. Humidity and clouds will vary the heat loss from the ground during the night but a peak is reached in heat loss just before sunrise.

The *advective freeze* occurs when an arctic cold mass moves in frequently dry and accompanied by winds. Many nights may have both radiation and invective factors operating. Orchard heating, of course, is made more difficult by cold arctic air which may last for several days when day temperatures seldom exceed 50°F. Most *orchard* heating equipment becomes non-protective with advective freezing.

Inversions, ceilings. An inversion occurs when a layer of warm air floats over cold air near ground level. In daytime the ground absorbs heat from the sun; air near ground level is warm then becomes cooler as you go up. On a cool clear, quiet night, however, some 50-800 ft. above ground the air is warmer than at ground level, hence, an inversion. The magnitude of this inversion varies from night to night, being strong or weak. Effectiveness of overtree wind machines and orchard heaters, of course, varies with the magnitude of the inversion. A *ceiling* is reached when the hot air from orchard heaters reaches the warm air layer above. Following warm days the night ceiling is low and less heater activity is needed. A high ceiling usually follows cold days and more heat is required to do the job. With an influx of cold arctic air and with wind or no wind, the ceiling tends to be very high, complicating orchard frost control.

Wind. Night winds more than 4 mph during an inversion tend to mix the warm and cold air and the temperature drop is slow, or, if the wind is strong the orchard temperature may actually rise. During advective freezes winds have no warming effect due to cold air continually moving in.

Clouds and Smoke. The diagram in Fig. 2 describes how clouds and smoke influence orchard heating.

Dewpoint is the temperature at which moisture begins to condense from the air mass. The more water vapor in the air, the higher the dewpoint temperature. As water vapor condenses and changes back to liquid water it releases latent stored heat. Thus, when the dewpoint is above the critical temperature (freezing of tissue) of the crop, the fruit grower benefits by a slower temperature drop due to latent heat being released from water vapor as it condenses to dew or frost. If the dewpoint is several degrees below the critical temperature of the crop, the temperature drop is faster. Orchard dewpoints in arid regions that are higher than 30°F are considered high; less than 20°F are low. Dewpoints below 0°F are rare. Dewpoints in the lower ranges indicate dry air and difficult heating conditions. Thus, the temperature drops fast at the lower dewpoints, making it difficult to light up heaters fast enough. Temperature may drop as much as 10°F in 15 minutes.

Weather Monitoring Equipment, Frost Alarms. The temperature-sensitive unit should be located in a low area of the fruit planting with the buzzer in the grower's home. A good system is a mercury sensor with a permanent pre-determined temperature switch. As the mercury column drops below the set temperature electrical current is broken and the buzzer sounds. This safeguards against broken lines in the orchard; hence, if a line is accidentally broken in some manner, the buzzer sounds. Alarms in the early 1970's cost from $40-$150. A standby battery that automatically cuts in is suggested in case the electrical power source is interrupted. Thermostat units in the orchard should be in a *standard thermometer shelter,* protected from dust, sprays, insects, etc., which may interfere with the bimetal points. Just before the frost season, have them checked for accuracy and electrical circuitry. Use two double-check thermometers and place the sensor in an ice-water slush for checking accuracy at 32°F, after stirring.

The *thermometer* recommended is one with a straight-tube alcohol registering minimum with an etched scale on the tube, called a "standard orchard thermometer." At least two thermometers are used, one in the coldest location and another nearby outside the heated area to indicate when

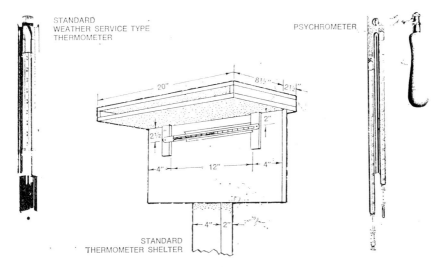

STANDARD
WEATHER SERVICE TYPE
THERMOMETER

PSYCHROMETER

20"

8½"   2½"

2"

2½"

4"   12"   4"

4"   2"

STANDARD
THERMOMETER SHELTER

Figure 3. A standard weather service type thermometer is on the left; a standard thermometer shelter with dimensions for construction is in the center; and a sling psychrometer with wet and dry bulb thermometers for determining dewpoint is at right.

to stop firing. Orchard size and topography govern the numbers of thermometers needed. They *must* be placed in *standard thermometer shelters* (Fig. 3), and after the frost season stored upright with bulb-down in a cool place. National Weather Service stations will test thermometers for accuracy. You should always watch for alcohol separation in the column, shaking the thermometer, bulb down to eliminate the separation, or place the bulb in a pan of water, slowly heating the water until the separations come together, then reduce the water temperature slowly.

Sling psychrometers. Since dewpoints are not stable during the night, some weather stations, on request, will broadcast hourly readings of dewpoints. Where this is not available, a sling psychrometer can be used (Fig. 3), which has two thermometers, the bulb of one having muslin (kept clean and renewed often) over it dipped in water. The thermometers are twirled by holding the handle; the difference between the readings on the wet and dry bulb thermometers (conversion to dewpoint) can be read from a chart that comes with the equipment, or, can be obtained from the Weather Bureau. U.S. Weather Service Bull. 235, obtainable from the U.S. Supt. of Documents, Washington, D.C., has this and other usable information. Dewpoint readings below 32°F are a bit complicated and directions are given.

Heating Fuels and Equipment. Any heating system should have the capacity to lift the temperature at least 7°F; from 20-40 heaters/A will be required, depending upon site. Grower experience on a site determines this. It is a proven fact that many small fires are more effective than a few large ones. High-density hedgerows may require more heaters than

641

standard trees. Heat should be directed horizontally toward the trees; radiant heat from heaters varies from 20-70% of the total heat output. Hence, the upright stack design tends to direct the heat toward the trees.

A listing of the types of orchard *heaters* is given below; see Fig. 4:

Return Stack. This is the best of individual type heaters, burning 0.3-0.6 gal/hr, not exceeding the smoke ordinance, radiant heat is 1/3 the total output, using plastic covers when under-tree sprinklers are used.

Large cone. Advantages are: slightly more radiant heat than the return stack; lower profile making its handling in and out of the orchard easier; resists taking in sprinkling water. It does soot up faster, necessitating cleaning, and burns 0.7 gal of oil/hr.

Short stack. Stacks vary from 6-30 inches high; the 20-inch high ones burn clean at the one-hole setting but vent holes soot up requiring cleaning. The heater has a lower efficiency than those above.

Open oil pots. These are too smoky to meet most local smoke ordinances. They have low initial cost, dependable fuel supply but high labor costs for firing and filling and the radiant fraction is 0.6% of total output.

Pressurized Oil Systems. Diesel fuel oil No. 2 is delivered to jets under high pressure through plastic lines from a central point. Automatic electric ignition saves labor. Advantages are: great operational efficiency, converting 99% of the usable energy; and stack heaters and some oil pots can be converted to the system and meet smoke ordinances. Disadvantages are: fruit loss can occur if pump, filter or motor should fail; a broken buried plastic line under 200 lbs/sq in pressure can discharge enough oil harmful to trees; above ground lines must be gopher proof; a check valve for each heater is needed to prevent after-burn damage to nozzles. An off-season shed storage is needed.

Gas Heaters. Natural gas, if a source is nearby, is the best source of fuel. It requires no tanks, pumps or filters and burns with a minimum of heater maintenance, but meter charge is for 12 months a year.

Liquid propane (L.P.) is used in the Northwest, but it is the most expensive on a heat unit basis and may have problems in delivery and handling. Its increasing popularity among growers, however, indicates distinct advantages over other orchard fuels. One should be acquainted with its characteristics. It turns from a liquid to a gas at -44°F. Rate of vaporization of gas, which passes into the orchard plastic pipe system, depends upon the size of storage tank, outside air temperature, and total demand of the heaters. If the system calls for more vapor than the tank can supply the liquid cools and slows its vaporization. Also, as the L.P. level in the tank drops, vaporization slows (tank must not be filled over 82% of its capacity for safety reasons). Hence, some growers provide extra large tanks (Fig. 5) to circumvent these problems, in addition to having an adequate fuel supply on hand and obtaining it at reduced rates or, special vaporization equipment is used to heat the L.P. either by hot

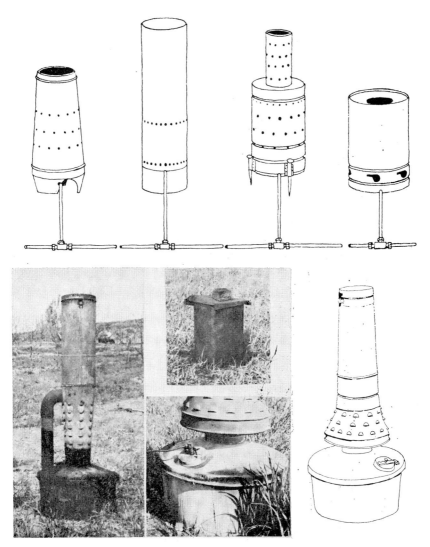

Figure 4. (Top) A row of oil pressure type orchard heater systems that use diesel fuel oil No. 2 through jets. Automatic electric ignition is available. (Lower left) The return-stack oil heater is the queen of all individual type heaters (Middle) The open oil pot (with cover) is initially economical but has many disadvantages. (Lower middle) Return stack oil heater converted to a pressure-line jet system. (Lower right) The large cone heater emits slightly more radiant heat than the return-stack but requires cleaning and burns more oil.

water or indirect fire to increase vaporization. Since L.P. gas is heavier than air, it will flow along the ground from a leak to a low area in the orchard or near the tank and is *highly explosive*.

About 500 gals of L. P. is required/A as a safe minimum for two nights of firing. A 30,000 gal tank has merits for protecting an orchard of 60 acres or more. Combustion chambers are available on the market or the

643

grower can make his own from various pipes, pails, or U.S. Army shell casings.

With L.P. the grower can operate the system on "pilot light" standby in anticipation of a frost, then increase flame as needed. This prevents over-heating and saves fuel in comparison with a system using oil or solid fuel.

Solid Fuels. These include petroleum bricks, paraffin, wood, and compressed sawdust logs. Coal and old tires have not proven satisfactory. A minimum of capital is needed to get involved, but if more than two light-ups per season are required, the economic advantage is lost. There is little or no flexibility in heat output, a longer warm-up period is required, labor is excessive and paraffin "candles" may be difficult to extinguish. Pallet-ized water-proofed petroleum bricks can be distributed in advance and if not used can be re-palletized and stored.

There are situations where use of solid fuels should be considered: (a) relatively frost-free areas where heating is rarely needed; (b) where supplemental heating may be needed on extremely cold nights; and (c) when a grower wants to "hold-off" a year to plan a permanent heating system.

Heating procedures. Light the orchard borders first on the windward or upslope side, then light every other heater or row, and with L.P., light all heaters as a "pilot" standby. Patrol the orchard and be careful not to overheat at first causing a cold-air influx particularly along the borders.

Five problems common to growers in the Northwest and suggested solutions are described below by Alan Jones, National Weather Service, Wenatchee, Washington:

1. The critical temperature is reached. You've made your first lighting of heaters. Occasional light puffs of wind are noticeable and you observe a sudden temperature rise. This may be delayed air drainage. If erratic, it probably won't last, particularly if it is still several hours before sunrise. You may reduce heat, but patrol the thermometers regularly. Winds oc-curing several hours before sunrise can quit again. Your thermometers are your guideline for turning the heat up or down.

2. The critical temperature is reached. The first lighting is made and the temperature suddenly rises. This time you observe a cloud drifting over. Leave your heaters as is, unless a solid cloud bank is moving in.

3. The sun has risen after a long, arduous night of firing. Check your outside thermometer before turning the heaters off. It takes time for the natural temperature rise to take over, particularly if the low level air is smoky. If you have a normal cold air drainage into the orchard, you may observe a sudden drop in temperature after sunrise.

4. The frost alarm rings. You prepare to light but the thermometers all read 3 to 5 degrees above the critical temperature. The sky is clear and winds have subsided. The forecaster predicted a low dewpoint of 15°F.

Figure 5. (Upper left) A row of commercially made liquid propane (L.P.) heaters connected by an above-ground gas line: some gas lines are sunken. (Upper right) heaters are covered with plastic for protection against irrigation spray. (Lower left) A simple home-made L P. heater, using scrap materials and a little ingenuity. (Low center) A 30,000 gal. L.P. oil-pressure storage tank with hot air warmer. (Low right) One of the better orchard heaters available.

with a high ceiling. This means a fast temperature drop. With cold air masses over the district, temperature drops of 9 degrees in 15 minutes have been observed. With an abnormally low dewpoint, you will have trouble holding the temperature above critical. It is better in this case to fire a little early.

5. An advective freeze is upon you. You have done everything right and still the temperature falls. This tells you your heating system is inadequate for future severe situations. For the time being, keep the heat going. You will get some damage but not as much as if you give up and turn the heat off.

Wind Machines. When there is an inversion of warm air above and cold air near the ground, downward tilted wind machines are effective in blowing the warm air among the trees. Actually, wind machines provided with heating devices have proved less effective than those without. Added heat makes the air more bouyant, causing it to rise. If the warm layer is out of reach of the machine, no benefit is gained by turning it on.

A 50 ft. pole with instant reading electronic thermometers at 5, 30, and 50 ft. will help determine whether to use the machine. It is difficult to predict the usefulness of a wind machine. If the site consistently has a 3°F warmer inversion at the 30 to 50 ft layer, a wind machine may be worth trying. Costs have been around $5,000+ each. One machine can handle from 6-10 acres, but this depends on the site, size of machine and nearness to other wind machines. Two machines tend to enhance their single effectiveness. Over 250 machines have been in use in the Yakima Valley alone.

Overtree Sprinkling. This technique of frost protection has been world tested, is convenient, clean, and operational costs are lower than any other method, but there are complications which account for greater risk than heat application.

With continuous water application, the tree tissue temperature remains at or above 31.5°F, even though a layer of ice is forming. If water application stops, the ice and plant tissue become colder than the air because of the cooling effect of evaporating water. Ice is a poor insulator.

Water application must continue until ice begins to thaw (at dawn). The big problem is excessive weight of the ice which may break limbs. Hedgerow dwarf trees, (particularly those on trellis), have the advantage of taking this weight over standard-size trees. An exposed thermometer in the sprinkling area gives a better indication of the plant protection than one outside the area.

The minimum water application rate to carry protection down to 20°F is 0.15 to 0.20 inch/hr, depending upon the average dewpoint and wind speed. Experience has shown that at a low dewpoint with wind, water can be applied at 0.15 inch/hr and protect blossoms to 20°F. This is the minimum at which all economically justified heating systems begin to fail. In the Northwest U.S., such conditions occur only about once in 10 years at around bloom time. The 0.2 inch/hr could be used on the upwind side of the planting where more evaporation cooling occurs. A rate of 0.15 requires 67.3 gal/A/minute or 4,038 gal/A/hr. accumulating 1½ inches in a 10-hr run. Water supply should be adequate for several successive (at least 3) 10-hr night runs. If irrigation water has not been turned into the canals, special wells or holding ponds may be good insurance.

Equipment. An *even* distribution of water over the tree is important. The system must be large enough to sprinkle the entire planting; hence, larger mainlines, pump and motor will be needed vs. use for irrigation block-rotation. Engineering specialists must be consulted. Sprinkler heads must rotate at least once a minute, and two is better. Design of sprinkler heads must not permit ice buildup around the activator spring. Pump must be capable of operating far below freezing. Breakdowns for only a few minutes may result in loss of crop.

Sprinkler Spacing. A 40 x 40 ft. spacing is better than wider spacing. Full protection and overlap must be provided around the borders. In general, the maximum spacing between sprinklers should not exceed 50% of the wetted diameter.

Operation. Start sprinkling when the temperature reaches 33°F on

646

the protected thermometer in the coldest spot of the planting. This is the margin of safety against water freezing in the system. Cease sprinkling when the temperature reaches 33°F after dawn.

Precautions. Central leader trees will support more ice than open-vase ones. Spur, twig, limb breakage and bending of branches is greatest the first season of sprinkling. Roping or some form of branch support may be needed on obviously weak main limbs. Water should be well filtered to be free of sand, silt and debris. Due to a muddy condition in the orchard at frost sprinkling time, it may be well to arrange to apply sprays by plane or helicopter. Also, excessive water application may leach N, B and other key nutrient elements from the rooting area, necessitating additional applications to take care of tree needs.

Artificial Fogs. No satisfactory technique has been devised to provide a fog or cloud blanket above the orchard to arrest outgoing heat radiation to the sky.

Critical Temperature. This is defined as the temperature on a properly exposed orchard thermometer at which the buds, flowers, or fruits will endure 30 minutes or less without injury. Under the tree-fruit discussion in this book, temperatures are given at which a 10 or 90% kill of flower buds may occur at different stages of development. Many factors, however, may alter the ability of flower buds to remain alive at the various stages and temperatures, such as wind, humidity, variety, tree vigor, rate of thawing of tissue that has been frozen, and cool-temperature conditioning of tissue before the freeze, and other factors.

DROUTH — IRRIGATION

Most deciduous fruits are grown between 25° and 55° latitude both north and south of the equator. Annual precipitation (mainly rain and snow) varies from less than 5 in/yr, as in certain regions of North Africa and Southwestern United States, to more than 100 inches. Where precipitation is generally less than 20 in/yr, irrigation is necessary, and in regions of 20 to 30 inches some supplementary water application is needed most years. Where 30 to 50 inches occur, fruit trees usually can survive periodic drouths but growers may lose money once every 4 to 6 years due to small apples, poorer quality, and reduced yields. The trees may be damaged in an extended drouth so that recovery, if at all, is slow and subsequent monetary loss occurs. Hence, today many tree fruit growers, particularly those with the shallow-rooted dwarf trees as well as the berry growers are providing some means of water application to protect the crops. The irrigation equipment, if of the sprinkler type, also can be used for frost control, cooling the plants in hot weather for better fruit quality and for application of pesticides, herbicides (late winter) and fertilizer as is being done in some Northwestern U.S. orchards.

During the winter months when trees are without leaves, they use very little water. Much of the winter precipitation is stored in the soil if it is deep and has a moderate supply of clay particles that retain moisture well. Hence, soil depth, its water holding capacity, and the evaporating power of the air will determine the need for irrigation where the yearly average of precipitation may be more or less adequate but where its distribution is erratic.

Root Distribution, Water Absorption. Roots of decidious fruit and nut trees will be extensive in deep well-drained soil which is free of an impervious layer or a high-water table. Depth of rooting in California may be 16 feet for apricots, 12 feet for walnut and 6 feet for peach and plum. Apple roots have been found 30 to 35 feet deep in the uniform wind-blown loess soil of Nebraska. In New York in a well-drained uniform brown soil, cherry and peach roots will extend to 5 ft, and apple and prune to 6 ft. If there is a mottled grey poorly-drained layer, however, apple, peach or cherry roots will not penetrate it but prune roots have been found to do this which may account for prunes and plums performing better under such conditions where other fruits except possibly pear perform poorly.

Roots have been found to extend laterally 2 to 3 times the branch spread in sandy soil and 1.5 times in loam or clay soils. Where roots are deep and extend well laterally and the soil holds a good supply of winter precipitation, there will be less need for or frequency of irrigation. Where rooting is shallow the tree is likely to become water-deficient, even during short periods of rainfall deficiency. *Hence, it must be emphasized that the need for irrigation and its frequency will be greater for the dwarf high-density trees than for the larger low-density ones.*

The number of the small so-called feeder roots of a tree become fewer with increasing distance from the trunk both vertically and laterally. Maximum density of these roots is in the upper 3 ft. of soil beneath the branch spread and, in fact, 80 to 90% may be found in the upper foot with an established program of mulching.

Water absorption from the soil by roots increases as the leaf surface of the tree increases in spring and most of the water comes from the upper soil layer which is warmer and has greater feeder-root penetration.

If a portion of the root system is in a soil mass at the wilting percentage (% water in a soil when a plant such as sunflower wilts), water uptake by the roots in that area is reduced and under high transpiration (water-vapor loss by leaves) conditions, a water deficit will occur in the tree, depending upon the percentage of the root system involved.

Water status within a tree changes from day to day and hour to hour, while soil water changes slowly. Tree usage of water and transpiration increase with increased air temperature mainly and also with increased air movement and sunlight intensity and lowered relative humidity. A water deficit may occur in a tree when transpiration is quite high, even though soil water is adequate. For example, with adequate soil moisture the water in apple leaves may decrease 6 to 7% from early morning to noon on a warm clear dry day while bark water will decrease 3%. Maximum water deficit in the leaf usually occurs around 2 p.m. on a clear day and the reverse about 2 a.m. Soluble solids are highest at about 3 p.m. and lowest at 6 a.m. Water accumulates in the tree overnight.

Stomatal Activity and Leaf Processes. Stomata are the pores in the epidermis (skin) of a leaf (see cross-leaf diagram, Chap. IV) through which carbon dioxide, oxygen and water vapor pass in the processes of photosynthesis (food manufacture), respiration (energy and heat release) and transpiration (water-vapor loss). Water, and soluble solids content, pH, light and other factors govern the opening and closing of these pores. In peach, prune and apricot, which is typical of most fruit trees, their maximum degree of opening occurs between 9 a.m. and noon after which they begin to close. Stomata are open less wide and a shorter time on trees (a) in a dry soil vs those in a moist soil and (b) on trees during a high temperature and low relative humidity vs those on a cool humid day. When dryness is acute, stomata may not open at all and thus help to conserve water in the tree.

When stomata are less active or closed due to dryness, both photosynthesis and transpiration are reduced as much as 40% before the leaves show wilting, and over 90% at wilting. Food and energy loss by respiration increase during drouth conditions.

In a soil with inadequate water, the bark of a fruit tree may show 10-15% more sugar and 25% less starch than in a tree with adequate water. Effects of auxin sprays such as 2, 4, 5-T may be enhanced by irrigation when needed, resulting, e.g., in larger apricot fruit that mature sooner than fruits not so-treated.

Vegetative Growth and Water. Water deficiency is associated with reduced shoot length and leaf size, particularly with an early season drouth. If, however, there is adequate stored soil moisture early in the season, shoot growth may be equally good in non-irrigated orchards due to shoot growth being completed within about six weeks after growth begins. Trunk diameter of fruit and nut trees, however, likely will be reduced by a mid- or late-summer drouth. In fact, trunk growth measurements with very sensitivie equipment are a more exact indicator of hourly and day and night water fluctuations in a tree than fruit growth measurements.

Observations indicate that roots will not grow into dry soil at the wilting percentage; in fact they grow very slowly in soil just above the WP.

Fruiting. During a dry or moderately dry season researchers agree that the number of fruit buds initiated on apple and pear, e.g., will be increased appreciably, thus giving a good bloom the following spring. The biennial bearing habit on apple, however, can be reduced by regular application of water when needed in adequate but not excessive amounts.

Little or no data are available on the effect of irrigation on fruit set.

Little water is used during winter months; hence, adequate water usually is available shortly after growth starts at fruit setting time. Irrigation the previous season when needed, however, helps to develop strong flower buds that are more likely to set than weak buds that develop during a drouth. It is doubtful under orchard conditions if an early season dry period will affect the usual so-called "June drop" of small fruit one to two months after bloom.

Fruit growth, as measured by its circumference increase has been used as a sensitive and practical measurement of water stress in the tree. The different fruits and nuts may respond differently to water stress, depending upon the time the stress occurs; this is because they have different patterns of growth. If water is ample, the fruit growth rate of apples and pears is almost uniform to maturity. In the lighter sandy soils of California apple and pear growth may be unaffected as long as the soil water is above the wilting percentage. In medium to heavy loams, however, in the New England area of the U.S., the number of 3-inch apples has been shown to decrease when the available soil water drops below 25% of the field capacity of the soil.

Seasonal growth of stone fruits follows a double sigmoid curve (see chart in XIV) when there is little or no fruit swelling during pit hardening, after which growth may be rapid to maturity. Once a fruit falls behind in growth due to drouth, it never will attain the ultimate size of a fruit receiving ample water.

In peach about two-thirds of the final fruit volume is attained the last 30 days on the tree and, hence, ample water supply is critical during this period. In cherry about 80% of the "final swell" occurs during the last 25 days. Plums, prunes, and apricots show similar double-sigmoid growth curves.

With nuts there is no "final swell" period. Ultimate size is reached about mid-summer, when the kernel begins to fill and mature. Full size of almonds is reached in about 50 days after bloom in California. Kernel development occurs mainly during the latter 2 months on the tree. Early soil water stress affects the size of the nut whereas late stress can affect kernel development. This also holds true with pecan and walnut.

Fruit cracking may be due to rapid increase in fruit size, due to rapid absorption of water through the roots or the skin. Cherry cracking is associated with rapid absorption of water through the skin from rain or irrigation. In apple, grape, and pecan, cracking may occur when water is supplied by rain or by irrigation following a rather extended dry period. Irrigated and nonirrigated fig trees may show no difference in cracking.

Plum fruits may show end or side cracking. Cracks on the side of the fruit may develop at the beginning of the "final-swell" regardless of irrigation practices, whereas end cracks may occur any time during fruit development with water application after a dry period, except at the end of the "final-swell" period.

A *preharvest drop* of peaches may occur on trees that have been under water stress and then irrigated near harvest. Apple drop just before harvest and poor fruit coloring are common on trees suffering from drouth, at which time effectiveness of "stop-drop" sprays such as NAA is reduced. Preharvest drop of hazel nuts has been reduced or stopped by regular application of water where needed. Pecan leaves have been noted to drop before the fruit during an extreme drouth.

Yield, Quality. Any tree subjected to WP conditions can be expected to have a reduced *yield* and poorer quality of fruits or nuts. An ample water supply is more important with a heavy crop than a light one. Quality of canned cling peaches may be tough and leathery, and fresh peaches dry and bitter when grown under dry soil conditions. Pears may be hard and green after the ripening period, prunes sunburned, and nut kernels poorly filled during a drouth.

Irrigated apple, peach, and plum fruits tend to be lower in soluble solids (sugar) and higher in water; apples are less firm and acidic but juicier; and apples and peaches may show more storage problems. However, when soil water is maintained above its wilting point, soluble solids are likely to be higher and water less in fruit than when soil water is held at a high level. Over-irrigation can be quite harmful.

Drouth, Defoliation and Winter Injury. Trees under water stress tend to drop their leaves early and if a rain occurs or water is applied late in the season, growth may start, some bloom appear and, hence, the crop reduced the following year.

The dry cold air of winter may dessicate tree tissues resulting in winter injury or freezing if the tree enters dormancy under dry soil conditions. An irrigation in arid country is suggested to alleviate this sitiuation, while under humid conditions an irrigation at ths time was found to enhance winter injury. Trees in soil with about ⅓ available water have shown less frost damage during bloom than trees in soil held at a higher moisture level.

Drouth, Diseases and Insects. Figs and walnut are subject to sunburn under drouth conditions which may invite the branch-wilt fungus. Increasing soil moisture is associated with increased fire blight on pear. The apricot gummosis fungus has shown little relation to level of soil moisture, as some workers had suspected.

Mites will increase rapidly under dry conditions and over-tree irrigation is one way of reducing them. Such irrigation, however, may increase crown rot of apple, scatter the fire blight infection from higher to lower parts of a tree and favor fruit rots and twig infections particularly on stone fruits. Under-tree irrigation will solve some of these problems.

Drouth and Nutrient Supply. Any problems associated with a marginal or deficient supply of a nutrient such as boron usually is aggravated by a drying soil; less water is available as a carrier of the nutrient from the soil particles into the tree roots. Excess irrigation or an over water supply, however, may decrease the percentage of a nutrient in the tree tissue.

When a nutrient such as nitrogen, boron, magnesium or potassium is highly soluble in water, excess rains or irrigation can leach the nutrient downward below the rooting zone and result in a deficiency of the elements in the tree.

After a series of dry years in California, leaf scorch on apricot occurred due to excess absorption of sodium from the soil. It took double the usual water application to leach out the sodium and reduce the injury.

Irrigation water high in boron, bicarbonate and calcium, may result in chlorosis and toxicity to tree. In irrigated orchards, incipient leaf chlorosis (yellowing) sometimes can be reduced by merely reducing the frequency of irrigations.

IRRIGATION METHODS

The main methods of applying water to orchards are (a) basin or flood, (b) furrow, and (c) sprinkler. A fourth method (d) is under wide testing—trickle irrigation, which somewhat resembles the old canvas-ooze or eyelet hose system.

The *basin* or *flood* system is economical and used when the land is fairly level and the flood basins are level and of acceptable area (see photo Chap. XVII). Small dikes are built with special equipment along contour lines and the area within dikes flooded with several acre-inches of water. The soil must be able to hold or store from 4 to 8 acre-inches of water.

In the *furrow type,* the water runs between the trees in furrows spaced usually about 3-4 ft. apart; closer in sandy soils. There must be a gentle slope of the furrows. Tree rows remain dry. If slope is too great, water accumulates at the ends of furrows; if the soil is too sandy or there is too little slope, too much water sinks in near the source and over-irrigates some trees. Hence, even distribution of the water over the entire orchard is the goal and initial engineering assistance is needed.

Sprinkler irrigation has been increasing rapidly over the years with the light-weight, portable aluminum pipe or over- and under-ground (18-24") plastic pipe, and with small sprinkler heads becoming available. Under-tree or over-tree sprinkler application of water has the advantages of (a) more uniform and complete coverage of an orchard block, (b) applicable to rolling land and/or sandy or gravelly soils and (c) is adapted in humid regions having only periodic drouths during a growing season. Portable pipe is usually placed under the trees, with once or twice daily moves to new spots, allowing cultivation, harvesting, etc., in one direction. Permanent over-tree sprinkler equipment (just high enough to clear trees) is in use in the arid Northwest; growers are using it for application of pesticides, frost control, herbicides (dormant season), fertilizers, and for cooling the trees in particularly hot weather. Main disadvantages are (a) higher initial cost, (b) the need for pumping equipment and the over-tree type may increase some disease problems, but, of course, it will reduce mites. Growers in humid areas are studying similar uses under their conditions. Application rates vary from 1/10" to 25/100 inch/hr depending upon crop and soil with pressures of 40 and 70 psi. Nozzle spacings are about 50% of the diameter coverage along the line and about 70% of the coverage diameter between lines.

Several sprinkler manufacturers now supply automatic equipment for the permanent-set system where the controllers automatically turn the sprinklers off and on at predetermined periods, as well as change from a long sprinkling period to a short cooling period which is determined by a pre-set thermostat. The thermostat will turn the sprinklers on for short periods ranging from 2½ minutes to 5 minutes or longer and up to 30 to 60 minutes off in a continuous cycle until the thermostat is "satisfied" at the pre-set thermostat setting. The sprinkling cycle, again then is returned automatically by the controller and proceeds through the cycle to allow the full irrigation. The equipment will, also, turn sprinklers on for frost control by a thermostat pre-set. The thermostat also can automatically turn the sprinklers off at the predetermined setting of the thermostat; however, it is suggested that the system should be turned off after the orchard is inspected to make sure that most of the ice has melted or is melting rapidly. If frost protection is desired, 50 to 60 gallons per minute per acre should be applied continuously during the frost period. The sprinklers should be turned on before the freezing period is reached—generally, to be safe, at temperatures from 34° degrees to 38°F., depending upon the dewpoint. The lower the dewpoint, the earlier the sprinklers should be turned on and left running continuously until the ice is melted or rapidly melting.

Trickle irrigation is relatively recent and shows promises in both arid and humid regions, with some limitations which time and experience will define. "Drip" (Israel) or "Daily Flow" (Australia) are two other names given to the more popular U.S. name, "Trickle Irrigation." This type irrigation refers to the best use of a limited or expensive supply of water to *prevent moisture stress* (rather than correct it) in at least a portion of the root system area. Water is supplied near the tree or plant base through perforated plastic hose lines under about 15 lbs pressure at 1 to 2 gals/hr (gph) to hold the soil at or near its *field capacity* (amount of water it will hold against gravity).

This approach has proven workable since moisture to the top of a plant or tree tends to equalize throughout the plant. Only different organs such as leaves, fruit and growing points respond differently when moisture stress occurs. For example, W. H. Chandler in Missouri back in 1914 showed

Figure 6. Trickle irrigation may be used where water is scarce, costly and salt accumulation at soil surface is not a problem (arid areas). (Upper left) A microtube (0.076 inch dia.). Flow rate is adjusted by tube diameter and length which operates at 5-10 psi. (Right) A "Uniflow" emmitter giving about 1 gal./hr. at 20-30 psi. (Lower) Hydrant water sometimes is used if convenient and inexpensive. Note filters, valve, shutoff, pressure regulator and meter. (Courtesy Roy Rom, Univ. of Ark., Fayetteville).

that the osmotic situation in a leaf had a stronger drawing power for water than in the frut and, hence, during a dry period water was withdrawn from the fruit to the leaves until the fruit shrivelled. About one-fourth of the root system if supplied with adequate water can prevent moisture stress throughout the tree.

An efficient trickle irrigation system should provide equal water delivery from each emitter[1]. Hence, friction loss as water moves down the plastic pipes, amount of head pressure, varied elevations in the planting and any other factor affecting flow of water must be considered in designing the entire system.

In a model system tested in several orchards by A. L. Kenworthy of Michigan State University, he used the Australian system of microtube emitters at the tree because they were easy to install, available and economical. A ¾-in solenoid value and time clock were installed to activate the system for a predetermined time each day. From the valve, a 2-in. black plastic main line, usually buried, was run to about the highest level point in the orchard. A 100-mesh in-line screen and pressure regulator were installed, beyond which the 2 in. line was continued as a header to which the ½ inch above ground plastice in-row lateral lines were attached as indicated in Fig. 6. Ends of the ½ inch lines were closed by folding back and holding them secure with clamps. The microtube outlet inside diameter

---

[1]Contact John Bean Div., FMC Corp., 1305 Co. Cedar St., Lansing, Mi., 48910; Chapin Watermatics, Inc., No. Colo. Ave., Watertown, N. Y. 13601; Drip-Eze, Inc., Box 953, El Cajon, Ca. 92022; Submatic, Inc., Box 246, Lubbock, Tex. 79408. Also see Amer. Fruit Grower Magazine, a recent July issue.

(ID) was 0.036 in. or about the size of a thin-lead mechanical pencil. Length of the microtube was adjusted to get the desired delivery rate at a given pressure. Microtubes were inserted in a hole in the ½ in. line made by (provided) hand equipment and held in place by friction.

Rate of Water Application.   From 1-2% of the orchard floor area is irrigated for newly planted orchards and 10-50% for mature orchards. Hence, conventional means of measuring soil moisture cannot be used as an index of when to irrigate. Experience in Israel and Australia indicate that evaporation rate of water from a free-water surface is the best index. The mid-summer month of July in Michigan showed the greatest 20-yr evaporation average of 0.243 in/day or 6598 gals/A (1 A-inch=27,154 gals). For June it was 6408 and for August, 5620 gal/A/day.

Based on these figures Kenworthy draws the following calculations: (1) Assuming the mature trees occupy 50% of the orchard floor and that we need to replace 75% of the evaporation from a free water surface, the following can be calculated for July:

6598 divided by 2=3299
3299 multiplied by 0.75=2474 gal per day

Thus, in July, the irrigation should supply 2474 gal per day (103 gph or 1.7 gallons per minute (gpm) per acre) with average rainfall.

For convenience, a need for 2400 gal per acre per day or 100 gph per acre can be assumed.   This would require a continuous flow of 1 gph for 100 trees per acre; if 200 trees per acre—0:5 gph per tree.   (3) To allow time for soil moisture equalization or drainage, a program of no more than 12 hr irrigation, rather than continuous flow, would be desirable.   Thus, in a mature orchard with 100 trees per acre, a flow rate of 2 gph per tree for 12 hr daily would be required.

The time interval for irrigation should vary with tree age or size and number of emitters per acre.   Using 100 trees per acre with one emitteer per tree as a base, the time interval for irrigation should be scaled down to perhaps 1 hr daily in newly planted orchards.

This suggests daily irrigation for 1 hr for each year of tree age up to 12 hr. If lesser amounts are required because of above normal rainfall, the calculated amount of irrigation should be in ratio to tree age; 1 for newly planted orchards and 12 for mature orchards.

Acreage and Well Capacity. From the above figures it is evident that a low-capacity well or small reservoir for trickle irrigation will be needed for a given acreage vs. sprinkler, flood, or other irrigating systems. A 10-gpm well should provide 14,400 gal/day. If friction loss in the pipes does not reduce water flow this would irrigate 6.7 acres (14,400÷2400).

A well can be used to full capacity by applying water to a given area on a 12-hr/day basis, then shifting to another block the next day.

Elevation Changes. Water pressure in a line obviously will change with elevation in the orchard. This factor is critical with the low-pressure system in trickle irrigation. Hence, a change of elevation of 2.3 ft will cause a gain or loss in pressure of 1 lb. For example, if the friction loss in a given pipe at a given flow is 1 lb/100 ft of pipe, a 2.3 ft drop in elevation will equalize this loss.

As the rate of flow of water increases through a pipe, there is more turbulence and the friction loss increases with each successive increase in flow. These figures are available in tables in Kenworthy's Michigan Research Report 165, May 1972, or they may be supplied by sales people to assist in laying out a trickle system.

Microtubes per Acre and Tree. In trickle irrigation the rate of movement of water laterally in the soil from an emitter or microtube is important. Particle size in the soil governs this, being slower in coarse (sandy) particle size vs. small size (silt, clay). If free water is present, lateral movement is greater. Hence, water application must exceed penetration. This combined with duration of flow, results in one microtube wetting a relatively large soil mass, or at least 25% of the root system of a tree.

Tests have shown that in most orchard soils a flow of 2 gph water for 6-12 hrs. can wet a soil mass of 12-20 ft. diameter, not wetting the upper 6-12 in so well but mostly at the 12-36 in depth. The wetting pattern in silt loam soils is balloon-shaped with an elongated shape for sandy soils. With a sub-clay layer, the balloon is flattened at the base.

With 100 trees/A, there would be 100 emitters; or with 200 trees, 200 emitters and flow rate would be cut in half.

For dwarf trees, one microtube/2 trees may be adequate. For example, a 10 lb pressure giving a 2 gph flow would require a microtube 11.2 inches long; for a 1.5 gph flow an 18.4-inch microtube is needed; and at 1.0 gph the microtube should be 35.2 inches long.

How Much Water to Apply. Since rate of evaporation varies so much from one area to another, the grower should keep an evaporation record in his own orchard. This helps you to make the most efficient use of water. The following inexpensive technique should help you to make reasonably accurate measurements.

(a) Obtain a rigid plastic or metal container having a minimum diameter of 10 in. and a minimum depth of 12 in. The container should not taper appreciably from top to bottom. (A 30-lb can as used for frozen cherries is close to these dimensions.)

(b) Install the container in the open. Elevate or enclose the container to prevent use by animals.

(c) Fill the container with water to within 2 in. of the top and record the depth with a ruler. (If daily measurements are made, a hole may be drilled 2 in. below the top and used as an overflow.)

(d) Measure the water depth again at a set time each day (or week) and adjust the water level to the original depth.

(e) Calculate *net water loss* on a weekly basis by subtracting inches of rainfall from inches of evaporation. This *net water loss* indicates the amount of water to be applied the following week.

(f) The amount of irrigation for the following week can be calculated as follows.

a) Following the assumed need to replace 75% of the evaporation on 50% of the area, we find that each 1 in. of net water loss requires 10,183 gal of water per acre for the next week of 1,455 gal per acre per day.

Dividing 1,455 by the number of emitters per acre will provide gallons per day per emitter. Dividing gallons per day per emitter by the gph delivery will provide hours of daily irrigation. With 100 microtubes or emitters per acre and delivery at 2 gph this would be:

$$1{,}455 \div 100 = 14.55 \text{ gal per emitter per day}$$
$$14.55 \div 2 = 7.28 \text{ hr irrigation each day}$$

g) If there is no net water loss or if less than 1 hr irrigation each day is required, the irrigation system can be turned off for the week.

Observations from Israel indicate that trickle irrigation permits use of water having a higher salt content than can be used in sprinkler or furrow irrigation. Accumulated salt is leached to the edge of the wetted soil mass and trickle irrigation takes the highest salt concentration away from the tree or plant. Furrow irrigation results in an opposite action.

Few wells and lakes used as a water source for orchard operations have water of high salt content. Also, of the system installed in 1971, only one well resulted in plugging of the 100-mesh screen. On all others no deposit was seen on the 100-mesh screen.

When to Start Irrigation. June, July and August in the northern temperate climate are the high evaporation months, but May and September can be dry months for fruit plants in some years. With adequate winter rains the soil usually is well supplied with moisture in the rooting zone. Start taking water-loss data (described above) as growth begins in spring. When water-loss accumulates to about 3 inches, irrigation can start particularly for sandy soils. A silt loam soil with good depth has greater water-holding capacity and, hence, irrigation may be started at a somewhat later date.

Water Quality and Source. Water from a well, pond, river or other sources may be used, but it should be reasonably free of solid particles that will not plug the system. Water from sources other than a well should be screened by a 100-mesh filter before the pump. Place the suction pipe in a gravel or sand bed, or build a box 3 ft. on a side and cover it with fine nylon cloth to keep out algae, moss, and other particles.

Somewhat higher salt content in the water can be used for trickle irrigation vs. sprinkler, flood or furrow irrigation. Trickle irrigation moves the highest soil salt content away from the tree. Furrow irrigation does the opposite. Few wells and lakes have high salt content. Well water ordinarily does not plug the filter with particles.

Plugged Microtubes or Filters. Some types of emitters under the trees are adjustable and are self-flushing. However, a 100-mesh filter, recommended regardless, will screen particles and prevent plugging. When the pump is shut down, water will drain from the highest level microtubes to the lowest. Hence, soil may be pulled into the tubes; bore a hole through a short stake and insert the microtube through it to keep it off the ground.

Fertilizer Application Through Irrigation. A suitable injection pump which operates on hydraulic pressure or on an electric circuit can be used to inject fertilizer solution into the main line after the water pump. In arid regions this approach of fertilizer supply to plants is essential since rainfall is not adequate to wash soil-surface-applied fertilizer into the rooting zone. The economy of this technique has not been determined for humid areas, but is under study.

Miscellaneous Suggestions. The 80-*lb black plastic pipe* is more than adequate for most trickle systems and does not need to meet drinking-water standards. Do not mix grades of plastic pipe; avoid light-weight thin-walled grades.

Black plastic pipe can be manipulated best when warm; it stiffens and shrinks when cold. Hence, it is wise to slowly flush cold water through the system as the microtubes are cut to proper length and holes in the ½ in. laterals are punched for the microtube insertion. Also, insert the microtubes on the header (water-source) side of the tree so it will not be pulled closer to the trunk if the header line shrinks in cooler weather.

Clamps in initial installations have been provided at all couplings. The friction fit of coupling should hold after it has been subjected to maximum cold contraction. Clamps are desirable on sections of the main line but may not be necessary on the laterals or header.

T-Connectors. T-connectors where the ½ in. line enters the main line may not be necessary. Drill a hole in the header line 1/16 in. smaller than the outside diameter of the lateral (OD 0.742 for ½ in. pipe; or 0.944 for ¾ in. pipe). This friction fit can withstand about 50 lbs pressure. Use a slant cut on the end of the ½ in. lateral for insertion.

Winter Effects. It is doubtful if cold itself will harm the black plastic pipe, but traffic and rodents may harm the small ½ in. laterals.

Planning Installations. The layout for a trickle irrigation installation will vary so much from orchard to orchard that it is difficult to give general cut-and-dried instructions. A system to cover 5 to 10 acres for each pressure regulator and header line is known to be easier to manage, at least based on present experience. This is particularly true if microtubes are used. Where the slopes are appreciable, smaller blocks may be needed.

For a larger acreage, a 3- to 4-in. main line may be used to deliver water to the orchard and a 2-in. header line may be used for each block. Thus, each block to be covered would have a 2-in. header line and pressure regulator. If water is limited for irrigation of the entire block at once, a manual or automatic means will be needed to change water flow from one block to another.

In case the number of rows in each block exceed the capacity of the pressure regular for each header, the main line can be run down the center of the orchard with header lines taken off both sides.

Illustrations of Installation Systems. Many questions will arise when planning an installation. Dr. Kenworthy of Michigan State University has posed several basic problems and solutions. *Questions and answers follow each example based on tables* (1-23) *given in his Mich. Res. Rpt.* 149 (*request recent edition or seek library copy to solve your specific orchard problems.*)

Problem:
The orchard is planted 20 x 25 ft. The well is 1500 ft away and operates at 50 lb pressure. Irrigation is wanted at the rate of 2 gph per tree with 10 lb pressure on the header.

Using a 2-in. main line, 2-in header and ½-in laterals, what is the maximum number of trees that can be irrigated?

Solution:

1) The limiting factors will be friction loss in the main-line, header line and the laterals. Also, the capacity of the pressure regulator will limit irrigation capacity.

2) Table 1 shows that a 2-in. pressure regulator with an initial pressure of 50 lb and a delivery pressure of 10 lb has a capacity of 1848 gph.

3) With a flow rate of 1748 gph through the main line, Table 16 shows a friction loss of 1.3 lb per 100 ft or 19 lb for the 1500 ft.

4) Thus, the pressure at the regulator would be 30 lb rather than 50 lb. This reduces the pressure regulator capacity to 1512 gph (Table 1).

5) Next, the maximum number of trees per row is calculated as shown in the following table. Since friction loss accumulates, calculations start at the far end of the row and proceed back toward the header. On the first line of the table enter the gph for laminar flow in a ½-in pipe (Table 2).

Now calculate gph emitted per 100 ft. Dividing 100 by tree spacing equals trees per 100 ft. Trees per 100 ft multiplied by gph per tree equals gph per 100 ft. (In this illustration $100 \div 5.0 \times 2 = 10$). In column 1, list gph flow in increments of gph per 100 ft (10 in example).

In column 2, list pounds of friction loss (Table 11) for each value in column 1. In column 3, tabulate totals or accumulated friction loss for each increment. The table ends when this equals the delivery pressure at the regulator. In column 4, enter the number of trees each flow increment will irrigate (5 in this example). The total of column 4 equals the maximum number of trees per lateral.

Flow (a) (gph)	Friction Loss—lb	Total Friction Loss—lb	Number of Trees
60			30
70	1.1		5
80	1.5	2.6	5
90	1.8	4.4	5
100	2.2	6.6	5
110	2.6	9.2	5
		Total — 55	

(a) Laminar plus increments in amount used per 100 ft.

6) Thus, with no elevation change, a maximum of 55 trees per row can be irrigated. With a flow of 1512 gph into the header, there is enough water for 756 trees. With 55 trees per row, this would permit covering 13 rows plus 41 trees.

Question 1:

How is the length of microtube determined from the calculations (item 5 of the above solution)?

Answer:

A second table is made to show the pressure at each emitter starting from the header. The values for number of trees (in increments of trees per 100 ft) in column 4 of the first table are reversed and listed in column 1. The tree numbers are shown in column 2. The values for friction loss (column 2 of the first table) are used to reduce pressure from the header. Thus, for trees 1-5, the pressure would reduce 2.6 lb or from 10 to 7.4 lb. This continues for each 100 ft down the row until laminar flow is reached. The calculations are listed in column 3.

Next, the range of pressure drop is proportioned and listed for each tree in column 4. This is done by determining the pressure drop by number of trees ($2.6 \div 5 = .5$) and subtracting the amount (0.5) for each tree. The results are as follows:

No. Trees	Tree No.	Pressure	Proportioned Pressure
5	1-5	10.0-7.4	10.0, 9.5, 9.0, 8.5, 8.0
5	6-10	7.4-5.2	7.5, 7.1, 6.6, 6.1, 5.6
5	11-15	5.2-3.4	5.2, 4.9, 4.5, 4.1, 3.7
5	16-20	3.4-1.9	3.4, 3.1, 2.8, 2.5, 2.2
5	21-25	1.9-0.8	1.9, 1.7, 1.5, 1.3, 1.1
30	26-55	0.8	0.8

Next, using Table 22, a table of microtube lengths is made up as follows:

Tree Numbers	Respective Microtube Lengths
1-5	11.25, 10.61, 9.97, 9.33, 8.70
6-10	8.08, 7.58, 6.97, 6.36, 5.77
11-15	5.29, 4.94, 4.48, 4.02, 3.58
16-20	3.24, 2.92, 2.59, 2.28, 1.96
21-25	1.66, 1.46, 1.26, 1.07, 0.79
26-55	0.75

Since it may be desirable to have the lengths in fractions of inches rather than decimal of inches, the conversion may be made using the following decimal equivalents:

$\frac{1}{8} =$ .125		$\frac{1}{2} =$ .500	
$\frac{1}{4} =$ .250		$\frac{5}{8} =$ .675	
$\frac{3}{8} =$ .375		$\frac{3}{4} =$ .750	
		$\frac{7}{8} =$ .875	

If the microtubes are cut to the nearest $\frac{1}{8}$-in. the following table would be used:

Tree Numbers	Respective Microtube Lengths
1-5	$11\frac{1}{4}$, $10\frac{5}{8}$, 10, $9\frac{3}{8}$, $8\frac{3}{4}$
6-10	8, $7\frac{1}{2}$, 7, $6\frac{3}{8}$, $5\frac{3}{4}$
11-15	$5\frac{1}{4}$, 5, $4\frac{1}{2}$, 4, $3\frac{1}{2}$
16-20	$3\frac{1}{4}$, 3, $2\frac{1}{2}$, $2\frac{1}{4}$, 2
21-25	$1\frac{5}{8}$, $1\frac{1}{2}$, $1\frac{1}{4}$, 1, $\frac{3}{4}$
26-55	$\frac{3}{4}$

Question 2:

How can adjustments be made for changes in elevation?

Answer:

A 2.3 ft change in elevation causes a change in pressure of 1 lb. Thus, if any part of the system is on a grade, pressure will decrease 1 lb for each 2.3 ft of rise and increase 1 lb for each 2.3 ft of fall.

Question 3:

How does this affect the number of trees that may be irrigated with a $\frac{1}{2}$-in. lateral

Answer:

Let us assume a uniform grade of 2.3% (2.3 ft/100 ft). This will cause an increase or decrease of 1 lb pressure per 100 ft. Preparing a table as in step 5 (page 659), we find that:

a) Going up-grade, the gain in pressure must be added to friction loss. This is, the friction loss and the increase in pressure accumulate as follows:

Flow (gph)	Friction Loss—lb	Total Friction Loss—lb	Number of Trees
60		6.0(*)	30
70	2.1	8.1	5
74	0.9	9.0	2
		TOTAL—37	

(*) Since 30 trees are accounted for, the lateral involved would be 600 ft long. This would cause a 6 lb increase in friction loss equivalent. Also, since the lateral is going up-grade, the total friction loss values represent pressure at the beginning of each distance involved. Note that the line was terminated at 9.0 lb. This was done so there would be 1 lb pressure at the end of the lateral. This added to the pressure range values in the following table.

b) The table for pressures proportioned for each emitter would be as follows:

No. Trees	Tree No.	Pressure Range	Proportioned Pressures				
2	1-2	10.0-9.1	10.0,	9.5			
5	3-7	9.1-7.0	9.1,	8.7,	8.3,	7.9,	7.5
30	8-37	7.0-1.0	7.0,	6.8,	6.6,	6.4,	6.2
			9.1,	8.7,	8.3,	7.9,	7.5
			7.0,	6.8,	6.6,	6.4,	6.2

$$6.0, \quad 5.8, \quad 5.6, \quad 5.4, \quad 5.2$$
$$5.0, \quad 4.8, \quad 4.5, \quad 4.4, \quad 4.2$$
$$4.0, \quad 3.8, \quad 3.6, \quad 3.4, \quad 3.2$$
$$3.0, \quad 2.8, \quad 2.6, \quad 2.4, \quad 2.2$$
$$2.0, \quad 1.8, \quad 1.6, \quad 1.4, \quad 1.2$$

c)   Going down-grade, there is a gain in pressure of 1 lb for each 100 ft. That is, friction loss is decreased 1 lb for each 100 ft of lateral.

Flow (gph)	Friction Loss—lb	Total Friction Loss—lb	Number of Trees
60		6.2(*)	30
70	.2	.2	5
80	.5	.7	5
90	.8	1.5	5
100	1.2	2.7	5
110	1.6	4.3	5
120	2.1	6.4	5
130	2.6	9.0	5
132	0.6	9.6	1
		Total—66	

(*) Since 30 trees or 600 ft of lateral is involved there is a gain in pressure of 6 lb. Also since the lateral is going down-grade, the total friction loss values represent pressure at the end of each distance involved (same as on zero grade).

d)   The table for pressure proportioned for each emitter would be as follows:

No. Trees	Tree No.	Pressure Range	Proportioned Pressures				
1	1	10.0-9.6	10.0				
5	2-6	9.6-7.0	9.6,	9.1,	8.6,	8.0,	7.5
5	7-11	7.0-4.9	8.0,	6.6,	6.2,	5.8,	5.2
5	12-16	4.9-3.3	4.9,	4.7,	4.4,	4.0,	3.7
5	17-21	3.3-2.1	3.3,	3.1,	2.8,	2.6,	2.4
5	22-26	2.1-1.3	2.1,	1.9,	1.7,	1.5,	1.4
5	27-31	1.3-0.8	1.3,	1.2,	1.1,	1.0,	0.9
5	32-36	0.8-0.6	0.8,	0.8,	0.7,	0.7,	0.7
30	37-66	0.6-6.6	0.6,	0.8,	1.0,	1.2,	1.4
			1.6,	1.8,	2.0,	2.2,	2.4
			2.6,	2.8,	3.0,	3.2,	3.4
			3.6,	3.8,	4.0,	4.2,	4.4
			4.5,	4.8,	5.0,	5.2,	5.4
			5.6,	5.8,	6.0,	6.2,	6.4

The proportioned pressures show that for trees 30 to 38 the pressure is less than 1 lb. Table 22 shows the microtube length for a minimum of 1 lb is 0.79 in. For trees 30 to 38, the microtube should be equal at 0.75 (¾) in.

Note that the proportioned pressure for the last 30 trees (trees 37-66) was not equal as in item 5 (page 659). It is necessary to proportion the 6.5 lb increase in pressure between the trees.

Question 4:

What would be the effect of going down a greater grade; for example a 4.6% (4.6 ft per 100 ft) grade?

Answer:

The calculations would be made the same way as in the answer to Question 3. However, going down-grade, the gain of 2.0 lb per 100 ft would tend to eliminate friction loss until a flow rate of 94 gph is reached (See Table 11). Table 3 shows a maximum flow of 144 gph through a ½-in. pipe at 10 lb pressure. When this flow rate is reached the total friction loss is only 6.8 lb. Therefore, the length of the lateral is determined by maximum flow rate rather than friction loss. Also, the calculations will show that minimum pressure along the lateral would be 3.2 lb and the pressure at the end of the lateral would be approximately 12.6 lb.

Question 5:

What effect would using ¾-in laterals have?

Answer:

This would increase the number of trees per row and reduce the number of rows. Using Table 12, the trees per row would increase to 92. The number of rows would decrease to 8 plus 20 trees.

Question 6:

What would be the effect of using a ½-in. lateral with 15 lb delivery pressure?

Answer:

This would not increase the flow through the pressure regulator (See Table 1). Therefore, the total number of trees would not change. However, the maximum number of trees per row would increase to 63. Also, microtube lengths would increase.

Question 7:

If my rows were 25 trees long, what effect would this have?

Answer:

If there are 25 trees per row, a total of 50 gph per row would be required. Laminar flow through ½-in. pipe is 60 gph (See Table 2). Therefore, the number of rows can be calculated by dividing 25 into the maximum number of trees (756). Thus 30 rows plus 6 trees could be irrigated. Also, with no elevation changes, the microtube lengths would be equal for all trees (11.2 in. for 10 lb. and 18.0 in. for 15 lb—see Table 19 or 22).

Question 8:

What would be the effect of using 1.0 or 1.5 gph per tree rather than 2.0?

Answer:

Following the procedure outlined in item 5 (page 659), a table could be made up for 1.0 and 1.5 gph per tree using Table 11.

For 10 gph per tree, this would show a maximum of 92 trees per row and 16 rows plus 24 trees.

For 1.5 gph per tree, this would show a maximum of 74 trees per row and 13 rows plus 46 trees.

Thus, the comparison as follows:

gph per Tree	Trees per Row	No. Rows
1.0	93	16 (plus 24 trees)
1.5	74	13 (plus 46 trees)
2.0	55	13 (plus 41 trees)

If each row had only 25 trees, the comparison would be as follows:

gph per Tree	No. Rows
1.0	60 (plus 12 trees)
1.5	40 (plus 18 trees)
2.0	30 (plus 6 trees)

Question 9:

Why not use adjustable emitters rather than calculating microtube lengths?

Answer:

Adjustable emitters are satisfactory. However, each emitter will need calibration by catching the flow and adjusting the setting. This can be done using the following relationships (approximate):

1 ml per sec = 1 gph
1 fluid oz per 28 sec = 1 gph
⅛ cup per 28 = 1 gph
Fluid oz per min

$$\frac{\text{Fluid oz per min}}{2} = \text{gph}$$

Cups per min x 4 = gph

Also, the relative cost of microtubes and adjustable emitters should be considered. Microtubes may cost as little as 1 cent per foot. Adjustable emitters may cost from 15 cents to 1 dollar each. It is not possible to preset adjustable emitters to exact flow rates at varying pressures.

Question 10:

These calculations are rather complicated. Is there a simple ratio between percent grade and microtube lengths that can be used?

Answer:

If we had a 2.3% grade (2.3 ft per 100 ft), pressure would increase 1 lb per 100 ft going down-grade and decrease 1 lb per 100 ft going up-grade.

Following the original requirements of 2 gph per tree and trees 20 ft apart, laminar flow of 60 gph for ½-in. pipe (Table 2) would supply 30 trees and result in 600-ft laterals. With an initial pressure of 10 lb, the terminal pressure would be 4 lb going up-grade and 16 lb going downgrade.

Table 22 shows that microtube length increases 3.9 in. (from 7.35 to 11.25 in.) with a pressure change from 4 to 10 lb. With a pressure change from 10 to 16 lb the microtube length increases 11.25 in. (11.25 to 22.5 in.). These increases of 3.9 and 11.25 in. are required to compensate for a 6 lb change in pressure (from 10 lb) or a 13.8 ft change in elevation. This is an average decrease of 0.53 in. in microtube length for each ft of rise and an average increase of 0.81 in. for each ft of fall.

If the precision of water delivery illustrated previously is not desired, a value of approximately 0.75 (¾) in. change in microtube length for each foot of elevation change could be followed on installations not exceeding laminar flow in the laterals. This would result in unequal water delivery to the trees but, unless excessive, may not be of great consequence.

Question 11:

No reference has been made regarding friction loss in the header line. Should this be considered?

Answer:

Yes, if laminar flow in the header was exceeded. Table 2 shows laminar flow in a 2-in. pipe equals 628.2 gph.

In our example, the pressure regulator limited flow into the header to 1512 gph. Table 16 shows a friction loss of about 1 lb per 100 ft until laminar flow is reached. This may not be sufficient to be concerned about.

One way to reduce friction loss in the header line is to have the main line delivering water at the center of the header or block. Thus, the header line would go in both directions from the main line. Water flow would be cut in half and friction loss in the header would be negligible.

It is possible to use this principle on the laterals. By doing so, the row length could be increased for each installation. The limiting factor, however, would be the amount of water delivered to the header.

THE IRRIGATION PROGRAM[1]

Water Usage. Amount of water needed by trees obviously will vary with their size, density of planting and evaporating power of the air. Large trees require 7 to 9 acre-inches/mo in mid-summer in arid regions. Water need in spring and fall is less. Large trees require about 40 total acre-inches a year under arid conditions.

In warm humid areas about 4- to 5-acre inches in mid-summer are needed for low-density apple trees; peaches need somewhat less. In the cooler climates as in Canada and northern Europe, less water is needed.

Irrigation Timing. Factors governing the timing of irrigations are amount of water available, rooting depth, rate of use by trees, evaporating power of the air, seasonal stage of fruit and tree development, the water quality, and other "interfering" orchard operations.

---

[1]For a complete up-to-date well-written book on irrigation of agricultural crops, purchase a copy or refer to "Irrigation of Agricultural Lands," by a team of experts and published by Amer. Soc. of Agron., Inc., Segoe Rd., Madison Wis., USA 53711. 1179 pp. 1967.

Tests with sensitive instruments such as soil tensiometers, trunk dendro-meters, and soil gypsum blocks have shown that trees should be supplied with supplemental water when the soil moisture reaches 50% of the available water (water in the soil between its field capacity and WP).

When trunk dendrometers are used on apple, water is applied when the rate of trunk expansion falls below 80% of that of the frequently irrigated trees (see Verner). For peach, 20 fruits are tagged on a few frequently watered trees and compared in growth rate every 3 days with 20 tagged fruits in the rest of the orchard, as follows: apply water during pit harden-ing when 80% of the fruits stop growing, and when in "final swell" 50% of the fruits stop growing, and in the last 4 weeks before harvest when 50% of the fruits show less than 0.1 cm increase/day.

Rate of evaporation of water from an open pan (receives rain also) can be used against established equations to determine need for water vs aver-age precipitation for a particular month or accumlative for the season.

QUESTIONS

1. Describe and differentiate between (a) a radiation frost (freeze) and (b) an advective freeze.
2. Discuss weather-monitoring equipment for the orchard and how it is installed and operated.
3. List and compare (a) orchard heating equipment and (b) fuels for heating.
4. Describe over-tree irrigation systems and how effective they are, relative costs, general usefulness, and principles of operation.
5. Define, "critical temperature" in an orchard.
6. Discuss air movement through plantings of fruit trees planted (a) on the square, (b) in hedgerows, (c) across an incline, (d) rows up-and-down the incline and (e) when near wooded areas.
7. Define (a) wilting point, (b) field capacity of soils and (c) available water in soils.
8. List 3 commercial methods of applying water to fruit plants and their relative merits.
9. Discuss "Trickle Irrigation," materials used and how it is installed and operated. What are its chief advantages, disadvantages?
10. Discuss effects of water deficiency on (a) fruit bud formation, (b) fruit set, (c) fruit drop and (d) fruit growth of apple, peach and nuts.
11. Discuss water deficiency and fruit (a) splitting, (b) yield, (c) size and (d) quality.
12. Discuss the relationship between irrigation and insects, diseases and nutrient supply to fruit trees.

SUGGESTED COLLATERAL READINGS

FROSTS AND FREEZE PREVENTION

Alleweldt, G. Physiology of frost resistance Agr. Meteorol., 6(2):97-110 (in Ger-man. (1969).

Davis, G. R. and Gerber, J. F. Radiant heat: general properties and its production by four types of grove heaters. Proc. Fla. State Hort. Soc. 1970.

Georg, J. G. An objective minimum temperature forecasting technique using the economical net radiometer. J. Appl. Meteorol. 9:711-713. 1970.

Gubbels, G. H. Frost protection of crops by sprinkler irrigation. Can. J. Plant Sci. 49:715-718. 1969.

Hewett, E. W. Water sprinkling and prevention of frost damage. Orchard: New Zealand. 42:271-276. 1969.

Huovila, S. and Valmari, A. Artificial ventilation for prevention of radiation frost. Geophysics. Helsingfors, 8:303-312. 1966.

Kramar, L. M. Analysis of risk of frost in the Nahimovskij fruit and grape state farm. Gl. Geofyz. Obs., Leningrad, T. Vyp. 264:82-89. 1970.

Lovelidge, B. U. S. diesel heater gives encouraging results (against frost). Grower 75(22):1315. 1971.

McCarthy, C. D. Minimum temperatures: hedgerow versus open-planted citrus. Calif. Citrograph, 53:438; 453-454. 1968.

Mihara, Y. Protection against cold and frost by an artificial fog. Rept. Coop. Res. Disaster Prevention, 6:33-46 (in Japanese). 1966.

Oke, T. R. Temperature profile near ground on calm clear nights. Quart. J. Roy. Meteorol. Soc., 96:15-29.

Patric, J. H. and Fridley, B. D. Device for measuring soil frost. U. S. Dept. Agr. Forest Serv. Res. Note NE-94:7 pp. 1969.

Smock, R. M. Facts and fancies on freezing damage to apples. Proc. N. Y. State Hort. Soc., 1970. 115:199-203. 1970.

Soderberg, M. E. Advance frost warning procedures, W. Mich. U. S. Dept. Commerce/Environ. Sci. Serv. Admin. Tech. Memo. WBTM-CR-28, 1969.

Solov'eva, M. A. Frost damage to fruit trees: protective and remedial measures. Sadovodstvo, 10:37-39. (in Russian). 1969.

Frost and the prevention of frost damage. USDC, National Oceanic and Atmospheric Admin. 35 pp. Revised 1972.

Valli, V. J. Freeze and the prevention of freeze damage. Mountaineer Grower. W. Va. 283:2-23. 1969.

Valli, V. J. Appalachian orchard heating with petroleum coke based fuel blocks to prevent freeze damage. Mountaineer Grower, W. Va. 286-1-10. 1969.

Valli, V. J. Natural gas heating to prevent spring freeze damage. Agr. Meteorol. 7(6):481-486. 1970.

Valli, V. J. Basic principles of freeze occurrence and the prevention of freeze damage. (good bulletin). Spot heaters, Sunnyside, Wash. 98944. 20 pp.

WMO. Protection against frost damage. Technical Note 51, WMO Secretariat, Geneva, Switzerland. 1963.

Van Den Brink, C. et al. Growing Degree Days in Mich. Mich Res. Rpt. 131, 48 pp. 1971.

Yelenosky, G., Horanic, G., and Galena, F. Frost conditions and damage to citrus during two consecutive radiation freezes. Proc. Fla. State Hort. Soc. 1969. 82: 60-62. 1970.

IRRIGATION

Ackley, W. B. Seasonal and diurnal water contents of pear leaves. Plant. Phys. 29: 445-448. 1954.

Alben, A. O. Irrigation of pecan trees in Texas. S. E. Pecan Growers Assn. Proc. 51:61, 63, 65, 67-8. 1958.

Aldrich, W. W. Irrigation studies on Anjou pear. Oregon State Hort. Soc. 25th Annu. Rep. p. 30-35. 1933.

Ballinger, W. E., et al. Irrigation, nitrogen and pruning interrelationships of peach in North Carolina. ASHS Proc. 83:248-258. 1963.

Batjer, L. P. and M. N. Westwood. Relation of size of peach at thinning to size at harvest. ASHS 72:102-105. 1958.

Bowman, F. T. and J. R. Davison. Irrigation, soil management of prune, Agr. Gaz., New South Wales 52:543-4. 585-8. 1941.

Branton. D., et al. Soil moisture on apricot leaf composition. ASHS 77:90-96. 1961.

Brown, D. S. Irrigation on apricot flower bud development and fruiting. ASHS Proc. 61:119-124. 1953.

Butijn, J. Water requirements of pome fruits (in Eng. with Ital., French and Ger. summaries). From Irrigazione 8(3): 40-51. 1961.

Cockroft, B. Irrigation timing in orchards. J. Agr. Victoria, Australia. 61:492-5, 521. 1963.

Crane, J. C. and K. Uriu. Irrigation, 2, 4, 5-T on apricot fruits. ASHS Proc. 86:88-94. 1965.

Cripps, J. Orchard irrigation. J. Agr., W. Aust. Services. 3:7:127-128. 1958.

Davis, L. D. Split-pits in peach. ASHS 39:183-189. 1941.

Degman, E. S., et al. Soil moisture and apple fruit bud formation. ASHS 29:199-201. 1932.

Donoho. C. W. Jr., et al. Apple irrigation and mulch. Ohio Farm Home Res. 49 (3):40-41, 43. 1964.

(See additional references under Chapter XIX Appendix)

CHAPTER XX

Grape Growing

◆ ◆

Grapes are popular in home gardens the country over. They are grown commercially in 13 of the 50 States. The industry is separated into three general regions[1] over the country according to the type of grape grown: (a) regions with European-type grapes (*Vitis vinifera*), including mainly California, Arizona, and lower Texas; (b) regions with native American-type varieties (*V. labrusca,* or its hybrids with *V. vinifera*), consisting of an area east of the Rocky Mountains and north of the Gulf states plus the Northwest and California which have significant commercial acreages; and (c), regions with Muscadine grapes (*V. rotundifolia*), including the South Atlantic and Gulf states.

The *vinifera* grape, largely grown in California, comprises about 93 per cent of the grapes produced in the United States. This grape is exemplified by the Tokay variety commonly seen on the fresh-fruit markets in the East. *Vinifera* grapes are characterized by a relatively thick skin that adheres to a firm pulp which is sweet throughout. Most *viniferas* require a mild climate, such as found in California. Certain varieties are used principally for raisins, others for wine or for table use. A U.S. boom planting of grapes for wine occurred in the early 70's due to an appreciable increase in U.S. and world wine consumption.

The native American- or Fox-type grape, which is grown principally in the lower Great Lakes region of the United States and Canada, is the second-most important grape, commercially. Concord is the leading and

---

[1] These have been further divided by Loomis into 9 regions according to climate and variety. See his reference.

Ronald B. Tukey, Wash. State Univ., Pullman; H. K. Fleming, retired, and C. W. Haeseler, Penn. State Univ., Northeast; and A. N. Kasimatis, Univ. of California, Davis; Nelson Shaulis, N. Y. Agr. Exp. Sta., Geneva, and Garth Cahoon, Ohio, Agr. Res. Center, Wooster, assisted in the chapter revision.

typical variety. It has a relatively thin skin that adheres loosely to the pulp; the pulp is soft and relatively acid near the seeds. The American grapes require a temperate climate such as found near the Great Lakes.

The Muscadine grapes are exemplified by the Scuppernong variety which is long lived, remarkably disease resistant, and vigorous in vine. The bunches are relatively small and the berries have a strong musky odor, large seeds, ripen unevenly and tend to shatter from the bunches when ripe.[1] The fruit is adapted to home use, wine making, and culinary purposes, but not to distant marketing as a dessert grape.

Over 80 percent of the 290 million grapevines (1970 census) in the United States are located in the state of California. California in some years may produce as much as 95 percent of the total grape production. The relative importance of California is shown in Figure 2. The 1969-71 average annual grape production in tons by the five leading states was: California, 3,289,000; New York, 157,666; Michigan, 56,333; Washington, 67,666; Pennsylvania, 42,200; and Ohio, 13,100. Two thirds of the *vinifera* grapes grown in California are raisin varieties, whereas the other portion is divided 21% wine and 14% table varieties. U.S. grape production has shown a marked increase the past decade (Figure 3), with prospects of continued planting increases.

About 77% of the World grape production goes into wine and about 18% into raisins; the balance is grown largely for table grapes, juice, and other products. The *vinifera* type grape predominates. Approximate World grape production by country and in 1000's of metric tons is given below for the early 1970's.

Country[1]	Production	Country	Production
Italy	11,700	Germany (FR)	770
France	9,200	Chili	720
Spain	3,800	Australia	630
Turkey	3,600	Brazil	510
Argentina	3,600	Japan	380
U. S.	3,200	Austria	350
Greece	1,600	Morocco	300
Portugal	1,400	Iran	290
Yugoslavia	1,300	Syria	230
Bulgaria	1,200	Tunisia	140
Algeria	1,100		
Rumania	1,100	Total world	52,454
Hungary	900	Wine	39,890
South Africa	810	Raisins	9,187

[1]Other countries producing grapes in approximate order from 130,000 to 50,000 metric tons annually are: Switzerland, Uruguay, Lebanon, Czechoslovakia, Cyprus, Mexico, Israel, Jordan. Peru and Canada.

The American-type grapes (with its hybrids), the Muscadine and the European types of grapes will be discussed separately in this order.

---

[1]A few varieties are now available which do not shatter from the bunch.

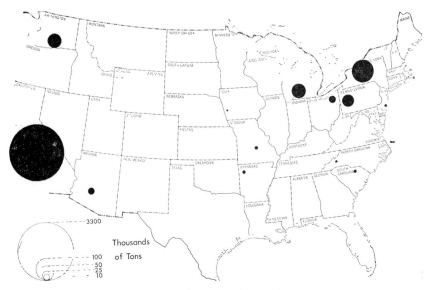

-3300

Thousands of Tons

100
50
25
10

Kenneth A. Wightman, Rutgers University

Figure 2. California produces 90 to 95 per cent of the grapes in the United States, consisting almost entirely of the European-type grape (Vitus vinifera). The American-type grape or its hybrids with American and Viniferas are grown mainly in the central and northeastern states, while the Muscadine (V. rotundifolia) is grown in the Gulf and South Atlantic states. New York, Michigan, Washington, Pennsylvania, Ohio, Arizona and Arkansas rank in order after California. California has over 255 million grapevines, or about 80% of the United States total. New York ranks second with about 20 million vines. Grapes from eastern areas are mainly consumed fresh or made into juice. In California, grapes used for raisins are grown around Fresno, wine grapes come mainly from San Francisco Bay area, and table grapes come from vineyards in the Sacramento and San Joaquin valleys and from the southern section of the state.

THE VINEYARD LOCATION

The three natural factors which largely govern where an American bunch type vineyard can be located properly are (a) climate, (b) site, and (c) soil.

Climate. Grape varieties have rather exact requirements with respect to total and mean temperatures of the growing season. Also, the number of days required for proper maturity of the wood and fruit varies with the variety. Most of the American-type grapes will mature in about 165 frost-free days provided summer heat is adequate; *labrusca-vinifera* hybrids require a longer period and *viniferas* require at least 175 days. Largest production is located along the shores of the Great Lakes because of the tempering effect of the large bodies of water and the lengthening of the growing season. These areas are especially adapted to such long-season varieties as Catawba. Concord requires fewer days than Catawba for maturity and will generally succeed in areas where the average length of the growing season is about 170 days; it is of doubtful success in regions of 157 days and generally unsuccessful at 145 days. Commercial plantings of grapes should be

668

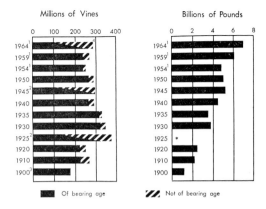

Millions of Vines   Billions of Pounds

U.S. Census, adapted by K. A. Wightman
Figure 3. Grape production in the United States and number of vines is shown from 1900 to 1964. It is interesting to note a rise in production over the years on a reducing number of vines. Super numbers mean: (1) farms of 20 vines or less not included; (2) bearing, non-bearing vines combined; (3) nonbearing data unavailable; (4) number of vines based on bearing vines acreage.

■ Of bearing age   ▨ Not of bearing age

confined to favorable sites in established areas (see your local experiment station bulletins or Loomis' U.S.D.A. bulletin for details).

Site. In the East, there are many small vineyards outside the commercial regions which supply grapes for local markets and for home use. Special attention should be given to selection of a frost-free site and the use of adapted varieties. The vineyard should be somewhat above the surrounding country. The ground may be almost level provided there is opportunity for cold air to drain on one or two sides. Air drainage through and away from the vineyard not only reduces the danger from late-spring and early-fall frosts, but also is highly important in the control of many diseases of grapes. In the southern extensions of the industry, the tempering effect of large bodies of water is not such an important factor, but air drainage is of primary consideration. There appears to be no advantage in having the land slope in a particular direction. Steep land without bench terracing is undesirable due to soil erosion factor.

Soil. The best vineyards in the East are growing on moderately fertile, well-drained, sandy, or gravelly loam soil (four to six feet rooting area) which contains a good supply of organic matter. Grapes will grow on a wide variety of soils both in the East and West, including the heavy clays provided they contain plenty of organic matter and are *well drained*. In general, the lighter sandy type of soils promote earlier ripening and higher sugar content of the grapes than do heavy soils.

SELECTION OF VARIETIES

Only those varieties should be planted in a commercial vineyard that are adapted to the region and have proven their value over many varied seasons.

Vareties of the American-type grape and its hybrids are grown mostly in commercial plantings.

Varieties of the species *V. riparia* (frost grape), are adapted to the more northerly areas, are extremely cold hardy and mature fruit in a short growing season. Many are excellent wine varieties.

669

Most varieties adapted to the South belong to the species *V. champini,*
V. lincecumi, V. rupestris, and *V. bourquiniana.*

Many varieties are hybrids of two or more species. American species
have been crossed with the *vinifera* grape to develop bunch grape varieties with superior fruit quality, larger berries, and larger fruit clusters.
However, these varieties are less cold hardy and less resistant to nematodes,
diseases and phylloxera.

After the American varieties, the French-American varieties are an important part of the table grape and wine industries in the eastern U. S.
French hybrids rank first, *viniferas* second in the eastern U. S. table wine
interests. Dutchess, Steuben and Diamond show promise. See Cornell Ext.
Bull. 1201 on grape varieties.

American-type grapes which are generally recommended for commercial
plantings in the Great Lakes regions are in the order of ripening: Niagara
(white), Delaware (red), Concord (blue), and Catawba (red).

Niagara has large compact bunches of high quality yellow-green
berries. The vigorous vines are adapted to a wide variety of soils. Since
white grapes are limited in market demand, they should be planted in
amounts to suit local requirements. Two disadvantages of Niagara are
tenderness to winter cold and the fruit and leaves are somewhat more
susceptible to fungus diseases than those of Concord. *Delaware* is a standard
midseason variety, hardy, one of the highest-quality table grapes, ships and
stores well, and makes good wine. Bunches, berries, and vines are relatively small. Delaware is a slow-growing grape which should be planted
closer than most varieties (about eight feet) and requires good soil management and fertilization with relatively close pruning. *Concord* is the
standard blue grape in the East. It succeeds under a wide variety of
soil and climatic conditions. The vine is vigorous, hardy, highly productive, and resistant to downy mildew and phylloxera galling. The fruit ripens
evenly, stands reasonable shipment and storage, and is highly prized for
juice, jelly, and table use. It is used in blending dry table wines and there
is a growing market in frozen concentrates. Probably over 85 per cent
of the varieties grown in the Great Lakes region consist of Concord, and
more are being planted. *Catawba* requires a longer growing season than
Concord. Berries and bunches are of medium size, ship well, and can
be stored until almost midwinter under proper conditions; the vines are
fairly productive and hardy, medium in vigor, but foliage and fruit are
relatively susceptible to fungous diseases.

A few *V. vinifera* varieties have "limited" acreage in New York, notably
White Riesling and Pinot Chardonnay. The best sites and management
must be used. Other varieties for the home and local market are: Schuyler,
Van Buren, Ontario, Seneca, Bath, Buffalo, N. Y., Muscat, Steuben, Gold-
en Muscat, Vinered, Sheridan, Yates and Urbana. Seedless varieties include Interlaken Seedless, Himrod, Romulus and Concord Seedless.

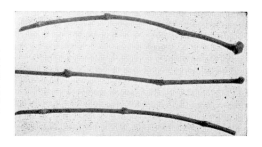

Ohio State University

Figure 5. Grape cuttings for propagating new vines in the nursery. (Top) Mallet-type cutting is frequently used, consisting of current season cane with small section of 2-year wood at base. (Middle) Type of cane most commonly used. (Bottom) Cuts on this cane are improperly made.

Commercial varieties of limited acreage include Elvira, Fredonia, Ives, Missouri Riesling, Dutchess, Clinton and Isabella. French hybrids (*V. vinifera* x wild American species) suggested primarily for wine are: Aurora, Marechal Foch, Seyval, Seibel 9110, 1000, 9549, 5898, Baco Noir and Chelois.

In the Northwest[1], Concord comprises 90% of all commercial grapes (juice, "Cold Duck" wine); some Diamond, Delaware for wine; wine varieties (10% of acreage) are Riesling, Chardonnay, Chenin Blanc, Semillion, Cabernet Sauvignon, Pinot Noir, Gamay Beaujolais and Pearlette; for home use Concord, Seneca, Campbell Early, Diamond and Delaware and some *V. vinifera* types.

PROPAGATION OF GRAPES

Cuttings. Growers can propagate their own cuttings by selecting dormant, pencil-sized, mature wood as shown in Fig. 5 in early winter, tie in bundles of 25, and bury base-up in a well-drained spot. Cover with 3 inches of soil and 6 inches of straw for winter protection.

Set the best plants in early spring in loose friable soil about 6 inches apart in rows 3 ft apart (Fig. 6). Leave the top bud exposed, firm the soil, and keep the planting free of weeds by cultivation and/or herbicides. An average stand is a 50-60% take. Set the larger better plants to the vineyard the following spring.

Layering. The principal value of layering is to replace missing vines in the vineyard. Plants started by layering in an established vineyard usually grow faster than one-year plants secured from the nursery. As shown in Figure 7, a vigorous cane from the nearest vine is covered with soil with 3 tip buds exposed at the location of the missing vine.

Grafting. Most varieties of American grapes are on their own roots. Own-rooted Concord usually performs satisfactorily on new sites but on replant sites it performs best when grafted on N. Y. "virus-free" Couderc 3309 roots. This stock is resistant to the phylloxera insect pest.

In New York, own-rooted Clinton, Concord, Baco No. 1 and Catawba are satisfactory on new sites, but should be grafted on resistant

Se: Wash. Ext. Serv. EB-635. January 1972.

Figure 6. (Left) Grape cuttings in an Ohio nursery in July will be sold as 1-year plants the next spring. Mulch prevents heaving in cold climates; cuttings are set directly to nursery in fall or spring in mild climates. (Right) Own-rooted Concord vines at New York Agr. Exp. Substation, Fredonia, are short plants; on either side are Concord taller vines grafted on resistant Couderc 3309; both planted in May on a replant site, photographed in early November. Own-rooted Concords perform satisfactorily on non-replant sites. Resistance is to root parasites or unfavorable soil conditions.

stocks for old grape sites, whereas Delaware, Ives, and *vinifera* types always should be grafted on resistant roots, which are available. At least 6 species of *Vitis* comprise parentage of American hybrids grown in New York, ranging from the highly resistant *V. riparia* to the highly susceptible *V. vinifera*, accounting for the varied resistance cited above.

PLANTING THE VINEYARD

Nursery stock. One-year-old No. 1 grape plants with well-developed root systems are most satisfactory for planting (Figure 8). Two-year plants may be unsatisfactory for several reasons. Most eastern grape growers secure their planting stocks from near-by reputable nurserymen rather than to attempt to grow their own plants and cuttings.

Plant the rooted vines as soon after arrival as possible. Early spring planting is recommended in the northern states. If the plants arrive before convenient planting time, they should be heeled-in immediately on a well-drained site, preferably near the north side of a building. Prepare a furrow deep enough to accommodate the roots, untie the bundles, separate the plants, and distribute them along the furrow. Pack the soil thoroughly around the roots so there are no air spaces. Cover most of the tops with soil, then cover with a wet burlap or moist soil to keep them dormant in case the weather turns warm suddenly.

Preparation of soil for planting. Plow and harrow the soil for early spring plantings. Sod land to be used for a vineyard should be planted to a cultivated crop for at least a year before setting the vines. Contour planting is suggested to avoid soil erosion on sloping land (Figure 9). Grape rows must be cultivated in a commercial vineyard, so every precaution must be taken to avoid soil erosion losses. Where available, an application of six to eight tons per acre of barnyard manure before plow-

672

ing is recommended to improve growth of both vines and cover crop.

Planting. Rows can be lined out with a three-foot guide stick at each end and as many stakes in between as are needed on long rows. A straight furrow is then plowed out along row lines. After row lines have been plowed out, a heavy chain or other suitable marker can be dragged at

Ohio State University

Figure 7. A simple and effective method for replacing missing vines is to layer a vigorous cane from the neighboring vine. Stake serves to locate layered cane during cultivation.

right angle across the furrows to mark the points where plants are to be set. Planting distances vary with variety and type of soil. Vigorous varieties such as Niagara, Concord, Fredonia, and Sheridan on good soils should have the rows spaced about nine feet apart with the plants seven to nine feet apart in the row. Less vigorous varieties as Catawba and Delaware may be set seven to eight feet apart in the row. If plants are set nine by nine feet, 534 plants will be required per acre; if nine by eight feet, 605 plants; and if nine by seven feet, 691 plants.

Rows spaced nine feet apart are desirable to facilitate spraying and cultivating and for convenient hauling at harvest. In large commercial vineyards, it is desirable to provide cross alleyways to facilitate the movement of machinery. Alleyways should be spaced at intervals of about 300 to 400 feet.

Before setting the plants, prune the roots only enough to cut away broken portions and ragged ends, as shown in Figure 8. Place and arrange roots well in the hole, firming the soil around and over them. The top is cut back to two buds on the best single cane after planting.

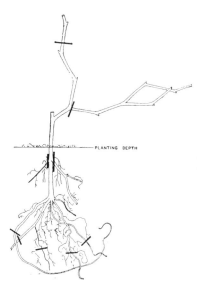

PLANTING DEPTH

Figure 8. Before planting a rooted grape cutting the tops and roots are pruned as indicated by black marks. The planting depth is shown.

SOIL MANAGEMENT

Cultivation. Growth and yields are improved by frequent *shallow* cultivation beginning as early in spring as soil can be worked and continuing

673

J. T. Bregger, U.S. Soil Conservation
Service

**Figure 9. On rolling land there is op-
portunity for surface erosion in spite
of good cultural management. If the
vineyard is planted on the contour,
erosion is reduced to a minimum, and
considerably more rainfall is retained
in the vineyard.**

through early summer. If the season is dry and the crop large, cultivation
should be prolonged to keep down weeds and conserve moisture. If moisture is plentiful, discontinue cultivation to induce early maturing of wood
and fruit. It is important that the wood enter the winter well-ripened to
avoid freezing injury and a consequent crop reduction the following year.
If a winter cover of rye has been used, it should be disked in while rye is
leafy and before it has become tough fibrous and jointed. Continue cultivation with a disk or spring-tooth harrow to kill weeds and prevent soil from
baking, and to level the vineyard until time for seeding the cover crop.
However, on heavier loams and clay where surface drainage is slow,
one or more rounds should be made with a shallow plow, one-way-
throw disk or grape hoe, in late fall (Figure 11), throwing the soil in a
ridge under the wires. The ridge should be high enough to provide surface drainage away from the grape row during the winter and prevent
heaving damage to the vines. Soil can be pulled away or left, using strip
herbicide treatment under the wires. (See Chap. XVIII for weed control
suggestions).

Cover crops. Since more cultivation is practiced in vineyards than in
orchards, it is highly important that soil organic matter be maintained by
the growing of winter crops and the application of strawy manure and
waste hay. To invigorate weak plantings Ohio experiments favor mulching, particularly for small plantings where source of adequate mulch may
not be a problem.

Wheat, rye or ryegrass are common cover crops in the Great Lakes
region. In young vineyards, two cover crops a year often are grown. Soybeans can be planted shortly after bloom and disked under in late August
when the vineyard then is drilled to a rye cover crop. When the vineyard
has become established and is in full bearing, a single cover crop, such as
oats or rye sown at the time of last cultivation in late July or early August
and turned under the following spring, provides a cover crop which is quite
satisfactory for most soil types. Another cover crop in the Great Lakes region
is domestic ryegrass which can be sown earlier than rye. It makes a larger
root system but less top growth in the spring than rye and can be worked
down later.

674

Courtesy J. H. Dawson, W. J. Clore, V. F. Burns, Wash. State Univ., Prosser.

Figure 10. Chemical weed control is the best and most economical weed control under trellis wires in a commercial vineyard. Monuron and Diuron kept plots nearly free of weeds all year (foreground). Vetch cover in row middles had been mowed recently.

If at all possible, cover crops such as wheat, rye, and ryegrass should be drilled in order to confine the cover crop to the middles between the rows (Figure 11). To facilitate grape harvest, the cover crop of rye can be flattened with a roller or planker just before the grapes are harvested. Where a cover crop is desired which kills overwinter, oats or buckwheat sown in midsummer are worth considering.

Liming. Rye and rye grass will grow in a relatively acid soil. It usually is not necessary to add lime, unless the pH is below 5.0, magnesium deficiency is apparent in the leaves, or it may benefit the cover crop. Dolomite is used to correct Mg deficiency at one ton/A. Too much lime may induce Mn or other trace element deficiencies.

Chemical weed control. Grapes are highly sensitive and almost permanently stunted or killed by 2, 4-D and 2, 4, 5-T; they should not be used in fields anywhere near grapes to avoid drift or in spray equipment to be used in vineyards. MCP, TCA (sodium-triichloroacetate) are detrimental or fatal to grapes. Monuron, Diuron, or Simazine are used in vineyards (see Chapter XVIII). Karmax and fortified aromatic petroleum oil emulsions have been found satisfactory for weed control in grapes. Contact local authorities for current recommendations which change rather frequently.

Figure 11. Cover crops are important in good vineyard management. (Left) Rye cover crop early in May in northern Ohio. Rye cover is almost ready to be disked. (Right) A drilled wheat cover crop photographed in September in northern Ohio. Modern heribicidal treatment will keep soil bare under vines.

Mechanical weed control. Aside from herbicide usage in-the-row (Figure 10), the best in-row cultivating equipment is the PTO or tractor-pulled grape hoe with a rotating-disc soil-stirrer, hydraulically activated by a metal whisker to move around the vine trunks. (Friday Tractor Co., Hartford, Mich.).

MANURE AND FERTILIZERS

Manure. Strawy manure is probably the best general all-around fertilizer for grapes. Applied during the winter or very early spring at the rate of six to eight tons per acre, manure may increase yield by 30 per cent, but it has become too limited for large scale use.

Commercial fertilizers. Grapes in general have not responded as readily to nitrogen fertilizer applications as other fruit crops, except perhaps on exhausted soils. This may be due in part to the heavy annual pruning given the grapevine. However, when growth becomes unsatisfactory to support the proper number of buds per vine after pruning, nitrogen fertilizer applications are usually beneficial. Nitrogen shows the most immediate and greatest effect on vines on sandy and gravelly soils. On the heavier soils, it may require two or three years before a response is indicated from nitrogen . Applications can be made in late fall or early spring. For vines of moderate vigor, use 150 lbs. ammonium nitrate or equivalent per acre or 500 lbs. 10-10-10 mix. On the basis of a single vine, this would be about 0.3 pound of ammonium nitrate, or the equivalent in nitrogen in another source for vines of moderate vigor. For weak vines, about one-half pound per vine is recommended. Drill the fertilizer in strips on either side of the grape row for benefit of vines if nitrogen is used alone; if a complete fertilizer and lime (for legumes) are applied to benefit the cover crop, they should be broadcasted.

A 6-ton grape crop per acre removes about 120 lbs/A of N, P, K, Mg, Ca, S, Fe, Mn, B, Zn, Cu and Mo. Nutrient deficiencies in humid

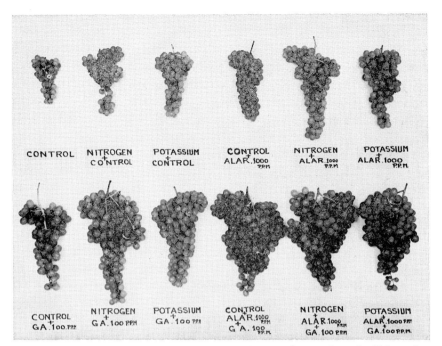

Figure 12. Himrod grape bunches and berry size are shown above in Ohio as in-fluenced by: Control (no Treatment); ammonium nitrate, ½ lb/vine; potassium sulphate, 1½ lbs/vine; Alar, 1000 ppm first bloom and GA (Pro-Gibb) 100 ppm, shatter stage. Researchers also are studying Ethephon sprays as a means of getting better more uniform coloring and maturity of grapes with less sourness. (Photo courtesy Garth A. Cahoon, Ohio ARDC, Wooster.)

areas that have been noted in vineyards are N, K, Mn, Mg, Fe and B. Ca and certain trace elements may become deficient under special conditions or in sandy low-organic matter soils. In arid regions, N, Zn, K, B, Mn and Fe may be found, rarely Cu. Deficiencies vary from area to area, farm to farm and within the same farm area.

When deficiencies become moderate to acute, they can be recognized in the leaves, fruit and growth characters. Marginal deficiencies occur, however, and are not apparent except in reduced yield and quality. The modern approach is to have the grape leaf petioles ("leaf stems") chemically analyzed for their level of essential nutrient elements. Equipment to do this is expensive and, hence, one state experiment station well equipped will service several area states at a cost of up to about $10/sample— N. Y., Pa., Ohio, Me., Fla., Mich., Colo., Calif., Ore. to name a few. Standards have been established for "normal" levels of each element for satisfactory vigor and yield of good quality.

Briefly, visual symptoms of deficiencies frequently found in grapes are: *Nitrogen* deficiency causes low vigor and yield, light green foliage, small leaves. If 60-90% of the trellis is covered with dark green foliage for 8 ft. spaced vines and 3 lbs of prunings are removed, N may not be needed.

Other factors causing light green foliage are drouth, sun scald, leafhoppers, mildew, dead arm, winter injury, certain herbicides and others. Low *potassium* appears as a marginal and interveinal scorch on mid-shoot leaves; as black leaf, low vigor and yield, small berries and delayed maturity (Fig. 13a). Apply 300 lbs KCL or 360 lbs K_2SO_4/acre. *Magnesium* shortage may occur on low pH soils, affecting the older leaves. Light green to whitish areas occur between the main views as shown in Fig. 13a. About a ton of dolomite/A should help and/or 16 lbs/100 gals of $MgSO_4$ (epsom salts) at 200 gals/A in 2 post-bloom sprays. Low *Manganese* may appear on high-lime or pH (7.0) soils as interveinal light greening on shaded more exposed leaves. One-half to 1 lb. $MnSO_4$/vine banded under the trellis, or 5 lbs/100 gal. spray should correct it. Low *Iron* appears as a yellowish-whitening of the younger leaves, frequently on high lime or pH (7.0) soil or poorly drained "cold" soils. Ammonium sulfate as the N source is suggested in N. Y. Iron chelate at manufacturers recommendations to the soil is suggested in some areas. Low *boron* results in deformed leafing out in spring, split shoots, shot berries (small), or no fruit at all. Be careful not to over-apply B. About 10 lbs borax per acre every other year is suggested in So. Carolina. Sprays of 1-2 lbs. borax or equivalent/100 gals once or twice may be needed in soils of high pH. Low *zinc* is common in arid regions and may be found in humid areas, particularly in sandy soils (Fig. 14). Paint pruning wounds during pruning with 1 lb. Zn SO_4/gal water, or spray with Zn chelate at mfg. recommendation. See Dr. J. A. Cook's grape chapter in Childers' *Fruit Nutrition* book.

THE TRELLIS

The plants should be staked during the first growing season after planting, and the strongest shoot for each vine trained to the stake. The trellis should be in place at the beginning of the second season, if possible. While the trellis is an important item in the expense of establishing a vineyard, a strong durable support system set at the start will be more economical in the long run.

Posts. Posts should be set from 24 to 30 feet apart with three vines between the posts. Exact distance between the posts will depend upon whether the planting distance between the vines in the row is eight, nine, or ten feet. Posts should consist of durable wood, such as white oak, locust, or cedar, preferably creosote-treated to prolong life. Metal posts are being used in some vineyards, and although the initial cost of these posts is higher than wood, they are more durable, relatively free from frost heaving, drive and handle better in the ground, and look neater. End wood posts should be heavier and longer than line posts with a top diameter of five to eight inches, and a length of about 10 feet to permit setting four feet in the soil, as shown in Figure 16. Reinforced concrete sometimes is used for end posts.

(Upper) A. F. Wilhelm, Freiburg, Germany; (Lower) L. E. Scott, Univ. of Md.

Figure 13a. (Upper) Marginal scorch of older grape leaves due to potassium deficiency. (Lower) Magnesium deficiency whitish yellowing between main veins of older grape leaves.

Line posts can be somewhat lighter, or at least three inches in top diameter and about eight feet long to permit driving two feet in the ground where the Kniffin system of training is used. If the wooden posts are sharpened, they can be driven into the ground with a heavy 12 to 14 pound maul while the operator stands on a truck bed.

End posts will require sturdy bracing. A satisfactory bracing system can be employed where a four by four-inch brace is run from near the top of

John Quail, Cal. Agr. Ext. Serv., Fresno

Figure 14. Zinc deficiency on grape causes straggly bunches with small berries (above, control on left), and a whitish chlorosis and general stunting of the leaves.

Figure 15. Trellis end posts are particularly strong when braced as shown. Life of posts is increased by soaking lower ends in creosote before setting. Wood reel may be used with ratchet for tightening wire. Recent experience has shown that end posts hold better if 10 ft. in length, sunk 4 ft. in the ground instead of 3 ft. as shown here.

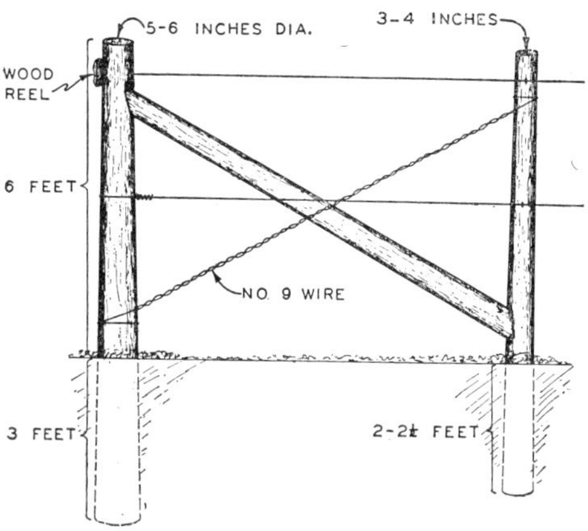

the end post obliquely toward the ground and fitted against a short post set about eight feet back in the row from the end post. A second method of bracing is to carry a heavy brace wire from the top of the endpost to a large rock or log ("dead-man") buried about two feet in the ground beyond the end post. Objection to this bracing method is that the brace wire is frequently caught by cultivating tools. A third method is shown in Figure 15, in which a second post is set six to eight feet back in the row from the end post. An end-post brace for Geneva double-curtain training system is shown in Figure 16.

Wires. If the Kniffin system of training is used (Figure 20), a two-wire trellis is satisfactory with the upper wire consisting preferably of the heavier No. 9 gauge wire and the lower wire of No. 10 gauge. For the Fan system of training (Figure 23), two or three wires of No. 10 or 11 gauge may be used. A durable galvanized wire is preferred. The amount of wire needed can be calculated from the table below.

Gauge of Wire	Feet per Pound
9	17.05
10	20.57
11	25.82

For the Kniffin system, the upper wire is located from five and one-half to six feet from the ground.

Long staples are used for securing the wires to line posts. The wire should be loose in the staples, so that it can be tightened at the end posts as needed. Wires are more secure if placed on the windward side of the posts, or on the upper side in hillside vineyards. Iron wires contract during cold weather and should be loosened in the fall to prevent undue strain on the end posts. In spring after pruning is completed and before the canes are tied, the posts should be driven down where necessary and the wires tightened, using a common wire stretcher. Each wire should be fastened

681

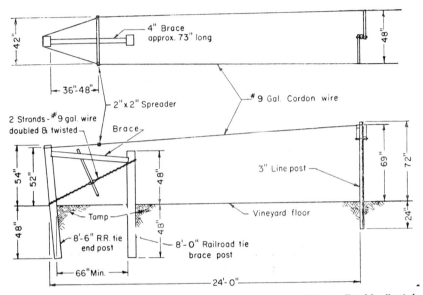

Figure 16. Suggested end-post and brace construction for Geneva Double-Curtain trellis system. Keep the cordon wire and brace sufficiently high. Construction success depends on the deep setting of the wide surface railroad ties. (Courtesy Nelson Shaulis, N. Y. Agr. Exp. Sta., Geneva).

securely to the end posts; a good method is shown in Figure 15. A ratchet-type of tightener often is used.

Another method for tightening wires is to cut the wire midway between end posts and use a wire stretcher, then splice the wire after it is drawn taut.

Trellis for contour rows. On the sharper curves in the contour planting system, extra posts should be used, some of which are set deeper or set in concrete to help absorb the extra strain encountered at these points. No bracing other than at the end posts is needed. If terraces are used with contour planting, the trellises should be established on the ridges. For establishing contour lines and terraces, see Chapter III.

PRUNING AND TRAINING

Growth and fruiting habits of vines. Grape clusters are borne laterally near the base of leafy shoots which arise from the buds on one-year wood or canes as shown in Figure 17. Shoots which arise from wood older than one year are unproductive.

For good grape production, it is important that the vines be pruned annually so that an adequate amount of one-year wood conveniently placed is available from year to year near the trunk of the vine. Average yield for a Concord vine grown under good conditions is about 15 pounds. A bunch of Concord grapes averages about 0.16 lb. About 100 bunches are needed to produce the 15 pounds of fruit. If each fruit-bearing shoot produces from one to three bunches, the vine after pruning should produce

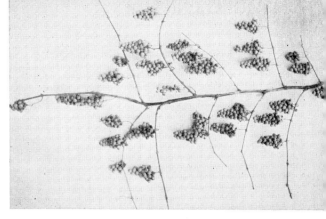

Figure 17. A defoliated fruiting Catawba cane showing location of best clusters and where most fruit is produced. On the average, the fifth, sixth, and seventh buds from the base of main cane develop most productive shoots.

15 pounds easily from 50 buds. Relatively heavy annual pruning is necessary because a vine before pruning contains an excessive number of buds. Heavy pruning also is necessary to prevent an undesirable amount of old wood from accumulating and to select a proper number and length of desirable fruiting canes from year to year.

Parts of vine defined. *Trunk*: The main unbranched stem of the vine. *Arm*: Short branch of old wood extending from the trunk. *Old wood*: Parts of the vine older than one year. *Shoot*: Leafy growth developing from a bud, which may support blossoms and later, fruit. During the growing season, such growths are called shoots; after the leaves have dropped they are called canes. *Canes*: The dormant shoots which have become woody and which carry buds or eyes.

Lateral: Side branch of a shoot or cane. *Spur or renewal spur*: A cane which has been cut back to a short stub carrying one or two buds and placed to develop a shoot to be used as a fruiting cane the following year (Figure 20). *Node*: The joint on a shoot or cane where leaves, tendrils, or buds are located. *Internode*: The portion of the shoot or cane between the nodes. *Eye*: The compound bud at each node on the cane. *Primary bud*: Largest and most important bud of the eye at a node. *Secondary buds*: The smallest buds at a node which often develop into shoots when the primary buds fail due to frost injury. Such a shoot is less productive than a shoot from a primary bud. *Sucker*: A shoot which arises from below the ground. *Water sprout*: A shoot which arises along the trunk or arm.

Season for pruning. In the northern states the best time to prune is after danger from heavy freezes and until the buds begin to swell. Canes will "bleed" sap from cut ends if pruned after the sap starts to run and while the buds are swelling. While bleeding may annoy the worker, it is not serious. Pruning should be completed as early as possible. Vines should never go without annual pruning. Pruning is not recommended during the growing season, since grape berries do not require direct sunlight to develop color. Large high-quality bunches are possible only with full development of healthy leaves. During the summer, it may be desirable at two-to-four-week intervals to tie back any stray shoots growing on the ground or toward the row middles with the Kniffin training system. Summer tying of shoots is necessary with the upright training systems such as the Fan, Chautauqua, and Keuka and is the key reason for disappearance of these training systems.

PRUNING YOUNG VINES

There are several systems of pruning grapes, including those which the shoots are allowed to droop (single or Y-trunk Kniffin with four to six or more canes, Umbrella, and Munson systems), and those in which the shoots are tied to upper wires during the growing season (Fan, Chautauqua, and Keuka High renewal). Although the latter three systems are said to be specially adapted to weak-growing varieties such as Delaware, the four-arm single-trunk Kniffin system appears to have more advantages and has proven quite satisfactory for all varieties. For this reason, most emphasis will be placed on the four-arm Kniffin system as shown in Figure 20.

First year. Immediately after planting, remove all but the strongest cane and cut it back to two buds. As shoots become woody in early summer, special attention should be given to pruning the young vines to develop a single vigorous shoot. Each vine should be trained to a five-foot stake, about 2 x 2 inch size, to aid in developing a straight trunk.

Second year. Assuming that the trellis is ready at the beginning of the second year, remove all side branches on the vigorous cane and tie it to the lower wire, and with an extension string anchor the tip to the top wire. If the cane reaches above the top wire, it should be pruned about three inches above the wire. If the trellis is not ready at the beginning of the second year, it is best to stake the canes if they have not already been staked to develop and maintain a straight trunk. If at the beginning of the second year, the cane growth is weak or less than three feet, cut off all but the best single cane and cut this back to two buds as recommended after planting.

Third year. A vigorous vine at the beginning of the third year can carry about 25 buds after pruning. Select two of the best canes near each wire level (making four canes in all) and prune away the rest, leaving one renewal spur with two buds near the base of each selected cane, as shown in Figure 20. Cut the canes to about a six-bud length on the lower wire and a four-to-five bud length on the upper wire. The two canes at each wire level, one trained to the right and the other to the left, can be spiraled around the wire and tied loosely to it in one or two places. These canes when cut back the following year become the arms (Figure 20) from which fruiting canes are selected for each wire level in later years.

PRUNING MATURE VINES

Purpose of pruning old vines annually is to maintain the trunk and arms so that the minimum amount of old wood supports the desirable type,

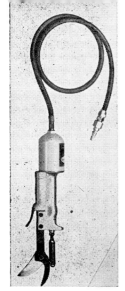

(Left) Miller-Robinson Co., Los Angeles, Calif.; (right) A. N. Kasimatis, Univ. of Calif., Davis.

Figure 19. In grapes, as in all fruit growing enterprises, there is a continuing effort to reduce labor costs. Power pruning is shown in a vinifera vineyard in California. A tractor-powered pneumatic system, self-guided by furrow, is at top right; a smaller unit is below. In addition to the shears at left, there is a power saw tool to remove large "fruited-out" trunks.

length, number, and distribution of canes. The renewal spurs are provided near the base of the fruiting canes to give a source of desirable new canes for fruiting the following year.

The canes selected for fruiting should be stocky, and carrying plump, vigorous buds. Concord canes and other varieties of similar vigor should measure ¼ inch in diameter between the fifth and sixth nodes from the base of the cane. Canes with eight to ten buds after pruning are the most desirable length. These canes should arise as near the trunk of the vine as possible and renewal spurs should be provided near the base of each cane, as shown in Figure 20. Remove all surplus wood, leaving only fruiting canes and spurs. Then tie the fruiting canes to the trellis with jute twine, light wire, or light wire set in strips of tough paper,[1] using a loose tie. Plastic chains are durable for tying trunks and cordons to wires.

Each vine provides a different problem. In every vineyard, one will find weak and strong vines; pruning must be adapted to the age, vigor, and to the individual canes on the vine. Vigorous Concord vines in well-managed vineyards may carry 40 or more buds after pruning, whereas with weaker-growing vines and varieties, half this number of buds may result in better fruiting. Usually the fifth, sixth, and seventh buds, counting from the base of a vigorous cane (Figure 17), will develop the most

---

[1] Commercial tying materials are available from Kwik-Way Products, 1350 E. Camino Ave., N. San Francisco, California, or A. M. Leonard and Son, Piqua, Ohio.

685

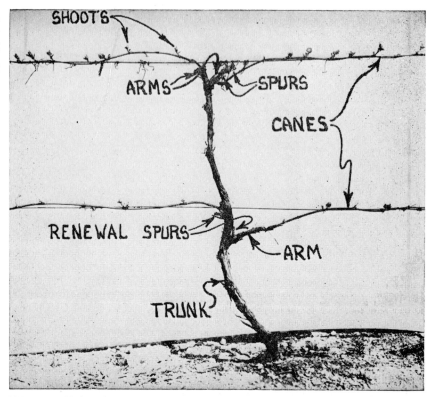

Figure 20. The 4-cane single-trunk Kniffin system is well adapted to vigorous varieties of grapes such as Concord, Niagara, and Fredonia. The vine is pruned to 4 canes, totaling 35 to 40 buds. A renewal spur with two buds is left near the base of each cane in order to renew the fruiting wood next year.

productive shoots, and such canes pruned to eight and ten buds are very desirable for fruiting.

Four-Arm Kniffin System. This has been the more popular training system with Concord and similar varieties. It is described basically in Figure 20, insofar as the training and maintenance of the vine is concerned from year to year.

Umbrella Kniffin. This system is similar to the four-arm Kniffin system of training except that the two lower canes and arms are removed and the upper canes are left long enough to bear the entire crop. This is because the best fruiting wood usually is found in the upper part of the vine. The same type of trellis is used. See Figure 21.

In the mature vine trained to the umbrella Kniffin system, the canes growing in opposite directions are bent gently over the upper wire and extended rather sharply downward to the lower wire to which they are tied. Renewal spurs are left at the head of the trunk. The general shape of the

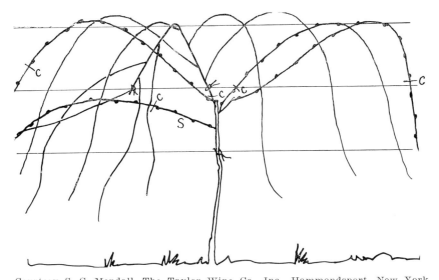

Courtesy S. C. Mendall, The Taylor Wine Co., Inc., Hammondsport, New York

Figure 21. This is a 4-year Concord vine trained to the Umbrella Kniffin system, showing where winter cuts would be made at "C." Canes and trunk can be tied loosely by reusable plastic chains, obtainable at most supply houses.

pruned vine resembles an umbrella. Canes are bent over the upper wire so the outer bark cracks. Shoots arising back of the bend are vigorous and excellent for fruiting the following year. If canes are drooped over the top wire and tied without a sharp bend, shoots at the tip of the cane usually grow best and it is difficult to obtain good fruiting canes that originate below the top wire. In recent tests in New York, the yields of Concord and Fredonia trained to the umbrella Kniffin system have been as good as or better than from vines trained to the four-arm Kniffin system.

Balanced pruning. N. L. Partridge of the Michigan Experiment Station, and N. J. Shaulis of the New York Experiment Station, Geneva, have suggested the balanced pruning system for grapes by which the number of buds left on a vine after pruning is kept proportionate to the vigor of the vine (Figure 24). This is done by weighing all the one-year wood pruned from the vine. Shaulis found the weight of this wood to vary from one to four pounds or more. For Fredonia, where more than one pound of wood is removed because of its inherent vigor, at least 40 fruiting buds are left on the vine. Ten buds then should be left for each extra pound of wood removed. For example, if three pounds total is removed from Fredonia, then 40 plus 10, plus 10 fruiting buds, or 60 buds in all, are left on the vine. For practical purposes, it is suggested that the grower estimate the weight of one-year wood on the vine, prune the vine, and weigh the one-year wood removed. This can be repeated on ten or more vines until the pruner comes to know the appearance of one, two, three, or four pounds of wood on a vine. Then he can

687

again estimate, prune, and weigh several vines until he becomes adept at estimating wood weight. By this balanced pruning Shaulis has been able to lift the yields per acre by double or more, as compared with leaving approximately the same number of buds on every vine in a vineyard, regardless of its individual vigor.

For the Concord variety, 30 buds are left for the initial pound of one-year prunings, plus ten buds for each additional pound of one-year prunings. For both Concord and Fredonia, the Four-Cane Kniffin system of training, combined with balanced pruning, was found to work satisfactorily.

The Geneva Double-Curtain (GDC) System. This training system (Fig. 24) was developed by Nelson Shaulis of the New York Agricultural Experiment Station, Geneva, for grape varieties with vine growth like Concord, Niagara, Catawba and Delaware, used primarily for processing; it is adapted to mechanical harvesting. Yields may be increased 50 per cent for vigorous vines and soluble solids may be increased significantly by about one per cent due apparently to better light exposure.

Conversion from a Kniffin to a GDC system has shown a labor cost in the mid 1960's of $300/A for vine and trellis, plus cost of growing the crop the first year. Trellising and tying materials cost an additional $135 an acre if wooden trellis arms were used, and about $300 per acre if metal trellis arms were used. Cost of new and/or replacement posts are not included since this varies considerably with the condition of the existing trellising system and the individual operator. Much of this conversion the first year must be considered a capital investment for subsequent years.

Labor cost to grow the crop the year after conversion averaged $175/A. As more experience is gained with this system, however, it is likely that conversion costs can be lowered below the above costs. Experience has shown that cultural operations, such as weed control, insect and disease control, cultivation, and hand harvesting, cost about the same for GDC as for other training systems. With the GDC system, more fertilizer may be needed in humid climates, particularly for nitrogen and potassium. Varieties grafted on resistant stock is important with this system to get the vigor needed.

Trellis construction has the important feature of T-top or Cordon wires (Fig. 24). One vine is trained for about 16 feet along one of these wires while an adjacent vine in the same row is trained 16 feet along the parallel wire. Trellis space per vine is about doubled over other training systems. Two trunks per vine is suggested; five-bud spurs and one-bud renewal spur should be maintained on each cordon or branch. Each year, the shoots from these spurs are positioned by hand so that they grow vertically downward to form a curtain of foliage suspended from each cordon wire, hence, a double curtain of foliage is the final effect from each row of grapes with good light exposure.

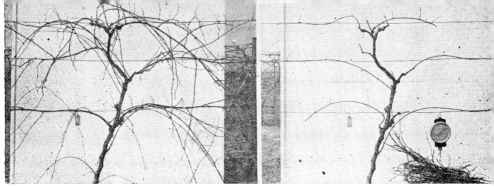

James M. Beattie, Ohio Agricultural Experiment Station, Wooster

Figure 23. This is "balanced pruning" on a six-cane kniffin trained Concord Vine (before pruning, left). The Vine was pruned by the "30 plus 10" formula (leave 30 buds for first pound of one-year wood removed plus 10 buds for each additional pound of such wood removed). Removed from this relatively vigorous vine were 3.4 lbs. of one-year wood, leaving 54 buds to produce the new crop.

Increase in net returns per acre should offset the additional cost of building the trellis and positioning the shoots each year. For details, consult the references by Nelson Shaulis *et al.*

Other training systems. The *Hudson River Umbrella* system is a modification of the umbrella kniffin in which the arms, at least 2 ft. long, rest along the top wire. From these arms, or cordons, the spurs arise and canes which grow or can be bent downward are tied to the bottom wire. The system (Fig. 25a) is productive and suggested for a variety like Concord.

The *Munson* system is suited to home vineyards where there are several varieties in the planting. The trellis resembles a T-type telephone pole arrangement with three wires on the cross bar on which the vines are trained. A person can cross from one row to another under the trellis in cultivation, spraying, and harvesting. Small fruits which are tolerant of some shade such as currants, gooseberries, and raspberries, can be planted in the row between the vines.

The *arbor* system for grapes frequently is used in the home landscape. Placement of trunks, canes, and spurs is similar to that for the Kniffin system, except more wood is left to provide shade at the sacrifice of some fruiting (Figure 25).

PRUNING NEGLECTED VINES

If mature vines have been neglected for a year or more, they become rangy with too much old wood. The best fruiting wood will be found a long distance from the base of the vine. Select from four to six reasonably desirable canes for fruiting as near to the central trunk of the vine as possible. Remove also any additional old wood coming from near the base of the vine or the main trunk, which will not be needed in fruiting in subsequent years. After two or three years of renewal pruning and selecting

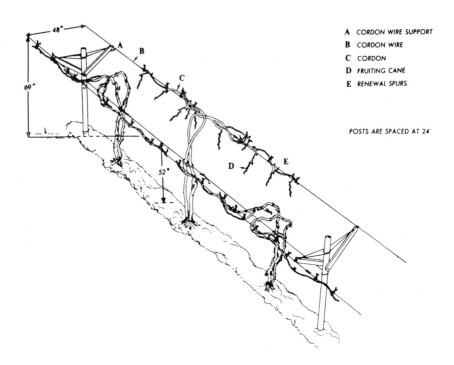

A CORDON WIRE SUPPORT
B CORDON WIRE
C CORDON
D FRUITING CANE
E RENEWAL SPURS

POSTS ARE SPACED AT 24'

(Upper) Nelson Shaulis N. Y. Agr. Exp. Sta., Geneva; (Lower) Mr. Cary, Mr. Whitford, CSIRO, Australia.

Figure 24. (Upper) With the Geneva Double-Curtain system of training, the shoots and leaves receive more light and air circulation, resulting in higher yields. (Lower) Tests are underway with cutter-bar mowing of trellised grapes to reduce labor. In Australia one swipe (left) is made to facilitate hand harvesting of table grapes; another swipe is made in winter to reduce wood and hand pruning. Fruiting is essentially on "spur canes."

690

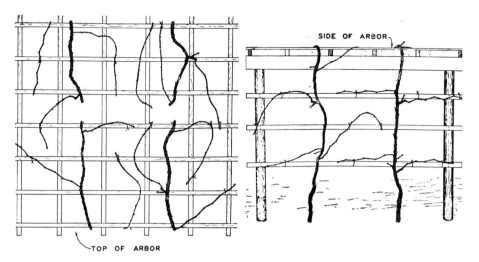

TOP OF ARBOR

SIDE OF ARBOR

Figure 25. On backyard arbors, more fruiting canes are left than for trellis pruning because shade as well as fruit are desired. A modification of the Single-Trunk-Kniffin plan of training can be used. The diagram shows vines after pruning.

fruiting canes closer and closer to the main trunk, neglected vines can be brought back within bounds to a fairly manageable pattern.

Sometimes it is possible to select a sucker arising from the base of the trunk for training straight to the upper wire to be used as a future central trunk for the new vine, eventually removing the old trunk.

COST OF GROWING GRAPES

Labor and material costs for growing grapes vary from season to season and from one location to another. Cost of producing a ton of grapes varies markedly with yield and quality—the higher the yield and quality the lower the costs. Following is a table showing costs of growing an acre of grapes by the GDC training system in New York, vs. the Umbrella Kniffin system.

TABLE 1

TABLE 1. GROWING COSTS/A OF GRAPES ON GENEVA DOUBLE CURTAIN VS. UMBRELLA KNIFFIN TO HARVEST. 1971. (T. D. TAYLOR, CORNELL, ITHACA, N. Y.)

Item	Geneva Double Curtain	Conventional Umbrella Kniffin
	Dollars	
Vineyard overhead	99	69
Fertilizer	21	11
Spray and dust materials	15	13
Labor (@ $2.50/hr.)	233	141
Tractor (8.6 hrs. @ $1.25/hr.)	11	11
Other equipment (including truck)	19	19
Interest	27	12
All other	41	41
Total	466	317

691

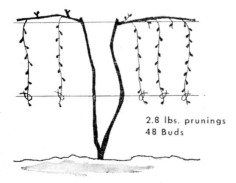

2.8 lbs. prunings
48 Buds

Figure 25a. The Hudson River Umbrella is a modification of the Umbrella Kniffin. Arms to left and right are at least 2 ft. long. (Courtesy Nelson Shaulis, N Y. Agr. Exp. Sta., Geneva).

Another survey by T. D. Taylor in New York (1972) showed that GDC training system of grapes yielded 10.5 T/A vs. the average yield of 4.5T by the Umbrella Kniffin system. Net returns over and above growing ($466/A) and harvesting costs ($26/T) with total returns @ $125/T were $574/A GDC vs. $129/A for the Umbrella Kniffin system.

In 1962, a survey of nine vineyards in Northwest Pennsylvania showed production costs/A to be about $77/Ton for 4.07 T/A yield, which can be adjusted to the current price level.

In 1971, Washington State University economists R. T. Dailey, et al. reported a 3-year cost study of mechanical harvesting of Concords. Conclusions were:

"Mechanical harvesting requires a large capital investment; about $54,-000 for a typical operation with $27,000 for the harvester. Annual fixed costs for operation were $12,260 or $7.40/ton. The variable costs/T were $5.15." As tonnage harvested per machine increased, variable costs remained constant at $5.15/T, while fixed costs decreased from $24.52/T at 500T harvested to $4.09/T on a 3,000-T harvest. Total costs were $29.67 and $9.24/T for those two respective harvesting rates."

Operating efficiency, that is the time a harvester was actually picking grapes, averaged nearly 65%. These harvesters (9) picked about 1,760 T of grapes on 245A and operated 568 hrs. during a 29-day harvest season." With a per hr. harvesting rate of 2 T and 200 hrs of use per season, the per T cost was $35.80. However, with a picking rate of 6 T/hr. and a 400-hr. picking season, the cost per T was $10.26."

HARVESTING AND MARKETING GRAPES

Stage of maturity. It is a common mistake to pick grapes too early. Unlike most fruits, there is practically no increase in color and sugar in grapes after they have been removed from the vines. Sour, poorly colored grapes on the market discourage subsequent sales.

The time for picking grapes depends upon the particular way in which they will be used. For jelly making, the fruit should be picked somewhat early in order to obtain light clear jelly free from crystals. For table use, grapes are picked when color and flavor are at the peak and before berries begin to shatter from the bunch, which varies with the variety. For juice, the grapes should be allowed to hang until full maturity is attained. Full maturity of grapes for wine or juice is judged by the soluble solids — sugar ratio, using a hand refractometer or Balling hydrometer (see Mrak's references). Indications often used to judge maturity other than by taste are browning and slight shrivelling of the stem, ease of separation of the berries, browning of the seeds, freeness of the seeds from the pulp, and a reddening or browning of the wood. Grapes have more natural resistance to storage rots if picked as soon as fully mature and before they are wet by rain.

Containers. Containers should be ordered well in advance of the picking season. The number and type needed obviously will depend upon the amount and quality of the yields. Yields vary tremendously with variety and growing conditions. Concords may vary from one to eight tons per acre. An average commercial yield in the better northern Ohio vineyards is about two and one-half tons with some growers obtaining yields up to six tons per acre. Profit is doubtful with yields under two tons. Weak-growing varieties such as Delaware and Catawba average around one to two tons per acre, occasionally reaching four tons. These varieties were demanding double or more the price of Concords, but in recent years the price difference has been disappearing, causing acreage of these varieties to be reduced.

The climax baskets of the two-, four-, and twelve-quart sizes are popular for use with the bunch grapes. The wooden baskets with the wire handles or the cardboard baskets with single or double-weight walls and a wooden handle are used in the Great Lakes regions. Cardboard containers are light, somewhat more economical, and better suited to advertising copy on the sides (Figure 27). The two- and four-quart containers are used for table grapes, whereas the twelve-quart basket and the bushel or half-bushel basket are employed for juice or wine purposes. The shallow-depth bulk boxes or wheel trailers are being used with or without mechanical harvesters to collect and carry grapes to the winery or juice plants. See Fig. 34.

Hand Picking and packing. Grapes for table use should be handled carefully from the time they are picked until sold. Preserve the powdery bloom on the berries as much as possible. Handle the bunches by the stems and do not pull them from the vines. Remove bunches with special shears or a sharp knife. The better bunches on a vine are picked first and packed as Fancy or Number 1 grapes,[1] whereas the im-

---

[1] For all government grade specifications for Eastern and Western grapes, contact the Agricultural Marketing Service, U.S. Dept. of Agr., Washington, 25 D.C. These include U.S. Standards for (a) Table Grapes, (b) Sawdust Pack Grapes, (c) American Bunch Grapes (Eastern) for Processing and Freezing, (d) Juice Grapes and (e) American (Eastern) Bunch Grapes.

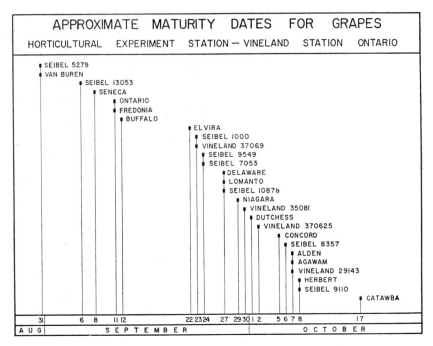

APPROXIMATE MATURITY DATES FOR GRAPES

HORTICULTURAL EXPERIMENT STATION — VINELAND STATION ONTARIO

O. A. Bradt, Hort. Exp. Sta., Vineyand Sta., Ontario

Figure 26. This chart gives the ripening order of grape varieties, from left to right, grown in Ontario, Canada. This same ripening order for varieties such as Fredonia, Delaware, Niagara, Concord, and Catawba should more or less hold in other regions where these varieties are grown.

perfect bunches are picked later and packed as Number 2 grapes. The poorer small bunches may be placed in a separate container for juice. In packing the basket, it is placed on the picking stand (Figure 29) in a slanting position and the corner nearest the picker is filled first with the stems pointing downward. The picker then proceeds to fill the basket from bottom to top until the farthest corner is filled last. The baskets are carefully packed to about an inch above the rim, after which they are placed in the shade of the vine until taken to the shelter house, which should be as soon as possible. Allow the grapes to settle from four to six hours before basket tops are applied. Many baskets are sold, however, without tops.

For the higher grade packages, the small, poorly colored, diseased, or insect-infested berries can be removed at picking and packing time, provided the current price will justify the extra labor. Cloudy dry days are best for picking. Decay is likely to occur if grapes are picked wet.

Mechanical Harvesting. To reduce harvesting labor costs, mechanical harvester machines are being perfected primarily for processing grapes for wine, juice, and other products. The Geneva-Double-Curtin

694

Dick Meister, American Fruit Grower magazine, Cleveland.

Fiigure 27. An exciting display of northern Ohio Concord and Niagara grapes in a Cleveland supermarket. The two-quart cartons with wooden handles are attractive; polyethylene wraps will preserve freshness and add attraction.

training system is well adapted to mechanical harvesting by certain types of machines. A machine is available, also, for the standard-trained grapes as shown in Figure 28. Grapes must be washed and processed as soon after harvesting as possible to avoid deterioration and self-crushing in the relatively large collection trailers. Most commercial vineyards are now mechanically harvested. See also mechanical harvesting under vinifera grapes. Labor union entrance into the grape and other agricultural enterprises has stimulated increased grower and engineer efforts to replace much of the migrant and other labor with automated equipment, particularly in harvesting.

Marketing. It is important that the grapes be taken to market on the day they are picked, or not later than the next day. The less they are handled from picking until they reach the consumer, the better. If a roadside stand is available near the main highway, a portion of the crop can be disposed of through this channel. It is possible to save on container costs by removing the grapes from the cartons and placing them in paper bags for the customer. Large retail stores sometimes will return the containers for repeat use but they may stretch with age.

During seasons of keen competition when labor costs are not out of reason, it may prove profitable to mix red, white, and blue grapes together with apples, peaches, pears and other fruits in a 2-qt family container.

The average housewife is canning and preserving less grapes than heretofore, reducing fresh sales of grapes and diverting more to processing.

Grape juice and wine offer large outlets for grapes (Figures 28, 29). Grapes made into wine approximate 700 thousand tons in the U.S.; annual frozen packs of juice vary between 4 and 10 thousand tons, depending upon carryover stocks. These marketing channels are extremely valuable during seasons when there is a heavy supply of grapes on the fresh-fruit market. The northern states ship large quantities of table grapes by refrigerator cars and trucks to the states farther south. Specific instructions for packing grapes for shipment can be obtained from the local freight station. It is important that grape baskets be packed solidly; a load of loose baskets is a juice factory on wheels.

Storing grapes. Eastern-type grapes cannot be stored successfully for more than about one or two months (Table 2). Controlled atmosphere (CA) storage shows promise of more than doubling this period. During a season when there is a heavy supply of grapes, it may be desirable to store a portion of the crop for later marketing. Grapes should be stored immediately after picking, using only the Fancy or No. 1 grapes which

TABLE 2. STORAGE LIFE OF LABRUSCA BUNCH-TYPE GRAPES IN WEEKS.

Concord	4-7	Catawba	5-8
Niagara	3-6	Worden	3-5
Delaware	4-7	Moore	3-6

are in sound condition. They preferably should be placed in cold storage at 31° to 32° F. with a humidity of 80 to 85 per cent. Stack the containers with frequent aisles running both vertically and laterally in order to provide free air circulation. To reduce mold development it is a common practice to spray the storage room and picking boxes with a solution of two pounds copper sulfate with 50 gallons of water several days before picking starts. The better keeping varieties are Delaware, Diamond, Concord, Agawam, Catawba, Sheridan, Vergennes, and Caco. The red grapes are usually somewhat better keepers than the black, white or blue varieties. The eastern varieties are not fumigated with sulfur dioxide, as western varieties, because of their susceptibility to damage.

Controlling insects and disease. Insect and disease problems vary in different vineyards. It is impossible to recommend a spray schedule for grapes that will have a general application. For a given vineyard, it seems desirable to study the quality of the crop previously produced and the type of insect or disease injury, if any, which was present. If one or more insects or diseases persist in appearing year after year, the spray or sprays designed to correct these troubles should be used. Thorough application of spray to both the upper and lower surfaces of the leaves, properly timed, and using the proper materials is highly important in producing good-quality grapes.

The following is a brief description of the common diseases and insects in eastern grape-growing regions. *Grape-berry moth*: Small brown worms that develop in the fruit, causing it to color prematurely. Infested berries later crack open or shrivel and drop from the bunch. *Grapevine flea beetle*: Small, steel-blue jumping beetles that eat the opening buds in spring and destory the new canes and fruit. The dark brown larvae feed on upper surface of the leaves in early summer. *Grape root worm*: Small, grayish-brown beetles which eat chain-like marks in the upper surface of the

(Top) Loren D. Tukey, Penn. State University, University Park and Chisholm Ryder Co., Inc., Niagara Falls, N. Y. 14305. (Bottom left) Welch Grape Juice Co., Westfield, N. Y. (Bottom right) Wine Institute, San Francisco.

Figure 28. (Top) This harvester for processing grapes, known as the "slapper type," knocks off and catches the grapes on a belt, blows off leaves and debris, and carries them up and over parallel row by belt to tractor-drawn trailer (see also Figure 35 for vinifera grapes). (Bottom) This is a processing plant for Concord grapes for juice in western New York. Grapes are unloaded, government inspected, washed in fresh water, picked up on cleats, thoroughly rinsed, and elevated to stemmers, then to hydraulic presses shown in bottom-left photo. In bottom-right picture is a common-type hydraulic grape press used in California wineries.

leaves in early summer. Larvae feed on grape roots. *Rose chafer*: Long-legged, yellowish-brown beetles about one-half inch long; they eat blossom buds, newly-set fruit, and foliage, and are limited principally to sandy areas of vineyards. *Climbing cutworms*: Brown cut worms that hide on the ground near canes by day and feed at night on the opening buds in early spring. *Leafhoppers*: Very small elongate pale green insects marked with

Figure 29. A light portable picking stand is convenient for filling baskets along the trellis. It should be about waist high to discourage pickers from dropping bunches into containers.

697

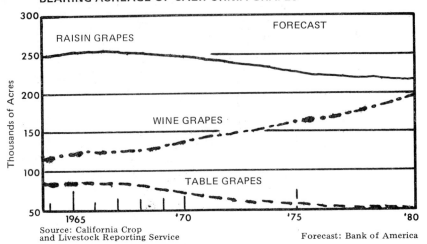

BEARING ACREAGE OF CALIFORNIA GRAPES

Source: California Crop
and Livestock Reporting Service

Forecast: Bank of America

Figure 29. This chart showing acreage trends in wine, raisin, and table grapes in California is probably more or less typical of trends in other countries. Due to hand and harvesting labor-union problems and others, table grapes will show a decline whereas wine (and juice) grapes mechanically harvested will show an increase, with raisin grapes showing a decline. Wine consumption over the world, and particularly in the U.S., is showing an increase, probably due to world travelling of people and the adoption of European wine-drinking customs. Wine consumption in France (32 gals/capita) and Italy, is continuing to increase. About 77% of the world grapes are made into wine. U.S. wine consumption is over 160 million gallons annually, or about 2 gallons/capita of which 93% is produced in the United States.

yellow and red, which jump from the leaves when disturbed. They suck sap from underside of leaves, causing speckled or rusty appearance of upper surface of leaves (Figure 30). *Black rot*: The fruit rots, then blackens, shrivels, and is covered with tiny black pimples. Leaves show brown spots having gray centers with black pimples (Figure 31). *Downy mildew*: Leaves have indefinite yellowish areas above, with white downy patches beneath. Young shoots are covered with white downy mildew. Fruit has poor size, color, and flavor while some berries cease development and show gray mold on the surface. If almost mature, they shrivel, dry completely, and turn brown. *Powdery mildew* is similar but whitish mainly on the upper leaf surface.

Dead arm is spreading in the East. Caused by a fungus, it weakens or eventually kills one or more sides of the vine. In early summer the leaves are yellowish, stunted, crimpled and curled on one or more canes. Cut and burn canes well back of injured areas as soon as noticed. Apply 6-6-100 Bordeaux or 2 lbs. of ferbam when shoots are a foot long; later black rot sprays will help control the disease. *Lightning* in grapes may wipe out an entire row. Partially injured plants may show a distinct marginal necrosis on the leaves. *Hail* may wipe out an entire crop, but the vines usually recover within a year or so.

(Top) George W. Still U.S.D.A. Grape Insect Laboratory, Sandusky, Ohio

Figure 30. The grape leaf on the left has been fed upon by a large population of leafhoppers; the one on the right was taken from a vine sprayed properly. A nymph and adult grape leafhopper are shown at lower right; normal length of adult is about ⅛ inch.

NYMPH   ADULT

The microscopic *bud mite* may cause serious crop loss in Western States. Symptoms are short basal internodes, scarification of bark, flattened canes, dead terminal buds, zigzag shoots, and absence of fruit. There is no known effective control.

Modern spray chemicals and machinery (Chap. XVIII) have simplified and increased control of grape pests and diseases immensely. (Fig. 32).

Inasmuch as spray recommendations for grapes vary considerably from region to region and vineyard to vineyard, it is wise to follow the spray program outlined by your local experimental station or agricultural extension service.

Spray machinery. No spraying is usually required during the time the vineyard is coming into production and in some cases during the early years of bearing. As the vineyard becomes older, however, diseases and insects tend to accumulate and may become a more serious problem. From 100 to 150 gallons of spray are required per acre of grapes for proper coverage. (See Chapter XVIII and Figure 32).

A few grapes in the home garden can be developed with practically no insects or diseases by placing paper bags around the bunches when the berries are about half grown. The bags should be fastened tightly around the stems by using paper clips, a stapling clamp, or string. Bagging is too expensive for commercial use.

Frost Control, Irrigation. If a late-spring frost severely injures new grape growth, remove all new growth ("stripping"). Grape buds are compound and this will force the secondary bud to develop, giving a partial crop. If shoot growth is long and only terminal tips and leaves are frosted, it is probably safer not to strip. These vines should produce a partial

Figure 31. Black rot fungus is one of the worst diseases of Labrusca grapes. It appears on leaves during rainy periods in June and July. Spots are small, translucent in center, browning toward the outside with concentric rings, pinhead black pimples and a blackline margin encircling the spot. (Left) Berries infected with black rot shrivel into hard black mummies covered with numerous tiny pimples. Most mummies shell and fall to the ground.

American Fruit Grower magazine, Willoughby, Ohio

crop without stripping; stripped vines never produce more than a partial crop.

California cost data showed for a 40A vineyard in 1971 a total investment of about $650 or $700/A for a combination of movable or tower-mounted wind machines, resp., with heaters. Annual costs/A in depreciation, interest on investment (7%) on ½ the cost, and cash outlay were about $141 vs. $146 for movable vs. tower-mounted wind machines with heaters. Investment costs per acre of a permanent sprinkler system installed for frost and irrigation for 40A totalled about $1,100 with either the liquid propane gas (LPG) engine or electric motor. Annual costs per acre were $108 for the LPG engine system and $115 for the electric motor. The sprinkler system is the best investment if water is available at reasonable cost. Trellised grapes can take the weight of ice accumulation well. Some growers are using surface trickle irrigation or underground (14-inch depth) through in-row plastic pipe distribution to save water but these systems, of course, cannot be used in frost control.

GROWING MUSCADINE GRAPES

The growing of Muscadine grapes in the southeastern states is limited to areas where the temperature rarely goes lower than 10° F., and practically never reaches 0° F. With legalized wine since 1933, a number of large Muscadine vineyards have developed for wine manufacture which is the largest single outlet. Other uses are in preserves, jellies, jams, and blending in fruit juice; the canned grapes are used in pies. Most varieties belong to *V. rotundifolia;* two other species are *V. munsoniana* and *V.*

700

Figure 32. These two sprayers are designed to cover grapes or hedgerow dwarf tree fruits faster and with less gallonage per acre. Upper FMC sprayer has 20 gpm pump; 300-500 gal stainless steel or coated epoxy or metalized tank that "takes" most chemicals (check herbicides with FMC); PTO or engine driven; lower is a Kinkelder PTO mist sprayer. (Courtesy FMC., Jonesboro, Arkansas and Marwald, LTD., Burlington, Ontario.)

popenoei. Upper boundary of growing area in southeastern U. S. extends from eastern North Carolina to southeast Missouri (excluding most of Tennessee) to central Oklahoma and south to Houston, Texas.

Propagation. Layering is the common practice; it is generally more successful than by cuttings. A 25 per cent or less "take" with Muscadine cuttings is due to a very hard wood that does not callus or root freely. It may prove more satisfactory to purchase vines from the nursery, requesting two-year plants rooted by layering. Concord and Delaware, *labrusca* grapes, can be grown successfully in the south on Dog Ridge stocks (*V. Champini*). See Overcash reference.

Varieties. Muscadine grape varieties are described in Table 3.

Magoon is an early mid-season, vigorous vine, self-fertile, medium reddish black berry of good quality being suggested in Alabama. North Carolina-USDA workers introduced Albemarle, Pamlico, Chowan, Roanoke and Magnolia for trial. All are superior producers and self-fertile.

701

TABLE 3. CHARACTERISTICS OF IMPORTANT MUSCADINE GRAPE[1] VARIETIES.

Variety	Color	Vigor[2]	Quality[2]	Berry size	Yield per vine	Maturity[3]	Sugar as total soluble solids
				Grams	Pounds	Harvest date	Percent
Burgaw[4]	Dark	7	5	4.0	33	Sept. 21	16.8
Creek	do	10	6	3.9	61	Oct. 5	17.3
Dearing[4]	Light	8	7	3.4	57	Sept. 27	19.2
Dulcet	Dark	9	8	3.6	44	Sept. 17	17.3
Higgins	Light	7	6	9.5	52	Oct. 1	16.0
Hunt	Dark	9	8	5.8	70	Sept. 17	17.1
Magoon[4]	Dark	8	7	4.1	64	Oct. 3	17.9
Scuppernong	Light	7	8	5.4	43	Sept. 23	16.8
Topsail	Light	10	10	5.9	46	Oct. 1	21.8
Yuga	do	8	7	4.1	64	Oct. 3	17.9

[1]Except for Higgins, ratings and figures for all varieties are averages in a 5-year test conducted at Raleigh, N. C. Higgins was tested 2 years. Vines were 4 years old at beginning of test.

[2]Rating: 2, very poor; 4, poor; 6, good; 8, very good; 10, excellent. A rating of 6 is as low as would be suitable for general planting.

[3]Average date of maximum maturity at Raleigh; date would be about 2 weeks earlier in Georgia and Mississippi. Most varieties have some ripe fruit 10 days before given maximum maturity dates.

[4]Perfect flowered. Other varieties are pistillate, and require pollinizers.

The Blue Lake bunch grape is grown in Florida. It's male parent was Caco x Concord; the female parent was an open-pollinated seedling of *V. smalliani*. Lake Emerald is another Florida variety.

Planting distances. Rangy varieties like Scuppernong on vertical trellises may be planted ten feet apart in the row with rows ten feet apart, later thinning the plants in the row to 20 feet. For less vigorous varieties, the plants may be set 15 feet apart in rows ten feet apart. The overhead training system (Figure 34) for Scuppernong is laid out with posts 20 feet apart on the square. Vines are planted ten feet apart and thinned over a five- to ten-year period as crowding occurs, leaving permanent vines 20 feet apart at the posts. Intercropping is a common practice with Muscadine grapes.

Soil Management. Apply annually in late winter about ½ lb 8-8-8 or equivalent N up to 4-6 lbs. On young vines apply an additional ½ lb sodium nitrate ringed a ft from the trunk one month after growth starts. A winter cover of crimson clover or a rye-vetch mixture can be grown in the middles; weed control is practiced under the wires with a chemical such as simazine.

Training and pruning. Muscadine grapes are trained to either a vertical or overhead trellis. A standard two-or three-wire vertical trellis is adapted to strong or weak varieties, resp., trained by either the *four-cane Kniffin* or *fan* system of the vertical six-arm renewal system (resembling the four-cane Kniffin system). The vertical trellis system has the advantages of

(Top left) R. D. Dickey, Florida Agr. Sta. (Top right, bottom left, bottom right) H. E. Jacob, Calif. Agr. Exp. Sta.

Figure 33. Methods for pruning Muscadine and Vinifera grapes. (Top left) Seven-foot high overhead trellis is used for Muscadine grapes in southern home and commercial vineyards. Two-wire vertical trellis is more popular, however. (Top right) A mature horizontal bi-lateral Cordon-pruned Vinifera vine system for table and spur-pruned wine varieties, giving earlier better yields and easier harvesting. Bottom left) A cane-pruned Vinifera vine on a two-wire trellis. The system is used primarily for raisin and wine varieties in California. (Bottom right) A head-pruned mature vine. The system used for vinifera varieties which bear well on spurs, including most wine grapes, the raisin Muscat, and a few table grapes, notably the Tokay. Note placement of trunk, arms, spurs, and canes from which fruiting shoots develop.

being less expensive to construct than the overhead system and the vines are more convenient to spray, prune, harvest, and intercrop with small fruits and vegetables. See Kniffin and fan training systems for *labruscas*.

The overhead trellis may be used for vigorous varieties (Figure 33), such as Scuppernong. It consists of durable posts and ten-gauge wire, affording a seven-foot clearance which permits cross-cultivation and grazing underneath by livestock; vines trained by this system are more likely to succeed under neglect. The posts are placed about 20 feet apart. The end posts are well braced with guy wires. A wire system is arranged across the tops of the posts so that four wires are attached to the top of each inner post, two running at right angles across the field and two running diagonally and at right angles to each other. This provides sufficient wires, radiating from the top of a post like the spokes on a wheel, to accommodate eight fruiting arms. If one old arm is cut back and renewed each year, this will mean that each of the eight arms will be renewed once in eight years. The canes in pruning are cut back to spurs about six inches long, each spur carrying from four to six buds. One arm, depending upon age, is capable of carrying many of these spurs.

Pruning can be done at any time when the vines are bare of foliage. The best time is after danger of freezing weather and before the buds start to swell. Pruning details are in USDA Farmers Bull. 2157.

Pests. Muscadines have a few pests. Black rot, bitter rot, grape flea beetle, berry moth and curculio may be problems; contact the local agricultural service for recent control measures.

Harvesting and handling. The average variety receiving good care should give 25 to 30 bushels of grapes per acre from four-year vines, 50 to 75 bushels from five-year vines, and 100 to 150 bushels from vines in full bearing. On the basis of 60 pounds per bushel, this is about three to six tons per acre. Varieties such as Scuppernong yield less than James and Thomas. Grapes for the winery or culinary purposes are harvested with a 6-8 ft long canvas catching frame hung on the wires (see USDA Farmers Bull. 2157). Mechanical harvesting machines may be profitable in large plantings. (Figure 34). Grapes for table use, including those that shatter from the cluster as well as those that remain attached to the cluster, are harvested carefully by hand and placed on the market in two- and four-quart climax baskets and the ordinary strawberry crates.

Store at 56-60° F to prolong berry life; CA storage extends quality further.

GROWING VINIFERA GRAPES

Vinifera grapes comprise most of the World grape production. About 72% of all grapes are produced in Europe, 13% in North and South America, 6% in Africa, 7% in Middle East, and 2% in Australia.

In the U. S. *viniferas* are grown in the semiarid warm-temperate and subtropical regions of California, Arizona, and lower Texas along the Rio Grande River. The vines require a hot dry summer and a cool wet winter (rain may be replaced or supplemented by irrigation). A mean daily winter temperature of between 35° and 50°F., gradually rising to between 70° and 85°F. in summer is favorable. An average yearly rainfall of 20 to 25 inches is usually sufficient if well distributed during the autumn, winter, and spring.

Varieties. Importance of varieties in the U. S. is exemplified by approximate acreage (000's) of 20 leading varieties in California: Thompson Seedless (RT)[1], 235; Emperor (T), 31.5; Carignane (rW), 27; Zinfandel (rW), 24; Tokay (T), 23.5; Muscat of Alexandria (R & W), 20;

James A. Cook, Univ. of California, helped revise the *Vinifera* section.

[1]R-raisin; T-table; r-red; W-wine; w-white.

Grenache (rW), 14.5; Alicante Bouschet (rW), 10; Mission (rW), 9; Palomino (wW), 9; Ribier (T), 8; Malaga (wW), 5; Petite Sirah (rW), 4.5; Cardinal (T), 4; Perlette (T), 3.5; Red Malaga (T), 3; Burger (wW), 3; Mataro (rW), 3; French Colombard (wW), 2.5; Salvador (rW), 2.5. Cabernet Sauvignon (claret of France) is a high-quality dinner wine. To emphasize, Thompson Seedless can be used for raisins, wine and table and makes up about 40% of the state's over 3 million tons. See reference for variety details.

Propagation. Rooted cuttings of the desired fruiting varieties can be used only in soils not infested with the phylloxera insect or nematodes. In soils infested with these pests, cuttings of resistant rootstocks must be grafted to the desired fruiting variety either before (whip-graft) or after rooting (by whip-, cleft-, or groove-grafting or chip budding). Soil fumigants such as DBCP can be applied by flooding to established plantings for controlling most (ectoparasitic) nematodes. Use rootstocks resistant to phylloxera and nematodes, particularly on replant sites and on deep coarse sandy low-fertility drouthy soils. The University of California and USDA have developed indexed vines of 34 table and raisin varieties, 50 wine and 14 rootstock varieties (available through Calif. Dept. of Agr. Nursery Serv., Sacramento) which have earlier and larger production, uniform vigorous vines and fruit with full color and maturity. Certified heat-treated "virus-free" stock should be sought to avoid destructive viruses.

Planting distances. One hundred square feet or more are required per vine in fertile soils and hot climates where vines grow large. For cooler climates, less fertile soils or for smaller growing varieties, about 80 square feet or even less may suffice. Trellised vigorous raisin varieties are planted 8 by 12 feet. With modern machinery, rows mostly are 12 ft apart, with avenues of 18 to 20 feet at intervals of 300 to 600 feet, or equivalent to the length of the irrigation furrows.

Vine supports. Varieties trained to the vase-form are supported by sticks four to six feet long. The sticks are removed after six to ten years when the vines become self-supporting. For a simple two-wire trellis, a substantial six-foot stake at each vine is sufficient with two No. 11 or No. 12 smooth galvanized fencing wires stretched along the row at 34 and 46 inches from the ground. For large-growing varieties, such as Thompson Seedless, a "wide top" trellis is often constructed by tying a cross-arm (two by two inches by three feet) to the top of each alternate stake and bracing the lower end to hold the cross-arm at an angle of about 30° from the horizontal. Three wires are used on the cross-arms and one just beneath on the stake. Advantages of this system are more fruiting wood, clusters better exposed to light and air, better distribution of wood and bunches, and cultural and mechanical harvesting operations are facilitated. The Duplex system of training is shown in Figure 34 which facilitates mechanical harvesting and increases yields and also soluble solids (by about one percent) with

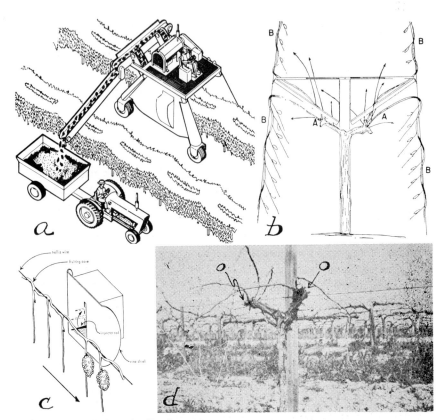

University of California, Davis.

Figure 34. Vinifera grapes for processing are mechanically harvested to cut labor costs and get grapes to the processor rapidly. (a) Shows essential principles of mechanical harvesting equipment; improvements are being made annually. The "slapper" type machine knocks the grapes off of standard trellises onto moving belts and escalators, thence to trailer alongside. The "impactor" type harvester (c) is designed to shake bunches apart and onto a belt (gondola training system). The "Duplex" or Geneva Double-Curtain training system shown in "b to d" is adapted to the impactor-type harvester. In "b", "A" shows replacement zone to furnish fruiting canes; the selected shoots remaining after spring deshooting and deflorating are indicated with arrows. "B" shows fruit-bearing zone or wires, the pendant shoots with flower clusters arising from fruiting canes. The "d" photo shows a cordon-pruned Palomino variety vine, 8 years, after conversion to the "duplex" system, showing shortening of side trunks at "o" and the canes saved to be wrapped on wires after assembly in "b" is in place. At "c" is the strong "needle" of the impactor-type harvester that extends out in the mid-wire section and shakes off bunches onto moving belt.

earlier maturity.   Machines are available, however, that will harvest vines trained on vertical trellises.   Conversion of old vines to the Duplex system is shown in Figure 34 and described in detail in a California bulletin AXT-274.   Table grapes are still harvested by hand.

Pruning.   Principles of pruning are similar to those for the Eastern grape. Three popular systems of training and pruning are shown in Figure 34, each adapted to the growth and fruiting habits of certain varieties. Head pruning is almost always used for wine grapes that bear well with short spur pruning, also for the Flame Tokay table grape and the Muscat raisin grape. Cane

706

Courtesy J. Lamaar Anderson, Utah State University, Logan.

Figure 35. (Upper) Thompson seedless grapes in Utah showing effects of spraying with gibberlic acid (GA) and girdling of vines. Largest bunches and berries (lower right) were obtained by thinning clusters to 12/vine and spraying with GA on June 13 at 20 ppm (blossom) and on June 23 at 40 ppm (shatter stage), plus girdling the trunk on June 23. Grapes were harvested August 24. (Lower left) a special knife to remove strip of back. A girdle made previous year below has heeled over. (Lower right) Treated bunch on left is compared with untreated at right.

pruning is universally used for *vinifera* varieties that do not have fruitful buds near the base of the canes, such as Thompson Seedless, and also for such small-clustered wine-grape varieties as Sauvignon Blanc, Pinot Noir, and Chardonnay. Cordon pruning is used for practically all of the seeded table grapes except Tokay and some White Malaga. Pruning is done annually during the dormant season. Pneumatic power pruning has reduced labor by at least 30% and also fatigue (Figure 19). Labor can be reduced further by trimming off canes of spur-pruned varieties by tractor mowing far ahead of subsequent detail pruning.

Fruit Thinning. Three types of fruit thinning are used on *vinifera* grapes; namely, flower-cluster thinning, cluster thinning, and berry thinning. Each type of thinning results in a reduction in the number of flowers or fruits and better growth and development of those which are left. The method of thinning used depends upon the type of fruit produced by a vineyard of a variety. *Flower-cluster thinning* is used on varieties which develop loose straggly clusters, such as Muscat of Alexandria and Dattier. The vines should be pruned with long spurs or fruit canes and some flowers removed as soon as possible after the clusters appear. *Cluster thinning,* or the removal of entire clusters soon after berries are set, is the most widely used. Enough wood is left at pruning time each year to produce a crop in so-called poor years, but if a good year later is in prospect, the overload is then removed by cluster thinning which results in large regular crops almost every year. *Berry thinning* is practiced by cutting off the end of the main stem and several branches of the cluster, or by cutting off enough of the main stem to leave only the desired number of berries. It is limited to varieties which set very compact or very large clusters. Berry thinning is practiced as soon as the berries have set.

Some of the kinins (SD-8339), growth regulators, have been found to promote protein synthesis among other things and increase cluster and berry size and berry roundness (Black Corinth) when treated with 1000 ppm spray shortly after bloom.

Girdling. The removal of a $\frac{3}{16}$-inch strip of bark from around the main trunk at blooming time increases the set of seedless berries. Girdling improves the yield of Black Corinth which normally sets straggly small clusters of mostly tiny seedless berries. Girdling is practiced on Thompson Seedless vines for increasing berry size of table grapes; it is performed as soon as possible after berries have set. (Figure 35).

Gibberellins. This group of growth regulators, which occurs naturally in grapes and other plants, can be sprayed on certain varieties of grapes at specific times to enlarge berries and loosen clusters (Figure 35). With girdling, use of GA (gibberellic acid, or commercial Gibrel)[1] has become standard practice on Thompson Seedless, the leading variety. Spraying before bloom has reduced bunch rot in some wine varieties; spraying in bloom has loosened bunches of Thompson Seedless and has replaced girdling in production of Zante currants. Use of kinins, Ethrel (Amchem 66-329), morphactins, 4-CPA, Alar, dormant sprays of 2, 4-D, and other growth regulators has given interesting results (see ref-

[1]Merck and Co., Inc., Rahway, New Jersey.

erences) in quality improvement, fruit set, delay in bud opening, and berry release for mechanical harvesting. Use of these chemicals is in the developmental stage. See Figures 16, 35.

Fertilizer. Nitrogen, at 200 to 400 pounds per acre, is usually the only nutrient to which these grapes respond in California. Economically, favorable responses to phosphorus and potash are rare. Ten to twenty tons per acre of manure or winery pomace, if available at low cost, are good fertilizers. Zinc deficiency may be a problem in some areas. Treatment consists of painting the pruning wounds at pruning with a solution of one pound of zinc sulfate in one gallon of water.

Weed Control. With strip-row chemical weed control, little in-row cultivation is being practiced in *vinifera* vineyards. Annual weeds are no problem but perennials such as Johnson and Bermuda grasses must be controlled by *timely* applications. Some growers are using complete ground coverage with chemicals. (See Chap. XVIII).

Irrigation. Irrigation is practiced in California chiefly in the interior valleys, and there are undoubtedly many vineyards in the south and north coast regions which would benefit from it. The entire rooting area should be wetted by each irrigation checking penetration with a probe. Some soils hold less than 1 inch of water/ft depth, others 2+ inches. Application can be by basin, checks (Fig. 36), furrows (most common), or sprinklers (on rough contour). See reference and Chapter XIX.

Experimental "off-on" automatic misting of field *viniferas* in California has been found to reduce irrigation water needed and cool the grapes, lifting yield and quality.

Harvesting. *Table grapes.* Most California table grapes are marketed 2,000 miles or more from the vineyards. Transportation is by refrigerated rail cars or by air; time for rail shipping is 7 to 11 days, only hours by air. Proper time of harvesting is judged by the sugar content, using a hydrometer (saccharimeter) as described by Jacob. By experience, the picker judges maturity roughly by: (a) color and condition of the cluster stem; when top of cluster stem is brown and woody or when framework stems of cluster are light or straw yellow, (b) taste of the berries (used only at intervals due to a dulling of the taste), and (c) the characteristic change in color of berries of different varieties which is recognized only with experience. It is usually necessary to go over a vine three or more times in order to harvest most of the table grapes at the proper stage. *Wine grapes.* The picking time for wine grapes varies with the kind of wine to be made. Grapes are picked earlier for dry wines than for sweet wines. Grapes for dry wines are picked when the sugar content tests 18° to 23° Balling, while grapes for sweet wines are harvested usually at 24° Balling or more. For ordinary wine, the entire crop is harvested at a single picking which is the usual practice in California.

For weed control commercial literature, contact E. I. Du Pont, Wilmington, Dela., and Geigy Agr. Chem., Saw Mill River Rd., Ardsley, N. Y.

Several pickings are made for very fine wine. The grapes are mechanically harvested (Figure 34) and taken to the processing plant and crushed as soon as possible. Grapes for raisins are picked at 23° Balling or more. The degree of maturity at which raisin grapes are picked is usually a compromise between leaving the grapes as long as possible for better quality and heavier yield and yet to avoid the possibility of early fall rains which may interfere with sun drying. If the grapes are to be dehydrated in special ovens, weather conditions are a minor factor in picking, but the grapes must be removed before early rains cause deterioration on the vine.

In mechanical harvesting, a breeding program is needed to develop varieties with bunches that "fall apart" easily on shaking and with berry scars (where pedicel is attached to berry) that do not break open readily.

Insect and disease resistance of *V. rotundifolia* has been transferred to the *V. vinifera* good fruit quality and vine fertility by backcrossing hybrid *V. rotundifolia* x *V. vinifera* to *vinifera* in California.

Temperature and storage conditions. Recommended storage temperatures for *vinifera* (California type) grapes are 30° to 31° F., according to W. F. Allen, formerly University of California. Although temperatures as low as 28° F have not been injurious to well-matured fruit of some varieties, other varieties of low sugar content have been damaged by exposure to 29°F. A humidity of 87 to 92% at temperatures of 30° to 31° F is recommended.

Some storage plants in California have precooling rooms where grapes are cooled to 36° to 40°F in 20 to 24 hours before they are placed in storage. In most plants all of the cooling is done in the storage rooms, but only a few have sufficient air movement to cool the fruit as quickly as desired. Experience has indicated that about 4,000 to 6,000 cfm per carload of fruit is needed in rooms used for precooling. A carload of about 1000 lugs occupies a space of 2000 cu. ft. After the fruit has been precooled, the air velocity should be reduced to that which will maintain uniform temperature throughout the room and distribute the SO_2 evenly.

TABLE 3. STORAGE LIFE OF VINIFERA TABLE GRAPES.

Emperor, Ohanez, Alphonse Lavallee (Ribier)	3-5 months
Malaga, Castiza (Red Malaga), Cornichon	2-3 months
Sultanina (Thompson Seedless)	1-2½ months
Flame Tokay, Alexandria (Muscat)	1-1½ months

In the storage of grapes there is no need for ventilation except to provide for exhausting sulfur dioxide-laden air following fumigations, as will be described later. Accumulation of carbon dioxide would not be objectionable and might benefit the grapes. Grapes do not give off appreciable amounts of ethylene or other substances that accelerate ripening as do apples, pears, and some other fruits.

The normal change that takes place in grapes in storage involves chiefly loss of water. The most noticeable effect of this is drying and browning of stems and pedicels and shriveling of the fruit. Grapes become slightly sweeter during storage due to concentration of sugar by loss of moisture, but the total amount of sugar present slowly diminishes as does the acid content as well.

Since the turgidity of grapes increases as the temperature is lowered, they sometimes split in storage. With prolonged holding, moisture loss eventually causes the fruit to lose its turgidity and to soften. During storage the pedicel attachment becomes weakened, probably as a result of changes in pectic substances; consequently shattering (loss of berries from the stem) is sometimes a problem on susceptible varieties such as Sultanina (Thompson Seedless). The color of red or blue varieties gradually becomes darker in storage. White varieties, such as Ohanez, Sultanina, and Malaga, may turn brown. This browning becomes worse with longer storage and cannot be prevented by storing at 36°F instead of 31°F. Browning of white varieties also is sometimes associated with over-maturity, and fruit from one vineyard may be affected more severely than that from another.

Fumigation. Grapes are usually stored in rooms by themselves, for if they are to be held more than a few weeks they should be fumigated for mold control with sulfur dioxide, which is injurious to other storage commodities. (See references for detail procedure).

The normal storage life of the principal varieties of California table grapes at 30° to 31° F is shown in Table 3. Under exceptional conditions sound fruit will keep longer than indicated; for example, Emperor grapes have been held in good condition for seven months, and Sultanina for four months.

The storage life of grapes is affected in large degree by the attention given to selecting and preparing the fruit. Grapes should be picked at the best maturity for storage, especially Sultanina and Ohanez. Stems and pedicels should be well developed and the fruit should be firm and mature. Soft and "weak" fruit should not be stored. The display lug is a satisfactory package for storage since it can be cooled and fumigated easily. Sawdust packages cannot be fumigated effectively, so that it is necessary to fumigate the grapes before they are packed. South African packs of wrapped bunches in excelsior have proved to be good storage packages. Precooling to 40° to 45°F is advised for grapes that are to be in transit a day or two before reaching storage. (See USDA Agr. Handbook 159 on storage problems of grapes by Ryall and Harvey.)

Diseases and pests. These include powdery mildew, black measles, black knot, Pierce's disease, little-leaf, Phylloxera, nematode, grape leafhopper, cutworms, red spider, grape leaf roller, rabbits, and gophers. Ozone is a by-product in exhaust fumes causing brown stipple on young or mature leaves in fall in southern California; laws making muffler filters mandatory have reduced damage.

Researchers are integrating the effects of natural control agents, chemi-

These are backyard gardens, mostly grapes, grown on terraces in the Alps of Switzerland. The time is late spring. (Courtesy Geigy Chemical Corp., Ardsley, N. Y. 10502).

cal use, and cultural practices in an attempt to cut costs of pest control in California. Contact local government services for control charts.

Marketing. Fresh *Vinifera* grapes are sold in conventional wood boxes, costing 94c to $1.08 per box to pack. Hale and Stokes prepackaged in poly-face fiberboard units in master containers in California before shipment East and found the cost of about 50c more to be justified. Grapes arrived with less damage (1.5%) and received less damage on the counters. Better shipment is obtained when the 28-lb. box or containers are vibrated before shipment to avoid a loose-pack condition (see Pear Chap.). One to 3 lb meshed colored plastic boxes are attractive containers on the counter.

Review Questions

1. Indicate the approximate regions where the European-, American- and Muscadine-type grapes are grown in the United States.
2. What is the relative commercial importance of the above three types of grapes in the United States?
3. What are the five leading states in grape production? How do you account for the heavy production in these states? What World countries lead in grapes?
4. What is the chief method for propagating the native American-type grapes?
5. Discuss leading *V. Labrusca* varieties in your area.
6. Briefly describe a soil management system for a (a) young and (b) mature vineyard in your locality, including recommendations for cultivation, cover crops, and manures or commercial fertilizers.
7. Diagram the Geneva Double-Curtain method of training grapes. Advantages? Disadvantages?

8. Diagram, label, and briefly describe the 4-cane Kniffin system of pruning a mature Concord vine; the fan system; what is "balanced" pruning?
9. How does pruning grapes on arbors differ from that described in the previous question?
10. How do you judge picking maturity for table grapes?
11. What type of spray equipment is most effective in insect and disease control in commercial vineyards in the East?
12. Discuss *current* aspects of mechanical harvesting of grapes.
13. Essentially, how do Muscadine grapes differ from the native American-type in berry and cluster, vigor, training systems and use?
14. For the *Vinifera* grape, as grown in California, e.g., discuss the modern concepts of 4 of the following topics: varieties, rootstocks, harvesting techniques, GA use to improve marketability, SO_2-treatment of harvested grapes, training systems for vines, pruning mature vines, drying for raisins, scoring or girdling the vines, and storage requirements. Check references for additional details on some topics.

Suggested Collateral Readings

LABRUSCA TYPE

Abbott, A. J. and R. A. Webb. Achene spacing of strawberries as an aid to calculating potential yield. Nature. Vol. 225. pp. 663-664. Feb. 14, 1970.

Abdalla, D. A. and H. J. Sefick, N, P, and K effects on yield, chemical composition, juice quality of Concord in South Carolina. ASHS 87:253-258. 1965.

Balerdi, C. F. and J. A. Mortensen. Performance of muscadine grapes (*Vitis rotundifolia* Mich.) in central Florida. HortSci. Vol. 4 (3):252-253. 1969.

Barritt, B. H. Fruit set in seedless grapes treated with growth regulators Alar, CCC and Gibberellin. J. ASHS. 95(1):58-61. Jan. 1970.

Beattie, J. M. and M. P. Baldauf. Soil management effects on yield, quality Concord grape juice. Ohio Agr. Exp. Sta. Res. Bull. 868, 35 pp. Oct. 1960.

Bernstein, L., C. F. Ehlig and R. A. Clark. Effect of grape rootstocks on chloride accumulation in leaves. J. ASHS. 94(6):584-590. Nov. 1969.

Bottrill, D. E. and J. S. Hawker. Chlorophylls and their derivatives during drying of sultana grapes. J. Sci. Fd. Agric. Vol. 21:193-196. April. 1970.

Bradt, O. A. and J. Wiebe. Four-arm vs. 6-arm Kniffin for Catawba. 46-48 pp. Hort. Res. Inst., Vineland, Ont. Ann. Rpt. 1970.

Bradt, O. A. and A. Hutchinson. Grape rootstock studies. Vineland, Ont. Ann. Rpt. 28-44. 1970.

Bradt, O. A. and R. A. Cline. Interrelated effect of pruning severity, growth and nutrition on yield of Concord grapes. Hort. Res. Inst. of Ontario. Rpt. 1969. pp. 53-58.

Cahoon, G. A. and C. W. Donoho, Jr. Alar effects on yield, quality, Concord. Jour. ASHS 94 (in Press) about 1969.

Cook, James A. Grape nutrition. Chap. in Fruit Nutrition book, edited by N. F. Childers. 777-812. Hort. Publ., Nichol Ave., New Brunswick, New Jersey, 1966.

Clore, W. J. *et al.* Composition of Washington-produced Concord grapes and juices. Wash. Agr. Exp. Sta. Tech. Bull. 48, 21 pp. 1965.

Dawson, J. H., W. H. Clore and V. F. Bruns. Weed control in grapes with Monuron, Diuron and Simazine. Wash. Agr. Exp. Sta. Bull 680, 10 pp. 1967.

Diener, R. G. and J. H. Levin. Grape trellis wire strength tested. Mich. Quart. Bull. 50:2, 197-203. Nov. 1967

Eskew, R. K. *et al.* Powdered grape juice. Food Tech. 8, 27-28. 1954.

Fleming, H. K. Age of vine and Concord grape production. Pa. Exp. Sta. Bull. 648. 13 pp. June, 1959.

Fleming, H. K. and R. B. Alderfer. Cultivation and Concord grape production. Pa. Agr. Exp. Sta. Bull. 616. 18 pp. January, 1957.

Fulton, R. H. Small fruit diseases in Michigan. Mich. Agr. Ext. Serv. Bull. 370. 75 pp. 1960.

Growing American bunch grapes USDA Farmers Bull. 2123. 21 pp. 1968.

Haeseler, C. W. and H. K. Fleming. Day temperature effects on Concord vines. Pa. Agr. Exp. Sta. Bull. 739, 17 pp. 1967.

References continued in Appendix under grape

CHAPTER XXI

Strawberry Growing

❖ ❖ ❖ ◇ ❖ ◈ ◆ ◆ ◆ ◆ ◆ ◆ ◆ ◆ ◆ ◆ ◆ ◆ ◆ ◆ ◆ ◆ ◆ ◆

The strawberry is among the first of the fresh fruits on the market in spring. It is in great demand locally in all regions in which it is grown. Due to its wide adaptation to climate and soils, the strawberry is available fresh from the tropics to the subarctic the year round. The growing air-freight business has spread the fresh strawberry to almost any World market every month of the year. World production of strawberries by countries is given in Table 1.

From the concentrated areas of U. S. production in Figure 1, considerable quantities of strawberries are shipped to distant markets. In the eastern United States, the first commercial berries are harvested in Florida near Homestead, December 1, and as the season progresses northward,

TABLE 1. APPROXIMATE WORLD PRODUCTION OF STRAWBERRIES IN 000'S OF METRIC TONS, EARLY 1970's.

Country	Production	Country	Production
United States	224	Hungary	21*
Japan	115	Canada (Ont.,	
Mexico	110	B. C., Que. N. S.)	19
Poland	100	Czechoslovakia	15*
Italy	74	Denmark	11
France	57	Norway	10
Yugoslavia	56*	Spain	8
United Kingdom	50	Greece	5
Germany (FR & E)	49*	Lebanon	5
Netherlands	32	New Zealand	4
Bulgaria	30	Australia	3
Belgium	25	Finland	3
		Israel	2

[1] Countries with an asterisk (*) list only berries, but this figure in most cases refers largely to strawberries. No data are available for the USSR, but production is known to be high with some plantings as large as 250 acres on government farms. There is little interest in small fruits in the general area of China where only fruits with peel are preferred for sanitary reasons. No data are available from Africa and South America, although appreciable production occurs in South Africa in the provinces of Transvaal, Natal, and Cape of Good Hope, and particularly near the large cities as Capetown and Johannesburg. Strawberries are grown widely in South America in small plantings near large cities.

Donald H. Scott, U. S. Dept. of Agr., Beltsville, Md., assisted in this chapter revision.

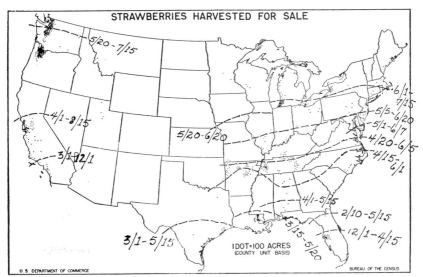

STRAWBERRIES HARVESTED FOR SALE

I DOT=100 ACRES
(COUNTY UNIT BASIS)

U S DEPARTMENT OF COMMERCE

BUREAU OF THE CENSUS

U. S. Bureau of Census

Figure 1. Strawberries are grown commercially from subtropical Florida and Texas to Minnesota, Maine, and Alaska. Concentrated areas of commercial production are shown in such states as Florida, Louisiana, Arkansas, Missouri, Tennessee, Illinois, New Jersey, California, Washington, and Oregon. Lines and dates show the approximate shipping season for each section. Shipments start about December 1 in Florida and continue to July 15 in New York, Michigan, and Washington. California harvests strawberries most of the year.

strawberries are shipped from Louisiana, North Carolina, Arkansas, Tennessee, Missouri, Kentucky, Maryland, and New Jersey. Among the last strawberries to ripen are those in the regions of the Upper New England States, New York, Wisconsin, and Washington.

The commercial strawberry industry is probably more equally distributed among southern and northern states than any other important fruit. The (a) average acreage (1970-72), (b) yield/A in lbs., and (c) production (1000 lbs), respectively, for the seasonal strawberry crop is about as follows in the U.S.: *Winter*, (Fla.), 1800, 9500, 15,200; Spring (California), 8200, 35,200, 288,000; *Early Spring* (La., Tex.), 3300, 27,200, 9000; *Mid-Spring* (Ill., Mo., Md., Va., N.C., Ky., Tenn., Ark. Okla.) 9050, 2920, 26,400; *Late Spring,* 28,890, 5100, 147,7000; *Total:* 50,047, 9700, 484,600. Total value of the United States crop in 1970 was about 100 million dollars. About 44 per cent of the crop comes from California. Around 42 per cent of the U.S. crop is processed.

Due to labor problems in the United States, strawberry production in both Mexico and Canada increased markedly in the 1960's, then leveled. Most of the crops go to processing and have had an effect on the U. S. strawberry market. Fresh berries from the U. S. now are being airfreighted to foreign markets and harvesting machines, though expensive, likely will minimize peak labor tensions in large plantings contracted for processing.

715

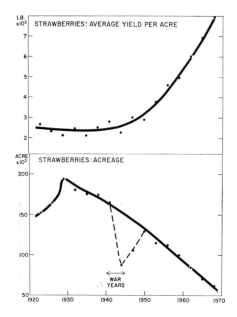

Figure 2. Note the marked increase in average yield/A of strawberries and the accompanying drop in acreage in the U. S. from the 1920's to 1970. This more or less continuing trend is typical of the strawberry regions throughout the world. Rise in yield/A is due mainly to the relatively "virus-free" plants, breeding programs for better yielding and quality, and general improvement in cultural techniques. The strawberry is an intensive crop, requiring considerable hand and back-breaking labor which accounts in part for the drop in acreage. Horticulturists and engineers, however, are developing automated equipment and techniques to reduce this labor as much as possible. (Courtesy Cecil H. Wadleigh, USDA, Beltsville, Md.)

LOCATING THE PLANTATION

Factors of first importance in locating a commercial strawberry plantation are: (a) accessibility of markets, (b) transportation facilities, (c) adequate labor supply, (d) community interest, and (e) climate. If strawberries are to be grown for the general market, it is usually best to select a site among other growers. Thus, it is easier to obtain experienced pickers, and co-operative handling and buying of supplies are possible. Also, shipments can be made where several growers combine their crops; otherwise, small shipments may need to be made at relatively greater expense.

Before producing strawberries on a large scale, the grower should have reasonable assurance that there will be an adequate supply of labor, especially during the harvesting season. Under nonirrigation conditions, it requires the time of one man for each four or five acres up to harvest, whereas under irrigation it requires one man for each acre. From five to ten pickers per acre are needed during harvest. Failure to secure labor during picking may result in severe losses.

Important factors in selecting the site are water and air drainage, slope, exposure of the land, and character of the soil. Because the strawberry grows close to the ground, the blossoms may be killed by spring frosts in years when fruit trees are unharmed. For this reason, it is particularly important to have good air drainage in frost regions. In California, frosts are of limited concern. (Figure 7).

The strawberry requires frequent cultivation and, consequently, sites with a slight slope are better than those with a steep slope. If steep slopes are used, contour plantings should be made with or without terraces in order to

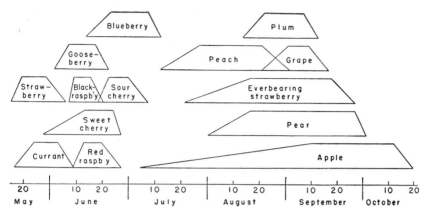

W. P. Judkins, Virginia Polytechnic Institute

Figure 4. The strawberry is the first fresh fruit on the local market in most states east of the Rockies. If grown and marketed attractively it finds a ready sale. These ripening dates for important fruits are for the general area of Virginia, but the relative order of ripening should more or less hold elsewhere.

conserve soil and moisture; in fact, contour planting is considered good practice on sites with only a slight slope (Figure 7). Southern exposures absorb more sun heat and the berries may ripen several days earlier than those growing on a northern slope in the same locality. A succession of ripening can be obtained by placing berries on both the northern and southern slopes.

The strawberry can be grown on almost any type of soil, from poor sand to heavy clay, provided it is well supplied with moisture and organic matter and is well drained. Berries ripen somewhat earlier on sandy soil than on clay soils, other conditions being similar. There is a definite varietal adaptation to soils, some growing better on heavy soils and others growing better on light soils. There is less difference, however, within a variety when grown on different soils, provided the soils are all high in humus. In the West, it is well to avoid alkali soils, since strawberries are sensitive to this condition.

CHOOSING VARIETIES

The strawberry variety picture has been changing rapidly in almost every key area, even within a 10-year period. In the next 10 to 20 years this pace may slow down somewhat with virus-nematode-free stock and varieties relatively more resistant to problem diseases. However, the several breeders in this field are busy and there is no doubt about there being room for improvements.

The variety selected will depend upon the climate, soil, and the purpose for which the crop is grown. Experience of the growers in a given locality is one of the best guides in selecting profitable varieties. Some varieties bear firm berries well adapted to long-distance shipping. Others bear large attractive berries of excellent quality but too soft for shipment and thus

717

TABLE 1a. The 20 Most Imortant Strawberry Varieties in the U.S., Based on Estimated Total Weight of Fruit, 1970. (After D. H. Scott, USDA).

Variety	% Total Crop[1]	Region[2] Grown	Variety	% Total Crop	Region Grown
Tioga	25.0	I, VIII	Tenn. Beauty	1.3	V
Northwest	17.0	VII	Sparkle	1.2	III, IV
Shasta	12.2	VIII	Marshall	1.0	VII
Fresno	10.1	VIII	Florida 90	0.9	I
Goldsmith	6.1	VIII	Pocahantas	0.8	I, II,V
Midway	4.9	II, IV	Raritan	0.8	II, III
Ned's Pride	4.0	VIII	Blakemore	0.7	I, V
Surecrop	1.9	II, III, IV, V	Jerseybelle	0.7	II, III
Dabreak	1.4	I	Robinson	0.7	III, IV
Hood	1.3	VII	Sunrise	0.7	II, V

[1]Total U. S. crop in 1970 was 494,700,000 lbs.
[2]Regions above cover areas about as follows: I, Southeastern and Gulf Coast; II, East-central Coast; III, Northeastern; IV, North Central; V, South Central; VI, Plains and Rocky Mt. States; VII, Northwestern; VIII, California and Southwestern United States to Gulf Coast of Texas.
See 1969 edition this book p. 718 for changing variety picture, 1946-1965.

suitable only for local trade or home use. Many federal and local experiment stations in the U. S. and abroad have breeding programs where special varieties are developed for each region. Importance of varieties in an area may change rather rapidly (see 1969 MFS book). Strawberry varieties popular in an area or state are given in Table 1b. For a detailed description of varieties and the regions in which they are best adapted, see Darrow and Scott. Also, contact the local state college or experiment station (see appendix for addresses). Table 2 gives important varietal characteristics, some of which may change with more experience.

In the home garden, it is desirable to have varieties of excellent dessert quality which ripen in succession over a long season. For market gardeners who sell the berries closeby, or for berries to be frozen, the majority of the berries may consist of a variety not especially adapted to shipping. However, when local markets become overloaded, it may be wise to have one or two later ripening varieties adapted to shipping or to freezing, for berries cannot be stored fresh more than about ten days.

When strawberries are raised for the general market, it is important to include only two or three varieties, since buyers prefer to obtain full truckloads of one variety, rather than loads of mixed varieties which may differ in shipping quality and may have different flavors, colors, and shapes. In large shipping regions, not over three varieties are grown. In regions where spring frosts are a factor, it may be wise to raise more than one variety so that if blossoms of one variety are killed, those of a later blooming sort may escape.

In a typical strawberry breeding program the objectives in the late

TABLE 1b. VARIETIES BY AREA AND STATE, 1967 (ADAPTED FROM CARTER R. SMITH, 1969).

Area or State	Varieties, Order of Importance[1]	Area or State	Varieties, Order of Importance
Special Areas		Mid Spring (Con't)	
California		Oklahoma	4, 46, 45, 10a
Central Coast	41, 47, 19, 40, 39	Tennessee	46, 4, 32, 9, 45
Central Valley	47, 20	Virginia	9, 32, 1, 45, 10a
Santa Maria	47, 16, 48, 19, 40	Late Spring	
Southern Calif.	16, 2, 42	Connecticut	25, 38, 30, 5, 43, 49
Florida	14, 8, 48, 47, 39, 15	Indiana	32, 30, 45
Early Spring		Maine	43, 5, 45, 28
Louisiana	23, 8	Massachusetts	25, 5, 43, 49, 10
Texas	14, 32, 9	Michigan	30, 38, 43, 45
Mid Spring		New York (L.I.)	25, 30a, 45, 35
Alabama	9, 32, 1, 27, 8, 23, 10	New York	5, 43, 30, 10, 11, 17, 18
Arkansas	46, 4, 45, 1, 9, 10a	New Jersey	25, 30, 44, 32, 45, 35, 36
Illinois	45, 30, 32, 44	Ohio	30, 32, 45, 38, 35
Kansas	45, 32, 43, 18, 13	Oregon	31, 29, 24, 41
Kentucky	32, 46, 45, 10, 44, 7	Pennsylvania	5, 38, 49, 45
Maryland	45, 10, 32, 44	Washington	31, 24, 29, 34
Mexico (D.F.)	26(So. Calif. var.)	Wisconsin	38, 30, 43, 25, 44, 3
Missouri	45, 32, 4, 44	Canada	
No. Carolina	1, 46, 10a	Ontario	37(33, 10, 6, 21, 45, 5, 12, 43, 22)[2]

[1]/Key to Varieties:							
1. Albritton	13. Fletcher	26. Klondike	37. Redcoat
2. Aliso	14. Florida 90	27. Klonmore	38. Robinson
3. Badgerbelle	15. Florida 113	28. Maine 55	39. Salinas
4. Blakemore	16. Fresno	29. Marshall	40. Sequoia
5. Catskill	17. Gala	30. Midway	41. Shasta
6. Cavalier	18. Garnet	30a. Midland	42. Solana
7. Citation	19. Goldsmith	31. Northwest	43. Sparkle
8. Dabreak	20. Gresno	32. Pocohontas	44. Sunrise
9. Dixiland	21. Grenadier	33. Premier	45. Surecrop
10. Earlidawn	22. Guardsman	(Ont. strain)	46. Tennessee Beauty
10a. Earlibelle	23. Headliner	34. Puget Beauty	47. Tioga
11. Empire	24. Hood	35. Raritan	48. Torrey
12. Erie	25. Jersevbelle	36. Redchief	49. Vesper

[2]/Redcoat for general planting; those in parenthesis for limited planting.
All Canada production (Ont., Queb., B.C., N.S.) totals about 16.000T.

1960's, as examples of the market needs, were: (a) Develop a series of varieties earlier than Midland and later than Jerseybelle that generally look alike to the customer (this eliminates the need of trying to sell the customers on each type of berry as the ripening season progresses), (b) develop a large productive berry for mechanical harvesting and processing that peak ripens heavily with easy removal of green calyx, (c) a low chilling requirement to break rest is important in mild climates, (d) develop firm high quality varieties, superior to ones now available, resistant to wet seasons and that hold up well in shipping and on the sales counter, (e) breed firmer and better quality everbearing varieties primarily for home garden, and (f) develop varieties resistant to key diseases and pests such as red stele, verticillium wilt, leaf scorch, powdery mildew, viruses, red mite, bacterial blight and other key and local pests. The several races of the red stele fungus make the problem difficult. A variety may be resistant to some races, not others. Red-stele-resistant Redchief (USDA-Md.) may be an improvement over Surecrop.

PROPAGATION

Strawberries are propagated commercially by runner plants. The Rockhill (Wayzata) variety, a poor plant producer and a minor variety, is one of the few propagated by dividing the crowns of older plants. This method is too tedious and expensive for varieties that produce runner plants readily. Plants raised from seed are undesirable because strawberry seedlings are too

TABLE 2. SOME CHARACTERISTICS OF STRAWBERRY VARIETIES IN AREAS WHERE ADAPTED (SCOTT, DARROW, LAWRENCE. USDA FARMERS' BULL. 1043. 1972.)

Variety	Plant Disease Resistance					Ripening Season: Days After Midland	Fruit Characteristics				
	Leaf Spot	Leaf Scorch	Red Stele	Verticillium Wilt	Virus Tolerance		Size	Flesh Firmness	Skin Firmness	Dessert Quality	Processing Quality For Freezing
Albritton	Resistant	Very Resistant	Susceptible	Susceptible	Susceptible	12	Large	Very Firm	Firm	Excellent	Good
Aliso	Unknown	Unknown	Susceptible	Susceptible	Unknown	7	Large	Medium	Medium	Good	Good
Apollo	Resistant	Very Resistant	Susceptible	Susceptible	Unknown	7	Large	Very Firm	Firm	Good	Good
Armore	Susceptible	Susceptible	Susceptible	Unknown	Unknown	10	Large	Medium	Soft	Good	Poor
Atlas	Resistant	Very Resistant	Susceptible	Intermediate	Unknown	3	Very Large	Firm	Firm	Good	Poor
Badgerbelle	Resistant	Susceptible	Susceptible	Unknown	Unknown	14	Large	Soft	Soft	Fair	Fair
Blakemore	Susceptible	Very Resistant	Susceptible	Resistant	Tolerant	3	Small	Firm	Firm	Fair	Good
Catskill	Susceptible	Resistant	Susceptible	Very Resistant	Very Susceptible	7	Very Large	Soft	Soft	Good	Fair to Good
Citation	Very Susceptible	Intermediate	Susceptible	Unknown	Unknown	7	Large	Medium	Medium	Good	Good
Columbia	Resistant	Resistant	Resistant	Unknown	Tolerant	18	Medium	Medium	Firm	Fair	Good
Cyclone	Resistant	Unknown	Susceptible	Unknown	Tolerant	3	Large	Soft	Soft	Very Good	Good
Dabreak	Very Resistant	Resistant	Susceptible	Unknown	Tolerant	0	Medium	Medium	Medium	Good	Good
Dunlap	Susceptible	Unknown	Susceptible	Unknown	Tolerant	7	Medium	Soft	Soft	Very Good	Fair
Earlibelle	Very Resistant	Very Resistant	Susceptible	Susceptible	Tolerant	3	Large	Very Firm	Very Firm	Good	Very Good
Earlidawn	Susceptible	Intermediate	Susceptible	Susceptible	Susceptible	0	Large	Medium	Medium	Fair	Very Good
Empire	Intermediate	Intermediate	Susceptible	Very Resistant	Unknown	7	Large	Soft	Soft	Very Good	Fair
Fairfax	Resistant	Resistant	Susceptible	Unknown	Susceptible	7	Medium	Firm	Soft	Excellent	Fair
Fletcher	Resistant	Very Resistant	Susceptible	Resistant	Unknown	7	Medium	Medium	Soft	Very Good	Good
Florida Ninety	Susceptible	Very Susceptible	Susceptible	Susceptible	Unknown	5	Very Large	Soft	Soft	Very Good	Fair
Fresno	Intermediate	Unknown	Susceptible	Susceptible	Intermediate	7	Very Large	Firm	Firm	Fair	Fair
Gala	Resistant	Unknown	Susceptible	Resistant	Unknown	0	Large	Soft	Soft	Very Good	Good
Garnet	Resistant	Unknown	Susceptible	Unknown	Unknown	12	Large	Soft	Soft	Good	Good
Gem	Susceptible	Resistant	Susceptible	Unknown	Unknown	7	Small	Soft	Soft	Fair	Fair
Guardian	Resistant	Resistant	Resistant	Very Resistant	Unknown	7	Very Large	Firm	Firm	Good	Fair
Headliner	Resistant	Unknown	Susceptible	Unknown	Unknown	7	Large	Medium	Medium	Good	Good

720

Variety											
Hood	Resistant	Resistant	Resistant	Resistant	Susceptible	14	Large	Medium	Medium	Very Good	Good
Howard 17 (Premier)	Resistant	Resistant	Resistant	Resistant	Tolerant	3	Medium	Soft	Soft	Good	Poor
Jerseybelle	Very Susceptible	Susceptible	Susceptible	Susceptible	Susceptible Very	14	Very Large	Soft	Firm	Fair	Poor
Marshall	Susceptible	Resistant	Unknown	Susceptible	Susceptible	7	Large	Soft	Soft	Excellent	Very Good
Midland	Resistant	Susceptible	Resistant	Resistant	Susceptible	0	Large	Firm	Soft	Excellent	Very Good
Midway	Very Susceptible	Resistant	Resistant	Intermediate	Unknown	10	Large	Firm	Medium	Good	Very Good
Northwest	Susceptible	Susceptible	Intermediate	Resistant	Unknown	14	Medium	Medium	Medium	Good	Very Good
Ogallala	Unknown	Unknown	Intermediate	Unknown	Tolerant	7	Medium	Soft	Soft	Good	Good
Ozark Beauty	Resistant	Unknown	Unknown	Resistant	Unknown	14	Medium	Medium	Medium	Very Good	Good
Pocahontas	Resistant	Intermediate	Susceptible	Resistant	Unknown	7	Large	Medium	Medium	Good	Very Good
Puget Beauty	Resistant	Resistant	Unknown	Susceptible	Susceptible	10	Large	Medium	Soft	Very Good	Very Good
Quinault	Resistant	Resistant	Unknown	Resistant	Unknown	7	Medium	Soft	Soft	Good	Fair
Raritan	Susceptible	Susceptible	Susceptible	Susceptible	Unknown	7	Large	Firm	Medium	Fair	Fair
Redchief	Resistant	Resistant	Resistant	Resistant	Unknown	7	Large	Firm	Firm	Good	Very Good
Redglow	Susceptible	Intermediate	Susceptible	Intermediate	Unknown	3	Large	Firm	Firm	Very Good	Very Good
Redstar	Susceptible	Resistant	Unknown	Resistant	Tolerant	18	Large	Firm	Firm	Good	Good
Robinson	Intermediate	Susceptible	Resistant	Susceptible	Tolerant	10	Large	Soft	Soft	Fair	Poor
Rockhill	Intermediate	Unknown	Unknown	Unknown	Unknown	7	Medium	Soft	Soft	Very Good	Good
Salinas	Unknown	Unknown	Resistant	Unknown	Tolerant	0	Large	Medium	Medium	Good	Unknown
Sequoia	Unknown	Unknown	Susceptible	Susceptible	Tolerant	0	Very Large	Soft	Soft	Very Good	Unknown
Shasta	Susceptible	Unknown	Susceptible	Susceptible	Tolerant	7	Large	Medium	Medium	Good	Good
Shuksan	Unknown	Unknown	Resistant	Unknown	Tolerant	16	Medium	Soft	Medium	Good	Good
Siletz	Resistant	Resistant	Resistant	Resistant	Tolerant	7	Medium	Medium	Soft	Very Good	Good
Sparkle	Susceptible	Intermediate	Resistant	Susceptible	Susceptible	12	Small	Medium	Soft	Very Good	Very Good
Sunrise	Susceptible Very	Resistant	Resistant	Intermediate	Susceptible	0	Small	Soft	Medium	Very Good	Very Good
Surecrop	Resistant	Susceptible	Resistant	Resistant	Unknown	5	Large	Firm	Firm	Good	Fair
Suwannee	Resistant	Resistant	Resistant	Very Resistant	Tolerant	7	Large	Firm	Medium	Good	Good
Tenn. Beauty	Resistant	Resistant	Unknown	Unknown	Susceptible	12	Medium	Soft	Soft	Excellent	Good
Tioga	Susceptible	Resistant	Unknown	Unknown	Tolerant	10	Small	Firm	Firm	Good	Good
Torrey	Unknown	Unknown	Susceptible	Susceptible	Intermediate	14	Very Large	Firm	Firm	Good	Good
Totem	Unknown	Unknown	Resistant	Resistant	Tolerant	14	Large	Medium	Medium	Fair	Fair
Trumpeter	Susceptible Very	Unknown	Unknown	Susceptible	Tolerant	10	Medium	Soft	Soft	Good	Very Good

Figure 5. Excellent improvement in the vigor and production of strawberries has been accomplished by U.S.D.A. techniques in conquering the virus problem. This is a screen house at the New Jersey Agricultural Experiment Station where plants are kept free of aphis vector and virus, and propagated in fumigated nematode-free soil for distribution to nurserymen.

variable. For this reason, old strawberry beds may have many untrue-to-name seedlings undesirable for propagation.

Where virus and nematodes are present, and this is likely to be true in most commercial areas, the growth and production of plants may be reduced by half or more. Strawberry plants that are substantially free from disease-causing viruses (at present there is no practical way of knowing that a plant is free from all viruses) are available from nurseries the country over. In addition, the plants from most nurseries have been raised in fumigated soils to get commercial control of nematodes. Growers who plant virus-free, nematode-free stock and keep it clean protect themselves from two common causes of serious strawberry losses. Viruses weaken plants and cut runner formation, as well as reduce yields. Nematodes, tiny eel-like worms, feed on the roots.

Most plants now are cold-storage spring-set or summer-set (Calif.) and are purchased from reputable nurserymen who sell certified virus-nematode-free stock. This stock is propagated in screen houses to prevent aphis from spreading the viruses, or is grown in isolated fields (about a mile from wild or cultivated strawberries) which are dusted or sprayed to control aphis. Growers should locate new plantings as far away from older plantings as feasible. If aphid-free stock is set, it may not pay most growers to dust. However, where aphids are abundant, as on the Pacific Coast, some control measure is needed. Dust twice or more in early spring and twice or more in the fall. Check with the local county agricultural agent for details.

In southern states, because of nematodes and the need of the plants for a cold rest period to produce runners, growers obtain a limited number of plants each year from northern nurseries. Plants are set during the winter

Michigan Orchard Supply Co., South Haven

Figure 6. With wider ownership of portable irrigation equipment by strawberry growers, who also frequently are vegetable and/or peach growers, it is possible to make double usage of the system. Here it is being used for frost control in Michigan. See wind machine used in California in Figure 7.

about three feet apart in rows four feet apart, and serve as mother plants for propagation. Some growers obtain all plants each year from northern nurseries and are convinced they obtain better results than by using their home-propagated stock.

In southern California, plants for setting to the field are obtained from northern California nurseries because some dormant period is needed in the strawberry for vigorous growth later.

Pot-grown plants are popular in home gardens. The pots are sunk in the ground near the parent plants and the first runners to appear are rooted in them. Good results can be obtained by this method because there is little or no shock in transplanting the strawberries to the field.

SOIL PREPARATION

Formerly it was advisable to cultivate for one to two years, previous to planting strawberries to free the land of white grubs and quack grass or similar persistent weeds. The use of 10 lbs. of actual chlordane per acre, once in five years, controls white grubs, wireworms, ants that harbor root aphis, and many other pests. Sod land can be plowed, harrowed, and planted at once. If the soil is nematode infested, and this is true of most U. S. strawberry land, fumigation with such chemicals as dichloropene, ethyl dibromide, or dibromochloropropane at the manufacturer's recommendation, is usually advisable before planting. Nematodes can stunt plants and reduce yields appreciably. See McGrew under "Pests."

Lime supplies calcium and magnesium, and also ties up toxic aluminum. In a humid region if the pH is 4.5 to 5.3, apply ½ to 1 ton of dolomite per acre to raise the pH from 5.5 to 6.5. It is best to lime a year ahead of planting. In arid areas avoid soil above pH 7.5, sites with more than 10% slope and requiring excessive leveling.

Strawberries ordinarily should not follow peas, tomatoes, white potatoes, and beets, because of possible injury from diseases common to both crops, nor should they follow corn, because of root aphis. A suggested rotation for

(Top left) G. M. Darrow, USDA; (top right) Merle H. Jensen, Univ. of Arizona; (low right) Dept. of Agr., Victoria, Australia.

Figure 7. (Top left) Strawberries are planted here in double-row hills and under overhead permanent irrigation; (top right) double-row hills in raised beds with poly mulch in central California, contoured for between-bed surface and gravity irrigation; (low left) wind machine in level area in California for frost control where air temperature inversion is likely to occur; and (low right) double-row raised beds, poly mulch, showing spray operation in Auchland, New Zealand. A major problem is Botrytis rot; verticillium is a soil borne problem.

the eastern states is (a) plow in autumn and sow rye and vetch or crimson clover; (b) plow in the spring and raise hoed vegetables other than those listed above; (c) plow again in autumn and sow rye and vetch. Plow under the cover crop the following spring and plant strawberries.

If it is the practice to grow strawberries on the same land for two or more years, the humus content of the soil should be increased before setting each new planting. This can be done best by applying eight to ten tons of manure to the crop preceding strawberries. If no manure is available, two green manure crops preceding the strawberries, both turned under, may be advisable on soils of low humus content.

Before planting strawberries, the land should be pulverized thoroughly and in most cases, leveled. Where ridges are needed on level, somewhat poorly drained areas, they can be made by throwing two or more plow furrows together and leveling the top with a drag plank. In California, special mechanical equipment is described in their bulletins (contact the Univ. of Calif., Davis) for building and leveling the ridges shown in Figure 7.

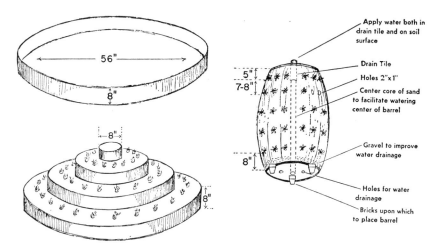

Elwood G. Fisher, Cornell University

Figure 10. For home gardens the strawberry pyramid (left) or barrel (right) are space-saving convenient methods of growing berries for the table. A hose or water pipe with sprinkler nozzle can be run up through the center of the pyramid for easy watering.

A large number of extra plants should be ordered for replanting if there is danger of loss from grubs, drought, or other factors. A field with many blank spaces is too costly to maintain on the basis of value of the crop obtained.

Care of plants on arrival. Plants are prepared at the nursery in bunches of about 25 and packed in different size slatted crates, or bare-root in boxes with poly liners. If, on arrival, the plants cannot be set immediately, place them in a refrigerator or cold storage. Roots on good plants should be fresh and slightly yellowish in color, or somewhat dark if grown on muck soil. Old and undesirable plants can be distinguished from young plants by their black and dead roots. Plants coming from the nursery should be protected from the sun and wind by covering them with a piece of wet burlap or other wet material. Bare-rooted plants in poly bags can be stored at 31-32° F. CA storage at 12% CO_2, 6% O_2 and 32° F will hold plants in better condition.

Setting the plants. The plant in Figure 11 has a healthy vigorous root system, is trimmed properly, and all but one good leaf has been removed. It is ready for planting. Two things are important in setting strawberry plants: (a) Set each plant so that the crown is even with the surface of the soil after it has been packed about the roots (see dash mark in Figure 11); and (b) firm the soil well around and over the root system. Plants may be set either by hand with a dibble, spade, or punch (Figure 11), or with a two-wheel planting machine used for large-scale setting of vegetable plants.

One man working by himself may set around 5,000 plants a day. If he has a boy helper who carries the plants in a bucket of water and hands them

(Top left photos) USDA; (Top right) Ohio Exp. St.; (Bottom) The Holland Transplanter Co., Holland, Michigan.

Figure 11. Planting strawberries. (Top left) Types of dibbles and trowels used in transplanting strawberries. (Top middle) Strawberry plant ready to set with long roots shortened and with all but one healthy leaf removed. Proper depth of planting is indicated by broken line. (Top right) Remove flowers the first season; the hormone sprays tested are not effective. For everbearing varieties, blossoms can be left after about July 1 for full crop. (Bottom) Commercial transplanters are available for one, two or three-row simultaneous setting of plants. A three-row machine with six operators can set one to two acres an hour. Discs open the furrow, paired men set plants alternately, starter solution is supplied from tank and paired wheels firm the soil about the plants.

to him, his capacity is increased by three or four thousand in a ten-hour day. A short-handled hoe in one hand is convenient to open the hole for planting.

With a planting machine, about 25,000 plants or three to four acres can be planted in a ten-hour day. One person drives the tractor or team and two others are seated at the rear of the planting machine close to the ground where they can drop plants alternately as the machine opens and closes the furrow and applies soluble fertilizer from a large barrel (see Fig. 11 and

730

starter solutions, page 735). In machine setting, plants must be relatively uniform in size, roots straight, trimmed, and arranged in one direction in the plant holders. One man is needed to follow the machine to tamp the soil about the roots, straighten misplaced plants and to plant the gaps. Good results have been obtained with these machines, but a more careful job usually can be done by hand.

COMPANION CROPS

Under intensive cultivation and in home gardens where the greatest possible returns per unit of ground is desired, vegetables are sometimes grown between the strawberry rows during the first season. Most vegetables can be used and the extra cultivation and fertilization given them also will benefit the strawberries. Quick-maturing plants such as lettuce and radishes, can be grown between the rows. Onion sets are sometimes grown in the rows. The vegetables should be removed before the strawberry plants begin to send out runners. Companion crops, such as potatoes, beans, and, cabbage, may be set about six inches to one side of the berry rows in the southern regions where the growing season is longer. This system is not adapted to the north because the season is not long enough to mature the vegetables and also allow the strawberry plants to develop sufficiently to bear a full crop the following year. With companion crops, such as potatoes and beans, the strawberry rows are often set four or four and one-half feet apart with the vegetables placed in the center of the cultivated area. In northern districts with a shorter growing season, the mat of strawberry plants must be more narrow than in southern regions when this system of management is used.

Strawberries can be used as an intercrop between rows of fruit trees, but it is good practice to plant only a few rows between the tree rows, and these should not be left longer than two or three years. Adequate space should be left on either side of the tree rows to cultivate with a disk. This is because strawberries are mulched and not cultivated early the second season during a period when young fruit trees need cultivation most. The straw also causes a reduction in available nitrogen to the trees.

CULTURE DURING FIRST SUMMER

Removing flowers. Flower stems should be removed as they appear on the plants the first summer after setting (Figure 11). Otherwise, the flowers will create a severe drain on the vitality of the plants, reducing the number and size of daughter plants and the subsequent crop of berries. The removal of flower stems from varieties which naturally produce a small number of daughter plants will increase greatly the number of runners and plants set.

Thinning and spacing plants. With the hill system of culture, the runners should be cut as soon as they appear, using a sharp hoe or a circular

731

cutter blade (made from blade of crosscut saw) about eight or ten inches in diameter and equipped with an upright handle. Also, considerable hand labor can be saved by equipping the cultivator with two rolling disk cutters attached just far enough apart to cut runners along the outside borders of the rows. This cutter cannot be used, however, in stony land or where there is straw mixed with the soil.

With the spaced-row system of culture (Figure 8), the runners are moved into place and the tips covered with soil as they begin to enlarge. The work must be done by hand. The first daughter plant is placed in the row between the mother plants. The next ones are placed the length of the runner out from the original row on either side. This makes three rows of plants and either all runners thereafter may be removed or additional runners may be rooted until a wide bed has been formed with plants spaced six to twelve inches apart, or as desired. Thereafter, all other runners should be cut. With this system, the plant-spacing and weed-hoeing jobs both can be done at the same time.

A machine is available that lifts the runners up by suction and cuts them off.[1] It cannot be used on pebbly soil.

With the matted-row system, surplus plants should be removed from the outsides of the rows during late summer or autumn, using a cultivator equipped with a special disk, described above, and by hand hoeing in the row. Some growers run a spike-toothed harrow down the middle of the row in late summer or autumn with the teeth slanting backward so that only the weaker, poorly rooted plants are dislodged. The harrow must be tried carefully first, however, to make sure it is not loosening too many plants. Another practice is to run a bull-tongue plow with a four- or five-inch-wide point down the center of the row, tearing up the center plants and dividing the matted row into two parts.

Cultivation. The strawberry field must be kept clean during the first season by cultivation, herbicides and/or hoeing to kill weeds and conserve moisture. Work the soil toward the plants in hoeing and cultivating. Moist soil must be kept around the crowns continuously, but not covering them. Cultivator teeth should be shortened so as to stir only the upper one or two inches of soil. Cultivation should be continued until the first hard frost or until the mulch is applied in regions where it is used. Weeds should not be allowed to start growing in the fall; otherwise, they will give severe competition early the next spring. A field free of weeds the first season will have few if any developing prior to harvest the next season. If weeds are present during the months when the fruits are sizing, they interfere with honeybee movements and proper pollination of the blossoms, causing many "nubbins"

---

[1]S. S. Simons Machine Works, Cornwells Hghts., Penna. 19020

to develop. Only a moderate amount of weeds has been known to reduce yield by 1200 quarts per acre.

Plastic film. Black plastic film (Fla., La., clear plastic, Calif.) is used as a mulch for the hill system to control weeds and conserve moisture, but some scalding of berries may occur on hot days. Berries are kept clean, and rots and mold are reduced. Bloom may be speeded up, exposing them to early frost, where frost is a problem.

The film is laid down over newly set plants and held in place by soil laid on the edges. Plants are pulled through slits cut in the film with a knife. Runners must be removed with knives or shears. Cost of the film was $150 to $175 per acre in the 1960's. In California and Florida there has been considerable success reported with plastic film.

Weed Control. Hand weeding and machine cultivation of strawberries are expensive and, in California, e.g., may cost about 1 cent/lb of marketed fruit or range from $100-$500/A. Annual weeds from seed are the main problem; they may "take over" during rainy periods making cultivation difficult or impossible. Common problems are chickweed, henbit, lambsquarters, vetch, nettle, purslane, shepherds-purse, annual bluegrass, and certain perennials such as morning glory and nutgrass. The perennials may need separate treatment. Nutgrass has no completely and economically effective chemical or manual control.

Pre-planting soil fumigation for nematodes, when needed, often also gives fair to good control of weeds.

Herbicides are used in strawberry growing to control weeds. In Chapter XVIII the recommendations are given as of the early 1970's. Since the techniques and chemicals are undergoing continual improvement, contact your local governmental extension service for latest recommendations.

Growth, Flowering Regulators. Any chemical that advances and/ or concentrates the peak ripening date, improves firmness, color and/or quality/and increases yield or saves labor is always viewed with interest. Potassium gibberellate at 10 ppm weekly just before fruit bud formation was found by Carter R. Smith of Rutgers University to advance peak ripening of Sparkle and Jerseybelle by about one week. An Alar spray of 5000 ppm on Fresno plants, tops cut off, applied on October 1 in California gave the most productive plants with least transplanting shock when dug October 29 and planted 3 days later (Puffer *et al.*). Ethrel (ethephon) sprays show promise of speeding the ripening of berries and giving more ripe berries at peak harvest for the one-cut mechanical harvesting system. Maleic hydrazide (MH) sprays properly timed will stunt runner growth. Most of these and other chemicals, however, have yet to be labeled by FDA for use and, also, their real value in a commercial program as yet must be demonstrated.

FERTILIZERS

Before the strawberry plants are set, much can be done to insure high production by placing the soil in the best possible state of fertility. As pointed out earlier, high organic matter content in addition to the fertilizer elements is of paramount importance.

When strawberries follow cultivated crops, they ordinarily do not show response to fertilizers because there is sufficient in the soil left from fertilization of the previous crops. If the strawberry leaves are dark green and the foliage abundant, no fertilizer should be applied unless trial plots for the particular soil have shown their value. The kind, amount, and time of applying fertilizers vary in different regions with the kind of soil, amount of rainfall, market and transportation conditions, varieties, and other factors.

Soils in most states vary greatly in fertility. With the help of your agricultural agent, test your soil to find the specific fertilizer needs. Strawberries need adequate nitrogen and water early the first year to build runners and strong crowns and develop fruit buds in the fall for next year's crop. Recommendations in Michigan are typical. If soil fertility and organic matter are low, a green manuring program is suggested for one to two years before planting. Otherwise use a 1-4-4 or 1-4-2 fertilizer, depending upon soil test. If growth is weak, apply a 1-1-1 fertilizer four weeks after setting plants, using 30 to 35 lbs. actual N per acre. Repeat in three to four weeks if growth is still weak.

Strawberries in the North Carolina region respond well to nitrogen application because the soils tend to be lower in available nitrogen than those to the north. There are some areas, however, farther north along the coast where strawberries respond well to the equivalent of 60 pounds per acre of actual nitrogen in organic or inorganic form, applied about August 15 in Maryland and around September 1 in New Jersey and Virginia. If nitrogen is added where not needed, it tends to cause a vigorous top growth with a decrease in yield and shipping quality of berries. Strawberries on acid soils definitely respond better to nitrate of soda than to ammonium sulfate. This is particularly true in the Atlantic Coast states, whereas in the Central states more of the soils are near the neutral point and thus response is better to ammonium sulfate.

In the spring of the fruiting year, an application of nitrogen on fertile soils will either show little or no response or may produce excess foliage and reduce the crop. On poor soils, however, nitrogen application in early spring may be worthwhile.

Nitrate of soda shows the best response when applied during the latter part of August. Stable manure may be used in place of, or, in addition to nitrate of soda. If free from weed seed, stable manure can be applied as a strawy mulch to protect the plants from heaving during severe winter weather. The nitrogen, humus, and other elements in manure tend to stimulate leaf growth the following year which aids in supporting a large crop of berries.

The addition of phosphoric acid in the Mississippi Valley region, ranging from 100 to 800 pounds per acre of superphosphate has increased yields greatly. The amount needed for a specific soil can be determined best by small trial plots. In the East and Northwest the importance of phosphorus has been demonstrated. In fact, the strawberry is more like vegetables in its phosphorus requirement than woody fruit plants. A 1-2 ratio of N-P is in common use in the East. See B. R. Boyce and D. L. Matlock's review of strawberry nutrition literature in Childers' *Fruit Nutrition* book.

On most soils, potash shows little or no response. Application ranges from 50 to 300 lbs. per acre of muriate of potash, depending upon response obtained in local test plots. In some areas of western Washington boron is applied *broadcast* at the rate of two lbs. of actual boron per acre.

Soils vary tremendously in fertilizer needs, not only from one region to the next, but from one field to the neighboring field. Thus, it is sound practice for a large grower to maintain small test plots to determine the relative value of manure, phosphoric acid, potash, nitrogen, and possibly magnesium and trace elements if his soil is sandy and low in organic matter. Also, the advice of the local state experiment station and the experience of neighboring growers should be carefully considered.

Time to apply. Fertilizers may be applied at three different times: (a) At time of planting, (b) during the first summer, and (c) just before blossoming in the fruiting season. Growers make only application (a) above in some regions, whereas in others (a) and (c) are made, or all three.

Potash and phosphoric acid, if needed, may be applied prior to the setting of the plants, but nitrogen should be applied 5 to 7 weeks before the frost date at the end of the first growing season except as noted for sandy soils above. Potash and phosphorus may be broadcast or drilled where the plant rows will be located. Later application of these materials and nitrogen either may be scattered on the plants or drilled along the side of the rows. When applied to the plants by hand, which is the common practice, the plants should be dry and later brushed or dragged over to remove the fertilizer from the leaves and prevent foliage burning. If the plantation is being renewed for a second or third fruiting, fertilizer should be applied at the time of renewal in midsummer.

Starter solutions. On plant-setting machines, use a starter solution

(Top left and right) M. S. Anderson, U.S.D.A. (Middle left and right) J. E. Christiansen, University of California. (Bottom left) Ohio Agr. Exp. Sta. (Bottom right) Dept. of Pomology, Cornell University

Figure 13. Strawberries are shallow rooted and require adequate moisture for high yields. Several systems of irrigation are used. (Top left) A portable, inexpensive, light weight, jiffy-coupling irrigation system with rotating sprinklers. Water is being supplied to system by pump shown in photo at top right. (Middle left) Contour ridges irrigated by the furrow and wooden-flume system in California, utilizing alleyways. (Middle right) Oscillating-type sprinkling system in California. (Bottom left) Ooze hose on straw mulch in the spring of fruiting year in Ohio. (Bottom right) Temporary sprinkler system installed in young McIntosh orchard in New York.

instead of water only. Apply about one cup per plant of a completely soluble 13-26-13 at the rate of 3 lbs. in 50 gallons of water. If a 5-10-5 is used, dissolve 8 lbs. in 50 gallons.

Leaf Analysis. Modern diagnosis of fertilizer needs of agricultural crops is by leaf and soil analysis in commercial or government labora-

736

Ernest H. Casseres, Inter-Amer. Inst. Agr. Sci., Mexico 6, D. F., Mexico.

Figure 14. Strawberry growing, mainly for freezing, has increased markedly, then leveled, in northern Mexico. This operation is under furrow irrigation in Irapuato area, Sonora state of Mexico, where the Klondike has been the principal variety. But Tioga is favored in recent years.

tories. The following are leaf analysis data based on research on strawberries to date.

TABLE 3a. APPROXIMATE RANGE OF LEAF CONTENT OF NUTRIENTS IN HEALTHY STRAWBERRY PLANTS THAT FRUITED SATISFACTORILY.

(Compiled by Carter R. Smith, Rutgers University).[1]

N	P	K	Mg	Ca	Mn	B	Zn	Cu	Fe
%	%	%	%	%	ppm	ppm	ppm	ppm	ppm
2.35	0.178	1.10	0.28	1.25	129	111	58	6.2	70
to	to	to	to	to	to	to	to	to	to
2.93	0.238	1.70	0.34	1.48	170	170	73	7.0	80

[1]Note: More data are needed from first-year and fruiting-year field plants to refine these data. Variety differences also can be a factor. Strawberries are sensitive to B excess; figures from literature above seem high, but this plant may tend to accumulate B. No data are available for Mo and S. N, P and K data from Bould et al.,1966; Mg, Ca, Mn, Zn, Cu and Fe data are from Webb and Hollas, 1966.

Lime. Lime not only reduces the acidity, but serves as a source of calcium. If dolomitic lime is used, magnesium also is added to the soil. According to Darrow, strawberries grow well on soils having a pH of 5.7 to 6.5. However, if the organic matter content is high, they will grow satisfactorily at a wider pH range of 5.0 to 7.0. Lime applied at the rate of 1000 to 2000 pounds per acre on acid soil tends to tie up free aluminum which is particularly toxic to strawberry plants; it also makes calcium and magnesium readily available, and induces better tilth of the soil. The lime should be applied a year or two in advance of planting strawberries. Lime is usually beneficial on the acid soils of the Atlantic Coast states, but not commonly needed in the Mississippi Valley and the Pacific Coast states. A word of caution should be made against overliming. Too much lime may induce manganese and other trace element deficiencies. Manganese deficiency can

(Leaf photos) D. R. Hoagland, University of California; (fruit photo) F. A. Gilbert, University of Wisconsin

Figure 15. This is boron deficiency on strawberry under controlled conditions. Crinkled, stunted, chlorotic tip leaves are characteristic. Misshapen small fruits on left are boron deficient; the two on the right received too much boron, whereas the second row from the right received a normal supply.

be corrected by spraying the plants with manganese sulfate, 3 lbs./100 gallons, or placing it in the irrigation water at 15 lbs. per acre.

IRRIGATION

In regions where droughts occur frequently during the early part of the season, in early fall, and at harvest, irrigation should be provided. Lack of proper water supply is probably responsible for more low yields and failures in strawberry growing than almost any other factor. Also, it is usually in drought years when an irrigation system pays well, because of local or widespread shortage of berries. Under irrigation, strawberries must be grown intensively because the cost of installing an irrigation system is such that the grower must make every square foot of ground count to make the enterprise successful financially. An irrigation system is a permanent improvement on a farm, but it should not be installed until the grower is assured that adequate local labor will be available. An abundant water supply must be available for an irrigation plant from either a well or a stream that does not run dry during the severest of droughts.

Overhead systems. The overhead sprinkling or spray systems, as sparsely employed throughout the eastern states for vegetables, have been found profitable, although it is being replaced by portable aluminum pipe systems. The investment in these systems is greater than for portable aluminum pipe systems. The overhead spray irrigation system, shown in Figure 13, has been responsible for 8000-quart yields per acre in years when only 3000 quarts were obtained for the same variety in neighboring fields without irrigation. Some varieties such as Sparkle respond particularly well to irrigation.

Surface irrigation. Furrow irrigation can be used only where the soil, or particularly the subsoil, is heavy, and where the slopes are uniform and gentle (Figure 7). Irrigation furrows 200 to 250 feet long are used frequently in commercial plantations. Shallow furrows are made in the alleyways during the first season and in alternate alleyways during the harvest season to facilitate the harvesting. Victor Voth in California uses a 60-inch bed (U. S. standard 40-inch) with one irrigation furrow serving 2 adjacent beds, reducing space used by irrigation furrows and increasing production with other advantages.

Portable Pipe and Hose. On sandy soils or irregular land, the portable aluminum pipe system, porous hose (Figure 13), or eyelet hose are well-adapted. The porous, or ooze-hose will irrigate only one row at a time, whereas the eyelet hose with holes spaced about two feet apart will irrigate three or four rows at one placement, both good also for home gardens.

The portable aluminum pipe system (Figure 13) is most widely used and is gaining in popularity because it is economical and can be shifted readily to sweet corn, potatoes, peaches, and other crops. It also can be set up quickly for frost control.

Trickle Irrigation. This system is used to reduce initial and operation costs and where water is scarce. See Chap. XIX. In arid California, e.g., it is little used because water is relatively inexpensive and salt accumulation may become a problem.

COLD PROTECTION

The strawberry leaves become hardened with the cooler temperatures in early fall and often can withstand a temperature of 15°F. without injury in late fall or early winter. If the temperature falls to 0°F. or below during the winter with no blanket of snow over the plants, they may be damaged severely. Also, alternate freezing and thawing of the soil, especially the heavier soils, will heave the plants out of the soil, causing severe damage or death by the beginning of the next growing season. The use of mulch is effective in minimizing this injury. Mulching also has the advantages of smothering the weeds, keeping the berries clean, and conserving moisture. In the South and West where winter cold protection is unnecessary, mulching with pine needles, straw, etc. has been largely replaced with plastic mulch which conserves moisture, controls weeds, and keeps the berries clean.

Mulching with marsh hay, grain straws, sawdust, or pine needles and ferns is recommended on the dates shown in Figure 16 for the respective regions. Marsh or salt hay and pine needles are free from weed seed which makes them particularly desirable. In the upper Mississippi Valley region, about six tons of straw per acre should provide sufficient protection. In the rest of the country where mulch is needed, two to two and one-half tons per acre are sufficient. The straw should be as free from weed seed as possible. If straw is scarce, Sudan grass can be raised for mulching material; but it should be cut before becoming coarse. Oats may be sown thickly in

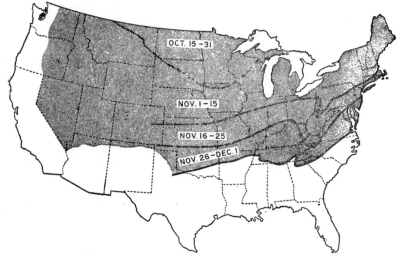

G. M. Darrow, U.S.D.A.

Figure 16. Map showing areas in which cold injury to strawberry plants may be expected often enough to make mulching pay. Growers in each area should be ready to put on the mulch by the first date listed and should have applied the mulch by the latter date.

the alleys at the rate of one and one-half to two bushels per acre. Oats kill down in early winter and help furnish a thin mulch.

Straw distributing machines, as used in highway grass seeding, are available for quick spreading on large acreages.

When growth starts in spring, surplus mulch should be pulled from the tops of the plants and placed in the alleyways. A light covering of straw can be left on the plants since they can come through readily. Mulch may delay ripening by a few days to a week, depending upon the thickness of the mulch on the plants.

Frosts usually destroy the earliest and most valuable blossoms and berries. While mulching is effective in frost control, if left on too late in spring it delays the crop. Infra-red heating units are too expensive; smudge pots are effective only when air is "layered." In Michigan and New Jersey most of the strawberry acreage is protected by portable-pipe irrigation. Lines are spaced 70-90′ apart with sprinklers 60′ apart in the line. Special "fogging" frost nozzles are used at 70 lbs. plus pressure. Start fogging when temperature near plants in low areas is 34°F. Continue fogging as long as ice forms. Smudge systems and petroleum bricks also are used; read labels carefully.

If an unseasonable spring frost is expected, it may be advisable to pull the straw from the alleyways back over the plants again. While this involves extra labor cost, it may prove the difference of crop or no crop where irrigation is not available.

If the region is particularly susceptible to frost injury, everbearing varieties

740

(Upper) American Air Lines, (lower) United Air Lines

Figure 22. Shipment of fresh strawberries and other fruits by jet airplane is on the increase. Firm-ripe berries from the South and West can be placed on northern markets the day after picked. North American fresh strawberries now are being shipped to Europe and other foreign markets. Upper photo shows outline and size of freight planes in the 1970's compared with the 1960's. Note palletized handling.

give a basis for estimating cost of growing strawberries the first and second years under average conditions. High yields are needed for good profits as indicated in Table 4. Adjust costs to present price levels.

It cost the typical Washington strawberry grower 9.5 cents per lb. to produce berries in Whatcom County in 1958. He had a capital investment of $1,552 per acre in 16 acres of strawberries. He got 108,000 lbs. of berries from this acreage. The typical grower had about 40 acres of cropland; 16 acres in strawberries, 19 acres planted to grass, and the remaining 5 acres waste. The life of a strawberry field was 4 years (producing 3 years). Hence, out of the 16 acres of berries, 4 acres were replaced each year. Bearing strawberries of the variety now being used yielded 4½ tons per acre. Table 5 gives a cost breakdown. Adjust costs to present-day levels.

TABLE 3b

AVERAGE COSTS OF PRODUCTION FOR FIVE TYPICAL STRAWBERRY GROWERS
IN SOUTHWEST MICHIGAN BASED ON 1956 PRICES.
(AFTER BELL, MANDINGO, AND CARLSON).

First year cost per acre up to picking time (2nd year)	*1 acre*
Plants $10.00 per M. 7,000 plants per acre	$ 70.00
Planting at rate of 22,000 per 10-hour day	14.00
Hand hoeing	22.50
Pinching blossoms	7.50
Power hoeing and late season cultivation ($ 6.60 per acre)	66.00
Spraying cost	33.40
Fertilizer at 1,000 lbs. per acre	34.00
Sidedress with starter solution, $4.00 labor; $4.00 materials	8.00
Preparing of ground for planting	12.00
Machine mulching	9.00
1½ tons straw at $20.00 per ton	30.00
Fall application of chemical weed spray, $7.30 materials; $3.00 labor	10.30
Hand weeding previous to picking	12.00
Irrigation	40.00
Frost prevention	15.00
Total first year production costs	$383.70
Cost from first year harvest up to second year harvest:	
Post-picking rototilling @ $8.00 per acre	$ 8.00
Cultivation (2 times) @ $7.00 per acre	14.00
Post-picking hoeing	36.00
Early and late fertilizers	18.00
Mulching (total cost)	39.00
Frost prevention (twenty hours)	15.00
Irrigation average of 3 acre inches per year @ $10.00	30.00
Spraying	25.00
Total second year production costs	$185.00

DISEASES

With strawberries it is possible to rotate the ground frequently and consequently, diseases and insects are not likely to become as serious a problem
as where the fruit crop occupies the ground for many years. The following
diseases (see also Figure 21) are among the most common. For more
specific control measures, the reader is referred to his local agricultural
experiment station and to a special bulletin by McGrew.

Leaf spot (Mycosphaerella fragariae) occurs in almost all regions where
strawberries are grown, particularly in some Gulf-state regions. Varieties
vary in susceptibility; Howard 17 is very resistant. Captan and fermate are
suggested which also control *Botrytis,* a fruit rot. *Leaf scorch (Diplocarpon
earliana),* dark purplish spots one-quarter inch across, can be reduced with

TABLE 4

EFFECT OF YIELDS ON COSTS OF PRODUCING MICHAGAN STRAWBERRIES.
(AFTER BELL, MANDIGO, AND CARLSON).

Item	Cost/qt. (cents)	Cost/lb. (cents)
First Year Production Costs		
140 crates* (3,080 lbs.†) per acre	17.2	12.4
200 crates (4,400 lbs.) per acre	11.9	8.7
400 crates (8,800 lbs.) per acre	5.9	4.4
Second Year Production Costs		
140 crates	8.3	6.0
200 crates	5.7	4.2
400 crates	2.8	2.1
Overhead Costs (land, machinery, buildings, etc.)	2.5	2.0
Harvest Costs		
Picking	6.0	7.0‡
Packing and supervision	1.0	.5
Crates and cups	4.4	——
Total Harvest Cost	11.4	7.5

*16-quart crates.
†After stems have been removed, a quart box of strawberries weighs about 22 ounces; a 16-quart crate, thus would weigh about 22 lbs, and 140 crates x 22 lbs.=3,080 lbs.
‡Includes cost of capping.

dithane or copper mixes. *Leaf blight (Dendrophoma obscurans)* is characterized by large red to brown spots surrounded by purplish margins; it occurs largely on old fruited plants, not young ones. Remedies are not warranted. *Crinkle,* a virus disease, is commonly found in Pacific Coast states, occasionally in the East. Leaves may be distorted, wrinkled, lighter shade of green, petioles short with leaves lying flat on the ground, giving the plants a dwarfed appearance. Use certified virus-free stock on isolated fields away from crops harboring aphids (the vectors), and dust or spray for aphids. *Yellows (Xanthosis),* a virus transmitted by strawberry aphis, is prevalent from Puget Sound to southern California and is frequently present in the East. Affected plants are dwarfed and somewhat yellow, occurring in strips in a row. Leaves may be cupped with less point at the tips, and showing dull green centers with yellow edges. See control for crinkle virus. *June yellows* is due to a hereditary factor. Leaves show mottling and streaking with yellow and green. The markings differ with the variety and season. Blakemore, Premier, Dixiland are susceptible. Species of *nematodes* are responsible for a summer dwarf appearing during high summer temperatures, and for a spring dwarf appearing early in the season (Figure 21). Control is by rigid state inspection of nursery plants and soil fumigation. *Red Stele* root disease is caused by a fungus occurring largely in the northeastern states, resulting in stunting and dwarfing in spring and wilting and dying of older leaves. Fungus invades central cylinder (stele) of root, causing it to turn dark

TABLE 5

Item	Total	Per Acre	Per lb.[1]
Interest on Investment at 5%			
Land	$ 240.00	$ 15.00	
Building and Power Line[2]	37.00	2.31	
Machinery[2]	263.00	16.44	
Strawberries[2]	162.00	9.50	
Depreciation			
Machinery	821.00	51.31	
Building and Power Line	75.00	4.69	
Taxes			
Real	60.00	3.75	
Personal Property	60.00	3.75	
License	60.00	3.75	
Subtotal	$1,768.00	$110.50	
Insurance	200.00	12.50	
Machine Repair	251.00	15.69	
Fertilizer	592.00	37.00	
Insecticides and Herbicides	398.00	24.88	
Fuel	162.00	10.13	
Oil and Grease	20.00	1.25	
Rye Seed	10.00	.63	
Strawberry Plants	300.00	18.75	
Electricity	26.00	1.63	
Phone	20.00	1.25	
Labor	2,254.00	140.87	
Picker Transportation	445.00	27.81	
Custom Work			
Spray Aldrin	12.00	.75	
Planting	54.00	3.38	
Cut Blooms	16.00	1.00	
Harvesting	3,780.00	252.50	
Subtotal	$ 8,540.00	$533.75	
TOTAL COST	$10,308.00	$644.25	.095

[1]Expected yield from 16 acres (12 acres bearing) 120,000 lbs. [2]Interest calculated on ½ of recorded investment.

red with outer part of root appearing healthy. Disease is aggravated by cold wet soils. Varieties differ in susceptibility; Surecrop, Redchief, Guardian and Sunrise are resistant; Sparkle usually. Nursery inspection is the recommended control. It is aggravated by poor soil drainage. *Blackseed fungus* (*Mycosthaerella fragariae*) causes black spots around one or a few seeds on a fruit, marring appearance. Use spray schedule for leaf spot. Verticillium Wilt (*V. alboatrum*) causes wilt in midsummer

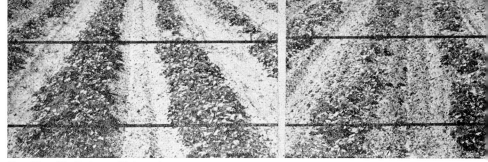

Lee Merrill, Rutgers University

Figure 23. Nematodes may be a problem in some soils and strawberry growing areas, particularly the sandy soils in the East and South. Delineated plot on the left was fumigated with D-D before planting; plot on right was not fumigated. Photo taken late the first season.

with outermost leaves dying. New leaves are stunted and plant lies flat; Guardian, Siletz, Catskill, Surecrop are highly resistant. Soil fumigation with 2 to 1 proportion of methyl bromide/chloropicrin under poly tarpaulin (machine laid) is used in the West and East. Crop rotation also is suggested in the East. Strawberries should not be planted on soil where potato, pepper, eggplant or other crops showing the disease have been planted recently. Use clean stock.

INSECTS

White grubs (*Phyllophaga* or *Lachmosterna*) may cause considerable trouble by feeding on the strawberry roots, as discussed previously. *Leaf roller* (*Ancylis competana fragariae*) larvae roll the leaves after feeding for a short time in the spring and continue to feed from within the enclosed chamber; serious losses sometimes occur. *Strawberry weevil* (*Anthonomus signatus*) lays eggs in flower buds, and then girdles the stem. Larvae feed in buds, destroying them. Injury may become serious in some regions. The *Cyclamen Mite* (*Tarsonemus pellidus*) occurs widely in the northern states and in California and Canada, causing dwarfing and/or loss of entire crop. Nursery planting stock treated for mites is available. New plantings should be made some distance from old infested fields. The *Spittle bug* (*Philaenus leucophthalmus*) frequently found in Oregon and Washington, also is becoming common in the East.

The accompanying spray schedule for strawberries for Ohio gives information on materials and techniques for controlling the common pests in that area. Each state can supply specific recommendations through the county agricultural agent.

EVERBEARING STRAWBERRIES

Everbearing varieties of strawberry bear fruit at the usual time followed by a period of little or no production until late summer when another crop is harvested throughout the fall if growing conditions are favorable. Everbearers, principally Rockhill, Ozark Beauty, Gem, are valuable in valleys

751

TABLE 6

Strawberry Insect and Disease Control

(Ohio Agricultural Extension Service and Experiment Station, Columbus and Wooster.)

Pest	Symptoms of Injury	Control
STRAWBERRY LEAF ROLLER	Leaflets folded and webbed together with a small green larva feeding within.	Spray with 2 lbs. 50% TDE (Rhothane) wettable powder in 100 gals. water, or dust with 5% TDE powder. Apply once late in August. Repeat in 15 days to destroy hibernating larvae. If treatment is delayed until spring, it should be applied when first blossoms appear.
ROOT WORMS (Strawberry leaf beetle)	Small beetles at numerous holes in leaves. Larvae feed on roots.	Plow down infested beds in July to kill larvae. Rotate beds with new plantings at some distance from old ones. If beetles do appear, spray or dust with dieldrin at the rate of 13 lbs. of actual toxicant per acre in early spring before bloom.
CROWN BORER	Crown of plants hollowed out by white legless grubs about ⅓ inch in length.	Same as for root worms.
SPITTLEBUGS	White frothy masses ½ inch or more in diameter covering small green insects on stems and leaves.	Spray with Thiodan 1 lb (50% wettable) per 100 gals with sticker-spreader. A 1% rotenone dust (30-40 lbs./acre) is suggested for control of spittlebugs during picking.
TARNISHED PLANT BUG	Feeds on buds before bloom and deforms fruits causing 'button berries.'	Spray with 2 lbs. of 50% DDT, or dust with 5% chlordane just before blossoms open.
WHITE GRUBS	Large fleshy white grubs that attack roots of new plants.	Don't plant in newly plowed sod or where grubs are abundant unless a soil insecticide is used. Cultivate soil, apply in advance of planting either aldrin or dieldrin 3 lbs., or chlordane 6 lbs. of actual toxicant per acre.
TWO-SPOTTED SPIDER MITE	Leaves curl and lose color. Silken webs may occur on lower surface.	Spray with Kelthane (18.5% emulsion) 1-½ pints per 100 gallons of water. Can be used 2 days prior to harvest. Malathion (4% dust) can be used up to 3 days of harvest. Aramite (5% dust) can be used before berries form, or after harvest. Dusts should be applied at the rate of 20-40 lbs. per acre depending on the age of the planting; sprays at the rate of 100-300 gallons per acre depending on the age of the planting.
CYCLAMEN MITE	Leaves and blossom clusters distorted. Fruits stunted.	Spray with Thiodan or Kelthane. Use Thiodan 1 lb. (50% WP) per 100 gallons of water plus spreader-sticker. Apply as a pre-bloom application in the spring and repeat after harvest if mites are present.

Pest/Disease	Description	Control
		Kelthane (18.5% emulsion) should be applied at the rate of 1-½ pints per 100 gallons of water. Kelthane may be used 2 days prior to harvest, if necessary. Cover the foliage thoroughly using 100-300 gallons of dilute spray per acre depending on the age of the planting.
SLUGS	Burrow into ripening fruits leaving slimy trails.	Apply a commercial metaldehyde bait according to directions on the container.
(1) LEAF SPOT	(1) Leaves show purplish spots, with gray centers.	Varieties differ greatly in susceptibility to the leaf diseases. When feasible select varieties which are least susceptible. Where control is necessary, spray new plantings at 10-day intervals with 2 lbs. per 100 gallons of either ferbam or captan. Spray second year plantings after harvest with same materials. Repeat at 2-week intervals if necessary.
(2) LEAF BLIGHT	(2) Reddish purple, almost circular, sometimes elliptical spots on leaflets. If spots occur on a prominent vein, fan-shaped injured areas extend to margin of leaflet. No gray or white centers are evident. When infection is on calyx, stemend rot of berries may occur.	Spray thoroughly.
(3) SCORCH	(3) Large, irregular-shaped purplish spots without light centers. Badly infected leaves often curl and 'burn.' Infection may also occur on leaf petioles, fruit pedicels, and on the sepals of the calyx.	Dodine 65 WP at 1½ lbs per 100 gals at 300 gals an acre. Zineb and captan are second best.
FRUIT ROT	Decay of blossoms, green and ripening fruits, and harvested berries. Most damaging in wet seasons.	Spray or dust plantings thoroughly every 5 to 7 days from start of blossoming until first fruit picking. Apply 3 lbs. of actual captan, or thiram per acre.
RED STELE ROOT ROT	Plants wilt and die, usually just preceding or during harvest. Roots of plants decay and show red cores. Roots devoid of fibrous, lateral rootlets, giving the roots a 'rat-tailed' appearance.	Set only disease-free plants on well-drained, porous, fertile soil which is uncontaminated by red stele fungus. Rotate crops with at least four years between strawberry crops. Use only red stele resistant varieties whenever feasible, especially if trouble with red stele disease has been experienced. Sparkle, Midway, Siletz and Surecrop are the more common resistant varieties now available.
VIRUS DISEASES Transmitted by Aphids	Reduced runner formation and decreased vigor and yields of plantings. No conspicuous symptoms.	Set only virus-free 'registered' plants. Virus-free stock of most varieties is now available. If planting is from virus-free stock and will be used for plant production, dust with Thiodan at above rate every 10-14 days. Make first application as soon as growth starts in spring and continue until frost in fall, except do not apply malathion during harvest.

Note: Cultivars resistant to, e.g., stele, verticillium, mildew, leaf scorch and leaf spot are available in some areas and should be used.

753

of western states where spring frosts may kill blossoms of standard varieties. They are used in the home garden in sections of the United States north of North New Jersey and in the higher Appalachian range. The present varieties are not adapted to the South. Everbearing strawberries are not considered profitable for the general market, although Dr. Wesley P. Judkins both in Ohio and Virginia (2000 feet altitude) has obtained good yields and profits from everbearers.

Best berries are obtained in the fall following the spring planting and many fields are kept only for one season. Deblossoming should be discontinued about the first part of July to obtain a fall crop the first year. If the bed is kept a second season, the fruit is borne at the normal time, followed by a rest period and then by further bearing, but the fruit may be small both in size and yield. Everbearing varieties need a very fertile soil and adequate soil moisture in order to develop berry size and satisfactory yields. They may be planted by the matted-row or hill system, depending upon the runner-forming habit of the variety. The culture, otherwise, is similar to that recommended for standard varieties.

The New Jersey Station is attempting to breed better size, flavor, and particularly keeping and handling quality into present everbearer varieties.

Spaced-Plant Sawdust-Mulch System for Everbearers. Karl Michener, Burton City, Ohio, and W. P. Judkins (See reference) were able to produce as high as 9,000 quarts per acre of everbearers, or 5,000 quarts with little difficulty by this system. The Gem (Brilliant or Superfrction) variety was best adapted. Wayzata, Streamliner, Brune's Marvel, Mastodon, and Gemzata did not yield enough berries to cover the cost of production and harvesting. The system also is well adapted to backyard gardens. An area 40 by 15 feet, with 500 plants, should produce 100 quarts of berries the first growing season and a similar or larger crop the second year. The 4-row-bed-type planting, with plants set a foot apart in the row and between rows with a 2-foot alley, gave the largest yields, greatest ease and economy of operation, and highest profits.

The plants should be set as early as possible in spring on fertile well-drained soil which has been under cultivation for a year or two. Two to three weeks after planting, remove the first crop of weeds by hoeing, then cover the entire area with a layer of sawdust, one inch thick. This conserves moisture and supresses weed growth. Weeds coming through the sawdust should be pulled and not hoed. After the first weed-pulling job, weed control should be relatively easy the rest of the season. All blossoms appearing on the newly-set plants should be removed until midsummer. If plants are growing vigorously, blossom removal may be discontinued two to three weeks earlier; if growing poorly due to drought, a late start, or other factors, blossom removal should be continued later. Harvesting starts in late summer and can continue twice a week until frost.

All runners must be removed from the fruiting plantation as fast as they develop. This is highly important if highest yields are to be secured. Hard or soft wood sawdust in a fresh or weathered condition can be used. If a slight nitrogen deficiency develops (fading of green leaves) shortly after application, this can be corrected by applying a quickly available source of nitrogen, such as sodium nitrate.

About 150 cubic yards of sawdust will be needed to cover an acre of land one inch deep. About 2 cubic yards will be needed to mulch a 40 by 15 foot home garden strawberry patch.

This method of growing strawberries requires a relatively large amount of hand labor, but growers have demonstrated in small and medium size plantations that a patch carefully managed will give good profits. Most commercial plantings do not exceed one acre in area. Larger plantings could be made, but adequate labor must be available.

Review Questions

1. Discuss the leading commercial strawberry production areas in the United States and foreign areas and indicate trends in outlets and shipping, including air freight.
2. Why is it possible to grow strawberries under so widely differing soil and climatic conditions?
3. Describe a desirable location and site for a commercial strawberry enterprise in your region.
4. What factors are paramount in selecting a strawberry variety for local market? For distant market?
5. Discuss precautions needed in getting good planting stock in strawberries.
6. Describe preparations necessary for growing strawberries on land which has been in sod.
7. Why is early planting of strawberries in the upper eastern states so important?
8. Describe briefly, by diagram if necessary, how the hill system of training straw-berries differs from the spaced-row and matted-row systems.
9. What is the proper depth for setting strawberry plants?
10. Describe a desirable cultivation and fertilization program for strawberries during the first season in your locality. Discuss value and use of herbicides.
11. Of what value is lime in strawberry culture?
12. In almost all regions where strawberries are grown, irrigation is frequently the deciding factor in successful strawberry production. Why is this true?
13. In mulching strawberries in your region, if practiced, what materials can be used, when are they applied, and why?
14. How would you handle a pick-your-own operation?
15. What instructions would you give your picking crew to reduce damage to the fruits as much as possible? Discuss the key aspects of mechanical harvesting.
16. List an important insect and disease of strawberries in your region and modern control.
17. Under what conditions should a strawberry plantation be renewed?
18. Give briefly the steps for renewing a plantation trained to the matted-row system; the system used in California.
19. Discuss the strawberry virus and nematode situation, their possible effect on yields, and how to control them.
20. Discuss strawberry containers and storage and marketing problems.

Suggested Collateral Readings

Anderson, William. The strawberry - a world bibliography - 1966. Scarecrow Press, Inc. P.O. Box 656, Metuchen, N. J. 08840. 731 pp. 1969.

Abbott, A. J., et al. Relation of achene number to berry weight in strawberry. J. HortSci. 46(3):215-222. July 1970.

Antoszewski, R., et al. Studies on K, Na and P (labelled) mobility in strawberry peduncle. Acta Societatis Botanicorum Poloniae. 37(3):433-441. 1968.

Bell, H. K. and J. D. Downes. Blossom removal effects on runners, berry size, yield of Robinson strawberry. Mich. Agr. Exp. Sta. Quar. Bull. 44:4. 619-624. May 1962.

Blatt, C. R. Effects of nitrogen forms, rates, pH levels on Arcadia strawberry. (Canada). J. Am. Soc. Hort. Sci. 92:346-353. 1968.

Bobb, A. C. Everbearing strawberries in the home garden. Conn. Agr. Ext. Serv. Leaflet 55-4. March 1960.

Boyce, B. and C. R. Smith. Winter hardiness studies with strawberry. Am. Soc. Hort. Sci., 91:261-266. 1968.

Brand Jr., H. J. and P. L. Hawthorne. Cold protection for strawberries. La. Exp. Sta. Bull. 591. 1965.

Bringhurst, R. S. and T. Gill. Fragaria polyploids. II. Unreduced and double unreduced gametes. Amer. J. Bot. 57(8):969-976. 1970.

Bunyard, E A. The history and development of the strawberry. Jour. Royal Hort. Soc. 39:541-552. 1914.

California Strawberry Advisory Board (under State Dir. of Agr., P.O. Box 269, Watsonville, Calif. 95076) issues frequent newsletter advice to growers, others, from planting to marketing.

Chaplin, C. E., et al. Breeding behavior of mite-resistant strawberries. J. ASHS 95 (3):330-333. 1970.

Collins, W. B. and C. R. Smith. Soil moisture effects on the rooting, early development of strawberry runners. J. ASHS 95(4):417-419. 1970.

Cooke, I. J. Some effects of light and nutrition in the forcing of strawberries. ASHS 44(1):49-55. 1969.

Crow, Howard M. The sprinkler (irrigation) story. PermaRain Irrigation Systems, P. O. Box 957, Lindsay, Calif. 40 pp. Request recent edition.

Darrow, G. M. Exploration in South America for strawberries and other small fruits. Fruit Varieties and Hort. Digest 12:5-7. 1957.

Darrow, G. M. Strawberry varieties, past, present, and future. Fruit Varieties and Hort. Digest 14:7-10. 1959.

Darrow, G. M. The strawberry: history, breeding, physiology, 447 pp. Holt, Rinehart and Winston. New York, Chicago, San Francisco, USA. 1966.

Denisen, E. L. and W. F. Buchele. Mechanical harvesting of strawberries. J. Am. Soc. Hort. Sci. 91:267-273. 1968.

Dennis, C. C. Strawberry purchases-trends, purchaser characteristics. Mich. Agr. Exp. Sta. Quart. Bull. 42:4, 859-870. May 1960.

Dennis, C. C. Strawberry prices and marketing margins. Mich. Agr. Exp. Sta. Quart. Bull. 43: No. 3. 648-659. 1960.

Droge, J. H. Radiation-pasteurizing fresh strawberries and other fresh fruits and vegetables: estimates of costs and benefits. USDA-ERS. 225. 21 pp. March 1965.

Eaton, G. W. and L. I. Chen. Strawberry achene set and berry development as affected by captan sprays. J. ASHS 94 (6):565-568. Nov. 1969.

Eddy, Roger. Mexico's strawberry "Boomtown." Am. Fr. Grower Mag. 12, 13, 32. June 1968.

Egger, D. A. Strawberry bloom protection from frosts with liquid foam. HortSci. 3: (1). Spring 1968.

Foster, James C., and Jules Janick. Variable branching patterns in the strawberry inflorescence. J. ASHS 94(4):440-443. 1969.

Fry, B. O. and E. F. Savage. Cultural effects on strawberry yields. Ga. Agr. Exp. Sta. Bull. N. S. 172. 27 pp. 1966.

Goble, W. E. Costs of processing strawberries for freezing in Tennessee. Tenn. Agr. Exp. Sta. Bull. 378, 62 pp. 1964.

Goble, W. E. and S. W. Cooler. Hydrocooling strawberries. Tenn. Agr. Exp. Sta. Bull. 344, 34 pp. 1962.

Hansen, C. M. Strawberry mechanization. Amer. Fruit Grower, June 1972.

Hard, M. M. and M. M. Weller. Properties of fresh frozen strawberries in stores. Wash. Bull. 740. 1971.

Harvey, J. N., et al. Air transport of Calif. strawberries by modified atmospheres. USDA Mkt. Res. Rpt. 920. 10 pp. 1971.

Hill, R. G., Jr. Growing strawberries in Ohio. Ohio Coop. Ext. Serv. Bull. 436, 16 pp. 1967.

Holland, A. H. et al. Strawberry production in southern California. Calif. Agr. Ext. Serv. AXT-50, 16 pp. Nov. 1967.

Jacobson, M. and M. M. Weller. Freezing Washington strawberries-shape retention, texture, flavor, color. Wash. Agr. Exp. Sta. Bull. 678, 13 pp. 1967.

Jonkers, H. Flower formation, dormancy and early forcing of strawberries. Hort. Agricultural University, Wageningen, The Netherlands, Publ. No. 265, 70 pp. (in English). 1965.

Judkins, W. P. and V. Patterson. Small fruit production in Ohio. O. Agr. Ext. Serv. Bull. 310. 24 pp. 1950.

Kamali, Abdul R. Strawberry culture in Lebanon (in Arabic). Publ. 6, Institut de Recherches Agronomiques, Liban, 40 pp. 1967.

Kattan, A. A. et al. Yield and quality of strawberries "once over" mechanically harvested. Ark. Farm Res. 3-4, July-Aug. 1967.

Keane, Eunice M. and W. E. Sackston. Effects of boron and calcium nutrition of flax on Fusarium wilt. Canadian J. Plant Sci. 50(4):145.

Kidder, E. H. and J. R. Davis. Frost protection with sprinkler irrigation. Mich. Ext. Bull. 327, 1956.

Kwong, S. S. Micro-elements in strawberry leaves. J. Am. Soc. Hort. Sci. 91: 257-260. 1968.

Lee, V. Antoine Nicholas Duchesne — first strawberry hybridist. Amer. Hort. Mag. 43:80-88. 1964.

Linton, R. E. and B. A. Dominick, Jr. Strawberry costs and returns, Long Island and western New York. Cornell Agr. Econ. Res. Mimeo. 84. Request recent data.

Lockhart, C. L. and C. A. Eaves. CA storage of strawberry plants. Can. J. of Pl. Sci. 46:151-154. 1966.

Longley, A. E. Chromosomes and their significance in strawberry classification. Jour. Agr. Res. 32:559-568. 1926.

Maxie, E. C. and N. F. Sommers. Strawberry preservation by irradiation. Calif. Agr. 24(12):13-14. 1970.

McConnell, G. E. Pick-your-own-strawberries. Amer. Fruit Grower. May 1972.

Mcgrew, J. R. Strawberry diseases, USDA Farmers' Bull. 2140. 27 pp. Recent edition.

Mitchell, H. G., et al. Handling fresh market strawberries. Calif. Cir. 527.

Montelaro, Joseph, W. F. Wilson, Jr. and D. A. Spurlock. Growing Louisiana strawberries. La. Agr. Ext. Serv. 1096, 21 pp 1962.

Moore, J. N. Insect pollination of strawberries. J. ASHS 94(4):362-364. 1969.

Moore, J. N. and Elvin Brown. Yield and maturity of strawberries in relation to time of once-over harvest. J. ASHS 95(5):519-522. Sept. 1970.

Moore, J. N. and H. L. Bowden. Date of planting effects on strawberries. J. Am. Soc. Hort. Sci. 91:231-235. 1968.

Morrison, W. W. Preparing strawberries for market. USDA Farmers' Bull. 1560. 16 pp. 1968.

New shipping trays speed berry handling in Florida. Am. Fr. Grower Mag., Aug. 1964.

Okasak, K. A. et al. Graftage to induce verticillium wilt resistance in susceptable strawberry. J. Am. Soc. Hort. Sci. 91:363-368. 1968.

Ourecky, D. K. and G. L. Slate. Everbearing characteristics in strawberries. J. Am. Soc. Hort. Sci. 91:236-241. 1968.

Redit, W. H. and A. A. Hamer. Precooling and shipping Louisiana strawberries. USDA-AMS Res. Rep. 358, 39 pp. 1959.

Ricketson, C. L. Plant spacing in solid-bed strawberry plantings. Hort. Res. Inst. of Ontario. Rpt. 1969. pp. 59-68.

Ricketson, C. L. The strawberry in Ontario. Ont. Dept. of Agr. Publ. 513, 47 pp. 1963.

Ross, S. T., et al. Cytological effects of juice, puree from irradiated strawberries. J. Food Sci. 35:549. 1970.

Ryan, J. J. Flavonol glycosides in strawberry. J. Food. Sci. Sept.-Oct. 1971.

Saxena, G. K. and S. J. Locascio. N and K effects on strawberry fruit quality. J. Am. Soc. Hort. Sci. 91:354-362. 1968.

Scott, D. H. Breeding and improvement of the strawberry in the United States of America — a review. Hort. Res. 2:35-55. 1962.

757

Scott, D. H. and A. D. Draper. Longevity of strawberry seed in storage HortSci. 5(5). Oct. 1970.

Scott, D. H., et al. Guardian: root-rot resistant strawberry. Fruit Var. & Hort. Digest. July 1970.

Scott, D. H. *et al.* Strawberry varieties in the U. S. USDA Farmer's Bull. 1043. 16 pp. 1972.

Singh-Dhaliwal T. *et al.* Strawberries in the central western mountainous region, Puerto Rico. J. Agr. of Univ. of Puerto Rico, 48-4. 337-351. 1964.

Stang, Elden J., and E. L. Denisen. Inflorescence and fruit development in concentrated and non-concentrated ripening strawberries. J. ASHS 95(2):207-210. 1970.

Staudt, G. Taxonomic studies on the genus *Fragaria*. Can. Jour. Bot. 40: 869-889. 1962.

Stoltz, L. P., *et al.* Mineral nutrition of strawberry plants in relation to mite injury. J. ASHS 95(5):601-603. 1970.

Symposium — Small Fruits (no grapes) in Yugoslavia (culture, pests, disease, harvesting, marketing: summaries in English). Covers strawberries, raspberries, blueberries and red currant. Fruit Growing Inst., Cacak, Yugoslavia. 243pp. 1969.

Taksdal, Gudmund. Reduction of strawberry fruit malformation by chemical control of *Plagiognathus arbustorum*. Fabr. (Heteroptera, Miridae). The J. of Hort. Sci. 46(1):51-54. Jan. 1971.

Thompson, P. A. Chilling and chemical effects on germination of strawberry achenes. J. Hort. Sci. 44(2):201-210. April 1969.

—————————. Environmental effects on pollination and receptacle development in the strawberry. J. Hort. Sci. 46(1):1-12. Jan. 1971.

Titan Strawberry. No. Carolina State Univ., Raleigh-USDA release. Dec. 1971.

Voth, Victor *et al.* Effect of high N in strawberries. J. Am. Soc. Hort. Sci. 91: 249-256. 1968.

Voth, Victor *et al.* Bed system, bed height, clear polyethylene mulch, effects on yield, soil salt and temperature in California strawberries. J. Am. Soc. Hort. Sci. 91:242-248. 1968.

Voth, Victor and R. S. Bringhurst. Pruning, polyethylene mulching of summer-planted strawberries, southern California. J. Am. Soc. Hort. Sci. 78:275-280. 1961.

Wallace, T. Modern Commercial Fruit Growing. 384 pp., Chap. XIX. Strawberries. 297-316. Country Life Ltd., London WC-2. 1956.

Worthington, John T. Successful response of cold-stored strawberry plants dug in the fall. J. ASHS 95(3):262-266. 1970.

Zubeckis, E. Evaluation of strawberry varieties for juice making. Ont. Dept. of Agr. Hort. Exp. Sta., Vineland, Ontario, Canada, 104-108. 1964.

CULTURE

Anonymous. Soft fruit-growing—strawberries. Ministry of Agriculture, Fisheries, and Food Bull. 95. 44 pp. Her Majesty's Stationary Office, London, 1955.

Barritt, B. H., et al. Shuksan strawberry. Wash. Cir. 530. 1970.

Bell, Harry K., J. H. Mandigo, R. F. Carlson, Ray Hutson and R. H. Fulton. Strawberries in Michigan—culture, insects, and diseases. Mich. Agr. Ext. Serv. Bull. 156. 55 pp. 1958.

Blair, D. S., L. P. S. Spangelo, H. B. Heeney, and A. W. Hunter. Strawberry culture in eastern Canada. Canada Dept. of Agr. (Ottawa) Pub. 1005 19 pp. 1957.

Bould, C., E. G. Bradfield and W. J. Redmond. A factorial NPK field experiment with strawberry, var. Royal Sovereign. J. Hort. Sci. 41:165-167 1966.

California Agriculture, published by Univ. of Calif., Davis, has monthly items regarding strawberries. Examples are: Effects of Alar and top removal on yield of Fresno strawberries at three digging dates, Feb. 1968; Sequoia and Tioga, new California strawberry varieties, May 1968, April 1964 respectively; preplant fertilizers on winter planted strawberries, Oct. 1963; water penetration in strawberries aided by seeding grain in furrows, Apr. 1966: control of strawberry powdery mildew, Feb. 1967; nematodes on strawberries, June 1952; California strawberry industry in a changing economic marketing situation, Nov. 1963.

Carlson, R. F., J. E. Moulton, and G. S. Rai. Field control of strawberry runners in the fall with maleic hydrazide. Mich. qtrly. Bull. 42:3. 622-628. 1960.

Childers, Norman F. Fruit Nutrition. Chapter 13. Strawberry nutrition by Bertie R. Boyce and D. L. Matlock. pp. 518-548. Horticultural Publication. Rutgers University. New Brunswick, N. J. 1966.

References continued in Appendix under Strawberry

758

CHAPTER XXII

Bush Fruits

❖ ❖

Included among the bush berry fruits of commercial importance are the brambles, gooseberry, currant, and blueberry. The blueberry has shown a marked increase in popularity in recent years, but it, like the cranberry, is of commercial importance only in localized areas in the United States. The cranberry also is briefly discussed in this chapter, but actually, it is too prostrate to be considered as a bush fruit in the strict sense of the term.

THE BRAMBLES[1]

The brambles are perennial plants that have a biennial growth and fruiting habit. They include the raspberry (red, black, and purple), blackberry, trailing dewberry, and their hybrids and sports. The brambles differ somewhat in climatic requirements. Where one succeeds, the other may produce poorly or not at all. Thus, more than half of the raspberry acreage in the United States, according to the U. S. Census, is confined to four northern states; namely Michigan, 8,070 acres; Oregon, 5700; Washington, 3350; and New York, 2,103 (see Figure 1). Raspberry acreage in the South is limited to the high cool elevations, although there is a tropical black raspberry (*Rubus albescens*), grown in south Florida, cultivars Mysore, Ceylon, or Hill. The loganberry, probably a red-fruited sport of the wild blackberry, is confined more or less to the Pacific Coast where more than two-thirds of the acreage is located in the Willamette Valley of Oregon. Most loganberries are canned or crushed into juice, whereas most reds and blacks are used fresh, in jams and jellies or frozen for pies.

Dr. Robert G. Hill, Jr., Ohio Agr. Res. and Devel. Center, Wooster, and Dr. Perry C. Crandall, Wash. State Univ., substation, Vancouver, assisted in the revision of this section.

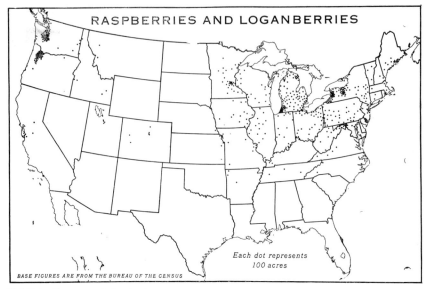

U.S.D.A. Bureau of Agricultural Economics

Figure 1. Raspberries thrive better in the upper-cool states. Michigan, Oregon, Washington, and New York lead. Loganberries are grown in the West, principally the Willamette Valley of Oregon. The lower Fraser River Valley, British Columbia, is important in red raspberries as is the cool coast area south of San Francisco, California.

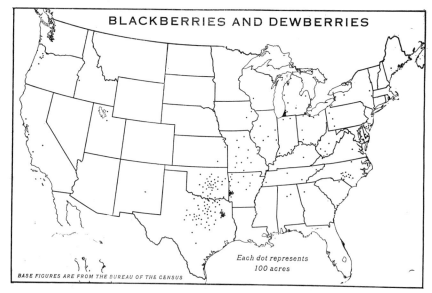

U.S.D.A. Bureau of Agricultural Economics

Figure 2. Blackberries are grown in a warmer climate than raspberries. Leading states are Oregon and Texas. Leading areas for the dewberry or trailing blackberry are Berrien County, Michigan; Hudson River Valley, New York; and North Carolina. All blackberries in Oregon are the trailing type; in the southern U. S., they are erect.

760

Figure 3. Eldorado black-berry is the leading variety in the East. Fruit ripens after raspberries.

The general decline in production of brambles the past several years is largely due to abandonment of marginal plantings and reduced harvesting by hand of wild acreage. Bramble production is likely to increase in the future with better-managed commercial plantings and the use of herbicides, "virus-free" stock, and mechanical and pick-your-own harvesting.

World raspberry production by leading countries in 100's of metric tons is approximately as follows: U.S., 325; Germany (all), 225; U.K., 165; Yugoslavia, 160; Hungary, 125; Poland, 110; Canada, 85; Netherlands, 50; France, 45; Norway, 25; and Australia, 15.

Blackberries can withstand more heat and dryness than raspberries and hence, a lot of acreage is located in Texas (Fig. 2) although Oregon is in the lead. Acreage in Oklahoma and Arkansas has dropped markedly, as is true in most blackberry-growing areas. United States rank is Oregon, Texas, Washington and Michigan. For boysen-, logan-, and youngberries, the rank of states is: Oregon, California, and Arkansas. A limited acreage of blackberries is found on a line from Maine to Missouri. Commercial dewberry sections are Berrien County, Michigan; the Hudson River Valley of New York; and North Carolina.

The red raspberry produces fruit on leafy shoots of erect slender canes. It is propagated by suckers which arise from the roots of the parent canes. Typical reds are Latham, Taylor, Cuthbert, Willamette. The yellow- and white-fruited raspberries are variants of the red type and are seen occasionally in home gardens. Golden Queen is a common yellow variety, although the Golden West, introduced by the Washington State Station is a better variety in the Northwest. Amber, from the New York Station, is a large conic berry. Typical everbearers are September, Durham.

The black raspberry, often called "blackcap," bears black and somewhat more seedy and aromatic fruit than the red raspberry. Canes of the black raspberry, as contrasted with the red, become arched in late summer and take root at the tips. These rooted tips can be cut away from the parent plant and used for propagation material. Black raspberries in general are not as hardy as some red raspberries and, hence, cannot be grown as far north. Varieties are Cumberland, Bristol, Allen, Dundee, Huron, Pearl, Bl. Hawk.

Purple-fruited raspberries are hybrids between the red and black sorts. They are more vigorous and productive than either of the parents, but resemble the black raspberry in growth habit and in method of propagation. Varieties are Clyde, Marion and Sodus.

The erect blackberries grow wild in most sections of the country and this has impeded to some extent the cultivation of the improved varieties which have firmer and better-keeping fruit than the wild sorts. Also, the season of cultivated varieties starts earlier and ends later than for the wild varieties. Eldorado, E. Wonder, Brazos, Dallas, Darrow, Smoothstem are examples.

The trailing blackberry (sometimes called "running" or "ground" blackberry or dewberry) has a prostrate growth habit. Actually, all commercial trailing blackberries are crosses between the trailing and erect blackberries. Thus, as one would expect, some hybrid varieties are semi-erect, as the Marion and the Thornless Evergreen blackberry varieties. Lucretia is the popular trailing blackberry for the North. The Young and Boysen lead in the West and South. The black raspberry differs from the blackberry in that it separates from the receptacle on harvesting. There are no commercially good everbearing black raspberries.

Bramble culture in the United States is limited to rather definite regions due to sensitiveness to extremes of heat, cold, and excess or deficiencies of moisture. One should determine from the accompanying figures, the foregoing discussion, and his neighbor's experience, which of the brambles is most likely to succeed in his locality. Most commercial growers rarely plant more than 10 to 50 acres, usually less than 20. Fresh sales are more or less limited to local towns and cities, but in larger producing areas considerable amounts (95%) are preserved by the frozen-pack method and canning. Since the fruit is soft and highly perishable, the crop must be either disposed of quickly in the fresh state or preserved. Many growers are planting brambles specifically for the pick-your-own trade.

Selecting the site and soil.   Good air drainage is important in reducing danger from spring frosts, winter injury, and diseases in regions where troublesome. A northern slope is not necessary but preferred, because the brambles naturally respond well to cool areas somewhat protected from the hot sun. Areas subjected to heavy drifting of snow are undesirable due to breakage of the canes, although some snow cover will help to protect the canes from winter injury. Brambles will grow on a wide range of soils from coarse sand to medium loams, provided they are *well drained* to a depth of at least three feet, preferably deeper. It has been shown that the leaves of brambles lose moisture more rapidly than those of most fruit plants, and, thus, provision for adequate soil moisture throughout the season is one of

(Bottom right) Ohio Agr. Exp. Sta., (Others) G. M. Darrow, U.S.D.A,

Figure 4. (Top left) Bundle of 27 Ranere (St. Regis) red raspberries as shipped from nursery. These should be heeled in, as shown at top right if they are not to be planted immediately. (Bottom left) All three are good nursery plants. Note difference between Ranere red raspberry, left, Columbian purple raspberry, center, and Cumberland black raspberry, right. (Bottom right) Raspberry plants should be fertilized with ammonium sulfate or a complete fertilizer about one month after planting, using two medium-sized handfuls per plant and distributed as shown. In the bottom left photo, the right plant has been propagated by a cane tip being covered by soil and taking root (tip layerage).

the most important factors in successful bramble culture. The incorporation of organic matter to help attain this desirable moisture situation, as recommended for the strawberry in the previous chapter, is most important. In general, the red, black, and purple raspberries and the erect blackberry perform best on medium loams, while the trailing blackberry will tolerate

763

heavier soils. Select *Verticillium* free soils and isolate the black raspberries from the reds to deter mosaic transfer.

Isolation of bramble blocks is important *to deter mosaic transfer* by insects; also select area of soil *free* of *Verticillium wilt.*

Planting time.   Best results generally are obtained by early spring planting. Fall planting for some brambles is practiced in the southern areas, but the plants should be protected during the winter by mounding with soil. On the Pacific Coast they should be set in early spring.

Propagation.   The best and safest source of planting stock is from reliable nurserymen who sell inspected certified plants, free from root rot and destructive virus diseases. Stock obtained from old plantations or neighboring growers should be selected with extreme care to avoid areas which have shown mosaic, anthracnose, and other diseases in excess.

As pointed out earlier, the red raspberry produces new plants from the roots of the parent plant. One-year plants are dug and bundled in spring for shipment by the nurserymen, as shown in Figure 4. Black raspberries and purple raspberries, are propagated from tips of canes which have bent over and taken root. If a large number of plants are desired for propagation, the canes at "squirrel ear" stage of tips are inserted two inches into the soil in mid-summer. They soon will root and be ready for transplanting the following spring, as illustrated in Figure 4.

Blackberries can be propagated from shoots from the roots as in the case of the red raspberry, using one-year plants. They are also propagated by root cuttings. In the fall, moderate to large roots of the blackberry are dug by nurserymen and cut into pieces two to four inches long. They are stored over winter in moist but not wet sand or sawdust in a cool place not subject to freezing. In the spring these roots are laid four to eight inches apart in furrows three to four inches deep and covered with friable soil. Under good cultivation and care the first season, the plants should be ready for sale and transplanting the following spring. Root cuttings can be made in the spring, but the percentage take is often considerably less. The plants also develop more slowly.

The trailing blackberry must be propagated from tip cuttings; root cuttings are thorny.

When ordering from the nursery, specify No. 1 grade state-inspected stock with vigorous root systems. Some varieties of raspberry have been heat-treated by USDA specialists, as with strawberry, to free them of the troublesome viruses. Virus-free raspberry varieties should be specified where available and a program of planting and dusting followed to keep them free. The availability of virus-free stock[1] may serve as a stimulus to the raspberry industry bringing back this crop in areas where it has been failing because of unprofitable yields and relatively poor quality. If the

---

[1] Most nurseries handling brambles have "virus-free" stock available. The New York Fruit Testing Association, Geneva, N. Y. 14456, was a pioneer in offering this stock for sale.

plants cannot be set to the field immediately on arrival, they should be heeled-in, as shown in Figure 4, or stored at 32°F in plastic bags.

Bramble varieties vary with the region, depending upon hardiness of canes, productiveness, and ways in which the fruit will be utilized. Darrow and Waldo make the following varietal suggestions for the raspberry: Varieties ripening over a long season in western New York may consist of June for early and Latham or Taylor for a late red variety; for black varieties, the Cumberland or Bristol; and for a purple variety, the Sodus. In the middle west, the red varieties should include Latham as the main sort, with Chief or Sunrise as early varieties and Taylor for trial to follow Latham. For black varieties, the Plum Farmer and Cumberland are best; in Iowa the Black Hawk shows promise. In Washington and Oregon, the Willamette, Meeker, Fairview and Matsqui are being planted commercially with Heritage for fall fruiting. Canby shows promise. Plum Farmer and Munger are the only blackcaps being planted in the Northwest. In central California, the Ranere, and in southern California, the Surprise red raspberries are among the best. The Latham and Ranere are grown in New Jersey, the Marlboro is popular in Colorado, and the Latham in Minnesota, inasmuch as the latter variety was developed by the Minnesota Agricultural Experimental Station. In some localities, other red varieties may be desirable, especially the new ones, such as Taylor, Marcy, and Newburgh, although the latter variety has shown too much susceptibility to winter injury in Michigan and Wisconsin. Where fall-fruiting varieties are desired, Ranere, September, Durham and Indian Summer are possibilities in the Northeast whereas LaFrance, as well as Ranere, are receiving attention in California. Tennessee Autumn and Durham are promising varieties in Tennessee and New Hampshire, respectively.

Care should be taken in selecting blackberries to obtain varieties that are sufficiently hardy in the northern states. Eldorado answers this requirement best if stock true-to-name can be obtained. The acreage of cultivated blackberries has declined in recent years because it is difficult to get plants of true varieties. Unknowingly, nurseries sold virus-infected plants that produced little fruit, or they have sold wild plants as known varieties.

Erect blackberry varieties include: Alfred (Mich.); Bailey, Darrow, Hedrick (N. Y.); Eldorado (general, not extreme South); Flint, Early Harvest, Georgia Thornless (Southeast); Himalaya (Calif.); Thornfree (Northwest); Jerseyblack, Nanticoke, Ranger, Raven, Smoothstem and Thornfree (Mid Atlantic Coast).

Trailing varieties include: Advance, Aurora, Boysen, Chehalem, Logan, Olallie, Young (Pacific Coast); Oklawaha, Olallie, Young, Gem, Flordagrand, Boysen (Gulf States); Mayes (Tex.); Marion, Thornless Evergreen (Northwest); Lucretia (general - needs severe winter protection).

The grower should keep in close touch with his local governmental experiment station for new variety developments.

W. R. O'Brien, U.S. Soil Conservation Service, Benton Harbor, Mich.

Figure 5. A contour-planted red raspberry plantation in Michigan. Note fine tilth of soil and special furrow cultivation to increase water retention and absorption. Adequate soil moisture is a most important factor in successful raspberry growing. Present-day use of herbicides in the row is a tremendous improvement in soil management of raspberries. (See Chap. 18).

Soil Preparation.   Soil preparation as described for the strawberry is equally desirable for the brambles. The soil should be in clean cultivation the year before to reduce the perennial weed problem as much as possible and to get the soil into good tilth. High organic matter content is of particular importance in successful bramble culture. This can be attained by turning under green manure crops the previous year or by the addition of eight to ten tons per acre of strawy manure before planting. Run soil tests the season before planting and apply fertilizer and lime accordingly; also, use herbicides to control difficult weeds as quack grass.

Planting plans.   The grower should consider the type of tools available for cultivation in laying out the raspberry plantation. Plants set somewhat farther apart than necessary to accommodate available cultivating equipment will be less expensive to handle than plants set close and requiring considerable hand labor. If the land is sloping, contour planting is suggested (Figure 5). The main planting systems are the *hill, hedgerow,* and *linear.* With the *hill* system, it is possible to cultivate both ways across the field. Dewberries are frequently grown in hills, as with any of the brambles. The total yield is reduced as compared with the hedgerow system, but the fruits are large and usually of higher quality and are more easily harvested. A source of low-price stakes should be available. The hill system is suggested only on level or gently sloping land where erosion will not be a factor. The *hedgerow* system consists of a continuous row of canes covering a strip of ground about one to two feet wide at the base. It is adapted to the blackberry and to short-cane red raspberries such as Sunrise and Latham, which tend to throw many suckers from the roots, making it difficult to maintain the plants in hills. Other varieties adapted to this training system are King, and Herbert. Cuthbert and Ranere have slender stems which are often cut back lightly in spring so that they can better support their crop. Also, varieties with weak or relatively tall canes are supported by different types of trellises.

The *linear* training system is more or less a modification of both the hill and hedgerow systems, in which no suckers are allowed to develop and the width of the row is restricted to the parent plants. The field, however, is cultivated one way only. Black and purple raspberries and some red raspberries are grown by this method. It is about the only system used in Washington where canes of the Willamette and Meeker are grown quite tall and trellises are used.

Red raspberries are planted three feet apart in rows seven to eight feet apart for the hedgerow system or five to six feet apart each way where the hill system is used. This width is adapted to the use of small garden tractors which are in common use in average-size plantations. The possibility of skips in the hill system can be avoided to some extent by setting two plants 18 inches apart and two more 18 inches apart at a distance of four or five feet in the row. The two plants 18 inches apart are trained to the same post set halfway between. These planting distances are suggested for average vigor and soil fertility. The distances may be more or less, depending upon these conditions.

The black raspberry has a spreading and drooping growth habit and thus requires somewhat more space than the red raspberries. They are set as an average 2½ to 3 ft. in rows 8 to 10 ft. apart (Mech. Harv.). Purple raspberries are more vigorous than the black varieties and thus require about ten feet between rows. The trailing blackberry is set 5 to 8 ft. apart in the row.

Planting brambles. Plow out furrows in one direction deep enough to accommodate the root systems, and cross-mark the field in the other direction at points where the plants will be set. The plants can be carried to the field in tubs of water and distributed from pails containing muddy water. Plants should be dropped only a short distance ahead of the planters to protect the roots from drying. Dull cloudy days with little or no wind are the best for planting. The plants are placed against the straight side of the furrow about two inches deeper than they grew in the nursery. Soil is pulled around the roots and well firmed with the foot. The growing tip of the black and purple raspberry plants, which is curled upward, should not be covered with soil. Another system for planting is to use a spade which is pushed into the ground and shoved forward. The plant is inserted while shaking out the roots, the spade withdrawn, and the soil well firmed with the foot. Only the vigorous well-rooted plants should be used, as illustrated in Figure 4. Vegetable planters as shown in the Strawberry Chapter 21 are used for large commercial plantings.

Soil management. Work the soil toward the plants while cultivating. Except for contour plantings, cultivate both ways frequently during the first season to reduce weed competition and increase soil aeration and rainfall penetration. Any practice which increases or maintains moisture supply among brambles is an important factor in success with these crops. The brambles are all shallow-rooted and are the first to show the effects of drought. In-row herbicides (e.g. dinoseb, simazine) now are widely used (Chap. 18).

Cultivation should cease around the first of September and the hoe used thereafter to eliminate weeds, except in the colder northern states where even hoe weeding may induce succulent cane growth susceptible to winter injury. Cultivated vegetables, except for tomatoes (*Verticillium* wilt), may be grown between the bramble rows the first year, but they should be removed by around the first of September for the same reason. The better the weeds are controlled the previous year, the less the difficulty with them during the fruiting season.

Shallow cultivation should be practiced after the first year. This is especially true next to the rows with the red raspberry and blackberry which sucker more freely if the roots are frequently cut and broken. Teeth of a spike-tooth harrow can be set at more of an angle next to the rows to accomplish this. Hand removal of the suckers is highly effective in reducing sucker growth, but expensive. A spring-tooth harrow with some of the teeth removed can be used for making shallow furrows for collecting moisture on a contour-planted field, as shown in Figure 5. One cultivation during the harvesting period may be desirable, provided the soil is not too dry and dusty. If the canes are drooping into the rows, cultivation will have to wait until after harvest. Rototillers are increasingly popular for caneberries.

In most sections, a cover crop is sown, or, preferably drilled in late summer. If the crop lives over winter, such as rye, it should be kept well away from the rows and disked down before it joints the next spring. A method often used for killing rye is to plow toward the row about April 1 and pull the soil away from the row two weeks later with a disc or old-type grape hoe. Oats seeded at the rate of three bushels per acre will make a good cover and die over winter. Other crops often used are cowpeas, vetch, millet, and the different clovers.

Mulching with straw or leaves to a depth of six to eight inches each year frequently is practiced to maintain moisture supply. Where mulch is used, either manure or a nitrogen fertilizer should be applied to avoid a nitrogen

Figure 6. "Die back" of raspberries on a sandy loam soil in New Zealand was found to be due to boron deficiency, corrected by ½ oz. borax per bush. The raspberry is fairly tolerant to boron, but caution must be used against excessive use. Probably 5 pounds of borax per acre per year is a safe maintenance program. Newly planted raspberries in New York have been injured following high boron requirement crops such as broccoli which have been fertilized with 25 or more pounds per acre of borax.

deficiency. Manure with a high percentage of straw and free of weed seed makes an excellent mulch when available. Mulch may increase yields by three to five times, but it is a fire hazard in large commercial fields in dry seasons. Mulch partially offsets cultivation and cover-crop costs.

Herbicides. See Chapter XVIII for chemical weed control suggestions. Also, keep in touch with your local governmental services since chemicals for weed control change from year to year. Herbicides are now a key factor in commercial bramble culture.

Irrigation. Provision for irrigation is good insurance against drought in almost all regions. Irrigation is a necessary practice in the arid and semiarid sections of the Southwest and Pacific Coast. In the humid sections of the East, good crops may be grown without irrigation, but even in this area there are frequently periods when irrigation would increase the crop considerably. The furrow, portable sprinkler, or "trickle" systems as described for strawberries may be used. Brambles do well in a 4 ft. depth rooting area, well drained, applying water whenever 50 to 65% of the available water in this zone is utilized. Hence, in Oregon, e.g., 4-5 acre inches will be needed 2-4 times a year, depending on rainfall and evaporation.

Fertilization. The importance of additions of large quantities of organic matter to bramble plantations cannot be overemphasized. The moisture-holding capacity, tilth, and aeration of the soil is improved greatly by organic matter. In addition to a heavy application of barnyard manure at the time the land is plowed and prepared, about eight to ten tons of manure, if avail-

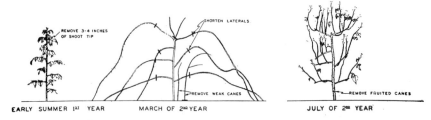

Figure ·7. **Black and purple raspberries produce shoots from the roots early in the growing season. When shoots attain proper height, summer pinching induces vigorous laterals which are shortened the following early spring. Bearing canes are removed immediately after harvest. Note tips of long laterals have taken root in center plant. New plants can be obtained by this means. Tips of laterals are covered in August with two inches of soil to induce rooting, and they are removed from the mother plant the next spring, leaving about six inches of mother cane for convenience in transplanting. New shoots from the roots should complete the diagram on right.**

able, applied per acre each year thereafter is one of the most effective means of maintaining vigorous growth and high fruit production.

Specific fertilizer recommendations for each bramble are difficult to make because soil conditions vary tremendously from one region to another and from one location to the next. It is highly recommended, therefore, that the grower maintain small test plots to determine the value of nitrogen, phosphorus, and potassium together and separately. It is known generally that black raspberries usually show the most response to fertility — the more fertile the soil, the stronger the growth and the larger the crop. Fertilizer requirements of purple raspberries are similar to those for the black varieties. While red raspberries respond to a fertile soil, their fertilizer requirements are not so well understood. Michigan studies have indicated that the larger the cane diameter, the more productive the canes; branched canes produced more than unbranched canes. Darrow and Waldo report that the best yields of red raspberries in the United States are obtained where annual application of two to 15 tons of stable manure per acre are made in addition to 400 to 500 pounds of a complete fertilizer. Judkins shows a 20 to 40 per cent increase in yield of Latham red raspberries receiving 500 pounds per acre of ammonium sulfate in the spring of each year in Ohio. If manure is not available, 200 pounds of nitrate of soda per acre applied to black raspberry fields at blossom time is suggested for trial on medium loam soils. Five hundred pounds of cotton seed meal is often used in place of 10 to 15 tons of manure. A 5-10-10 with magnesium and trace elements (see Chapter XIV for suggested formula) may be needed on light sandy soils low in organic matter, and in humid regions (Figure 6).

Blackberries have shown a greater response to nitrogen in the southern limits of the industry. Where manure, 20 tons per acre, is not available, Darrow suggests trying 600-1000 pounds of a 5-10-5 or similar ratio fertilizer. Less manure or fertilizer will be needed where green manure crops are turned under each year between the rows.

For trailing blackberries in North Carolina, two applications of fertilizer

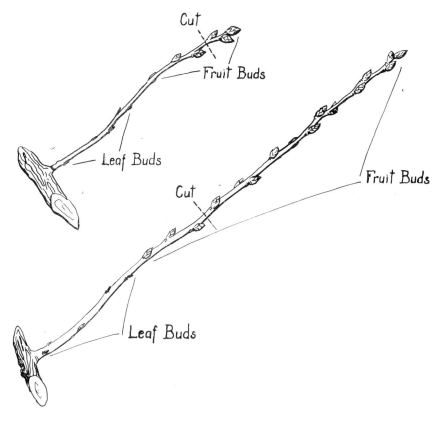

C. A. Doehlert, New Jersey Agr. Exp. Sta.

Figure 18. (Top) Lateral sprout of Cabot blueberry and (bottom) Sam showing amount of trimming back needed for varieties of these growth and fruiting characteristics.

with screen or netting. *Stem* canker is a serious problem in North Carolina. Varieties resistant to the fungus, *Botryosphaeria corticis,* have been developed in order for the industry to exist in this region.

Cranberry fruit worms (and other fruit worms) cause relatively unimportant fruit damage, but a few of these worms crawling over the fruit under cellophane packs is unsightly and may condemn sales. Dust with 1% parathion or 4% Malathion, 40 lbs. per acre about May 29 in New Jersey and 7-12 days later. *Cranberry weevil* may damage or destroy the blossoms, reducing the crop 50 per cent in some blueberry areas. Other insects of less importance include the blueberry bud worm, forest tent caterpillar, fall webworm, Tatana worm, and leaf rollers, blueberry mite, scale insects, stem gall, stem borer, and cranberry root worm. For detailed descriptions and controls, call upon your local experiment station or county

TABLE 7. PERCENTAGE OF CROP PICKED EACH WEEK DURING THE RIPENING SEASON FOR SEVERAL BLUEBERRY VARIETIES IN EASTERN NORTH CAROLINA, SOUTHERN NEW JERSEY, AND MICHIGAN (AFTER DARROW)....................

State and Variety	Week of Season													
	1 [a]	2	3	4	5	6	7	8	9	10	11	12	13	14
North Carolina														
Morrow	80	20	—	—	—	—	—	—	—	—	—	—	—	—
Angola	60	30	10	—	—	—	—	—	—	—	—	—	—	—
Wolcott	30	50	20	—	—	—	—	—	—	—	—	—	—	—
Weymouth	30	35	35	—	—	—	—	—	—	—	—	—	—	—
Croatan	20	50	30	—	—	—	—	—	—	—	—	—	—	—
Jersey	—	—	30	30	30	10	—	—	—	—	—	—	—	—
New Jersey														
Earliblue	—	—	—	—	40	60	—	—	—	—	—	—	—	—
Weymouth	—	—	—	—	50	35	15	—	—	—	—	—	—	—
Collins	—	—	—	—	—	50	50	—	—	—	—	—	—	—
Blueray	—	—	—	—	—	30	40	30	—	—	—	—	—	—
Bluecrop	—	—	—	—	—	20	40	30	10	—	—	—	—	—
Berkeley	—	—	—	—	—	—	20	30	30	20	—	—	—	—
Jersey	—	—	—	—	—	—	—	50	40	10	—	—	—	—
Herbert	—	—	—	—	—	—	—	20	40	30	10	—	—	—
Darrow	—	—	—	—	—	—	—	30	40	30	—	—	—	—
Coville	—	—	—	—	—	—	—	—	20	30	30	20	—	—
Michigan														
Earliblue	—	—	—	—	—	—	—	10	40	50	—	—	—	—
Stanley	—	—	—	—	—	—	—	—	20	30	40	10	—	—
Bluecrop	—	—	—	—	—	—	—	—	—	30	30	40	—	—
Berkeley	—	—	—	—	—	—	—	—	—	—	40	30	30	—
Herbert	—	—	—	—	—	—	—	—	—	—	40	30	20	10
Jersey	—	—	—	—	—	—	—	—	—	—	40	30	20	10

[a]May 15-22 in North Carolina.

agricultural agent. Ask for local spray schedule from governmental agency.

For detailed information on blueberry growing in North America, the reader is referred to *Blueberry Culture,* edited by Paul Eck and Norman F. Childers, 378 pp., Rutgers University Press, New Brunswick, New Jersey 08903.

CURRANT AND GOOSEBERRY CULTURE

Currants and gooseberries grow best in the northern United States where conditions are relatively moist and cool. In the South, the summers are too long and hot, and often too dry, particularly in the Southwest. In the Pacific Northwest and in the region of Colorado and Utah, they may grow

Design News, Canners Publ. Co., Wabash Ave., Chicago, 60603

Figure 19. The Harvey Harvester, developed by USDA, Michigan State University and industry, harvests up to 3,000 lbs/hr of berries for processing, cutting costs to less than 2 cents/lb as compared with 8 to 10 cents/lb hand-picked. All machine harvesters are in developmental stages, being improved each year so that eventually a portion of the crop may be acceptable to the fresh market trade. This heavy machinery may eventually pose a problem of soil compaction and ways of correcting it in blueberry plantings.

satisfactorily provided irrigation is available. The main area for commercial currant production is in a line from southern Michigan to the Hudson River Valley of New York. Other regions are around San Francisco, the Willamette Valley of Oregon, and the Puget Sound in Washington. Acreage of both currants and gooseberries in the U. S. is less than 1000 each.

Figure 20. (Left) An air-specific gravity berry cleaner that removes debris and immature berries. Fruit is graded on belt. (Right) Blueberry packing line at Cutts Bros., Chatsworth, New Jersey. Picking flats are dropped at left from field flatbed trucks, women hand grade berries, and cover pints with polyethylene and arrange in 12-pint flats (foreground).

Black currants, followed by red currants, gooseberries, and white currants are popular in Europe. Much of the black currant is made into juice. Germany (FR) produces, in 000's of metric tons, about 110; United Kingdom, 30; and Poland, 30; followed by Netherlands, France, Belgium, Australia and New Zealand. Russia's plantings are largely in home gardens with some commercial plantings near large cities. *Ribes* grows wild in upper China but is not accepted in the diet.

Currants and gooseberries are extremely resistant to low temperature and with windbreaks will even survive in the northern Great Plains area. Gooseberries can be grown somewhat farther south than currants because they are more resistant to heat. The limits of currant and gooseberry growing can be extended or altered somewhat by higher altitudes or provision for irrigation.

Four main factors limit production of currants and gooseberries in the United States; namely, summer heat, lack of adequate soil moisture, the currant maggot which is difficult to control, and the white-pine blister rust. Before making a commercial or home planting of currants or gooseberries, the nursery inspection department of the local state department of agriculture should be consulted. The reason for this is because gooseberries and currants, particularly the black currants, are alternate hosts to the white-pine blister rust which is a very destructive disease of the five-leaf pines. If currants and gooseberries are destroyed in regions where the white pine is

---

Figure 21. Harvesting Blueberries. (Top left) School children and instructors, as supervisors, are transported in early morning for blueberry picking. (Top right) Pint picking-baskets are fastened to the belt. (Middle left) Harvesting scene at Whitesbog, New Jersey, in July. (Top middle right) Late Elizabeth C. White, New Jersey pioneer in blueberry varieties and large commercial producer. (Bottom middle right) Twelve-pint trays are inspected by forewoman for any green and damaged berries; picker's card is punched if berries are satisfactory. (Bottom left) Most blueberries are marketed in crates and may be shipped long distances under refrigeration. Fiberboard and wood braced crates are used also. Cellophane improves appearance and prolongs keeping. (Bottom right) Branch showing fruiting habit of blueberries.

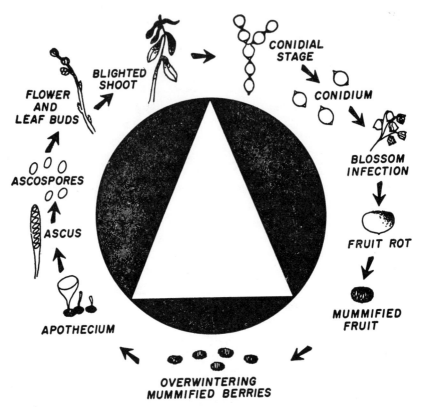

CONIDIAL STAGE

CONIDIUM

BLIGHTED SHOOT

FLOWER AND LEAF BUDS

BLOSSOM INFECTION

ASCOSPORES

FRUIT ROT

ASCUS

MUMMIFIED FRUIT

APOTHECIUM

OVERWINTERING MUMMIFIED BERRIES

R. H. Fulton, formerly of Michigan Agr. Exp. Sta.

Figure 22. This is the life cycle of the mummy berry fungus on blueberry, one of the more troublesome diseases.

grown, the disease is checked. Obviously, the value of the white pine crop far exceeds that of the currant or gooseberry. All citizens should co-operate in this program.

Varieties. Most desirable currants are the red varieties which have an erect vigorous growth habit, are easy to cultivate and pick, and have large-sized firm compact clusters. Following varieties are recommended in the United States: Red Lake, Perfection, Wilder, Red Cross, and White Imperial for the northeastern section; London Market, Wilder, Red Cross, Red Lake, Prince Albert, Perfection for Michigan, Middlewest; Perfection, London Market, Red Cross, Wilder, Fay, and Victoria for the Pacific Coast. Red Lake is tops in some regions and increasing in popularity in others. Red Lake has larger cluster size and is easier to pick than Wilder, but the latter will yield better under most conditions. White and black currants receive limited attention because of color and the peculiar flavor of the blacks; the black currant also is highly susceptible to the white-pine blister rust. This rust disease may be largely responsible for the marked reduction in currant acreage since 1929. White Grape is a white currant variety.

The Minnesota Station introduced the Welcome gooseberry in 1957 which has two "welcome" characteristics—the bush is nearly unarmed and is relatively resistant to troublesome diseases. It is a seedling of Poorman.

American varieties of gooseberries are most desired because they are more productive, hardier, and have better quality. European varieties are larger and sell better, but are more susceptible to mildew. The Poorman is widely planted in the North; Glenndale succeeds in Virginia, Tennessee, and Arkansas. Abundance, Perry, and Pixwell are recommended in the region of North Dakota. All of these are full or part American parentage.

Establishing the plantation. Currants and gooseberries bloom very early in spring. Northern exposures are desirable, especially in the southern extensions of the industry. Air drainage and circulation are important against frost damage and also for disease control, especially with gooseberries. A deep fertile loam retentive of moisture is the best soil.

Currants and gooseberries should follow a cultivated crop, if possible; plow and disk the soil well, and add manure and fertilizer as recommended for raspberries. Fall planting is suggested for most areas because these fruits start growth so early in the spring. Spring planting is suggested in the northcentral area, in which case fall plowing is desirable.

The nursery is probably the best source for plants; they are shipped as one- or two-year plants in bundles of about 25 (Figure 23). If a grower desires to extend his planting of a preferred variety, this may be done by cuttings. Eight-inch cuttings from one-year wood are selected any time during the dormant season. They are tied in bundles of a dozen and placed base up in a box of moist sand or peat in a cool basement. In early spring, cuttings are set to the garden or nursery at a depth of six inches with a spacing of six inches in rows three feet apart. Gooseberries can be propagated by bending branches downward in the fall and partly covering them with soil.

Gooseberries and currants also can be propagated by mound layerage; from 50 to 100 rooted cuttings can be obtained from a single plant. All branches are cut off about three inches aboveground in early spring. In July, soil is mounded around the vigorous shoots, covering half their length. The rooted shoots are removed in fall or spring and set to the nursery for one year before planting permanently in the field.

These fruits are set four to five feet apart in rows five to ten feet apart, depending upon cultivation equipment available. In planting, damaged roots are removed, the branches cut back to five inches, and the plants set with the lowest branches just below the ground surface in order to encourage a bushlike plant. Dig holes for each plant in heavy soil; in light soil, a shovel may be inserted and moved back and forth to form a V-shaped opening into which the plant is set.

In home gardens, currants can be planted between and in grape rows, but

(Top right) New York Agr. Exp. Sta., (Others) G. M. Darrow, U.S.D.A.

Figure 23. (Top left) Bundle of 27 vigorous gooseberry plants (currants are similar) as received from nursery. (Top right) Left rows in the currant plantation were sprayed with Bordeaux mixture with sticker-spreader for leaf spot; right rows unsprayed. (Bottom left) Imported currant worm may cause serious damage. (Bottom right) Curling of leaves caused by currant aphid on underside.

cultivation must be done either by hand or narrow machinery or herbicides, of course, can be used. Also, currants may be planted in tree rows, provided fertility and moisture are maintained sufficiently high for both crops.

Soil management. Frequent shallow cultivation should be practiced until shortly after picking when weeds are allowed to develop or a locally adapted cover crop is sown. These fruits respond well to a heavy mulch of straw or similar material. A double application of nitrogen fertilizer is needed with mulch to avoid nitrogen deficiency. A mouse poisoning program is necessary with mulching practice (Chapter V). No winter protection is needed, except perhaps to tie the bush in a bunch to prevent breakage from ice and snow. Currants are sensitive to chloride; use potassium sulfate instead of muriate (KCl).

Currants and gooseberries respond well to a fertile soil and to additions of manure at the rate of 10 to 20 tons per acre. In the absence of manure, apply 200 pounds per acre of ammonium sulfate or nitrate of soda, or 150 pounds of ammonium nitrate. The manure or fertilizer should be applied as a side dressing early in spring about two or three weeks before growth starts. In the light sandy or low-fertility soils, it may be wise to establish small fertilizer test blocks, using N, P, K, and/or Mg and trace elements alone or in combination. See Childers' *Fruit Nutrition* book, Chap. V, Bush Fruits, for leaf analysis data and techniques. Chemical weed control in the row can be practiced as described for blueberries.

See Chapter XVIII for herbicide suggestions.

Pruning. Plants are pruned to a bush form, varying in height from three to five feet. Best fruit with currants is produced on spurs of two- and three-year wood, although some fruit is borne near the base of one-year canes. Older wood produces inferior fruit. Prune in early spring before the buds begin to swell. The object is to remove branches over three years of age and, by thinning, select the proper kind and number of canes and branches to maintain a productive bush. Age of the wood can be judged by counting back annual growth rings from the tip (note change in color of bark and character of growth for each year). After pruning, the well-pruned dormant bush will have about three upright growths each of three-, two-, and one-year wood. With mature vigorous bushes, a few more upright growths of each age can be left (Figure 24). Thin the surplus slender weak wood. Branches growing horizontal and close to the ground should be removed to avoid dirty fruit. Pruning increases cluster size.

Gooseberries are often pruned similarly to currants, although they tend to bear heavier on one-year canes than do currants. Thus, the wood is sometimes removed after it is about two years old, or after it has borne a year from spurs.

Insects and diseases. *San Jose scale* appears as grayish crust formations on the older growth, resulting in a yellowish unthrifty dying condition. The *imported currant worm* (Figure 23) may appear shortly after the leaves expand in spring and destroy almost the entire foliage in a day or so. *Currant aphid* (Figure 23) attacks undersides of leaves, causing them to curl. In order to hit aphids, spray should be applied before leaf curling is pro-

Figure 24. (Left) A Red Lake currant before pruning. (Right) After pruning. Tall growth was cut back; low horizontal branches and most of wood older than 3 years was eliminated. One-year canes were thinned to three or four vigorous canes.

nounced. *Currant fruit fly* or *maggot* is destructive to the berries, particularly in the West and Canada; no control is known. *Leaf spot* may result in defoliation (Figure 23), the leaves falling during mid- to late season, reducing production the following year. *Anthracnose* appears as numerous small brown spots on upper leaf surface causing foliage to turn yellow and drop. Other diseases include cane wilt, white-pine blister rust, viruses and powdery mildew which is particularly destructive on gooseberries. Contact your local government service station for spray recommendations.

Harvesting and marketing. Currants for jelly should be picked slightly underripe when the pectin content is high. Currants can be picked fully ripe over a long period of time if they are to be stewed, spiced, or used in jams. For the market, they should be picked with extreme care when an occasional berry on each bunch is slightly green. Pinch off the main cluster stem at the base, using the forefinger and thumb. Do not crush the berries. Injured berries exude juice which collects dust and dirt and may develop mold quickly, especially if they are held shortly under damp conditions. Currants can be stored for a short time under cool dry ventilated conditions.

Gooseberries are mostly picked green at maximum size; harvesting may extend over a period of four to six weeks. For processing, berries can be stripped from the bushes with a cranberry scoop or heavy gloves, later separating the leaves by a grain-fanning mill. Gooseberries for the general market must be picked carefully to prevent injury and spoilage. Keep gooseberries in the shade to prevent sunscald. They can be held in storage much longer than currants.

Both gooseberries and currants are marketed in 12-pint corrugated or fiberboard boxes and flats or 16-quart crates. Some wood containers are

Figure 24a. Multipurpose self-propelled concentrate sprayer useful in bush fruits, grapes and full dwarf trees. The 8 nozzles are independently adjustable. (Courtesy KWH, Vandermolen Corp., Dorsa Ave., Livingston, N. J.)

still in use. For the canner, six- to eight-pound grape baskets are standard.

Yields may average 100 bushels per acre for European gooseberries, and 300 bushels per acre for varieties of American or partly American parentage. In England, 1½ tons/A is average, but to "break even" a grower should get 2 tons, and for satisfactory profit, 3 tons/A of black currants. In New York in the 1960's, only 3 of 17 growers profited at a production cost of 10.5c/lb average. Higher yields, sales promotion and new products are needed to boost the industry.

For the processor, it is possible that machine harvesting, as for brambles, could be used on a commercial scale to cut production costs.

CRANBERRY CULTURE[1]

The cranberry is native to North America. It is largely consumed in the United States and Canada with few exports. Cranberry growing is a highly specialized industry confined to acid bog or swamp areas and, thus, limited to a few states. Massachusetts produces almost half of the world's supply, bringing the state $10 million or more in good years. The 1970-71 average production for the United States was over 1,742,000 barrels utilized. Leading states for the 1970-71 period were: Massachusetts, 800,000 barrels; Wisconsin, 578,000; New Jersey, 170,000; Washington, 122,000 and Oregon, 64,700, utilized. (409,200 bbl. were set aside by marketing

[1]Dr. Paul Eck, Specialist in Cranberry and Blueberry Culture, Rutgers University, New Brunswick, N. J., assisted in this section revision.

Massachusetts Agr. Exp. Sta., (Lowest photos) Rutgers University

Figure 25. **(Top left)** A long, narrow, well-kept cranberry bog on Cape Cod, Mass., showing proper grading and ditching and the sand supply banks on either side. **(Top right)** After harvest, field is flooded, floater berries assembled with planks, and gathered for canneries. **(Middle) left)** A view of Early Black cranberries ready for harvest. **(Middle center)** An upright branch showing how berries are borne. **(Middle right)** Picking with a "snap" machine in young planting. Larger two-hand cranberry scoops are frequently used, holding one-half bushel. Power-driven harvesting machines are used by the larger growers. **(Lowest photos)** Water harvesting, developed in Wisconsin, is low-cost, efficient, and combs loose most of the berries with little vine damage and berry bruising. Berries are floated and accumulated by waves in a corner of bog and lifted to dump trucks by cleated loading belts.

order plus other quantities not utilized). Scattered fields are in Maine, New Hampshire, Rhode Island, Connecticut, Virginia, Minnesota, Michigan, and Long Island. Canada has a limited acreage in Nova Scotia, New Brunswick, Prince Edward Island, Quebec and British Columbia. U. S. cranberry production and prices have increased markedly in recent years due to an excellent product research and promotion program by the Ocean Spray, Inc., headquarters, Hanson, Massachusetts.

Several factors should be considered before developing a cranberry bog. Cost per acre is rather high to clear and properly level and ditch the bog,

Figure 26. In cranberry culture, like other fruit industries, a major effort is being made to reduce labor and grow a better quality product. Airplanes and helicopters are in common use for fertilizer and spraying applications. Man at far left is "flagging" the plane to designate the new strip for each "run."

install water pumping systems and dams, and to make the planting. There is also necessary upkeep for the first three years before the crop comes into bearing. Alkaline peat and ordinary garden and farm soils are not suitable. A large supply of water is needed for irrigation and flooding for protection against winter injury, untimely frosts, and insects. The site must permit drainage of the bog to a depth of 18 inches. A large supply of readily available clean sand is necessary. A climate, such as near Cape Cod, Massachusetts, and in Wisconsin is most desirable. A climate warmer than New Jersey induces more berry rotting and disease problems. Cranberry growing north of Nova Scotia is limited because the summers are too short and too cool. Cloudy weather during ripening, such as frequently occurs in Washington and Oregon, results in uneven maturity of berries. To establish cranberry fields in new sections, it requires years of work to develop new varieties, to train local people in the business, and to learn the peculiarities of the industry.

A good bog site for cranberry growing is shown in Figure 25. Long narrow bogs are the most desirable with adequate air circulation on all sides, good sun exposure, and with potentialities of quick flooding and quick drainage of the field. Steps involved in the preparation of the field include: (a) clearing the field of trees and brush, (b) cutting the turf into squares, turning them over, and removing and burning roots of all weeds and obnoxious plants, (c) construction of ditches around and through the field, (d) grading the field level to facilitate quick flooding and drainage, (e) construction of dams for sectional flooding of the field if it is large or the grade is relatively marked, (f) construction of flood gates and installation of pumping equipment, (g) covering the field with three to four inches of white coarse sand free of small stones, (h) planting the cuttings in the early spring about a foot apart both ways, and (i) flooding the bog for a day or so immediately after planting.

Leading varieties in Massachusetts are Early Black and Howes; in New Jersey, the Jersey, Howes, and Early Black; in Wisconsin, the McFarlin, Searles, and Stevens; and in Washington and Oregon, the McFarlin which comprises most of the crop. Improved cranberry hybrids released by USDA for commercial trial are: Beckwith, Stevens, Wilcox, Bergman, Franklin and Pilgrim. Stevens is adapted to water harvesting (Fig. 25).

Special attention to weeding is necessary for the first three years until the vines cover the ground. The bog is flooded to cover the vines with about 18 inches of water when the ground freezes in fall; it is drained about April 1 in Massachusetts, but may be left several weeks later if insects are a problem. Short floodings are necessary during the spring and fall for protection against frosts. Frost protection is being provided in some bogs with rotating sprinklers and overhead irrigation systems. Flooding is also timed during the early season to kill injurious insects, and is used occasionally for irrigation purposes during summer droughts. Some bogs are resanded periodically as needed, adding a one-quarter to one-inch layer for protection against frost, the girdler insect, the green spanworm, and the tip worm. This is done by hand from special wheelbarrows, or by dump trucks on the ice while the bog is frozen over.

No fertilizer is usually needed for peat-bottom bogs unless growth becomes poor. Nitrate of soda and superphosphate are recommended on bogs in Massachusetts with sand or clay underneath, using 150 and 300 pounds per acre, respectively, applied when the vines are beginning to bloom in late spring. In New Jersey, an 8-8-8 fertilizer is used applying 150 lbs. in May and 150 lbs. about August 15. Manures are likely to contain weed seed. Simazine (Princep 80W) can be applied in fall, winter or immediately after flood removal to control ferns, annuals and some grasses, rushes and sedges. Dalapon will control most weeds that are not killed by simazine, is applied after harvest, but bloom is lost for next year's crop in areas where used. Dalapon also is used in the ditches. See your local specialist for recommendations; follow them explicitly.

Berries may be harvested with the fingers, with hand scoops or by special motor-driven harvesting machines. A foreman, 13 scoopers, and two helpers are needed in Massachusetts to harvest a 15-acre bog. Average acre-yields for the 1970-71 period were: 67, 93, 120, 142 and 183 barrels/acre for New Jersey, Massachusetts, Wisconsin, Washington and Oregon, respectively. The field is flooded after harvest, and the floater berries are gathered and sold to the canneries (Figure 25). Water harvesting in large commercial bogs has become standard in Wisconsin and New Jersey (Figure 25).

Excessive runners are trimmed with a special knife-rake or pruner after harvest. On fertile bogs, the vines may need to be mowed if too deep and dense.

Cranberries can be stored in common storage in a screen house or in cold storage at 35°F., the latter being the better. The berries are first sent through a separator which removes chaff, then directed over bounding boards to separate decayed from sound fruits, and finally over grading belts for hand grading. Cranberries are sold by the hundredweight barrel box. Price per hundredweight varies from $10.00 to $15.00. Almost 80% of the crop is processed as sauce or made into beverages. Some cranberries are quick frozen. There is a good demand for cranberries at Thanksgiving and Christmas and a much better year-round market has been developed with fowl and all types of dinners in recent years. See Seelig and Roberts for review of growing, history, botany, processing and marketing of cranberries.

Diseases include *early rot* of the flowers, young berries, and stored berries and *false blossom* or rose bloom, a virus carried by the leafhopper. There are several troublesome insects. The *cranberry fruit worm* is sometimes found in a third of the crop; the *black-headed fireworm* feeds on the foliage; the *blunt-nosed leafhopper* carries false-blossom virus; the *root grub* causes dead spots over the field; the *gypsy moth* feeds on the foliage; and the *girdler* weakens or destroys plants by feeding on the underside of runners. The false army worm, brown spanworm, and other insects may become troublesome at times. For detail and up-dated control measures, see references at the end of this chapter and your local governmental service offices.

Well-managed cranberry fields are practically permanent.

Review Questions

BRAMBLES

1. To what regions of the United States are the following brambles commercially adapted: red, black, and purple raspberries, erect and trailing blackberries, and loganberries? What generally is the world production situation?

2. Describe a suitable site and soil for red raspberries.

3. State briefly how the following brambles are propagated: red, black, and purple raspberries, blackberries, and dewberries.

4. How do the three main planting systems for brambles differ and to what brambles is each particularly adapted?

5. Outline a good soil management program for red raspberries in your locality Would you include irrigation and, if so, why? Herbicides?

6. Which brambles are summer topped (pinched) and why?

7. How does dormant pruning of black raspberries differ from that for red raspberries?

8. When are trellises desirable for red raspberries and for blackberries?

9. How does dormant pruning for the upright blackberry differ from that for the trailing blackberry or dewberry?

10. Differentiate between anthracnose and a virus disease of raspberries.
11. At what stage of maturity should raspberries, blackberries, and dewberries be picked? Describe machine harvesting and its main value commercially.
12. Discuss mechanical harvesting of brambles. (Please check key references.)
13. For what brambles and in what regions is winter protection advisable? How is it provided?

BLUEBERRIES

14. What are the leading states in cultivated blueberry production?
15. Which of the blueberries are propagated for cultivation, and which is the most important commercially?
16. What are the climatic and soil requirements of the highbush blueberry?
17. List three leading varieties of the highbush blueberry.
18. How are blueberries propagated?
19. Outline a soil management program for a young and mature commercial plant ing of blueberries on a soil of medium to low fertility, having a pH of 5.0.
20. How would you prune a mature blueberry bush (a) with a spreading growth habit, (b) with an upright habit?
21. At what stage of maturity, how often, and over how long a period are high-bush blueberries harvested in a given region? Discuss machine harvesting.
22. List an important insect and disease of blueberries.

CURRANTS AND GOOSEBERRIES

23. What are the soil and climatic requirements for gooseberries and currants?
24. Where in the United States and World are commercial currants largely grown? Where is the black currant grown and why? The red currant?
25. How are the gooseberry and currant propagated?
26. Give 2 leading varieties of gooseberry and currant.
27. On what type and age wood are currants and gooseberries largely borne?
28. Briefly describe how to prune a mature currant bush.
29. What is a leading disease and insect of currants and gooseberries?

CRANBERRIES

30. Indicate where cranberries are grown in North America.
31. Briefly list the important factors to consider before establishing a cranberry planting.
32. What are the reasons for flooding a cranberry bog?
33. What varieties are most popular in the East, Midwest, and in the West?
34. Discuss methods and precautions for weed control in cranberries.
35. How are cranberries harvested, graded, and utilized?

Suggested Collateral Readings

BRAMBLES (ELDERBERRY INCLUDED)

Barritt, B. H. Fruit rot susceptibility of red raspberry cultivars. 55(2):135. Plant Disease Reporter. Feb. 1971.
Bould, C. Leaf analysis as a guide to the nutrition of fruit crops. VII. Sand culture NPK Mg experiments with red raspberry (Rubus idaeus). J. Sci. Food & Agric. 19(8):457-464. 1968. (England).
Bould, C., E. G. Bradfield and G. M. Clarke. N, P, K, Ca and Mg in raspberry as influenced by soil treatments. Journ. Sci. of Food and Agr., 5:359-364. 1963.
Brown, W. S. Influences of irrigation upon important small fruits. Oreg. Agr. Exp. Sta. Bull. 347. 1936.

Moore, J. N. Blueberry variety performance in Arkansas. Agriculture Exp. Sta. Univ. of Arkansas, Fayetteville, Ark. Rpt. series 186. June 1970.

Moore, J. N. et al. Fruit size and seed size and number of blueberry. HortSci. 7:3. 268-269. 1972.

Moore, J. N. and D. H. Scott. Blueberry breeding in northeast U. S. ASHS 88: 331-337. 1966.

Moore, James N. and N. F. Childers (Editors). Blueberry research — 50 years of progress. Proc. Conf. State and Fed. workers. Rutgers Univ., New Brunswick, N. J. 1960.

Neunzig, H. H. and J. M. Falter. Insect and mite pests of blueberry. No. Car. Agr. Exp. Sta. Bull 427, 34 pp. May 1966.

Pellatier, E. N. and M. T. Hilborn. Blossom and twig blight of lowbush blueberries. Me. Agr. Exp. Sta. Bull. 529. 27 pp. June, 1954.

Perkins, Frederick A. New container boosts blueberry sales. Produce Marketing, April 1964.

Schwartze, C. D. and A. S. Myhre. Growing blueberries in the Pugent Sound region of Washington. Wash. Agr. Exp. Sta. Cir. 245. 11 pp. 1954.

Shutak, V. G. and E. P. Christopher. Sawdust mulch for blueberries R. I. Agr. Exp. Sta. Bull. 312. 18 pp. 1952.

Shutak, V. G., R. Hindle, Jr., and E. P. Christopher. Growth studies of the cultivated blueberry. R. I. Agr. Exp. Sta. Bull. 339. 18 pp. 1957.

Taylor, Jack and Wesley Witcher. Blueberry diseases, North Carolina. No. Car. Agr. Ext. Serv. Circ. 466. 11 pp. 1965.

Townsend, L. R., et al. Chemical composition of rhizomes and associated leaves of the lowbush blueberry. Proc. ASHS 93:248-253. 1968.

Townsend, L. R. Soil acidity, growth, nutrient composition of highbush blueberry. Canadian Journal of Plant Science p. 385-290. 1971.

Trevett, M. F. Nutrition and growth of the lowbush blueberry. Me. Agr. Exp. Sta. Bull. 605, 151 pp. May 1962.

Trevett, M. F. Growth studies of the low-bush blueberry. Me. Agr. Exp. Sta. Bull. 581. 58 pp. 1959.

Turner, Darrell. Fertilization of evergreen huckleberry. Wash. Agr. Exp. Sta. Circ. 383, 6 pp. 1961.

Welker, William V. Jr. and J. L. Brogdon. Longtime use of diuron and simazine on highbush blueberries. Weeds 16:3. 303-305. July 1968.

Wood, G. W. Evidence of increased fruit set in lowbush blueberry by using honeybees. HortSci. 4(3):211-212. 1969.

CRANBERRIES

Chiriboga, C. and F. J. Francis. An anthocyanin recovery system from cranberry pomace. J. ASHS 95 (2):233-236. 1970.

Devlin, R. M., et al. Preharvest applications of malathion and indole-3-acetic acid on red color of cranberries. J. ASHS 94(1):52-55. Jan. 1969.

Eaton, G. W. Effect of N, P, and K fertilizer applications on cranberry leaf nutrient composition, fruit color and yield in a mature bog. J. ASHS. 96(4):430. July 1971.

——————. Effects of NPK fertilizers on the growth and composition of vines in a young cranberry bog. J. ASHS 96(4):426. July 1971.

Eaton, G. W., et al. Effect of preharvest malathion sprays upon cranberry fruit color. J. ASHS 94(6):590-592. Nov. 1969.

Eck, Paul. Cranberry growth and composition as influenced by nitrogen treatment. HortSci. 6(1):38. Feb. 1971.

——————. Cranberry yield and anthocyanin content as influenced by Ethephon, SADH, and Malathion. J. ASHS. 97(2):213. March 1972.

——————. Effect of preharvest sprays of Ethrel, Alar, Malathion on anthocyanin content of Early Black cranberry (*Vaccinium macrocarpon* Ait.). HortSci. 4(3):224-226. 1969.

Forsyth, F. R. and I. V. Hall. Oxygen absorption and ethylene production by developing cranberry fruit. Canadian J. Plant Sci. 47:153-156. 1967.

Greidanus, Ted, et al. Essentiality of ammonium for cranberry nutrition. J. ASHS 97(2):272. March 1972.

Hall, I. V., et al. Growing cranberries. Canada Dept. of Ag. Publ. 1282. Res. Station, Kentville, Nova Scotia. Revised.

Hicks, Judith L., et al. Growth of cranberry plants in pure stands and in weedy areas under Nova Scotian conditions. Hort. Res. 8(2):104-112. 1968.

Lees, D. H. and F. J. Francis. Standardization of pigment analyses in cranberries. HortSci. 7(1):83. Feb. 1972.

Leschyson, M. A. and G. W. Eaton. Effects of urea and nitrate nitrogen on growth and composition of cranberry vines. J. ASHS 96:597-599. 1971.

Medappa, K. C. and M. N. Dana. Tolerance of cranberry plants to manganese, iron and aluminum. J. ASHS 95(1):107-110. 1970.

Rigby, Bruce and Malcolm N. Dana. Flower opening, pollen shedding, stigma receptivity and pollen tube growth in the cranberry. HortSci. 7(1):84. Feb. 1972.

―――――――――. Rest period and flower development in cranberry. J. ASHS 97 (2):145. March 1972.

Rigby, Bruce, et al. Seed number and berry volume in cranberry. HortSci. 6(5). 1971.

Rigby, Bruce, et al. Ethephon sprays and cranberry fruit color. HortSci. 7(1):82. February 1972.

Stark, R., et al. Cranberries evaluated fruit and processing quality, after reduced oxygen storage. Res. Sta., Can. Dept. of Ag., Kentville, Nova Scotia.

Torio, Joyce C. and Paul Eck. Nitrogen, phosphorus, potassium and sulphur nutrition of the cranberry in sand culture. J. ASHS 94(6):622-625. November 1969.

CURRANTS AND GOOSEBERRIES

Baker, E. A., et al. Growth retardants' effects on cuticle of black currant. Ann. Rpt. Long. Ash. Res. Sta. (England). p. 116-121. 1967.

Branfield, E. G. Nutrient supply effects on growth, yield and leaf composition of black currant in sand culture. J. Hort. Sci. 44(2):211-218. April 1969.

Coker, E. G. The root development of black currants under straw mulch and clean cultivation. J. Hort. Sci. 33:21-28. 1958.

Currants and Gooseberries. Check the annual rpts. of the Long. Ashton Ag. & Hort. Res. Sta. (England) where research often is reported.

Darrow, George M. and S. B. Detwiler. Currants and gooseberries: Their culture and relation to white pine blister rust. U. S. Dept. of Agr. Farmers' Bull. 1398. (Rev.) 1946.

Gould, C. Leaf analysis as a guide to the nutrition of fruit crops. VIII, sand culture, NPK Mg experiments with black currant. J. Sci. Food & Agr. 20:172. March 1969.

Knight, R. L. and E. Keep. Abstracts and bibliography of fruit breeding and genetics —Rubus and Ribes—a survey Tech. Communication 25. Commonwealth Bureau of Horticulture and plantation crops. E. Malling, Kent, England. 1955.

Ljones, Bjarnes. Bush Fruits Nutrition. In Fruit Nutrition. Hort. Publications, Rutgers Univ., New Brunswick, N. J., edited by N. F. Childers 1966.

Ourecky, D. K. Blackberries, currants and gooseberries. Cornell Ext. Bull. 1216. 1969.

Posnette, A. F. New virus diseases of Ribes. Ann. Rpt. E. Malling Res. Sta. 133-135. 1951. (1952).

Skerrett, E. J. and O. J. Pritchard. Endrin residues on black currants. Ann. Rpt., Long Ash. Agr. & Hort. Res. Sta. 143-144. 1967.

Spangelo, L. P. S., et al. Combining ability analysis and interrelationships between thorniness and yield traits in gooseberry. Can. J. of Plant Sci. 50(4):439. July 1970.

Stark, R., et al. Cranberries, evaluated for fresh fruit and processing quality, after reduced oxygen storage. Rpt. Res. Sta.. Can. Dept. of Ag., Kentville, Nova Scotia.

Tinklin, I. G., et al. Factors affecting flower initiation in the black currant, Ribes nigrum (L.) J. HortSci. 45(3):275-282. July 1970.

Torio. Joyce C. and Paul Eck. Nitrogen, phosphorus, potassium and sulphur nutrition of the cranberry in sand culture. J. ASHS 94(6):622-625. November 1969.

Wilson, D. Black currant breeding: a progeny test of four cultivars and a study of inbreeding effects. J. Hort. Sci. 45(3):239-247. July 1970.

Bibliography continued in Appendix under "Currants and Gooseberries" and "Cranberries."

GENERAL

Harris, R. E. The Saskatoon (a Canadian bush with small fruits. A shadbush). Amelanchier alnifolia. Can. Dept. Agr., Ottawa. KIA, OC 7, 1972.

Ritter, C. M. and G. W. McKee. The elderberry — history, classification and culture. Pa. Agr. Exp. Sta. Bull. 709, 22 pp. Mar. 1964.

Appendix

SUGGESTED POMOLOGY LABORATORY EXERCISES[1]

A "Modern Fruit Science Laboratory Manual" is available for class use. This Manual has a total of 370 pages covering 31 laboratory exercises with a full color front cover and bound with a plastic ring so that the pages open flat on the laboratory table.

There is an itinerary of advance jobs for the instructor to do in preparation for each laboratory.

Students are asked to complete diagrams, tables, study and interpret charts, plant material and chemical herbicide and pesticide samples, answer questions, and read and abstract outside references. There are a variety of exercises for a basic and/or advanced course in fruit science. See list of exercises below.

Copies of the Manual are available through Horticultural Publications, Nichol Ave., Blake Hall, New Brunswick, N. J. 08903. A copy is mailed gratis to instructors planning to use the manual in classes of 5 or more students.

Laboratory No.	Title	Page
1	Sources of Information	1
2	World Fruit Production Survey	9
3	Classification of Fruit and Nut Crops	24
4	Climate and Fruit Production	30
5	Frost and Frost Protection	46
6	Production Machinery	59
7	Flowering, Fruiting and Growth Habits	71
8	Breeding	88
9	Propagation	101
10	Rootstocks	114
11	Grafting and Budding	133
12	Site Selection	140
13	Orchard Planning and Planting	152
14	Tree Fruits — Pruning & Training	167
15	Planting, Training and Pruning Small Fruits	178
16	Fruit Thinning	188
17	Fertilizers and Nutrient Deficiencies	199
18	Pests and Their Control	209
19	Irrigation	221
20	Determining Fruit Maturity	237
21	Grading, Sizing and Packing	245
22	Storage of Fruits	260
23	Interviewing a Leading Grower	277
24	Identification and Judging*	281
25	Sensory Evaluations	288
26	Tour of Experiment Station Research	298
27	Transportation and Marketing	301
28	Orchard Accounting	318
29	Processing Fruit and Nut Products	333
30	Less Widely Grown Fruits and Nuts	348
31	Job Opportunities	361

*See Chapter XIX, 1969 and previous editions of this book, for detail references, procedures.

815

TEACHER EVALUATION BY HIS STUDENTS

This teacher and course evaluation is used by Alpha Zeta, honorary fraternity of agriculture, on the Rutgers University campus to evaluate teachers and their courses (by their permission) a week to 10 days before the course is concluded. Summary evaluations are circulated to teachers and students during the following semester. Answers to questions, A to D, are shown only to the respective teachers.

INSTRUCTIONS TO STUDENTS:

Mark the answer sheet with a No. 2 pencil only (furnished each student by fraternity representative). Each evaluation characteristic is numbered for computer analysis. For each numbered characteristic you should select and mark a rating category from 1 to 5, e.g. 1=Excellent; 2=Good; 3=Average; 4=Fair; 5=Poor.

DO NOT MARK YOUR EVALUATIONS ON THESE SHEETS. USE THE ANSWER CARD (DESIGNED FOR COMPUTER). SAMPLE CARD AVAILABLE FROM RUTGERS INSTRUCTION DEAN.

PERSONAL TRAITS AND CHARACTERISTICS:

(1) fairness; (2) sympathy; (3) knowledge of subject; (4) firmness; (5) patience; (6) interesting; (7) enunciation; (8) willingness to help.

TEACHING ABILITY:

(17) preparation of lessons; (18) success in getting attention; (19) motivation—creating a need; (20) statement of lesson objectives; (21) use of varied techniques.

PRESENTATION:

(29) organization; (30) method of presentation; (31) ability to explain concepts; (32) extent and quality of questioning; (33) quality of review; (34) use of visual aids and devices; (35) ability to "stick to" topic.

ASSIGNMENTS:

(45) adequate time to complete; (46) understandable; (47) pertinence to lessons.

CLASS MANAGEMENT:

(57) care of physical conditions (lighting, ventilation, etc.); (58) ability to get things done; (59) fairness in grading.

LABORATORY MANAGEMENT (IF APPLICABLE):

(69) effciency of organization; (70) fairness in grading; (71) preparation by laboratory instructor; (72) laboratory instructor's knowledge of subject.

LABORATORY WORK (IF APPLICABLE):

(85) integration with text; (86) presentation of new and interesting ideas; (87) aid in better understanding course material; (88) encouragement to investigate on own.

LIBRARY AND CURRICULUM:

(97) Have you used the agricultural library relative to this course. If no, mark the 1. If yes, mark the 2 for one time, the 3 for two times, the 4 for three times, or the 5 for four or more times used: (101) Is this course required in your curriculum? If no, mark the 1; if yes, mark the 2.

OVERALL COURSE EVALUATION:

(113) My "learning experience" from the lecture; (114) My "learning experience" from the lab; (115) my "learning experience" from the course; (125) Expected grade: score 1, 2, 3, 4, or 5.

PLEASE ANSWER THE FOLLOWING ON THE BACK SIDE OF THE ANSWER SHEET.

A. Name one or two things which you especially like about this professor.

B. Give one or two suggestions for the improvement of this professor (objectionable, mannerisms, etc.).

C. Name one or two things you especially like about this course.

D. Give one or two suggestions for the improvement of this course.

RATE YOURSELF BEFORE YOU CHOOSE A PLANTING PROGRAM

By first evaluating ourselves, we can more correctly choose a planting system that suits our capabilities. Our commitment, ability, knowledge, financial status, and future goals are as important in planning our orchards as the rootstock, variety, or type of soil.

You be the judge . . . which system fits you best?

LOW DENSITY:

Spacing — wide working space around each tree.
Training and Pruning — minimum to grow a good tree.
Tree Size Control — None beyond rootstocks and regular practices.
Work Time Required — Least
Knowledge of Tree Growth — Minimum
Grower Commitment — Least
Investment Per Acre — Least
Yield Per Acre — Least
    (1st 15 years of orchard life)
Return Per Acre — Least
    (1st 15 years of orchard life)

MEDIUM DENSITY:

Spacing — Trees at least 4' closer than low density — work only one way.
Training and Pruning — Average training — short pruning
Tree Size Control — Rootstocks — Reduce by 4' with training and pruning
Work Time Required — Moderate — 30% more than low density in developing years.
Knowledge of Tree Growth — Average
Grower Commitment — Average — Committed to control tree size
Investment Per Acre — Average — $70 to $100 more than low density (1st year)
Yield Per Acre — 50% more than low density
    (1st 15 years of orchard life)
Return Per Acre — 200% greater than low density
    (1st 15 years of orchard life)

MEDIUM HIGH DENSITY:

Spacing — At least 6' closer than low density — hedgerow
Training and Pruning — Important — central leader training — short pruning
Tree Size Control — Rootstocks — Reduce by 6' through training and pruning
Work Time Required — Careful attention to details — 60% more than low density in developing years.
Knowledge of Tree Growth — Understand tree management
Grower Commitment — Committed to careful supervision and tree management
Investment Per Acre — $125 to $160 more than low density (1st year)
Yield Per Acre — 100% more than low density
    (1st 15 years of orchard life)
Return Per Acre — 300% plus more than low density
    (1st 15 years of orchard life)

HIGH DENSITY:

Spacing — Over 300 trees per acre — Systems: spindle bush; double hedgerow; triple hedgerow; trellis; etc.
Training and Pruning — Very important — fit system to planting — summer work necessary
Tree Size Control — Rootstocks — Maintain size by summer pruning — tiedowns — promote early fruiting
Work Time Required — Much — 200% more than low density in developing years.
Knowledge of Tree Growth — Good Understanding
Grower Commitment — Completely committed
Investment Per Acre — $500 to $3,000 more than low density in 1st year
Yield Per Acre — Highest potential — 500% greater than low density
    (1st 15 years of orchard life)
Return Per Acre — Greatest return — 600% more than low density
    (1st 15 years of orchard life)

Courtesy Hilltop Orchards Co., Hartford, Michigan, 49057. Note: additional planting information may be obtained from the yearly catalogues of leading nurseries. See recent July issues of Amer. Fruit Grower Magazine for a listing of nurseries.

AGRICULTURAL EXPERIMENT STATIONS AND COLLEGES
IN THE UNITED STATES

A list of available bulletins, circulars, and other information regarding temperate fruit growing can be obtained by writing to the agricultural editor of your agricultural experiment station or college.

State	City	State	City
Alabama	Auburn 36830	New Jersey	New Brunswick 08903
Alaska	College 99701	New Mexico	State College 99701
Arizona	Tucson 85721	New York	
Arkansas	Fayetteville 72701	College and	
California	Berkeley 94720	station	Ithaca 14850
	Davis 95616		
	L. Angeles 90024		
	Riverside 92502		
Colorado	Fort Collins 80521	Station	Geneva 14456
Connecticut		North Carolina	Raleigh 27607
College and		North Dakota	Fargo 58102
station	Storrs 06268	Ohio	
Station	New Haven 06504	College	Columbus 43210
Delaware	Newark 19711	Station	Wooster 44691
Florida	Gainesville 32601	Oklahoma	Stillwater 74074
	Tallahassee 32307		
	Lake Alfred 33850		
	Homestead 33030		
Georgia		Oregon	Corvallis 97331
College	Athens 30601	Pennsylvania	University Park 16802
Station	Experiment 30212	Puerto Rico	
Hawaii	Honolulu 96822	Insular Station	Rio Piedras 00928
Idaho	Moscow 83840	College and	
Illinois	Urbana 61801	Federal Station	Mayaguez 00708
Indiana	Lafayette 47907	Rhode Island	Kingston 02881
Iowa	Ames 50010	South Carolina	Clemson 29631
Kansas	Manhattan 66502	South Dakota	Brookings 57006
Kentucky	Lexington 40506	Tennessee	Knoxville 37901
Louisiana	University Station 70803	Texas	College Station 77843
Maine	Orono 04473	Utah	Logan 84321
Maryland	College Park 20740	Vermont	Burlington 05401
	Beltsville, USDA 20705		
Massachusetts	Amherst 01002	Virginia	Blacksburg 24061
			Winchester 22601
Michigan	East Lansing 48823	Washington	Long Beach 98631
			Mt. Vernon 98273
			Prosser 99350
			Pullman 99163
			Puyallup 98371
			Vancouver 98660
			Wenatchee 98801
Minnesota	St. Paul 55101	West Virginia	Morgantown 26506
Mississippi	State College 39762	Wisconsin	Madison 53706
Missouri	Columbia 65201	Wyoming	Laramie 82070
Montana	Bozeman 59715	United States	
Nebraska	Lincoln 68503	Department of	Washington
Nevada	Reno 89507	Agriculture[1]	D.C. 20250
New Hampshire	Durham 03824		

[1] A list of Federal agricultural publications arranged by subjects can be obtained by requesting Miscellaneous Publication No. 60 from the Division of Publications, Office of Information, U.S. Department of Agriculture, Washington, D.C. 20250.

A published list of state and federal staff at the above experiment stations, Handbook No. 305, can be obtained from Cooperative State Research Service, U. S. Dept. of Agri., Washington, D. C. 20705 for $1.25. The central government of each world country should have similar lists. Amer. Soc. Hort. Sci., P.O.B. 109, St. Joseph, Mich. publishes list of 3000+ world horticulturists, addresses.

SCIENTIFIC NAMES OF SOME DECIDUOUS FRUITS

COMMON NAME	SCIENTIFIC NAME
Almond	*Prunus amygdalus* Batsch. (*Amygdalus communis* L.)
Apple (Common)	*Malus pumila* Mill. (*Malus silvestris* Hort., *Pyrus malus* L.)
Apricot (Common)	*Prunus armeniaca* L. (*Armeniaca vulgaris* Lam.)
Apricot (Japanese)	*Prunus mume* Sieb. and Zucc. (*Armeniaca Mume* Sieb.)
Apricot, Siberian or Russian apricot	*Prunus sibirica* L. (*Armeniaca sibirica* Lam.)
Apricot, (Purple or Black)	*Prunus dasycarpa* Ehrh. (*Prunus armeniaca* var. *dasycarpa* K. Koch)
Blackberry (European)	*Rubus thyrsoideus* Wimm. (*Rubus candicans* Weihe)
Blackberry (Evergreen thornless)	*Rubus ulmifolius* var. *inermis* (Willd.) Focke
Blackberry (High or black-long berry or Allegany or Mountain Blackberry)	*Rubus allegheniensis* Porter (*Rubus nigrobaccus* (Bailey)
Blackberry (Himalaya)	*Rubus procerus* P. J. Muell
Blueberry, (Highbush or Swamp blueberry or High blueberry)	*Vaccinium corymbosum* L.
Blueberry (Lowbush)	*Vaccinium angustifolium* Ait.
Blueberry (rabbiteye)	*Vaccinium ashei* Reade
Blueberry, (Evergreen or box)	*Vaccinium ovatum* Pursh
Blueberry (Mountain)	*Vaccinium membranaceaum* Dougl.
Blueberry, (Dryland or low)	*Vaccinium pallidum* Ait.
Blueberry, (European or Whortleberry or Billberry)	*Vaccinium myrtillus* L.
Butternut (or American butternut)	*Juglans cinerea* L.
Cherry, (Bird or Pin cherry or Wild red cherry)	*Prunus pensylvanica* L.
Cherry, (Flowering of Japan)	*Prunus pseudocerasus* Lindl.
Cherry, (Duke)	*Prunus effusa* (Host.) Schneid: P. gondouini (Poit. & Turpin Rehd.) (Hybrid between *Prunus avium* L. and *Prunus cerasus* Linn.)
Cherry, (Mahaleb or Saint Lucie cherry)	*Prunus mahaleb* Linn. (*Cerasus mahaleb* Mill.)
Cherry, (Manchu or Nanking cherry)	*Prunus tomentosa* Thunb. (*Cerasus tomentosa* Wall., *Cerasus trichocarpa* Bunge)
Cherry, (Sour or Pie cherry)	*Prunus cerasus* L. (*Cerasus caproniana* Ser.)
Cherry (Sweet or Mazzard)	*Prunus avium* L. (*Prunus cerasus* var. *avium* L.)
Cherry (Western sand)	*Prunus besseyi*, Bailey (*Prunus pumila* var. *besseyi* Waugh., *Prunus rosebudii* Reagan *Prunus prunella* Daniels)

[1]Standardized Plant Names (Joint Committee), Second Edition, J. H. McFarland Co. 675 pp. Harrisburg, Pa.; Manual of Cultivated trees and shrubs, The Macmillan Co., New York City, used as authorities. To name and register a cultivar, consult "How to Name a New Plant", Bull. of Amer. Assn. of Nurserymen, Inc., 835 Southern Bldg., Wash., D. C. 20005. Dr. Peter A. Hyypio, Extension Botanist, Bailey Hortorium, Cornell University, checked these names.

COMMON NAME	SCIENTIFIC NAME

Chestnut, (Allegany chinkapin or Eastern chinkapin or Chinquapin) — *Castanea pumila* (L.) Mill.

Chestnut, (American) — *Castanea dentata* (Marsh.) Borkh. (*Castanea americana* Raf.)

Chestnut, (Chinese or Hairy chestnut) — *Castanea mollissima* Blume

Chestnut, (European or Spanish chestnut) — *Castanea sativa* Mill. (*Castanea vesca* Gaertn., *Castanea vulgaris* Lam.)

Chestnut, (Japanese) — *Castanea crenata* Sieb. and Zucc.

Cranberry, (Large or American) — *Vaccinium macrocarpon* Ait.

Cranberry, (Small or European) — *Vaccinium oxycoccos* L.

Currant, (Common red or Garden currant) — *Ribes sativum* (Reichenb.) Syme (*Ribes domesticum* Jancz., *Ribes hortense* Hedlund, *Ribes vulgare* Jancz.)

Currant, (European black) — *Ribes nigrum* L.

Currant, (Northern red) — *Ribes rubrum* L. (*Ribes sylvestre* DC.)

Dewberry (California or Western dewberry or Grapeleaf California dewberry) — *Rubus ursinus* Cham. and Schlecht.

Dewberry (Northern) — *Rubus flagellaris* Willd. (*Rubus villosus* Bailey, *Rubus procumbens* Muhl., *Rubus canadensis* Torr.)

Dewberry (Southern) — *Rubus trivialis* Michx. (*Rubus carpinifolius* Rydb., *Rubus continentalis* Bailey)

Fig, (Common) — *Ficus carica* L.

Filbert, (American Hazelnut) — *Corylus americana*, Marsh.

Filbert, (Beaked) — *Corylus cornuta* Marsh.

Filbert, (California or Western filbert) — *Corylus californica* Rose: (cornuta var. californica (A. DC.) Rose

Filbert, (European) — *Corylus avellana* L.

Filbert, (Giant) — *Corylus maxima* Mill.

Filbert, (Japanese or Siberian hazelnut) — *Corylus heterophylla* Fisch. ex Traut v.

Filbert, (Turkish) — *Corylus colurna* L.

Gooseberry, (American or Hairystem gooseberry) — *Ribes hirtellum* Michx. (*Grossularia hirtella* Spach.)

Gooseberry, (European, English) — *Ribes uva-crispa* L., (*Ribes grossularia* L., *Ribes grossularia* var. *pubescens* Koch.) *Ribes uva-crispa* var. *reclinata*

Grape, (European or Wine grape) — *Vitis vinifera* L.

Grape, (Fox or Northern grape fox) — *Vitis labrusca* L.

Grape, (Muscadine or Bullace or Southern Fox Grape) — *Vitis rotundifolia* Michx.

Grape, (Mustang of Florida or Bird grape or Everbearing grape or Everlasting grape) — *Vitis munsoniana* Simson

Hickory, (Big shellbark) — *Carya laciniosa* (Michx. f.) Loudon (*Carya sulcata* Pursh *Hicoria laciniosa* (Michx. f.) Sarg.)

Hickory, (Pignut) — *Carya glabra* (Mill.) Sweet. (*Hicoria glabra* Brit., *Carya porcina* Michx. f.)

820

COMMON NAME	SCIENTIFIC NAME
Hickory, (Red or Sweet pignut)	*Carya ovalis* (Wang.) Sarg. (*Hicoria microcarpa,* Brit., *Hicoria ovalis* Ashe.)
Hickory, (Shagbark)	*Carya ovata* (Mill.) K. Koch. (*Hicoria ovata* Brit., *Carya alba* Nutt.)
Nectarine, (Smooth skinned peach, L. H. B., a single gene mutation from peach)	*Prunus persica* var. *nectarina* (Ait.) Maxim. (*Prunus persica* var. *nucipersica* Borkh.)
Peach, (Common)	*Prunus persica* (L.) Batsch (*Amygdalus persica* L. *Persica vulgaris* Mill.)
Pear, (Chinese white)	*Pyrus bretschneideri* Rehd.
Pear, (European or Common)	*Pyrus communis* L.
Pear, (Sand)	*Pyrus pyrifolia* (Burm.) Nakai
Pear, (Snow or French Snow pear)	*Pyrus nivalis* Jacq.
Pear, (Manchurian or Ussurian)	*Pyrus ussuriensis* Maxim.
Pecan	*C. illinoinensis* (Wang.) K. Koch (*Carya pecan* Engl. and Graebn.)
Persimmon, (American)	*Diospyros virginiana* L.
Persimmon, (Kaki or Oriental)	*Diospyros Kaki* L. (*Diospyros chinensis* Blume, *Diospyros roxburghi* Carr.)
Persimmon (Dateplum)	*Diospyros lotus* L.
Plum, (Beach)	*Prunus maritima* Marsh.
Plum, (Big tree)	*Prunus mexicana* S. Wats. (*Prunus australis* Munson ex Waugh, *Prunus polyandra* *Prunus arkansana* Sarg.)
Plum, (Bullace or Damson plum)	*Prunus institia* L. (*Prunus domestica* var. *institia* Bailey,)
Plum, (Canada)	*Prunus nigra* Ait. (*Prunus pensylvanica* L. *Prunus mollis* Torr. *Prunus americana* var. *nigra* Waugh.)
Plum, (Chickasaw or Mountain cherry)	*Prunus angustifolia* Marsh. (*Prunus chicasa* Michx. *Prunus stenophylla* Raf.)
Plum, (Common)	*Prunus domestica* L. (*Prunus communis* Huds.)
Plum, (Common wild)	*Prunus americana* Marsh. (*Prunus latifolia* Moench., *Prunus hiemalis* Michx.)
Plum, (Hortulan)	*Prunus hortulana* Bailey (*Prunus hortulana* var. *waylandii* Bailey)
Plum, (Japanese)	*Prunus salicina* Lindl. (*Prunus triflora* Roxburg., *Prunus japonica* Hort.)
Plum, (Myrobalan or Cherry plum)	*Prunus cerasifera* Ehrh. (*Prunus domestica* var. *myrobalan* L.)
Plum, (Oklahoma)	*Prunus gracilis* Engelm. and Gray
Plum, (Pacific)	*Prunus subcordata* Benth.
Plum, (Simon or Apricot plum)	*Prunus simonii* Carr. (*Persica simonii* Decne.)
Plum, (Wild goose)	*Prunus munsoniana* Wight and Hedr.

821

COMMON NAME	SCIENTIFIC NAME
Plumcots	Hybrids between *Prunus salicina* and *Prunus armeniaca*
Pomegranate, (Common)	*Punica granatum* L.
Quince	*Cydonia oblonga* Mill. (*Cydonia vulgaris* Pers., *Pyrus cydonia* L.)
Raspberry, (Black or Blackcap raspberry)	*Rubus occidentalis* L.
Raspberry (European red)	*Rubus idaeus* L.
Red Raspberry, (American)	*Rubus idaeus* var. *strigosus* (Michx.) Maxim.
Raspberry (Purple cane)	*Rubus neglectus* Peck. (A hybrid between *Rubus strigosus* and *Rubus occidentalis*)
Strawberry (Chilean or Beach Strawberry)	*Fragaria chiloensis* (L.) Duch. *Fragaria* X *ananassa* Duch.
Strawberry (Cultivated)	Hybrid between different *Fragaria* species, mostly between *Fragaria viginiana* Duch. and *Fragaria chiloensis* (L.) Duch.
Strawberry (Virginia or Wild Meadow Strawberry)	*Fragaria virginiana* Duch.
Walnut (Black or Eastern black walnut)	*Juglans nigra* L.
Walnut (Bolivian black)	*Juglans boliviana* Dode
Walnut (California black or Southern California black walnut)	*Juglans californica* S. Wats.
Walnut (Cathay or Chinese walnut)	*Juglans catheyensis* Dode
Walnut (English or Persian walnut)	*Juglans regia* L.

SOME SCIENTIFIC AND POPULAR FRUIT PUBLICATIONS[1]

Following is a list of the world publications which frequently or regularly contain articles pertaining to fruit growing. A more detailed list can be obtained from Bailey Hortorium, Cornell University, Ithaca, N. Y., entitled "Bibliography of current horticultural publications." Request latest edition. If a more complete address is needed, go to or write your nearest state or federal agricultural library. Most of these publications, or records of them will be found there.

Become a member or read regularly the Journal of the American Society for Horticultural Science, P.O. Box 109, St. Joseph, Mich., 49085, to keep up-to-date on latest research trends and findings in the U.S.A. Read the Journ. of Pomology and Hort. Sci., London WC-2, for British work. Scientists should consult Horticultural Abstracts, Farnham Royal, Bucks, England for world research reports. P.O.B. 31

INSIDE THE UNITED STATES

Agriculture Chemicals (m)
P.O. B. 31
Caldwell, N. J. 07006

Agricultural Situation, or
Agricultural Prices, or
Agricultural Marketing
U.S.D.A. AMS (m)
Washington, D.C. 20250

Agronomy Soc. of Amer. Journal (m)
Madison, Wis. 53711

American Bee Journal (m)
Hamilton, Illinois, 62341

Amer. Cranberry Growers Assn.
a—Proc. of Ann. Meeting
b—Ann. Blueberry Open House
Pemberton, New Jersey. 08068

American Fruit Grower (m)
Willoughby, Ohio. 44094

Amer. Jour. of Botany (m)
City College of New York
N. Y. 31, N. Y.

Amer. Jour. of Path. (bm)
Ann Arbor, Mich.

[1] w—weekly; bw—biweekly; m—monthly; bm—bimonthly; q—quarterly; a—annually; i—irregular; no./yr.—number of issues per year or month (m).

Amer. Nurseryman (sm)
343 So. Dearborn St.,
Chicago, Illinois 60604

Amer. Soc. Hort. Sci. Journ.
P. O. Box 109, St. Joseph,
Michigan 49085

Annals of Applied Biol. (q)
London NW 1, Eng. or
New York 22, N. Y.

Annals Mo. Bot. Garden (q)
St. Louis, Mo.

Ann. Rev. of Pl. Phys. (a)
Palo Alto, California

Better Fruit-Better Vegetables (bm)
P. O. Box 7105
Salem, Ore. 97303

Blue Anchor, The (q)
P. O. Box 15498
Sacramento, Calif 95813

Botanical Gazette (q)
5750 Ellis Ave.,
Chicago, Ill. 60637

Botanical Review (m)
N. Y. Bot. Garden
New York, N. Y. 10458

Calif. Avocado Soc. Yrbk. (Calavo) (a)
4833 Everett Ave.,
Los Angeles, Calif. 90058

Calif. Citrograph (m)
5380 Poplar Blvd.
Los Angeles, Calif. 90032

Canner and Freezer (bw)
Chicago 3, Illinois

Canning Trade (w)
Baltimore 2, Md.

Citrus Industry (m)
Bartow, Florida 33830

Citrus World (m)
P. O. Box 823
Winter Haven, Fla. 33880

Cold Storage Rpt. (m)
U.S.D.A. AMS
Washington, D. C. 20250

Contrib. Boyce Thompson Inst. (q)
1086 No. Broadway
Yonkers, New York 10701

Cranberries (m)
Kingston, Massachusetts 02360

Crop Production (m)
U.S.D.A. AMS
Washington, D. C. 20250

Demand and Price Situation (m)
U.S.D.A. AMS
Washington, D. C. 20250

Diamond Walnut News (bm)
Calif. Walnut Grws. Assn.,
P. O. Box 1727,
Stockton 1, Calif.

Eastern Fruit Grower (m)
Drawer 127,
Boyce, Va. 22620

Ecology (q)
College Station
Durham, N. C.

Economic Botany (q)
N. Y. Bot. Garden,
N. Y., N. Y. 10458

Farm Income Situation (5/yr)
U.S.D.A. AMS
Wash., D. C. 20250

Farm Prod. Disposition and Value (i)
U.S.D.A. AMS
Washington, D. C. 20250

Florida Grower and Rancher (m)
P. O. Box 6429,
Nashville, Tenn. 37212

Food and Agri. Org. of U. N. (Yrbk)
Rome, Italy

Foreign Agri. Trade of U. S. (m)
Foreign Agricultural Service
Washington 25, D. C.

Foreign Crops and Markets (w)
Foreign Agricultural Service
Washington, D. C. 20250

Food Packer (m)
Chicago 2, Illinois

Food Research (bm)
Champaign, Illinois

Fruit Situation (4/yr.)
U.S.D.A. AMS
Wash., D. C. 20250

Fruit and Vegetable Rev. (m)
Orange Savings Building
Orange, California

Fruit Varieties and Hort. Digest (q)
Amer. Pomological Soc.,
Hort. Dept., Mich. State Univ.,
E. Lansing, Mich. 48823

Good Fruit Grower (bw)
11 So. 7th Ave.
Yakima, Washington

The Great Lakes Fruit Growers
News (m). Very good.
Sparta, Michigan 49345

Hilgardia (i) Univ. of Calif.
Berkeley, Calif.

Hort. Soc. Proc. (annual)
of imp. fruit states in U. S.
(Contact resp. Exper. Sta.)

Jour. of Econ. Entom. (bm)
Wash. 5, D. C.

Jour. of Heredity (bm)
Wash. 5, D. C.

Marketing and Transp. Situation (q)
U.S.D.A. AMS Wash., D. C. 20250

Nat. Food Situation (q)
U.S.D.A. AMS Wash., D. C. 20250

Nat. Hort. Magazine (q)
Plant Ind. Sta.,
Beltsville, Md. 20705

Northern Nut Growers' Assn. Rpt. (i)
4518 Holston Hills Rd.,
Knoxville, Tenn. 37914

Packer, The (w)
201 Dela. St.,
Kansas City, Mo. 64105

Phytopathology (m)
Baltimore, Maryland

Plant Disease Reporter (m)
U. S. Dept. of Agr.
Beltsville, Md. 20705

Plant Physiology (bm)
Smithsonian Inst.,
Washing., D. C. 20250

Produce Marketing (m)
251 Kearny Street
San Francisco, Calif. 94108

Produce News, The (w)
6 Harrison Street
New York, N. Y. 10013

Refrigerating Engineering (m)
New York 1, N. Y.

Rural New Yorker (m)
and Amer. Agriculturist
Ithaca, N. Y. 14850

Science (w)
Am. Assn. Adv. Sci.,
Washington 5, D. C.

Soil Science (m)
Rutgers Univ.,
New Bruns., N. J. 08903

Sour Cherry Report (a)
U.S.D.A. AMS
Wash., D. C. 20250

Virginia Fruit (m)
Va. Hort. Soc.,
Staunton, Virginia 24401

Western Fruit Grower (m)
P. O. Box 1877,
Salinas, Ca. 93901

Some U. S. Newsletters and Member Proceedings

Appalachian Apple Serv. (i)
123 S. Church St. Martinsburg, W. V.

Apple Institute News (m)
N. Y.—N. Eng. Apple Inst. Inc.
Kingston, New York

Appleland News (w)
324 W. Yakima Ave., Yakima, Wash.

Apple Peelings
201½ East Grand Rv. E. Lansing, Mich.

Cherry Talk (m)
272 Alexander Ave., Rochester 7, N. Y.

Conn. Pomological Soc. (a) Proc. and
(b) Pointers (q)
Univ. of Conn., Storrs, Conn.

Empire State Canner (m)
226 1st Fed. Sav. Bldg. Rochester 4, N. Y.

Fruit Ed.—Fruit and Veg. Mkting. (m)
Univ. of Conn., Storrs, Sonn.

Fruit Notes (m)
Univ. of Mass., Amherst, Mass.

Fruit and Vege. Mkting. Inf. (m)
Penn. State Univ., Univ. Park, Penn.

Peachtime USA (bm)
Nat. Peach Coun.
P. O. Box 1085
Martinsburg, W. Va. 25401

Fruit and Nut Crop Rev. (w)
104 Extension Hall, Corvallis, Ore.

Horticultural News (bm)
N. J. State Hort. Soc.,
New Brunswick, N. J. 08903

Ill. State Hort. Soc.
a—Transactions and Proc. (a)
b—Illinois Hoticulture
302 W. Walnut St., Carbondale, Ill.

Indiana State Hort. Soc.
a—Proceedings (a)
b—Hoosier Hort. Newsletter (m)
W. Lafayette, Indiana

International Apple Inst. (i)
2430 Penna Ave., N.W.
Wash., D. C. 20037

Maine State Hort. Soc. Annual Rpt. (a)
Livermore Falls, Maine

Maryland State Hort. Soc.
a—Proceedings (a)
b—Newsletter (q)
c—The Maryland Fruit Grower (q)
College Park, Maryland 20740

Mass. Fruit Growers Assn. (a)
French Hall, Amherst, Massachusetts
01002

Mich. State Hort. Soc. Rpt. (a)
E. Lansing, Mich. 48823

Available water. That portion of the soil moisture supply, mainly the capillary fraction, which the plant can absorb.

Availability. Being in such physical form and chemical combination that it can be absorbed by plants.

Axil. Angle above the junction of a leaf-blade, petiole, peduncle, or pedicel, with the branch or stalk from which it springs.

Bark. Tough, external covering or investment of a woody perennial stem or root, consisting of tissues external to the cork cambium, which on being cut off from food supplies will soon die and dry.

Branch. A shoot or secondary stem growing from the main stem. Or, a stem larger than a shoot growing on a tree or similar plant from the trunk or from a bough.

Basin. The depression at the apex or blossom end (opposite the stem end) of fruits such as the apple.

Beaked. Ending in a prolonged tip.

Berry. A pulpy, indehiscent fruit with few or many seeds. Technically, the pulpy or fleshy fruit resulting from a single pistil, containing one or more seeds, such as the blueberry or the orange.

Biennial. (a) Those plants which bear fruit only after two seasons of growth, as raspberry. (b) Biennial bearing of a tree is bearing heavy crops one year and little or none the next in a cycle.

Bisexual. A plant or variety that produces both staminate (male) and pistalate (female) flowers.

Bitter Pit. Physiological disease appearing as small, round, dead depressions of the epidermis, hypodermis, and other first layers of the fruit, as in apple. Spots may have a bitter taste. Caused by calcium deficiency.

Blackheart. Physiological disease which causes the inner layers of woody stems to decay causing a loss in ability of all or part of the conducting tissue to perform their functions, often caused by low-winter temperatures.

Blade. The expanded portion of a leaf.

Blight. Disease causing general killing of stems, leaves or branches.

Bloom. The delicate white or powdery substance on the surface of some fruits, or on the canes of vine and bramble-fruits.

Blush. An unbroken red tint on the surface of a fruit.

Bog Soils. Soils arising from decay of swamp vegetation having very high organic matter content. Surface is usually muck or peat with underlying layer of peat, used, e.g., in cranberry production.

Bound water. Water held tenaciously in the form of extremely thin film surrounding very small solid particles.

Bract. Reduced or modified leaf which can be large and very showy in some flowers, as poinsettia, or small and inconspicuous as at base of an apple leaf petiole.

British Thermal Units (BTU). The quantity of heat required to raise the temperature of one avoirdupois pound of water one degree Fahrenheit at or near 39.2°F, the temperature at its maximum density.

Broadcast application. Application of agricultural chemicals over an entire area rather than in strips, beds or middles.

Brush. The bundle of fibers connecting the pedicel with the berry of the grape.

Bud scales. Scale-like leaf which forms the external covering of a bud in winter and may have dense coatings of hair, gum, or resin.

Bud Sport (Mutation). A branch, flower or fruit which arises from a bud differing genetically from the "mother" plant. Usually caused by a spontaneous mutation of cell genes.

Bulb. A large fleshy bud-like structure as e.g. head lettuce, onion, tulip.

Callus. Parenchyma tissue which grows over a wound or a graft, protecting it against drying or other damage.

Cambium. Undifferentiated meristematic tissue in the form of a very thin layer between bark and wood.

Cane. A shoot which bears but once, particularly one which arises from the crown or root, as in brambles.

Capillary. Hair-like.

Capri Fig. The uncultivated wild fig, sometimes called the "male" fig.

Carbohydrate. A compound produced by plants containing chemically bonded energy composed of carbon, oxygen and hydrogen.

Carbon - Nitrogen Ratio (Relationship). Relative proportion, by weight, of carbon to nitrogen in the soil, organic matter or plant tissue.

Carotenoids. Yellow coloring pigments found in the leaves and fruits of plants. ($C_{26}H_{38}$).

Cationic. Having a positively charged molecule.

Cellulose. Any of several fibrous compounds found in cell walls and fibrous products of plants; a complex polymeric carbohydrate ($C_6H_{10}O_5$)x.

Chalaza. The place where seed-coat and kernel of a seed connect.

Chamagamy. Pollination only after the opening of the flower.

Chemotropism. Movement of the plant by bending or twisting in response to a chemical stimulus.

Chimera. A mixture of tissues of different genetic constitution in the same plant. **Periclinal chimera**-tissues of one element completely encircles another, as in some thornless blackberries; once formed, is stable. **Mericlinal chimera** - the different tissue is one layer deep and may occur, e.g., as a wide dark red stripe on an apple, unstable, common. **Sectorial chimera** - the genetically different tissue penetrates all three meristematic layers or occurs as a large segment (pie shape) of the trunk or branches. Some may be graft-chimeras from a mixed adventituous bud at the union of stock and scion; uncommon, unstable.

Chloroplast. Structure in a leaf called a plastid which contains chlorophyll.

Cleistogamy. Self pollination without the flower being open, as in violet.

Cluster base. Enlarged sections of a spur as in apple or pear to which the apple peduncle or flower pedicles were attached.

Colloid. Usually an uncrystalline semisolid which is capable of slow diffusion through a membrane.

Compatibility. (a) In sex cells, the ability of male and female forms to unite to form a fertilized egg that will continue to grow to maturity. (b) Ability of the scion and stock to unite in grafting and form a strong union.

Compound (leaf). Leaf which has the blade divided into separate leaflets.

Connivent. Coming into contact or to a point as the sepals on a Winesap apple.

Contact Herbicide. A chemical that kills the portion of the weed or plant upon coming in contact with it. A non-selectrive herbicide. Example is sodium arsenite.

Cordate. Heart-shaped, with the point upward.

Cork Spot (York Spot, drouth spot). Physiological (or virus?) disorder of apples appearing as slightly flattened areas on the apple having a water-soaked appearance, with deeper discoloration of the skin at the site of spot formation. Brown "corky" areas may form beneath the spotted skin. Boron, calcium and possibly other deficiencies or nutrient off-balances may be associated with the problem.

Corky Core. Disorder in apples, probably physiological, with symptoms of browning and corky textured areas around the core due to cell death; sometimes accompanied by a bitter taste. Boron deficiency is usually associated with the disorder.

Corymb. A flat-topped or convex open flower-cluster.

Cotyledons. The foliar portion or first leaves (one, two, or more) of the embryo as found in the seed.

Crenate. Dentate, with the teeth much rounded as on a leaf.

Crinkle. Apple disorder manifested by roughened skin on the fruit; a supposed form of drouth injury.

Cyme. A usually broad and flattish determinate inflorescence, with its central or terminal flowers blooming earliest.

Cytokinesis. Cytoplasmic changes involved in mitosis, meiosis, and fertilization, as distinguished from nuclear changes.

Deciduous (leaves). Falling of leaves after one season of growth.

Dehiscent. Opening regularly by valves, slits, etc., as a capsule or anther.

Dehorn. This refers to cutting of fruit trees back into 3- or 4-year wood during the dormant season to renew the top, usually following a freeze, as in case of peaches. Practice has not been encouraged in recent years.

Dentate. Toothed, usually with the teeth directed outward as in a leaf.

Dichogamy. When the stamens shed pollen and the pistils of a flower are receptive at different times; as in avacado.

Dieback. A psysiological or pathological disorder of plants characterized by the death and/or failure of the younger areas of the plant to grow.

Dieocious. The male and female flowers found on separate plants.

Dimorphism. Presence of two forms of leaves, flowers, or other organs upon the same plant, or upon other plants of the same species, such as pigmented or unpigmented fruit or deciduous or permanent branches.

Dioecious. Having the androecium (male flower) and gynoecium (female flower) on separate plants.

Dormant. Plants or buds which are not actively growing but can be made to grow with favorable environmental conditions.

Drupe (Stone Fruit). A fruit developed from a single carpel with a fleshy exocarp and a hard stony endocarp containing a single seed. Some stone fruits are multicarpellate with one to several seeds, as in raspberry.

Drupelet. A diminutive drupe, as in a raspberry fruit.

Emasculation. Removal of male parts of the flower by artificial means. Used by plant breeders to control pollination.

Embryo. The rudimentary plantlet within the seed.

Embryo Sac. Region of cell in the ovule where the embryo is formed.

Emulsion. Suspension of one liquid in another - oil and water is a common emulsion.

Endocarp. The inner layer of the pericarp, ripened ovary or fruit, as the pit of a peach.

Endodermis. The innermost layer of the cortex which abuts the stele.

Endosperm. The nourishment for the embryo, which surrounds the embryo in the plant seed.

Entire (leaves). Without any indentations or division.

Epicarp (exocarp). The outer layer of the pericarp, the ripened ovary or fruit coat, as the skin of a peach or apple.

Epigynous (flowers). Attached to the surface of the ovary so as to be apparently inserted upon the top of it, as in case of the attachment of stamens, petals or sepals. The apple fruit is an example.

Epinasty. Downward bending or drooping of leaves caused by stresses at the petiole changing the direction of growth, as induced by some fruit thinning chemicals on a variety like Wealthy.

Erosion. Wearing away, or carrying away of the surface of land by agents of wind, water or other natural agents.

Exanthema (fruit trees). A dieing back of younger wood in fruit trees due sometimes to copper deficiency which may be induced by excessive nitrogen fertilizer.

Exocarp. The outer layer of the pericarp, ripened ovary or the fruit coat, as the peel of an apricot.

Exocortis. A sluffing off of the bark of trees.

Extine. Outer layer of the pollen grain.

Eye. The calyx of a pome fruit; a compound bud of a grape; or the hole in an immature fig through which the wasp passes in pollination.

Family. A natural assemblage of plants placed together because of resemblances, as Rosaceae, which includes many pome fruits, rose, etc.

Fasciation. Flattening of the stem due to multiple terminal buds growing in the same place.

Fecundity. Ability of flowers to produce viable seed.

Feeder Roots. Fine roots and root branches with an unusually large absorbing area. Feeder roots are aided in uptake of water and minerals by their root hairs.

Fertility (in flowers). Ability to produce seeds that are viable (will germinate).

Fertilization. (a) In flowers, the fusion of the male and female gametes to form a zygote or new cell. (b) Also a term used to describe the process of applying fertilizers.

Filament. The anther supporting stalk in the flower.

Flaccid. Without rigidity. Wilted.

Floret. A small flower, usually one of a dense cluster, as in a sunflower.

Flower bud. A bud in which flower parts are contained.

Foliar feeding. Act of mineral fertilization of a plant through the surface of the leaves, usually in sprays.

Foxiness. The peculiar smell and taste in some grapes, particularly the native Labruscas.

Frenching. Physiological disease of leaves characterized by interveinal color loss.

Fruiting habit. Manner and location of fruit on a tree, bush or plant.

Fruit Set. Development of the parts of the ovary after fertilization of the egg(s) and swelling of the ovary is discernable.

Fungi. Organisms having no leaves, flowers or chlorophyll, and reproducing by means of spores.

Fungicide. Chemical agent used to control the infection and spread of fungi on crops.

Fusiform. Spindle-shaped; swollen in the middle and narrowing toward each end.

Gamete. A unisexual cell, male or female, which when fused with another gamete, forms a zygote, producing another individual.

Genus. A group of plants comprising a greater or less number of closely related species; plural is genera.

Glabrous. Smooth; not rough, pubescent or hairy.

Glaucous. Covered with a bloom, as a McIntosh fruit before harvest (powdery covering).

Growth Regulator. A chemical substance capable of altering the growth characteristics of a plant. There are four groups of growth regulators recognized by plant scientists: auxins, gibberellins, kinins and inhibitors.

Gum Spot. In stone fruits, small local deposits of gum in and on the tissue of fruit.

830

Gummosis. Disorder in citrus and stone fruits recognized by copious extrusions of sticky sappy substances on the stems and trunks of the tree.

Gynoecium. The pistils collectively, or the aggregate of carpels.

Hairy Root. Excessive production and grouping of weak roots.

Hardpan. A subsoil horizon which has become hard or cemented by compaction. Minerals such as iron oxide, organic material, silica, calcium carbonate can be the cause of or associated with this cementing action. Compaction also may be associated with use of heavy machinery over the soil.

Herb. A plant with no persistent woody stem above ground.

Herbicide. A chemical which will kill plants on coming in contact with them, usually weeds, or slow their growth.

Hermaphrodite. Flower with both male (stamen) and female (pistil) parts.

Hesperdium. A berry of the type found in sectioned fruit like that of an orange.

Hirsute. Pubescent with rather coarse or stiff hairs.

Homogamous. A condition of flowers all of one sex or two-sexed, having stamens and pistils that mature at the same time, allowing for self-pollination.

Hopperburn. Disorder of leaves which is manifested by curling, yellowing and browning of leaves, caused by leafhoppers.

Hormone. A chemical substance formed in cells which are produced in one area of a plant and transported or transferred to another where they affect the activity of those cells.

Horticulture. The art and science of growing fruits, vegetables and flowers or ornamental plants; a division of agriculture.

Hybrid. A cross-breed of two species.

Hybridizing. The operation or practice of crossing between species.

Hydrophyte. Those plants which grow naturally in water, as the water hyacinth or lily.

Hyphae. The interwoven hair-like growth of a fungus making up the mycelium.

Hypogynous (flowers). Refers to the structure of a flower where appendages such as sepals, petals and stamens are inserted upon the flower axis below the gynoecium or ovary and free from it. An example, orange.

Imbibition. Process of absorption of liquids by surface tension pull, usually by a solid such as blotting paper absorbing ink.

Imbricate. Overlapping.

Imperfect (flowers). Term referring to flowers in which either functionable stamens or pistils are present, not both.

Incompatibility. (a) Inability of sex cells to unite to form a fertilized egg that will grow to maturity. (b) Failure of the scion and stock to unite and form a strong union which will continue to grow.

Indehiscent. Not opening by halves.

Indexing. A means of determining the presence of disease, such as a virus, in a stock by removing buds and grafting them into a readily susceptible variety of closely related species that readily "shows" the virus.

Indigenous. Original to the region.

Inflorescence. The flowering part of a plant, flower-cluster. more accurately the mode of flowering.

Internode. That portion of a stem between two nodes.

Intersterility. The inability of one variety of fruit to set fruit and produce seeds that will germinate when pollinized by another variety of the same fruit.

Intine. The inner layer of a pollen grain.

Involucre. A whorl of small leaves or bracts found below and very near to a flower or clusters of flowers as in all composites (sunflower).

Involute. Rolled inward.

June Drop. Abscission of partially mature fruit (usually occurring in June in Northeastern U. S.).

Juvenile stage. Early or vegetative phase of growth characterized by carbohydrate utilization.

King blossom. This is the first blossom to appear and is usually the strongest in a cluster of flowers, as for example in apple and pear.

Latent Bud. Dormant bud, usually hidden, which is over a year old and may remain dormant indefinitely.

Leaching. Washing of soluable nutrients downward through the soil or from a leaf.

Leaflet. One of the divisions of a compound leaf.

Lesion. A localized spot of diseased tissue.

Long-day (plants). Period of daylight longer than 14 hours. Plants require a non-interrupted dark period of 12 hours or more to initiate flowering, as potato and spinach. Apple shows relatively little response to length of dark and light periods.

Low-Headed Tree. Trees which have primary branches low on the trunk.

Mamme. First crop of the capri fig or "male fig" which matures early in the spring. Fruits usually overwinter as oversized fruit.

Maturity. Stage of development in fruit when eating or processing quality is at its maximum.

Megasporophyll. A sporophyll or leaf or leaf-like appendage producing only megasporangia [give rise to gametophyte (female plant) as in ferns].

Meristematic. Cells which are capable of division, or a region of plant where rapid cell division takes place.

Mesocarp. The middle layer of the pericarp, as the edible flesh of a peach between the exocarp (skin) and endocarp (pit).

Metaxenia. Effect of pollen on tissue characteristics outside of the embryo.

Mildew. Plant disease (a fungus) coating the surface of plant parts, as powdery mildew.

Monecious. The male and female flowers are on the same plant, as in corn.

Monocotyledonous. A plant which produces seeds with a single cotyledon, e.g., corn, coconut.

Mulch. Materials placed on the soil surface or mixed in the soil such as straw to promote moisture retention, temperature control, provide cleaner fruit as in strawberries, weed control, and, if the mulch is plant material, supply nutrients as the mulch decomposes.

Mutation. Genetic change in a mother plant or stock which may influence the character of the offspring, buds or coins removed from the plants.

Mycorrhiza. Symbiotic association of the mycelium or hyphae of certain fungi (class **Basidiomycetes**) with the roots of the seed plant as in case of the cranberry and orchid.

Necrosis. Death of plant tissue due to psysiological, nutrient or pathological disorders or other causes.

Nectary. Any place or organ which secretes nectar.

Nematocide. Chemicals used to control nematodes.

Node. Area on a stem from which leaves and/or fruits develop.

Non-ionic. Having no electrical charge on the molecule, or it is commonly known as electrically neutral.

Nut. A hard indehiscent 1-celled and 1-seeded fruit, though usually resulting from a compound ovary.

Nutrients. Elements which are necessary and available for plant growth such as C, H, O and certain mineral elements.

Oblique. Unequal sided or slanting as a York Imperial fruit.

Obovate. Inverted ovate.

Obtuse. Blunt or rounded at the end.

Osmosis. Passage of materials through a semi-permeable membrane from a higher to a lower concentration.

Ovary. In angiosperms, it is the enlarged (usually the basil) portion of the pistil or gynoecium containing ovules or seeds.

Ovicide. A chemical used to destroy the eggs of insects.

Parthenocarpic. Physiological phenomena in fruit in which the fruit develops without seed production, as in the Thompson Seedless grape.

Pedicel. The support of a single flower in a cluster.

Peduncle. A primary flower-stalk, supporting either a cluster or a solitary flower (the stem of an apple fruit).

Pericarp. The ripened and variously modified walls of the ovary. It sometimes exhibits three distinct structural layers, the endocarp, mesocarp and epicarp.

Perigynous (flowers). When stamens, petals and sepals, as an example, are attached to a ring or cup of the flower axis, which is loose from and surrounding the pistil, as in the peach, plum and cherry.

Pesticide Tolerance. Pre-determined quantity of a pesticide which may legally remain on the harvested crops and products sold in interstate commerce, USA.

Petals. Rather showy structures around the reproductive organs of the flower which help to attract insects.

pH. An expression of acidity or alkalinity as a scale of numbers from 1 (very acid) to 14 (alkaline); pH 7.0 is neutral representing the reciprocal of the hydrogen ion concentration and expressed in gram atoms per liter of a solution.

Phloem. Region of tissue in the plant, as in the stems or veins of leaves, composed of sieve tubes and parenchyma which translocate food elaborated by the leaves.

Photoperiodism. Response of plants in growth and flowering to varying quantities and qualities of light.

Phylloclade. Leaf-like stem containing chlorophyll which performs photosynthetic action as in leaves.

Phyllody. A type of disorder in which the shoot or branch forms more leaves than is normal.

Phytotoxic. Poisonous to plants.

Pinnate (leaf). Compound, with the leaflets arranged on each side of a common petiole.

Pistil. Female part of the flower usually consisting of the ovules, ovary, style and stigma.

Pith. The tissue occupying the central part of stems, usually made up of soft parenchyma cells.

Pitted. Marked with small depressions or pits, as the fruit skin of some apple varieties.

Plumule. The bud or growing point of the embryo.

Pollen. Spore-like particles which are in the anther and contain the male gametophyte.

Pollination. Transfer of pollen from the anther to the stigma as by bees, wind or rain.

Polyploid. Containing one or more extra sets of chromosomes. Those plants having a 2N chromosome number or greater.

Pome. Fleshy fruits, usually of a perennial woody plant, which have an embedded core and seeds such as the apple, pear, and quince.

Pomology. The science and practice of fruit growing.

Primordia. Area in plants as the tips of stems and roots where initials or beginnings of plant structures are formed.

Procumbent. Lying on the ground or trailing but without rooting at the nodes.

Profichi. One of the crops of the capri fig or "male" fig which is the second to mature during the growing season. The fruit appear to be very small "buttons" in the late fall or early winter months.

Pruning. The proper and judicious removal of such plant parts as leaves, twigs, shoots, buds, branches or roots of a plant to increase its usefulness.

Pubescent. Covered with hairs, especially if short, soft and down-like.

Pyriform. Pear-shaped.

Quarantine. A legal action preventing the sale or shipment of plants, seed, or reproductive parts to prevent the accompanying invasion and infestation of a disease or insect pest.

Raceme. A simple inflorescence of pediceled flowers upon a more or less elongated axis, opening from the base.

Receptacle (torus). The apex of the pedicel or the stem of the flower, generally swollen, which bears the organs of a flower. If, for example, an apple forms, the pedicel becomes a peduncle or stem on the fruit.

Reflexed. Abruptly bent or turned downward as in calyx of apple.

Reniform. Kidney-shaped.

Respiration. The oxidation of food materials by plants and the release of energy in which oxygen is absorbed and carbon dioxide is released as a by-product.

Rest Period. Period of non-visible growth, controlled by internal factors, and when growth will not occur even when environmental conditions are favorable.

Reticulate. In the form of network; net-veined.

Rhizome. A rootlike stem under or along the ground, usually horizontal, which may send roots from its lower surface and leafy shoots from its upper surface.

Rib. A primary or prominent vein of a leaf; a ridge on a pome fruit.

Ringing. Removal of a narrow strip of bark of the stem, branch or trunk of a plant to prevent the downward translocation of food beyond the point of incision.

Root Hair. Lateral extension of an epidermal cell of a root.

Rootstock. Root material to which other varieties of fruit are grafted to produce a commercially acceptable tree or vine.

Rosette. Leaves having a bunched or clustered appearance due to a shortening of the internodes of leaves on a branch or stem, as in zinc and boron deficiencies.

Rugose. Wrinkled or uneven, as a leaf.

Salt. A compound produced by the reaction of a base with an acid, as sodium chloride or potassium nitrate.

Sapwood. Outer younger more porous region of the tree beneath the bark where there is active growth.

Scaffold branches. The larger branches arising from the central portion or trunk of a tree.

Scarf-skin. The roughened outer skin of a pome fruit; wax like and whitish.

Scarification. Injury by scratching, chemicals, cutting or removing of the seed coat to promote germination of seed.

Scion (cion). Part of plant which is grafted or budded to an acceptable understock.

Seed. A fertilized and ripened ovule containing an embryo capable of developing by germination into an individual.

Seedling. A young plant grown from a seed without the intervention of any method of grafting.

Selective Herbicide. A chemical, which upon coming in contact with a weed or plant, is absorbed by it and translocated throughout the plant, causing it to succumb slowly. An example is 2, 4-D.

Self-Pollinated. Pollinated with the pollen of the same plant or a plant exactly like it.

Sepals. Leaf-like structures encasing a flower bud and later subtending the open flower.

Serrations. Teeth-like indentations at the margin of a leaf.

Sessile. Without footstalk of any kind.

Simple. Of one piece; not compound as in a leaf.

Shoot. Current season's stem growth which bears leaves and buds.

Short-Day (plants). Plants requiring at least 12 continuous hours of uninterrupted dark period to induce flowering, such as poinsettia and salvia.

Shrub. A woody perennial, smaller than a tree, usually with several stems.

Slurry. A suspension made up of an insoluable material and water which is usually very thick in nature.

Sod Culture. Type of orchard management in which a permanent perennial ground cover is kept at all times. The cover, as grass, is mowed periodically during the growing season to keep the growth of the perennials in check.

Soft Fruits. Generally denotes those fruits which tend to be soft at maturity such as the stone fruits and brambles.

Soil sterilants. Materials which prevent the growth of plants when present in soils. It may also be of sufficient toxicity to destroy all other living organisms as well.

Soursap. Disorder characterized by a fermentation of tree sap associated with disorders of root and prolonged orchard wetting conditions.

Spore. Resting unicellular stage of a fungus capable of propagation.

Spraydrift. Movement of airborne spray particles from area of origin to areas not intended to be covered.

Spur. Short woody stem or branch which is a principal fruiting area for most fruit trees, sometimes arbitrarily said to be 4 inches or less, a twig being 4" or more.

Stamen. The male part of a flower consisting of an anther containing pollen and a filament.

Staminate (Flower). Flowers having stamens but no pistils; a male plant.

Starter Solution. A solution of soluable nutrients used to aid plants in surviving transplanting.

Stele. Group of vascular tissues in a stem, root and related plant part, including pericycle, phloem, xylem and pitch.

Stellate, stelliform. Star-shaped; said of star-like dots on the apple fruit.

Sterile flower. Without pistils or otherwise unable to accomplish fertilization.

Stigma. Upper surface of the pistil where the pollen grain settles and germinates.

Stolon. Horizontal stem or shoot near the surface of the soil that gives rise to new plants at its tip, as in strawberry.

Stomach poisons. Insecticides or chemicals which are ingested by insects into the stomach, eventually killing them.

Stomate. Pore or opening in the epidermis of a leaf through which gases and water vapor pass.

Stratification (seeds). Process of subjecting seeds to an after-ripening period to break the rest period. The seeds are usually placed in layers of a well aerated media under varying temperatures.

Stone (Pit). The center portion of stone (drupe) fruits or the pit, endocarp or pyrene found in many of the prunus plants.

Subordination (pruning). A method of restoring apical dominance on a plant by heading back all but one of multiple leaders.

Succulent. Juicy; fleshy.

Sucker. Shoot arising from the roots or lower part of the plant stem.

Sunscald. Injury or destruction of outer tissue due to excess sun heat, as on the exposed side of an apple, limbs or trunk.

Superior. Said of the ovary when it is free; above, in position.

Surfactant. Materials which tend to modify the surface tension of spray droplets, causing them, e.g., to spread out on a leaf forming a thin film; e.g. a detergent such as Tide.

Suture. A line formed by the union of two adjacent margins, as the suture line (union of folded fleshy modified leaf) on a peach fruit.

Synergism. When two agencies act simultaneously to produce a total effect greater than the sum of their individual effects, as growth regulators and certain plant nutrients.

Systemic herbicide. A compound which is translocated throughout a plant and has its effects on the entire plant system, modifying its growth habit or killing it.

Tap-root. The perpendicular main root of a tree which is characteristic for the species and penetrates deeply into the ground and possesses but few laterals, as in case of the pecan. Relatively difficult to transplant.

Temperature inversion. Meteorological phenomenon whereby the air temperature becomes warmer with altitude instead of becoming cooler as is normal.

Tendril. The coiled thread-like organ by which some vines clasp an object.

Terminal. The end of a shoot, spur, stem or twig.

Testa. The outer commonly hard and brittle seed-coat.

Topworking. Changing the variety of a tree by inserting buds or grafts of the new variety on its trunk and/or branches.

Translocated herbicide. A chemical absorbed through one part of the plants and exerts toxic effects in other parts.

Translocation. Physical movement of water, nutrients, or chemicals such as a herbicide or elaborated food within a plant.

Transpiration. Water loss by evaporation from the internal surface of the leaves and through the stomata.

Tropism. An involuntary response in the form of movement of a plant, the direction of which is determined by the source of the stimulus.

Trunk. The main stem or body of a tree apart from limbs and roots.

Turgidity. Pressure caused by fluids in the cell pressing against the cell wall giving shape to the cell.

Twig. Small short shoot or branch; arbitrarily said to be more than 4 inches in length.

Variety. A group of closely related plants of common origin which have characteristics not sufficiently different to form separate species.

Vein (leaf). One of the vascular bundles forming the fibrous framework of a leaf and through which food, water and nutrients are translocated.

Viscid. Sticky material, such as sap.

Volatile. Property of liquids which allow it to change easily from a liquid to a gas. Some herbicides will do this, causing a drift problem on nearby unsprayed plants.

Water Berries. Grape disorder characterized by watery fruits and failure to ripen.

Water Core. A disorder of, e.g., apple, which gives the area near the core a watery or glassy appearance. It may disappear after a time in cold storage.

Water logged. Soil which has poor drainage and lacks the necessary O_2 for proper root functioning.

Watersprouts. Rapidly growing shoots or sprouts that grow from adventitious or latent buds on branches or trunks of trees.

833

Wilting Coefficient. Percentage of moisture in the soil when the permanent wilting of a plant is reached (plant will not recover when placed in atmosphere of 100% humidity).

Windburn. Disorder of leaves recognizable by dead, torn and browned margins and areas of leaves.

Woody (plants). Plant tissue having many xylem tubes and fiber which are resilient. A non-herbaceous plant.

Xerophyte. Plants which can endure extreme moisture stress, as in the desert. A cactus plant.

Xylem. Tough fibrous vessels formed from heavy walled elongated cells which are responsible for the upward movement of water and nutrient salts from roots to the entire plant.

Zygote. A cell formed by the union of two gametes (male and female), or a fertilized egg or zygospore from which an individual will develop.

SUGGESTED POMOLOGY BOOK LIST

Following is a partial list of pomology books and other books related to the fruit growing industry, which fruit growers and technical workers may wish to consider for their library. Books of possible interest only to professional workers are listed separately.

Anderson, H. W. Diseases of fruit crops. McGraw-Hill Book Co., Inc., N. Y. City, 501 pp. 1956.

Beach, S. A. The apples of New York. Vol. I,, Vol. II. Out-of-print, available only from retiring horticulturists, second-hand stores. Color plates, history, variety descriptions. Early 1900's.

Castle, Emery and Manning Becker. Farm Business Management. The Macmillan Co., New York City. 400 pp. 1962.

Chandler, W. H. Deciduous orchards. Lea & Febiger Co., Phila., Pa. 492 pp. 1957.

Chandler, W. H. Fruit growing (excellent literature review to 1925). Houghton, Mifflin Co., N. Y. City, 777 pp. 1925.

Childers, N. F. (Editor) Fruit Nutrition — Temperate to Tropical (covers important deciduous and tropical woody plants and strawberries). Hort. Publ., Rutgers Univ., Nichol Ave., New Brunswick, N. J. 888 pp. 8½ x 12 inches. 1966.

Childers, Norman F., L. G. Albrigo and E. G. Christ. The peach — varieties, culture, marketing, pest control. Conf. Rpt. of 70 Researchers at Rutgers University, Hort. Dept., New Brunswick, N. J. 281 pp. 1965. (Out-of-print; see libraries.)

Common Poisonous Plants of New England. Public Health Serv. Publ. 1220. Apr. 1964. Supt. of Documents, U. S. Gov. Printing Office, Wash., D. C. 20402.

Darrow, George M. The strawberry — history breeding and physiology. Holt-Rinehart & Winston, N. Y. City. 447 pp. 1966.

Eck, Paul and Norman F. Childers. Blueberry Culture. Rutgers Univ. Press, New Brunswick, N. J. 378 pp. 1966.

Frey, K. J. (Ed.) Plant Breeding (a Symposium) Iowa Univ. Press, Ames. 430 pp. 1966.

Garner, R. J. The grafter's handbook. Faber and Faber Ltd., 24 Rosswell Sq., London, Eng., 260 pp. 1958.

Hartmann, H. T. and D. E. Kester. Plant propagation. 702 pp. Prentiss-Hall, Inc., Englewood Cliffs, N. J. 1968.

Hedrick, U. P. Peaches. Plums. Pears. Cherries. Small Fruits. (Separate books.) Of New York. Color plates, history, variety descriptions. Available only from retiring horticulturists, second-hand stores. N. Y. Agr. Exp. Sta., Geneva. Early 1900's.

Janick, Jules. Horticultural Science, W. H. Freeman and Co., San Francisco, London. 472 pp. 1963.

Journal American Society for Horticultural Science (Two volumes annually to members), technical papers from 3,000 members. P.O. Box 109, St. Joseph, Michigan, U.S.A. 49085.

Marshall, Roy E. Cherries and cherry products. Interscience Publ., Inc., N. Y., N. Y. 283 pp. 1954.

Metcalf, C. L. and W. P. Flint. Destructive and useful insects — their habits and control. McGraw-Hill Book Co., Inc., N. Y. City. 980 pp. (1962). Request recent edition.

Morettini, Alessandro. Frutticoltura — Generale Especials. (In Italian) Ramo Editoriele Degli Agricoltori, Publ., Rome, Italy. 692 pp. 1963.

Muenscher, Walter Conrad. Poisonous plants of the United States. The Macmillan Company, New York. Revised Edition 1962.

Perkins, H. O. Espaliers and vines for the home gardener. B. Van Nostrand Co., Inc., Princeton, N. J. 206 pp. 1964.

Proceedings International Horticultural Congress (Published every 2-4 years). Excellent 4-volume set in 1966, XVII Congress at College Park, Md. (H. B. Tukey, Sr., Dept. Hort., Mich. State Univ., East Lansing, Mich.)

Shoemaker, J. S. Small fruit culture. McGraw-Hill Co., Inc., N. Y., N. Y. 3rd Edition. 1955.

Smith, C. R. and N. F. Childers. The strawberry — varieties, culture, marketing, pests, Conf. Rpt. of 75 Researchers at Rutgers University, Horticulture Dept., New Brunswick, N. J. 184 pp. 1963.

Smock, R. M. and A. M. Neubert, Apples and apple products. Interscience Publ., Inc., N. Y. City. 486 pp. 1950.

Stiles, W. C. and N. F. Childers. Factors affecting fruit condition. Conf. Rpt. of 30 Researchers at Rutgers University, Hort. Dept., New Brunswick, N. J. 181 pp. 1961.

Teskey, B. J. E. and J. S. Shoemaker. Tree Fruit Production Deciduous, 2nd Ed. 336 pp. Avi Publ. Co., Westport, Conn. 1972.

Tukey, Harold B. Dwarfed fruit trees (an excellent book). The Macmillan Co., N. Y. City. 562 pp. 1964.

Upshall, W. H. (Ed.) North American Apples — varieties, rootstocks outlook. Mich. State Univ. Press., E. Lansing, 197 pp. 1970.

Wallace, T. Diagnosis of mineral deficiencies in plants by visual symptoms (color atlas and guide), 2nd Edition, Chemical Publ. Co., Inc., 212 5th Ave., N. Y., N. Y. 1961.

Wallace, T. and R. G. Bush. Modern commercial fruit growing (England). Country Life Publ. Ltd., London, England, 384 pp. 1956.

Winkler, A. J. General Viticulture. (A good book) Univ. of Calif. Press, Berkeley. 633 pp. 1962.

Woodroof, J. G. Tree nuts — production, processing, products. Vol. I — Almond, Brazil nut, cashew, chestnut, filbert, macadamia, 356 pp. Vol. II — Pecan, pine nut, pistachio, black walnut, English walnut, 373 pp. The Avi Publ. Co., Inc., Westport, Conn. 1967.

Woolrich, W. R. Handbook of refrigerating engineering. Vol. I, fundamentals; Vol II, applications. 460 and 410 pp., resp. 1965, 1966.

Zielinski, Q. B. Modern systematic pomology. Wm. C. Brown Co., Dubuque, Iowa. 296 pp. 1955.

FOR PROFESSIONALS

Baldini, B. et al. Apples (in Italian). Color plates, descriptions. 412 pp. 1967.

Briggs, F. N. and P. F. Knowles. Introduction to plant breeding. Reinhold Publ. Co., New York City. 426 pp. 1967.

Brooks, R. D. and H. P. Olmo. Register of new fruit and nut varieties, 1920-1950, Univ. of Calif. Press, Berkley. A supplement for 1950-70 is available from Amer. Soc. Hort. Sci., St. Joseph, Mich., Box 109. 49085.

Caillavet H. and J. Southy. Monograph of the principal varieties of peaches. (In French) Societe Bordelaise D'Imprimerie, Bordeau, France. 416 pp. 1950.

Chandler, W. H. Evergreen orchards. Lea & Febiger Co., Phila., Pa., 452 pp. 1950.

Chapman, H. D. (Editor). Diagnostic criteria for plants and soils. Univ. of Calif. Press, Berkeley. 1966.

Chatt, E. M. Cocoa — cultivation, processing analysis. Interscience Publ., Inc. N. Y., 300 pp. 1953.

Collins, J. L. The pineapple — botany, cultivation and utilization. Leonard Hill (books) Ltd., London, England, 296 pp. 1960.

Constantinescu, N. and A. Negriala, and N. Ghena. Pomicultura, Vol. I, 575 pp., Vol. II, 345 pp., Editura Angra - Silvica, Bucharest Czechoslovakia (In Slovac). 1967.

Darlington, C. D. and A. P. Wylie. Chromosome Atlas. The Macmillan Co., New York City. 519 pp. 1956.

Dowson, V. H. W. and A. Aten. Dates — handling, processing and packing. Food and Agr. Org. of United Nations, Rome, Italy, 392 pp. 1962.

Esau, Katherine. Plant Anatomy. John Wiley & Son, Inc., New York City; Chapman & Hall, Ltd. London. 735 pp. 1953. A later smaller edition is available.

Gangolly, S. R. et al. The mango. Indian Counc. of Agr. Res., New Delhi, India, 530 pp. 1957.

Gardner, V. R. Principles of Horticulture. (Tropical examples included). Michigan State University Press, East Lansing, 650 pp. 1966.

Hewitt, E. J. Sand and water culture methods in plant nutrition studies. Commonwealth Agricultural Bureau, Maidstone, Kent, England. 547 pp. 1966.

Hulme, A. C. Bio-chemistry of fruits and their products. Academic Press, London, N. Y. Vols. I & II, 620, 788 pp. 1970, 1971.

Kelsey, H. P. and W. A. Dayton. Standardized plant names. 2nd Edition. J. H. McFarland Publ. Co., Harrisburg, Pa. 675 pp. 1942.

Kolesnikov, V. Fruit biology. Mir Publ. Co., Moscow, Russia (in English) 338 pp. 1966.

Kolesnikov, V. Root systems of fruit plants (in English), Mir Publishers. Moscow, USSR. 269 pp. 1971.

Levitt, J. The hardiness of plants. Academic Press, Inc., Publishers. New York City, 274 pp. 1956.

Menon, K. P. V. and K. M. Pandalai. The coconut — a monograph. Indian Central Coconut Committee, Ernakulam, South India, 385 pp. 1958.

Meyer, B. S. and D. B. Anderson. Plant physiology. D. Van Nostrand Co., Inc., Princeton, N. J. 785 pp. Request late edition.

Morettini, A. et al. Monografia delle Principali Cultivar di Pesco (in Italian). Color plates, descriptions of peach varieties. 633 pp. 8-½ x 12 inches. Consig. Naz. delle Ric., Centro Miglio. Pianta da Frutto e da Orto, Firenze. 1962.

Mutation and Plant Breeding, a Symposium (at Cornell Univ.). Leading scientists. Nat. Acad. Sciences, Nat. Res. Coun. Publ. 891, Wash., D. C., 523 pp. 1961.

Pieniazek, S. A. Sadownictwo (on fruit growing, in Polish) Panstwowe Wydawnictwo Rolnicze 1 Lesne, Warszawa, Poland. 733 pp. 1968.

Reuther, Walter, L. D. Batchelor and H. J. Webber (Editors). The citrus industry, Vol. I (Later volumes to come), History, world distribution, botany, varieties, culture. 610 pp. Univ. of Calif. Press, Berkeley, Calif. 1967.

Simmonds, N. W. Bananas. Longmans, Green & Co., Inc., 119 W. 40th St., N. Y., N. Y. 1959.

Sinclair, W. B. The orange — its biochemistry and physiology. Univ. Calif. Press, Riverside, Calif. 1961.

Style Manual for Biological Journals. Am. Inst. of Bio. Sci., 2000 P. St. NW., Wash., D. C. 20036, 117 pp. 1964.

Thorne, Gerald. Principles of nematology. McGraw-Hill Publ., Inc., N. Y. City, 548 pp. 1961.

Transeau, E. N. et al. Textbook of botany, 812 pp. Harper & Bros., Publ., N. Y. City. Request recent edition.

Upshall, W. H. No. Amer. apples: varieties, rootstocks, outlook. Mich. St. Univ. Press, E. Lansing. 198 pp. 1970.

Urquhart, D. H. Cocoa. John Wiley & Sons, Inc., N. Y. City, 294 pp. 1961.

Virus diseases and other disorders with viruslike symptoms of stone fruits in North America, USDA Agr. Handbook 10, 276 pp. Apr. 1951.

Wickizer, V. D. Coffee, tea and cocoa — an economic and political analysis. Stanford Univ. Press, Stanford, Calif., 487 pp. 1951.

ADDITIONAL REFERENCES

NOTE. These references, in addition to those at the end of each chapter, should give the reader and particularly the researcher, key works which also have sets of references that can be read for thorough investigation of a subject. Obviously some important works will be missed but it is hoped in future years the author can improve and up-date the list with the help of his colleagues.

Alderman, W. H. Fruit breeding—past, present, and future. Proc. A.S.H.S. 51, 670, 1948.

Bradt, O. A. et al. Fruit varieties for Canada. Ontario Dept. of Agriculture & Food, Toronto, 80 pp. Publ. 430. 1969.

Brooks, R. M. and H. P. Olmo. New orchard varieties. Proc. A.S.H.S. 45, 467, 1944; 47, 544, 1946; 50, 426, 1947; 53, 573, 1949; 56, 509, 58, 386, 60, 497, 62, 513, 64, 535, 66, 445, 1955; 611, 1956; 557, 1957; 519, 1958; 758, 1959; see also their book covering to 1950.

Brown, D. S., C. O. Hesse, and E. C. Koch. Red sports of Delicious apple. California Agr. p. 3, 10. October 1959.

Camp, W. H., V. R. Boswell and J. R. Magness. The world in your garden (color photos, history, of flowers, vegetables, fruits). Nat. Geographic Soc. book, Wash., D. C., USA. 231 pp. 1957.

Crane, M. B. The genetics and breeding of fruit trees. Rpt. of the 13th International Hort. Cong. 2: 687-695. 1952.

Crane, M. B. and W. J. C. Lawrence. The genetics of garden plants. 4th edition. London, Macmillian & Co., 1952.

Darrow, G. M. Polyploidy in fruit improvement. Proc. A.S.H.S. 54, 523, 1949.

Dayton, D. F. Genetic heterogeneity in the histogenic layers of apple. ASHS 94:(6) 592-595 pp. November 1969.

Deciduous Fruit Board. Ann. Rpt., London Office, 105 Strand St., London, England WC-2.

Derman, H. Chimeral apple sports. J. Hered. 39, 235, 1948.

Derman, H. The pattern of tetraploidy in flowers and fruits of cytochimeral apples. J. Hered. 44, 31, 1953. See also Tetraploid from 2-2-4 chimeral Winesap 46, 244, and Tetraploid from giant applesports, Am. J. Bot. 42, 837, 1955.

Einset, J. and B. Imhofe. Chromosome numbers of apple varieties and sports II. Proc. A.S.H.S. 53, 197, 1949.

Einset, J. The occurrence of spontaneous triploids and tetraploids in apples. Proc. A.S.H.S. 51, 61, 1948.

Einset, J. Spontaneous polyploidy in cultivated apples. Proc. A.S.H.S. 59, 291, 1952.

Einset, J. and B. Lamb. Chromosome numbers of apple varieties and sports. Proc. A.S.H.S. 58, 103, 1951.

Fisher, D. V. Growing fruits in B. C. Summerland Res. Sta. 58 pp. Feb. 1962.

Guinea, Emilio. Apples of Spain (in Spanish) 209 pp. Nat. Inst. of Agron. Invest. Madrid, 1957.

Hall, D. and M. B. Crane. The apple. M. Hopkinson, Ltd., London. pp. 44-45:85-106. 1933.

Hartman, F. O. and F. S. Howlett. An analysis of the fruit characteristics of seedlings of Rome Beauty, Gallia Beauty and Golden Delicious parentage. Proc. Amer. Soc. Hort. Sci. 40: 241-244. 1942.

Howlett, F. S. and J. H. Gourley. Characteristics of the progeny obtained from utilizing standard commercial varieties in apple breeding. Proc. Amer. Soc. Hort. Sci. 48: 121-132. 1946.

Klein, L. G. Apples of yesteryear. Farm Research. N. Y. Agr. Exp. Sta. Jan. 1956.

Knight, R. L. Abstract bibliography of fruit breeding and genetics to 1960 for Malus and Pyrus. Technical communication #29, Commonwealth Bureau of Hort. and Plantation Crops, E. Malling, Maidstone, Kent, England. 1961.

Koch, E. C. et al. Commercial Apple Growing in California. Agr. Ext. Serv. Cir. 538. Request recent edition.

Kon, K. Results of the apple breeding work. Aomori Apple Exp. Sta., Bull. 4. 1951 (in Japanese with English summary).

LaMont, T. E., Albion, N.Y., edited by. High-density apple planting using clonal rootstock. N. Y. State Horticultural Society Newsletter. Vol. XXVI No. 3, April 1970 supplement.

Magness, J. R. Progress in apple improvement. U.S.D.A. Yearbook 575-614. 1937.

Mori, H. Studies on the inheritance of the main characters of deciduous fruit trees (peach, Japanese pear and Japanese persimmon). Japan National Institute of Agricultural Sciences, Series E, No. 2. 1953 (in Japanese with English summary).

National Program for Conservation of Crop Germ Plasm (Federal-State Cooperation). USDA, Plant Industry Station, Beltsville, Md. 73pp.

New Fruits from breeding programs. Contact New York, New Jersey, Illinois, Minnesota, Ohio, Virginia, British Columbia, USDA, Ontario, and Quebec central agricultural experiment stations for cooperative fruit testing catalogues, bulletins or circulars.

Nilsson, F. Fruit growing in Sweden. Hort. Abs. 16, abs. No. 1268, 1946, and 17, abs. 1162, 1947.

Norton, Richard L. Western N. Y. Coop. Ext. Spec. High-Density Apple Planting Using Clonal Roostocks. N.Y. (Cornell) Agr. Exp. Sta., 1971 (Several spot reports)

Seilig, R. A. Apples. United Fruit and Vegetable Assn. Rpt. 40 pp. Wash., D. C. 20005.

Seitzer, Josef. Apple variety descriptions (in German) 112 pp. Verlag Eugen Ulmer, Stuttgart. 1956.

Schneider, G. W. Progenies from some apple crosses. Proc. A.S.H.S. 53, 205, 1949.

Sinnott, E. W. and L. C. Dunn. Principles of genetics. New York, The McGraw-Hill Company, 1939.

Skard, O. Fruit growing in Norway. Hort. Abs. 17, abs. 1161, 1947.

Stebbins, G. L. Apomixis in the Angiosperms. Bot. Rev. 7: 507-542. 1941.

Upshall, W.H. North American Apples: Varieties, Rootstocks, Outlook. Mich. State Univ. Press. E. Lansing. 197 pp. 1970.

Varieties. Each state has a recommended list of varieties. Contact your local County Agricultural Agent or government experiment station.

PRUNING, ASSOCIATED PHYSIOLOGY (Chap. IV)

Asami, Y. Fundamentals of Fruit Growing (Kajyu Saibai Hanron). Part 1—Pruning and thinning, Yokendo Co., Tokyo. 1942; Part 2—Fruit setting, Yokendo Co., Tokyo. 1950. Part 3—Soil and fertilization, Yokendo Co., Tokyo. 1951. (In Japanese).

Aaron, I. Dormant and adventitious buds. Science, 104, 329, 1946.

Aaron I. and W. W. Clarke. Breakage of apple trees. Proc. A.S.H.S. 54, 57, 1949.

Badizadegan, M. and R. F. Carlson. Effect of N^6 benzyladenine on seed germination and seedling growth of apple. ASHS 91. 1-8. 1967.

Bloch, R. Wound healing in higher plants, II. Bot. Rev. 18, 655, 1952.

Bohning, R. H. Time course of photosynthesis in apple leaves exposed to continuous illumination. Pl. Physiol. 24: 222-240, 1949.

Christopher, E. P. The pruning manual. Macmillan Co. New York, 1954.

Crowdy, S. H. Regulators in lanolin and apple wound healing. Annls. Appld. Biol. 40, 197, 1953.

Cutting, C. V. and L. C. Luckwill. The physiology of tree crops, Proceedings of a symposium held at Long Ashton Research Station, University of Bristol, 392 pp. 1969, 1970.

Davis, E. A. Regulators and wound healing. Proc. A.S.H.S. 53, 233, 1949.

Dennis, F. G., Jr. Effects of gibberellins and naphthaleneacetic acid on fruit development in seedless apple clones. J. ASHS. 95(1):125-128. 1970.

Edgerton, L. J. and W. J. Greenhalgh. Absorption, translocation and accumulation of labeled (Alar) in tissues. ASHS 91:25-30. 1967.

Edgerton, L. J. and M. B. Hoffman. Some psysiological responses of apple to N-dimethylaminosuccinamic acid and other growth regulators. ASHS 86: 28-36. 1965.

Gaston, H. P. The "Thin Wood" Method of Pruning Bearing Apple Trees. Mich. Agr. Expt. Sta. Cir. Bul. 179, 1942.

Gunckel, J. E. and K. V. Thimann. Auxin production in shoot growth. Am. J. Bot. 36, 145, 1949.

Hansen, C. M., R. P. Larsen and G. Monroe. Hedge pruning of fruit trees. Mich. Agr. Exp. Sta. Quart. Bull 50, No. 3. pp. 331-341. Feb. 1968.

Heinicke, A. J. and M. B. Hoffman, The rate of photosynthesis of apple leaves under natural conditions. Cornell Agr. Exp. Sta. Bul. 577, 1933.

Heinicke, A. J. and N. F. Childers. The daily rate of photosynthesis, during the growing season of 1935, of a young apple tree of bearing age. Cornell Univ. Agr. Exp. Sta. Memoir 201, 1937.

Heinicke, D. R. Characteristics of McIntosh and Red Delicious apples as influenced by exposure to sunlight during the growing season. ASHS 89:10-13. 1966.

Heinicke, D. R. The effect of natural shade on photosynthesis and light intensity in Red Delicious apple trees. ASHS 88:1-18. 1966.

Heinicke, D. R. The micro-climate of fruit trees. III. The effect of tree size on light penetration and leaf area in Red Delicious apple trees. ASHS 85:33-41. 1964.

Heinicke, D. R. Foliage and light distribution patterns in apple trees. ASHS 83:1-11. 1963.

Jackson, J. E., et al. Shade effects on apple fruit size, color, storage quality. J. HortSci. 46(3):277-287. July 1971.

Jackson, J. E. and C. H. W. Slater. An interesting photometer for outdoor use particularly in trees. J. Appl. Ecol. 4:421-424.

Kender, Walter J. and Stephen Carpenter. Stimulation of lateral bud growth of apple trees by 6-Benzylamino purine. J. ASHS 97 (3): 377. May 1972.

Letham, D. S. and M. W. Williams. Regulators of cell division in plant tissues. VIII. The cytokinins of the apple fruit. Phys. Plantarum Vol. 22. p. 925-936. 1969.

Leiser, A. T. et al. Staking, pruning on trunks young trees (ornamentals). J ASHS 97:4. 498-502. 1972.

Lumby, R., et al. Photosynthesis. Annl. Rev. Plant Phys. 5, 271, 1954.

MacDaniels, L. H. and F. F. Cowart. Development and structure of the apple leaf. Cornell Univ. Agr. Exp. Sta. Memoir, 258, 1944.

Martin, G. C., Max W. Williams, and L. P. Batjer. Movement and fate of labeled N-dimethylaminosuccinamic acid (B-9), a size controlling compound, in apple seedlings. ASHS 84:7-13. 1964.

Martin, G. C. and Max W. Williams. Breakdown products of C^{14} labeled N-Dimethylaminosuccinamic acid (Alar) in the apple tree. ASHS 89:1-9. 1966.

Meyer, B. S. and D. B. Anderson. Plant physiology. New York, D. Van Nostrand Company. Seek latest edition.

Mullins, M. G. and W. S. Rogers. Effects of stem orientation, bud position on apple shoot growth. J. HortSci. 46(3):313-321. July 1971.

Nelder, J. A., R. B. Austin, J. K. A. Bleasdale and P. J. Salter, An approach to the study of yearly and other variation in crop yields. Jour. Hort. Sci. 35: 73-82, 1960.

Reiter, R. F. Proceedings Eastern Golden Delicious Marketing Conference, 1971. Dept. Agr., Commonwealth of Pennsylvania, Harrisburg. 1972.

Phillipson, W. R. The ontogeny of the shoot apex in dicotyledons. Cambridge Phil. Soc. Biol. Rev. 24, 21, 1949.

Roberts, R. H. Pruning for fruit size. Proc. A.S.H.S. 59, 184, 1952.

Skoog, F. Bud inhibition by indoleacetic acid. Am. J. Bot. 26, 702, 1939.

Skoog, F. and C. Tsui. Chemical growth control. Am. J. Bot. 35, 782, 1948.

Storer, T. I. Control of field rodents in California. Calif. Agr. Ext. Serv. Cir. 138. (Request revised edition).

Upshall, W. H. Pruning the Tree Fruits. Ontario Dept. of Agr., Publication 392, Revised February, 1960.

Verner, L. Hormone and apple tree training. Idaho Agr. Exp. Sta. Res. Bull. 28, 1955.

SITES, ROOTSTOCKS, PROPAGATION (CHAP. III AND VIII)

Bark, L. Dean. When to expect late-spring and early-fall freezes in Kansas. Kansas Agr. Exp. Sta. Bull. 415, 23 pp. December 1959.

Barton, L. V. Some effects of treatment of seeds with growth substances on dormancy. Contrib. Boyce Thompson Inst. Plant Res. 11: 229. 1940.

Beakbane, A. B., and E. C. Thompson. Anatomical studies of stems and roots of hardy fruit trees. II. The internal structure of the roots of some vigorous and some dwarfing apple rootstocks and the correlation of structure with vigor. Jour. Pom. 17: 141-149. 1939.

Beakbane, A. B. and E. C. Thompson. Anatomical studies of stems and roots of hardy fruit trees. IV. The root structure of some new clonal apple rootstocks budded with "Cox's Orange Pippin." Jour. Pom. and Hort. Sci. 23: 206-211. 1947.

Blair, D. S. Rootstocks and intermediate pieces. Sci. Agr. 19 (2), 85, 1938.

Blaser, H. W. and J. Einset. Flower structure in periclinal chimeras of apple. Am. J. Bot. 37, 297, 1950.

Brooks, F. A., et al. Wind machines in orchards. Calif. Agr. 2, No. 12, 5-12, 1948.

Chang, W. Studies in incompatibility between stock and scion, with special reference to certain deciduous fruit trees. Jour. Pom. and Hort. Sci. 15: 267-325. 1937.

Colby, H. L. Stock-scion chemistry and the fruiting relationships in apple trees. Pl. Physiol. 10: 483-498. 1935.

Collins, C. M. Nova Scotia apples. Nova Scotia Dept. Agr. Bull. 4, 1941.

Curtis, O. F., Jr. and D. R. Rodney. Ethylene injury to nursery trees in cold storage. Proc. A.S.H.S. 60, 104, 1952.

Dutcher, R. D. and L. E. Powell. Apple shoots from buds *in Vitro*. J. ASHS: 97-4, 511-14, 1972.

Day, L. H. and W. P. Tufts. Nematode resistant rootstocks for deciduous fruit trees. Calif. Agr. Exp. Sta. Cir. 359, 1944.

Dwarf fruit trees. Agricultural Research Service, Hort. Crops Research Branch. U. S. Dept. Agr. Leaflet 407. 1956.

Faust, Miklos and C. B. Shear. Fine structure of the fruit surface of three apple cultivars. J. ASHS 97(3):351. May 1972.

Frith, H. J. Frost protection in orchards using air from temperature inversion. Aust. J. Agr. Res. 2, 24, 1951.

Gardner, F. E., et at. Lethal effects of certain apple scions on Spy 227 stock. Proc. A.S.H.S. 48, 195, 1946.

Garner, R. J. and E. S. J. Hatcher. Behavior of some apple and plum cuttings. J.H.S. 30, 116, 1955.

Greve, E. W. Variability among own-rooted and seedling-rooted apple trees. Proc. A.S.H.S. 42, 337, 1943.

Haut, I. C. The effect of various low temperatures upon the after-ripening of fruit seeds. Proc. Amer. Soc. Hort. Sci. *30*: 365-367. 1934.

Haut, I. C. After ripening and germination of fruit-tree seed. Maryland Agr. Exp. Sta. Bull. 420, 1938.

Herrero, J. Studies of compatible and incompatible graft combinations with special reference to hardy fruit trees. Jour. Hort. Sci. *26*: 186-237. 1951.

Hitchcock, A. E. and P. W. Zimmerman. Rooting leafy apple cuttings. Proc. A.S.H.S. 40, 292, 1942.

Hoffman, M. B. The home fruit planting. Cornell Agr. Ext. Serv. Bull. 913. 32 pp. 1957.

Hutchinson, Aleck. Dwarf Apple Trees on EMIX Rootstock: 30 year trial. Ann. Rpt. Hort. Res. Inst., Vineland, Ontario. 1970.

Ibrahim, I. M. and M. N. Dana. Gibberellin-like activity in apple rootstocks. HortSci. 6(6):541. Dec. 1971.

Johansson, E. Apple variety rootstock trials. Medd. Trädgardsförs Malmo 59, 10, 1950.

Kobayashi, A. Principles of fruit growing (Kajyu Engei Soron). Environment, fruit setting and nutrition, Yokendo Co., Tokyo (in Japanese). 1954.

Kolesnikov, V. A. The root system of fruit plants. Mir Publishers, Moscow USSR, 269 pages, 1971.

Lagasse, F. A., et al. Fruit variability from seedling and budded Tung. Proc. A.S.H.S. 52, 107, 1948.

Lasheen, A. M. and R. G. Lockard. Dwarfing stocks, stems on amino acid-protein in apple roots, J. ASHS 97:443.5. 1972.

Luckwell, L. C. and A. I. Campbell. The use of apomictic seeding rootstocks for apples. Progress report. Bristol Univ. Agr. and Hort. Res. Sta. Annu. Rpt. 1953: 47-52. 1953.

Luckwell, L. C. Growth inhibiting and growth promoting substances in relation to the dormancy and after-ripening of apple seeds. J. Hort. Sci. *27*: 53-67. 1952.

Luckwell, L. C. Hormone production by the developing apple seed. J.H.S. 28, 14, 1953.

Maney, T. J., H. H. Plagge and B. S. Pickett. Stock and scion effects in top-worked apple trees. Proc. Amer. Soc. Hort. Sci. *33*: 332-335. 1936.

Martin, D. Variation among apple fruits. Aust. J. Agr. Res. 4, 235, 1953; Between trees, 5, 9, 1954.

Modlibowska, I. Frost injury to apples. Jour. of Pomology *22*: 46-50. 1946.

Mori, H., Editor. Science of apple growing (Ringo Saibai Zensho). Asakura Co., Tokyo (in Japanese). 1958.

Mosse, B. Bridge tissue in ring-grafted apple stems. J.H.S. 28, 41, 1953.

Nagasawa, K. Modern fruit growing (Kajyu Engei Shinsetsu). Asakura Co., Tokyo (in Japanese). 1953.

Nelson, S. H. and H. B. Tukey. Temperature responses of apple rootstocks. J.H.S. 31, 55, 1956.

Partridge, N. L. and J. O. Veatch. The relationship between soil profile and root development of fruit trees. Mich. Agr. Quar. Bull. Vol. XIV. 1932.

Perkins, Frederick A. Organization and management of 42 Maine commercial apple farms. Maine Agr. Exp. Sta. Bull. 589, 34 pp. February, 1960.

Preston, A. P. Apple rootstock studies: Malling-Merton rootstocks. Jour. Hort. Sci. *30*: 25-33. 1955.

Preston, A. P. Five new apple rootstocks. Rpt. E. Malling Res. Sta. 179-170. 1952.
Preston, A. P. Malling-Merton rootstocks. J.H.S. 30, 25, 1955.
Proebsting, E. L. Soil temperature and root distribution. Proc. A.S.H.S. 43, 1, 1943.
Proebsting, E. L. Structural defects of the graft union. Bot. Gaz. 86, 82, 1928.
Roach, W. A. Rootstocks and mineral nutrition. Ann. Rept. East Malling Res. Sta. for 1946, 88.
Roach, W. A. and E. C. Thompson. Dye injection to study stock-scion incompatibility. J. Pom. and H. S. 23, 212, 1947.
Roberts, A. N., and W. M. Mellentin. Propagating clonal rootstocks. Oregon Agr. Exp. Sta. Cir. 578. May, 1957.
Roberts, R. H. Theoretical aspects of graftage. Bot. Rev. 15: 423-463. 1949.
Rogers, W. S. Some aspects of spring frost damage to fruit and its control. Jour. Royal Hort. Soc. 79: 29-36. 1954.
Rogers, W. S. Growth and cropping of clonal-root apple trees on five soils. J. Pom. and H. S. 22, 209, 1946.
Rogers, W. S., et al. Water sprinkling against frost. J.H.S. 29, 126, 1954.
Sax, K. Asiatic malus species as possible rootstocks. Proc. A.S.H.S. 53, 219, 1949.
Sax, Karl. Interstock effects in dwarfing fruit trees. Proc. A.S.H.S. 62: 201-204. 1953.
Sax, K. Stock and scion relationship in graft incompatibility. Proc. Amer. Soc. Hort. Sci. 64: 156-158. 1954.
Sax, K. The control of tree growth by phloem blocks. Havard Univ., Jour. Arnold Aboretum. 35: 251-259. 1954.
Sax, K. The use of Malus species for apple rootstocks. Proc. Amer. Soc. Hort. Sci. 53: 219-220. 1949.
Shaw, J. K. Malling rootsocks and American apple trees. Proc. A.S.H.S. 48, 166, 171, 1946.
Simons, Roy. Frost injury on Golden Delicious apples—morphological and anatomical characteristics of russeted and normal tissue. A.S.H.S. 69: 48-55. 1957.
Snyder, J. C. and R. D. Bartram. Grafting fruit trees. Pacific Northwest Bull. 62, 18 pp. Jan. 1965.
Swarbrick, T., D. Blair, and Sham Singh. Studies in the physiology of rootstock and scion relationships. Jour. Pom. and Hort. Sci. 22: 51-61. 1946.
Swingle, C. F. Regeneration and vegetative propagation. Bot. Rev. 18, 1, 1952.
Thomas, L. A. Influence of an intermediate stem piece. J.H.S. 29, 150, 1954.
Thomas, L. A. Stock and scion investigations. X. Influence of an intermediate stempiece upon the scion in apple trees. Jour. Hort. Sci. 29: 150-152. 1954.
Thompson, E. C. et al. Reinvigoration by inarching. J.H.S. 29, 175, 1954.
Thompson, E. C., W. A. Roach, and A. P. Preston. The reinvigoration of apple trees by inarching. Journ. of Hort. Sci. 29. No. 3, pp. 175-183. 1954.
Tiscornia, J. R. and F. E. Larsen. Rootstocks for apple and pear — a literature review. Wash. Agr. Exp. Sta. Cir. 421. 45 pp. mimeo. July, 1963.
Tuebner, F. G. Identification of the auxin present in the apple endosperm. Science 118, 418, 1953.
Tukey, H. B. and K. D. Brase. Dwarfing by intermediate stem piece. Proc. A.S.H.S. 42, 357, 1943.
Tukey, H. B. Stock and scion terminology. Proc. Am. Soc. Hort. Sci. 35: 378-392. 1937.
Tukey, H. B. and K. D. Brase. The dwarfing effect of an intermediate stem-piece of Malling IX. apple. Proc. Am. Soc. Hort. Sci. 42: 357-364, 1943.
Tukey, R. B., et al. Malling rootstocks during 12 years. Proc. A.S.H.S. 64, 146, 1954.
Upshall, W. H. Malling and French crab apple stocks. Sci. Agr. 28, 454, 1948.
Upshall, W. H. The new orchard. Ont. Dept. of Agr. Bull. 528, 15 pp. 1959.
Van Overbeek, J., et al. The leaf and rooting of cuttings. Am. J. Bot. 33, 100, 1946.
Vardar, Y. Transport of plant hormones. 457 pp. North-Holland Publishing Co., Amsterdam, Wiley Interscience Div., John Wiley & Sons, Inc., New York 1968.
Vyvyan, M. C. Interrelation of scion and rootstock in fruit-trees. Ann. Bot. 19: 401-423. 1955.
Welch, M. F. and G. Nylund, Virus heat treatment in apple clones, Can. J. Pl. Sci. 45: 443-454. 1965.
Yerkes, G. E. and W. W. Aldrich. Behavior of apple varieties on certain clonal stocks. Proc. A.S.H.S. 48, 227, 1946.
Young, Floyd D. Frost and the prevention of frost damage. U. S. Dept. Agr. Farmers' Bull. 588. 1947.
Zeiger, Donald C. and H. B. Tukey. An historical review of the Malling apple rootstocks in America. Mich. Agr. Exp. Sta. Cir. Bull. 226. 74 pp. 1960.

Allen, F. W. Influence of sugar, nitrogen, fertilizers and ringing Gravenstein apple trees upon color, and maturity of the fruit. Proc. Amer. Soc. Hort. Sci. *32*: 52-55. 1934.

Agarwala, S. C. and E. J. Hewitt. Molybdenum as a plant nutrient. J.H.S. 30, 151 and 163, 1955.

Anthony, R. D., N. F. Farris, and W. S. Clarke. Effect of certain cultural treatments on orchard soil and water losses and on apple tree growth. Penn. State Agr. Exp. Sta. Bull. 493. 1948.

Archibald, J. A. Orchard soil management. Ontario Dept. of Agr. Pub. 457. Revised 1960.

Arnon, D. I. Mineral nutrition of plants. Ann. Rev. Biochem. 12, 493, 1943.

Arnon, D. I. Copper enzymes. Plant Phys. 24, 1, 1949.

Assaf, L. R. and B. Bravdo. Irrigation, water up-take from soil layers. J ASHS:97-4. 521-6, 1972.

Baker, C. E. The relation of nitrogen and soil moisture to growth and fruitfulness of apple trees under different systems of soil management. Purdue Univ. Agr. Expt. Sta. Bull. 414. 1936.

Batjer, L. P., et al. Nitrogen intake of dormant apple trees at low temperature. Proc. A.S.H.S. 42, 69, 1943.

Batjer, L. P., et al. N, P, K, Ca, and Mg utilization by apple trees from a rich but fertilized soil. Proc. A.S.H.S. 60, 1, 1952.

Beattie, J. M. High nitrogen for Baldwin apples. Proc. A.S.H.S. 63, 1, 1954.

Blake, M. A., L. J. Edgerton and O. W. Davidson. Importance of environment for growing apples. N. J. Agr. Expt. Sta. Cir. 498. 1949.

Blasberg, C. H. Apple trees and Urea foliar sprays. Proc. A.S.H.S. 62, 147, 1953.

Boald, C., et al. Grass and uptake of P by trees. J.H.S. 29, 301, 1954.

Boald, C. and J. Tolhurst. Magnesium sulphate sprays on deficient trees. Ann. Rept. Long Ashton Agr. and Hort. Res. Sta. for 1948, 51.

Boynton, D. Leaf analysis for nutrient deficiencies. Soil Sci. 59, 369, 1945.

Boynton, D. Magnesium nutrition of apple trees. Soil Sci. 63, 53, 1947.

Boynton, D., et al. Soil and seasonal influences on nutrients in apple leaves. Proc. A.S.H.S. 44, 15, 1944.

Boynton, D., et al. Leaf color and leaf nitrogen. Proc. A.S.H.S. 52, 40, 1948.

Boynton, D., et al. McIntosh apple trees, N response. Cornell Univ. Memoir 290, 1950.

Boynton, D., et al. Hay mulch and N supply. Proc. A.S.H.S. 59, 103, 1952.

Boynton, D., et al. N metabolism in McIntosh apple trees sprayed with Urea. Proc. A.S.H.S. 62, 135, 1953.

Boynton, D. and O. C. Compton. Oxygen concentration and new root formation. Proc. A.S.H.S. 42, 53, 1943.

Brown, J. B. (Revised by J. C. Marr). The contour-check method of orchard irrigation. Calif. Agr. Ext. Ser. Cir. 73. 1949.

Brown, J. G. and O. Lilleland. Determining potassium and sodium by flame photometry. Proc. A.S.H.S. 48, 341, 1946. Calcium and magnesium by quartz spectrophotometer. Proc. A.S.H.S. 52, 1, 1948.

Brown, R. T. and G. F. Potter. Fertilizer applied to cover crop in Tung orchard. Proc. A.S.H.S. 54, 53, 1949.

Broyer, T. C. et al. Chlorine: A micronutrient element for higher plants. Plant Phys. 29, 526, 1954.

Cain, J. C. Interrelation of Ca, Mg, and K in young apple trees. Proc. A.S.H.S. 51, 1, 1948.

Cain, J. C. N and K fertilizers and minerals in apple trees. Proc. A.S.H.S. 62, 46. 1953.

Cain, J. C. and D. Boynton, Nitrogen fertilization influence on mineral composition of leaves. Proc. A.S.H.S. 51, 13, 1948.

Carne, W. M. The non-parasitic disorders of apple fruits in Australia. Aust. Council Sci. and Indus. Res. Bull. 238, 1948.

Chandler, W. H., D. R. Hoagland and J. C. Martin. Zinc and copper deficiency in corral soils. Proc. A.S.H.S. 47, 15, 1946.

Chapman, H. D. Diagnostic criteria for plants and soils, (Book) Univ. of Calif. Berkeley, 1966.

Childers, N. F. (Editor) Fruit Nutrition — Temperate to tropical. Hort. Publ. Rutgers University, New Brunswick, N. J. USA. 888 pp. 1966.

Cooper, R. E. and A. H. Thompson. Solution culture investigations of the influence of manganese, calcium boron, and pH on internal bark necrosis of 'Delicious' apple trees. J. ASHS 97(1):138. Jan. 1972.

Dickey, R. D. and M. Drosdorf. Manganese deficiency in Tung trees. Proc. A.S.H.S. 42 , 74, Copper deficiency in Tung trees. 42, 79, 1943.

Drake, F., F. W. Southwick, J. E. Steckel, and W. D. Weeks. The effect and sources of nitrogen, phosphorus and potassium on the mineral composition of McIntosh foliage and fruit color. Proc. Amer. Soc. Hort. Sci. 60: 11-21. 1952.

Drosdorf, M. and D. C. Nearpass. Quick tests for potassium and magnesium in Tung leaves. Proc. A.S.H.S. 50, 131, 1947.

Eaves, C. A. and A. Kelsall. Composition of Cortland apple leaves and nutritional treatment. J.H.S. 29, 59, 1954.

Eggert, D. A. and A. E. Mitchell. Russeting of Golden Delicious apples as related to soil applications of sodium nitrate. ASHS 90:1-8. 1967.

Eggert, R., et al. Apple leaf and root absorption of radioactive P. Proc. A.S.H.S. 64, 47, 1954.

Ellenwood, C. W. and J. H. Gourley. Cultural systems for the apple in Ohio. Ohio Agr. Exp. Sta. Bull. 580. 1937.

Faust, Miklos and C. B. Shear. Corking disorders of apples, physiological and biochemical literature review. Bot. Rev. 34:441-469. 1968.

Faust, Miklos, et al. Calcium accumulation in fruit of certain apple crosses. HortSci. 6(6):542. Dec. 1971.

Faust, M. and C. B. Shear. Ca on apple respiration. JASHS:97-4. 437-9, 1972.

Fernandez, C. E. and N. F. Childers. Molybdenum deficiency of apple. Proc. Amer. Soc. Hort. Sci. 75: 32. 1960.

Ferree, M. E. and J. A. Barden. Influence of strains and rootstocks on photosynthesis, respiration and morphology of 'Delicious' apple trees. J. ASHS 96(4):453.

Fisher, E., et al. Nitrogen as leaf sprays with urea. Proc. A.S.H.S. 51, 23, 1948.

Fisher, E. G. Apple foliar application of N as Urea. Proc. A.S.H.S. 59, 91, 1952.

Fisher, E. G. and D. R. Walker. Apple leaf absorption of Mg and P applied to lower surface. Proc. A.S.H.S. 65, 17, 1955.

Ford, Elsie M. Apple rootstock nutrition studies V. Magnesium deficiency symptoms in relation to magnesium supply. Annals of Bot. 32:125. 45-56. 1963.

Forde, H. L. and E. L. Proebsting. Utilization of ammonia supplied to peaches and prunes at different seasons. Hilgardia, 16, 411, 1945.

Ford, H. W., et al. The effect of iron chelate on root development of citrus. Proc. A.S.H.S. 63, 81, 1954.

Garner, R. J. and W. A. Roach. Comparative susceptibilities of plants to trace element deficiencies. Rpt. E. Mall, Res. Sta. for 1944 (1945) 72-3.

Gauch, H. G. and W. M. Duggar, Jr. The role of boron in the translocation of sucrose. Plant Phys. 28, 457, 1953. See also Maryland Agr. Exp. Bull. A-80, 1954.

Gauch, H. G. Inorganic plant nutrition, 487 pp. Dowden, Hutchinison and Ross, Inc., Stroudsburg, Pa. 18360. 1972.

Geigy Chemical Corporation, Ardsley, N. Y. 10502. Contact for latest weed control chemicals for fruits and for chelated trace elements for fruits.

Gilbert, F. A. The place of sulfur in plant nutrition. Bot. Rev. 17, 671, 1951.

Goodall, D. W. Apple leaf mineral composition. J. Pom. and H. S. 21, 90, 1945.

Gourley, J. H. and E. F. Hopkins. Nitrate fertilization and keeping quality of apple fruits. Ohio Agric. Expt. Sta. Bull. 479. 1931.

Gray, A. S. Sprinkler irrigation handbook. Latest edition. Rain Bird Sprinkler Mfg. Corp., Glendore, Calif. 1967.

Greenham, D. W. P. Long-term manurial trial on apple trees. J. Hort. Sci. 40 213-35, 1965.

Greenham, D.W.P. and G. C. White. Effects of grass sward, straw mulch, cultivation on Laxton's Superb trees. Rpt. E. Mall. Res. Sta. for 1967 (1968) 121-8.

Gulick, A. Phosphorus as a factor in the origin of life. American Scientist 43, 479, 1955.

Haller, M. H. and P. L. Harding. Relation of soil moisture to firmness and storage quality of apples. Proc. Amer. Soc. Hort. Sci. 36: 205-211. 1938.

Harley, C. P., et al. Nutrient reserves in apple trees. Proc. A.S.H.S. 53, 1, 1949.

Harley, C. P., et al. Nutrients from a mulch. Proc. A.S.H.S. 57, 17, 1951.

Hewitt, E. J. Role of mineral nutrients. Annl. Rev. Plant Phys. 2. 25, 1951.

Hewitt, E. J. Metal interrelationships in plant nutrition. J. Exp. Bot. 4, 59, 1953; and 5, 110, 1954.

842

Hildreth, A. C., and C. G. Brown. Repellents to protect trees and shrubs from damage by rabbits. USDA Tech. Bull. 1134:31 pp. 1955.

Hoagland, D. R. Tree deficiencies of molybdenum and copper. Proc. A.S.H.S. 38, 8, 1941.

Hoagland, D. R. Lectures on inorganic nutrition of plants. Waltham, Mass. Chronica Botanica Co., 1944.

Holland, D. A. Estimating leaf area on a tree. Rpt. East Malling Res. Sta. for 1967, pp. 101-104. 1968.

Huberty, M. R. and H. E. Pearson. Some effects of water rather high in sodium. Proc. A.S.H.S. 53, 62, 1949.

Hulme, A. C. Studies in nitrogen metabolism of apple fruits. Biochem. J. 43, 343, 1948.

Jacobson, L. Iron in chloroplasts and in other activity. Plant Phys. 20, 233, 1945.

Jones, W. W. Biuret toxicity from Urea sprays. Science 120, 499, 1954.

Judkins, W. P. and I. W. Wander. Photoelectric reflection meter for N estimation. Plant Phys. 25, 78, 1950.

Kelley, W. P., et al. Soil salinity in relation to irrigation. Hilgardia, 18, 635, 1949.

Kenworthy, A. L. and C. Bould. Nutrient analysis of plant tissue by use of the electron microprobe x-ray analyzer. Journ. ASHS (In press) About 1969.

Kenworthy, A. L. Plant analysis and interpretation of analysis for horticultural crops. Soil Anal. and Plant Anal. II. Soil Sci. Soc. of Amer., Inc., So. Segoe Rd., Madison, Wis. 53711.

Kidder, E. H. and R. Z. Wheaton. Supplemental irrigation in Michigan. Mich. Agr. Ext. Bull. 309. 39 pp. June 1963.

Kidson, E. B. Potassium and magnesium in each leaf along a shoot. J. Pom. and H. S. 23, 178, 1947.

Kirby, A.H.M. and T. M. Warman. Influence of Mg SO_4 on physiochemical properties of orchard pesticides. Rpt. E. Mall. Res. Sta. 1966 (1967), 177-80.

Kirby, A.H.M. and T. M. Warman. Physiochemical compatibility of $CaNO_3$ with orchard sprays. Rpt. E. Mall. Res. Sta. 1965 (1966) 174-82.

Kirsch, R. K. Effects of sawdust mulches. I. Soil properties. Oregon Agr. Exp. Sta., Tech. Bull. 49, 15 pp, October, 1959.

Kolesnikov, V.A. Root system of fruit plants. Mir Publishers, Moscow, USSR. 269 pages. 1971.

Kramer, P. J. Absorption of water by plants. Bot. Rev. 11, 310, 1945.

Kramer, P. J. Water relations of plant cells. Annl. Rev. Plant Phys. 6, 253, 1955.

Latimer, L. P. Relation of weather to prevalence of internal cork of apples. Proc. Amer. Soc. Hort. Sci. *38*: 63-69. 1941.

Latimer, L. P. and G. P. Percival. Sawdust, hay, and seaweed mulch. Proc. A.S.H.S. 50, 23, 1947.

Leonard, C. D. and I. Stewart. An available source of iron for plants. Proc. A.S.H.S. 62, 103, 1953. See also I. Stewart and C. D. Leonard. Chelated metals. Fruit nutrition, p. 775 Hort. Publ., New Brunswick, N. J., 1954.

Lessler, M. A. Effect of a temperature gradient on distribution of water in apples. Bot. Gaz. 109, 90, 1947.

Lilleland, O. and J. G. Brown. Potassium in peach leaves. Proc. A.S.H.S. 38, 37, 1941. Fruit tree and field crop yield in phosphorus deficient soil. Proc. A.S.H.S. 40, 1 and 41, 1, 1942.

Lindner, R. C. Arsenic injury of peach trees. Proc. A.S.H.S. 42, 275, 1943.

Lord, W. J. et al. Accumulation of simazine in mulch residue under apple trees. Hort. Sci. Vol. 5, No. 4, August 1970.

Lord, W. J., et al. Phytotoxicity of soil-incorporated 2, 6-Dichloro-Benzonitrile to clonal apple rootstocks. J. ASHS 97(3):390. May 1972.

Lord, W. J., L. F. Michelson and D. L. Field. Response to irrigation and soil moisture by McIntosh apple trees in Massachusetts. Mass. Agr. Exp. Sta. Pub. 537. 23 pp. November 1963.

Magness, J. R., et al. Apple-tree response to nitrogen applied at different seasons. J. Agr. Res. 76, 1, 1948.

Magness, J. R., E. S. Degman, and J. R. Furr. Soil moisture and irrigation investigations in Eastern apple orchards. USDA. Tech. Bull. 491. 1935.

Martell, A. E. and M. Calvin. Chemistry of metal chelate compounds. Prentice-Hall, Inc., New York, 1952.

Martin, D., et al. Calcium sprays on stored Sturmer apples. Field Station Record, Div. of Plant Indus. C.S.I.R.O. (Aust.) Vol. 7. p 10-21. 1971.

Martin, D. et al. Tree sprays to control bitter pit, scald. Fld. Sta. Res. Rpt., Div. Pla. Ind. CSIRO (Aust); 45-64. 1969.

843

Martin, D. et al. High levels of N on disorder incidence in Jonathan. Comm. Sci. Ind. Res. Org., Australia 1970.

McCall, W. W. What's in that fertilizer bag? Hawaii Agr. Ext. Serv. Cir. 441, 1970.

McElroy, W. D. and A. Nason. Nutrient elements in enzyme systems. Annl. Rev. Plant Phys. 5, 1, 1954.

Merrill, S., Jr. et al. N, P, and K effects in a Tung orchard. Proc. A.S.H.S. 65, 41, 1955.

Merrill, T. A. Soil management practices in the orchard. Mich. State Cir. Bul. No. 199. 1946.

Michelson, L. F. et al. Differential placement of N and K on apple. Hort.Sci. Vol. 4 (3) 249-250. 1969.

Michelson, L.F. et al. Response of apple trees to soil injections of lime. Hort.Sci. Vol. 4 (3) 251-252. 1969.

Miller, R. J. and E. Schultz. Trickle Irrigation; Fraser Valley. Canadian Horticulture and Agriculture. Sept. 1971. Contact Canada Research Sta., Summerland, B.C.

Millikan, C. R. and B. C. Hanger. Distribution of Zn in pear trees following bark injection. Reprint Aust. J. Agric. Res. 18: 85-93. 1967.

Misic, P. and M. Gravrilovic. Effects of Malling Rootstocks on some apple varieties. Jour. for Sci. Agric. Res. (Yugoslavia) 20:68, 2-28. 1967.

Moon, H. H., et al. Early-season symptoms of magnesium deficiency in apple. Proc. A.S.H.S. 59, 61, 1952.

Mokrzecki S. 1904. A cure of chlorosis. The Gardner's Chronicle January 16th, London.

Morita, Y. Studies on orchard soils. Japan National Institute of Agr. Sci., Series E. No. 4, 5. 1955 (in Japanese with English summary).

Mortvedt, J. J. et al. (eds.). Micro-nutrients in agriculture—Zn, Fe, B, Mo, Cu, Mn. Soils Sci. Soc. of Amer., Madison, Wisconsin. 665p. 1972.

Myers, A. T. and B. C. Brunstetter. Spectographic study of nutrients in Tung leaves. Proc. A.S.H.S. 47, 169, 1946.

Nicholas, D. J. D. Rapid chemical test for nutrients in plants. J.H.S. 24, 72, 106, 1948.

Nour, Moshen. Nutritional status of apple orchards in New Mexico. New Mexico Agr. Exp. Sta., Bull. 443, 23 pp, October, 1959.

Nutritional Charts. Eleventh Edition. Pittsburgh, Pa. H. J. Heinz Co., 1942.

Painter, J. H., et al. Nutrients and mulches for Tung trees. Proc. A.S.H.S. 52, 19, 1948.

Pirson, A. Functional aspects in mineral nutrition of green plants. Annl. Rev. Plant Phys. 6, 71, 1955.

Proebsting, E. L. Effect of time of application of nitrogen on size and maturity of stone fruit. Proc. Amer. Soc. Hort. Sci. 46: 178-182. 1945.

Proebsting, E. L. Some effects of long-continued cover cropping in a California orchard. Proc. A.S.H.S. 60, 87, 1952.

Proebsting, E. L. and J. G. Brown. Leaf analysis of differently covercropped deciduous fruit trees. Hilgardia 23, 125, 1954.

Proebsting, E. L. Fertilizers and cover crops for deciduous orchards in California. Univ. of Calif. Agr. Exp. Sta. Cir. 354. 1959.

Potassium in Horticulture — A Symposia. Hort. Sci. 4 (1):33-48. 1969.

Profitable use of poultry manure. Penn. State Univ., Coll. of Agr., Special Ciircular 146. About 1965.

Reed, H. S. Boron deficiency. Hilgardia, 17, 377, 1947.

Reitz, H. J. and W. C. Stiles. Fertilization of high-producing orchards. In Changing Patterns in Fertilizer Use. Soil Sci. Soc. of Amer., Madison, Wis., 53711.

Reuther, W. and F. W. Burrows. Manganese deficiency and photosynthesis in Tung leaves. Proc. A.S.H.S. 40, 73, 1942.

Richer, A. C. and J. W. White. Apple tree soil organic material and nitrogen. Penn. Agr. Exp. Sta. Bull. 483, 101, 1946.

Ries, S. K., H. K. Bell, H. Davidson and R. P. Larsen. Chemical weed control for horticultural crops. Mich. Agr. Ext. Bull. E-433. April 1964.

Roach, W.A. Mineral Nutrition and the rootstock-scion effect. (Appendices on methods of analysis by A.C. Mason and F. H. Vanstone). Rep. E. Mall. Res. Sta., 1946 (1947), 88-94.

Roberts, A. N., and Mellenthin, W. M. Effects of sawdust mulches. Oregon Agr. Exp. Sta., Tech. 50, 34 pp., October, 1959.

Rodney, D. R. Entrance of N compounds through the epidermis of apple leaves. Proc. A.S.H.S. 59, 99, 1952.

Rogers, W. S., et al. Cover crops. Journ. Hort. Sci. 24, 228, 271, 1948.

Roll of Phosphorus in Plant Growth — A Symposia. Hort. Sci. 4 (4):309-324. 1969.

Roos, J.T.H. and W. J. Price. Determination of several major and trace metals in fruit. J. Sci. Fd. Agric., Vol. 21 (1):51-52. 1970. 14 Belgrave Square, London, SW.

Saidak, W. J. and W. M. Rutherford. Tolerance of young apple trees to amitrole, diuron, and simazine. Canadian Jour. Pl. Sci. 43:113-118. April 1963.

Sato, K. Studies on leaf analysis of fruit trees. Japan National Institute of Agr. Sci.. Series E, No. 1-6, 1952-58 (in Japanese with English summary).

Sauchelli, Vincent, Trace elements in Agriculture. Van Nostrand-Reinhold, NYC, 1969. 249 p. Illus.

Sell, H. M., et al. Chemical changes in developing Tung fruits. J. Agr. Res. 73, 319, 1946.

Sequestrene micronutrient chelates — coating on granular fertilizer. Ciba-Geigy Tech. Bull. Ciba-Geigy Corp., Ardsley, N. Y. 10502. 1972.

Serr, E. F. Phosphorus deficiency in walnut on volcanic soils. Calif. Agr. p. 6. June 1960.

Shannon, L. M. Internal bark necrosis of the Delicious apple. Proc. A.S.H.S. 64, 165, 1954.

Shear, C. B. Calcium Deficiency on Leaves and Fruit of 'York Imperial' apple. ASHS Vol. 96, No. 4, July 1971. pp. 415.

Shear, C. B., et al. Nutrient balance and leaf analysis. Proc. A.S.H.S. 51, 319, 1948.

Shibukawa, J. Studies on the sod-mulch system as a method of soil management of the apple orchard. Aomori Apple Exp. Sta., Bull. 5. 1960 (in Japanese with English summary).

Sisler, E. C., et al. Boron in translocation of organic compounds. Plant Phys. 31, 11, 1956.

Sitton, B. G. Nitrogen, phosphorus, and potassium, for bearing Tung trees. Proc. A.S.H.S 52, 25, 1948. Young trees. 54, 22, 1949.

Skoog, F. Zinc and auxin in plant growth. Am. J. Bot. 27, 939, 1940.

Smith, Cyril B. A five-year nutritional survey of Pennsylvania apple, peach, and sour cherry orchards. Penn. Agr. Exp. Sta. Bull. 717. 16 pp. March 1965.

Smith, C. B. Magnesium nutrition of apple trees as affected by a wide range of fertilizer materials. Journ. ASHS (In press; presented by 1968 ann. meeting). 1969.

Smith, P. F. and A. W. Specht. Heavy metal nutrition and iron chlorosis of citrus seedlings. Plant Phys. 28, 371, 1953.

Smock, R. M. and D. Boynton. The effects of differential nitrogen treatments in the orchard on the keeping quality of McIntosh apples. Proc. Amer. Soc. Hort. Sci. 45: 77-86. 1944.

Smock, R. M. Apple fruit respiration off the tree. JAS HS: 97-4. 509-11. 1972.

Southwick, R. W. Pressure injecting nutrient solutions. Proc. A.S.H.S. 46, 27, 1945.

Stebbins R. L. and D. H. Dewey. Transpiration on Ca_{45} in apple. J ASHS:97-4.471-7. 1972.

Spencer, P. and J. S. Titus. Translocation of Glutamate 14C and Aspartate 14C by intact apple trees. ASHS Vol. 96, No. 2, March 1971.

Stahly, E. A. and M. Williams. TIBA-induced pitting of Golden Delicious. Hort. Sci. Vol. 5 (1):45-46. February 1970.

Stevenson, I. L. and F. E. Chase. Nitrification in an orchard soil under three cultural practices. Soil Sci. 76, 107, 1953.

Stewart, I. and C. D. Leonard. Molybdenum deficiency. Proc. A.S.H.S. 62, 111, 1953.

Stiles, W. C. (with H. J. Reitz) Changing patterns in fertilizer use. pp. 353-378. Soil Sci. Soc. Amer., L. B. Nelson (Ed.). 1968.

Storer, T. I. and E. W. Jameson, Jr. Field rodents on California farms. Calif. Ext. Serv. Circ. 535, 50pp. 1965.

Sudds, R. H. and R. S. Marsh. Fall application of nitrogen and winter injury to tree trunks. Proc. A.S.H.S. 42, 293, 1943.

Sudds, R. H., and R. S. Marsh. Calcium cyanamid injury to trees. Proc. A.S.H.S. 43, 25, 1943.

Titus, J. S. and D. Boynton. Soil and leaf analyses in 80 orchards. Proc. A.S.H.S. 61, 6, 1953.

Toenjes, W., R. J. Higlow and A. L. Kenworthy. Soil moisture used by orchard sods. Mich. Agr. Expt. Sta. Article 39-34. 1956.

Toenjes, Walter. The first twenty years' results in a Michigan apple orchard, cultivation cover-crop versus sod-mulch culture. Mich. State Coll. Special Bull. 313. 1941.

Tolhurst, J. and C. Boald. Urea foliar sprays. Annl. Rept. Long Ashton Agr. & Hort. Res. Sta. for 1952, 55.

845

Tsui, C. Zinc and auxin synthesis and water relations. Am. J. Bot. 35, 172, 309, 1948.

Tukey, H. B. The uptake of nutrients by leaves and branches of fruit trees. Rept. Int. Hort. Cong. 13, 297, 1952.

Unrath, C. R. Cooling effects of sprinkler irrigation on Apples. J. ASHS 97(1):55. Jan. 1972. Quality of apples as affected by sprinkler irrigation. J. ASHS 97(1):58. Jan. 1972.

Veihmeyer, F. J. and A. H. Hendrickson. Essentials of irrigation and cultivation of orchards. Calif. Agr. Exp. Sta. Cir. 486. 22 pp. 1960.

Verner, Leif, W. J. Kochan, D. O. Ketchie, A. Kamal, R. W. Braun, J. W. Berry, Jr., and M. E. Johnson. Trunk growth as a guide in orchard irrigation. Idaho Agr. Exp. Sta. Res. Bull. No. 52. 32 pp. October 1962.

Viney, R. Mineral deficiencies in fruit trees. N. Z. J. Agr. 76, 467, 1948.

Wadleigh, C. H. Mineral nutrition in plants. Ann. Rev. Biochem. 18, 655, 1949.

Walker, J. H. Forty years work at East Malling. Rep. E. Malling Res. Sta. for 1953 (1954) 223-7.

Wallace, A., et al. Behavior of chelating agents in plants. Proc. A.S.H.S. 65, 9, 1955.

Wander, I. W. and J. H. Gourley. Effect of heavy mulch in an apple orchard upon several soil constituents and the mineral content of foliage and fruit. Proc. Amer. Soc. Hort. Sci. 42: 1-6. 1943.

Wander, I. W. and J. H. Gourley. Potassium penetration from mulch. Proc. A.S.H.S. 46, 21, 1945.

Weeks, W. D., et al. Soil nutrients 10 years after heavy mulch. Proc. A.S.H.S. 56, 1, 1950.

White, G. C. and R. I. C. Holloway. Grass, cultivation, mulch, herbicide treatment and growth of Cox's orange on M.26. Jour. Hort. Sci. 42: 377-89. 1967.

Wiggans, C. C. Depletion of Subsoil moisture by apples trees and other woody species. Neb. Agr. Exp. Sta. Res. Bull. 216. 32 pp. April 1964.

Wightman, K. et. al. Ca., B. and NAA sprays on cork spot. ASHS 95 (1):23-27. January 1970.

Wilcox, J. C., and C. H. Ferries. A comparison of furrow and sprinkler irrigation in the Okanagan Valley. Canada Dept. of Agr. Publ. 954. Ottawa, Ontario, 1955.

Yamazaki, T., H. Mori, H. Yokomizo and H. Fukuda. Relation of bitter pit to mineral nutrition of apples. Effects of calcium and nitrogen supplies. Bull. of Tohoku Nat. Agr. Exp. Sta. No. 23. Pages 152-196. Jan. 1962.

Yocum, W. W. Root development of young Delicious apple trees as affected by soil and by cultural treatments. Univ. of Neb. Research Bul. 90. 1937.

Flowering, Alternate Bearing (Chap. VI)

Avery, G. S., Jr. and E. B. Johnson. Hormones and Horticulture. New York, McGraw-Hill Book Co., 1947.

Bonner, J. and S. G. Wildman. Auxin in physiology. 6th Growth Symposium. 51. 1947.

Dermen, H. Aposponic parthenogenesis in a triploid apple, *Malus hupehensis*. Journal of Arnold Arboretum *17*: 90-105. 1936.

Edgerton, L. J., and W. J. Greenhalgh. Regulation of growth, flowering and fruit abscission of apples and peaches with Amchem 66-329. Journ. ASHS (In press; presented at 1968 ann. meeting).

Free, J. B. Honey bee efficiency in pollinating apple flowers. J. Hort. Sci. *41*:91-4. 1966.

Free, J. B. Pollination of fruit trees. Bee World. Vol. 41. pp. 141-151 & 169-186. 1960.

Free, J. B., Y. Spencer-Booth. Honey bee foraging on dwarf apple trees. J. Hort. Sci. *39*:78-83. 1964.

Greenhalgh, W. J. and L. J. Edgerton. Interaction of Alar and Gibberellin on growth and flowering of the apple. ASHS 91:9-17. 1967.

Griggs, W. H., et al. Hand-collected and bee-collected pollen storage. Proc. A.S.H.S. 62, 304, 1953.

Guttridge, C. G. GA inhibition on apple fruit bud formation. Nature *196*:4858. p. 1008. Dec. 8, 1962.

Harley, C. P., et al. Cause of Alternate bearing by apple trees. U. S. Dept. Agr. Tech. Bull. 792, 1942.

Hartman, F. O. and F. S. Howlett. Fruit setting of Delicious apple. Ohio Agr. Exp. Sta. Res. Bull. 745, 1954.

Hemphill, D. D. The effects of plant growth-regulating substances on flower bud development and fruit set. Mo. Agr. Exp. Sta. Res. Bul. 434, 1949.

Jaycox, E. R. Evaluating honey bee colonies for pollination. Univ. of Ill. Ag. Ext. Serv. Fruit Growing 20. Revised 1969.

——————. Pollen inserts for apple pollination. Ill. Ag., Fruit Growing 22. Making and using pollen insets. Fruit Growing 23, 1969.

Kremer, J. C. Viability of pollen from bees' pellets. Proc. A.S.H.S. 53, 153, 1949.

Lang, A. The Physiology of flowering. Annl. Rev. Plant Phys. 3, 265, 1952.

Lewis, D. Chemical control of flower formation. J. Pom. and H. S. 22, 175, 1946.

Lewis, D. and L. K. Crowe, Induction of self-fertility. J.H.S. 29, 220, 1954.

Lu, C. S. and R. H. Roberts. Effect of temperature on the setting of Delicious apples. Proc. A.S.H.S. 59, 177, 1952.

Luckwell, L. C. Apple seed hormone that induces tomato parthenocarpy. J.H.S. 24, 19, 32, 1948.

Luckwell, L. C. NAA and fruit set and development. J.H.S. 28, 25, 1953.

Maggs, D. H. Apple tree growth reduction due to fruiting. J. Hort. Sci. 38s 2. p. 119-128. 1963.

Martin, D. and T. L. Lewis. Cells and respiration of light and heavy crop fruit. Aust. J. Sci. Res., Ser. B. Biol. Sci. 5, 315, 1952.

McDaniels, L. H. and A. J. Heinicke. Factors affecting apple fruit set. Cornell Bull. 407. 1930.

Meeuse, B. J. D. The story of pollination. The Ronald Press Co., New York City. 242 pp. 1961.

Modlibowska, I. Apple and pear pollen tube growth. J. Pom. and H. S. 21, 57, 1945.

Modlibowska, I. Regulators and apple fruit setting. East Malling Res. Sta. A 34, 65, 1950.

Murneek, A.E. Growth substance sprays and tomato fruit setting. Proc. A.S.H.S. 50, 254, 1947.

Murneek, A. E. The nature of shedding of immature apples. Mo. Agr. Exp. Sta. Res. Bull. 201. 1933.

Noel, A. R. A. The girdled tree (a review). Bot. Gaz. 36:2. 162-195. 1970.

Pearce, S. C. Statistical techniques in fruit tree research. Biometrice-Praximetrie, 6. 79-92. 1965.

Pearce, S. C. and A. P. Preston. Temperature effects on apple blossom forecasts. Ann. Rpt. E. Malling Res. Sta. p. 133. June 1954.

Percival, Mary S. Floral biology. First edition. Pergamon Press Ltd., London W. 1. 243 pp. 1965.

Preston, A. P. Apple blossom morphology and bee visits. Ann. Rpt. E. Malling Res. Sta. P. 64. 1949.

Preston, A. P. An observation on apple blossom morphology in relation to visits from honey bees (Apis mellifera). Rep. E. Malling Res. Sta. for 1948 (1949) 64-7.

Reece, P. C., et al. Mango flower induction. Am. J. Bot. 36, 734, 1949.

Roberts, R. H. and B. E. Struckmeyer. Notes on pollination with special references to Delicious and Winesap. Proc. A.S.H.S. 51, 54, 1948.

Singh, L. B. Bud rubbing, blossom thinning, and alternate bearing. J.H.S. 24, 159, 1948.

Singh, Sardar. Behavior studies of honeybees in gathering nectar and pollen. Cornell Univ. Agr. Exp. Sta. Ithaca, N. Y. Mem. 288. April 1950.

Singh, S. and D. Boynton.Viability of pollen bees' pellets. Proc. A.S.H.S. 53, 148, 1949.

Snyder, J. C. Commercial hand pollination of apples. Proc. A.S.H.S. 41, 183, 1942.

Struckmeyer. B.E. and R. H. Roberts. Wealthy apple blossom induction. Proc. A.S.H.S. 40, 113, 1942.

Sullivan, D. T. and F. B. Widmoyer. Succinic acid, 2, 2-dimethylhydrazide (Alar) on bloom delay, fruit development, Delicious apples. HortSci. 5(2):91-92. 1970.

Thompson, A. H. and L. P. Batjer. Boron and pollen growth. Proc. A.S.H.S. 56, 227, 1950.

Toenjes, Walter. The effect of trunk girdling on inducing bearing of Northern Spy Apple trees. Mich. Qtrly. Bull. Vol. 32. No. 1. pp. 23-27. Aug. 1949.

Tukey, H. B. and J. O. Young. Development of the apple flower and fruit. Bot. Gaz. 104, 1. Abs. Proc. A.S.H.S. 41, 104, 1942.

Tukey, R.B. et al. Chemical aids to apple tree fruiting. Wash. E.M. 3517. Jan. 1972.

Verheij. I. E. W. M. Competition in apple, as influenced by Alar sprays, fruiting, pruning, tree spacing. Publ. 73. 54 pp. Instituut Voor Tuinbouwtechniek, Wageningen, Holland. 1972.

Vyvyan, M. C. and G. F. Trowell. NAA sprays to reduce June drop in Cox orange. E. Malling Res. Sta. A 34, 111, 1951.

Wildman, S. G. and J. Bonner. Auxin and proteins in leaves. Archives Biochem. 14, 381, 1947.

847

Wildman, S. G. and R. M. Muir. Auxin formation. Plant Phys. 24, 84, 1949.

Williams, Max W. and D. S. Letham. Effect of gibberellins and cytokinins on development of parthenocarpic apples. HortSci. Vol. 4 (3) 215-216. 1969.

Williams, R. R. Hand-pollination studies in fruit trees. Long Ashton Res. Sta. 79, 142-149. 1968; 23-28, 1969.

Zimmerman, Richard H. Flowering in crabapple seedlings: Methods of shortening juvenile phase. J. ASHS 96: (4) p. 404. July 1971.

Fruit Thinning, Growth Regulators (Chap. VII)

Abbot, D. L. The effects of seed removal on the growth of apple fruitlets. Ann. Rept. Long Ashton Res. Sta. 1958: 52-56. 1958.

Audus, L. J. Plant growth substances. Leonard Hill, London, 1953.

Avery, G. S., Jr. and Elizabeth B. Johnson. Hormones and Horticulture. McGraw Hill Co. Inc. New York City, N. Y. 1947.

Bain, J. M. and R. N. Robertson. Cell size and cell number in apple fruit development J. Sci. Res. B: Biol. Sci. 4, 75, 1951

Batjer, L. P. and M. B. Hoffman. Chemical thinning. U. S. Dept. Agr. Cir. 867, 1951.

Batjer, L. P. and A. H. Thompson. 2,4-D sprays and Winesap apple drop. Proc. A.S.H.S. 49, 45, 1947. Also: Transmission of Naphthaleneacetic acid spray effect from leaves to fruit pedicels. Proc. A.S.H.S. 51, 77. Also: Naphthaleneacetic acid vs. 2, 4-D. Proc. A.S.H.S. 51, 71, 1948.

Batjer, L. P. and A. H. Thompson. Chemical fruit thinning. Proc. A.S.H.S. 52, 164, 1948.

Batjer, L. P. and M. N. Westwood. 1-Naphthyl N-methylcarbamate, a new chemical for thinning apples. Proc. Amer. Soc. Hort. Sci. 75 p. 1. 1960.

Blasberg, C. H. Spraying pollen onto apple trees. Proc. A.S.H.S. 58, 23, 1951.

Bonner, J. and R. S. Bandurski. Auxin Physiology. Annl. Rev. Plant Phys. 3, 59, 1952.

Fisher, D. V., et al. Chemical fruit thinning with concentrate spray machines. Proc. A.S.H.S. 61, 144, 1953.

Flory, W. S. and R. C. Moore. Apple blossom thinning with elgetol. Proc. A.S.H.S. 45, 45, 1944.

Gordon, S. A. Occurrence, formation, and inactivation of auxins. Annl. Rev. Plant Phys. 5, 341, 1954.

Gustafson, F. G. Inducement of fruit development by growth-promoting chemicals. Proc. Natl. Acad. Sci. 22: 628-636. 1936.

Gustafson, F. G. The cause of natural parthenocarpy. Amer. Jour. Bot. 26: 135-138. 1939.

Gustafson, F. G. Auxin distribution in fruits and its significance in fruit development. Am. J. Bot. 26: 189-193. 1939.

Harley, C. P., J. R. Magness, M. P. Masure, L. A. Fletcher, and E. S. Degman. Investigations on the cause and control of biennial bearing of apple trees. U.S. Dept. of Agr. Tech. Bull. 792. March, 1942.

Kelley, V. W. NAA and transpiration. Proc. A.S.H.S. 66, 65, 1955.

Leopold, A. C. Auxins and plant growth. UCLA Press, Los Angeles, Calif. 1955.

Longley, R. P. A Study of the Relationship Between the Amount of Bloom and Yield of Apples. Reprinted Canadian Jour. Plant Sci. 40: 52-57, January, 1960.

Luckwell, L. C. The hormone content in relation to endosperm development and fruit drop in the apple. J. Hort. Sci. 24: 32-34. 1948.

Luckwell, L. C., and D. Woodcock. A preliminary investigation into the nature of the hormone produced by developing apple seeds. Ann. Rep. Long Ashton Res. Sta. for 1950: 23-31. 1950.

Luckwell, L. C. Studies of fruit development in relation to plant hormones I. J. Hort. Sci. 28: 14-24. 1953.

Luckwell, L. C. Studies of fruit development in relation to plant hormones. The effect of NAA on fruit set and fruit development in apples. Journ. Hort. Sci. 28: pp. 25-40. 1953

Luckwell, L. C. The auxins of the apple seed and their role in fruit development. Proc. VII Th. Int. Bot. Congr. Paris Sec. 11: 377-379. 1954.

Luckwell, L. C. Parthenocarpy and fruit development in relation to plant regulators. Plant Regulators in Agriculture 81-98. J. Wiley & Sons, Inc. 1954.

Luckwell, L. C. and L. E. Powell, Jr. Absence of Indoleacetic Acid in the apple. Sci. 225-6. 1956.

Luckwell, L. C. Hormonal aspects of fruit development in higher plants. In. Symp. Soc. Exp. Biol. 11: 63-85. 1957.

848

Claypool, L. L. and F. W. Allen. Oxygen supply and fruit respiration. Proc. A.S.H.S. 51, 103, 1948.

Claypool, L. L., et al. Aeration and fruit respiration. Proc. A.S.H.S. 66, 125, 1955.

Comin, D. and S. V. Ting. Harvest maturity and amount of scald in Rome Beauty apples. Proc. A.S.H.S. 57, 95, 1951.

Crandall, P. C. Maleic hydrazide and Delicious storage. Proc. A.S.H.S. 65, 71, 1955.

Dewey, D. H., Raphael, H. J., and Goff, J. W. Polyethylene covers for apples stored in bushel crates on pallets. Article 42-19, Reprinted Mich. Agr. Exp. Sta. Quart. Bull. 42:(1)197-209, August, 1949.

Dilley, D. R., D. C. MacLean and R. R. Dedolph. Aerobic and anaerobic CO_2 production by apple fruits following air and controlled atmosphere storage. ASHS 84:59-64. 1964.

Eaves, C. A. and J. S. Leefe. Orchard nutrition and acidity of Cortland apples. J.H.S. 30, 86, 1955.

Eggert, F. P. Stowage of apples in storage in relation to their cooling. Proc. Amer. Soc. Hort. Sci. 71: 32-35. 1958.

Ezell, B. D. and F. Gerhardt. Respiration and oxidase and catalase activity of apples in relation to maturity and storage. Jour. Agr. Res. 65: 453-471. 1942.

Faust, Miklos, Betty R. Chase and L. M. Massey, Jr. The effect of clonizing radiation and diphenylamine treatment on glucose metabolism and membrane permeability of Cortland apples. ASHS 90:25-32. 1967.

Fidler, J. C. Volatile organic production of metabolism of fruits. Jour. Sci. Food Agr. 6: 293-295. 1955.

Fisher, D. V. and N. E. Looney. Growth, fruiting and storage response of five cultivars of bearing apple trees to N-dimethylaminosuccinamic acid (Alar). ASHS 90:1-19. 1967.

Ford, H. W. and E. K. Alban. The influence of certain wax emulsions on the weight loss and respiration rate of Rome Beauty and Golden Delicious apples. Proc. Amer. Soc. Hort. Sci. 58: 99. 1951.

Francis, F. J., Patricia M. Harney and Pamela C. Bulstrode. Color and pigment changes in the flesh of McIntosh apples after removal from storage. Proc. Amer. Soc. Hort. Sci. 65: 211-113. 1955.

Frenkel, Chaim, Isaac Klein and D. R. Dilley. Protein synthesis in relation to ripening of pome fruits. Pl. Phys. 43:7, 1146-1153. 1968.

Gerhardt, F. and D. F. Almendinger. Naphthaleneacetic acid spray and fruit durability in storage. Jour. Agr. Res. 73, 189, 1946.

Goldstein, J. L. and T. Swain. Changes in tannins in ripening fruits. Phytochemistry. Vol. 2. pp. 371-383. Pergamon Press Ltd., England. 1967.

Griffin, J. H. and Z. I. Kertesz. Ascorbic acid, hydrogen peroxide, and apple softening. Bot. Gaz. 108, 279, 1946.

Griffiths, D. C. and N. A. Potter. Apple volatiles in gas storage. J.H.S. 25, 10, 1949.

Hall, W. C. Ethylene in plant tissue. Bot. Gaz. 113, 55, 1951.

Haller, M. H. and J. M. Lutz, Apple storage losses at 36° F. U. S. Dept. Agr. Tech. Bull. 776, 1941..

Haller, M. H. and Batjer, L. P. Storage quality of apples in relation to soil application of boron. Jour. Agr. Res. 73: 243-253. 1946.

Hansen, E. Ethylene production by apple varieties. Plant Phys. 20, 631, 1945.

Hardenburg, R. E. and H. W. Siegelman. Effect of polyethylene box liners on scald, firmness, weight loss, and decay of stored Eastern apples. Proc. Amer. Soc. Hort. Sc. 69: 75-83. 1957.

Hardenburg, R. E. Polyethylene liners and covers for storage of Golden Delicious apples. ASHS 82:77-82. 1963.

Howe, G. H. and W. B. Robinson. Ascorbic acid in apples. Proc. A.S.H.S. 48, 133, 1946.

Huelin, F. E. and R. A. Gallop. Studies in the natural coatings of apples. Aust. Jour. Sci. Res. B. Biol. Ser. 4, 526 and 533, 1951.

Huelin, F. E. and G. B. Tindale. The gas storage of Victorian apples. J. Dept. Agr. Vict. 45, 74, 1947.

Hulme, A. C. Studies in the nitrogen metabolism of apple fruits. The climacteric rise in respiration in relation to changes in the equilibrium between protein synthesis and breakdown. Jour. Expt. Bot. 5: 159. 1954.

Hulme, A. C. Apple respiration and protein content. J.H.S. 29, 98, 1954.

Hyde, J. F. and M. Ingle. Size of apple bruises as affected by cultivar, maturity and time in storage. ASHS. 92: 733-738. 1968.

Johansson, Jan. Concentrations of volatiles in controlled atmosphere storage and their relation to some storage operations. ASHS 80:137-145. 1962.

Kidd, F. and C. S. Hanes. Hydrogen-ion concentration in apples. Rept. Food Invest. Bd. (Gt. Britain) for year 1936: 133. 1936.

Kidd, F. and C. West. Respiratory activity and duration of life of apples gathered at different stages of development and subsequently maintained at a constant temperature. Plant Physiol. *20*: 467-504. 1945.

Lord, W. J. and F. W. Southwick. Delicious strains and physiological disorders. ASHS *84*:65-71. 1964.

Lord, W. J. and R. A. Damon, Jr. Internal breakdown development in water-cored Delicious apples during storage. ASHS 88: 94-97. 1966.

Lord, W. J., F. W. Southwick and R. A. Damon, Jr. The influence of Alar on flesh firmness and on some pre-and post-harvest physiological disorders of Delicious apples. ASHS 91: 829-832. 1967.

Lott, R. V. Relation of skin color of Golden Delicious apples to quality changes during maturation and ripening. ASHS 86:61-69. 1965.

Lott, R. V. Skin color and quality changes in Golden Delicious apples. ASHS *86*s 61-69. 1965.

Leife, J. S. and C. A. Eaves. The variability of foliar nutrient levels and storage behavior of apples from commercial orchards. ASHS 73:52-56. 1959.

Looney, N. E., *et al.* Factors influencing the level of succinic acid-2, 2-dimethylhydrazide residues in apple fruits. J. ASHS 97 (3):323. May 1972.

Lott, R. V. The levulose, dextrose, and sucrose content of fifteen Illinois apple varieties. Proc. Amer. Soc. Hort. Sci. *43*: 56-58. 1943.

Magness, G. R. and F. L. Overley. Effect of fertilizers on storage qualities of apples. Proc. Amer. Soc. Hort. Sci. *26*: 180-181. 1930.

Mason, Jack. Spartan apple breakdown and calcium spray control. Contact Can. Exp. Sta., Summerland, B. C. 1972.

Mattus, G. E. Bitter pit and similar fruit spots. Virginia Fruit 59 (3): 77-83. 1971.

Mattus, G. E. Extending the sales period for Golden Delicious. Proc. State Hort. Assoc. of Pa. Pa. Fruit News 49 (4): 12-18. 1970.

Mattus, G. E. and G. R. Williams. Apple scald control. Va. Ext. Pub. 313. 1969.

Maxie, E. C. and C. E. Baker. Fruit storage filtration. Proc. A.S.H.S. 64, 235, 1954.

McMahon, M. L. Reducing apple water loss in storage. Proc. A.S.H.S. 50, 31, 1947.

Meigh, D. F. Volatile compounds produced by apples. I. Aldehydes and Ketones. Jour. Sci. Food. Agr. *6*: 396. 1956.

Merritt, R. H., W. C. Stiles, A. Vaughn Havens, and L. A. Mitterling. Effects of preharvest air temperature on storage scald of Stayman apples. ASHS 78:24-34. 1961.

Meyer, A. A study of the skin structure of Golden Delicious apples. Proc. A.S.H.S. 45, 105, 1944.

Millerd, A., et al. The climacteric rise in fruit respiration as controlled by phosphorylative coupling. Plant Phys. 28, 521, 1953.

Murneek. A. E. and S. H. Wittwer. Some factors affecting ascorbic acid content of apples. Proc. Amer. Soc. Hort. Sci. *51*: 97-102. 1948.

Neal, G. E. and A. C. Hulme. The organic acid metabolism of Bramley's seedling apple peel. Jour. Expt. Bot. *9*(25): 142-157. 1958.

Palmer, R. C. Apple bitter pit. Proc. A.S.H.S. 43, 63, 1943.

Pearson, J. A. and R. N. Robertson. The climacteric rise in respiration of fruit. Aust Jour. Sci. 15, 99, 1952.

Pentzer, W. T. and P. H. Heinze. Post-harvest physiology of fruits. Annl. Rev. Plant Phys. 5, 205, 1954.

Pflug, I. J. and D. H. Dewey. A theoretical relationship of the variables affecting the operation of controlled-atmosphere storage rooms. Mich. Agr. Expt. Sta. Quart. Bull. *39*(2): 353-359. 1956.

Phillips, W. R., et al. McIntosh storage behavior at near 32 degrees F. Proc. A.S.H.S. 65, 214, 1955.

Pieniazek, S. A. Nature of the apple skin and rate of water loss. Plant Phys. 19, 529, 1944.

Pierson, C. F., M. J. Ceponis and L. P. McColloch. Market diseases of apples, pears and quinces. U.S.D.A. Agr. Handbook 376. 1971.

Porritt, S. W. O_2 and low CO_2 effects on quality of CA apples. Can. J. Plant Sci. *46*:317-321. 1966.

Reyneke, J. and H. L. Pearse. Oil treatment, respiration, and physical condition of apples and pears. J. Pom. and H. S. 21, 8, 1945.

856

Roberts, E. A. *et al.* CO₂ and O₂ effects on Jonathan apple. Aust. J. Exp. Agi. & Anim. Husb. 5:161-165. 1965.

Schomer, H. A. and P. C. Marth. Growth-substances and apple scald. Bot. Gaz. 107, 284, 1945.

Schomer, H. A. and C. F. Pierson. Waxing apples and pears, Wash. St. Hort. Assn. Proc. 198-200. 1967.

Schomer, H. A. and L. P. McColloch. Ozone in relation to storage of apples. U. S. Dept. Agr. Cir. 765, 1948.

Scott, L. E. and S. Tewfik. Atmospheric changes occurring in film-wrapped packages of vegetables and fruits. Proc. Amer. Soc. Hort. Sci. *49*: 130. 1947.

Seelig, R. A. Apples. United Fresh Fruit and Veg. Assoc. Wash., D.C. 1965.

Shutak, V. G., et al. Role of cutin in storage scald. Proc. A.S.H.S. 61, 228, Mineral oil and scald 233, 1953.

Shutak, V. G. and E. P. Christopher. Role of apple cuticle in development of storage scald on Cortland apples. ASHS 77:106-11. 1960.

Shutak, V. G. and J. T. Kitchin. Effect of time of harvest and apple color on storage scald. ASHS 88: 89-93. 1966.

Shutak, V. G. and J. T. Kitchin. Storage scald, time of harvest and apple color. ASHS *88*:89-93. 1966.

Stegelman, H. W. and H. A. Schomer. Effect of scald on apple skin respiration. Plant Physiol. *29*: 429. 1954.

Sims, E. T., Jr. The influence of Diphenylamine, light and warming on color changes in the skin of apple fruit. ASHS 82:64-67. 1963.

Sinclair, W. B. and D. M. Eny. The organic acids of lemon fruits. Bot. Gaz. *107*: 231-242. 1945.

Smith, T. B. and J. W. Browning. Fresh fruit and vegetable prepackaging. U. S. Dept. Agr. Agr. Mktg. Serv. Market Research Rept. No. 154. 1957.

Smock, R. M. Chemicals for apple red color increase before and after harvest. ASHS *83*:162-171. 1963.

Smock, R. M. and F. W. Southwick. Some factors affecting apple scald disease. Sci. *95*: 576-577. 1942.

Smock, R. M. Influence of controlled-atmosphere storage on respiration of McIntosh apples. Bot. Gaz. *104*: 178. 1942.

Smock ,R. M. and G. D. Blanpied. O₂ reduction rate, temperature, and McIntosh quality. ASHS *83*:135-138. 1963.

Smock, R. M. The influence of stored apples on the ripening of other apples stored with them. N. Y. Agr. Expt. Sta. Bull. 799. 1943.

Smock, R. M. Eliminating ethylene from apple storage rooms. Proc. A.S.H.S. 44, 134, 1944.

Smock, R. M. The physiology of deciduous fruits in storage. Bot. Rev. 10, 560, 1944.

Smock, R. M. and D. Boynton. Nitrogen and keeping of McIntosh apples. Proc. A.S.H.S. 45, 77, 1944.

Smock, R. M. and F. W. Southwick. Studies on storage scald of apples. N. Y. Agr. Expt. Sta. Bull. 813. 1945.

Smock, R. M. Brown core of McIntosh. Proc. A.S.H.S. 47, 67, 1946.

Smock, R. M. Recent advances in controlled atmosphere storage of fruits. HortScience 1 (1): 13-15. 1966.

Smock, R. M. "Spot" of Northern spy. Proc. A.S.H.S. 50, 95, and controlled atmosphere storage for McIntosh. 109, 1947.

Smock, R. M. and C. R. Gross. The effects of some hormone materials on respiration and softening rates of apples. Proc. Amer. Soc. Hort. Sci. *47*: 84-90. 1947.

Smock, R. M. and C. R. Gross. Growth substance sprays and fruit respiration and softening. Proc. A.S.H.S. 49, 67, 1947.

Smock, R. M. and F. W. Southwick. Air purification in apple storage. Cornell Univ. Agr. Exp. Sta. Bull. 843. 1948.

Smock, R. M. Maturity indices for McIntosh. Proc. A.S.H.S. 52, 176, 1948.

Smock, R. M. and C. R. Gross. Studies on respiration of apples. N. Y. Agr. Expt. Sta. Memoir 297. 1950.

Smock, R. M. Climate and apple keeping quality. Proc. A.S.H.S. 62, 272, 1953.

Smock, R. M., et al. Regulators with respiration inhibitors and apple maturity. Proc. A.S.H.S. 63, 211, 1954.

Smock, R. M. Apple volatiles and their significance at storage temperatures. Proc. Amer. Soc. Hort. Sci. *66*: 111-117. 1955.

Smock, R. M. and G. D. Blanpied. A comparison of controlled atmosphere storage and film liners for the storage of apples. Proc. Amer. Soc. Hort. Sci. *71*: 36-44. 1958.

Smock, R. M. and G. D. Blanpied. Effect of modified technique in CA storage of apples. ASHS 87:73-77. 1965.

Smock, R. M. and G. D. Blanpied. Some effects of temperature and rate of oxygen reduction on the quality of controlled atmosphere stored McIntosh apples. ASHS 83:135-138. 1963.

Smock, R. M. and L. Yatsu. Removal of CO_2 from controlled atmosphere storages with water. ASHS 76:-53-60. 1960.

Smock, R. M. and G. D. Blanpied. A comparison of controlled atmosphere storage and film liners for the storage of apples. ASHS 71:36-44. 1958.

Smock, R. M. Laboratory studies on the effects of chemicals on the coloration of apples. Journ. ASHS (In press; presented at 1968 ann. meeting).

Southwick, F. W. Removal of organic emanations from apple store rooms. Jour. Agr. Res. 71, 297, 1945.

Southwick, F. W. Methyl bromide in storage rooms and fruit respiration and softening. Proc. A.S.H.S. 46, 152, 1945.

Southwick, F. W. Methyl A-naphthaleneacetate and fruit ripening. Proc. A.S.H.S. 53, 169, 1949.

Southwick, F. W. and R. M. Smock. Activated carbon for fruit storage air purification. Proc. A.S.H.S. 52, 219, 1948.

Southwick, F. W. Nitrogen level and apple ripening response to 2, 4, 5-Tp. Proc A.S.H.S. 63, 225, 1954.

Teskey, B. J. E. and F. J. Francis. Color changes in skin and flesh of stored McIntosh apples sprayed with 2, 4, 5 Trichlorophenoxypropionic acid. Proc. Amer. Soc. Hort. Sci. *63*: 220-224. 1954.

Thompson, A. H. 2, 4, 5-TP against preharvest drop. Proc. A.S.H.S. 60, 175, 1952.

Thompson, A. R. Volatile products in apples. Aust. Jour. Sci. Res. B. Biol. Sci. 4, 283 and 544, 1951.

Van Doren, A. Physiological studies with McIntosh apples in modified atmosphere cold storages. Proc. Amer. Soc. Hort. Sci. *37*: 453-458. 1940.

Van Doren, A. Air purification trial in a Wenatchee apple storage. Proc. A.S.H.S. 52, 205, 1948; also, 55, 239, 1950.

Van Overbeek, J. Growth regulating substances in plants. Ann. Rev. Biochem. 13, 631, 1944.

U.S.D.A. Agr. Res. Service. A review of literature on harvesting, handling, storage and transportation of apples. U.S.D.A. ARS 51-4. 1965.

West, C. and S. S. Zilva. Synthesis of vitamin C in stored apples. Biochem. Jour. *38*: 105-108. 1944.

Wilcox, J. C. and C. G. Woodbridge. Some effects of excess boron on the storage quality of apples. Sci. Agr. 23, 332, 1943.

Wilkinson, B. G. Some effects of storage under different conditions of humidity on the physical properties of apples. Jour. Hort. Sci. 40:58-65. 1965.

Woolrich, W. R. Handbook of refrigerating engineering. Volume I — Fundamentals, Volume II — Applications. 460 pages and 410 pages respectively. 1965 and 1966.

Workman, M. CA storage of Turley apples. ASHS *83*:126-134. 1963.

Workman, M. and Max E. Patterson. The value of alkaline potassium permanganate air scrubber to reduce volatile levels in apple storage rooms and maintain apple quality. ASHS 74:106-112. 1959.

Workman, Milton. Controlled atmosphere studies on Turley apples. ASHS 83: 126-134. 1963.

Zahradnik, John W., and Southwick, Franklin W. Design details and performance characteristics of a Douglas Fir Plywood CA apple storage. Mass. Agr. Exp. Sta. Bull. 505, 16 pp. August, 1958.

Marketing Tree Fruits, Nutritive Value (Chap. XII)

Brunk, Max E. How the apple industry can strengthen its selling. Cornell University Agr. Econ. Mimeo. Rpt. MB *60*: 24, June, 1960.

Farrell, Harry. The Salinas Valley Power Struggle (Chavez vs growers). San José Mercury Newspaper, San José, Calif. July, 1971.

Frye, R. E. and V. D. Grubbs. Promotion of farm products by Agric. groups, U. S. D. A. — MRR 380. 27 pp. January, 1960.

Marketing agreements for fruits and vegetables. U. S. Dept. Agr. AMS-230. May, 1958.

Milmoe, J. J. Farm roadside marketing in the United States. Del. Ext. Serv., Univ. of Del. 118 pp. 1965.

O'Rourke, Desmond. Challenge of marketing Washington fresh apples in the 70's. Wash. Agr. Exp. Sta. Cir. 538. 23pp. 1971.

Potter, M. T. The vitamin A content of yellow-tissued and white-tissued apples. Jour. Nutrition. *6*: 99. 1933.

Proceedings of the fifteenth National conference of bargaining cooperatives. USDA, Farmer Cooperative Service. Jan. 10-11, 1971. 72pp.

Prospects for foreign trade in fruits, vegetables, tree nuts. USDA For. Agr. Ser. 30 pp. July 1964.

Publications of the transportation and facilities research div. (a reference list) USDA Agr. Res. Ser., Trans. & Fac. Res. Div., Federal Center Bldg., Hyattsville, Md. 20782. (August 1969).

Pujdak, J. S. South American and South African Deciduous Fruit imports. The Blue Anchor, May 1961, p. 7-9.

Redit, W. H. and A. A. Hamer. Protection of rail shipments of fruits and vegetables. USDA Agr. Handbook No. 195. 108 pp. Request recent editions.

Roadside marketing annual conference reports are available from universities of Ohio, New Jersey (Rutgers), Indiana and others.

Rogers, John L. Automatic vending — merchandising, catering. Food Trade Review. 105 pages. 1958.

Shadburne, R. A. Loading methods for truck shipments of apples in fiberboard boxes. USDA Agr. Mkt. Ser. 321. 27 pp. July, 1959.

Shepherd, G. S. and Gene A. Futrell. Marketing farm products, Iowa State Univ. Press, Ames. 510pp. 1970.

Smith, D. L. and D. J. Ricks. Applesauce price relationships. Mich. AER-210. 1972

Stembridge, E. and G. Morell, GA, etc., on shape, set apple. J ASHS:97-4. 464-7. 1972.

Thompson, E. R. and Robert C. Gross. Canned and dried fruits on the London market. USDA For. Agr. Rept. No. 120. 48 pp. Jan., 1962.

Thornton, N. C. Carbon dioxide storage XI. The effect of carbon dioxide on the ascorbic acid (Vitamin C) content of some fruits and vegetables. Proc. Amer. Soc. Hort. Sci. *36*: 200-201. 1938.

Todhunter, E. N. Some factors influencing ascorbic acid (Vitamin C) content of apples. Food Res. *1*: 435. 1936.

Todhunter, E. N. The nutritive value of apples. Wash. Agr. Expt. Sta. Pop. Bull. 152. 1937.

Todhunter, E. N. Further studies on the vitamin A and C content of Washington grown apples. Wash. Agr. Exp. Sta. Bull. 375. 1939.

Ulrey, I. W. Economics of farm products transportation. USDA-MRR-843, 95pp. March 1969.

Valko, L. Co-op. fruit growers association in Washington. Wash. Agr. Exp. Sta. Cir. 316. 17 pp. 1957.

Wagley, H. O., Jr. Deciduous fruit canning in Australia. USDA, FAS M-240. 12pp. 1972.

PEAR (CHAP. XIII)

Ackley, W. B. Water deficits in Bartlett pear leaves. Plant phys. 29, 445, 1954.

Ackley, W. B. Water deficits and pear fruit hard end. Proc. A.S.H.S. 64, 181, 1954.

Aldrich, W. W., et al. Pruning Anjou pear trees. Ore. Agr. Exp. Sta. Bull. 436, 1945.

Allen, F. W. Regulator sprays and pear maturity and breakdown. Proc. A.S.H.S. 62, 279, 1953.

Allen, F. W. and L. L. Claypool. Modified atmosphere storage of Bartlett pears. Proc. A.S.H.S. 52, 192, 1948.

Allen, F. W. and A. E. Davey. Growth substance sprays and pear keeping. Calif. Agr. Exp. Sta. Bull. 692, 1945.

Batjer, L. P. and A. H. Thompson. Boric acid spray and pear fruit set. Proc. A.S.H.S. 53, 141, 1949.

Batjer, L. P. and M. Uota. 2,4,5-TP flower sprays and fruit set of pears and apples. Proc. A.S.H.S. 58, 33, 1951.

Brock, R. D. Pear-apple hybrids. Heredity 8, 421, 1954.

Brown, D. S., W. H. Griggs and B. T. Iwakiri. Effect of winter chilling on Bartlett pear and Jonathan apple trees. California Agriculture, Feb. 1967.

Claypool, L. L. Further studies on controlled atmosphere storage of Bartlett pears. Journ. ASHS (In press. About 1969).

Crandall, O. C., and C. G. Woodbridge. Foliar absorption of boron by Bartlett pears. Journ. ASHS (In press. About 1969).

Crane, M. B. and E. Marks. Pear-apple hybrids. Nature 170, 1017, 1952.

Cropley, R. Decline and death of pear on quince rootstocks caused by virus infection. Journ. Hort. Sci. 42:113-15. 1967.

Degman, E. S. Boron sprays on pears. Proc. A.S.H.S. 62, 167, 1953.

Degman, E. S. and L. P. Batjer. Delayed effects of 2, 4, 5-TP on Anjou pears. Proc. A.S.H.S. 66, 84, 1955.

Fish, V. B., et al. Ascorbic acid in some apple varieties. Proc. A.S.H.S. 44, 196, 1944. Also 43, 73, 1943.

Fisher, D. V. and S. W. Porritt. Some recent studies in late harvesting and delayed cold storage of Bartlett pears. Proc. Amer. Soc. Hort. Sci. 65: 223-230, 1955.

Gerhardt, F. Rates of emanation of volatiles from pears and apples. Proc. A.S.H.S. 64, 248, 1954.

Griggs, W. H., et al. Effect of 2, 4, 5-TP flower spray on fruit set and seed content of some pear varieties. Proc. A.S.H.S. 58, 37, 1951.

Griggs, W. H. and B. T. Iwakiri. Pollination and parthenocarpy in Bartlett pears. Hilgardia 22, 643, 1954.

Hansen, E. Ethylene and pear respiration and ripening. Bot. Gaz. 103, 543, 1942. Also, Proc. A.S.H.S. 43, 69, 1943.

Hansen, E. Effect of 2, 4-D on rate of pear ripening. Plant Phys. 21, 588, 1946.

Hansen, Elmer. Factors affecting post-harvest color development in pears. Proc. Amer. Soc. Hort. Sci. 66: 118-124. 1955.

Hansen, E. Reactions of Anjou pears to carbon dioxide and oxygen content of the storage atmosphere. Proc. Amer. Soc. Hort. Sci. 69: 110-115. 1957.

Harris, R. W. and W. H. Griggs, Copper and streptomycin and russetting of pears. Proc. A.S.H.S. 65, 155, 1955.

Kidd, F. and C. West. Refrigerated gas storage of Conference, Comice, and Bartlett pears. J. Pom. and H. S. 19, 243, 1942.

Marks, G. E. Giant bud sports in pears. J.H.S. 28, 141, 1953.

Mattus, G. E. Bartlett pear respiration and volatile production after storage in air vs. in controlled atmosphere. Proc. A.S.H.S. 55, 199, 1950.

Murneek, A. E. Embryo and endosperm and fruit development. Proc. A.S.H.S. 64, 573, 1954.

Pierson, C. F. and H. A. Schomer. Anjou scald — chemical, non-chemical control. Hort. Sci. 2:(4). Winter 1967.

Proebsting, E. L. Concentration of N, P, K, Ca, and Mg in pear leaves. Proc. A.S.H.S. 61, 27, 1953.

Reimer, F. C. Genetic bud mutation of the pear. J. Hered. 42, 93, 1951.

Ryall, A. L. and D. H. Dewey. 2,4,5-T vs. Ethylene for hastening harvested pear softening. Proc. A.S.H.S. 61, 251, 1953.

Toenjes, W. The response of Bartlett pear trees under sod mulch and clean culture systems of soil management. Mich. Agr. Quar. Bu. Article 37-42.

Toyama, S. and S. Hayashi. Studies on the fruit development of Japanese pears. Jour. of Hort. Assoc. of Japan. Vol. 25 no. 4, pp. 274-282. 1957 (In Japanese with English summary).

Tukey, R. B. et al. Predicting harvest size of Bartlett pears. Wash. Tree Fruit production Series E. M. 3403. June 1970

Wang, C. Y. and E. Hansen. Differential response to ethylene in respiration and ripening of immature Anjou pears. J. ASHS 95(3):3140316. 1970.

Wang, C. et al. Maturation of "Anjou" pears in relation of chemical composition and reaction to ethylene. J. ASHS. 97:1. January 1972. P. 9.

Wang, C. Y. and W. M. Mellenthin. Temperature and premature ripening, pear. J ASHS:97-4. 1972.

Westigard, P. H., M. N. Westwood, and P. B. Lombard. Host preference and resistance of *Pyrus* species to the pear Psylla, *Psylla pryricola Foerster*. J. ASHS. 95:1. 34-36. Jan. 1970.

Westwood, M. N. *et al.* Long-term soil management test of pears in clay soil. Ore. Tech. Bull. 82. 39 pp. 1964.

Westwood, W. N., F. C. Reimer and V. L. Quackenbush. Yield, tree size of pears on five rootstocks (decline noted) ASHS 83: 103-108. 1963.

Westwood, M. N., H. R. Cameron, P. B. Lombard and C. B. Cordy. Effects of trunk and rootstock on decline, growth and performance of pear. J. ASHS 96:2. March 1971.

Westwood, M. N. and J. Grim. Pollenizer placement and pear yields. ASHS 81:103-107. 1962.

Westwood, M. N. and N. E. Chestnut. Rest period of pear and rootstock effects. ASHS 84: 82-87. 1964.

Williams, Max W., H. D. Billingsley and L. P. Batjer. Early season harvest size prediction of "Bartlett" pears. J. ASHS. 94:6. 596-598. Nov. 1969.

Woodbridge, C. G., A Carney, and H. R. McLarty. A boron deficiency in pear growing in soil having an adequate content. Sci. Agr. 32: 440-442. Aug. 1952.

Woodbridge, C. G. Calcium level of pear tissue with cork and black-end. Hort-Sci. vol. 6, No. 5, 1971.

PEACH, APRICOT, ALMOND (CHAP. XIV)

Albrigo, L. G., L. L. Claypool, and K. Uriu. Nitrogen level and apricot fruit maturity. ASHS 89:53-60. 1966.

Baker, G. A. and R. M. Brooks. Effect of almond fruit thinning. Bot. Gaz. 108, 550, 1947.

Benner, Barbara. Peaches — botany to marketing. Fruit & Veg. Facts and Pointers. United Fresh Fruit & Vegetable Assoc. 25 pp. Nov. 1963.

Baumgardner, R. A. et. al. Alar on peach. J ASHS:97-4. 485-88. 1972.

Boyes, W. W. and D. J. R. De Villiers. Prestorage treatment of peaches with acetylene gas. Fmg. in S. Afr. 24, 9, 1949 .

Bradley, M. V. and J. C. Crane, 2,4,5-T and apricot cell and nuclear size. Am. J. Bot. 42, 273, 1955.

Bradt, O. A. Peach breeding at the Hort. Res. Inst. of Ont. 1957-1968. Ontario Dept. of Agric. & Food, 54-60.

Brooks, R. M. Origin of the almond flower. Hilgardia, 13, 249. 1940.

Brown, D. S. Temperature and apricot fruit growth. Proc. A.S.H.S. 62, 173, 1953.

Brown, J. D. and J. C. Elrod. Interregional competition with Georgia peach industry. Ga. Agr. Exp. Sta. Res. Bul. 24, 46 pp. Dec. 1967.

Brown, J. W., et al. Salinity injury in Prunus spp. Proc. A.S.H.S. 61, 49, 1953.

Byers, Ross E., et al. Effect of succinic acid - 2, 2-Dimethylhydrazide (SADH) and other growth regulating chemicals on peach fruit maturation. J. ASHS. 97(3):420. May 1972.

Bullock, R. M., et al. Peach trees and Urea sprays. Proc. 60, 77. 1952.

Bullock, R. M. and N. R. Benson. Boron deficiency in apricots. Proc. A.S.H.S. 51, 19, 1948.

Gambrell, C. E. et al. Comparison of Yunnan, Shalil and S-37 nematode-resistant rootstocks for Dixigem peach trees during 14 seasons. South Car. Exp. Sta. Bull. 534. 8pp. July 1967.

Gambrell, C. E. et al. Response of peaches to Alar as an aid in mechanical harvesting. HortSci. Vol. 92, No. 2. March 1972. p. 265.

Campbell, R. W. Winter injury to peach wood. Proc. A.S.H.S. 52, 117, 1948.

Carlson, R. F. Apricot scion rootstock incompatability in Michigan. Mich. Quart. Bul. 48: No. 1. pp. 23-29. 1965.

Carlson, R. F. and M. Badizadegan. Peach seed germination and growth. Mich. Quart. Bul. 49, No. 3, pp. 276-282. Feb. 1967.

Chaplin, C E. Freezing of peach buds. Proc. A.S.H.S. 52, 121, 1948.

Ginn, J. L. Comparison of shipping packages for peaches. USDA MRR No. 533, 27 pp. 1962.

Claypool, L. L. et al. Horticultural aspects in mechanical peach harvesting. ASHS 86:152, 165. 1965.

Cooper, J. R. Factors that influence production, size, and quality of peaches. Ark. Agr. Expt. Sta. Bul. 547. 1955.

Craft, C. C. Evaluation of maturity indices based on pressure-test readings for Eastern-grown peaches, 1954. USDA AMS-34. 1955.

Crane, J. C. 2,4,5-T increased frost resistance and reduced drop of injured apricots. Proc. A.S.H.S. 64, 225, 1954.

Crane, J. C. 2,4,5-T and frost resistance and survival of apricot fruits. Proc. A.S.H.S. 64, 225, 1954; and size and date of maturity, 65, 75, 1955.

Crane, J. C. and R. M. Brooks. 2,4,5-T and growth of apricot fruits. Proc. A.S.H.S. 59, 218, 1952.

Cummings, G. A. and W. E. Ballinger. Influence of longtime nitrogen, pruning and irrigation treatments upon yield, growth and longevity of 'Elberta' and 'Redhaven' peach trees. HortScience. Vol. 7, No. 2, April 1972, p. 133.

Davis, L. D. and M. M. Davis. Size in canning peaches. Proc. A.S.H.S. 51, 225, 1948.

Day, L. H. and E. F. Serr. Deciduous orchard rootstocks and meadow nematodes. Proc. A.S.H.S. 57, 150, 1951.

Dewey, D. H. and W. T. Pentzer. Ultra-violet light against stone-fruit rots. Proc. A.S.H.S. 53, 181, 1949.

Dorsey, M. J. and R. L. McMunn. Tree-conditioning the peach crop. Ill. Agr. Exp. Sta. Bull. 507, 1944.

Edgerton, L. J. Fluctuations in cold resistance of peach flower buds. Proc. A.S.H.S. 64, 175, 1954.

Edgerton, L. J. and M. B. Hoffman. Early chemical thinning and cold resistance of peach flower buds. Proc. A.S.H.S. 60, 155, 1952.

Fisher, D. V. Time of blossom bud induction in apricots. Proc. A.S.H.S. 58, 19, 1951.

Fogle, H. W. Winter hardiness of apricot variety crosses. Proc. Wash. State Hort. Soc. 46, 19, 1950.

Ford, H. W. and W. P. Judkins. N supply to peach trees and respiration and maturity of the fruit. Proc. A.S.H.S. 57, 73, 1951.

Frear, D. E. H., et al. Potassium in parts of peach trees. Proc. A.S.H.S. 52, 61, 1948.

Gilmore, A. E. Pot experiments related to the peach replant problem. Hilgardia 34, No. 3, pp. 63-78. March 1963.

Gleason, B. L. and F. L. O'Rourke. Tests of peach rootstocks. American Nurseryman 96 (5), 10; see also 96 (4), 30, 1952.

Griggs, W. H. Almond blossoms and frost. Proc. A.S.H.S. 53, 125, 1949.

Hale, P. W. and E. D. Mallison. Shipping containers for eastern peaches. USDA MRR 737, 11 pp. 1966.

Haller, M. H. and P. L. Harding. Effect of storage temperatures on peaches. U. S. Dept. Agr. Tech. Bull. 680, 1939.

Hansen, C. J. Boron toxicity and rootstocks. Proc. A.S.H.S. 51, 239, 1948.

Hansen, C. J. Peach and almond rootstocks and boron injury. Proc. A.S.H. 65, 128, 1955.

Harris, R. W. and D. Boynton. Control of available nitrogen for yield and quality of New York peaches. Proc. A.S.H.S. 59, 36, 1952.

Havis, L. Studies in peach thinning. Proc. A.S.H.S. 49, 55, 1947.

Havis, L., Pruning peach trees at different periods in Spring. Proc. A.S.H.S. 58, 14, 1951.

Havis, L. and F. P. Cullinan. Peach cover crop trials. Proc. A.S.H.S. 48, 27, 1946.

Havis, L. and A. L. Gilkeson. N, K, and pruning and fruiting of peach trees. Proc. A.S.H.S. 57, 24, 1951.

Hayward, H. E., et al. Chloride and sulphate salts and peach trees. U. S. Dept. Agr. Tech. Bull. 922, 1946.

Helton, A. W. and S. H. S. Fenwick. Coryneum blight of stone fruit trees. Idaho Ext. Serv. Bull. 365, 11 pp. 1961.

Hendrickson, A. H. and F. J. Veihmeyer. Use of water by almond trees. Proc. A.S.H.S. 65, 133, 1955.

Hendershott, C. H. and L. F. Bailey. Growth inhibitor in dormant peach flower buds. Proc. A.S.H.S. 65, 85, 1955.

Hesse, C. O. and A. E. Davey. Sprays against fruit drop in apricots and peaches. Proc. A.S.H.S. 40, 55, 1942.

Hesse, C. O. Apricot culture in California. Calif. Agr. Exp. Sta. Cir. 412. 57 pp. Request recent edition.

Hesse, C. O. and D. E. Kester. Germination of prunus sp. embryos. Proc. A.S.H.S. 65, 251, 1955.

Hibbard, A. D. Peach pruning trials. Proc. A.S.H.S. 52, 131, 1948.

Hibbard, A. D. and A. E. Murneek. Thinning peaches with hormone sprays. Proc. A.S.H.S. 56, 65, 1950.

Higdon, R. J. 2,4,5-T and development and ripening of peaches. Proc. A.S.H.S. 58, 73, 151.

Hill, Robert G., Jr. Sod effects on growth and yield of peach. Ohio Ag. Exp. Sta. Bul. 903, 35 pp. 1962.

Hirano, S. Studies on peach sick soil. Jour. of Hort. Assoc. of Japan. Vol 26 no. 4, pp. 53-58. 1957   (In Japanese with English Summary).

Inoue, H. and M. J. Bukovac. Peach fruit deformation induced with 2-(n-chlorophenoxy)-propionamide. J. ASHS. Vol. 96, No. 6. November 1971. p. 728.

Jeffrey, C. W. Dinitro-cresol against delayed bud break. Dept. Agr. S. Afr. Sci. Bull. 325, 1951.

862

Jensen, R. E., E. F. Savage and R. A. Hayden. Effect of certain environmental factors on cambium temperatures of peach trees. J. ASHS 95(3).286-292. 1970.

Johnston, Stanley and R. Paul Larsen, Peach culture in Michigan. Mich. Agr. Ext. Bul. 509, 1965. (One of the best bulletins.)

Jones, R. W. Selection of incompatible almond and root knot, nematode resistant peach rootstock as parents for production of hybrid rootstock seed. J. ASHS 94:289-91. March 1969.

Kamali, Abdul R., and Norman F. Childers. Growth and fruiting of peach in sand culture as affected by boron and a fritted form of trace elements. J. ASHS 95(5):-652-656. 1970.

Kelley, V. W. Time for NAA spray in peach thinning. Proc. A.S.H.S. 66, 70, 1955.

Kester, D. E. and C. O. Hesse. Peach embryo culture. Proc. A.S.H.S. 65, 265, 1955.

Koch, L. W. The peach replant problem in Ontario. I. Symptomology and distribution. Canadian Journ. of Bot. 33: 450-460. 1955.

Kochba, J. and R. M. Samish. Effect of growth inhibitors on root-knot nematodes in peach roots. J. ASHS Vol. 92, No. 2. March 1972. p. 178.

Kochba, J. and R. M. Samish. Level of endogenous cytokinins and auxin in roots of nematode-resistant and susceptible peach rootstocks. J. ASHS Vol. 97, No. 1. Jan. 1972. p. 115.

Lasheen, Aly M. and Carl E. Chaplin. Biochemical comparison of seasonal variations in three peach cultivars differing in cold hardiness. J. ASHS. 95(2):177-181. 1970.

Lee, Y. N. and P. S. Luh. CPA residues in canned apricots and grapes. Jour. Food Sci. 33, pp. 104-108. 1968.

Lesley, J. W. and J. Bonner. Seeds of early maturing peach varieties. Proc. A.S.H.S. 60, 238, 1952.

Lott, R. V. Peach fruit growth. Ill. Agr. Exp. Sta Bull. 493, 1942.

Martin, George C. and M. Nelson. Peach thinning with ethylene. HortSci. Vol. 4(4):328-29. 1969.

Martin, George C. and M. Nelson. The thinning effect of 3-chlorophenoxy-a-propionamide (3-CPA) in Paloro peach. Hort-Sci. Vol. 4(3):206-208. 1969.

Marth, P. C., et al. 2,4,5-T and peaches. Proc. A.S.H.S. 55, 152, 1950.

Marth, P. C., L. Havis, and V. E. Prince. Effects of growth regulating substances on development and ripening of peaches. Proc. Amer. Soc. Hort. Sci. 55: 152-158. 1950.

Maximos, S. E., L. E. Scott. Na and K nutrition of the peach. Proc. A.S.H.S. 64, 71, 1954.

McClintock, J. A. Peach on Marianna plum roots. J. Agr. Res. 77, 253, 1948.

McClung, A. C. Magnesium deficiency in peach orchards. Proc. A.S.H.S. 62, 123, 1953.

Morris, J. R. et al. Peach production in Arkansas. 48 pp. Cir. 449 (Rev.) 1967.

Mort, C. H. Almonds in New South Wales. Agr. Gaz. N. S. W. 60, 246, 1949.

Norton, R. A. and N. F. Childers. Urea sprays on peach trees. Proc. A.S.H.S. 63, 23, 1954.

National Peach Council, monthly "It's Peach Time, U.S.A." This up-to-date report covers pertinent talks at annual meetings and current developments in the peach business. Distributed to Council Members, P.O. Box 1085, Martinsburg, W. Va. 25401.

Norton, R. A. et al. Peach and nectarine rootstocks. Calif. Ag. Ext. Serv. Leaflet 157. 1963.

O'Reilly, H. J., Armillaria root rot of fruit plants. Calif. Ag. Exp. Sta. Cir. 525, 15 pp. 1963.

Overcash, J. P. and J. A. Campbell. Daily warm periods and total chilling-hour requirements to break the rest in peach twig. Proc. A.S.H.S. 66, 87, 1955.

Overcash, J. P. et al. Peach fertilizer and pruning experiments. Miss. Ag. Exp. Sta. Bul. 596, 23 pp. May 1960.

Parker, K. G. et al. Combating replant problems in orchards. Cornell Univ. Bul. 1169. 19 pp. 1966.

Parker, K. G. et al. X-disease of peach and cherry and control. Cornell Ext. Bul. 1100, 12 pp. 1963.

Parker, K. G. Verticillum wilt of stone fruit trees, control. Cornell Ext. Bul. 1072, 8 pp. 1961.

Patrick, Z. A. Toxic products of peach root decomposition. Canad. J. Bot. 33, 4161, 1955.

Peach packing equipment. FMC Corp. Woodstock, Va.

863

Peach production costs, Pennsylvania — 1959-63. Pa. Farm Manage. Mimeo. 19, 20 pp. 1964.

Pest and disease control program for peaches and nectarines (issued each year) Calif. Ag. Exp. Sta. Bul. 20 pp. Check your local experiment station.

Prince, V. E. and B. D. Horton. Influence of pruning at various dates on peach tree mortality. J. ASHS. 97(3):303. May 1972.

Proebsting, E. L. Distribution of nitrogen in peach trees. Proc. A.S.H.S. 49, 15, 1947.

Proebsting, E. L., Jr. Yield, growth, and date of maturity of Elberta peaches as influenced by soil management systems. Proc. A.S.H.S. 72: 92-101. 1958.

Proebsting, E. L., Jr. and H. H. Mills. Standardized temperature-survival curve for dormant Elberta peach fruit buds. ASHS 89:85-90. 1968

Raese, J. T. A further report on blossom delay of tung trees with alar in spray oil. HortSci. Vol. 6, No. 6. December 1971. p. 543.

Reed, A. D. Almond production costs in California. Calif. Ext. Serv. Mimeo. M-24, Feb. 1968.

Redit, W. A., M. A. Smith, and P. L. Benfield. Tests in hydrocooling and refrigeration of peaches in transit from Georgia and South Carolina, 1954. U. S. Dept. of Agr. AMS-62: 24 pp. July 1955.

Reeves, John and George Cummings. The influence of some nutritional and management factors upon certain physical attributes of peach quality. J. ASHS. 95(3):338-341. 1970.

Ritter, C. M. Peach nutrition and cultural methods. pp. 3, 4, 5, 16-19. Hort. News (New Brunswick, N. J.) Jan. 1968.

Ritzert, R. W. et al. Indole-3-Acetic Acid oxidase activity from developing peach seeds and its inhibition by extractable catechin. J. ASHS, 97(1). Jan. 1972. p. 48.

Rogers, B. L. Peach irrigation studies. Md. Ag. Exp. Sta. Bul. A-148, 29 pp. 1967.

Rogers, Ewell. Mineral content of peach trees as affected by nitrogen source and rate. J. ASHS. 94(4):352-353, 1969. Effects of N sources on peach. Colo. Tech. Bull. 116. 1971. Iron Chelates on peach; iron-induced Mn deficiency; Colo. Prog. Rpts. 72-8, Jan. 1972, 71-25, 72-11, 72-2.

Rom, R. C. and E. H. Arrington. Peach variety evaluation for Arkansas. 22 pp, Ark. Agr. Exp. Sta. Rpt. Series 122. 1963.

Rood, Paul. Development and evaluation of objective maturity indices for California freestone peaches. Proc. Amer. Soc. Hort. Sci. 70: 104-112. 1957.

Ross, N. W. and A. D. Rizzi. Thinning, irrigating, varieties, sites and establishing cling peach orchards. Mimeo. Pubs. AXT-44,-16-5, 38,-15, 1961-66.

Ryugo, Kay and L. D. Davis. Seasonal changes in acid content of fruits and leaves of selected peach and nectarine clones. Proc. Amer. Soc. Hort. Sci. 72: 106-112. 1958.

Savage, E. F. et al. Pruning of Elberta and effect on growth and yield. Ga. Ag. Exp. Sta. Bul. NS 127. 11 pp. 1964.

Savage, E. F. Root rot of peaches. Amer Fruit Grower. pp. 16, 42, 43. April 1953.

Scott, D. H. and F. P. Cullinan. Freezing peach buds. J. Agr. Res. 73, 207, 1946.

Serr, E. F. and L. H. Day. Lesion Nematodes. Proc. A.S.H.S. 53, 134, 1949.

Serr, E. F. and H. I. Forde. Sprays to control preharvest drop of Peerless almonds Proc. A.S.H.S. 60, 193, 1952.

Sharpe, R. H. and C. O. Hesse, B. F. Lownsberry and C. J. Hansen. Breeding peaches for root-knot nematode resistance. Journ. ASHS (In press) About 1969.

Sharpe, R. H. Peaches and nectarines in Florida. Fla. Ag. Exp. Sta. Cir. 299, 19 pp. 1966.

Shoemaker, J. S. Experiments on thinning peaches. Ohio Agric. Exp. Sta. Bul. 541. 1934.

Snyder, John C., D. H. Brannon, and M. K. Harris. Picking peaches for profit. (Color plates showing proper maturity) Wash. Ext. Bull. 393. 12 pp. 1949.

Sherman, W. B., D. W. Buchanan and J. B. Aitken. Endosperm development in 'Maygold' peach. HortSci. Vol. 5 (1):41. Feb. 1970.

Sims, E. T., Jr., C. E. Gambrell, Jr. and J. T. McClary, Jr. Alar on Peach Quality. J. ASHS. 96(4):527. July 1971.

Snapp, O. I. Insect pests of the peach east of the Rocky Mountains. USDA Ag. Inf. Bul. 272. 32 pp. 1963.

Springer, J. K., L. A. Miller and L. D. DeBlois. Bacterial spot survey-variety susceptibility. HortNews, N. J. State Hort., New Brunswick, N. J. 08903. Jan. 1970.

Stahly, E. A. and A. H. Thompson, Auxin levels of developing Halehaven peach ovules. Maryland Agr. Expt. Sta. Bul. A-104. 1959.

Stembridge, G. E. and C. E. Gambrell, Jr. Thinning peaches with 3-chlorophenoxy-a-propionamide. J. ASHS. Vol. 94, No. 6. p. 570-573. Nov. 1969.

Taylor, B. K. and L. G. Isbell. Superphosphate effects on newly planted peach trees. J. ASHS 46:3, 251-261. July 1971.

The Fruit Situation. U. S. Dept. of Agr.—AMS Reports issued monthly. Washington 25, D. C. This covers important commercial deciduous fruits, including the peach.

Thomas, W. H. et al. Bulk shipping containers for peaches. S. Car. Agr. Exp. St. Bul. 486, 15 pp. July 1960.

Trieb, Dr. S. E. (Cy). Part I. Structure, trends and consumption projections to 1980. U. S. Peach Industry. U. S. Dept. of Agr. Econ. Rpt. No. 200 March 1971. (Part II also available).

Tufts, W. P. and R. H. Harris. Pruning deciduous fruit trees. Calif. Agr. Exp. Sta. Cir. 444. 47 pp. 1955.

Tufts, Warren P. Interesting facts about apricots. Blue Anchor 12-14, May, 1960.

Tukey, H. B. Growth pattern of plants developed from immature embryos in artificial culture. Bot. Gaz. 99: 630-665. 1938.

Tukey, H. B.. and R. F. Carlson. Abnormal peach seedlings and seed after-ripening. Proc. A.S.H.S. 46, 203, 1945.

Tukey, H. B. and R. F. Carlson. Breaking the dormancy of peach seed by treatment with thiourea Plant Phys. 20, 505, 1945.

Tukey, L. D. Periodicity in growth of apple, peach and sour cherry fruits. Pa. Agr. Exp. Sta. Bul. 661, 21 pp. 1959.

Tunsuwan, Tragool, and H. H. Bowen. Effects of alternating 40°F with higher temperatures on satisfying the chilling requirements of peach trees. Journ. ASHS (In press) About 1969.

United States standards for peaches (1952), Fresh peaches for freezing or pulping (1946), fresh freestone peaches for canning (1946), nectarines (1958), apricots (1958) U. S. Dept. of Agr. AMS, Washington 25, D. C. (Request recent edition).

Wadsworth, J. I., et al. Flaking process could protect profits on rejected peaches. Canner-Packer, October 1966.

Wahtley, James A. New developments in processing peaches and competition in processing peaches (plus other crops). ARS-U. S. Dept. of Agri. 72-82. December 1970. Conference held at New Orleans, La. March 16-17, 1970.

Weinberger, J. H. Temperature and breaking of rest in peach flower buds in Calif. ASHS 91:84-89. 1967.

Weinberger, J. H. Temperature and peach fruit development. Proc. A.S.H.S. 51, 175, 1948.

Weinberger, J. H. 2,4,5-T and peach ripening. Proc. A.S.H.S. 57, 15, 1951.

Weinberger, J. H. 2,4,5-T sprays and ripening of peaches. Proc. A.S.H.S. 57, 115, 1951.

Weinberger, J. H. Winter injury to peach trees on Yunnan stock. Plant Disease Reptr. 36, 307, 1952.

Weinberger, J. H., et al. Urea spray on peach leaves. Proc. A.S.H.S. 53, 26, 1949.

Wise, K. O. and J. C. Thompson. Guide for a peach packing cooperative. Ga. Ag. Exp. Sta. Bul. NS 89, 34 pp. 1962.

Wittiver, S. H. and A. D. Hibbard. Nitrogen and vitamin C in peaches. Proc. A.S.H.S. 49, 116, 1947.

Woodroof, J. G. et al. Popular drink from surplus peaches. Canner-Packer. May 1965.

Woodroof, J. G. et al. Preparation of peaches for freezing. Ga. Exp. Sta. Bull. 251. 70 pp. 1947.

Van Blaricom, L. O. The effect on decay of adding various reagents to the water for hydrocooling peaches. South Carolina Agr. Exp. Sta., Cir. 124, July, 1959.

Zielinski, Q. Ascorbic acid in thirty-three peach varieties. Proc. A.S.H.S. 52, 143, 1948.

Zielinski, Q. B. et al. Peach varieties for Oregon. Ore. Ag. Exp. Sta. Bul. 589, 30 pp. 1963.

Apricot & Almond

Almond Industries of Italy and Spain. U. S. Dept. of Agr. Foreign Agr. Serv. FAS-M 228. May 1971.

Anstey, T. H. Predicting bloom date of apple, pear, cherry, peach, apricot from air temperature data. ASHS 88:57-66. 1966.

Bryan, H. C. Almonds in Spain. USDA — FAS — M - 165, 19 pp. 1965.

Crane, Julian C., and M. M. Nelson. Apricot fruit growth and abscission as affected by Maleic hydrazide-induced seed abortion. J. ASHS 95(3):302-306. 1970.

865

Crane, J. C. and K. Uriu. Effect of irrigation on response of apricot fruits to 2, 4-5-L application. ASHS 86:88-94. 1965.

English, W. H. *et al.* Apricot dieback — Cytosporina. Calif. Ag. Ext. Leaflet 165, Oct. 1963.

Foytik, J. Apricot industry in California. Calif. Ag. Ext. Serv. Cir. 495, 29 pp. 1961.

Johnston, S. *et al.* Apricot growing in Michigan. Mich. Ag. Ext. Serv. Bul. 533, 9 pp. 1966.

Kester, D. E. Almond orchards — combination plantings. Calif. Ag. Ext. Serv. Leaflet 150. Oct. 1962.

Kester, D. E. Almond varieties for California. Calif. Ag. Ext. Serv. Leaflet 152. 1963.

Kester, Dale E. Non-infections bud-failure in almond, a nontransmissible inherited disorder. III. Variability if BF potential within plants. J. ASHS 95(2):162-165. 1970.

Madsen, H. F. and L. B. McNelly. Apricot pests. Calif. Ag. Exp. Sta. Bul. 783. 40 pp. 1961.

Meith, C. and A. D. Rizzi. Establishing the almond orchard — Part 1. Care of almond orchard — Part 2. Calif. Ext. Serv. Mimeo. AXT-29,-83 (Butte County) 1965, 1966.

Meith, C. and A. D. Rizzi. Chemical strip weed control in almond orchards. Univ. of Calif. Ag. Ext. Ser. Pub. AXT-164. 1964.

Norton, R. A. *et al.* Apricot rootstocks in California. Calif. Ag. Ext. Leaflet 156. March 1963.

Pons Canals, D. Antonio y D. B. Simonet Salas. Planificacion del cultivo del Almendro. 60pp. Jefatura Agronomica de Baleares. Palma de Mallorca. (Bolletin buena). 1970.

Ramsay, Juan and George C. Martin. Isolation and identification of a growth inhibitor in spur buds of apricot. J. ASHS 95(5):574-577. 1970.

Ramsay, Juan and George C. Martin. Seasonal changes in growth promoters and inhibitors in buds of apricot. J. ASHS 95(5):569-570. 1970.

Ramsay, Juan, George C. Martin and Dillon S. Brown. Determination of the time of onset of rest in spur and shoot buds of apricot. HortSci. Vol. 5, No. 4. August 1970. p. 270.

Spiegel, P. *et al.* Performance and moisture use of apricot trees under runoff farming. J. ASHS Vol. 96, No. 6. November 1971. p. 696.

Summers, F. M. Insect and mite pests of almonds. Calif. Ag. Ext. Serv. Cir. 513, 16 pp. 1966.

Uriu, K., G. E. Martin, and Robert M. Hagan. Radial trunk growth of almonds by 2, 4-D. J. ASHS 94(4):370-372. 1969.

Uriu, K., G. E. Martin, and Robert M. Hagan. Radial trunk growth of almonds as affected by soil water and crop density. J. ASHS 95(2):166-169. 1970.

Wankier, B. N., D. K. Salunkhe, and W. F. Campbell. Effects of controlled atmosphere storage on biochemical changes in apricot and peach fruit. J. ASHS. 95(5):604-609. 1970.

Weinberger, J. W. Growing apricots. USDA. Home & Garden Bull. 1971.

General

Guillou, Rene. Coolers for fruits and vegetables, Calif. Ag. Exp. Sta. Bull. 773, 66 pp. 1960.

Madson, B. A. Winter cover crops. Calif. Ag. Exp. Serv. Circ. 174. 23 pp. 1951.

Proceedings of XVII International Horticultural Congress, Volume 4 (contains papers on world production practices of fruits). Meetings held at Beltsville, Md., USA, 1966.

Proebsting, E. L., Sr. Fertilizers and cover crops for California orchards. Calif. Ag. Ext. Serv. Circ. 466, 19 pp. 1958.

PLUMS (CHAP. XV)

Bailey, J. S. The Beach plum in Massachusetts. Mass. Agr. Exp. Sta. Bull. 422, 1944.

Bowman, F. T. Sugar prune fruit removal and tree composition. J. Pom. and H. S. 19, 34, 1941.

Boyes, W. W., et al. Storage tests with plums. Fmg. S. Afr. 27, 299, 1952.

Brierley, W. G. and J. S. McCartney. Cold resistance of European plums. Proc. A.S.H.S. 55, 254, 1950.

Cain, J. C. and D. Boynton. Nutrients and a leaf mottle and fruit drop on Italian prune trees. Proc. A.S.H.S. 59, 53, 1952.

Claypool, L. L. and F. W. Allen. The influence of temperature and oxygen level on the respiration and ripening of Wickson plums. Hilgardia *21*: 129-160. 1951.

de Goede, Cornelis. The dried prune industry of Australia. USDA FAS-M-97. Oct. 1960.

Gaston, H. P., S. L. Hedden and J. H. Levin. Mechanizing the Harvest of Plums. Mich. Agr. Expt. Sta. Quarterly Bul. Vol. *42*: No. 4. 779-783. 1960.

Gerdts, M., *et al.* Mechanical and chemical thinning of shipping fruits. Blue Anchor. March 1969. p. 7-10.

Griggs, W. H. and C. O. Hesse. Pollination requirements of Japanese plums. Calif. Leaflet 163, 9 pp. 1963.

Hansen, C. J. and E. L. Proebsting. Boron requirements of plums. Proc. A.S.H.S. 53, 13, 1949.

Harris, R. W. and C. J. Hansen. 2,4,5-T and prune growth and maturity. Proc. A.S.H.S. 66, 73, 1955.

Helton, A. W. Cytospora canker of prunes. Univ. of Idaho Agr. Exp. Sta. Bull. 254: 12 pp. 1956.

Hendrickson, A. H. and F. J. Veihmeyer. Irrigation experiments with prunes. Calif. Agr. Exp. Sta. Bull. 573. 1934.

Herrero, J. Incompatibility between stock and scion. I. The behavior of some reciprocal graft combinations. An Aula Dei (Zaragoza) 4: (1-2) 149-166. 1955.

Hesse, C. O. and Claypool, L. L. Some promising plums. Blue Anchor, 15, 16, 40, May, 1960.

Kochan, Walter J., Leif Verner, Abdul Kamal and Ronald Braun. Control of fruit-dropping in Italian prunes by foliar sprays of 2, 4, 5-TP. Idaho Agr. Exp. Sta. Bull. 378. March 1962.

Lee, Frank A., *et al.* New York State dried prunes. N. Y. State Ag. Exp. Sta., Cornell Univ., Geneva. Cir. II. July 1968.

Lilleland, O., and J. N. Fiske. Spray thinning prunes. Western Fruit Grower. April, 1951. p. 25.

Lin, C. F. and A. A. Boe. Effects of some endogenous and exogenous growth regulators on plum seed dormancy. J. ASHS. Vol. 97, No. 1. Jan. 1972. p. 41.

Lyon, T. L., A. J. Heinicke, and B. D. Wilson. The relation of soil moisture and nitrates to the effects of sod on plum and cherry trees. Cornell Univ. Agr. Exp. Sta. Mem. 91. 1925.

Maxie, E. C., Betty J. Robinson and P. B. Catlin. Effects of various oxygen concentrations on the respiration of Wickson plum fruit and fruit tissues. Proc. Amer. Soc. Hort. Sci. *71*: 145-156. 1958.

Mitchell, F. G., *et al.* Tight-fill fruit packing. Div. of Ag. Sci., Univ. of Calif., Cir. 548. Dec. 1968.

Mosse, B., and R. J. Garner. Growth and structural changes induced in plum by an additional scion. J.H.S. 29, 12, 1954.

Nehr, Stanley. The Yugoslav dried prune industry. U. S. Dept. of Agr. FAS Rpt. 86. 19 pp. August 1955.

Norton, R. A. *et al.* Rootstocks for plums and prunes in California. Calif. Leaflet 158, March 1963.

Overcash, J. P. Heat units required for plum varieties to bloom. Miss. Inf. Sheet 759, April 1962.

Pest and disease control program for plums and prunes. Div. of Ag. Sci., Univ. of Calif. January 1972.

Phillips, E. L. and George D. Oberle. Plums for Virginia. Virginia Coop. Ext. Serv., VPI, Blacksburg 24061. Cir. 784. Nov. 1966.

Posnette, A. F. and C. E. Ellenberger. The line-pattern virus disease of plums. Ann. Applied Bot. *45*: No. 1, 74- 80. March 1957.

Proebsting, E. L., Jr., and Harlan H. Mills. Effects of 2-chloroethane phosphonic acid and its interaction with gibberellic acid on quality of 'Early Italian' prunes. J. ASHS 94(4):443-446. 1969.

Roberts, A. N. and L. A. Hammers. Pacific plum. Oregon Agr. Exp. Sta. Bull. 502. 1951.

Roberts, A. N. and L. A. Hammers. The native Pacific plum in Oregon. Ore. Sta. Bul. 502, 22 pp. 1951.

Roberts, Kim O. *et al.* Prune maturity tests for harvest timing. Ag. Ext. Serv., Univ. of Calif. July 1965.

Smith, W. H. Some observations on ripening of plums by ethylene. J. Pom. and Hort. Sci. 21, 53, 1945.

867

Smith, W. H. Storage of Victoria plums. J. Pom. and Hort. Sci. 23, 92, 1947.

Southwick, L. and A. P. French. The identification of plum varieties from nonbearing trees. Mass. Agr. Exp. Sta. Bull. 413. 1944.

Slate, G. L. Plum growing. Cornell Ext. Bull. 1010. 15 pp. April 1958.

Symposium on plums in Yugoslavia. (Culture, economics, pests, storage processing). 303 pp. (summaries in English). Inst. for Fruit Growing. Cacak, Yugoslavia. 1968.

Swanson, J. P. et al. Production costs of cherries, peaches, pears and plums. Wash Sta. Circ. 452, 28 pp. Request recent data. Also, contact Univ. of Calif., Davis.

Tanaka, Hirosato and M. W. Miller. Microbial spoilage of dried prunes — yeasts, molds, osmophilic, nature and relative humidity relationships. Hilgardia 34:6, 167-190. 1963.

Tehrani, G., and D. R. Logan. Propagation of six plum rootstocks by basal heating of hardwood cuttings. Hort. Res. Inst. of Ontario. Rpt. for 1969. p. 27-36.

Thompson, M. M. and L. J. Liu, Pollination - alt. bearing, prune. J ASHS:97-4. 489-91. 1972.

Truscott, J. H. L. and Margaret Simpson. The quality of dried prunes from Niagara-grown fruit. Hort. Prod. Lab. (Vineland, Ontario) Ann. Rpt. pp. 75-76. 1951-52.

Tufts, W. P. and R. W. Harris. Pruning deciduous fruit trees. Calif. Agr. Ext. Serv. Cir. 444. 47 pp. 1955.

Uota, M. Effects of temperature and ethylene on evolution of carbon dioxide, ethylene, and other oxidizable volatiles from three varieties of plum. Proc. Amer. Soc. Hort. Sci. 65: 231-243. 1955.

U. S. Standards for fresh plums and prunes. U. S. Dept. of Agr. AMS. 5 pp. Request recent addition.

Verner, Leaf et al. Internal browning of fresh Italian prunes. Ida. Res. Bul. 56, 38 pp. 1962.

Verner, Leif and Delance F. Franklin. Training and pruning Italian prune trees. Idaho Agr. Exp. Sta. Bull. 335. Aug. 1960.

Zielinski, Q. B., et al. 2,4,5-T and maturing of prunes. Proc. A.S.H.S. 58, 65, 1951.

Verner, L. Pruning Italian prunes. Ida. Agr. Exp. Sta. Bull. 335. 1960.

Weber, John H. The Idaho prune industry production costs. Ida. Sta. Bul. 400, 23 pp. Request recent work.

Zielinski, Q. B. and W. A. Sistrunk and T. P. Davidson. Plum varieties for Oregon. Ore. Sta. Publ. 582, 22 pp. 1961.

CHERRY (CHAP. XVI)

Boynton, D., et al. Manganese deficiency and interveinal leaf chlorosis. Proc. A.S.H.S. 57, 1, 1951.

Bukovac, M. J., and R. P. Larsen and C. E. Kesner. Chemical promotion of cherry fruit abscission. Journ. ASHS (In press) About 1969.

Bullock, R. M. A study of some inorganic compounds and growth promoting chemicals in relation to fruit cracking of Bing cherries at maturity. Proc. Amer. Soc. Hort. Sci. 59: 243-253. 1952.

Chaplin, M. H. and A. L. Kenworthy. The influence of N-dimethylaminosuccinamic acid (Alar) on growth of the sweet cherry, Prunus avium. Journ. ASHS (In press; presented at 1968 ann. meeting).

Clarke, W. S. and R. D. Anthony. Strains of Mazzard and Mahaleb rootstocks. Proc. A.S.H.S. 48, 200, 1946.

Coe, F. M. Cherry rootstocks. Utah Agr. Exp. Sta. Bull. 319, 1945.

Cullinan, F. P. Improvement of stone fruits. U. S. Dept. of Agr. Yearbook. 1588. 1937.

Davison, R. M. and M. J. Bukovac. The distribution of an inhibitor similar to abscisic acid in young fruits of peach and cherry. Journ. ASHS (In press). 1969

Day, L. H. Cherry rootstocks in California. Calif. Agr. Expt. Sta. Bull. 725. 1951.

Day, L. H. Cherry rootstocks in California. Calif. Agr. Exp. Sta. Bull. 725. 31 pp. 1951 and Calif. Leaflet 159 by Norton, R. A. et al., 1963.

Dennis, F. G. Promotion of germination by warm periods during stratification of cherry and plum pits. Journ. ASHS (In press), New York. About 1969.

Downing, D. L., et al. Review of handling tarts for processing. Food Sciences (N.Y. Exp. Sta., Geneva). May 1971.

Edgerton, J. and A. H. Hatch. Absorption and metabolism of ^{14}C (2-chloroethyl) phosphonic acid in apples and cherries. J. ASHS. 97 (1). Jan. 1972. 112.

Fitch, L. B., et al. Tree shaker thinning of French prunes. Calif. Agr., Apr. 1972.

Fleming, H. K. Growth and mortality in a young sweet cherry orchard. Penna. Agr. Exp. Sta., Bull. 662, 11 pp, November, 1959.

Fogle, H. W., et al. Growing sour cherries. USDA, Beltsville, Md. New handbook. 1973.

Fogle, H. W. Character inheritance in sweet cherry crosses. ASHS 78: 76-85. 1961.

Fogle, H. W. Sweet cherries: production, marketing, processing. New USDA Handbook. 1973.

Fountain, J. B. and P. G. Chapogas. Evaluation of shipping containers for Washington cherries. USDA-MRR 426, 26 pp. 1960.

French, A. P. Plant characters of cherry varieties. Mass. Agr. Exp. Sta. Bull. 401. 1943.

Gardner, V. R. Studies in the nature of clonal variety. III Permanence of strain and other differences in Montmorency cherry. Mich. Tech. Bull. 186. June 1943.

George, J. A. and T. R. Davidson. Virus assay of seed from selected Montmorency cherry trees. Canada Jour. Pl. Sci. Vol. 46:501-505. 1966.

Gerhart, F., et al. Respiration, internal atmospheres and moisture studies of sweet cherries during storage. Proc. A.S.H.S. 41, 119, 1942.

Gerhardt, F., et al. Sweet cherry cracking and decay and surface moisture. Proc. A.S.H.S. 46, 191, 1945.

Gilmer, R. M., K. D. Brase and K. G. Parker. Virus disease control of stone fruit nursery trees in New York. N. Y. Agr. Exp. Sta. Bull 779, 53 pp. 1957.

Graham, S. O. Factors in propagating presumably virus-free *Prunus* understock clones by softwood cuttings. Wash. Agr. Exp. Sta. Bull. 581. 34 pp. 1958.

Griggs, W. H. and W. T. Iwakiri. Pollen dispensers for pollination of almond, sweet cherry and apple. ASHS 75: 114-128. 1960.

Grubb, N. H. Cherries. Crosby Lockwood, London, 1949.

Hansche, P. E. and V. Beres. Analysis of environmental variability in sweet cherry. ASHS 88: 167-172. 1966.

Harrington, W. O. *et al.* Cultural practices and processed cherry quality. ASHS 88:184-189. 1966.

Hart, R. The new Merton cherries. J. Pom. and H. S. 23, 112, 1947.

Hedrick, U. P. Cherries of New York. N. Y. Agr. Exp. Sta. N. Y. State Dept. of Agr. J. B. Lyon Co., Albany, N. Y. 1925.

Iwagaki, H. On the formation and early development of the flowers in the cherry referring to the age of bouquet spur and to the basal bud of new shoot. Jour. of Hort. Assoc. of Japan. Vol 16, no. 3, pp. 197-202. 1947 (in Japanese).

Kennard, W. C. Defoliation of Montmorency sour cherry trees in relation to winter hardiness. Proc. Amer. Soc. Hort. Sci. *53*: 129-133. 1949.

Kenworthy, A. L. Effect of sods, mulches, fertilizers on production, soluble solids, leaf and soil analysis of cherry. Mich. Tech. Bull. 243, 39 pp. June 1954.

Kenworthy, A. L. and A. E. Mitchell. Soluble solids in Montmorency cherries at harvest as influenced by soil management practices. Proc. Amer. Soc. Hort. Sci. *60*: 91-96. 1952.

Kirkpatrick, J. D. and W. F. Mai. *Pratylenchus penetrans*—serious pest of fruit tree roots. Farm Research (N. Y. Exp. Sta., Geneva) 10-11. June 1958.

Kirkpatrick, J. D. and E. G. Fisher. Sour cherry affected by soil potassium level. Farm Research (N. Y. Exp. Sta., Geneva). September 1958.

Kwong, S. S. K relation to acids in sweet cherries. ASHS 86:115-119. 1965.

LaBelle, R. L. *et al.* Tart cherry fruit recovery from repeated bruising. ASHS 84: 103-109. 1964.

LaBelle, R. L. Post-harvest texture changes in Montmorency cherries. (New York) Journ. ASHS (In press) About 1969.

Larsen, F. E. Sweet cherry dwarfing rootstocks. Good Fruit Grower (Canada). Feb. 1, 1972.

Langer, C. A. and V. J. Fisher. Effect of wax sprays and fungicides on size, color, and composition of cherries. Proc. A.S.H.S. 54, 163, 1949.

Levin, J. H., H. P. Gaston, S. L. Hedden and R. T. Whittenberger. Mechanizing the harvest of red tart cherries. Mich. Agr. Expt. Sta. Quarterly Bul. Vol. *42*: 656-685. 1960.

Lewis, F. H. Quality tart cherries. Pa. Hort. News. L:2. 6 pp. Feb. 1971.

Lune, T. R. "Blood bank" of virus disease-free fruit trees. Wash. Sta. Circ. 401, 12 pp. 1962.

Lyon, T. L., A. J. Heinicke and B. D. Wilson. The relation of soil moisture and nitrates to the effects of sod on plum and cherry trees. Cornell Agr. Exp. Sta. Memoir 91 (New York). 1925.

869

Marshall, R. E. Cherries and cherry products. Interscience Publishing, Inc., N. Y. 283 pp. 1954.

Micke, W. C. *et al.* Pruning methods for bearing sweet cherry trees. Calif. Ag. May, 1968.

Milbrath, J. A. Selecting stone fruit trees free from virus diseases. Ore. Agr. Exp. Sta. Bull. 522. 1952.

Milliken, Jr., D. F. Stone fruit (cherry) virus investigations. Mo. Agr. Exp. Sta. Res. Bull. 582. 1955.

Neff, J. A. and R. T. Mitchell. The rope firecrackers. U. S. Dept. of Interior. Wildlife Leaflet 365. 8 pp. April 1955.

Parker, K. G., L. J. Edgerton and K. D. Hickey. GA treatment for yellows of sour cherry. Farm Res. (N. Y. Ag. Exp. Sta., Geneva). Jan. - Feb. 1964.

Parker, K. G., K. D. Hickey, K. D. Brase and R. M. Gilmer. Planting practices for control of cherry yellows virus complex. N. Y. Ag. Ext. Bull. 1066. 8 p. 1961.

Patchen, G. O. and H. O. Schomer. Cooling, shipping cherry gift packages. USDA-ARC. 52-66. 7 p. Aug. 1971.

Pest control of cherries. Contact your local government experiment station or agricultural extension agent for up-to-date recommendations.

Philip, G. L. Cherry culture in California. Cal. Agr. Ext. Serv. Cir. 46, 1947.

Pollack, R. L. *et al.* Respiration of tart cherry during growth. ASHS 78:86-95. 1961.

Pollack, R. L. *et al.* Studies on cherry scald. Part I and Part II. Food Technology *12*: No. 2. pp. 102-105, 106-108. 1958.

Porritt, S. W. and J. L. Mason. CA storage of sweet cherries. ASHS 87:128-130. 1965.

Porritt, S. W., et al. Storage surface pitting of sweet cherries. Canadian Jour. of Pl. Sci. 51: (5) p. 409-414. Sept. 1971.

Posnette, A .F. and R. Cropley. A canker disease of cherry trees caused by virus infection. Plant Pathology 6: (3) pp. 85-87. 1957.

Processing of cherries. Contact food technology departments at Oregon State Univ., Corvallis; N. Y. Ag. Exp. Sta., Geneva; Hort. Res. Instit. of Ontario, Vineland, Canada; Mich. Sta. Univ., E. Lansing.

Proebsting, E. L., Jr. and A. L. Kenworthy. Mineral nutrition, solar radiation, and cherry tree growth. Proc. A.S.H.S. 63, 41, 1954.

Rebeiz, C. A. and J. C. Crane. Parthenocarpy induced in Bing cherry. ASHS 78:69-75. 1961.

Ryugo, Kay. Alar effects on red color in sweet cherry. ASHS 88: 160-166. 1966.

Sawada, E. Studies on the cracking of cherries. Agr. and Hort., Vol. 6 no. 6. pp. 3-30. 1931 (in Japanese with English summary).

Schomer, H. A. and K. L. Olsen. Storage of sweet cherries in controlled atmospheres. USDA-AMS-529. 7 p. 1964.

Siegelman, H. W. Brown discoloration and shrivel of cherry stems. Proc. A.S.H.S. 61, 265, 1953.

Smith, C. B. *et al.* Fertilizer and soil management effects on leaf composition, performance of tart cherry trees. Pa. Ag. Exp. Sta. Bull. 683, 12 pp. June 1961.

Smith, R. B. and F. I. Cook. Weight-to-volume relationship of cherries suspended in water. Hort. Res. Inst., Vineland, Ontario 1970 rpt.

Stanberry, C. O. and W. J. Clore. Nitrogen, phosphorus, and Bing cherry maturity. Proc. A.S.H.S. 56, 40, 1950.

Stosser, R. and H. P. Rasmussen, and M. J. Bukovac. (*Prunus cerasus* L.) Abscission layer development in the tary cherry. Journ. ASHS (In press) about 1969.

Taylor, O. C. and A. E. Mitchell. Changes in sour cherries during the season of harvest. Proc. A.S.H.S. 62, 267, 1953.

Tillay, D. T. N. *et al.* Factors affecting germination of cherry seeds. ASHS 86:102-107. 1965.

Tufts, W. P. and R. W. Harris. Pruning deciduous fruit trees. Calif. Agr. Exp. Sta. Serv. 444. 47 pp. 1955.

Tukey, L. D. Night temperature and growth of sour cherry fruits. Bot. Gaz. 114, 155, 1952.

Unrath, C R., A. L. Kenworthy and C. L. Bedford. The effect of Alar on fruit maturation, quality and vegetative growth of sour cherries. cv. "Montmorency." J. ASHS 94(4):387-391. 1969.

Unrath, C. R. and A. L. Kenworthy. The effects of Alar on red tart cherries (*Prunus cerasus* L.). Journ. ASHS (In press; presented at 1968 ann. meeting).

U. S. Standards for sweet cherries, and for sweet cherries for export, for sulphur brining, U. S. Dept. of Agr. AMS. Washington, D. C. Request latest report.

Virgo, B. B. Sweet cherry bird damage. Canadian Jour. of Pl. Sci. 51:(5) p. 415. 1971.

Walker, D. R. and E. G. Fisher. Urea sprays on sour cherries. Proc. A.S.H.S. 66, 21, 1955.

Whittenberger, R. T. *et al.* Electric sorting machines for tart cherries. USDA-ARS 73-45 (2116) Oct. 1964.

Worley, R. E. et al. Growth, yield, nutritional correlation, pecan. JASHS:97-4. 514-21. 1972.

Yang, H. Y., E. Ross and J. E. Brekke. Cherry brining. Wash. Agr. Exp. Sta. Cir. of Inform. 597. April 1959. (See also Wash. Agr. Exp. Sta. Cir. 340 (mimeo) 3 pp. September 1958.

Zagaya, S. W. Effect of germination temperatures on development of seedlings from immature embryos. Bull. Acad. Polon. Sci. Cl. V. 9:591-592. 1963.

Zielinski, Q. B. Fruit cracking of sweet cherry as related to variety. ASHS 84:98-102. 1964.

Zielinski, Q. B., W. A. Sistrunk, and W. A. Mellenthin. Sweet cherries for Oregon. Ore. Agr. Exp. Sta. Bull. 570. 20 pp. 1959.

Zielinski, Q. B. and R. G. Garren. 2,4-D and NAA effects on fruit setting and maturity and fruit bud formation in Montmorency cherry. Bot. Gaz. 113, 147, 1951.

Nuts, Minor Tree Crops (Chap. XVII)

Alben, A. O. Zinc chelate for pecan trees. Proc. A.S.H.S. 66, 28, 1955.

Alben, A. O., et al. Some nutrient deficiency symptoms of the pecan. Proc. A.S.H.S. 41, 53, 1942.

Alben, A. O. and H. E. Hammar. Pecan rosette cured with zinc sulphate, manure, and sulphur. Proc. A.S.H.S. 45, 27, 1944.

Alben, A. O. and B. G. Sitton. Thinning trees in a pecan orchard. Proc. A.S.H.S. 56, 98, 1950.

Anonymous. Chestnut blight and resistant chestnuts. U. S. Dept. Agr. Farmer's Bull. 2068, 1954.

Batchelor, L. D., O. L. Braucher and E. F. Serr. Walnut production in California. Agr. Exp. Sta. Cir. 364, 1945.

Blackmon, G. H. Experiments with growth substances on pecans. Proc. A.S.H.S. 47, 147, 1946.

Blake, M. A. Chinese chestnuts. N. J. Agr. Exp. Sta. Bull. 717, 1945.

Blondeau, R. and J. C. Crane. Induction of parthenocarpy in figs. Plant Phys. 25, 158, 1950. See also: Crane, J. C. and R. Blondeau. Plant Phys. 24, 44, 1949.

Brooks, M. G. Juglans nigra root toxicity. West Va. Agr. Exp. Sta. Bull. 347, 1951.

Claypool, L. L., et al. Temperature, Co_2, respiration and storage of Mission figs, Proc. A.S.H.S. 60, 226, 1952.

Clements, J. R. and W. T. Pentzer. Response of figs to olive oil and other treatments. Proc. A.S.H.S. 55, 172, 1950.

Condit, I. J. The fig. Chronica Botanica Co., 1947.

Cooil, B. J. et al. Phosphorus effects on growth, yield, leaf composition of Macadamia nut. Hawaii Ag. Exp. Sta. Tech. Bull. 66, 71 pp. Dec. 1966.

Crandall, B. S. and W. L. Baker. A wilt disease of American persimmons. Phytopathology 40, 307, 1950.

Crane, J. C. Growth of fig fruits. Proc. A.S.H.S. 52, 237, 1948.

Crane, J. C. Ovary wall development in Calimyrna figs and regulators. Bot. Gaz. 114, 102, 1952.

Crane, J. C., and M. M. Nelson. Effects of crop load, girdling, and auxin application on alternate bearing of pistachio. J. ASHS 97(3):337. May 1972.

Crane, J. C. and R. Blondeau. Controlled growth of fig fruits by synthetic hormone application. Proc. A.S.H.S. 54, 102, 1949.

Crane, J. C. and J. G. Brown. Growth of Mission fig fruits. Proc. A.S.H.S. 56, 93, 1950.

Crosby, E. A. and J. C. Crane. The carbohydrate cycle and parthenocarpy in Mission and Adriatic figs. Proc. A.S.H.S. 59, 196, 1952.

Curtis, O. F., and Clark, A. K. The effect of a temperature gradient on the distribution of water in apples, tomatoes, oranges and potatoes. Proc. Amer. Soc. Hort. Sci. 35: 160. 1937.

English, H. Phomopsis canker of figs. Phytopathology 42, 513, 1952.

Gerdts, M. and G. Obenauf. Ethephon speeds maturity on figs. Calif. Agri. May, 1972.

Hammar, H. E. and J. H. Hunter. Nutrients in developing pecan leaves. Plant Phys. 24, 16, 1949. See also: Changes in composition of nuts. Plant Phys. 21, 476, 1946.

Hansen, C. J. and H. T. Hartman. Treatments for walnut grafts. Proc. A.S.H.S. 57, 193, 1951.

Hoffman, M. B. et al. NAA vs. its amide for apple thinning. Proc. A.S.H.S. 65, 63, 1955.

Horoschak, T. Walnut industries of the Mediterranean Basin. USDA, For. Agr. Serv. FAS M-245. April 1972.

Johnston, F. A. and H. M. Sell. Changes in chemical composition of Tung kernels during germination. Plant Phys. 19, 694, 1944.

Kadiura, M. The physiological dropping of fruits in the Japanese persimmon. National Hort. Exp. Sta. Res. Bull. 19. 1944 (in Japanese with English summary).

Klose, A. A., et al. Vitamin C content of walnuts (Persian) during growth and development. Plant Phys. 23, 133, 1948.

Loustalot, A. J. Effect of ringing the stem on photosynthesis, transpiration, and respiration of pecan leaves. Proc. A.S.H.S. 42, 127, 1943.

Loustalot, A. J. et al. Copper and zinc deficiency and photosynthesis in Tung. Plant Phys. 20, 283, 1945.

Manning, W. E. Flowers in Juglandaceae. Am. J. Bot. 27, 839, 1940 and 35, 606, 1948.

Maxie, E. C. and J. C. Crane. Effect of ethylene on growth and maturation of the fig. Journ. ASHS (In press; presented at 1968 ann. meeting).

McKay, J. W. Embryology of the pecan. J. Agr. Res. 74, 263, 1947.

National Pecan Conference, Dallas, Texas, 1970. (Tex. Pecan Growers' Assn., College Station). Covers research, marketing, mech. harvesting, Cheyenne var., taxes, rootstocks, etc. Published 1972.

Nayer, T. G. and K. M. Shetty. Curing persimmons. Ind. J. Hort. 6, 30, 1949.

Petrucci, V. E. and J. C. Crane. Fruit bud initiation and differentiation in the fig. Proc. A.S.H.S. 56, 86, 1950.

Preston, W. H., Jr. and Eugene Griffith. Use of apples to remove astringency from Persimmon fruits. Reprint from Northern Nut Growers Assn., Inc. 53rd Annual Report-1962. pp. 29-34.

Preston, W. H., Jr., and Eugene Griffith. Current status of the Oriental Persimmon in temperate eastern United States. Reprint from 57th Annual Rpt.—1966. Northern Nut Growers Association, Inc.

Proebsting, E. L. and R. Tate. Nitrate in fig leaves. Proc. A.S.H.S. 60, 7, 1952.

Proebsting, E. L. and R. M. Warner. Fertilizer experiments with fig trees. Proc. A.S.H.S. 63, 10, 1954.

Reed, C. A. Chinese chestnut. Proc. A.S.H.S. 49, 139, 1947.

Romberg, L. D. and C. L. Smith. Summer drop from self- and cross-pollinated flowers of pecan varieties. Proc. A.S.H.S. 47, 130, 1946.

Serr, E. F. and H. I. Forde. Paradox vs. J. hindsii as rootstock for walnuts. Proc. A.S.H.S. 57, 198, 1951.

Sparks, D. and C. E. Brack. Return bloom and fruit set of pecan from leaf and fruit removal. HortSci. 7: (2) April 1972. p. 131.

Van Horn, C. W. Rest period of some pecan varieties. Proc. A.S.H.S. 41, 65, 1942.

Whitehouse, W. E. and L. E. Joley. Pterocarya as rootstock for walnut. Proc. A.S.H.S. 52, 103, 1948.

Worley, R. E. Pecan leaf analysis service summary. 1965. Ga. Coastal Plain Exp. Sta., Tifton, Mimeo. Series N. S. 259, 9 pp. Oct. 1966.

Worley, R. E. Pecan leaf analysis summary, 1966. Ga. Coastal Plain Exp. Sta., Tifton., Research Rpt. 9, 19 pp. Sept. 1967.

Worley, Ray E., et al. Effect of Zn sources and methods of application on yield and leaf mineral concentration of pecan, Carya illinoensis, Koch. J. ASHS 97(3): 364. May 1972.

Wright, R. C. Investigations on the storage of nuts. U. S. Dept. Agr. Teach. Bull. 770, 1941.

PERSIMMON

Archer, C. J. The starch cycle in the Hachiya persimmon. Proc. Amer. Soc. Hort. Sci. 38:187-190. 1941.

Camp, A. F. and Harold Mowry. The cultivated persimmon in Florida. Fla. Agr. Ext. Service Bulletin 124. Revised 1945.

872

Crandall, B. S. Known range of persimmon wilt in 1939. U. S. Dept. of Agr. Plant Disease Reporter 24: 168-169. May 15, 1940.

Davis, W. B. and C. G. Chruch. The effect of ethylene on the chemical composition and the respiration of the ripening Japanese persimmon. Jour. Agr. Research 42:31. 165-182 Feb. 1931.

Dorsett, P. H. and J. H. Dorsett. Culture and outdoor winter storage of persimmons in the vicinity of Peking, China. U. S. Dept. of Agr. Circular 49. November, 1928.

Drain, B. D. The Japanese persimmon in Tennessee. Tenn. Agr. Expt. Sta. Circular 51. 1934.

Fruits and Tree Nuts, bloom, harvesting and mkting dates, etc., by states. USDA Hdbk. 186. July 1960.

Gould, H. P. The Oriental persimmon. U. S. Dept. of Agr. Leaflet 194: 1-8 May, 1940.

Hodgson, R. W. Girdling to reduce fruit drop in the Hachiya persimmon. Proc. Amer. Soc. Hort. Sci. 36: 405-409. 1939.

Hodgson, R. W. Floral situation, sex condition and parthenocarpy in the Oriental persimmon. Proc. Amer. Soc. Hort. Sci. 37: 250-252. 1940.

Hodgson, R. W. Rootstocks for the Oriental persimmon. Proc. Amer. Soc. Hort. Sci. 37: 338-339. 1940.

Hume, H. H. A kaki classification. Jour. of Heredity 5(9): 400-406. 1914.

Hume, H. H. Non-fruiting of Japanese persimmons due to lack of pollen. Science (U. S.) 30: 308-309. 1919.

Lloyd, F. E. Tannin-colloid complexes in the fruit of the persimmon, Diospyros. Biochem. Bull. 1(1): 7-14. September 1911.

Overholser, E. L. Some studies upon ripening and removal of astringency in Japanese persimmons. Proc. Amer. Soc. Hort. Sci.: 256-266. 1927.

Preston, W. H., Jr., and E. Griffith. Current status of Oriental persimmon in temperate eastern United States. Northern Nut Growers Assoc. 57th Ann. Rpt. 112-123. 1966.

Rizzi, A. D. The Oriental persimmon in California. Calif. Ag. Ext. Serv. Publ. AXT-87, 8 pp. 1964.

Terami, H. A method of identifying the species with the root in Diospyros kaki, D. lotus and D. virginiana. Jour. of Hort. Assn. Japan 9(2): 129-133. Sept. 1938.

MACADAMIA

Labanauskas, C. K. and M. F. Handy. The effects of iron and manganese deficiencies on accumulation of nonprotein and protein amino acids in macadamia leaves. J. ASHS 95(2):218-222. 1970.

Shigeura, Gordon T., James Lee and James A. Silva. The role of honey bees in macadamia nut production in Hawaii. J. ASHS. 95(5):544-546. 1970.

SPRAYING, PESTS (CHAP. XVIII)

GENERAL

Backyard fruits—pest control. Ohio Ext. Bull. L-1. (Good). Request recent edition.

Bethell, R. S. et al. Sex pheremone traps to reduce orchard sprays. Calif. Agric. May 1972.

Brann, James L., Jr. Factors affecting use of airblast sprayers. Transactions of the ASAE Vol. 7, No. 3:200-203. American Society of Agricultural Engineers, Saint Joseph, Mich. 1964.

Brann, James L., Jr., Factors affecting the thoroughness of spray application. Proc. of N. Y. State Hort. Soc., pp. 186-95. 1965.

Brann, James L., Jr., Paul Steiner and Donald Lisk. Comparison of spray deposits applied at 33X and 2X concentrations. Proc. of N. Y. State Hort. Soc., pp. 184-190. 1967.

Burkholder, C. L., et al. Cutting out center tops for better spraying. Proc. A.S.H.S. 42, 283, 1943.

Cation, Donald. Dwarf fruit and tree decline, a virus disease of apple. Mich. Agr. Expt. Sta. Quarterly Bul. Vol. 42: No. 4, 722-727. 1960.

Clore, W. J., W. E. Westlake, K. C. Walker and V. R. Boswell. Residual effects of soil insecticides on crop plants. Wash. State Univ. IAS Bull. 627, Apr. 1961.

Dayton, D. F., J. R. Shay and L. F. Hough. Apple scab resistance from R12740-70, a Russian apple. Proc. Amer. Soc. Hort. Sci. 62: 334-340. 1953.

Dominick, B. A., Jr. Costs regarding dusting by air or on ground. (A panel.) Eastern Fruit Grower. pp. 16,20,22,24,26,28,29. May 1960.

Flaherty, D., et al. Correcting spider mite imbalances, Southern Calif. Calif. Agr., Apr. 1972.

Helson, V. A. Effects of Ryania and Ryanodine on the apparent photosynthesis of McIntosh apple leaves. Canadian Jr. Plant Sci. *40*: 218-224. Apr. 1960.

Hesse, C. O. and W. H. Griggs. Peach leaf glands and surface wettability. Proc. A.S.H.S. 56, 173, 1950.

Hough, L. F., J. R. Shay and D. F. Dayton. Apple scab resistance from *Malus floribunda* Sieb. Proc. Amer. Soc. Hort. Sci. *62*: 341-347. 1953.

McMechan, A. D. and G. D. Halvorson. Operation and maintenance of air-blast orchard sprayers. Canada Dept. Agr., Res. Sta., Summerland, SP 23(5M) June, 1961.

Posnette, A. F. and R. Cropley. Indicator plants for latent virus infection in apple. J. Hort. Sci. 36:168-173. July 1961.

Powell, Dwight, Meyer, Ronald H., and Owen, Frank W. Pest control in commercial fruit plantings. Univ. of Ill. Ext. Serv., Cir. 821, May, 1960.

Scurfield, G. and D. E. Bland. The anatomy and chemistry of "rubbery" wood in apple var. Lord Lambourne. J. Hort. Sci. 38:297-306. 1963.

Shay, J. R., D. F. Dayton and L. F. Hough. Apple scab resistance from a number of *Malus* species. Proc. Amer. Soc. Hort. Sci. *62*: 348-356. 1953.

Stern, A. C. (Ed.) Air pollution and its effects, Vol. I. Analysis, monitoring and surveying, Vol. II. 694, 684 pp. resp. (Environ. Sci. and Monograph Ser.) Academic Press, New York and London. 1968.

Taylor, O. C. and A. E. Mitchell. Soluble solids, total solids, sugar content and weight of the fruit of the sour cherry (Prunus cerasus) as affected by pesticide chemicals and time of harvest. Proc. Amer. Soc. Hort. Sci. *68*: 124-130. 1956.

(CON'T. FROM SPRAY CHAPTER CITATIONS)

SOIL NEMATODES

Good, J. M. and A. L. Taylor. Plant-parasitic nematodes — chemical control. USDA Agr. Handbook 286, 28 pp. 1965.

Hedden, O. K. *et al.* Equipment for applying soil pesticides. USDA Agr. Handbook 297, 36 pp. 1966.

Jenkins, W. R. *et al.* Nematodes in the northeastern U. S. — literature review 1956-63, future outlook, N. J. Agr. Exp. Sta. Mimeo Bull. 805, 30 pp. 1963.

Wave, H. E. and W. C. Stiles. Influence of Superior Oil Sprays on Growth and Bark Necrosis of 'Delicious' Apple Trees. HortSci. 7: (2) April 1972. p. 171.

WEED CONTROL

Bunting, A. H. A symposium on British Weed Control. No. 2. 114 pp. Blackwell Scientific Publications, Oxford, England. 1963.

Clingman, G. C. Weed control: as a science. John Wiley and Son, Inc., New York City. 421 pp. 1961.

Craft, A. S. Herbicides — chemistry and mode of action. Interscience Publishers, New York City. 269 pp. 1961.

Fischer, B. and A. Lange. Herbicide residues—banding vs broadcasting. Calif. Agric. May. 1972.

Gebhardt, M. R. and C. L. Day. How to calibrate your sprayer. Univ. of Mo. Agr. Exp. Sta. B-848, 8 pp. May 1966.

Greig, J. K. *et al.* Chemical weed control in forestry and horticultural plants. Kan. Agr. Exp. Sta. Bull. 505, 27 pp. Request recent edition.

Herbicide catalogues. Weed and brush control; and Farm Weed Killer Manual, Amchem Prod., Inc., Ambler, Pa.

Lange, A. H. *et al.* Weed control in apples and pears. Prog. Rpt. Calif. Agr. Ext. Serv. Mimeo. Jan. 1967.

Ries, S. K. *et al.* Chemical weed control for horticultural crops. Mich. Agr. Ext. Bull. E-433. (Request recent edition)

Saidak, W. J. and W. M. Rutherford. Young apple tree tolerance to Amitrole, Diuron and Simazine. Can. Journ. of Plant Sci. 43:113-119. Apr. 1963.

Smika, D. E. and G. A. Wicks. Herbicides boost soil water storage. Farm Chem. 131:8. pp. 44-46. August 1968.

Sources of up-to-date weed control information for fruits: Univ. of California, Davis (most fruits); Washington St. Univ., Prosser (most fruits; cranberry at Long Beach, Wash.); Michigan St. Univ., E. Lansing (most fruits); Indiana (Purdue), Lafayette, small fruits; Univ. of Wisconsin, Sturgeon Bay (cherry);

Ohio Agr. Exp. St., Wooster (small fruits); Kansas St. Univ., Manhattan (most small and tree fruits); Pennsylvania St. Univ., University Park (most fruits); N. Y. Agr. Exp. Sta., Geneva (most fruits); and USDA cooperating with Rutgers Univ., New Brunswick, N. J. (most tree and small fruits, cranberry, blueberry).

VIRUS DISEASES

Campbell, A. I. Latent virus infections and growth and cropping of apple. Journ. of Hort. Sci. 38:1. 15-19. 1963.

Cation, Donald. Dwarf fruit and tree decline, a virus disease of apple. Mich. Quart. Bull. 42:4. 722-727. May 1960.

"Flat-limb" virus in apple. Aust. Journ. of Agr. Res. 15:4. 548-59. July 1964.

Fridlund, P. R. Temperature and viruses of *Prunes, Malus, Pyrus*. Wash. Agr. Exp. Sta. Bull. 726. 1970.

Gilmer, R. M., K. D. Brase and K. G. Parker. Control of virus diseases of stone fruit nursery trees in New York, N. Y. Agr. Sta. Bull. 779, 53 pp. 1957.

McCrum, R. C. *et al*. Apple virus diseases — illustrated review. Agr. Exp. Stations of Maine (Bull. 595) and New Hampshire (Tech. Bull. 101) 63 pp. June 1960.

Mink, G. I. and J. R. Shay. Latent viruses in apple. Purdue Agr. Exp. Sta. Res. Bull. 756, 23 pp. 1962.

Posnette, A. F. Virus diseases of apples and pears. Commonwealth Bureau of Hort. and Plantation Crops, E. Malling, Kent. Eng. Tech. Communication 30, 141 pp. 1963.

Posnette, A. F. and R. Cropley. Indicator plants for latent virus in apple. Journ. of Hort. Sci. 36:3. 168-173. July 1961.

Reeves, E. L. and R. C. Lindner. Some apple virus disease problems in Washington. Proc. Wash. State Hort. Assn. 117-119. Dec. 1959.

Reeves, E. L. and P. W. Cheney. Russet ring, a graft transmissible disease on Golden Delicious apples. Wash. State Hort. Assn. Proc. 55th Meeting. 157-158. 1959.

Scurfield, G. and D. E. Bland. "Rubbery" wood virus in apple — anatomy and chemistry. Journ. of Hort. Sci. 38:4. 299-306. 1963.

Thomas, H. Earl. Virus diseases of apples. Hilgardia 31:435-456. Nov. 1961.

Viruses of horticultural plants. Proc. XVII International Horticultural Congress Vol. III: 79-102. Univ. of Md., College Park, 1966.

Wadley, Bryce N. Stem pitting of apple in Utah. Farm and Home Sci. Dec. 1961.

Welsh, Maurice F. Control of fruit plant virus diseases (Canada). The Mountaineer Grower, W. Va. Hort. Soc. Proc. Dec. 1967.

AERIAL SPRAY AND DUST APPLICATIONS

Aerial applications of agricultural chemicals. USDA Agr. Handbook 287, 48 pp, 1965.

Carlton, James B. Electrostatic charging of sprays by airplane coverage. Farm Chem. 131:8. pp. 40-42. 1968.

Dominick, Jr., B. A. *et al*. Costs regarding dusting by air or on ground. A panel discussion. Eastern Fruit Grower. pp. 16-3. May 1960.

Haines, R. G. Controlling fruit insects by aircraft application. Mich. Qtrly. Bull. 41: 2, 410-420. Nov. 1958.

How to spray the aircraft way—a guide for farmers and spray-plane pilots. U. S. Dept. of Agr. Farmers Bull. 2062. 32 pp. 1954.

Nelson, G. S. and C. Lincoln. Airplane sprayers for spray applications. Ark. Agr. Exp. Sta. Bull. 730, 27 pp. 1968.

Szkolnik, Michael. Aircraft application of orchard fungicides. Farm Res. (N. Y. Agr. Exp. Sta.) Oct.-Dec. 1966.

AIR POLLUTION

Air Pollution. Proc. of the U. S. Tect. Conf. on Air Pollution. McGraw-Hill Publ. Co., Inc., New York City. 1952.

Daines, R. H., I. A. Leone and E. Brennan. Air pollution as it affects agriculture in New Jersey. N. J. Agr. Exp. Sta. Bull. 794. 14 pp. 1960.

Nyle, C. Brady. Agriculture and the quality of environment (a book on air pollution). Amer. Assoc. for Adv. Sci. Publ. No. 85. Wash. D. C. 460 pp. 1965.

Wilson, B. R., Ed. Environmental problems — pesticides, thermal pollution and environmental synergisms. J. B. Lippincott Co., Phila.-Toranto, 183 pp, 1968.

Dibble, J. E. *et al.* Concentrate spraying — questions and answers. Calif. Agr. Ext. Serv. Publ. AXT-131. 1966.

Dibble, J., et al. Concentrate spraying in Wash. orchards. Wash. Agr. Ext. Serv. EM 3430. 16 pp. 1971.

Howitt, A. J. and A. Psea. Ultra-low volume ground sprayers; development and evaluation. Mich. Agr. Exp. Sta. Quart. Bull. 48:2. 144-60. About 1967.

Kilgore, W. W., W. E. Yates and J. M. Ogawa. Concentrate and dilute ground air carrier and aircraft spray coverages. Hilgardia 35:19. 527-543. 1964.

Kresten, E. R. and C. Graham. Contact these authors for several reprints on equipment, techniques and materials in concentrate spraying. Univ. of Md. Field Sta., Hancock, Md.

Lewis, F. H. and Dean Asquith. Note: these men devote full time and publish on up-to-date spraying equipment, techniques, costs and materials for deciduous fruit crops. Contact them for recent publications at Fruit Res. Lab., Pa. State Univ., Biglerville, Pa.

Linde, J. E., Jr. High concentrate spraying (3x vs 33x). Equipment, costs, techniques, 1965-67. Trexler Orchards, Inc., Orefield, Pa. Hort. News, (N. Bruns., N. J.) May 1968.

Marshall, James. Concentrate spraying in deciduous orchards. Canada Dept. of Agr., Summerland, B .C., Publ. 1020. 47 pp. 1958.

Mitchell, A. E. 2-X or 30-X concentrate spraying in orchards. Amer. Fruit Grower Mag. 22, 47, 49. Feb. 1968.

Potts, S. F. Concentrate spray equipment, mixtures and application methods. Dorland Books. Caldwell, New Jersey. 1958.

Waddell, D. B. and J. M. McArthur. Effects of pruning on spray deposits from concentrate orchard sprayers. Can. Journ. of Agr. Sci. 34: 444-450. Sept.-Oct., 1954.

Wright, Earl J. Concentrate spraying in Pennsylvania Heisey orchards. Am. Fruit Grower. June 1968.

IRRIGATION (CHAP. XIX)

English, H. Canker and dieback of fig. Calif. Fig. Inst. Proc., 16th Ann. Res. Conf. p. 13-15. 1962.

Foott, J. H., *et al.* Walnut branch wilt. Calif. Agr. 9(10):11. 1955.

Forshey, C. G. Irrigating New York orchards. N. Y. State. Hort. Soc. Proc. 103rd Annu. Mtg. 90-93. 1958.

Fortier, S. Orchard irrigation. U.S.D.A. Bull. 1518. 27 p. 1940. ASHS 28:547-551. 1932.

Gamble, S. J. Does orchard irrigation pay? Ind. Hort. Soc. Trans., 103rd Ann. Mtg. 32-38. 1964.

Gammon, N. Jr., *et al.* Soil types, seasonal rainfall and Mg in pecan leaves. Soil Crop Sci. Soc., Fla. Proc. 20:154-8. 1960.

Gayner, F. C. H. Irrigation and injection effects on non-setting pears. E. Malling Res. Sta., Ann. Rep.: 1940. A24:36-41. 1941.

Goode, J. E. Soil moisture relationships in orchards. Ann. Appl. Biol. 44:525-30. 1956.

Goode, J. E. and K. J. Hyrycz. Soil moisture and apple tree response. J. Hort. Sci. 39:254-76. 1964.

Halsey, D. D., *et al.* Na-apricot-leaf scorch. Calif. Agr. 12(9):4-5. 1958.

Harley, C. P. and R. C. Lindner. Irrigation of apple and pear in Washington. ASHS 46:35-44. 1945.

Heinicke, A. J. and N. F. Childers. Water deficiency in photosynthesis and transpiration of apple leaves. ASHS 33:155-159. 1935.

Hendrickson, A. H. and co-workers. Prunus and water relations. Hilgardia 1:479-524. 1926; Water relations and clingstone peaches. ASHS 24:240-244. 1927; Dry soil on root extension. Plant, Physiol. 6:567-576. 1931; Irrigation of pears on clay adobe soil. ASHS Proc. 34:224-226. 1937; Factors affecting rate of pear growth. ASHS 39:1-7. 1941; Irrigation effects on French prunes. ASHS. Proc. 46:187-190. 1945; Nitrogen irrigation on walnut tree growth. Plant. Psysiol. 25:567-72. 1950a; Irrigation of apricots. ASHS Proc. 55:1-10. 1950b; Water use, rooting depth of almond trees. ASHS 65:133-8. 1955a.

Hibbard, A. D. and Mohsen Nour. P and K in leaves under moisture stress. ASHS. 73:33-39. 1959.

Hoffman, M. B. and L. J. Edgerton. NAA effects on apple drop under moisture stress. ASHS 48:48-50. 1946.

Houston, C. E. and J. L. Meyer. Apricot irrigation. Calif. Agr. 12(9):6. 1958.

Jensen, M. C., et al. Apple orchard irrigation. Wash. Agr. Exp. Sta. Circ. 402. 11 p. 1962.

Jones, I. D. Soil moisture, leaf area and fruit growth in peach. ASHS 28:6-14. 1932.

Kenworthy, A. L. Soil moisture and growth of apple trees. ASHS 54:29-39. 1949.

Lagache, P. and G. Pascaud. Irrigation water and chlorosis of fruit trees in France. (In French). UNESCO Arid Zone Res. 16:285-294. 1961.

Laycock, D. H. and L. J. Foster. Rainfall and biennial bearing in Tung. Nature 176:654. 1955.

Larson, K. L. and J. D. Eastin. Drouth Injury and resistance in crops. Soil Sci. Soc. of Amer., Madison, Wis. 88 pp. 1971.

Livingston, R. L. and T. B. Hagler. Irrigation on peaches. Assn. So. Agr. Workers, Proc. 54:179. 1957.

Magness, J. R. Moisture effects on pecan. Nat'l Pecan Assn. Proc. 30:18-23. 1931.

Magness, J. R., et al. Apple irrigation in eastern U. S. orchards. ASHS Proc. 29: 246-252. 1935.

Magness, J. R., et al. Carbohydrates in apple leaf, bark and wood and soil moisture. ASHS 29:246-252. 1933.

Mason, A. C. Apple leaf mineral content and soil moisture. J. Hort. Sci. 33(3): 202-211. 1958.

Mathews, C. D. Water and the Tasmanian apple. Tasmanian J. Agr. 31:346-351. 1960.

Ministry of Agriculture, London. Irrigation (3rd ed.) Bull. Min. Agr. 138. pp 88. 1962.

Modlibowska, I. Soil moisture and apple blossom frost resistance. J. Hort. Sci. 36 (3):186-196. 1961.

Morris, J. R., et al. Interactive effects of irrigation, pruning, and thinning on peach. ASHS. Proc. 80:177-189. 1962.

Nasharty, A. H. and I. M. Ibrahim. Irrigation frequency on quality and quantity of plums. Agr. Res. Rev. Cairo. 39:100-7. 1961.

Office of the Minister for Science. Irrigation in Great Britain. Natural Resources Tech. Comm. Rep. H. M. Stationery Office, London, 82 p. 1962.

Oskamp, Joseph. Rooting of fruit trees in different soils. ASHS 29:213-219. 1932.

Packer, W. J., et al. Irrigation of Jonathan apple. J. Agri. Victoria, Australia. 61: 453-60-475. 1963.

Parker, Johnson, Drough resistance in woody plants, Bot. Rev. 22:4. Apr. 52 pp. 1956.

Peikert, F. W. and R. T. Tribble. Irrigation effects on humidity in orchards. Mich. Agr. Exp. Quart Bull. 31:266-9. 1949.

Proebsting, E. L. Fruit tree rooting in California. ASHS Proc. 43:1-4. 1943.

Rogers, W. S. Apple root growth, rootstock, soil, seasonal factors. J. Pom. Hort. Sci. 17:99-130. 1939.

Rogers, W. S. and J. E. Goode. Irrigation requirements of fruit orchards. East. Malling Res. Sta. Annu. Rep. A. 36. p. 171-3. 1953.

Romberg, L. D. Pecan orchard irrigation. Southeastern Pecan Growers' Assn., Proc. 53:20, 22-50. 1960.

Ross, N. and J. L. Meyer. Almond irrigation timing. Almond Facts. 22(3):9. 1957.

Schneider, G. W. and N. F. Childers. Soil moisture on apple photosynthesis, respiration and transpiration. Plant Physiol. 16:565-583. 1941.

Shaw, L. Intercellular humidity and apple and pear fire blight. Cornell Agr. Exp. Sta. Mem. 181. 40 pp. 1935.

Simons, R. K. Irrigation and apple fruit abscission. ASHS Proc. 83:77-87. 1963.

Skepper, A. H. and A. E. Vincent. Orchard irrigation. New So. Wales Dept. Agr. Publ. 77 p. 1962.

Skepper, A. H., et al. Prune irrigation. Agr. Gaz. New So. Wales 72(4):199-202, 215. 1961.

Taerum, R. Soil moisture, climate, stomatal behavior, growth of apple. ASHS 85: 20-32. 1964.

Till. M. R. Nitrogen, irrigation on apricot. S. Australia Dept. Agr. J. 61(6):295-297. 1958.

Uriu, K. Post-Harvest soil moisture, subsequent apricot yield. ASHS Proc. 84:93-97. 1964.

Uriu, K., et al. Cling peach irrigation. Calif. Agr. 18(7): 10, 11. 1964.

Veihmeyer, F. J. and A. H. Hendrickson. Soil moisture, root distribution in orchards. Plant Physiol. 13:169-177. 1948; Basic soil concepts, soil moisture, and irrigation. Wash. State. Hort. Assn. Proc. 45:25-41. 1949; Soil moisture and fruit tree and vine responses. ASHS Proc. 55:11-15. 1950,; Soil moisture and plant growth. Ann. Rev. Plant Physiol. 1:285-304. 1950b; Soil moisture effects on fruit trees. Int. Hort. Congr. Rep. 13th, London 1:306-319. 1952.

Verner, L. and E. C. Blodgett. Cracking of sweet cherries. Idaho Agr. Exp. Sta. Bull. 184. 15 p. 1931.

Verner, L., et al., Trunk growth guide to orchard irrigation. Idaho Agr. Exp. Sta. Res. Bull. 52. 32 p. 1962.

Wahlberg, H. E. Pecan growing, Yuma Valley. Amer. Fruit Grower. 52(1):8-9. 1932.

Way, R. D. Winter hardiness, crop size and cultural practices of apple trees. ASHS 63:163-6. 1954.

Wiggans, C. C. Sub-soil moisture effects on orchard plants. ASHS 33:103-107. 1936.

Wilcox, J. C. Sprinkler irrigation in British Columbia orchards. Dept. Agr. Ottawa. Publ. 878. 72 p. 1953.

Wilcox, J. C. and C. H. Brownless. Tree fruit sprinkler irrigation, Okanagan Valley. British Columbia Dept. Agr. (Canada) Publ. 1121. 32 p. 1961.

Zioni, E. Cultivation, irrigation on hazel nut preharvest drop. (Ital. with Eng. and French summaries). Frutticoltura 25: 363-7. 1963.

GRAPES (CHAP. XX)

Amerine, M. A. Maturity studies with California grapes. II. The titratable acidity, pH, and organic acid content. Proc. Amer. Soc. Hort. Sci. *40*: 313-324. 1942.

Amerine, M. A. and A. J. Winkler. Maturity studies with California grapes. I. The Balling-acid ratio of wine grapes. Proc. Amer. Soc. Hort. Sci. *38*: 379-387. 1941.

Burlingame, B. B. et al. Frost protection costs for North Coast vineyards. Calif. Agr. Ext. Cir. 267. 10p. 1971.

Buttrose, M. S. Fruitfulness in grapevines: development of leaf primordia in buds in relation to bud fruitfulness. Bot. Gaz. 131(1):78-83. 1970.

Cahoon, G. A. and C. W. Donoho, Jr. Alar effects on yield, quality. Concord. Jour. ASHS 94 (in Press) about 1969.

Cahoon, G. A. and C. W. Donoho, Jr. The effect of Alar (N-dimethylamino succinamic acid) on yield and quality attributes of Concord grapes. Journ. ASHS (In press; presented at 1968 ann. meeting).

Canter-Visscher, T. W. Verticillium wilt of grapevine, a new record in New Zealand, New Zealand J. Agric. Res. pp. 359. 1970.

Carroll, D. E. Sugar and organic acid concentrations in cultivars of muscadine grapes. J. ASHS 96(6). Nov. 1971. p. 737.

Chamberlain, E. E., A. J. Over De Linden, and F. Berrysmith. Virus diseases of grapevines in New Zealand. N. Z. J. Agr. Res. p. 338. 1970.

Clore, W. J. and R. D. Fay. Effect of preharvest applications of Ethrel on Concord grapes HortSci. 5(1):21-23. Feb. 1970.

Clore W. J. et al. Composition of Washington-produced Concord grapes and juices. Wash. Agr. Exp. Sta. Tech. Bull. 48, 21 pp. 1965.

Clore, W. J. et al. Grape Varieties and wine making trials. Wash. Agr. Exp. Sta. Cir. 524. July 1970.

Cook, James A. Grape nutrition. Chap. in Fruit Nutrition book, edited by N. F. Childers. 777-812. Hort. Publ., Nichol Ave., New Brunswick, New Jersey, 1966.

Coulvillon, Gary A. and T. O. M. Nakayama. Effects of modified Munson training system on uneven ripening, soluble solids and yield of 'Concord' grapes. J. ASHS 95(2):158-161. 1970.

Crowther, R. F. and O. A. Bradt. Evaluation of grape cultivars for production of wine. Hort. Res. Inst., Ontario (Vineland). 1970 rpt.

————————————————. Grape cultivars for wine, Hort. Res. Inst. of Ontario, Vineland. 121-128. Ann. Rpt. 1970.

Dailey, R. T. et al. Costs, mechanical grape harvesters. Wash. Cir. 540. July 1971.

Dawson, J. H., W. J. Clore and V. F. Bruns. Weed control in grapes with Monuron, Diuron and Simazine. Wash. Agr. Exp. Sta. Bull 680, pp. 1967.

Dethier, B. E. and N. Shaulis. Cold hazard in N. Y. vineyards. Cornell Ext. Bull. 1127. 1964.

Diener, R. G. and J. H. Levin. Grape trellis wire strength tested. Mich. Quart. Bull. 50:2, 197-203. Nov. 1967.

878

Eguchi, T., T. Kato, and M. Koide. Flower bud differentiation and development of grapes. Jour. Hort. Assn. of Japan. Vol. 21 no. 1, pp. 46-52. 1952 (in Japanese with English summary).

Einset, Jr., et al. Grape varieties for N. Y. Cornell Ext. Bull. 1201. 1968.

Eskew, R. K. et al. Powdered grape juice. Food Tech. 8, 27-28. 1954.

Fay, R. and W. J. Clore. Plastic houses for propagating grape plants. Wash. E. M. 3501. Oct. 1971.

Fisher, D. V. et al. Location of fruit on grapevines in relation to cluster size and chemical composition. J. ASHS 96: (6). Nov. 1971. p. 741.

Fleming, H. K. and R. B. Alderfer. Cultivation and Concord grape production, Pr. Agr. Exp. Sta. Bull. 616. 18 pp. January, 1957.

Fuleki, T. Methods for tristimulus colorimetry of fruit juices. Hort. Res. Ins., Vineland, Ont. 1970 rpt.

Fulton, R. H. Small fruit diseases in Michigan, Mich. Agr. Ext. Serv. Bull. 370. 75 pp. 1960.

Grapes. Their Characteristics and Suitability for Production in Washington. Coop. Ext. Serv. Wash. State Univ., Pullman. EB-635, Jan. 1972.

Growing American bunch grapes USDA Farmers Bull. 2123. 21 pp. 1968.

Haeseler, C. W. and H. K. Fleming. Day temperature effects on Concord vines. Jan. 1970.

Haeseler, C. W. and H. K. Fleming. Day temperature effects on Concord vines. Pa. Agr. Exp. Sta. Bull. 739, 17 pp. 1967.

Hall, Carl W. Future of fruit industry in 2000 A.D. Blue Anchor. 47: (4) p. 24. Dec. 1970.

Hartmann, H. T. and D. E. Kester. Plant propagation — principles and practices (grape rootstocks and grafting). Prentice-Hall Inc., Englewood Cliffs, N. J. 07632. 700 pp. 1968.

Harvey, J. M. and W. T. Pentzer. Market diseases of grapes, small fruits. USDA-AMS Agr. Handbook 189, 45 pp. 1960.

Hewitt, W. B. and H. E. Jacobs. Zinc and fruit setting in Muscat grapes. Proc. A.S.H.S. 46, 256, 1945.

Kelly, B. W. Factors affecting grape production costs. Pa. Farm Manage. Mimeo. 14, 20 pp. 1962.

Kender, W. and G. Remaily. Regulation of sex expression and seed development in grapes wtih 2-chlorcethylphosphonic acid. Hort-Sci. 5: (6) p. 491. Dec. 1970.

Kliewer, W. M. et al. Effects of controlled temperature and light intensity on growth and carbohydrate levels of 'Thompson Seedless' grapevines. J. ASHS. 97: (2). March 1972. p. 185.

Kliewer, W. M. Effect of nitrogen on growth and composition of fruits from 'Thompson Seedless' grapevines. J. ASHS. 96: (6), Nov. 1971. p. 816.

Kliewer, W. Mark and J. A. Cook. Arginine and total free amino acids as indicators of the N status of grapevines. J. ASHS. 96:(5).581. 1971.

Kishi, M. and M. Tazaki. Response of grapes to gibberellin treatment. Agriculture and Horticulture, Vol. 35 no. 2, pp. 73-76. 1960 (in Japanese).

Larsen, R. P. et al. Effect of K, Mg, dolomitic lime on Concord grape. Mich. Quart. Bull. 45:3, 376-386. 1963.

Larsen, R. P. Chemical Concord defoliation for mechanical harvesting. Mich. Quart. Bull. 43:4, 830-838. May 1961.

Larsen, R. P., H. K. Bell, and Jerry Mandigo. Pruning grapes. Mich. Agr. Ext. Bull. 347, 16 pp. 1962.

Lider, L. A. and Nelson Shaulis. Resistant rootstocks in New York. N. Y. Agr. Exp. Sta.(Geneva) Res. Circ. 2. 1965.

Loomis, N. H. Growing American bunch grapes. U. S. Dept. of Agr. Farmers' Bull. (1936), 2123, 22 pp. (1959) 1968.

Mann, A. J. and F. W. Keane. The grape in the Okanagan Valley. Canada Agr. Exp. Sta., Summerland, British Columbia, mimeographed, no date.

Markarian, Deran. Genetic sources of winter hardiness in grapes. Jour. ASHS: 94: (in press) about 1969.

Mendall, S. C. and H. W. Tyler. Young vineyard culture, Finger Lakes area, 36 pp. Taylor Wine Co., Hammondsport, N. Y.

Moore, J. N. Cytokinin-induced sex conversion in male clones of Vitis species. J. ASHS 95(4):387-393. 1970.

Motts, G. N. Grape grader's manual. Mich. State Univ. Folder F-200. 1960's.

Moyer, J. C. Dirt content of grapes. Res. Circ. 6. N. Y. Agr. Exp. Sta., Geneva. July 1966.

Nelson, K. E. Packaging and handling trials on export grapes. Blue Anchor. 47(4):9. Dec. 1970.

Nesbitt, W. B. Seed-handling *V. rotundifolia* in breeding. Jour. ASHS 94: About 1969.

Overcash, J. P. Pruning, cluster thinning and potash fertilizer experiments with Concord and Delaware grapes growing on Dog Ridge rootstocks. Miss. Agr. Exp. Sta. Tech. Bull. 41. Apr., 1955.

Partridge, N. L. Fruiting habits and pruning, Concord. Mich. Agr. Exp. Sta. Tech. Bull. 69. 1925.

Partridge, N. L. Effect of crop and fertilizer on Concord maturity. Proc. ASHS 28: 147-150. 1931.

Paul, N. H. French-Amer. hybrid grape names. Finger Lakes Wine Growers Assn., Naples, N. Y. 14512. August 1970.

Pool, Robert M. and Robert J. Weaver. Internal browning of Thompson seedless grapes) J. ASHS 95(5):631-634. 1970.

Processing of grapes. For up-to-date information on Labrusca types, contact the agricultural experiment stations of New York, Geneva; Ohio, Wooster; Georgia, Griffin; Canada, Vineland, Ontario; Washington, Puyallup. For *vinifera* type, contact Univ. of California, Davis.

Saurer, W. and A. J. Antcliff. Polyploid mutants in grapes. HortSci. 4(3):226-227. 1969.

Shaulis, N. and R. G. D. Steel. Interaction of resistant rootstocks to the nitrogen, weed control, pruning and thinning effects on productivity of Concord grapevines. J. ASHS 95(4):422-429. 1969.

Shaulis, N. J. and T. D. Jordan. Cultural practices, New York vineyards. Cornell Ext. Bull. 805, 35 pp. 1960.

Shaulis, Nelson *et al.* Concord response to light, exposure, and Geneva Double-Curtain training. ASHS 89: 268-280. 1966.

Shaulis, Nelson *et al.* Controlled pruning effects on Concord grapes. ASHS 62: 221-227. 1953.

Shaulis, N., *et al.* Cultural practices for N. Y. vineyards. Cornell Ext. Bull. 805. 39 pp. 1966.

————. Growing cold-tender grapes in N. Y. Cornell Agr. Exp. Sta. Bull. 821. 16pp. 1968.

Shewfelt, A. L. Nature of red color in South Carolina Concord fruit. S. Car. Agr. Exp. Sta. Tech. Bull. 1025, 13 pp. 1966.

Slate, G. L. New York grape varieties, 1928-61. N. Y. Agr. Exp. Sta. Bull. 794, 50 pp. 1962.

Smit, C. J. B. and G. A. Couvillon Effect of modified Munson and 4-Arm Kniffin training systems on changes in pectic substances of 'Concord' Grapes. J. ASHS. 96(5) 1971 p. 547.

Snyder, J. C. and D. H. Brannon. Growing grapes in Washington. Wash. Agr. Ext. Bull. 271. 26 pp. 1961.

Soleimani, Abbas, *et al.* Influence of growth regulators on concentration of protein and nucleic acids in 'Black Corinth" Grapes. J. ASHS 95(2):143-45. 1970.

Sparks, D. and R. P. Larsen. Nitrogen effects on soluble solids of Concord. Mich. Quar. Bull. 48, No. 4:506-513. May 1966.

Stafford, E. M., J. E. Dibble, C. D. Lynn and W. B. Hewitt. Effects of oil sprays for controlling Pacific mite on grapevines. California Agriculture. May 1968.

Stover, L. H. Blue Lake, a new bunch grape for Florida home gardens. Florida Agr. Exp. Sta., Cir. S-120, January, 1960.

Thompson, C. R., *et al.* Effects of photochemical air pollutants on Zinfandel grapes. HortSci. 4(3):222-224. 1969.

Thompson, Robert. (ed.) California wine country. Sunset Lane Books. 95p. Menlo Park, California. 1968.

Tsuchiya, N. Modern Grape Growing (Budo Saibai Shinsetsu). Yokendo Co., Tokyo. 1956 (in Japanese).

Tukey, L. D. Post-year responses of Concord grape vines treated with N-dimethylamino succinamic acid. Journ. ASHS (In press; presented at 1968 ann. meeting).

Tukey, D. Relation of temperature and succinic acid, 2, 2-dimethyldrazide on berry set in the 'Concord' grape. HortSci. 5(6):481. Dec. 1970.

Tukey, L. D. and H. K. Fleming. Alar, fruit setting effect on grapes. Pa. Fruit News 46:6. 12-31. 1967.

Tukey, R. B., and W. J. Clore. Grape varieties for Wash. Wash. Coop. Ext. Serv. EB-635. Jan. 1972.

Vaile, J. E. Rootstock influence on yield, vigor of American grapes. ASHS 35: 471-474. 1938.

Way, R. D., F. G. Dennis and R. M. Gilmer. Propagating fruit trees, New York. N. Y. Agr. Exp. Sta. (Geneva) Bull. 817, 34 pp. 1967.

Weaver, Robert J. and M. Pool. Berry response of 'Thompson Seedless' and 'Perlette' grapes to application of Gibberellic Acid. J. ASHS. 96(2). March. 1971.

Weaver, R. J. and R. M. Pool. Induction of berry abscission in Vitis vinifera by morphactins. Journ. ASHS (In press; presented at 1968 ann. meeting).

Weaver, R. J. and A. J. Winkler. Effect of a regulator on the size of grapes. Plant Phys. 27, 626, 1952. See also Proc. A.S.H.S. 61, 135, 1953.

Winkler, A. J. Maturity tests for table grapes — The relation of heat summation to time of maturing and palatability. Proc. Amer. Soc. Hort. Sci. 51:295-298. 1948.

MUSCADINE TYPE

Bagby, John. Muscadine grapes, Alabama. Ala. Agr. Ext. Serv. Circ. P-25, 11 pp. 1965.

Carroll, D. E. et al. Chemical composition, muscadine grapes. Jour. ASHS 94: (in press) about 1969.

Fry, B. O. Chemical weed control in muscadine grapes. Ga. Agr. Exp. Sta. Leaflet NS-40, May 1963.

Hinrichs, H. A. Cimarron grape variety for fresh fruit, juice. Okla. Agr. Bull. B-597, 7 p. 1962.

Muscadine grapes for southern U. S. USDA Farmers Bull. 2157, 16 pp. 1961.

Stover, L. H. The Lake Emerald Grape. Fla. Agr. Exp. Sta. Cir. S-68. 12 pp. 1954. The Blue Lake grape, Fla. Agr. Exp. Sta. Cir. 1961.

Woodroof, J. G., S. R. Cecil, and W. E. DuPree. Processing Muscadine grapes. Ga. Agr. Exp. Sta. Bull. N. S. 17. 35 pp. 1956.

VINIFERA TYPE

Barrett, H. C. The French hybrid grapes. The National Horticultural Magazine. pp. 132-144. July, 1956.

Burlingame, B. B. et al. Frost protection costs, north coast vineyards. Calif. Agr. Ext. Serv. AXT-267. 13 pp. Feb. 1968.

Chambliss, S. E. Salinas (Calif.) Valley grape expansion. Am. Fruit Grower. May 1972.

California Agriculture is a monthly publication from Univ. of Calif., Davis, containing popular articles on agricultural research, including grapes. The articles following are examples. Loosening Thompson seedless bunches with bloom GA sprays, Nov. 1965; grape berry thinning with GA, Nov. 1966; GA timing for table grapes, Mar. 1966; irrigating Tokays, Apr. 1961; B deficiency in vineyards, Mar. 1961; grape leafhoppers-spray resistance, July 1961; grape mechanical harvesting, June 1962; grape container testing, July 1962; improving grape pruning labor, Mar. 1963; vineyard salinity, May 1963; kinins effects, Sept. 1963; grape leaf hopper parasite, Apr. 1965; bark-grafting grapes, Mar. 1965; soil management effects on vineyard irrigation, June 1968; Storage conditions, planting time on rooting Thompson Seedless cuttings, Dec. 1970. Spider mite situation in So. Joaquin on Thompson Seedless, Nov. 1971.

Christensen, Peter and A. N. Kasimatis. Zinc deficiency correction by soil injection. Amer. Jour. of Eno. and Vitic. 18:4. 217-224. 1967.

Clore, W. J. and R. B. Tukey. Trellising and training grapes. Wash. EB 637. 12pp. May 1972.

Combe, D. G. Growth retardants effects on V. vinifera fruit set. Nature 205: 4968. 305-306. 1965.

Delano Grape Story—growers' view re. Ceasar Chavez. So. Cent. Farmers Comm. P.O.B. 1094. Delano, Calif. 1969.

Folwel, R. J. et al. Table wine consumption in U.S. Wash. Agr. Exp. Sta. Cir. 519. June 1970.

Grape pest, disease control. Calif. Ext. Serv. Bull. 26pp. Request recent ann. edition.

Guillou, Rene. Coolers for fruits. Calif. Agr. Exp. Sta. Bull. 773. 66 pp. 1960.

Hale, C. R. and R. J. Weaver. Developmental stage effect on fruit translocation. V. vinifera. Hilgardia 33:3. 89-131. Oct. 1962.

Hale, P. W. and D. R. Stokes. Prepackaging California grapes at shipping point. U. S. Dept. of Agr., MRP-410. 35 pp. July, 1960.

Harmon, F. N. Rootstocks for vinifera grapes in the Napa Valley, California. ASHS 54: 157-162. 1949.

Harmon, F. N. and J. H. Weinberger. Chip-bud propagation of *vinifera* on root stocks. USDA Leaflet 513, 8 pp. July 1962.

Hendrickson, A. H. and F. J. Veihmeyer. Irrigation experiments with grapes. Calif. Agr. Exp. Sta. Bull. 728. 31 pp. 1951.

Hewitt, W. B. Some virus and virus-like diseases of grapevines. California Dept. of Agriculture (Sacramento) Ann. Bull. 1955.

Hoefert, L. L. and E. M. Gifford, Jr. Grape leaf-roll virus. Hilgardia 38:11. 403-426. Oct. 1967.

Kasimatis, A. N. *et al.* Economic review, California grape industry. Calif. Ext. Sev. M-17 Mimeo. 24 pp. Aug. 1967.

Kasimatis, A. N. *et al.* California offset-press leaflets as follows: grape rootstock varieties, AXT-47; standard wine varieties, AXT-59; Thompson seedless for table use, AXT-61; Thompson seedless for raisins and wine, AXT-60; non-irrigated, head-pruned varieties, AXT-158*; non-irrigated, head-pruned wine varieties, AXT-157*; irrigated, cane-pruned premium and wine varieties, AXT-156*; and 226*; standard wine varieties, AXT-55*; Emperor grapes, AXT-54*; drying fruits at home, HXT-80; producing quality raisins, AXT-235; vineyard irrigation, AXT-199; 1966-67. *These are cost-of-production pamphlets.

Lider, L. A. Nematode-resistant grape fruit stocks. Hilgardia 30:4. 123-139. July 1960.

Lider, L. A. *et al.* Effect of nematocide DBCP and irrigation on grapes on St. George rootstock. Amer. Journ. Eno. and Vitic. 18:1. 55-60. 1967.

Lider, L. A. *et al.* Pruning effects on vigorous grafted grapes. Jour. ASHS 94 (in Press) about 1969.

May, P. and A. J. Antcliff. Shading on fruitfulness of Sultana. Jour. Hort. Sci. 38:2. 85-94. 1963.

Mehr, S. Raisin industry of Iran. USDA-SASM-114, 37 pp. Apr. 1961.

Mehr, Stanley. Competition in world raisin market. USDA-FAS-136, 71 pp. June 1962.

Mosesian, R. M. and K. E. Nelson. Girdling and GA effects on Thompson Seedless. Amer. Journ. of Eno. and Vitic. 19: 1. 37-46. 1968.

Nelson, K. E. *et al.* Chemical and sensory variability in table grapes. Hilgardia 34:1. 1-42. 1963.

Olmo, H. P. Fertility in *vinifera-rotundifolia* hybrids. Jour. ASHS 94: (in press) about 1969.

Olmo, H. P. *et al.* Training and trellising grape vines for mechanical harvest. Calif. Agr. Ext. Serv. AXT-274. 16 pp. 1968.

Olmo, H. P. and A. Koyama. Rubired and Royalty varieties for concentrate and wine. Calif. Agr. Exp. Sta. Bull. 789, 13 pp. 1962.

Olmo, H. P. and A. Koyama. Niabell and Early Niabell grapes for commercial, home gardens. Calif. Agr. Exp. Sta. Bull. 790, 10 pp. Aug. 1962.

Raski, D. J., *et al.* Grape fan-leaf virus-nematode control by soil fumigation. Calif. Agr. Apr. 1971.

Raski, B. J. *et al.* Nematodes - vineyard control. Calif. Agr. Exp. Sta. Circ. 533, 23 pp. 1965.

Ryall, A. L. and J. M. Harvey. Cold storage of *vinifera* table grapes. USDA Agr. Handbook 159. 43 pp. 1959.

Seelig, R. A. (Editor) Grapes (inclusive review). Fruit and Vegetables Facts and Pointers, 28. pp. 777 14th St., N.W., Wash., D. C. 20005.

Shindy, W. W. *et al.* Growth regulator effects on acid and sugar transport in Muscat and Alexandria grapes. Journ. ASHS 94 (in press). About 1969.

Smith, L. M. and E. M. Stafford. Grape pests in California. Calif. Agr. Exp. Sta. Cir. 445. 63 pp. 1955.

Sullivan, D. T. and J. V. Enzie. New Mexico grape varieties. N. M. Agr. Exp. Sta. Bull. 475, 8 pp. 1963.

Thompson, V. (a) Calif. heat-treated grape plants. (b) Subirrigation saves water, increases yield, inhibits weeds in Calif. Goodgrape Grower (B. C. Canada). April 15, 1971.

Tukey, L. D. Subsequent effects of Alar on Concord. Jour. ASHS 94 (in press). About 1969.

Uota, M. and J. M. Harvey. SO₂ fumigation of grapes in RR refrigerator cars. USDA-AMS-MQRD. Rep. 642. 23 pp. Jan. 1964.

Weaver, R. J. and R. M. Pool. Morphactins and *vinifera* berry abscission. Jour. ASHS: 94 (in press) about 1969.

Weaver, R. J. *et al.* *Vinifera* response to 2, 4-D, related compounds. Hilgardia 31:5. 113-125. Aug. 1961.

Weaver, R. J. and S. B. McCune. Effect of GA on seeded and seedless *V. vinifera*. Hilgardia 30:15. 425-444. 1961.

Weaver, R. J. and O. J. Leonard. 2, 4-D dormant effects on pruned, non-pruned Tokay. Hilgardia 37:18. 661-675. Jan. 1967.

Weaver, R. and R. M. Pool. Effect of (2-Chloroethyl) phosphonic acid. (Ethephon) on Maturation of *Vitis vinifera*. J. ASHS. 96:(6). Nov. 1971. p. 725.

Weaver, R. J. and R. M. Pool. Thinning 'Tokay' and 'Ziinfandel' grapes by bloom sprays of Gibberellin. J. ASHS. 96:(6). Nov. 1971. p. 820.

Weaver, R. J., J. Van Overbeek, and R. M. Pool. Kinins effects on fruit set, yield, *V. vinifera*. Hilgardia 37:7. 181-201. Jan. 1966.

Weaver, R. J. and S. B. McCune. Girdling: Its relation to carbohydrate nutrition and development of Thompson Seedless Red Malaga, and Ribier grapes. Hilgardia 28: No. 1b. 421-457. 1959.

Winkler, A. J. Pruning Grapevines. Calif. Agr. Exp. Sta. Cir. 477. 11 pp. 1959.

Winkler, A. J. General Viticulture. Univ. of Calif. Press, Berkeley, 633 pp. 1962.

Wittwer, S. H. and M. J. Bukovac. Effects of GA on economic crops. Econ. Bot. 12:3. 213-255. 1958.

Yeou-Der, Kang, *et al.* Temperature-growth regulator effects on Tokay seed germination. Jour. ASHS 94: (in press). About 1969.

WINE

Amerine, M. A. and A. J. Winkler. Grape varieties for wine production. Calif. Agr. Exp. Sta. Leaflet 154. 1963.

Amerine, M. A. and A. J. Winkler. California wine grapes: composition and quality of their musts and wine. Calif. Agr. Exp. Sta. Bull. 794, 83 pp. 1963.

Amerine, M. A. and G. L. Marsh. Wine making at home. Wine Publ., 16 Beale St., San Fran., Calif. 94105. 32 pp. 1962.

Amerine, M. A., H. W. Berg, and W. V. Cruess. The technology of wine making. The Avi Publ. Co., Inc., Westport, Conn. 799 pp. 1967.

Amerine, M. A. and V. L. Singleton. Wine. An introduction for Americans. Univ. of Calif. Press, Berkeley and Los Angeles. 357 pp. 1965.

Barretts T. J. , *et al.* Induced malo-lactic fermentations of N. Y. wines. N.Y. Food and Life Sci. Jan.-Mar. 1972.

Castille, M. A. The "grapemobile" for rapid field testing of sugar content, processing grapes. Agricultural Marketing (USDA) 13: October 1968.

Clore, W. J. *et al.* Grape variety responses and wine making trials in central Washington. Wash. Ag. Exp. Sta. Circ. 477, 11 pp. 1967.

Hedrick, U. P. Grapes and wines from home vineyards. Oxford Univ. Press, London, N. Y., Toronto, 325 pp. 1945.

Joslyn, M. A. and M. A. Amerine. Dessert, appetizer and related flavored wines. The technology of their production. Div. Agr. Sci., Univ. of Calif., Berkeley. 483 pp. 1964.

Van Haarlem, J. R., R. F. Crowther, and J. H. L. Truscott. Variety tests of grapes for wine. Hort. Prod. Lab. Rpr., Ontario Dept. of Agr., 130-152. 1953-54.

Yang, H. Y., W. F. Steele, and H. B. Lagerstedt. Analysis of Oregon grapes for Oregon wines. Ore. Agr. Exp. Sta. Cir. 598. Sept., 1959.

STRAWBERRY (CHAP. XXI)

Anderson, J. F. and W. J. Lord. Small fruit culture. Mass. Agr. Ext. Serv. Publ. 17, 36 pp. 1968.

Arney, S. E. Studies in growth and development in the genus *Fragaria*. I. Factors affecting the rate of leaf production in Royal Sovereign strawberry. Jour. Hort. Sci. 28: 73-84. 1953.

Arney, S E., Studies of growth and development in the genus *Fragaria* II. The initiation, growth and emergence of leaf primordia. Ann. Bot. NS *17*: 477-492. 1953.

Arney, S. E. Studies of growth and development of the genus *Fragaria*. III. The growth of leaves and shoots. Ann. Bot. (n.s.) *18*: 349-365. 1954.

Arney, S. E. Studies of the growth and development in the genus *Fragaria*. IV. Winter growth. Ann. Bot. *19*: 265-267. 1955.

Arney, S. E. Studies of growth and development in the genus *Fragaria*. V. Spring growth. Ann. Bot. *19*: 277-287. 1955.

Arney, S. E. Studies of growth and development in the genus *Fragaria*. VI. The effect of photoperiod and temperature on leaf size. Jour. Exp. Bot. 7: 65-79. 1956.

Bain, Henry F. and J. B. Demaree. Red Stele Root Disease of the Strawberry Caused by *Phytophthora Fragariae*. Jour. Agr. Res. *70*: 11-30. 1945.

Ball, E. and C. E. T. Mann. Studies in Root and Shoot Growth of the Strawberry. III. The influence of time of planting on the development of the Strawberry. Jour. Pom. and Hort. Sci. 6: 87-103. 1927.

Brierley, W. G. and R. H. Landon. Studies on some factors relating to hardiness in the strawberry. Part III. The respiratory rate of the dormant strawberry plants. Minn. Agr. Exp. Sta. Bull. Pt. III 30-34. 1939.

Chesness, J. L., H. J. Braud, and P. L. Hawthorne. Freeze protecting strawberries with foam insulation. Journ. ASHS (In press; presented at 1968 ann. meeting).

Clark, J. H. Growth and composition of the strawberry plant as affected by source of nitrogen and pH value of the nutrient medium. N. J. Agr. Expt. Sta. Bull. 691. 1941.

Christopher, E. P. The influence of spacing on yield and grade of strawberries. R. I. Agr. Expt. Sta. Bull. 283. 1941.

Darrow, G. M. Development of runners and runnerplants in the strawberry. U.S.D.A. Tech. Bull. 122. 1929.

Darrow, G. M. Experimental studies on the growth and development of strawberry plants. Jour. Agr. Res. 41: 307-325. 1930.

Darrow, G. M. Inter-relation of temperature and photoperiodism in the production of fruit-buds and runners in the strawberry. Proc. Amer. Soc. Hort. Sci. 34: 360-363. 1936.

Darrow, G. M., and H. A. Borthwick. Fasciation in the strawberry. Inheritance and the relationship of photoperiodism. Jour. Hered. 45: 298-304. 1954.

Darrow, G. M., A. C. Goheen and P. W. Miller. The importance of virus diseases in the cultivation of strawberries in the United States. Proc. Amer. Soc. Hort. Sci. 63: 547-552. 1954.

Darrow, G. M., and G. F. Waldo. Responses of strawberry varieties to duration of the daily light period. U. S. Dept. Agr. Tech. Bull. 453. 1934.

Darrow, G. M. Strawberry culture—South Atlantic and Gulf Coast Regions. U. S. Dept. of Agr. Farmer's Bull. 1026. 36 pp. 1966.

Davis, M. B. Factors influencing strawberry production. Sci. Agr. 5: 196-198. 1925.

Davis, M. B., and H. Hill. Nutritional studies with Fragaria. Sci. Agr. 8: 681-692. 1928.

Davis, M. B., H. Hill and F. B. Johnson. Nutritional studies with Fragaria. II. A study of the effect of deficient and excess potassium, phosphous, magnesium, calcium and sulfur. Sci. Agr. 14: 411-432. 1934.

Demaree, J. B. and C. P. Marcus. Virus diseases of strawberries in the United States with special reference to distribution, indexing, and insect vectors in the east. Plant Dis. Reptr. 35: 527-537. 1951.

Dennis, Carleton C. Strawberry purchases. Mich. Agr. Expt. Sta. Quartely Bull. Vol. 42: No. 4. 859-870. 1960.

Denisen, E. L., R. H. Shaw, and B. F. Vance. Effect of summer mulches on yields of everbearing strawberries, soil temperature and soil moisture. Ia. State Coll. Journ. of Sci. 28:2. pp. 167-175. Nov. 15, 1953.

Dodge, J. C. and J. C. Snyder. Growing strawberries in Washington. Wash. Agr. Ext. Serv. Bull. 246. 19 pp. Request recent edition.

Fisher, E. G. and Ray Sheldrake. Growing strawberries for home use. Cornell Exten. Bull. 943. Request recent edition.

Friedman, B. A. and W. A. Radspinner. Vacuum cooling fresh vegetables and fruits. USDA AMS-107. 1956.

Greenslade, R. M. The migration of the strawberry aphis Capitophorus Fragaria Theob. Jour. and Hort. Sci. 19: 87-106. 1941.

Guttridge, C. G. Inflorescense initiation and aspects of the growth habit of the strawberry. Ann. Rep. Long Ashton Res. Sta. 1951, 42-48. 1952.

Guttridge, C. G. Observations on the shoot growth of the cultivated strawberry plant. Jour. Hort. Sci. 30: 1-11. 1955.

Harris, G. H. Sawdust as a mulch for strawberries. Sci. Agr. 31: 52-60. 1951.

Hartmann, H. T. Some effects of temperature and photoperiod on flower formation and runner production in the strawberry. Plant Physiol. 22: 407-420. 1947.

Hartmann, H. T. The influence of temperature on the photoperiodic response of several strawberry varieties grown under controlled environment conditions. Proc. Amer. Soc. Hort. Sci. 50: 243-245. 1947.

Havis, A. L. A developmental analysis of the strawberry fruit. Amer. Jour. Bot. 30: 311-314. 1943.

Hull, Jerome, Jr. Commercial strawberry culture in Michigan. Mich. Ext. Bull. E-682. Oct. 1970.

Hunter, A. W. S. The experimental induction of parthenocarpic strawberries. Can. Jour. Bot. C *19*: 413-419. 1941.

Johanson, Frank D. and R. B. Walker. Nutrient deficiencies and foliar composition of strawberries. Proc. Amer. Soc. Hort. Sci. 83:431-439. 1963. See also Johanson's deficiency symptoms in color: Wash. Ext. Bull. 561. 24 pp. 1965.

Judkins, W. P. The effect of training systems and irrigation on the yield of everbearing strawberries grown in sawdust mulch. Proc. Amer. Soc. Hort. Sci. *55*:277-284. 1950.

Kirsch, R. K. and T. L. Jackson. Fertilizing strawberries in the Willamette Valley. Ore. Exp. Sta. Cir. 594. 7 pp 1959.

Koehler, C. S., et al. Strawberry diseases, insects. Cornell Ext. Bull. 1120. 1967.

Lineberry, R. A. Influence of fertilizers on winter root growth of strawberries on Norfolk fine sandy loam in Eastern North Carolina. Commercial Fert. *61*: (4): 7-10. 1940.

Lineberry, R. A. and L. Burkhart. Nutrient deficiencies in the strawberry leaf and fruit. Plant Physiol. *18*:324-333. 1943.

Lineberry, R. A., L. Burkhart and E. R. Collins. Fertilizer requirements of strawberries on new land in North Carolina. Proc. Amer. Soc. Hort. Sci. *45*:283-292. 1944.

Mann, C. E. T. Studies in the root and shoot growth of the strawberry. V. The origin, development and function of the roots of the cultivated strawberry. Ann. Bot., Lond. *44*:55-86. 1930.

Mann, C. E. T. and E. Ball. Studies in the root and shoot growth of the strawberry. Jour. Pom. Hort. Sci. *5*: 149-169. 1925.

Mann, C. E. T. and E. Ball. Studies in the root and shoot development of the strawberry. II. Normal development in the second year. Jour. Pom. Hort. Sci. *6*: 81-86. 1927.

Mann, C. E. T. and E. Ball. Studies in the root and shoot development of the strawberry. IV. The influence of some cultural practices on the normal development of the strawberry plant. Jour. Pom. Hort. Sci. *6*: 104-112. 1927.

Marcus, C. P. Survey for virus-infected wild strawberry plants in eastern United States. Plant Dis. Reptr. *36*: 353-354. 1952.

McCrory, S. A. and William Lazaruk. Mulching strawberry plants for winter protection. So. Dakota Agr. Exp. Sta. Bull. 420. 18 pp. 1952.

McGrew, J. R. and D. H. Scott. Effect of Two Virus Complexes on the Responses of Two Strawberry Varieties. Plant Disease Reptr. *43*: 385-389. 1959.

Matlock, D. L. Strawberry Nutrition in Fruit Nutrition. Ed. by N. F. Childers. Horticultural Publications, New Bunswick, N. J. pp. 684-726. 1954.

Morrow, E. B. and G. M. Darrow. Relation of number of leaves in November to number of flowers the following spring in the Blakemore strawberry. Proc. Amer. Soc. Hort. Sci. *37*: 571-573. 1939.

Nitsch, J. P. Growth and morphogenesis of the strawberry as related to auxin. Am. J. Bot. 37, 211. 1950. Also excised ovaries in Vitro. 28, 566. 1951.

Norton, R. A. Winter protection of strawberry plants by physical and chemical methods. Journ. ASHS (In press; presented at 1968 ann. meeting).

Parker, M. M. *et al.* Commercial strawberry production in Eastern Virginia. Va. Truck Exp. Sta. Bull. 115, 71 pp. 1956.

Pest, disease control-strawberries. Calif. Agr. Exp. Sta. & Exp. Serv. Bull. 12 pp. Jan. 1972.

Robertson, M. Studies in the development of the strawberry. III. Flower-bud initiation and development in the large-fruited perpetual ("Remontant") strawberries. Jour. Hort. Sci. *30*: 62-68. 1955.

Robertson, M. and C. A. Wood. Studies in the development of the strawberry. I. Flower-bud initiation and development in early- and late-formed runners in 1951 and 1952. Jour. Hort. Sci. *29*: 104-111. 1954.

Robertson, M. and C. A. Wood. Studies in the development of the strawberry. II. Stolon production by first-year plants in 1952. Jour. Hort. Sci. *29*: 231-234. 1954.

Rogers, W. S. and Irena Modlibowska. Low temperature injury to fruit blossom III. Water sprinkling as an anti-frost measure. Rep. E. Malling Res. Sta. for 1949, 63-68. 1950.

Ruef, J. U. and H. W. Richey. A study of flower bud formation in the Dunlap strawberry. Proc. Amer. Soc. Hort. Sci. *22*: 252-260. 1925.

Rudnicki, R., J. Pieniazek and N. Pieniazek. Abscisin II in strawberry — role in dormancy, fruit ripening. Bull. de L'Academie Polonaise des Sciences *16*: No. 2. 127-130. 1968.

Schilletter, J. C. Fruit-bud differentiation in the Dunlap strawberry in relation to the age and position of the plant. Proc. Amer. Soc. Hort. Sci. 28: 216-219. 1931.

Scott, D. H., W. F. Jeffers. Resistance of strawberry varieties and selections to races of red stele. Proc. Amer. Soc. Hort. Sci. 62: 306-310. 1953.

Smeets, L. Runner formation on strawberry plants in autumn and winter. II. Influence of the light intensity on the photo-periodical behavior. Euphytica. 4: 240-244. 1955.

Smeets, L. Influence of the temperature on runner production in five strawberry varieties. Euphytica 5: 13-17. 1956.

Smeets, L. and H. G. Kronenberg. Runner formation on strawberry plants in autumn and winter. Euphytica 4: 53-57. 1955.

Smith, W. L. Jr., and P. H. Heinze. Effect of color development at harvest on quality of post-harvest ripened strawberries. Proc. Amer. Soc. Hort. Sci. 72: 207-211. 1958.

Sproat, B. B., G. M. Darrow and J. H. Beaumont. Relation of leaf area to berry production in the strawberry. Proc. Amer. Soc. Hort. Sci. 33: 389-392. 1936.

Varney, E. H., J. N. Moore and D. H. Scott. Field Resistance of Various Strawberry Varieties and Selections to Verticillium. Plant Disease Reptr. 43: 567-569. 1959.

Waldo, G. F. Fruit-bud formation in everbearing strawberries. Jour. Agr. Res. 40: 409-416. 1930.

Waldo, G. F. Fruit-bud development in strawberry varieties and species. Jour. Agr. Res. 40: 393-407. 1930.

Waldo, G. F. Investigations on the runner and fruit production of everbearing strawberries. U. S. Dept. Agr. Tech. Bull., 470. 1935.

White, P. R. Studies in the physiological anatomy of the strawberry. Jour. Agr. Res. 35: 481. 1927.

Wilcox, A. N., Weir, T. S., and Trantanella, Shirley, A new fruit introduction for 1960, the "Trumpeter" strawberry. Minn. Agr. Exp. Sta., Misc. Report 37, December, 1959.

(CON'T FROM STRAWBERRY CHAPTER CITATIONS)

Scott, D. H. Changing production patterns-strawberries. Amer. Fruit. Gr. Feb. 1971.

Smith, Carter R. and N. F. Childers. The strawberry: varieties, culture, marketing, pest control. Horticulture and Forestry Dept. Mimeo Rep. of National Conference of Research Workers. 184 pp. Rutgers Univ., New Brunswick, N. J. 1963.

Shoemaker, J. S. Small fruit culture. McGraw-Hill Book Co., Inc. New York, Toronto, London. Third Edition, 441 pp. 1955.

Slate, G. L. New strawberry varieties, N. Y. Agr. Exp. Sta. Bull. 762. 8 pp. March, 1954.

Strawberry culture: Eastern United States USDA Farmers' Bull. 1028. 20 pp. 1968.

Tompkins, J. Strawberry growing. Cornell Ext. Bull. 923. 23 pp. Mar. 1963.

Vaile, J. E. and A. T. McDaniel. Irrigation of strawberries—influence on development of beds and on yields. Ark. Agr. Exp. Sta. Bull. 568. March 1956.

Waldo, G. F. Commercial strawberry growing in the Pacific Coast States. Farmer's USDA Bull. 1027. Nov. 1968.

Webb, R. A. and D. G. Hollas. The effect of iron supply on strawberry, var. Royal Sovereign. J. Hort. Sci. 41:179-188. 1966.

Worthington, J. T. and D. H. Scott. Evaluation of stored and freshly dug strawberry plants for late summer and fall planting at Salisbury and Beltsville, Maryland. Transactions of Peninsula Hort. Soc. 1957.

FROST PROTECTION

Braud, H. J., Jr. and P. Hawthorne. Cold protection for Louisiana strawberries. La. State Univ. Bull. 591, 40 pp. 1965.

Eggert, Dean A. Liquid foam to prevent freeze injury to strawberry bloom. HortSci. 3:1. 11. Spring 1966.

Kidder, E. H. and J. R. Davis. Frost protection with sprinkler irrigation. Mich. Agr. Ext. Serv. Bull. 327. 1956.

Wheaton, R. Z. and E. H. Kidder. Frequency of sprinkler application on frost protection. Mich. Agr. Exp. Sta. Quart. Bull. 47:No. 3. 439-445. 1965.

PESTS

Allen, W. W. Strawberry pests in California—a guide for commercial growers. Calif. Agr. Exp. Sta. Circ. 484, 39 pp. 1959.

Campbell, Roy E. and E. A. Taylor. Strawberry insects—how to control them. USDA Farmers' Bull. 2184, 20 pp. 1965.

Darrow G. M., J. R. McGrew, and D. H. Scott. Reducing virus and nematode damage to strawberry plants. U. S. Dept. of Agr. Leaflet 414. 8 pp. 1957.

Demaree, J. B., and C. P. Marcus. Virus diseases of strawberries in the United States, with special reference to distribution, indexing, and insect vectors in the East. Plant Disease Reporter *35*: 12. pp. 527-537. Dec. 15, 1951.

Fulton, R. H. Small fruit diseases in Michigan. Mich. Agr. Ext. Serv. Bull. 370. 74 pp. January 1960.

Hamblen, M. L. and R. D. Riggs. Soil fumigation increases strawberry production in Arkansas. Down to Earth (Dow Chemical Co., Midland, Mich.) Winter 1962.

Horn., N. L. and P. L. Hawthorne. Control of *botrytis* rot of strawberries. La. State Univ. Bull. 547, 16 pp. 1961.

Huffaker, C. B. and C. E. Kenneth. Experimental studies on predation: predation and Cyclamen-mite population on strawberries in California. Hilgardia *26*: 4. pp. 191-222. October, 1956.

Jeffers, W. F. Cause and control of the red stele disease of strawberries. Md. Agr. Exp. Sta. Bull. 445. 8 pp. 1953.

McGrew, John R. Strawberry diseases. USDA Farmers' Bull. 2140, 27 pp. 1966.

Miller, P. W. and R. O. Belkengren. Elimination of certain virus complexes from strawberries by excision and culturing of apical meristems. Pl. Disease Reporter 47:4. 298-300. 1963.

Neiswander, R. B. Insect pests of strawberries in Ohio. Ohio Agr. Exp. Sta. Res. Bull. 763. 31 pp. 1955.

Overcash, J. P. and S. P. Crockett. Soil fumigation increases strawberry yields. Miss. Agr. Exp. Sta. Bull. 701, 7 pp. 1965.

Plakidas, A G. Strawberry diseases. La. State Univ. Studies Biol. Sci. Serv., Baton Rouge, 194 pp. 1964.

Schaefers, G. A. Deformed strawberries by tarnished plant bug. Farm Res. (N. Y. Ag. Exp. Sta., Geneva) June-Aug. 1963.

Schaefers, G. A. and W. W. Allen. Biology of strawberry aphids, cockerell, and P.T.H.R. Lambers in California. Hilgardia 32:393-431. 1962.

Spray schedules for strawberries: Contact your local, federal, provincial or state agricultural extension service or experiment station for up-to-date spray schedules. See also Chapter XVIII.

Varney, E. H., J. N. Moore, and D. H. Scott. Field resistance of various strawberry varieties and selections to *Verticillium*. Plant Disease Reporter 43:567-569. 1959.

Way, D. W. Further observations on the field performance of heat-treated strawberry clones. Journ. Hort. Sci. 40:No. 2., 167-174. Apr. 1965.

Wilhelm, Stephen. Diseases of strawberry—a guide for the commercial grower. Calif. Agr. Exp. Sta. Circ. 494, 28 pp. 1961.

WEED CONTROL

Anderson, J. Lamar. Chemical weed control in small fruits. Utah Farm and Home Sci. 5, 24. March 1964.

Collins, W. B. and C. F. Everett. Simazine for weed control in strawberries in Eastern Canada. Can. Journ. Pl. Sci. 45:541-547. 1965.

Haglund, W. A. Fumazone—a post plan fumigant for strawberries. Down to Earth, (Dow Chemical Co., Midland, Mich.), Spring 1966.

Ilnicki, R. D., C. R. Smith, and J. F. Ellis. The response of three varieties of strawberries to several herbicidal treatments. Proc. Northeast Weed Control Conf. 17:178-179. 1963.

Jones, T. H. Rotations for control of weeds in strawberries. Tenn. Agr. Exp. Sta. Bull. 267. 9 pp. 1957.

Lange, A. *et al.* Herbicide residues in soils. Calif. Agr. August 1968.

Leefe, J. S. Simazine on strawberries; effect on yield and labor. Can. Jr. Pl. Sci. 45:537-540. 1965; Soil pH and Simazine effects. Can. Jr. Pl. Sci. 48:424-425. 1968.

Ricketson, C. L. Effects of herbicides on growth and yield of strawberries. Ont. Hort. Exp. Sta. Rep. 6-13. 1965.

Note: See Chapter XVIII, Discussion and Bibliography. See previous editions of this book for earlier literature citations.

Bush Fruits (Chap. XXII)

Baker, E. A. *et al.* Growth retardants' effects on cuticle of black currants. Ann. Rpt. Long Ash. Res. Sta. (England) 116-121. 1967.

Brazos, a new erect blackberry for East Texas. Texas Agr. Exp. Sta. L-473, November, 1959.

Bunemann, G., D. H. Dewey and D. P. Watson. Anatomical changes in the fruit of the Rubel blueberry during storage in controlled atmospheres. Poc. Amer. Soc. Hort. Sci. *70*:156-160. 1957.

Currants and Gooseberries. Check the Ann. Rpts. of the Long Ash. Agr. & Hort. Res. Sta. (England) where research often is reported.

Fry, B. O. Early June, a new blackberry variety for Home Gardens. Georgia Agr. Exp Sta., Leaflet 21, October, 1959.

Garner, R. J. Propagation by cuttings and layers. Great Britain Bur. Hort. Plant Crops. Tech. Commun. 14, 1944.

Kennard, W. C., L. D. Tukey and D. G. White. Further studies with Maleic Hydrazide to delay blossoming of fruits. Proc. Amer. Soc. Hort. Sci. *58*:26-32. 1951.

Marth, P. C. and E. M. Meader. Regulators and blackberries. Proc. A.S.H.S. 45, 293, 1944.

Shutak, V. G., R. Hindle and E. P. Christopher. Factors associated with ripening of highbush blueberry fruits. Proc. Amer. Soch. Hort. Sci. *68*:178-183. 1956.

Skerrett, E. J. and O. J. Pritchard. Endrin residues on black currants. Ann. Rpt., Long Ash. Agr. & Hort. Res. Sta. (England) 143-144. 1967.

Zielinski, Q. B., et al. Regulators and blackberry size. Proc. A.S.H.S. 63, 182, 1954.

(CON'T FROM BUSH FRUITS CHAPTER CITATIONS)

Sanborn, P. C. Red currant cost production Western New York, 1962. Cornell Univ. Dept. Agr. Econ. Res. Rpt. 106, 22 pp. Nov. 1962.

Slate, G. L. Red currants and gooseberries. N. Y. Agr. Exp. Sta. (Geneva). Cir 112. Request late edition.

Thayer, Paul. The red and white currants: Their history, varieties, and classification. Ohio Agr. Exp. Sta. Bull. 371. 1923.

CRANBERRIES

American Cranberry Growers Association Proceedings. Distributed annually to members. (U. S. Cranberry Research, developments). Rutgers Univ. Substation. Pemberton, New Jersey.

Bergman, H. F. Disorders of cranberries. U. S. Dept. of Agr. Yearbook pp. 789-796. 1953.

Brannon, D. H. *et al*. Recommendations for cranberry production in Washington. Wash. Agr. Exp. Serv. Chart. Cir. 144. (Revised frequently).

Cain, J. C. and Paul Eck. Blueberry-cranberry nutrition, Chap. IV, Fruit Nutrition book, Editor N. F. Childers, Hort. Publ., Rutgers Univ., New Brunswick, N. J. 1966.

Chandler, F. B. Fertilizer for cranberries. Mass. Agr. Exp. Sta. Bull. 499, 15 pp. 1961.

Chandler, F. B. and I. E. Demoranville. Rest period for cranberries. Jour. Amer. Soc. Hort. Sci. 85:307-311. 1964.

Chandler, F. B. Cranberry varieties of North America. Mass. Agr. Exp. Sta. Bull. 513, 24 pp. 1959.

Cross, C. E. and I. E. Demoranville. Dalapon and Massachusetts cranberries. Down to Earth. Summer 1962.

Cross, C. E. Weeds of the Massachusetts cranberry bogs. Mass. Agr. Exp. Sta. Bull. 463. 55 pp. 1952.

Devlin, R. M., B. M. Zuckerman and I. E. Demoranville. Influence of preharvest applications of malathion on anthocyanin development in *Vaccinium macrocarpon*. (Mass.) Jour. ASHS (In press; presented at 1968 ann. meeting).

Doughty, C. C. *et al*. Cranberry storage longevity as influenced by growth retardants. ASHS 91: 192-204. 1967.

Eaton, E. L., K. A. Harrison, C. W. Marwell, and A. D. Pickett. The cranberry. Dom. of Canada, Dept. of Agr. Farmers' Bull. 151. Pub. 810, 35 pp. 1948.

Eaton, G. W. and D. P. Ormrod. Photoperiod effect on plant growth in cranberry. Can. Jr. Pl. Sci., 48:5. 447-450. Sept. 1968.

Eck, Paul. Cranberry culture (A book in preparation). Rutgers Univ. Press., New Brunswick, N. J. About 1971.

Filmer, R. S. and C. A. Doehlert, Use of honeybees in cranberry bogs. N. J. Agr. Exp. Sta. Bull. 764. 6 pp. 1952.

Franklin, Henry J. and Neil E. Stevens. Weather and water as factors in cranberry production. Mass. Agr. Exp. Sta. Bull. 433. 1946.

Greidanus, T. and M. N. Dana. Cranberry growth related to tissue concentration and soil test phosphorus. J. ASHS 97(3):326. May 1972.

Hovercraft. Shows promise in chemical applications to cranberry bogs without molesting the vines. Business Farming, p. 28, Mar. 1967. Contact Dept. of Aviation and Aeronautics, Princeton Univ., Princeton, N. J. for periodic U. S. developments.

Kaufman, J., P. L. Benfield, and P. R. Harding, Jr. Shipping tests with Massachusetts cranberries in conventional refrigerator cars with standard ventilation and in mechanically refrigerated cars. U. S. Dept. of Agr. AMS-187. 9 pp. 1955.

Kaufman, J., S. M. Ringel, A. A. Hamer, E. P. Atrops, and G. G. Ramsey. Effect of precooling on market quality of cranberries shipped by rail or truck. U. S. Dept. of Agr. AMS-287. 9 pp. 1958.

Mainland, C. M. and P. Eck. GA and Alar effects on cranberry fruit set, growth, yield. ASHS 92:296-300. 1968.

Norton, John S. Cleaning cranberry bog ditches — a new technique. Mass. Agr. Exp. Sta. Bull. 527, 9 pp. 1962.

Norton, John S. Sprinkler systems for cranberries. Mass. Agr. Exp. Sta. Bull. 532, 20 pp. 1962.

Patterson, M. E. et al. Bruising effects on cranberry fruit. ASHS 90:498-505. 1967.

Ringel, S. M., J. Kaufman and M. J. Jaffe. Refrigerated storage of cranberries. USDA-MRR 312, 17 pp. 1959.

Seelig, R. A. and Elise Roberts. Cranberries (complete survey, history, etc.). Fruit and Vegetable Facts and Pointers. Fresh Fruit and Vegetable Assoc., 777 - 14th St., NW, Wash., D. C. 15 pp. Nov. 1959.

Shawa, A. Y. et al. Fungicide effects on cranberry pollen germination, fruit set. ASHS 89:255-258. 1966.

Stevens, C. D., C. E. Cross, and W. E. Piper. Cranberry industry in Massachusetts. Mass. Dept. of Agr. (Boston), Bull. 157, 45 pp. 1957.

Zuckerman, B. M. et al. Juice, sauce from cranberry varieties. ASHS 89:248-254. 1966.

BLUEBERRIES

Ballinger, W. E., et al. Anthocyanins of ripe fruit of a "Pink-Fruited" hybrid of highbush blueberries, Vaccinium corymbosum L. J. ASHS 97(3):381. May 1972.

Frenkel, C. Isozymes in fruit ripening—pear, blueberry, Pl. Phys. 49. 757-63, 1972.

Knapp, F. W. Processing, evaluation of Florida blueberries. Proc. Fla. State. Hort. Soc. 84:247-249. 1971.

Mainland, C. and R. P. Rohrbach. Procedings—1971 Highbush Blueberry Mechanization Symposium. HortSci. Dept., No. Car. State Univ., Raleigh. 177p. 1971.

U. S. STANDARDS

U. S. Standards for (a) berries for processing, (b) blueberries for processing, (c) dewberries and blackberries, (d) currants for processing and (e) fresh cranberries for processing, can be obtained by writing the U. S. Dept. of Agr., Agr. Marketing Service, Washington 25, D.C.

PRODUCTION COSTS (FRUITS IN GENERAL)

Bontrager, H. L. and H. M. Hutchings. Cherry brining costs as affected by container type. Ore. Agr. Exp. Sta. Spec. Rpt. 191, 47 pp. Apr. 1965.

Doran, S. M. and J. M. Lange, Pear production costs in Washington. Wash. Mimeo EM—3553. June 1972.

Doran, S. M. and R. E. Hunter. Cost of establishing full-dwarf (EM-2834) semi-dwarf (EM-2833) and standard apple trees (EM-2832) in Wash. Wash. Agr. Ext. Serv. Mimeo pamphlets. 1967. See also 1972 follow-up reports.

Fitch, L. B. et al. Plum machine fruit thinning cost. Calif. Agric., 1972.

Greig, W. S. and A. D. O'Rourke. Apple packing costs in Wash. Wash. Agr. Exp. Sta. Bull. 755. May, 1972.

Norton, R. L. Costs of growing standard vs. compact apple trees. Proc. Va. State Hort. Soc., Roanoke, 1972.

Kearl, C. D. Cash crops and fruits, costs and returns from farm cost accounts, 39 farms, 1961. N. Y. Agr. Exp. Sta. AE Res. Rpt. 101, 17 pp. 1962.

Kelly, B. W. Cost of producing cherries in Pennsylvania 1959-62. Penna. Agr. Exp. Sta. Farm Management Bull. 13, 12 pp. 1963.

Lamborn, E. W. and Richard K. Hart. Processing costs in the frozen sour cherry industry. Utah County 1964. Utah Agr. Exp. Sta. Resources Series 35, 22 pp. 1966.

Myszkowski, E. J., Jr. Costs of producing red tart cherries in 58 western New York farms 1961. N. Y. Agr. Exp. Sta. AE Res. Rpt. 105, 20 pp. Nov. 1962.

Shieh, John T. and Carlton C. Dennis. The tart cherry industry: processing costs and efficiency. Mich. Agr. Exp. Sta. Res. Rpt. 27, 36 pp. 1965.

Stanton, B. F. and B. A. Dominick, Jr. Management and cost control in producing apples for fresh market. N. Y. Agr. Exp. Sta. Bull. 1001, 24 pp 1964.

Travis, Van and B. F. Stanton. Costs and use of labor in harvesting apples for fresh market. Hudson Valley 1959-60. N. Y. Agr. Exp. Sta. AE Res. Rpt. 63, 13 pp. Apr. 1961.

Zuroske, C. H. and J. A. Black. Sweet cherry production costs, central Washington, 1959. Wash. Agr. Exp. Sta. Circ. 378, 9 pp. 1960.

Note: For up-to-date cost-of-production data, write the departments of agricultural economics at the state experiment stations where the crop in question predominates in the country. States who have been issuing this type information rather regularly are: Cornell University, Ithaca, New York; Washington State University, Pullman; Michigan State University, East Lansing; Pennsylvania State University, University Park; University of California, Davis; Oregon State University, Corvalis; and Ohio State University, Columbus.

PROFIT SHARING
(Helps avoid labor problems)

Note: Following is a philosophy of orchard operation that may be of help to other orchard managers.

The key to a profitable orchard operation is a spirit of mutual trust, co-operation, and effort between management and labor. This is the philosophy of Henry W. Miller, Jr., president of the 1500-acre Consolidated Orchard Company of Paw Paw, W. Va. Beginning in 1939, Consolidated has encouraged a spirit of mutual interest through a profit-sharing plan for its employees. In addition to prevailing wages, paid semi-monthly, employees receive in cash, just before Christmas each year, a share of profits determined by the company's board of directors. Depending upon the market, production costs, and other economic factors, the plan has paid from 2 to 20% of each employee's yearly earnings during the 29 years it has been in effect; the average has been about 10% extra pay to all regular employees.

What happens under profit sharing in a year when there are no profits? Consolidated made small year-end payments three times during the course of the plan when the company had not made an operating profit. In 1951, after a heavy loss from hail storms, only 2% was paid and in 1957 and 1958, small distributions were made (6% and 5%) when the company just about broke even after being squeezed by a buyer's market, higher production costs, and adverse weather.

When year-end distributions are made, a personal letter from the company's president goes with each check, explaining in detail why it was possible to make the payment, how the enclosed check was figured, and how much the employee's friendly co-operation and good work has contributed to the success being shared by all.

To try to keep pace with changing trends in labor-management relations, Consolidated has from time to time also added some fringe benefits as the company became financially able to do so.

● The company covers a major part of the cost of a group insurance plan providing medical attention and hospitalization for employees and their families. The policy also provides for payment of $20 per week up to 26 weeks to employees unable to work due to illness and $1500 life insurance with double indemnity on the breadwinner. Regular employees are eligible without examination after having worked with the company more than one year.

● After a year's service, employees are also entitled to a one-week vacation with pay at the company's convenience—generally Christmas week.

● The company owns and maintains 36 comfortable homes for foremen and other key personnel. These homes are rent free.

● After one year's service, regular employees with a good work record can borrow up to $100 without collateral or interest. Repayment is generally made by $5 or $10 payroll deductions later on when the employee is better able to return the money.

Perhaps as important as the profit-sharing plan and fringe benefits at Consolidated is the company's attitude toward its employees. Henry Miller feels strongly that employees should be treated as neighbors and friends. An employee visiting his office or home receives the same pleasant and courteous consideration as a good customer. As Miller points out, a trained, interested employee is even more valuable to Consolidated than a good customer. Good employees under first-class management produce a good product, and a good product invariably attracts good customers—thus, the employee comes first.

As a result of close employee-management relationship at Consolidated, dissension and arguments between workers and management are practically non-existent and the company has thereby become known throughout the area as a good place to work. This is the major reason why the organization has never suffered from a shortage of good help. It has always been able to attract additional local help to harvest crops without resorting to the use of imported workers, even during World War II. All other large Appalachian orchardists have found it necessary to rely upon imported help to save their crops in recent years.

Occasionally someone indicates that Mr. Miller's plan is comparatively easy because the company operates in a depressed area where there is supposed to be a labor surplus. But Miller is quick to reply that this is an incorrect assumption because Consolidated's orchards are located in northeastern West Virginia and western Maryland, in a highly developed industrial section.

The Organization

Consolidated Orchard Company now carries about 80 year-round employees, including labor and management to man the orchards, cold storages, packing plant, shops, and offices. In September and October about 80 more employees are added to the payroll in a normal season.

The company owns and operates four large orchards which are called divisions — two in Allegany County, Maryland, and one each in Morgan and Hampshire counties, West Virginia — for a total of 1500 acres. Each division has a superintendent and two foremen.

The central packing plant and cold storages are in Paw Paw and these facilities are used about nine months each year. The company produces a substantial tonnage of summer apples and peaches and the regular apple packing season generally lasts until mid-March. All apples are packed fresh on order throughout the shipping season. Management in the plant consists of a packing superintendent and his assistant, plus a cold storage manager and his assistant.

A general workshop is maintained where all company machinery is kept in good working shape. During the winter months, four mechanics give trucks, tractors, sprayers, and other equipment a first-class overhauling. The shop foreman works full time at keeping up the equipment, however, his three wintertime helpers generally become truck, tractor, or fork-lift operators in the orchards and storages when the crop is being harvested.

After 29 years of experience with profit sharing, he is convinced that it is a sound business policy. He also is convinced that the plan has helped make it possible for Consolidated to produce and market a top-quality product that sells readily at premium prices. In Miller's opinion there is no sounder moral or business investment than profit sharing.

How Profits Are Shared

All employees on the payroll during the pay period ending December 15 of each year are eligible. Seniority is not a factor in distribution under the plan. (Seasonal workers are not on the payroll when profit-sharing payments are made and, therefore, do not participate in the plan.)

The total number of dollars set up for distribution at the end of each 12-month period is voted by the board of directors. In determining the amount to be distributed in a given year, the board first gives proper consideration to the company's general financial condition. When the company has had a financially satisfactory season, the board then sets aside a safe and proper share of the net operating earnings, before taxes, for distribution to eligible employees.

Actual distribution is allocated to employees in proportion to the basic salaries received during the year for which a given distributon is made. The basic wage scale, before profit sharing, is maintained at or above levels paid by other fruit producers in the area.

To illustrate, should the company make a distribution of say 10% as of the end of a given year, an employee having earned $3000 would receive $300; and an employee in a more responsible and better paying job of, say $4000, would get $400. All payments are made in cash. From American Fruit Grower.

FARM LABOR, PROTECTION OF PROPERTY RIGHTS

The following excerpts have been taken from McDermott, Frank X. "Guide to farm labor and the protection of property rights," circulated by the N. J. Farm Bureau, 168 W. State St., Trenton, 08608. Copies for details are available for $2.50. This informaion was distributed in the late 1960s. The farm labor regulations and trends are changing fast. It also should be recognized that these suggestions apply to the State of New Jersey and may vary elsewhere. They do give, however, a survey of the problems involved and suggested solutions.

Developing an Employee Program

"The most important thing you as a grower can do is to keep up with the prevailing wage rates and working conditions in your area and to have a personal awareness of the operation of your orchard. Keep abreast with the minimum wage from year to year.

A contract to pay less than the minimum wage is not enforceable, even if the worker signs a written agreement. However, reasonable deductions are permitted for the actual cost of food and lodging furnished. The grower who pays his employees the same wages which employees on neighboring farms receive and who provides comfortable living and working conditions is less likely to be singled out as the target of a strike or other union action on grounds that he is treating his employees in a substandard manner. In addition, the employer who knows the people who work for him and who shows an interest and awareness of their working conditions, is less likely to be organized by a union.

Check List For Good Employer-Employee Relations

This check list is designed to assist you in taking the pulse of employee morale. Questions which cannot be answered "yes" indicate areas where corrective action may be taken profitably.

Favoritism: Do you assign work to employees in a fair and equal manner? Are you impartial in your dealings with the people you supervise? Do you "play favorites"? Do you give some employees special privileges and deny them to others? Is overtime distributed fairly? Are your policies involving employee conduct administered in the same way to all employees?

Working Conditions: Have hazardous conditions been eliminated? Do working conditions compare favorably with other farms in the area? Are employees provided with convenient facilities which meet expected standards? Wash rooms? Fresh, cool water? Eating facilities? Are employees provided with proper work equipment and supplies?

Listening and Talking to Employees: Are employees kept informed on your plans, policies, "news," etc.? Do members of management make regular tours of the farm, and speak to employees? Are the suggestions and opinions of employees given careful consideration and, if not acted upon, the employees told why? Are employees encouraged to pass their thinking and reactions on to supervisors? Does your announcement system scoop the employees! "grapevine"?

Employees Attitudes: Do you know what employees really think about you, the farm, their jobs, and their supervisors? Are employee attitudes friendly and cooperative? Are you constantly alert to conditions of possible employee unrest? Is employee turnover at a low level? Do you know the real reasons for the voluntary quits? Are they chargeable to: poor supervision? lack of job security? pay levels or methods? working conditions? Are increases in the number of gripes and complaints carefully noted and considered? Are "don't care" attitudes at a minimum? Is efficiency at satisfactory levels? Are supervisors alert for—and do they keep you informed of—any change in the attitudes of employees? Does your farm rate high as a place to work in the community? Do employees have a sense of pride in working for you? Do they have a feeling of belonging?

Relationship Of The Crew Leader To The Farmer

An increasing number of farmers have come to depend upon the use of migrant labor. As a rule, these laborers are supplied by crew leaders who round up the workers, transport them to and from the farm, and receive money from the farmer to pay their wages. Inquiries are frequently made about the status of the crew leader with respect to the farmer and the migrant laborer, and their respective liabilities for payment of wages and withholding taxes. Although both the State and Federal governments have laws requiring the crew leader to register and to conform to a certain standard of conduct, neither government has a policy sufficiently definite to provide clear answers to these and other questions that arise. The Federal law is revised and modified frequently. Therefore, the following observations ultimately may become the subject of court litigation before firm answers can be given in the current gray areas.

Who is the Employer? In the usual situation, the farm pays the crew leader who makes the necessary deductions and distributes the wages to the employees, keeping the balance as his fee. In this case, the crew leader should really be considered the employer because his relationship to the farmer is not unlike that of an independent contractor who employs laborers to do the work called for under the provisions of his contract with the owner. Therefore, the responsibility for payment of the minimum wage and for withholding social security taxes properly falls upon the crew leader and not upon the farmer. In fact, it is the administrative policy of the Federal Government that the crew leader occupies this status as an independent contractor, with the obligation to keep records and forward social security taxes, unless the crew leader enters into a written agreement with the farmer creating an employer-employee relationship between themselves. In such a case, the duty of record keeping and responsibility for social security taxes would fall upon the farmer as well, because the migrant laborers then would become the employees of the farmer. Obviously, so long as the Federal Government maintains this position, it is in the best interests of the farmer to avoid entering into a written agreement which might create an employer-employee relationship between himself and a crew leader, thereby protecting himself from liability in case of a default by a crew leader.

It must be remembered that the Crew Leader Registration Act is relatively new and will undoubtedly undergo certain changes, both in interpretation and application, before it becomes settled law. A farmer who "keeps his nose clean" by advising his crew leader that he expects compliance with the law, and by refusing, either actively or passively, to condone unscupulous exploitation of migrant laborers, need not be alarmed when a Labor Department representative comes to make an investigation.

The Minimum Wage Law. The State Minimum Wage Law, however, places responsibility upon a person who "suffers and permits" another person to work for him. On this basis, the State Department of Labor takes the position that the farmer as well as the crew leader may be responsible for payment of the minimum wage. The question is one of fact, and because a violation must be "knowing and willing," a farmer who acts honestly and in good faith, and not in collusion with a crew leader, cannot be prosecuted for criminal violation of the Wage and Hour Law where his violation is unintentional. As the New Jersey Minimum Wage Law is recent, there is little experience upon which the farmer may rely at this time. Undoubtedly, in the near future, there will be administrative and court decisions which will define and establish more clearly the legal relationship existing between crew leaders and farmers, and their respective responsibilities under the Act.

Workmen's Compensation Law. For purposes of workmen's compensation, the responsibility to provide coverage is upon the farmer. The fact that the crew leader makes wage payments to the laborers does not necessarily remove the farmer from responsibility. Under the totality of circumstances the farmer, who makes the decisions regarding when, where and how much work there shall be, is viewed as the employer.

Ordinarily, workmen's compensation coverage does not apply when the employee is going to or coming from work, but where transportation is furnished by the employer, it is considered to be incidental to and arising out of the course of employment and therefore covered. In this instance coverage begins at the moment the worker steps onto the bus. However, the crew leader is required under Federal Law to carry personal injury insurance for the protection of the workers while they are being transported to and from the farm.

The question of injuries to employees resulting from fights has been the subject of considerable litigation. Fights between fellow employees resulting from personal animosities are not compensable because they are not work-connected. Similarly, injuries sustained by employees as a result of "skylarking" or "horseplay" are not compensable. However, an innocent bystander injured as a result of "skylarking" or "horseplay" of others during working hours would be covered.

Injuries which occur during lunch hours or after the working day is over, whether from a fight or an accident, generally are not compensable. However, subject to the above-mentioned limitations there may be coverage for injuries sustained during a lunch hour if the employee is paid for his eating time, or if he remains under the control of the employer during his lunch hour. Under the Workmen's Compensation Law the decisions generally favored the payment of benefits to injured employees housed on a farm during either working or non-working hours.

How A Union Organizes Workers

Union attempts at organizing farm workers are inevitable and perhaps imminent. This does not mean that the farm must sit back helplessly and allow the union to take over. The organizer has no right to come upon the farmer's property if he is unwanted, and he must leave if asked to do so. How, then, will the union attempt to organize the farm help?

The union organizer has two immediate objectives when he makes his first contacts with workers. He is looking for leadership for his campaign and information about the specific problems and complaints of the employees.

There is no blueprint for meeting individual workers and gaining their confidence—conversations can be started in restaurants and bars, through "leads" passed on by other union members, and by acquaintances made through social affairs. If there is any rule at all, it is that contacts are not made by suddenly appearing at the farm with a leaflet urging employees to sign a union authorization card and mail it to a post office box.

Most organizers are interested primarily in meeting with the type of employee who is respected by his fellow-workers and who has influence on the farm. Getting to know a few of these employees is more important—at this stage—than meeting with the maximum number of workers.

Developing Leadership. Once a potential leader has been contacted, it is important that the union organizer wins his confidence and trust. Time spent in developing this leader, answering his questions about the union, and explaining the benefits of collective bargaining will be well worthwhile after the organizing campaign gets underway and this leader becomes a union spokesman inside the company's premises.

Respected "inside leaders" are vital to any campaign. The union representative must be sure that they are not known as "gripers" or "soreheads" and that they are not motivated simply by a desire for revenge or a driving personal ambition.

In the "perfect" campaign, the organizer will find a leader in every group; a woman for the female workers, leaders within minority racial and national groupings, and spokesmen for the various work gangs. Since the "perfect" situation rarely exists, the union organizer must develop a leadership group as representative as possible.

If no potential leaders can be found, the union representative had better acknowledge the probability that he will not be able to wage a successful campaign. There is no sense wasting time and funds when all the influential employees are not interested in unionism or opposed to it. Employees must have the desire to organize themselves and, in fact, must do the real job of building their own local union. The organizer can utilize his experience and knowledge to help workers win their rights, but he cannot forcibly organize them.

The Organizer Takes Over. Once the key leaders have been found, the organizer—who has gotten to know each of them as an individual—usually calls his people together for their first meeting. By pooling the knowledge of his leaders, the organizer will, at this meeting, get his first complete breakdown of employees in the potential bargaining unit and a picture of the company policies and practices that are responsible for worker discontent.

As the complaints are discussed, the organizer gains a good opportunity to describe how similar problems have been settled by the union in other places. This meeting usually ends with an agreed upon time for another discussion. The organizer may distribute union membership cards to be given other employees who did not attend the meeting. The following meetings of the same group will be used to add new leaders selected by the organizer, to gain a more complete breakdown of the company's operations, and to secure the names of additional employees to be contacted.

Where will this meeting be? The most desirable place is on the farm itself, where the workers can be approached as a group. However, because the organizer would be trespassing if he simply walked up the main road to the farm in his normal business attire, and because the farmer would put him off the land quickly once his presence was discovered, it is reasonable to assume that the union organizer might try to disguise himself, perhaps as a hunter or as fisherman or even as a laborer, in order to get onto the property unnoticed. The farmer who follows the suggested procedure for protecting his property against trespassers and unwelcome visitors, to be discussed below, has his remedy available when the trespasser is found.

Property Rights Protection

By way of summary, it should be remembered that a property owner has the right to control who may and who may not come upon his property. He may place signs around his property forbidding trespassers to enter, or he may personally order trespassers off his land. He may permit people to come upon his property, giving permission either orally or in writing, and may revoke this permission whenever he chooses to do so. He is allowed to use a reasonable amount of self-help to eject trespassers or to take them into custody, and is given access to the Courts to protect his property rights. He must recognize, however, that certain government employees, in the exercise of their public duties, have a right to enter his property to perform that duty.

Points To Remember

1. You can and should deal with your own employees, but you are not compelled by law to deal with any union or other third party.

2. You do have the right of free speech and can freely discuss employment conditions with your employees. You can peacefully resist organizational union activity.

3. You can distribute and post information making your employees aware of the fact that they have a right to work. (See attached sample message.)

4. You can effectively protect yourself against illegal trespassing, violence or threats of violence affecting you or your property. You have a civil right to collect for damages to your property.

5. You should always have the phone number of your local police to report instances of violence or threats of violence concerning your land or your produce, while it is still on the land or while it is being transported.

6. As soon as any union activity is noted, you should phone or visit the State Farm Labor Coordinating Committee and ask for information and advice.

7. You should consult with your own neighbors and help each other through the harvest period but notice should always be given to every employee if there is a labor dispute in progress.

8. You should take down license numbers of cars and take notes and pictures of any disputes occurring on the farm or affecting your produce off the farm.

9. Do not participate in unplanned discussions on farm labor conditions with outsiders or in labor negotiations with union officials unless you have competent advice. Check with State Farm Labor Coordinating Committee before proceeding.

10. You should cooperate with newspapers, radio and T. V. people whenever possible. They are performing a public service by keeping the people informed about items of general interest. Naturally, no one has to put up with unwarranted "newshounding" where it invades the right of privacy.

A Message To My Employees*

YOU HAVE A RIGHT TO WORK

It is your American right to choose whether you want to work or not.

DON'T SURRENDER THAT RIGHT

No union pickets with a cardboard sign can stop you from working and earning a living for yourself and your family.

THE LAW IS ON YOUR SIDE

Law enforcement agencies have sworn to protect you and your property. Don't hesitate to contact your County Prosecutor.

YOU VIOLATE NO LAW WHEN YOU CROSS A PICKET LINE

Do not be frightened by the implications of threats.

Do not be fooled by union promises which cannot be fulfilled.

Work is available. The wages are good.

YOU CAN EARN MORE THAN THE UNION WANTS YOUR EMPLOYER TO PAY

You don't have to pay any union dues to get a job. All you have to do is present yourself and go to work.

....
Employer

*It is recommended that this type of message to employees not be used until difficulty is anticipated on your farm.

NOTE: For additional farm labor information and local laws, contact your Dept. of Labor, State Government offices and the Dept. of Labor, U. S. Government, Washington, D. C. for federal rulings. It is well to associate yourself now with a grower organization who will speak for growers in the formulation of future rulings.

IMPROVING MANAGEMENT IN THE FRUIT BUSINESS[1]

Management has been defined as containing elements of both an art and science. To argue the degree of each is pointless, but both must exist. Probably the most generally accepted definition is that management is the accomplishment of results through the efforts of other people. Managers have to decide what results are to be accomplished, and by what people. They must decide HOW and WHEN things should be done. They have to conclude whether the results have been obtained, and decide where to go from there.

Kinds of Managers

There are all kinds of managers — each with a unique personality. Some are harsh, some are lenient; some are disciplined, some are not. Some managers have organized work skills, some are casual, indefinite, and border on being confused.

Whatever a man's life style is, that style is quickly exposed to his employees through the daily contact of work supervision.

A manager cannot hide himself. His traits, characteristics, ambitions, fears and prejudices are all exposed. Try as we will to cover them, each of us exposes "bald spots," through our personal conduct — areas where improvement would be of benefit.

As a manager, the challenge is to improve his supervisory skill by improving himself in his dealings with others.

The Strong Manager

What does it take to work well through others? The following check-list is not all inclusive but outlines six characteristics of successful leadership.

1. CREATIVE ABILITY: One who can think (also called vision) — imaginative. Must think creatively, constructively and clearly.

2. JUDGMENT: Ability to judge justly or wisely, especially in matters which affect action.

3. ADMINISTRATIVE SKILLS: Ability to forecast events and needs — to plan. An outward manifestation of orderliness — one's life, working quarters, desk, etc. Being organized.

4. POSITIVE ATTITUDE: Optimistic. one who can inspire others. The manager's behavior—facial expressions, droop of shoulders, etc. — all are closely watched by employees. Starts with good health.

5. COURAGE: Managers must be willing to gamble or take chances; courage to delegate — a manager can never abdicate responsibility.

6. CHARACTER: The previous five traits in varying degrees. But, on the question of integrity, there can be no compromise. A manager must have the confidence of his associates; his actions will be the same whether he is being observed or not. This is integrity!

---

[1]This has been adapted from suggestions made to nurserymen in the "The Bulletin," California Association of Nurserymen, Sacramento.

894

The Weak Manager

By contrast, the weak manager inevitably lacks planning and organization with respect to supervising his people.

a. He chooses people and makes assignments arbitrarily and emotionally rather than by an objective evaluation of their abilities and skills;

b. He gives vague or incomplete instructions, showing he hasn't thoroughly analyzed the problem;

c. He keeps subordinates in the dark about company policy;

d. He is always too busy to train someone to fill his shoes.

Summary

With all the variety of orchard operations — both in scope and annual sales — and the wide range of management styles, each individual success is finally determined by the ability of each individual manager. His company becomes the lengthened shadow of himself. Since the subordinates are extensions of his own efforts, their errors are his errors, their successes his successes.

No matter how much work a man can do, no matter how engaging a personality he may be, he will not advance far in business if he cannot work through others.

HOW TO DEVELOP LEADERSHIP IN EMPLOYEES

Fruit growing normally does not attract employees highly skilled in sales motivation or work organization. Yet the fruit business depends upon these qualities for its very success.

It is apparent that chain stores, with centralized procedures, management-development programs and operating efficiencies can outdistance many of the independent orchard operations and their sales outlets.

Furthermore, it must be recognized that the chronic problem of low wages stems from the average low productivity of the workers involved.

One solution to this problem lies in the full development of latent abilities of employees. The challenge of the supervisor is to bring out the extra talents in his people.

It is enlightening to see the growth of people and the increased productivity of a work force when a supervisor, responding to leadership needs, develops a program of 1) training, 2) delegation, 3) correction, and 4) motivation. Ideas on how this can be done are as follows:

1. TRAINING — sessions should be held on a regular basis and by the manager. This should not be delegated to an outsider or held away from the premises except for unusual circumstances or opportunities.

There is a psychology that works strongly in the manager's favor when the men are brought together for training, discussion and commendation in the work environment. The feeling of acceptance and success that employees so badly need can only be conveyed by the man for whom they work. The core of these meetings should be **information and training.**

2. DELEGATION — If a manager organizes his operation into departments, usually by product lines or supporting functions, then delegating authority to his department heads naturally follows. However, there are some managers who go through the motions of delegation, but hug to themselves the essence of the job.

A manager with several orchard-block superintendents or department heads and still doing all the detail supervising is an example of this lack of real delegation. This often comes from the belief of some men that to have a job well done he must do it himself. How are others going to be developed? Real delegation defines clearly in a job description the subordinate's area of responsibility and then grants him the full right for decision in that area.

The manager is still accountable for any errors of his subordinates and should accept the fault for such errors. That is the risk and the courage of delegation.

3. CORRECTION — A good supervisor should develop a technique for effective correction. Properly used, correction is the most important single device in leadership.

Here is a procedure abstracted from a publication of the American Institute of Personnel Managers and modified to the needs of a farm manager.

a. Acquaint yourself with all the facts so that you will be fair.

b. Avoid correcting a person in the presence of anyone else.

c. Always begin with a question — WHY — not an accusation. Give the person an opportunity to discuss the subject of the interview.

d. Maintain your own calmness regardless of the other person's attitude.

e. Never reprimand in anger.

f. Always give reasons why you are making the correction.

g. Be specific.

h. Make suggestions as to how he can improve.

i. Do not threaten.

j. Try a "Criticism sandwich" (begin interview with a pleasant remark and close with a word of encouragement).

k. Separate the man from the problem — correct the problem without demeaning the self-esteem of the person involved.

l. Close interview pleasantly when all reasons for correction are thoroughly understood.

4. MOTIVATION — Motivation of subordinates is a most critical challenge to managers. Perhaps the most important to avoid are the three "C's."

a. Don't Criticize.

b. Don't Complain.

c. Don't Condemn.

All too often a manager builds resentment and encourages inactivity through fault-finding. What employees need is an abundance of praise, recognition and encouragement.

A recent study by a leading psychologist listed five employee wants and asked 1,000 workers to rate them according to their importance. Here's how the motivators were ranked. Note that wages were last on the list of five.

1. Recognition, appreciation for work well done.
2. Feeling "in" on things.
3. Help with personal problems.
4. Job Security.
5. Good wages.

It is such "psychic" values that managers must give their employees to achieve maximum productivity and good will.

In conclusion, an objective would be to strive to meet the increasing challenge to our market position by developing the latent capabilities of our employees through bolder and more aggressive leadership.

WHAT IS AN ORCHARD WORTH?

The drastic changes in the fruit industry over the past several years and the taking of land for public use have made the problem of orchard valuation of considerable interest. The statement has been made that orchard owners have no basis of determining value. This statement in itself is suspect since all property has some value to someone although value may be lower or higher depending on circumstances.

There are two general problems: (a) Determining value to set for a sales price. (b) Determining value under condemnation or land-taking for public use.

The problem of determining a value for a sales price is usually a matter for an appraisal either by the owner, his representative, or by a trained appraiser. An appraisal is always an opinion. An appraisal by a trained and experienced appraiser is usually a composite based on observation of the property in its present condition and experience of the appraiser. It frequently is a composite of many opinions on parts of the farm and its setting.

The value of an orchard is determined by the production after development and the cost of maintaining that production. Any orchard will be in one of three conditions: (a) A developing orchard—on the way up in production; (b) A producing orchard—in full production; and (c) A declining orchard—going down in production.

When reaching a value for a developing orchard it is necessary to determine whether development can continue until the orchard is a producing one. If this seems likely then there are some requirements for a successful orchard: (a) The soil is important and it should be suitable for the varieties being grown as well as the type of fruit—apple—peach—pear; (b) The orchard should be located in a fruit area where there are other successful orchards; (c) Markets should be established; (d) Some plan for replacement should be indicated; (e) Hazards of climate, drainage and requirements for irrigation should be minimum; (f) Wild trees, abandoned orchards and other pest and disease sources should be few and control of orchard damaging animals should be established; (g) Spacing and planting distances and varieties should meet accepted standards for the area; (h) Orchard layout should permit use of labor saving equipment in orchard care, spraying and harvesting; (i) Tree growth should be vigorous and evidence of good care should be present.

A **producing orchard** should meet all of the above tests plus having a record of high yields annually.

A **declining orchard** presents some additional problems. The property may have value for other uses. In this case the suitability of the soil for other crops becomes important and the cost of converting the orchard site for other uses becomes an item. If the reduced yields represent the start of a rather long period of declining yields, yield levels may still be such that continued operation is indicated and possible rehabilitation may be a consideration.

It is important in arriving at a value for a sales price to determine the stage of the orchard and then proceed to place a value on it by using all three of the generally accepted methods of determining value: (a) Values based on net income capitalization or "earning value"; (b) Values based on comparison with other property which has changed hands or where values have been established; and (c) Value based on reproduction cost.

Usually a sound answer to the question 'What is my orchard worth?' can be reached by considering all three of these and balancing them against each other to determine a basic value. The actual sales value then would be adjusted by comparison with sales prices of similar properties in the area.

The American Society of Farm Managers and Rural Appraisers has defined Present Market Value as follows: "It is the price at which, within a reasonable time and with a substantial down payment, the property may be expected to change hands from a willing, able and informed seller to a desirous, able and informed purchaser."

The problem of determining value under condemnation or land taking for public use is somewhat different from that of determining value for a sales price or present market value.

Taking private property for public use upon payment of just compensation is condemnation. The legal basis is called the "right of eminent domain." Under this procedure the people or the government take private property for public use when public needs cannot be provided for in some other manner.

The requirement that no person shall be deprived of private property without just compensation is a part of the "right of eminent domain." The courts by their decisions have varied in just what is "just compensation."

Under the "right of eminent domain" it follows that the injured party who is entitled to "just compensation" has the responsibility of determining values. The fact that the owner prefers the particular property to some other does not mean that he is thereby entitled to additional compensation. Legal precedent and usage have tended to favor the property owner.

In general, courts have held that market value is the guide to be followed in determining awards and further, again in general, the measure to be used in determining damages in condemnation cases is market value.

The courts have defined market value in these terms quite generally: "Market value is the highest price, estimated in terms of money, which the property will bring, if exposed for sale in the open market, with a reasonable time allowed to find a purchaser buying with knowledge of all uses and purposes to which it is best adapted, and for which it is capable of being used."

In some instances the term "fair market value" is used and then is defined as a situation where the sale can be made for cash or terms equivalent to cash, at a price agreed on by an informed seller willing but not obliged to sell to an informed buyer willing but not obliged to buy.

The attempt frequently made to value property taken under eminent domain or, for that matter, in attempting to arrive at a sales price by valuing the property by units and adding the unit values to get a value for the property, is likely to be very misleading. It is a good deal like trying to arrive at the value of a used car by placing values separately on the motor, the wheels, the tires, etc. and then adding the unit values together. The value needs to be determined for the whole property and it is the loss in value of the whole property as a result of the condemnation or partial sale, that needs to be determined. By Lawrence D. Rhoades, Department of Agricultural Economics, Univ. of Mass. Amherst.

ORCHARD CONDEMNATION VALUE

STATEMENT BY RUTGERS UNIVERSITY STAFF, NEW JERSEY[1]

. . . It should be emphasized that it is difficult to place a specific value on an individual fruit tree or group of trees killed by fire, or removed because of a highway or pipe line, or damaged or destroyed in other ways. Each case usually is different. Most important is the general effect on the grower's business. It takes 10 to 15 years to replace an apple, pear or cherry tree and 5-6 years for peach and dwarf trees. Trees removed from an orchard corner are not as serious to the business as those removed in a strip through the orchard. This cuts the orchard in two and makes it difficult to spray, harvest and conduct important operations. If his best block of trees is involved, his business is affected more than if his poorest block is involved. A grower who loses his trees during a prosperous period nationally may be affected more financially than if he lost trees during a depression. Also, fruit trees are worth more during a period when the fruits in question are not over-planted nationally.

It should be taken into consideration that old untended fruit trees on the right-of-way are a liability rather than an asset to the buyer, who must pay for the cost of their removal ($1.00 to $2.00 per tree or more depending upon total number and method of removal).

Age of the trees may not be so important under some conditions. If they are in full bearing at a relatively young age, full value to the trees can be given. Trees may be rather old and still be in good production and thus would be worth the full value. Apple trees usually reach peak production at about 15 years, whereas peaches may reach top production between 6 and 8 years.

In order to approach the problem of fruit tree appraisal, we have based decisions on one fact—a commercial grower who loses his fruit trees, by reason of condemnation proceedings for turnpikes or other reasons, not only loses the trees, but has his operations upset. His efficient use of men and equipment is reduced and the general plan of his orchard is changed. Therefore, we believe a grower is entitled to at least five years additional profit from each bearing tree destroyed for any reason, if it is beyond his control. If a tree produces an annual profit of $50.00 he would be entitled to 5 times $50.00 or $250.00 for the loss (based on early 1960s prices). This figure will include full value of tree and consequential damages to orchard operations. Correct figures below to your local conditions.[1]

Example: 20-Year McIntosh Tree

1. Cost of tree up to bearing age of 10-12 years—$60.00 (includes original cost, fertilizing, spraying, pruning, rodent and deer control, land improvements, etc.)

2. A McIntosh at 20 years has at least 15 years of good bearing yet to come. Grower is entitled to at least 5 years of additional profit.

3. Average cost of growing bushel of apples is a minimum of 55c maximum $0.95 to $1.00. Net profit most years will be 1/3 of gross income in this North Jersey area.

4. Health and condition will determine bearing capacity, life expectancy, etc.

5. McIntosh and Red Delicious are the most valuable apple trees in this area, followed closely by Cortland, Rome, Stayman, R. I. Greening, Kendall, etc.

6. Bearing capacity will be determined by health, general condition of tree.

7. $1,000 investment will yield $60.00 annually at 6% or $80.00 at 8%. Formula: 1/5 of investment worth plus cost of tree to bearing age plus 10% consequent damage equals full value of tree.

8. To get consequential damages, take 10% of (1/5 investment plus cost of tree) and add to the combination (see below) which equals full value of tree.

25 bushels of McIntosh apples should yield $50.00 profit. It will take an investment of $833.00 at 6% to give this annual yield.

1/5 of $833.00 equals .... $166.00 investment worth

$166.00 plus $60.00 (cost of growing to 10-12 years) $226.00

10% of $226.00 (consequential damage) .... $ 22.60

Full tree value $248.60

Formula For Determining Value of Apple Or Other Fruit Trees 35 Years Or Older To Maximum 45 Years

Take average yield of tree, multiply by average profit per bushel. Total figure represents annual profit per year. (1) First, determine what investment at 6% will give same annual income (investment worth so-called). (2) Next take 10% of investment worth. (3) Add; cost of growing tree up to 10 or 12 years old—$50.00 to $60.00 at least. (4) Add 10% consequenial damage (10% of total 2 and 3). (5) Add 2 and 3 and 4 for total value of tree.

---

[1]The reasoning and examples given here may apply to the New Jersey area, but not necessarily to other areas. Also, price levels will need to be adjusted according to current and local levels.

Example: McIntosh Tree 35 Years Old

1. Take average yield of tree, multiply by average net profit for that variety.
2. What investment at 6% will give same income annually.
3. Now take 10% of the investment worth.
4. Take 10% of the figure derived under step 3 and add to the figure for full value of tree.

Produced 30 bushels last few years.

30 x $2.00 - - - $60.00

$60.00 income equals an investment of $1,000 at 6%.

(1) 10% of $1,000 .... $100.00
(2) $100.00 + $60.00 .... $160.00
(3) 10% of $160.00 .... $ 16.00 added to $160.00 =
    Appraisal value of tree $176.00

Example: McIntosh Tree 49 Years Old

1. Average annual yield 30 bushels of marketable fruit.
   30 x $1.80 .... $54.00
   $54.00 will be derived from an investment of $900.00

2. 10% of $900.00 .... $90.00
3. 10% of $90.00 .... $ 9.00
4. $90.00 + $9.00 .... $99.00 Value of 49-year-old tree.

Example: Biennial Bearer—Baldwin—Age 50 Years

1. Produced 36 bushels in 1954
   Produced 12 bushels in 1955 — add the two figures and divide by 2.
      48 bushels ÷ 2 = 24 bushels average.
2. 24 × $1.50 = $36.00
3. $36.00 also can be secured from an investment of $600.00 (investment worth)
4. 10% of $600.00 = $60.00 value of tree.
5. 10% of $60.00 = $6.00 consequential damage
6. $60.00 plus $6.00 equals $66.00, the full value of 50-year Baldwin tree.

Example: Annual Bearer—50-Year McIntosh

Average production per year—28 bushels

1. 28 × $1.75 .... $49.00 annual net income.
2. $49.00 can be derived from an investment of $816.66.
3. 10% of $816.66 .... $81.67—value of tree
4. 10% of $81.67 .... $ 8.17 consequential damage
5. $81.67 plus $8.17 equals $89.94 full value of 50-year-old tree.

MINIMIZING ESTATE TAXES[1]

Many times the impact of the estate tax problem is not recognized until too late. Being human, we all tend to delay facing or ignore discussion of what must be decided by plan or by default after we are gone. Planning can save many thousands of dollars that otherwise will be confiscated by the tax. More often than not, the farm family is completely unaware of the fact that an estate tax problem exists. There are many situations in New Jersey where a farm has been owned by two or three generations. As the family grew, the needs of new families developed and adjoining land was purchased. What may have started as a farm of one hundred twenty acres may now be three hundred to five hundred acres. Urban development has crept in. The farm family has developed permanent assets over the years. There are friends in the community, schools, churches. In short, the roots of this family grow strong and deep in a community they consider their own. It would be expensive to replace the economic set-up. They have been offered high prices for the land, but they just do not want to sell, so they ignore the real estate man and go ahead planning for the children and grandchildren.

Grandfather bought one hundred twenty acres. Now that his three grandsons are farming, the acreage has expanded to 450 acres. Grandfather bought at $60 per acre. His son, the present owner, bought at $175, and for the last eight-five acres he paid $235 an acre in 1951. The boys, all married are living in homes on the land, have developed a fine system that gets the most out of the equipment and the hired help. Two years ago, someone offered them $500 an acre for the land, but they did not want to sell. The land has increased in value since then, but they are reluctant to sell and, besides, Dad owns the land, and they do not want him to think they are trying to get things away from him.

Here is the position they are in, and sentiment will not change it. Unless something is planned, and carried out now, when the parents of these three married men go to their reward, the three men may have to give up their business, or spend the rest of their lives paying off a mortgage with after-income-tax dollars. They do not need to waste this productivity if they plan now. For instance, for estate tax purposes, let us value the land at $500 per acre.

Land	$225,000
4 Homes	60,000
Equipment	50,000
Total	$335,000

[1]This discussion was given before New Jersey Fruit Growers and applies to N. J. laws, but other states have similar laws which would be well to investigate and heed.

We could add the value of storage, barns, bonds, etc.

The tax and settlement costs without planning could be about one-third or $105,700. By careful planning much or all of this cost can be eliminated.

There are four major methods of minimizing estate taxes:

1. Gifts
2. Consuming the estate during life
3. Sales of stock or land
4. Life Insurance

A combination of these is the method many people decide to follow.

To give away too much and be sorry is not wise. It is important to be sure we will never really need what we give to others. However, if we have the desire, we can often save 30c of each dollar by transferring these dollars to the persons we want to have them during our lifetime, rather than after we die.

To consume what we have created, to use it all up, is a plan that some may be willing to follow, but it could be dangerous. Not many of us want to take that chance.

To sell our land or our stock may be a good idea. However, some of us have a sentimental desire to keep in touch or hold onto what we have created. There are ways to do this through the use of corporate devices so we can maintain control and still reduce the gross taxable estate. However, it is important that competent legal advice be available in all of this planning.

Where life insurance fits, no other estate planning method conserves values better at less cost. It will accomplish things no other method can. Here, too, judgment and balance must play a major part. The planning team must be objective. To go off the deep end on the use of life insurance can become just as burdensome as doing too much for children or charities through gifts. In the end, a plan is a combination of opinion and judgment. There is no perfect plan.

A plan today that does an excellent job, may need serious revision two years from now. Children may be married, babies may be born, sales may occur, business may change, stocks may go down or up, people may die, or what we want today may be quite different from what we want two years hence.

One of the keys to any estate planning is a good will. It will cost you very little to have a will drawn up, but be sure to get a good lawyer. Do not do it yourself. Do you have a will?

In New Jersey, a man dying without a will leaves all his real estate to his children with a life interest in only ½ of the lands for the widow as dower. His personal property will go 1/3 to his wife and ⅔ to the children. If there are no children, the wife gets all the property purchased during the marriage, and only a life interest in half of any property purchased prior to the marriage. At her death, the residue goes to the husband's relations, brothers, sisters, parents. By these uncomplicated examples, you can see how important it is to write down what you want and have your lawyer put it into legal form. I cannot over-emphasize the importance of not doing it yourself.

You may have an estate tax problem and not know it. It is easy to find that the death costs will be as much as $300 of each $1,000 you thought were going to your heirs. You can save much or all of it by planning now. Get the best team you can. A good life insurance Estate Planner and a good lawyer can help you. A New Jersey Farmers Week Talk by Samuel C. DeCou, fruit grower and C.L.U., Haddonfield, New Jersey.

FARM ACCOUNTING BY COMPUTER

Many growers, particularly large growers and grower-corporations, now are using electronic computer systems to save time, labor and money in their business and provide better accounting information. The service is furnished by companies over the world so-specializing. The service is confidential and economical. The mail-in forms require around 30 minutes of the bookkeeper's time a week. The service provides a wide range of information, including machinery costs, labor costs of each worker, income tax, social security, credit accounts, household expenses, depreciation records, etc. The service will indicate strengths and weaknesses in the operation and the manager will be able to spot areas needing improvement. Records can be kept by variety and block, e.g., indicating which blocks or varieties are paying and those that are a liability. Summary information is sent to the grower each month. The followng column headings of a data sheet indicate the type of information recorded by day of the month and supplied at the end of the month to the service.

BASIC COMPUTER DATA SHEET

Page No. 11

Name: Horn-of-Plenty Fruitgrower   Acct. Number: 2987
Address: Orchardtown, N. J. 08850   Month: January 1974

Line No.	Day	Description and Source		Check No.	Enter-prize code	Alloc-ation No.	Item code	Credit code	Quantity Vol.	Unit	Dollar Amount
1	3	Baskets returned	Pathmark Store				356		3	Bu	1.50
2	7	Labor	Bill Jones	43			374		1	wk	95.50
3	9	Soc. Security 9%	" "					802			8.60
4	9	Total trees					301		989	No	
5	10	Fertilizer	FCA	44			205		10	Tons	500.00

Type of information received by the grower or corporation each month is: (a) a one-page summary of your business at a glance: breakdown of receipts and expenses, budget balance for the current month and year-to-date by general categories; (b) financial summary involving a classification of all receipts and expenses for the month (or report period) and cumulative totals for the year, quantities of items purchased and products sold for the period and year-to-date (lbs, hrs, numbers, etc.); (c) income and expense items separated for different enterprises and groups within enterprises if desired; (d) at the year-end you will receive (1) a tax summary of income

899

and expense items for preparing your income tax form; (2) depreciation and credit investment report which provides figures necessary for income tax reporting; (3) complete listing and classification of credit accounts (amounts paid, charged, borrowed and balances); (4) amount of income tax and social security withheld and deposits made with a running balance of liabilities; and (5) individual drawing accounts with special detail of household expenses to account for withdrawals and investments in the business. An annual summary analysis of the business is provided at the end of the year.

You can contact your local governmental agricultural extension service or Farm Bureau organization for information on how to obtain this service in your general area. THE FARM QUARTERLY has a 6 x 9 bulletin on "'The Farmer-Computer Team," 32 pp., a copy of which can be had by contacting the Quarterly at 22 E. 12th St., Cincinnatti, Ohio 45210. The bulletin gives a complete picture of how the service works for the farmer. AgData, Inc. P.O.B. 1077, Davis, Ca. 95616 also can provide information.

In order that the computer be of real service to the farmer, he must provide good management information. The computer can be no better than the information supplied to it. Good accounting information is not generally available from farmers and, hence, may be a good incentive to encourage fruit growers to keep better records. (Prepared by Fred Perkins and N. F. Childers, Rutgers University).

PUBLIC: PICK-YOUR-OWN FRUIT

With harvest-labor problems and increasing costs, many fruit growers are turning to the public-harvest--your-own system for moving certain of their fruit crops. Small fruits and grapes are well adapted since the public does not use ladders; full-dwarf trees also fall into this class.

The grower and his family should best be located near population centers where a good supply of customers are available. He and his family or help must enjoy and be able to handle crowds of people. Considerable thought and planning should be given to the project, including every detail, before advertising in the local paper or radio station.

Mr. John Bell, Jr. who has an orchard and attractive roadside market just west of Chicago at Barrington, Illinois has been quite successful in selling his entire crop most years through his market and on a "Pick-your-own basis." He gives the following pointers,

1. The average price per bushel he received for apples in the 1960s was about $3.00. For Red and Golden Delicious he received about 25c per bushel more.

2. He thinks that pick-your-own is the marketing method of the future in view of the increasing harvest labor problems.

3. Among the merits and requirements given are: (a) consumers will harvest apples on the weekend when picking labor is hard to get; (b) some advertising is needed at first to get people in the habit, but once they have taken part, post cards can be sent to the desirable customers each year announcing pick-your-own periods. People who have given some trouble are not invited back. (c) There is likely to be more leisure time among people in the future to do this type of thing; and (d) the grower must be reasonably free of competition in neighboring areas.

4. The fruit grower family must deal with hundreds of people, sometimes a thousand on a weekend; hence, the family all must be helpful and have personalities to deal with people effectively.

5. There must be adequate parking space which may be used for only a total of five or so days a year. Sunday is a big day.

6. Parking space must be fairly close to the trees to be harvested. Or, flat-bottom trailers must be provided to carry the people to and from the harvest area.

7. Dwarf or semi-dwarf trees would have a definite advantage in a pick-your-own deal. Ladders and chances of injury and insurance problems would be largely avoided.

8. If a pick-your-own procedure is used year after year, it might be well to bring the trees down in height by moderate to severe topping.

9. Orchards should be kept neat for pick-your-own people, which they like. They do not like a jungle.

10. A good ground cover is needed under the trees to protect windfalls and to protect against sun scald.

11. It is highly desirable to have a sequence of ripening of varieties so that when people come out to get apples, they will not be sent back without them.

12. It is desirable to have varieties that ripen fairly evenly over the tree, otherwise there is a problem of people picking the red apples on the southwest side first.

13. Once pick-your-own is started on the weekends, it is desirable to continue it week after week until the harvest is done rather than try to skip a weekend.

14. It is desirable to have annual producing varieties to keep the clientele built up and satisfied.

15. One advantage to hauling people to the trees by flat trailers is that they cannot hide apples in car trunks, car wells and oher places. Some system may be needed for checking these areas as the cars leave.

16. The Bell's have found it undesirable to place the Golden and Red Delicious together. The clientele may be tempted to pick either the Goldens or the Red when they are assigned to the other. In laying out the orchard, it is desirable to put the varieties in blocks so that neighboring blocks will ripen at widely different periods to discourage picking in unassigned rows or trees.

17. The Bell's have considered putting a man in a 14' tower and a bull horn to keep the crowd under control in a general area.

18. For a 50-acre orchard, the Bells estimate that an 8-acre area will be needed for parking cars in a pick-your-own deal. Since this 8 acres is used only a few days a year, there is some question how it can be used profitably the balance of the time. They are considering putting it in alfalfa.

19. See specific fruit chapters in this book for pick-your-own comments for a particular fruit.

"U-PICK" STRAWBERRIES IN WISCONSIN

By G. C. Klingbeil, The University of Wisconsin, Madison

Editor's Note: The Pick-Your-Own technique of harvesting particularly small fruits is a fast-growing method of planning, growing, harvesting and marketing of crops.

Not many years ago the commercial strawberry industry in Wisconsin had declined to near 1,000 acres and further reduction was imminent. Growers sales were at the mercy of a few fruit brokers, production costs were increasing, labor was high in cost and scarce in quantity due to laws that restricted the traditional use of women and children for harvest. Returns on investments were far from favorable. It was obvious that if strawberries were again to be a crop of economic significance in the state, a new and different approach to production and marketing must be developed.

Horticultural specialists from the College of Agricultural and Life Sciences and several key growers reviewed the problems facing the industry and then planned and implemented a program aimed at improving production and marketing. Two major projects developed—the Wisconsin Plant Improvement Program and the consumer harvest or "U Pick" method of harvesting and marketing. In the years that followed, Wisconsin growers shifted to those essentially virus-free varieties that have proven to be reliable producers and most desirable for the "U-Pick" trade.

In 1967 we harvested about 2,000 acres and the acreage is continuing to increase. The major reason,, however, for this vast improvement in the state's strawberry economy was the change in harvesting and marketing to the "U-Pick" program. Marketing procedures changed slowly at first but the obvious success of several growers in the "U-Pick" business encouraged others until the change was nearly complete. A decade ago, less than 10 percent of our berries were picked by consumers;   today about 98 percent are harvested by the "U-Pick" method. From a few producing-shipping locations in the early 1950's, we have expanded to commercial plantings in every county in the state and the number of acres is increasing yearly.

Let's look more closely at the "U-Pick" harvesting and marketing program. What does it take to be successful? Success in the method can be assured by careful attention to planning, production, people, parking, policing, pricing, protection, public relations, patience and most of all, profit. Horticulturally, success requires a good site, good soil, adequate fertility, the best varieties, irrigation, pest control, and the production management skill to produce a good crop consistently. The location is not too important although close proximity to centers of population is most favorable. Records show that the greatest number of customers are within a 25-mile radius although it is not uncommon for many to drive 75 to 100 miles for good fruit. Nearby customers come often and pick moderate quantities while those from greater distances may come only once but will take up to 100 pounds per customer. The average customer will take 20 quarts or around 28 pounds of berries each time. The amount harvested is generally in proportion to the kind of picking.

Productivity is a major criteria considered by all growers. Today, the main varieties in Wisconsin are Sparkle, Red Glow, Jerseybelle, Midway, Sunrise, and Badgerbelle with some Catskill and Robinson in localized plantings, but these are changing with experience and better cultivars. Growers should expect a minimum of 5,000 quarts per acre if they have irrigation. Some get 7,500 or more. Our yield trials indicate that 12,000 quarts per acre is not an unrealistic goal. The search for better varieties continues through variety trials and a breeding program aimed, in part, toward the development of varieties for the "U-Pick" trade.

One of the most important considerations for this kind of marketing is the provision for parking of customers' cars. Have plenty of space because many customers are senior citizens and women. They prefer not to walk far and will appreciate easy parking. A rule of thumb is to provide space for 200 cars for each 10 acres you expect to harvest. Provide a well-marked entrance and exit; one of each makes checkout easier. An early cut hay or mulch field is satisfactory.

It is desirable to have an area where youngsters can play. Youngsters supervised by a babysitter is an added incentive for many young housewives. Generally, children under 12 in the picking field are a liability. Post your rules such as picking hours and days, minimum age for pickers, prices and penalties. If customers know the rules, field supervision is easier. Customers tend to police themselves but a small battery powered portable loud speaker can be most helpful. Field supervisors, and you don't need many, should have a special hat or garb to identify them to the pickers.

We use a standard six-quart carrier. The use of quart cups and reliance on volume measurement is rapidly losing favor to a die-cut, corrugated, fold-up box that is used in the carrier in place of quart cups. It will hold 10 to 12 pounds of fruit. The use of this liner-box and a weight measurement speeds checkout, eliminates the arguments that arise over the interpretation of "full quart" and encourages larger sales. Pricing is about the same throughout the area.   An average was 25 to 30 cents per quart or 25 to 25 cents per pound in the late 1960's in Wisconsin.

Here are a few other suggestions:

(1) Protection — liability insurance for protection of the grower against personal injury and property damage claims is essential. We have had no difficulty with this problem yet, but an ounce of prevention is worth a pound of cure!

(2) Plan for a system of prompt banking and protection of cash receipts. Most all payments will be in cash and a large enterprise may collect several thousand dollars each day for several days.

(3) Establish and adhere to a daily time schedule for the picking operation. Most growers find 7:30 A.M. a convenient time to open the field for picking. Few growers find it necessary to continue daily picking after 3:00 P.M.

(4) Prepare a comprehensive plan of publicity and promotion through contact with communications media. A schedule of advertising rates for newspaper, radio and television outlets should be available to you. Our growers find that spot announcements on radio are an effective means of calling in customers and some have used this medium to discourage customers when the demand exceeded the supply of fruit. Roadside signs have not proven to be an effective means of reaching a mass audience for a short season of harvest.

(5) Develop a pleasant and patient approach to your customers. Your day as a hard-nosed, independent farmer may return after the strawberry season, but for 3 weeks the public are your

best friends and you better keep them contented and holding an easy hand on their pocketbook. IN SUMMARY, let me say that growing strawberries is one of the most exacting kinds of agriculture. To aid in the decision-making that will result in maximum yields of high quality fruit, production management skills are needed in planting, pest control, irrigation, plant nutrition, and frost protection. Wisconsin growers have proven that a well-managed "U-Pick" strawberry enterprise can be profitable and in addition contribute to the recreational pleasure of a large group of people that enjoy getting into a rural area and have the pleasure of taking part in the berry harvest.

ORGANICALLY GROWN FRESH PRODUCE AS A NEW MARKET

Walter Androsko, Cooperative Extension Agent, Westchester County, N. Y.[1]

"Organically" grown fresh produce offers a new market for some farm stand operators. There has always been a group of people interested in organic gardening and organically grown produce. With the emphasis on ecology, the concerns regarding the thousands of chemicals used in our society, and the new life style of the young, there is an increasing market for "organic foods." An examination of many home magazines will show glowing accounts and exotic recipes for "organic foods." Magazines and books have prolificated on the subject of natural foods, organic foods, the natural life, etc. Natural food stores are springing up in many communities.

Growers of fruits and vegetables have the opportunity of supplying some of these demands. All of you have used organic matter and organic fertilizers in the production of fruits and vegetables. It now becomes a management decision whether this market, with its possible premium prices, should be developed by you. This will mean some change in your farming practices. It may be that the organic fertilizers now used over the entire farm and then supplemented with commercial fertilizer will need be concentrated on one portion of the farm as the only nutrients used. It may be necessary that on some crops a change in pest control will be necessary. The term "organic foods" and organically produced foods mean different things to different people. It may be well for you to find out what is meant by these terms by your potential customers before you start a program of catering to this specific group.

Organic gardening and organic foods traditionally has meant the production of food without the use of commercial fertilizers. It may also mean the production of these foods without the use of pesticides of any kind. On the other hand, some organic gardeners feel that the use of plant type pesticides are in harmony with nature. These could be products such as Rotenone, Pyrethrum, tobacco products, Ryania, etc. There are other variations that could be mentioned but the point I make is that organic gardening and organic food does not mean the same to all people.

Roadstand operators have always been alert to the demands of their customers. If a certain portion of your customers are demanding organically grown foods and are willing to pay the price needed for you to produce them, it certainly behooves you to give consideration to these demands. It may also be that some of the "natural" food stores in your area would also be an outlet for these type products.

There are pitfalls that should be considered by anyone contemplating the production of these organic foods. One consideration is the mentioned fact that your production methods, no matter how well intentioned, may not conform to the standard of organic food some customers desire. You would also need to adjust your own standards of perfection in production and harvestin as there will be imperfections that may be tolerated by the organic trade that you likely would not consider selling in your normal merchandising program.

You will also need to review your pricing policy carefully. The changes in production and the yield at harvest will be such that a different pricing policy will be necessary. This is a specialized trade and higher prices will be expected. Finally, it should be remembered that this is a new project for you. There is at least some fad element involved among the buyers. It may be that once the product is put onto your merchandising counter the appeal of it in comparison to your own product will be less and the demands lower than expected. On the other hand, we could hope that the demands would be above expectations; but in either event caution and alertness should be followed with this new project. It will be an interesting departure for you. You will meet an entirely new clientele that will challenge you and I hope interest you.

You will find these customers for organically grown food different from your regular customers. Many of them are looking upon food purchases as an expression of their philosophy of living. They will question you and your practices, some will be overly zealous, others eager to learn. All will be interesting if you have the time and interest in their points of view. You must be alert to their wishes, to your cost of production and to the final figure that determines profit and loss which is so important to whether you continue this new enterprise, expand it or discontinue it. As with any new enterprise some patience will be necessary to allot time for the new products to catch on. Depending upon your own interests and enthusiasms, the growing of organic foods can present a challenge that will open up an entirely new farming experience for you.

NUT TREE NURSERIES

A list is available through the Northern Nut Growers' Association, S. Chase, Secretary, 2338 Parkview Avenue, Knoxville, Tenn. See also the recent July issue of Amer. Fruit Grower Magazine Willoughby, Ohio. 44094.

California does not permit entry of walnut scions or trees from areas east of the Rocky Mountains. A few of the western states do not permit entry of chestnut trees from east of the Mississippi River.

Grafted named Chinese chestnuts are sold by Nos. 4, 9, 14, 18, 21, 26, 33, and 35; butternuts from 2, 4, 7, and 24; heartnuts from 2, 3, 4, 12, and occasionally from 36 and 37; shagbark hickories from 2, 4, 10, 12, 22, and 24; Carpathian English walnuts from 2, 3, 4, 7, and 36.

1. Armstrong Nurseries, Ontario, California
2. Benton & Smith Nut Nursery, Route 2, Millerton, N. Y.[s]

[1]Presented at the 1972 N. Y. State Horticultural Society Meeting, Kingston.

3. Berhow Nursery, Huxley, Iowa*
4. Bernath's Nursery, Route 3, Poughkeepsie, N. Y.*
5. Bountiful Ridge Nurseries, Princess Ann, Maryland*
6. California Nursery Company, Niles, California*
7. Hebden H. Corsan, Route 1, Hillsdale, Michigan*
8. Eastern Shore Nurseries, Inc., Easton, Maryland
9. Louis Gerardi Nursery, Route 1, Caseyville, Illinois*
10. Felix Gillet Nursery, Nevada City, California*
11. Gold Chestnut Nursery, Cowen, West Virginia
12. Hazel Hills Nursery Company, 96 S. Wabasha, St. Paul, Minn.*
13. S. H. Graham, Route 5, Ithaca, New York*
14. Hirschi's Nut Nursery, 414 N. Robinson, Oklahoma City, Okla.*
15. Howell Nurseries, Sweetwater, Tennessee
16. Idaho Tree Farm, Spirit Lake, Idaho
17. Indiana Nut Nursery, Rockport, Indiana*
18. Inter-State Nurseries, Hamburg, Iowa
19. J. F. Jones Nursery, Box 136, Erie, Illinois*
20. Kelley Brothers Nurseries, Dansville, New York*
21. Leeland Farms, Box 128, Leesburg, Georgia*
22. Linn County Nursery (Snyder Brothers), Center Point, Iowa*
23. Linwood Nurseries, Route 2, Box 771, Turlock, California*
24. Michigan Nut Nursery, Box 33, Union City, Michigan*
25. New York State Fruit Testing Assn., Geneva, New York*
26. Nut Tree Nurseries, Downington, Pennsylvania*
27. H. L. Pearcy Nursery Co., Route 2, Salem, Oregon*
28. George Salzer, 169 Garford Road, Rochester 9, New York
29. Wm. N. Scarff's Sons, New Carlisle, Ohio*
30. Southern Nursery and Landscape Co., Winchester, Tennessee*
31. Spring Hill Nurseries, Tipp City, Ohio
32. Stark Brothers Nursery & Orchard Co., Louisiana, Missouri*
33. Sunny Ridge Nurseries, Swarthmore, Pennsylvania*
34. Lynn Tuttle Nursery, Clarkston, Washington*
35. Whitford Nursery, Farina, Illinois*
   Canada (An import permit is necessary to carry trees across the border.'
36. George H. Corsan, Toronto 18, Ontario*
37. J. U. Gellatly, Box 19, Westbank, B. C.
38. Papple Brothers, R. D. 3, Cainsville, Ontario
39. Bountiful Ridge Nurseries, Princess Ann, Maryland

SUGGESTED CRITICAL LEAF LEVELS FOR

FRUIT AND NUT TREES[1] (July Samples)

	% Nitrogen (N) [2]		% Potassium (K) [3]		% Calcium (Ca)	% Magnesium (Mg)	% Sodium (Na)	% Chlorine (Cl) [4]	Boron (B) (ppm)			Zinc (Zn) (ppm)
	Defic. Below	Adequate	Defic. Below	Adequate Over	Adequate Over	Over	Excess Over	Over	Defic. Below	Adequate	Excess Over	Defic. Below
Almonds	1.9	2.0 – 2.5	1.0	1.4	2.0	0.25	0.25	0.3	25	30–65	85	15
Apples	1.9	2.0 – 2.4	1.0	1.2	1.0	0.25	--	0.3	20	25–70	100	14
Apricots (ship)[2]	1.8	2.0 – 2.5	2.0	2.5	2.0	--	0.1	0.2	15	20–70	90	12
Apricots (can)[2]	2.0	2.5 – 3.0	2.0	2.5	2.0	--	0.1	0.2	15	20–70	90	12
Cherries (sweet)	--	'2.0 – 3.0	0.9	--	--	--	--	--	20	--	--	10
Figs	1.7	2.0 – 2.5	0.7	1.0	3.0	--	--	--	--	--	300	--
Olives	1.4	1.5 – 2.0	0.4	0.8	1.0	0.10	0.2	0.5	14	19–150	185	--
Nectarines and Peaches (freestone)	2.3	2.4 – 3.3	1.0	1.2	1.0	0.25	0.2	0.3	18	20–80	100	15
Peaches (cling)	2.4	2.6 – 3.5	1.0	1.2	1.0	0.25	0.2	0.3	18	20–80	100	15
Pears	2.2	2.3 – 2.8	0.7	1.0	1.0	0.25	0.25	0.3	15	21–70	80	15
Plums (Japanese)	--	2.3 – 2.8	1.0	1.1	1.0	0.25	0.2	0.3	25	30–60	80	15
Prunes	--	2.3 – 2.8	1.0	1.3	1.0	0.25	0.2	0.3	25	30–80	100	15
Walnuts	2.1	2.2 – 3.2	0.9	1.2'	1.0	0.3	0.1	0.3	20	36–200	300	15

· Adequate levels for all fruit and nut crops: Phosphorus (P) is 0.1 – 0.3%; Copper (Cu), over 4 ppm; Manganese (Mn), over 20 ppm.

[1]Leaves are from nonfruiting spurs on spur-bearing trees, fully expanded basal shoot leaves on peaches and olives, and terminal leaflet on walnut. (K. Uriu, J. Beutel, O. Lilliland, and C. Hansen, University of California, Davis)

[2]N % in August and September samples can be 0.2—0.3% lower than July samples and still be equivalent. N levels higher than underlined values will adversely affect fruit quality and tree growth. Maximum N for Blenheims should be 3.0% and for Tiltons, 3.5%.

[3]K level between deficient and adequate is considered "low" and may cause reduced fruit sizes in some years. Potash applications are recommended for deficient orchards but test applications only for "low" K orchards.

[4]Excess Na or Cl cause reduced growth at levels shown. Leaf burn may or may not occur when levels are higher. Confirm salinity problems with soil or root samples.

APPLE PRODUCTION COSTS IN NEW YORK

Note: Following the charts below is a summary of New York costs of production in 1971 for typical low-density (large) trees. Data were presented at the N. Y. State Horticultural Society Meeting, Kingston, 1972 by Dr. C. G. Forshey, Hudson Valley Laboratory of Cornell University, Highland, N. Y. 12528. For previous rather detailed cost-of-production data for large apple trees in New York and Washington, consult the 1969 edition of this book. Some charts in the 1969 edition are repeated here for New York from Cornell Bull. 1001, 27 pp. 1964, since they stress basic principles even though the price levels are for the early U. S. 1960's.

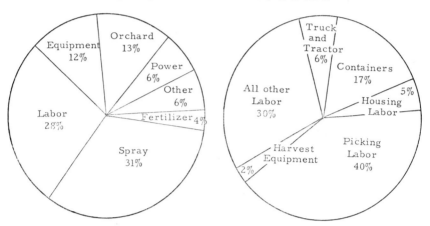

Distribution of growing costs in New York, 1962   Distribution of harvest costs

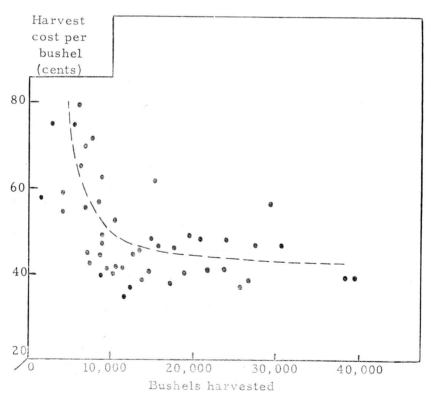

Harvest cost per bushel related to bushels harvested

904

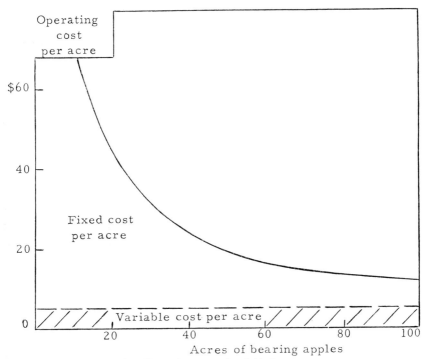

Operating costs per acre for air-blast sprayer

Address by Dr. Forshey: The problem of altering supply to fit demand can be approached from many angles. One of the most direct approaches is economic analysis. Over the past few years, this area has suffered chronic marketing problems with McIntosh apples. The problems have by no means been confined to this variety, but they have been most acute with McIntosh. There are actually two parts to the problem — overproduction and mediocre quality. Excessive supply has tended to depress McIntosh prices in general, and consumer reaction to unsatisfactory quality has compounded the problem. In addition, the poor pack-out of sub-standard fruit further reduces the returns to the producer. At today's prices, only the very best McIntosh will return a profit. The elimination of those orchards that consistently produce low quality McIntosh would improve the economic situation in 3 ways:

1. Reduce the total volume of McIntosh.

2. Improve the quality of apples available to the consumer.

3. Eliminate a source of direct financial loss to the producer.

Good financial records readily identify those orchards that should be replaced or eliminated entirely. Unfortunately, few growers keep detailed records that permit the identification of such problem areas. Because neither production costs nor returns are critically analyzed, many orchards that are consistent losers are being maintained. It is obvious at harvest that some blocks of McIntosh will not return the cost of harvesting, but they are harvested anyway, and they add an additional burden to a market that is already over-extended.

In an effort to focus attention on this problem, a cost survey was conducted in Eastern New York in 1971 with the following results:

Orchards included in the survey

Number of orchards	6
Acres of bearing apples	834
Fruit harvested in 1971-	312,717
Yield per acre - bu.	375

COST OF PRODUCTION

Orchard Overhead
Taxes ....$ 14.93/A
Interest 45.63/A
Rental 11.26/A
Total .... $ 71.82/A

Management
Salary ....$ 17.39/A
Accounting 1.80/A
Secretarial 1.35/A

Office 1.47/A
Total ....$ 22.01/A

Labor
Pruning and brush removal . $ 35.67
Spraying 7.73
Mowing 12.12
Other (spreading fertilizer, .. 17.66
applying herbicides, grubbing, etc.)

905

Total ....$ 73.18/A	TOTAL COST PER ACRE $288.23

Equipment

Investment per acre $142.06
Depreciation 15.01/A
Fuel 13.34/A
Repairs 14.93/A
Interest 7.52/A

Total ....$ 50.80/A

Materials

Spray and dust ....$ 53.74/A
Lime, fertilizer 5.13/A
Other (herbicides, growth
regulators, etc.) 11.55/A
Total ....$ 70.42/A

Cost per Bushel .... $ 0.77

HARVESTING COSTS

Equipment $0.03/bu
Containers .... .09/bu
Housing .... .04/bu
Picking .... .34/bu
Other labor (supervision and .... .08/bu
handling)
Other (fringe benefits, etc.) .... .03/bu
Total Harvesting Costs $0.61/bu

As a supplement to these cost figures, returns from different lots of fruit were collected as follows:

McINTOSH—LOT NO. 1

Pack	Number	Selling Price	Packing and Handling Cost	Return
12/3	122	$2.15	$ .90	$152.50
120	158	2.85	1.00	292.30
100	130	2.85	1.00	240.50
80	8	2.15	1.00	9.20
Utility	108	.80	.35	48.60
Cider	16	.50	.20	4.80
	542			$747.90

Average return per bushel—$1.38

McINTOSH—LOT NO. 2

Pack	Number	Selling Price	Packing and Handling Cost	Return
12/3	311	$2.15	$ .90	$388.75
120	120	2.85	1.00	122.10
100	22	2.85	1.00	40.70
80	1	2.15	1.00	1.15
Utility	212	.80	.35	95.40
Cider	50	.50	.20	15.00
	662			$663.10

Average return per bushel—$1.00

In Lot No. 1, utilities and ciders totalled 22%, but in Lot No. 2 this figure was 39%. After deducting harvesting costs of $ .61/bu, a yield of 374 bu/A would be required in Orchard No. 1 to cover the average growing costs of $288.23/A. The break-even point for the second orchard would be 739 bu/A. It must be emphasized that these figures do not include storage. If a charge of $ .35/bu is deducted for storage, the break-even yield for Lot No. 1 becomes 686 bu/A and for Lot No. 2, it becomes a practical impossibility. The orchard that produced the fruit in Lot No. 2 is a definite loser and should be purged immediately.

On the other hand, the returns from other varieties may be substantially greater. The returns for one lot of Delicious were as follows:

DELICIOUS

Pack	Number	Selling Price	Packing and Handling Cost	Return
12/3	75	$3.10	$ .90	$165.00
125	54	4.50	1.00	189.00
113	80	4.75	1.00	300.00
100	75	4.75	1.00	281.25
88	60	5.25	.95	258.00
80	19	5.25	.95	81.70
72	13	5.25	.95	55.90
64	8	5.25	.95	34.40
Utilities & Ciders	60	.50	.20	18.00
	444			$1383.25

Average return per bushel—$3.11

After harvesting costs of $ .61/bu and storage costs of $ .35/bu are deducted, there is a net of $2.15/bu to cover growing costs. This converts to a surprisingly low break-even yield of 134 bu /A.

It should not be inferred from these data that all McIntosh should be replaced with Delicious. However, it should be fairly obvious that McIntosh orchards that consistently produce fruit with 30-40% utilities cannot make money under today's conditions. Such orchards should be summarily replaced or eliminated because their continued existence can only aggrevate a situation that is already nearly intolerable.

COSTS: STANDARD VS. COMPACT APPLE TREES, NEW YORK

Richard L. Norton. Cornell Agricultural Extension Agent, Rochester, New York, has obtained data in western New York with apple growers converting from large apple trees to the compacts. Data are for the 1960's and early 1970's. Contact Mr. Norton for accumulative data each year on these trees.

TABLE 1. ESTABLISHMENT COST—HIGH DENSITY—ON WIRE—454 TREES/ACRE vs. ULTRA-HIGH DENSITY PLANTING—792 TREES/ACRE, N. Y. 1971

Items	Tractor/Hrs.		Man/Hrs.		Cost	
	HD*	UHD**	HD*	UHD**	HD*	UHD**
Plowing-Fitting	4	6	4	6	$ 26.00	$ 39.00
Marking	—	2	2	5	5.00	20.50
Setting trees	8	5	20	10	82.00	45.00
Setting posts	2	—	10	40	41.00	100.00
Installing wire	—	11	16	21	48.00	96.50
Cost of wire—14,400'	—	—	—	—	140.00	1188.00
Cost of trees	—	—	—	—	681.00	633.60
Cost of poles	18	24	52	82	228.00	
	—	—	—	—	$1251.00	$2122.60

*HD—High Density
**UHD—Ultra High Density; varieties Jonathan, Idared, Golden Delicious

TABLE 2.—YIELDS WITH ULTRA-HIGH DENSITY ON EM-IX: SET 1969. WESTERN N. Y., 1971

Variety	Planting System	Trees/ Acre	Lbs./ Tree	Bu./ Acre
Empire	11 x 5	792	33.9*	639.2
Empire	**11 x 6 x 4	1281	23.5	716.7
Golden Delicious	11 x 4	990	17.2	405.4
Golden Delicious	11 x 5 x 4	1361	14.7	476.3
McIntosh	11 x 6 x 5	1025	6.7	163.5

*Pollinator provided in each adjoining row.
**11 feet between tree rows/6 feet between double rows in bed/5 feet between trees in row.

TABLE 3. GOLDEN DELICIOUS YIELD (BU.) REQUIRED TO AMORTIZE AN EM-IX PLANTING: ULTRA-HIGH DENSITY, 1971, WESTERN N. Y.

Material and labor — planting	$2,294
Growing cost for 3 years	451
Interest for 3 years at 7%	571
	$3,316
Total	
Amortization over 15 years at 7%	$ 356
Amount per year	
Bushels of apples at	356
$1.00 above picking costs	237
$1.50 above picking costs	
Amortization over 25 years at 7%	$ 280
Amount per year	
Bushels of apples at	280
$1.00 above picking costs	187
$1.50 above picking costs	

Both the grower and his banker want to know whether the high cost of establishing an ultra-high density planting on EM-IX will pay. In the above table are shown the costs per acre at the end of the third growing season including interest at 7%. This amounts to $3,316.00 per acre. Significant yield was produced in the third year, so the cost was reduced by this amount. However, to amortize the full $3,316.00 over a period of 15 years with interest at 7% would amount to $356 per year per acre. To figure the extra bushels of apples required to pay this, one should take the price less the cost of picking. If this figure were $1.50 a bushel, it would take 237 bushels.

SUMMARY

It is obvious that there are certain financial advantages with the small trees employed in a properly designed intensive planting system.
My experiences illustrate to me that less labor per bushel and per acre is involved for the intensive system. Because of the small tree size in the intensive system, there is

a minimum requirement in pruning. Harvesting efficiency also is increased, reflecting another labor advantage. Quality-wise, fruit size and color has always been better and more uniform in the intensive planting using small size trees. Even using a conservative figure, the cost of spraying (one of the major growing costs) is reduced by one-third using EM-IX (454 trees per acre) compared with 116 trees per acre on MM-106. The higher initial cost, even at low fruit prices, has been more than adequately recovered either before or by the fifth growing season as a result of moving from 116 trees per acre to 454 trees per acre. The new question is, can we do equally as well moving from 454 trees per acre to 800-1,000 or more trees per acre? Indications look favorable. However, more years of data will be needed.

There is no doubt that the intensive planting, using a suitable rootstock and variety, has tremendous production advantages over less intensive plantings using larger trees. For this comparison, we have supporting data. However, today we have a new situation which makes the grower hesitate and question the advisability of setting new high density orchards and this is: too many apples and a price that is too low. When doubt exists that the fruit price in the future will come above a reasonable level, the question is not whether to plant more or less intensively, but rather if you should plant at all! If you intend to stay competitive and produce quality fruit—you **must** plant more intensively!

TABLE 4. McINTOSH TREE GROWTH: PLANTED 1963/MEASUREMENTS IN 1970.

Rootstock	Width/ Ft.	Height/ Ft.	Circ./ Cm
EM VII	17.3	13.2	41.6
EM IX	10.1	8.1	24.9
EM II	17.6	13.6	41.0
MM 106	18.5	15.4	47.2
MM 109	18.5	15.4	46.7
MM 104	18.5	15.7	47.7
MM 111	18.2	15.2	42.2
Seedling	18.4	15.1	44.5

TABLE 5. McINTOSH PRODUCTION ON STANDARD VS. COMPACT STOCKS, SET 1963. WESTERN N. Y. DATA 1967-71

Rootstock	Suggested Spacing	Tr./A	Bushels per Acre 1967/70	1971	Total
MM 106/EM IX	8' x 12'	454	5266	1407	6673
EM VII	12' x 22'	165	2327	1898	4225
MM 106	15' x 25'	116	2189	1786	3975
MM 109	15' x 30'	97	1597	1436	3033
EM II	15' x 30'	97	1276	1222	2498
MM 104	15' x 30'	97	1216	1135	2351
MM 111	15' x 30'	97	964	1232	2196
Seedling	18' x 35'	69	358	580	938

*No records were taken 1965-66, but the MM-106/EM-IX trees had significantly higher production.

TABLE 6. ROOTSTOCK EFFICIENCY, McINTOSH: SET 1963/MEASUREMENTS TAKEN 1970*

Rootstock	Lbs/Fruit/Cm2 Trunk Cross-Section
EM-IX/MM-106	3.12
EM-VII	2.54
EM-IX	2.43
EM-II	1.91
MM-106	1.86
MM-109	1.52
MM-104	1.25
MM-111	1.19
Seedling	.74

*In the above table, tree measurements were made in 1970 and correlated only with the 1970 yield. If the accumulative average yearly yield were used, EM-IX would show a much more favorable rating. However, it should be noted at this point that certain varieties are also more efficient than others on the same rootstock.

TABLE 7. PICKERS PERFORMANCE ON McINTOSH, STANDARD Vs. DWARFS, 1970: AGE—8 YEARS

Rootstock	Spacing	Ave. Bu./ Tree	Ave. Min./ Bu.	Ave. Bu./ Hr.	Height/ Feet
MM-106/EM-IX	10 x 15	4.1	2.4	25	8.0
EM-IX	8 x 12	2.0	2.6	23	8.1
MM-106	15 x 30	8.1	3.3	18	15.4
EM-VII	15 x 30	6.1	3.8	16	13.2
EM-11	15 x 30	6.7	4.2	14	13.6
MM-109	15 x 30	6.6	5.6	11	15.4
Seedling	15 x 30	2.6	7.1	8.4	15.1

TABLE 8. FRUIT GRADE IMPROVEMENT ON COMPACT TREES, McINTOSH, SAME WESTERN N. Y. FARM

%Grading	Standard Tree	Stem Piece EM IX/Sldg.
Fancy and Above	41%	88%
U. S. No. 1	48%	10%
Culls	5%	2%

TABLE 9. ORCHARD REMOVAL COST PER ACRE (Based on 40-50 Yr. Old Trees) WESTERN, N. Y.

Step No. 1	Bull Dozer ($22.00/hr.)	$56.00	
	Labor - Cleanup ($2.50/hr.)	5.00	
	Tractor and Wagon	10.00	
			$ 71.00
Step No. 2	Plowing (9.00/hr.)	$27.00	
	Picking up Roots - Labor	5.00	
	Tractor and Wagon	10.00	
			$ 42.00
Step No. 3	Disposing of debris (bulldozer)	$18.00	
	Tractor and Loader (5 hrs.)	40.00	
	Land Leveling ($9.00/hr.)	27.00	
			$ 85.00
			$198.00

TABLE 10. APPLE ORCHARD ESTABLISHMENT COST/ACRE, WESTERN, N. Y. 1972

Planting System	Cost per acre
Medium Density 116 Trees/A.	$ 210.00
High Density 454 Trees/A/	$1,155.00*
Ultra High Density 990 Trees/A	$2,568.85**

*on wire   **each tree staked

TABLE 7. NEW YORK STATE COST ACCOUNT FARMS— STANDARD LOW-DENSITY TREES

Item	1966	1969
Growing costs per acre	$197	$275
Harvesting costs per bushel	32c	57c
Storing and selling costs per bushel	16c	28c
Yield per acre (bu.)	498	323
Grower price per bushel	1.12	1.40
Net return per bushel	+24c	—30c
Net return per acre	+$1.21	—$97
Net return per farm	+8,172	—7,501
Number of acres of bearing apples per farm	68	77

Source: N. Y. Cost Account Farms — B. J. Dominick, Cornell Univ.

TABLE 11. TREE AGE, PLANTING DISTANCE AND PRUNING PERFORMANCE AND COST (McINTOSH), WESTERN, N. Y. EARLY 1970's.

Rootstock	Spacing	Age	Hours per Acre	Yield per Acre	Cost per Bushel
EM 1X	8' x 12'	6	9	901	.025c
MM 106	15' x 25'	6	12.5	340	.092c
EM IX	8' x 12'	7	8	1190	.017c
MM 106	15' x 25'	7	17.5	940	.046c
EM IX	8' x 12'	8	8	1340	.014c
MM 106	15' x 25'	8	28	1786	.039c
Standard	40' x 40'	25	31.5	400	.20c

TABLE 12. McINTOSH YIELDS ON DIFFERENT ROOTSTOCKS—TREES SET 1963, WESTERN, N. Y.

Rootstock	Bushel per tree 1967/70	1971	Total	Suggested Spacing	Tr./A	Bushels per acre 1967/70	1971	Total
EM VII	14.1	11.5	25.6	12 x 22	165	2327	1898	4225
MM 106	18.9	15.4	34.3	15 x 25	116	2189	1786	3975
MM 109	16.5	14.8	31.3	15 x 30	97	1597	1436	3033
EM 11	13.2	12.6	25.8	15 x 30	97	1276	1222	2498
MM 104	12.5	11.7	24.3	15 x 30	97	1216	1135	2351
MM 111	9.9	12.7	22.6	15 x 30	97	964	1232	2196
Seedling	5.2	8.4	13.6	18 x 35	69	358	580	938

TABLE 13. COST OF STORING FRUIT BELOW FANCY GRADE OUT

% Grade Out Below Fancy	1,000 Bu. Cold Stor. Cost at 40c	1,000 Bu. C. A. Stor. Cost at 70c
5	$ 20.00	$ 35.00
10	$ 40.00	$ 70.00
15	$ 60.00	$105.00
20	$ 80.00	$140.00
30	$120.00	$210.00

TABLE 14. EFFECT OF APPLE YIELD/A ON PROFITS; THREE GROWERS, WESTERN N. Y.* **

Grower	"A"	"B"	"C"
Production per acre/bus.	323	500	1,000
Cost: Growing/Acre	$275	$305	$356
Harvesting/Acre	$185	$200	$400
Storing and Selling/Acre	$90	$140	$280
Total Cost/Acre	$550	$645	$1,036
Returns: $1.40/bu.	$452	$700	$1,400
Net Gain or Loss/Acre	$-90	$+55	$+364

* Cornell Cost Account Records 1970
**Compact trees

TABLE 15. SIZE OF APPLE ORCHARD OPERATION AND PROFIT OR LOSS. WESTERN N. Y. 1970*

Grower	"A"	"B"	"C"
Yield per acre	323	500	1,000
Total acres	62	40	20
Total production	20,000	20,000	20,000
Cost: Growing	$17,050	$12,200	$7,120
Harvesting	$11,470	$8,000	$8,000
Storing & Selling	$5,600	$5,600	$5,600
Total Cost	$34,120	$25,800	$20,720
Returns: $1.40/bu.	$28,000	$28,000	$28,000
Net Gain or Loss	$-6,120	$+2,200	$+7,280

*Compact trees

ILLINOIS FRUIT YIELDS FROM GOLDEN DELICIOUS, STARKING AND JONARED ON EM-VII RESULTING FROM DIFFERENT CULTURAL PRACTICES. TREES WERE PLANTED IN 1963.
(Roy Simons, U. of Illinois, Urbana)

TREATMENTS	Average yield in pounds/tree with 30 trees/treatment and 3 varieties														
	1967			1968			1969			1970			4 Yr. Aver.		
	GD	SD	JR	GD	SD	JR	GD	SD	JR	GD	SD	JR	GD	SD	JR
Whole cobs;1	18	8	5	111	45	56	116	69	111	195	206	156	440	328	328
Whole cobs;2	16	5	9	150	37	53	114	43	138	338	197	165	618	282	365
Ground cobs;1	16	7	0	124	51	19	136	53	90	168	204	128	444	315	237
Ground cobs;2	15	4	12	142	42	46	133	75	165	363	221	173	653	342	396
Straw mulch;1	11	7	12	114	50	46	142	87	115	234	231	161	501	375	334
Straw mulch;2	21	6	13	145	51	74	128	78	163	326	207	162	620	342	412
No mulch;1	29	9	10	107	42	47	106	59	99	431	197	94	673	307	250
No mulch;2	30	6	13	111	33	74	89	63	138	258	160	153	488	262	378

1irrigated   GD Golden Delicious   JR Jonared
2non-irrigated   SD Starking Delicious   NOTE: Mulching gave best fruit finish.

910

COSTS: ESTABLISHING AN ORCHARD ON FULL AND SEMI-DWARFING STOCK WASHINGTON, USA

The following table was taken from the mimeo publication EM-2834 by S. M. Doran and R. S. Hunter, Washington State University. 1972. The full-dwarf trees were 7 x 14 feet, or 444 trees/A, rill-irrigated, 2/3 Red Delicious, 1/3 Golden Delicious, using 90% of the land with the rest in ditches, headlands, roads, etc.

APPLES: SUMMARY OF PER ACRE ESTABLISHMENT COSTS[a]

	First Year	Second Year	Third Year
	$	$	
Land prepartion	8.03		
Tree location	7.47		
Trees (544 at $1.70)	834.70	18.70	
Dig holes, plant, water	141.75	7.54	
PLANTING COSTS	1082.05	26.24	
Growing Costs			
Trellis		184.45	4.83
Prune, train, tie	6.75	71.74	108.80
Rodent control	13.24	12.25	13.24
Fertilizer		7.67	17.82
Irrigation - corrugate	13.67	13.67	18.26
- labor	40.50	40.50	40.50
Beating			9.30
Weed control - chemical		13.88	13.88
- mechanical	68.55	12.30	
Pest control	7.00	7.00	14.00
Cover crop			14.81
Fruit removal - chemical			5.96
- hand			15.75
GROWING COSTS	149.71	363.46	277.15
Cash Overhead			
Taxes	7.00	7.00	7.00
Water	10.00	10.00	10.00
General Overhead	56.00	15.00	9.00
Interest on Operating Cap.	53.00	14.00	9.00
TOTAL CASH & LABOR COSTS	1357.76	435.70	312.15
Deprec. of equip., bldgs.	8.16	8.56	21.40
Int. on equip., bldgs., land	57.16	57.40	64.04
Int. on Accum. Invest. (8%)		113.85	163.09
TOTAL ANNUAL COSTS	1423.08	615.51	560.68
Yield - tons per acre			
Crop value			
Annual Income			
ACCUMULATED INVESTMENT	1423.08	2038.59	2599.27

a/Based on establiishing a 24-acre apple orchard on full-dwarfing rootstock on a 300-acre diversified farm. Trees on EM IX and 26 rootstocks, 1971 data.

Following data were taken from Washington State University Bulletin EM-2833 by S. M. Doran and R. S. Hunter, 1972. Giving establishment costs for an orchard on **semi-dwarfing** rootstock. Comparable costs for establishing an orchard on **standard** rootstock may be found in Wash. EM-2832 Bulletin, 1972.

APPLES: SUMMARY OF PER ACRE ESTABLISHMENT COSTSa/
SEMI DWARFING STOCK (1971)

	First Year	Second Year	Third Year	Fourth Year	Fifth Year
Land preparation	$ 8.03	$	$		
Tree location	6.15				
Trees	455.60	8.50			
Dig holes, plant and water	56.80	3.73			
PLANTING COSTS	526.58	12.23			
Growing Costs					
Prune, train, and tie	4.50	13.40	93.80	127.30	120.60
Rodent control	10.90	11.30	11.30	11.30	11:30
Fertilize		18.72	18.72	17.41	25.40
Irrigation - corrugate	12.45	13.69	16.60	16.60	16.60
- labor	36.00	36.00	36.00	36.00	36.00
Beating			11.62	15.81	15.81
Weed control - chemical		11.74	11.74	11.74	11.74
- mechanical	50.86	12.30			
Pest control	7.00	7.00	14.00	82.12	82.12
Cover crop			15.89		
Thinning					
Fruit removal				6.58	6.58
Chemical			6.58	11.25	24.75
Hand					
GROWING COSTS	121.71	124.15	236.25	336.11	350.90
Picking				25.00	95.00
Hauling, bin distribution				20.00	76.00
Supervision harvest				6.00	6.75
Cleanup				2.08	4.15
HARVEST AND CLEANUP				53.08	181.90
Taxes	7.00	7.00	7.00	7.00	7.00
Water	10.00	10.00	10.00	10.00	10.00
General Overhead	29.00	5.00	9.00	15.00	25.00
Interest on Oper. Cap.	27.00	5.00	8.00	15.00	24.00
CASH AND LABOR COSTS	721.29	163.38	270.25	436.19	598.80
Deprec. of equip., bldgs.	9.08	9.40	14.24	25.80	25.80
Int. on equip., bldgs., land	57.24	57.44	59.28	66.20	66.20
Int. on Accum. Invest. (8%)		63.00	86.47	120.88	159.32
TOTAL ANNUAL COSTS	787.61	293.22	430.24	649.07	850.11
Yield - tons per acre				2.25	8.55
Crop value at $75 per ton				168.75	641.25
ANNUAL INCOME	-787.61	-293.22	-430.24	-480.32	-208.86
ACCUMLATED INVESTMENT	787.61	1080.83	1511.07	1991.39	2200.25

a/Based on establishing a 25-acre apple orchard on semi-dwarfing rootstock on a 300-acre diversified farm.

b/Thinning by hand, third year; hand and chemicals used, 4th and 5th years.

COSTS: ORCHARD INVESTMENT, ANNUAL COSTS AND RELATION TO YIELD IN WASHINGTON, USA

Space here is unpermitting. See data in Washington State University EM-3484 mimeo bulletin by S. M. Doran and J. M. Lange. 12 pp. 1971. About 2/3 were Delicious trees, 1/3 Golden Delicious.

REGIONAL USA COSTS OF HARVESTING, STORING AND PACKING APPLES

The following data were taken from USDA—Economic Research Service Bulletin ERS-496. 7 pp. 1971 November. See Source for more details.

Estimated 1970-71 costs to pack a box of Washington apples (From Wash. Agr. Exp. Sta. Bull 755, May 1972)

ITEMS	DELICIOUS Reds	DELICIOUS Goldens
Storage buildings and bulk bin overhead (depreciation, interest, taxes, insurance, repairs and a "normal" profit of 8% on equity). Plant operating at 80% utilization of capacity. Red Delicious 15% culls, Golden Delicious 25% cull—cost differences based on cullage.	.531	.603
Packing shed and packing equipment overhead. Plant operating at 80% utilization of capacity. Cost differences based on time requirement—Goldens one-half more time than Reds.	.267	.401
Overhead management costs. (Excluding the salaries of owners or managers and sales personnel).	.122	.143
Operating costs (electricity, water, gas, telephone, etc.). .7c to 1.5c box/month for 4.5 months.	.045	.045
Direct labor in packing: Reds (average size 122, average 1970-71 grade)2 9.54 man minutes per packed box at $2.25/hour.	.358	
Goldens (average size 113, average 1970-71 grade)2 13.89 man minutes per packed box at $2.25/hour.		.521
Container: Reds: Top wrap, tray pack (Size 100)	.600	
Goldens: Full wrap, tray-cell pack, poly liner (Size 100)		.750
Wax and fungicide	.030	.030
Federal-State inspection (approximate)	.028	.028
Apple Commission fees (approximate)	.050	.050
Tree Fruit Research Commission fees (approximate)	.002	.002
Totals	$2.03	$2.57

1Not included: General Manager's Salary. Any selling or brokerage fees.
Voluntary fees to Washington Growers Clearing House or to the Traffic Association.
Hauling into original storage and truck or car loading.

2Average grade in the cost study.

3Compliance inspection 1.87c/box.

Apple harvesting costs and storage charges, 5 major production regions, 1969/70 season, USA.

Region	Harvesting Picking	Harvesting Hauling	Harvesting Total	Storage charges Regular atmosphere	Storage charges Controlled atmosphere
	----------Dollars per bushel----------				
Northeast ....:	0.36	0.08	0.44	0.33	0.64
Lake States ....:	.37	.06	.43	.29	.57
Appalachia					
North 1/.............:	.33	.07	.40	.30	.63
South 2/.............:	.32	.10	.42	.35	---
All Appalachia ....:	.33	.08	.41	.30	.63
California ....:	.31	.05	.36	.23	.43
Northwest					
Wenatchee, Okanogan,					
Washington 3/........:	.24	.04	.28	.38	.75
Yakima, Wash. 3/......:	.23	.05	.28	.32	.65
Idaho, Oregon,					
Colorado ....:	.23	.11	.34	.35	.60
All Northwest ......:	.24	.05	.29	.35	.69

1/Virginia (North of Roanoke), Maryland, Delaware, West Virginia, and Pennsylvania.
2/Virginia (South of Roanoke), and North Carolina.
3/And other nearby points.

913

Apple packing and selling costs and charges, 5 major production regions, 1969/70 season, USA.

Region	Costs of packing and selling (Dollars per carton)											Packing and selling charges			
		Containers				Sell-ing 3/	Over-head	Totals				Totals			
	Labor	Tray packs 1/	Bag cartons 1/	Bulk cartons	Aver-age 2/			Tray packs	Bag cartons 1/	Bulk cartons	Aver-age 2/	Tray packs	Bag cartons 1/	Bulk cartons	Aver-age 2/
Northeast	0.35	0.58	0.46	0.32	0.49	0.26	0.15	1.34	1.22	1.08	1.25	1.34	1.23	1.09	1.25
Lake States	.32	.53	.46	.30	.48	.18	.14	1.17	1.10	.94	1.12	1.28	1.14	NA	1.18
Appalachia															
North 4/	.44	.60	.50	.36	.53	.18	.17	1.39	1.29	1.15	1.32	1.43	1.27	1.14	1.33
South 5/	.47	.53	.50	.38	.51	.16	.36	1.52	1.49	1.37	1.50	NA	NA	NA	1.78
All Appalachia ...	.44	.58	.50	.37	.53	.18	.20	1.40	1.32	1.19	1.35	1.43	1.29	1.13	1.34
California															
North of S.F.	.57	.64	.47	NA	.56	.16	.48	1.85	1.68	NA	1.77	NA	NA	NA	NA
South of S.F.	.28	NA	.48	.34	.40	.14	.18	NA	1.08	.94	1.00	NA	NA	NA	NA
All California ...	.40	.65	.48	.34	.47	.14	.31	1.50	1.33	1.19	1.32	NA	NA	NA	NA
Northwest															
Wenatchee-Okanogan Washington 6/ ...	.48	.61	.58	.36	.61	.15	.26	1.50	1.47	1.25	1.50	1.65	1.55	1.16	1.67
Yakima, Wash. 6/ .	.44	.62	.52	.35	.60	.13	.42	1.61	1.51	1.34	1.59	1.74	1.63	1.28	1.72
Idaho, Oregon, Colorado	.47	.72	.58	.39	.65	.15	.30	1.64	1.50	1.31	1.57	1.67	1.43	1.28	1.56
All Northwest	.46	.63	.55	.38	.62	.15	.34	1.58	1.50	1.33	1.57	1.70	1.60	1.27	1.68

1/ Average of all bags packed 10/4's, 12/3's, etc. In particular in the Appalachian area this includes some 15/3's and 12/4's.
2/ Includes cell packs and overwraps but excludes other bulk containers and other miscellaneous containers.
3/ Selling charge.
4/ Virginia (North of Roanoke), Maryland, Delaware, West Virginia and Pennsylvania.
5/ Virginia (South of Roanoke) and North Carolina.
6/ And nearby points.
NA—Not Available.

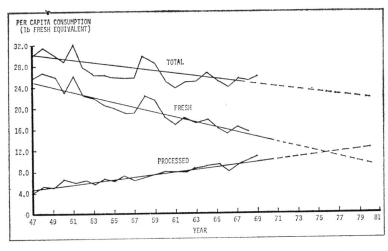

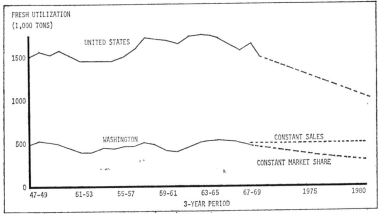

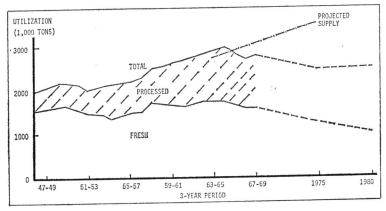

Projections to 1980 for (a) per capita consumption of apples; (b) fresh utilization of apples in the U.S. and Washington, and (c) fresh and processed utilization of apples in the U.S. (After A. O. O'Rourke, W. S. Greig and A. H. Harrington. Apple Marketing Research in the Seventies. (Wash. Agr. Exp. Sta. Bull. 754. Apr. 1972).

COSTS: CANNING PEACHES IN CALIFORNIA

Following two tables on canning peaches were prepared by N. Ross, D. Rough, V. Carlson and E. Yeary, Farm Advisory of Stanislaus, San Joaquin, Merced and State Wide counties, respectively, in the late 1960's and early 1970's. Additional data in subsequent years may be had by writing to the Extension Pomologist, University of California, Davis 95616.

SAMPLE COSTS TO ESTABLISH A CANNING PEACH ORCHARD
In Merced, Stanislaus & San Joaquin Counties, California

Based on 80 Acres Planted 108 Trees per Acre

	Year 1	2	3	4
Planting Costs				
Fumigate soil	50.00			
Land Preparation	44.00			
Layout and plant: 108 trees at 25¢	27.00			
Trees: 108 at 85¢	91.80			
Total Planting Costs	212.80			
Cultural Cost; Cash & Depreciation				
Prune	10.00	25.00	35.00	50.00
Brush Removal				4.25
Shred brush or disc			7.17	7.17
Fertilize	3.00	4.00	4.00	5.40
Fertilizer	5.00	10.00	20.00	24.00
Spray	5.00	10.00	15.00	21.08
Spray material	10.00	20.00	40.00	75.00
Cultivate 4X	14.34	14.34	14.34	14.34
Ridge and knock ridges	5.79	5.79	5.79	5.79
Irrigate	5.00	7.50	10.00	12.00
Water cost (variable)	8.00	8.00	8.00	8.00
Thin				100.00
Rope or wire			10.00	17.42
Hoe or spray	5.40	5.40	5.40	5.40
Re-plant		3.50	2.05	1.25
Misc. labor and tree care	3.50	8.00	10.34	10.34
Total Cultural Costs	75.03	121.53	187.09	361.44
Harvest Cost				
Harvest at $14 ton			42.00	98.00
Overhead				
Misc., office, car, etc.	17.27	7.30	15.42	30.06
Taxes	18.00	18.00	18.00	35.00
Marketing order			11.25	22.50
Interest	140.35	162.47	195.16	233.45
Management	30.00	30.00	30.00	30.00
Total Overhead	205.62	217.77	269.83	351.01
Total Cost	493.45	339.30	498.92	810.45
Income				
Yield: tons			3	7
Income at $75.00 ton			225.00	525.00
Net Cost Per Acre	493.45	339.30	273.92	285.45
Accumulated Cost Per Acre	492.45	832.75	1106.67	1392.12
Investment Per Acre				
Land	1350.00	1350.00	1350.00	1350.00
Trees		493.35	832.75	1106.67
Irrigation System	150.00	150.00	150.00	150.00
Buildings	120.00	120.00	120.00	120.00
Equipment	334.62	334.62	334.62	334.62
Total Investment	1954.62	2447.97	2787.37	3061.29

Total Cost of Developing an Orchard to the End of the 4th Year = $1392.12

Sample Costs to Produce Canning Peaches on the East Side (Cortez to Escalon) of Merced, San Joaquin & Stanislaus Counties

Based on an 80-acre orchard yielding 16-ton yield (No. 1 fruit) per acre
Labor at $1.90 and $2.40 per hour, which includes Social Security, Workman's Compensation Insurance and all benefits furnished by the grower.

Cash and Depreciation Costs per Acre

Operation	Hours per Acre	Labor	Fuel and Repairs	Depreciation	Materials — Kind	Amount	Cost	Total Cost
Pre-harvest								
Prune 108 trees @ $1.00 labor cost	1.0	108.00	5.90	.85				114.75
Limb removal	1.0	2.40	1.70	1.39				5.49
Disc or shred brush	1.0	2.40	1.85	2.24				6.49
Fertilize 2X Custom					Material & application		27.00	27.00
Spray 5X 350 gal.	2.0	6.70	8.30	6.08				21.08
					Materials		75.00	75.00
Ridge and knock down 6X	1.0	2.40	1.90	1.49				5.79
Cultivate 4X	2.0	4.80	5.30	4.24				14.34
Irrigate 6X	2.5	6.00	1.00	5.00	Water-variable; est.		8.00	20.00
Thin $1.40 tree; labor cost		151.20					2.00	153.05
Prop and wire	3.0	6.20	1.25	4.52				17.42
Spray or hoe weeds 5¢ tree		5.40						5.40
Misc. labor and tree care	4.00	8.10	4.70	.60				13.47
Re-plant	.2	.40					.85	1.25
Other			1.50	3.87				
Total Cultural Costs		304.00	33.40	30.28			112.85	480.53
Harvest Costs								
Pick 17-273 tons @ $14		247.33		2.08				249.41
Total Harvest Costs		247.33		2.08				249.41
Overhead Costs								
Misc., office, etc.				13.15	Variable		36.24	49.39
Taxes							35.00	35.00
Tree Depreciation				69.60				69.60
Marketing order					16 tons at $2.25		36.00	36.00
Total Overhead				82.75			107.24	189.99
Total Cash & Depreciation		551.33	33.40	115.11			220.09	919.95
Interest								164.36
Management 5% of 16 tons @ $75.00								60.00
Total Cost Per Acre								1144.29

Cost Per Ton @ 16 Ton Yield = $71.52

							Your Est.
Total D'Anjous trees per acre	93	93	93	93	93	93	
Bearing D'Anjous per acre	20	30	40	50	60	70	
Non-Bearing D'Anjous[a]	73	63	53	43	33	23	
Yield - loose boxes per Acre[b]	184	276	368	460	552	644	
	$	$	$	$	$	$	$
Non-Harvest Operations							
Pruning, brush disposal	55.00	66.00	78.00	89.00	101.00	113.00	
Tree replacement	54.00	54.00	54.00	54.00	54.00	54.00	
Sprays, spraying	133.27	133.27	133.27	133.27	133.27	133.27	
Mow, irrigate	22.00	22.00	22.00	22.00	22.00	22.00	
Propping (3.8¢ per box)	7.00	10.50	14.00	17.50	21.00	24.50	
Fall - cleanup, fertilize, etc.	31.86	31.86	31.86	31.86	31.86	31.86	
Fuel, repairs, supplies, etc.	87.89	87.89	87.89	87.89	87.89	87.89	
Supervision - non-harvest oper.[c]	15.32	15.78	16.26	16.72	17.20	17.69	
SUBTOTAL - per acre	406.34	421.30	437.28	452.24	468.22	484.21	
- per loose box	2.21	1.53	1.19	.98	.85	.75	
Harvest Operations							
Picking (24¢ per box)	44.16	66.24	88.32	110.40	132.48	154.56	
Yarding (2.7¢ per box)	5.00	7.50	10.00	12.50	15.00	17.50	
Hauling (57¢ per bin)	4.20	6.30	8.40	10.50	12.60	14.70	
Harvest supervision[c]	2.42	3.63	4.84	6.04	7.25	8.46	
SUBTOTAL - per acre	55.78	83.67	111.56	139.44	167.93	195.22	
- per loose box	.30	.30	.30	.30	.30	.30	
General Overhead							
OASI, Industrial Insurance	7.26	9.28	11.35	13.38	15.45	17.52	
Util.,office, irrig.water, etc.	38.21	38.21	38.21	38.21	38.21	38.21	
Taxes, Insurance	32.78	32.78	32.78	32.78	32.78	32.78	
Interest - operating capital	18.40	19.51	21.42	22.93	24.46	26.00	
- orchard, equip.	189.21	189.21	189.21	189.21	189.21	189.21	
Depreciation - equip., bldgs.	78.28	78.28	78.28	78.28	78.28	78.28	
Other supervision[c]	4.37	4.52	4.65	4.79	4.94	5.08	
SUBTOTAL - per acre	368.51	371.79	375.90	379.58	383.33	387.08	
- per loose box	2.00	1.34	1.02	.82	.69	.60	
TOTAL ANNUAL COSTS - per acre	830.63	876.76	924.74	971.26	1019.48	1066.51	
- per loose box[d]	4.51	3.18	2.51	2.11	1.85	1.66	

a/ Includes 12 first-year replacement trees.
b/ Based on 9.2 field boxes per bearing tree.
c/ Orchard supervision assessed at 5 percent of the cash costs.
d/ The equivalent costs per packed box would be about 50 percent more than the costs per loose box, because of weight differences and cullage.

CA STORAGE OPERATION AND CONSTRUCTION DETAILS

Note: This material is from Bulletin 433, West Virginia Agricultural Extension Service, Morgantoan 26506, prepared by A. W. Selders and L. M. Ingle. Information valid to 1973: contact authors for any suggested changes since 1973.

CONTROLLED ATMOSPHERE storage of apples is now a commercially accepted practice in many of the principal producing areas of North America and Europe. The method was developed in England over thirty-five years ago and has been used commercially in New York since the early 1940s. The principal characteristic of controlled atmosphere storage is a modification of the atmosphere in the storage room. While the atmosphere normally contains 20-21 per cent oxygen, 0.03 per cent carbon dioxide, and the balance nitrogen (with traces of other inert gases), apples can be stored for prolonged periods in atmospheres composed of 3 to 5 per cent oxygen and 0 to 5% carbon dioxide (with the balance in nitrogen). Because the method is based on modification of the atmosphere, the term "modified atmosphere" is sometimes used rather than "controlled atmosphere" or CA. While perhaps not as precise CA seems to be the most common term and will be used in this bulletin. Regular storage will mean the conventional refrigerated storage which is now used by most growers.

While all of the effects of this atmospheric modification on the psysiology of apple fruits are not known, it is clear that there is an overall reduction in the rates of the chemical reactions which normally occur in fruits stored in normal atmospheres at comparable temperatures. As a

918

ADDITIONAL CA STORAGE INFORMATION

Table 1. Atmospheric and temperature requirements for controlled atmosphere storage of different apple and pear varieties (After Smock, Cornell University).

Variety	Carbon dioxide	Oxygen	Temperature
APPLES	%	%	°F
Cortland	2 (1 month, then 5%)	3	38
Delicious	2*	3	30-32
Golden Delicious	2	3	30-32
Jonathan	5**	3	32
McIntosh	2 (1 month, then 5%)	3	38
N. Spy	2-3	3	32
Rome Beauty	2-3	3	30-32
Stayman	2-3	3	30-32
Turley	2-3	3	32
Yellow Newtown	7	3	38-40
PEARS			
Anjou	0.5-1	2-3	30-32
Bartlett	1-2***	2-3	30-32
Bosc	0.5-1***	2-3	30-32

* Washington State recomends less than 1%
** If stored with Delicious, the Delicious requirement must be met.
*** Based on limited tests at Oregon State University and Cornell University.

Precautions

1. The room does not have to ge gastight if modern gas mixing and injecting equipment is used.
2. The room must be filled with apples.
3. The fruit must be of high quality and of the proper degree of maturity to justify the added expense of this type of storage.
3a. Keep doors slightly open as temperature is lowered to prevent "cave-in" of walls or insulation
4. The room must be sealed up within 10-14 days after starting to fill it in the fall.
5. The proper atmospheric and temperature requirements must be followed for each variety.
6. The atmosphere must be checked twice daily.
7. The oxygen must never be allowed to go lower than 2.5 per cent. The carbon dioxide level must not be allowed to rise higher than that recommended for the variety.
8. Open port hole in the door when adding air to the room.
9. A relative humidity of 90-95 per cent must be maintained during the holding and unloading period. During the loading period it should be at least 85 per cent.
10. There must be good circulation of the atmosphere in the room. The apples must be properly stacked.
11. Never go into the room without an air mask or an oxygen mask.
12. The caustic soda solution used is harmful to the skin. It will also burn clothing. If it gets on the skin, wash it off immediately. Do not breathe the fumes of the caustic soda when making up the solution of the material with water.
13. Control odors in the room by some means.
14. Do not let the spent caustic soda or salt solutions come in contact with the roots of trees or other plants.
15. Air out the room well before removing the gastight door. Gas analyses should show 18-20 per cent oxygen before men work in the room to remove the fruit.

result, desirable quality levels can be maintained over a longer storage period. The effects of these altered rates of change usually can be observed only after ninety days or so; therefore, the common practice is to place part of the crop in regular storage for use during the first 90-123 days after harvest while the remainder of the crop is placed in CA for use after the regular-stored fruit has been exhausted.

About 12-15 per cent of the total U. S. apple crop is placed in CA. This represents over 20 per cent of the total volume of apples stored. The trend is slightly upward. In 1971-72 over 18 million U. S. apples were placed in CA storages. The Netherlands stores over half their crop in CA. In New York, some growers place as much as 50 per cent of their crop in CA. Packing and marketing are then extended until June or July. Over the last five years prices received for apples from CA have averaged about 80 cents per bushel higher than fruit from regular storage. Costs for CA storage exceed regular storage by 35 to 40 cents per bushel.

This discussion describes some of the methods and materials that have been used successfully in CA construction and operation. It is based primarily on inspection of commercial facilities and conversation with established growers and operators. The information is intended to help growers who are considering CA make some preliminary decisions. CA can be built and operated in several ways. Each prospective CA operator should carefully analyze many factors including his own objectives, present facilities, resources, and future production before proceeding to detailed plans. Considerable time also should be devoted to gathering cost data for the various materials and construction that ought to be used. It cannot be overemphasized that profitable CA storage requires attention to details of construction and operation. There are no short-cuts or cheap methods.

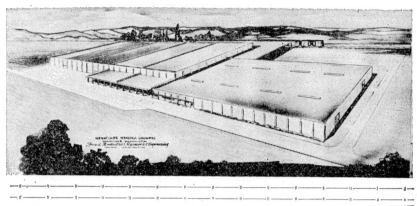

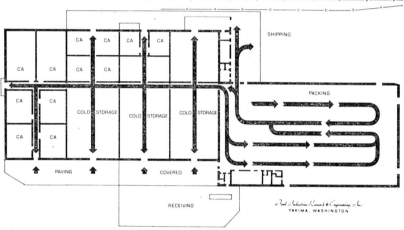

This is the largest controlled atmosphere fruit storage in the United States, completed in early 1973 by the Wenatchee Wenoka Growers Association in Wenatchee, Washington. This facility will increase the Association's capacity to over a half million bushels. (Food Industries Research and Engineering, Inc., Yakima, Washington).

STORAGE SCALD CONTROL

CA storage greatly increases the susceptibility of apples to a storage or superficial scald. This physiological disorder, however, can be effectively controlled with scald inhibitors. Apples to be placed in CA must be treated. If treatment facilities are not available at the proposed CA storage, plans must include the addition of adequate scald-treatment equipment. Scald control materials and methods are described in West Virginia Agricultural Experiment Station Current Report 47. Equipment for this operation is being improved constantly. Treatment of regular stored fruit, while not essential, is recommended.

CONSTRUCTION OF CA ROOMS

BASIC construction for CA storage rooms is not much different from that for conventional storage rooms. Structural requirements for foundations, floor, wall, roof, and other parts are the same as for regular refrigerated storage rooms. There is one additional requirement. A CA room must have a good gas seal on the inside or somewhere in the wall section. The gas seal must extend completely around the room and include the floor and ceiling. Wood frame, masonry, and steel buildings have all been used successfully for CA rooms. As noted above, with modern gas generating and mixing equipment, rooms do not have to be absolutely gas tight.

ROOM SIZE. There is probably no "best" size for CA rooms. Rooms may range in size from 1000 boxes to 50,000 boxes. The size of a room for a particular grower or operator will depend on several factors. One of these is the rate at which the room can be filled. Another is the rate at which fruit can be marketed once the room is opened. Some states have laws controlling CA storage and these laws specify time limits during which the room must be filled and the atmosphere established. The laws also specify that the apples must be left in the controlled atmosphere for certain period of time (usually 90 days), before they can be removed and marketed as CA apples.

920

Another factor to consider is the number of different varieties of apples to be stored. Because of varietal responses to different CA storage atmospheres and temperatures it is recommended that certain varieties not be stored together in the same room. If five or six varieties are to be stored in CA, it is best to provide at least two or three different rooms so that different atmospheres and temperatures can be provided. For most situations in West Virginia, an economical and practical room size would be about 12,000-16,000 boxes. Even though the construction cost for several smaller rooms is higher than for one large room, room size must be considered because of the practical management aspects.

INSULATION. In general, the same insulations are used for CA rooms as for conventional re-frigerated storage rooms. The one difference is that an adequate gas seal must be provided in a CA rooms. Certain foam-type insulations applied with proper mastics and coatings provide both a vapor barrier and an adequate gas seal. Granulated cork, corkboard, and loose or bat type insulations were used in the earliest CA rooms. Recently, expanded foam-type insulations have been used successfully. Spray-on insulations also are being used. If applied properly, spray-on insulation provides both a vapor barrier and a gas seal.

WOOD FRAME STRUCTURES. Wood frame structures with granular or bat insulation can be used for CA rooms. Wood structures usually consist of studded walls with the vapor barrier and siding on the outside and 28-gauge sheet metal on the inner surface to provide the gas seal. The wall space is filled with granulated cork, bat, or other type insulation. The metal is fastened with nails to either the rough lumber wall used to confine the insulation, or if no conforming wall is used, the metal is fastened to the studs or other nailing strips and serves as the confining wall for the insulation. A special caulking compound is often used to seal the joints and nail holes. It is important that the wall framing be structurally sound. Any movement in the wall section can crack or break the seal in the galvanized metal. In gable room construction, a wood ceiling is installed with loose fill or bat insulation laid over the ceiling. The sheet metal is nailed to the underside of the ceiling.

Aluminum sheets have been used for the gas seal. However, in some instances, aluminum has not been satisfactory because of corrosion from the salt brine spray from the refrigeration units. Some protection from corrosion can be provided by applying certain coatings to the aluminum, particularly in the area around the cooling unit.

A high-grade gun caulking compound which will not dry out is used to seal the metal joints. The sheets are butted or overlapped about 2 inches. If overlapped, caulking compound is laid down first under the sheet before it is fastened to the studs or wooden surface. Then another strip of caulking is laid down on top of the first sheet at the edge where an overlap will be made. The second sheet is fastened down with large-headed galvanized nails spaced every 2 to 3 inches. The caulking that oozes out is smoothed down over the overlap and all nail heads are covered with the caulking compound. If the sheets are butter, a space of ⅛ to ¼ inch is left between sheets. It is preferable to caulk under the sheets before they are fastened down. Then a gal-sheet metal moulding is slightly overfilled with caulking compound and is fastened with gal-vanized screws every 6 to 8 inches. The caulking that oozes out is smoothed down over the joints between the moulding and the metal sheet to provide a good seal.

FLOOR CONSTRUCTION. For floor construction a concrete pad is poured on a well prepared base. Two layers of 55 lb. asphalt-impregnated roofing paper are mopped in hot asphalt and ap-plied over the subfloor to make a good gas seal. The layers are put down so that the joints do not come directly under one another. Another method is to use roofer's felt (two or three layers), and make a typical built-up roof over subfloor. The wall seal must tie in with the floor seal. The wall can extend down far enough to allow it be flared 12 to 18 inches out on the floor and hot-mopped into the felt or roofing paper. Any metal that will come in contact with concrete should be coated with hot asphalt to check corrosion from the moist concrete. Rigid insulation having a com-pressive strength adequate to support the total floor loading is then applied over this asphalt or felt surface. A reinforced concrete wearing slab sufficient to carry the loads imposed on the floor is then poured over the insulation. A space of about ¾ inches is left between the concrete slab and the wall and filled with hot asphalt to make an expansion joint and to make certain that a good seal is obtained at the wall and floor juncture.

A concrete floor of at least 5 inches is recommended. The base floor should be poured on a good sand or gravel fill that has been properly drained and firmly compacted. Insulation in the floor may or may not be used. Most engineers recommend the use of at least 2 inches of floor insulation for CA rooms. Two inches or more of perimeter insulation extending 1 to 2 feet be-low the floor is recommended if the floor is not insulated. Where single wall construction is used the perimeter insulation can be a continuation of the wall insulation. Perimeter insulation for double wall construction can be provided by extending the double wall 12 inches below the bottom of the floor. A dense concrete floor slab which is fairly impermeable to gas has provided an adequate gas seal in some instances. However, it is generally recommended that a gas seal other than concrete be provided.

MASONRY STRUCTURES. Concrete block masonry construction is commonly used for storage rooms although reinforced precast concrete wall sections are coming into use in some areas. Con-ventional methods of supporting the wall with buttresses and horizontal reinforcing are employed. The walls are usually constructed with a single layer of concrete blocks with a board-form insu-lation, or with a double or cavity wall filled with loose-type insulation. In reinforced precast tilt-up construction the concrete is first poured and compacted into a dense monolithic mass in a horizontal position and is then erected with suitable equipment to form the vertical walls. A board-type insulation is usually used. The thickness of the insulation will vary with the material used but is usually equivalent to 4-6 inches of corkboard. Precast sandwich-type wall sections with the insulation between two layers of concrete also are available. These sections are fairly easy to erect and make an attractive building.

There are several methods and materials which may be used to apply rigid insulation to block or concrete walls. Depending on the type of insulation and the wall surface, various kinds of adhesives can be used to apply the insulation directly to the blocks. A special cement mortar mix has been used successfully to apply rigid polystyrene insulation to unprimed concrete block walls. For foamed glass insulation, hot dip asphalt is usually used. Masonry walls must be primed with a brush coat of asphalt priming paint and allowed to dry before applying foamed glass with a hot asphalt dip. Certain polystyrene and urethane foam insulations cannot withstand the high

921

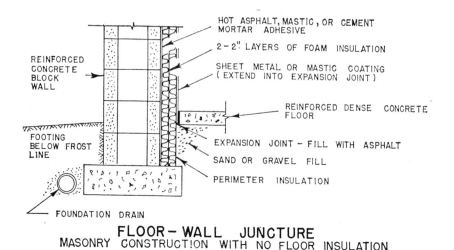

HOT ASPHALT, MASTIC, OR CEMENT MORTAR ADHESIVE

2-2" LAYERS OF FOAM INSULATION

SHEET METAL OR MASTIC COATING (EXTEND INTO EXPANSION JOINT)

REINFORCED CONCRETE BLOCK WALL

REINFORCED DENSE CONCRETE FLOOR

FOOTING BELOW FROST LINE

EXPANSION JOINT - FILL WITH ASPHALT

SAND OR GRAVEL FILL

PERIMETER INSULATION

FOUNDATION DRAIN

FLOOR - WALL JUNCTURE
MASONRY CONSTRUCTION WITH NO FLOOR INSULATION

temperature of the hot asphalt and must be applied with approved cold adhesives, mastics, or cement mortar mix. Insulation manufacturers can supply the proper materials for applying various insulations to different surfaces. Furring strips with special insulation nails also may be used for applying rigid insulation. Hanger rods and tee bars are available for ceiling installation.

Concrete block rooms can be made gastight by apply two coats of a special mastic over the insulation. A nylon membrane is applied between coatings for added strength and to help cracking of the mastic due to expansion and contraction of the wall section. These coatings are applied over the insulation with a trowel or hand application. This method of sealing masonry structures for CA rooms will prove satisfactory if good construction techniques are used. It is important that the insulation be properly applied and that the wall section be reinforced so that cracking does not occur. Insulation with a low coefficient of thermal expansion should be selected. If an insulation having a high coefficient of expansion is used the gas seal coating may crack at the joints of the insulation.

Galvanized sheet metal also may be used to provide the gas seal in masonry structures. Furring strips to which the sheet metal is nailed are anchored through the insulation to the block wall. Another method of attaching the furring strips to board insulation is to rout out an area of insulation equal to the area of the furring strip and then fasten the furring strip to the insulation with an adhesive. The sheet metal is then lapped at least -½ inch and nailed to the furring strips. All wood furring strips should be treated for decay resistance. The high humidity conditions required for satisfactory fruit storage are favorable for the development of rot and the deterioration of any wood used in masonry buildings. In general, no additional vapor barrier is needed with rigid foam insulation which is impervious to vapor penetration. All of the joints and nail heads of the sheet metal must be sealed with a caulking compound.

Many variations in roof framing have been used with masonry construction. Flat roof designs include combinations of wood and steel structural members, steel bar joists, and precast steel reinforced concrete roof decks such as T-beam, channel, and slab sections. Other roof designs use various shapes—tied arches, pitched trusses, and wooden bow-string trusses. Masonry construction provides adequate support for these different roof designs. The open web steel bar joist or the concrete roof are usually preferred for masonry structures in West Virginia although the cost of these types of roofs is usually higher than for wood joist and trussed roofs. Steel or concrete has the advantage of being fire resistant and less prone to deterioration because of moisture. Flat, arched, or gable-type steel trusses are available for widths up to 40 or 50 feet. Prestressed concrete T-beams are fairly economical for roof construction for widths up to about 50 feet.

Rigid insulation can be utilized as the roof deck with bar joist construction. The first layer of insulation is attached to the bar joists or purlins with metal fasteners and the second layer of insulation is then applied with adhesive or hot asphalt. A built-up roof is then applied over the insulation according to the roofing manufacturer's specification. Normally, a properly applied built-up roof will serve as a gas seal. However, it is sometimes difficult to get a good seal between the wall and the built-up roof. Some contractors prefer to apply two or three layers of asphalt roofing paper or felt between the two layers of insulation. This roofing paper is then folded around the end and under the bottom layer and mopped into the wall gas seal. If foamed glass insulation is used the roofing or felt can be hot-mopped directly on top of the first layer. The second layer and the built-up roof is then applied over the gas seal. If the insulation cannot be mopped with hot asphalt a cold-type adhesive must be used to apply the first layer of roofing paper.

Another method of providing a gas seal in bar joist roof construction involves the use of a suspended or false ceiling. Metal hanger rods suspended from the joists support a metal pan ceiling over suspended channel irons. The insulation is applied on the top surface of the metal ceiling and a gas seal is provided above, below, or between layers of insulation. The hanger rods should be insulated above the upper ceiling insulation layer for a distance of 12 inches.

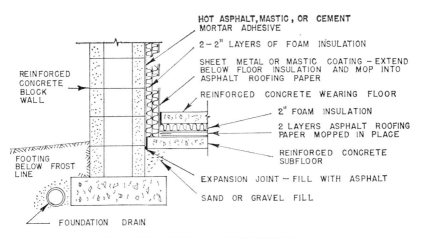

HOT ASPHALT, MASTIC , OR CEMENT
MORTAR ADHESIVE

2 – 2" LAYERS OF FOAM INSULATION

SHEET METAL OR MASTIC COATING – EXTEND
BELOW FLOOR INSULATION AND MOP INTO
ASPHALT ROOFING PAPER

REINFORCED CONCRETE WEARING FLOOR

2" FOAM INSULATION

2 LAYERS ASPHALT ROOFING
PAPER MOPPED IN PLACE

REINFORCED CONCRETE
SUBFLOOR

EXPANSION JOINT – FILL WITH ASPHALT

SAND OR GRAVEL FILL

REINFORCED
CONCRETE
BLOCK
WALL

FOOTING
BELOW FROST
LINE

FOUNDATION DRAIN

FLOOR – WALL JUNCTURE
MASONRY CONSTRUCTION WITH INSULATION

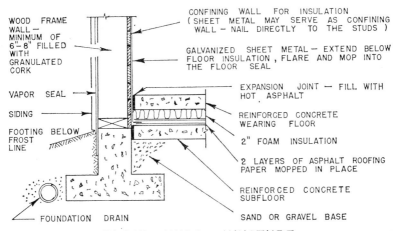

WOOD FRAME
WALL –
MINIMUM OF
6"– 8" FILLED
WITH
GRANULATED
CORK

VAPOR SEAL

SIDING

FOOTING BELOW
FROST LINE

FOUNDATION DRAIN

CONFINING WALL FOR INSULATION
(SHEET METAL MAY SERVE AS CONFINING
WALL – NAIL DIRECTLY TO THE STUDS)

GALVANIZED SHEET METAL – EXTEND BELOW
FLOOR INSULATION , FLARE AND MOP INTO
THE FLOOR SEAL

EXPANSION JOINT – FILL WITH
HOT ASPHALT

REINFORCED CONCRETE
WEARING FLOOR

2" FOAM INSULATION

2 LAYERS OF ASPHALT ROOFING
PAPER MOPPED IN PLACE

REINFORCED CONCRETE
SUBFLOOR

SAND OR GRAVEL BASE

FLOOR – WALL JUNCTURE
WOOD FRAME CONSTRUCTION WITH FLOOR INSULATION

Hanger rods and T-bars also can be used to support the ceiling insulation without the metal pan. A rabbit is cut out on the bottom edges of the upper layer of insulation so that the T-bar flange will fit snugly and permit flush lay-up of the second layer from underneath. The upper layer of insulation is bonded to the T-bar with adhesive or asphalt emulsion. The second layer is applied from below using wood skewers and latex cement adhesive. The hanger rods are insulated above the upper insulation layer. A mastic can be applied on the underside of the insulation for a gas seal.

Prestressed concrete T-beam construction is about the same as bar joist construction with the insulation and built-up roof on top. However, it is more difficult to get a gas seal between the roof and wall. The concrete beam may be sufficiently dense to serve as a gas seal. Sealing compounds can be used to seal the joints at the ends around the filler blocks. Asphalt mastics which remain flexible at 32°F should be used.

STEEL BUILDINGS. Steel buildings also are being used for CA storages. Board and spray-on type insulations are applied either on the inside or outside of the steel structure. For inside application, the first layer of board insulation is nailed to wood furring strips attached to the steel frame and the second layer is applied with mastic adhesive. Galvanized sheet metal or the mastic coating may be used for the gas seal. A disadvantage here is that wood nailing strips may deteriorate or rot due to the high moisture conditions. When galvanized sheet metal is to be used for gas seal furring strips for nailing the metal must be provided on the inside of the insulation. One method of doing this is to rout out an area in the outer lay of insulation equivalent to the

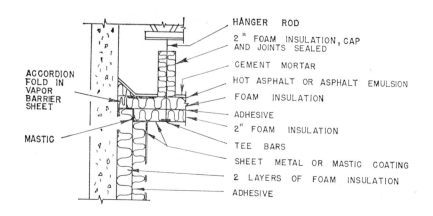

Labels (top diagram):
- HANGER ROD
- 2" FOAM INSULATION, CAP AND JOINTS SEALED
- CEMENT MORTAR
- HOT ASPHALT OR ASPHALT EMULSION
- FOAM INSULATION
- ADHESIVE
- 2" FOAM INSULATION
- TEE BARS
- SHEET METAL OR MASTIC COATING
- 2 LAYERS OF FOAM INSULATION
- ADHESIVE
- ACCORDION FOLD IN VAPOR BARRIER SHEET
- MASTIC

WALL – CEILING JUNCTURE
SUSPENDED T- BAR CEILING

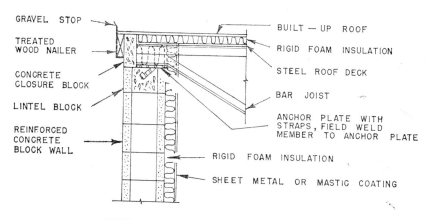

Labels (bottom diagram):
- GRAVEL STOP
- TREATED WOOD NAILER
- CONCRETE CLOSURE BLOCK
- LINTEL BLOCK
- REINFORCED CONCRETE BLOCK WALL
- BUILT — UP ROOF
- RIGID FOAM INSULATION
- STEEL ROOF DECK
- BAR JOIST
- ANCHOR PLATE WITH STRAPS, FIELD WELD MEMBER TO ANCHOR PLATE
- RIGID FOAM INSULATION
- SHEET METAL OR MASTIC COATING

WALL – CEILING JUNCTURE
BAR JOIST WITH STEEL DECKING

area of the nailing strip. The nailing strips are then glued to the insulation with a suitable material, juncture at the floor and wall is sealed in the same manner as with concrete and wood framing.

Spray-on insulation may be applied directly to the steel siding. Manufacturers claim that a spray-on insulation properly applied provides an adequate gas seal for CA rooms. The use of these materials is fairly new and their performance over a period of years needs to be evaluated before definite recommendations can be made.

Another innovation in insulating steel buildings for CA storage is spray-on insulation applied on the outside of corrugated metal siding. A 2- or 3-inch thickness of sprayed-on insulation is applied on both the roof and sides. A second layer of a protective coating spray-on material applied over the insulation is recommended. The outer coating provides weathering protection even in corrosive chemical environment. One type of coating is impregnated with nylon shreds to provide added strength and resistance to cracking.

The spray-on insulation can be used in the floor also. The desired thickness is applied to the concrete subfloor with the wearing pad poured on top of the insulation. Advantages claimed for spray-on insulation are that it provides an excellent gas and vapor seal, can be used to seal

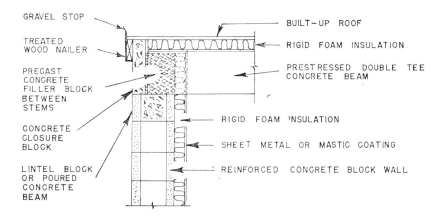

WALL – CEILING JUNCTURE
CONCRETE T – BEAM DECK

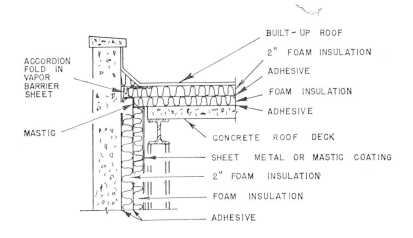

WALL – CEILING JUNCTURE
COLUMN SUPPORTED CONCRETE ROOF DECK

around pipes and electrical conduits going through the wall, can be applied over rough or uneven surfaces, and is easily applied with the proper equipment.

As with any type of construction, steel buildings for CA rooms must be structurally sound to eliminate any movement which can crack or break the gas seal. Proper attachment of the building to the foundation is very important. Special equipment usually will be required to erect framing for a steel building. As with concrete, the cost of steel construction may be slightly higher than for wood. However, since a CA storage is a functional building, the builder should be cautious of false economy as well as expensive frills. The most desirable type of building should provide satisfactory use and longevity at minimum per bushel storage cost.

DOORS. Doors for CA rooms should be large enough to accommodate a fork lift truck operation. The recommended size is approximately 6 to 8 feet wide by 8 to 10 feet high. Depending upon the storage layout and the number of rooms in one building it is best to have only one door per room if possible. Doors for CA rooms must be constructed so that they can be made gas tight. Sealing around the door is just as important as sealing the wall, floor, and ceiling.

Steel-clad insulated doors or a closure panel bolted to the walls from the inside are used in CA rooms. One preferred way to seal doors is to use a heavy galvanized sheet metal plate bolted

925

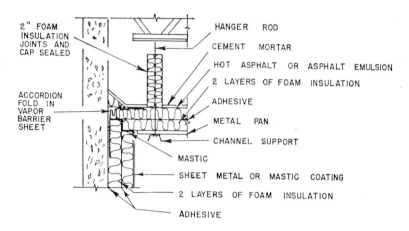

2" FOAM INSULATION JOINTS AND CAP SEALED

HANGER ROD

CEMENT MORTAR

HOT ASPHALT OR ASPHALT EMULSION

2 LAYERS OF FOAM INSULATION

ADHESIVE

METAL PAN

CHANNEL SUPPORT

ACCORDION FOLD IN VAPOR BARRIER SHEET

MASTIC

SHEET METAL OR MASTIC COATING

2 LAYERS OF FOAM INSULATION

ADHESIVE

WALL- CEILING JUNCTURE
SUSPENDED METAL PAN CEILING

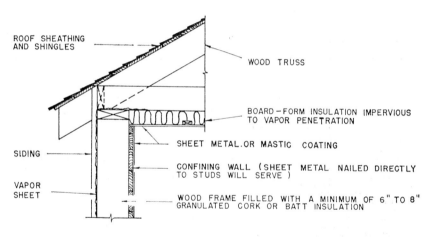

ROOF SHEATHING AND SHINGLES

WOOD TRUSS

BOARD—FORM INSULATION IMPERVIOUS TO VAPOR PENETRATION

SHEET METAL.OR MASTIC COATING

SIDING

CONFINING WALL (SHEET METAL NAILED DIRECTLY TO STUDS WILL SERVE)

VAPOR SHEET

WOOD FRAME FILLED WITH A MINIMUM OF 6" TO 8" GRANULATED CORK OR BATT INSULATION

WALL- CEILING JUNCTURE
WOOD ROOF TRUSS CONSTRUCTION

to the inside of the door opening. The metal door is uninsulated and a standard hinged cooler door is used on the outside. A window or porthole is provided in the door to observe the functioning of the equipment and to remove fruit samples. Sometimes the porthole is large enough to be used as the access door to permit a man to crawl through after sealing around the door from the inside. The preferred way is to provide two openings, one being an access window large enough for a man to crawl through with a smaller porthole about 6 to 8 inches in diameter through which fruit samples can be removed and through which observations can be made of the equipment to see that everything is functioning properly.

The porthole also may be used to add air into the enclosure when necessary. The porthole and access window may be used to observe thermometers which are placed strategically inside the enclosure. The access panel is fastened to the door with screws or bolts and a special sealing compound used to seal around the panel. A soft polybutene sealant may be used to seal the main door to the wall. After the main door is sealed workmen leave the enclosure through the access panel. Heavy glass or plexi-glass is used for the access panel and is sealed from the outside with petroleum jelly or caulking compound.

The framing required to fasten the gastight door on the inhide should not protrude into the door opening or should be such that it can be removed when not in use, so that it is not in the way when unloading and loading the room. The door is fastened down on knife-grade caulking compound with bolts spaced every 4 to 6 inches. The door also must be sealed at the floor level

926

Improvements made on farm land may be of three types:

(1) Farm business improvements subject to depreciation, such as farm buildings, silos, fences, and tile drains.

(2) Farm business improvements not depreciable, such as cost of clearing land, constructing open ditches, and soil and water conservation expenditures not deducted as expenses.

(3) Improvements to the farmer's personal dwelling which are depreciable for tax purposes.

Cost of these improvements is added to the original cost which is then reduced by the amount of all depreciation previously deducted or allowable. If any item has been deducted as an expense, such as soil and water conservation expenditures, it cannot be included in the cost basis. Thus it is important to have a complete record of all depreciation and capital expenditures during the entire period of ownership.

There is frequently a tax advantage in trading a farm for another farm, rather than selling one and buying another. In case of trade all or part of the tax liability is postponed. No gain is recognized for tax purposes unless a difference in cash or certain non-business property is received in the transaction.

In particular cases it may be more desirable in the long run to sell ,and pay taxes on the gains in order to get a higher cost basis on the new farm or business property. This might apply in case an unimproved farm is exchanged for a well improved farm or business property.

In selling a farm the tax liability on the gain can be spread over a period of years and in many cases can be reduced by use of the "installment sales" method. To qualify for such sale, the payments received in the year of sale must not exceed 30 per cent of the selling price.

In all cases where the farmer's personal dwelling is part of the farm which is sold, any gain realized on the dwelling is not recognized for tax purposes, if all of the proceeds from the dwelling are reinvested in a new dwelling, purchased and occupied by the farmer, within one year prior to or after the date of sale of his original dwelling.

4. Tax Planning In Buying A Farm

The year in which a farm is purchased is the time when many tax savings can be initiated. At the time of purchase the buyer should allocate the total cost of the farm to: (1) growing crops, if any, (2) depreciable improvements, (3) dwelling, and (4) land.

From a tax management viewpoint, the amounts allocated to the different items are handled differently. The "cost" of the growing crops is an offset against the selling price of the crop in the year of sale. Of course, the cost basis of the farm is reduced by the amount allocated to the crop.

The part of the "cost" allocated to land will not be recovered until the farm is sold, since land cannot be depreciated or amortized. So, too, the portion allocated to the dwelling is not depreciable if used as the buyer's personal residence. A tenant house is depreciable for tax purposes. Cost allocated to depreciable improvements will be recovered through depreciation. Recovery of cost is faster on short-lived improvements than on long-lived ones.

Of course, for management and tax purposes, the "cost" must be broken down and allocated to each particular structure or improvement. In allocating cost to depreciable improvements the following procedure may be helpful: (1) figure the present cost of replacing the improvement, (2) establish the years of normal useful life, (3) determine the age of the present improvement, (4) determine remaining years of life of the improvement, and (5) compute the present value of present improvement. The following is an example:

(1) Replacement cost of barn — $7500; (2) Useful life of new barn — 50 years; (3) Age of present barn — 30 years; (4) Remaining life of present barn — 20 years; and (5) Value of present barn — 20/50 of $7500==$3000.

Consideration of the utility value of a particular improvement to the farm may materially reduce the "present value" of the improvement. Another guide in allocating costs is the reasonable insurance values of insurable prpoerty. Care should be taken to see that in the final allocation the amount allocated to the bare land represents a reasonable value for similar land in the community.

The proper allocation of cost may help determine the price a buyer will pay for the farm. This is particularly true where the buyer is looking to future farm income after taxes to pay off the purchase price.

Closely related is the manner of payment of the purchase price. In computing taxable income the buyer deducts interest payments but not payments on principal. The seller treats interest as ordinary income, while principal payments are usually part return of capital and part capital gain. Thus, in particular cases, it might be wise for the buyer and seller to adjust the principal amount and interest rate to obtain the best tax results. It is generally true that if these allocation and payment provisions are within the bounds of reasonable judgment, they will stand up. In fact, revenue agents give great weight to written contracts setting forth these details.

MANAGING INCOME FOR INCREASED SOCIAL SECURITY BENEFITS

As older farmers approach retirement age they may wish to maximize their net farm income to as near $4800 as possible in order to secure maximum social security benefits. In so doing they will automatically increase their income taxes. However, they may prefer to pay these additional taxes for additional retirement benefits. Many of these farmers are far more interested in methods of increasing rather than decreasing their taxable income.

Some of the means for increasing income which should receive consideration are: (1) renting and operating additional land, (2) intensifying and expandng present enterprises, (3) adding new enterprises, (4) marketing forest products, (5) selling more young stock, (6) doing custom work or other off-farm work, and (7) contracting pasturage and services together, so that the income is recognized as self-employment income and not excluded as rental income.

Where choice of method of handling certain items of expense is optional, they may choose the method which gives the smaller deductions. Examples of such would include: (1) shifting from the rapid depreciation method to the slower straight-line method for improvements, machinery, etc., (2) electing to treat soil and water conservation costs as capital investments rather than as current operating expenses, (3) disposing of some depreciable capital items to reduce the total depreciation deductions, and (4) in general reducing operating costs to a minimum.

SUMMARY

Like other farm costs, income taxes can be reduced by good management. A good tax manager is one who "thinks taxes" all during the year. He does not rely on end-of-the-year planning alone. There is very little that can be done to reduce taxes after the close of the year's business.

A farmer need not be a tax expert, but he should know enough about taxes to recognize the income tax aspects of a farm decision. If he knows how to look for tax problems, he will know when he needs tax advice.

This section has discussed some of the major tax planning decisions that farmers must face. On the next pages there ts a list of tax items often overlooked by farmers, and a list of tax management ideas. Every idea that can be used on a particular farm is a tax dollar saving.

TAX REPORTING REMINDERS

1. Be sure that CCC loans are not counted as income twice (in one year when borrowed and next year when crop is sold).

2. If using the cash method, deduct cost of purchased livestock lost, strayed, or stolen or which died during the year.

3. If using the accrual method all purchases of livestock should be recorded. Make a "livestock number check" to see that the total number purchased, born, and on the beginning inventory equal the total number sold, died, butchered, and on the ending inventory.

4. Deduct cost of auto and truck licenses, insurance, etc.

5. Deduct as much expense of auto, utilities, telephone, etc., as is actually used in the farm business (half is not enough in many cases).

6. Take all depreciation allowable on depreciable improvements, machinery, equipment and on purchased draft, breeding and dairy livestock.

7. Keep records to insure deduction of easily overlooked items such as farm magazines, organization membership, bank service fees, overnight business trips, portion of dwelling used for farm use, losses on household goods used for hired help ,and cash outlay to board hired workers.

8. Itemize on bank deposit slips all gifts, borrowings, sale of bonds, etc., so that there is no chance that they will be considered farm income.

9. Keep records of all medical, dental, and hospital bills, including payments for accident and health insurance.

10. Keep exact records of dates of purchase, costs and date of sale on all items sold.

11. Do not include in income any indemnity for diseased animals if the payment has been or will be used to purchase "like or similar" animals within one year.

12. Deduct social security tax paid on farm laborers.

13. Do not report as income capital gains on sale of your dwelling if you plan, within a year to buy, or within 18 months to build, another dwelling that will cost as much or more than your selling price.

14. Keep all paid bills, invoices, cancelled checks, etc., for at least five years, including checks used to pay income taxes. Pay bills by check whenever possible. Write down all other payments at once in an account book. Get the bank statement each month and check it against the farm account book.

15. Establish a charge account at hardware store, elevator or other places where considerable business is done during the year. Pay this account by check upon receipt of monthly statements. This prevents the omission of many small expense items which might otherwise be paid by cash and tickets lost. Every dollar of cost not deducted will result in at least 20 cents of unnecessary income tax being paid.

TAX MANAGEMENT TIPS

1. Pay reasonable wages to children for farm work actually done by them, so long as there is a true employer-employee relationship.

2. If child is under 19 or regularly enrolled in school or on on-farm training program, he can earn over $600 and the father still gets an exemption for the child if the father pays over half of the child's support. This makes possible a double exemption.

3. Give income producing property to children, e.g., land, cattle, machinery, and let them report income from their work and capital. Family partnerships are sometimes used to do this. It is another way to spread family income over the lower brackets. Remember, gifts and partnerships must be legally sound to achieve tax savings.

4. If age 63 or 64, postpone income to age 65 to take advantage of the $1200 personal exemption. But persons qualifying for social security will probably want to maximize income in those years.

5. If nearing 65, plan income from rents, dividends, interest and pensions to qualify for the retirement income credit. If 65 or over, claim retirement income credit on $1200 of rents, dividends, interest and pensions (up to $240 in tax reduction).

6. Do not hold breeding stock used for production of market livestock too long. Farrowing only one or two litters from sows will qualify a larger percentage of sales for capital gain treatment.

7. Buy machinery and equipment in years of high income and take additional 20 per cent first year depreciation in addition to the regular depreciation allowable.

8. In replacing machinery, equipment, and draft, breeding or dairy stock decide whether it is better to trade or to sell outright and buy the replacement. Outright sale and new purchase may allow extra depreciation deductions that more than offset taxable capital gains.

9. If selling or cutting timber, plan to obtain special capital gains treatment.

10. Manage sales of farm machinery, equipment, land and capital gain livestock. These can result in capital gains or ordinary losses. Keep gain sales in another year to get lowest tax on gains, and use losses to offset other farm income. Livestock must be held for 12 months or more to qualify for capital gains treatment. Other depreciable items must be held more than 6 months.

11. Plan personal deductions. Many payments that are normally spread over two years can be paid in one year and itemized as deductions. In the next year the standard 10% deduction (up to $1000 per joint return) may be taken. Charitable contributions and medical expenses are examples. of such deductible items.

12. Plan to have enough income to use up the personal deductions that are allowed.

13. Avoid wide fluctuations in income from one year to the next.

14. Accelerated depreciation can be used in many cases as an income evener and as an aid in shifting income into the capital gains category.

15. Installment sales can be used to spread income over a period of five years and thus avoid a high income in one year.

16. The amount of income subject to capital gain treatment can frequently be increased on the accrual basis by setting up a depreciation schedule for draft, breeding, and dairy animals. By doing this the remaining cost is less at the time of sale.

17. Understand the effect of rapid depreciation on improvements, machinery and equipment.

932

Decide whether to recover costs quickly or spread them out against farm production over a longer period.

18. Check loss years in the past. Is there an unused net operating loss deduction? Remember that claims for refund may bring an audit.

19. Don't forget about social security in tax planning.

20. Use the tax estimate work sheets in Purdue Ext. Bull. 413 to plan tax savings. Send for a copy at Dept. of Farm Economics, Purdue Univ., Lafayette, Indiana.

W. P. Tufts, Univ. of Calif., Davis

The low-spreading Kadota fig trees are secured by pruning the outside branches long and the inside branches short to facilitate harvesting the fruit which is used fresh for the most part. Before pruning (above).

933

FRUIT-CROP-FROST-HAIL INSURANCE

By Paul W. Barden, Special Agent
Rain and Hail Insurance Bureau, U.S. Rt. 15, Camp Hill, Pa. 17011

When your local agent quotes you the premium cost of hail coverage, your current Crop-Hail rate is determined by past loss experience on that crop in your locality. Records for all companies are tabulated on IBM cards by the Crop-Hail Insurance Actuarial Association in Chicago for the years 1936-on for each crop, and recorded by township, by county, and by state. Also there are accurate records for most fruit states as to premiums and losses for the years 1913-1936, so you can readily see that we have an excellent picture of what has happened concerning frequency and intensity of storms and the resulting cost to the insurance companies.

In New Jersey, e.g., our experience is not as conclusive as for some of our other states like Virginia, New York and Pennsylvania, but last year crop hail rates were reduced by 20% in New Jersey which gives it the distinction of having the lowest crop-hail rates of any of the Northeastern states. The most frequently used contract is $4.00 per $100 of insurance per acre of apple in New Jersey as cohpared with $8.00 and $10 in New York State.

The all-time loss ratio on apples in several of our northeastern states is about 70%. Our administrative expense ratio was approximately 35% during this same period. From the preceding figures you easily can see that our companies had had a median loss of about 5% by writing apples in the northeastern states and all insurance companies, like other businesses, must have some pleasure of profit as a goal. So with these percentages in mind, it is only practical for us to adjust our rates as conditions change. Therefore, we make a complete review of all crops in all areas at least every three years.

I have traveled the northeastern states for the past twenty-four years and we have tried to adapt our contracts to the needs of the various areas because we know that conditions in the Champlain Valley of New York are not the same as they are in Western New York, where the canning plants are principally located. We are attempting to improve our contract to secure a reduced rate for those growers who are primarily growers of canning apples.

ADJUSTMENT PROCEDURE

In eastern New York, I still find growers who feel that we should pay 100% of a loss on all apples hit by hail irrespective of the degree of damage. Our adjustment procedure has always been based on U. S. standards for grades of apples, and our percentages have been based on a reduction in grade as follows:

U. S. No. 1 reduced to Utility 30%
U. S. No. 1 reduced to Canner 50%
U. S. No. 1 reduced to Cider or Cull 100%

This provides an excellent yardstick from which to measure the loss.

After selecting two average trees in a ten acre block of apples and having picked 50 apples from each of four sides and the top of the tree, a typical weighted average adjustment for this block would be as follows:

$$
\begin{array}{rcr}
25 \text{ x} & 0 = & 0 \\
100 \text{ x} & 30 = & 3000 \\
225 \text{ x} & 50 = & 11250 \\
150 \text{ x} & 100 = & 15000 \\
\hline
500 & & 29250
\end{array}
$$

$$\frac{500}{29250} = 58.5\%$$

If a grower had purchased $300 per acre of Crop-Hail Insurance (and he could have purchased up to $500), his return would be $300 x 58.5% = $175.50 for each acre damaged.

By this method of adjustment our policy contract provides better coverage for partial losses than does the unit contract of the Federal Crop Corporation.

In our low rated areas, Federal Crop Insurance is about twice as expensive as our Crop-Hail policy because of the widely different methods of computing loss payments used by the two programs. By using a little arithmetic, many growers would find that our program would have saved them money.

Who adjusts our losses? Our adjusters are orchardists who have graduated from agricultural colleges, college professors, extension specialists, and other commercial men who have had many years of experience and are authorities in their field. They are fair-minded and impartial in their interpretation of the policy contract, but when a specific question arises the grower's interest is uppermost in their final decision.

When are losses adjusted? Preliminary inspections are made at the time of loss and final adjustment is completed prior to harvest.

FROST OR HAIL LOSS

They say that people spend six days a week sowing wild oats and then go to church on Sunday and pray for a crop failure. I doubt that you will be praying for a crop failure, even though you have an "All Risk" Federal Crop policy, since 25% of the yield is deducted from coverage, thus removing the profit incentive. Also, in years with a relatively high yield, the percentage of damage must be severe before an indemnity is payable. Crop-Hail Insurance from stock companies may be purchased separately or in combination with Federal Crop Insurance in those areas where this is available. In the northeastern states, there are generally only two primary weather hazards: frost and hail. Once the frost-free date has passed, the only danger is from hail. You will have to decide which hazard reduces your profit the most. There is, I realize, a limit on the amount of protection you can afford to buy in a high-risk, high-rated area.

---

[1]Presented at the annual meeting of the N. J. State Horticultural Society, Atlantic City. 1970.

The Federal Crop Insurance Corporation, with unlimited resources of generous government subsidies, does have a value for all of us since they are able to accumulate statistics and experience which may be used in future years to encourage our stock companies to engage in the writing of All Risk crop insurance in this area. A new Multiple Peril crop insurance program was approved and was introduced by private companies in five states on specific crops for 1969. The areas and crops are: Washington—wheat and barley; North Carolina—tobacco; and Illinois, Indiana and Iowa—corn and soybeans. The coverage parallels that previously offered only by the Federal Crop Insurance Corporation.

Today we hear a lot about the "credit crunch, but apparently the Federal Crop Corporation, completely financed by your tax dollars, isn't particularly concerned because they do not require that premiums be paid until after harvest.

Credit is expensive and stock companies' Crop Hail Departments must operate in the black, especially when money can be invested at short term for 8%.

ORCHARD LABOR MANAGEMENT

By John Giunco, Fruit Grower, Freehold, N. J.

My brother and I operate approximately 350 acres of orchard. We have our home farm of 250 acres, 50 in peaches of which 35 acres are in production. About 200 acres are in apples, 50 acres of which are in young trees and all of which are semi-dwarfs. We also rent 100 acres of apple trees which are 20 years old. We operate our own packing plant. While it is not worked steadily, it is in operation from 10 to 12 months a year. We have our own cold storage, half of which is CA and one-half mile from our packing house. Two years ago we went into the retail business and this opened a whole new field to us.

LABOR—THE BIG PROBLEM

Labor is of course a big problem, perhaps our biggest. I break down our labor into four types: (1) permanent employees, (2) packing house workers, (3) pickers and (4) the retail stand staff. Each group is different and presents different problems. The permanent help are the people we depend upon the most. Without them we could not operate and we want them to know it. They present many problems. We have to build up a pride in their work and a sense of accomplishment. This sounds grand; but to do it, we have to hunt good workers and then try to keep them. To attract people we first have to pay them fairly well. All our steady help is paid on an hourly rate—6 paid holidays—time and a half after 45 hours—and paid vacation. I prefer our steady help to live off the farm but this does not always happen. We make adjustments to pay for those who live off the farm and those who live on the farm. The ones who live on the farm we try to give them the best accommodations we have.

To build pride in work, give him a job, whether it be pruning, mowing, what have you, tell him what has to be done, let him decide how best to do it, then impress on him the importance of the job by checking constantly; I question how the job is going, offer suggestions on how to do it, listen to his ideas, and try not to "boss" him.

Often, especially during harvest season, we get our picking foreman, mechanic, tractor and truck drivers together, and discuss how things are going when we are running into difficulties. We, also discuss the different pickers, who is good, who is bad. We try to give them an idea of how we are going to move from block to block. We believe this gives everyone a feeling of belonging and being a part of a team, because a farm operation is a team operation. Also, at some of these meetings we get some good ideas and suggestions. Incidently, a little praise, or even using a suggestion (even if you planted the idea yourself) can go a long way.

We always back up an orchard foreman 100%, in a dispute with a picker— but in the same vein, we have to watch for favoritism of an individual picker by a forman and attempt to adjust this before it causes trouble.

The second group, packing-house personnel, we consider our easiest group to get and to manage. The men during the summer and early fall are some of our steady people together, with school boys. The women are usually the wives and older daughters of some of our picking help. During late fall, winter, and spring, the men are our steady men. The women are all local housewives who want a part-time job.

We try to generate interest in the packing house operation by not running a secret service. We tell our people where and to whom the apples are going—if it is a special promotion of a supermarket.

IRREGULAR PACKING HOUSE SCHEDULE

The biggest problem in the packing house is the irregular work schedule, which is necessary because we do not pack ahead except in special cases. Some of the larger promotional orders necessitate the build up of a fairly large stock of packed apples. This irregular work schedule has in the past cost us some of our best packers and will probably continue to cost us people. Because of this we are always hunting for new people. We prefer a woman whose children are in school and does not mind working one day one week and five days the next week. The irregularity of the work forces us into understanding appointments made and kept, sick children and all sorts of excuses when we would really like to have that person working in the packing house.

PICKING HELP

Our picking help certainly generates the most trouble and the most public interest. To understand the problem, let us try to understand them. These people are migrants, southern negroes. They generally travel in a family group. By that I mean a man and a woman. We do not encourage children in our camp because of the extra problems in housing, school, and damage to the camp and themselves when left unattended. These migrants like to display their independence, but depend on us for many things. We lend money to them, save for them, give them advice on anything from cars to baby cribs. For this, we carefully plan any weekend harvesting we want to do. We never demand that they work on a Saturday or Sunday. Why put yourself in a bad position? Your best picker may be the one that does not show up Sunday morning. I always plan to be in the best and fastest picking for the weekend, a place where even a slow picker can do well. Sometimes it is a nice medium-size tree where there is a big crop, other times it is a processing variety where careful handling can be forgotten for speed.

All our pickers work on a piece-work basis which is broken down into several rates for different jobs;

(1) Peaches—Open baskets for resale, field run, field crates for packing.

(2) Apples—Color or size picking—into 2 boxes—red—green—strip trees—most picking is special jobs with varying rate—large yellows—small trees—light crop trees—all apples are picked in bulk bins except summer reds.

There are several rules I set for myself in handling the pickers: (1) close supervision, constant irregular checks in the orchard; and do not form habits of time or routine; (2) never yell at a man without others hearing. If someone is doing a poor job the rest of them know it and want the wrong-doer to get yelled at. This also helps keep the others from getting into the same habits. I try never to yell at a really good picker.

Perhaps most important is to know your pickers. Know which ones can be trusted to do a good job, which one has to be watched, and which one wants reassurance, bad or good.

To minimize lost or wasted time I try to plan our picking moves several days in advance. I always attempt to make the shortest possible move, consequently, losing the least amount of time. Also, we try to move the pickers in the morning. A mid-afternoon move for some pickers is a signal for the end of the day. On Friday afternoon I am unavailable until 5:00 o'clock, because that money has to be spent and the faster the pickers get started the better job they can do spending it.

RETAIL BUSINESS

A retail business is an entirely new ball game. Here we need people who are cheerful, courteous, clean, neat, and who can think. A sour-faced clerk can drive customers away faster than the plague. I always encourage our people to answer all questions—they may not be 100% correct, but they probably know more than the questioner anyway. Neatness and cleanliness are important. This is the picture you want your customer to have. I demand that all arithmetic be done on paper or an adding machine—no matter how simple. The customer may be like some of my relatives—2 plus 2 is a major undertaking. The one thing I try to impress on everyone involved with our stand is that we need the customers. They do not need us. There is another place two or four miles down the road in every direction.

Recruiting boys and girls for the stand is fairly easy for us. We have three teenage children with lots of friends. Perhaps the best piece of luck with the stand is having a retired uncle and his wife who both enjoy working there. This also gives a certain sameness to the place, since my brother and I cannot devote too much time to the stand.

Generally speaking, there are several rules I try to maintain in managing our help. I try not to give a man a job he cannot handle. This does occur and when it does I try to get the man out of trouble without him losing face. At the same time I try to demand a high degree of success. Try not to lose your temper, but if you do lose it, do it at the right time and place. It can do a lot of good. I have several people, some migrants and some of our steady people with whom I have to get angy almost on schedule; they seem to be waiting for it.

I always try to sell a new machine or a new method to those who will be using it or doing it. Everyone ends up happier this way, including myself.

Incidently, some of these machines or new concepts are going to take a better operator than we are accustomed to hiring. We have run into this with spraying. In the last few years we have gone from dilute spraying to 6x. The man who did the spraying for us for years just could not handle the more exacting ground speed and more care on turns and everything else that goes with concentrate spraying. We had to put him on a different job.

A part of the labor management and an important part is changing operations to fit the labor. We cannot do the impossible. Several years ago we switched from Puerto Rican to negro migrants. There were many reasons involved in this change. One of the biggest was that our apple plantings were growing up and our volume of apples was increasing with it. We were having trouble keeping enough help to finish apple harvest. By changing, we solved the apple problem. But we started to get into a problem with peaches. The migrant workers, No. 1, did not like to pick peaches; No. 2, they could not make enough money picking them and we found we could not do the job we wanted to do with peaches.

Our solution was to cut down on the peach production and cut back on the number of varieties we were growing, hoping to have a break between varieties to rest the crew and ourseves. In the last several years we have ended up with a peach operation we can handle with the available labor. And more important, we make a profit at it.

SUMMARY STATEMENT

Changes are going to continue to occur in the fruit business and we will have to cope with them. One of our biggest problems will be to fit in our existing labor and recruit new types of labor to do their present jobs. Machines will be important and will help, but machines will only be as good as the people who operate them.

I believe that the single most important thing in the managing of labor is to figure out beforehand what we are going to do every day and know it with definiteness before the people are standing in front of you in the morning.

BECOME A STOCKHOLDER—IT'S EDUCATIONAL

Reports to stockholders are often interesting reading. Especially when they contain very good or very bad news; or when they reflect major changes in company policy. For years, I have been suggesting that vegetable and fruit growers own at least one share of stock in every firm they sell to or buy from. You get the quarterly or annual reports without having to write for them; and sometimes you make a little money. But the greatest value is a glimpse into the economic health of the organization and occasionally a clear peek into the future of a firm in a related business. By John Carew, Michigan State University, East Lansing.

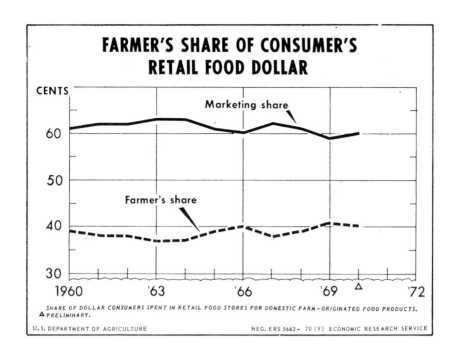

FARMER'S SHARE OF CONSUMER'S RETAIL FOOD DOLLAR

CENTS

Marketing share

Farmer's share

1960 '63 '66 '69 △ '72

SHARE OF DOLLAR CONSUMERS SPENT IN RETAIL FOOD STORES FOR DOMESTIC FARM-ORIGINATED FOOD PRODUCTS.
△ PRELIMINARY.

U. S. DEPARTMENT OF AGRICULTURE   NEG. ERS 5662 - 70 (9) ECONOMIC RESEARCH SERVICE

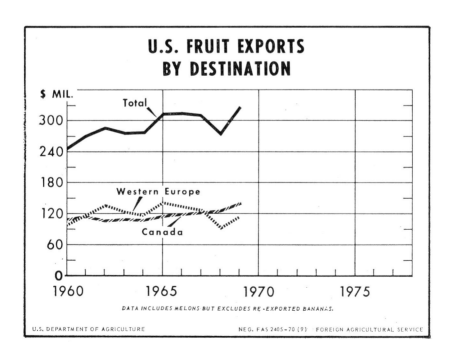

U.S. FRUIT EXPORTS BY DESTINATION

$ MIL.

Total

Western Europe

Canada

1960   1965   1970   1975

DATA INCLUDES MELONS BUT EXCLUDES RE-EXPORTED BANANAS.

U.S. DEPARTMENT OF AGRICULTURE   NEG. FAS 2405-70 (9)   FOREIGN AGRICULTURAL SERVICE

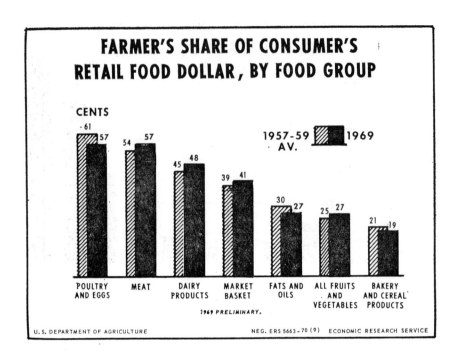

FARMER'S SHARE OF CONSUMER'S
RETAIL FOOD DOLLAR, BY FOOD GROUP

CENTS

1957-59 AV. / 1969

| POULTRY AND EGGS | MEAT | DAIRY PRODUCTS | MARKET BASKET | FATS AND OILS | ALL FRUITS AND VEGETABLES | BAKERY AND CEREAL PRODUCTS |

61 57 · 54 57 · 45 48 · 39 41 · 30 27 · 25 27 · 21 19

1969 PRELIMINARY.

U.S. DEPARTMENT OF AGRICULTURE   NEG. ERS 5663-70 (9)   ECONOMIC RESEARCH SERVICE

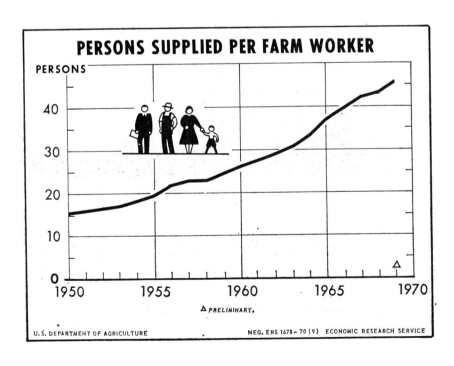

PERSONS SUPPLIED PER FARM WORKER

PERSONS

40

30

20

10

0

1950   1955   1960   1965   1970

△ PRELIMINARY.

U.S. DEPARTMENT OF AGRICULTURE   NEG. ERS 1678-70 (9)   ECONOMIC RESEARCH SERVICE

938

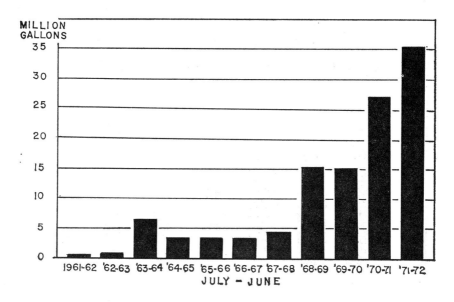

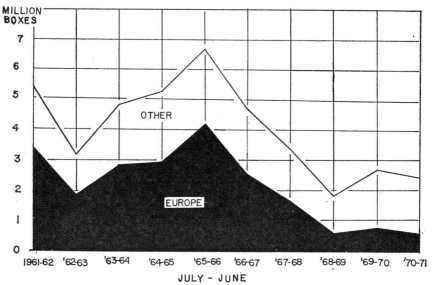

Foreign Agricultural Service, USDA

(Above) Imports of apple juice concentrate into the United States have increased markedly since 1961-2. Apple juice can be made into wine flavored with artificial fruit flavors. Sales are good but there are the questions of how long the popularity will ast and whether growers should plant trees for this outlet alone. A large California wine company has planted their own extensive orchard for this purpose.

(Below) Exports of fresh apples from the United States have been downward This has necessitated more effort in the U. S. to move apples through the local market outlets.

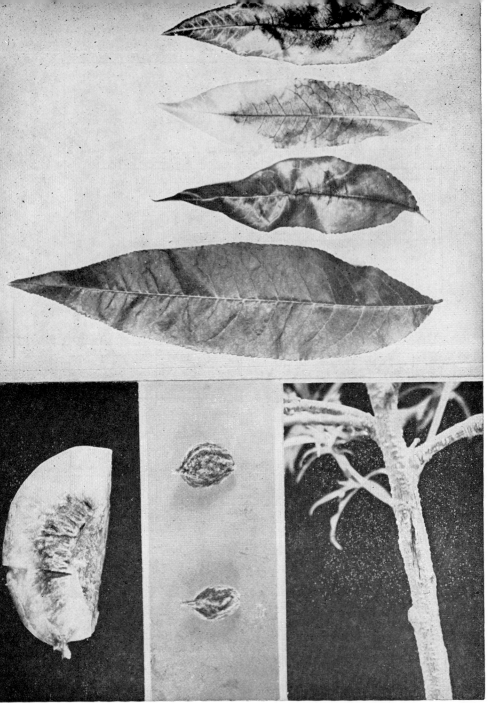

(Above) Hector R. Cibes, (below) Abdul Kamali; both formerly Rutgers University.

(Above) Calcium deficiency on peach under controlled conditions appears first on spur leaves. The leaves are smaller and show breakdown and necrosis of center of leaves. (Below) Boron deficiency in peach is characterized by brown corking of tissue near pit, shriveling and dropping of young fruits, and cracking of trunk bark with prominent lenticels.

(Above) Carlos E. Fernandez, formerly Rutgers University, New Brunswick, New Jersey; (Below) Long Ashton Research Station, Kent, England.

(Above) Molybdenum deficiency on apple under controlled conditions shows normal leaf on left, chlorotic shoot tip leaf in the middle and marginal scorch on mid or basal leaf. Mid-shoot leaves may show both chlorosis and marginal scorch. (Below) Copper deficiency on apple is characterized by dieback or shoot tips, ragged leaves and some whitish chlorosis.

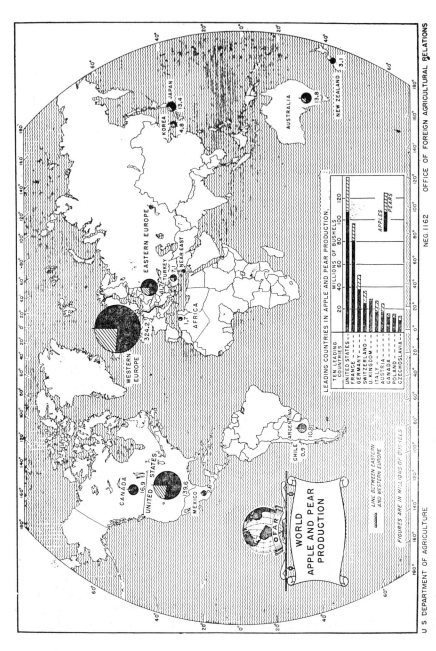

In World production of apples and pears the United States is second to Western Europe. These two deciduous fruits are confined to the temperate zones north and south of the Equator.

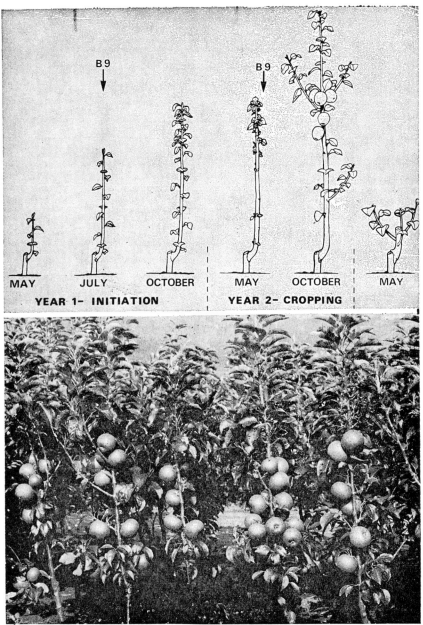

THE MEADOW ORCHARD. Dr. John Hudson, Director of the Long Ashton Research Station, Bristol, England, and his research team started working on the "Meadow Orchard" project in 1969, using a combination of chemical treatments and machine approach. They are using basically a single-shooted tree on full dwarfing stock as shown above. The tree is reduced to a single bud the third season. Trees are planted in beds 6 ft by 67 ft with trees spaced 12 inches in rows 18 inches apart, making 29,000 trees/A in a solid block. As experience is gained, adjustments will be needed in spacing and proposed management. A yield of 78 T/A may be obtained in alternate years. Contact Professor Hudson for year-by-year developments. The system shows possibilities. (From Western Fruit Grower, April 1972)

FARM DEFENSIVELY

By John Carew, Mich. State Univ., E. Lansing

Look for more environmental law suits against farmers. Livestock producers will be the hardest hit, but crop growers will also go to court. People no longer view farmers benevolently. Many regard farms as undesirable neighbors, sources of offensive odors and pollutants or competition for recreation land.

When the famous Michigan swine odor suit was settled, thousands of farmers smiled happily when the judge ruled in favor of the defendant whose farmer-neighbor claimed his pigs had a harmful smell. But the judge emphasized his decision was not to be regarded as a precedent. We can expect increased complaints against farm chemicals, odors, crop refuse, and noise.

Here are a few tips to individual growers for protecting against environmental law suits or court action:

● **Locate** all non-residential buildings, packing sheds, etc., in the middle of your property so as to provide wide buffer strips of land between you and your neighbors.

● **Pay attention** to state agricultural recommendations for building construction and the use of pesticides and fertilizers. The defense in the Michigan swine odor suit was strengthened considerably because the owner followed extension recommendations.

● **Train** employees to "Think and Act Environmentally": Pick up all pesticide and fertilizer containers. Do not spray in the wind. Dump nothing in streams. Burn only in compliance with local ordinances. Spread plant refuse on fields and disc it in.

● **Think** . . . before selling a home site on your farm. The man you sell to may be the one who takes you to court for polluting his air and water.

● **Develop** your personal public relations program. Deliberately, especially if they are not farmers. Invite them to visit your farm. Show them what you do and why. Point out, diplomatically, how your blsiness cnntributes to the community and the neighborhood; employment; your purchases of supplies and equipment; and the taxes you pay. Be certain to remind them that your cropland is also open space with living plants that serve as air conditioners in the summer and soil acts as a water reservoir in the winter. You might gently remind them that the alternatives to your continued farming could be selling the land as real estate for housing or industrial development.

● **Invite** public school teachers to bring classes to your farm. Show the children your contribution to food production and to their environment. Do the same with members of your town council: some of them may never have been on a real farm.

● **Become** involved in all environmental and zoning law discussions. Our nation abounds with well-meaning but often misinformed laymen and government employees. Many seek to ban most pesticides and fertilizers. The most effective place to oppose them is at the community level.

In summary: "Drive Defensively" is sound advice for people who drive. The car coming toward you may not be completely under control.

"Farm Defensively" can be sound advice for men who earn their living on the land. Farming practices generally influence the environment adjacent to farms as well as on them. Operate your farm as though you might be called to defend it.

RENT-A-TREE

Another way to retail some fruit has been launched recently by a Southwestern Michigan grower. He is Herbert Teichman of Eau Claire who has rented 25 apple trees on his farm to families living in Southwestern Michigan as well as others from Northern Indiana and Illinois.

Mr. Teichman said that he rents the trees for prices ranging from $15 to $30 per tree depending on the estimated tree yield, variety and quality. Varieties rented are Jonathan, Red Rome, Red Delicious and Fenton.

Mr. Teichman, who owns and operates the "Tree-Mendus" fruit farm also has developed recreational areas around the apple trees that are available for the season to the renters. These include picnic areas, scenic hiking trails and tall pine trees.

Advantages cited for the grower in such an operation are that a sale is secured, less labor and housing is needed to pick the fruit and the program can be operated in conjunction with the farm's pick-your-own crops as well as a retail market.

Some disadvantages would include extra weekend work for the grower, maintaining a park-like atmosphere around the orchard and grounds, increase insurance costs and the problems associated with extra correspondence and record keeping.

For the customer Mr. Teichman said the advantages are a guarantee of tree ripe fruit, the chance to earn a little extra cash by selling the crop from his tree, and the experience of watching a tree develop from bloom through fruit.

The customer has no responsibility for care of the tree which is done by Mr. Teichman.

Here is how the "rent-a-tree" operation works.

The customer selects the tree he wishes to lease for the season and the tree is marked as "sold" and a contract is written between Mr. Teichman and the customer. A number is placed on the tree, which corresponds with an identification number-card given to the customer.

The customer must present his I. D. card upon entering the orchard when visiting his family tree. The card entitles the customer to enter the grounds and any additional friends of the family will be charged 25 cents apiece to enter the grounds.

Persons who rent a tree are kept informed of its progress during the season, by postcard.

"This is only a trial year, and we are taking only a limited number of customers," Mr. Teichman said. "If the idea works out satisfactorily, we will be leasing family trees in the future." (From Great Lakes Fruit Growers News, Sparta, Mich.)

In Germany, Gerhard Hopp of Baulkhausen (near Frankfurt) placed an ad several years ago offering to rent individual trees for about $7 in American money per year. After he had rented 1200 of his 3500 trees, he had to stop. His weekend traffic got so heavy, with whole families driving out to see their tree, he could not get anything else done. The idea is popular in Germany, where the cost of picking had reached an all time high. Apples belong to the renters, of course, and not all of them are harvested.

944

In the Northwest apple growing region of the USA, much of the fruit crop is being dewaxed of natural covering and rewaxed with synthetic materials for attractiveness and better handling and storage qualities Water-dumping system is shown in the foreground with a Decco Waxer in the line. Tray packing is shown at left. (Courtesy Wallace & Tiernan Inc., Decco Division, Monrovia, California, 91016, and Paul Stark, Jr. nurseryman-grower, Wapato, Wash.)

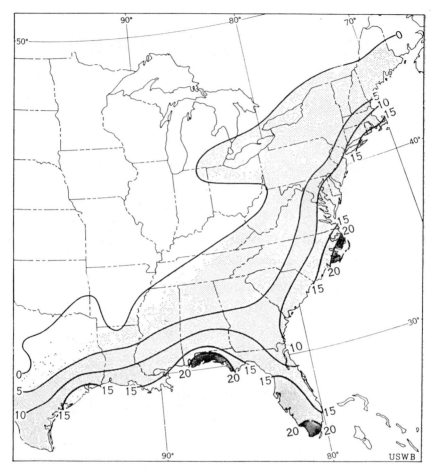

*Number of times destruction was caused by tropical storms in Eastern
United States, 1901-1955.*

THE WEATHER

Weather is a major factor in successful farming and **particularly** in fruit growing.
The fruit grower continuously is conscious and listening to weather predictions. His
entire business is dependent upon how he can "swing" with the weather, controlling
water supply by irrigation, controlling any freeze damage in the spring, fall and winter, dodging bad spraying and dusting days, adjusting his labor force to keep it busy
indoors or outdoors, and to plan for or repair repairable damage due to a heavy snow-
fall, rainfall, hurricane winds, freeze damage, or other acts of the weather.

The United States Environmental Science Service Administration of the U. S. Department of Commerce, Washington, D.C. or your local governmental weather service
can supply you with publications on details of past weather for many decades in your
particular area. Also, in recent years, this Service is giving more detailed information
on microclimate (near the soil surface) as well as other valuable information in local
fruit crop areas. This information is quite valuable to individual growers in their immediate planning to save their crops or make any needed precautions.

The chart above shows frequency of distructive storms in the Atlantic Coast region
of the United States. The hurricane that occurred in late summer of 1938 when leaves
were on fruit trees in the New England area was heavily distructive and was "felt"
for years afterward in weakened and/or dying trees. For details on this and other
hurricanes from the seasons they occur to how they are "born" and perform can be
found in "Hurricane — the Greatest Storm on Earth", ESSA/Pi 670009, Superintendent
of Documents, U. S. Printing Office, Washington, D. C., 20402. 65 cents.

NORTH AMERICAN POMOLOGISTS AND HORTICULTURISTS. Photographs of horticulturists dealing largely with deciduous fruits and presented here, were assembled by Dr. Donald V. Fisher, Director, Canada Dept. of Agr. Research Station, Summerland, B. C. for another publication. He kindly permitted their use here and also gave us his own portrait on request. (Upper, l. to r.) **Liberty Hyde Bailey,** 1858-1954; taxonomist, teacher, author, administrator; New York. **Marshall Pinckney Wilder.** 1798-1886; hybridizer, taxonomist, founder; Massachusetts. **William Terrill Macoun,** 1869-1933; breeder, administrator; Canada. **Arthur John Heinicke,** 1892-1971; physiologist, teacher, research, administrator; Missouri, New York. (Lower, l. to r.) **Ulyssis Prentiss Hedrick,** 1870-1951; taxonomist, author, teacher, administrator; Michigan, Oregon, New York. **Ezra Jacob Kraus,** 1885-1960; teacher physiologist, research, breeder, administrator; Illinois, New York, Michigan. **William Henry Chandler,** 1878-1970; physiologist, teacher, author, administrator; Missouri, New York, California. (Continued, next page).

NORTH AMERICAN POMOLOGISTS AND HORTICULTURISTS. (Upper, l. to r.) **Frank Patrick Cullinan**, 1895-, physiologist, teacher, administrator: New York, Illinois, Indiana, USDA (Md.). **Eugene Curtis Auchter**, 1889- about 1955, physiologist, teacher, author, administrator: New York, West Virginia, USDA (Md.), Hawaii. **George McMillan Darrow**, 1889-, breeding, physiology small fruits; Vermont, New York, USDA (Md.). **Maurice Adin Blake**, 1882-1947; tree fruit breeder, administrator, Massachusetts, New Jersey, (Lower, l. to r.) **Robert Mumford Smock**, 1908-, teacher, author, fruit storage; Ohio, California, New York, **Leon Fredric Hough**, 1915-, tree-small fruits breeder, physiologist; Michigan, New York, Illinois, New Jersey, **Luther Dent Davis**, 1895-, physiologist, teacher; Indiana, California. **Julian Creighton Miller**, 1895-'69, strawberry breeder, teacher, administrator; South Carolina, New York, North Carolina, Oklahoma, Louisiana. (Continued, next page).

WORLD POMOLOGISTS AND HORTICULTURISTS. (Upper l. to r.). The late **Nils Nybom**, 1925-69, administrator, teacher, author, fruit breeder, Kristianstad, Sweden. **L. C. Luckwill**, 1914-, physiologist, teacher, author, virologist, Bristol, England. **G. S. Roosje**, 1930-, culture, research, author, administrator. Wilhelminadorp, The Netherlands. **V. A. Kolesnikov**, 1891-, author, teacher, research, administrator. Russia. (Lower l. to r.). **G. Friedrich**, 1910-, grape and tree physiologist, teacher, author, administrator. Dresden, Germany. **Paul Stark Jr.**, 1916-, nursery man, propagator, industry administrator. New York, California, Washington, Missouri. **D. Martin**, 1911-, tree and post-harvest physiology, administrator. England, Tasmania. **Akira Kobayashi**, 1909-, physiology, research, teacher. Kyoto, Japan. (Continued, next page).

WORLD POMOLOGISTS AND HORTICULTURISTS. (Upper l. to r.). **R. G. Hatton**, 1886-1965, clonal rootstocks, research, administrator. **Freeman S. Howlett**, 1900-70, physiologist, breeder, teacher, author, administrator. New York, Ohio. **Donald V. Fisher**, 1914-, physiologist, storage, teacher, author, administrator. Iowa, British Columbia. **Arthur H. Thompson**, 1922-, teacher, physiologist, author, research. Minnesota, Washington, Maryland. (Lower l. to r.) **Orlando Rigitano**, 1916-, breeder of sub-tropical and temperate fruits. Brazil. **Sergio Sachs**, 1930-, deciduous fruit breeder, New Jersey, Brazil. **Norman H. Grubb**, 1882-1965, breeder, author. Bristol, England. **B. Budagovski**, 1910-, teacher, research in dwarf and cold-resistant rootstocks. Russia. (Continued, next page).

WORLD POMOLOGISTS. (Upper, l. to r.) **Warren Porter Tufts**, 1890-1968; research, teacher, author, administrator; Ohio, Oregon, California. **Victor Ray Gardner**, 1885-; physiologist, teacher, author, administrator; Michigan, Missouri, Iowa, Canada, Maine, Oregon, New Jersey Columbia (So. Am.), Florida. **Alfred Herman Krezdorn**, 1920-; research teacher, author, administrator; Texas, Florida. **Lawrence Paul Batjer**, 1907-1967; research physiologist, author, administrator. (Lower, l. to r.) **John Robert Magness**, 1893-; research physiologist, teacher, author, administrator; Michigan, Illinois, Oregon, Wisconsin, USDA. **Anthony P. Preston** 1918-; cultural, physiological research; England. **Ernest George Christ**, 1916-; extension fruit culture, author; New Jersey. **Malcolm Bancroft Davis**, 1890-; physiologist, teacher, administrator; Canada. (Continued, next page).

WORLD POMOLOGISTS. **Robert Paul Larsen,** 1926-; physiological, cultural extension, research, teaching, administrator, author; Utah, Kansas, Michigan, Washington. **Robert Fritz Carlson** 1909-; research, teacher, author, organizations; Sweden, Minnesota, New York, Michigan. **Alvin Lawrence Kenworthy,** 1915-; research, author, teacher; Oklahoma, Kansas, Washington, Michigan. **Stephen A. Pieniazek,** 1912-; research, teacher, author, traveler, administrator; New York, Rhode Island, Poland. (Lower, l. to r.) **Lawrence Leonard Claypool,** 1907-; postharvest, physiology, research, teacher; Washington, California. **Donald W. McKenzie,** 1930-; anatomy, breeding, viruses, rootstock, tree training, research and extension, New Zealand. **Joseph Harvey Gourley;** 1883-1946; physiologist, botanist, teacher, administrator; West Virginia, New Hampshire, Ohio. **Norman Franklin Childers,** 1910-; research, teacher, author, administrator; Idaho, Missouri, New York, Ohio, Puerto Rico, New Jersey. Additional photographs of pomologists will be included in future editions of this book.

Rootstocks, almond, 384; apple, 46-53; apricot, 382; cherry, 421; English walnut, 472; peach, 336; pear, 304; pecan, 456; persimmon, 500; plum, 396.

Rosette (see zinc deficiency).

Russeting, fruit, 563-8.

Rye, 111.

Scab, apple, control, 523-7; schedule, 538-43; selecting chemicals, 526; temperature required, 525; wet conditions required, 524.

Scab, pear control, 544-6.

Scab, pecan control, 466.

Scald, apple, 266-269; pear, 322; cherry, 437.

Scions, (cion), 162.

Self-incompatibility, 137

Semi-dwarf trees, apple, 44-53; peach, 338-9; pear, 301, 306.

Sevin, 154-55, 518.

Shuck-split, peach, 550.

Site selection, 36.

Sod in orchards, 102-7; seed mixtures, 107.

Soggy breakdown, apple, 269.

Soil, aeration, 37; excess water, 38-39; fertility, 40; peach, 355; pecan, 456; pH, 39, 122; selection, 37; shallow, 39; survey, 40; (see also each fruit).

Soil management, apples, bearing trees, 99, 102; cover crops, 108-14; advantages, 108; summer, 110; winter, 111; deficiency symptoms, K, 116; N, 101, 103, 106, 114; P, Mg, Ca, Cu, B, Zn, Fe, Mn, Mo, S, 116-17; dwarf trees, 100; fertilization, 118-21; frost damage, 101; herbicides, 101-2; growth desired, 115; high density trees, 121; intercropping, 101; irrigation, 124-6; leaf analysis, 121; liming, 122-3; manure, 119; mulching, 101-107; advantages, 102-109; cost, 106; limitations, 104; source, 106; nutrients needed, 114; objectives, 114-5; subsoiling, 108; timing fertilizers, 123; young trees, 100; almond, 385; apricot, 383; blueberry, 785; brambles, 768; cherry, 429; cranberry, 805-6; currant, 800; English walnut, 475; fig, 492; filbert, 485-6; gooseberry, 800; grapes, 673, 702, 709; nectarine, 380; peach, 350; pear, 310; pecan, 459; persimmon, 501; plum, 400; strawberry, 731-38; walnut, 475.

Soil analysis, 121.

Soybeans, 109-10.

Spray application, adjusting air-carrier sprayer, 615; air-blast, 612; compatibility of sprays, 536-7; concentrate, 617; custom spraying, 631; effect on color, quality, yield, 568; night spraying, 630; by over-tree irrigation, 634; size air-carrier needed, 614; time and amounts, 628.

Spray injury, 563-9; arsenical, 565; coppers, 564; varietal susceptibility, 563, weather, 563.

Spray machinery, agitators, 584; air-blast or speed sprayers, 586, 612, 619; airplane, 598, 605; application sprays, 610; atomization, 580, 586, 620; basic mechanics of, 574; brooms, 580; care of, 606, 607; costs, 629; dusting, 602; hand, 602; power, 603; guns, 580; hand sprayers, 584; helicopter, 595, 598, 604; history of, 570; low-volume concentrate, 617; air-blast, 619; droplet size, 620; liquid nozzles, 580, 620; machinery, 619; materials, 627; night spraying, 630; rate of travel, 624; mixing plants, 596; plungers, 578; power, sprayer, small, 585; large, 585; power take-off, 586, 592; pressure losses, 582, 607; pressure regulator, 578; pumps, types of, 574; size needed, 577, 614; refilling equipment, stationary plants, 597; tanks, 592, 594; towers, 595; trucks, wheel equipment 593; valves, 577; water supply, 594; weeds, 598.

Spray schedules, apple 538; pear, 544; peach, 540; blueberry, 792; brambles, 775; weeds, 554-62; young trees, 553.

Spur, 69, 81, 85, 833; (see pruning, each fruit).

Spur-type apples, 49.

Stamen, 129, 833.

Stigma, 129, 833.

Stocks, see grafting, rootstocks, 831, 832.

Stockholding ($), 936.

Stomach poisons, 513.

Storage, apples, 238; air circulation, 261; air-cooled, 244, 254; ammonia injury, 258; ceiling, 253; climacteric, 243; compression system, 257; condensors, 259; controlled atmosphere, 242, 244, 261; construction of 245, 251, 252, 918; costs, 264; diseases, 266; doors, 252; expension coils, 259; factors effecting, 241; floors, 253; fruit heat, 255; function of, 239; humidity control, 242, 262; insulation, 247; objectives, 238; refrigerants, 257; refrigerated, 255; refrigeration load, 255; respiration effects, 242; storage-life-apples, 241; temperature, 241; troubles in operation, 262; types of 243; vapor barriers, 251; ventilation, 243; walls, 252; blueberries, 792; brambles, 777; cherry, 441; grapes, 696, 704, 710; peach, 373; pear, 318; pecan, 467; plum, 409; strawberry, 745; walnuts, 480.

Strawberry, air shipment, 747; breeding objectives, 719; cold storage, 745; containers, 744-5; cost of growing, 746-8; diseases, 748; everbearing, 751; spaced-plant mulch, fertilizers, 734; leaf analysis, 737; time to apply, 735; starter solutions, 735; frost protection,

739; frozen pack, 745; gibberellins, 733; harvest dates over U.S., 715; harvesting, 742-44; insects, 751; irrigation, 738, Chap. XIX; liming, 737; locating planting, 716; mulching, 739, 754; nematodes, 751; planting time, 725; barrel, 728-9; care of plants, 729; cultivation, 732; marking rows, 728; plants per acre, 727; pyramid, 728-9; removing flowers, 731; setting plants, 729; thinning plants, 731; training systems, 725; plastic film, 733; production areas U.S., 715; pick-your-own, 901; propagation, 719; renewing plantation, 741; shipping, 744-7; soil preparation, 723; spray - herbicide schedule, 554; varieties, 717-19; characteristics, 720-21; relative importance, 718; virus free, 722; weed control, 554, 733; winter protection, 739-40; world production, 714; yields, 745.

Sudan grass, 109-10.

Students, entering pomology, 14.

Subsoiling, 108.

Sulphur, 520.

Sulphur deficiency, apple, 117; pecan, 463.

Sulphur dioxide, grape, 711; peach, 375.

Sun scald, apple, winter, 186.

Sunshine, 34.

Sweet clover, 109, 113.

Systemic pesticides, 514.

Tap root, 457-8, 473.

Taxes, estate, 898; farm, 927-33.

Temperature, in fruit growing, 32.

Temperature regions, minimum range for plants, USA and Canada, see 1961-66 editions of this book.

Terrace planting, 57; construction, 58.

Thinning of fruits, apple, 146; alternate bearing, effects on, 151; chemical thinning, 151-61; fruit color effects, 149; easy-difficult-to-thin conditions, 160; fruit size effects, 147-8; defruiting trees, 160; limb breakage, 149; nitrogen-pruning interrelation, 150; objects, 147; pest control, 150; quality effects, 149; yield effects, 150; cherry, 434; grape, 708; peach, 362-5; pear, 312; pecan, 463; plum, 399-400.

Thin-wood pruning, apple, 70.

TIBA, 96, 132.

Timothy, 109.

Top-working, apple, 141, 167; peach, 367; pear, 306.

Tree, planting specifications, apple, 52; cherries, 47; dwarf trees, 49, 50-53; nuts, 53; pear, 53.

Trunk splitting, 187.

Turnpike condemnation, 897.

Umbrella system, grapes, 686, 689.

Unions, 890-4.

Universities in the U.S., 918; see 1961 edition for foreign universities.

Urea nitrogen sprays, 119.

Value, sprayers, 577, 896-8.

Varieties, apples, 16-30; general, 25, 41; (see each fruit).

Vegetative propagation, 46-53.

Vitamins, 468, 495, 502.

Walnuts, black species, 468; English (Persian), 470-482; boron deficiency, 477; climate, 470; copper deficiency, 477; dehydration, 480; ethephon, 480; ethylene usage, 479; fertilization 476; harvesters, mechanical, 478; hulling, 479; intercrops, 476; irrigation, 476; manganese deficiency, 477; marketing, 480; nutritive value, 482; packaging, 480; pest control, 478; planting, 473; production, 468; regions, 468-9; propagation, 473; pruning trees, 477; rootstocks, 472; soil, 470; soil management, 475; training trees, 474; varieties, 471; washing, 480; zinc deficiency, 477; walnut, Japanese, 469.

Waxing apples, 228, 945.

Weed control, see herbicides, 554, each crop.

Water, ground level, 39.

White washing trees, 186.

Wholesale prices, farm products, 5.

Wild game control, 97;

Wind machines, 33.

Windbreaks, 35.

Winds, heavy, 34, 946.

Winter injury, apple, treatment, 189; peach, 346; see each fruit.

Zinc deficiency, apple, 114, 116, 117; cherry, 431; English walnut, 476; grape, 678, 680; peach, 353; pear, 311; pecan, 460-2; plum, 402.